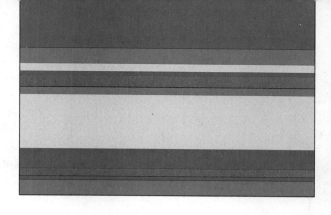

THIRD EDITION

FINANCIAL ACCOUNTING

Loren A. Nikolai, Ph.D., CPA

Ernst & Young Professor, School of Accountancy
University of Missouri–Columbia

John D. Bazley, Ph.D., CPA

Professor, School of Accountancy
University of Denver

PWS-KENT PUBLISHING COMPANY • BOSTON

PWS–KENT
Publishing Company

Senior Editor: Rolf A. Janke
Assistant Editor: Deirdre A. Lynch
Production Editor: Eve B. Mendelsohn
Interior Designer: Catherine L. Johnson
Cover Designer: Lindgren Design Associates
Cover Pen: Courtesy of S. T. Dupont
Cover Photographer: Bindas Studios
Manufacturing Coordinator: Margaret Sullivan Higgins
Compositor: Graphic Typesetting Service
Text Printer and Binder: Arcata Graphics/Hawkins
Cover Printer: New England Book Components

PWS-KENT Publishing Company is a division of Wadsworth, Inc.

Printed in the United States of America
1 2 3 4 5 6 7 — 94 93 92 91 90

Material from FASB documents copyright by Financial Accounting Standards Board, 401 Merritt 7,
P.O. Box 5116, Norwalk, Connecticut, 06856-5116, U.S.A. Reprinted with permission. Copies of the
complete documents are available from the FASB.

Material from *Accounting Research Bulletins, Accounting Principles Board Opinions, Accounting Principles
Board Statements, Accounting Interpretations,* and *Accounting Terminology Bulletins* is reprinted with the
permission of the American Institute of Certified Public Accountants, Inc., copyright © 1968, 1969,
1970, 1971, 1972, 1973, 1974, 1975, 1976, 1977, 1978, 1979, 1980, 1981, 1982, 1983, 1984, 1985, 1986, 1987,
1988, and 1989.

Library of Congress Cataloging-in-Publication Data

Nikolai, Loren A.
    Financial accounting / Loren A. Nikolai, John D. Bazley,
    — 3rd ed.
        p.   cm.
    ISBN 0–534–92017–9
        1. Accounting.   I. Bazley, John D.   II. Title
    HF5635.N692   1989   89–36385
    657—dc20   CIP

About the Authors

Loren A. Nikolai

Loren A. Nikolai, Ph.D., CPA, is the Ernst & Young Professor in the School of Accountancy at the University of Missouri, Columbia. He received his M.B.A. from St. Cloud State University and his Ph.D. from the University of Minnesota. Professor Nikolai has taught at the University of Wisconsin at Platteville and at the University of North Carolina at Chapel Hill. He has received awards for outstanding teaching at both the University of Wisconsin at Platteville and the University of Missouri. He holds a CPA certificate in the state of Missouri and previously worked for the 3M Company. Professor Nikolai is the lead author of *Intermediate Accounting* Fourth Edition and *Principles of Accounting* Third Edition and coauthor of *Financial Accounting: Concepts and Uses* (PWS-KENT Publishing Company). He has published numerous articles in *The Accounting Review, Journal of Accounting Research, The CPA Journal, Management Accounting, Policy Analysis, Academy of Management Journal, Journal of Business Research,* and other professional journals. He was also lead author of a monograph published by the National Association of Accountants. Professor Nikolai is the Faculty Vice President of the Beta Alpha Psi chapter at UMC. He is a member of the American Accounting Association, the American Institute of Certified Public Accountants, and the Missouri Society of CPAs. He has chaired or served on several American Accounting Association committees and was Director of Education for 1985–87.

John D. Bazley

John D. Bazley, Ph.D., CPA, is Professor of Accounting in the School of Accountancy at the University of Denver, where he has received the Alumni Award for Faculty Excellence. He earned a B.A. from the University of Bristol in England and an M.S. and Ph.D. from the University of Minnesota. Professor Bazley has also taught at the University of North Carolina at Chapel Hill and holds a CPA certificate in the state of Colorado. He has taught national professional development classes for a major CPA firm, and was a consultant for another CPA firm. Professor Bazley is the lead author of *Financial Accounting:*

Concepts and Uses and coauthor of *Intermediate Accounting* Fourth Edition and *Principles of Accounting* Third Edition (PWS-KENT Publishing Company). Professor Bazley has published numerous articles in professional journals, including *The Accounting Review, Management Accounting, Accounting Horizons, The Practical Accountant,* and *The Academy of Management Journal.* He is also a coauthor of a monograph on Environmental Accounting published by the National Association of Accountants. He is a member of the American Institute of Certified Public Accountants, the Colorado Society of Certified Public Accountants, and the American Accounting Association.

Preface

Purpose

Our goal in writing this introductory financial accounting textbook is to provide students with a solid foundation in the dynamic and growing field of accounting. The book is intended for students who wish to develop a comprehensive understanding of the meaning of accounting information, whether they are accounting majors or not. Accounting majors using this book will obtain a sound understanding of financial and managerial accounting fundamentals. These students will have a thorough preparation for the move from beginning to intermediate and advanced courses. Nonaccounting majors will find the solid grounding in accounting and the explanations of the uses of accounting information presented in this text to be valuable in their future careers as investors, managers, bankers, or perhaps as owners of their own businesses.

General Overview

Financial Accounting Third Edition has been written for a one-semester (two quarter) sequence in introductory financial accounting. Our goal is to include the most educationally effective blend of theory and practice. Whereas practice is the main focus, we discuss accounting concepts and the uses of accounting information as they apply to the topics in each chapter. The textbook is organized in a fairly traditional manner. We do not feel that rearranging the order of coverage just for the sake of being different is sound pedagogy. On the other hand, we have chosen to combine the treatment of some topics (e.g., current and noncurrent investments, inflation and international accounting) while reducing that of other topics (e.g., consolidations). We believe this blend of topics will provide a more realistic and useful introduction to accounting.

Pedagogy

Although accounting principles are sometimes difficult for beginning students, we believe they can be made more understandable and interesting by using a clear, direct, building-block discussion that anticipates a student's learning process and that is written at the student's reading level. Each chapter begins with a set of learning objectives—what the student should understand after reading the chapter—and an introduction that presents the topics to be covered. Each topic is then discussed in a logical order. Generally, each topic is introduced by a brief practical or conceptual overview, followed by a discussion of the related accounting practices. This discussion often includes the use of visuals; i.e., flowcharts, diagrams, or sets of steps designed to facilitate the student's understanding of the material. After the discussion, an example is presented to reinforce the student's learning process. Each example is straightforward, fully explained, and avoids gaps that might confuse the student. Illustrations of journal entries, supporting schedules, and financial statements are abundant and meaningful. A conceptual summary concludes the discussion of many topics.

Within each chapter, headings separate the material into logically ordered, understandable portions for the student. Key definitions and concepts are **bold-faced;** *italics* are used for emphasis. An overall summary tied to the learning objectives is included at the end of each chapter. Each chapter also has a glossary of key terms, carefully developed to be a concise but complete reference for the student. A review problem (and solution) is included at the end of each chapter except Chapter 6. Illustrations of real companies are often used to relate the discussion to actual practice. The 1988 annual report of the Black & Decker Corporation is included in Appendix A at the end of the text.

Coverage

The text consists of 20 chapters divided into four parts: I. The Accounting Process, II. Accounting for Assets and Liabilities, III. Business Entities, and IV. Financial Statements: Additional Aspects of Financial Reporting. For those instructors not wishing to cover all chapters, the text is designed to allow coverage of topics in a variety of ways. For instance, the internal control, special journals, and electronic data processing topics of Chapter 6 are independent units enabling deferral or omission of one or more topics. Since partnership accounting is covered in a separate chapter (13) from corporations, it may be deleted without disruption of the remaining material. Chapters 14 and 15 on corporations may be covered after Chapter 6 for a corporate approach to the text. Because present value is discussed as a separate unit in Chapter 16, this topic and related applications may be omitted if desired. Finally, the statement of cash flows, analysis and interpretation of financial statements, and accounting for changing prices and international operations are covered in separate chapters (18, 19, and 20) so that selected coverage may be assigned.

Specific Features

In our combined 40 years of teaching experience we have identified many aspects of sound pedagogy that have been incorporated into this textbook. Some of the major features are summarized here.

1. *Source documents.* In Part I the role of source documents is emphasized to give students a better understanding of where the information comes from for recording transactions (and for internal control). The importance of source documents is reinforced throughout the text.

2. *Uses of financial statements.* In Chapters 2 and 3, the discussion of the balance sheet and income statement includes an introductory explanation of liquidity, financial flexibility, return on investment, risk, and operating capability.

These concepts are also discussed in regard to the analysis and interpretation of financial statements in Chapter 19.

3. *Nontechnical GAAP.* Broad, generally accepted accounting principles (GAAP) are introduced and explained in Chapter 1; others are introduced and explained in later chapters as specific topics arise. GAAP is presented in understandable, nontechnical language without repeatedly quoting formal pronouncements.

4. *Revenue and expense transactions.* Discussion of revenues and expenses is deferred until Chapter 3, after a clear discussion of simple balance sheet transactions (Chapter 1) and accounts, journal entries, and postings for balance sheet transactions (Chapter 2), causing less confusion for the students.

5. *Corporations.* Parts I and II focus primarily on sole proprietorships, although many of the basic principles also apply to partnerships and corporations. Chapter 5, however, includes a section that identifies the basic accounting differences between sole proprietorships and corporations, allowing the instructor the flexibility of taking a more corporate approach throughout Part II. Partnerships and corporations are then fully discussed in Chapters 13, 14, and 15.

6. *Internal control and EDP systems.* Chapter 6 provides a comprehensive discussion of internal control, highlighting the importance and use of an efficient and effective accounting system. This includes internal control as it relates to authorizing, executing, and recording transactions, and overall accountability for assets. The EDP section includes a discussion of various software programs, as well as internal control for an EDP system.

7. *EDP demonstration and homework disk.* An illustration of electronic data processing is included on a demonstration disk for an IBM personal computer so that students can "work through" the illustration. This Instructor's Disk for Students is available at no charge to instructors who adopt the text. In addition, Exercise 6-14 and Problems 6-8A and 6-8B deal with elementary EDP accounting systems. These are also included on the disk. Complete instructions for both the illustration and the homework are provided in an appendix to Chapter 6.

8. *Receivables and liabilities.* Accounts receivable and notes receivable are thoroughly discussed together in Chapter 8; current liabilities (including payroll) are also covered in one chapter (Chapter 10). This arrangement lessens the confusion often found in many books that try to discuss the accounting principles for both receivables and payables at the same time.

9. *Income tax issues integrated.* Rather than devoting an entire chapter to the specifics of income taxes (which many instructors do not cover in a principles course, given the complex and changeable nature of tax), a brief discussion of income tax is integrated in each chapter where it applies to specific topics (e.g., inventories and depreciation). This enables students to understand the general relationship of accounting principles and income taxes while leaving the detailed discussion of specifics to a separate tax course, often taken by both accounting and nonaccounting majors.

10. *Bonds payable and present value.* Bonds payable and the straight-line method for premiums or discounts are discussed *before* present value. After present value is fully discussed, the effective interest method is described. This

arrangement allows flexibility for the instructor and a more logical organization for the student.

11. *Present value concepts and techniques.* Present value is carefully introduced at an elementary level in Chapter 16 and later applied to bonds, leases, mortgages, and investments, allowing a more realistic and relevant understanding of these topics.

12. *Consolidated financial statements.* In accordance with the recommendations of reviewers and a survey of principles instructors, only the underlying concepts and basic practices of this very technical topic are presented (as part of Chapter 17), rather than devoting a full chapter to it as in many texts. The important items affecting financial statements (e.g., goodwill and minority interest) are discussed while the complexities of preparation are not. This enables valuable class time to be devoted to other topics more appropriate for the beginning level.

13. *Statement of cash flows.* Chapter 18 includes several useful diagrams for helping students understand operating, investing, and financing cash flows. Both the direct and indirect methods of reporting operating cash flows are discussed. The indirect method is explained in the main part of the chapter; the direct method is explained in an appendix to the chapter.

14. *Assignment materials.* An abundance of end-of-chapter assignment materials is included, divided into questions, exercises, problems (Parts A and B), and decision cases. A **boldfaced** description beside each assignment indicates the subject at issue. The questions address key concepts and terms; each exercise reinforces a topic at an elementary level. The problems either combine a number of topics or focus on a more in-depth study of a single topic. Many problems also require short discussion-type answers. The decision cases require the students to integrate the topical materials, and many are based on actual companies.

Major Changes

Preparation of the third edition involved a careful and extensive research program. Reviews of the entire second edition as well as selected chapters were obtained from both users and nonusers of the text. Several "focus groups" evaluated these reviews and also addressed common pedagogical issues. Based on results of this research, numerous changes have been made in the third edition. Several of the major changes are summarized as follows:

1. *Expansion of learning objectives and summary.* To improve pedagogy, the learning objectives at the beginning of each chapter have been modified to be more carefully linked to the major chapter topics. Each learning objective is repeated beside the related textual material. Finally, a summary keyed to these learning objectives has been added to the end of each chapter.

2. *Expansion of decision cases.* In order to enhance the "user" orientation of the text, many new decision cases have been added. Most chapters now have four decision cases, many of which involve analysis of an excerpt from an actual corporation's annual report.

3. *Increased use of visual aids.* Many new visual aids have been added throughout the book to help in the students' learning process. These visual aids include such items as diagrams, flowcharts, equations, numbered lists, and

T-accounts. They are designed to help explain complex topics, reinforce key ideas, and break up the text into more manageable segments.

4. *Rearrangement of introductory discussion.* The coverage in Chapter 1 has been rearranged to facilitate the introduction of basic accounting concepts and procedures. The FASB "conceptual framework" and accountancy profession discussions have been moved to the end of the chapter to provide more flexibility in coverage.

5. *Better linkage of text to exhibits.* To facilitate students' comparisons of text discussion to related exhibits, notations have been added to several exhibits. For instance, step numbers have been added to Exhibit 4-3 to correspond to the steps listed in the text to complete the worksheet.

6. *Addition of alternative closing entry procedures.* The coverage of closing entries for merchandising companies in Chapter 5 has been expanded to include alternative approaches. This expansion provides greater flexibility for those instructors who prefer to emphasize a certain approach.

7. *Elimination or reduction of coverage of selected topics.* In response to reviewers' concerns that the previous edition included several "intermediate" level topics, coverage of certain topics has been eliminated or reduced. The topics eliminated include the liquidation of LIFO layers, premiums and coupons, self-construction of assets, and sales-type leases of lessors. Reduced coverage has been given to inflation accounting, pensions, deferred income taxes, segment reporting, interim worksheets, and convertible bonds. For those instructors interested in covering LIFO liquidation, self-construction of assets, and sales-type leases or extending the coverage of pensions and deferred taxes, discussion material and homework is included in the *Instructor's Manual* that accompanies the text.

8. *Rearrangement of certain topics.* For more cohesive coverage, the discussion of several topics has been rearranged in selected chapters. For instance, Chapter 16, "Noncurrent Liabilities," includes leases of the lessee, mortgages, deferred income taxes, and pensions, in addition to bonds payable. Chapter 17, "Investments," covers the lower of cost or market method, equity method, and consolidations. Chapter 20, "Accounting for Changing Prices and International Operations," includes coverage of both topics.

9. *Addition of discussion of contingencies.* In response to reviewers' suggestions, a brief discussion of contingencies has been added to Chapter 10.

10. *Revised chapter on statement of cash flows.* Because the statement of cash flows has replaced the statement of changes in financial position, Chapter 18 has been completely revised.

11. *Modification of ACRS discussion.* The discussion and explanation of the Accelerated Cost Recovery System (ACRS) presented in Chapter 11 has been modified to include the current income tax rules. An ACRS table has been added to simplify the discussion.

12. *Omission of redundancies.* In response to reviewers' suggestions, certain redundancies concerning sales and purchases discounts have been removed from Chapters 8 and 10.

13. *Modification of company names in homework.* To enhance realism, over 50 percent of the company names in the homework have been modified to include

the company's business function. In many cases, the company's accounts have been similarly modified. For instance, Talleby Company is now Talleby Photo Developing Company and acquires developing equipment instead of office equipment.

14. *Expanded and revised homework assignments.* Additional homework items have been added to various chapters. The numbers (and solutions) have been changed in over 70 percent of the homework material.

Design

The new design and physical appearance of this edition is the result of careful planning and market research. Over forty instructors of Principles and Financial Accounting were surveyed to determine their preferences for color, layout, and exhibit design. Responding to these suggestions and working closely with our publisher, we have adopted an entirely new design that will enhance learning by making material clear and easy to follow. The larger page size allows an open and accessible format. Color has been used with a pedagogical purpose rather than solely for aesthetic embellishment: learning objectives are red, headings are green, and financial material is blue. Diagrams and charts make use of blue and green to emphasize and distinguish elements.

Supplementary Material

For the Instructor

- **Instructor's Manual.** A list of objectives, synopsis, lecture outline, general notes, and content analysis of exercises, problems, and decision cases are included for each chapter.

- **Solutions Manual.** This includes a list of suggested assignments, content analysis, and complete solutions to all questions, exercises, problems, and decision cases. Many solutions include helpful notes to the instructor concerning difficult areas within each problem.

- **Test Bank.** David Gotlob, University of Wisconsin–Oshkosh, and Jerry Kreuze, Western Michigan University, have prepared an expanded test bank that includes approximately 50 multiple-choice questions and 10 short-answer problems for each chapter. Sufficient examination material permits the development of numerous tests without repetition of questions. An answer key for all questions and problems is located at the end of each chapter for easy reference. Where applicable, supporting computations are shown for the problem solutions.

- **Computerized Test Bank.** The same test material appearing in the printed *Test Bank* is available on disk for use with the IBM PC or compatible.

- **Check Figures.** This features a checklist of the key answers to the exercises and problems. Two sets are available for distribution to students, one for problems and one for exercises.

- **Customized Transparencies.** A complete set of transparencies, including the solutions to all questions, exercises, problems, and decision cases, set in large type is available. Four-color teaching transparencies for lecture or illustrative purposes are also included. The transparencies are divided into topical groups; adopters may order specific groups or a complete set. A bound set of printed transparency masters is available for reference and review. It includes a form to be used for ordering the actual acetate transparencies.

- **EDP Demonstration and Homework Disk.** This features a demonstration file of the review problem from Chapter 3 and files to complete selected problems from Chapter 6 in the text. The completely menu-driven disk includes programs for entering journal entries into a transactions file, updating the master file, and printing the transactions file, an adjusted trial balance, and financial statements. The disk may be copied for student use with the IBM PC or compatible.

For Both the Instructor and Student

- **Source Documents.** This innovative teaching tool is a collection of actual input, transaction, control, and output documentation used for preparing accounting records and generating financial statements. Lawrence Ponemon of the State University of New York at Albany designed this package to provide "hands on" experience with real company documents. The accompanying booklet explains each document's operations in the accounting scheme.

For the Student

- **Study Guide.** This was prepared by David Gotlob, University of Wisconsin–Oshkosh; Jerry Kreuze, Western Michigan University; and Loren Nikolai to help students master terms, concepts, and practices introduced in the text and to provide a means of testing this mastery. It includes a list of learning objectives, a chapter synopsis, numerous self-evaluation exercises with answers, and a three-part posttest corresponding to each text chapter.

- **Working Papers.** This includes partially completed working papers for all problems.

Manual Practice Sets

- **Boone Office Supply.** Developed by David Gotlob and Loren Nikolai, this focuses on accounting for a sole proprietorship retailing company and is designed for use after completing Chapter 6.

- **Crockett Automotive Parts.** This practice set, also prepared by David Gotlob and Loren Nikolai, deals with accounting for a wholesaling corporation and is to be used anytime after Chapter 18.

- **Healthy Grocer, Inc.** This was developed by Elliot Levy of Bentley College. It presents transactions for a corporate retailer and allows students to complete an accounting cycle. It is appropriate for use after discussion of financial statements, the accounting cycle, and merchandise accounting.

- **Virginia Equipment Company.** Prepared by Harry Dickinson of Virginia Commonwealth University, this puts students in the role of decision maker by allowing a choice of accounting methods to be used to complete various transactions. It is to be used after coverage of inventory and cost of goods sold.

Computerized Materials

- **Principles of Accounting Applications and Extensions Using Lotus 1-2-3.** Prepared by E. Lewis Bryan of Clemson University, this computer package teaches students the basics of how to manipulate data, save and print files, and design logical spreadsheet formats using Lotus 1-2-3. It includes three levels of problems (A, B, and C) in progressing difficulty, with many problems requiring value and formula input. The program promotes decision making and conclusive thinking by requiring students to prepare a written analysis of output. Basic Lotus functions are explained and demonstrated for students with no prior knowledge of the program.

- **Tutorial Disk and Booklet.** Developed by Ted Bainbridge of Concordia College, this menu-driven tutorial consists of selected problems from the text for use on the microcomputer. This package allows students to interact with the computer during all phases of computations. The program provides explanations for answers, both correct and incorrect, thereby teaching the student the hows and whys of an accounting method. It is usable with the IBM PC or compatible.

- **A Review of the Accounting Cycle for the IBM PC.** Annette Pearson, Neilson, Inc., and Frederic Stiner, University of Delaware, designed this program to help students review the accounting cycle using a computerized practice set. Students manually record transactions and post journal entries to a ledger to track the flow of information through each step of the process, then use the computer to perform the simple mathematical steps involved in the preparation of trial balances, adjusting entries, and financial statements. This package requires students to assume responsibility for both the analysis and entry of accounting information. No computer experience is necessary. This is designed for use with the IBM PC/XT/AT or compatible.

- **McGee: A Computerized Accounting Information System.** Prepared by Earl Weiss and Donald Raun, both of California State University–Northridge, this user-friendly microcomputer tutorial is a comprehensive accounting information system as well as a learning aid that helps reinforce principles concepts. This package follows two accounting cycles of the McGee Company, as a service operation and as a merchandising operation, for a period of over two months. Students are able to analyze business transactions using actual source documents and enter them into the accounting cycle. Sensitivity or "what if" analysis can be performed using a spreadsheet and a cash-and-profit forecast. This is designed for use with the IBM PC or compatible.

Acknowledgments

We wish to thank our second edition users and reviewers for their useful comments in this revision. We are particularly grateful to Joe Silvoso and Ken Harmon, University of Missouri, for their constructive criticism. A special thanks is due to Steve Sutton for his valuable computer technical assistance. We also wish to thank our graduate and undergraduate students including Beth Adair, Lynn Hartman, Charlotte Agee, Teresa Hickam, and Trish Nikolai for their invaluable technical assistance in the preparation of the book and supporting materials. We are sincerely indebted to our typists, Lisa Copeland, Anita Blanchar, and Mary Thomas, whose quality work and perseverance enabled us to complete the manuscript in a timely and orderly fashion. Appreciation is also extended to our editorial and production staffs, including Richard A. Pellagrini, Eve Mendelsohn, Tina Samaha, Marcia Cole, Deidre Lynch, and Sue Purdy.

We are grateful to our respective Schools of Accountancy for their support and to the American Institute of Certified Public Accountants, the Financial Accounting Standards Board, and the many companies for granting us permission to quote from their pronouncements and financial statements. We are also grateful to our wives, children, and friends who provided us with considerable moral support and understanding during the entire manuscript production process.

Loren A. Nikolai   John D. Bazley

Note from the Publisher

In order to produce a Financial Accounting text best suited to current market needs, we conducted an extensive and on-going research program throughout the three-year development of this edition. Over fifty-five highly qualified educators who teach Financial Accounting participated in our research.

The development program began with a questionnaire that defined the market, competition, and existing reputation of the Nikolai text; a number of indepth reviews of the second edition were also solicited at this time. Then, in the spring of 1988, we conducted three Focus Groups at the Western, Midwestern, and Eastern Regional Meetings of the AAA.

The initial manuscript was written to incorporate these preliminary suggestions. It was then reviewed extensively one more time and revised before the final manuscript was released to production. Every reviewer involved in this process greatly aided us in creating the most effective teaching and learning package possible. *Financial Accounting* has been improved immeasurably through their perceptive insights and helpful comments about how the book could best fill the needs of both students and teachers.

We acknowledge with gratitude the help, advice, and support of the following professionals whose involvement, past and present, has greatly enhanced this edition.

Richard C. Crews
Editor-in-Chief

Final Reviewers

Linda J. Benz
Jefferson Community
College

Phillip G. Buchanan
George Mason University

Gyan Chandra
Miami University

Willard C. Clark, Jr.
University of Dayton

Larzette G. Hale
Utah State University

Thomas Largay
Husson College

Mary Loyland
University of North
Dakota

Edward O. Lutz
Brooklyn College

Rebecca L. Phillips
University of Louisville

Donald F. Putnam
California State
Polytechnic University

Alan Rainford
Greenfield Community
College

Patrick J. Roche, Jr.
Northern Essex
Community College

Stephen D. Willits
Bucknell University

Preliminary Reviewers

Gyan Chandra
Miami University

Lee H. Nicholas
University of Northern
Iowa

Leo A. Ruggle
Mankato State University

Special Reviewers of End-of-Chapter Problem Sets

Elizabeth Baer
Miami University

Marcia Halvorsen
University of Cincinnati

Peggy O'Kelly
Northeastern University

Mayda Shorney
University of Lowell

Questionnaire Respondents

David D. Bame
Pepperdine University

Gyan Chandra
Miami University

Alan E. Davis
Community College of
Philadelphia

Dean S. Eiteman
Wright State University

Albert H. Frakes
Washington State
University

Ralph M. Grieco
Northeastern University

Cynthia L. Holloway
Terrant County Junior
College

Thomas Largay
Husson College

Michael Lawrence
Portland Community
College

James Jay Mackie
Drexel University

Janet S. Omundson
University of Texas at
El Paso

Reginald N. Rezec
Texas Woman's
University

David Skougstad
Metropolitan State
College

Focus Groups Participants

David D. Bame
Pepperdine University

Peter E. Battelle
University of Vermont

Philip Conklin
Springfield College

Andrew J. DeMotses
Fairfield University

John P. Fertakis
Washington State
University

Robert R. Garrett
American River College

Leon J. Hanouille
Syracuse University

Judith A. Kamnikar
Auburn University at
Montgomery

Jerry G. Kreuze
Western Michigan
University

Anthony T. Krzystofik
University of
Massachusetts at
Amherst

Edward O. Lutz
Brooklyn College

Daniel M. Norris
Iowa State University

Donald F. Putnam
California State
Polytechnic University

Kent E. St. Pierre
James Madison
University

George M. Sanderson
Moorhead State
University

Scott Sandstrom
College of the Holy Cross

Stephen V. Senge
Western Washington
University

Hope J. Siino
Los Mendanos College

Jacob Wambsganss
University of South
Dakota

Design Survey Participants

Ron Burrows
University of Dayton

Willard C. Clark, Jr.
University of Dayton

John W. Devine
Murray State University

Kirsten M. Ely
University of California
at Los Angeles

Debbie Gilliard
Metropolitan State
College

Alan S. Glazer
Franklin and Marshall
College

Jack O. Hall, Jr.
Western Kentucky
University

Roger G. Hehman
University of Cincinnati

Ken Neet
Aims Community
College

Ron Summers, CPA
Oklahoma City
Community College

Philip H. Vorherr
University of Dayton

Brief Contents

Contents

PART TWO

ACCOUNTING FOR ASSETS AND LIABILITIES

PART THREE
BUSINESS ENTITIES

PART FOUR

FINANCIAL STATEMENTS: ADDITIONAL ASPECTS OF FINANCIAL REPORTING

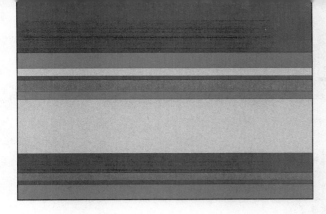

P A R T   O N E

THE ACCOUNTING PROCESS

1

Accounting: Its Uses, Principles, and Practices

LEARNING OBJECTIVES

1. Describe accounting and its use in decision making.

2. Identify the three types of business organizations.

3. State the basic concepts of accounting.

4. Explain the purpose of (a) an income statement, (b) a statement of cash flows, and (c) a balance sheet.

5. Define assets, liabilities, and owner's equity.

6. Explain the (a) accounting equation and (b) double entry rule.

7. Record balance sheet transactions.

8. Prepare a balance sheet.

9. Define generally accepted accounting principles (GAAP).

10. Describe the FASB conceptual framework and list its characteristics.

11. Identify the specialty areas of public accounting.

12. Identify the accounting activities of a managerial accountant.

The traditional joke, "old accountants never die, they just lose their balance," is as outdated as the image of an accountant wearing a green eyeshade and working at a dimly lit desk. Although some accounting still involves the computation of balances, a large part of accounting is the communication of information for use in many important decisions. There are now more than 700,000 professional accountants and they are engaged in several interesting areas of accounting specialties, many of which involve high levels of responsibility and may require national and worldwide travel.

We begin our study of accounting in this chapter by defining what accounting is and showing how accounting information affects decision making. Next we introduce some fundamental background information that is important for understanding the accounting process. Then we explore several basic practices in the accounting process. Finally we explain additional general concepts of accounting and the various areas of the accountancy profession.

Accounting and Decisions

To understand the role of accounting in business, we must know what accounting involves and when accounting is used in the decision-making process. These topics are discussed in this section.

Accounting Defined

1. Describe accounting and its use in decision making.

Accounting is an information system. It has been defined in many different ways and by combining these definitions we arrive at the following: **Accounting is the process of providing quantitative information about economic entities to aid users in making decisions concerning the allocation of economic resources.** This definition is quite long and can be best understood by briefly studying each phrase of the definition.

The process of providing means that there is a series of activities leading up to and including the communication of accounting information. These activities are (1) identifying the information, and then (2) measuring, (3) recording, (4) retaining, and (5) communicating it by means of an accounting system. *Quantitative* means that the information is communicated by using numbers; in accounting, numbers are usually numbers of *dollars*. *Economic entities* means that accounting not only applies to all types of businesses but also to churches, hospitals, charitable organizations, municipalities, governments, and other organizations.

Decisions concerning the allocation of economic resources include, among others, whether to buy, sell, or hold investments, whether to extend credit to a company desiring a loan, whether to manufacture and sell a particular product, or whether to modify the income tax regulations to stimulate business activities. Accounting information is used in making each of these decisions.

As suggested by the variety of decisions listed here, there are many *users* of accounting information. Users may be categorized into two groups, external users and internal users. **External users are persons and groups outside the business or other economic entity who need accounting information to decide**

whether or not to engage in some activity with the entity. They include individual investors, persons such as stockbrokers and financial analysts who offer investment assistance, consultants, bankers, suppliers, employees, labor unions, and the local, state, and federal governments. **Internal users are persons within the business or other economic entity who need accounting information to make decisions concerning the operations and activities of the entity.** These users include all levels of management, including departmental supervisors, divisional and regional managers, and "top management," in areas such as sales, advertising, production, personnel, finance, and computers.

Decision Making by Internal and External Users

Decision making, whether by external or internal users, can be viewed as a four-stage process as shown in Exhibit 1-1.

The first step for the decision maker is to recognize that a problem exists for which a decision must be made. For example, assume a company applies for a bank loan of a certain amount for a specified time. When this request is made the banker (an *external* user of accounting information) recognizes that a decision must be made about granting the loan. Or in the case of an *internal* user, a manager of the business may need to decide whether or not to manufacture and sell Product X.

The second step is to identify the alternatives. For the banker there are many alternatives, including refusing the bank loan, granting a loan of a smaller or greater amount for a shorter or longer time, or granting the loan as requested. For the internal manager the alternatives include not manufacturing and selling the product, manufacturing and selling a few units of the product, or manufacturing and selling many units.

The third step is to evaluate the alternatives. Accounting information is used for this purpose. The banker must have information concerning the cash in the checking and savings accounts of the business, the cash the business must spend to pay its bills and the amount it expects to collect from its customers, the timing of these payments and collections, and the way in which the bank loan would be used. By gathering the related accounting information the banker can evaluate whether the business needs the bank loan, the amount and length of time of the loan, and the likelihood that the loan will be repaid. For the manager, accounting information concerning the cost to manufacture and sell the product, the expected selling price and number of units sold, and the financial impact on the manufacture and sales of existing products must be known in order to evaluate the alternatives.

Once the alternatives have been evaluated a decision may be made. The banker makes the loan decision and the manager makes the product decision

EXHIBIT 1-1
Four Stages in
Decision Making

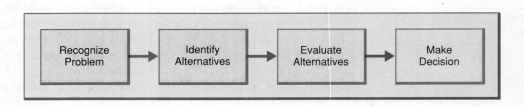

based, to a great extent, on the accounting information gathered in the *alternative evaluation* stage. Although these examples of decisions are overly simplified, we can see that accounting information is used by both internal and external users in the decision-making process.

Accounting Information and Decision Making

The role of accounting information in the decision-making process is further illustrated by Exhibit 1-2. This exhibit shows the interactive nature of the accounting process; that is, accounting information about economic entities is accumulated (identified, measured, recorded, and retained) and communicated to both internal and external users to assist them in decision making. Their decisions, in turn, have an impact on the economic entity, and the accounting information accumulation and communication process is repeated again. For the bank loan and product decisions, we can see that the decisions by both the internal and external users will affect the accounting information accumulated and communicated about the business. *Prior* to either decision, the information communicated would be the information needed to make the decisions as discussed earlier. *After* the decisions, whether or not the bank loan is granted and whether or not the product is manufactured and sold will change the future activities of the business and, in turn, result in different accounting information about the business.

EXHIBIT 1-2   Accounting Information and Decision Making

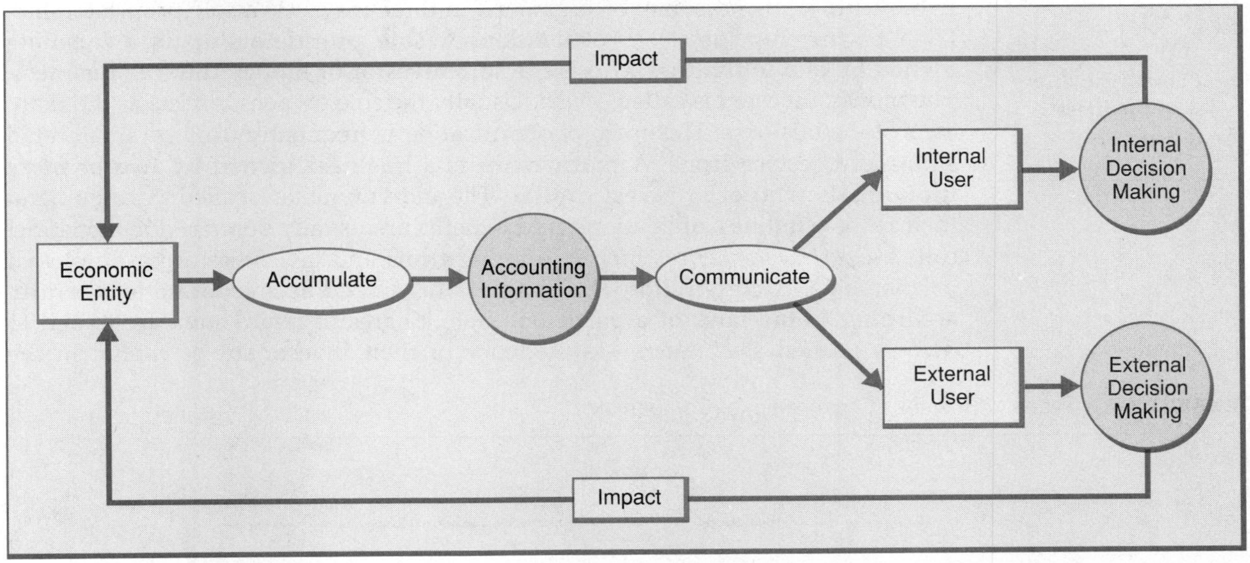

Fundamental Background Information

At this point we have a general understanding of the accounting process and the role of accounting information in decision making. Now we turn to the *fundamentals* to begin our study of the technical and conceptual aspects of accounting.

Accounting has been called the language of business. Throughout our early education, we learned the vocabulary and other basic elements of the English language so that we would be able to communicate effectively. The same is true for accounting. Many students using this textbook will not become accountants, although they may be employed by or own businesses, become managers, consultants, stockbrokers, bankers, or investors and will use accounting information. In order to understand and to use accounting information most effectively, they must have a solid grounding in its fundamentals. For students who plan to pursue a career in accounting, a thorough understanding of accounting fundamentals is needed for more advanced study. Thus the emphasis of this textbook is on the basics of accounting. An inquisitive mind, however, must also ask "why" and "why not," and these aspects of accounting information are discussed as well.

To orient our discussion we will narrow our study to business organizations, compare the meanings of the terms accounting and bookkeeping, identify the differences between financial and managerial accounting, and explain several basic concepts of accounting.

Business Organizations

2. Identify the three types of business organizations.

Although there are several types of organizations that prepare accounting information for use in decision making, the emphasis in this textbook is on business organizations. These organizations are a significant aspect of the United States economy and are intended to earn a profit for their owners. As shown in Exhibit 1-3, a business may be organized in three ways: (1) a sole proprietorship, (2) a partnership, or (3) a corporation. **A sole proprietorship is a business owned by one individual who is the sole investor of money into the business.** The money invested is called *capital*. Usually the sole owner also acts as the manager of the business. This form of organization is frequently used by small retail stores and service firms. **A partnership is a business owned by two or more individuals who each invest capital.** The individuals are called partners, and their responsibilities, obligations, and benefits are usually described in a contract called a *partnership agreement*. Accounting firms and law firms are examples of partnerships. **A corporation is a business organized as a separate legal entity according to the laws of a particular state.** Shares of *capital stock* are issued to owners—called *stockholders*—as evidence of their investment of capital in the

EXHIBIT 1-3 Types of Business Organizations (Companies)

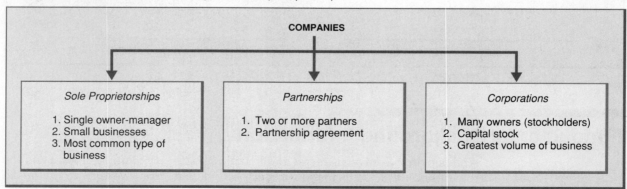

corporation; these shares are easily transferable. A corporation may be owned by a few or by many stockholders; certain large corporations have thousands of stockholders. Examples of large corporations are General Motors and IBM Corporation.

The sole proprietorship is the most common type of business because it is easiest to organize and simplest to operate. The corporation, on the other hand, has the greatest volume of business in the United States. Its organization and legal structure are complex, requiring complex accounting procedures as well as complex decision making by internal and external users. Most basic accounting principles apply to all types of businesses; therefore, in our discussion we use the general term *company* to apply to any business, unless the topic relates only to a specific type of business. In these cases we identify the type of business. *"Company" applies, therefore, to a sole proprietorship, partnership, or corporation.* Because the sole proprietorship is a simpler type of business, in the first part of the book we mainly study this type of business.

Accounting Versus Bookkeeping

The term *bookkeeping* has sometimes been confused with accounting. Accounting includes external and internal auditing, management advisory services, income tax planning and preparation of tax returns, budgeting, and the design and operation of an accounting system, as discussed later in the chapter. Recall that the accounting process includes several phases, including identifying, measuring, recording, retaining, and communicating information. **Bookkeeping is the process of recording accounting information for a company according to a standard set of steps.** Thus bookkeeping is only one phase (i.e., the *recording* phase) in the accounting process. A person who understands bookkeeping may not necessarily be knowledgeable about accounting, but an accountant must always have a thorough knowledge of bookkeeping. In addition, a user of accounting information will find a basic knowledge of bookkeeping helpful in understanding the accounting information about a company.

Differences Between Financial and Managerial Accounting

A common way of viewing accounting is to separate it into two types, financial accounting and managerial accounting. **Financial accounting is the aspect of accounting that involves the recording, accumulation, and communication of a company's accounting information for external users in their various decisions.** In contrast, **managerial accounting involves the recording, accumulation, and communication of a company's accounting information for internal users in their managerial decision making.**

Much accounting information that is useful to an external user in making a decision (e.g., whether or not to extend a bank loan to a company) is not useful to a manager within the company in making a decision (e.g., should a certain product be produced and sold). Thus one set of accounting information is prepared for the external user and another set is prepared for the internal user, although at least some of the accounting information needed by the internal user is also helpful to the external user, and vice versa. (For example, the product may not be produced unless there is sufficient money to do so, and the likelihood of repayment of the bank loan may depend upon current and future sales of the product.) The different external and internal needs for accounting information and the overlap of this information are characteristics of an accounting system. In this text, we discuss the relationship between financial and managerial accounting information.

Basic Concepts of Accounting

There are several basic concepts of accounting that you need to know to better understand the accounting process. These include:

1. **Transactions**
2. **Source documents**
3. **Monetary unit concept**
4. **Historical cost concept, and**
5. **Entity concept**

These items are explained here; more general concepts are discussed later in the chapter.

3. State the basic concepts of accounting.

Although not strictly concepts, business transactions and source documents are very important in the overall financial accounting process. The identification, measurement, and recording phases of the accounting process usually begin as a result of a business transaction. **A transaction is an exchange of property or services by a company with an external party.** For example, the purchase of office supplies by a company involves an exchange of cash for property (the supplies). Events or activities other than a transaction may be recorded in the accounting process; they are discussed later in the text.

A source document is a business record that serves as evidence that a transaction has occurred. A source document may be a canceled check, a sales receipt, a bill from a supplier, a bill sent to a customer, a payroll timecard, or a record of the miles driven in the company's delivery truck. Although the accounting process begins when a transaction occurs, identifying, measuring, and recording the accounting information are based on an analysis of the source document. For instance, a review of a check written by a company would show the date of the transaction, the dollar amount, the payee, and possibly the reason for the check. Several source documents may be used as evidence of a single transaction. In the early part of this textbook, as we discuss the accounting for various transactions, the source documents used in the analysis are identified.

In the exchange of property or services, a unit of exchange value is used. Information about these transactions must be recorded and communicated in a form that is understood by both external and internal users. This requirement has led to the concept of the monetary unit. **The monetary unit concept means that the results of transactions are recorded and communicated in monetary terms.** In the United States the monetary unit is the dollar, and therefore financial statements are expressed in dollars. In other countries the monetary unit is the national currency of the particular country. The use of a monetary unit does not stop the reporting of other important, but nonmonetary, information. This information may be expressed in numbers and descriptions as shown in later sections of this textbook.

Another important concept related to the monetary concept is the historical cost or, simply, the cost concept. **The historical cost concept means that transactions are recorded on the basis of the dollars exchanged (i.e., the cost) in the transaction,** as evidenced by the related source documents. Once a transaction is recorded the *cost* involved in the transaction is usually retained in the accounting records regardless of whether the *value* of the property or services owned increases (or decreases). For instance, a company may acquire land for $10,000. Several years later the land may have increased in value to $13,000. Under the historical cost concept the company would continue to show the land in its accounting records at $10,000, the acquisition cost.[1]

We noted earlier that individuals may own several types of companies, including sole proprietorships, partnerships, or corporations. Furthermore, one individual may own all or part of several companies. From an accounting standpoint each company is treated as a separate economic entity. **An entity is considered to be separate from its owners and from any other company.** Thus each company has its own accounting system and accounting records for identifying, measuring, recording, retaining, and communicating its accounting information. An owner's personal financial activities are *not* included within the accounting records of the company owned unless this activity has a *direct* impact upon the company. For instance, the purchase by an owner of an automobile for personal use would not affect the company's accounting records, but the purchase by the owner with personal funds of a delivery van to be used in the company would affect its records. We now turn to a discussion of the financial statements of a company.

Financial Statements

Companies operate to achieve various goals. They may be interested in providing a healthy work environment for their employees, in achieving a high level of pollution control, or in making contributions to civic and social organizations and activities. To meet these goals, however, a company must achieve two *primary* objectives: (1) to earn a satisfactory profit and (2) to remain solvent (be able to pay its debts). If a company fails to meet either of these primary objectives, it will not be able to survive in the long run. To earn a satisfactory profit, a company engages in earnings activities. *Earnings activities* involve acquiring and selling inventory (goods) or providing services to customers. *Remaining solvent* involves having cash on hand or having cash available through such items as bank loans to pay debts as they come due.

Financial statements are accounting reports used to summarize and communicate financial information about a company. Three major financial state-

---

[1]Later in the book we discuss the *supplemental* reporting of the effects of inflation and other "price level" changes. Until then, both the monetary unit and historical cost concepts are followed.

ments, the income statement, the statement of cash flows, and the balance sheet, are used to report information about the company's primary objectives discussed in the previous paragraph. These financial statements are the end product of the accounting system. Each of these statements summarizes certain information that has been identified, measured, recorded, and retained during the accounting process.

Income Statement

4(a). Explain the purpose of an income statement.

An income statement is a financial statement summarizing the results of a company's earnings activities for a specific time period. It shows the revenues, expenses, and net income (or net loss) of a company for this time period. *Revenues* are the prices charged to a company's customers for goods or services provided. *Expenses* are the costs of providing the goods or services. The *net income* is the excess of revenues over expenses; a *net loss* arises when expenses are more than revenues. An example of an income statement for one type of company is shown in Exhibit 1-4. We defer further discussion of the income statement until Chapter 3.

EXHIBIT 1-4
Income Statement

JACKSON ADVERTISING AGENCY Income Statement For Month Ended July 31, 1991		
Revenues:		
Advertising revenues		$44,000
Expenses:		
Rent expense	$ 9,600	
Salaries expense	11,700	
Office supplies expense	2,300	
Utilities expense	1,800	
Total expenses		(25,400)
Net income		$18,600

Statement of Cash Flows

4(b). Explain the purpose of a statement of cash flows.

A statement of cash flows is a financial statement summarizing a company's cash receipts, cash payments, and net change in cash for a specific time period, in a manner that reconciles the beginning and ending cash balances. The net cash provided by operating activities is summarized in the *net cash flow from operating activities* section of the statement. The cash receipts and cash payments for investing activities are summarized in the *cash flows from investing activities* section of the statement. The cash receipts and cash payments for financing activities are summarized in the *cash flows from financing activities* section of the statement. An example of the statement of cash flows for a company is shown in Exhibit 1-5. Because the preparation of a statement of cash flows requires a thorough understanding of the income statement and balance sheet, we defer further discussion until Chapter 18.

EXHIBIT 1-5
Statement of
Cash Flows

CROW SUPPLY COMPANY Statement of Cash Flows For Year Ended December 31, 1991		
Net Cash Flow from Operating Activities		
Net income	$ 13,200	
Adjustments for differences between net income and cash flows from operating activities:		
Add: Depreciation expense	4,700	
Net cash provided by operating activities		$17,900
Cash Flows from Investing Activities		
Payment for purchase of equipment	$(19,800)	
Proceeds from sale of land	3,100	
Net cash used for investing activities		(16,700)
Cash Flows from Financing Activities		
Proceeds from bank loan	$ 2,000	
Net cash provided by financing activities		2,000
Net Increase in Cash		$ 3,200
Cash, January 1, 1991		900
Cash, December 31, 1991		$ 4,100

Balance Sheet

4(c). Explain the purpose of a balance sheet.

A balance sheet summarizes a company's financial position on a given date. It is alternatively called a *statement of financial position*. A balance sheet lists the company's assets, liabilities, and owner's equity. A balance sheet for Turner's Laundry is shown in Exhibit 1-6. This balance sheet is discussed in more detail so that later we can explain the accounting process used in preparing the balance sheet.

Note that the balance sheet has a heading consisting of three lines: the name of the company, the title of the financial statement, and the date for which it was prepared. Note also that the balance sheet consists of three segments: the assets section, the liabilities section, and the owner's equity section. Finally observe that the information is expressed in monetary terms and that the total (indicated

EXHIBIT 1-6
Balance Sheet

TURNER'S LAUNDRY Balance Sheet December 31, 1991			
Assets		*Liabilities*	
Cash	$ 1,000	Accounts payable	$ 4,000
Laundry supplies	800	Notes payable	12,000
Prepaid insurance	700	Total Liabilities	$16,000
Land	9,000		
Building	21,000	*Owner's Equity*	
Laundry equipment	3,500	P. Turner, capital	$20,000
		Total Liabilities and	
Total Assets	$36,000	Owner's Equity	$36,000

by a double ruled line) of the assets ($36,000) is equal to the sum of the liabilities ($16,000) plus the owner's equity ($20,000). The balance sheet is so named, in fact, because both sides must be in balance (equal to each other).

5. Define assets, liabilities, and owner's equity.

Assets.   **Assets are the economic resources of a company that are expected to provide future benefits to the company.** A company may own many assets, some of which are physical in nature such as land, buildings, supplies to be used in the business, and goods (*inventory*) that the company expects to sell to its customers. Other assets do not possess physical characteristics but are economic resources because of the legal rights they convey to the company. These assets include, for example, amounts owed by customers to the company (*accounts receivable*), the right to insurance protection (*prepaid insurance*), and investments made in other companies.

Liabilities.   **Liabilities are the economic obligations (debts) of the company.** The external parties to whom the economic obligations are owed are referred to as the *creditors* of the company. Legal documents often serve as evidence of liabilities. These documents establish a claim (*equity*) by the creditors (the *creditors' equity*) against the assets of the company. Liabilities include such items as amounts owed to suppliers (*accounts payable*), amounts owed to employees for wages (*wages payable*), taxes payable, and mortgages owed on the company's property. A company may also borrow money from a bank on a short- or long-term basis by signing a legal document called a *note,* which specifies the terms of the loan. Amounts of such loans would be listed as *notes payable.*

Owner's Equity.   **The owner's equity of a company is the owner's current investment in the assets of the company.**[2] (For a partnership, the owners' equity might be referred to as the *partners' equity;* for a corporation, *stockholders' equity.*) As is shown later the owner's equity is affected by the capital (assets) invested into the company by the owner, by the company's earnings from its operations, and by withdrawals of capital (assets) by the owner from the company. For a sole proprietorship, the owner's equity is shown by listing the owner's name, the word *capital,* and the amount of the current investment. The owners' equity of a partnership (partners' equity) and of a corporation (stockholders' equity) is shown slightly differently as discussed later. Owner's equity is sometimes referred to as *residual equity* because creditors have first legal claim to a company's assets. Once the creditors' claims have been satisfied, the owner is entitled to the remainder (residual) of the assets. Sometimes the total of the liabilities (creditors' equity) is combined with the owner's equity and the result is referred to as the *total equity* of the company.

---

[2]Because we focus primarily on sole proprietorships in the first part of this text, the singular *owner's* equity is usually used throughout the early chapters. Generally the discussion is equally applicable to partnerships and corporations, in which case the plural *owners' equity* is appropriate.

Accounting Equation and Double Entry Rule

We now turn to a discussion of the accounting process leading up to a balance sheet. As noted on the Turner's Laundry balance sheet shown in Exhibit 1-6, the total of the assets is equal to the total of the liabilities plus the owner's equity. This is true for any balance sheet because **a company's economic resources are financed either by its creditors or by its owners.** As a result two concepts are important in the recording and reporting of accounting information. These concepts are the accounting equation and the double entry rule.

Accounting Equation

The equality of the assets to the liabilities plus owner's equity may be shown in equation form. **The basic** *accounting equation* **(sometimes referred to as the** *balance sheet equation*) **is as follows:**

$$\text{Assets} = \text{Liabilities} + \text{Owner's Equity}$$

6(a). Explain the accounting equation.

In the case of Turner's Laundry, the equation in monetary terms is:

$$\$36,000 = \$16,000 + \$20,000$$

Like any equation, the components may be transposed. A common way of showing the equation is:

$$\text{Assets} - \text{Liabilities} = \text{Owner's Equity}$$

or

$$\$36,000 - \$16,000 = \$20,000$$

In this form of the equation, the left-hand side (i.e., assets minus liabilities) is referred to as the *net assets*. In this book we will use the first form of the equation. Regardless of what form of the equation is used, **the accounting equation must always remain in balance—the two sides must always be equal.** This equality rule is one of the basic rules in accounting. Since a transaction normally begins the accounting process, each transaction must be recorded so that this equality is maintained.

Double Entry Rule

6(a). Explain the double entry rule.

A second rule, which complements the equality rule, is the double entry rule. **The double entry rule means that in recording a transaction at least two changes must be made in the assets, liabilities, or owner's equity.** These changes are made as *entries* in the accounting records; thus a double entry must always be made. For instance, if the owner invested $20,000 into the company, assets (cash) would be increased by $20,000 and owner's equity (owner's capital) would be increased by $20,000. The double entry rule is observed and the accounting equation is in balance.

The rule about a double entry does not mean that a transaction will always affect both sides of the equation—or even two components of the equation. For example, a transaction may affect only one side by increasing one asset and decreasing another asset for the same amount. A transaction could also affect only the right side. The rule does not specify in which direction a change is made. The left and right side totals may increase, decrease, or even remain the same. If assets and liabilities both go up, for example, the total of the equation increases, and if both go down, it decreases. But if one asset increases and another asset decreases, the total assets remain unchanged. It is essential, however, that the accounting equation as a whole remains in balance after the transaction.

The balance sheet shows the equality of the accounting equation. A balance sheet can be prepared at any point in the operations of a company, even following each transaction, and it should *always* show total assets equal to the total of the liabilities and owner's equity.

Example of Recording Transactions

7. Record balance sheet transactions.

Let us assume that Anne Dixon opens a travel agency on January 1, 1991, by writing a $30,000 personal check and depositing the money in the checking account of the Dixon Travel Agency. This company checking account is separate, of course, from her personal account because of the entity concept. She decides to establish a simple accounting system by listing assets, liabilities, and owner's equity as headings of separate columns with subheadings for specific kinds of assets, liabilities, and owner's equity. Each transaction is recorded by entering the amounts in the appropriate columns. The source documents for the first transaction are Anne Dixon's check and the receipt issued by the Dixon Travel Agency to Dixon for her check. Anne Dixon's check does *not* serve as the only source document for the Dixon Travel Agency because the company's records are kept separate from the owner's, in accordance with the entity concept. This transaction is recorded as follows:

Trans.	Date	Assets Cash	=	Liabilities	+	Owner's Equity A. Dixon, Capital
(1)	1/1/1991	+$30,000	=			+$30,000

As a result of this first transaction the company now has an asset, Cash, worth $30,000 and owner's equity, A. Dixon, Capital, shows the $30,000 investment by the owner. Note that two entries were made to record this transaction—one to an asset and one to owner's equity—and that the accounting equation is in balance because both sides of the equation were increased by the same amount.

To conduct its operations, the Dixon Travel Agency purchased land for $3,000 and a small office building for $15,000 on January 2, 1991, paying $18,000 cash. Since such a major cash outlay is paid by check, the Dixon Travel Agency check and the legal documents relating to the purchase of the land and building serve as the source documents for this transaction. This second transaction is recorded as follows:

		Assets			=	Liabilities	+	Owner's Equity
Trans.	Date	Cash	Land	Building				A. Dixon, Capital
(1)	1/1/1991	+$30,000						+$30,000
(2)	1/2/1991	− 18,000	+$3,000	+$15,000				
		$12,000 +	$3,000 +	$15,000	=	-0-	+	$30,000

The land and building are economic resources expected to provide future benefits to the company by providing parking and space for conducting its business. As a result the land and buildings are separate assets and are recorded as increases in the new assets, Land and Building, for $3,000 and $15,000, respectively. Because cash was paid out, the asset Cash must be decreased by the total amount paid, $18,000. This amount is subtracted from the previous amount of Cash to show the new amount, $12,000. After recording the transaction, the accounting equation must be checked to see that it remains in balance. This is done by adding the assets ($12,000 + $3,000 + $15,000) and comparing this figure to the total of the liabilities ($0) plus owner's equity ($30,000). Thus the balance is maintained.

On January 5, 1991, Dixon Travel Agency purchased $700 of office supplies from City Supply Company, agreeing to pay for half the supplies on January 15 and the remainder on February 15. The *invoice* (a document listing the items purchased, the cost of each item, and the total cost) received with the supplies is the source document for the information recorded as follows:

		Assets				=	Liabilities	+	Owner's Equity
Trans.	Date	Cash	Land	Building	Office Supplies		Accts. Payable		A. Dixon, Capital
(1)	1/1/1991	+$30,000							+$30,000
(2)	1/2/1991	− 18,000	+$3,000	+$15,000					
(3)	1/5/1991				+$700		+$700		
		$12,000 +	$3,000 +	$15,000 +	$700	=	$700	+	$30,000

Because the office supplies will be used to conduct business, they are recorded as an asset, Office Supplies. This asset is increased by $700. Cash is not reduced, however, because none was paid out. Since Dixon Travel Agency has agreed to pay for half of the supplies on January 15 and the remainder on February 15, it has incurred a debt, or a liability. The liability is labeled Accounts Payable—because it is an amount to be paid by the company—and is increased for the total amount ($700). Note that the increase in the company's assets was financed by a creditor (the supply company), not the owner. As a result no change was recorded in owner's equity. The accounting equation must remain in balance, however, and therefore the increase in assets on the left side is matched by an increase in liabilities on the right side. Also note that the total of the assets remains equal to the total of the liabilities and owner's equity.

On January 12, 1991, Dixon Travel Agency purchased office equipment from Ace Equipment Company at a cost of $3,000. It paid $1,000 down and signed a note, agreeing to pay the remaining $2,000 at the end of one year. The invoice, check, and note are used to record this fourth transaction as follows:

				Assets			=	Liabilities		+	Owner's Equity
Trans.	Date	Cash	Land	Building	Office Supplies	Office Equipment		Accts. Payable	Notes Payable		A. Dixon, Capital
(1)	1/1/1991	+$30,000									+$30,000
(2)	1/2/1991	− 18,000	+$3,000	+$15,000							
(3)	1/5/1991				+$700			+$700			
(4)	1/12/1991	− 1,000				+$3,000			+$2,000		
		$11,000 +	$3,000 +	$15,000 +	$700 +	$3,000	=	$700 +	$2,000 +		$30,000

Because the office equipment is an economic resource to be used in the business, the asset, Office Equipment, is increased by the total cost of $3,000. The asset Cash is decreased by the amount paid, $1,000. Since a $2,000 liability is incurred and a legal note has been issued, the liability, Notes Payable, is increased by this amount. Observe that this transaction affected two assets and a liability but the accounting equation remains in balance.

On January 15, 1991, Dixon Travel Agency paid the City Supply Company half the amount owed for the supplies purchased on January 5, 1991, by issuing a check for $350. This fifth transaction is recorded as follows:

				Assets			=	Liabilities		+	Owner's Equity
Trans.	Date	Cash	Land	Building	Office Supplies	Office Equipment		Accts. Payable	Notes Payable		A. Dixon, Capital
(1)	1/1/1991	+$30,000									+$30,000
(2)	1/2/1991	− 18,000	+$3,000	+$15,000							
(3)	1/5/1991				+$700			+$700			
(4)	1/12/1991	− 1,000				+$3,000			+$2,000		
(5)	1/15/1991	− 350						− 350			
		$10,650 +	$3,000 +	$15,000 +	$700 +	$3,000	=	$350 +	$2,000 +		$30,000

Because the debt owed to City Supply Company was reduced, the liability Accounts Payable was decreased by $350. Because the company made a cash outlay, the asset Cash was decreased by $350. This transaction caused a decrease of the same amount in both sides of the accounting equation, and therefore the equation remained in balance.

Finally, on January 28, 1991, the Dixon Travel Agency decided that it did not need a desk that it had purchased on January 12. This desk had cost $400 and it was sold for this price to James Baker, an insurance agent, for use in his office. The insurance agency agreed to pay for the desk on February 7. This sixth transaction is recorded as follows:

Trans.	Date	Cash	Land	Building	Office Supplies	Office Equip.	Accts. Rec.	Accts. Payable	Notes Payable	A. Dixon, Capital
					Assets			= Liabilities	+	Owner's Equity
(1)	1/1/1991	+$30,000								+$30,000
(2)	1/2/1991	− 18,000	+$3,000	+$15,000						
(3)	1/5/1991				+$700			+$700		
(4)	1/12/1991	− 1,000				+$3,000			+$2,000	
(5)	1/15/1991	− 350						− 350		
(6)	**1/28/1991**					− 400	+$400			
Balances	1/31/1991	$10,650 +	$3,000 +	$15,000 +	$700 +	$2,600 +	$400 =	$350 +	$2,000 +	$30,000

Because the company sold one of its economic resources, the asset Office Equipment is decreased by $400, the cost of the desk. Since the amount to be received from the agent in February is a different economic resource for the Dixon Travel Agency, it also records an increase of $400 in the asset, Accounts Receivable. Again, note the equality of the accounting equation.

We have now recorded six typical transactions for the Dixon Travel Agency. In each case we identified, measured, recorded, and retained the monetary information from the transactions. Our accounting system now contains all the information relating to the company's financial position at the end of January. We can now summarize and communicate this information in a balance sheet. The January 31, 1991, balance sheet of the Dixon Travel Agency is shown in Exhibit 1-7.

EXHIBIT 1-7
Balance Sheet

DIXON TRAVEL AGENCY
Balance Sheet
January 31, 1991

Assets		Liabilities	
Cash	$10,650	Accounts payable	$ 350
Accounts receivable	400	Notes payable	2,000
Office supplies	700	Total Liabilities	$ 2,350
Land	3,000	*Owner's Equity*	
Building	15,000	A. Dixon, capital	$30,000
Office equipment	2,600	Total Liabilities and	
Total Assets	$32,350	Owner's Equity	$32,350

8. Prepare a balance sheet.

The balance sheet lists the ending amounts for each item of assets, liabilities, and owner's equity recorded in the accounting system. Although Accounts Receivable was the last column in the assets section of our simple accounting system, the ending amount of Accounts Receivable is shown directly after Cash on the balance sheet. This procedure is typical because assets are listed in the order of their liquidity. *Liquidity* is the ease of converting assets into cash. Office supplies are listed next because they will be used in the business more quickly than the land, building, or office equipment. As we noted throughout the example, in recording each transaction the double entry rule was followed to maintain the equality of the accounting equation. The result is that total assets ($32,350) are equal to the total of the liabilities ($2,350) and the owner's equity ($30,000).

In the Dixon Travel Agency example, for simplicity we assumed that the company did not engage in any earnings activities. In addition, we studied only basic balance sheet transactions. In the next chapter we introduce more complex transactions involving balance sheet items. Income statement transactions are introduced in Chapter 3. At this point you should be familiar with the basic concepts and principles underlying the accounting process, as well as the elementary procedures involved in completing this process. We now turn to a discussion of several broad concepts.

General Principles and Concepts of Financial Accounting

9. Define generally accepted accounting principles.

Earlier we introduced several concepts basic to the accounting process. Accounting, however, is a dynamic and growing field, keeping pace with the rapidly changing business and economic environment. Over the years, because of the activities of several professional accounting organizations, a set of broad guidelines for financial accounting has evolved. These guidelines are referred to as generally accepted accounting principles. **Generally accepted accounting principles, or GAAP, are the currently acceptable principles, procedures, and practices that should be used for financial accounting.**

Organizations Influential in Establishing GAAP

The organizations that have had a significant influence in establishing generally accepted accounting principles in the United States are the American Institute of Certified Public Accountants (AICPA), the Financial Accounting Standards Board (FASB), the Securities and Exchange Commission (SEC), the Governmental Accounting Standards Board (GASB), and the Cost Accounting Standards Board (CASB).

The AICPA is the national professional association of CPAs. In 1938 the AICPA formed the Committee on Accounting Procedures, which issued fifty-one *Accounting Research Bulletins* identifying GAAP. This committee was replaced in 1959 by the Accounting Principles Board (APB) of the AICPA. The APB issued thirty-one *APB Opinions* before it was phased out in 1973. At that time the FASB was created as an independent board of professionals experienced in accounting. The FASB currently establishes GAAP for companies; as of July 1, 1989 the FASB had issued 102 *Statements of Financial Accounting Standards*, 38 *Interpretations*, and

6 *Statements of Financial Accounting Concepts.* The SEC is an agency of the federal government created to administer legislation (including the filing of certain accounting reports) concerning the initial sale and later trading of corporate securities. The SEC establishes accounting principles in its *Financial Reporting Releases.* The GASB establishes accounting principles for state and local governments by issuing *Statements of Governmental Accounting Standards.* The CASB establishes accounting principles for defense contracts with the U.S. government by issuing *Cost Accounting Standards.*

Most of these pronouncements involving generally accepted accounting principles are still in effect, and many of them are complex and very technical in nature. As we discuss specific accounting issues in this textbook, the applicable generally accepted accounting principles are summarized in a manner that is easily understood. In addition, only the basic aspects of generally accepted accounting principles are introduced. It is important to recognize, however, that these principles do change; they are modified as business practices and decisions change and as better accounting techniques are developed. Before we discuss the specific principles in the rest of the book, an explanation of several general underlying concepts of financial accounting is useful.

Conceptual Framework

10. Describe the FASB conceptual framework and list its characteristics.

As an aid in establishing generally accepted accounting principles, the FASB has established a conceptual framework. **The FASB conceptual framework is a theoretical foundation of concepts intended to provide a logical structure for financial accounting.** In this conceptual framework, the general objective of financial accounting is to provide information that is useful to external users as they make decisions. Therefore, **decision usefulness is the primary purpose of financial accounting information.** To be useful, financial accounting information must be relevant and reliable. Closely related to relevance and reliability are materiality and validity. These general concepts are discussed next and illustrated in Exhibit 1-8 along with the basic concepts explained earlier.

EXHIBIT 1-8
General Concepts
Affecting Useful
Financial Accounting
Information

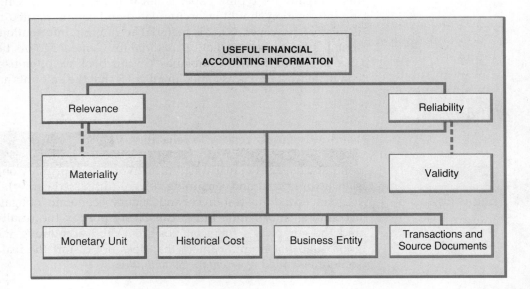

Relevance

The accounting information communicated to users must be relevant to their decision-making process. **Relevance is the capacity to influence a user's decision.** As we saw in the bank loan decision discussed earlier, the amount of cash in the company's checking and savings account and the cash it expected to collect and to pay were relevant information for the banker's decision. On the other hand, the cost of the typewriters owned by the company is probably not relevant to the banker and this accounting information would not be communicated. Relevance is a very important concept to be considered in accumulating and communicating accounting information.

Reliability

In their decision-making process users must have confidence that the information they are using is reliable. **Reliable accounting information is factual and capable of being verified.** Reliability does not necessarily imply certainty. For instance, estimates can be reliable. Source documents and recorded transactions (discussed earlier) play an important part in establishing and confirming the reliability of accounting information in the *auditing* process (discussed later). To evaluate the fairness of a company's financial statements, an auditor verifies that the recorded transactions are supported by evidence in the form of source documents so that the resulting reported information is reliable.

Materiality

Materiality is like relevance in that both concepts are defined in terms of what influences or makes a difference to a user of accounting information. **Materiality is the concept that accounting information is useful when the monetary amount involved is large enough to make a difference in a user's decision.** Thus in the bank loan decision the amount of cash to be paid by the company for its employees' wages is material to the banker's decision. The cash to be paid by the company for typing paper is not material, however. Only material accounting information should be accumulated and communicated to users. Materiality is relative, however. What is material accounting information about a local automobile parts store may not be material for General Motors because of the difference in size of the two companies. (In this book we often use small numbers for convenience, but it is assumed in all cases that the amounts are material.)

Validity

Validity is closely related to reliability. **Validity is the concept that accounting information presents a realistic picture of what it is meant to represent.** A company engages in many activities involving its primary objectives of earning a satisfactory profit and remaining solvent (discussed earlier). To do so it acquires various economic resources and incurs economic obligations. To be valid, accounting information must realistically portray the results of these activities and the company's financial position. Valid accounting information is like a good snapshot from a camera that does not distort the real picture. Validity is sometimes called *representational faithfulness*.

Relationship Among Concepts of Financial Accounting

We have discussed several important general and basic concepts of financial accounting that affect the information accumulated and communicated in the accounting process. These concepts were presented in Exhibit 1-8 and should be kept in mind as we discuss the accounting process. Not all of the concepts affecting financial accounting have been introduced here; others will be presented as they apply to topics discussed later in the book. We now turn to a discussion of the accountancy profession.

The Accountancy Profession

Accountancy has emerged as a profession, alongside the professions of medicine and law. The study and practice of accountancy require a broad understanding of concepts in such areas as business, economics, sociology, psychology, and public administration as well as in-depth knowledge of specialized accounting areas. The two main fields of accountancy include (1) public accounting and (2) managerial accounting, each of which has several accounting specialty areas. These areas are summarized in Exhibit 1-9 and briefly discussed here, along with the accounting activities in governmental and quasi-governmental organizations.

EXHIBIT 1-9
The Accountancy Profession

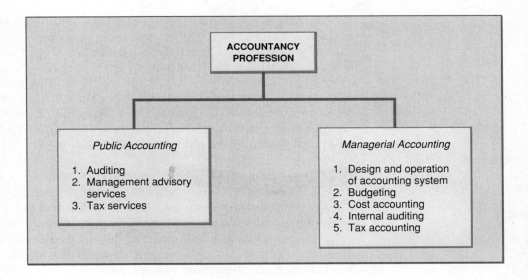

Public Accounting

A public accountant is an independent professional who provides accounting services to clients for a fee. Most of them are **certified public accountants** (CPAs), having met certain state requirements. In order to practice accountancy, each CPA must hold a license issued by the state in which the CPA works. Licensing is designed to help to ensure that high-quality, professional service is provided by accountants. Although the licensing requirements vary from state to state, all CPAs must pass the Uniform CPA Examination, a national examination given by the AICPA twice a year across the United States. In addition, states often have minimum educational and practical experience requirements. Several specialty areas of public accounting are discussed next.

11. Identify the specialty areas of public accounting.

Auditing.   Accounting information may be communicated in many different ways. One way is through the issuance of financial statements. Both the New York Stock Exchange and the American Stock Exchange, as well as the Securities and Exchange Commission, require certain companies to issue an annual report. **An annual report is a report published by a company once a year that contains its audited financial statements.** In addition, banks may require a company to provide its audited financial statements when applying for a loan. Other types of economic entities, such as universities and charitable organizations, also issue audited financial statements.

Auditing involves examining the accounting records of a company and the resulting financial statements to attest to the fairness of the accounting information in the financial statements. Auditing is necessary because financial statements are prepared by the management of the company issuing the statements. Because of the potential bias of management, external users of the financial statements need assurance that the statements present fairly the accounting information about the company. Consequently, these financial statements must be audited by an *independent* CPA because a CPA is the only person licensed to do so.

Auditing is the primary professional service offered by a CPA, who is an independent and unbiased observer. Based upon the evidence gathered in the auditing process, the CPA expresses a professional opinion as to the fairness of the financial statements. Because many external users rely on the CPA's opinion, auditing plays an important role in society. Most CPAs work in CPA firms, and auditing is done by many local and regional CPA firms. In addition, the large size of many companies, some of which span the United States as well as the world in their activities, has led to the growth of large CPA firms with offices in most major United States and international cities.

Management Advisory Services.   During an audit by a CPA firm, a careful study is made of the accounting records kept by the company, which are part of its *management information system.* Thus the CPA firm has a good knowledge of the strengths and weaknesses of the operating activities and information system of the company. In addition to auditing departments, many CPA firms have separate management advisory services departments to offer organizations constructive criticism about how to improve their internal operations, and to conduct special studies to aid management in their various activities.

Management advisory services in CPA firms include the design or improvement of the financial accounting system for identifying, measuring, recording, retaining, and reporting accounting information. These services also may include assistance in developing cost control systems, planning manufacturing facilities, and installing computer operations. Providing these services requires CPA firms to hire people with specialties other than accounting, for example, lawyers, industrial engineers, and systems analysts.

Tax Services. The federal government as well as most state governments require the filing of income tax returns and the payment of taxes. Because of the high tax rates, complex tax regulations, and special tax incentives today, most companies (and individuals) can benefit from carefully planning their activities to minimize or postpone their tax payments. Many CPA firms have separate tax services departments that employ tax professionals who are experts in the various federal and state tax regulations to assist these companies and individuals in tax planning. Similarly, company or individual income tax returns, reflecting the results of these tax planning activities, are frequently prepared by the tax services department of the CPA firms.

Managerial Accounting

A managerial accountant is employed by a company to perform its internal (managerial) accounting activities. A high-level manager usually coordinates these activities. This manager frequently reports directly to the top management of the organization such as the vice president of finance, which is an indication of how important the accounting functions are to the company's operations.

Another indication of the importance of managerial accounting is the Certificate in Management Accounting (CMA). The CMA is granted to persons who meet specific educational and professional standards and who pass a uniform CMA examination, administered twice yearly by the Institute of Management Accounting of the National Association of Accountants. Although the CMA is not required as a license to practice, accountants holding the CMA are recognized as professional experts in the area of managerial accounting.

Managerial accounting activities encompass several areas: (1) design and operation of accounting systems, (2) budgeting, (3) cost accounting, (4) internal auditing, and (5) tax accounting. Each of these areas is briefly discussed here.

12. Identify the accounting activities of a managerial accountant.

Design and Operation of Accounting System. **An accounting system is a means by which accounting information about a company's activities is identified, measured, recorded, and retained so that it can be reported in an accounting statement.** One duty of the managerial accountant is to design and operate a company's accounting system. This function is sometimes referred to as *general accounting* because of the wide variety of activities involved. These activities include, among others, determining the portion of the accounting system that will be manually or computer operated, integrating the accounting activities for different departments, and designing accounting procedures, forms, and reports.

Budgeting. The management of a company includes two functions: planning and controlling. *Planning* means developing a plan of action for the short-, mid-, and long-term future of the company. **Budgeting is the process of quantifying the plans of management to show their impact on the company's operating activities.** The quantification of a plan is known as a *budget* (or *forecast*). Frequently included in a budget are *forecasted* (or *projected*) financial statements. *Controlling* is the process of making sure, to the extent that is reasonable, that the actual operations of the various parts of the company achieve the established plans. As an aid in the control function, another aspect of budgeting is the frequent comparison of actual quantified results to the budget so that differences between actual and planned results may be seen and corrective action may be taken when necessary.

Cost Accounting. **Cost accounting is the process of determining and accumulating the costs of certain activities within a company.** Cost accounting is primarily concerned with product costs, that is, determining the cost of producing a unit of a product. Cost accounting may also involve calculating the cost of operating a particular department, a manufacturing process, or a marketing technique.

Internal Auditing. One part of the design of an accounting system is establishing good internal control. **Internal control involves the procedures to safeguard a company's economic resources and to promote the efficient and effective operation of its accounting system.** Internal auditing is a part of the internal control procedures and reviews operations to ensure that these procedures are being followed throughout the company. Internal auditing is becoming increasingly important because the procedures for the external audit depend, to a great degree, on the quality of the internal control. As evidence of professionalism in internal auditing, an accountant may earn a Certificate of Internal Auditing (CIA) awarded by the Institute of Internal Auditors, Inc. Although it is not a license to practice, the certificate states that the holder has met strict educational and practical experience requirements and has passed a uniform CIA examination.

Tax Accounting. Although companies often assign their tax work to the tax services department of a CPA firm, many of them still maintain their own tax departments. This department is staffed by accountants with expertise in the tax laws relating to the company. These accountants handle income tax planning and the preparation of state and federal income tax returns. They also work on real estate taxes, personal property taxes, such as taxes on inventories, and other taxes.

Governmental and Quasi-Governmental Accounting

Certain governmental and quasi-governmental agencies also employ accountants. The Internal Revenue Service (IRS) is responsible for administering the collection of federal income taxes. State revenue agencies also perform similar functions. Administrators of other federal, state, and local government agencies are responsible for the control of both tax revenues and tax expenditures. Accountants are hired by these agencies to provide accounting information for use in the administration of these activities.

Administrators of federal, state, municipal, and other not-for-profit organizations such as colleges and universities, hospitals, and mental health agencies are responsible for their efficient and effective operations. The accounting information needed by these organizations is similar to that needed by companies. But because they are not-for-profit organizations financed in part by public funds, they are required to use somewhat different accounting procedures (sometimes called *fund* accounting). Accountants hired by these organizations design and operate their accounting systems.

Several other governmental organizations are involved in accounting activities. The Securities and Exchange Commission (SEC) has the responsibility of overseeing the financial statements of certain companies and has the legal authority to establish accounting regulations for them. The SEC employs accountants to identify appropriate accounting procedures and to verify that existing regulations are being followed. The General Accounting Office (GAO) has the responsibility of cooperating with various agencies of the federal government in the development and operation of their accounting systems to improve the management of these agencies. Other federal and state agencies, such as the Interstate Commerce Commission, the Environmental Protection Agency, and the Federal Communications Commission, also prepare and use accounting information.

You should now have a general understanding of the accounting process and the role of accounting information in users' decision making. You should also be familiar with the general and basic concepts and practices of an accounting system, as well as the specialty areas needed to satisfy users' needs. In the next chapter we will expand our discussion of the components of an accounting system for processing accounting information.

Chapter Summary

Review of Learning Objectives

1. **Describe accounting and its use in decision making.**

   Accounting is the process of providing quantitative information about economic entities to aid users in making decisions concerning the allocation of economic resources. The activities of accounting include identifying, measuring, recording, retaining, and communicating quantitative information. Economic entities include both businesses and other organizations. Users include both external users (outside the economic entity) and internal users (inside the entity). Allocation decisions include, for example, whether to buy, sell, or hold investments (external user), and whether to manufacture and produce a product (internal user).

2. **Identify the three types of business organizations.**

   The three types of business organizations are: (1) *sole proprietorship,* owned by one individual, (2) *partnership,* owned by two or more individuals (partners), and (3) *corporation,* incorporated as separate legal entity and owned by numerous stockholders who hold capital stock in the corporation.

3. **State the basic concepts of accounting.**

   The basic concepts include: (1) *transactions,* which are exchanges of property or services by a company with an external party; (2) *source documents,* which are business records that serve as evidence that transactions have occurred; (3) *monetary unit concept,* which means that the results of transactions are recorded and communicated in monetary terms; (4) *historical cost concept,* which means that transactions are recorded on the basis of the dollars exchanged; and (5) *entity concept*, which means that a company is considered to be separate from its owners and from any other company.

4. **Explain the purpose of (a) an income statement, (b) a statement of cash flows, and (c) a balance sheet.**
Financial statements are accounting reports used to summarize and communicate financial information about a company. There are three major financial statements. An *income statement* summarizes the results of a company's earnings activities for a specific time period. A *statement of cash flows* summarizes a company's cash receipts, cash payments, and net change in cash for a specific time period. A *balance sheet* summarizes a company's financial position on a given date.

5. **Define assets, liabilities, and owner's equity.**
Assets are the economic resources of a company that are expected to provide future benefits to the company. *Liabilities* are the economic obligations (debts) of the company. The *owner's equity* of a company is the owner's current investment in the assets of the company.

6. **Explain the (a) accounting equation and (b) double entry rule.**
The *accounting equation* is: Assets = Liabilities + Owner's Equity. This equation must always remain in balance (i.e., the two sides must always be equal) whenever accounting information is recorded and reported. The *double entry rule* means that in recording a transaction at least two changes (entries) must be made in the assets, liabilities, or owner's equity. By following the double entry rule, the accounting equation will always remain in balance.

7. **Record balance sheet transactions.**
For each transaction, identify which asset, liability, or owner's equity items are affected. Record the date and list the dollar amount of increase or decrease in the related asset, liability, or owner's equity item. Be sure that the double entry rule is followed so that the accounting equation remains in balance.

8. **Prepare a balance sheet.**
To prepare a balance sheet, first list the heading consisting of the company name, title (balance sheet), and date. Then on the left side list the asset items and their amounts according to their liquidity. Sum these amounts to determine the total assets. Next, on the right side list the liability items and their amounts. Sum these amounts to determine the total liabilities. Finally, list the owner's equity amount and add it to the total liabilities to determine the amount of total liabilities and owner's equity. This amount must be equal to the total assets.

9. **Define generally accepted accounting principles (GAAP).**
Generally accepted accounting principles (GAAP) are the currently acceptable principles, procedures, and practices that should be used in financial accounting.

10. **Describe the FASB conceptual framework and list its characteristics.**
The FASB conceptual framework is a set of concepts that provide a logical

structure for financial accounting. The primary purpose of financial accounting is to provide information that has decision usefulness to external users. To be useful, accounting information must be relevant and reliable as well as material and valid. In addition, accounting information must be based on transactions and source documents, and communicated in dollar amounts recorded on the basis of historical cost.

 11. **Identify the specialty areas of public accounting.**
Public accounting is performed by certified public accountants (CPAs) and includes auditing, management advisory services, and tax services.

 12. **Identify the accounting activities of a managerial accountant.**
A managerial accountant is employed by a company to perform its internal accounting activities. These activities include the design and operation of the company's accounting system, budgeting, cost accounting, internal auditing, and tax accounting.

Review Problem

On December 31, 1991, the following alphabetical list of items was contained in the records of the Chriszim Company:

Accounts payable	$ 4,000
Accounts receivable	3,700
Cash	2,600
Building	25,000
Equipment	10,400
G. Chriszim, capital	27,000
Land	7,000
Notes payable	20,000
Prepaid insurance	1,000
Supplies	1,300

REQUIRED Prepare a December 31, 1991, balance sheet for the Chriszim Company.

Solution to Review Problem

CHRISZIM COMPANY
Balance Sheet
December 31, 1991

Assets		Liabilities	
Cash	$ 2,600	Accounts payable	$ 4,000
Accounts receivable	3,700	Notes payable	20,000
Supplies	1,300	Total Liabilities	$24,000
Prepaid insurance	1,000		
Land	7,000	*Owner's Equity*	
Building	25,000	G. Chriszim, capital	$27,000
Equipment	10,400	Total Liabilities and	
Total Assets	$51,000	Owner's Equity	$51,000

Glossary

Accounting. The process of providing quantitative information about economic entities to aid users in making decisions. *Financial accounting* provides accounting information for external users. *Managerial accounting* provides accounting information for internal users.

Accounting Equation. Assets = Liabilities + Owner's Equity. This equation must always remain in balance (the two sides must always be equal).

Accounting System. Means by which accounting information is identified, measured, recorded, and retained so that it can be reported in an accounting statement.

Accounts Payable. Liability showing amounts owed *by* a company to its suppliers.

Accounts Receivable. Asset showing amounts owed *to* a company by its customers.

Annual Report. A yearly report published by a company that contains its audited financial statements.

Assets. Economic resources of a company that are expected to provide future benefits to the company.

Auditing. The primary professional service offered by a CPA. Involves examining the accounting records and resulting financial statements of a company to attest to the fairness of the financial statements.

Balance Sheet. A financial statement used to summarize the financial position (assets, liabilities, and owner's equity) of a company on a given date. Also called a *statement of financial position*.

Certified Public Accountant (CPA). A licensed professional accountant who has met specific educational requirements, had certain practical experience, and passed the licensing examination.

Corporation. A company organized as a separate legal entity according to the laws of a particular state.

Decision Usefulness. Overall characteristic of useful financial accounting information.

Double Entry Rule. Rule stating that for each transaction at least two entries must be recorded in the components of the accounting equation to maintain its equality.

Entity Concept. The concept that a company is considered as separate from its owners and from any other company.

FASB Conceptual Framework. Theoretical foundation of concepts intended to provide a logical structure for financial accounting.

Financial Accounting Standards Board (FASB). An independent board of professionals experienced in accounting that currently establishes generally accepted accounting principles for companies.

Financial Statements. Accounting reports (income statement, statement of cash flows, and balance sheet) used to summarize and communicate financial information about a company.

Generally Accepted Accounting Principles (GAAP). The currently acceptable accounting principles, practices, and procedures that should be used in financial accounting.

Historical Cost Concept. Concept that all transactions are recorded at the cost involved in the transaction and that this cost is retained in the accounting records.

Income Statement. A financial statement summarizing the results of a company's earnings activities for a specific time period.

Liabilities. Economic obligations of a company that have been incurred as a result of a transaction and which can be measured in monetary terms.

Materiality. Concept that accounting information should be communicated only when the monetary amount is large enough to make a difference (be useful) in a user's decision.

Monetary Unit. The concept that the results of transactions are recorded and communicated in monetary terms.

Notes Payable. Liability showing amounts owed by a company as a result of issuing legal documents called *notes*.

Owner's Equity. The owner's current investment in the assets of a company.

Partnership. A company owned by two or more individuals called *partners*.

Prepaid Insurance. Asset showing amount paid for legal right to insurance protection in the future.

Relevance. Capacity to influence a user's decision. Important aspect of accounting information.

Reliable. Factual and capable of being verified. Important aspect of accounting information.

Sole Proprietorship. A company owned by one individual.

Source Document. A business record that serves as evidence that a transaction has occurred.

Statement of Cash Flows. A financial statement summarizing a company's cash receipts, cash payments, and net change in cash for a specific time period, in a manner that reconciles the beginning and ending cash balances.

Transaction. An exchange of property or services by a company with an external party.

Validity. Concept that accounting information presents a realistic picture of what it is meant to represent. Sometimes called *representational faithfulness*.

Questions

QUESTION 1-1 Define accounting. Briefly discuss each of the phrases included in your definition.

QUESTION 1-2 Who are external users? Give two examples of an economic decision made by an external user.

QUESTION 1-3 Who are internal users? Give two examples of an economic decision made by an internal user.

QUESTION 1-4 Draw a diagram of the decision-making process. Briefly discuss the steps in the process and indicate where in the process accounting information is used.

QUESTION 1-5 Differentiate accounting from bookkeeping.

QUESTION 1-6 Differentiate financial accounting from managerial accounting. How are they similar?

QUESTION 1-7 Identify and define the three types of companies. Which type is the most numerous? Which type conducts the greatest volume of business?

QUESTION 1-8   What is a transaction? A source document? Why are they important in accounting?

QUESTION 1-9   What are the monetary unit and historical cost concepts?

QUESTION 1-10   What is the entity concept and how does it affect the accounting for a specific business?

QUESTION 1-11   What is an income statement? Define the items included in an income statement.

QUESTION 1-12   What is a statement of cash flows? What are the three major sections of this statement?

QUESTION 1-13   What is a balance sheet? What is included in the heading of a balance sheet? What are the three segments of a balance sheet?

QUESTION 1-14   Define assets. Give four examples.

QUESTION 1-15   Define liabilities. Give two examples.

QUESTION 1-16   Define owner's equity. What items affect owner's equity?

QUESTION 1-17   What is the accounting equation? Why must it always be in balance?

QUESTION 1-18   What is the double entry rule? How does this rule relate to the accounting equation?

QUESTION 1-19   What are generally accepted accounting principles?

QUESTION 1-20   Identify the five organizations that have established generally accepted accounting principles in the United States. List the pronouncements used for this purpose by each organization.

QUESTION 1-21   What is the FASB conceptual framework? What is the primary purpose of financial accounting information?

QUESTION 1-22   Define relevance and materiality. How do these concepts relate to each other?

QUESTION 1-23   Define reliable accounting information. How do source documents relate to reliability in auditing?

QUESTION 1-24   What is validity? What must accounting information accurately portray?

QUESTION 1-25   What is auditing? Why is an audit important to the external users of a company's financial statements?

QUESTION 1-26   List and briefly explain the specialty areas of public accounting.

QUESTION 1-27   What is internal control and how does it relate to internal auditing?

Exercises

EXERCISE 1-1 **Accounting Equation.** Each of the following cases is independent of the others:

Case	Assets	Liabilities	Owner's Equity
1	A	$19,000	$42,000
2	$65,000	B	36,000
3	28,000	13,000	C

REQUIRED Determine the amounts of A, B, and C.

EXERCISE 1-2 **Change in Accounting Equation.** At the beginning of the year the Ellis Security Guard Company had total assets of $61,000 and total liabilities of $20,000. During the year total assets increased by $14,000. At the end of the year owner's equity totaled $56,000.

REQUIRED Determine (1) the owner's equity at the beginning of the year and (2) the total liabilities at the end of the year.

EXERCISE 1-3 **Manipulate Accounting Equation.** At the end of the year a company's total assets are $75,000 and its total owner's equity is $48,000. During the year the company's liabilities decreased by $11,000 while its assets increased by $7,000.

REQUIRED Determine the company's (1) ending total liabilities, (2) beginning total assets, and (3) beginning owner's equity.

EXERCISE 1-4 **Balance Sheet.** On August 31, 1991, the Hernandez Engineering Company's records contained the following items (listed in alphabetical order):

Accounts payable	$ 3,700
Accounts receivable	4,000
Cash	5,200
L. Hernandez, capital	?
Notes payable	6,000
Office equipment	7,500
Office supplies	600
Prepaid insurance	800

REQUIRED Prepare a balance sheet for the Hernandez Engineering Company at August 31, 1991. Insert the correct amount for L. Hernandez, capital.

EXERCISE 1-5 **Balance Sheet.** Listed in random order are all the items included in the Ridge Rental Company balance sheet on December 31, 1991:

Land	$ 2,200
Accounts receivable	3,500
Cash	?
Supplies	900
Accounts payable	4,600
Building	19,000
A. Ridge, capital	?
Rental equipment	5,600
Notes payable	5,700

Total assets on December 31, 1991, are $32,600.

REQUIRED   Prepare a balance sheet for the Ridge Rental Company on December 31, 1991. Insert the correct amounts for Cash and A. Ridge, capital.

EXERCISE 1-6   **Impact on Accounting Equation.**   The following transactions are taken from the records of the Lee Dating Service:

	Assets	Liabilities	Owner's Equity
(a) C. M. Lee, the owner, invested $12,000 cash in the business.			
(b) Paid $6,000 cash to acquire land and a small building for the business.			
(c) Received $650 cash from A. B. Jacobs, as payment for office equipment that Jacobs purchased from the company on credit last month.			
(d) Issued a $1,200 check in payment of a note issued last month.			

REQUIRED   Determine the overall effect of each transaction on the assets, liabilities, and owner's equity of the Lee Dating Service. Use the symbols *I* for increase, *D* for decrease, and *N* for no change. Also show the related dollar amounts.

EXERCISE 1-7   **Recording Transactions.**   The Wilman Duplicating Company entered into the following transactions during the month of June:

Date	Transaction
6/1	T. Wilman deposited $10,000 in the company's checking account.
6/10	Purchased $750 of office supplies from Timmer Supplies, agreeing to pay for half the supplies by June 30 and the remaining balance by July 15.
6/15	Purchased a 3-year fire insurance policy on a building owned by the company, paying $600 cash.
6/30	Paid Timmer Supplies half the amount owed for supplies purchased on June 10.

REQUIRED   Record the above transactions using the following accounting system (use subheadings for the specific kinds of assets, liabilities, and owner's equity):

Date	Assets	=	Liabilities	+	Owner's Equity

EXERCISE 1-8   **Examples of Transactions.**   A transaction of a company may change the balances of the assets, liabilities, and owner's equity of the company.

REQUIRED   Give a transaction that will result in the following changes in the contents of a balance sheet:

(*a*) Increase in an asset and increase in a liability.

(*b*) Decrease in an asset and decrease in a liability.

(c) Increase in an asset and decrease in another asset.

(d) Increase in an asset and increase in owner's equity.

EXERCISE 1-9   **Source Documents.**   Source documents are used by companies as a basis for recording business transactions.

REQUIRED   Name the source documents for each of the following transactions:

(a) Receipt of cash from the owner for additional investment in the business.

(b) Payment by check to purchase office equipment.

(c) Purchase of office supplies on credit.

(d) Sale of office equipment at its original purchase price to a local attorney.

(e) Purchase of fire and casualty insurance protection.

Problems

Part A

PROBLEM 1-1A   **Recording Transactions and Source Documents.**   Parsons Fashion Designers was established on June 1, 1991. The following transactions occurred during the month of June:

(a) E. Parsons, owner, started the business by investing $28,000 cash.

(b) Design equipment was purchased. The cash price of $2,600 was paid by writing a check to the supplier.

(c) Land and an office building were acquired at a cost of $5,000 and $18,000, respectively. The company paid $6,000 down and signed a note for the remaining balance of $17,000. The note is due in 6 months.

(d) Office supplies totaling $250 were purchased on credit. The amount is due in 30 days.

(e) One piece of design equipment was sold for $600 cash to a real estate agent. The equipment had been purchased earlier this month at a cost of $600.

(f) Purchased a 1-year fire insurance policy for $800.

REQUIRED   1.   Record the transactions for Parsons Fashion Designers.

2.   List the source documents that you would normally use in recording each of the transactions.

PROBLEM 1-2A   **Recording Transactions and Preparing Balance Sheet.**   L. Snider, a young CPA, started an accounting practice on September 1, 1991. During the month of September, the following transactions took place:

(a) L. Snider invested $35,000 cash to start the new business.

(b) Land and building were purchased for the business at a cost of $6,000 and $24,000, respectively. The company made a down payment of $9,000 and signed a note for the remaining balance of $21,000. The note is due in 1 year.

(c) Office equipment totaling $3,500 was purchased for cash.

(d) One piece of office equipment was sold to D. Popper. The selling price, $570, was the same as the cost at which the office equipment was originally purchased. Popper agreed to pay the $570 at the end of October.

(e) Office supplies were purchased for a total price of $1,700. The amount was paid by writing a check to the supplier.

REQUIRED   1. Record the transactions for the company, L. Snider, CPA.

2. Prepare a September 30, 1991 balance sheet for the company, L. Snider, CPA.

PROBLEM 1-3A   **Recording Transactions and Preparing Balance Sheets.** The Envoy Investment Company was recently established by the owner, G. Envoy. The following transactions took place during April:

(a) On April 1 G. Envoy set up the business by transferring $20,000 cash from his personal checking account to the newly opened checking account of the Envoy Investment Company.

(b) On April 3 land and a building were acquired to be used as the office. A note for the entire purchase price of $28,000 (land, $4,500; building, $23,500) was signed and given to the seller. The note is due in 1 year.

(c) On April 6 several pieces of office equipment were purchased for a price of $4,200. A check for that amount was written and given to the seller.

(d) On April 15 office supplies totaling $740 were purchased on credit. The amount is due at the end of May.

(e) On April 23 one piece of office equipment was sold at a selling price equal to its original cost of $730. The amount was collected in cash.

REQUIRED   1. Record the transactions for the Envoy Investment Company.

2. Prepare a balance sheet after each transaction has taken place (a total of five balance sheets is required).

PROBLEM 1-4A   **Analyzing Cash Transactions.** All the transactions that took place during the month of February for the Van Tassel Insurance Agency are as follows:

(a) On February 1 L. Van Tassel started the business by investing $40,000 in the company. A checking account was opened in the name of the Van Tassel Insurance Agency and the entire $40,000 was deposited in the newly opened account.

(b) Land and an office building were purchased for $23,000. A down payment of $8,000 was paid by writing a check; a note was signed for the remaining $15,000. The note is due in 3 months.

(c) A $4,340 check was written to pay for the entire purchase price of office equipment.

(d) A check in the amount of $620 was written to acquire office supplies.

(e) One piece of office equipment was sold to D. Clark at its original purchase price, and the cash collected was deposited in the company's checking account.

REQUIRED   Assuming all the transactions of the Van Tassel Insurance Agency in the month of February were properly recorded and the balance of the checking account at the end of February was found to be $28,030, compute the selling price of the piece of equipment sold in (e). Show your calculations.

PROBLEM 1-5A   **Identifying Transactions from Successive Balance Sheets.** The bookkeeper of the Smith Company prepares a balance sheet immediately after each transaction is recorded. During March, the first month of operations, the following five balance sheets were prepared:

(a)

SMITH COMPANY
Balance Sheet
March 1, 1991

Assets		*Liabilities and Owner's Equity*	
Cash	$80,000	Jan Smith, capital	$80,000
		Total Liabilities and	
Total Assets	$80,000	Owner's Equity	$80,000

(b)

SMITH COMPANY
Balance Sheet
March 4, 1991

Assets		*Liabilities and Owner's Equity*	
Cash	$75,000	Notes payable	$15,000
Land	3,000	Jan Smith, capital	80,000
Building	17,000	Total Liabilities and	
Total Assets	$95,000	Owner's Equity	$95,000

(c)

SMITH COMPANY
Balance Sheet
March 7, 1991

Assets		*Liabilities and Owner's Equity*	
Cash	$75,000	Accounts payable	$ 1,300
Office supplies	1,300	Notes payable	15,000
Land	3,000	Total Liabilities	$16,300
Building	17,000	Jan Smith, capital	80,000
		Total Liabilities and	
Total Assets	$96,300	Owner's Equity	$96,300

(d)

SMITH COMPANY
Balance Sheet
March 8, 1991

Assets		*Liabilities and Owner's Equity*	
Cash	$68,500	Accounts payable	$ 1,300
Office supplies	1,300	Notes payable	15,000
Land	3,000	Total Liabilities	$16,300
Building	17,000	Jan Smith, capital	80,000
Office equipment	6,500	Total Liabilities and	
Total Assets	$96,300	Owner's Equity	$96,300

(e)

```
┌─────────────────────────────────────────────────────────────────────────┐
│                          SMITH COMPANY                                    │
│                          Balance Sheet                                    │
│                          March 29, 1991                                   │
│                                                                           │
│            Assets                        Liabilities and Owner's Equity   │
│   Cash ............................ $69,030   Accounts payable ................ $ 1,300 │
│   Office supplies ...................  1,300  Notes payable ...................  15,000 │
│   Land ............................   3,000     Total Liabilities ...............  $16,300 │
│   Building .........................  17,000  Jan Smith, capital ..............  80,000 │
│   Office equipment ...............   5,970      Total Liabilities and         │
│      Total Assets ..................  $96,300      Owner's Equity ..............  $96,300 │
│                                                                           │
└─────────────────────────────────────────────────────────────────────────┘
```

REQUIRED   Describe the nature of the five transactions that took place during the month of March.

PROBLEM 1-6A   **Identifying Transactions.**   The five transactions that occurred during June, the first month of operations for Brown's Gym, were recorded as follows:

Trans.	Date	Assets					= Liabilities		+ Owner's Equity
		Cash	Gym + Supplies +	Land +	Building +	Gym + Equipment =	Accts. Payable +	Notes Payable +	Tom Brown, Capital
(a)	6/01/1991	+$25,000							+$25,000
(b)	6/04/1991	− 8,000		+$5,000	+$23,000			+$20,000	
(c)	6/07/1991	− 270	+$270						
(d)	6/17/1991	− 4,000				+$10,000		+ 6,000	
(e)	6/26/1991		+ 480				+$480		
Balances	6/30/1991	$12,730 +	$750 +	$5,000 +	$23,000 +	$10,000 =	$480 +	$26,000 +	$25,000

REQUIRED   1.   Describe the nature of the five transactions that took place during the month of June.

2.   Prepare a balance sheet at June 30, 1991.

Problems

Part B

PROBLEM 1-1B   **Recording Transactions and Source Documents.**   The Johnson Drafting Company was established on October 1, 1991 to draw blueprints for building contractors. The following transactions occurred during the month of October:

(a) M. Johnson, the owner, started the business by investing $40,000 cash.

(b) Land and an office building were acquired at a cost of $4,200 and $20,000, respectively. A down payment of $8,000 was made and a note for $16,200 was signed. The note is due in 1 year.

(c) Several pieces of drafting equipment were purchased for a cash price of $4,600. The amount was paid immediately.

(d) Drafting supplies totaling $850 were purchased on credit. The amount is due in early December.

(e) Two pieces of drafting equipment that had been acquired earlier in the month at a cost of $1,300 were sold to T. Jackson. The selling price of $1,300 was received in cash.

(f) Purchased a 1-year fire insurance policy for $400.

REQUIRED

1. Record the transactions for the Johnson Drafting Company.

2. List the source documents that you would normally use in recording each of the transactions.

PROBLEM 1-2B **Recording Transactions and Preparing a Balance Sheet.** F. Ryan, a young attorney, decided to start a law firm on December 1, 1991. During the month of December the following transactions took place:

(a) F. Ryan invested $30,000 cash to start the new business.

(b) Land and an office building were purchased for $5,000 and $19,000, respectively. Out of the total purchase price of $24,000, $6,000 was paid in cash and a note for the remaining balance of $18,000 was signed and given to the seller. The note is due in 3 months.

(c) Office equipment was purchased for a cash price of $5,600.

(d) Office supplies were purchased on credit from a local supplier. The purchase price of $660 is due next month.

(e) One piece of office equipment that had been purchased earlier was sold at its original cost of $470. A check in the amount of $470 was received.

REQUIRED

1. Record the transactions for the company, F. Ryan, Attorney.

2. Prepare a December 31, 1991 balance sheet for the company, F. Ryan, Attorney.

PROBLEM 1-3B **Recording Transactions and Preparing Balance Sheets.** The Lawrence Travel Agency was established by the owner, K. Lawrence. The following transactions took place during July:

(a) On July 1 K. Lawrence set up the business by transferring $33,000 cash from his personal checking account to the newly opened checking account of the Lawrence Travel Agency.

(b) On July 7 land and a building were acquired for a price of $5,000 and $27,000, respectively. A down payment of $7,000 was made and a note in the amount of $25,000 was signed. The note is due in 6 months.

(c) On July 13 office equipment was purchased for a total price of $5,500. A cash payment of $1,500 was made and the remaining balance of $4,000 is due in 30 days.

(d) On July 24 office supplies totaling $880 were purchased on credit. The amount is due at the end of August.

(e) On July 31 one piece of office equipment was sold at its original cost of $1,040. The amount was collected in cash.

REQUIRED

1. Record the transactions for the Lawrence Travel Agency.

2. Prepare a balance sheet after each transaction has taken place (a total of five balance sheets is required).

PROBLEM 1-4B   **Analyzing Cash Transactions.** All the transactions that took place during the month of November for the Patrick Painting Company are as follows:

(a) On November 1 T. Patrick set up the company by investing $50,000 in the business. A checking account in the name of the company was opened and the entire $50,000 was deposited in that account.

(b) A building and land were purchased for the new business. A check in the amount of $6,500 was written to pay for the down payment and a 3-month note for the remaining $18,500 was signed.

(c) A check in the amount of $7,700 was written to pay for the entire purchase price of painting equipment.

(d) One piece of painting equipment that had been purchased earlier was sold to J. Collins at its original cost of $1,200. The $1,200 was collected and deposited in the company's checking account.

(e) Painting supplies were purchased, and a check was written for the purchase price.

REQUIRED   Assuming all the transactions of the Patrick Painting Company in the month of November were properly recorded and the balance of the checking account at the end of November was found to be $34,900, compute the purchase price of the painting supplies in (e). Show your calculations.

PROBLEM 1-5B   **Identifying Transactions from Successive Balance Sheets.** Lisa Wallace, owner of the Wallace Company, believes that current information is necessary for successful business operations. Accordingly, she requires that a balance sheet be prepared and submitted to her immediately after each transaction takes place. During the month of August, the following five balance sheets were prepared and submitted to her by the company's bookkeeper:

(a)

WALLACE COMPANY
Balance Sheet
August 1, 1991

Assets		*Liabilities and Owner's Equity*	
Cash	$65,000	Lisa Wallace, capital	$65,000
		Total Liabilities and	
Total Assets	$65,000	Owner's Equity	$65,000

(b)

WALLACE COMPANY
Balance Sheet
August 2, 1991

Assets		*Liabilities and Owner's Equity*	
Cash	$59,000	Notes payable	$15,000
Land	5,000	Lisa Wallace, capital	65,000
Building	16,000	Total Liabilities and	
Total Assets	$80,000	Owner's Equity	$80,000

(c)

```
┌──────────────────────────────────────────────────────────────────────────┐
│                          WALLACE COMPANY                                   │
│                           Balance Sheet                                    │
│                          August 5, 1991                                    │
│                                                                            │
│            Assets                          Liabilities and Owner's Equity  │
│ Cash ..........................  $59,000   Accounts payable ...........  $ 1,400 │
│ Office supplies ...............    1,400   Notes payable ..............   15,000 │
│ Land ..........................    5,000     Total Liabilities ........  $16,400 │
│ Building ......................   16,000   Lisa Wallace, capital ......   65,000 │
│                                              Total Liabilities and               │
│      Total Assets .............  $81,400     Owner's Equity ...........  $81,400 │
└──────────────────────────────────────────────────────────────────────────┘
```

(d)

```
┌──────────────────────────────────────────────────────────────────────────┐
│                          WALLACE COMPANY                                   │
│                           Balance Sheet                                    │
│                          August 9, 1991                                    │
│                                                                            │
│            Assets                          Liabilities and Owner's Equity  │
│ Cash ..........................  $56,000   Accounts payable ...........  $ 1,400 │
│ Office supplies ...............    1,400   Notes payable ..............   23,000 │
│ Land ..........................    5,000     Total Liabilities ........  $24,400 │
│ Building ......................   16,000   Lisa Wallace, capital ......   65,000 │
│ Office equipment ..............   11,000     Total Liabilities and               │
│      Total Assets .............  $89,400     Owner's Equity ...........  $89,400 │
└──────────────────────────────────────────────────────────────────────────┘
```

(e)

```
┌──────────────────────────────────────────────────────────────────────────┐
│                          WALLACE COMPANY                                   │
│                           Balance Sheet                                    │
│                          August 23, 1991                                   │
│                                                                            │
│            Assets                          Liabilities and Owner's Equity  │
│ Cash ..........................  $53,100   Accounts payable ...........  $ 1,400 │
│ Office supplies ...............    4,300   Notes payable ..............   23,000 │
│ Land ..........................    5,000     Total Liabilities ........  $24,400 │
│ Building ......................   16,000   Lisa Wallace, capital ......   65,000 │
│ Office equipment ..............   11,000     Total Liabilities and               │
│      Total Assets .............  $89,400     Owner's Equity ...........  $89,400 │
└──────────────────────────────────────────────────────────────────────────┘
```

REQUIRED   Describe the nature of the five transactions that the bookkeeper recorded during the month of August.

PROBLEM 1-6B   **Identifying Transactions.**   The following transactions were recorded by the Sutton Systems Design Company for the month of May, its first month of operations:

Trans.	Date	Cash	Office + Supplies	+ Land	+ Building	Office + Equipment	= Accts. Payable	Notes + Payable	Steve Sutton, + Capital
(a)	5/01/1991	+$55,000							+$55,000
(b)	5/02/1991	− 8,000		+$6,000	+$18,000			+$16,000	
(c)	5/07/1991	− 3,500				+$7,500		+ 4,000	
(d)	5/10/1991		+$1,100				+$1,100		
(e)	5/22/1991	+ 300				− 300			
Balances	5/31/1991	$43,800	+ $1,100	+ $6,000	+ $18,000	+ $7,200	= $1,100	+ $20,000	+ $55,000

REQUIRED

1. Describe the nature of the five transactions that were recorded during the month of May.

2. Prepare a balance sheet at May 31, 1991.

Decision Cases

DECISION CASE 1-1   **Financial Statements.**   A friend of yours, Mary Stolle, has never had an accounting course. Her speech class instructor has assigned a short speech in which Mary must describe the "financial statements" of a company. Mary has come to you for help. She says, "Please describe what financial statements are, what the major financial statements are, and what each financial statement includes."

REQUIRED   Prepare a written response to Mary's request.

DECISION CASE 1-2   **FASB Conceptual Framework.**   A friend of yours has recently completed a course in bookkeeping at his high school. He has been browsing through this chapter of your book and noticed the heading "conceptual framework." He says, "We never had a conceptual framework in our bookkeeping class. What is this framework anyhow? Please tell me about its qualities or characteristics, and define each one."

REQUIRED   Prepare a written response to your friend's question.

DECISION CASE 1-3   **Balance Sheet.**   At the beginning of December 1991, Anna Ashley started the Anash Company by depositing $20,000 in the company's checking account. The company immediately used 40% of this cash to make a down payment on some land and an office building, financing the remaining purchase price with a 20-year mortgage. The cost of the land was 15% of the purchase price and the cost of the building was 85% of the purchase price. The company then purchased some office equipment, paying $2,000 down and signing a 2-year note payable for the remaining balance of $4,000. Finally, office supplies were purchased for $1,000 cash. At the end of the month, the cash balance was 20% of the total assets.

REQUIRED   Based on the preceding information, prepare a balance sheet for the Anash Company at December 31, 1991. Show supporting calculations.

2

Recording and Reporting Accounting Information

LEARNING OBJECTIVES

1. Define an account and a general ledger.

2. State the meaning of a debit entry and a credit entry.

3. Explain how asset, liability, and owner's equity accounts are increased and decreased.

4. Describe the double entry rule.

5. Define a general journal and a journal entry.

6. Prepare journal entries for asset, liability, and owner's equity accounts.

7. Complete the posting process.

8. Prepare a trial balance.

9. Prepare a balance sheet from a trial balance.

10. List the steps and documents in an accounting system.

n Chapter 1 we used a simple columnar accounting system to record transactions and to prepare a balance sheet. Although this system was helpful for explaining the accounting process, it is not very practical in today's business world. Within the period of a month most companies have hundreds or thousands of transactions involving many assets, liabilities, and owner's equity items. These transactions not only affect the balance sheet but also the other financial statements. Setting up a column for recording transactions affecting all the assets, liabilities, and owner's equity items of most companies would result in a very large accounting record, which would not be very useful for an actual business.

A better system for processing accounting information is needed. This system would include a set of accounting procedures and documents for recording, retaining, and reporting all the information about each transaction. In this chapter we introduce a system for transactions affecting the balance sheet. After you have attained a good understanding of the accounting system described in this chapter, we extend the system in Chapter 3 to include income statement transactions. The accounting system shown here can be used for either manual or computer information processing. For ease of learning, the discussion in this textbook mostly involves manual processing. Computer information processing is briefly discussed in Chapter 6.

Accounts

1. Define an account and a general ledger.

We defined an accounting system as a means by which accounting information about a company's activities is identified, measured, recorded, and retained so that it can be reported in an accounting statement. In the example in the last chapter we used a separate column to record and retain the increases and decreases in each asset, liability, and owner's equity item. In an accounting system in the business world, an account is used for this purpose. **An account is a business document used to record and retain the monetary information from a company's transactions.** Separate accounts are used for each asset, liability, and owner's equity item. For example, a company may have accounts for Cash, Accounts Receivable, Notes Receivable, Office Supplies, Prepaid Insurance, Office Equipment, Delivery Equipment, Land, Buildings, Accounts Payable, Notes Payable, and A. Dixon, Capital, to name only a few. The number, types, and names of the accounts for each company depend upon the particular company's operations, whether it is a sole proprietorship, partnership, or corporation, and the types of assets it owns and liabilities it has incurred. **A general ledger is the entire set of accounts for a company.** For this reason, sometimes accounts are referred to as *general ledger accounts*.

An account can take several physical forms. It might be a location on a computer disk or tape, or a standardized business paper in the case of a manual system. The general ledger might be a computer disk or tape, or a loose-leaf binder containing all the accounts of a manual system. Regardless of the physical form, all accounts are used for recording and retaining accounting information.

Components of an Account

No matter what physical form is used, the same logical format is used throughout for recording and retaining accounting information in the accounts. This format is easiest to understand for a manual system. A simple format for the accounts in a manual system is called a *T-account* because it looks like the capital letter T. As shown below, each T-account has three basic parts: (1) a place at the top for the *title* of the particular asset, liability, or owner's equity item, (2) a *left* side, called the *debit* side, and (3) a *right* side, called the *credit* side. The title of each account describes the nature of the account (e.g., Buildings, Notes Payable). The left (debit) and the right (credit) sides of each account are used for recording and retaining the monetary information from transactions. **A debit entry is a monetary amount recorded (debited) in the left side of an account. A credit entry is a monetary amount recorded (credited) in the right side of an account.**

2. State the meaning of a debit entry and a credit entry.

Title of Account	
Left (debit) side	Right (credit) side

Debit and Credit Rules

Each account accumulates information about both increases and decreases from various business transactions. There are two rules for recording these increases and decreases in the accounts. The first rule is that **for each account all increases are recorded in one side of the account and all decreases are recorded in the other side of the account.** This rule makes it easy to determine the total increases and decreases for a particular account. It does not indicate, however, whether the increases or decreases should be recorded in the debit (left) or credit (right) side of the account. A second rule is *the debit and credit rule.* This rule relates to the basic accounting equation; it states:

3. Explain how asset, liability, and owner's equity accounts are increased and decreased.

Asset accounts (accounts on the left side of the accounting equation) are increased by debit entries (i.e., recorded amounts on the left side) and decreased by credit entries.

Liability and owner's equity accounts (accounts on the right side of the equation) are increased by credit entries (i.e., recorded amounts on the right side) and decreased by debit entries.

This rule[1] and its relationship to the accounting equation are illustrated as follows.

Assets		=	Liabilities		+	Owner's Equity	
Asset Accounts			*Liability Accounts*			*Owner's Equity Accounts*	
(debit) Increase +	(credit) Decrease −		(debit) Decrease −	(credit) Increase +		(debit) Decrease −	(credit) Increase +

---

[1]This rule is stated in the singular *owner's* equity because we are discussing a sole proprietorship. The rule also applies to partnerships and corporations, as discussed in later chapters. For these companies, the plural *owners'* equity is appropriate.

This rule is essential for understanding how to record business transactions. It may be separated into parts as follows:

1. **Assets**
   (a) An increase in an asset is recorded in the left (debit) side of the asset account, by a debit entry.
   (b) A decrease in an asset is recorded in the right (credit) side of the asset account, by a credit entry.

2. **Liabilities**
   (a) An increase in liability is recorded in the right (credit) side of the liability account, by a credit entry.
   (b) A decrease in a liability is recorded in the left (debit) side of the liability account, by a debit entry.

3. **Owner's Equity**
   (a) An increase in owner's equity is recorded in the right (credit) side of the owner's equity account, by a credit entry.
   (b) A decrease in owner's equity is recorded in the left (debit) side of the owner's equity account, by a debit entry.

Balance of an Account

The balance of an account is the difference between the total increases and decreases recorded in the account. Usually the balance of each account is computed when the accounting information is to be communicated in an accounting report, such as a balance sheet. Each asset account normally has a debit balance because the total increases (debits) exceed the total decreases (credits) in the account. Each liability and owner's equity account normally has a credit balance because the total increases (credits) exceed the total decreases (debits) in each account.

To illustrate, look at the Cash account (numbered 101, discussed later) shown here:

				Cash		No. 101
6/1/91 Balance	2,000		6/3/91			900
6/4/91	5,000		6/10/91			3,000
			6/26/91			700
6/30/91 Balance	2,400					

Note that on June 1, 1991, the account had a $2,000 debit balance (this was the ending balance for May, the difference between the total debits and credits in the account to that date). On June 4 a transaction occurred that increased (debited) the Cash account by $5,000, while on June 3, 10, and 26 the Cash account was decreased (credited) by $900, $3,000, and $700, respectively. The debit balance of the Cash account is $2,400 on June 30, 1991, because the total debits ($7,000) exceed the total credits ($4,600). The debit and credit entries in accounts are discussed in more detail later in the chapter.

Double Entry Rule

4. Describe the double entry rule.

In Chapter 1 we introduced the double entry rule, which stated that to record a transaction, at least two entries must be made in the components of the accounting equation to keep both sides of the equation equal. At that time we had not discussed the debit and credit rule. The double entry rule is now modified as follows: **The double entry rule states that when recording each transaction, the total amount of the debit entries must be equal to the total amount of the credit entries for that transaction.** Thus for each recorded transaction there must be at least one debit entry and one credit entry (although there could be more entries of each type), and the total amounts must be equal. For example, suppose a company purchased land for cash at a cost of $2,000. To record this transaction, an asset account Land would be increased by a debit entry for $2,000 and another asset account Cash would be decreased by a credit entry of $2,000. Thus the total debits equal the total credits in this transaction.

It is important to understand the consistent relationship between the accounting equation, the debit and credit rule, and the double entry rule. Recall that the accounting equation must always be in balance. Recall also that when recording a transaction, it is not necessary to affect both sides of the equation or even two components of the equation. It is possible to record a transaction as affecting only the left side, the right side, or both sides of the equation provided that the equation remains in balance. If the debit and credit rule and the double entry rule are followed, the accounting equation will *always* remain in balance. For instance, in the land example just given, the debit entry *increased* the Land account while the credit entry *decreased* the Cash account. The total debits equaled the total credits, and thus the double entry rule was followed. Only the left side of the accounting equation (the asset component) was affected, but the equation remained in balance because there was no change in *total* assets. The left side of the equation therefore remained equal to the right side of the equation. Additional examples are presented later in the chapter.

Checklist of Important Rules

Up to this point we have stated several important rules that must be followed in an actual accounting system. These rules are summarized as follows to help you remember them and their relationship:

1. **The accounting equation (assets equal liabilities plus owner's equity) must always remain in balance.**

2. **All increases in an account are recorded on one side of the account; all decreases are recorded on the other side of the account.**

3. **The debit and credit rule states that:**
   (a) **Asset accounts are increased by debit entries and decreased by credit entries.**
   (b) **Liability and owner's equity accounts are increased by credit entries and decreased by debit entries.**

4. **Asset accounts normally have debit balances. Liability and owner's equity accounts normally have credit balances.**

5. **The double entry rule states that for all recorded transactions, the total amount of the debit entries must be equal to the total amount of the credit entries.**

Illustration of Rules

To illustrate the rules that have been stated in this chapter, we use the Dixon Travel Agency example from Chapter 1. The agency entered into six transactions during January 1991. Presented next are the date and description of each transaction, an analysis of the transaction, the applicable debit and credit rules, a summary of the entries to record the transaction, and the T-account debit and credit entries. The arrows show that the total amount of the debit and credit entries is equal for each transaction.

Transaction 1 (1/1/1991). Anne Dixon opened a travel agency by depositing a $30,000 personal check in the Dixon Travel Agency checking account.

Analysis: The asset account Cash is increased by $30,000 and the owner's equity account A. Dixon, Capital is increased by $30,000.

Debit and Credit Rules: Asset accounts are increased by debit entries; owner's equity accounts are increased by credit entries.

Summary of Entries: Cash is debited for $30,000 and A. Dixon, Capital is credited for $30,000.

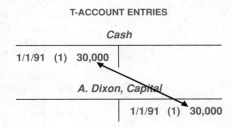

Transaction 2 (1/2/1991). Land ($3,000) and office building ($15,000) are purchased for $18,000.

Analysis: The asset accounts Land and Building are increased by $3,000 and $15,000, respectively, and the asset account Cash is decreased by $18,000.

Debit and Credit Rules: Asset accounts are increased by debit entries; asset accounts are decreased by credit entries.

Summary of Entries: Land and Building are debited for $3,000 and $15,000, respectively, and Cash is credited for $18,000.

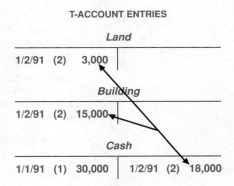

Transaction 3 (1/5/1991). Office supplies costing $700 are purchased on account from City Supply Company. Half the amount owed is to be paid for on January 15; the remainder is due on February 15.

Analysis: The asset account Office Supplies is increased by $700 and the liability account Accounts Payable is increased by $700.

Debit and Credit Rules: Asset accounts are increased by debit entries; liability accounts are increased by credit entries.

Summary of Entries: Office Supplies is debited for $700 and Accounts Payable is credited for $700.

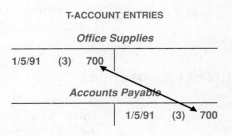

Transaction 4 (1/12/1991). Office equipment costing $3,000 is purchased from Ace Equipment Company by making a $1,000 down payment and signing a $2,000 note due at the end of one year.

Analysis: The asset account Office Equipment is increased by $3,000. The asset account Cash is decreased by $1,000 and the liability account Notes Payable is increased by $2,000.

Debit and Credit Rules: Asset accounts are increased by debit entries and decreased by credit entries. Liability accounts are increased by credit entries.

Summary of Entries: Office Equipment is debited for $3,000. Cash is credited for $1,000 and Notes Payable is credited for $2,000.

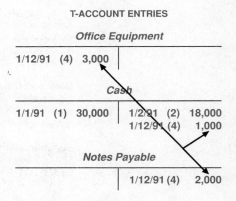

Transaction 5 (1/15/1991). $350 is paid to City Supply Company in partial payment of Accounts Payable.

Analysis: The liability account Accounts Payable is decreased by $350 and the asset account Cash is decreased by $350.

Debit and Credit Rules: Liability accounts are decreased by debit entries; asset accounts are decreased by credit entries.

Summary of Entries: Accounts Payable is debited for $350 and Cash is credited for $350.

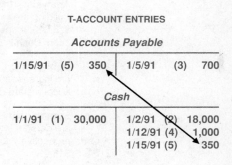

Transaction 6 (1/28/1991). Office equipment (desk) that cost $400 is sold for $400 on account, the purchaser agreeing to pay the full amount on February 7.

Analysis: The asset account Accounts Receivable is increased by $400 and the asset account Office Equipment is decreased by $400.

Debit and Credit Rules: Asset accounts are increased by debit entries and decreased by credit entries.

Summary of Entries: Accounts Receivable is debited for $400 and Office Equipment is credited for $400.

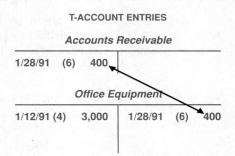

T-ACCOUNT ENTRIES

Accounts Receivable

1/28/91 (6) 400

Office Equipment

1/12/91 (4) 3,000 | 1/28/91 (6) 400

Note that the double entry rule was followed in recording each transaction. Now look at a summary of the impact of each transaction on the accounting equation (*dr* and *cr* in parentheses refer to debit and credit, respectively; they are common abbreviations and are used frequently throughout this textbook).

Transaction Number	Assets	=	Liabilities	+	Owner's Equity
1	+$30,000 (dr) Cash				+$30,000 (cr) A. Dixon, Capital
2	+ 3,000 (dr) Land				
	+ 15,000 (dr) Building				
	− 18,000 (cr) Cash				
3	+ 700 (dr) Office supplies		+$ 700 (cr) Accounts payable		
4	+ 3,000 (dr) Office equipment				
	− 1,000 (cr) Cash		+ 2,000 (cr) Notes payable		
5	− 350 (cr) Cash		− 350 (dr) Accounts payable		
6	+ 400 (dr) Accounts receivable				
	− 400 (cr) Office equipment				
Totals	$32,350	=	$2,350	+	$30,000

In this summary see that for each transaction the total debits always equaled the total credits. This was true even when there was more than one debit or credit entry (transaction 2 had two debit entries and transaction 4 had two credit entries). See also that the accounting equation always remained in balance, even though (1) only one side of the equation may have been affected by a particular transaction and (2) a transaction may have caused an increase, a decrease, or no change in the equation. Furthermore, the total of each side of the equation is $32,350. Although we could compute the account balances and prepare a balance sheet at this point as we did in Chapter 1, first we will introduce several other accounting procedures.

General Journal and Journalizing

Our example of the Dixon Travel Agency had only six transactions and each was summarized to keep the example simple. The agency had only nine accounts in which we directly recorded the transactions. In reality a company engages in hundreds or thousands of transactions and has many more than nine accounts. When the transactions occur they are not summarized as shown in the example. Recording the transactions directly in the accounts would lead to a high chance for error because of the numerous accounts in the general ledger. In addition, if the accountant reviews a debit entry in an account and wants to see the related credit entry of the transaction, it would not be possible. Finally, no written description of the transactions would exist if the transactions were recorded directly in the accounts. For these reasons, transactions are *not* initially recorded directly in a company's accounts. The recording, retaining, and reporting of information from transactions is discussed throughout the rest of the chapter. The following diagram provides an overview of the documents used in this process and explained in the following sections.

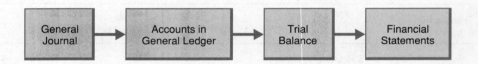

| General Journal | → | Accounts in General Ledger | → | Trial Balance | → | Financial Statements |

General Journal

5. Define a general journal and a journal entry.

The business transactions of a company are first recorded in a journal, after which the information is transferred to the company's accounts. **A general journal is a business document in which are recorded the date of the transaction, the accounts to be debited and credited, the amounts of the debit and credit entries, and an explanation of each transaction.** In a manual accounting system the general journal is a book of columnar pages.

A general journal can be used to record all types of transactions. It is the main journal used throughout this textbook. Many companies have a number of *special journals,* each of which is designed to record a particular type of business transaction. For instance, one special journal is the Cash Receipts Journal used to record all receipts of cash. Special journals are discussed in an appendix to Chapter 6. The following discussion applies to all types of journals.

A journal entry is the recorded information for each transaction. Journalizing is the act of preparing the journal entry. A journal is often referred to as the *document of original entry* because each transaction is first, or originally, entered in the journal. (Before computers were widespread, a journal was called the *book* of original entry. But since a journal today may be a magnetic tape or disk as well as a book of columnar pages, the term *document* is more appropriate than the term book.)

There are many advantages in using a journal to initially record a company's transactions.

1. Use of a journal helps to prevent errors. Since the accounts and the debit and credit amounts for each transaction are initially recorded on a single journal page rather than directly in the many accounts, this method makes it easier to prove that the debits and credits are equal.

2. All the information about the transactions (including the explanation) is recorded in one place, thereby providing a complete "picture" of the transaction. This is very useful during the auditing process or if an error is discovered later in the accounting process, because the accountant can look in the journal to see all of the accounts involved and find an explanation for the transaction.

3. The transactions are recorded chronologically (day by day), so that the journal also provides a chronological "history" of the company's financial transactions.

Key Procedures in Journalizing

Throughout this text you will study many journal entries. You will also prepare many journal entries in the general journal for your homework assignments. It is very important that you understand the form of the general journal and carefully learn the procedures for journalizing each transaction, as well as understand the impact of the transaction on the accounting equation. A completed general journal page is shown in Exhibit 2-2; a blank partial page is shown here:

	GENERAL JOURNAL			Page 9
Date	Account Titles and Explanations	Acct. No.	Debit	Credit

The following list outlines the journalizing procedures for each column of the general journal. Study it carefully, referring to the partial general journal page or to Exhibit 2-2.

1. The month, day, and year of the first transaction are entered in the "Date" column, with the year written above the month. It is not necessary to repeat the month and the year of subsequent transactions until a new journal page is begun or transactions for the next month are recorded.

2. The *exact* title of the account to be debited is entered at the far left of the column entitled "Account Titles and Explanations." The amount of the debit to

6. Prepare journal entries for asset, liability, and owner's equity accounts.

this account is entered in the "Debit" column. Dollar signs are typically not used in the debit (or credit) column.

3. The *exact* title of the account to be credited is entered on the next line below the title of the debited account. The title of the credit account is indented slightly to the right so that when looking at the journal page a reader can easily identify which account titles are to be credited and debited. The amount of the credit to this account is entered in the "Credit" column.

4. As you have already seen, a transaction may be recorded that involves two or more debits, two or more credits, or both. (Remember that for each transaction the *total* amount of the debit entries must be equal to the *total* amount of the credit entries.) This type of entry is called a *compound entry*. When recording a compound entry, all the accounts (and amounts) to be debited are listed first (with each account listed on a separate line), followed by all the accounts to be credited (indented and also listed on a separate line). The January 2, 1991, transaction in Exhibit 2-2 is an example of a compound journal entry and is discussed later.

5. A brief explanation is entered on the line below the last credit entry of each transaction. The explanation is entered at the far left of the column entitled "Account Titles and Explanations." A line is left blank before beginning another journal entry to set off each entry.

6. During the process of journalizing, a number is *not* recorded in the column entitled "Acct. No." (Account Number). A number will be entered in this column later.

Once the debit and credit entries of a transaction have been journalized, the next transaction for the day is journalized and the process continues until all the transactions are recorded. **By strictly following these journalizing procedures, the chance of error is minimized.**

Illustration of Journal Entries

To illustrate the general journal and journalizing, the six transactions of the Dixon Travel Agency for January 1991 are recorded in Exhibit 2-2, but first the transactions are briefly summarized in Exhibit 2-1. The source documents from which the accounting information was obtained for each transaction are also included.

Exhibit 2-2 shows the journal entries in the Dixon Travel Agency general journal for each of the six transactions. In studying Exhibit 2-2 you should review each transaction listed in Exhibit 2-1, form a picture in your mind of the accounting information on the source documents, understand the impact on the accounting equation, determine the debit and credit entries, think of the journalizing procedures, and compare these procedures to the journal entries made in Exhibit 2-2.

To illustrate the journalizing process, we look at the January 2, 1991, transaction (the purchase of the land and office building). To start the process, we examine the source documents, the Dixon Travel Agency check for $18,000 and the legal documents related to the event. The legal documents (deed, contract, etc.)

EXHIBIT 2-1
Source Documents
and Summary of
Transactions

Transaction Number	Date	Source Document	Transaction
1	1/1/1991	Receipt issued by DIxon Travel Agency	Anne Dixon invests $30,000 in the Dixon Travel Agency.
2	1/2/1991	Check and legal documents	Land costing $3,000 and office building costing $15,000 are purchased for $18,000.
3	1/5/1991	Invoice received with supplies	Office supplies costing $700 are purchased on account from City Supply Company. Half of this amount is to be paid on January 15; the remainder is due on February 15.
4	1/12/1991	Invoice received with office equipment, check, and note	Office equipment costing $3,000 is purchased from Ace Equipment Company by making a $1,000 down payment and signing a 1-year note for $2,000.
5	1/15/1991	Check	$350 is paid on account to City Supply Company.
6	1/28/1991	Written agreement summarizing sale and payment terms	Office equipment (desk) costing $400 is sold for $400 on account to James Baker. The full amount is due on February 7.

verify that the check was written for the purchase of the land costing $3,000 and the building costing $15,000. In the accounting equation, two assets (Land and Building) were increased while one asset (Cash) was decreased. The asset accounts Land and Building should be debited (increased) for $3,000 and $15,000, respectively, while the asset account Cash should be credited (decreased) for $18,000. Thus, as discussed earlier in item 4 of the journalizing procedures, we must make a compound journal entry because the transaction involves two debit entries and one credit entry. Skipping a line after the previous transaction, we enter the date and the exact account title (Land) and amount ($3,000) of the first account to be debited. On the next line, we enter the exact title (Building) and amount ($15,000) of the next account to be debited. We indent the next line and enter the exact account title (Cash) and amount ($18,000) to be credited.[2] On the next line we write a brief explanation of the journal entry. In this explanation we could include the reference numbers (e.g., check number) to the source documents that are available. This is helpful in the auditing process

---

[2]We have not used a "cents" column in the debit and credit amount columns to avoid unnecessary detail. Both dollars and cents would be recorded in the general journal for actual transactions, however.

EXHIBIT 2-2
Dixon Travel Agency
General Journal

			GENERAL JOURNAL			Page 1
Date			Account Titles and Explanations	Acct. No.	Debit	Credit
1991 Jan.	1		Cash		30,000	
			A. Dixon, Capital			30,000
			To record investment by owner of cash into business.			
	2		Land		3,000	
			Building		15,000	
			Cash			18,000
			To record purchase of land and office building for use in operating the travel agency.			
	5		Office Supplies		700	
			Accounts Payable			700
			To record purchase of office supplies on account from City Supply Company; agreed to pay half of the amount owed on January 15 and the remainder on February 15.			
	12		Office Equipment		3,000	
			Cash			1,000
			Notes Payable			2,000
			To record purchase of office equipment from Ace Equipment Company; made cash down payment and signed 1-year note.			
	15		Accounts Payable		350	
			Cash			350
			To record payment to City Supply Company of half the amount owed for office supplies purchased on January 5.			
	28		Accounts Receivable		400	
			Office Equipment			400
			To record sale of desk that cost $400 to James Baker on credit for $400; the full amount is to be collected on February 7.			

or in the case of an error, where a review of the original source documents would be useful. This process is followed for each transaction, and all the source documents are then filed in the company's records.

Accounts and Posting

In the journalizing process each transaction is initially entered in one record, the journal, to (1) minimize errors, (2) have all the debit and credit information for each transaction in one place, and (3) have a chronological list of all the company's financial transactions. However, the accounting information from each transaction is not yet recorded in the accounts, the so-called "storage units" for the company's accounting information. To do so we must post the accounts from the journal to the ledger accounts. **Posting is the process of transferring the debit and credit information for each journal entry to the proper accounts in the general ledger.**

Account Formats

Earlier in the chapter we used T-accounts to show the process of recording and retaining information. Throughout the text we often use T-accounts as examples of ledger accounts because they are simple and easy to understand. In a manual accounting system in the actual business world, however, an account usually has a format as shown in Exhibit 2-3.

EXHIBIT 2-3
Illustration of a
Typical Account
Format

				CASH			Acct. No. 101
Date		Explanation		Jr. Ref.	Debit	Credit	Debit Balance

In this format the columns for the date, explanation, and journal reference (Jr. Ref.) are the first three columns in the account. The debit and credit columns are on the right-hand side. A column entitled "balance," which shows a running total of the debit or credit balance in the account, is at the far right side of the account. The column entitled "explanation" is used for only unusual and complicated entries, since an explanation of each entry in the account has already been made in the journal The use of the journal reference column is explained later when posting is discussed.

Account Numbers and Chart of Accounts

To help in posting (and later accounting procedures), each account of a company is assigned a number. This number is listed to the right of the account title for both a T-account and the account format shown in Exhibit 2-3. The number is obtained from the company's chart of accounts. **The chart of accounts is a num-**

bering system designed to organize the accounts efficiently and to reduce errors in the recording and retaining process. The chart of accounts is generally set up so that the Cash account is given the lowest number, followed in order by all the other asset accounts, all the liability accounts, and then by the owner's equity account. Within the asset accounts, after Cash the remaining assets are given higher numbers in the order of their *liquidity* (i.e., their ease of conversion into cash) and according to their usual placement on the company's balance sheet. The physical assets such as land, buildings, and equipment generally are given the highest asset numbers because they are usually the last assets listed on the balance sheet. A similar scheme is used for the liability and owner's equity accounts. The accounts are then included in the general ledger in the order in which they are listed in the chart of accounts. The chart of accounts must be flexible enough so that as new asset, liability, or owner's equity accounts are needed, they can be properly placed in the general ledger.

The chart of accounts of the Dixon Travel Agency is listed in Exhibit 2-4. Notice that the asset account numbers begin at 101, the liabilities at 201, and owner's equity at 301. This numbering system is used to help identify and classify accounts. (Some large corporations use numbers as high as six digits for classifying their accounts and even use decimals to further subclassify their accounts.) Note also that the accounts are not consecutively numbered. This procedure is followed because any new asset, liability, and owner's equity accounts can be inserted in the chart of accounts (and general ledger) later and given account numbers in their proper balance sheet order.

EXHIBIT 2-4
Dixon Travel Agency
Chart of Accounts

Account Title	Account Number
Cash	101
Accounts Receivable	103
Office Supplies	107
Land	120
Building	122
Office Equipment	124
Accounts Payable	201
Notes Payable	204
A. Dixon, Capital	301

Summary of Posting Process

Recall that the posting process involves transferring the information recorded in the general journal to the accounts in the general ledger. In a manual system posting is usually done at the end of each work day. As in the journalizing process, a set of key procedures should be learned for posting to the individual accounts. These procedures are summarized as follows:

7. Complete the posting process.

1. In the general ledger locate the first account of the first transaction in the general journal to be posted. This is done by looking at the account title in the general ledger.

2. Enter the month, day, and year of the transaction (as listed in the general journal) in the "Date" column of the account. It is not necessary to repeat the year and month until a new account page is begun or a transaction for the next month is posted.

3. Enter the debit amount (as listed in the general journal) in the "Debit" column of the account and compute the new account balance. (Caution: Remember that assets have debit balances and liability and owner's equity accounts have credit balances.)

4. In the Journal Reference ("Jr. Ref.") column, enter the *page number* of the general journal on which the journal entry was recorded. This is done to provide a *cross reference* between the general journal page and the posting to the account. This cross reference is useful in the auditing process or when an error has been discovered. (Caution: Remember that this procedure is completed *after* the amount is posted in the account.)

5. Go back to the general journal and enter in the Account Number ("Acct. No.") column the number of the account in which the debit amount was posted. A number listed in the Account Number column indicates that the posting process has been completed for that *line* of the general journal; it is the last step before continuing with the posting of the next line. (Caution: Remember that this procedure is completed *after* the amount is posted in the account.)

6. For the next line of the transaction in the general journal (usually the credit entry, unless a compound entry is involved) repeat steps 1 through 5, except that the amount to be credited is recorded in the "Credit" column of the appropriate account.

Once the debit and credit entries for the first transaction have been posted to the related accounts, the next journal entry for the day is posted and the process continues until the daily postings are completed. **By strictly following these posting procedures, the chance of error is minimized.**

Illustration of Posting Process

The posting process is illustrated in Exhibit 2-5 for the January 1, 1991, transaction of the Dixon Travel Agency. The arrows numbered 1, 2, 3, 4, and 5 refer to steps 1 through 5 (for both the debit and credit entries) in the preceding list of posting procedures.

Note that the date of the transaction is transferred from the general journal to each ledger account. The amount of the debit ($30,000) is posted in the debit

EXHIBIT 2-5
Illustration of Posting

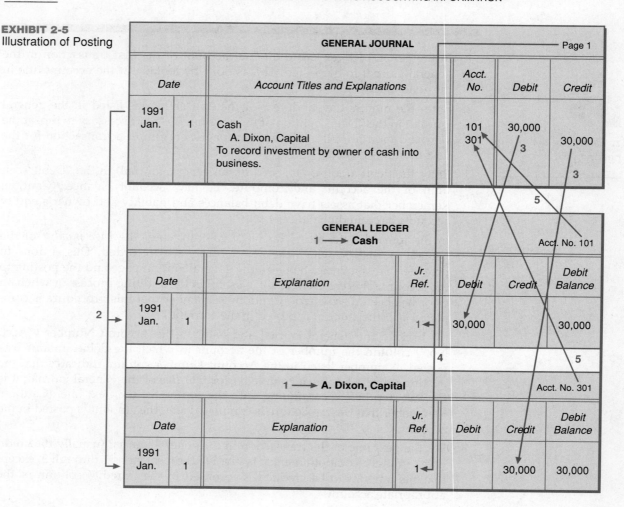

column[3] of the Cash account and the new balance is computed. (Since this is the first posting to the account, the balance is the same as the debit entry.) The credit entry ($30,000) and the new balance are posted in the A. Dixon, Capital account. The page number (1) of the general journal on which the transaction is journalized is listed in the journal reference column of each account, and the account numbers (101 and 301) are listed in the account number column of the general journal.

The posting process is completed at the end of each day of January. The accounts at the end of January are shown in Exhibit 2-6. They are listed as they would appear in the general ledger, which is according to the chart of accounts shown in Exhibit 2-4. You should study the postings to the accounts, referring to the journal entries listed in Exhibit 2-2. Note that in Exhibit 2-2 the account

---

[3]To avoid unnecessary detail, we again omitted the "cents" column in the debit and credit columns of the accounts. Both dollars and cents would be recorded in an actual account, however.

EXHIBIT 2-6
Dixon Travel Agency
Postings and Account
Balances

Cash — Acct. No. 101

Date		Explanation	Jr. Ref.	Debit	Credit	Debit Balance
1991 Jan.	1		1	30,000		30,000
	2		1		18,000	12,000
	12		1		1,000	11,000
	15		1		350	10,650

Accounts Receivable — Acct. No. 103

Date		Explanation	Jr. Ref.	Debit	Credit	Debit Balance
1991 Jan.	28		1	400		400

Office Supplies — Acct. No. 107

Date		Explanation	Jr. Ref.	Debit	Credit	Debit Balance
1991 Jan.	5		1	700		700

Land — Acct. No. 120

Date		Explanation	Jr. Ref.	Debit	Credit	Debit Balance
1991 Jan.	2		1	3,000		3,000

Building — Acct. No. 122

Date		Explanation	Jr. Ref.	Debit	Credit	Debit Balance
1991 Jan.	2		1	15,000		15,000

Office Equipment — Acct. No. 124

Date		Explanation	Jr. Ref.	Debit	Credit	Debit Balance
1991 Jan.	12		1	3,000		3,000
	28		1		400	2,600

continued

EXHIBIT 2-6
continued

Accounts Payable   Acct. No. 201

Date		Explanation	Jr. Ref.	Debit	Credit	Credit Balance
1991 Jan.	5		1		700	700
	15		1	350		350

Notes Payable   Acct. No. 204

Date		Explanation	Jr. Ref.	Debit	Credit	Credit Balance
1991 Jan.	12		1		2,000	2,000

A. Dixon, Capital   Acct. No. 301

Date		Explanation	Jr. Ref.	Debit	Credit	Credit Balance
1991 Jan.	1		1		30,000	30,000

number column had not been completed when the journal entry was made but would have been completed during the posting process. You should think of the numbers that would be listed in this column based on the account numbers in Exhibit 2-6.

Trial Balance

In discussing the journalizing and posting process we have set up procedures so that the double entry rule is followed; that is, the total amount of the debit entries is equal to the total amount of the credit entries. By following these procedures the accounting equation remains in balance and errors are minimized.

People can make mistakes, however, and therefore it is desirable to reduce the chance that a journalizing or posting error may be included in the financial statements used to communicate the accounting information. If we follow the double entry rule in journalizing and posting each transaction, the total of the debit balances in all the accounts should be equal to the total of the credit balances in all the accounts. Before preparing the financial statements, it is useful to perform an additional procedure to check for errors. This procedure involves proving the equality of the debit and credit account balances by preparing a trial balance.

8. Prepare a trial balance.

A trial balance is a schedule that lists the titles of all the accounts in the general ledger, the debit or credit balance of each account, and the totals of the debit and credit balances. To prepare a trial balance, the balance of each account in the general ledger is computed if this has not already been done. Next the accounts and debit or credit balances are listed on the trial balance according to the order in which the accounts are listed in the general ledger. Finally, the debit and credit columns are totaled to determine their equality. The trial balance of the Dixon Travel Agency is shown in Exhibit 2-7.

The trial balance is an accounting working paper used to prove the equality of the debit and credit account balances in the accounts. It is *not* a formal accounting statement but rather a type of source document. After it is prepared it is kept in the accounting records for future reference if necessary.

EXHIBIT 2-7
Trial Balance

DIXON TRAVEL AGENCY Trial Balance January 31, 1991		
Account Titles	*Debits*	*Credits*
Cash	$10,650	
Accounts receivable	400	
Office supplies	700	
Land	3,000	
Building	15,000	
Office equipment	2,600	
Accounts payable		$ 350
Notes payable		2,000
A. Dixon, capital		30,000
Totals	$32,350	$32,350

Error Detection

If a trial balance does not balance (i.e., the total debits are not equal to the total credits), an error has been made. To find the error, the debit and credit columns of the trial balance should be readded. If the column totals still do not agree, the amounts in the debit and credit columns should be checked to be sure that a debit or credit account balance was not mistakenly listed in the wrong column.

If the error is still not found, the difference in the column totals should be computed and divided by 9. When the difference is evenly divisible by 9, there is a good chance that a *transposition* or a *slide* has occurred. **A transposition occurs when two digits in a number are mistakenly reversed.** For instance, if the $2,600 Office Equipment balance had been listed as $6,200 in Exhibit 2-7, the debit column would have totaled $35,950 instead of $32,350. The difference, $3,600, is evenly divisible by 9. **A slide occurs when the digits are listed in the correct order but are mistakenly moved one decimal place to the left or right.** For instance, if the $350 Accounts Payable balance had been listed as $35 in Exhibit 2-7, the credit column would have totaled $32,035 instead of $32,350. The $315 difference is evenly divisible by 9.

If a transposition or slide has occurred, the error may have been made when transferring the account balances from the accounts to the trial balance or when the account balances were initially computed. Thus the account balances listed on the trial balance should be compared with the account balances listed in the ledger. Then the ledger account balances should be recomputed, and if no error is found, the postings should be double checked. Finally, the journal entries should be reviewed for accuracy.

If the trial balance is in balance (i.e., the total debits are equal to the total credits), it is likely that:

1. equal debit entries and credit entries were recorded for each transaction;
2. the debit and credit entries were posted to the accounts; and
3. the account balances were correctly computed.

The equality of the debit and credit totals, however, does not necessarily mean that the information in the accounting system is error free. Several types of errors are not found by a trial balance:

1. An entire transaction may not have been journalized.
2. An entire transaction may not have been posted to the accounts.
3. Equal debits and credits, but of the wrong amount, may have been recorded for a transaction.
4. A transaction may have been journalized to a wrong account. For instance, the purchase of land may have been debited to the Building account instead of the Land account.
5. A journal entry may be posted to the wrong account. For instance, the debit in a journal entry to the Office Supplies account may be posted as a debit to the Office Equipment account.

These potential errors illustrate why it is very important that you carefully study each transaction and always follow the set procedures in the journalizing and posting process.

Balance Sheet

9. Prepare a balance sheet from a trial balance.

Once the trial balance has been completed, the financial statements may be prepared. Since we have discussed only balance sheet transactions up to this point, the focus here is on this financial statement. Recall from Chapter 1 that **a balance sheet summarizes a company's financial position on a given date.** The balance sheet (or statement of financial position) reports on a company's resource structure (i.e., assets) and its financial structure (i.e., liabilities and owner's equity). **The information in a balance sheet (e.g., Exhibit 2-8) is intended to be useful by providing information about liquidity, financial flexibility, and owner's capital.** The *liquidity,* or "nearness to cash," of a company's assets is important for its ability to pay debts that are coming due. *Financial flexibility* refers to the ability of a company to adapt to change. Financial flexibility is important

EXHIBIT 2-8
Balance Sheet

DIXON TRAVEL AGENCY
Balance Sheet
January 31, 1991

Assets			*Liabilities*		
Cash	$10,650		Accounts payable	$ 350	
Accounts receivable	400		Notes payable	2,000	
Office supplies	700		Total Liabilities	$ 2,350	
Land	3,000		*Owner's Equity*		
Building	15,000		A. Dixon, capital	$30,000	
Office equipment	2,600		Total Liabilities and		
Total Assets	$32,350		Owner's Equity	$32,350	

because it allows a company to increase operations to take advantage of new business activities or to reduce operations due to, say, a slowdown in the economy. The types and amounts of a company's assets and liabilities can provide useful information about its financial flexibility. The *capital* of a company is the owner's current investment. As noted in Chapter 1, one of the primary objectives of a company is to earn a "satisfactory" profit. Knowledge of the owner's capital is important because a satisfactory profit involves both maintaining this capital and providing for a return on the capital so that withdrawals can be made. This topic is discussed more in Chapter 3.

To prepare the balance sheet, recall that the accounts and account balances are listed on the trial balance in the order that they appear in the general ledger according to the chart of accounts. Recall also that the chart of accounts is set up so that assets are listed first, followed by the liability and owner's equity accounts. Thus the listing of the accounts on the trial balance follows the order in which the accounts will appear on the balance sheet.

Another advantage of the trial balance is that it aids in the preparation of the balance sheet. The accounts and account balances as shown on the trial balance are simply recopied in a balance sheet format. The balance sheet of the Dixon Travel Agency shown in Exhibit 2-8 was prepared directly from the trial balance listed in Exhibit 2-7.

Components of an Accounting System

10. List the steps and documents in an accounting system.

We have now completed a simple accounting process for an accounting system. The steps in the process included examining source documents, journalizing, posting, preparing a trial balance, and completing a balance sheet. The business documents in the system include source documents, a general journal, ledger accounts, a trial balance, and the balance sheet. They are important steps and documents in any manual accounting system; their relationship is shown in Exhibit 2-9.

EXHIBIT 2-9
Accounting System:
Documents and Process

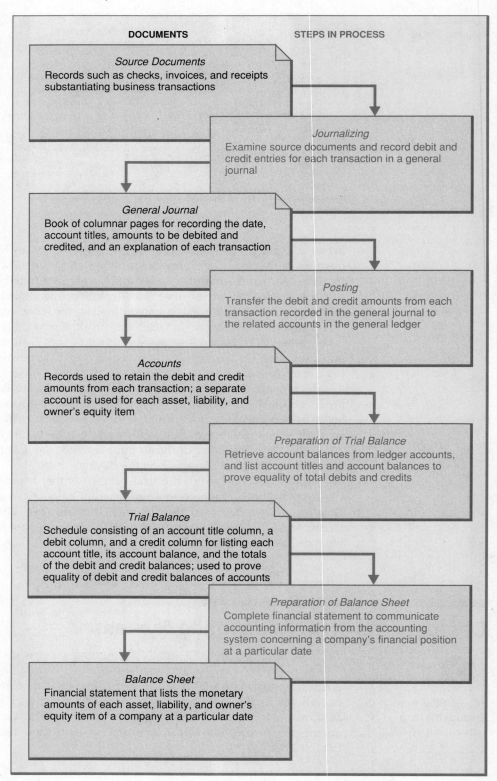

DOCUMENTS   **STEPS IN PROCESS**

Source Documents
Records such as checks, invoices, and receipts substantiating business transactions

Journalizing
Examine source documents and record debit and credit entries for each transaction in a general journal

General Journal
Book of columnar pages for recording the date, account titles, amounts to be debited and credited, and an explanation of each transaction

Posting
Transfer the debit and credit amounts from each transaction recorded in the general journal to the related accounts in the general ledger

Accounts
Records used to retain the debit and credit amounts from each transaction; a separate account is used for each asset, liability, and owner's equity item

Preparation of Trial Balance
Retrieve account balances from ledger accounts, and list account titles and account balances to prove equality of total debits and credits

Trial Balance
Schedule consisting of an account title column, a debit column, and a credit column for listing each account title, its account balance, and the totals of the debit and credit balances; used to prove equality of debit and credit balances of accounts

Preparation of Balance Sheet
Complete financial statement to communicate accounting information from the accounting system concerning a company's financial position at a particular date

Balance Sheet
Financial statement that lists the monetary amounts of each asset, liability, and owner's equity item of a company at a particular date

The documents and steps in Exhibit 2-9 should be studied carefully. They are the main parts of each accounting system[4] and are important to understanding the remaining topics in this textbook.

Chapter Summary

Review of Learning Objectives

1. **Define an account and a general ledger.**
   An account is a business document used to record and retain monetary information from a company's transactions. Separate accounts are used for each asset, liability, and owner's equity item. A general ledger is the entire set of accounts for a company.

2. **State the meaning of a debit entry and a credit entry.**
   A *debit* entry is a monetary amount recorded (i.e., debited) in the left side of an account. A *credit* entry is a monetary amount recorded (i.e., credited) in the right side of an account.

3. **Explain how asset, liability, and owner's equity accounts are increased and decreased.**
   Asset accounts are increased by debit entries and decreased by credit entries. Liability and owner's equity accounts are increased by credit entries and decreased by debit entries.

4. **Describe the double entry rule.**
   The double entry rule means that when recording each transaction the total amount of the debit entries must be equal to the total amount of the credit entries. For each recorded transaction there must be at least one debit and one credit entry, and the totals must be equal.

5. **Define a general journal and a journal entry.**
   A general journal is a business document in which a company's transactions are recorded. A journal entry is the recorded information for each transaction. It includes the date, the accounts and amounts to be debited and credited, and an explanation of each transaction. The process of preparing a journal entry is called *journalizing*.

6. **Prepare journal entries for asset, liability, and owner's equity accounts.**
   To prepare a journal entry, first enter the month, day, and year in the date column of the general journal. Then enter the title and amount of the

---

[4]As we shall see, there are more documents (e.g., the income statement) and processes in an accounting system; they are discussed in Chapter 3.

account to be debited in the appropriate columns. Indent the next line and enter the title and amount of the account to be credited in the appropriate columns. Finally, write a brief explanation on the line directly below the credit entry.

7. **Complete the posting process.**
   Posting involves transferring the debit and credit information for each journal entry to the proper accounts in the general ledger. To post a line from the general journal, first find the proper account. Second, enter the month, day, and year in the date column of the account. Then, enter the debit (or credit) amount in the debit (or credit) column. Next, enter the page number of the general journal in the journal reference column of the account. Finally, go back to the general journal and enter the account number in the account number column.

8. **Prepare a trial balance.**
   To prepare a trial balance, first compute the balance of each account in the general ledger. Then, write the company name, trial balance, and the date on a working paper. Next, list the accounts and debit or credit balances in their respective columns on the trial balance, in the order in which they appear in the general ledger. Finally, total the debit and credit columns to determine their equality.

9. **Prepare a balance sheet from a trial balance.**
   Remember that the listing of the account balances in the trial balance follows the order in which the accounts are to appear on the balance sheet. Thus to prepare a balance sheet, first list the proper heading. Then copy the accounts and account balances shown on the trial balance in a balance sheet format, making sure that the total of the assets is equal to the total liabilities and owner's equity.

10. **List the steps and documents in an accounting system.**
    In an accounting system, first journalize the transactions in a general journal based on the related source documents. Then, post the amounts for each transaction from the general journal to the accounts in the general ledger. Next, prepare a trial balance of the account balances to prove the equality of the total debits and credits. Finally, prepare a balance sheet listing the amount of each asset, liability, and owner's equity account on that date.

Review Problem

During the month of March 1991, Paul Campbell started the Campbell Insurance Agency, a sole proprietorship, and the company entered into the following transactions.

Date	Transaction
3/4/1991	Paul Campbell formed the Campbell Insurance Agency and invested $20,000 into the company.
3/6/1991	The company purchased land and a building for $35,000. The land was valued at $8,000 and the building at $27,000. The company made a $5,000 down payment and signed a 20-year mortgage for the remaining balance.
3/11/1991	The company purchased office equipment for $2,000 from the Tiger Office Supply Company, paying $500 down and agreeing to pay the remaining balance in 30 days.
3/14/1991	The company purchased a 2-year comprehensive insurance policy on the building and its contents, paying $300.
3/18/1991	The company sold half of the land purchased on March 6, 1991 for $4,000. The purchaser (Ace Realty Company) made a $1,000 down payment and signed a note requiring payment of the balance at the end of 1 year.
3/22/1991	The company purchased $600 of office supplies from the Tiger Office Supply Company on account; it agreed to pay the amount owed by the end of the month.
3/30/1991	The company paid Tiger Office Supply Company $600 for the supplies purchased on March 22.

The company established the following chart of accounts.

Account Title	Account Number
Cash	101
Notes Receivable	104
Office Supplies	105
Prepaid Insurance	106
Land	120
Building	121
Office Equipment	123
Accounts Payable	201
Mortgage Payable	205
P. Campbell, Capital	301

REQUIRED (1) Prepare journal entries to record the March transactions, (2) post the journal entries to the proper accounts, (3) prepare a trial balance at the end of March, and (4) prepare a March 31, 1991, balance sheet.

Solution to Review Problem

REQUIREMENT 1 General Journal Entries. (Note: The Acct. No. column is completed *after* posting to the accounts.)

			Acct.		
		GENERAL JOURNAL			Page 1
Date		*Account Titles and Explanations*	*Acct. No.*	*Debit*	*Credit*
1991 Mar.	4	Cash	101	20,000	
		P. Campbell, Capital	301		20,000
		To record investment by owner of cash into business.			
	6	Land	120	8,000	
		Building	121	27,000	
		Cash	101		5,000
		Mortgage Payable	205		30,000
		To record purchase of land and building. Made cash down payment and signed a 20-year mortgage for the balance owed.			
	11	Office Equipment	123	2,000	
		Cash	101		500
		Accounts Payable	201		1,500
		To record purchase of office equipment from Tiger Office Supply Company, by making cash down payment and agreeing to pay balance owed in 30 days.			
	14	Prepaid Insurance	106	300	
		Cash	101		300
		To record purchase of a 2-year comprehensive insurance policy on building and contents.			
	18	Cash	101	1,000	
		Notes Receivable	104	3,000	
		Land	120		4,000
		To record sale of half of the land purchased on March 6, 1991, to Ace Realty Company; received a cash down payment and accepted a 1-year note for the balance owed.			
	22	Office Supplies	105	600	
		Accounts Payable	201		600
		To record purchase of office supplies from the Tiger Office Supply Company, agreeing to pay the balance owed by the end of the month.			
	30	Accounts Payable	201	600	
		Cash	101		600
		To record payment to Tiger Office Supply Company of amount owed on account for office supplies purchased on March 22.			

REQUIREMENT 2 Postings to the Accounts.

Cash   Acct. No. 101

Date		Explanation	Jr. Ref.	Debit	Credit	Debit Balance
1991 Mar.	4		1	20,000		20,000
	6		1		5,000	15,000
	11		1		500	14,500
	14		1		300	14,200
	18		1	1,000		15,200
	30		1		600	14,600

Notes Receivable   Acct. No. 104

Date		Explanation	Jr. Ref.	Debit	Credit	Debit Balance
1991 Mar.	18		1	3,000		3,000

Office Supplies   Acct. No. 105

Date		Explanation	Jr. Ref.	Debit	Credit	Debit Balance
1991 Mar.	22		1	600		600

Prepaid Insurance   Acct. No. 106

Date		Explanation	Jr. Ref.	Debit	Credit	Debit Balance
1991 Mar.	14		1	300		300

Land   Acct. No. 120

Date		Explanation	Jr. Ref.	Debit	Credit	Debit Balance
1991 Mar.	6		1	8,000		8,000
	18		1		4,000	4,000

continued

Building   Acct. No. 121

Date		Explanation	Jr. Ref.	Debit	Credit	Debit Balance
1991 Mar.	6		1	27,000		27,000

Office Equipment   Acct. No. 123

Date		Explanation	Jr. Ref.	Debit	Credit	Debit Balance
1991 Mar.	11		1	2,000		2,000

Accounts Payable   Acct. No. 201

Date		Explanation	Jr. Ref.	Debit	Credit	Credit Balance
1991 Mar.	11		1		1,500	1,500
	22		1		600	2,100
	30		1	600		1,500

Mortgage Payable   Acct. No. 205

Date		Explanation	Jr. Ref.	Debit	Credit	Credit Balance
1991 Mar.	6		1		30,000	30,000

P. Campbell, Capital   Acct. No. 301

Date		Explanation	Jr. Ref.	Debit	Credit	Credit Balance
1991 Mar.	4		1		20,000	20,000

REQUIREMENT 3 Preparation of Trial Balance.

CAMPBELL INSURANCE AGENCY
Trial Balance
March 31, 1991

Account Titles	Debits	Credits
Cash	$14,600	
Notes receivable	3,000	
Office supplies	600	
Prepaid insurance	300	
Land	4,000	
Building	27,000	
Office equipment	2,000	
Accounts payable		$ 1,500
Mortgage payable		30,000
P. Campbell, capital		20,000
Totals	$51,500	$51,500

REQUIREMENT 4 Preparation of Balance Sheet.

CAMPBELL INSURANCE AGENCY
Balance Sheet
March 31, 1991

Assets		Liabilities	
Cash	$14,600	Accounts payable	$ 1,500
Notes receivable	3,000	Mortgage payable	30,000
Office supplies	600	Total Liabilities	$31,500
Prepaid insurance	300		
Land	4,000	*Owner's Equity*	
Building	27,000	P. Campbell, capital	$20,000
Office equipment	2,000		
		Total Liabilities and	
Total Assets	$51,500	Owner's Equity	$51,500

Glossary

Account. Document used to record and retain the monetary information from a company's transactions. A separate account is used for each asset, liability, and owner's equity item.

Account Balance. The difference between the total increases and total decreases in an account. Asset accounts have debit balances; liability and owner's equity accounts have credit balances.

Account Number. The number assigned to each account from the company's chart of accounts.

Balance Sheet. A financial statement used to summarize the financial position of a company on a given date. Also called a *statement of financial position.*

Chart of Accounts. A numbering system for a company's accounts in its general ledger. Helps reduce errors in the recording and retaining of the company's accounting information.

Compound Entry.   A journal entry in which two or more debit entries, two or more credit entries, or both, are made.

Credit Entry.   Monetary amount recorded (credited) in the right side (or credit column) of an account or the credit column of a journal.

Cross Reference.   Page number of general journal listed in the *journal reference (Jr. Ref.)* column of an account. Used to link the account entry to the general journal for auditing purposes and error detection.

Debit and Credit Rule.   Rule that states that all asset accounts are increased by debits and decreased by credits and all liability and owner's equity accounts are increased by credits and decreased by debits.

Debit Entry.   Monetary amount recorded (debited) in the left side (or debit column) of an account or the debit column of a journal.

Double Entry Rule.   Rule that states that for all recorded transactions, the total amount of the debit entries must be equal to the total amount of the credit entries.

General Journal.   A business document in which each transaction is initially recorded.

General Ledger.   The set of accounts of a company listed in order according to the chart of accounts.

Journal Entry.   An entry made in a journal listing the date, the account titles and amounts to be debited and credited, and an explanation of a transaction.

Journalizing.   The process of recording a journal entry

Posting.   The process of transferring the debit and credit entries recorded in each journal entry to the related accounts in the general ledger.

T-Account.   An account that looks like the capital letter T. The left side is used for recording debit entries and the right side for recording credit entries. T-accounts are used for illustrative purposes.

Trial Balance.   Schedule used to prove the equality of the debit and credit account balances. It lists the titles of all the accounts, the debit or credit balance of each account, and the totals of the debit and credit columns.

Questions

QUESTION 2-1   What is an accounting system?

QUESTION 2-2   Define an account. What are the parts of a T-account? What is a set of accounts called?

QUESTION 2-3   What is the debit and credit rule? How does this rule relate to the accounting equation?

QUESTION 2-4   What is a debit entry? A credit entry?

QUESTION 2-5   How is an account balance computed? What accounts usually have debit balances and what accounts usually have credit balances?

QUESTION 2-6   What is a general ledger? What is a chart of accounts?

QUESTION 2-7   Explain the double entry rule. How (if at all) is this rule changed in the case of a compound entry?

QUESTION 2-8   What is a general journal (in a manual accounting system)? Why is a journal often referred to as a document of original entry?

QUESTION 2-9   List the advantages of initially recording all transactions in a journal.

QUESTION 2-10   What is journalizing? Briefly describe the journalizing process.

QUESTION 2-11   What is posting? Briefly describe the posting process.

QUESTION 2-12   What is a trial balance? What are the advantages of preparing a trial balance? In what order are the accounts listed on a trial balance? Why?

QUESTION 2-13   Describe the process that should be completed if a trial balance does not balance.

QUESTION 2-14   List the types of errors that would *not* be detected by a trial balance.

QUESTION 2-15   What is a balance sheet? What is liquidity, financial flexibility, and owner's capital, and why is each important?

QUESTION 2-16   List the steps involved in completing the accounting process in their proper order. Relate these steps to the documents involved in the accounting system.

QUESTION 2-17   Indicate which accounts would be debited and credited in the following events:

(a) Increase in asset and increase in owner's equity

(b) Increase in asset and increase in liability

(c) Increase in asset and decrease in another asset

(d) Decrease in liability and decrease in asset

(e) Decrease in liability and increase in owner's equity

Exercises

EXERCISE 2-1   **Ending Cash Balance.** On March 1 Kaw Counseling Services showed a balance of $12,000 in its cash account. During the month it entered into the following transactions affecting cash:

Date	Transaction
Mar. 2	Purchased a building and land for $9,500.
15	Owner deposited an $18,000 personal check in the Kaw Counseling Services checking account.
21	Office equipment costing $2,500 was purchased by making a $1,000 down payment and signing a $1,500 note due at the end of 1 year.
28	Paid March telephone bill in the amount of $212.

REQUIRED   Set up a T-account for Cash and, based on the information given, enter the beginning balance, record the changes in the account, and calculate the ending balance.

EXERCISE 2-2   **Reconstruct Journal Entries.**   The general ledger of the Keller Tutoring Company showed the following T-accounts on September 30 after all the transactions for the month of September had been recorded and posted.

Cash					Accounts Receivable		
9/1	16,000	9/7	12,000		9/28	830	
		9/11	1,500				
		9/16	450				

Office Supplies			Land		
9/16	450		9/7	3,000	

Building			Office Furniture			
9/7	9,000		9/11	6,500	9/28	830

Notes Payable			W. A. Keller, Capital		
	9/11	5,000		9/1	16,000

REQUIRED   Prepare the journal entries that the company recorded during September.

EXERCISE 2-3   **Accounting Equation and Debits and Credits.**   In each of the following situations, the total debits or credits for one component of the accounting equation are missing:

(a)   Assets debited for $9,400; liabilities credited for $3,200.

(b)   Liabilities debited for $2,000; owner's equity credited for $10,000.

(c)   Assets credited for $6,200; owner's equity debited for $12,500.

(d)   Owner's equity credited for $27,500; liabilities debited for $5,715.

(e)   Assets debited for $12,600; owner's equity debited for $25,750.

REQUIRED   Using Assets: $60,000 = Liabilities: $20,000 + Owner's Equity: $40,000 as the beginning accounting equation, for each of the preceding situations determine (1) the total debits or credits for the missing component of the equation and (2) the amount of each component in the *ending* accounting equation. Treat each situation independently.

EXERCISE 2-4   **Accounting Equation and Debits and Credits.**   The total debits or credits for one component of the accounting equation are missing in each situation that follows:

(a)   Assets credited for $12,000; liabilities debited for $6,500.

(b)   Owner's equity debited for $15,750; assets credited for $7,500.

(c)   Liabilities credited for $1,000; owner's equity debited for $5,000.

(d)   Owner's equity credited for $20,000; assets debited for $9,650.

REQUIRED   Using Assets: $45,000 = Liabilities: $15,000 + Owner's Equity: $30,000 as the beginning accounting equation, for each of the preceding situations determine (1) the total debits or credits for the missing component of the equation and (2) the amount of each component in the *ending* accounting equation. Treat each situation independently.

EXERCISE 2-5 **Journal Entries.**   During the month of July the Sands Realty Company entered into the following transactions:

Date	Transaction
July 1	Nancy Sands deposited a $40,000 personal check in the company's checking account.
10	Purchased land and an office building at a cost of $2,000 and $21,000, respectively, paying $8,000 down and signing a $15,000 note due at the end of the year.
25	Purchased office supplies costing $800 on account.

REQUIRED   *1.* Prepare the journal entries necessary to record the preceding transactions.

2. List the source documents normally used in recording each of these transactions.

EXERCISE 2-6 **Journal Entries.**   Albert Mitchell started Worldwide Travel Service on April 1 of the current year, and the company engaged in the following transactions during the month of April:

Date	Transaction
Apr. 1	Albert Mitchell opened the business by depositing a $35,000 personal check in the new company's checking account.
3	Purchased land and a small office building for $2,500 and $28,000, respectively, paying $10,500 down and signing a 1-year note for $20,000.
20	Purchased office equipment at a cost of $6,000. Half of the cost was paid in cash and the remainder is due at the end of May.

REQUIRED   *1.* Prepare the necessary journal entries to record the preceding transactions.

2. List the source documents normally used in recording each of these transactions.

EXERCISE 2-7 **Journal Entries.**   Wiley Cato started Cato's Tax Service on January 1 of the current year, and the company engaged in the following transactions during the month of January:

Date	Transaction
Jan. 2	Wiley Cato deposited a $16,000 personal check in the company's checking account to start the business.
2	Purchased land and building at a cost of $4,000 and $19,000, respectively, paying 15% down and signing a 10-year mortgage for the balance.

3	Purchased office equipment costing $2,000 by paying $500 cash and signing a 90-day note for $1,500.
4	Purchased $540 of office supplies on account.
6	Purchased a 3-year insurance policy for $480 cash.
10	Purchased office furniture at a cost of $800, paying 25% down with the balance due at the end of the month.
15	Paid the amount due for office supplies purchased on January 4.
30	Paid balance due on office furniture purchased on January 10.

REQUIRED   Prepare the necessary journal entries to record the preceding transactions.

EXERCISE 2-8   **Posting and Trial Balance.**   The general journal and chart of accounts of the Miffler Company on May 31, 1991, are shown below:

GENERAL JOURNAL					Page 1
Date		Account Titles and Explanations	Acct. No.	Debit	Credit
1991 May	1	Cash J. R. Miffler, Capital To record investment by owner of cash into business.		29,000	29,000
	6	Land Cash To record purchase of land for future use.		5,000	5,000

	10	Office Equipment
		    Cash
		    Accounts Payable
		To record purchase of office equipment from Hav-all Supply Company, by making cash down payment and agreeing to pay balance at end of month.
				2,700	500
					2,200

	15	Land
		Building
		    Cash
		    Mortgage Payable
		To record purchase of land and building; made 10% down payment and signed a 10-year mortgage.
				3,000
				30,000
					3,300
					29,700

	31	Accounts Payable Cash To record payment of amount owed to Hav-all Supply Company on account for office equipment.		2,200	2,200

MIFFLER COMPANY CHARTS OF ACCOUNTS

Account Title	Account Number
Cash	101
Land	110
Building	112
Office Equipment	115
Accounts Payable	201
Mortgage Payable	205
J. R. Miffler, Capital	301

REQUIRED   1. Prepare general ledger accounts for each of the accounts in the chart of accounts.

2. Post the journal entries to the proper accounts and prepare a trial balance.

EXERCISE 2-9   **Recording in T-Accounts.**   The Waterloo Investigations Company began operations on January 2, 1991. During the month of January it entered into the following transactions:

Date	Transaction
Jan. 2	Ken Waterloo deposited $24,000 cash in the company's checking account.
7	Purchased land and a building for $1,000 and $8,000, respectively; $3,000 was paid in cash and a 10-year mortgage was signed for the remaining balance.
23	Office supplies were purchased at a cost of $2,100.
30	Surveillance equipment was purchased at a cost of $4,500, paying $1,500 down and signing a note for $3,000.

REQUIRED   1. Set up T-accounts for each of these accounts: Cash, Office Supplies, Land, Building, Surveillance Equipment, Mortgage Payable, Notes Payable, and Ken Waterloo, Capital.

2. Record each of the preceding transactions directly in the T-accounts set up in Requirement 1.

EXERCISE 2-10   **Prepare Trial Balance from Accounts.**   On May 31, 1991, the Broden Delivery Company showed the following account balances (listed in random order).

L.A. Broden, capital	$41,500
Accounts receivable	3,900
Delivery equipment	14,500
Cash	15,700
Mortgage payable	22,000
Buildings	25,000
Accounts payable	6,400
Prepaid insurance	1,000
Delivery supplies	4,300
Land	5,500

REQUIRED   Prepare in good form a trial balance for the Broden Delivery Company on May 31, 1991.

EXERCISE 2-11   **Correction of Errors.**   The trial balance of the Jordan Company that follows does not balance:

JORDAN COMPANY
Trial Balance
March 31, 1991

Account Titles	Debits	Credits
Cash	$ 6,000	
Notes receivable	3,000	
Office supplies	750	
Land	9,500	
Building	21,000	
Office equipment	3,750	
Accounts payable		$ 1,150
Jim Jordan, capital		43,000
Totals	$44,000	$44,150

Upon investigation, the following errors were discovered:

(a) On March 22, the company purchased office equipment at a cost of $1,500. The purchase was recorded by a debit of $1,500 to office equipment and a credit to accounts payable of $150.

(b) On March 30 the bookkeeper mistakenly posted a debit of $750 in cash to the credit side of the cash account.

REQUIRED   Assuming there are no other errors, prepare a corrected trial balance for the Jordan Company at March 31, 1991.

EXERCISE 2-12   **Balance Sheet.**   The following trial balance was prepared by the Cooper Dance Studio on June 30, 1991:

COOPER DANCE STUDIO
Trial Balance
June 30, 1991

Account Titles	Debits	Credits
Cash	$ 5,400	
Accounts receivable	4,700	
Office supplies	840	
Prepaid insurance	560	
Land	4,000	
Building	29,000	
Stereo equipment	6,500	
Accounts payable		$12,000
Susan Cooper, capital		39,000
Totals	$51,000	$51,000

REQUIRED   Prepare a balance sheet for the Cooper Dance Studio at June 30, 1991.

Problems

Part A

PROBLEM 2-1A **Recording in T-Accounts.** On August 1, 1991, Judy Kimberly started the Nu-Way Advertising Agency and the company engaged in the following transactions during August:

Date	Transaction
Aug. 1	Judy Kimberly deposited a $23,000 personal check into the agency's checking account.
2	Acquired land and an office building at a cost of $2,000 and $22,000, respectively. A down payment of $4,000 was made and a 1-year note was signed for the balance.
14	Purchased several pieces of office equipment at a cost of $1,500. The entire amount is due September 15.
26	Purchased office supplies at a cost of $850 cash.

REQUIRED

1. Prepare T-accounts for the following accounts: Cash, Office Supplies, Land, Building, Office Equipment, Accounts Payable, Notes Payable, and J. Kimberly, Capital.

2. Enter the preceding transactions directly in the T-accounts from Requirement 1.

3. List the source documents normally used in recording each of the transactions.

4. Prepare a trial balance for the Nu-way Advertising Agency at August 31, 1991.

PROBLEM 2-2A **Journal Entries and Posting.** The Cameron Copy-Quick Company was recently set up by Joseph Cameron. The company's transactions during October, the first month of operations, were as follows:

Date	Transaction
Oct. 3	Joseph Cameron deposited $32,000 in the company's checking account.
4	Acquired land and a building for $3,000 and $42,000, respectively, paying $5,000 cash and signing a 5-year mortgage.
15	Copy equipment costing $8,000 was purchased on account from Tailor Equipment Company.
20	Office supplies costing $1,600 were purchased for cash.
24	Purchased office furniture costing $2,300 from Freddy's Furniture, paying $300 cash. The balance of $2,000 is due in 30 days.
28	Purchased a 3-year insurance policy for $900 cash.
31	Paid balance due to Tailor Equipment Company for copy equipment purchased on October 15.

REQUIRED

1. Set up the following general ledger accounts (and account numbers): Cash (101), Office Supplies (105), Prepaid Insurance (106), Land (110), Building (112), Copy Equipment (114), Office Furniture (118), Accounts Payable (201), Mortgage Payable (220), and J. Cameron, Capital (301).

2. Record the preceding transactions in a general journal.

3. Post the journal entries to the general ledger accounts.

PROBLEM 2-3A   **Journal Entries, Posting, and Trial Balance.** On July 1, 1991, B. Bonzor started Bonzor's Barbeque Pit. During the month of July the company entered into the following transactions:

Date	Transaction
July 1	B. Bonzor deposited $40,000 cash into the business checking account.
2	Purchased building and land for $35,000, making a $5,000 down payment and signing a 15-year mortgage for the remaining balance. The land was valued at $8,000.
3	Purchased all necessary kitchen equipment for $10,000 cash.
5	Purchased tables and booths for the dining area at a cost of $6,500 by signing a 1-year note for the entire amount.
10	Purchased $500 of supplies on account from Gelone's Restaurant Supplies.
23	Purchased dining room equipment for $600 cash.

REQUIRED   1. Set up the following general ledger accounts (and account numbers): Cash (101), Supplies (106), Land (110), Building (112), Kitchen Equipment (114), Tables and Booths (115), Dining Room Equipment (116), Accounts Payable (201), Notes Payable (210), Mortgage Payable (220), and B. Bonzor, Capital (301).

2. Record the preceding transactions in a general journal.

3. Post the journal entries to the general ledger accounts.

4. Prepare a trial balance for Bonzor's Barbeque Pit at July 31, 1991.

PROBLEM 2-4A   **Journal Entries and Trial Balance.** The general ledger of Humphrey's Fishing Guide Service shows the following T-accounts on April 30, 1991 (all the transactions during April have been properly recorded and posted):

Cash				Accounts Receivable	
4/1	44,000	4/2	5,000	4/29	400
		4/8	3,500		

Boating Supplies		Land	
4/5	900	4/2	7,000

Building		Boating Equipment		
4/2	18,000	4/8	8,500	4/29	400

Accounts Payable		Notes Payable	
	4/5	900	4/8	5,000

Mortgage Payable		R. Humphreys, Capital	
	4/2	20,000	4/1	44,000

REQUIRED   1. Prepare the journal entries that the company recorded during April.

2. List the source documents normally used in recording each of the journal entries.

3. Prepare a trial balance for Humphreys Fishing Guide Service at April 30, 1991.

PROBLEM 2-5A   **Trial Balance and Balance Sheet.**   The following are the account balances of the Sheetel Company on May 31, 1991 (listed in random order):

Mortgage payable	$14,200
Notes receivable	940
P. Sheetel, capital	26,000
Office supplies	2,450
Land	8,500
Cash	9,550
Prepaid insurance	1,360
Accounts payable	1,000
Building	22,500
Notes payable	?

REQUIRED   1. Prepare a trial balance in the proper order for the Sheetel Company at May 31, 1991 (insert the correct amount for Notes Payable).

2. Prepare a balance sheet for the Sheetel Company at May 31, 1991.

PROBLEM 2-6A   **Correction of Errors.**   On July 31, one month after the Salisbury Credit Bureau was established, the company's accounting records showed the following trial balance:

SALISBURY CREDIT BUREAU
Trial Balance
July 31, 1991

Account Titles	Debits	Credits
Cash	$ 6,100	
Accounts receivable	600	
Office supplies		$ 1,300
Building	8,400	
Office equipment	6,700	
Notes payable		4,100
James Salisbury, capital		20,000
Totals	$21,800	$25,400

The following errors were found upon examination of the records:

(a) One piece of office equipment was sold at its original cost of $700 on July 16. In posting, the building account was credited erroneously instead of office equipment. The debit was posted correctly.

(b) When posting, $1,300 of supplies purchased on July 9 were entered erroneously in the credit side of the office supplies account. The cash payment was posted correctly.

(c) An addition error was made when determining the ending cash account balance on July 31. The error overstated the credit entries to cash by $1,000.

REQUIRED

1. Prepare a corrected trial balance for the Salisbury Credit Bureau at July 31, 1991.

2. Prepare a balance sheet for the company at July 31, 1991.

PROBLEM 2-7A   **The Accounting Process.**   During the month of June 1991, E. Fliey established Fliey Secretarial Services, and the company entered into the following transactions:

Date	Transaction
June 3	E. Fliey deposited $40,000 cash in the company's checking account.
10	The company purchased land and a building for $26,500. The land was valued at $6,000 and the building at $20,500. A down payment of $6,875 was made and a 10-year mortgage signed for the balance.
11	The company purchased data processing equipment for $5,000, paying $500 down and agreeing to pay the balance due in 30 days.
19	The company purchased $1,200 of office supplies for cash.
29	The company purchased a 2-year comprehensive insurance policy on the building, paying $600.

REQUIRED

1. Set up the following general ledger accounts (and account numbers): Cash (101), Office Supplies (105), Prepaid Insurance (106), Land (110), Building (112), Data Processing Equipment (114), Accounts Payable (201), Mortgage Payable (220), and E. Fliey, Capital (301).

2. Prepare the necessary general journal entries to record the preceding transactions.

3. Post the journal entries to the proper accounts.

4. Prepare a trial balance at June 30, 1991.

5. Prepare a balance sheet at June 30, 1991.

Problems

Part B

PROBLEM 2-1B   **Recording in T-Accounts.**   On June 1, 1991, Jody Weis started the Weis Company. The company engaged in the following transactions during June:

Date	Transaction
June 1	Jody Weis deposited $27,000 cash in the company's checking account.
3	Purchased land and an office building for $6,000 and $33,500, respectively, paying $9,500 down and signing a 10-year mortgage for the balance.
18	Purchased $2,000 of office equipment, paying $1,000 and agreeing to pay the remaining $1,000 in 30 days.
24	Purchased office supplies for $1,600 cash.

REQUIRED

1. Prepare T-accounts for the following accounts: Cash, Office Supplies, Land, Building, Office Equipment, Accounts Payable, Mortgage Payable, and Jody Weis, Capital.

2. Enter the preceding transactions directly in the T-accounts set up in Requirement 1.

3. List the source documents normally used to record each of the transactions.

4. Prepare a trial balance for the Weis Company at June 30, 1991.

PROBLEM 2-2B **Journal Entries and Posting.** The Polar Cold Storage Company was recently set up by P. T. Polar. During November 1991, the first month of operations, the company entered into the following transactions:

Date	Transaction
Nov. 1	P. T. Polar deposited $20,000 in the company's checking account.
4	Acquired land and building for $18,500. The land was valued at $3,500 and the building at $15,000. A $3,700 down payment was made and a 5-year mortgage was signed for the balance.
18	Freezer equipment costing $4,300 was purchased on account from Weller's Company.
21	Office supplies costing $900 were purchased for cash.
22	Purchased a 2-year insurance policy for $600 cash.
27	Purchased $2,600 of office furniture by signing a 90-day note for $1,800 and paying $800 cash.
29	Paid Weller's Company $2,000 on account for freezer equipment purchased on June 18.

REQUIRED

1. Set up the following general ledger accounts (and account numbers): Cash (101), Office Supplies (105), Prepaid Insurance (106), Land (110), Building (112), Freezer Equipment (114), Office Furniture (116), Accounts Payable (201), Notes Payable (210), Mortgage Payable (220), and P. T. Polar, Capital (301).

2. Record the preceding transactions in a general journal.

3. Post the journal entries to the general ledger accounts.

PROBLEM 2-3B **Journal Entries, Posting, and Trial Balance.** P. Talleby started the Talleby Photo Developing Company on August 1, 1991, and the company entered into the following transactions during the month of August:

Date	Transaction
Aug. 1	P. Talleby deposited $12,000 into the company's checking account.
5	Purchased land and a building for $5,000 and $28,000, respectively. The company made a $3,300 down payment and signed a mortgage for the balance.
8	Purchased a 3-year insurance policy on the building and its contents, paying $450 cash.
12	Purchased developing equipment for $1,350 from Belle's Photo Equipment Company, paying $350 cash and agreeing to pay the balance at the end of the month.
19	Purchased $800 of office supplies on account from Joe's Office Supplies.
30	Paid balance due Belle's Photo Equipment Company for developing equipment purchased on August 12.

REQUIRED

1. Set up the following general ledger accounts (and account numbers): Cash (101), Office Supplies (106), Prepaid Insurance (108), Land (110), Building (112), Developing Equipment (114), Accounts Payable (201), Mortgage Payable (220), and P. Talleby, Capital (301).

2. Record the preceding transactions in a general journal.

3. Post the journal entries to the general ledger accounts.

4. Prepare a trial balance for the Talleby Photo Developing Company at August 31, 1991.

PROBLEM 2-4B   **Journal Entries and Trial Balance.** The general ledger of the Lanards Electrical Engineering Company shows the following T-accounts on October 31, 1991 (all the transactions during October have been properly recorded and posted):

Cash				Accounts Receivable		
10/1	35,000	10/2	6,500	10/28	350	
		10/8	1,000			

Office Supplies		Land	
10/7	450	10/2	9,000

Building		Office Equipment		
10/2	37,500	10/8	4,500	10/28	350

Accounts Payable		Notes Payable	
	10/7 450		10/8 3,500

Mortgage Payable		R. S. Lanards, Capital	
	10/2 40,000		10/1 35,000

REQUIRED

1. Prepare the journal entries that the company recorded during October.

2. List the source documents normally used to record each of the journal entries.

3. Prepare a trial balance for the Lanards Electrical Engineering Company at October 31, 1991.

PROBLEM 2-5B   **Trial Balance and Balance Sheet.** The following are the account balances of the Letel Company on March 31, 1991 (listed in random order):

Notes payable	$ 6,120
Building	53,500
Accounts payable	?
Prepaid insurance	2,700
Cash	4,500
Land	15,000
Office supplies	2,900
R. Letel, capital	40,000
Notes receivable	1,650
Mortgage payable	31,100

REQUIRED 1. Prepare a trial balance in the proper order for the Letel Company at March 31, 1991 (insert the correct amount for Accounts Payable).

2. Prepare a balance sheet for the Letel Company at March 31, 1991.

PROBLEM 2-6B **Correction of Errors.** After the February 28, 1991, trial balance was prepared, the owner of Chatam Laundry Service suspected the cash account was in error. The balance shown for the cash account was $18,750, whereas the February 28 bank statement for the company showed a balance of $16,280. Upon investigation the following errors were discovered in the company's records:

(a) When calculating the ending cash balance the bookkeeper made a mathematical error that overstated the balance by $200.

(b) On February 6 the company purchased office supplies for $650 cash. However, the bookkeeper erroneously credited Accounts Payable instead of Cash for $650.

(c) On February 18 the company sold laundry equipment at its original cost of $970 for cash. The bookkeeper erroneously debited Cash and credited Laundry Equipment for $790.

(d) When posting to the general ledger the bookkeeper carelessly entered a credit entry for cash of $900 to the debit side of the cash account.

REQUIRED Starting with the cash account balance in a T-account make corrections in the account necessary to reconcile the difference between the cash balance and the balance shown on the bank statement. Assume the bank statement is accurate and current to date.

PROBLEM 2-7B **The Accounting Process.** During the month of August 1991, Z. Peeley established Peeley's Driving Range, and the company entered into the following transactions:

Date	Transaction
Aug. 1	Z. Peeley deposited $15,000 cash in the company's checking account.
6	Purchased land and a building for $23,000. The land was valued at $18,400 and the building at $4,600. A down payment of $6,000 was made and a 5-year mortgage signed for the balance.
9	Purchased golf equipment for $4,000, paying $400 down and agreeing to pay the balance due in 30 days.
19	Purchased $600 of golf supplies for cash.
30	Purchased a 2-year comprehensive insurance policy on the building and equipment, paying $300.

REQUIRED 1. Set up the following general ledger accounts (and account numbers): Cash (101), Golf Supplies (105), Prepaid Insurance (106), Land (110), Building (112), Golf Equipment (114), Accounts Payable (201), Mortgage Payable (220), and Z. Peeley, Capital (301).

2. Prepare the necessary general journal entries to record the preceding transactions.

3. Post the journal entries to the proper accounts.

4. Prepare a trial balance at August 31, 1991.

5. Prepare an August 31, 1991, balance sheet.

Decision Cases

DECISION CASE 2-1   **Stolen Checkbook.**   On March 8, 1991, Peter Bailey started his own company by depositing $10,000 in the Bailey Company checking account at the local bank. On March 14, 1991, the Bailey Company checkbook was stolen. During that period of time the Bailey Company had entered into several transactions, but unfortunately it had not established an accounting system for recording the transactions. Bailey did save numerous source documents, however, which had been put into an old shoebox.

In the shoebox is a fire insurance policy dated March 12, 1991, on a building owned by the Bailey Company. Listed on the policy was an amount of $300 for 1 year of insurance. "Paid in Full" had been stamped on the policy by the insurance agent. Also included in the box was a deed for land and a building at 800 East Main. The deed was dated March 11, 1991, and showed an amount of $40,000 (of which $8,000 was for the land). The deed indicated that a down payment had been made by the Bailey Company and that a mortgage was signed by the company for the balance owed.

The shoebox also contained an invoice dated March 12, 1991, from the Ace Office Equipment Company for $600 of office equipment sold to the Bailey Company. The invoice indicates that the amount is to be paid at the end of the month. A $34,000 mortgage, dated March 11, 1991, and signed by the Bailey Company, for the purchase of land and a building is also included in the shoebox. Finally, a 30-day, $4,000 note receivable is included in the shoebox. It is dated March 14, 1991, and is issued to the Bailey Company by the Ret Company for "one-half of the land located at 800 East Main."

The Bailey Company has asked for your help in preparing a balance sheet as of March 14, 1991. Peter Bailey indicates that company checks have been issued for all cash payments. Bailey has called its bank. The bank's records indicate that the Bailey Company's checking account balance is $9,500, consisting of a $10,000 deposit, a $200 canceled check made out to the Finley Office Supply Company, and a $300 canceled check made out to the Patz Insurance Agency.

You notice that the Bailey Company has numerous office supplies on hand. Peter Bailey indicates that a company check was issued on March 8, 1991, to purchase the supplies, but none of the supplies had been used.

REQUIRED   Based on the preceding information prepare a balance sheet for the Bailey Company on March 14, 1991. Be prepared to support each amount shown.

DECISION CASE 2-2   **Components of an Accounting System.**   The new owner of a small company has come to you for advice in setting up an accounting system for his business. Having had bookkeeping in high school, he vaguely remembers T-accounts but has no idea about the other components of an accounting system.

REQUIRED   Explain the components of an accounting system (e.g., the steps in the accounting process and the business documents related to each step).

DECISION CASE 2-3   **Erroneous Trial Balance.**   P. Seftly recently opened Seftly's Watch Repair. Since opening the business, he has recorded all the transactions relating to the business directly in T-accounts without dating or referencing the transactions in any way. Upon preparation of a trial balance Mr. Seftly discovered that the trial balance is "out of balance" by $2,700 and he has no idea where the problem lies.

REQUIRED   What suggestions would you make to Mr. Seftly in order to find the error? What suggestions would you make in order to prevent this type of problem from occurring in the future? Even if the trial balance had been in balance, could Mr. Seftly be certain that his accounting system is error free? Why or why not?

DECISION CASE 2-4   **Ending Balance Sheet.**   At the beginning of July 1991, Patti Dwyer established PD Company by investing $25,000 cash in the business. On July 5, the company purchased land and a building, making a $6,000 down payment (which was 10% of the purchase price) and signing a 10-year mortgage for the balance owed. The land was 20% of the cost and the building was 80% of the cost. On July 16, the company purchased $3,800 of office equipment on account, agreeing to pay half the amount owed in 10 days and the remainder in 30 days. On July 26, the company paid the amount due on the office equipment. On July 30, the company sold $900 of the office equipment that it did not need to another company for $900. The company signed a note requiring payment of the $900 at the end of 1 year.

REQUIRED   Based on the preceding information, prepare a balance sheet for the PD Company on July 31, 1991. Show supporting calculations.

DECISION CASE 2-5   **Projected Balance Sheet.**   Bart Brock is thinking about starting his own company, BB's. At the beginning of October 1991, he plans to invest $15,000 into the business. During the first month of business, the company will purchase land, a small building to house the business, some office equipment, and some supplies. Bart has found land and a building that would be suitable for the company. The purchase price of both the land and building is $50,000. Bart estimates that the cost of the land is 15% of the total price and the building is 85% of the total price. Bart wants the company to "finance" this purchase through its bank. The bank would require BB's to make a 20% down payment and would also require the company to sign a mortgage for the balance. Bart has determined that there is too much land, however, so that if BB's purchased the land and building, it would sell one quarter of the land to another company to use as a parking lot. The other company has agreed to buy the land at a price equal to the cost paid by BB's and to sign a note requiring payment of this cost at the end of 2 years. Bart has found some used office equipment which could be purchased by BB's for $4,500 on account, to be paid in 60 days. He also expects that BB's will need $800 of office supplies, which the company would purchase for cash.

    Before the bank will lend BB's the money to buy the land and building, it has requested a "projected" balance sheet for the company as of October 31, 1991, based on the preceding plans. Bart Brock has asked for your help.

REQUIRED   Based on the preceding information, prepare a projected balance sheet for BB's as of October 31, 1991. Show supporting calculations.

3

Revenues, Expenses, and the Income Statement

LEARNING OBJECTIVES

1. Define net income, revenues, and expenses.
2. Describe (a) an accounting period, (b) matching, and (c) accrual accounting.
3. Describe an income statement.
4. Explain the relationship of net income, investments, and withdrawals to owner's equity.
5. Explain the debit and credit rules for revenues, expenses, and withdrawals.
6. Record and post revenue and expense transactions.
7. Explain the purpose of adjusting entries.
8. Describe the relationships between the financial statements.
9. Prepare closing entries.
10. List the steps and documents in an accounting system.

n Chapter 2 we introduced an accounting system, the accounting process, and accounting documents. The intent of any accounting system is to identify, measure, record, retain, and communicate the accounting information from business transactions. Until now we have focused on only a few types of transactions (e.g., purchase of land for cash) affecting only the balance sheet accounts.

Companies also enter into other types of transactions to earn income, which is a major goal of every business enterprise. In this chapter we focus on these income-producing (earnings) transactions. We do not change the basic accounting rules established in the previous chapter; instead, we extend these rules as they apply to additional types of transactions.

Net Income and the Income Statement

A major goal of a company is to sell goods or services to customers at prices that are higher than the costs of providing the goods or services and, as a result, earn satisfactory income (profit) for the owners. Users of financial statements need income information to evaluate a company's operating results. By recording the transactions of a company's day-to-day operations, accountants are able to develop this income information.

1. Define net income, revenues, and expenses.

The income of a company is commonly referred to as net income. **Net income is the excess of revenues over expenses for a particular time period.** Net income is sometimes called *net profit, net earnings,* or simply *earnings.* **Revenues are the prices charged to a company's customers for goods or services provided during a particular time period. Expenses are the costs of providing the goods or services during the time period.** Net income may be shown in an equation as follows:

If expenses are more than revenues, the resulting negative amount is called *net loss,* instead of net income. Because net income (net loss) is the difference between revenues and expenses, it is important to understand these items and their relationship.

Revenues

Revenues may be thought of as the "accomplishments" of a company during a particular time period. Because revenues are prices charged to customers, **revenues result in increases in assets or decreases in liabilities** (as is shown later). When goods or services are provided, either the company receives cash from the customer or the customer agrees to pay at a later date, and the company thus acquires an account receivable. In either case, (1) revenue has resulted and (2) assets (either cash or accounts receivable) have increased.

It is very important to understand that the definition of revenue is *not* directly related to the inflow of cash. **The inflow of cash is *not* a requirement to record a revenue;** that is, a revenue may be earned whether or not there is an inflow of cash. (This issue is discussed more fully in Chapter 4.) Also, **there may be an inflow of cash without earning a revenue.** For instance, cash would increase as a result of borrowing money from a bank and signing a note payable to be repaid at a future date, or after a sale of goods to a customer on accounts receivable when the receivable is collected. In either case, even though there is an increase in cash, no revenue would be recorded. In the first case the cash increased as a result of an increase in a liability. In the second case, the cash increased as a result of a decrease in another asset, accounts receivable. (The revenue was recorded at the time of the sale; a common mistake among beginning accounting students is to record the revenue again at the time of the cash collection.) The requirement for recording revenue is that assets must have increased (or liabilities decreased) as a result of providing goods or services to customers.

Expenses

Expenses may be thought of as the "efforts" or "sacrifices" of a company during a particular time period. Examples of expenses include the wages and salaries of employees, the cost of products sold, advertising, heat, light, and power expenditures, property taxes, and delivery costs. Because expenses are the costs of providing goods or services, **expenses result in decreases in assets or increases in liabilities.** When current wages are paid to employees, for instance, an expense has resulted and an asset (Cash) has decreased.

It is important to remember two issues in regard to expenses. First, **the outflow of cash is *not* a requirement to record an expense;** that is, an expense may be incurred whether or not there is an outflow of cash. (This issue is discussed more fully later in the chapter.) Also, **there may be an outflow of cash without incurring an expense** (e.g., the purchase of office equipment for cash). The important point is that assets must have decreased (or liabilities increased) because of providing goods or services in a time period.

Second, **it is important to distinguish between the terms *cost* and *expense*.** Recall from Chapter 1 that accounting is based upon the historical cost principle; that is, business transactions are recorded on the basis of the monetary value exchanged (i.e., the cost) in the transaction. Thus the term *cost* refers to the amount at which a transaction is recorded. The nature of the transaction determines *how* a cost is recorded in an accounting system. The cost involved in a transaction can be recorded as either (1) an asset or (2) an expense. A cost is recorded as an asset when, in a transaction, the company acquires an economic resource that is expected to provide future benefits to the company. A cost is recorded as an expense if it results from providing goods or services to customers in a time period. This difference in recording costs is illustrated in Exhibit 3-1.

When a cost is recorded as an asset, it may be referred to as an unexpired cost, and when it is recorded as an expense, it may be referred to as an expired cost. What is important to remember at this point is that assets do not provide future benefits forever. Most assets eventually lose their potential for providing

EXHIBIT 3-1   Cost: Asset or Expense

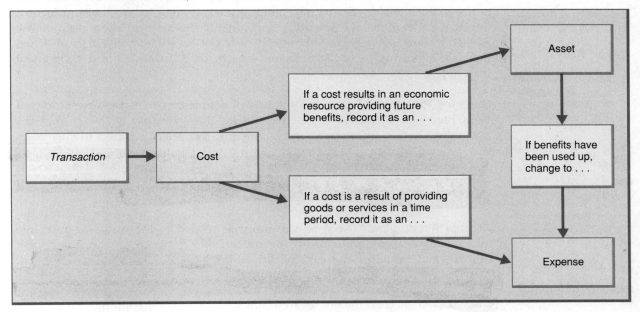

future benefits, and their status must be changed from an unexpired cost (asset) to an expired cost (expense). This concept is illustrated in the right column of Exhibit 3-1 and is also discussed later in the chapter.

Accounting Principles Related to Net Income

Three principles are important for understanding the measurement of net income. They include the concept of an accounting period, the matching principle, and accrual accounting. These principles are consistent with the conceptual framework and basic concepts (e.g., relevance, reliability, historical cost) introduced in Chapter 1.

2(a). Describe an accounting period.

Accounting Period.   Companies typically operate for many years. Financial statement users, however, need net income information on a regular basis in order to make economic decisions. Earlier, when defining net income, we referred to a *particular time period*. **An accounting period is the period of time for which the revenues and expenses of a company are computed.**

For financial accounting, a company usually uses a twelve-month accounting period called a fiscal year or *fiscal* period. The fiscal year is often the same as the calendar year; however, a company whose operations are seasonal may use a year that corresponds more closely to its seasonal operating activities. For instance, a company may use July 1, 1991, through June 30, 1992, as its accounting period. Certain companies are now required to compute and report their net income on a quarterly basis. These accounting periods (and others shorter than a year) are referred to as *interim* periods.

For managerial accounting, most companies use a month as the accounting period, which enables the management of the company to have current income information available for operating decisions. In this text we often use a month as our accounting period. Although it may not be realistic in terms of actual financial reporting, it saves time and space for illustrations and assignment material.

2(b). Describe matching.

Matching Principle. In the computation of net income, expenses are subtracted from revenues. Another way of expressing this principle is to say that the expired costs (i.e., efforts) are *matched* against the prices charged to customers (i.e., accomplishments) to determine net income. **The matching principle states that to determine the net income of a company for an accounting period, the total expenses involved in obtaining the revenues of the period must be computed and deducted from the revenues recorded in that period.**

2(c). Describe accrual accounting.

Accrual Accounting. Accrual accounting is related to the matching principle and to our earlier discussion of the relationship between revenues and cash inflows, and expenses and cash outflows. **In accrual accounting, revenue and expense transactions are recorded in the accounting period when the goods or services are provided, regardless of whether cash is received or paid by the company.** To accrue means to accumulate. In accrual accounting a company must be certain that all revenues have been recorded at the end of each accounting period. Thus it must record all revenues even if no cash inflow has been received. Similarly, the company must be certain that all expenses that should be matched against the revenue have been recorded even if no cash outflow has been made.

To illustrate this point, suppose a company purchased a two-year insurance policy at the beginning of 1991. At that time it properly recorded the cost as an asset, Prepaid Insurance, because the insurance policy was an economic resource that would provide benefits to the company for 1991 and 1992. At the end of 1991 only one year of insurance coverage from the policy remains. Part of the insurance cost was for insurance coverage in 1991, an expense of doing business in that year. Thus, as we discussed earlier, a portion of the cost originally recorded as an asset (unexpired cost) must be recorded as an expense (expired cost) and reported on the income statement for 1991. The remaining cost must be recorded as an asset (unexpired cost) and reported on the balance sheet at the end of 1991.

Accrual accounting is important because it links the revenues of a company to the accounting period in which they were earned, and it matches the expenses against the revenues in the same period. This procedure makes the resulting accounting information especially useful to users in evaluating the performance of a particular company. The accounting procedures related to accrual accounting are discussed later in the chapter.

Some companies, particularly smaller companies, do not use accrual accounting. Instead they use cash basis accounting. **In cash basis accounting, the net income for the accounting period is computed by subtracting the cash payments from the cash receipts for operations.** This method may result in a misleading evaluation of a company's operating results. The receipt and payment of cash may occur much earlier or later than the sale of goods or the provision of services to customers and the related costs. Accrual accounting eliminates distortions of a company's operating results due to the timing of cash transactions. Accrual accounting recognizes the economic substance of the earnings transactions and is appropriate for companies of all sizes. For convenience, however, cash basis accounting is often used for small companies with a few employees in which the owner-manager finances all the operations. However, generally accepted accounting principles require the use of accrual accounting.

Income Statement

An income statement is a financial statement summarizing the results of a company's earnings activities for its accounting period. Recall from Chapter 1 that a company's earnings activities involve acquiring and selling inventory (goods) or providing services to customers. Thus an income statement shows the revenues, expenses, and net income (or net loss) for this time period. This statement is alternatively referred to as a *statement of income, statement of earnings, profit and loss statement,* or *statement of operations.* The income statement is an expansion of the income equation presented earlier.

Net Income = Revenues – Expenses

The income statement is considered by many users to be the most important financial statement. This importance arises because the statement is used to determine how well a company has achieved one of its primary goals, which is to earn a profit. That is, the income statement reports on the company's accomplishments (i.e., revenues), its efforts (i.e., expenses) to achieve these accomplishments, and the resulting net income (or net loss). The income statement is also used in conjunction with the balance sheet to determine whether a "satisfactory" profit has been made. An owner invests *capital* into a company to earn a profit. The profit, or earnings, is sometimes referred to as making a *return on investment.* Before a company can provide a satisfactory return on investment, as discussed in Chapter 2, the owner's capital (i.e., owner's equity[1]) first must be maintained. Then the earnings must be compared with the capital invested to determine whether a satisfactory profit has been earned.

Related to the preceding concepts, income statement information is also used to evaluate a company's risk, financial flexibility, and operating capability. **Risk is the uncertainty about the future earnings potential of a company.** Users can look at the current and past income statements of a company to predict its future earnings. As discussed in Chapter 2, **financial flexibility refers to a company's ability to adapt to change.** The relationship of expenses to revenues can reveal useful information about a company's financial flexibility. **Operating capability refers to a company's ability to maintain a given physical level of operations.** A review of the types and amount of current expenses can provide insights about a company's operating capability.

---

[1]Recall that the singular *owner's* equity is used throughout this chapter because we are focusing primarily on sole proprietorships.

Owners, potential owners, creditors, and other users of accounting information rely on the information in the income statement to make important economic decisions concerning the current and likely future operating performance of a company. This topic is discussed further in Chapter 19.

In this chapter we focus the discussion on the income statements of *service companies* (companies such as marketing research firms, travel agencies, and laundries) which sell a service instead of a product. (In Chapter 5 we extend the discussion to include the income statements of *merchandising companies*, which sell products.)

3. Describe an income statement.

An illustration of a typical income statement for a service company is shown in Exhibit 3-2. An income statement always has a heading consisting of three lines: the company's name, the title of the statement (i.e., *income statement*), and the accounting period for which the income statement is prepared. The dating for the accounting period includes both the length of the period and the date at the end of the period. Within the income statement are two sections; one is for revenues and the other for expenses. In the revenues section the types and amounts of revenues for the period are listed. These amounts are summed to determine the total revenues. A service company often has only a single revenue (e.g., Travel Commissions Revenue or Laundry Revenue). In the expenses section the various types and amounts of expenses for the period are listed. These amounts are summed to determine the total expenses. Total expenses are then subtracted from total revenues to determine net income. Note that parentheses are used to indicate a subtraction or negative item. (When total expenses exceed total revenues the format of the income statement is the same, although the resulting negative difference is entitled *net loss*.)

Each income statement is a result of a company's accounting system. To understand the accounting information contained in the income statement better, we return to the identifying, measuring, recording, and retaining processes

EXHIBIT 3-2
Income Statement

NORSTED LAUNDRY AND DRY CLEANING		
Income Statement		
For Year Ended December 31, 1991		
Revenues:		
Laundry revenues		$28,200
Dry cleaning revenues		49,700
Total revenues		$77,900
Expenses:		
Employees' wages	$22,400	
Heat, light, and power	8,100	
Property taxes	1,200	
Depreciation expense: washers and dryers	2,600	
Depreciation expense: dry cleaning equipment	3,900	
Rent expense on building	9,600	
Insurance expense	500	
Supplies	4,300	
Total expenses		(52,600)
Net income		$25,300

that must be completed before the preparation of the income statement. First, however, we briefly discuss withdrawals and the relationship of net income to owner's equity.

Withdrawals

When an owner invests in a company the owner contributes cash or other assets, and an increase is recorded in the company's assets and in owner's equity. This investment in assets is used in the company's operations in order to earn a satisfactory net income for the owner. In many businesses the owner is also the full-time manager. While operating the business the owner may require cash for personal expenditures or other investment opportunities. Cash may be periodically withdrawn from the company for this purpose.

Care must be taken to account properly for the owner's withdrawals of assets from a business. A withdrawal should be recorded in a manner opposite to that of recording an investment by the owner; that is, a withdrawal is recorded as a decrease in a company's assets and as a decrease in the company's owner's equity. Withdrawals should not be confused with expenses. **Withdrawals are not expenses, just as investments are not revenues.**

This treatment of withdrawals is consistent with the business entity concept introduced in Chapter 1, in which we noted that a company is considered to be an economic entity separate from its owner. We observed that an owner's personal financial activities are not included within the accounting system of the company unless the activity has a direct impact on the business. The direct impact of a withdrawal is a *disinvestment* of assets by the owner. It is not considered an expense, but is instead treated as a direct reduction of assets and owner's equity. Withdrawals are therefore *not* included in an income statement. We discuss the recording and reporting of withdrawals later in this chapter.

Relationship of Net Income, Investments, and Withdrawals to Owner's Equity

In Chapter 1 we introduced the accounting equation: assets equal liabilities plus owner's equity. We noted that the equation must always remain in balance because assets are financed either by a company's creditors or by its owner. We have observed that owner's equity may increase as a result of the initial and subsequent investments by the owner. It may decrease as a result of withdrawals by the owner.

In this chapter we relate revenues to increases in assets (or decreases in liabilities) as a result of providing goods or services to customers during an accounting period. We relate expenses to decreases in assets (or increases in liabilities) from providing the goods or services. When revenues exceed expenses, resulting in net income, an increase in net assets (net assets are assets minus lia-

4. Explain the relationship of net income, investments, and withdrawals to owner's equity.

bilities) also occurs. Since the net income of a company belongs to its owner, it is recorded as an increase in owner's equity (thereby keeping the accounting equation in balance).

We may now summarize the components of owner's equity. Owner's equity is increased by the initial and subsequent investments of the owner and by net income (revenues greater than expenses). Owner's equity is decreased by the withdrawals of the owner and by a net loss (expenses greater than revenues). This relationship is shown in Exhibit 3-3.

It is important to understand the relationship of the components (revenues and expenses) of net income to owner's equity. Exhibit 3-3 shows that net income increases owner's equity. Since revenues increase net income, it follows that *revenues increase owner's equity.* Since expenses decrease net income, it follows that *expenses decrease owner's equity.* In the case of a net loss a decrease in owner's equity occurs because expenses (which decrease owner's equity) exceed revenues (which increase owner's equity). The relationship of revenues and expenses to owner's equity plays an important part in the recording process for these items.

EXHIBIT 3-3
Components of
Owner's Equity

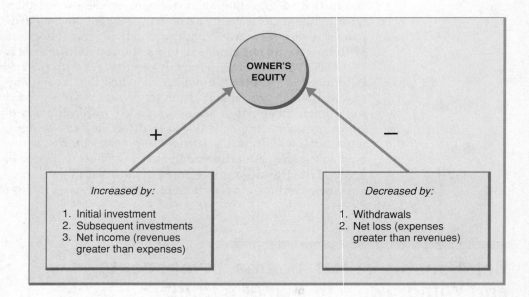

Recording, Retaining, and Reporting Net Income and Withdrawals Information

Since net income affects owner's equity, it would be possible to record all the transactions of a company affecting revenues and expenses directly in the owner's capital account. Remember, however, that only the balance of an account is reported on a financial statement. Reporting the ending balance of the owner's capital account may be useful for certain purposes, but it would not be useful in reporting the company's net income. What is needed are additional accounts in the company's accounting system in which to record and retain the monetary amounts of the revenue and expense transactions so that an income statement for the accounting period can be prepared. These accounts are called *temporary* (or *nominal*) accounts because they are used only to compute the net income for the accounting period. These accounts are different from the accounts that are listed on the balance sheet, which are called *permanent* (or *real*) accounts.

Withdrawals could also be deducted directly from the owner's capital account. It is important, however, to report the total withdrawals for the accounting period so that the owner will know exactly how much has been taken out of the business during the period. A *temporary* withdrawals account is used for this purpose.

Debit and Credit Rules

5. Explain the debit and credit rules for revenues, expenses, and withdrawals.

We already have several rules for a typical accounting system. They include maintaining the equality of the accounting equation, the debit and credit rules for assets, liabilities, and owner's equity accounts, and the double entry system. In creating new revenue and expense accounts and a withdrawals account, these accounts must *fit* into the accounting system so that none of these rules will be broken. Thus debit and credit rules have been made for revenues, expenses, and withdrawals based on their relationship to owner's equity. These rules are summarized later in Exhibit 3-4 and are explained as follows.

Recall that the owner's capital account is on the right side of the accounting equation. It is therefore increased by credit entries and decreased by debit entries. Since revenues increase owner's equity, all revenue accounts are increased by credit entries and decreased by debit entries. Expenses, however, decrease owner's equity. As expenses increase, owner's equity decreases. Thus the debit and credit rule for expenses is the opposite of that for owner's equity; that is, increases in expense accounts are recorded by debit entries and decreases in expense accounts are recorded by credit entries. Withdrawals similarly reduce owner's equity. An increase in the withdrawals account is recorded by a debit entry and a decrease in the withdrawals account is recorded by a credit entry.

The entire set of debit and credit rules, as they relate to the permanent asset, liability, and owner's equity accounts and to the temporary withdrawals, revenue, and expense accounts, are summarized as follows:

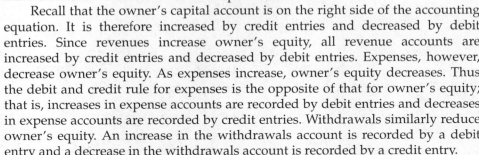

1. **Asset accounts are increased by debit entries and decreased by credit entries.**
2. **Liability accounts are increased by credit entries and decreased by debit entries.**

3. **Permanent owner's equity (capital) accounts are increased by credit entries and decreased by debit entries. Temporary owner's equity accounts have the following rules:**
   (a) **Withdrawal accounts are increased by debit entries and decreased by credit entries.**
   (b) **Revenue accounts are increased by credit entries and decreased by debit entries.**
   (c) **Expense accounts are increased by debit entries and decreased by credit entries.**

The remaining rules that have already been made are still used in the accounting system; that is, the accounting equation must always remain in balance and the double entry rule must be followed in recording all transactions. The debit and credit rules, as they relate to the accounting equation, are illustrated in Exhibit 3-4.

EXHIBIT 3-4   Accounting Equation and Debit and Credit Rules

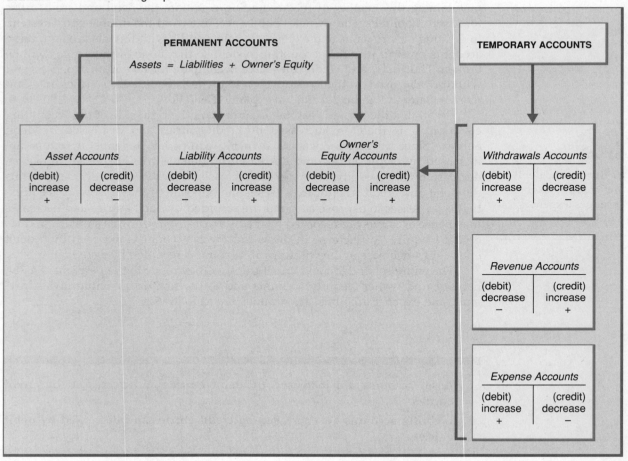

As a result of using the debit and credit rules along with maintaining the equality of the accounting equation, **the accounts will have these** *normal* **balances during the accounting period:**

Accounts	Normal Balance
Assets	Debit
Liabilities	Credit
Owner's capital	Credit
Owner's withdrawals	Debit
Revenues	Credit
Expenses	Debit

Recording and Posting Transactions

6. Record and post revenue and expense transactions.

The rules for recording and posting also apply to revenue and expense transactions. That is, for each transaction the source documents are examined to determine the types of accounts affected and the monetary amount of the transaction. The transaction is initially recorded in the general journal by listing the date, the account to be debited and the amount, the account to be credited (remember this item is indented slightly) and the amount, and an explanation of the journal entry. Compound entries are recorded as discussed earlier.

The postings to the general ledger follow the same procedures as before. The journal entry is posted, line by line, to the related accounts. In the account is listed the date, the amount of the debit or credit entry, and the page number of the journal on which the transaction was initially recorded. The number of the account is listed in the "account number" column of the general journal to complete the posting for that line. The posting is continued until each line for all the journal entries has been posted.

Chart of Accounts and Account Titles

As explained in Chapter 2, the chart of accounts is established so that the asset, liability, and owner's equity accounts are listed in order in the general ledger. **Because withdrawals, revenue, and expense accounts are temporary accounts affecting owner's equity, they are located in the general ledger** *after* **the permanent owner's equity accounts and are assigned higher account numbers.** The withdrawals account typically follows directly after the owner's capital account. Then all the revenue accounts are included, followed by the expense accounts. As you will see shortly, ordering the accounts in the general ledger in this way helps in the preparation of the income statement and the balance sheet. The title of each revenue and expense account is usually very descriptive. Thus Legal Fees Earned or Accounting Services Revenues might be titles used for the revenue accounts of a lawyer and CPA, respectively. Salaries Expense and Rent Expense are examples of the titles of expense accounts.

Illustration of Accounting for Withdrawals, Revenues, and Expenses

To illustrate the accounting for withdrawals, revenue, and expense transactions, we continue with the Dixon Travel Agency example introduced in Chapter 1 and continued in Chapter 2. In Chapter 2 we journalized and posted six transactions during January 1991. The January journal entries for these transactions are shown in Exhibit 3-5.

At the beginning of February 1991 the Dixon Travel Agency hired one employee at a monthly salary of $600, payable at the end of each month, and

EXHIBIT 3-5
General Journal
Entries for
January 1991

GENERAL JOURNAL				Page 1
Date	Account Titles and Explanations	Acct. No.	Debit	Credit
1991 Jan. 1	Cash	101	30,000	
	A. Dixon, Capital	301		30,000
	To record investment by owner of cash into business.			
2	Land	120	3,000	
	Building	122	15,000	
	Cash	101		18,000
	To record purchase of land and office building for use in operating the travel agency.			
5	Office Supplies	107	700	
	Accounts Payable	201		700
	To record purchase of office supplies on account from City Supply Company; agreed to pay half of the amount owed on January 15 and the remainder on February 15.			
12	Office Equipment	124	3,000	
	Cash	101		1,000
	Notes Payable	204		2,000
	To record purchase of office equipment from Ace Equipment Company; made cash down payment and signed 1-year note.			
15	Accounts Payable	201	350	
	Cash	101		350
	To record payment to City Supply Company of half the amount owed for office supplies purchased on January 5.			
28	Accounts Receivable	103	400	
	Office Equipment	124		400
	To record sale of desk that cost $400 to James Baker on credit for $400, the full amount is to be collected on February 7.			

began its operations. It added the following accounts and account numbers to its chart of accounts:

Account Titles	Account Numbers
Accumulated Depreciation: Building	123
Accumulated Depreciation: Office Equipment	125
A. Dixon, Withdrawals	304
Income Summary	306
Travel Commissions Revenues	401
Salary Expense	501
Telephone Expense	502
Utilities Expense	503
Office Supplies Expense	504
Depreciation Expense: Building	505
Depreciation Expense: Office Equipment	506

During February it entered into eight transactions. These transactions are summarized and analyzed in Exhibit 3-6.

Journal Entries. The journal entries to record the February transactions are listed in Exhibit 3-7. Notice that the January 1991 journal entries completely filled page 1 of the Dixon Travel Agency general journal and therefore the February transactions are recorded on page 2. Also remember that the Acct. No. (account number) column has been filled in because the journal entries have been posted to the respective accounts (shown in Exhibit 3-8).

The February 4 and 11 journal entries involve revenue transactions. In both cases assets were increased as a result of services performed and revenues were recognized.[2] The February 4 entry involved Cash while the February 11 entry involved Accounts Receivable. On February 27 and 28 three expense transactions were recorded as a result of providing services. The first two transactions involved a decrease in the asset, Cash, while the third transaction resulted in an increase in a liability, Accounts Payable.

Note that the February 20 withdrawal was *not* recorded as an expense but rather in the Withdrawals account. Although the February 7 and 15 journal entries involved a receipt and payment of cash, respectively, neither was a revenue nor an expense. The February 7 entry related to the collection of an account receivable while the February 15 entry involved a payment of an account payable.

Posting. The postings of journal entries to the appropriate accounts for the February transactions are shown in Exhibit 3-8. Notice that the beginning February balance for each permanent (balance sheet) account is the ending balance for January (as computed in Chapter 2). Also notice that the Jr. Ref. (journal

---

[2]In accounting, the terms *recognized* and *recorded* are often used interchangeably. We will do so in this text.

EXHIBIT 3-6   Analysis of Transactions

Date	Source Document	Transaction	Analysis
2/4/1991	Receipts issued to customers and related paperwork	Made travel arrangements for several customers and collected $620 in commissions for services performed.	The asset Cash is increased as a result of services performed. Debit (increase) Cash and credit (increase) the revenue account, Travel Commissions Revenues.
2/7/1991	Check from James Baker	Collected $400, the amount owed by Baker for desk purchased on January 28.	The asset Cash is exchanged for the asset Accounts Receivable. No revenue is involved. Debit (increase) Cash and credit (decrease) Accounts Receivable.
2/11/1991	Bills sent to customers and related paperwork	Made travel arrangements for several customers. Customers agreed to pay the $680 commissions by March 11, 1991.	The asset Accounts Receivable is increased as a result of services performed. Debit (increase) Accounts Receivable and credit (increase) Travel Commissions Revenues.
2/15/1991	Check issued to supplier	Paid City Supply Company $350 on account for supplies purchased on January 5, 1991.	The liability Accounts Payable is paid. No expense is involved. Debit (decrease) Accounts Payable and credit (decrease) Cash.
2/20/1991	Check issued to Anne Dixon	Anne Dixon withdrew $450 cash from the business for her personal use.	The asset Cash is decreased as a result of withdrawal (disinvestment) by owner. Debit (increase) A. Dixon, Withdrawals and credit (decrease) Cash.
2/27/1991	Check issued to employee	Employee was paid $600 monthly salary.	The asset Cash is decreased as a result of an expense. Debit (increase) Salary Expense and credit (decrease) Cash.
2/28/1991	Bill from phone company	Paid phone company $100 for phone charges for month of February.	The asset Cash is decreased as a result of an expense. Debit (increase) the expense account Telephone Expense and credit (decrease) Cash.
2/28/1991	Utility bill	Received the $170 utility bill (heat, light, and water) for February, to be paid by March 5, 1991.	The liability Accounts Payable is increased as a result of an expense. Debit (increase) Utilities Expense and credit (increase) Accounts Payable.

reference) in each account is to page 2 of the general journal and that the account numbers are listed in the general journal (Exhibit 3-7) as evidence that the postings are completed.

Trial Balance.   At the end of February a trial balance may be prepared to prove the equality of the debit and credit balances in the ledger accounts. This trial balance is shown in Exhibit 3-9.

EXHIBIT 3-7
Journal Entries

		GENERAL JOURNAL			Page 2
Date		Account Titles and Explanations	Acct. No.	Debit	Credit
1991 Feb.	4	Cash Travel Commissions Revenues To record travel arrangements made for customers and collection of cash.	101 401	620	620
	7	Cash Accounts Receivable To record collection of cash from James Baker as amount owed for desk purchased in January.	101 103	400	400
	11	Accounts Receivable Travel Commissions Revenues To record travel arrangements made for customers on account. Customers agreed to pay amounts owed by March 11, 1991.	103 401	680	680
	15	Accounts Payable Cash To record payment to City Supply Company for balance owed on account from purchase of office supplies on January 5.	201 101	350	350
	20	A. Dixon, Withdrawals Cash To record withdrawal of cash by owner for her personal use.	304 101	450	450
	27	Salary Expense Cash To record payment of employee's salary for February.	501 101	600	600
	28	Telephone Expense Cash To record payment of phone bill for the month of February.	502 101	100	100
	28	Utilities Expense Accounts Payable To record utilities for February to be paid by March 5, 1991.	503 201	170	170

Adjusting Entries

Earlier in the chapter when discussing accrual accounting, we pointed out that at the end of a company's accounting period the company must be certain that all revenues and expenses have been recorded. We stated that in journalizing a transaction, a *cost* may be recorded as an expense (expired cost) or as an asset (unexpired cost). We also observed that most assets eventually lose their potential for providing future benefits and must be changed to an expense. An adjusting entry is used for this purpose.

EXHIBIT 3-8
Postings and
Account Balances

Cash Acct. No. 101

Date		Explanation	Jr. Ref.	Debit	Credit	Debit Balance
1991						
Jan.	1		1	30,000		30,000
	2		1		18,000	12,000
	12		1		1,000	11,000
	15		1		350	10,650
Feb.	4		2	620		11,270
	7		2	400		11,670
	15		2		350	11,320
	20		2		450	10,870
	27		2		600	10,270
	28		2		100	10,170

Accounts Receivable Acct. No. 103

Date		Explanation	Jr. Ref.	Debit	Credit	Debit Balance
1991						
Jan.	28		1	400		400
Feb.	7		2		400	0
	11		2	680		680

Office Supplies Acct. No. 107

Date		Explanation	Jr. Ref.	Debit	Credit	Debit Balance
1991						
Jan.	5		1	700		700

Land Acct. No. 120

Date		Explanation	Jr. Ref.	Debit	Credit	Debit Balance
1991						
Jan.	2		1	3,000		3,000

Building Acct. No. 122

Date		Explanation	Jr. Ref.	Debit	Credit	Debit Balance
1991						
Jan.	2		1	15,000		15,000

continued

EXHIBIT 3-8
continued

Office Equipment — Acct. No. 124

Date		Explanation	Jr. Ref.	Debit	Credit	Debit Balance
1991 Jan.	12		1	3,000		3,000
	28		1		400	2,600

Accounts Payable — Acct. No. 201

Date		Explanation	Jr. Ref.	Debit	Credit	Credit Balance
1991 Jan.	5		1		700	700
	15		1	350		350
Feb.	15		2	350		0
	28		2		170	170

Notes Payable — Acct. No. 204

Date		Explanation	Jr. Ref.	Debit	Credit	Credit Balance
1991 Jan.	12		1		2,000	2,000

A. Dixon, Capital — Acct. No. 301

Date		Explanation	Jr. Ref.	Debit	Credit	Credit Balance
1991 Jan.	1		1		30,000	30,000

A. Dixon, Withdrawals — Acct. No. 304

Date		Explanation	Jr. Ref.	Debit	Credit	Debit Balance
1991 Feb.	20		2	450		450

Travel Commissions Revenues — Acct. No. 401

Date		Explanation	Jr. Ref.	Debit	Credit	Credit Balance
1991 Feb.	4		2		620	620
	11		2		680	1,300

continued

EXHIBIT 3-8
continued

Salary Expense						Acct. No. 501
Date		Explanation	Jr. Ref.	Debit	Credit	Debit Balance
1991 Feb.	27		2	600		600

Telephone Expense						Acct. No. 502
Date		Explanation	Jr. Ref.	Debit	Credit	Debit Balance
1991 Feb.	28		2	100		100

Utilities Expense						Acct. No. 503
Date		Explanation	Jr. Ref.	Debit	Credit	Debit Balance
1991 Feb.	28		2	170		170

EXHIBIT 3-9
Trial Balance

DIXON TRAVEL AGENCY
Trial Balance
February 28, 1991

Account Titles	Debits	Credits
Cash	$10,170	
Accounts receivable	680	
Office supplies	700	
Land	3,000	
Building	15,000	
Office equipment	2,600	
Accounts payable		$ 170
Notes payable		2,000
A. Dixon, capital		30,000
A. Dixon, withdrawals	450	
Travel commissions revenues		1,300
Salary expense	600	
Telephone expense	100	
Utilities expense	170	
Totals	$33,470	$33,470

7. Explain the purpose of adjusting entries.

Adjusting entries are journal entries made at the end of an accounting period in order to bring the revenue and expense account balances up to date and to show the correct ending balances in the asset and liability accounts. There are many different types of adjusting entries, and they are discussed in detail in Chapter 4. Adjusting entries are briefly introduced here because they are necessary for an up-to-date income statement and balance sheet.

In the Dixon Travel agency example we will assume that the month of February is the accounting period. Three adjusting entries must be made at the end of the month. These adjusting entries are shown in Exhibit 3-10 along with the postings and account balances. A further illustration is provided in the review problem at the end of the chapter. The adjusting entries are explained in the following paragraphs.

EXHIBIT 3-10
Adjusted Entries
and Postings

		GENERAL JOURNAL			Page 2
Date		Account Titles and Explanations	Acct. No.	Debit	Credit
1991 Feb.	28	Office Supplies Expense	504	30	
		Office Supplies	107		30
		To record office supplies used during February.			
	28	Depreciation Expense: Building	505	50	
		Accumulated Depreciation: Building	123		50
		To record depreciation of office building.			
	28	Depreciation Expense: Office Equipment	506	27	
		Accumulated Depreciation: Office Equipment	125		27
		To record depreciation of office equipment.			

		GENERAL LEDGER Office Supplies				Acct. No. 107
Date		Explanation	Jr. Ref.	Debit	Credit	Debit Balance
1991 Jan.	5		1	700		700
Feb.	28		2		30	670

		Accumulated Depreciation: Building				Acct. No. 123
Date		Explanation	Jr. Ref.	Debit	Credit	Credit Balance
1991 Feb.	28		2		50	50

		Accumulated Depreciation: Office Equipment				Acct. No. 125
Date		Explanation	Jr. Ref.	Debit	Credit	Credit Balance
1991 Feb.	28		2		27	27

continued

EXHIBIT 3-10
continued

			Office Supplies Expense			Acct. No. 504	
Date		Explanation	Jr. Ref.	Debit	Credit	Debit Balance
1991 Feb.	28		2	30		30

			Depreciation Expense: Building			Acct. No. 505	
Date		Explanation	Jr. Ref.	Debit	Credit	Debit Balance
1991 Feb.	28		2	50		50

			Depreciation Expense: Office Equipment			Acct. No. 506	
Date		Explanation	Jr. Ref.	Debit	Credit	Debit Balance
1991 Feb.	28		2	27		27

Office Supplies Expense.   Office supplies expense is the cost of the office supplies used during the accounting period. When the office supplies costing $700 were purchased on January 5, they were recorded as an asset, Office Supplies. By the end of February some of these supplies had been used in the operations of the travel agency. The office supplies used are an expense of doing business while the remaining supplies are still an asset. The expense amount and the reduction in the asset is recorded in an adjusting entry.

If the office supplies used during February amount to $30, the adjusting entry involves a debit (increase) to the expense account, Office Supplies Expense, for $30 and a credit (decrease) to the asset account, Office Supplies, for $30. It is important to understand that when the $30 credit to the Office Supplies account is subtracted from the $700 debit balance, a $670 ending debit balance results, which is the amount of office supplies still on hand at the end of February.

Depreciation Expense: Building.   When the office building was purchased, the asset account, Building, was increased for the $15,000 cost. The building was acquired for use in the operations of the travel agency. One expense of operating the agency involves the cost of using the building during the accounting period. **Depreciation expense is the part of the cost of a physical asset allocated as an expense to each accounting period in which the asset is used.**

Assume the depreciation expense for the office building is $50 per month.[3] The adjusting entry involves a $50 debit (increase) to Depreciation Expense:

---

[3]The method of computing this amount is discussed in Chapter 4. Although land is a physical asset, depreciation expense is *not* recorded for land because it is not considered to have a limited useful life. This concept is discussed more fully in Chapter 4.

Building and a $50 credit (increase) to Accumulated Depreciation: Building. The Accumulated Depreciation: Building account is used to record the portion of the cost of the office building that has expired to date and has been assigned as depreciation expense. This account has a *credit* balance (and therefore is increased by a credit entry) because it is deducted from the Building account on the balance sheet to show the book value of the building. **The book value of an asset is the remaining unexpired cost of the physical asset (i.e., cost less accumulated depreciation).** The book value is also called the *carrying value.*

The remaining unexpired cost (book value) of the building on February 28, 1991, is $14,950. This amount would be reported on the Dixon Travel Agency balance sheet for that date as follows:

Building	$15,000	
Less: Accumulated depreciation	(50)	14,950

The complete balance sheet is shown in Exhibit 3-14. Each month, as the depreciation adjusting entry is recorded and posted, the Accumulated Depreciation account balance increases and causes the book value of the building to decrease.

It is important to understand the usefulness of the Accumulated Depreciation account. The $50 credit in the adjusting entry *could* have been made directly to the Building account. In that case the Building account would have been listed on the balance sheet at its ending balance of $14,950. The reader of the balance sheet, however, would have no way of determining that the building had originally cost $15,000, with the $50 being assigned to date as depreciation. By using an Accumulated Depreciation account much more useful information can be presented on the balance sheet. This procedure is explained more fully in Chapter 4.

Depreciation Expense: Office Equipment. When the office equipment was purchased the $2,600 cost was recorded as an asset. The office equipment was purchased to be used in the operations of the travel agency. As in the case of the building, a part of the cost of the office equipment must be assigned as depreciation expense in order to show all the operating expenses for the February accounting period.

Assume that the monthly depreciation for the office equipment is $27. The adjusting entry to record the depreciation involves a $27 debit (increase) to Depreciation Expense: Office Equipment and a $27 credit (increase) to Accumulated Depreciation: Office Equipment. The Accumulated Depreciation account balance is subtracted from the Office Equipment account balance on the February 28, 1991, balance sheet (see Exhibit 3-14) to report the $2,573 book value of the office equipment on that date.

Adjusted Trial Balance

After the adjusting entries have been journalized and posted, all the account balances are up to date for the accounting period. Before preparing the financial statements, it is useful to prepare an adjusted trial balance. **An adjusted trial balance is a schedule prepared after the adjusting entries have been made to prove the equality of the debit and credit balances in the ledger accounts.** Like the trial balance, an adjusted trial balance is the accountant's working paper and not a financial statement.

An adjusted trial balance helps to prevent debit and credit errors from being included in the financial statements. (If the debit and credit columns do *not* balance, the procedures recommended in Chapter 2 should be followed.) An adjusted trial balance also makes it easier to prepare the financial statements. As we will see shortly, since the adjusted trial balance lists the accounts according to their place in the chart of accounts, different parts of the adjusted trial balance are used to prepare each financial statement. The adjusted trial balance of the Dixon Travel Agency is shown in Exhibit 3-11.

EXHIBIT 3-11
Adjusted Trial Balance

DIXON TRAVEL AGENCY
Adjusted Trial Balance
February 28, 1991

Account Titles	Debits	Credits
Cash	$10,170	
Accounts receivable	680	
Office supplies	670	
Land	3,000	
Building	15,000	
Accumulated depreciation: building		$ 50
Office equipment	2,600	
Accumulated depreciation: office equipment		27
Accounts payable		170
Notes payable		2,000
A. Dixon, capital		30,000
A. Dixon, withdrawals	450	
Travel commissions revenues		1,300
Salary expense	600	
Telephone expense	100	
Utilities expense	170	
Office supplies expense	30	
Depreciation expense: building	50	
Depreciation expense: office equipment	27	
Totals	$33,547	$33,547

Financial Statements

8. Describe the relationships between the financial statements.

After completing the adjusted trial balance, the financial statements for the accounting period are prepared. The income statement is prepared first because the amount of net income (or net loss) affects the owner's capital account on the balance sheet. For a sole proprietorship the statement of changes in owner's equity, a supporting schedule to the balance sheet, is often prepared next. Finally the balance sheet is prepared.[4] A discussion of each statement follows.

Income Statement.   An income statement is the financial statement that summarizes the earnings activities (i.e., revenues, expenses, and net income) of a

---

[4]A statement of cash flows would also be prepared, as briefly introduced in Chapter 1 and more fully discussed in Chapter 18.

EXHIBIT 3-12
Income Statement

DIXON TRAVEL AGENCY
Income Statement
For Month Ended February 28, 1991

Revenues:
  Travel commissions revenues $1,300

Expenses:
  Salary expense $600
  Telephone expense 100
  Utilities expense 170
  Office supplies expense 30
  Depreciation expense: building 50
  Depreciation expense: office equipment 27
    Total expenses .... (977)
Net income .... $ 323

company for its accounting period. The income statement of the Dixon Travel Agency for the month of February is shown in Exhibit 3-12.

The Dixon Travel Agency income statement was prepared from the accounts listed on the lower part of the adjusted trial balance shown in Exhibit 3-11. Because the revenue and expense accounts are listed at the end of each company's chart of accounts (and, therefore, its general ledger), these accounts are always listed in the lower portion of every company's adjusted trial balance. This procedure simplifies preparation of the income statement. The Dixon Travel Agency net income for February is $323, computed by deducting (matching) the $977 total expenses from the $1,300 total revenues.

Statement of Changes in Owner's Equity. In order to disclose the impact on the owner's equity of any additional investments, the net income, and the withdrawals during the accounting period, a statement of changes in owner's equity is often prepared. This statement is presented as a supporting schedule to the owner's capital account balance listed on the balance sheet. The schedule starts with the beginning balance in the owner's capital account. To this balance are added the additional investments (if any) by the owner and the net income[5] for the accounting period. From the resulting subtotal the amount of the owner's withdrawals for the period is subtracted to determine the ending balance in the owner's capital account. A similar schedule would be prepared for a partnership or a corporation. The Dixon Travel Agency statement of changes in owner's equity is shown in Exhibit 3-13.

Because withdrawals were more than net income for February, owner's equity decreased from $30,000 to $29,873. Although this decrease is undesirable, it is not unusual in the first month or even the first several months of the operation of a business. A good sign for future success is that the travel agency earned a net income in its first month of operations. Many small businesses fail and go bankrupt early in their operations because they cannot earn a net income or cannot keep a positive cash balance.

---

[5]A net loss for the accounting period would be subtracted in the computation.

EXHIBIT 3-13
Statement of Changes
in Owner's Equity

DIXON TRAVEL AGENCY
Statement of Changes in Owner's Equity
For Month Ended February 28, 1991

A. Dixon, capital, February 1, 1991	$30,000
Add: Net income for February	323
	$30,323
Less: Withdrawals for February	(450)
A. Dixon, capital, February 28, 1991	$29,873

Balance Sheet.   A balance sheet reports the financial position of a company on a particular date. The balance sheet of the Dixon Travel Agency as of February 28, 1991, is shown in Exhibit 3-14.

Use of the adjusted trial balance makes the preparation of the balance sheet very easy. The assets, liabilities, and owner's capital account are the first accounts in a company's chart of accounts and in its general ledger. Therefore these accounts are always listed in the upper portion of the company's adjusted trial balance. It should be noted, however, that the amount listed as the owner's capital on the adjusted trial balance is *not* the amount to be listed on the ending balance sheet because it has not been updated for the company's net income or withdrawals. The ending amount of owner's capital is obtained instead from the statement of changes in owner's equity. In Exhibit 3-14 the $29,873 amount listed for A. Dixon, Capital was obtained from the statement of changes in owner's equity shown in Exhibit 3-13.

The balance sheet shown in Exhibit 3-14 is presented in report form. **In the report form of the balance sheet, the assets are presented first, directly fol-**

EXHIBIT 3-14
Balance Sheet
(Report Form)

DIXON TRAVEL AGENCY
Balance Sheet
February 28, 1991

Assets

Cash		$10,170
Accounts receivable		680
Office supplies		670
Land		3,000
Building	$15,000	
Less: Accumulated depreciation	(50)	14,950
Office equipment	$ 2,600	
Less: Accumulated depreciation	(27)	2,573
Total Assets		$32,043

Liabilities

Accounts payable		$ 170
Notes payable		2,000
Total Liabilities		$ 2,170

Owner's Equity

A. Dixon, capital		29,873
Total Liabilities and Owner's Equity		$32,043

lowed by the liabilities and owner's equity. An alternative format is the account form of the balance sheet, as used in Exhibit 2-8 of Chapter 2. **In the account form of the balance sheet, the assets are presented on the left side and the liabilities and owner's equity are presented on the right side.** Both forms of balance sheets are commonly used today.

The relationships of the items on the adjusted trial balance, income statement, statement of changes in owner's equity, and balance sheet are shown in Exhibit 3-15.

EXHIBIT 3-15   Relationship of Financial Statements

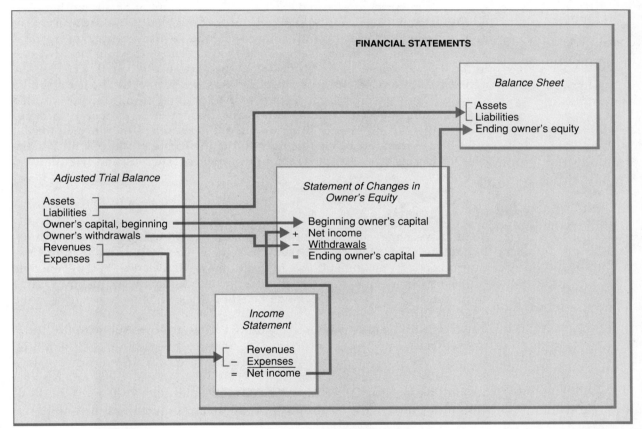

Closing Entries

Earlier we noted two points. First, the revenue, expense, and withdrawals accounts are *temporary* accounts. These accounts are used to determine the changes in the owner's equity in the current accounting period as a result of net income (or net loss) and withdrawals. Second, the owner's capital account balance listed on the adjusted trial balance was *not* used in preparing the balance sheet because this account balance was not up to date for the net income and withdrawals of the accounting period.

To begin the next accounting period, it is important to (1) show the current balance in the owner's capital account and (2) show zero balances in the revenue, expense, and withdrawals accounts. The owner's capital account balance should be up to date to show the owner's current investment in the assets of the company. The revenue, expense, and withdrawals accounts will be used in the next accounting period to accumulate the net income and withdrawals *for that period*. It is important, therefore, to start with a zero balance in each of these accounts at the beginning of the period so that at the end of the period, the balances in the accounts will show the revenues, expenses, and withdrawals for only one period.

9. Prepare closing entries.

Closing entries are journal entries made at the end of an accounting period to create a zero balance in each revenue, expense, and withdrawals account and to transfer these account balances to the owner's permanent capital account. Closing entries are made like any journal entry. They are recorded first in the general journal and then posted to the respective accounts. The revenue and expense account balances are not closed directly to the owner's capital account. These account balances are first transferred to an account entitled Income Summary. **The Income Summary account is a temporary account used in the closing process to accumulate the amount of net income (or net loss) before transferring this amount to the owner's capital account.** We discuss the closing of each type of account (revenues, expenses, and withdrawals) separately.

Closing the Revenue Accounts

Recall that each revenue account normally has a credit balance (prior to closing). In order to reduce this credit balance to zero, a debit entry is made in the revenue account for an amount *equal* to that of the credit balance. At the same time this revenue amount is transferred to the Income Summary account by a credit entry to that account. These debit and credit entries are initially recorded in the general journal.

To illustrate the preparation of closing entries, we continue with the Dixon Travel Agency example. In reviewing the adjusted trial balance of Exhibit 3-11, we see that the company has one revenue account, Travel Commissions Revenues, with an ending balance of $1,300. The journal entry to close this account is a debit to Travel Commissions Revenues for $1,300 and a credit to Income Summary for $1,300, which is as follows:

GENERAL JOURNAL					Page 3
Date		Account Titles and Explanations	Acct. No.	Debit	Credit
1991 Feb.	28	Travel Commissions Revenues Income Summary To close the revenue account.		1,300	1,300

The journal entry and the postings (identified by the arrows labeled A and B) are also shown in Exhibit 3-16. After the revenue closing entry has been journalized and posted, the Travel Commissions Revenues account has a zero balance and is ready to accumulate the revenues for the next accounting period. The total revenues of $1,300 have been transferred as a credit to the Income Summary Account. If a company has more than one revenue account, it is typical to close all of the revenue accounts in a single compound journal entry.

Closing the Expense Accounts

Each expense account has a debit balance (prior to closing). To reduce each debit balance to zero, a credit entry is made in each expense account for an amount *equal* to that of the debit balance. This expense amount is transferred to the Income Summary account by a debit entry. Companies typically have many expense accounts, and therefore it is usual to close all the expense accounts by making a compound journal entry crediting each expense account for its balance and debiting the Income Summary account for the *total* expenses. (Remember, however, that the debit entry is always listed first in the general journal.)

The adjusted trial balance in Exhibit 3-11 shows six expense accounts with debit balances at the end of February. The journal entry to close these accounts involves a debit to Income Summary for $977 and a credit to each of the six expense accounts for the respective balance. This journal entry is as follows:

		GENERAL JOURNAL			Page 3
Date		Account Titles and Explanations	Acct. No.	Debit	Credit
1991 Feb.	28	Income Summary		977	
		Salary Expense			600
		Telephone Expense			100
		Utilities Expense			170
		Office Supplies Expense			30
		Depreciation Expense: Building			50
		Depreciation Expense: Office Equipment			27
		To close the expense accounts.			

The journal entry and postings (identified by the arrows labeled C through I) are also shown in Exhibit 3-16. After the expenses closing entry has been journalized and posted, each of the expense accounts has a zero balance and is ready to accumulate the respective expenses for the next accounting period. The $977 total expenses has been transferred as a debit to Income Summary. The $323 *credit* balance in the Income Summary account represents the *net income* for February because the revenue credit entry of $1,300 exceeds the expenses debit entry of $977.

EXHIBIT 3-16
Dixon Travel Agency
Closing Entries,
Postings, and
Account Balances

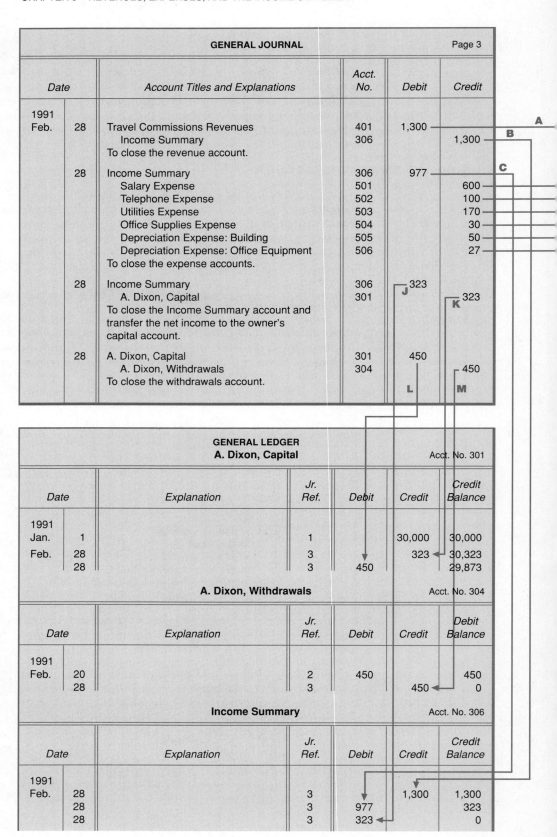

GENERAL JOURNAL					Page 3
Date		Account Titles and Explanations	Acct. No.	Debit	Credit
1991 Feb.	28	Travel Commissions Revenues	401	1,300	
		Income Summary	306		1,300
		To close the revenue account.			
	28	Income Summary	306	977	
		Salary Expense	501		600
		Telephone Expense	502		100
		Utilities Expense	503		170
		Office Supplies Expense	504		30
		Depreciation Expense: Building	505		50
		Depreciation Expense: Office Equipment	506		27
		To close the expense accounts.			
	28	Income Summary	306	323	
		A. Dixon, Capital	301		323
		To close the Income Summary account and transfer the net income to the owner's capital account.			
	28	A. Dixon, Capital	301	450	
		A. Dixon, Withdrawals	304		450
		To close the withdrawals account.			

A B C J K L M

GENERAL LEDGER
A. Dixon, Capital   Acct. No. 301

Date		Explanation	Jr. Ref.	Debit	Credit	Credit Balance
1991 Jan.	1		1		30,000	30,000
Feb.	28		3		323	30,323
	28		3	450		29,873

A. Dixon, Withdrawals   Acct. No. 304

Date		Explanation	Jr. Ref.	Debit	Credit	Debit Balance
1991 Feb.	20		2	450		450
	28		3		450	0

Income Summary   Acct. No. 306

Date		Explanation	Jr. Ref.	Debit	Credit	Credit Balance
1991 Feb.	28		3		1,300	1,300
	28		3	977		323
	28		3	323		0

Travel Commissions Revenues   Acct. No. 401

Date		Explanation	Jr. Ref.	Debit	Credit	Credit Balance
1991 Feb.	4	A	2		620	620
	11		2		680	1,300
	28		3	1,300		0

Salary Expense   Acct. No. 501

Date		Explanation	Jr. Ref.	Debit	Credit	Debit Balance
1991 Feb.	27		2	600		600
	28	D	3		600	0

Telephone Expense   Acct. No. 502

Date		Explanation	Jr. Ref.	Debit	Credit	Debit Balance
1991 Feb.	28	E	2	100		100
	28		3		100	0

Utilities Expense   Acct. No. 503

Date		Explanation	Jr. Ref.	Debit	Credit	Debit Balance
1991 Feb.	28	F	2	170		170
	28		3		170	0

Office Supplies Expense   Acct. No. 504

Date		Explanation	Jr. Ref.	Debit	Credit	Debit Balance
1991 Feb.	28		2	30		30
	28	G	3		30	0

Depreciation Expense: Building   Acct. No. 505

Date		Explanation	Jr. Ref.	Debit	Credit	Debit Balance
1991 Feb.	28		2	50		50
	28	H	3		50	0

Depreciation Expense: Office Equipment   Acct. No. 506

Date		Explanation	Jr. Ref.	Debit	Credit	Debit Balance
1991 Feb.	28		2	27		27
	28	I	3		27	0

Closing the Income Summary Account

After the revenue and expense accounts have been closed to the Income Summary account, the balance in this account is the net income (or net loss). A credit balance indicates that the company has earned a net income for the accounting period because revenues exceeded expenses. A debit balance indicates a net loss because expenses exceed revenues.

The net income (or net loss) amount is now transferred to the owner's permanent capital account. For net income, the journal entry is a debit to the Income Summary account for its balance and a credit to the owner's capital account for a like amount. The debit to Income Summary reduces the account balance to zero, making it ready for the closing entries of the next accounting period. The credit to the owner's capital account increases the account for the net income. A net loss would be handled in an opposite manner, that is, a debit to the owner's capital account for the amount of the net loss and a credit to the Income Summary account to reduce it to zero. The journal entry to close the $323 credit balance in the Income Summary account of the Dixon Travel Agency is as follows:

GENERAL JOURNAL					Page 3
Date		Account Titles and Explanations	Acct. No.	Debit	Credit
1991 Feb.	28	Income Summary A. Dixon, Capital To close the Income Summary account and transfer the net income to the owner's capital account.		323	323

The journal entry and postings (identified by the arrows labeled J and K) are shown in Exhibit 3-16. After posting this closing entry, the Income Summary account has a zero balance and the A. Dixon, Capital account is up to date for the net income of the accounting period, but *not* for the withdrawals.

Closing the Withdrawals Account

The debit balance of the withdrawals account is closed *directly* to the owner's permanent capital account, since withdrawals are *disinvestments* by the owner. The closing entry is a debit to the owner's permanent capital account and a credit to the withdrawals account for the total withdrawals of the period. The debit entry brings the owner's capital account balance up to date at the end of the period. The credit to the withdrawals account reduces the account balance to zero so that it can accumulate the withdrawals of the next period. The withdrawals account is *never* closed to the Income Summary account because withdrawals are not part of net income.

The withdrawals by Anne Dixon totaled $450 during February, as shown in the adjusted trial balance of Exhibit 3-11. The journal entry to close the A. Dixon, Withdrawals account is shown on the next page.

The journal entry and postings (identified by the arrows labeled L and M) are shown in Exhibit 3-16. After posting the withdrawals closing entry, the end-

GENERAL JOURNAL					Page 3
Date		Account Titles and Explanations	Acct. No.	Debit	Credit
1991 Feb.	28	A. Dixon, Capital A. Dixon, Withdrawals To close the withdrawals account.		450	450

ing balance in the A. Dixon, Capital account is $29,873, the amount listed on the February 28, 1991, balance sheet shown in Exhibit 3-14. The $450 credit entry in the A. Dixon, Withdrawals account reduces the account balance to zero and completes the closing entries.

Illustration of Complete Closing and Posting Process

All of the closing entries, postings, and account balances for the Dixon Travel Agency are shown in Exhibit 3-16. The closing entries are the same as those discussed earlier in the separate sections on closing the revenue accounts, expense accounts, Income Summary account, and Withdrawals account.

Post-Closing Trial Balance

After the closing entries have been journalized and posted, the only accounts with nonzero balances should be the permanent accounts, that is, the assets, liabilities, and owner's capital accounts. As a check to make sure that no debit or credit errors were made during the closing entries, a post-closing trial balance is prepared. **A post-closing trial balance is a schedule prepared after the closing entries have been made to prove the equality of the debit and credit balances in the asset, liability, and owner's capital accounts.** It can only contain permanent accounts because all the temporary accounts have zero balances due to the closing process. The post-closing trial balance of the Dixon Travel Agency is shown in Exhibit 3-17.

EXHIBIT 3-17
Post-Closing
Trial Balance

DIXON TRAVEL AGENCY
Post-Closing Trial Balance
February 28, 1991

Account Titles	Debits	Credits
Cash	$10,170	
Accounts receivable	680	
Office supplies	670	
Land	3,000	
Building	15,000	
Accumulated depreciation: building		$ 50
Office equipment	2,600	
Accumulated depreciation: office equipment		27
Accounts payable		170
Notes payable		2,000
A. Dixon, capital		29,873
Totals	$32,120	$32,120

Summary of Closing Process

The steps in the closing process at the end of each accounting period are as follows:

1. Close all the revenue accounts to a zero balance by debiting each revenue account for its balance and crediting the Income Summary account for the total revenues.

2. Close all the expense accounts to a zero balance by crediting each expense account for its balance and debiting the Income Summary account for the total expenses.

3. Compute the balance in the Income Summary account after completing steps 1 and 2. Close a credit balance (net income) in the account by debiting Income Summary and crediting the owner's capital account for the amount of the net income. Close a debit balance (net loss) in the account by crediting Income Summary and debiting the owner's capital account.

4. Close the owner's withdrawals account by crediting the account and debiting the owner's capital account for the balance of the withdrawals account.

5. Prepare a post-closing trial balance to prove the equality of the debit and credit balances in the asset, liability, and owner's capital account balances.

The closing entries for a partnership and a corporation are similar to the entries discussed for a sole proprietorship except that they are modified to apply to the particular type of business entity. They are discussed in later chapters.

The Accounting Process

10. List the steps and documents in an accounting system.

In Exhibit 2-9 of Chapter 2 we listed a set of steps and business documents in the accounting process. In this chapter we added several new steps and documents. The complete set shown in Exhibit 3-18 makes up a typical manual accounting system designed to identify, measure, record, retain, and report accounting information. A good understanding of the sequence of steps, the business documents, and their relationships is very important for further study in this text.

EXHIBIT 3-18
Accounting System:
Documents and Process

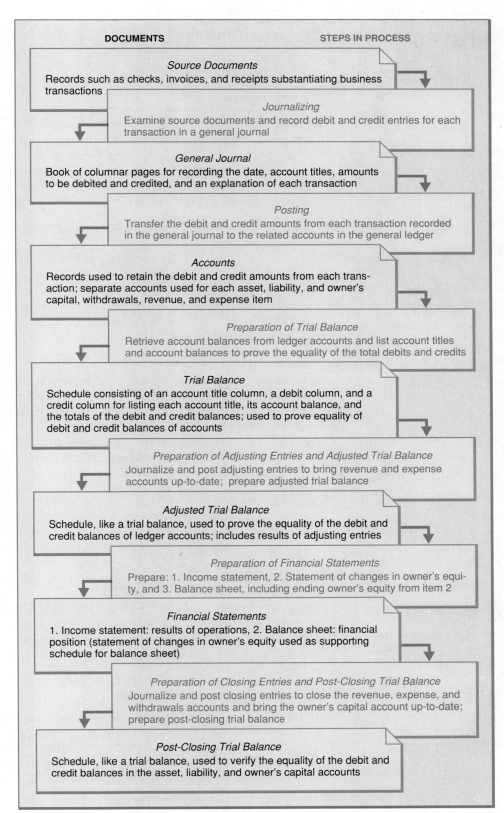

DOCUMENTS

STEPS IN PROCESS

Source Documents
Records such as checks, invoices, and receipts substantiating business transactions

Journalizing
Examine source documents and record debit and credit entries for each transaction in a general journal

General Journal
Book of columnar pages for recording the date, account titles, amounts to be debited and credited, and an explanation of each transaction

Posting
Transfer the debit and credit amounts from each transaction recorded in the general journal to the related accounts in the general ledger

Accounts
Records used to retain the debit and credit amounts from each transaction; separate accounts used for each asset, liability, and owner's capital, withdrawals, revenue, and expense item

Preparation of Trial Balance
Retrieve account balances from ledger accounts and list account titles and account balances to prove the equality of the total debits and credits

Trial Balance
Schedule consisting of an account title column, a debit column, and a credit column for listing each account title, its account balance, and the totals of the debit and credit balances; used to prove equality of debit and credit balances of accounts

Preparation of Adjusting Entries and Adjusted Trial Balance
Journalize and post adjusting entries to bring revenue and expense accounts up-to-date; prepare adjusted trial balance

Adjusted Trial Balance
Schedule, like a trial balance, used to prove the equality of the debit and credit balances of ledger accounts; includes results of adjusting entries

Preparation of Financial Statements
Prepare: 1. Income statement, 2. Statement of changes in owner's equity, and 3. Balance sheet, including ending owner's equity from item 2

Financial Statements
1. Income statement: results of operations, 2. Balance sheet: financial position (statement of changes in owner's equity used as supporting schedule for balance sheet)

Preparation of Closing Entries and Post-Closing Trial Balance
Journalize and post closing entries to close the revenue, expense, and withdrawals accounts and bring the owner's capital account up-to-date; prepare post-closing trial balance

Post-Closing Trial Balance
Schedule, like a trial balance, used to verify the equality of the debit and credit balances in the asset, liability, and owner's capital accounts

Chapter Summary

Review of Learning Objectives

1. **Define net income, revenues, and expenses.**

   Net income is the excess of revenues over expenses for an accounting period. (*Net loss* occurs when expenses exceed revenues for the period.) *Revenues* are the prices charged to customers for goods or services provided during the accounting period, and result in increases in assets or decreases in liabilities. *Expenses* are the costs of providing the goods or services during the period, and result in decreases in assets or increases in liabilities.

2. **Describe (a) an accounting period, (b) matching, and (c) accrual accounting.**

   An *accounting period* is the period of time for which net income (revenues and expenses) is computed. *Matching* involves computing the total expenses and deducting (matching) that amount from the total revenues to determine the net income for the period. *Accrual accounting* involves recording revenues and expenses in the period when the goods or services are provided, regardless of whether cash is received or paid.

3. **Describe an income statement.**

   An income statement is a financial statement summarizing the results of a company's earnings activities for its accounting period. An income statement has a heading and two sections. In the revenues section, the types and amounts of revenues are listed and totaled. In the expenses section, the types and amounts of expenses are listed and totaled. The total expenses are subtracted from the total revenues to determine the net income (or net loss).

4. **Explain the relationship of net income, investments, and withdrawals to owner's equity.**

   Net income (revenues greater than expenses), initial investments, and subsequent investments increase owner's equity. Net loss (expenses greater than revenues) and withdrawals decrease owner's equity.

5. **Explain the debit and credit rules for revenues, expenses, and withdrawals.**

   Revenues increase owner's equity. Therefore all revenue accounts are increased by credit entries and decreased by debit entries. Expenses and withdrawals decrease owner's equity. Therefore all expense and withdrawals accounts are increased by debit entries and decreased by credit entries.

6. **Record and post revenue and expense transactions.**

   To record a revenue or expense transaction, first, list the date in the general journal; then, record the account and amount to be debited; next, record the account and amount to be credited; and finally, provide an explanation of the journal entry. Each debit and credit entry in the general journal is posted to the appropriate account. In the account, first, list the date, then, record the debit or credit amount; next, list the page number of the general journal; and finally, record the number of the account in the account number column of the general journal.

7. **Explain the purpose of adjusting entries.**

Adjusting entries are made at the end of the accounting period to bring the revenue and expense accounts up to date and to show the correct ending balances in the asset and liability accounts. They are needed in order to report the correct net income on the income statement for the period and the correct financial position on the balance sheet at the end of the period.

8. **Describe the relationships between the financial statements.**

The financial statements are prepared after the completion of the adjusted trial balance. First, the income statement is prepared; in this the expenses are deducted from the revenues to determine the net income. The statement of changes in owner's equity is prepared next, and involves adding the net income to, and subtracting withdrawals from, the beginning owner's equity to determine the ending owner's equity. Finally, the balance sheet is prepared to report the assets, liabilities, and owner's equity at the end of the accounting period.

9. **Prepare closing entries.**

Closing entries are made at the end of an accounting period to create a zero balance in each revenue, expense, and withdrawals account and to update the balance of the owner's permanent capital account. The first closing entry involves a debit to each revenue account and a credit to the Income Summary account for the total revenues. The second closing entry involves a debit to the Income Summary account for the total expenses and a credit to each expense account. The third closing entry involves a debit to the Income Summary account and a credit to the owner's capital account for the balance (net income) of the Income Summary account. (A net loss would be closed in the opposite way.) The final closing entry involves a debit to the owner's capital account and a credit to the owner's withdrawals account for the balance of the withdrawals account.

10. **List the steps and documents in an accounting system.**

Based on source documents, first journalize (record) each transaction in the general journal. Second, post the transactions from the general journal to the accounts in the general ledger. Third, prepare a trial balance based on the account balances at the end of the accounting period. Fourth, journalize and post adjusting entries, and then prepare an adjusted trial balance. Fifth, prepare the financial statements. Sixth, journalize and post closing entries. Finally, prepare a post-closing trial balance.

Review Problem

John Thompson operates Ace Insulating Company from a small rented office; he installs insulation for customers in their houses and buildings. The company has been in business for several years. On March 31, 1991, it prepared the following post-closing trial balance:

ACE INSULATING COMPANY
Post-Closing Trial Balance
March 31, 1991

Account Titles	Acct. No.	Debits	Credits
Cash	101	$ 1,000	
Accounts receivable	103	3,000	
Insulating supplies	105	2,400	
Prepaid rent	107	300	
Trucks	125	12,000	
Accumulated depreciation: trucks	126		$ 3,800
Accounts payable	201		1,200
J. Thompson, capital	301		13,700
Totals		$18,700	$18,700

In addition to the preceding accounts and account numbers, the following accounts are listed in the company's chart of accounts:

Account Titles	Account Numbers
J. Thompson, Withdrawals	302
Income Summary	303
Insulating Revenues	401
Salaries Expense	501
Utilities Expense	502
Insulating Supplies Expense	503
Gas, Oil, and Maintenance Expense	504
Rent Expense	505
Depreciation Expense: Trucks	506

During April 1991 the company engaged in the following transactions:

Date	Transaction
Apr. 2	Collected $700 on account from a customer for insulating work completed in March.
8	Installed insulation for customer and collected $1,200 for services performed.
10	Paid $600 on account for insulating supplies purchased in March.
15	Thompson withdrew $500 cash for his personal use.
18	Paid $80 to service station for gas, oil, and routine maintenance on trucks during April.
20	Installed insulation for customer; customer agreed to pay the contract price of $1,500 in 30 days.
29	Paid $40 for April utilities bill.
29	Paid $450 to employees for April salaries.

At the end of April, the following information is available:

1. The company pays rent on its office for several months in advance. At the time of payment, the cost is recorded (debited) as an asset Prepaid Rent because it represents the legal right to use the office in the future. For April $50 of prepaid rent is now an expired cost and must be recorded as rent expense.

2. Insulating supplies used during April cost $580.

3. Depreciation expense on the trucks totals $200 for April.

REQUIRED   For April 1991, (1) journalize and post entries to record the transactions, (2) journalize and post adjusting entries (a trial balance is not prepared here to save space), (3) prepare an adjusted trial balance, (4) prepare financial statements, and (5) journalize and post closing entries.

Solution to Review Problem

REQUIREMENTS 1, 2, and 5.   Journalize transactions, adjusting entries, and closing entries. (Note: The Acct. No. column is completed after posting to the accounts.)

		GENERAL JOURNAL			Page 9
Date		Account Titles and Explanations	Acct. No.	Debit	Credit
1991 Apr.	2	Cash Accounts Receivable To record collection of cash on account.	101 103	700	700
	8	Cash Insulating Revenues To record installation of insulation and collection of contract price.	101 401	1,200	1,200
	10	Accounts Payable Cash To record payment of cash on account.	201 101	600	600
	15	J. Thompson, Withdrawals Cash To record withdrawal of cash by owner for personal use.	302 101	500	500
	18	Gas, Oil, and Maintenance Expense Cash To record payment of April bill owed to service station.	504 101	80	80

		GENERAL JOURNAL			Page 10
Date		*Account Titles and Explanations*	*Acct. No.*	*Debit*	*Credit*
1991 Apr.	20	Accounts Receivable	103	1,500	
		Insulating Revenues	401		1,500
		To record installation of insulation; customer agreed to pay contract price in 30 days.			
	29	Utilities Expense	502	40	
		Cash	101		40
		To record payment of April utilities.			
	29	Salaries Expense	501	450	
		Cash	101		450
		To record payment of employees' April salaries.			
		Adjusting Entries			
	30	Rent Expense	505	50	
		Prepaid Rent	107		50
		To record rent expense for April.			
	30	Insulating Supplies Expense	503	580	
		Insulating Supplies	105		580
		To record insulating supplies used during April.			
	30	Depreciation Expense: Trucks	506	200	
		Accumulated Depreciation: Trucks	126		200
		To record depreciation expense for April.			
		Closing Entries			
	30	Insulating Revenues	401	2,700	
		Income Summary	303		2,700
		To close revenue account.			
	30	Income Summary	303	1,400	
		Salaries Expense	501		450
		Utilities Expense	502		40
		Insulating Supplies Expense	503		580
		Gas, Oil, and Maintenance Expense	504		80
		Rent Expense	505		50
		Depreciation Expense: Trucks	506		200
		To close expense accounts.			
	30	Income Summary	303	1,300	
		J. Thompson, Capital	301		1,300
		To close net income to the owner's capital account.			
	30	J. Thompson, Capital	301	500	
		J. Thompson, Withdrawals	302		500
		To close withdrawals account.			

REQUIREMENT 3

ACE INSULATING COMPANY
Adjusted Trial Balance
April 30, 1991

Account Titles	Debits	Credits
Cash	$ 1,230	
Accounts receivable	3,800	
Insulating supplies	1,820	
Prepaid rent	250	
Trucks	12,000	
Accumulated depreciation: trucks		$ 4,000
Accounts payable		600
J. Thompson, capital		13,700
J. Thompson, withdrawals	500	
Insulating revenues		2,700
Salaries expense	450	
Utilities expense	40	
Insulating supplies expense	580	
Gas, oil, and maintenance expense	80	
Rent expense	50	
Depreciation expense: trucks	200	
Totals	$21,000	$21,000

REQUIREMENT 4

12,400

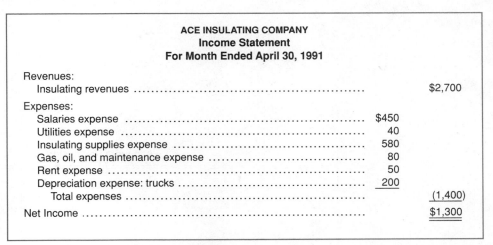

ACE INSULATING COMPANY
Income Statement
For Month Ended April 30, 1991

Revenues:		
Insulating revenues		$2,700
Expenses:		
Salaries expense	$450	
Utilities expense	40	
Insulating supplies expense	580	
Gas, oil, and maintenance expense	80	
Rent expense	50	
Depreciation expense: trucks	200	
Total expenses		(1,400)
Net Income		$1,300

ACE INSULATING COMPANY
Statement of Changes in Owner's Equity
For Month Ended April 30, 1991

J. Thompson, capital, March 31, 1991	$13,700
Add: Net income for April	1,300
	$15,000
Less: Withdrawals for April	(500)
J. Thompson, capital, April 30, 1991	$14,500

ACE INSULATING COMPANY
Balance Sheet
April 30, 1991

Assets			*Liabilities*		
Cash		$ 1,230	Accounts payable		$ 600
Accounts receivable..............		3,800			
Insulating supplies		1,820			
Prepaid rent		250			
Trucks	$12,000			*Owner's Equity*	
Less: Accumulated			J. Thompson, capital		$14,500
depreciation	(4,000)	8,000	Total Liabilities and		
Total Assets		$15,100	Owner's Equity		$15,100

Accounts after posting April transactions, adjusting, and closing entries:

Cash   Acct. No. 101

Date		Explanation	Jr. Ref.	Debit	Credit	Debit Balance
1991						
Mar.	31					1,000
Apr.	2		9	700		1,700
	8		9	1,200		2,900
	10		9		600	2,300
	15		9		500	1,800
	18		9		80	1,720
	29		10		40	1,680
	29		10		450	1,230

Accounts Receivable   Acct. No. 103

Date		Explanation	Jr. Ref.	Debit	Credit	Debit Balance
1991						
Mar.	31					3,000
Apr.	2		9		700	2,300
	20		10	1,500		3,800

Insulating Supplies   Acct. No. 105

Date		Explanation	Jr. Ref.	Debit	Credit	Debit Balance
1991						
Mar.	31					2,400
Apr.	30		10		580	1,820

Prepaid Rent — Acct. No. 107

Date		Explanation	Jr. Ref.	Debit	Credit	Debit Balance
1991 Mar.	31					300
Apr.	30		10		50	250

Trucks — Acct. No. 125

Date		Explanation	Jr. Ref.	Debit	Credit	Debit Balance
1991 Mar.	31					12,000

Accumulated Depreciation: Trucks — Acct. No. 126

Date		Explanation	Jr. Ref.	Debit	Credit	Credit Balance
1991 Mar.	31					3,800
Apr.	30		10		200	4,000

Accounts Payable — Acct. No. 201

Date		Explanation	Jr. Ref.	Debit	Credit	Credit Balance
1991 Mar.	31					1,200
Apr.	10		9	600		600

J. Thompson, Capital — Acct. No. 301

Date		Explanation	Jr. Ref.	Debit	Credit	Credit Balance
1991 Mar.	31					13,700
Apr.	30		10		1,300	15,000
	30		10	500		14,500

J. Thompson, Withdrawals — Acct. No. 302

Date		Explanation	Jr. Ref.	Debit	Credit	Debit Balance
1991 Apr.	15		9	500		500
	30		10		500	0

Income Summary   Acct. No. 303

Date		Explanation	Jr. Ref.	Debit	Credit	Credit Balance
1991 Apr.	30		10		2,700	2,700
	30		10	1,400		1,300
	30		10	1,300		0

Insulating Revenues   Acct. No. 401

Date		Explanation	Jr. Ref.	Debit	Credit	Credit Balance
1991 Apr.	8		9		1,200	1,200
	20		10		1,500	2,700
	30		10	2,700		0

Salaries Expense   Acct. No. 501

Date		Explanation	Jr. Ref.	Debit	Credit	Debit Balance
1991 Apr.	29		10	450		450
	30		10		450	0

Utilities Expense   Acct. No. 502

Date		Explanation	Jr. Ref.	Debit	Credit	Debit Balance
1991 Apr.	29		10	40		40
	30		10		40	0

Insulating Supplies Expense   Acct. No. 503

Date		Explanation	Jr. Ref.	Debit	Credit	Debit Balance
1991 Apr.	30		10	580		580
	30		10		580	0

Gas, Oil, and Maintenance Expense   Acct. No. 504

Date		Explanation	Jr. Ref.	Debit	Credit	Debit Balance
1991 Apr.	18		9	80		80
	30		10		80	0

Rent Expense						Acct. No. 505

Date		Explanation	Jr. Ref.	Debit	Credit	Debit Balance
1991 Apr.	30		10	50		50
	30		10		50	0

Depreciation Expense: Trucks						Acct. No. 506

Date		Explanation	Jr. Ref.	Debit	Credit	Debit Balance
1991 Apr.	30		10	200		200
	30		10		200	0

Glossary

Account Form.   Form of balance sheet on which assets are reported on the left side and liabilities and owner's equity are reported on the right side.

Accounting Period.   Period of time for which the revenues and expenses of a company are computed and reported on an income statement. Stated in the heading of the income statement.

Accrual Accounting.   The principle that revenue and expense transactions are recorded in the accounting period when goods or services are provided, regardless of whether cash is received or paid.

Adjusted Trial Balance.   A schedule prepared to prove the equality of the debit and credit balances in the ledger accounts after the adjusting entries have been made.

Adjusting Entries.   Journal entries made at the end of an accounting period to bring the revenue and expense account balances up to date and to show the correct ending balances in the asset and liability accounts.

Cash Basis Accounting.   Accounting practice in which net income of a company is computed by subtracting the cash payments from the cash receipts for operations during the accounting period.

Closing Entries.   Journal entries made at the end of an accounting period to create a zero balance in each revenue, expense, and withdrawals account and to transfer these account balances to the owner's capital account.

Cost.   The amount at which a transaction is recorded. A cost may be recorded as an expense (expired cost) or as an asset (unexpired cost).

Expenses.   Costs of a company to provide goods or services during an accounting period.

Income Statement.   Financial statement summarizing the results of a company's earning activities for its accounting period. Also called *statement of income, statement of earnings, profit and loss statement*, or *statement of operations*.

Income Summary Account.   A temporary account used during the closing process to accumulate the revenue and expense balances before transferring the net income (or net loss) to the owner's capital account.

Matching Principle. States that expenses of an accounting period are subtracted from (matched against) the revenues earned during that period to determine net income.

Net Income. The amount by which the revenues of a company exceed the expenses during an accounting period. Also called *net profit, net earnings,* or *earnings.*

Net Loss. The amount by which the expenses of a company exceed the revenues during an accounting period.

Permanent Accounts. Asset, liability, and owner's capital accounts that are not closed at the end of each accounting period. Also called *real* accounts.

Post-Closing Trial Balance. Schedule prepared to prove the equality of the debit and credit balances in the asset, liability, and owner's capital accounts after the closing entries have been made.

Report Form. Form of balance sheet in which assets are listed first, after which liabilities and owner's equity are reported directly below the assets.

Revenues. Prices charged to a company's customers for goods or services provided during an accounting period.

Temporary Accounts. Revenue, expense, and withdrawals accounts used to determine the net income and withdrawals during an accounting period. These accounts are closed at the end of each accounting period. Also called *nominal* accounts.

Withdrawals Account. Account used to accumulate the amounts of assets withdrawn from a sole proprietorship by its owner during an accounting period.

Questions

QUESTION 3-1   How is net income computed? Where (if at all) do withdrawals fit into the net income calculation?

QUESTION 3-2   Define revenues. Define expenses. What is meant by *matching* expenses against revenues?

QUESTION 3-3   What is cost? When is a cost an asset and when is it an expense?

QUESTION 3-4   What is an accounting period? How long is a usual accounting period in actual financial reporting?

QUESTION 3-5   What is accrual accounting? What is cash basis accounting? Which is more useful?

QUESTION 3-6   Explain the matching principle and how it relates to the computation of net income.

QUESTION 3-7   Define an income statement. What are the two sections of an income statement?

QUESTION 3-8   What are return on investment, risk, financial flexibility, and operating capability? How can the income statement be used to evaluate each of these items?

QUESTION 3-9   What are withdrawals? How are they recorded?

QUESTION 3-10   Give the debit and credit rules for revenue, expense, and withdrawals accounts.

QUESTION 3-11   Why are revenue, expense, and withdrawals accounts called *temporary* accounts? What are *permanent* accounts?

QUESTION 3-12   Where are revenue, expense, and withdrawals accounts included in a company's chart of accounts? Why is the chart of accounts useful in preparing financial statements?

QUESTION 3-13   What are adjusting entries? Why are they necessary?

QUESTION 3-14   What is the book value of a physical asset? Show how the book value of a building would be reported on a balance sheet.

QUESTION 3-15   What is an adjusted trial balance? How is it used in preparing financial statements?

QUESTION 3-16   What is a statement of changes in owner's equity? Show the format of this schedule.

QUESTION 3-17   How does a report form of a balance sheet differ from an account form of a balance sheet?

QUESTION 3-18   What are closing entries? Describe how (a) revenue accounts, (b) expense accounts, and (c) the withdrawals account are closed.

QUESTION 3-19   What is a post-closing trial balance?

QUESTION 3-20   List the steps and related business documents in a manual accounting system.

Exercises

EXERCISE 3-1   **Income Statement.**   On June 30, 1991, the Robinskon Barber Shop showed the following revenue and expense account balances for June:

Barbering revenues	$1,900
Salaries expense	1,100
Telephone expense	30
Barber supplies expense	120
Utilities expense	90
Rent expense	350
Depreciation expense: barber equipment	35

REQUIRED   Prepare the June 1991 income statement for the Robinskon Barber Shop.

EXERCISE 3-2   **Income Statement.** The adjusted trial balance for the Benzer Diaper Service on February 28, 1991 (the end of its monthly accounting period) is as follows:

BENZER DIAPER SERVICE
Adjusted Trial Balance
February 28, 1991

Account Titles	Debits	Credits
Cash	$13,745	
Supplies	5,000	
Land	2,000	
Building	11,500	
Accumulated depreciation: building		$ 530
Equipment	10,000	
Accumulated depreciation: equipment		420
Accounts payable		1,560
B. D. Benzer, capital		39,000
B. D. Benzer, withdrawals	1,000	
Diaper service revenues		7,900
Salaries expense	4,000	
Supplies expense	1,250	
Telephone expense	45	
Utilities expense	785	
Depreciation expense: building	53	
Depreciation expense: equipment	32	
Totals	$49,410	$49,410

REQUIRED   Prepare the February 1991 income statement for the Benzer Diaper Service from the preceding adjusted trial balance.

EXERCISE 3-3   **Owner's Equity Account.** Four independent cases related to the owner's equity account of the Cox Company are as follows:

Case	Laura Cox, Capital May 1, 1991	Net Income May 1991	Withdrawals in May	Laura Cox, Capital May 31, 1991
1	$ A	$2,700	$1,000	$26,700
2	37,000	B	1,720	40,250
3	28,200	900	C	24,800
4	34,000	1,820	1,500	D

REQUIRED   Determine the amounts of A, B, C, and D.

EXERCISE 3-4 **Assets and Expenses.**   During the month of October the Wilson Company incurred the following costs:

(a) Paid $500 to an insurance company for a 2-year comprehensive insurance policy on the company's building.

(b) Purchased office supplies costing $970 on account from Bailey's Office Supplies.

(c) Paid the telephone company $110 for telephone service during the month of October.

(d) Paid the $970 owed to Bailey's Office Supplies.

(e) The owner withdrew $1,200 for personal use.

(f) Found that of the $970 of office supplies purchased in (b), only $900 remained at October 31.

REQUIRED Which of the preceding transactions would be recorded as expenses by the Wilson Company for the month of October? Explain.

EXERCISE 3-5   **Revenues.**   Gertz Rent-A-Car is in the business of providing customers with quality rental automobiles at low rates. The following transactions were engaged in by the company during the month of March:

(a) J. Gertz deposited an additional $1,900 of his personal cash into the agency's checking account.

(b) Collected $1,050 in car rental fees for the month of March.

(c) Borrowed $7,000 from the 1st National Bank to be repaid in 1 year.

(d) Completed arrangements to provide fleet service to a local company at a price of $18,000 per year; this amount was collected in advance.

REQUIRED Which of the preceding transactions would be recorded as revenues by Gertz Rent-A-Car for the month of March? Explain.

EXERCISE 3-6 **Journal Entries.**   The Both Plumbing Company entered into the following transactions during the month of May:

Date	Transaction
May 4	Installed plumbing in new house under construction; contractor agreed to pay contract price of $1,700 in 30 days.
15	Made plumbing repairs for customer and collected $85 for services performed.
28	Paid $79 for May telephone bill.
31	Paid $800 to employees for May salaries.
31	Received $100 utility bill, to be paid in early June.

REQUIRED *1.* Prepare the necessary journal entries to record the preceding transactions.

2. List the source documents normally used to record these transactions.

EXERCISE 3-7 **Journal Entries.**   The Aline Taxi Service entered into the following transactions during the month of September.

Date	Transaction
Sept. 1	Paid $450 rent on garage for the month of September.
15	Cash receipts for taxi fares for the first half of the month totaled $1,640.
23	Paid $980 for September fuel bill from Wildcat Oil Company.
29	P. L. Aline withdrew $400 for personal use.
30	Paid salaries amounting to $1,200 to employees.
30	Cash receipts for taxi fares for the second half of the month totaled $1,340.

REQUIRED

1. Prepare journal entries to record the preceding transactions.

2. List the source documents normally used to record these transactions.

EXERCISE 3-8   **Adjusting Entries and Adjusted Trial Balance.**   On June 30, 1991, the Washington Background Music Company showed the following trial balance:

Account Titles	Debits	Credits
Cash	$10,150	
Office supplies	368	
Sound system	6,500	
Accounts payable		$ 295
D. L. Washington, capital		15,000
Music system revenues		3,198
Salary expense	1,000	
Rent expense	300	
General expenses	175	
Totals	$18,493	$18,493

The following adjustments are needed:

(a) Office supplies used during the month of June totaled $58.

(b) Depreciation expense for the month of June on the sound system totaled $75.

June was the first month of operations for the Washington Background Music Company.

REQUIRED

1. Prepare the necessary adjusting entries to record the preceding adjustments.

2. Prepare the June 30, 1991, adjusted trial balance for the Washington Background Music Company.

EXERCISE 3-9   **Statement of Changes in Owner's Equity.**   The beginning balance in the R. L. Barnun, Capital account on October 1, 1991 was $20,000. The Barnun Company reported total revenues for October of $3,000 and total expenses of $1,250. In addition, R. L. Barnun withdrew $1,200 for his personal use on October 25.

REQUIRED   Prepare a statement of changes in owner's equity for the month of October for the Barnun Company.

EXERCISE 3-10   **Closing Entries and Post-Closing Trial Balance.**   The adjusted trial balance of the Larkin Marketing Research Company on May 31, 1991 (the end of its monthly accounting period) is as follows:

Account Titles	Debits	Credits
Cash	$ 9,440	
Accounts receivable	1,630	
Equipment	4,200	
Accumulated depreciation: equipment		$ 140
Accounts payable		1,500
Joseph Larkin, capital		12,000
Joseph Larkin, withdrawals	900	
Marketing research revenues		4,635
Salaries expense	1,600	
Rent expense	300	
Depreciation expense: equipment	70	
Utilities expense	78	
Telephone expense	57	
Totals	$18,275	$18,275

REQUIRED
1. Prepare the closing entries for the company on May 31, 1991.

2. Prepare the post-closing trial balance for the company on May 31, 1991.

EXERCISE 3-11 **Closing Entries.** The Cobbler Company shows the following revenue, expense, and withdrawals account balances on December 31, 1991, before closing:

	Debits	Credits
A. B. Cobbler, withdrawals	$1,750	
Shoe service revenues		$4,720
Salaries expense	2,300	
Utilities expense	226	
Supplies expense	147	
Rent expense	550	
Depreciation expense: equipment	28	

REQUIRED Prepare closing entries.

EXERCISE 3-12 **Balance Sheet.** Use the information in Exercise 3-10.

REQUIRED Prepare a balance sheet (account form) for the Larkin Marketing Research Company on May 31, 1991.

EXERCISE 3-13 **Financial Statement Relationships.** The financial statement information of the Trish Aerobics Center for 1991 is as follows:

Revenues	$62,500
Trish, capital, 1/1/1991	30,700
Net income	29,700
Trish, withdrawals	1
Assets, 12/31/1991	79,000
Expenses	2
Trish, capital, 12/31/1991	35,400
Liabilities, 12/31/1991	3

REQUIRED Fill in the blanks numbered 1 through 3. All the necessary information is listed. (Hint: It is not necessary to do your answers in numerical order.)

Problems

Part A

PROBLEM 3-1A   **Journal Entries.**   The Riles Landscaping Service entered into the following transactions during the month of March:

Date		Transaction
Mar.	1	Paid 3 months' rent in advance at $270 per month.
	2	Provided landscaping service for customer, collecting $575 cash.
	5	Purchased $50 of repair parts on account from LT's, a small engine service company, to be used immediately in repairing one of the company's mowers.
	6–10	Provided landscaping service for customer; customer agreed to pay the contract price of $2,450 in 15 days.
	15	Paid $50 due to LT's for repair parts purchased on March 5.
	25	Collected $2,450 from customer for service provided on March 6–10.
	31	Paid $40 for March utilities bill.
	31	Paid $1,800 to employees for March salaries.
	31	Received $82 March telephone bill, to be paid in early April.

REQUIRED   1. Prepare the necessary journal entries to record the preceding transactions.

2. List the source documents normally used to record these transactions.

PROBLEM **3-2A**   **Journal Entries, Postings, and Trial Balance.**   The Jardine Tax Services Company was established on January 2, 1991 to help clients with their tax planning and preparation of their tax returns. The company engaged in the following transactions during January.

Date	Transaction
Jan. 2	D. Jardine set up the company by investing $32,000 cash in the company's checking account.
3	Acquired land and a building at a cost of $3,000 and $21,000, respectively. A $6,000 down payment was made and a mortgage was signed for the remaining balance.
4	Purchased office equipment costing $7,000 by signing a note due in 1 year.
10	Office supplies costing $735 were purchased for cash.
21	Performed tax planning services for customer and collected $3,020.
31	Paid $1,450 for employee's salary.
31	Paid utilities bill for January of $88.
31	D. Jardine withdrew $850 cash for personal use.

REQUIRED *1.* Set up the following accounts (and account numbers): Cash (101), Office Supplies (105), Land (110), Building (112), Office Equipment (115), Notes Payable (220), Mortgage Payable (221), D. Jardine, Capital (301), D. Jardine, Withdrawals (302), Tax Service Revenues (401), Salary Expense (501), Utilities Expense (502).

2. Prepare the necessary journal entries to record the preceding transactions.

3. Post the journal entries to the accounts.

4. Prepare a trial balance at January 31, 1991.

 **PROBLEM 3-3A** **Financial Statements and Closing Entries.** The adjusted trial balance for the Swire Interior Decorating Company on November 30, 1991 (the end of its monthly accounting period) is as follows:

Account Titles	Debits	Credits
Cash	$ 7,082	
Accounts receivable	4,394	
Office supplies	1,074	
Prepaid insurance	1,540	
Land	6,000	
Building	29,400	
Accumulated depreciation: building		$ 130
Office equipment	2,880	
Accumulated depreciation: office equipment		40
Accounts payable		1,580
Mortgage payable		10,000
A. Swire, capital		40,000
A. Swire, withdrawals	800	
Interior decorating revenues		3,145
Salaries expense	850	
Insurance expense	140	
Telephone expense	177	
Utilities expense	276	
Office supplies expense	112	
Depreciation expense: building	130	
Depreciation expense: office equipment	40	
Totals	$54,895	$54,895

REQUIRED *1.* Prepare a November income statement, statement of changes in owner's equity, and a November 30, 1991, balance sheet (account form) for the Swire Interior Decorating Company.

2. Prepare the closing entries on November 30, 1991.

3. Prepare a post-closing trial balance.

PROBLEM 3-4A **Closing Entries and Post-Closing Trial Balance.** On February 28, 1991 (the end of the first month of operations), the following adjusted trial balance for the Gammon Employment Agency was prepared:

Account Titles	Debits	Credits
Cash	$15,920	
Accounts receivable	575	
Office supplies	1,526	
Prepaid insurance	792	
Land	5,000	
Building	16,600	
Accumulated depreciation: building		$ 60
Office equipment	5,280	
Accumulated depreciation: office equipment		55
Accounts payable		875
Notes payable		15,000
M. Gammon, capital		30,000
M. Gammon, withdrawals	2,400	
Employment commissions revenues		3,762
Salaries expense	950	
Insurance expense	72	
Telephone expense	170	
Utilities expense	268	
Office supplies expense	84	
Depreciation expense: building	60	
Depreciation expense: office equipment	55	
Totals	$49,752	$49,752

REQUIRED

1. Set up the following T-accounts: M. Gammon, Capital, M. Gammon, Withdrawals, Employment Commissions Revenues, Salaries Expense, Insurance Expense, Telephone Expense, Utilities Expense, Office Supplies Expense, Depreciation Expense: Building, Depreciation Expense: Office Equipment, Income Summary. Enter the account balances as listed on the adjusted trial balance.

2. Prepare closing entries for the Gammon Employment Agency on February 28, 1991.

3. Post the closing entries to the T-accounts.

4. Prepare a February 28, 1991, post-closing trial balance.

PROBLEM 3-5A   **Financial Statements.**   On May 31, 1991, the bookkeeper of Marina Boat Storage prepared the following closing entries for the month of May:

(a) Storage Revenues	4,060	
Income Summary		4,060
(b) Income Summary	2,724	
Depreciation Expense: Building		140
Depreciation Expense: Equipment		110
Supplies Expense		233
Salaries Expense		1,650
Telephone Expense		92
Utilities Expense		264
Insurance Expense		235
(c) Income Summary	1,336	
L. Marina, Capital		1,336
(d) L. Marina, Capital	830	
L. Marina, Withdrawals		830

In addition, the following post-closing trial balance was prepared:

Account Titles	Debits	Credits
Cash	$ 6,120	
Accounts receivable	4,989	
Supplies	1,117	
Land	16,000	
Building	25,200	
Accumulated depreciation: building		$ 140
Equipment	10,560	
Accumulated depreciation: equipment		110
Accounts payable		2,350
Notes payable		7,000
Mortgage payable		20,000
L. Marina, capital		34,386
Totals	$63,986	$63,986

REQUIRED

1. Prepare an income statement for the month ended May 31, 1991.

2. Prepare a statement of changes in owner's equity for the month ended May 31, 1991.

3. Prepare a May 31, 1991, balance sheet (report form).

PROBLEM 3-6A **Accounting Process.** The June 30, 1991, trial balance of the Ruff Furniture Refurbishment Center is as follows:

Account Titles	Debits	Credits
Cash	$ 1,425	
Accounts receivable	152	
Supplies	1,400	
Equipment	6,160	
Accumulated depreciation: equipment		$ 986
Accounts payable		208
J. Ruff, capital		8,600
J. Ruff, withdrawals	850	
Refurbishment revenues		935
Rent expense	400	
Telephone expense	55	
Utilities expense	287	
Totals	$10,729	$10,729

Additional Information:

(a) The temporary accounts reflect only June transactions.

(b) The supplies used during the month totaled $197.

(c) Depreciation expense on the equipment totals $62 for June.

REQUIRED

1. Prepare adjusting entries on June 30, 1991.

2. Prepare a June 30, 1991, adjusted trial balance.

3. Prepare closing entries on June 30, 1991.

4. Prepare a statement of changes in owner's equity for the month ended June 30, 1991.

5. Prepare a June 30, 1991, post-closing trial balance.

PROBLEM 3-7A   **Interrelationships.** The financial statement information of the Leon Appraisal Company for 1991 and 1992 is as follows:

	1991	1992
Assets, 12/31	1	$308,900
Expenses	$ 47,400	51,600
Additional investments	10,000	12,000
Net income	2	39,700
Liabilities, 12/31	153,500	5
Leon, capital, 1/1	3	117,200
Revenues	82,600	6
Withdrawals	24,000	7
Leon, capital, 12/31	4	138,900

REQUIRED   Fill in the blanks numbered 1 through 7. All the necessary information is listed. (Hint: It is not necessary to do your answers in numerical order.)

Problems

Part B

PROBLEM 3-1B   **Journal Entries.**   Stevel Stor-All rents storage facilities to customers. It entered into the following transactions during the month of April:

Date	Transaction
Apr. 1	Purchased a 3-year insurance policy on the company's building for $480 cash.
6	Purchased office supplies on account at a cost of $94.
14	Paid $30 on account for supplies purchased on April 6.
15	Collected storage fees totaling $720 for the first half of the month.
30	Paid April telephone bill of $82.
30	Collected storage fees totaling $750 for the last half of the month.
30	Paid $600 to employee for April salary.
30	Received $98 April utility bill, to be paid in early May.

REQUIRED   1. Prepare the necessary journal entries to record the preceding transactions.

2. List the source documents normally used to record these transactions.

PROBLEM 3-2B   **Journal Entries, Postings, and Trial Balance.** The Salanar Answering Service Company was established on March 1, 1991, to answer the phones of doctors, lawyers, and accountants when they are away from their offices. The company entered into the following transactions during March:

Date	Transaction
Mar. 1	P. Salanar set up the company by investing $15,000 cash in the company's checking account.
4	Acquired land and a building at a cost of $6,000 and $25,000, respectively. A $5,000 down payment was made and a mortgage was signed for the remaining balance.
7	Purchased telephone equipment costing $5,000 by signing a note due in 1 year.
8	Office supplies costing $330 were purchased for cash.
20	Collected $3,964 from customers for services performed.
31	Paid $845 for employee's salary.
31	Paid $82 for March utilities bill.
31	P. Salanar withdrew $1,000 cash for personal use.

REQUIRED

1. Set up the following accounts (and account numbers): Cash (101), Office Supplies (106), Land (112), Building (113), Telephone Equipment (116), Notes Payable (221), Mortgage Payable (222), P. Salanar, Capital (301), P. Salanar, Withdrawals (302), Answering Service Revenues (401), Salary Expense (501), and Utilities Expense (502).

2. Prepare the necessary journal entries to record the preceding transactions.

3. Post the journal entries to the accounts.

4. Prepare a trial balance at March 31, 1991.

PROBLEM 3-3B   **Financial Statements and Closing Entries.**   The adjusted trial balance on June 30, 1991 (the end of the first month of operations), for Tellet Musicians Booking Agency is as follows:

Account Titles	Debits	Credits
Cash	$ 6,420	
Accounts receivable	892	
Office supplies	940	
Land	3,075	
Building	13,300	
Accumulated depreciation: building		$ 65
Equipment	1,440	
Accumulated depreciation: equipment		20
Accounts payable		832
Mortgage payable		6,000
C. Tellet, capital		20,000
C. Tellet, withdrawals	700	
Musicians' booking revenues		1,468
Salaries expense	675	
Telephone expense	109	
Utilities expense	247	
Rent expense	415	
Office supplies expense	87	
Depreciation expense: building	65	
Depreciation expense: equipment	20	
Totals	$28,385	$28,385

REQUIRED

1. Prepare a June income statement, statement of changes in owner's equity, and a June 30, 1991, balance sheet (report form) for Tellet Musicians' Booking Agency.

2. Prepare the closing entries on June 30, 1991.

3. Prepare a June 30, 1991, post-closing trial balance.

PROBLEM 3-4B   **Closing Entries and Post-Closing Trial Balance.**   The October 31, 1991, adjusted trial balance for Casey's Cleaners is as follows:

Account Titles	Debits	Credits
Cash	$ 3,677	
Accounts receivable	920	
Cleaning supplies	2,289	
Land	4,240	
Building	29,000	
Accumulated depreciation: building		$ 90
Equipment	7,920	
Accumulated depreciation: equipment		82
Accounts payable		1,950
Notes payable		20,500
R. Casey, capital		25,000
R. Casey, withdrawals	1,500	
Cleaning service revenues		5,082
Salaries expense	1,775	
Telephone expense	158	
Utilities expense	232	
Rent expense	510	
Cleaning supplies expense	311	
Depreciation expense: building	90	
Depreciation expense: equipment	82	
Totals	$52,704	$52,704

REQUIRED

1. Set up the following T-accounts: R. Casey, Capital, R. Casey, Withdrawals, Cleaning Service Revenues, Salaries Expense, Telephone Expense, Utilities Expense, Rent Expense, Cleaning Supplies Expense, Depreciation Expense: Building, Depreciation Expense: Equipment, Income Summary. Enter the account balances as listed on the adjusted trial balance.

2. Prepare closing entries on October 31, 1991.

3. Post the closing entries to the T-accounts.

4. Prepare an October 31, 1991, post-closing trial balance.

PROBLEM 3-5B   **Financial Statements.**   On September 30, 1991, the bookkeeper of Kerrel Lawn Service prepared the following adjusted trial balance (the temporary accounts reflect only September transactions):

Account Titles	Debits	Credits
Cash	$ 940	
Supplies	852	
Prepaid rent	1,100	
Land	12,000	
Trucks	28,900	

Accumulated depreciation: trucks		$ 105
Lawn equipment	7,920	
Accumulated depreciation: lawn equipment		82
Accounts payable		1,300
Notes payable		6,400
T. Kerrel, capital		43,200
T. Kerrel, withdrawals	1,250	
Lawn service revenues		4,364
Salaries expense	715	
Gas and oil expense	500	
Supplies expense	200	
Telephone expense	67	
Utilities expense	270	
Rent expense	550	
Depreciation expense: trucks	105	
Depreciation expense: lawn equipment	82	
Totals	$55,451	$55,451

REQUIRED   *1.* Prepare an income statement for the month ended September 30, 1991.

2. Prepare a statement of changes in owner's equity for the month ended September 30, 1991.

3. Prepare a September 30, 1991, balance sheet (report form).

PROBLEM 3-6B   **Accounting Process.** The July 31, 1991, trial balance for the Cane Motivational Consulting Agency is as follows:

Account Titles	Debits	Credits
Cash	$ 1,210	
Accounts receivable	3,634	
Office supplies	1,000	
Office equipment	14,820	
Accumulated depreciation: office equipment		$ 2,520
Accounts payable		1,446
D. Cane, capital		16,000
D. Cane, withdrawals	1,000	
Motivational consulting revenues		2,942
Telephone expense	170	
Rent expense	800	
Utilities expense	274	
Totals	$22,908	$22,908

Additional Information:

(a) The temporary accounts reflect only July transactions.

(b) The office supplies used during the month totaled $80.

(c) The depreciation expense on the office equipment amounted to $210 for the month.

REQUIRED   *1.* Prepare adjusting entries on July 31, 1991.

2. Prepare an adjusted trial balance on July 31, 1991.

3. Prepare closing entries on July 31, 1991.

4. Prepare a statement of changes in owner's equity for the month ended July 31, 1991.

5. Prepare a July 31, 1991, post-closing trial balance.

PROBLEM 3-7B   **Interrelationships.**   The financial statement information of the Charles Adjusting Company for 1991 and 1992 is as follows:

	1991	*1992*
Charles, capital, 12/31	$ 83,500	*4*
Withdrawals	*1*	24,000
Revenues	*2*	65,000
Charles, capital, 1/1	69,400	*5*
Liabilities, 12/31	*3*	116,800
Net income	24,100	*6*
Additional investments	8,000	*7*
Expenses	35,200	39,800
Assets, 12/31	184,500	211,500

REQUIRED   Fill in the blanks numbered 1 through 7. All the necessary information is listed. (Hint: It is not necessary to do your answers in numerical order.)

Decision Cases

DECISION CASE 3-1   **Erroneous Financial Statements.**   The bookkeeper for the Powell Import Service Agency was confused when he prepared the following financial statements.

POWELL IMPORT SERVICE AGENCY
Profit and Expense Statement
December 31, 1991

Expenses:		
Salaries expense	$21,000	
Utilities expense	3,400	
Accounts receivable	1,600	
C. Powell, withdrawals	20,000	
Office supplies	1,500	
Total expenses		$(47,500)
Revenues:		
Service revenues	$47,000	
Accounts payable	1,100	
Accumulated depreciation: office equipment	1,800	
Total revenues		49,900
Net Revenues		$ 2,400

POWELL IMPORT SERVICE AGENCY
Balancing Statement
For Year Ended December 31, 1991

Liabilities		*Assets*	
Mortgage payable	$27,000	Building	$44,000
Accumulated depreciation:		Depreciation expense:	
building	6,400	building	1,600
Total Liabilities	$33,400	Office equipment	9,700
		Depreciation expense:	
C. Powell, capital[a]	27,000	office equipment	900
Total Liabilities and		Cash	4,200
Owner's Equity	$60,400	Total Assets	$60,400

[a] $24,600 beginning capital + $2,400 net revenues

C. Powell has asked you to examine the financial statements and related accounting records. You find that, with the exception of office supplies, the debit or credit *amount* of each account is correct even though the account might be incorrectly listed in the financial statements. You determine that the office supplies used during the year amount to $800 and the office supplies on hand at the end of the year amount to $700.

REQUIRED

1. Review each financial statement and indicate any errors you find.

2. Prepare a corrected 1991 income statement, statement of changes in owner's equity, and ending balance sheet.

DECISION CASE 3-2

Confusion About Debit and Credit Rules. A friend of yours in this accounting class is confused and says, "I just don't understand revenues and expenses. I learned in the previous chapter that assets are increased by debits and liabilities are increased by credits. Now I read in this chapter that expenses are increased by debits and revenues are increased by credits. So the way I look at it, expenses must be assets and revenues must be liabilities. But then this book says that revenues increase assets and expenses decrease assets. And, if that isn't confusing enough, the book goes on to say that not all increases in assets are revenues and not all decreases in assets are expenses. Wow! Does this make sense to you?"

Your friend continues, "And these closing entries boggle my mind. Why are they necessary? The company isn't going to close down its business. How do I know which accounts to close? At first I thought *all* accounts are closed at the end of each accounting period but now I'm not so sure. And after learning that expenses are increased by debits (like assets) and revenues are increased by credits (like liabilities), I look at the closing entry example. There the revenues were debited and the expenses were credited! Furthermore, I thought withdrawals were expenses but then why isn't the withdrawals account listed with the expenses in the closing entries? Please help me! I know I need a good understanding of these issues before I read any further in the book."

REQUIRED

Prepare a written explanation for each issue raised by your friend. Use examples where needed.

DECISION CASE 3-3   **Projected Income Statement.** Cara Agee owns a hair styling shop, Air Hair Company. It is now November of 1991. Although she has never developed a "projected" income statement before, Cara is interested in preparing one for 1992. She understands that to do so she must make a "best guess" of her 1992 revenues and expenses based upon past activities and future estimates. She asks for your help and provides you with the following information.

1. Styling revenues for 1991 were $80,000. Cara expects these to increase by 10% in 1992.

2. Air Hair employees are paid a total "base" salary of $20,000 plus 20% of all styling revenues.

3. Styling supplies used have generally averaged 15% of styling revenues; Cara expects this relationship to be the same in 1992.

4. Air Hair has recently signed a 2-year rental agreement on its shop, requiring payments of $400 per month payable in advance.

5. The cost of utilities (heat, light, phone) is expected to be 25% of the yearly rent.

6. Air Hair owns styling equipment that cost $12,000. Depreciation expense is estimated to be $2,000 on this equipment for 1992.

REQUIRED   Prepare a 1992 projected income statement for the Air Hair Company. Show supporting calculations.

DECISION CASE 3-4   **Missing Records.**   The Gray Service Company had a fire and lost some of the accounting records it needed to prepare its 1991 income statement. Stan Gray, the owner, has been able to determine that his capital in the business was $32,000 at the beginning of 1991 and $33,000 at the end of 1991. During 1991 he withdrew $14,000 from the business. Stan has also been able to remember or determine the following information for 1991.

1. Cash service revenues were twice the amount of net income; credit service revenues were 40% of cash service revenues.

2. Rent expense was $250 per month.

3. The company has one employee who was paid a salary of $14,000 plus 10% of the service revenues.

4. The supplies expense was 15% of the total expenses.

5. The utilities expense was $100 per month for the first 9 months of the year and $200 per month during the remaining months of the year due to the cold winter.

Stan also knows that the company owns some service equipment, but cannot remember the cost or amount of depreciation expense.

REQUIRED   Based on the preceding information, prepare the 1991 income statement of the Gray Service Company.

4

Adjusting Entries and the Worksheet

LEARNING OBJECTIVES

1. Explain the purpose of adjusting entries.

2. Describe a depreciable asset and calculate depreciation expense.

3. Record depreciation expense and show the resulting book value.

4. Define a prepaid expense and record the related adjusting entry.

5. Define an unearned revenue and record the related adjusting entry.

6. Define an accrued expense and record the related adjusting entry.

7. Define an accrued revenue and record the related adjusting entry.

8. Describe a worksheet and list the steps needed to complete a worksheet.

9. Use a worksheet to complete the accounting process.

10. List the steps in the accounting process.

APPENDIX

A-1 Explain the purpose of reversing entries.

n the first three chapters we developed an accounting system for recording, retaining, and reporting information about transactions. The discussion involved a company operating as a service business and entering into simple transactions. In this chapter we look at transactions that lead to more complex adjusting entries at the end of the period. We also introduce the worksheet, an accounting working paper designed to aid in several steps of the accounting process.

Adjusting Entries

1. Explain the purpose of adjusting entries.

Most companies use the *accrual* basis of accounting, in which revenues are recorded in the accounting period when products are sold or services are performed for customers and not necessarily when cash is collected. All the related expenses are then matched against these revenues, regardless of the inflow or outflow of cash. In many cases not all revenue and expense account balances are up to date at the end of the accounting period. As introduced in Chapter 3, certain amounts must be *adjusted* to report the correct net income on the income statement and the correct ending financial position on the balance sheet. These adjustments are made by adjusting entries. **Adjusting entries are journal entries made at the end of the accounting period to bring the revenue and expense account balances up to date and to show the correct ending balances in the asset and liability accounts.**

An adjusting entry ordinarily affects both a permanent (balance sheet) and a temporary (income statement) account. Adjusting entries may be grouped into two types. The types of entries and the affected balance sheet accounts are listed as follows:

1. Apportionment of depreciable, prepaid, and unearned items:
    (a) Depreciable assets
    (b) Prepaid expenses
    (c) Unearned revenues
2. Recording of accrued items:
    (a) Accrued expenses
    (b) Accrued revenues

A discussion of the adjusting entries and illustrations for each category are presented in the following sections.

Apportionment of Depreciable Assets

In Chapter 3 we discussed the differences between the terms *cost, asset,* and *expense.* We illustrated these differences in the diagram in Exhibit 3-1, which is repeated here as Exhibit 4-1. The cost refers to the amount at which a transaction is recorded. This cost may be recorded as an asset (unexpired cost) when a company acquires an economic resource that is expected to provide future benefits to the company. The cost may be recorded as an expense (expired cost) if it relates to selling goods or providing services to customers in an accounting period. If a

EXHIBIT 4-1   Cost: Asset or Expense

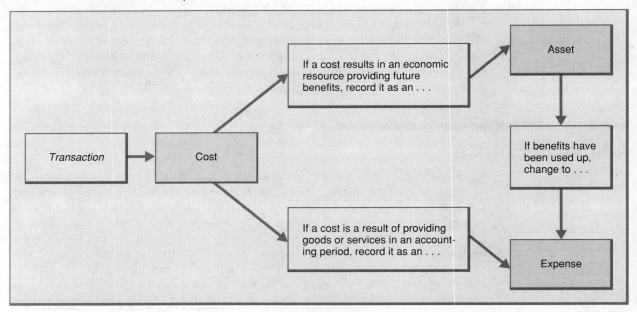

cost is recorded as an asset, part or all of the related cost must be changed from an asset (unexpired cost) to an expense (expired cost). This procedure is necessary because most assets eventually lose their potential for providing future benefits. Another way of stating this concept is to say that the cost must be *apportioned* (allocated) between the assets (portion remaining) at the end of an accounting period and the expenses incurred (portion used up) during that period.

Companies frequently acquire physical economic resources that they expect to use for many years in their operating activities. These resources are recorded as assets at the acquisition cost. Examples of these assets are land, buildings, office equipment, trucks, machinery, and automobiles. These long-term physical assets are commonly called *property and equipment*. Alternative terms for these assets are *fixed assets* and *operational assets*. Most of these assets are also depreciable. **A depreciable asset is a long-term physical asset whose expected economic benefits expire over the useful life of the asset.** In accordance with Exhibit 4-1, the cost of a depreciable asset must be apportioned as an expense in the accounting period during which it is used. This expense is called depreciation expense. **Depreciation expense is the part of the cost of a long-term physical asset allocated as an expense to each accounting period in the asset's useful life.**[1] An adjusting entry is made at the end of the accounting period to record depreciation expense. The amount is calculated as discussed next.

2. Describe a depreciable asset and calculate depreciation expense.

Calculation of Depreciation Expense.   There are several methods for computing depreciation expense, and these methods are fully discussed in Chapter 11.

---

[1]Although land is a physical asset, it is not depreciable because it is not considered to have a limited useful life.

One method of depreciation is referred to as the straight-line depreciation method. **The straight-line method records an equal portion of the cost of the asset as depreciation expense in each accounting period in which the asset is used.** The equation for computing *annual* straight-line depreciation is:

$$\text{Annual Depreciation Expense} = \frac{\text{Cost} - \text{Estimated Residual Value}}{\text{Estimated Useful Life in Years}}$$

To compute *monthly* depreciation, the annual depreciation is simply multiplied times 1/12.

The *cost* is the amount recorded in the account for the physical asset. Thus the depreciable asset account balance serves as the starting point for the depreciation calculation. The *estimated residual value* is the amount for which the asset is expected to be disposed of at the end of its useful life. Because of difficulties in making this estimate accurately, companies often assign a nominal or zero amount to the residual value. In this chapter we assume the residual value is zero for all the depreciation calculations in the discussions and homework materials. The *estimated useful life* is the number of years the asset is expected to be used before its disposal. This estimate is also difficult to make, but management has the responsibility for developing the best estimate possible.

To illustrate the calculation of depreciation, the adjusting entries for depreciation, and the resulting book values, we discuss the 1991 depreciation for two physical assets of the Stalley Company, which are described here.

1. *Building.* On January 1, 1983, the company purchased a building at a cost of $60,000. The estimated useful life was 25 years at that date.

2. *Store Equipment.* On December 1, 1991, the company purchased store equipment at a cost of $12,000. The estimated life was 10 years on that date.

The company computes its 1991 depreciation expense (assuming a zero residual value) as shown here.

BUILDING:

$$\text{Annual Depreciation Expense} = \frac{\$60,000 - \$0}{25 \text{ years}}$$

$$\text{1991 Depreciation Expense} = \underline{\$2,400}$$

STORE EQUIPMENT:

$$\text{Annual Depreciation Expense} = \frac{\$12,000 - \$0}{10 \text{ years}}$$

$$= \$1,200$$

$$\text{1991 Depreciation Expense} = \$1,200 \times 1/12$$

$$= \underline{\$100}$$

For the store equipment, it would be incorrect to record $1,200 annual depreciation expense for 1991 because the store equipment was used only 1 month during that period. Instead the 1991 depreciation of the store equipment is $100, computed by multiplying the $1,200 times 1/12 (the fraction of time the asset was used during the year).

Many companies prepare financial statements for accounting periods shorter than a year (e.g., for interim reports or for monthly budgeting purposes).

These companies would compute the depreciation expense for the shorter period based on a fraction of the year.

Depreciation Adjusting Entry.   The adjusting entry to record the depreciation expense for Buildings, for example, involves a debit (increase) to the expense account Depreciation Expense: Buildings and a credit (increase) to the account Accumulated Depreciation: Buildings. The last word of the account titles would be changed for other depreciable assets (e.g., Depreciation Expense: Store Equipment).

To illustrate this concept, the adjusting entries of the Stalley Company for the depreciation expense on the building and store equipment are recorded as follows based on the amounts calculated earlier.[2]

3. Record depreciation expense and show the resulting book value.

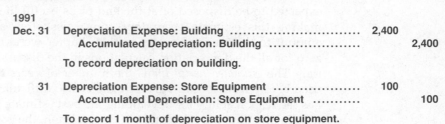

1991
Dec. 31   Depreciation Expense: Building   2,400
                  Accumulated Depreciation: Building   2,400

          To record depreciation on building.

      31   Depreciation Expense: Store Equipment   100
                  Accumulated Depreciation: Store Equipment   100

          To record 1 month of depreciation on store equipment.

Each Depreciation Expense account is listed on the income statement to compute the net income for the accounting period. Each Depreciation Expense account is then closed to Income Summary at the end of the period.

Book Values.   Each Accumulated Depreciation account is a permanent account and is a contra (negative) account to its related physical asset. **A contra account is an account whose balance is subtracted from another related account in order to determine a resulting amount.** A contra account always has a balance opposite of the account to which it is related. The debit and credit rule that applies to a contra account is also the opposite of the rule that applies to the related account. Thus each Accumulated Depreciation account is increased by credit entries (and decreased by debit entries) and has a credit balance. The credit balance of each Accumulated Depreciation account is subtracted from the debit balance of its related long-term physical asset account on the ending balance sheet for the accounting period to determine the remaining *unexpired* cost. This unexpired cost is referred to as the book value of the asset. **The book value (or carrying value) is the cost of a depreciable asset less its related accumulated depreciation.** Each year, after the depreciation expense has been recorded for a physical asset, the related Accumulated Depreciation account balance increases and the book value decreases. The accounting equation remains in balance, however, because the decrease in the book value of the asset is accompanied by a decrease in owner's equity due to the closing of the Depreciation Expense account. Eventually, at the end of the asset's life, the Accumulated Depreciation account credit balance will be equal to the related asset account debit balance

---

[2]Throughout the remainder of the book, we will use a simpler format for general journal entries, which omits the column headings, account number column, and transaction date (unless the date is critical to the discussion).

(assuming no residual value), and therefore the asset will have a zero book value.

To illustrate this procedure consider the depreciation adjusting entries recorded earlier for the Stalley Company. After the adjusting entry for the depreciation on the building has been posted to the general ledger accounts, the Accumulated Depreciation: Buildings account has an ending balance of $21,600. This amount results from having depreciated the building for 8 years (1983 through 1990) at $2,400 per year totaling $19,200 at the beginning of 1991, and adding $2,400 depreciation for 1991. The resulting book value of the building on December 31, 1991, is $38,400 ($60,000 − $21,600). This book value would be reported on the company's December 31, 1991, balance sheet as follows:

Building	$60,000	
Less: Accumulated depreciation	(21,600)	$38,400

Note that the book value of the building has decreased from $40,800 ($60,000 − $19,200) on December 31, 1990, to $38,400 ($60,000 − $21,600) on December 31, 1991, because the Accumulated Depreciation account balance was increased by $2,400 in 1991. Note also that the $38,400 book value will be reduced to a book value of zero after $2,400 annual depreciation has been recorded in each of the remaining 16 years of the building's estimated useful life.

After the depreciation adjusting entry for the store equipment has been posted, the Accumulated Depreciation: Store Equipment account has an ending balance of $100 (since this is the first month that the store equipment was used). The resulting book value of the store equipment on December 31, 1991, is $11,900 and would be reported on the company's balance sheet for that date as follows:

Store equipment	$12,000	
Less: Accumulated depreciation	(100)	$11,900

As has been illustrated, by using an Accumulated Depreciation account instead of reducing (crediting) the asset account directly for the depreciation, the original cost of each long-term physical asset is retained in the accounts and reported on the balance sheet. In addition, the total unexpired cost (the book value) and the total expired cost (the Accumulated Depreciation) that have been recorded over the current and all previous accounting periods are also reported on the balance sheet. In this way the reader of the balance sheet can see the original cost of the physical assets. By observing the book value, the Accumulated Depreciation, and the changes in these amounts each accounting period, the reader can also gain insights into the age of the physical assets. This information is helpful to users of the balance sheet in evaluating the need for the company to replace its physical assets and the likely timing of this replacement.

Apportionment of Prepaid Expenses

A prepaid expense is an economic resource that is expected to be used in the near future. Prepaid expenses are similar in several ways to depreciable assets; that is, they are economic resources that a company has acquired and expects to use in its current and future operating activities. Prepaid expenses differ from depreciable assets because they may or may not be physical in nature and are

4. Define a prepaid expense and record the related adjusting entry.

expected to provide economic benefits for only a short period of time. Examples of prepaid expenses include prepaid insurance, prepaid rent, office supplies, and store supplies.

When goods or services involving a prepaid expense are acquired, the cost is recorded as an asset. At the end of the accounting period a part of the goods or services has been used in order to earn revenues. In accordance with Exhibit 4-1, the expired cost must be matched, as an expense, against the revenues of the period, while the unexpired cost remains as an asset on the ending balance sheet. The apportionment (allocation) of the cost of each prepaid expense between an expense and an asset is recorded in an adjusting entry at the end of the accounting period.

Prepaid Expense Adjusting Entry.   When a prepaid expense has been initially recorded as an asset, the related end-of-period adjusting entry involves a debit (increase) to an appropriately titled expense account (e.g., Rent Expense, obtained from the company's chart of accounts) and a credit (decrease) directly to the asset account (e.g., Prepaid Rent). A contra account, like Accumulated Depreciation, is *not* used with each prepaid expense because of the relatively short expected life of the asset.

The calculation of the amount of the adjusting entry depends upon the type of prepaid expense. In the case of prepaid insurance, for example, the total cost of insurance coverage (as determined by a review of the insurance policy source document) is apportioned on a *straight-line* basis similar to depreciation. The cost, however, is usually divided by the number of *months* of insurance coverage acquired instead of years. The resulting monthly insurance expense is then multiplied times the number of months in the accounting period that the insurance coverage was in force to determine the insurance expense for the period. In the case of prepaid rent, the total rent expense for the period is computed by multiplying the monthly rent (determined by a review of the rental agreement source document) times the months in the accounting period. For office supplies and store supplies, a physical count is made of the supplies and related costs on hand at the end of the accounting period. The difference between the cost of the supplies on hand at the end of the accounting period and the cost of the supplies available for use during the period is the supplies expense for the period.

To illustrate the accounting for prepaid expenses, assume that the Stalley Company acquires two prepaid expenses during 1991, summarized as follows:

1. *Office Supplies.* On January 1, 1991, the company had $240 of office supplies on hand. On May 8, 1991, the company acquired an additional $80 of office supplies. A physical count on December 31, 1991, determines that $170 of office supplies are on hand on that date.

2. *Prepaid Insurance.* On November 1, 1991, the company paid $540 for a 1-year comprehensive insurance policy.

The year-end adjusting entries based on this information for office supplies and prepaid insurance are explained next.

Office Supplies.   The office supplies purchased on May 8, 1991, were an economic resource to the company and were recorded as an asset by debiting (increasing) Office Supplies for $80 and crediting (decreasing) Cash for $80. After posting this entry, the Office Supplies account had a balance of $320 ($240 + $80), the office supplies available for use. On December 31, 1991, $170 of office supplies were still on hand. Since $320 of office supplies were available for use and $170 of office supplies were left, $150 ($320 − $170) of office supplies were used during the year. The December 31, 1991, adjusting entry to record the office supplies expense is as follows:

```
1991
Dec. 31   Office Supplies Expense  .........................................  150
              Office Supplies  ..................................................          150
          To record office supplies expense.
```

After the journal entry is posted, the $150 amount in the Office Supplies Expense account is listed as an expense on the 1991 income statement. Note that after the $150 credit (decrease) to the Office Supplies account is deducted from the previous $320 debit balance, it results in a $170 ending debit balance that is listed as an asset on the December 31, 1991, balance sheet. These amounts are shown in the following T-accounts.

Office Supplies Expense		Office Supplies			
12/31/91	150	1/1/91	240	12/31/91	150
		5/8/91	80		
		Balance	170		

Prepaid Insurance.   On November 1, 1991, when the company paid $540 for the 1-year insurance policy, the right to the insurance protection was an economic resource to the company. At that time the transaction was recorded by debiting (increasing) the asset account Prepaid Insurance for $540 and crediting (decreasing) Cash for the same amount. No further entries were made in the Prepaid Insurance account during the rest of the accounting period. At the end of the year a review of the insurance policy related to this account reveals that 2 months of insurance protection (for November and December) or $90 [($540 ÷ 12) × 2 months] has expired and 10 months of insurance protection or $450 [($540 ÷ 12) × 10] remains in force (unexpired). The December 31, 1991, adjusting entry to record the insurance expense is as follows:

```
1991
Dec. 31   Insurance Expense  ...................................................  90
              Prepaid Insurance  .................................................          90
          To record insurance expense.
```

After the journal entry is posted, the $90 debit (increase) is included as insurance expense to the 1991 income statement. When the $90 credit (decrease) to Prepaid Insurance is deducted from the $540 debit balance, it results in a $450 ending debit balance. This balance is listed as an asset on the December 31, 1991, balance sheet. These amounts are shown in the following T-accounts.

Insurance Expense				Prepaid Insurance			
12/31/91	90			11/1/91	540	12/31/91	90
				Balance	450		

Alternative Accounting Procedures. As a way of standardizing its accounting process, a company may choose to establish a policy of *initially* recording the entire prepayment of a cost as an *expense* (expired cost) *instead* of as an *asset* (unexpired cost). In this case an adjusting entry is still necessary at the end of the accounting period but it is different from the entries discussed earlier. The proper adjusting entry procedure is to calculate the correct ending balance that *should be* in the asset account and adjust the accounts accordingly. The adjusting entry must *reduce* the expense account and *increase* the asset account by this amount. For simplicity, in this book generally we will record prepayments as *assets*.

Apportionment of Unearned Revenues

In Chapter 3 we defined revenues as the prices charged to customers for goods or services provided during an accounting period. We also noted that the inflow of cash and the recording of revenue are not always directly related.

In some cases customers may make an advance payment to a company for goods or services to be provided in the future. At the time of the transaction, even though an asset, Cash, has increased, the company has not earned revenue because the goods or services have not yet been provided. Instead the company has incurred a liability because it has an obligation to provide the future goods or services. **An unearned revenue is an advance receipt for goods or services to be provided in the future and it is recorded as a liability.** The liability is frequently entitled, *Unearned,* and is followed by an explanatory term (e.g., *Unearned Legal Fees*). At the end of each accounting period all such liabilities and related source documents must be examined to determine whether the goods or services have been provided. If so, an adjusting entry must be made to reduce the liability and increase the revenues of the period. The journal entry involves a debit (decrease) to the unearned liability account (e.g., Unearned Legal Fees) and a credit (increase) to a related revenue account (e.g., Legal Fees Earned). As a result, the income statement shows all the revenues in the period in which they are earned and the ending balance sheet reports the remaining liabilities of the company.

5. Define an unearned revenue and record the related adjusting entry.

Example of Adjustment of Unearned Revenue. To illustrate, assume the building that the Stalley Company owns is too large for its current operations and therefore the company rents a portion of the building to another company. On December 1, 1991, the other company pays $720 in advance for 6 months rent ($120 per month). Upon receipt of the money, the Stalley Company incurred an economic obligation (liability) to provide the use of the rented space to the other company for 6 months. No revenue should be recorded at this point because no service has been provided. Thus the Stalley Company recorded this transaction as a debit (increase) to Cash for $720 and a credit (increase) to a liability account, Unearned Rent, for $720. No further entries were made in the Unearned Rent account during the accounting period. At the end of the period a review of this account and the rental agreement reveals that 1 month of rent revenue or $120 has been earned and 5 months or $600 ($120 × 5) is still unearned. The December 31, 1991, adjusting entry to record the rent revenue is as follows:

```
1991
Dec. 31   Unearned Rent ......................................................  120
               Rent Revenue ..................................................             120

          To record rent earned.
```

After the journal entry is posted, the $120 rent revenue is included on the 1991 income statement. When the $120 debit (increase) to Unearned Rent is deducted from the $720 credit balance, it results in a $600 ending credit balance. This balance is listed as a liability on the December 31, 1991, balance sheet. These amounts are shown in the following T-accounts.

Unearned Rent				Rent Revenue	
12/31/91 120	12/1/91 720			12/31/91 120	
	Balance 600				

Alternative Accounting Procedures.   Instead of following the preceding procedures, to standardize its accounting process a company may choose to establish a policy of *initially* recording the receipt of an advance payment for future goods or services as a revenue (instead of as a liability). In this case an adjusting entry must be made at the end of the accounting period to *reduce* the revenue and *increase* a liability for the amount of goods or services that have not yet been provided. For simplicity, in this book generally we will record receipts in advance as *liabilities*.

Recording of Accrued Expenses

6. Define an accrued expense and record the related adjusting entry.

Most of a company's expenses are recorded when payment is made. At the end of an accounting period some expenses of the company usually have not yet been recorded, however. These expenses are called accrued expenses. **An accrued expense is an expense that has been incurred during the accounting period but has been neither paid nor recorded.** The most common type of accrued expense is unpaid employees' wages and salaries. Other common accrued expenses include unpaid interest, taxes, and utility bills. In order to match all expenses against revenues and to report all the liabilities at the end of the period, an adjusting entry must be made for each accrued expense. The journal entry involves a debit (increase) to an appropriately titled expense account and a credit (increase) to an appropriately titled liability account. Two accrued expenses, salaries and interest, are discussed further. The accounting principles that apply to these accrued items also apply to the others.

Accrued Salary Expense.   Companies have different policies for payment of their employees' salaries. Employees are seldom paid in advance, and they are usually paid after completion of their duties in the pay period. Some employees of a company may be paid weekly, some twice a month, and others monthly.

Seldom does an accounting period end on the same day as the salary payment date for all of the employees. Nevertheless, the salaries earned by the employees from the date of the last salary payment through the end of the accounting period are an *expense* of the period even though they will be *paid* in the next accounting period. An adjusting entry must be made at the end of the period to record the salary expense and liability. The journal entry is a debit (increase) to Salaries (or Wages) Expense and a credit (increase) to Salaries (Wages) Payable. The amount is determined by a review of the payroll records.

To illustrate, assume that the Stalley Company has six employees, each of whom earns $300 per week for a 5-day work week (Monday through Friday). The employees are paid every Friday at the end of the day. December 31, 1991, is on Tuesday. The employees' salaries totaling $720 ($300 $\times$ 6 $\times$ 2/5) for the Monday and Tuesday of the last week in December are an expense of 1991 even though they will not be paid until 1992. The December 31, 1991, adjusting entry to record the expense and the liability[3] is as follows:

```
1991
Dec. 31   Salaries Expense ................................................    720
              Salaries Payable ................................................            720
          To record accrued salaries.
```

After the journal entry is posted, the Salaries Expense account includes the total employees' salaries for all of the 1991 accounting period and is listed on the 1991 income statement. The $720 of Salaries Payable is listed as a liability on the December 31, 1991, balance sheet.

When a company has recorded accrued salaries at the end of an accounting period it must be careful to record the correct journal entry when the salaries are paid in the *next* accounting period. The journal entry must record the part of the total salaries for the new period as Salaries Expense and the part for the salaries of the previous period as a reduction of Salaries Payable. To illustrate, the Stalley Company will pay $1,800 ($300 $\times$ 6) of salaries on Friday, January 3, 1992. Of this amount, $1,080 ($300 $\times$ 6 $\times$ 3/5) is for the 3 workdays of January and is an expense of 1992. The remaining $720 is for the 2 workdays of December that was accrued in the adjusting entry on December 31, 1991. The January 3, 1992, journal entry for the payment of the weekly salary would be recorded as follows:

```
1992
Jan. 3    Salaries Expense ................................................   1,080
          Salaries Payable ................................................     720
              Cash ........................................................          1,800
          To record salaries expense and eliminate accrued salaries.
```

After posting, the Salaries Expense account has a debit balance of $1,080 for the 3 days of salaries for the new 1992 accounting period. (Remember that the Salaries Expense account was closed at the end of 1991.) The Salaries Payable account has

---

[3]In reality, a company would also record certain payroll taxes related to such items as unemployment benefits and social security. For simplicity, these items are ignored in this chapter but they are discussed in Chapter 10.

a zero balance because the $720 liability recorded at the end of 1991 has now been eliminated.

Accrued Interest Expense.   Many companies enter into transactions involving the issuance or receipt of a note. **A note is a written legal document in which one party (the issuer) agrees to pay another party a certain amount of money (the principal) on an agreed future date (the maturity date).** Notes may be exchanged for cash or for goods or services. Most notes are interest bearing. An *interest-bearing note* is a note for which the issuer is charged interest on the principal. The *annual* interest rate is included on the note. In the case of an interest-bearing note, the issuer may pay both the principal and the interest on the maturity date. Between the date that the note is issued and the maturity date, interest accumulates (accrues) daily on an interest-bearing note. This relationship is illustrated in the following diagram.

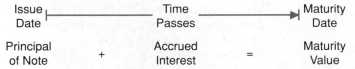

If a company issues an interest-bearing note, the interest is an expense of doing business. Even though the interest accrues daily, however, interest expense is normally recorded when the note is paid on the maturity date. When a company has issued a note in the current accounting period but the maturity date is not until the next accounting period, part of the interest expense applies to the current period and part to the next period. An adjusting entry must be made at the end of the current period to record the accrued interest as an expense of the period and as a liability at the end of the period. The journal entry is a debit (increase) to Interest Expense and a credit (increase) to Interest Payable.

The amount of interest that has accrued on a note at any time is computed by multiplying the principal times the annual interest rate for the length of time the note has been issued. The information necessary to make this computation is determined by a review of the note. The computation of interest is discussed more fully in Chapter 8. For our purposes here you need only a basic understanding of the interest calculation.

To illustrate, assume that on November 1, 1991, the Stalley Company borrowed $12,000 from a local bank. The company signed (issued) a $12,000, 3-month, 10% note requiring it to repay the principal plus $300 interest ($12,000 × 10% for 3/12 year) on February 1, 1992. At the date of issuance the company recorded the transaction by debiting (increasing) Cash for $12,000 and crediting (increasing) Notes Payable for $12,000. No further entries were made for the note during the accounting period. At the end of the period a review of the note reveals that an adjusting entry must be made to record the interest that has accrued but has not been recorded. Since two of the three months life of the note have passed, the amount of accrued interest is $200 ($300 total interest × 2/3). The journal entry to record the accrued interest is as follows:

1991
Dec. 31   Interest Expense 200
           Interest Payable   200
       To record accrued interest on note payable.

The Interest Expense is listed on the 1991 income statement and the Interest Payable is listed as a liability on the December 31, 1991, balance sheet.

Recording of Accrued Revenues

7. Define an accrued revenue and record the related adjusting entry.

Most revenues of a company are recorded at the time goods or services are provided to a customer. At the end of an accounting period, some revenues of a company may not yet have been recorded. These revenues are called accrued revenues. **An accrued revenue is a revenue that has been earned during the accounting period but has been neither collected nor recorded.** An adjusting entry must be made for each accrued revenue at the end of the period in order to record all the revenues for the period and the ending assets of the period. The journal entry involves a debit (increase) to an appropriately titled asset account and a credit (increase) to an appropriately titled revenue account. The amount is determined by a review of the accounting records and related source documents. There are not many types of accrued revenues. One common accrued revenue is the interest that has accumulated on a note *received* by a company.

Example of Accrued Revenue. Assume that on May 1, 1991, the Stalley Company sold some land to the Trage Company for $9,000. The land had originally cost $9,000 and was recorded by the Stalley Company as an asset at the time it was purchased. The Trage Company paid $1,000 down and signed a 1-year, 12% note for the $8,000 balance. At that time the Stalley Company recorded the transaction by debiting (increasing) Cash for $1,000, debiting (increasing) Notes Receivable for $8,000 and crediting (decreasing) Land for $9,000. No further entries were made for the note during 1991. At the end of the accounting period an adjusting entry must be made to record the interest revenue that has accrued on the note but which will not be collected until the maturity date. The note has been issued for 8 months (May through December), and therefore the accrued interest amounts to $640 ($8,000 × 12% for 8/12 year). The journal entry to record the accrued interest is as follows:

```
1991
Dec. 31   Interest Receivable  ...............................................   640
             Interest Revenue  ...............................................           640
          To record accrued interest on note receivable.
```

The $640 of Interest Revenue is included in the 1991 income statement and the $640 of Interest Receivable is reported as an asset on the December 31, 1991, balance sheet. The journal entries to record the collection of the note and interest are discussed in Chapter 8.

When all the adjusting entries have been journalized and posted, an adjusted trial balance is prepared to prove the equality of the debit and credit account balances. After the adjusted trial balance is completed the financial statements and closing entries are prepared. To aid in these steps of the accounting process a worksheet may be prepared.

Summary of Adjusting Entries

At the beginning of the section on adjusting entries, we identified the various types of entries and the affected balance sheet accounts. We then described and illustrated each type of adjusting entry. For convenience, Exhibit 4-2 summarizes the adjusting process by listing each adjustment and providing an example (without amounts) of the related adjusting entry.

EXHIBIT 4-2
Summary of
Adjusting Entries

Type of Adjustment	Example of Adjusting Entry		
Depreciation of long-term physical asset	Depreciation Expense Accumulated Depreciation	xxx	 xxx

Apportionment of prepaid expense
    (*asset* initially debited)
	Insurance Expense
	    Prepaid Insurance
		xxx	
			xxx

Apportionment of unearned revenue
    (*liability* initially credited)
	Unearned Rent
	    Rent Revenue
		xxx	
			xxx

Recording of accrued expense	Salaries Expense Salaries Payable	xxx	 xxx
Recording of accrued revenue	Interest Receivable Interest Revenue	xxx	 xxx

Worksheet

8. Describe a worksheet and list the steps needed to complete a worksheet.

At the end of an accounting period a company must prepare adjusting entries, closing entries, and its financial statements. A worksheet is often prepared to aid in these accounting activities. **A worksheet is an accounting working paper used for initially preparing the trial balance, adjustments, adjusted trial balance, income statement, and balance sheet at the end of an accounting period.** A worksheet, which is a large columnar paper, is used to (1) minimize errors, (2) simplify the journal recording of the adjusting and closing entries, and (3) make it easier to prepare the financial statements. Note that a worksheet is *not* a substitute for any formal accounting records or financial statements; it is an accounting working paper used only for the purposes just mentioned.

There are four steps in the completion of a worksheet. They are:

Step 1: Prepare a trial balance.

Step 2: Prepare the worksheet adjustments.

Step 3: Prepare the adjusted trial balance.

Step 4: Prepare the worksheet financial statements.

A completed worksheet of the law practice of D. Jones, Attorney for the year ended December 31, 1991, is shown in Exhibit 4-3. Each step in the completion of the worksheet is listed on Exhibit 4-3 and discussed next.

EXHIBIT 4-3
Worksheet

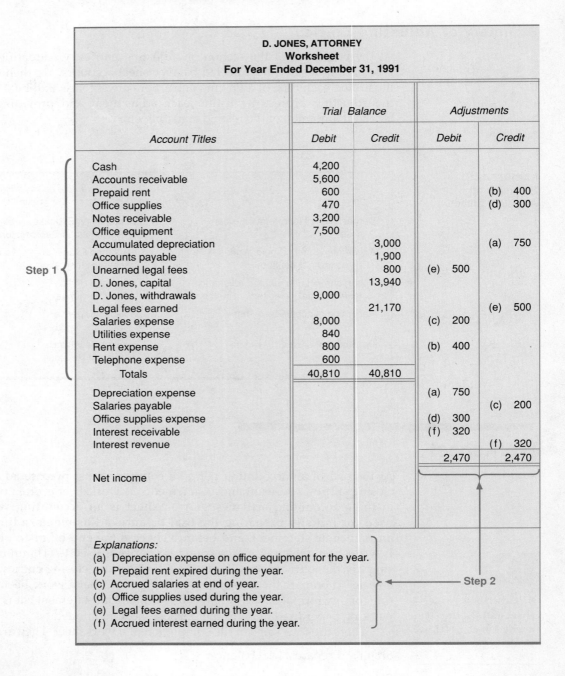

D. JONES, ATTORNEY
Worksheet
For Year Ended December 31, 1991

Account Titles	Trial Balance Debit	Trial Balance Credit	Adjustments Debit	Adjustments Credit
Cash	4,200			
Accounts receivable	5,600			
Prepaid rent	600			(b) 400
Office supplies	470			(d) 300
Notes receivable	3,200			
Office equipment	7,500			
Accumulated depreciation		3,000		(a) 750
Accounts payable		1,900		
Unearned legal fees		800	(e) 500	
D. Jones, capital		13,940		
D. Jones, withdrawals	9,000			
Legal fees earned		21,170		(e) 500
Salaries expense	8,000		(c) 200	
Utilities expense	840			
Rent expense	800		(b) 400	
Telephone expense	600			
Totals	40,810	40,810		
Depreciation expense			(a) 750	
Salaries payable				(c) 200
Office supplies expense			(d) 300	
Interest receivable			(f) 320	
Interest revenue				(f) 320
			2,470	2,470
Net income				

Step 1 (bracket covering Cash through Totals)

Step 2 (arrow pointing to Adjustments totals)

Explanations:
(a) Depreciation expense on office equipment for the year.
(b) Prepaid rent expired during the year.
(c) Accrued salaries at end of year.
(d) Office supplies used during the year.
(e) Legal fees earned during the year.
(f) Accrued interest earned during the year.

Preparation of Trial Balance (Step 1)

The first step in completing a worksheet is the preparation of a trial balance. All the account titles and account balances (prior to adjustments) are obtained from the general ledger. The account titles are listed in the Account Titles column of the worksheet. (Frequently, a company will use a preprinted worksheet in which all of its account titles are already listed.) The debit or credit balance of each

Adjusted Trial Balance		Income Statement		Balance Sheet	
Debit	Credit	Debit	Credit	Debit	Credit
4,200				4,200	
5,600				5,600	
200				200	
170				170	
3,200				3,200	
7,500				7,500	
	3,750				3,750
	1,900				1,900
	300				300
	13,940				13,940
9,000				9,000	
	21,670		21,670		
8,200		8,200			
840		840			
1,200		1,200			
600		600			
750		750			
	200				200
300		300			
320				320	
	320		320		
42,080	42,080	11,890	21,990	30,190	20,090
		10,100			10,100
		21,990	21,990	30,190	30,190

Step 3

Step 4

account is listed in the debit or credit column of the Trial Balance on the worksheet; the columns are then *footed* to prove the equality of the debit and credit totals. **To foot means to total a vertical column on the worksheet.** Double lines are drawn under the totals to indicate their equality. For D. Jones, Attorney, the account titles and balances were taken from the company's general ledger. The debit and credit columns of the trial balance total $40,810, as shown on Exhibit 4-3.

Preparation of Worksheet Adjustments (Step 2)

The second step involves analyzing the accounts to determine the adjustments needed at the end of the accounting period. These adjustment are made directly on the worksheet in the Adjustments columns. For each adjusting entry a letter of the alphabet is listed in front of the debit and credit amount to provide a cross reference and thus to reduce the chance of error. If an adjusting entry involves an account that is not included in the trial balance, the account title is written on the first available line below the other account titles. An explanation for each entry (identified by the same letter of the alphabet) is also included at the bottom of the worksheet. The explanation may include the calculations for the adjusting entry. After all the adjusting entries are made on the worksheet, the Adjustments debit and credit columns are footed (totaled) to prove the equality of the debit and credit totals. It is important to understand that the entering of the adjusting entries on the worksheet is *not* the same as the preparation of adjusting entries in the general journal. As discussed later the worksheet adjusting entries must be copied into the general journal and posted to the general ledger accounts to bring the actual account balances up to date.

The worksheet adjusting entries of D. Jones, Attorney are shown in Exhibit 4-3. A summary of each adjusting entry is as follows:

(a) Jones owns office equipment costing $7,500. The office equipment has a 10-year life and a zero residual value; therefore annual depreciation is $750. Since the account Depreciation Expense is not yet listed on the worksheet, this account title is written on the first available line and $750 is entered on that line in the debit column of the Adjustments. $750 is entered in the credit column of the Adjustments on the line entitled Accumulated Depreciation.

(b) On September 1, 1991, Jones had paid $600 for 6 months rent in advance for office space. (The previous 8 months rent had been paid monthly and recorded as Rent Expense.) At year end, 4 months rent ($400) has expired. Rent Expense is debited for $400 and Prepaid Rent is credited for $400 in the Adjustments columns of the worksheet.

(c) On December 31, 1991, salaries had accrued in the amount of $200. Salaries Expense is debited for $200 on the worksheet. Since the Salaries Payable account is not listed on the worksheet, it is listed on the first available line and $200 is entered on the line in the credit column of the Adjustments.

(d) Office supplies used during 1991 totaled $300. The account title Office Supplies Expense is entered on the worksheet and $300 is recorded in the debit column of the Adjustments. Office Supplies is credited for $300.

(e) During 1991 Jones had collected $800 of legal fees in advance and recorded them as Unearned Legal Fees. A review of the accounting and legal records shows that $500 of these fees are earned at the end of 1991 and the rest will be earned in 1992. In the Adjustments columns of the worksheet, Unearned Legal Fees is debited for $500 and Legal Fees Earned is credited for $500.

(f) On January 1, 1991, a client had issued Jones a $3,200, 2-year, 10% note for legal services recently provided. The interest is to be collected on the maturity date. To date, $320 ($3,200 × 10%) has been earned. Both the Interest Receivable and Interest Revenue account titles must be listed on the worksheet and debited and credited in the Adjustments columns for the $320, respectively.

The Adjustments debit and credit columns both total $2,470, proving the equality of the debit and credit entries of the adjustments.

Preparation of Adjusted Trial Balance (Step 3)

After completing the adjustments on the worksheet, an adjusted trial balance is prepared. The trial balance debit or credit amount of each account is combined with the amount of any debit or credit adjustment to that account to determine the new account balance. **Crossfooting is the combining of these amounts for each account.** Care must be taken when crossfooting. For instance, when the debit balance of an account is combined with a credit entry in the adjustments, the credit entry must be *subtracted* to determine the new debit balance of the account. Each new account balance is listed in the correct debit or credit column of the Adjusted Trial Balance on the worksheet. The Adjusted Trial Balance columns are footed to prove the equality of the debit and credit totals.

In Exhibit 4-3 each line is crossfooted and the resulting account balance is listed in one of the Adjusted Trial Balance columns. For instance, no adjustments were made to the Cash or Accounts Receivable accounts and therefore their balances of $4,200 and $5,600 are listed as debits in the Adjusted Trial Balance. The $600 debit balance of the Prepaid Rent account is combined with the $400 credit from adjusting entry (b) and the resulting $200 debit balance is listed in the debit column of the Adjusted Trial Balance. This process is continued until the last account balance (Interest Revenue of $320) has been listed in the Adjusted Trial Balance. Each column of the Adjusted Trial Balance is then footed. The columns total $42,080, proving the equality of the debit and credit totals.

Preparation of Worksheet Financial Statements (Step 4)

After the Adjusted Trial Balance has been completed, the income statement and balance sheet are prepared on the worksheet. The preparation of these statements involves several parts including transferring each account balance listed in the Adjusted Trial Balance columns to its respective Income Statement or Balance Sheet column, subtotaling the columns, computing net income (or net loss), and totaling the columns.

Transfer Balances to Balance Sheet Columns. The asset, liability, and owner's capital, as well as the owner's withdrawals, account balances are transferred to the Balance Sheet columns. For instance, in Exhibit 4-3 the $4,200 Cash account balance is listed in the Balance Sheet debit column while the $1,900 Accounts Payable balance is listed in the credit column. The transfer of the $9,000 D. Jones, Withdrawals account to the Balance Sheet *debit* column needs further explanation. Recall that a statement of changes in owner's equity is prepared as a supporting schedule to the *ending* owner's capital account balance listed on a company's balance sheet. This ending owner's capital account balance is computed by adding net income to and subtracting withdrawals from the beginning balance. The owner's capital account balance on the worksheet is the *beginning* balance. Since no columns of the worksheet are included for preparing the statement of changes in owner's equity (this would make the worksheet too wide), the net income and withdrawals must be included in the Balance Sheet columns of the worksheet. The withdrawals account is listed in the Balance Sheet debit column because it is a subtraction from the beginning credit balance of the capital account.

Transfer Balances to Income Statement Columns.   The revenue and expense account balances are transferred to the Income Statement columns. For instance, in Exhibit 4-3 the $21,670 Legal Fees Earned account balance is listed in the Income Statement credit column. The $8,200 Salaries Expense balance is listed in the debit column. Although the revenue and expense accounts are listed in the lower part of the Adjusted Trial Balance, some of the items in this lower part may *not* belong on the income statement. Recall that in preparing the adjusting entries on the worksheet, if an account title was not listed in the trial balance, it was written on the first available line of the worksheet. Worksheet adjusting entries often require listing an asset (e.g., the Interest Receivable of $320) or a liability (e.g., the Salaries Payable of $200) in the lower part of the worksheet. Care must be taken to transfer these asset and liability items to the Balance Sheet instead of the Income Statement on the worksheet, as shown in Exhibit 4-3.

Subtotal Columns.   After the account balances have been transferred to the Income Statement and Balance Sheet columns, each column is subtotaled. In Exhibit 4-3 the Income Statement debit and credit column subtotals are $11,890 and $21,990, respectively. The Balance Sheet debit and credit column subtotals are $30,190 and $20,090, respectively. Note that the subtotal of the Income Statement debit column does *not* equal the subtotal of the Income Statement credit column. In addition, the subtotal of the Balance Sheet debit column does *not* equal the subtotal of the Balance Sheet credit column. **The net income (or net loss) for the accounting period is the difference between the column subtotals of each financial statement.**

Compute Net Income and Total Columns.   The $21,990 subtotal of the Income Statement credit column is the total revenues for the period. The $11,890 subtotal of the Income Statement debit column is the total expenses for the period. The difference is a $10,100 net income. To make these columns balance, the term *Net Income* (or when expenses are more than revenues, *Net Loss*) is written on the next line below the subtotals. The amount of net income ($10,100) is listed directly under the Income Statement debit column subtotal (a net loss would be listed under the credit column subtotal) and added to the subtotal to determine the $21,990 total of the Income Statement debit column. The Income Statement credit column subtotal is extended down to the same line as the debit total and it is listed as the $21,990 total of the Income Statement credit column. These two totals are now equal and a double line is drawn below the totals.

The Balance Sheet subtotals are not equal because the net income has not yet been transferred to the owner's capital account. All the amounts listed in the Balance Sheet columns are ending account balances except for the owner's capital account, which shows a beginning credit balance. Net income must be added and withdrawals subtracted to determine the ending balance. Since withdrawals are already included in the debit column of the Balance Sheet, net income must be added to the credit column to bring the owner's capital account balance up to date (i.e., to make the balance sheet "balance"). The amount of net income ($10,100) is listed directly under the Balance Sheet credit column subtotal (a net loss, which decreases owner's equity, would be listed under the debit column subtotal) and added to the subtotal to determine the $30,190 total of the Balance Sheet credit column. The Balance Sheet debit column subtotal is extended down to the same line as the credit column total and listed as the $30,190 total of the Balance Sheet debit column. These two totals are now equal and a double line is inserted below the totals. The worksheet is now complete.

Checking for Errors

There are several ways of reducing the chance of errors in the worksheet. The Trial Balance columns, Adjustments columns, and Adjusted Trial Balance columns are footed at the end of each step to prove the equality of the debit and credit column totals. If any of these sets of column totals are not equal, the error causing the inequality must be corrected before going on to the next step. This usually involves double checking, in reverse order, the work done in the previous step. For instance, if the Trial Balance and Adjustments columns are in balance (e.g., the column totals are equal) but the Adjusted Trial Balance column totals are not equal, the debit and credit columns should be re-added to prove their accuracy. If no error is found, each debit and credit account balance should be checked to be sure it has been listed in the correct debit or credit column. If the error still is not found, the mistake must be in the crossfooting of the accounts.

Sometimes the worksheet will not balance because an error has been made in completing the financial statement columns. This imbalance occurs when the computed net income amount is added to the balance sheet credit column subtotal and the resulting credit column total does not equal the total of the debit column. This inequality does not always mean that an error was made in transferring the accounts from the adjusted trial balance to the Balance Sheet columns. An error could have been made in transferring accounts to the Income Statement columns, in which case an incorrect net income would have been computed. To correct for an error in the Income Statement or Balance Sheet columns the mathematical accuracy of each of the four columns should be checked. Each debit and credit account balance should be reviewed next to be sure it has been listed in the correct debit or credit column. Finally each account title should be checked to be sure its balance has been listed in the correct financial statement.

Completing the Accounting Process from the Worksheet

Earlier we mentioned that the worksheet is used to aid in journalizing the adjusting and closing entries and in preparing the financial statements. We now discuss completing the accounting process from the information in the worksheet.

9. Use a worksheet to complete the accounting process.

Adjusting Entries.   Adjusting entries must be journalized in the general journal and posted to the general ledger to bring the account balances up to date at the end of the accounting period. The journalizing of the adjusting entries is very simple once a worksheet has been prepared. Each adjusting entry included in the worksheet is simply copied from the worksheet into the general journal. The explanation of each adjusting entry in the worksheet is used to prepare the explanation of the adjusting entry in the general journal. The posting of the adjusting entries is completed in the usual manner. The adjusting entries for D. Jones, Attorney are shown in Exhibit 4-4.

EXHIBIT 4-4
D. Jones, Attorney
Adjusting and Closing
Entries for 1991

			GENERAL JOURNAL		Page 87
Date			Account Titles and Explanations	Debit	Credit
			Adjusting Entries		
1991 Dec.	31		Depreciation Expense	750	
			Accumulated Depreciation		750
			To record depreciation of office equipment.		
	31		Rent Expense	400	
			Prepaid Rent		400
			To record prepaid rent expired during the year.		
	31		Salaries Expense	200	
			Salaries Payable		200
			To record accrued salaries at end of year.		
	31		Office Supplies Expense	300	
			Office Supplies		300
			To record office supplies used during the year.		
	31		Unearned Legal Fees	500	
			Legal Fees Earned		500
			To record legal fees earned during the year.		
	31		Interest Receivable	320	
			Interest Revenue		320
			To record accrued interest earned during the year.		
			Closing Entries		
	31		Legal Fees Earned	21,670	
			Interest Revenue	320	
			Income Summary		21,990
			To close the revenue accounts.		
	31		Income Summary	11,890	
			Salaries Expense		8,200
			Utilities Expense		840
			Rent Expense		1,200
			Telephone Expense		600
			Depreciation Expense		750
			Office Supplies Expense		300
			To close the expense accounts.		
	31		Income Summary	10,100	
			D. Jones, Capital		10,100
			To close the Income Summary account and transfer net income to the owner's capital account.		
	31		D. Jones, Capital	9,000	
			D. Jones, Withdrawals		9,000
			To close the withdrawals account.		

Closing Entries.   Closing entries must also be journalized and posted to bring the revenue, expense, and withdrawals accounts to zero and update the ending balance in the owner's capital account. The worksheet also aids in preparing the closing entries. The amounts of all the accounts listed in the Income Statement credit column of the worksheet (i.e., the revenue accounts) are debited in the first closing entry and the subtotal of the credit column is credited to Income Summary. Next the amounts of all the accounts listed in the Income Statement debit column (i.e., the expense accounts) are credited in the second closing entry and the subtotal of the debit column is debited to Income Summary. The amount of the net income listed on the worksheet is used to close the Income Summary account to the owner's capital account in the third closing entry. Finally the amount of the withdrawals account listed in the Balance Sheet debit column is closed as a reduction (debit) to the owner's capital account. The posting of the closing entries is completed in the usual manner. The closing entries for D. Jones, Attorney are shown in Exhibit 4-4.

Financial Statements.   The information on the worksheet also aids in preparing the financial statements. The income statement is prepared from the information contained in the Income Statement columns of the worksheet. The 1991 income statement of D. Jones, Attorney is shown in Exhibit 4-5. Note that the income statement includes two parts, an Operating Income section and an Other Revenues and Expenses section. The Operating Income section of an income statement includes all the revenues earned and expenses incurred in the normal day-to-day operations of a company. The Other Revenues and Expenses section of an income statement includes any revenues and expenses that are not related to the primary operations of the company. A more detailed discussion of the sections of the income statement is presented in Chapter 5.

EXHIBIT 4-5
Income Statement

D. JONES, ATTORNEY Income Statement For Year Ended December 31, 1991		
Revenues:		
Legal fees earned		$21,670
Expenses:		
Salaries expense	$8,200	
Utilities expense	840	
Rent expense	1,200	
Telephone expense	600	
Depreciation expense	750	
Office supplies expense	300	
Total expenses		(11,890)
Operating Income		$ 9,780
Other Revenues and Expenses:		
Interest revenue		320
Net Income		$10,100

The balance sheet is prepared from the information contained in the Balance Sheet columns of the worksheet, with one exception. Recall that the owner's capital account balance listed on the worksheet is the beginning balance. A separate supporting schedule, the statement of changes in owner's equity, must be completed to determine the ending balance of the owner's capital account. The net income and withdrawals information for this schedule is included on the worksheet. This schedule is shown in the lower part of Exhibit 4-6. In completing the balance sheet, the items in the lower part of the Balance Sheet columns of the worksheet must be put in the correct section of the balance sheet. The 1991 ending balance sheet of D. Jones, Attorney is shown in the upper part of Exhibit 4-6.

EXHIBIT 4-6
Balance Sheet and
Statement of Changes
in Owner's Equity

D. JONES, ATTORNEY
Balance Sheet
December 31, 1991

Assets		Liabilities	
Cash	$ 4,200	Accounts payable	$ 1,900
Accounts receivable	5,600	Unearned legal fees	300
Office supplies	170	Salaries payable	200
Prepaid rent	200	Total Liabilities	$ 2,400
Notes receivable			
(due 1/1/1993)	3,200		
Interest receivable			
(due 1/1/1993)	320	Owner's Equity	
Office equipment $7,500		D. Jones, capital (see	
Less: Accumulated		Schedule A)	15,040
depreciation ..... (3,750)	3,750	Total Liabilities and	
Total Assets	$17,440	Owner's Equity	$17,440

D. JONES, ATTORNEY
Schedule A
Statement of Changes in Owner's Equity
For Year Ended December 31, 1991

D. Jones, capital, January 1, 1991	$13,940
Add: Net Income	10,100
	$24,040
Less: Withdrawals	(9,000)
D. Jones, capital, December 31, 1991	$15,040

Interim Statements.   Companies normally use a year as their accounting period and journalize and post adjusting entries at the end of the year. Many companies also prepare interim financial statements. **Interim financial statements are financial statements prepared for a period of less than one year.** Interim financial statements for each quarter of the year are common. When a company prepares interim financial statements, the accounting information that is being gathered for the yearly accounting period should not be affected by actually journalizing and posting the adjusting entries for the interim period. Use of a worksheet is ideal for the preparation of interim financial statements. The interim period adjusting entries can be made only on the worksheet, without actually journalizing the entries. The interim financial statements can then be prepared from the worksheet information. It is not necessary to prepare closing entries since the accounts will be used to accumulate the accounting information for the rest of the year. By using a worksheet, interim financial statements can be prepared without affecting the yearly accounting process.

Summary of Accounting Process

In Exhibit 2-9 of Chapter 2 we listed a set of steps in the accounting process, and the related business documents. We expanded on the steps and documents in Exhibit 3-18 of Chapter 3 to include those pertaining to the income statement. The steps in Exhibit 3-18 are a complete set for a company that does not use a worksheet or prepare reversing entries (discussed in the appendix). If a company uses a worksheet and prepares reversing entries, the steps in the accounting process are modified as follows:

10. List the steps in the accounting process.

1. Journalize the daily transactions.
2. Post each transaction to the related ledger accounts.
3. Prepare a trial balance on the worksheet.
4. Enter the adjusting entries on the worksheet.
5. Prepare an adjusted trial balance on the worksheet.
6. Complete the financial statement columns on the worksheet.
7. Journalize and post the adjusting entries from the worksheet.
8. Journalize and post the closing entries from the worksheet.
9. Prepare the financial statements from the worksheet.
10. Prepare a post-closing trial balance from the ledger accounts.
11. Journalize and post any reversing entries (dated the first day of the next accounting period).

If a company issues interim financial statements, steps 1 through 6 are completed on a monthly or quarterly basis, after which the interim financial statements are prepared. Steps 7 through 11 are then completed at the end of the year to prepare annual financial statements and to prepare the accounting records for the next accounting period.

APPENDIX: Reversing Entries

After the accounts have been adjusted and closed for the current accounting period, the accounting process is begun for the next period. Before journalizing the daily transactions of the new accounting period in the general journal, some companies prepare reversing entries. **A reversing entry is a journal entry that is the exact reverse (both account titles and amounts) of an adjusting entry.**

A-1. Explain the purpose of reversing entries.

Reversing entries are usually made at the same time as closing entries but are dated the first day of the *next* accounting period. Not all adjusting entries are reversed. Reversing entries are *optional* and have one purpose, to simplify the recording of a later transaction related to a particular adjusting entry. Reversing entries allow the later transaction to be recorded in a routine way, without the need for considering the impact of the related adjusting entry from the previous year.

To illustrate the preparation and use of reversing entries consider the December 31, 1991, adjusting entry presented earlier in regard to the $720 accrued salaries of the Stalley Company and the subsequent $1,800 payment of the salaries on January 3, 1992. These entries are reproduced in Exhibit 4-7. At the time of payment we noted that (if a reversing entry is not made) a careful analysis must be made to determine the portion of the $1,800 salaries relating to salaries expense ($1,080) for 1992 and the salaries payable ($720) for 1991. The use of a reversing entry eliminates this analysis. The payment of the salaries on January 3, 1992, is recorded in the usual manner as a debit for the entire amount ($1,800) to Salaries Expense and a credit to Cash, as shown in Exhibit 4-7.

EXHIBIT 4-7
Illustration of Reversing Entry

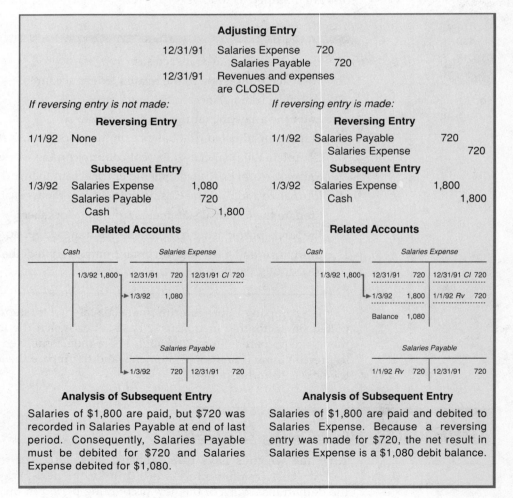

It is a matter of judgment whether or not to make a reversing entry. The important consideration is whether or not the reversing entry will simplify the recording of a later transaction related to the adjusting entry. If it will do so, the reversing entry should be made. As a general rule a reversing entry should be made for any adjusting entry that creates a new balance sheet account.

Therefore, reversing entries *should be* made for:

1. Adjusting entries that establish accrued expenses or revenues to be paid or collected in the next accounting period (e.g., salaries payable, interest receivable).

2. Adjusting entries related to prepayments of costs initially recorded as *expenses* or receipts in advance initially recorded as *revenues*.

Reversing entries *should not* be made for:

1. Adjusting entries related to prepayments of costs initially recorded as assets or receipts in advance initially recorded as liabilities (e.g., prepaid rent, unearned legal fees).

2. Adjusting entries for depreciation.

Except where indicated in the homework materials at the end of this chapter, reversing entries are *not* used in this textbook.

Chapter Summary

Review of Learning Objectives

1. **Explain the purpose of adjusting entries.**
   Adjusting entries are journal entries made at the end of the accounting period to bring the revenue and expense account balances up to date and to show the correct ending balances in the asset and liability accounts. They are needed to report the correct net income on the income statement and the correct financial position on the balance sheet at the end of the period.

2. **Describe a depreciable asset and calculate depreciation expense.**
   A depreciable asset is a long-term physical asset whose expected economic benefits expire over the useful life of the asset. Depreciation expense is the part of the cost of a depreciable asset that is allocated as an expense to each accounting period in the asset's useful life. Annual depreciation expense is calculated by dividing the cost minus the estimated residual value by the estimated useful life in years.

3. **Record depreciation expense and show the resulting book value.**
   Depreciation expense is recorded by a debit to the Depreciation Expense account and a credit to the Accumulated Depreciation account. The book value of a depreciable asset is determined by deducting the total accumulated depreciation to date from the cost of the depreciable asset.

4. **Define a prepaid expense and record the related adjusting entry.**
   A prepaid expense is an economic resource that is expected to be used in the near future. The related adjusting entry involves a debit to an expense account and a credit to the prepaid expense account.

5. **Define an unearned revenue and record the related adjusting entry.**
   An unearned revenue is an advance receipt for goods or services to be provided in the future that is recorded as a liability. The related adjusting entry involves a debit to the unearned revenue (liability) account and a credit to a revenue account.

6. **Define an accrued expense and record the related adjusting entry.**
   An accrued expense is an expense that has been incurred during the accounting period but has been neither paid nor recorded. The related adjusting entry involves a debit to an expense account and a credit to a liability account.

7. **Define an accrued revenue and record the related adjusting entry.**
   An accrued revenue is a revenue that has been earned during the accounting period but has been neither collected nor recorded. The related adjusting entry involves a debit to an asset account and a credit to a revenue account.

8. **Describe a worksheet and list the steps needed to complete a worksheet.**
   A worksheet is an accounting working paper used for initially preparing the trial balance, adjustments, adjusted trial balance, income statement, and balance sheet at the end of an accounting period. There are four steps needed to complete a worksheet. First, prepare a trial balance on the worksheet. List the accounts and their respective debit and credit balances. Total (foot) the debit and credit columns to prove their equality. Second, analyze the accounts and prepare appropriate adjusting entries on the worksheet. Write any new account title on the first available line below the other account titles. Include an explanation at the bottom of the worksheet. Total (foot) the adjustments debit and credit columns to prove their equality. Third, prepare an adjusted trial balance on the worksheet. Combine (crossfoot) the amounts from the trial balance with the amounts from the adjustments. Total (foot) the adjusted trial balance debit and credit columns to prove their equality. Fourth, prepare the worksheet financial statements. Transfer each account balance from the adjusted trial balance to its respective debit or credit column of the income statement or balance sheet on the worksheet. Subtotal each column. The subtotals of the income statement columns and the balance sheet columns will not be equal; the difference is the net income (or net loss). Write net income on the next line below the subtotals. List the amount of net income under the subtotal of the income statement debit column and under the subtotal of the balance sheet credit column. Total the columns to prove the equality of each set of columns. The worksheet is now complete.

9. **Use a worksheet to complete the accounting process.**
   Based on the information from a worksheet, the accounting process may be completed as follows. First, record adjusting entries in the general journal and post to the accounts based on the adjustments prepared on the work-

sheet. Second, record closing entries in the general journal and post to the accounts based upon the revenue and expense account balances listed in the income statement columns of the worksheet. Finally, prepare the financial statements based on the account balances listed in the income statement and balance sheet columns of the worksheet.

10. List the steps in the accounting process.

If a company uses a worksheet and prepares reversing entries (Appendix), there are eleven steps in the accounting process. These include: (1) journalizing the daily transactions; (2) posting these transactions; (3) preparing a trial balance; (4) entering the adjusting entries; (5) preparing an adjusted trial balance; (6) completing the financial statement columns on the worksheet; (7) journalizing and posting the adjusting entries; (8) journalizing and posting the closing entries; (9) preparing the financial statements from the worksheet information; (10) preparing a post-closing trial balance; and (11) journalizing and posting any reversing entries.

A-1. Explain the purpose of reversing entries (Appendix).

A reversing entry is a journal entry that is the exact reverse (both account titles and amounts) of an adjusting entry. The purpose of a reversing entry is to allow a later transaction related to a particular adjusting entry to be recorded in a routine way. That is, the transaction can be recorded without having to consider the impact of the adjusting entry from the previous period.

Review Problem

The December 31, 1991, trial balance of the Sparkle Company included the following accounts and account balances:

Account Titles	Debits	Credits
Notes receivable	$ 2,000	
Office supplies	600	
Prepaid insurance	216	
Building	30,000	
Accumulated depreciation: building		$12,000
Unearned rent		2,400

A review of the accounting records and related source documents reveals the following information for 1991:

1. Interest of $100 has accrued on the notes receivable.

2. Office supplies on hand at year end total $80.

3. The prepaid insurance is for a 2-year insurance policy purchased on May 1, 1991.

4. The building was acquired at the beginning of 1985 and is being depreciated over a 15-year life (no residual value).

5. The unearned rent is for 1 year of rent ($200 per month) collected in advance from the renter on October 1, 1991.

6. Accrued salaries total $500 at the end of 1991.

REQUIRED Prepare 1991 year-end adjusting entries to record the preceding information.

Solution to Review Problem

GENERAL JOURNAL				Page 38
Date		*Account Titles and Explanations*	*Debit*	*Credit*
1991 Dec.	31	Interest Receivable Interest Revenue To record accrued interest earned during the year.	100	100
	31	Office Supplies Expense Office Supplies To record office supplies used ($600 — $80) during the year.	520	520
	31	Insurance Expense Prepaid Insurance To record insurance expense [($216 ÷ 24) x 8].	72	72
	31	Depreciation Expense: Building Accumulated Depreciation: Building To record depreciation of building ($30,000 ÷ 15).	2,000	2,000
	31	Unearned Rent Rent Revenue To record rent earned [($2,400 ÷ 12) x 3].	600	600
	31	Salaries Expense Salaries Payable To record accrued salaries at year end.	500	500

Glossary

Accrued Expense. Expense that has been incurred during the accounting period but has been neither paid nor recorded. An example is unpaid employees' salaries.

Accrued Revenue. Revenue that has been earned during the accounting period but has been neither collected nor recorded. An example is uncollected interest.

Adjusting Entries. Journal entries made at the end of an accounting period to bring the revenue and expense account balances up to date and to show the correct ending balances in the asset and liability accounts.

Book Value. The cost of a depreciable asset less its related accumulated depreciation. Also called *carrying value*.

Contra Account. Account whose balance is subtracted from another related account to determine a resulting amount. An example is accumulated depreciation.

Crossfooting. Combining the amount of an account with a debit or credit adjustment to the account on a worksheet. Horizontal addition or subtraction.

Depreciable Asset. Long-term physical asset whose expected economic benefits expire over the useful life of the asset. The related cost must be apportioned as depreciation expense in the accounting periods during which the asset is used.

Depreciation Expense. The part of the cost of a long-term physical asset allocated as an expense to each accounting period in the asset's useful life.

Foot. To total a vertical column of a worksheet.

Interest. Amount charged for the use of money. For an interest-bearing note the interest is computed by multiplying the principal times the annual interest rate for the length of time the note has been issued.

Interest Rate. Rate of interest charged on the principal of a note. Expressed as an annual percentage.

Interim Financial Statements. Financial statements prepared for a period of less than one year.

Prepaid Expense. Economic resource that is expected to be used in the near future. Examples are prepaid rent and office supplies.

Principal. Amount of a note.

Reversing Entry. Journal entry that is the exact reverse (both account titles and amounts) of an adjusting entry. Dated the first day of the new accounting period. It is optional and used to simplify the recording of a later transaction related to the adjusting entry.

Straight-Line. Method of depreciation that records an equal portion of the cost of a long-term physical asset as depreciation expense in each accounting period in which the asset is used.

Unearned Revenue. Advance receipt for goods or services to be provided in the future. Recorded as a liability at the time of receipt. An example is unearned rent.

Worksheet. A large columnar accounting paper for initially preparing the trial balance, adjustments, adjusted trial balance, income statement, and balance sheet at the end of an accounting period.

Questions

QUESTION 4-1 What are adjusting entries? Why are they necessary?

QUESTION 4-2 What is a depreciable asset? How is annual straight-line depreciation expense computed?

QUESTION 4-3 What is a contra account? What is a book value? Show how the book value of a building costing $14,000 and having accumulated depreciation of $5,000 would be listed in a balance sheet.

QUESTION 4-4 What is a prepaid expense? Give an example of the journal entries to record the initial transaction and adjusting entry for a prepaid expense (dollar amounts are not necessary).

QUESTION 4-5 What is an unearned revenue? Give an example of the journal entries to record the initial transaction and adjusting entry for an unearned revenue (dollar amounts are not necessary).

QUESTION 4-6 What is an accrued expense? Give an example of an adjusting entry for an accrued expense (dollar amounts are not necessary).

QUESTION 4-7 Discuss the journal entry that would be made to record the salaries paid to employees at the beginning of a new accounting period if part of the salaries were accrued at the end of the last period. Assume reversing entries are not used.

QUESTION 4-8   What is an accrued revenue? Give an example of an adjusting entry for an accrued revenue (dollar amounts are not necessary).

QUESTION 4-9   When preparing adjusting entries why is it important to know if a company initially recorded the receipt of an advance payment from a customer as a liability or a revenue?

QUESTION 4-10   For an interest-bearing note define the following: (a) interest, (b) principal, (c) rate. How is interest computed?

QUESTION 4-11   What is a worksheet? Why is it used?

QUESTION 4-12   List and very briefly discuss the steps that must be completed in the preparation of a worksheet.

QUESTION 4-13   Briefly discuss what to do if a worksheet does not "balance."

QUESTION 4-14   What are interim financial statements? Why is a worksheet helpful in their preparation?

QUESTION 4-15   What steps in the accounting process are completed *after* a worksheet is prepared?

QUESTION 4-16   List the steps in the accounting process, assuming a worksheet is used and reversing entries are prepared.

QUESTION 4-17   (*Appendix*). What are reversing entries? Why are they used? For what kinds of adjusting entries should they be made?

QUESTION 4-18   (*Appendix*). A company accrues salaries at the end of 1991 in the amount of $500. Salaries paid to its employees in the first pay period of 1992 total $1,800. Show the journal entry to record the 1992 payment assuming that: (a) reversing entries are not used and (b) reversing entries are used (also show the reversing entry).

Exercises

EXERCISE 4-1   **Depreciation.**   On January 1, 1991, McCartney Photographers purchased photography equipment for $5,400 cash. The equipment has an estimated useful life of 9 years and a residual value of zero. The company uses the straight-line depreciation method.

REQUIRED   1. Prepare journal entries to record:
   (a) The purchase of photography equipment on January 1, 1991.
   (b) The necessary adjusting entry at the end of 1991.

2. If the adjusting entry had *not* been made in Requirement 1(b), discuss what effect this error would have on the accounts and totals listed in the income statement and the balance sheet.

EXERCISE 4-2   **Prepaid Expense.**   On October 1, 1991, the Bourdon Company paid $480 for a 2-year comprehensive insurance policy on the company's building.

REQUIRED   1. Prepare the journal entry to record:
   (a) The purchase of this insurance policy.
   (b) The adjusting entry at the end of 1991.

2. If the adjusting entry had *not* been made in Requirement *1(b)*, discuss what effect this error would have on the accounts and totals listed in the income statement and balance sheet.

EXERCISE 4-3 **Unearned Revenues.** On October 1, 1991, the Sagir Appraisal Company received $1,500 in advance for 6 months rent of office space to the Land-Ho Real Estate Agency.

REQUIRED 1. Prepare the Sagir Appraisal Company journal entries to record:
  (a) The receipt of the payment.
  (b) The adjustment for rent revenue at the end of 1991.

2. If the adjusting entry had *not* been made in Requirement *1(b)*, discuss what effect this error would have on the accounts and totals listed in the income statement and balance sheet.

EXERCISE 4-4 **Accrued Expense.** The Clinkscales Tuxedo Rentals Company employs five employees, each of whom earns $220 per week for a 5-day work week (Monday through Friday). The employees are paid every Thursday. September 30, 1991, the end of the company's fiscal year, falls on Monday.

REQUIRED 1. Prepare the necessary adjusting entry for salaries on September 30, 1991.

2. Prepare the journal entry for the payment of salaries on October 3, 1991.

EXERCISE 4-5 **Accrued Interest Expense and Revenue.** On October 1, 1991, the Scotch Company purchased 2 acres of land from the Irist Company at a cost of $10,000. The Scotch Company signed (issued) a 1-year, 10% note requiring it to repay the $10,000 principal plus $1,000 interest on October 1, 1992, to the Irist Company. The Irist Company had originally purchased the land for $10,000.

REQUIRED Based on the preceding information, prepare the October 1, 1991, entry and the adjusting entry for interest at the end of 1991 for:

1. The Scotch Company

2. The Irist Company

EXERCISE 4-6 **Adjusting Entries.** The following partial list of accounts and account balances has been taken from the trial balance and the adjusted trial balance of the Mane Lettering Company:

	Trial Balance		Adjusted Trial Balance	
Account Titles	Debit	Credit	Debit	Credit
Accumulated depreciation		$5,000		$6,500
Interest payable		0		230
Prepaid insurance	$360		$240	
Salaries payable		0		590

REQUIRED Prepare the adjusting entry that caused the change in each account balance.

EXERCISE 4-7   **Adjusting Entries.**   At the end of the current year Rulem Hair Styling provides you with the following information:

(a)   Depreciation expense on styling equipment totals $1,240 for the current year.

(b)   Accrued interest on a note payable issued on October 1 amounts to $850 at year end.

(c)   Unearned revenue in the amount of $1,000 has become earned (all receipts in advance are recorded in an unearned revenue account).

(d)   Hair styling supplies used during the year total $210 (all purchases of supplies are recorded in an asset account).

REQUIRED   Prepare adjusting entries at the end of the current year based on the preceding information.

EXERCISE 4-8   **Worksheet.**   The June 30, 1991, trial balance for Shelen Stockbrokers is shown on the following partially completed worksheet.

SHELEN STOCKBROKERS
Worksheet
For Month Ended June 30, 1991

Account Titles	Trial Balance Debit	Trial Balance Credit	Adjustments Debit	Adjustments Credit	Adjusted Trial Balance Debit	Adjusted Trial Balance Credit	Income Statement Debit	Income Statement Credit	Balance Sheet Debit	Balance Sheet Credit
Cash	30,000									
Accounts receivable	3,740									
Prepaid rent	2,100									
Office supplies	450									
Office equipment	6,000									
Accumulated depreciation		600								
Accounts payable		1,200								
F. Shelen, capital		40,000								
F. Shelen, withdrawals	1,000									
Service revenues		5,435								
Salaries expense	3,575									
Utilities expense	230									
Telephone expense	140									
Totals	47,235	47,235								

Additional Information:

(a)   Prepaid rent in the amount of $300 has expired during June.

(b)   Salaries at month end that have accumulated but have not been paid total $570.

(c)   Monthly straight-line depreciation on office equipment is based on a cost of $6,000, an estimated useful life of 5 years, and no residual value.

(d)   Office supplies used during the month of June totaled $60.

REQUIRED   Complete the worksheet for the month of June.

EXERCISE 4-9   **Worksheet.**   The September 30, 1991 trial balance for the Conrad Company is shown on the following partially completed worksheet.

	CONRAD COMPANY Worksheet For Month Ended September 30, 1991										
	Trial Balance		Adjustments		Adjusted Trial Balance		Income Statement		Balance Sheet	
Account Titles	Debit	Credit	Debit	Credit	Debit	Credit	Debit	Credit	Debit	Credit
Cash	40,000									
Accounts receivable	1,000									
Supplies	6,500									
Building	90,000									
Accumulated depreciation: building		10,000								
Accounts payable		3,280								
Unearned rent revenues		4,500								
D. Conrad, capital		95,500								
Rent revenues		26,900								
Salaries expense	2,200									
Utilities expense	400									
Telephone expense	80									
Totals	140,180	140,180								

Additional Information:

(a)   Monthly depreciation on the building is computed on a straight-line basis with an estimated life of 15 years and no residual value.

(b)   Supplies on hand on September 30, 1991, total $5,810.

(c)   Unearned rent revenue that was earned during September totaled $800.

REQUIRED   Complete the worksheet for the month of September.

EXERCISE 4-10   **Adjusting and Closing Entries from Worksheet.**   At the end of 1991 the Crandle Window Cleaning Company prepared the worksheet on the following page.

REQUIRED   *1.*   Prepare adjusting entries from the worksheet.

2.   Prepare closing entries from the worksheet.

CRANDLE WINDOW CLEANING COMPANY
Worksheet
For Year Ended December 31, 1991

Account Titles	Trial Balance Debit	Trial Balance Credit	Adjustments Debit	Adjustments Credit	Adjusted Trial Balance Debit	Adjusted Trial Balance Credit	Income Statement Debit	Income Statement Credit	Balance Sheet Debit	Balance Sheet Credit
Cash	7,145				7,145				7,145	
Accounts receivable	2,400				2,400				2,400	
Prepaid rent	750			(b) 375	375				375	
Supplies	1,310			(d) 1,270	40				40	
Cleaning equipment	5,000				5,000				5,000	
Accumulated depreciation		1,000		(a) 1,000		2,000				2,000
Accounts payable		475				475				475
Unearned cleaning revenue		1,000	(e) 950			50				50
G. Crandle, capital		10,000				10,000				10,000
G. Crandle, withdrawals	7,000				7,000				7,000	
Cleaning revenue		22,180		(e) 950		23,130		23,130		
Salaries expense	9,000		(c) 600		9,600		9,600			
Utilities expense	800				800		800			
Rent expense	750		(b) 375		1,125		1,125			
Telephone expense	500				500		500			
Totals	34,655	34,655								
Depreciation expense			(a) 1,000		1,000		1,000			
Salaries payable				(c) 600		600				600
Supplies expense			(d) 1,270		1,270		1,270			
			4,195	4,195	36,255	36,255	14,295	23,130	21,960	13,125
Net Income							8,835			8,835
							23,130	23,130	21,960	21,960

Explanations:
(a) Depreciation expense on equipment for the year.
(b) Prepaid rent expired during the year.
(c) Accrued salaries at end of year.
(d) Supplies used during the year.
(e) Unearned cleaning fees earned during the year.

EXERCISE 4-11   Financial Statements.   Refer to the data in Exercise 4-10 for the Crandle Window Cleaning Company.

REQUIRED   From the information on the worksheet:

1. Prepare a 1991 income statement.

2. Prepare a 1991 statement of changes in owner's equity.

3. Prepare a December 31, 1991, balance sheet (account form).

EXERCISE 4-12   (Appendix) Reversing Entries.   On December 31, 1991, the Bluen Company made the following adjusting entries for its annual accounting period:

Depreciation Expense	1,500	
Accumulated Depreciation: Equipment		1,500
To record depreciation on equipment.		
Interest Receivable	110	
Interest Revenue		110
To record interest on note receivable due on February 1, 1992.		
Salaries Expense	470	
Salaries Payable		470
To record salaries accumulated but not paid.		
Rent Expense	400	
Prepaid Rent		400
To record expired prepaid rent.		

REQUIRED Prepare whatever reversing entries are appropriate.

Problems

Part A

PROBLEM 4-1A   **Adjusting Entries.** The trial balance of Halsey Architectural Consultants on December 31, 1991 (the end of its annual accounting period), included the following account balances *before* adjustments:

Note receivable	$14,000	debit
Prepaid insurance	1,560	debit
Building	92,000	debit
Drafting equipment	12,000	debit
Unearned rent	6,240	credit
Note payable	10,000	credit
Supplies	1,500	debit

In reviewing the company's recorded transactions and accounting records for 1991, you find the following data pertaining to the December 31, 1991, adjustments:

(a) On July 1, 1991, the company had accepted a $14,000, 1-year, 10% note receivable from a customer. The interest is to be collected when the note is collected.

(b) On October 1, 1991, the company had paid $1,560 for a 3-year insurance policy.

(c) The building was acquired on January 1, 1983, and is being depreciated using the straight-line method over a 20-year life with no residual value.

(d) The drafting equipment was purchased on December 1, 1991. It is to be depreciated using the straight-line method over an 8-year life with no residual value.

(e) On July 1, 1991, the company had received 2 years rent in advance for a portion of its building rented to the Shields Company.

(f) On November 1, 1991, the company had issued a $10,000, 3-month, 9% note payable to a supplier. The $225 total interest is to be paid when the note is paid.

(g) On January 1, 1991, the company had $200 of supplies on hand. During 1991 the company purchased $1,300 of supplies. A physical count on December 31, 1991, revealed that there are $90 of supplies still on hand.

REQUIRED   Prepare the adjusting entries that are necessary to bring the Halsey Architectural Consultants accounts up to date on December 31, 1991. Each journal entry explanation should summarize your calculations.

PROBLEM 4-2A   **Adjusting Entries.**   Several transactions of Paribus Janitorial Services that occurred during 1991 and which were recorded in balance sheet accounts are as follows:

Date	Transaction
Jan. 1	Purchased cleaning equipment for $12,000, paying $3,000 down, and issuing a 2-year, 12% note payable for the $9,000 balance. The equipment has an estimated life of 10 years and a zero residual value. The interest on the note will be paid on the maturity date.
May 24	Purchased $340 of office supplies. The office supplies on hand at the beginning of the year totaled $145.
June 1	Purchased a 2-year comprehensive insurance policy for $960.
Sept. 2	Received 6 months rent in advance at $350 per month and recorded the $2,100 receipt as unearned rent revenue.
Oct. 1	Accepted a $3,000, 6-month, 10% note receivable from a customer. The $150 total interest is to be collected when the note is collected.

Additional Information:

(a) On December 31, 1991, the office supplies on hand totaled $58.

(b) All employees work Monday through Friday. The weekly payroll of Paribus Janitorial Services amounts to $6,000. All employees are paid at the close of business each Friday for the previous 5 working days (including Friday). December 31, 1991, falls on a Tuesday.

REQUIRED   On the basis of the preceding information prepare journal entries to record whatever adjustments are necessary on December 31, 1991. Each journal entry explanation should show any related computations.

PROBLEM 4-3A   **Adjusting Entries.**   A partial list of accounts and account balances taken from the December 31, 1991, trial balance and adjusted trial balance of the Rowland Billboard Company is as follows:

Account Titles	Trial Balance		Adjusted Trial Balance	
	Debit	Credit	Debit	Credit
Supplies	$1,200		$316	
Prepaid insurance	500		150	
Accumulated depreciation: building		$5,000		$6,700
Accumulated depreciation: equipment		800		1,100
Interest payable		0		96
Salaries payable		0		673
Unearned rent		2,250		750

REQUIRED Prepare the adjusting entry that caused the change in each account balance.

PROBLEM 4-4A **Worksheet and Closing Entries.** Shown as follows is the December 31, 1991, worksheet (partially complete) for Gundy's Repair Service.

GUNDY'S REPAIR SERVICE
Worksheet
For Year Ended December 31, 1991

Account Titles	Trial Balance Debit	Trial Balance Credit	Adjustments Debit	Adjustments Credit	Adjusted Trial Balance Debit	Adjusted Trial Balance Credit	Income Statement Debit	Income Statement Credit	Balance Sheet Debit	Balance Sheet Credit
Cash	34,650				34,650				34,650	
Prepaid rent	2,100			(a) 2,100						
Prepaid insurance	500			(d) 250	250				250	
Supplies	3,100			(c) 1,900	1,200				1,200	
Notes receivable	8,000				8,000				8,000	
Equipment	40,000				40,000				40,000	
Accumulated depreciation		4,000		(b) 2,000		6,000				6,000
Accounts payable		3,970				3,970				3,970
H. Gundy, capital		50,000				50,000				50,000
H. Gundy, withdrawals	18,000				18,000				18,000	
Repair service revenues		101,500				101,500		101,500		
Salaries expense	50,000				50,000		50,000			
Utilities expense	2,160				2,160		2,160			
Telephone expense	960				960		960			
Totals	159,470	159,470								
Rent expense			(a) 2,100		2,100		2,100			
Depreciation expense			(b) 2,000		2,000		2,000			
Supplies expense			(c) 1,900		1,900		1,900			
Insurance expense			(d) 250		250		250			
Interest receivable			(e) 960		960				960	
Interest revenue				(e) 960		960		960		
			7,210	7,210	162,430	162,430				

Explanations:
(a) Prepaid rent expired during the year.
(b) Depreciation expense on equipment for the year.
(c) Supplies used during the year.
(d) Prepaid insurance expired during the year.
(e) Accrued interest earned during the year.

REQUIRED 1. Complete the worksheet.

2. Prepare an income statement for the year ended December 31, 1991.

3. Prepare closing entries on December 31, 1991.

PROBLEM 4-5A **Worksheet.** The McKinnon Company prepared a trial balance on the following partially completed worksheet for the year ended December 31, 1991.

McKINNON COMPANY
Worksheet
For Year Ended December 31, 1991

Account Titles	Trial Balance		Adjustments		Adjusted Trial Balance		Income Statement		Balance Sheet	
	Debit	Credit	Debit	Credit	Debit	Credit	Debit	Credit	Debit	Credit
Cash	9,050									
Accounts receivable	15,500									
Prepaid insurance	1,000									
Supplies	3,000									
Building	35,000									
Accumulated depreciation: building		8,750								
Equipment	15,000									
Accumulated depreciation: equipment		6,250								
Accounts payable		850								
Note payable		10,000								
Unearned service revenues		1,200								
Z. McKinnon, capital		40,000								
Z. McKinnon, withdrawals	17,000									
Service revenues		75,000								
Salaries expense	45,000									
Utilities expense	960									
Telephone expense	540									
Totals	142,050	142,050								

Additional Information:

(a) The equipment is being depreciated on a straight-line basis over a 12-year life, no residual value.

(b) The building is being depreciated on a straight-line basis over a 20-year life, no residual value.

(c) Salaries accrued but not recorded total $800.

(d) Supplies on hand at December 31, 1991, total $845.

(e) On October 1, 1991, the company had paid $1,000 for a 1-year comprehensive insurance policy.

(f) On July 1, 1991, the company borrowed $10,000 from a local bank. The company signed (issued) a $10,000, 1-year, 12% note. The $600 year-end accrued interest is to be paid when the note is paid.

(g) Unearned service revenues that were earned by the end of the year totaled $285.

REQUIRED   Complete the worksheet.

PROBLEM 4-6A   **Comprehensive.** The Dickinson Employment Agency has prepared a trial balance on the following partially completed worksheet for the year ended December 31, 1991.

Additional Information:

(a) Prepaid rent expired during the year totaled $2,000.

DICKINSON EMPLOYMENT AGENCY Worksheet For Year Ended December 31, 1991										
Account Titles	Trial Balance		Adjustments		Adjusted Trial Balance		Income Statement		Balance Sheet	
	Debit	Credit	Debit	Credit	Debit	Credit	Debit	Credit	Debit	Credit
Cash	1,105									
Prepaid rent	3,000									
Supplies	2,800									
Equipment	17,400									
Accumulated depreciation		1,200								
Accounts payable		1,245								
P. Dickinson, capital		15,000								
P. Dickinson, withdrawals	6,500									
Employment service fees		25,320								
Salaries expense	10,400									
Utilities expense	960									
Telephone expense	600									
Totals	42,765	42,765								

(b) Supplies on hand on December 31, 1991, totaled $1,600.

(c) Depreciation expense on equipment for the year amounted to $600.

(d) Salaries accrued but not recorded total $525.

REQUIRED

1. Complete the worksheet.

2. Make any adjusting entries needed on December 31, 1991.

3. Prepare an income statement for the year ended December 31, 1991.

4. Prepare a statement of changes in owner's equity for the year ended December 31, 1991.

5. Prepare a balance sheet (account form) at December 31, 1991.

6. Prepare closing entries on December 31, 1991.

7. (*Appendix*) Prepare whatever reversing entries are appropriate.

Problems
Part B

PROBLEM 4-1B   **Adjusting Entries.**   The trial balance of the Cronell Antique Refinishing Company on December 31, 1991 (the end of its annual accounting period), included these account balances before adjustments:

Note receivable	$6,000	debit
Prepaid rent	4,320	debit
Supplies	2,000	debit
Refinishing equipment	10,000	debit
Unearned service revenues	1,025	credit
Note payable	5,000	credit

Upon reviewing the company's accounting records, you find the following data pertaining to the December 31, 1991, adjustments:

(a) On October 1, 1991, the company had accepted a $9,000, 6-month, 12% note receivable from a major customer. The $540 total interest is to be collected when the note is collected.

(b) On January 2, 1991, the company paid for 1 year of rent in advance at $360 per month.

(c) On January 1, 1991, $400 of supplies were on hand. During 1991 the company purchased $1,600 of supplies. A physical count on December 31, 1991, revealed that there are $330 of supplies on hand.

(d) The refinishing equipment was purchased on January 1, 1991. It is to be depreciated using the straight-line method over a 5-year life with no residual value.

(e) On October 1, 1991, the company received $1,025 in advance for services to be rendered. On December 31, 1991, $125 remained unearned.

(f) On April 1, 1991, the company had issued a $5,000, 1-year, 10% note payable to a supplier. Interest is to be paid when the note is paid.

REQUIRED   Prepare the adjusting entries necessary to bring the Cronell Antique Refinishing Company accounts up to date on December 31, 1991. Each journal entry explanation should summarize your calculations.

PROBLEM 4-2B   **Adjusting Entries.**   Several transactions of Marlin Medical Laboratory that occurred during 1991 and which were recorded in balance sheet accounts are as follows:

Date	Transaction
June 14	Purchased $750 of office supplies. The office supplies on hand at the beginning of 1991 totaled $250.
July 1	Received 6 months rent in advance at $300 per month and recorded the $1,800 receipt as unearned rent revenue.
Nov. 1	Accepted a $4,000, 6-month, 12% note receivable from a major customer. The $240 total interest is to be collected when the note is collected.
Dec. 2	Purchased laboratory equipment for $18,000 paying $6,000 down and issuing a 1-year, 10% note payable for the $12,000 balance. The equipment has an estimated life of 12 years and a zero residual value. The interest on the note will be paid on the maturity date.

Additional Information:

(a) On December 31, 1991, the office supplies on hand totaled $270.

(b) All employees work Monday through Friday. The weekly payroll of the company amounts to $6,000. All employees are paid at the close of business each Thursday for the previous 5 working days (including Thursday). December 31, 1991, falls on a Tuesday.

REQUIRED   On the basis of the preceding information, prepare journal entries to record whatever adjustments are necessary on December 31, 1991.

PROBLEM 4-3B   **Adjusting Entries.**   A partial list of accounts and account balances taken from the December 31, 1991, trial balance and adjusted trial balance of the Triton Company is as follows:

	Trial Balance		Adjusted Trial Balance	
Account Titles	Debit	Credit	Debit	Credit
Office supplies	$ 675		$236	
Prepaid rent	3,300		550	
Accumulated depreciation		$1,000		$1,800
Interest receivable	0		120	
Salaries payable		0		325
Unearned revenue		1,275		275

REQUIRED   Prepare the adjusting entry that caused the change in each account balance.

PROBLEM 4-4B   **Worksheet and Closing Entries.** The following is the December 31, 1991, worksheet (partially complete) for Sundal Travel Agency:

SUNDAL TRAVEL AGENCY
Worksheet
For Year Ended December 31, 1991

Account Titles	Trial Balance		Adjustments		Adjusted Trial Balance		Income Statement		Balance Sheet	
	Debit	Credit	Debit	Credit	Debit	Credit	Debit	Credit	Debit	Credit
Cash	8,270				8,270					
Prepaid rent	5,400			(a) 2,700	2,700					
Supplies	1,300			(c) 1,100	200					
Equipment	4,000				4,000					
Accumulated depreciation		1,000		(b) 500		1,500				
Accounts payable		2,970				2,970				
T. Sundal, capital		14,000				14,000				
T. Sundal, withdrawals	2,000				2,000					
Travel arrangement fees		16,430				16,430				
Salaries expense	10,000				10,000					
Utilities expense	950				950					
Telephone expense	2,480				2,480					
Totals	34,400	34,400								
Rent expense			(a) 2,700		2,700					
Depreciation expense			(b) 500		500					
Supplies expense			(c) 1,100		1,100					
			4,300	4,300	34,900	34,900				

Explanations:
(a) Prepaid rent expired during the year.
(b) Depreciation expense on equipment for the year.
(c) Supplies used during the year.

REQUIRED

1. Complete the worksheet.

2. Prepare an income statement for the year ended December 31, 1991.

3. Prepare closing entries on December 31, 1991.

PROBLEM 4-5B   **Worksheet.**   The Conon Advertising Service Company prepared a trial balance on the following partially completed worksheet for the year ended December 31, 1991.

	CONON ADVERTISING SERVICE COMPANY Worksheet For Year Ended December 31, 1991										
	Trial Balance		Adjustments		Adjusted Trial Balance		Income Statement		Balance Sheet	
Account Titles	Debit	Credit	Debit	Credit	Debit	Credit	Debit	Credit	Debit	Credit
Cash	8,020									
Accounts receivable	7,240									
Prepaid rent	3,000									
Office supplies	2,500									
Note receivable	5,000									
Office equipment	7,500									
Accumulated depreciation		3,125								
Accounts payable		1,250								
Unearned revenues		2,000								
Q. Conon, capital		30,000								
Q. Conon, withdrawals	3,000									
Advertising service revenues		20,625								
Rent expense	4,000									
Salaries expense	15,600									
Utilities expense	660									
Telephone expense	480									
Totals	57,000	57,000								

Additional Information:

(a) The office equipment is being depreciated on a straight-line basis over a 12-year life, no residual value.

(b) On October 1, 1991, the company accepted a $5,000, 6-month, 14% note from a customer. The $350 total interest is to be collected when the note is collected.

(c) Salaries accrued but not recorded total $250.

(d) Office supplies on hand on December 31, 1991, total $700.

(e) On September 1, 1991, the company had paid 6 months rent in advance at $500 per month.

(f) Unearned revenues that were earned by completing advertising services during the year total $850.

REQUIRED   Complete the worksheet.

PROBLEM 4-6B   **Comprehensive.**   The following is the December 31, 1991, trial balance prepared on a partially completed worksheet for the Raffensager Consulting Agency.

Account Titles	Trial Balance Debit	Trial Balance Credit	Adjustments Debit	Adjustments Credit	Adjusted Trial Balance Debit	Adjusted Trial Balance Credit	Income Statement Debit	Income Statement Credit	Balance Sheet Debit	Balance Sheet Credit
RAFFENSAGER CONSULTING AGENCY Worksheet For Year Ended December 31, 1991										
Cash	1,295									
Accounts receivable	3,570									
Office supplies	3,000									
Building	17,000									
Accumulated depreciation: building		2,500								
Office equipment	6,000									
Accumulated depreciation: office equipment		1,500								
Accounts payable		2,645								
F. Raffensager, capital		18,000								
F. Raffensager, withdrawals	5,000									
Consulting revenues		28,100								
Salaries expense	14,600									
Utilities expense	1,080									
Telephone expense	1,200									
Totals	52,745	52,745								

Additional Information:

(a) Depreciation expense on the building for the year amounts to $500.

(b) Depreciation expense on the office equipment for the year amounts to $300.

(c) Salaries accrued but not recorded total $650.

(d) Supplies on hand on December 31, 1991, total $1,200.

REQUIRED   *1.* Complete the worksheet.

2. Prepare the necessary adjusting entries on December 31, 1991.

3. Prepare an income statement for the year ended December 31, 1991.

4. Prepare a statement of changes in owner's equity for the year ended December 31, 1991.

5. Prepare a balance sheet (account form) at December 31, 1991.

6. Prepare closing entries on December 31, 1991.

7. (*Appendix*) Prepare whatever reversing entries are appropriate.

Decision Cases

DECISION CASE 4-1

Faulty Financial Statements. Ray Young owns and operates a repair service called Ray's Rapid Repairs. It is the end of the year and his bookkeeper has recently resigned to move to a warmer climate. Knowing only a little about accounting, Ray prepared the following financial statements, based upon the ending balances in the company's accounts on December 31, 1991:

RAY'S RAPID REPAIRS
Income Statement
For Year Ended December 31, 1991

Repair service revenues		$29,000
Operating expenses:		
Rent expense	$ 3,800	
Salaries expense	9,900	
Utilities expense	1,100	
R. Young, withdrawals	16,000	
Total operating expenses		(30,800)
Net Loss		$ (1,800)

RAY'S RAPID REPAIRS
Balance Sheet
December 31, 1991

Assets		Liabilities and Owner's Equity	
Cash	$ 1,600	Accounts payable	$ 2,600
Repair supplies	2,300	Note payable (due 1/1/1993)	10,000
Repair equipment	15,000	Total Liabilities	$12,600
		R. Young, capital[a]	6,300
		Total Liabilities and	
Total Assets	$18,900	Owner's Equity	$18,900

[a]Beginning capital — net loss.

Ray is upset and says to you, "I don't know how I could have had a net loss in 1991. Maybe I did something wrong when I made out these financial statements. Could you help me? My business has been good in 1991. In these times of rising prices, people have been getting their appliances and other items repaired by me instead of buying new ones. I used to have to rent my repair equipment, but business was so good that I purchased $15,000 of repair equipment at the beginning of the year. I know this equipment will last 10 years even though it won't be worth anything at the end of that time. I did have to sign a note for $10,000 of the purchase price, but the amount (plus 12% annual interest) will not be due until the beginning of 1993. I still have to rent my repair shop, but I paid $3,800 for 2 years of rent in advance at the beginning of 1991, so I am OK there. And besides, I just counted my repair supplies and I have $1,000 of supplies left from 1991 which I can use in 1992."

He continues, "I'm not too worried about my cash balance. I know that customers owe me $700 for repair work I just completed in 1991. These are good customers and always pay, but I never tell my bookkeeper about this until I collect the cash. I am sure I will collect in 1992, and that will also make 1992 revenues look good. In fact, it will just about offset the $600 I collected in advance (and recorded as a revenue) from a customer for repair work I said I would do in 1992. I still have to write a check to pay my bookkeeper for his last month's salary, but he was my only employee in 1991. In 1992 I am only going to hire someone on a part-time basis to keep my accounting records. You can have the job, if you can determine whether the net loss is correct, and if not, what it should be and what I am doing wrong."

REQUIRED

1. Prepare any adjusting entries you think are appropriate for 1991. Show any calculations in your explanations.

2. Prepare closing entries for 1991.

3. Prepare a corrected 1991 income statement, statement of changes in owner's equity, and ending balance sheet (report form).

4. Write a brief report to Ray Young summarizing your suggestions for improving his accounting practices.

DECISION CASE 4-2   **Effects of Adjusting Entry Errors.**   During the current accounting period the bookkeeper for the Nallen Company made the following errors in the year-end entries:

| | | | Effect of Error on: | | | |
| | Revenues | Expenses | Net Income | Assets | Liabilities | Owner's Equity |
Error						
Example: Failed to record $200 of accrued salaries	N	U $200	O $200	N	U $200	O $200
1. Failed to adjust prepaid insurance for $400 of expired insurance.						
2. Failed to record $500 of interest expense that had accrued during the period.						
3. Inadvertently recorded $300 of annual depreciation twice for the same equipment.						
4. Failed to record $100 of interest revenue that had accrued during the period.						
5. Failed to reduce unearned revenues for $600 of revenues that were earned during the period.						

REQUIRED   Assuming that the errors are not discovered, indicate the effect of each error on revenues, expenses, net income, assets, liabilities, and owner's equity at the end of the accounting period. Use the following code: O = Overstated, U = Understated, and N = No effect. Include dollar amounts. Be prepared to explain your answers.

DECISION CASE 4-3

Purchase of Company. On January 3, 1991, Ken Harmot agreed to buy the Ace Cleaning Service from Janice Steward. They agreed that the purchase price should be five times the 1990 net income of the company. To determine the price, Janice prepared the following condensed income statement for 1990.

Revenues	$ 48,000
Expenses	(36,000)
Net Income	$ 12,000

Janice said to Ken, "Based on this net income, the purchase price of the company should be $60,000 ($12,000 × 5). Of course, you may look at whatever accounting records you would like." Ken examined the accounting records and found them to be in order, except for several balance sheet accounts. These accounts and their December 31, 1990, balances are: Prepaid Rent, $2,400; Equipment, $4,800; Accumulated Depreciation, $1,200; and Unearned Cleaning Service Revenues, $0.

Ken gathered the following information about the company related to these accounts. The company was started on January 2, 1988. At that time, the company rented space in a building for its operations and purchased $4,800 of equipment. The equipment had an estimated life of 8 years and no residual value. On July 1, 1990, the company paid 1 year of rent in advance at $200 per month. On September 1, 1990, customers paid $600 in advance for cleaning services to be performed by the company for the next 12 months. Ken asks for your help. He says, "I do not know how these items affect net income, if at all. I want to pay a fair price for the company."

REQUIRED

1. Discuss how the 1990 net income of the Ace Cleaning Service was affected, if at all, by each of the items.

2. Prepare a corrected condensed 1990 income statement.

3. Compute a fair purchase price for the company.

DECISION CASE 4-4

Correcting Net Income. The Lawrence Modeling Company reported net income of $15,300 in 1990 and $16,700 in 1991. In 1992, the company discovered that it had mistakenly not recorded the following accrued expenses and accrued revenues in 1990 and 1991. The expenses and revenues that were not recorded in the proper year were paid or collected, respectively, in the following year. The company also found that it had mistakenly recorded the following prepaid expenses and unearned revenues as expenses and revenues, respectively, in the year of payment or collection. These expenses and revenues were incurred and earned, respectively, in the following year.

	1990	1991
Accrued expenses	$ 400	$ 300
Accrued revenues	600	800
Prepaid expenses	700	1,100
Unearned revenues	1,300	1,000

The company has asked for your help in determining the correct amount of its 1990 and 1991 net income.

REQUIRED Compute the correct net income for 1990 and 1991 using the following form:

	1990	1991
Reported net income	$15,300	$16,700
Adjustments:		
Correct net income		

5

Accounting for a Merchandising Company

LEARNING OBJECTIVES

1. Describe a merchandising company.

2. Record transactions involving (a) sales revenues, (b) sales returns and allowances, and (c) sales discounts.

3. Describe the (a) perpetual and (b) periodic inventory systems.

4. Calculate cost of goods sold under the periodic inventory system.

5. Record transactions involving (a) purchases, (b) purchases returns and allowances, (c) purchases discounts, and (d) transportation-in.

6. Describe classified financial statements.

7. Prepare a classified (a) income statement and (b) balance sheet.

8. Prepare closing entries for a merchandising company.

9. Complete a worksheet for a merchandising company.

1. Describe a merchandising company.

n the first four chapters we developed an accounting system and accounting process for companies. In Chapter 3, we focused on the income statements of service companies. Recall that a *service company* provides a service to its customers and records the related revenues and expenses to determine its net income. Two other types of business entities, the manufacturing company and the merchandising company, are very important in business today. A *manufacturing company* is a business entity that makes products for sale to its customers in order to earn a net income. Generally, a manufacturing company's "customer" is a merchandising company. **A merchandising company is a business entity that purchases goods (*merchandise*) for resale to its customers in order to earn a net income.** Merchandising companies can be *retailers*, such as shoestores, department stores, or automobile dealerships, which sell their goods directly to the final customer. Or they can be *wholesalers*, such as plumbing supply stores, electrical suppliers, or beverage distributors, which primarily sell their goods to retailers or other commercial users. The relationship between manufacturing companies and merchandising companies is shown in the following diagram.

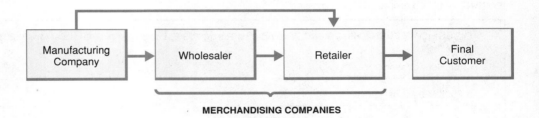

Whether merchandising companies are retailers or wholesalers, the accounting systems used are similar to, but more extensive than, systems used for service companies. An accounting system for a merchandising company must record, retain, and report information about the purchase and sale of its merchandise. These accounting topics are the main focus of this chapter.

Sales

A merchandising company sells goods to customers either for cash or on account. Occasionally these goods are returned by customers or are found to be damaged. When goods are sold on credit some merchandising companies offer an incentive for prompt payment. These aspects of sales are discussed next.

Sales Revenues

Whether a customer buys goods for cash or on credit, most merchandising companies use a revenue account entitled *Sales Revenues*, or simply, *Sales*, to record the transaction. For instance, a cash sale of merchandise for $300 is recorded as:

2(a). Record transactions involving sales revenues.

```
1991
May 9   Cash ...................................................................  300
            Sales ...............................................................        300
        To record the cash sale of merchandise.
```

Alternatively, if the same sale is made on account it is recorded as:

```
1991
May 9   Accounts Receivable ................................................  300
            Sales ...............................................................        300
        To record the sale of merchandise on account.
```

The source document for a sale on account is called a sales invoice, or simply, an invoice. **An invoice is a business document that lists the terms of a sale, including the customer's name and address, date of sale, items sold and selling price, total amount, payment terms, and other information.** (The source document for a purchase, which is discussed later, is the same invoice made out by the supplier.) An example of an invoice is shown in Exhibit 5-1.

EXHIBIT 5-1   Example of Sales Invoice

GIBBS HOME FURNISHINGS, INC., Providence Plaza, 203 E. Leslie Lane, Columbia, Mo. 65201, (314) 449-1716

SOLD TO

Mr. Roger Younger

2802 Middlebush Drive

Columbia, Missouri 65203

SHIPPED TO

Same

Date	Date Shipped	Shipped Via	Your Order No.	F.O.B.	Terms	Invoice No.
3/2/91	Same	Local	—	Destination	n/30	**002676**

Quantity	Description	Price	Amount
1	43411-120 Triple Dresser 43411-220 Mirror 43411-311 Chest 43411-120 H Board } Reg. $1,198.00 Sale	$ 799.00	
1	5/0 Mattress }	278.00	
1	5/0 Box Spring		
1	R. O. Bed Frame W/Center Support	36.00	
	Subtotal	$1,113.00	
	Sales Tax	51.48	
	Total		$1,164.48

Reprinted with permission.

Sales Returns and Allowances

When merchandise is sold to a customer, it is assumed by both the merchandising company and the customer that the merchandise is not damaged and is acceptable to the customer. Occasionally, upon checking the merchandise after purchase, the customer may find that it is damaged, of inferior quality, or simply the wrong size or color. Most merchandising companies have a *satisfaction guaranteed* policy and allow the customer to return the merchandise or make an adjustment in the sales price. **A sales return is the return of previously purchased merchandise by a customer.** The effect of a sales return is to cancel the sale. **A sales allowance occurs when the customer agrees to keep the merchandise, and an adjustment (reduction) is made in the original sales price.** In either case a source document called a credit memo is prepared by the merchandising company and issued to the customer. **A credit memo is a business document that lists the information for a sales return or allowance.** A credit memo includes the customer's name and address, how the original sale was made (cash or on account), the reason for the sales return or allowance, the items returned or upon which the allowance is given, and the amount of the return or allowance.

When the merchandise was originally sold, the revenue account Sales was increased (credited) for the amount of the sale. For a sales return the Sales account could be decreased (debited) for the amount of the return. For a sales allowance the Sales account also could be decreased for the amount of the allowance. Both transactions are reductions of sales recorded earlier. Most merchandising companies do *not* reduce the Sales account directly, however. **A Sales Returns and Allowances account is used to record the total sales returns and allowances.** This account is a contra account to the Sales account and thus has a debit balance and is increased by debit entries and decreased by credit entries. The Sales Returns and Allowances account and the related credit memos provide useful information about customer dissatisfaction with the company's merchandise to the sales manager of a merchandising company and to other users.

The credit memo is used as the source document to record the return or allowance. The amount is listed on the credit memo. If the original sale had been made for cash, a cash refund is typically given to the customer. If the original sale had been made on account and the account has not been collected, the customer's account is reduced (credited) by the amount of the return or allowance. (The source document is called a *credit* memo because it lists the *credit* to the Cash or Accounts Receivable account.)

To illustrate this procedure assume that a customer returns merchandise that had been sold to the customer for $100 on account. The following journal entry is made by the merchandising company to record the return:

2(b). Record transactions involving sales returns and allowances.

1991			
June 7	Sales Returns and Allowances	100	
	Accounts Receivable		100

To record return of merchandise originally sold on account.

Assume that another customer purchased goods for $80 cash and, upon unpacking the goods, found that they had been slightly damaged. The customer agrees to keep the goods but is allowed a $20 reduction (i.e., allowance) in the original sales price. A cash refund is given and the following journal entry is made:

1991			
July 19	Sales Returns and Allowances	20	
	Cash		20
	To record allowance given to customer for damaged merchandise.		

The recording of sales returns and allowances, as discussed, is consistent with the definition of revenues. Revenues include the prices charged to a company's customers for goods sold during an accounting period. When sales returns or allowances are recorded in the Sales Returns and Allowances account, since this account is a contra account to Sales, revenues are reduced because part (or all) of the prices charged to customers is returned to them.

Sales Discounts

When merchandise is sold on account the terms of payment are normally listed on the sales invoice. These terms vary from company to company, although most competing companies tend to have similar credit terms. Many companies offer a cash discount as an incentive for early payment of accounts by customers. **A cash discount is a percentage reduction of the invoice price for payment of the invoice within a specified time period.**

The payment terms for an invoice are usually expressed in a standard format. For instance, a common payment term is n/10/EOM. This term means that the total amount (n) of the invoice is due 10 days after the end of the month (EOM) in which the sale occurred. Thus if a credit sale is made on July 8, 1991, payment of the invoice is due by the 10th of August.

In the previous example no cash discount was allowed for early payment. Cash discount terms might read 2/10, n/30. The first number is the percentage discount (2%) and the second number (10) is the number of days in the discount period. **The discount period is the period of time from the date of the invoice within which the customer must pay the invoice to receive the cash discount.** The term n/30 means that full payment of the invoice is due within 30 days of the invoice date. Thus 2/10, n/30 is read as "a 2% discount is allowed if the invoice is paid within 10 days and the total amount of the invoice is due within 30 days." If a $500 sale on account is made with terms of 2/10, n/30 and the customer pays the invoice within 10 days, $490 would be collected [$500 − (0.02 × $500)].

When a sale is made on account and the terms of payment include cash discount terms, Accounts Receivable is increased (debited) and Sales is increased (credited) for the full invoice price because the merchandising company does not know whether the customer will pay within the discount period. If the customer pays the invoice (less the discount) within the discount period, the cash collected from the sale is less than the accounts receivable initially recorded. **A Sales Discounts Taken account is used to record the amount of cash discounts deducted by customers in the accounting period.** The Sales Discounts Taken account is a contra account to Sales, and therefore it has a debit balance.

To illustrate this procedure assume that on March 15, 1991, a customer purchased $1,000 of merchandise on account, with terms of 3/10, n/30. The customer remitted a check for $970 [$1,000 − (.03 × $1,000)] on March 25, 1991. The

2(c). Record transactions involving sales discounts.

journal entries made by the merchandising company to record the sale and collection are as follows:

```
1991
Mar. 15   Accounts Receivable  .........................................  1,000
              Sales  .......................................................        1,000
          To record sales on account.

     25   Cash  ........................................................   970
          Sales Discounts Taken  .....................................    30
              Accounts Receivable  ...................................         1,000
          To record collection of March 15 invoice, less 3%
          cash discount.
```

Two additional points are important for sales discounts. First, if a sales return or allowance is allowed on an invoice, the cash discount terms apply to the amount owed on the invoice *after* deducting the return or allowance. This is because the cash discount is allowed only on the amount of the goods actually purchased by the customer. Second, if a customer pays for an invoice after the discount period has expired, the collection of the total invoice price is recorded in the usual manner by a debit (increase) to Cash and a credit (decrease) to Accounts Receivable.

Net Sales

Because contra accounts for sales returns and allowances and sales discounts are used to reduce the total amount of sales revenues, the revenues section of a merchandising company's income statement must be expanded to include these items. On the income statement both the Sales Returns and Allowances account and the Sales Discounts Taken account are deducted from the Sales account to determine Net Sales. The Sales account is frequently entitled *Gross Sales* on the income statement to show that it is not the same as the Net Sales. Exhibit 5-2 illustrates the revenues section of a typical merchandising company.

Since the Sales Returns and Allowances and Sales Discounts Taken accounts are used to accumulate the returns and allowances and discounts *during* the accounting period, they are temporary accounts. These accounts are closed along with the Sales account at the end of the period. Closing entries for a merchandising company are discussed later in the chapter.

EXHIBIT 5-2
Partial Income Statement

HINES DEPARTMENT STORE		
Partial Income Statement		
For Year Ended December 31, 1991		
Revenues:		
Gross sales		$89,200
Less: Sales returns and allowances	$2,900	
Sales discounts taken	3,600	(6,500)
Net sales		$82,700

Cost of Goods Sold

In the previous section we discussed the additional issues involved in recording the revenues of a merchandising company. In this section we focus on the issues involving the expenses of a merchandising company. Expenses are the costs of providing goods or services during an accounting period. These expenses are matched against the revenues of the period to determine the net income. One of the major expenses of a merchandising company is the cost of goods sold. **Cost of goods sold is the cost a merchandising company has incurred for the merchandise (goods) it has sold to customers during an accounting period.** The way a merchandising company determines the amount of cost of goods sold that it reports on its income statement depends upon whether the company uses a perpetual inventory system or a periodic inventory system. **Inventory is the merchandise being held for resale by a merchandising company.** Some companies use the term *merchandise inventory* to refer to these goods.

Perpetual Inventory System

3(a). Describe the perpetual inventory system.

Some merchandising companies use a perpetual inventory system. **A perpetual inventory system is a system in which a continuous record is kept of the cost of inventory on hand and the cost of inventory sold.** When an item of inventory is purchased for resale a journal entry is recorded to increase (debit) the asset account, Inventory (or Merchandise Inventory), for the invoice cost of the merchandise. When merchandise is sold, a journal entry is made to record the sale in the usual way. A journal entry is also made to reduce (credit) the Inventory account and to increase (debit) an expense account entitled Cost of Goods Sold. Hence the Inventory and Cost of Goods Sold accounts are perpetually up to date. In addition, a written record is also kept of the physical quantities of inventory purchased and sold, and therefore the physical quantity of inventory on hand is always known.

To illustrate this procedure assume that on April 4, 1991, a merchandising company makes a $2,000 cash purchase of goods for resale. On April 8, 1991, it sells $500 of these goods to customers at a cash selling price of $900. If the company used a perpetual inventory system, the following journal entries would be made to record the purchase and subsequent sale of the goods:

1991			
Apr. 4	Inventory	2,000	
	Cash		2,000
	To record the purchase of merchandise.		
8	Cash	900	
	Sales		900
	To record the cash sale of merchandise.		
8	Cost of Goods Sold	500	
	Inventory		500
	To record the cost of merchandise sold.		

Note that on April 8 the company made two journal entries. The first was made to record the inflow of assets and revenue based on the *selling price* of the merchandise. The second was made to record the outflow of assets and the expense based on the *cost* of the merchandise that was sold.

The ending balance of the Cost of Goods Sold account would be listed on the income statement in a separate section as a deduction from Net Sales. Since the Cost of Goods Sold account is a temporary account used to accumulate the expense of the merchandise sold during the period, the account is closed at the end of each accounting period. Both the income statement and closing entries are discussed later in this chapter.

The perpetual inventory system is more common when a merchandising company sells relatively few items at a high selling price and the cost of each item sold is easily determined. Examples of merchandising companies using this system are automobile dealers, jewelers, and appliance retailers. A periodic system is more common when a merchandising company sells a high volume of low-priced items because the cost of each item may not be easily determined, although modern computer systems often make it practical to use a perpetual system. Perpetual inventory systems are discussed in more detail in Chapter 9. The remainder of this section deals with the accounting for a merchandising company that uses a periodic inventory system.

Periodic Inventory System

3(b). Describe the periodic inventory system.

4. Calculate cost of goods sold under the periodic inventory system.

A periodic inventory system is a system in which a continuous record of the inventory on hand is not kept and a physical count of the inventory is taken periodically at the end of each accounting period.[1] The only time that the cost of the inventory on hand is known is when the periodic inventory is taken. Each time a sale is made, a record of the cost of goods sold is *not* made. The cost of goods sold for the accounting period is calculated by deducting the ending inventory from the cost of goods available for sale during the period. The items that are included in this calculation are as follows:

Cost of Goods Available for Sale = Beginning Inventory + Purchases
– Purchases Returns and Allowances
– Purchases Discounts Taken
+ Transportation-In

Cost of Goods Sold = Cost of Goods Available for Sale
– Ending Inventory

These calculations are shown directly on the income statement, as illustrated in Exhibit 5-3. Each component of cost of goods sold is discussed next.

Inventory. In the periodic inventory system a physical count of the inventory is taken at the end of each accounting period. At that time the goods on hand are counted and their costs determined. This amount is then recorded in the Inventory account during the closing process. (This procedure is discussed later.) Thus, as opposed to the perpetual inventory system, the Inventory account in a periodic system is up to date only at the time of the periodic count at the end of

[1]The process of taking inventory is discussed in Chapter 9.

EXHIBIT 5-3
Partial Income
Statement

> **HINES DEPARTMENT STORE**
> **Partial Income Statement**
> **For Year Ended December 31, 1991**
>
> Cost of Goods Sold:
> Inventory, January 1, 1991 .... $10,300 *A*
> Purchases $47,200
> Less: Purchases returns and allowances .... (1,800)
> Purchases discounts taken .... (3,100)
> Plus: Transportation-in 4,300
> Net purchases .... *C NP* $46,600
> Cost of goods available for sale .... $56,900 *B*
> Less: Inventory, December 31, 1991 .... (11,600) *C*
> Cost of Goods Sold .... *DCOGS* $45,300

the accounting period. This ending inventory of the current period is also the beginning inventory of the next period. Thus in Exhibit 5-3 the January 1, 1991, beginning inventory of $10,300 was the December 31, 1990, ending inventory on the 1990 income statement. The December 31, 1991, ending inventory of $11,600 will also be the January 1, 1992, beginning inventory on the 1992 income statement. Inventories, as well as the other components of cost of goods sold, are discussed in more detail in Chapter 9.

Purchases.   The cost of merchandise purchased by a merchandising company during an accounting period is not recorded directly in the Inventory account. A temporary account is used instead. **The Purchases account is used in a periodic inventory system to record the invoice cost of the merchandise acquired for resale during an accounting period.** Since the Purchases account is used to increase cost of goods sold (an expense of operations), the Purchases account has a debit balance and is increased by debit entries. All purchases of merchandise for resale, whether for cash or on account, are included in the Purchases account. The source document used to record the purchase is an invoice from the supplier.

To illustrate this procedure assume that on June 7 and 10, 1991, a company purchased merchandise costing $400 and $700, respectively. The first purchase was for cash, and the second was on account. The journal entries made by the merchandising company to record these purchases are as follows:

5(a). Record
transactions
involving purchases.

1991			
June 7	Purchases	400	
	Cash		400
	To record cash purchases.		
10	Purchases	700	
	Accounts Payable		700
	To record purchases on account.		

It is important to remember that the Purchases account shows only the invoice cost of the goods purchased for resale during the accounting period. The balance or change in the account at any time or for any period does *not* disclose any information about whether the goods purchased during the period are still on hand or have been sold. The Purchases account is closed at the end of each accounting period.

Purchases Returns and Allowances. When merchandise for resale is purchased from a supplier both the supplier and the merchandising company assume that the goods will be of acceptable quality. For various reasons, after a purchase has been recorded, it may be discovered that certain merchandise is unacceptable to the merchandising company. (Often this discovery is made when a customer of the merchandising company is granted a sales return or allowance.) **A purchases return is a return of the merchandise to the supplier.** The effect of a purchases return is to cancel the purchase. **A purchases allowance is an adjustment (reduction) in the purchase price that is made when the merchandising company agrees to keep the goods.** In either case a debit memo is prepared by the merchandising company and issued to the supplier. **A debit memo is a business document that lists the information for a purchases return or allowance.** A debit memo includes the supplier's name and address, the terms of the original purchase, the reason for the purchases return or allowance, and the items and amount involved.

Control of purchases returns and allowances is very important to the efficient management of a merchandising company. Customer satisfaction with the quality of goods offered for sale by a merchandising company is directly affected by the quality of merchandise purchased from suppliers. In addition, the return (or allowance) of purchased merchandise is a time-consuming and costly process. An initial step in this control process is to keep an accurate record of the cost of any purchases returns and allowances. **A Purchases Returns and Allowances account is used to record the total purchases returns and allowances.** This account is used instead of reducing Purchases directly for these costs. The Purchases Returns and Allowances account is a contra account to Purchases, and therefore it has a credit balance.

The debit memo (so called because it lists the *debit* to Cash or Accounts Payable) is used as the source document to record the return or allowance. If the original purchase was for cash, a cash refund is received from the supplier. If the purchase was on account, accounts payable is reduced (debited). To illustrate this procedure suppose that merchandise which had been previously purchased on account is found to be of inferior quality and the supplier grants an allowance of $80. The merchandising company records the allowance as follows:

5(b). Record transactions involving purchases returns and allowances.

```
1991
Feb. 4   Accounts Payable .....................................................   80
                Purchase Returns and Allowances ..............................        80
         To record allowance given by supplier for inferior
         merchandise.
```

If $60 of goods previously purchased for cash are returned to a supplier, a cash refund would be received and the following journal entry recorded:

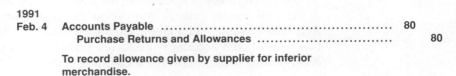

```
1991
Nov. 8   Cash ................................................................   60
                Purchase Returns and Allowances ..............................        60
         To record inferior goods returned to supplier for cash refund.
```

Since the Purchases Returns and Allowances account is used to accumulate the total returns and allowances for the accounting period, it is deducted from Purchases on the income statement and is closed at the end of the period.

Purchases Discounts Taken.   When merchandise is purchased on account, the payment terms are listed on the invoice. Many suppliers offer a cash discount[2] if payment is made within the specified discount period. These terms are expressed as discussed earlier, for example, 2/10, n/30. All cash discounts on purchases should be taken because of the high annual interest rate involved, and many companies establish procedures designed to make sure that this is done. The interest rate and payment procedures are discussed in Chapters 9 and 10.

When a purchase is made on account and cash discount terms are involved, Purchases is increased (debited) and Accounts Payable is increased (credited) for the full invoice amount.[3] If payment is made within the discount period the Purchases account is not directly reduced. **A Purchases Discounts Taken account is used to record all cash discounts taken.** This account is a contra account to Purchases, and therefore it has a credit balance.

To illustrate this procedure assume that on October 11, 1991, a merchandising company purchased $2,000 of goods from a supplier on account, with terms 2/10, n/30. The company remitted (issued) a check for $1,960 [$2,000 − (.02 × $2,000)] on October 21, 1991. The journal entries made by the merchandising company to record the purchase and payment are as follows:

5(c). Record transactions involving purchases discounts.

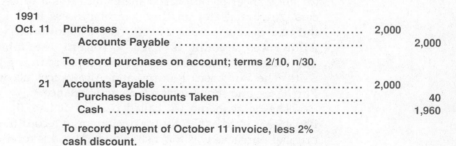

```
1991
Oct. 11  Purchases ..................................................  2,000
             Accounts Payable ..........................................      2,000
         To record purchases on account; terms 2/10, n/30.

     21  Accounts Payable ...........................................  2,000
             Purchases Discounts Taken .............................         40
             Cash ......................................................      1,960
         To record payment of October 11 invoice, less 2%
         cash discount.
```

Two additional points are important for purchases discounts. First, if a purchases return or allowance is granted on an invoice, the cash discount terms apply to the amount owed on the invoice *after* deducting the return or allowance. Second, if payment is made after the discount period has expired, the payment of the total invoice price is recorded in the usual manner as a debit (decrease) to Accounts Payable and a credit (decrease) to Cash. The balance of the Purchases Discounts Taken account is deducted from Purchases on the income statement and is closed at the end of the accounting period.

---

[2]Another type of discount is the trade discount. **Trade discounts are reductions in the list or catalog price of a merchandise item, and are usually shown as a percentage of the list price.** For example, if goods with a list price of $1,000 subject to a 20% trade discount are purchased, the invoice price is $800 [$1,000 − (0.20 × $1,000)]. Trade discounts are *not* recorded by the merchandising company; thus the preceding purchase would be recorded at $800. Trade discounts are discussed more fully in Chapter 9.

[3]Some companies initially record their purchases and accounts payable at the net amount after deducting the cash discount. This method of handling cash discounts is discussed in Chapter 9.

Transportation Costs. When merchandise is purchased for resale it must be shipped from the supplier to the merchandising company. Shipping costs can be very significant. Whether the supplier or the purchaser is responsible for payment of the freight charges associated with purchased merchandise depends upon the terms agreed to at the time of purchase. These terms are typically included on the purchase invoice.[4] When the merchandising company agrees to pay the freight charges, these costs are, in effect, a cost of purchasing the merchandise. **Transportation-In (or Freight-In) is an account used to record the freight charges incurred for shipments of merchandise purchased from suppliers.** This account is used instead of including the freight charges directly in the Purchases account. The Transportation-In account has a debit balance since it increases the total cost of purchases for the period. The freight bill presented by the freight company is the source document used to record the transportation charges.

To illustrate this procedure suppose that a merchandising company agrees to pay freight charges on goods purchased from a supplier. The merchandising company is billed $70 by the freight company for the delivered merchandise. The journal entry made by the merchandising company to record the payment of the freight charges on August 9, 1991, is as follows:

5(d). Record transactions involving transportation-in.

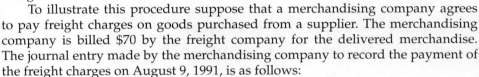

1991
Aug. 9   Transportation-In 70
         Cash 70

To record payment of freight charges on purchases.

The balance of Transportation-In is added to Purchases on the income statement and is closed at the end of the accounting period.

It is important to distinguish clearly between the payment of freight charges on purchased goods from the payment of freight charges on goods sold to customers. When the merchandising company agrees to pay the freight charges on shipments of merchandise *to* customers, these freight charges are a delivery expense of the accounting period. **Transportation-Out (or Freight-Out) is the account used to record the freight charges incurred for shipments of merchandise sold to customers.**

To illustrate this procedure suppose that a merchandising company ships merchandise to customers and is billed $40 by the freight company for the delivery. The journal entry made by the merchandising company to record the payment of the freight charges on May 2, 1991, is as follows:

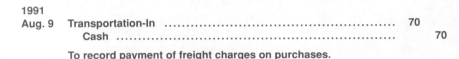

1991
May 2   Transportation-Out 40
         Cash 40

To record payment of freight charges on merchandise shipped to customers.

---

[4]As can be seen in Exhibit 5-1, the freight terms are expressed as *FOB destination*, which means the supplier is responsible for paying the freight. Alternatively, the freight terms could be expressed as *FOB shipping point*, which means the purchaser is responsible for payment of the freight charges. These terms are discussed more fully in Chapter 9.

Transportation-Out is a selling expense (discussed later) on the income statement and is closed at the end of the accounting period.

Cost of Goods Available and Sold.   As we noted in the previous discussion, in a periodic inventory system Transportation-In is added to Purchases and Purchases Returns and Allowances and Purchases Discounts Taken are subtracted. These calculations are shown on the income statement, and the result is entitled *Net Purchases.* The net purchases are added to the beginning inventory (remember that this inventory is the ending inventory of the previous accounting period) to determine the Cost of Goods Available for Sale during the current accounting period. The ending inventory (determined by a physical count at the end of the period) is subtracted from the cost of goods available for sale to derive Cost of Goods Sold. These calculations were shown in Exhibit 5-3.

Classified Financial Statements

6. Describe classified financial statements.

In the early chapters we used only a limited number of accounts in our discussion. Regardless of whether a business entity is a service company or a merchandising company, as a general rule the larger the company the more accounts it needs in its chart of accounts. These accounts are necessary to record and retain the financial information from the many types of transactions of the company. When a *service* company or a *merchandising* company prepares its financial statements, it is useful to group the accounts on each financial statement in a way that will help the readers of the financial statement in decision making. **A classified financial statement is a statement in which the accounts are grouped into selected categories to provide more useful information for the users of the statement.** Most companies prepare classified financial statements. The groupings in a classified financial statement will depend upon the way the company is organized and its type of operations. Basic classifications have been developed, however, and the way in which they apply to a merchandising company is the focus of this section.

Classified Income Statement

7(a). Prepare a classified income statement.

Recall from Chapter 3 that a company's income statement is used to compare its efforts and accomplishments. It is also useful for evaluating the company's return on investment, risk, financial flexibility, and operating capability. To help provide information about these items, a classified income statement of a company has two parts: an *operating income* component and an *other revenues and expenses* component. **Operating income includes all the revenues earned and expenses incurred in the primary day-to-day operating activities of the company.** This is true regardless of whether a business is a merchandising or service company. The operating income component of a classified income statement for a merchandising company is usually much more complex than that of a service company and has three sections: (1) revenues, (2) cost of goods sold, and (3) operating expenses. **Other revenues and expenses include any items of rev-**

enue and expense that are not related to the primary operations of the company. This section includes such items as interest revenue and interest expense. The complete 1991 classified income statement of the Hines Department Store is presented in Exhibit 5-4. The items on the income statement are discussed next.

EXHIBIT 5-4
Income Statement

HINES DEPARTMENT STORE
Income Statement
For Year Ended December 31, 1991

Revenues:			
Gross sales			$89,200
Less: Sales returns and allowances		$ 2,900	
Sales discounts taken		3,600	(6,500)
Net sales			$82,700
Cost of Goods Sold:			
Inventory, January 1, 1991		$10,300	
Purchases	$47,200		
Less: Purchases returns and allowances	(1,800)		
Purchases discounts taken	(3,100)		
Plus: Transportation-in	4,300		
Net purchases		46,600	
Cost of goods available for sale		$56,900	
Less: Inventory, December 31, 1991		(11,600)	
Cost of goods sold			(45,300)
Gross profit			$37,400
Operating Expenses:			
Selling expenses:			
Depreciation expense: store equipment	$ 1,400		
Depreciation expense: building (sales space)	2,700		
Utilities expense (sales space)	800		
Advertising expense	2,900		
Sales salaries expense	4,200		
Transportation-out	1,100		
Store supplies used	600		
Total selling expenses		$13,700	
General and administrative expenses:			
Depreciation expense: office equipment	$ 1,300		
Depreciation expense: building (office space)	900		
Utilities expense (office space)	400		
Office salaries expense	2,300		
Administrative salaries expense	3,500		
Office supplies expense	800		
Insurance expense	200		
Total general and administrative expenses		9,400	
Total operating expenses			(23,100)
Operating income			$14,300
Other Revenues and Expenses:			
Interest revenue		$ 1,300	
Rent revenue (from specialty shop in store)		900	
Interest expense		(700)	
Nonoperating income			1,500
Net Income			$15,800

Revenues.   The revenues section includes the revenues earned from the sale of merchandise to customers. This section begins with gross sales from which sales returns and allowances given to customers and sales discounts taken by credit customers are subtracted. The result is entitled net sales and amounts to $82,700 for the Hines Department Store.

Cost of Goods Sold and Gross Profit.   Cost of goods sold is the total cost of the merchandise that has been sold to customers during the accounting period. Because the cost of goods sold is such an important expense of a merchandising company, it is listed in a separate section of the income statement, directly below the revenues section and above the operating expenses section. A service company would not have a cost of goods sold section because it sells a service rather than a product. For a merchandising company using a perpetual inventory system, the amount of cost of goods sold is the ending balance in the cost of goods sold account. For companies using a periodic inventory system, the amount of cost of goods sold is calculated directly on the income statement, as shown in Exhibit 5-4. The amount of cost of goods sold is subtracted from net sales to determine the *gross profit* (or *gross margin*). For the Hines Department Store the $45,300 cost of goods sold is deducted from the $82,700 net sales to derive a gross profit of $37,400.

A merchandising company's gross profit may range from 30 to 50% of net sales depending on the types of products it sells. **This gross profit percentage is calculated by dividing the gross profit by the net sales.** In the case of the Hines Department Store the gross profit percentage is 45.2% ($37,400 ÷ $82,700). The managers of a merchandising company keep a close watch on the company's gross profit because a small percentage change may have a great impact on the percentage change in net income. For example, a $1,000 increase in cost of goods sold for the Hines Department Store would decrease the gross profit by 2.7% ($1,000 ÷ $37,400), causing net income to decrease by 6.3% ($1,000 ÷ $15,800).

The gross profit is sometimes referred to as the portion of profits remaining to cover the operating expenses. Although cost of goods sold is shown separately from the other expenses to determine gross profit, nonetheless it is still an expense. Although some expenses are more "avoidable" than cost of goods sold, *all* expenses must be covered in order to earn a net income and there is no priority in the coverage of expenses.

Operating Expenses.   The operating expenses are the expenses (other than cost of goods sold) incurred in the primary day-to-day operations of a merchandising or service company. The operating expenses section of the income statement is frequently separated into two parts, selling expenses and general and administrative expenses. **Selling expenses are the operating expenses directly related or allocated to the sales activities of a company.** Sales activities are activities involved in the actual sale and delivery of merchandise to customers. Selling expenses include such items as sales salaries expense, advertising expense, and transportation-out. **General and administrative expenses are the operating expenses directly related or allocated to the general management of a company.** They include such items as office salaries expense, insurance expense, and office supplies expense.

Sometimes an operating expense is not directly related to either the sales activities or the general management of the company. The total expense, however, may be allocated to selling expenses and general and administrative expenses on a reasonable basis. For instance, many merchandising companies that have their sales floor and offices in the same building will allocate the depreciation expense and utilities expense for the building between selling expenses and general and administrative expenses based upon the proportion of the floor space used for sales activities and office activities. This type of allocation may be useful in internal decision making by helping to determine the profitability of various departments in the company, such as the sales department or the purchasing department. This allocation method is followed by the Hines Department Store in Exhibit 5-4.

The total selling expenses are added to the total general and administrative expenses to determine the total operating expenses. The total operating expenses are deducted from gross profit to determine operating income. The selling expenses of the Hines Department Store total $13,700 while the general and administrative expenses amount to $9,400. The total operating expenses of $23,100 are deducted from the $37,400 gross profit to determine the operating income of $14,300.

Other Revenues and Expenses.   The other revenues and expenses (sometimes called the *nonoperating income*) section of the income statement includes the revenues and expenses that are not related to the primary operations of the company. Included in this section are revenues and expenses related to financing the company's operations (e.g., interest revenue and interest expense), revenues and expenses (called gains and losses) from selling depreciable assets for more or less than their book value, and other incidental items (e.g., miscellaneous rent revenue, losses due to theft or fire). These items are discussed more fully later in the book.

Net Income.   The total amount of the other revenues and expenses (nonoperating income) is added to the operating income to determine the net income of a sole proprietorship or partnership. The net income of the Hines Department Store (a sole proprietorship) is $15,800, which was determined by adding the $1,500 nonoperating income to the $14,300 operating income.

Evaluation of Profitability   To evaluate the profitability of a company, many users (including the company's management) will compute its profit margin. **A company's profit margin is determined by dividing its net income by its net sales.** A higher profit margin for a company compared to previous years or to other companies indicates the company is doing a good job of controlling its expenses in relation to its sales or of selling its products at higher prices. Users may also compute a company's return on total assets. In its simplest form, **a company's return on total assets is determined by dividing its net income by its total assets.** The return on total assets measures how well a company is using its economic resources to achieve a profit, and can be compared to the results of previous years or other companies. The profit margin of the Hines Department Store is 19.1% ($15,800 ÷ $82,700), while the return on total assets is 12.3%

[$15,800 ÷ $128,600 (from Exhibit 5-5)]. These and other *ratios* are discussed more fully in Chapter 19.

Modifications of Income Statement for Corporations.   Sole proprietorships and partnerships are not subject to income taxes (although, of course, the owners are taxed on the income from the business, which is included in their personal income). Corporations, however, must pay income taxes because they are separate legal entities. These income taxes are an expense of doing business and are computed as a percentage of income before income taxes (the total of operating and nonoperating income). Income tax expense is deducted as the last item in the computation of a corporation's net income. Since a corporation *pays* its income taxes in the next period,[5] income taxes are also shown as a liability on the balance sheet (discussed later).

Since the owners of a corporation hold shares of capital stock, a corporation also reports earnings per share on its income statement, which is shown directly below net income. **Earnings per share is the net income divided by the number of capital shares held by stockholders.** To illustrate earnings per share and income taxes, assume that the Hines Department Store is a corporation that has issued 4,000 shares of capital stock to its owners, has earned income before income taxes of $15,800 in 1991, and is subject to a 40% income tax rate. The journal entry that the Hines Department Store would make to record its income taxes is as follows:

1991			
Dec. 31	Income Tax Expense ($15,800 x 0.40)	6,320	
	Income Taxes Payable		6,320
	To record income taxes for the year.		

The lower portion of the Hines Department Store's income statement shown in Exhibit 5-4 would be modified to include the income tax expense as follows:

Income before income taxes	$15,800
Income tax expense	(6,320)
Net Income	$ 9,480
Earnings per share (4,000 shares)	$ 2.37

The $6,320 income taxes payable would be reported as a liability on the balance sheet of the corporation. These and other items in a corporation's income statement and balance sheet are discussed more fully in Chapter 15. Because corporations are taxed at such a high rate (over 40% in many cases involving federal and state income taxes), in later chapters we frequently discuss the impact of accounting practices upon the income taxes of corporations.

---

[5]Many corporations actually have to pay their income taxes four times a year, but these payments are beyond the scope of this text. We will assume that all the income taxes for a current period are paid in the next period.

Classified Balance Sheet

7(b). Prepare a classified balance sheet.

Recall from Chapter 2 that a company's balance sheet reports on its resource structure and financial structure. It is used to provide information about the company's liquidity, financial flexibility, and capital invested by the owner. To report on these items, a classified balance sheet (i.e., statement of financial position) of a sole proprietorship has three major sections: the assets, liabilities, and owner's equity. Within each section the items are classified in an informative manner. Regardless of whether a business entity is a *service* company or *merchandising* company, a common classification scheme on its balance sheet is as follows:

1. *Assets*
   (a) **Current assets**
   (b) **Long-term investments**
   (c) **Property and equipment**

2. *Liabilities*
   (a) **Current liabilities**
   (b) **Noncurrent liabilities**

3. *Owner's equity*
   (a) **Owner's capital account**

Even though not every company uses all of these classifications, a discussion of the classification scheme helps in understanding the contents of a classified balance sheet. Each classification is briefly discussed next, and the items within each section are more fully discussed in later chapters. An example of a classified balance sheet (report form) for the Hines Department Store is presented in Exhibit 5-5.

Current Assets. **Current assets are cash and other assets that are expected to be converted into cash, sold, or consumed within 1 year or the normal operating cycle, whichever is longer.[6] An operating cycle is the average time taken by a company to spend cash for inventory, sell the inventory, and collect the receivables, converting them back into cash.** Most companies have operating cycles of a year or less. A few companies such as lumber, distillery, and tobacco companies have operating cycles that are longer than 1 year. In this case the longer time period should be used to determine the current assets. In this textbook we use 1 year unless stated otherwise. The following items are typically classified as current assets: (1) cash, (2) marketable securities, (3) receivables, (4) inventory, and (5) prepaid items. These items are presented in the current assets section in the order of their liquidity; that is, according to how quickly they can be converted into cash.

    Cash includes cash on hand and in checking and savings accounts. *Marketable securities* are items such as government bonds and capital stock and bonds (these securities are a type of legal note that pays interest) of corporations in which the company has temporarily invested. Alternative captions are *tempo-*

---

[6]"Restatement and Revision of Accounting Research Bulletins," *Accounting Research and Terminology Bulletins*, Final Edition, No. 43 (New York: AICPA, 1961), ch. 3, sec. A, par. 4.

EXHIBIT 5-5
Balance Sheet

HINES DEPARTMENT STORE
Balance Sheet
December 31, 1991

Assets

Current Assets			
Cash		$ 5,200	
Marketable securities		4,400	
Receivables			
Accounts receivable		22,900	
Notes receivable (due 7/1/1992)		5,000	
Interest receivable (due 7/1/1992)		200	
Inventory		11,600	
Prepaid items			
Insurance	$500		
Store supplies	400		
Office supplies	900	1,800	
Total current assets			$ 51,100
Long-Term Investments			
Government bonds (due 12/31/1998)		$ 6,000	
Notes receivable (due 12/31/1993)		4,000	
Total long-term investments			10,000
Property and Equipment			

	Cost	Accumulated Depreciation	Book Value
Land	$ 8,200	—	$ 8,200
Building	49,000	$10,900	38,100
Store equipment	15,500	3,600	11,900
Office equipment	11,700	2,400	9,300
Totals	$84,400	$16,900	$67,500

Total property and equipment		67,500
Total Assets		$128,600

Liabilities

Current Liabilities		
Accounts payable	$19,100	
Salaries payable	300	
Notes payable (due 3/1/1992)	3,000	
Interest payable (due 3/1/1992)	100	
Unearned rent	800	
Total current liabilities		$ 23,300
Noncurrent Liabilities		
Note payable (due 12/31/1996)	$ 7,000	
Mortgage payable	19,800	
Total noncurrent liabilities		26,800
Total Liabilities		$ 50,100

Owner's Equity

T. Hines, capital (see Schedule A)	78,500
Total Liabilities and Owner's Equity	$128,600

rary investments and *short-term investments*. *Receivables* include accounts receivable, notes receivable, and interest receivable with maturity dates of less than 1 year. *Inventory* is goods held for resale. *Prepaid items* such as insurance, rent, office supplies, and store supplies will not be converted into cash but will be consumed. In theory prepaid items should not be classified as current assets in the sense that they are not convertible into cash (i.e., not liquid) and do not directly enter into the operating cycle. They are included as current assets, however, because if they had not been paid in advance, cash would have been paid out within the cycle. Furthermore even though a 2-year prepayment of insurance would extend over more than an annual operating cycle, the payment is usually classified as a current asset for convenience. The current assets of the Hines Department Store total $51,100 as shown in Exhibit 5-5.

Assets that are not classified as current assets are called noncurrent assets. Noncurrent assets include long-term investments and property and equipment.

Long-Term Investments. Long-term investments include items such as notes receivable, government bonds, and bonds of corporations with maturity dates more than a year in advance, capital stock of corporations, and other securities. Sometimes these are called *noncurrent marketable securities*. To be classified in the long-term investments section the company must intend to hold the investment for more than 1 year or the operating cycle, whichever is longer. The long-term investments of Hines Department Store total $10,000 as shown in Exhibit 5-5.

Property and Equipment. The property and equipment section of the balance sheet includes all the physical, long-term assets used in the operations of the company. Often these assets are referred to as the *fixed assets* or *operating assets* because of their relative permanency in the company's operations. Assets that have a physical existence, such as land, buildings, equipment, and furniture, are listed in this category. Except for land, all the fixed assets are depreciable. Land is listed at its original cost while the remaining fixed assets are listed at their book values. A contra account, accumulated depreciation, is used to reduce the fixed assets to their book values while still reporting the historical cost.

Certain long-term lease contracts relating to leased property and equipment are also included in this section. Long-term leases of assets have become a popular way by which a lessee company may acquire the rights to the use of the assets without the initial cash outlay to finance the acquisitions. Since certain leases give the lessee company relatively unrestricted rights to the use of an asset for an extended period of time, the rights are economic resources to the company and an asset is recorded even though the asset is not legally owned. The property and equipment section of the Hines Department Store totals $67,500 as shown on Exhibit 5-5.[7]

Current Liabilities. **Current liabilities are obligations that are expected to be paid within 1 year (or the operating cycle, if longer) and whose payment is expected to require the use of existing current assets.**

---

[7]Some companies, primarily manufacturing firms, have another section of noncurrent assets entitled "Intangible Assets." This section is presented below Property and Equipment and includes such items as patents and copyrights, which are reported at their book values. This topic is discussed in Chapter 12.

The following types of liabilities should be included as current liabilities:

1. Obligations for items (goods or services) that have entered the operating cycle. These obligations would include such items as accounts payable and salaries payable.

2. Advance collections for the future delivery of goods or performance of services, for instance, unearned rent and unearned legal fees. These items are referred to as unearned revenues.

3. Other obligations that will be paid within 1 year or the operating cycle, such as short-term notes payable and interest payable, the portions of noncurrent liabilities that will become due during this period, and income taxes payable (for corporations).[8]

The current liabilities of the Hines Department Store total $23,300 as shown in Exhibit 5-5.

Noncurrent Liabilities. Noncurrent liabilities are obligations that are not expected to require the use of current assets within the next year or operating cycle (if longer than a year). Noncurrent liabilities are also called *long-term* liabilities because usually these obligations are outstanding for several years. Included in this category are such items as long-term notes payable, obligations for long-term lease contracts, mortgages payable, and bonds payable (in the case of corporations). The noncurrent liabilities of the Hines Department Store are $26,800 as shown in Exhibit 5-5.

Owner's Equity. Owner's equity is the current investment of the owner in the assets of the company; that is, the equity of the owner is the company's assets less the liabilities. For a sole proprietorship, whether the business entity is a service or merchandising company, the total ending owner's equity is listed in a single *capital* account. For a partnership the total ending owners' equity is divided into separate partner's capital accounts. The ending balance in the capital account(s) may be affected by additional investments, net income, or withdrawals. To report these items, a separate schedule, the statement of changes in owner's equity (for a sole proprietorship) or the statement of changes in partners' equity (for a partnership) is prepared. This schedule is a supporting schedule to the balance sheet. An example is presented in Exhibit 5-6. The Hines Department Store owner's equity totals $78,500 as shown in Exhibit 5-5.

EXHIBIT 5-6
Statement of Changes in Owner's Equity

HINES DEPARTMENT STORE Schedule A Statement of Changes in Owner's Equity For Year Ended December 31, 1991	
T. Hines, capital, January 1, 1991	$70,700
Add: Net income	15,800
	$86,500
Less: Withdrawals	(8,000)
T. Hines, capital, December 31, 1991	$78,500

---

[8]Op. cit., par. 7.

Modifications of Owner's Equity for Corporations.   A corporation is a separate legal entity that must adhere to the laws of the state in which it is based. Many state laws affect the accounting for stockholders' equity (the term used for owners' equity) on the balance sheet of a corporation. To adhere to these laws stockholders' equity is separated into two sections, contributed capital and retained earnings.

Contributed capital is the total dollar amount of investments made by stockholders into the corporation. Various types of stock are issued to the owners (called stockholders); collectively they are called capital stock. **Capital stock is the term used for shares issued to the owners of a corporation as legal evidence of their ownership.** Accounting for capital stock transactions is fully discussed in Chapter 14. Here it is sufficient to know that for certain capital stock, the total amount invested by stockholders in the corporation is reported in a separate account called Capital Stock. Thus, in the contributed capital section of stockholders' equity, the item Capital Stock, $26,000, means that stockholders have invested this amount in the corporation.

Retained earnings is the total lifetime earnings (net income or net loss) of a corporation that have not been distributed to stockholders as dividends. Dividends are the amounts distributed to stockholders as a reward (incentive) for investing in the corporation. Each corporation has a Retained Earnings account and may have a Dividends account. The Retained Earnings account has a credit balance that is reported on a corporate balance sheet in the stockholders' equity section. A Dividends account for a corporation has a debit balance and is similar to the Withdrawals accounts of a sole proprietorship or partnership.

The ending balance in the Capital Stock account is affected by additional stockholders' investments. The ending balance in the Retained Earnings account is affected by the net income and dividends of the current period. To report these items a separate schedule, the statement of changes in stockholders' equity, is prepared as a supporting schedule to the balance sheet of a corporation. This schedule is not illustrated in this chapter but is discussed in Chapter 14.

If the Hines Department Store had been a corporation instead of a sole proprietorship, the stockholders' equity section of the balance sheet in Exhibit 5-5 might appears as follows:

Stockholders' Equity

Contributed capital	
Capital stock	$26,000
Retained earnings	46,180
Total Stockholders' Equity	$72,180

It is important to note that the total stockholders' equity of $72,180 is *not* the same as the $78,500 owners' equity shown in Exhibit 5-5. This is because the net income of the corporation is only $9,480 (as computed earlier) compared to the $15,800 net income shown in Exhibit 5-4, due to the income taxes of $6,320. The balance sheet still "balances," however, because the $6,320 would be listed as a current liability, income taxes payable. Thus as a corporation the Hines Department Store would list current liabilities of $29,620 ($6,320 + $23,300) and total liabilities of $56,420 ($29,620 + $26,800). The total liabilities and stockholders' equity would be $128,600 ($56,420 + $72,180), the same amount as shown in Exhibit 5-5.

Working Capital. The working capital of a company relates primarily to the financial resources utilized in its operating cycle. **Working capital is the excess of a company's current assets over its current liabilities.** Although working capital is seldom disclosed on the balance sheet, it is an indicator of the short-run liquidity of the company and is often computed by creditors and other users. Often a slightly different computation, the current ratio, is used for the same purpose. **The current ratio is the current assets divided by the current liabilities.** A common "rule of thumb" is that a company's current ratio should be around 2 to 1. A satisfactory current ratio depends upon the type of company, however. Some companies have current assets that are more "liquid" (more easily converted into cash) than other companies. For instance, a company with a high percentage of prepaid items is not as liquid as a company without any prepaid items. The working capital of the Hines Department Store is $27,800 ($51,100 − $23,300) while its current ratio is 2.2 to 1 ($51,100 ÷ $23,300).

Annual Report

Recall from Chapter 1 that a company's *annual report* contains its audited financial statements. A complete set of audited financial statements from the 1988 annual report of the Black & Decker Corporation is shown in Appendix A. Included with the financial statements are numerous notes. **A note (footnote) explains additional information about certain items in the financial statements.** Some of the items included in the financial statements and related notes are discussed in the later chapters of the book. In reviewing these financial statements, however, you should recognize that we have introduced many of the items in these first five chapters.

Closing Entries

Because of the many contra accounts and the importance of cost of goods sold, the closing entries for a merchandising company are more complex than for a service company. The objective is still the same, however, to close the temporary income statement and withdrawals accounts and to update the permanent balance sheet accounts. The 1991 closing entries of the Hines Department Store, a sole proprietorship using a periodic inventory system, are shown in Exhibit 5-7 (based on the account balances shown in Exhibit 5-4) and are discussed next. The closing entries of partnerships are discussed in Chapter 13; the closing entries of corporations are discussed briefly later in this section.

Cost of Goods Sold Closing Entries (Periodic System)

Because cost of goods sold is such an important operating expense, a merchandising company that uses a *periodic* inventory system may use a Cost of Goods Sold *closing* account in addition to the Income Summary account. (Remember that a company has a Cost of Goods Sold account during the accounting period only if it uses a *perpetual* inventory system.) For a periodic inventory system all of the accounts used to compute cost of goods sold are first closed to the Cost of Goods Sold account.[9] The balance of the Cost of Goods Sold account is then closed with the remaining expenses to the Income Summary account.

8. Prepare closing entries for a merchandising company.

The first two closing entries in Exhibit 5-7 are used to compute the 1991 cost of goods sold. The first closing entry closes the temporary accounts with debit balances (Purchases, Transportation-In, and beginning Inventory) to the Cost of Goods Sold account. It is important to understand the handling of the Inventory account in the closing entries of a company using a periodic inventory system. Under this system the beginning Inventory account balance (remember that this amount is the ending inventory of the previous period) has not changed throughout the entire accounting period. The actual cost of inventory on hand is not known until the end of the accounting period when the periodic inventory is taken. At this point the beginning Inventory account balance is outdated and must be replaced by the cost of the ending inventory. To do this, the first step is to close out the beginning inventory by crediting the Inventory account for its beginning balance ($10,300 in this case).

The second closing entry closes the temporary accounts with credit balances (Purchases Returns and Allowances and Purchases Discounts Taken) and records the cost of the ending inventory (as determined by the physical count in the periodic inventory) in the Inventory account. After the two journal entries have been posted, the Purchases, Transportation-In, Purchases Returns and Allowances, and Purchases Discounts Taken accounts all have zero balances as shown in the following diagram (where *Bal.1* is balance of account before closing, *Cl.* is closing amount, and *Bal.2* is balance after closing).

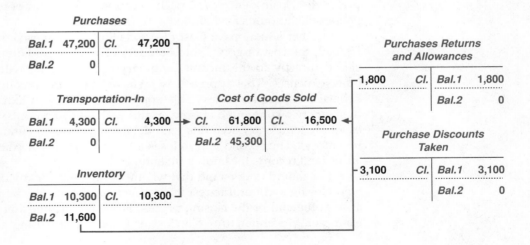

The Cost of Goods Sold account has a $45,300 debit balance ($61,800 − $16,500), which is the 1991 cost of goods sold as shown in the income statement in Exhibit 5-4. The Inventory account has a debit balance of $11,600, the cost of the

---

[9]Alternative approaches to closing entries, including closing the cost of goods sold accounts directly to Income Summary, may be used. These approaches are briefly discussed later in the chapter.

ending inventory. This is the result of closing out the beginning balance and establishing the ending balance in the closing entries.

Remaining Closing Entries

Once the Cost of Goods Sold account balance has been determined it is closed to the Income Summary account along with the rest of the revenue and expense accounts.[10] These closing entries for a merchandising company are the same as the entries for a service company, except that they also include the additional contra accounts, Sales Returns and Allowances and Sales Discounts Taken, and the Cost of Goods Sold account. The remaining closing entries for the Hines Department Store are shown in Exhibit 5-7 below the cost of goods sold closing entries (the $8,000 withdrawals information was obtained from Exhibit 5-6).

Alternative Closing Entries.   A slightly different approach may be used in preparing the closing entries of merchandising companies. For instance, the inventory balance may be "adjusted" as part of the adjusting entry process. That is, at the time the adjusting entries are made the Cost of Goods Sold account is debited and the Inventory account is credited to eliminate the beginning inventory balance. Then the Inventory account is debited and the Cost of Goods Sold account is credited to establish the ending inventory balance. Finally the remaining cost of goods sold accounts are closed during the closing entry process. You should understand that it is a matter of preference whether the Inventory account balance is brought up to date as part of the closing entry process or as part of the adjusting entry process. Both approaches have *identical* results; the ending inventory amount is listed as the balance of the Inventory account. We prefer the closing entry approach because under this approach all the cost of goods sold accounts are handled at the same time.

In other situations, a Cost of Goods Sold closing account may not be used. Instead, the cost of goods sold accounts (including updating the inventory) are closed directly to the Income Summary account along with the revenues and other expenses. This approach is preferred by some accountants because they believe it is simpler to use. This approach is shown in Exhibit 5-8. Notice that there are two compound closing entries with many accounts. The first entry closes all the temporary accounts with debit balances (and eliminates the beginning inventory). The second entry closes all the temporary accounts with credit balances (and records the ending inventory).

You should understand that whether or not a company uses a Cost of Goods Sold closing account, the results are *identical*; the Income Summary account balance at the end of the closing process is the net income amount ($15,800 in our example). We prefer to use a Cost of Goods Sold closing account because we

---

[10]If the Hines Company had been using a *perpetual* inventory system, it would show a $45,300 debit balance in its Cost of Goods Sold account and an $11,600 debit in its Inventory account in the general ledger at the end of the accounting period. In this case, the first two cost of goods sold closing entries in Exhibit 5-7 would not be necessary and the Cost of Goods Sold account would be closed to the Income Summary account as shown in the fourth entry of Exhibit 5-7. This procedure is discussed more fully in Chapter 9.

EXHIBIT 5-7
Hines Department
Store Closing Entries

Date		Account Titles and Explanations	Debit	Credit
		Closing Entries		
1991 Dec.	31	Cost of Goods Sold	61,800	
		Purchases		47,200
		Transportation-In		4,300
		Inventory (January 1, 1991)		10,300
		To close merchandise costs to cost of goods sold.		
	31	Purchases Returns and Allowances	1,800	
		Purchases Discounts Taken	3,100	
		Inventory (December 31, 1991)	11,600	
		Cost of Goods Sold		16,500
		To close the accounts that reduced the merchandise costs and to establish the ending inventory.		
	31	Sales	89,200	
		Interest Revenue	1,300	
		Rent Revenue	900	
		Income Summary		91,400
		To close the revenue accounts.		
	31	Income Summary	75,600	
		Cost of Goods Sold		45,300
		Sales Returns and Allowances		2,900
		Sales Discounts Taken		3,600
		Depreciation Expense: Store Equipment		1,400
		Depreciation Expense: Building (sales and office space)		3,600
		Utilities Expense (sales and office space)		1,200
		Advertising Expense		2,900
		Sales Salaries Expense		4,200
		Transportation-Out		1,100
		Store Supplies Used		600
		Depreciation Expense: Office Equipment		1,300
		Office Salaries Expense		2,300
		Administrative Salaries Expense		3,500
		Office Supplies Expense		800
		Insurance Expense		200
		Interest Expense		700
		To close the temporary accounts with debit balances.		
	31	Income Summary	15,800	
		T. Hines, Capital		15,800
		To close Income Summary account and transfer net income to owner's capital account.		
	31	T. Hines, Capital	8,000	
		T. Hines, Withdrawals		8,000
		To close the withdrawals account.		

GENERAL JOURNAL   Page 92

EXHIBIT 5-8
Alternative Closing
Entries

	GENERAL JOURNAL		Page 92
Date	**Account Titles and Explanations**	**Debit**	**Credit**
	Closing Entries		
1991 Dec. 31	Income Summary	92,100	
	Inventory (January 1, 1991)		10,300
	Sales Returns and Allowances		2,900
	Sales Discounts Taken		3,600
	Purchases		47,200
	Transportation-In		4,300
	Depreciation Expense: Store Equipment		1,400
	Depreciation Expense: Building (sales and office space)		3,600
	Utilities Expense (sales and office space)		1,200
	Advertising Expense		2,900
	Sales Salaries Expense		4,200
	Transportation-Out		1,100
	Store Supplies Used		600
	Depreciation Expense: Office Equipment		1,300
	Office Salaries Expense		2,300
	Administrative Salaries Expense		3,500
	Office Supplies Expense		800
	Insurance Expense		200
	Interest Expense		700
	To close the temporary accounts with debit balances and eliminate the beginning inventory.		
31	Inventory (December 31, 1991)	11,600	
	Sales	89,200	
	Interest Revenue	1,300	
	Rent Revenue	900	
	Purchases Returns and Allowances	1,800	
	Purchases Discounts Taken	3,100	
	Income Summary		107,900
	To close the temporary accounts with credit balances and record the ending inventory.		
31	Income Summary	15,800	
	T. Hines, Capital		15,800
	To close Income Summary account and transfer net income to owner's capital account.		
31	T. Hines, Capital	8,000	
	T. Hines, Withdrawals		8,000
	To close the withdrawals account.		

think it follows a more logical step-by-step process. It also accumulates in the Cost of Goods Sold closing account an amount that can be "cross checked" for accuracy with the cost of goods sold amount listed on the income statement. Unless told otherwise, you should use a Cost of Goods Sold closing account and update your inventory as part of the closing process.

Modifications of Closing Entries for Corporations. As discussed earlier, a corporation pays income taxes to the government and dividends to its stockholders. As a result the corporation has a debit balance in both its Income Tax Expense account and its Dividends account at the end of the accounting period, prior to making its closing entries. Both of these accounts are temporary accounts. The corporation also has a permanent Retained Earnings account with a credit balance that is reported as part of the stockholders' equity section on its balance sheet. In a corporation's closing entries the balance of the Income Tax Expense account is closed in the usual manner to Income Summary along with the other revenues and expenses. The balance of the Income Summary account (which equals the corporation's net income or loss) is then closed to the Retained Earnings account. The balance of the Dividends account (which is similar to a withdrawals account) is also closed (as a reduction) to Retained Earnings.

To illustrate, if the Hines Department Store had been a corporation, as part of its closing entries Income Summary would have been debited and Income Tax Expense would have been credited for $6,320 (the amount of its income taxes, as computed earlier). These closing entries, in turn, would have resulted in a credit balance of $9,480 in the Income Summary account, representing the net income for 1991. Consequently, Income Summary would have been debited and Retained Earnings would have been credited for $9,480. After debiting Retained Earnings and crediting the Dividends account for $8,000 (the amount of the 1991 dividends), the Retained Earnings account would have an ending balance of $46,180, as illustrated in the stockholders' equity section presented earlier.

Worksheet for Merchandising Company

A merchandising company may use a worksheet to aid in preparing its adjusting entries, closing entries, and financial statements. The steps in completing a worksheet for a merchandising company that uses a periodic inventory system are almost identical to the steps shown in Chapter 4 for a service company. An extra step must be included for a merchandising company, however. The six steps to be completed for this worksheet are discussed as follows as they relate to Exhibit 5-9:

Step 1: Prepare the trial balance in the trial balance columns. List the account titles and ending account balances from the general ledger. Remember that the Inventory account in the trial balance is the *beginning* balance because no entries have been made in this account during the year. The trial balance for the Cohen Company in Exhibit 5-9 totals $128,300.

9. Complete a worksheet for a merchandising company.

Step 2: Prepare the worksheet adjusting entries. Analyze the accounts and make whatever adjusting entries are necessary to bring the accounts up to date at the end of the period. Use letters of the alphabet to identify each entry and list an explanation for each entry at the bottom of the worksheet. Total the adjustments columns to prove the equality of the total debits and credits. In Exhibit 5-9 two adjusting entries for $1,500 depreciation and $200 accrued salaries were made. The adjustments columns total $1,700.

EXHIBIT 5-9
Worksheet for a
Merchandising
Company

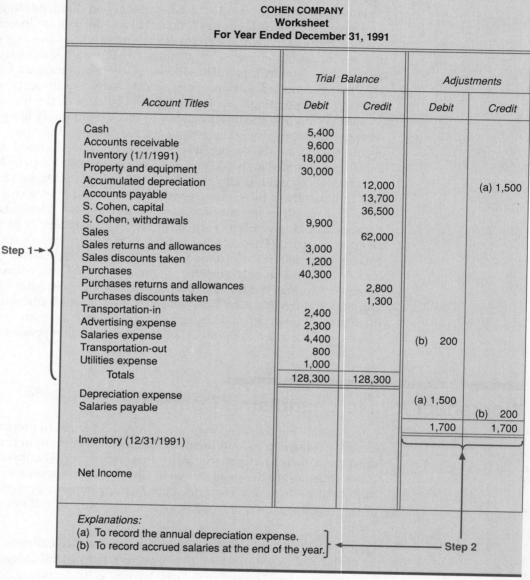

COHEN COMPANY
Worksheet
For Year Ended December 31, 1991

Account Titles	Trial Balance		Adjustments	
	Debit	Credit	Debit	Credit
Cash	5,400			
Accounts receivable	9,600			
Inventory (1/1/1991)	18,000			
Property and equipment	30,000			
Accumulated depreciation		12,000		(a) 1,500
Accounts payable		13,700		
S. Cohen, capital		36,500		
S. Cohen, withdrawals	9,900			
Sales		62,000		
Sales returns and allowances	3,000			
Sales discounts taken	1,200			
Purchases	40,300			
Purchases returns and allowances		2,800		
Purchases discounts taken		1,300		
Transportation-in	2,400			
Advertising expense	2,300			
Salaries expense	4,400		(b) 200	
Transportation-out	800			
Utilities expense	1,000			
Totals	128,300	128,300		
Depreciation expense			(a) 1,500	
Salaries payable				(b) 200
			1,700	1,700
Inventory (12/31/1991)				
Net Income				

Step 1→ (bracket for trial balance rows)

Explanations:
(a) To record the annual depreciation expense.
(b) To record accrued salaries at the end of the year. ⟵———— Step 2

Step 3: Prepare an adjusted trial balance. Crossfoot (combine) the trial balance amount of each account with any adjustments to the account. The adjusted trial balance columns total $130,000 in Exhibit 5-9.

Step 4: Transfer each account balance listed in the adjusted trial balance columns to its respective income statement or balance sheet column. The beginning inventory account balance is transferred to the *income statement* debit column instead of to the balance sheet. This may be seen for the

Step 4

Adjusted Trial Balance		Income Statement		Balance Sheet	
Debit	Credit	Debit	Credit	Debit	Credit
5,400				5,400	
9,600				9,600	
18,000		18,000			
30,000				30,000	
	13,500				13,500
	13,700				13,700
	36,500				36,500
9,900				9,900	
	62,000		62,000		
3,000		3,000			
1,200		1,200			
40,300		40,300			
	2,800		2,800		
	1,300		1,300		
2,400		2,400			
2,300		2,300			
4,600		4,600			
800		800			
1,000		1,000			
1,500		1,500			
	200				200
130,000	130,000				
		21,000	21,000		
		75,100	87,100	75,900	63,900
		12,000			12,000
		87,100	87,100	75,900	75,900

Step 3

Step 5

Step 6

$18,000 beginning inventory in Exhibit 5-9. It is important to understand why this is the case. Recall that the inventory listed on the adjusted trial balance is the *beginning* inventory. The beginning inventory is added to purchases on the income statement in the calculation of cost of goods available for sale. Therefore it is listed in the income statement debit column. The *ending* inventory will be included on the balance sheet as shown in Step 5.

In transferring the accounts to the respective financial statement columns, special attention should be paid to the new accounts introduced in this chapter (Sales Returns and Allowances, Sales Discounts, Purchases, Transportation-In and -Out, Purchases Returns and Allowances, and Purchases Discounts Taken). All of them are income statement accounts; many of them are contra accounts. A common error is to list one of these account balances in the wrong income statement column (e.g., debit instead of credit column) or to include it in the balance sheet. Be careful when transferring these accounts!

Step 5: Enter the ending inventory on the worksheet. This is the additional step for a merchandising company using a periodic inventory system. The term *Inventory* (and the ending date) is written in the account titles column on the first line below the totals of the adjustments columns and the adjusted trial balance columns. The ending inventory amount (as determined by a physical count) is entered in two columns. First, it is entered in the *credit* column of the income statement. Second, it is entered in the *debit* column of the balance sheet. This may be seen in Exhibit 5-9 for the $21,000 ending inventory (12/31/1991) of the Cohen Company.

It is important to understand why the ending inventory is included in both the income statement and balance sheet. The ending inventory is included in the income statement credit column because it is deducted from cost of goods available for sale in computing cost of goods sold. Since the beginning inventory and purchases (which are used to determine cost of goods available for sale) are listed in the income statement debit column, it is necessary to list the ending inventory in the credit column in order to determine accurately the cost of goods sold and net income. The amount of the ending inventory is listed in the debit column of the balance sheet because this amount will replace the beginning inventory when the closing entries are prepared and will be included in the ending balance sheet.

Step 6: Complete the financial statement columns on the worksheet. Subtotal the income statement columns and the balance sheet columns. The difference between the subtotals of each set of columns is the net income (or net loss). Enter the term *Net Income* in the account titles column. List the amount of the net income directly below the income statement debit column subtotal and the balance sheet credit column subtotal and total each set of columns.[11] The net income of the Cohen Company is $12,000 as shown in Exhibit 5-9. The worksheet is now complete.

Once the worksheet is completed, the adjusting entries, closing entries, and financial statements are prepared. The adjusting entries are copied from the worksheet to the general journal (the explanations from the worksheet are used to prepare the explanations in the general journal). The closing entries (as discussed earlier) are prepared in the general journal based on the amounts in the income statement columns (and the withdrawals amount). The financial statements (including the statement of changes in owner's equity) are prepared from the information in the income statement and balance sheet columns of the worksheet.

---

[11] A net loss would be listed below the income statement *credit* column subtotal and the balance sheet *debit* column subtotal.

Chapter Summary

Review of Learning Objectives

1. **Describe a merchandising company.**

   A merchandising company is a business entity that purchases goods (*merchandise*) for resale to its customers in order to earn a net income. A merchandising company can be a *retailer* that sells its goods directly to the final customer, or a *wholesaler* that primarily sells its goods to retailers or other commercial users.

2. **Record transactions involving (a) sales revenues, (b) sales returns and allowances, and (c) sales discounts.**

   Net sales are affected by cash or credit sales, sales returns and allowances, and sales discounts. The following is a summary of the journal entries to record these items.

Item	Journal Entry	
Sales for cash or on account	Cash (or Accounts Receivable) xx	
	Sales	xx
Sales returns and allowances	Sales Returns and Allowances xx	
	Cash (or Accounts Receivable)	xx
Sales discounts	Cash xx	
	Sales Discounts Taken xx	
	Accounts Receivable	xx

3. **Describe the (a) perpetual and (b) periodic inventory systems.**

   A *perpetual* inventory system is one in which a continuous record is kept of the cost of inventory on hand and the cost of inventory sold. This system is more common when a few items are sold at a high selling price and the cost of each item sold is easily determined. A *periodic* inventory system is one in which a continuous record of the inventory on hand is not kept and a physical count of the inventory is taken periodically at the end of each accounting period. This system is more common when a high volume of low-priced items is sold.

4. **Calculate cost of goods sold under the periodic inventory system.**

   Under the periodic inventory system, cost of goods sold is calculated by deducting the ending inventory from the cost of goods available for sale. The calculations are as follows:

	Beginning Inventory		Cost of Goods Available for Sale
+	Purchases	–	Ending Inventory
–	Purchases Returns and Allowances	=	Cost of Goods Sold
–	Purchases Discounts Taken		
+	Transportation-In		
=	Cost of Goods Available for Sale		

5. **Record transactions involving (a) purchases, (b) purchases returns and allowances, (c) purchases discounts, and (d) transportation-in.**
Net purchases are affected by cash and credit purchases, purchases returns and allowances, purchases discounts, and transportation-in. The following is a summary of the journal entries to record these items.

Item	Journal Entry	
Purchases for cash or on account	Purchases	xx
	Cash (or Accounts Payable)	xx
Purchases returns and allowances	Cash (or Accounts Payable)	xx
	Purchases Returns and Allowances	xx
Purchases discounts	Accounts Payable	xx
	Purchases Discounts Taken	xx
	Cash	xx
Transportation cost for purchases	Transportation-In	xx
	Cash	xx

 6. **Describe classified financial statements.**
A classified financial statement is a statement in which accounts are grouped into selected categories to provide more useful information for the users of the statement.

 7. **Prepare a classified (a) income statement and (b) balance sheet.**
In a *classified income statement,* cost of goods sold is deducted from net sales to determine gross profit. Then the total of the operating expenses (classified as selling expenses or general and administrative expenses) is deducted from gross profit to determine operating income. Finally the total of the other revenues and expenses is added to (or deducted from) operating income to determine net income. In a *classified balance sheet,* the totals of the current assets, long-term investments, and property and equipment are added to determine the total assets. Then the totals of the current liabilities and noncurrent liabilities are added to determine the total liabilities. Finally the total liabilities are added to the total owner's equity to determine the total liabilities and owner's equity, which must be equal to the total assets. Slight modifications are made in the classified income statement and balance sheet of a corporation.

 8. **Prepare closing entries for a merchandising company.**
Under a periodic inventory system, the first closing entry involves a debit to the Cost of Goods Sold account and credits to the Purchases, Transportation-In, and beginning Inventory accounts for their respective balances. The second closing entry involves debits to the Purchases Returns and Allowances, Purchases Discounts Taken, and ending Inventory accounts for their respective balances and a credit to the Cost of Goods Sold account. After the Cost of Goods Sold account balance is determined, it is closed to the Income

Summary account in the usual manner, along with the rest of the revenue and expense accounts.

9. **Complete a worksheet for a merchandising company.**
The six steps involved in completing a worksheet for a merchandising company are as follows: (1) Prepare the trial balance in the trial balance columns. (2) Prepare the worksheet adjusting entries in the adjustments columns. (3) Prepare an adjusted trial balance in the adjusted trial balance columns. (4) Transfer each account balance listed in the adjusted trial balance columns to its respective income statement or balance sheet column. Be sure to transfer the beginning inventory account balance to the income statement *debit* column. (5) List the ending inventory account in the account titles column and enter the ending inventory amount in the income statement *credit* column and the balance sheet *debit* column. (6) Complete the financial statement columns. Subtotal the columns and list Net Income in the account titles column. Compute the difference between the subtotals of each set of columns and list this amount as the net income in the income statement debit column and the balance sheet credit column. Total each set of columns to complete the worksheet.

Review Problem

The Houston Company has the following adjusted trial balance on December 31, 1991:

Account Titles	Debits	Credits
Cash	$ 1,000	
Accounts receivable	2,700	
Inventory (January 1, 1991)	5,100	
Prepaid insurance	800	
Land	3,200	
Buildings and equipment	31,000	
Accumulated depreciation		$15,000
Accounts payable		3,300
Salaries payable		420
Notes payable (due July 1, 1993)		5,000
Interest payable (due July 1, 1993)		400
Unearned rent		360
A. Roe, capital		16,020
A. Roe, withdrawals	1,200	
Sales		30,000
Sales returns and allowances	2,100	
Rent revenue		1,440
Purchases	15,900	
Purchases returns and allowances		1,240
Freight-in	1,780	
Selling expenses	4,800	
General and administrative expenses	3,200	
Interest expense	400	
Totals	$73,180	$73,180

In addition, the company took its annual physical inventory on December 31, 1991. It determined that its ending inventory is $5,600.

REQUIRED   Prepare the following items for 1991:

1. A classified income statement
2. A statement of changes in owner's equity
3. A classified ending balance sheet (report form)
4. Closing entries

Solution to Review Problem

REQUIREMENT 1

HOUSTON COMPANY
Income Statement
For Year Ended December 31, 1991

Revenues:			
Sales			$30,000
Less: Sales returns and allowances			(2,100)
Net sales			$27,900
Cost of Goods Sold:			
Beginning inventory, 1/1/1991		$ 5,100	
Purchases	$15,900		
Less: Purchases returns and allowances	(1,240)		
Plus: Freight-in	1,780		
Net purchases		16,440	
Cost of goods available for sale		$21,540	
Less: Ending inventory, 12/31/1991		(5,600)	
Cost of goods sold			(15,940)
Gross profit			$11,960
Operating Expenses:			
Selling expenses		$ 4,800	
General and administrative expenses		3,200	
Total operating expenses			(8,000)
Operating income			$ 3,960
Other Revenues and Expenses:			
Rent revenue		$ 1,440	
Interest expense		(400)	
Nonoperating income			1,040
Net income			$ 5,000

REQUIREMENT 2

HOUSTON COMPANY
Schedule A
Statement of Changes in Owner's Equity
For Year Ended December 31, 1991

A. Roe, capital, January 1, 1991	$16,020
Add: 1991 net income	5,000
	$21,020
Less: 1991 withdrawals	(1,200)
A. Roe, capital, December 31, 1991	$19,820

REQUIREMENT 3

HOUSTON COMPANY
Balance Sheet
December 31, 1991

Assets

Current Assets		
Cash		$ 1,000
Accounts receivable		2,700
Inventory		5,600
Prepaid insurance		800
Total current assets		$10,100
Property and Equipment		
Land	$ 3,200	
Buildings and equipment	$31,000	
Less: Accumulated depreciation	(15,000)	16,000
Total property and equipment		19,200
Total Assets		$29,300

Liabilities

Current Liabilities		
Accounts payable		$ 3,300
Salaries payable		420
Unearned rent		360
Total current liabilities		$ 4,080
Noncurrent Liabilities		
Notes payable (due 7/1/1993)	$ 5,000	
Interest payable (due 7/1/1993)	400	
Total noncurrent liabilities		5,400
Total Liabilities		$ 9,480

Owner's Equity

A. Roe, capital (see Schedule A)		19,820
Total Liabilities and Owner's Equity		$29,300

REQUIREMENT 4

		GENERAL JOURNAL		Page 79

Date		Account Titles and Explanations	Debit	Credit
		Closing Entries		
1991 Dec.	31	Cost of Goods Sold	22,780	
		Purchases		15,900
		Freight-In		1,780
		Inventory (January 1, 1991)		5,100
		To close merchandise costs to cost of goods sold.		
	31	Purchases Returns and Allowances	1,240	
		Inventory (December 31, 1991)	5,600	
		Cost of Goods Sold		6,840
		To close account that reduced merchandise costs and to establish the ending inventory.		

31	Sales		30,000	
	Rent Revenue		1,440	
	Income Summary			31,440
	To close the revenue accounts.			
31	Income Summary		26,440	
	Cost of Goods Sold			15,940
	Sales Returns and Allowances			2,100
	Selling Expenses[a]			4,800
	General and Administrative Expenses[a]			3,200
	Interest Expense			400
	To close temporary accounts with debit balances.			
31	Income Summary		5,000	
	A. Roe, Capital			5,000
	To close net income to the owner's capital account.			
31	A. Roe, Capital		1,200	
	A. Roe, Withdrawals			1,200
	To close the withdrawals account.			

[a]Each selling expense and general and administrative expense would normally be listed separately on the income statement and closed separately in the closing entries. To save space in this review problem only the totals are listed and closed.

Glossary

Capital Stock. Term used for shares issued to the owners of a corporation as legal evidence of their ownership.

Cash Discount. Percentage reduction of the invoice price for payment within the discount period.

Contributed Capital. Total dollar amount of investments made by stockholders into a corporation. Reported in the stockholders' equity section of the corporation's balance sheet.

Cost of Goods Available for Sale. Beginning inventory plus purchases and transportation-in, less purchases returns and allowances and purchases discounts taken.

Cost of Goods Sold. Cost a merchandising company has incurred for the merchandise (goods) that it has sold to customers during an accounting period. For a periodic inventory system, cost of goods sold equals cost of goods available for sale less ending inventory.

Credit Memo. Business document used to list the information for a sales return or allowance. Called a credit memo because it shows the amount of the credit (decrease) to cash or accounts receivable.

Current Assets. Cash and other assets that are expected to be converted into cash, sold, or consumed within 1 year or the normal operating cycle, whichever is longer. Current assets include cash, marketable securities, receivables, inventory, and prepaid items.

Current Liabilities. The obligations that are expected to be paid within 1 year (or the operating cycle, if longer) and whose payment is expected to require the use of existing current assets. Examples are accounts payable and salaries payable.

Current Ratio. Current assets divided by current liabilities. Indicator of short-run liquidity of a company.

Debit Memo. Business document used to list the information for a purchases return or allowance. Called a debit memo because it shows the amount of the debit to cash or accounts payable.

General and Administrative Expenses. Section on a classified income statement. Includes operating expenses directly related or allocated to the general management of a company.

Gross Profit. Net sales less cost of goods sold.

Gross Profit Percentage. Gross profit divided by net sales.

Income Tax Expense. Account used to record the income tax expense of a corporation for the accounting period. Deducted from income before income taxes to determine net income.

Inventory. Merchandise (goods) being held for resale by a merchandising company. Sometimes referred to as *merchandise inventory.*

Invoice. Business document used to list the information for a sale of merchandise.

Long-Term Investments. Section on a classified balance sheet for investments in items that a company intends to hold for more than 1 year or the operating cycle, whichever is longer. Examples are investments in government bonds, noncurrent notes receivable, and capital stock and bonds of corporations.

Manufacturing Company. Business entity that makes products for sale to its customers.

Merchandising Company. Business entity that purchases goods (merchandise) for resale to its customers. May be a retailer or wholesaler.

Net Sales. Sales less sales returns and allowances and sales discounts taken.

Noncurrent Assets. Assets not classified as current assets. Included are long-term investments and property and equipment.

Noncurrent Liabilities. Obligations that are not classified as current liabilities. Examples are long-term notes payable and mortgages payable.

Note (Footnote). Explains additional information about certain items in the financial statements.

Operating Cycle. Average time taken by a company to spend cash for inventory, sell the inventory, and collect the receivables, converting them back into cash.

Operating Income. Section of classified income statement that includes all the revenues earned and expenses incurred in the normal day-to-day operating activities of the company.

Other Revenues and Expenses. Section of classified income statement that includes any items of revenue and expense that are not related to the primary operations of the company.

Periodic Inventory System. System in which a continuous record is *not* kept of the cost of inventory on hand and sold during the accounting period. Ending inventory is determined by a physical count.

Perpetual Inventory System. System in which a continuous record is kept of the cost of inventory on hand and the cost of inventory sold during the accounting period.

Profit Margin. Net income divided by net sales.

Purchases. Account used in a periodic inventory system to record the cost of goods purchased for resale to customers.

Purchases Discounts Taken. Contra account to the Purchases account. Used to record the reduction in the amount paid for purchases on account as a result of payment within the discount period.

Purchases Returns and Allowances. Contra account to the Purchases account. Used to record the cost of goods returned to suppliers or the adjustments (reductions) given by suppliers in the cost of goods purchased because of inferior quality.

Retained Earnings.   Total lifetime earnings of a corporation that have not been distributed to stockholders as dividends. Reported in the stockholders' equity section of the corporation's balance sheet.

Return on Total Assets.   Net income divided by total assets.

Sales.   Revenue account used to record the selling price of goods sold for cash or on account to customers during an accounting period.

Sales Discounts Taken.   Contra account to the Sales account. Used to record the cash discounts deducted by credit customers for payment of an invoice within the discount period.

Sales Returns and Allowances.   Contra account to the Sales account. Used to record the selling price of goods returned by customers or allowances (reductions in the sales price) made to customers because of dissatisfaction with the goods.

Selling Expenses.   Section on a classified income statement. Includes operating expenses directly related or allocated to the sales activities of a company.

Transportation-In.   Account used to record the freight charges incurred for shipment of goods purchased *from* suppliers. Also referred to as *Freight-In*.

Transportation-Out.   Selling expense. Account used to record the freight charges incurred for shipments of merchandise sold *to* customers. Also referred to as *Freight-Out*.

Working Capital.   Current assets minus current liabilities. Indicator of short-run liquidity of a company.

Questions

QUESTION 5-1   What is a merchandising company? Distinguish between a retailer and a wholesaler.

QUESTION 5-2   List and define the components of net sales.

QUESTION 5-3   Give and explain the debit and credit rules for recording sales returns and allowances and sales discounts taken.

QUESTION 5-4   What is the difference between a sales return and a sales allowance?

QUESTION 5-5   What is a cash discount? A discount period? Explain the meaning of the terms 2/10, n/30, and n/15/EOM.

QUESTION 5-6   Distinguish between a perpetual and a periodic inventory system. Which is more useful?

QUESTION 5-7   For a periodic inventory system give the equations for (1) cost of goods available for sale and (2) cost of goods sold.

QUESTION 5-8   List and define the components of net purchases.

QUESTION 5-9   Give and explain the debit and credit rules for recording purchases returns and allowances and purchases discounts taken.

QUESTION 5-10   What is the difference between transportation-in and transportation-out? Where is each reported on the income statement?

QUESTION 5-11   What are classified financial statements?

QUESTION 5-12   List the sections of a classified income statement for a merchandising company (sole proprietorship). What items are included in each section? Assume the use of a periodic inventory system.

QUESTION 5-13   How does the lower portion of the income statement for a corporation differ from that of a sole proprietorship? Where are income taxes payable reported in the classified financial statements of a corporation?

QUESTION 5-14   List the major sections of assets and liabilities in a classified balance sheet. What items are included in each section?

QUESTION 5-15   What are the major items included in current assets? Current liabilities? What is working capital? How is the current ratio computed?

QUESTION 5-16   How is the owners' equity of a (a) sole proprietorship, (b) partnership, and (c) corporation shown on a balance sheet?

QUESTION 5-17   For a corporation define the following terms: (a) earnings per share, (b) contributed capital, (c) capital stock, (d) retained earnings, and (e) dividends.

QUESTION 5-18   Discuss how the amounts of the beginning and ending inventory are entered on a worksheet.

Exercises

EXERCISE 5-1   **Sales and Sales Returns.**   On April 6 Piper Car Shop sold $582 of merchandise to a customer. On April 8 the customer returned $76 of the merchandise purchased on April 6 because it was defective.

REQUIRED   1. Prepare the journal entries to record this information assuming:
   (a) The merchandise was sold for cash.
   (b) The merchandise was sold on account.

2. What source documents would be used to record each transaction?

EXERCISE 5-2   **Sales Discounts.**   On June 4 the Shearson Shelving Company sold $1,500 of merchandise on account to a customer, with terms of 3/10, n/30.

REQUIRED   Prepare journal entries to record the sale and later payment assuming:

1. The customer remits payment on June 13.

2. The customer remits payment on June 30.

EXERCISE 5-3 **Sales Returns and Discounts.** On May 8 Hernandez Camera Store sold $1,200 of merchandise on account to a customer, with terms of 2/10, n/30. On May 12 the customer returned $200 of the merchandise.

REQUIRED

1. Prepare journal entries to record the sale, return, and collection assuming:
   (a) The customer remits payment on May 17.
   (b) The customer remits payment on May 29.

2. What source documents would be used to record each transaction?

EXERCISE 5-4 **Purchases and Purchases Allowances.** On July 1 the Nikko Company purchased merchandise costing $14,000. Upon inspection of the merchandise some of it was found to be of inferior quality. Instead of returning the merchandise to the supplier the Nikko Company was granted an allowance of $1,700, and it planned to sell the merchandise at its annual "sidewalk sale." The Nikko Company uses a periodic inventory system.

REQUIRED

1. Prepare journal entries to record this information assuming:
   (a) The merchandise was purchased for cash.
   (b) The merchandise was purchased on account.

2. What source documents would be used to record each transaction?

EXERCISE 5-5 **Purchase Discounts.** On September 2 the Morgan Furnace Company purchased $8,000 of merchandise from a supplier on account, with terms 4/10, n/30. The Morgan Furnace Company uses a periodic inventory system.

REQUIRED Prepare journal entries to record this information assuming:

1. The Morgan Furnace Company remits payment on September 12.

2. The Morgan Furnace Company remits payment on September 30.

EXERCISE 5-6 **Purchases Returns and Discounts.** On June 4 the Klein Balloon Company purchased $3,000 of merchandise on account, with terms of 2/10, n/30. On June 6 Klein returned $300 of the merchandise to the supplier. The Klein Balloon Company uses a periodic inventory system.

REQUIRED

1. Prepare journal entries to record the purchase, return, and payment assuming:
   (a) The Klein Balloon Company remits payment on June 12.
   (b) The Klein Balloon Company remits payment on June 25.

2. What source documents would be used to record each transaction?

EXERCISE 5-7 **Cost of Goods Sold.** You are given the following information:

Ending inventory	$15,000
Purchases	62,000
Transportation-in	4,000
Beginning inventory	16,000
Sales returns and allowances	5,000

REQUIRED Compute the cost of goods sold.

EXERCISE 5-8   **Cost of Goods Sold.** The following data are available for the Arnhold Horn Company for the year:

Beginning inventory	$ 43,000
Ending inventory	50,000
Purchases	102,000
Purchases returns and allowances	4,000
Purchases discounts taken	500
Transportation-in	5,000

REQUIRED   Prepare a schedule that computes the cost of goods sold for the year.

EXERCISE 5-9   **Perpetual Inventory System.** On July 1 Drexel's Appliance purchased $5,000 of goods for resale. On July 15 it sold $2,600 of these goods to customers at a selling price of $4,000. The company uses the perpetual inventory system and all transactions are for cash.

REQUIRED   Prepare journal entries to record this information.

EXERCISE 5-10   **Closing Entries.** The following are various accounts related to the income statement and owner's equity of the Lynn Company (a sole proprietorship) for the current year.

Beginning inventory	$ 25,000
P. Lynn, withdrawals	30,000
Salaries expense	31,400
Transportation-in	8,100
Delivery expense	9,300
Utilities expense	14,700
Sales	200,400
Depreciation expense	5,600
Purchases	74,900
Sales returns and allowances	10,900
Ending inventory	24,900
Purchases returns and allowances	6,300

REQUIRED   From the information given, prepare the December 31 closing entries.

EXERCISE 5-11   **Income Statement.** The following are items that appeared in the income statement of the Harburg Hobby Shop for the month ended October 31, 1991. The company is a sole proprietorship and uses the periodic inventory system.

Beginning inventory	?
Sales	$93,000
Purchases	42,000
Purchases returns and allowances	1,500
Ending inventory	10,000
Cost of goods sold	53,000
Sales returns	5,000
Selling expenses	7,000
General and administrative expenses	?
Transportation-in	500
Net income	16,000

REQUIRED From the information given determine the amounts of the beginning inventory and general and administrative expenses. (Hint: Preparation of an income statement will help you determine the answers.)

EXERCISE 5-12 **Classified Income Statement.** The following are selected accounts and account balances of Foile's Music Store for the year ended December 31, 1991. The company is a sole proprietorship, uses the periodic inventory system, and has made all necessary adjusting entries.

Beginning inventory	$ 7,300
Depreciation expense: office equipment	1,600
Ending inventory	5,200
Interest revenue	725
Interest expense	250
Purchases	58,000
Purchases returns and allowances	2,000
Sales	98,000
Sales returns and allowances	2,900
Transportation-in	1,300
Office supplies expense	600
Depreciation expense: store equipment	2,400
Office salaries expense	4,000
Sales salaries expense	8,200
Advertising expense	360
Rent expense	1,800

Of the rent expense, 5/6 is applicable to the store and 1/6 is applicable to the office.

REQUIRED Prepare, in good form, a classified income statement for Foile's Music Store for the year ended December 31, 1991.

EXERCISE 5-13 **Classifying Accounts.** At the end of 1991 the Jaffray Juke Box Company showed the following accounts on its post-closing trial balance:

Accounts payable
Accounts receivable
Buildings and equipment
Accumulated depreciation: buildings and equipment
Cash
Marketable securities
Inventory
Prepaid insurance
Notes payable (due 12/31/1993)
Government bonds (due 12/31/1994)
Salaries payable
Unearned rent
P. Jaffray, capital

REQUIRED Using the common classifications presented in the chapter prepare a classified balance sheet (report form) for the Jaffray Juke Box Company on December 31, 1991. Use XXX's for dollar amounts.

EXERCISE 5-14 **Worksheet.** The trial balance of the Becker Company for the year ended December 31, 1991, is shown on the following partially completed worksheet.

	BECKER COMPANY Worksheet For Year Ended December 31, 1991									
	Trial Balance		Adjustments		Adjusted Trial Balance		Income Statement		Balance Sheet	
Account Titles	Debit	Credit	Debit	Credit	Debit	Credit	Debit	Credit	Debit	Credit
Cash	2,100									
Accounts receivable	4,000									
Inventory, 1/1/1991	6,800									
Prepaid rent	3,600									
Equipment	30,000									
Accumulated depreciation		12,000								
Accounts payable		3,100								
E. Becker, capital		24,400								
E. Becker, withdrawals	1,000									
Sales		45,000								
Purchases	22,400									
Salaries expense	7,100									
Utilities expense	2,900									
Advertising expense	4,600									
Totals	84,500	84,500								

Additional Information:

(a) The equipment is being depreciated on a straight-line basis over a 15-year life, with no residual value.

(b) On January 1, 1991, the company had paid 2 years rent in advance at $150 per month.

(c) The December 31, 1991, inventory is $10,000.

REQUIRED   Complete the worksheet.

EXERCISE 5-15   **Corporation's Net Income.**   For the year ended December 31, 1991, the Newhard Corporation had operating income of $32,000 and other revenues of $2,800. The company is subject to a 40% income tax rate and currently has 10,000 shares of capital stock held by stockholders.

REQUIRED   1. Prepare the journal entry on December 31, 1991, to record the Newhard Corporation's 1991 income taxes.

2. Prepare a partial 1991 income statement for the Newhard Corporation, starting with operating income.

EXERCISE 5-16   **Stockholders' Equity.**   On January 1, 1991, the ACE Corporation showed the following account balances:

Capital stock $100,000
Retained earnings 59,700

During 1991, the following events occurred:

(a) The company issued $30,000 of additional capital stock.

(b) Net income for the year was $39,000.

(c) Dividends in the amount of $12,000 were paid to stockholders.

REQUIRED Prepare the stockholders' equity section of the ACE Corporation's balance sheet on December 31, 1991. (Hint: The beginning balance of capital stock and retained earnings must be changed for the events occurring during the year.)

EXERCISE 5-17 **Corporation's Closing Entries.**   The Erin Corporation shows the following account balances at the end of 1991, prior to preparing closing entries:

Operating expenses	$21,000
Dividends	5,000
Sales	70,000
Income tax expense	8,000
Retained earnings	71,000
Cost of goods sold	29,000
Capital stock	42,000

REQUIRED Prepare the December 31, 1991, closing entries for the Erin Corporation. Assume the corporation uses a perpetual inventory system.

Problems

Part A

PROBLEM 5-1A **Journal Entries.**   Morg Building Supplies sells building supplies and small tools to retail customers. It entered into the following transactions (the company uses the periodic inventory system) during September:

Date	Transaction
Sept. 1	Purchased $2,000 of building supplies on account from the Doe Company, with terms 2/10, n/30.
2	Returned $150 of defective building supplies purchased on September 1 from the Doe Company for credit.
5	Sold $800 of small tools to customers for cash.
6	Purchased $350 of small tools for cash.
6	Granted $70 allowance to customer for minor defects found in small tools sold on September 5.
10	Paid balance due to Doe Company for purchase of September 1 and related transaction.
21	Sold $1,500 of building supplies on account to R. Bailey, with terms 1/10, n/30.
30	Received balance due from R. Bailey for building supplies purchased on September 21.

REQUIRED 1. Prepare the necessary journal entries to record these transactions.

2. What were the net sales for the month?

3. What were the net purchases for the month?

PROBLEM 5-2A **Journal Entries.** The Steed Art Supplies Company sells various art supplies to local artists. It entered into the following transactions during the month of August (the company uses the periodic inventory system):

Date	Transaction
Aug. 1	Purchased $1,000 of art supplies for cash.
4	Sold $2,200 of art supplies on account to P. Tarlet, with terms n/15. The Steed Art Supplies Company agreed to pay all shipping charges.
4	Paid freight charges incurred in the shipping of merchandise sold to P. Tarlet, $80.
6	Purchased $5,000 of art supplies on account from the Rony Company, with terms n/20. The Steed Art Supplies Company agreed to pay all freight charges.
6	Paid freight charges related to merchandise purchased from the Rony Company, $150.
10	Returned, for credit, $300 of defective merchandise purchased on August 6 from the Rony Company.
12	Sold $450 of art supplies to customers for cash.
13	Granted $60 allowance to customer for damaged merchandise sold on August 12.
15	Received balance due from P. Tarlet for merchandise sold on account on August 4.
25	Paid balance due to the Rony Company for purchase on August 6.

REQUIRED Prepare the necessary journal entries to record these transactions.

PROBLEM 5-3A **Income Statement Calculations.** The income statement information, for 1991 and 1992, of the Weeden Furniture Company is as follows:

	1991	1992
Beginning inventory	$ 1	$ 4
Sales	200,000	5
Purchases	120,000	130,000
Purchases returns and allowances	5,000	4,000
Ending inventory	52,000	6
Sales returns and allowances	3,000	17,000
Gross profit *NS− CGS*	2	95,000
Cost of goods sold	103,000	100,000
Operating expenses	50,000	7
Transportation-in	1,000	6,000
Net income	3	66,000

REQUIRED Fill in the blanks numbered 1 through 7. All the necessary information is listed. (Hint: It is not necessary to do your answers in numerical order.)

PROBLEM 5-4A **Income Statement and Closing Entries.** The adjusted trial balance of the Werthiem Carpet Company on December 31, 1991, is as follows (the company uses the periodic inventory system):

Account Titles	Debits	Credits
Cash	$ 6,400	
Accounts receivable	9,700	
Inventory (1/1/1991)	16,500	
Property and equipment	40,000	
Accumulated depreciation		$ 15,000
Accounts payable		13,900
T. Werthiem, capital		45,000
T. Werthiem, withdrawals	8,800	
Sales		70,000
Sales returns and allowances	3,000	
Purchases	41,500	
Purchases returns and allowances		2,500
Transportation-in	2,600	
Advertising expense	5,000	
Salaries expense	7,000	
Telephone expense	940	
Utilities expense	960	
Depreciation expense	4,000	
Totals	$146,400	$146,400

The inventory on December 31, 1991, amounted to $24,000.

REQUIRED
1. Prepare an income statement for the year ended December 31, 1991 (do *not* separate the operating expenses section into two parts).

2. Prepare closing entries on December 31, 1991.

PROBLEM 5-5A **Classified Income Statement.** The December 31, 1991, adjusted trial balance and other accounting records of Lyon's Hardware showed the following items (the company is a sole proprietorship and uses the periodic inventory system):

Advertising expense	$ 4,300
Beginning inventory	?
Depreciation expense: store equipment	1,600
Depreciation expense: building (store)	3,700
Depreciation expense: office equipment	2,300
Depreciation expense: building (office)	1,100
Ending inventory	10,000
Interest revenue	1,700
Interest expense	900
Insurance expense	350
Sales returns and allowances	4,020
Freight-out	1,400
Sales	108,000
Cost of goods sold	63,900
Office supplies expense	480
Sales discounts taken	2,040
Purchases	52,000
Store supplies expense	800

Sales salaries expense	5% of sales
Freight-in	5,300
Office salaries expense	2,600
Purchases returns and allowances	600
Utilities expense (store)	1,500
Utilities expense (office)	400

REQUIRED

1. Prepare, in good form, a classified income statement for Lyon's Hardware for the year ended December 31, 1991 (insert the correct amount for the beginning inventory).

2. Compute the profit margin for 1991. If the profit margin for 1990 was 10.5%, what can be said about the 1991 results?

PROBLEM 5-6A **Classified Balance Sheet.** The following accounts and account balances appeared in the accounting records of the Merkin Office Equipment Company on December 31, 1991:

Accounts receivable	$ 3,900
Accounts payable	2,900
Building	30,000
Cash	1,400
Delivery equipment	12,000
Inventory (12/31/1991)	7,500
Accumulated depreciation: delivery equipment	2,000
L. Merkin, capital	34,700
Mortgage payable	29,000
Marketable securities	2,000
Accumulated depreciation: office equipment	1,600
Notes payable (due 10/1/1992)	10,000
Office supplies	2,300
Land	6,000
Notes receivable (due 12/31/1993)	7,000
Accumulated depreciation: building	6,000
Office equipment	8,000
Prepaid insurance	1,700
Notes payable (due 12/31/1993)	11,000
Interest payable (10/1/1992)	1,000
Unearned revenue	3,000
Government bonds (due 12/31/1998)	20,000
Salaries payable	600

All necessary adjustments have been made.

REQUIRED

1. Prepare, in good form, a classified balance sheet (report form) on December 31, 1991.

2. The Merkin Office Equipment Company is applying for a short-term loan at a local bank. If you were the banker would you grant a loan to the company? Explain your decision. (Hint: Look at such items as the current ratio and working capital of the company.)

PROBLEM 5-7A **Worksheet and Financial Statements.** The Bulse Clothing Company, a retail clothing store, prepared the following partially completed worksheet for the year ended December 31, 1991:

	BULSE CLOTHING COMPANY Worksheet For Year Ended December 31, 1991									
	Trial Balance		Adjustments		Adjusted Trial Balance		Income Statement		Balance Sheet	
Account Titles	Debit	Credit	Debit	Credit	Debit	Credit	Debit	Credit	Debit	Credit
Cash	3,000									
Accounts receivable	5,000									
Inventory (1/1/1991)	8,000									
Store supplies	550									
Prepaid insurance	1,000									
Property and equipment	30,000									
Accumulated depreciation		3,000								
Accounts payable		1,160								
H. Bulse, capital		42,000								
H. Bulse, withdrawals	8,500									
Sales		79,000								
Sales returns and allowances	3,650									
Purchases	48,000									
Purchases returns and allowances		1,000								
Transportation-in	2,600									
Salaries expense	13,700									
Advertising expense	960									
Utilities expense	840									
Telephone expense	360									
Totals	126,160	126,160								

Additional Information:

(a) The property and equipment is being depreciated using the straight-line method with an estimated life of 15 years and no residual value.

(b) Store supplies on hand at December 31, 1991, totaled $250.

(c) Prepaid insurance expired during the year in the amount of $600.

(d) Inventory on December 31, 1991, totaled $15,000.

REQUIRED

1. Complete the worksheet.

2. Prepare an income statement for the year ended December 31, 1991 (do *not* separate the operating expenses section into two parts).

3. Prepare a statement of changes in owner's equity for the year ended December 31, 1991.

4. Prepare a December 31, 1991 balance sheet (report form).

5. Compute the return on total assets for 1991. If the return on total assets for 1990 was 25.3%, what can be said about the 1991 results?

PROBLEM 5-8A **Corporation.** The Finestein Corporation showed the following balances on January 1, 1991:

Capital stock (5,000 shares)	$50,000
Retained earnings	$64,000

On January 2, 1991, the company issued 1,000 shares of capital stock for $10,000. For the year ended December 31, 1991, the company had sales revenues of $102,000, cost of goods sold of $48,000, operating expenses of $17,000, and other revenues of $3,000. In addition, the company paid dividends of $6,000 on December 31. The Finestein Corporation is subject to a 40% income tax rate and uses a perpetual inventory system.

REQUIRED 1. Prepare the journal entry on December 31, 1991, to record the Finestein Corporation's 1991 income taxes.

2. Prepare an income statement for the year ended December 31, 1991. Include earnings per share information based on the total capital stock for 1991.

3. Prepare the stockholders' equity section of the December 31, 1991, balance sheet. (Hint: The beginning balances of capital stock and retained earnings must be changed for the events occurring during the year.)

4. Prepare the December 31, 1991, closing entries.

Problems

Part B

PROBLEM 5-1B **Journal Entries.** Nomura Sales, a medical supplies wholesaler, entered into the following transactions (the company uses the periodic inventory system):

Date	Transaction
Aug. 1	Purchased $5,300 of medical supplies on account from the Nead Company, with terms 3/10, n/30.
3	Returned $200 of defective medical supplies purchased on August 1 from the Nead Company for credit.
5	Sold $2,000 of medical supplies on account to P & H Drugs, with terms 2/10, n/30.
8	Granted $300 credit to P & H Drugs for return of medical supplies purchased on August 5.
9	Purchased $1,000 of medical supplies for cash.
10	Paid balance due to the Nead Company for purchase of August 1 and related transaction.
15	Received balance due from P & H Drugs for medical supplies purchased on August 5.
30	Sold $800 of merchandise to customers for cash.

REQUIRED   *1.* Prepare the necessary journal entries to record these transactions.

2. What were the net sales for the month?

3. What were the net purchases for the month?

PROBLEM 5-2B   **Journal Entries.**   The Kerem Heater Company sells portable heaters and related equipment. The company entered into the following transactions during the month of July (the company uses the periodic inventory system):

Date	Transaction
July 1	Sold $480 of heaters for cash.
3	Purchased $1,900 of heater equipment for cash from the Jokem Supply Company.
5	Received $250 cash allowance from the Jokem Supply Company for defective merchandise purchased on July 3.
6	Sold $1,400 of heater equipment on account to Q. Reemy with terms n/10. The Kerem Heater Company agreed to pay all transportation charges.
6	Paid $60 in transportation charges to ship merchandise sold to Q. Reemy.
8	Q. Reemy returned $90 of defective merchandise sold on July 6 for credit.
12	Purchased $1,500 of heaters on account from Duwell Supplies, with terms n/15. The Kerem Heater Company agreed to pay all transportation charges.
12	Paid transportation charges related to merchandise purchased from Duwell Supplies, $100.
16	Received balance due from Q. Reemy for merchandise sold on July 6.
25	Paid balance due to Duwell Supplies for merchandise purchased on July 12.

REQUIRED   Prepare the necessary journal entries to record these transactions.

PROBLEM 5-3B   **Income Statement Calculations.**   The income statement information of the Lernette Sauna Company for 1991 and 1992 is as follows:

	1991	1992
Ending inventory	$ 75,000	$ 4
Sales	299,000	315,000
Freight-in	1,500	9,000
Sales returns and allowances	4,500	5
Purchases returns and allowances	7,500	6,000
Beginning inventory	76,000	6
Operating expenses	1	46,000
Purchases	2	195,000
Gross profit	128,500	142,500
Net income	59,000	7
Cost of goods sold	3	152,000

REQUIRED   Fill in the blanks numbered 1 through 7. All the necessary information is listed. (Hint: It is not necessary to do your answers in numerical order.)

PROBLEM 5-4B   **Income Statement and Closing Entries.**   The adjusted trial balance of the Hyphon Wallpaper Company on December 31, 1991, is as follows (the company uses the periodic inventory system):

Account Titles	Debits	Credits
Cash	$ 8,800	
Accounts receivable	12,125	
Inventory (1/1/1991)	31,230	
Property and equipment	45,000	
Accumulated depreciation		$ 17,000
Accounts payable		17,375
T. Hyphon, capital		56,250
T. Hyphon, withdrawals	12,000	
Sales		94,820
Sales returns and allowances	3,750	
Purchases	49,900	
Purchases returns and allowances		3,125
Freight-in	3,250	
Advertising expense	4,140	
Salaries expense	10,000	
Telephone expense	1,175	
Utilities expense	2,200	
Depreciation expense	5,000	
Totals	$188,570	$188,570

The inventory on December 31, 1991, amounted to $29,745.

REQUIRED   1. Prepare an income statement for the year ended December 31, 1991. (Do *not* separate the operating expenses section into two parts.)

2. Prepare closing entries on December 31, 1991.

PROBLEM 5-5B   **Classified Income Statement.**   The December 31, 1991, adjusted trial balance and other accounting records of the Oppenel Bowling Supply Company showed the following items (the company is a sole proprietorship and uses the periodic inventory system):

Purchases returns and allowances	$ 4,400
Office salaries expense	5,200
Transportation-in	5,600
Sales salaries expense	10% of sales
Store supplies expense	900
Purchases	51,000
Sales discounts taken	2,000
Office supplies expense	500
Cost of goods sold	50,100
Sales	87,000
Transportation-out	1,600
Advertising expense	4,800
Beginning inventory	16,300
Depreciation expense: store equipment	4,100
Depreciation expense: building (store)	2,900
Depreciation expense: office equipment	800
Depreciation expense: building (office)	1,200

Ending inventory	?
Interest revenue	2,260
Interest expense	1,060
Insurance expense	700
Sales returns and allowances	3,700
Utilities expense (store)	1,300
Utilities expense (office)	600

REQUIRED

1. Prepare, in good form, a classified income statement for the year ended December 31, 1991. Insert the correct amount for the ending inventory.

2. Compute the profit margin for 1991. If the profit margin for 1990 was 4.6%, what can be said about the 1991 results?

PROBLEM 5-6B **Classified Balance Sheet.** The following accounts and account balances appeared in the accounting records of the Rigons Incinerators Company on December 31, 1991:

Salaries payable	$ 1,100
Accounts receivable	11,300
Government bonds (due 12/31/1995)	30,000
Accounts payable	7,700
Unearned revenue	1,000
Building	45,000
Interest payable (due 9/1/1992)	200
Cash	6,100
Notes payable (due 12/31/1993)	15,000
Store equipment	18,000
Prepaid insurance	900
Office equipment	12,000
Inventory (12/31/1991)	13,200
Accumulated depreciation: store equipment	3,000
Accumulated depreciation: building	9,000
Notes receivable (due 12/31/1994)	8,000
P. Rigons, capital	84,300
Land	4,000
Mortgage payable	22,500
Office and store supplies	2,700
Marketable securities	2,000
Notes payable (due 9/1/1992)	7,000
Accumulated depreciation: office equipment	2,400

All necessary adjustments have been made.

REQUIRED

1. Prepare a classified balance sheet (report form) on December 31, 1991.

2. The Rigons Incinerators Company is applying for a $2,000 short-term loan at a local bank. If you were the banker would you grant a loan to the company? Explain. (Hint: Look at such items as the company's current ratio and working capital.)

PROBLEM 5-7B **Worksheet and Financial Statements.** The Amary Sporting Goods Company prepared the following partially completed worksheet for the year ended December 31, 1991:

AMARY SPORTING GOODS COMPANY
Worksheet
For Year Ended December 31, 1991

Account Titles	Trial Balance Debit	Trial Balance Credit	Adjustments Debit	Adjustments Credit	Adjusted Trial Balance Debit	Adjusted Trial Balance Credit	Income Statement Debit	Income Statement Credit	Balance Sheet Debit	Balance Sheet Credit
Cash	4,200									
Accounts receivable	6,900									
Inventory (1/1/1991)	15,200									
Supplies	870									
Prepaid insurance	1,400									
Property and equipment	42,000									
Accumulated depreciation		4,200								
Accounts payable		6,200								
B. Amary, capital		56,000								
B. Amary, withdrawals	7,700									
Sales		108,624								
Sales returns and allowances	5,110									
Purchases	68,000									
Purchases returns and allowances		1,400								
Transportation-in	3,640									
Salaries expense	18,380									
Advertising expense	1,344									
Utilities expense	1,176									
Telephone expense	504									
Totals	176,424	176,424								

Additional Information:

(a) The property and equipment is being depreciated using the straight-line method with an estimated life of 20 years and no residual value.

(b) Supplies on hand at December 31, 1991, totaled $250.

(c) Prepaid insurance expired during the year in the amount of $350.

(d) Inventory on December 31, 1991, totaled $18,500.

REQUIRED

1. Complete the worksheet.

2. Prepare an income statement for the year ended December 31, 1991. (Do *not* separate the operating expenses section into two parts.)

3. Prepare a statement of changes in owner's equity for the year ended December 31, 1991.

4. Prepare a December 31, 1991, balance sheet (report form).

5. Compute the return on total assets for 1991. If the return on total assets for 1990 was 20.6%, what can be said about the 1991 results?

PROBLEM 5-8B   **Corporation.**   The following are the various accounts related to the income statement and stockholders' equity of the Garrett Corporation at the end of 1991, prior to preparing closing entries. The corporation uses a perpetual inventory system.

Sales	$80,000
Capital stock (4,000 shares)	40,000
Operating expenses	17,000
Dividends	4,000
Cost of goods sold	35,000
Retained earnings	57,000
Income tax expense	10,000

REQUIRED

1. Prepare an income statement for the year ended December 31, 1991.

2. Prepare the stockholders' equity section of the December 31, 1991, balance sheet. (Hint: The balance of retained earnings must be changed for the events occurring during the year.)

3. Prepare the December 31, 1991, closing entries.

Decision Cases

DECISION CASE 5-1   **Financial Statements from Incomplete Records.** On January 1, 1991, Paula Randolph opened a boutique called P.R.'s Boutique. At that time she invested $30,000 cash in the business. With this cash the business immediately purchased $8,000 of inventory and $16,000 of store equipment, and paid two years rent in advance for store space. Paula estimated the store equipment would last for 8 years and after that it would be worthless.

During the year the boutique appeared to operate successfully. Paula did not know anything about accounting, although she did keep an accurate checkbook. Her checkbook showed the following summarized items on December 31, 1991:

Payment of 2 years rent for store space	$ 2,400
Receipts from cash sales	38,000
Payments for purchases of merchandise	15,000
Payments for operating expenses	12,000
Withdrawals of cash for personal use	11,000

Paula has asked for your assistance. She says, "The ending cash balance in the company checkbook is $3,600. Since the beginning cash balance was $30,000, the company seems to have had a net loss of $26,400. Something must be wrong. I am sure the company did better than that. Please find out what the company's earnings were for 1991 and its financial position at the end of 1991."

You agree to help Paula. She has just finished "taking inventory" and indicates the cost of the ending inventory is $8,000. She has kept copies of invoices made out to customers who purchased merchandise on account. These uncollected invoices total $12,000. Paula also has a file of unpaid invoices of suppliers. These unpaid invoices add up to $8,000. Just as you begin your calculations, Paula says, "Oh yes, I also owe my employees $700 of salaries that they have earned this week."

REQUIRED   Prepare a 1991 income statement and a December 31, 1991, balance sheet for P.R.'s Boutique. Include explanations for all amounts shown.

DECISION CASE 5-2   **Corrections to Balance Sheet.** The bookkeeper of the Washet Company prepared the following balance sheet as of December 31, 1991:

```
                          WASHET COMPANY
                           Balance Sheet
                   For Year Ended December 31, 1991

Working capital ................  $ 27,100   Noncurrent liabilities ............  $ 25,400
Other assets ....................   117,900   Owner's equity ................   119,600
       Total .........................  $145,000         Total .........................  $145,000
```

Your analysis of these items reveals the following information (the amounts in parentheses indicate deductions from each item):

(a) Working capital consists of:

Equipment	$ 30,000
Land	10,000
Accounts due to suppliers	(28,000)
Inventory, including office supplies of $3,700	34,700
Salaries owed to employees	(2,600)
Note owed to bank (due December 31, 1993)	(17,000)
	$ 27,100

(b) Other assets include:

Cash	$ 6,000
Prepaid insurance	1,900
Buildings	70,000
Long-term investment in government bonds	30,000
A. Washet, withdrawals	10,000
	$117,900

(c) Noncurrent liabilities consist of:

Mortgage payable	$ 33,000
Accumulated depreciation: equipment	16,000
Accounts due from customers	(16,600)
Notes receivable (due December 31, 1994)	(7,000)
	$ 25,400

(d) Owner's equity includes:

A. Washet, capital	$104,900
Accumulated depreciation: buildings	24,000
Securities held as a temporary investment	(11,000)
Interest payable (due July 1, 1992)	1,700
	$119,600

REQUIRED Based on your analysis prepare a properly classified December 31, 1991, balance sheet (report form) for the Washet Company.

DECISION CASE 5-3 **Inaccurate Income Statement.** Jay Ryan owns "Jay's Skate Board Shop," which he opened on April 1, 1991. At that time Jay invested $20,000 cash into the company. With this money, the shop immediately purchased store equipment for $8,000. Jay estimated that this equipment would last 10 years and would have no value after that time. The shop also purchased $6,000 of inventory for cash and paid $1,800 for one year of store rent in advance. During the year the shop was open for business 6 days a week. Over the 9-month period in 1991, Jay withdrew $1,000 per month for his personal expenses. He employed one part-time helper and paid the shop's bills by company check. For most of the year the shop made only cash sales, and paid for purchases before they were shipped from its supplier. However, near the end of the year the shop began to sell items on credit to a few "responsible customers." Jay kept a small notebook of the amounts of these credit sales. They totaled $3,000 at the end of 1991, and none had been collected yet. Because the shop was such a good customer, its suppliers allowed the shop to purchase $4,000 of inventory on credit near the end of 1991. These purchases had not yet been paid at the end of 1991.

At the end of 1991 Jay wanted to know how well the shop was doing, so he prepared the following "income statement."

INCOME STATEMENT FOR 1991

Cash receipts:		
Cash sales		$40,000
Cash payments:		
Salary to part-time help	$ 3,200	
Cash purchases	14,000	
Rent expense	1,800	
Utilities expense	1,300	
Withdrawals	9,000	(29,300)
Net income		$10,700

He did not feel comfortable with this information and came to you, a small business consultant, for help. He said, "The shop shows net income of $10,700 but there is $16,700 in the company's checking account, so cash went down by $3,300. I do not understand. I just 'took inventory' and it amounts to $5,000 (including the credit purchases), but the shop owes $400 of salary to my employee. I want to know how much the shop earned in 1991 and where the shop stands financially at the end of 1991. Please prepare a report for me to answer these questions."

REQUIRED   Prepare a report for Jay that includes a 1991 income statement and a December 31, 1991 balance sheet. Include explanations for all amounts shown.

DECISION CASE 5-4   **Forecasted Financial Statements.**   Ava Mendleson operates a small fabric shop. She has been earning a satisfactory profit, but is short of cash. Following is an accurate but unclassified balance sheet of the store on December 31, 1990.

MENDLESON'S FABRIC SHOP
Balance Sheet
December 31, 1990

Cash		$ 2,500
Store equipment	$ 8,000	
Less: Accumulated depreciation	(1,600)	6,400
Inventory		9,500
Accounts receivable		3,000
Total Assets		$21,400
Accounts payable		$ 4,500
Ava Mendleson, capital		16,900
Total Liabilities and Owner's Equity		$21,400

On January 2, 1991, Ava went to her bank to get a loan for her company. The bank agreed to loan her $5,000 under the following conditions. First, the note payable would be a 10%, 2-year note, so that the company would repay $5,000 plus $1,000 interest on December 31, 1992. Second, she must prepare a "forecasted" classified income statement for 1991 that shows that the company expects to earn a net income of at least $12,000. Finally, she must prepare a "forecasted" classified balance sheet as of December 31, 1991 that shows that the company expects to have cash on hand at that date of at least $10,000 (including the cash from the bank loan).

Ava has never prepared any forecasted financial statements. She understands, however, that they are prepared using the best estimates she can make, based upon the store's previous operations and her future expectations. Ava has come to you for help, having gathered the following information:

1. Sales for 1991 are expected to be $80,000. Of these, half will be cash sales and half will be credit sales. There are no cash discounts. Of the credit sales, 10% will not be collected until 1992. The accounts receivable on December 31, 1990 will be collected in 1991.

2. Purchases for 1991 are expected to be $50,000. All purchases are on credit; there are no cash discounts. Of the purchases, 12% will not be paid until 1992. The accounts payable on December 31, 1990 will be paid in 1991.

3. Sales returns and purchases returns are expected to be insignificant.

4. The company's gross profit percentage has been 40% of gross sales, and this rate is expected in 1991.

5. The store rents store space in a local mall. The rent is $200 per month; the rent for the whole year is due on January 6, 1991.

6. The store equipment has a 10-year estimated life with no residual value.

7. Ava pays her one salesperson a basic salary of $5,000 per year, plus 1% of gross sales. The total salary for 1991 will be paid in cash by the end of the year.

8. Ava expects to withdraw $7,000 during 1991 to cover her personal living expenses.

9. Other operating expenses are expected to be $1,600 in 1991; these will be paid in cash by the end of the year.

You determine that the information Ava has gathered is "reasonable" and includes her best estimates.

REQUIRED

1. Prepare a forecasted classified income statement for 1991. Show supporting calculations.

2. Prepare a forecasted classified balance sheet as of December 31, 1991. Show supporting calculations.

3. Indicate whether the company has met the bank's conditions.

6

Internal Control, Special Journals, and EDP Systems

LEARNING OBJECTIVES

1. Define internal control and identify its subgoals.

2. List and describe the four important factors in good internal control.

3. Describe a subsidiary ledger and list the reasons for its use.

4. Identify the two most common control accounts and state the basic rule for each.

5. State the general principles of good internal control.

6. Define a special journal and list the major journals.

7. Describe the (a) sales journal, (b) purchases journal, (c) cash receipts journal, (d) cash payments journal, and (e) general journal.

8. List the advantages of special journals.

9. Describe a computer and list the hardware components.

10. Define a computer program and software.

11. List the modifications of internal control principles for an EDP system.

APPENDIX

A-1. Solve assigned homework using a personal computer.

I n Chapter 1 we defined an **accounting system as a means by which accounting information is identified, measured, recorded, and retained so that it can be reported in an accounting statement.** We also said that internal control involved procedures to safeguard a company's economic resources and to promote the efficient and effective operation of the accounting system. In Chapters 2 through 5 we introduced a manual accounting system using a general journal, first as it applied to a service company and then as it applied to a merchandising company. We limited our discussion of internal control to the use of source documents as evidence of a company's transactions.

In this chapter we extend our discussion to the assignment of responsibilities, documentation, and routines and procedures needed for sound internal control. Next, we discuss how a company might use special journals in addition to its general journal to make its accounting system more efficient. Then, we briefly look at how a company's accounting system and internal control would be different if it used electronic data processing (EDP) (i.e., a computer) in its operations. Finally, in an appendix we demonstrate how to use a personal computer to operate an EDP system.

Internal Control

The definition of internal control can be expanded slightly from that given in Chapter 1. **Internal control consists of the policies and procedures used to safeguard a company's assets and to ensure that reliable financial statements are the end result of an efficient accounting system.** Safeguarding assets means that a company's assets are protected against loss from unintentional or intentional errors (involving fraud and theft) in processing transactions and handling the assets.

Establishing and maintaining a good system of internal control is the responsibility of the management of a company. Accountants can assist in fulfilling this responsibility. The purpose of this section is to discuss several general principles of good internal control. In later chapters we discuss the aspects of internal control that apply to specific assets or parts of the accounting system.

To meet the goal of safeguarding assets and having an efficient accounting system, there are **four subgoals of internal control:**

1. Define internal control and identify its subgoals.

1. To ensure that transactions are carried out according to management's general and specific policies.
2. To ensure that transactions are recorded as needed so that (a) financial statements are prepared according to generally accepted accounting principles (GAAP) and (b) specified employees are held accountable for the various assets of the company.
3. To ensure that only authorized individuals have access to assets.

4. **To ensure that the accounting records of the company's assets agree with the actual existing assets under the company's control.**[1]

The term *to ensure* does not mean that management always uses internal control procedures to protect each and every asset. Promoting an efficient accounting system and protecting assets costs time and money. The advantages of doing so must be greater than the costs incurred. Management must make sure, *within reason,* that efficiency is promoted and assets are protected. For instance, it is more important to safeguard a personal computer than a box of paperclips even though both are assets.

Because transactions are the basis of a company's operations, they are the main concern of internal control. Transactions not only include exchanges with external parties but also include the use of assets (or services) within a company. Revenue and expense transactions are also included because they involve assets (e.g., sale of items from inventory for cash or accounts receivable, incurrence of an expense by payment of cash). In establishing good internal control, consideration must be given to:

2. List and describe the four important factors in good internal control.

1. Authorizing transactions

2. Executing transactions

3. Recording transactions

4. Maintaining accountability for the resulting assets

These factors are discussed in the following sections.

Authorization for Transactions

The final authority for business transactions is the owner or owners of a company. The owner frequently delegates authority to different managers in the company, however. **Authorization means permission to exchange or use assets for specific purposes under given conditions**. Good internal control must include policies that indicate who can enter into different kinds of transactions and provide guidelines about the price, quantity, timing, and other aspects of each transaction.

For instance, general policies may indicate who is authorized to make sales to customers, who may make purchases of inventory, who may enter into transactions to acquire equipment, buildings, and marketable securities, and who may purchase office supplies. Such policies assign responsibilities for certain transactions to specific employees and help to prevent other employees from making unauthorized purchases or sales. Authorization policies may also be specific and include guidelines for the selling price to each customer, whether some customers are entitled to a cash discount, which customers can make purchases on account, when to reorder inventory, which suppliers to purchase from, and how many alternatives must be considered when a major product is pur-

---

[1]"Communication of Internal Control Structure Related Matters Noted in an Audit," *Statement on Auditing Standards No. 60* (New York: AICPA, 1988), Appendix D, par. 2.

chased. These policies ensure that similar procedures are followed for similar transactions and minimize the chance of an unintentional error (such as giving a trade discount to a customer not entitled to a lower selling price).

Execution of Transactions

The execution of transactions refers to the set of steps needed to complete the exchange of assets or use of assets in the company. A well-established set of steps to be followed for each major type of transaction is important to good internal control. Two common transactions, the sale of merchandise and the purchase of merchandise, are used to illustrate these steps.

Sale of Merchandise. The routine procedures for the sale of merchandise to a customer vary from company to company, depending upon the size and type of company, size of customer, size of order, and so on. A general description of the steps for good internal control can be presented, however. Assume that a wholesaler accepts orders from retailers through the mail. The steps would include accepting the order, assembling, packing and shipment of the inventory, and billing and collection of the sales price.

Acceptance of the order would begin with the receipt of a retailer's order form, a source document, in the mail. Since retailers normally purchase on account, approval would first be obtained from the wholesale company's credit department (a department in the company responsible for checking potential and current customer's *credit ratings* and collecting past due accounts) before proceeding. This credit check helps to avoid the unintentional error of making a credit sale to a customer that has been late in paying its account. Upon credit approval, a sales invoice (illustrated in Chapter 5) indicating the items ordered is prepared by the accounting department. An original invoice and three copies of the invoice are typically prepared and used for internal control, as illustrated in Exhibit 6-1.

Copies 1 and 2 are sent to the inventory department where the ordered items are assembled and packed for shipment. Copy 1 is included in the shipment. Copy 2 is initialed by the employees who assembled and packed the items and is returned to the accounting department. Copy 3 is retained by the accounting department. The accounting department enters the items shipped (based on Copy 2), price, discount terms, and other information on Copy 3 and the original invoice. The original invoice is then mailed as a bill to the retailer and Copy 3 is used to record the sales transaction.

Copies 2 and 3 are kept in the company's records. They indicate that the asset (inventory) has been shipped and identify which employees were responsible for the asset as it went through the company's assembling, packing, and shipping operations. Copy 3 is also used later as a source document for preparing and mailing a monthly statement to the retailer and recording the collection of the retail customer's account. These steps help to ensure that operations are run efficiently, that only authorized individuals have access to the company's assets (inventory and accounts receivable), and that these assets are protected from theft or misplacement throughout the execution of the sale, assembly, shipment, billing, and collection activities.

EXHIBIT 6-1
Flow of Sales Invoice
Copies for Internal
Control

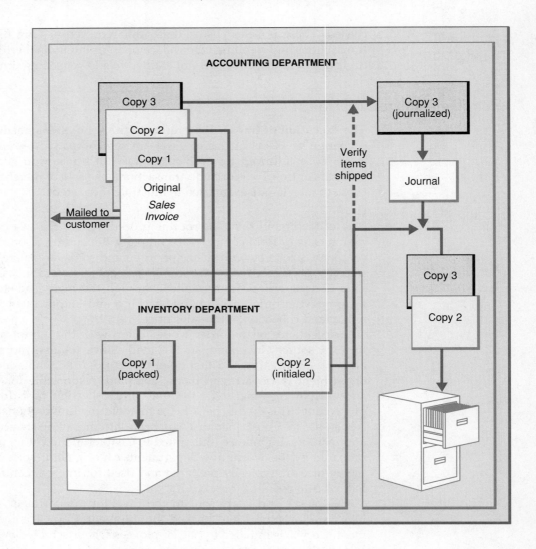

EXHIBIT 6-1
Flow of Sales Invoice Copies for Internal Control

Purchase of Merchandise.   The procedures for purchases of merchandise also vary from company to company. A general description is presented for a retailer purchasing inventory on credit from a wholesaler. The steps include preparing a requisition of the inventory, issuing the purchase order, receiving the inventory, and paying the purchase price.

Processing of the order begins with a purchase requisition. **A purchase requisition is an internal business document requesting that certain items of inventory be purchased.** This document is usually prepared by the manager in charge of the department selling the inventory items. The purchase requisition is sent to the purchasing department, which then prepares a purchase order. **A purchase order is a business document authorizing a supplier to ship the items listed at a specified price.** Exhibit 6-2 shows an example of a purchase order.

EXHIBIT 6-2
Purchase Order

Purchase Order

Order No. 129

Jay Sports Company
1200 East Main Street
Columbia, Missouri

To: Smith Supply Company   Date   5/18/1991
      3000 South James Street   Shipping Instructions   UPS
      Kansas City, Missouri   Authorization: *Al Knox*

Please ship the following items:

Description	Quantity	Price	Total
#472 Tennis racket	10	$20.00	$200.00
# 68 Tennis balls (24 cans per box)	20 boxes	24.00	480.00
#124 Nylon racket covers (12 per box)	2 boxes	18.00	36.00
			$716.00

An original and three copies of the purchase order are usually prepared by the purchasing department. The original purchase order is mailed to the wholesaler, Copy 1 is sent to the receiving department (the department responsible for receiving and unpacking inventory shipped from suppliers), Copy 2 is kept by the purchasing department, and Copy 3 is sent to the accounting department.

The multiple copies of the purchase order are used for internal control as shown in Exhibit 6-3. When the inventory is received by the receiving department from the wholesaler, the quantity and condition are checked. Copy 1 of the purchase order (sometimes called the *receiving report*) is initialed and sent with the inventory to the sales department. An employee in the sales department checks the inventory for quality and style, initials Copy 1 of the purchase order, and sends it to the accounting department. The accounting department notifies the purchasing department that the order is received and collects Copy 2 of the purchase order. Copies 1 and 2 are compared with Copy 3 to verify that the items ordered have been received in the proper condition. By this time the original invoice from the supplier should have been received in the mail. The accounting department checks the invoice against Copy 3 of the purchase order for accuracy and approves (1) the recording of the purchase transaction and (2) the payment of the invoice (less any applicable cash discounts) on the due date.

These steps help to ensure that purchasing activities are efficient, that no unauthorized individual has access to the assets (inventory and cash), and that the company's assets are protected from theft or misplacement throughout all the purchase activities. They also help to ensure that the company's accounting records show the actual existing assets under the company's control. Similar internal control steps for the acquisition and disposal of operating assets such as office equipment and sales equipment are also important for the safeguarding of assets and the proper operation of the accounting system.

EXHIBIT 6-3
Flow of Purchase Order
Copies for Internal
Control

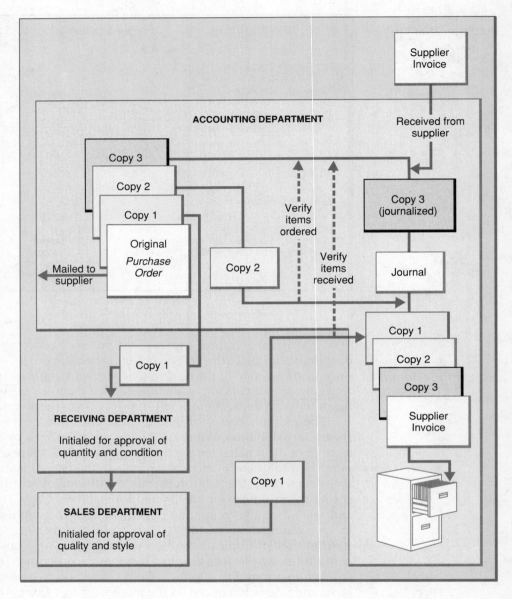

Recording of Transactions

Recording includes journalizing and posting transactions, and keeping up-to-date records of a company's assets. There are several concerns important to internal control: (1) that all executed transactions are recorded in the correct amounts and the correct accounting period, (2) that no unauthorized transactions are recorded, and (3) that the transactions are recorded in the proper accounts. Good internal control procedures for recording transactions are independent of the method of data processing used. Thus these procedures apply equally to manual or electronic data processing. Besides protecting a company's assets, good internal control for recording transactions helps to ensure that the resulting financial statements are prepared according to generally accepted accounting principles.

Three factors, the use of source documents, subsidiary ledgers, and special journals, help in the internal control for recording transactions. The first two factors are discussed next. Special journals are discussed later in the chapter.

Source Documents.   Source documents play an important part in recording transactions. As we have often mentioned in the first five chapters, all recorded transactions must be supported by source documents. Source documents help to ensure that all executed transactions are recorded in the correct amounts, accounts, and accounting period. They also provide evidence that no unauthorized transactions have been recorded.

We have discussed many source documents in previous chapters. These source documents include sales invoices, canceled checks, freight bills, sales returns and allowances credit memos, purchases returns and allowances debit memos, legal notes, and purchase requisitions, to name a few. As a general rule, source documents prepared by *independent* external parties are more useful in internal control than documents prepared internally. Thus an invoice received from another company for inventory delivered is better evidence of an executed transaction than simply a purchase order prepared within the company. Assembling several source documents for a transaction is the best evidence, however. For instance, in our earlier example the wholesaler's invoice combined with the retailer's purchase order provide strong evidence for recording the purchase transaction and the resulting payment for the purchase by the retailer.

Subsidiary Ledgers and Control Accounts.   Recall from Chapter 2 that a company's general ledger includes all the accounts listed in its chart of accounts. As a company increases in size, its general ledger also increases because of the additional accounts needed to record the accounting information. A larger company, for example, is likely to own more and different types of physical assets. In addition, it will have more customer accounts for sales on credit and supplier accounts for purchases on credit.

3. Describe a subsidiary ledger and list the reasons for its use.

In order to (1) reduce the size of the general ledger, (2) minimize errors, (3) improve efficiency in recording transactions, and (4) keep up-to-date records of dealings with charge customers and suppliers, a company sets up subsidiary ledgers. **A subsidiary ledger is a group of similar accounts that are taken out of the general ledger and that show the detail of one specific company activity.** Most companies have separate subsidiary ledgers for accounts receivable and accounts payable. These ledgers enable a company to have better information about the amounts due from customers and the amounts owed to suppliers.

The *accounts receivable* **subsidiary ledger contains the individual accounts of all the company's charge (credit) customers;** that is, all of the individual customer accounts are taken out of the general ledger and are included in the accounts receivable subsidiary ledger. The customer accounts can be listed either alphabetically or numerically in the subsidiary ledger. Whenever a credit sale is made to a customer the increase (debit) in the customer's account is recorded in this subsidiary ledger. When a customer pays its account the decrease (credit) in the customer's account is recorded in this ledger. Thus at all times the balance in each customer's account is known. This information is very helpful in deciding whether or not to extend additional credit to a customer and in determining which customers need to be reminded to pay their bills.

4. Identify the two most common control accounts and state the basic rule for each.

Since the individual customer accounts normally have debit balances (because sales on account are made before collections on the accounts), it follows that the accounts receivable subsidiary ledger has a *total* debit balance. When an accounts receivable subsidiary ledger is used, a single Accounts Receivable account is still kept in the general ledger (to keep the general ledger in balance in accordance with the accounting equation). **The Accounts Receivable account is referred to as a control account because it takes the place of (controls) the individual customer accounts, which have been removed and placed in the subsidiary ledger.** *The debit balance of the Accounts Receivable control account must always be equal to the debit total of the accounts receivable subsidiary ledger on each balance sheet date.* Thus after a company records a sale on account (or collection of an account or a credit sales return or allowance) in its general journal, *two* postings must be made for the receivable. One posting is made to the *control account* in the general ledger and another is made to the *subsidiary ledger.* To illustrate this procedure suppose a $1,000 credit sale was made to James Franklin. The journal entry and postings are shown here. The check mark ($\sqrt{}$) in the general journal indicates the posting has been made in the subsidiary ledger. (In this and following examples as well as the exercises and problems, the accounts in the subsidiary ledgers are listed alphabetically so that no account number is necessary. In more complex accounting systems subsidiary account numbers would be used.) The accounting equation remains in balance because the $1,000 debit to Accounts Receivable is equal to the $1,000 credit to Sales (since the James Franklin customer account is *not* in the general ledger, the $1,000 debit in the subsidiary ledger does not affect the accounting equation). The balance of the control account remains in agreement with the balance of the subsidiary ledger because a $1,000 debit entry was recorded in each.

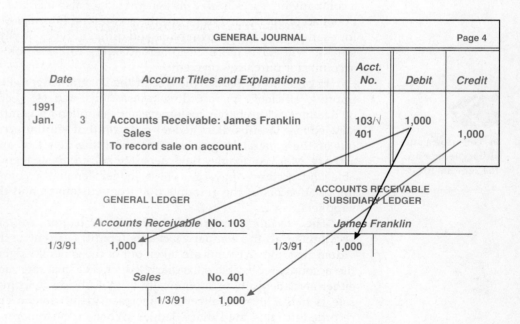

Before preparing a trial balance, at the end of each accounting period a schedule is prepared that lists the balance of each customer account in the accounts receivable subsidiary ledger. These balances are totaled and the total is

EXHIBIT 6-4
Accounts Receivable
Control Account and
Subsidiary Ledger
Totals

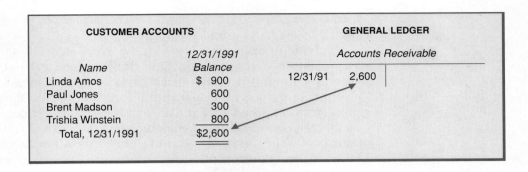

compared with the balance of Accounts Receivable to prove the equality of the control account and subsidiary ledger. Exhibit 6-4 shows a schedule and comparison for a company's accounts receivable.

The *accounts payable* **subsidiary ledger contains the individual accounts of all the company's charge (credit) suppliers** and works in the same manner as an accounts receivable subsidiary ledger. Whenever a purchase on account or a payment of a supplier account is made it is recorded in the individual supplier account in the subsidiary ledger. **An Accounts Payable** *control account* **is kept in the general ledger to control the individual supplier accounts in the subsidiary ledger.** *The credit balance of the Accounts Payable control account must always be equal to the credit total of the accounts payable subsidiary ledger on each balance sheet date.* Thus after recording credit purchases, credit purchases returns and allowances, or payments on account in the general journal, *two* postings must be made for the payable, one to the *control account* and the other to the *subsidiary ledger.* (Note that since the Trale Supply Company account is *not* in the general ledger, the $800 credit in the subsidiary ledger does not affect the accounting equation.)

At the end of the period, before preparing the trial balance a schedule is prepared listing the balance of each supplier account in the subsidiary ledger. The

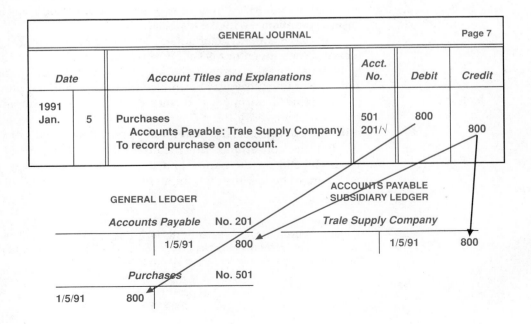

total is compared to the Accounts Payable balance to prove the equality of the control account and subsidiary ledger.

Subsidiary ledgers are also used by many companies for such major items as property and equipment, selling expenses, and general and administrative expenses. Control accounts again replace the individual asset and expense accounts in the general ledger and the accounting procedures are similar to the procedures discussed earlier. For a subsidiary ledger for property and equipment, each piece of physical equipment is listed, along with its cost, acquisition date, book value, residual value, life, and depreciation method. In addition, the individual employee responsible for the control of each piece of physical equipment is usually listed. This procedure is an added feature of internal control because the accounting records report who is accountable for each physical asset of the company.

Subsidiary ledgers are desirable in internal control for recording transactions because they help to ensure that similar transactions are recorded in a similar way in the proper accounts.[2] They also help to minimize errors and improve the efficiency of the accounting system because one person can be trained to, say, record all accounts receivable transactions. Subsidiary ledgers are also helpful in internal control, because up-to-date records are kept of a company's assets and the individuals accountable for the assets. Subsidiary ledgers may be used with or without special journals, as discussed later.

Accountability for Assets

In internal control, **accountability involves keeping track of assets from the time of their acquisition in one transaction until their disposal or use in another transaction.** These procedures ensure that the assets are used for their intended purpose, are not misplaced, are maintained in proper operating condition, and are not stolen. Therefore adequate records must be kept of who is responsible for each asset and periodic checks must be made to ensure that the records agree with the actual assets. Policies must be established concerning which individuals are authorized to have access to assets; periodic checks must be made to ensure compliance with these policies.

We have already mentioned several internal control procedures in this regard. When inventory is sold, for instance, employees in the inventory department must initial a copy of the sales invoice to verify that the correct amount and type of inventory was assembled and shipped. For a purchase, employees in the receiving department and sales department must initial a copy of the purchase order to verify the receipt of the inventory. The property and equipment subsidiary ledger lists the individual responsible for each physical asset.

Policies concerning which individuals are authorized to have access to assets depend on the nature and importance of the assets and how likely the assets are to be lost through unintentional errors or fraud or theft. Because cash

---

[2]For simplicity, in the remainder of the text (except Chapters 8 and 10 dealing with accounts receivable and accounts payable, respectively) when general journal entries are used to illustrate transactions, subsidiary ledger accounts will not be shown.

is very easy and tempting to steal, for instance, very strict policies should be established for its control (these policies are briefly discussed later in the chapter and more fully in Chapter 7). Some items of inventory, such as thin gold necklaces or other jewelry, are also easy to misplace or steal; careful internal control policies for these items (such as always keeping them in locked display cases or drawers) are also important. On the other hand, an inventory of items like wastebaskets or cement blocks needs less restrictive policies of internal control.

The frequency of periodic checks on the agreement of the accounting records with the actual assets also depends on the nature and importance of the assets and the likelihood of loss. A comparison of a company's cash records and its bank account records, for example, is usually made on a monthly basis. Companies on a perpetual inventory system normally take a physical count of their inventory at least once a year. For certain kinds of inventory, such as gold jewelry, this physical count may be made much more often. Checks of operating assets are made at regular intervals, the time depending in part on whether the assets are likely to break down or malfunction if not properly maintained. Comparisons of the accounting records with the actual office desks of a company may be made every several years, whereas checks of the office typewriters and calculators may be made over shorter time periods.

Internal Control Principles

Internal control is concerned with protecting assets from unintentional errors as well as from fraud or theft, which may arise in authorizing, executing, or recording transactions or in controlling the use of the assets. Several principles have been developed that help in promoting good internal control. They are general principles not necessarily relating to a single aspect of internal control and are briefly discussed next.

5. State the general principles of good internal control.

Competent and Responsible Employees. The key to a good system of internal control lies in the employees of the company. Responsibilities must be clearly defined and employees must be technically competent for their assigned tasks and willing to accept responsibility for their performance. It is helpful if they understand the importance of strong internal control procedures and the need to follow these procedures in all cases. Employees must have high integrity because dishonest employees can undermine even the best internal control system. Technical competence, willingness to accept responsibility, and high integrity can be identified through sound personnel hiring programs and can be improved by ongoing employee training programs.

Separation of Duties. An important principle of internal control is that one person should *not* be responsible for both recording transactions involving an asset and for control of that asset. Anyone who has both responsibilities is in a position to make an unintentional error (e.g., misplacing the asset) or an intentional error (e.g., stealing the asset) that is difficult to detect. For instance, an employee who is responsible for both depositing customer checks and recording the receipt of the checks might inadvertently lose a customer's check and fail to record it. Or an employee responsible for authorizing payments for purchases as well as writing checks may prepare a fictitious invoice, write a company check to a fictitious supplier, and cash the check. Assets are better protected by separating the recording duties from the asset control duties, whether for cash, marketable securities, inventory (as discussed earlier), or other assets. The employee responsible for the recording duties serves as a monitor or double check over the employee controlling the asset, thus reducing unintentional errors and also minimizing intentional errors. This procedure helps to prevent theft or fraud unless collusion exists between two or more employees. It is a commonly held belief that two (or more) people acting together are less likely to commit theft or fraud than one person acting alone.

Rotation of Duties.   When practical, duties should be rotated among employees because rotation can uncover unintentional or intentional errors. The knowledge that an employee's duties soon will be performed by another employee is likely, in fact, to encourage the employee to follow established policies and procedures. Employees should also be required to take annual vacations so that their duties will be taken over by another employee for the vacation period. This procedure also helps to uncover errors. Any rotation, of course, must always involve competent employees with technical knowledge of the duties.

Rules for Control of Assets.   In addition to the separation of duties, rules are useful in keeping good internal control over assets. For instance, rules may be established that identify who may use specific physical assets and who has access to an inventory warehouse. Many companies restrict employees from bringing purses, coats, and bags into working areas to discourage theft of company property.

Other rules are helpful in controlling cash. For cash receipts the rule is to deposit all cash receipts daily in the company's bank. This reduces the amount of cash on hand and results in a double record of cash inflows, one in the company's cash records and the other in the bank's records. Another policy involves establishing a maximum cash balance that a company should keep in its checking account. When this balance is exceeded many companies require that the excess cash be invested in short-term marketable securities. This makes efficient use of the excess cash and discourages misuse. Cash payments should be made only by check, using a check-writing machine and accompanied by independent source documents. This discourages unauthorized cash payments. Accounts payable should also be arranged and filed according to due date so that all cash discounts can be taken. Additional internal control procedures for cash receipts and payments are discussed in Chapters 7 and 10.

Well-Designed Source Documents.   Each type of source document used in the company should be properly designed, including preprinting the source documents, having spaces for authorization signatures, and using serial numbers. Invoices, checks, purchase orders, purchases return and allowance debit memos and sales return and allowance credit memos, as well as other frequently used forms, should each be serially numbered when they are printed. In this way all source documents must be accounted for. If a check or invoice is misplaced or stolen, the missing number in the sequence will highlight the discrepancy.

Internal Auditing.   Many companies have an internal auditing staff, which consists of accountants who establish the internal control procedures and who review operations to ensure that these procedures are being followed throughout the organization. This staff is an important element of internal control because improvements can be made on a regular basis to the internal control system. In addition, employees who know that their activities are being monitored are more likely to follow prescribed procedures.

This form of control is also important to the CPA firm that audits the company in order to be able to express an opinion concerning the fairness of the company's financial statements. If the CPA firm knows that the company has a good internal auditing staff, it can feel more confident that the financial statements fairly present the accounting information about the company.

Diagram of Internal Control

Exhibit 6-5 shows a diagram of the goals and subgoals in internal control, the concerns of internal control in regard to transactions, and the general principles of good internal control. We will discuss more internal control principles as they apply to different topics throughout the book.

EXHIBIT 6-5
Internal Control

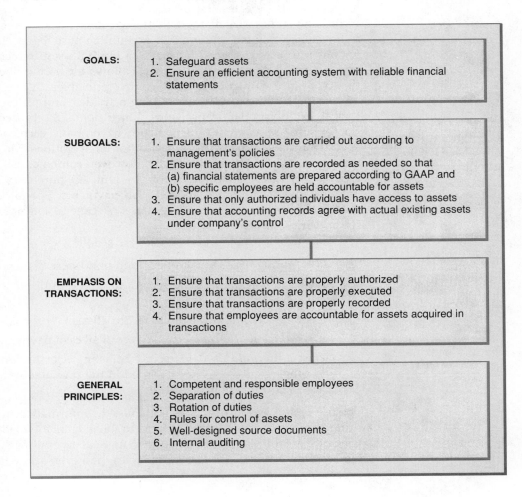

GOALS:	1. Safeguard assets 2. Ensure an efficient accounting system with reliable financial statements
SUBGOALS:	1. Ensure that transactions are carried out according to management's policies 2. Ensure that transactions are recorded as needed so that (a) financial statements are prepared according to GAAP and (b) specific employees are held accountable for assets 3. Ensure that only authorized individuals have access to assets 4. Ensure that accounting records agree with actual existing assets under company's control
EMPHASIS ON TRANSACTIONS:	1. Ensure that transactions are properly authorized 2. Ensure that transactions are properly executed 3. Ensure that transactions are properly recorded 4. Ensure that employees are accountable for assets acquired in transactions
GENERAL PRINCIPLES:	1. Competent and responsible employees 2. Separation of duties 3. Rotation of duties 4. Rules for control of assets 5. Well-designed source documents 6. Internal auditing

Limitations of Internal Control

The design of an internal control system should be based on the current operations of the company. Regardless of how careful management is in establishing internal control, however, there are always limitations. Unintentional errors may still arise from a misunderstanding of instructions, mistakes of judgment, personal carelessness, distractions, or fatigue. Theft and fraud, even with the separation of duties, can still occur if collusion takes place. Finally, a good internal control system for efficient current operations may become weak because of changes in future operating conditions. These conditions may arise from increasing sales that require additional purchases of inventory and different operating assets. Management must always be alert for improvements in its internal control and accountants should make every effort to assist in this activity.

Special Journals

A general journal can be used to record all the transactions of a company. However, just as a company's increasing size causes the need for subsidiary ledgers, it also creates the need for internal control procedures to efficiently record and summarize many daily transactions. Regardless of whether a company is using a manual or computer accounting system, special journals are used for this purpose. **A special journal is a journal used to record major recurring transactions.** Use of these journals (1) allows the accounting task to be divided (in accordance with good internal control principles), (2) reduces the time needed to complete the various accounting activities, and (3) provides for a chronological list of similar transactions. Since operating procedures and business transactions are different from company to company, each company organizes its special journals in the way that is best for its operations. Most recurring transactions for a merchandising company, however, can be classified into one of four types: (1) sales of merchandise on account, (2) purchases of merchandise on account, (3) cash receipts, and (4) cash payments. Special journals are usually established to record these transactions. A general journal is still necessary to record various other transactions.

6. Define a special journal and list the major journals.

The major journals and their uses are as follows:

1. *Sales Journal.* Used to record all (and only) sales of merchandise on account.
2. *Purchases Journal.* Used to record all (and only) purchases of merchandise on account.
3. *Cash Receipts Journal.* Used to record all cash receipts.
4. *Cash Payments Journal.* Used to record all cash payments.
5. *General Journal.* Used to record adjusting, closing, and reversing entries and other transactions not recorded in the special journals (such as the purchase of equipment on account).

The use of special journals does not affect the information in the general or subsidiary ledgers, although the postings to the ledgers are made at different times. Each of these journals is discussed for a manual accounting system in the following sections. Many of the same principles, however, apply to an electronic data processing system.

Sales Journal

7(a). Describe the sales journal.

Companies make sales of merchandise on credit or for cash. **The sales journal is used to record all sales of merchandise on account** (cash sales are recorded in the cash receipts journal, which is discussed later). Recall that recording a sale on credit increases (debits) an individual customer's account (account receivable) and increases (credits) the Sales account. A sales journal has columns for the date, customer account debited, invoice number, posting reference, and the amount of the sale. A sales journal[3] is shown in Exhibit 6-6. A sale on credit is recorded by simply listing the date, the customer's name, the invoice number, and the amount. For example, on June 1 a $400 credit sale was made to Ann Alcott on sales invoice number 229.

EXHIBIT 6-6
Sales Journal and Postings

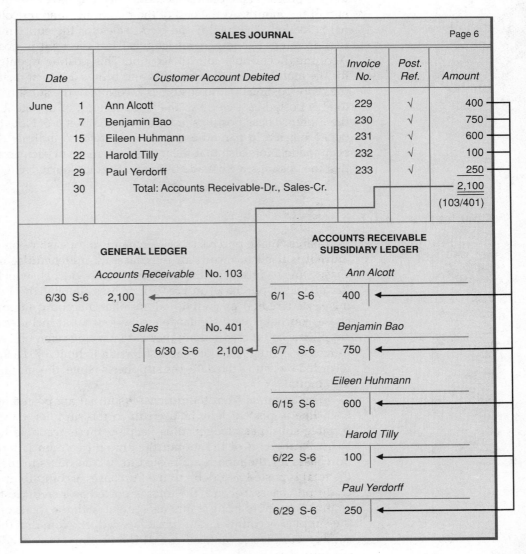

---

[3]It should be noted that in this and later journals, for simplicity, only a few transactions are shown. In reality, however, each journal could have hundreds of recorded transactions.

The amounts from the sales journal are posted at two different times. Since each credit sale increases (debits) a customer's account, each line in the sales journal is posted daily as a debit to the customer's account in the accounts receivable subsidiary ledger, as shown in Exhibit 6-6. By using this posting procedure each customer account balance is always current. A check mark (√) is placed in the posting reference column to indicate that the daily posting has been made to the customer account.

Except for decisions involving the extension of credit and efforts to collect cash from credit customers, the balances in a company's accounts need be up to date only when the company prepares its financial statements. Most companies prepare interim financial statements on a monthly basis for managerial accounting purposes. Therefore the accounts need to have current balances only at the end of the month. At the end of the month the amount column of the sales journal is totaled. The total is the credit sales for the entire month and is posted to two accounts in the general ledger. First, the total is posted as a debit to the Accounts Receivable control account. This posting updates the control account for the monthly customer charges and brings it into agreement with the totals of the daily postings to the customer accounts in the subsidiary ledger. Second, the total is posted as a credit to the Sales account to update it for the credit sales of the month. These postings are shown in Exhibit 6-6. Note that the account numbers are listed in parentheses below the total to indicate that the postings have been made. Note also that the journal reference in each account is S-6, indicating that the postings were made from the Sales (S) journal, page 6.

Purchases Journal

7(b). Describe the purchases journal.

Companies make purchases of merchandise for cash or on credit. The **purchases journal is used to record all purchases of merchandise on account** (cash purchases are recorded in the cash payments journal, which is discussed later). Recall that a purchase on credit increases (debits) the Purchases account and increases (credits) an individual supplier's account (account payable). A purchases journal is very similar to a sales journal. It includes columns for the date, supplier account credited, invoice date, posting reference, and the amount of the purchase. A purchases journal is shown in Exhibit 6-7. Each purchase on credit is recorded by listing the date, the supplier's name, the supplier's invoice date, and the amount.

The amounts from the purchases journal are posted at two different times. Each line is posted daily as a credit to the supplier's account in the accounts payable subsidiary ledger, thus keeping these accounts up to date on a daily basis. At the end of the month the amount column is totaled. The total credit purchases for the month are posted to two accounts in the general ledger. First, the total is posted as a debit to the Purchases account to update it for the current credit purchases. Second, the total is posted as a credit to the Accounts Payable control account to bring it into agreement with the totals of the daily postings to the supplier accounts in the subsidiary ledger. Note that the journal reference in each account is P-8, indicating that the postings were made from the Purchases (P) journal, page 8.

EXHIBIT 6-7
Purchases Journal
and Postings

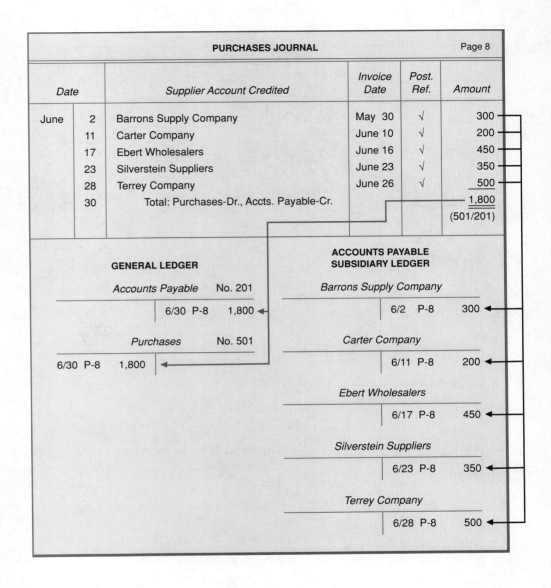

Cash Receipts Journal

7(c). Describe the cash
receipts journal.

All transactions involving the receipt of cash are recorded in the cash receipts journal. A Cash debit column is used for this purpose. Since many transactions involve cash receipts, each company determines exactly which accounts are frequently credited and accordingly establishes column headings for these accounts. A Miscellaneous credit column is then used for recording the credit amounts of infrequent transactions. Because many cash receipts are from cash sales and collections of accounts receivable (less the sales discounts), column headings are frequently provided for these accounts. Columns for the date, explanation, and posting references complete the cash receipts journal. A cash receipts journal is shown in Exhibit 6-8.

EXHIBIT 6-8   Cash Receipts Journal and Postings

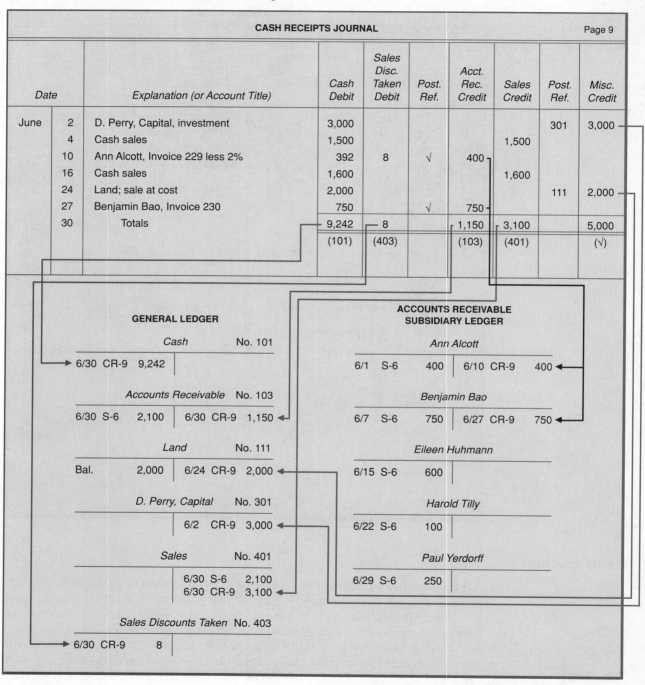

To record a cash receipt transaction, it is necessary to list the title of the account to be credited only if the amount of the credited account must be listed in the Miscellaneous credit column or if an individual customer account is credited in the subsidiary ledger. For instance, on June 2 D. Perry invested $3,000 into the company. Since no credit column is used for the D. Perry, Capital account, the account title is listed and the $3,000 credit is listed in the Miscellaneous credit column. A similar recording is made for the sale of land on June 24. On June 10 and 27 two customers paid their accounts and the customer account titles in the accounts receivable subsidiary ledger are listed. Account titles are *not* needed for amounts listed in the columns set up for specific accounts in the general ledger; explanations are usually provided, however. For the June 4 and 16 entries, explanations indicate these amounts are for cash sales.

Certain items in the cash receipts journal are posted on a daily basis and the remaining items are typically posted monthly. The entries to the individual customer accounts are posted daily. This daily posting keeps the customer account balances in the subsidiary ledger up to date. A check mark is placed in the accounts receivable posting reference column to indicate that the postings have been completed. In Exhibit 6-8 the June 10 and 27 credit entries are posted on those dates, respectively, as reductions to the Ann Alcott and Benjamin Bao customer accounts as shown (note the debit entries in the accounts from the sales journal). The individual amounts in the Miscellaneous credit column are typically posted daily (or at convenient intervals during the month) to the account titles listed. Thus the $3,000 credit to D. Perry, Capital on June 2 and the $2,000 credit to Land on June 24 are posted on the respective dates. The account numbers are listed in the posting reference column to indicate that the postings have been completed.

At the end of the month all the columns are totaled, and the total of the debit columns is compared with the total of the credit columns to prove their equality. The totals of the Cash and Sales Discounts Taken columns are posted as debits to each of these accounts, respectively. The total of the Accounts Receivable column is posted as a credit to the control account to bring it into agreement with the subsidiary ledger. [Note the debit posting in the control account from the sales journal; also note that the debit and credit postings in the control account total $950 ($2,100 – $1,150), the same amount as the total of the postings to the subsidiary ledger accounts.] Finally, the total of the Sales column is posted as a credit to the Sales account to record the total cash sales. (The $3,100 cash sales, when combined with the $2,100 credit sales posted from the sales journal, amount to $5,200 total sales for June.) The total of the Miscellaneous column is *not* posted since the individual miscellaneous accounts were previously posted. The account numbers are listed below the column totals to indicate that the totals have been posted. A check mark is shown under the Miscellaneous column to indicate that it was not posted. The CR-9 listed beside each posting in the accounts indicates that the amount came from the cash receipts (CR) journal, page 9.

Cash Payments Journal

7(d). Describe the cash payments journal.

All transactions involving the payment of cash are recorded in the cash payments journal. The form of this journal as well as the entry and posting procedures are similar to the cash receipts journal. A Cash credit column is used to record the amount of each cash payment. Column headings are established for accounts that are frequently debited, and Miscellaneous debit and credit columns are used to record amounts of infrequent transactions. Since cash payments often involve cash purchases and payments of accounts payable (less the purchases discounts taken) column headings are usually provided for these accounts. Columns for the date, explanation, and posting references complete the cash payments journal. A cash payments journal is shown in Exhibit 6-9. Note that the *credit* columns are listed *before* the debit columns because so many credit entries are recorded in the Cash credit column. (The totals of the debit and credit entries, however, must still be equal.) By placing the Cash credit column and the other credit columns on the left side, time is saved in recording cash payment transactions.

To record a cash payment transaction the account title is listed only if the amount must be recorded in the Miscellaneous debit or credit column or if an individual supplier account is debited in the subsidiary ledger. For instance, on June 18 the purchase of the equipment requires a debit to Equipment for $4,500 and credits to Notes Payable and Cash for $3,500 and $1,000, respectively. Both the Equipment and the Notes Payable account titles must be listed since the respective amounts are recorded in the Miscellaneous columns (two lines are needed for this transaction). Similar entries are made for the Salaries Expense on June 20 and the Sales Returns and Allowances on June 22. On June 8 and June 21 payments are made to suppliers, and each supplier's account title in the subsidiary ledger is listed. Explanations are provided for amounts listed in the columns established for specific accounts in the general ledger (see the June 3 and 28 entries).

Certain items in the cash payments journal are posted daily, whereas other items are posted monthly. The entries to the individual supplier accounts are posted daily to keep the accounts payable subsidiary ledger up to date. In Exhibit 6-9 the June 8 and 21 debit entries are posted on those dates to the Barrons Supply Company and Carter Company supplier accounts as shown (note the credit entries in the accounts from the purchases journal). The individual amounts in the Miscellaneous debit and credit columns are typically posted daily (or at convenient intervals during the month) to the account titles as shown.

At the end of the month all the columns are totaled, and the total debits are compared with the total credits to prove their equality. The totals of the Cash and Purchases Discounts Taken columns are posted as credits to these accounts. The Accounts Payable column total is posted as a debit to the control account to bring it into agreement with the subsidiary ledger. [Note the credit posting in the control account from the purchases journal; also note that the $1,300 ($1,800 − $500) difference in the postings to the control account is the same as the total of the postings to the subsidiary ledger accounts.] Finally, the debit total of the Purchases column is posted to the Purchases account. (The $1,800 credit purchases from the purchases journal combined with the $600 cash purchases amounts to $2,400 total purchases for June.) The totals of the Miscellaneous columns are not posted since the individual amounts in these columns were previously posted. The CP-7 listings indicate that each posting came from the cash payments (CP) journal, page 7.

General Journal

The general journal is required even when special journals are used. In this situation, **the general journal is used to record adjusting, closing, and reversing entries, as well as for certain other transactions that do not occur very often.**

EXHIBIT 6-9 Cash Payments Journal and Postings

		CASH PAYMENTS JOURNAL									Page 7
Date		Explanation (or Account Title)	Cash Credit	Purch. Disc. Taken Credit	Post. Ref.	Misc. Credit	Post. Ref.	Acct. Pay. Debit	Purch. Debit	Post. Ref.	Misc. Debit
June	3	Cash purchases	200						200		
	8	Barrons Supply Co., no discount	300				√	300			
	18	Equipment	1,000							114	4,500
		Notes Payable			203	3,500					
		Purchased with note and cash down payment.									
	20	Salaries expense	900							511	900
	21	Carter Company, less 2% discount	196	4			√	200			
	22	Sales Returns and Allow- ances for cash	34							402	34
	28	Cash purchases	400						400		
	30	Totals	3,030	4		3,500		500	600		5,434
			(101)	(503)		(√)		(201)	(501)		(√)

GENERAL LEDGER

Cash   No. 101

6/30 CR-9 9,242 | 6/30 CP-7 3,030

Equipment   No. 114

6/18 CP-7 4,500

Accounts Payable   No. 201

6/30 CP-7   500 | 6/30 P-8   1,800

Notes Payable   No. 203

| 6/18 CP-7 3,500

Sales Returns & Allowances   No. 402

6/22 CP-7   34 |

Purchases   No. 501

6/30 P-8 1,800
6/30 CP-7   600

Purchases Discounts Taken   No. 503

| 6/30 CP-7   4

Salaries Expense   No. 511

6/20 CP-7   900 |

ACCOUNTS PAYABLE SUBSIDIARY LEDGER

Barrons Supply Company

6/8 CP-7 300 | 6/2 P-8   300

Carter Company

6/21 CP-7 200 | 6/11 P-8   200

Ebert Wholesalers

| 6/17 P-8   450

Silverstein Suppliers

| 6/23 P-8   350

Terrey Company

| 6/28 P-8   500

7(e). Describe the
general journal.

These transactions include purchases returns and allowances on account, sales returns and allowances on account, and also the purchase or sale of assets (other than merchandise) on account. The journalizing and posting process is the same as that described in earlier chapters, but with one exception. If subsidiary ledgers are used, any debit or credit to accounts receivable or accounts payable must be posted *twice*, once to the appropriate control account and once to the individual subsidiary account that is not part of the double-entry system.

For example, suppose that a $50 purchase allowance is granted on June 30 by Ebert Wholesalers for goods purchased on account on June 17. This entry would be recorded in the general journal. (If a *cash* purchase allowance had been given, the entry would have been recorded in the cash receipts journal.) The journal entry and postings are as follows (the other amounts in the control account and supplier account are from the cash payments and purchases journals; the G-5 refers to general (G) journal, page 5):

GENERAL JOURNAL					Page 5
Date		Account Titles and Explanations	Acct. No.	Debit	Credit
June	30	Accounts Payable: Ebert Wholesalers Purchases Returns and Allowances **To record purchase allowance on June 17 invoice.**	201/√ 502	50	 50

GENERAL LEDGER

Accounts Payable   No. 201

6/30	CP-7	500	6/30	P-8	1,800
6/30	G-5	50			

ACCOUNTS PAYABLE SUBSIDIARY LEDGER (PARTIAL)

Ebert Wholesalers

6/30	G-5	50	6/17	P-8	450

Purchases Returns and Allowances   No. 502

		6/30	G-5	50

Modifications in Special Journals

As indicated earlier special journals are designed to fit the needs of each company. They are based on each company's common transactions; that is, the more often a company records transactions in a specific account, the more useful it is to establish a column for that account in the appropriate special journal. For instance, a company might include a Sales Tax column in its sales journal. It might also include a Sales Returns and Allowances column in its sales journal, or it might create a separate special journal for these items. Similar adjustments could be made to the purchases journal for purchases returns and allowances or transportation-in.

The cash payments journal might include additional columns for the Selling Expenses control account and the General and Administrative Expenses control account if these accounts are used. Or the Purchases column might be omitted from the cash payments journal if a company makes almost all its purchases on account. In fact, if a company uses a voucher system as discussed in Chapter 7, the purchases journal is greatly expanded into a special journal called a *voucher register*. In addition, the columns in the cash payments journal are reduced in number, and this journal is then called a *check register*. The important point to remember is that although the special journals illustrated in this chapter are commonly used, each company designs its own special journals to fit its needs.

Advantages of Special Journals (with Subsidiary Ledgers)

There are several advantages in using special journals in conjunction with subsidiary ledgers. Some of the advantages are as follows:

8. List the advantages of special journals.

1. *Time Is Saved in Recording.* Usually only one line is used in recording each journal entry. Since the column headings list the main accounts to be debited or credited, this procedure reduces the amount of recording required. In addition, no explanations are needed in the sales and purchases journals.

2. *Time Is Saved in Posting.* In the sales and purchases journals only two postings for the monthly totals are made in the general ledger. In the cash receipts and cash payments journals, postings are also reduced because only monthly postings are needed for most columns.

3. *Customer and Supplier Accounts Are Always Up to Date.* Since postings are made daily to the subsidiary ledgers from the special journals, the current balance is always known for each customer or supplier account. Current customer account balances are useful to the credit department in (a) determining whether or not to extend additional credit to a customer; (b) watching for slow-paying customers so that they can be contacted about paying their accounts; and (c) answering customer questions about their account balances. Current supplier account balances are useful in ensuring that all cash discounts are taken and that payments are made when invoices are due.

4. *Similar Transactions Are Listed in Chronological Order.* All sales on credit and purchases on credit are listed in chronological order in the sales and purchases journals. This procedure is useful in tracing inconsistencies between the records of a company and the records of its customers or suppliers when disagreements have arisen. It is also useful in the auditing process of verifying the total amounts of the sales and purchases transactions.

5. *Division of Accounting Tasks.* Since several special journals are usually used, this procedure allows several employees to journalize and post at the same time in the separate journals. It also allows employees to "specialize" in recording certain transactions, thereby making the accounting process more efficient and minimizing errors.

Electronic Data Processing

Throughout this text we have used and will continue to use a manual accounting system for convenience. In the business world, however, because of the (1) lower cost of acquiring a computer, (2) reduced physical size of a computer, (3) increased speed of a computer, and (4) increased "user-friendliness" of many aspects of computers, many companies are using electronic data processing for their accounting information. **In electronic data processing (EDP) a computer is used to record, retain, and report a company's financial and managerial accounting information.** The basic elements of an EDP system are (1) hardware and (2) software. Because many students already have experience with computers, these elements are only briefly discussed in this section. A computer application is included in the appendix at the end of the chapter.

Hardware

9. Describe a computer and list the hardware components.

A computer is a high-speed electronic machine that can record, retain, process, and report information on the basis of a set of stored instructions. Computers range in size from small *microcomputers* (frequently called *personal computers*), to medium size *minicomputers*, to the largest and most powerful *mainframes*. A computer, however, is only one part of an EDP system. The equipment (or **hardware**) of an EDP system consists of three main components: (1) input devices to transfer information and instructions into the central processing unit, (2) a central processing unit (the computer), and (3) output devices to transfer information out of the central processing unit.

Input devices are necessary in an EDP system to transfer information and instructions to the computer. An input device can be a terminal or a reader of magnetic tapes and disks. *Terminals* are keyboard devices by which information is sent directly to the central processing unit. Examples of terminals are cash registers (referred to as "point-of-sale" terminals) used by retail companies such as Sears and J. C. Penney. *Readers* "read" information from physical input items such as magnetic tapes and disks and send this information to the central processing unit. Examples of readers are *scanners* that scan certain items such as uniform product codes (UPC systems), optical characters (OCR systems), and magnetic ink (MICR systems).

The central processing unit (CPU) of an EDP system consists of three parts: (1) the control unit, (2) the arithmetic unit, and (3) the memory (storage) unit. The *control unit* reads, interprets, and carries out the instructions given in the computer program (discussed later). The *arithmetic unit* does the actual computing; that is, it adds, subtracts, multiplies, divides, and performs other computations (at extremely fast speeds). The *memory unit* stores program instructions and accounting information (e.g., results of recorded transactions, account balances).

Output devices are necessary in an EDP system to transfer information out of the computer. Output devices include magnetic tape and disk drives, CRT (cathode ray tube) screens, and printers. Tape or disk *drives* record output information on magnetic tapes or disks. CRT *screens* show the output on a television-like screen. *Printers* can print out accounting information in whatever form is programmed into the computer. For financial accounting this information would include trial balances, financial statements, adjusting and closing entries, and so on. Printers can also print source documents such as sales invoices, purchase orders, and payroll checks.

Regardless of what type of hardware a company is using in its financial accounting applications, the company must provide instructions to the computer for the processing of the related information. These instructions are briefly discussed in the next section.

Software

10. Define a computer program and software.

In the previous section, we indicated that input devices are used to communicate with a computer. In financial accounting the information contained in the physical input items (tapes or disks) may be data from transactions, data from accounts, or computer programs. **A computer program is a detailed set of instructions (commands) to the computer about how to record, retain, process, and report information.** The type, quality, and quantity of work done by a computer depends on the quality of the programs (instructions) and other input that the operator communicates to the computer.

Software is the set of computer programs used to operate the computer.[4] Computer software consists of two types: systems software and applications software. *Systems software* includes the programs that are designed to coordinate the operations of the various parts of the computer itself. *Applications software* includes the programs designed to allow the user to complete specific tasks in the computer (i.e., recording, retaining, processing, and reporting information). In this section we are concerned with applications software developed for financial accounting.

Software packages have been developed by software companies for the financial accounting functions, such as accounts receivable, accounts payable, inventory, payroll, and the general ledger. In addition, "spreadsheet" packages have been developed to serve a variety of accounting needs. Each of these software packages is used with computer hardware to produce accounting reports and business documents, as shown in Exhibit 6-10. Each package is briefly described next.

Accounts Receivable.   Because a company generates much of the cash needed for its operations from the collection of accounts receivable, the software program for accounts receivable is a very important aspect of an EDP system. Accounts receivable software is generally designed to provide continually current balances in customers' accounts by recording new invoices and cash receipts from customers; print out monthly statements (bills) for customers; monitor sales returns and allowances as well as sales discounts taken by customers; generate a credit history of each customer to help avoid uncollectible accounts; and provide projections of future cash inflows.

---

[4]Some people would also include the related documents (e.g., flowcharts and procedures manuals) as part of the software.

EXHIBIT 6-10   EDP System

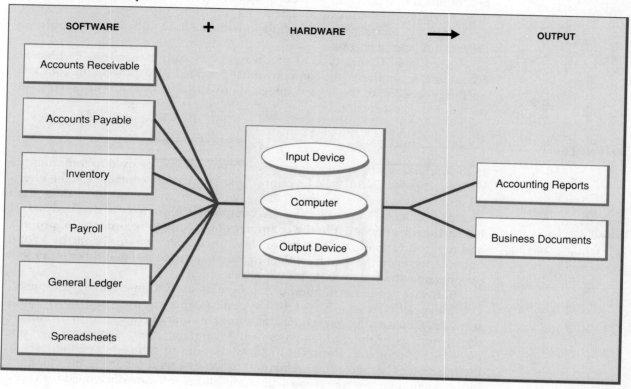

Accounts Payable.   Accounts payable software is concerned with monitoring and controlling the cash paid to suppliers. In the case of a merchandising company payments for purchases of inventory for resale is the primary activity. The software for accounts payable is generally designed to provide continually current balances in suppliers' accounts by recording purchase orders and cash payments to suppliers; generate a verification listing of the quantity and unit price of an order when it is received from a supplier; monitor purchases returns and allowances and purchases discounts; write checks; and provide projections of future cash outflows.

Inventory.   Inventory is a very important asset for a merchandising company. Most inventory software programs are interrelated to a company's accounts receivable and accounts payable software. Inventory software generally is designed to provide a continually current count of the number of units of each item of inventory by recording all unit purchases and sales; highlight when a minimum or maximum stock level has been reached for each item of inventory; print price tags for newly acquired inventory; prepare reports on slow-moving or obsolete inventory items; and provide unit prices when a physical count of the inventory is taken.

Payroll.   Software for payroll was one of the first to be developed. Payroll software can be very complex because of the various federal, state, and local tax laws. Payroll software may be designed to compute the salaries earned by each employee based on pay rates and overtime; allocate the salaries across departments in the company; calculate federal, state, and local withholding taxes; compute other voluntary withholdings, such as for investments in U.S. savings bonds; print payroll checks; generate comparisons of actual with projected salaries; and prepare various tax-withholding reports.

General Ledger.   A general ledger software package is broader than the name implies and includes many aspects of an accounting system. General ledger software usually includes all special journals and the general journal for recording transactions, a chart of accounts, and the ledger accounts on disks or tapes for storing the recorded information. Usually, the software is capable of preparing a trial balance and financial statements at any point in time. Frequently, supporting schedules (e.g., depreciation) and budgets may also be generated. The general ledger software of a company is usually linked to its accounts receivable, accounts payable, inventory, and payroll software.

Spreadsheets.   Spreadsheets are "electronic worksheets." They are laid out as a manual worksheet would appear on a large sheet of paper; the key difference is that they appear on a CRT screen and the computer performs all the mathematical calculations defined by the user of the program. Spreadsheet software is "general purpose" because it is modified and programmed by a user for a particular purpose. Spreadsheets are, perhaps, more useful in managerial accounting. There they can be used, for example, to forecast sales, predict operating costs, and establish budgets for different levels of operations. Spreadsheet software is also used in financial accounting for preparing worksheets and financial statements and for developing schedules involving such items as depreciation and interest computations.

Internal Control for an EDP System

Whether a company uses a manual or EDP system, the steps that must be completed to record, retain, and report accounting information are the same. There are, however, two primary differences between these systems. The first difference lies in the *way* in which the steps are completed. In a manual system the steps are done by hand and are usually based on a set of written procedures. In an EDP system the steps are performed electronically by a computer and are based on software written in computer language. The second difference between manual and electronic data processing is the *form* of the accounting documents used in the process. In a manual system, from the time a source document is used to first record a transaction until the time the accounting information is reported in a financial statement, accounting documents are listed on pieces of paper. These documents are easily read by individuals and include the general journal, general ledger accounts, trial balances, and worksheets. In an EDP system the documents are tapes and disks, which are easily read by a computer but not by a person.

Although the goals and subgoals of internal control are the same regardless of whether a company uses a manual or an EDP system, certain internal control principles must be modified because of these two differences. These modifications are briefly discussed as follows:

11. List the modifications of internal control principles for an EDP system.

1. *Competent and responsible employees.* Whether a company uses a manual or EDP system, competent and responsible employees are critical to internal control. Competency, however, is likely to involve different specialties in the EDP system. Competent employees in an EDP system must have adequate knowledge of both accounting and computer systems.

2. *Separation of duties.* Under an EDP system, separation of duties is not always possible because the computer is capable of almost instantaneously performing many functions. For instance, in regard to the accounts payable software discussed earlier, one computer operator may initiate the recording of a purchase and the payment of the related invoice. In such cases, *input*, *processing*, and *output* controls may be substituted for separation of duties. These types of controls deal with the detection of operator input errors, the testing of software reliability, and the evaluation of the "reasonableness" of the computer output.

3. *Rotation of duties.* The rotation of duties may be more difficult in the case of an EDP system, where technical competence may be of a higher level or of a different type than in a manual system. On the other hand, data processing duties in an EDP system are typically allocated among several individuals to enhance internal control. For instance, it is common for a company to have a *data processing manager* responsible for management of the EDP system; a *systems analyst* responsible for the general design of the EDP system; a *programmer* responsible for developing flowcharts, preparing and testing the related computer programs, and documenting the results; and a *computer operator* responsible for entering data into the computer based upon carefully specified instructions.

4. *Rules for control of assets.* In addition to the rules discussed earlier for the internal control of physical assets, further controls must be established in the case of an EDP system. These controls pertain to both the hardware and software. Large EDP systems are often kept in locked, air-conditioned rooms to prevent vandalism and deterioration. Furthermore a *librarian* is frequently given the responsibility for maintaining physical control over the software and other computer records to avoid intentional or unintentional misuse. In addition, all users of the system should be required to "sign-on" using an assigned password, and the system should maintain a record of the times and duration of all uses.

5. *Well-designed source documents.* Although well-designed source documents are an important aspect of internal control for both a manual and an EDP system, some source documents are eliminated in an EDP system. For instance, the purchase requisition and purchase order may be combined in an inventory software program. In addition, since accounting data are recorded, processed, and stored by a computer in a form that is not readable by a person, source documents such as accounts are not available. Procedures manuals (source documents of a different type) dealing with systems, programs, and operating instructions documentation are used as a substitute for the traditional source documents. Furthermore, *hardware* controls

are built into computer hardware by the manufacturer to detect equipment failure.

6. *Internal auditing.* In an EDP system, the internal auditing staff is generally expanded to include experts in the design and operation of a computer system. These individuals evaluate the effectiveness and efficiency of each aspect of the EDP system, including the clarity of the procedures manuals and the adequacy of the input, processing, and output controls.

Summary

Although computers are very efficient machines, they are machines nevertheless. The sizes of computers and numbers and sophistication of computer programs may vary from company to company. The quality of the accounting information (the output), however, depends on the quality of the computer programs and the quality of the employees operating the system. There is an old saying, "garbage-in, garbage-out," which is very true for EDP systems. In addition, many experts argue that EDP systems cannot prevent unauthorized access by someone with sufficient skill and time. Therefore special attention must be placed on evaluating the strength of internal control for these systems in the auditing process.

APPENDIX: Using a Personal Computer for Applications of an EDP Accounting System

To illustrate the accounting process, the review problem and solution at the end of Chapter 3 show manual journalizing in the general journal, posting of several transactions in the general ledger, and preparation of an adjusted trial balance and financial statements. In this Appendix, we discuss a demonstration problem that shows the completion of the accounting process for the same review problem using an EDP accounting system for a personal computer. In addition, instructions are provided for completing several homework assignments on a personal computer using this system.

Copying Instructor's Disk for Students

Your instructor has been provided with a programmed disk and instructions for its use. This disk is to be used with an IBM personal computer (or a compatible computer). The disk contains a demonstration file of the review problem from Chapter 3; files for Exercise 6-14, Problem 6-8A, and Problem 6-8B; and an accounting software program for your use in completing these exercises and problems. You will need to provide your own blank floppy disk. Any single- or double-sided, double-density disk will work.

The first step is for your instructor to prepare the Instructor's Disk for Students for you to use with your computer. Instructions for this procedure are given in Chapter 6 of the Solutions Manual and the Instructor's Manual. Once this preparation is completed, the next step is for you to copy the Instructor's Disk for Students. To do this, you need to complete the following steps:

(1) Insert the Instructor's Disk for Students into the A-Drive of the Computer

If your IBM-PC (or compatible computer) has dual floppy drives, there will be two slots in the front of the computer. The A-drive is the slot on the left side (or top) as you face the computer; the B-drive is the slot on the right side (or bottom). If your computer has only a single floppy drive, then that drive is the A-drive. Being careful not to touch the unprotected areas of the disk or to bend the disk, insert the Instructor's Disk for Students into the A-drive, open side first and label side up. If you are working on a dual floppy drive computer, place your blank disk into the B-drive, again open side first and label side up.

(2) Turn the Computer On

As you sit facing the computer, the on-off switch for the IBM-PC is located toward the back of the right-hand side of the computer. This switch is orange colored, about 1 inch wide, and needs to be flipped upward to turn the computer on. Now flip the switch up. The computer will come on with a blinking cursor on the monitor screen, then will prompt you for a response by a printing on the screen similar to the following:

```
CURRENT DATE IS TUE 1-01-1980
ENTER NEW DATE:
```

You should type today's date in the form: 01-22-1991 and enter this date by depressing the enter ($\leftarrow$) key. The computer will then respond with the time in the form:

```
CURRENT TIME IS 0:00:15:54
ENTER NEW TIME:
```

You do not have to enter the time; simply depress the enter key. The computer will then display a message about the system on the screen, followed by the A-prompt, which looks like this: **A>**.

(3) Make the Copy

Now you are ready to copy the Instructor's Disk for Students onto your own blank disk. Depending on whether you have a dual floppy drive or single floppy drive computer, complete the appropriate directions as follows:

Dual floppy drive computer: To copy, type the command: **DISKCOPY A: B:** and depress the enter key. The computer will respond with:

```
INSERT SOURCE DISKETTE IN DRIVE A:
INSERT TARGET DISKETTE IN DRIVE B:
STRIKE ANY KEY WHEN READY
```

Now, since the source (Instructor's) and target (your blank) disk are already in drives A and B, simply depress any key and the computer will copy the Instructor's Disk information onto your disk.

Single floppy drive computer: To copy, type the command: **DISKCOPY A: A:** and depress the enter key. During the copy process, you will be prompted by the computer to insert the source (Instructor's) and target (your blank) disk at various times. Simply follow those instructions to complete the copy process.

With either a single floppy drive or dual floppy drive computer, the computer will display on the screen the following message upon completion of the copying process:

```
COPY COMPLETE
COPY ANOTHER (Y/N)?
```

Now you should depress the **n** key on your keyboard. The computer will respond to this command by displaying the A-prompt (**A>**).

At this point you should remove both disks from the drives, return the Instructor's Disk for Students to its place of storage, and turn the computer off by flipping the orange switch down.

Demonstration Problem

Now that you have successfully copied the Instructor's Disk for Students onto your disk, insert your disk in the A-drive of your computer to see a demonstration of the review problem from Chapter 3. Turn the computer on with the orange switch. When you see: **Enter new date** on your screen, type: **04-30-1991** and depress the enter key. The computer will respond with: **Enter new time;** depress the enter key again. The screen will display the A-prompt. To work the demonstration problem (**CAUTION**[5]), type:

demo

Depress the enter key. The screen will now briefly display the copyright symbol. Following this symbol, the computer will display the *options menu*, shown as follows, for working the problem.[6]

```
┌──────────────────────────────────────────────────────────┐
│               EDP ACCOUNTING SYSTEM                      │
│                                                          │
│      F1 - ENTER JOURNAL ENTRIES INTO TRANSACTIONS FILE   │
│      F2 - UPDATE MASTER FILE & PRINT TRANSACTIONS FILE   │
│      F3 - PRINT ADJUSTED TRIAL BALANCE                   │
│      F4 - PRINT FINANCIAL STATEMENTS                     │
│      F5 - EXIT PROGRAM                                   │
└──────────────────────────────────────────────────────────┘
```

[5]You must complete the entire demonstration problem before you shut off the computer, or you will have to start over. Please allow 20 minutes to do so.

[6]In the options menu and the program, the *transactions file* is an area on the disk where the journal entries are stored, while a *master file* is where the account balances are stored.

The F-keys (function keys) are located on the left-hand side (or across the top) of the IBM-PC and have been preset by the program to do certain operations. Now depress the F1 key. The following *headings* will appear on the screen:

```
ACCOUNT NUMBER          ACCOUNT NAME      DEBIT        CREDIT
```

The Journal Entries for the demonstration problem will then be automatically displayed on the screen. These journal entries will look slightly different from those of a manual system. Once the entries are completely displayed, study the entries and compare them with those in the review problem of Chapter 3. After this review, depress the enter key, which will return you to the options menu. At this point be sure that your computer is connected to a printer, that the printer is turned on and on-line[7], and that your paper is properly aligned in the printer. Depress the F2 key and you will receive a warning message telling you to be sure the printer is turned on. After this message, depress the enter key. The Transactions File (Journal Entries) will be printed, and you will be returned to the options menu screen. Depress the F3 key, and you will receive another warning message at the bottom of the screen. When your printer is on and on-line, depress the enter key and the Adjusted Trial Balance will be printed, after which you will again be returned to the options menu screen. Depress the F4 key and another warning message will appear. Depress the enter key and the printer will print the Financial Statements, and you will again be returned to the options menu screen. At this point the demonstration problem is complete; depress the F5 key, and the program will return you to the A-prompt. Remove your disk from the A-drive, turn the computer off by flipping the orange switch down, and remove your output from your printer.

Instructions for Exercise 6-14, Problem 6-8A, and Problem 6-8B

Instructions for preparing solutions to Exercise 6-14, Problem 6-8A, and Problem 6-8B on your computer are included in this section. Although the instructions are presented as they apply to Exercise 6-14, they are also applicable to Problems 6-8A and 6-8B. First, insert your disk into the A-drive. Turn the computer on by flipping up the orange switch. When the computer prompts you to enter the date, type: **05-31-1991** and depress the enter key. This information is the date of the adjusted trial balance you are to prepare for Exercise 6-14. If you are solving one of the Problems, *type and enter the date of that problem's adjusted trial balance* in the same form. At this point, the computer will prompt you to enter the time. This is not necessary; simply depress the enter key. The computer will then display the A-prompt. You should now type:

acctng

Depress the enter key, and the computer screen will first display the copyright symbol and then display the *problem selection menu:*

---

[7]"On-line" means that the printer is ready to print. This condition is indicated when all the green lights on the printer are lit.

```
┌────────────────────────────────────────────────────────────┐
│                   PROBLEM SELECTION MENU                     │
│                                                              │
│              F1 - EXERCISE 14 (E6-14)                        │
│              F2 - PROBLEM 8A (P6-8A)                         │
│              F3 - PROBLEM 8B (P6-8B)                         │
│              F4 - EXIT PROGRAM                               │
└────────────────────────────────────────────────────────────┘
```

A-1. Solve assigned homework using a personal computer.

Depress the F1 key for Exercise 6-14 (F2 for Problem 6-8A; F3 for Problem 6-8B). The computer will now display the *options menu* illustrated earlier. Depress the F1 key, and the screen will now show the *headings* illustrated earlier. You are now ready to enter the transactions and adjusting entries (**CAUTION**[8]). To enter the first transaction, type the account number: **101** and depress the enter key. The computer screen will display the account title: **Cash** for you, and the cursor will move to under the debit column. Next, type: **8000** in the debit column (**Note:** Do *not* use a dollar sign or insert commas in your amounts or the computer will not accept your input!) and depress the enter key. The cursor will now move to the next line. Now you are ready to enter the credit side of the journal entry. Type the account number: **301** and depress the enter key. The computer will display the account title: **S. Watts – Capital** for you. Depress the enter key again, and the cursor will move to under the credit column. Now type: **8000** in the credit column and depress the enter key. The cursor will move to the next line, and the first transaction will be complete. At this point the first transaction will appear as follows:

ACCOUNT NUMBER	ACCOUNT NAME	DEBIT	CREDIT
101	CASH	8000	
301	S. WATTS-CAPITAL		8000

Note that no dates appear because you are entering in a *batch mode* (i.e., all at one time). Enter the rest of the transactions and adjusting entries in exactly the same manner.

After entering *each* transaction, check your work. To correct an error simply reverse the entire line where the error occurred. That is, if you make an error in a line containing a *debit* entry, simply enter the line again as a *credit* entry. This entry cancels (i.e., "reverses") your incorrect entry, and you are now ready to reenter the entire correct line of the debit entry. As an example, suppose that when reviewing the debit and credit entries for the first transaction, you find that you have entered the credit amount as $6,000 (instead of $8,000). The incorrect credit line would appear on your screen as follows:

301	S. WATTS-CAPITAL		6000

To reverse this error, you should enter the following debit line:

301	S. WATTS-CAPITAL	6000	

---

[8]This program allows you to stop in the middle of completing the exercise (or problem). However, you must at least record the transactions and adjusting entries (F1) and print the Transactions File (F2), before you shut off the computer. When you begin again, you must type and enter the appropriate date and time, type and enter **acctng**, make the proper selection from the problem selection menu, and begin *exactly* where you stopped.

This debit entry "cancels out" your incorrect credit entry. Then you should reenter the entire correct credit line as follows:

```
301   S. WATTS-CAPITAL                                        8000
```

Be sure to carefully check your entries as they appear on the screen.

When you have entered all the entries and have checked for errors, depress the enter key again, and the computer will display the options menu illustrated earlier. Depress the F2 key, making sure your printer is on and on-line and the paper is aligned in response to the warning. Then depress the enter key, and the Transactions file (Journal Entries) will be printed. After the file is printed, you will be returned to the options menu screen. Before proceeding, check the printout and correct any errors.[9] Now depress the F3 key to print the Adjusted Trial Balance. You will receive a warning message to make sure your printer is on and on-line; depress the enter key to continue. After the screen has returned to the options menu, check the printout again and correct any errors.[10] Now depress the F4 key to print the Financial Statements. You will again receive a warning message; depress the enter key to continue. After they have been printed, the screen will again display the options menu. At this point depress the F5 key to exit the program because you have finished the exercise (or problem). The computer will now display the A-prompt. Remove your disk, turn the computer off, and remove your output from your printer.

Chapter Summary

Review of Learning Objectives

1. **Define internal control and identify its subgoals.**
   Internal control consists of the policies and procedures used to safeguard a company's assets and to ensure that reliable financial statements are the end result of an efficient accounting system. The four subgoals of internal control are to ensure that: (1) transactions are carried out according to management's general and specific policies; (2) transactions are recorded as needed so that (a) financial statements are prepared according to GAAP and (b) specified employees are held accountable for the various assets of the company; (3) only authorized individuals have access to assets; and (4) the

---

[9]To correct an error in the Transactions File, depress the F1 key again. Your computer will now show a blank screen except for the *headings* for the journal entries. Now correct your error as discussed earlier, by first entering a line that cancels (i.e., reverses) the incorrect line and then reentering the correct line. Then depress the enter key again to return to the options menu. Depress the F2 key (making sure your printer is on and the paper is aligned) and the enter key to update your master file and print your correcting entries.

[10]This is the last time you can correct an error. To do so, depress the F1 key again and then make your corrections as discussed in footnote 9. Then depress the enter key to return to the options menu. Depress the F2 key and the enter key to update your master file and print your correcting entries. After this printing, depress the F3 and the enter key to print a corrected Adjusted Trial Balance.

accounting records of the company's assets agree with the actual existing assets under the company's control.

2. **List and describe the four important factors in good internal control.**
   The four important factors include: (1) authorizing transactions, (2) executing transactions, (3) recording transactions, and (4) maintaining accountability for the resulting assets. *Authorization* means permission to exchange or use assets for specific purposes under given conditions. *Execution* of transactions means the set of steps needed to complete the exchange of assets or use of assets in the company. *Recording* of transactions includes journalizing and posting, as well as keeping up-to-date records of a company's assets. *Accountability* for assets involves keeping track of assets from the time they are acquired until their disposal or use in another transaction.

3. **Describe a subsidiary ledger and list the reasons for its use.**
   A subsidiary ledger is a group of similar accounts that are taken out of the general ledger and that show the detail of one specific company activity (e.g., accounts receivable and accounts payable). A subsidiary ledger is used to (1) reduce the size of the general ledger, (2) minimize errors, (3) improve efficiency in recording transactions, and (4) keep up-to-date records of dealings with charge customers and suppliers.

4. **Identify the two most common control accounts and state the basic rule for each.**
   The two most common control accounts are the Accounts Receivable account and the Accounts Payable account. The debit balance of the Accounts Receivable control account must always be equal to the debit total of the accounts receivable subsidiary ledger on each balance sheet date. The credit balance of the Accounts Payable control account must always be equal to the credit total of the accounts payable subsidiary ledger on each balance sheet date.

5. **State the general principles of good internal control.**
   There are six general principles of internal control. They include: (1) competent and responsible employees, (2) separation of duties, (3) rotation of duties, (4) rules for control of assets, (5) well-designed source documents, and (6) internal auditing.

6. **Define a special journal and list the major journals.**
   A special journal is a journal used to record major recurring transactions. There are five major journals when special journals are used: (1) sales journal, (2) purchases journal, (3) cash receipts journal, (4) cash payments journal, and (5) general journal.

7. **Describe the (a) sales journal, (b) purchases journal, (c) cash receipts journal, (d) cash payments journal, and (e) general journal.**
   The *sales journal* is used to record all (and only) sales of merchandise on account. The *purchases journal* is used to record all (and only) purchases of merchandise on account. The *cash receipts journal* is used to record all transactions involving the receipt of cash. The *cash payments journal* is used to record all transactions involving the payment of cash. The *general journal* is used to record adjusting, closing, and reversing entries and other transactions not recorded in the special journals.

8. **List the advantages of special journals.**
    The advantages of special journals are (1) time is saved in recording, (2) time is saved in posting, (3) customer and supplier accounts are always up to date, (4) similar transactions are listed in chronological order, and (5) the accounting task is divided.

9. **Describe a computer and list the hardware components.**
    A *computer* is a high-speed electronic machine that records, retains, processes, and reports information on the basis of a set of stored instructions. The *hardware* of an EDP system includes: (1) input devices, (2) the central processing unit (i.e., computer), and (3) output devices.

10. **Define a computer program and software.**
    A *computer program* is a detailed set of instructions (commands) to the computer about how to record, retain, process, and report information. *Software* is the set of computer programs used to operate the computer.

11. **List the modifications of internal control principles for an EDP system.**
    The modifications include: (1) competent employees must know computer systems; (2) input, processing, and output controls may be substituted for separation of duties; (3) data processing duties may be allocated among a data processing manager, a systems analyst, a programmer, and a computer operator; (4) more rules are used for control of assets, including locked rooms, a librarian to maintain physical control over the software, and assigned passwords; (5) procedures manuals are used as substitutes for traditional source documents, and hardware controls are used to detect equipment failure; and (6) internal auditing is expanded to include evaluation of the EDP system.

A-1. **Solve assigned homework using a personal computer.**
    An Instructor's Disk may be copied so that you can view a demonstration problem as well as work several homework assignments on a personal computer. Follow the instructions in the Appendix to copy the Instructor's Disk onto your disk. After doing so, the demonstration problem on your disk is contained in the *demo* file. The files to complete Exercise 6-14, Problem 6-8A, and Problem 6-8B are contained in the *acctng* file.

Glossary

Accounting System.   Means by which accounting information is identified, measured, recorded, and retained so that it can be reported in an accounting statement.

Authorization.   Permission to exchange or use assets for specific purposes under given conditions in a company. Used for internal control purposes.

Cash Payments Journal.   Special journal used to record all cash payments.

Cash Receipts Journal.   Special journal used to record all cash receipts.

Computer.   High-speed electronic machine that can record, retain, process, and report information on the basis of a set of stored instructions.

Computer Program.   Detailed set of instructions to the computer about how to record, retain, process, and report information.

Control Account. Account in the general ledger that takes the place of certain accounts that have been removed and placed in a subsidiary ledger. Examples are Accounts Receivable and Accounts Payable.

Electronic Data Processing (EDP). Use of a computer to record, retain, and report a company's accounting information.

Execution. The set of steps needed to complete the exchange of assets or use of assets in a company. Used for internal control purposes.

Hardware. The equipment of an EDP system. Consists of input devices, a central processing unit (the computer), and output devices.

Internal Control. Policies and procedures used by a company to safeguard its assets and to ensure that reliable financial statements are the end result of an efficient accounting system.

Purchase Order. Business document authorizing a supplier to ship the items listed at a specified price.

Purchase Requisition. Internal business document requesting that certain items of inventory be purchased.

Purchases Journal. Special journal used to record all purchases on account.

Recording. Includes journalizing and posting transactions, and keeping up-to-date records of a company's assets. Used for internal control purposes.

Sales Journal. Special journal used to record all sales on account.

Software. Set of computer programs used to operate a computer.

Special Journal. Journal used to record major recurring transactions. Examples are sales journal, purchases journal, cash receipts journal, and cash payments journal.

Subsidiary Ledger. Group of similar accounts that are taken out of the general ledger and that show the detail of one specific company activity. Examples are accounts receivable and accounts payable subsidiary ledgers.

Questions

QUESTION 6-1 What is the definition of internal control? What is meant by "safeguarding assets"?

QUESTION 6-2 List the four subgoals of internal control.

QUESTION 6-3 For internal control, what is meant by (1) authorizing, (2) executing, and (3) recording transactions? What internal control policies would be established for each of them?

QUESTION 6-4 List the major concerns of internal control in regard to recording transactions.

QUESTION 6-5 What is a subsidiary ledger? What is a control account? Why are subsidiary ledgers used for accounts receivable and accounts payable?

QUESTION 6-6 Reply to this statement: "When all the customer accounts are taken from the general journal and placed in a subsidiary ledger, the general journal will no longer balance."

QUESTION 6-7 What is meant by "accountability for assets"? Why is it important for internal control?

QUESTION 6-8   List the general principles of good internal control.

QUESTION 6-9   What is a special journal? When special journals are used, list the major journals and the transactions recorded in each journal.

QUESTION 6-10   How are transactions journalized in the sales journal? When is the sales journal posted?

QUESTION 6-11   How are transactions journalized in the purchases journal? When is the purchases journal posted?

QUESTION 6-12   Discuss the recording and posting process for the cash receipts journal.

QUESTION 6-13   Discuss the recording and posting process for the cash payments journal.

QUESTION 6-14   Which types of journal entries are recorded in a general journal when a company uses special journals?

QUESTION 6-15   List and briefly discuss the advantages of using special journals.

QUESTION 6-16   What is electronic data processing? Define: hardware, computer program, and software.

QUESTION 6-17   List and briefly discuss the three main components of hardware for an EDP system.

QUESTION 6-18   Name the three parts of a central processing unit (CPU) of an EDP system. For what is each part used?

QUESTION 6-19   Define software. What are systems software and applications software?

Exercises

EXERCISE 6-1   **Completion: Internal Control.**   The following are several definitions of factors related to internal control.

A. _____ includes journalizing and posting transactions, and keeping up-to-date records of a company's assets.

B. _____ means permission to exchange or use assets for specific purposes under given conditions.

C. _____ involves keeping track of assets from the time of their acquisition in one transaction until their disposal or use in another transaction.

D. _____ means the set of steps needed to complete the exchange of assets or use of assets in the company.

REQUIRED   Fill in the word that completes each definition.

EXERCISE 6-2   **Separation of Duties.**   The Leonibus Company is concerned about maintaining internal control over selected accounting duties. The company has three competent employees (Employees A, B, and C) who must perform the following tasks:

(a) Write checks to suppliers.

(b) Record transactions in the sales journal and the accounts receivable subsidiary ledger.

(c) Deposit customers' checks received in payment of their accounts.

(d) Issue credit memos to customers for sales returns and allowances on account.

(e) Record transactions in the purchases journal and the accounts payable subsidiary ledger.

(f) Issue debit memos to suppliers for purchases returns and allowances on account.

REQUIRED   1. Explain what is meant by *separation of duties*. Why is it important for internal control?

2. Show how you would divide the preceding tasks among Employees A, B, and C for *good* internal control. Explain your reasoning.

3. Show how you would divide these tasks among Employees A, B, and C for *poor* internal control. Explain your reasoning.

EXERCISE 6-3   **Internal Control Weaknesses.**   The following are several internal control weaknesses of a retail store:

(a) Sales invoices are not prenumbered.

(b) Credit sales of a large dollar amount can be approved by any sales employee.

(c) One employee is responsible for recording purchases in the purchases journal and for writing checks.

(d) Some purchases are made by phone and no purchase order is written up.

(e) Employees are allowed to bring coats, bags, and purses into working areas.

(f) One employee is responsible for depositing customer checks and for recording their receipt in both the cash receipts journal and the accounts receivable subsidiary ledger.

(g) The inventory of gold jewelry for sale is kept in unlocked display cases.

(h) Whenever inventory is low, any sales employee can prepare a purchase order to reorder the items and send the purchase order to the purchasing department.

REQUIRED   1. For each internal control weakness explain how the weakness might result in a loss of the company's assets or an inefficient accounting system.

2. For each internal control weakness explain what action could be taken to correct the weakness.

EXERCISE 6-4   **Journalizing and Posting Control Accounts.**   The Axel Computer Store uses subsidiary ledgers and control accounts for both accounts receivable and accounts payable. No cash discounts are available. The following is information relating to these items at the beginning of January.

GENERAL LEDGER		SUBSIDIARY LEDGERS	
Accounts receivable, 1/1	$4,500	Accounts receivable:	
		B. Mont,	$3,600
		C. Rail,	900
Accounts payable, 1/1	$5,700	Accounts payable:	
		Dorn Co.,	$3,100
		True Co.,	2,600

At the beginning of January, the company's Cash account had a balance of $3,900. During January, the following transactions occurred:

Date	Transaction
Jan. 3	Sold $300 of merchandise on credit to C. Rail.
10	Paid $1,200 on account to True Company.
17	Purchased $800 of inventory on credit from Zorro Company.
26	Collected $1,600 on account from B. Mont.

REQUIRED

1. Set up T-accounts for the accounts receivable and accounts payable subsidiary ledgers, and the following T-accounts (and account numbers) in the general ledger: Cash (101), Accounts Receivable (103), Accounts Payable (201), Sales (401), and Purchases (501).

2. Journalize the January transactions in a general journal and post to the accounts.

3. Prepare schedules that list the totals of the accounts receivable and accounts payable subsidiary ledgers at the end of January.

EXERCISE 6-5

Matching Transactions with Special Journals. The following journals are used by a company:

A. Cash Receipts

B. Cash Payments

C. Sales

D. Purchases

E. General

During a month the company entered into the following transactions:

1. Returned defective merchandise to supplier for adjustment to account.

2. Purchased equipment with note payable and cash down payment.

3. Prepared closing entries.

4. Purchased merchandise for cash.

5. Purchased land by issuing note payable.

6. Paid cash to customer for return of faulty merchandise previously sold to the customer.

7. Sold merchandise for cash.

8. Purchased merchandise on account.

9. Returned defective merchandise for cash refund.

10. Owner invested an additional $5,000 in the company.

11. Paid utilities expense.

12. Sold merchandise on account.

REQUIRED   Match each of these transactions with the appropriate journal (A through E) in which it would be recorded.

EXERCISE 6-6   **Special Journals and Accounts.** The following are ten transactions of a company that uses special journals:

Transaction	Journal	Accounts
(a) Return of defective merchandise to supplier for adjustment to account	_____	_____
(b) Payment on accounts payable	_____	_____
(c) Purchase of merchandise for cash	_____	_____
(d) Payment of advertising expense	_____	_____
(e) Sale of merchandise for cash	_____	_____
(f) Purchase of merchandise on account	_____	_____
(g) Sales allowance for cash	_____	_____
(h) Preparation of adjusting entries	_____	_____
(i) Sale of merchandise on account	_____	_____
(j) Purchase of equipment for cash	_____	_____

REQUIRED   In the space provided:

1. Indicate in which of the following journals the transaction would be recorded: sales, purchases, cash receipts, cash payments, and general journal.

2. Indicate the accounts that would be debited or credited in the journal for each transaction.

EXERCISE 6-7   **Special Journals and Accounts.** The following are ten transactions of a company that uses special journals:

Transaction	Journal	Accounts
(a) Purchase of merchandise for cash	_____	_____
(b) Payment of telephone expense	_____	_____
(c) Additional investment by owner	_____	_____
(d) Sale of merchandise on account	_____	_____
(e) Preparation of closing entries	_____	_____
(f) Purchase of merchandise on account	_____	_____
(g) Payment of salary expense	_____	_____
(h) Purchase of equipment by issuing note payable	_____	_____
(i) Sale of merchandise for cash	_____	_____
(j) Payment on account payable, less discount	_____	_____

REQUIRED

1. Indicate in which of the following journals the transaction would be recorded: sales, purchases, cash payments, cash receipts, and general journal.

2. Indicate the accounts that would be debited or credited in the journal for each transaction.

EXERCISE 6-8   **Cash Receipts Journal.**   The Boggler Pre-Fab Fireplace Store entered into the following transactions during the month of May:

Date	Transaction
May 1	Sold $3,000 of merchandise to W. Moehler for cash.
5	Received payment from P. Ott on account receivable of $450 less 2% discount.
13	Sold land at its original cost of $1,800.
24	T. Boggler invested an additional $1,000 cash in the company.
30	Received payment from V. Sidnel on account receivable in the amount of $500.

REQUIRED   Using the format shown in the text prepare a cash receipts journal and record the Boggler Pre-Fab Fireplace Store transactions in it.

EXERCISE 6-9   **Cash Payments Journal.**   The Foily Outdoor Clothing Store entered into the following transactions during the month of April:

Date	Transaction
Apr. 2	Refunded $60 cash to a customer, Tolley Company, for faulty merchandise returned.
5	Purchased $1,500 of merchandise for cash.
15	Paid advertising expense of $200 for the first two weeks of the month.
20	Purchased $1,300 of store equipment making a $300 cash down payment and signing a $1,000 note.
26	Paid $1,000 account payable to Caner Company, less 2% discount.

REQUIRED   Using the format shown in the text prepare a cash payments journal and enter the Foily Outdoor Clothing Store transactions in it.

EXERCISE 6-10   **Posting from Journals.**   The sales journal and purchases journal of Atheon Jewelers for July are as follows:

SALES JOURNAL				Page 8
Date	Customer Account Debited	Invoice No.	Post. Ref.	Amount
July 1	Van Haley	640		71
6	Faye Dunday	641		103
14	Howard Carren	642		63
29	Gayle Francis	643		206
31	Total			443

PURCHASES JOURNAL					Page 4
Date		Supplier Account Credited	Invoice Date	Post. Ref.	Amount
July	3	Lalel Company	June 30		400
	12	Deiter's Supply Company	July 12		100
	24	Foiler Suppliers	July 22		200
	30	Longaker Company	July 29		300
	31	Total			1,000

The company shows the following accounts in its general ledger:

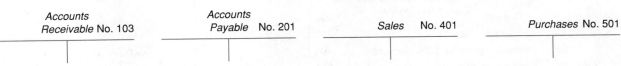

Accounts Receivable No. 103   Accounts Payable No. 201   Sales No. 401   Purchases No. 501

REQUIRED   Assuming that Atheon Jewelers uses subsidiary ledgers for accounts receivable and accounts payable, make the necessary daily and monthly postings to the appropriate accounts.

EXERCISE 6-11   **Posting from Cash Receipts Journal.**   The cash receipts journal of TR Appliances for May is as follows:

CASH RECEIPTS JOURNAL									Page 2
Date		Explanation (or Account Title)	Cash Debit	Sales Disc. Taken Debit	Post. Ref.	Acct. Rec. Credit	Sales Credit	Post. Ref.	Misc. Credit
May	3	Cash sales	250				250		
	10	P. Tari, Invoice 302 less 2%	588	12		600			
	20	Randall Quepy, Invoice 306	300			300			
	28	Land; sale at cost	5,000						5,000
	31	Totals	6,138	12		900	250		5,000

The company uses a subsidiary ledger for accounts receivable, and it shows the following accounts in its general ledger:

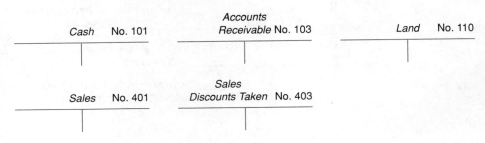

Cash No. 101   Accounts Receivable No. 103   Land No. 110

Sales No. 401   Sales Discounts Taken No. 403

REQUIRED Make all the necessary postings from the cash receipts journal.

EXERCISE 6-12 **Posting from Cash Payments Journal.** The cash payments journal used by the Polex Company follows. The company uses a subsidiary ledger for accounts payable and shows the following accounts in its general ledger.

CASH PAYMENTS JOURNAL											Page 6
Date		Explanation (or Account Title)	Cash Credit	Purch. Disc. Taken Credit	Post. Ref.	Misc. Credit	Post. Ref.	Acct. Pay. Debit	Purch. Debit	Post. Ref.	Misc. Debit
May	1	Land — Purchase with note and									5,000
		Notes — cash down payment									
		Payable	1,000			4,000					
	10	Utilities Expense	210								210
	20	Porter Company, less 2% discount	490	10				500			
	30	Cash purchases	520						520		
	31	Barrows Company	700					700			
	31	Totals	2,920	10		4,000		1,200	520		5,210

Account Title	Account Number
Cash	101
Land	110
Accounts Payable	201
Notes Payable	210
Purchases	501
Purchases Discounts Taken	503
Utilities Expense	521

REQUIRED Set up T-accounts for the Polex Company account titles and the accounts payable subsidiary ledger and make all the necessary postings from the cash payments journal.

EXERCISE 6-13 **Completion: EDP.** The following are several statements that relate to EDP systems.

A. The basic elements of an EDP system are _____ and _____ .

B. The _____ of an EDP system consists of input _____ , a CPU, and _____ devices.

C. Computer software consists of two types, _____ software and _____ software.

D. _____ software includes the programs designed to allow the user to complete specific tasks with the computer.

E. _____ software includes the program designed to coordinate the operations of the various parts of the computer itself.

REQUIRED   Fill in the word(s) that completes each statement.

EXERCISE 6-14   **(Appendix) EDP Accounting System.**   The Watts Service Company was established on May 1, 1991. It created the following chart of accounts:

Acct. No.	Account Title	Acct. No.	Account Title
101	Cash	301	S. Watts—Capital
105	Office Supplies	302	S. Watts—Withdrawals
108	Prepaid Rent	401	Service Revenue
110	Land	501	Salary Expense
115	Office Equipment	502	Utilities Expense
116	Accumulated Depreciation:	503	Office Supplies Expense
	Office Equipment	505	Rent Expense
201	Accounts Payable	506	Depreciation Expense: Office Equipment
220	Notes Payable	510	Interest Expense
221	Interest Payable		

During May, the company engaged in the following transactions:

Date	Transaction
May 1	S. Watts set up the company by investing $8,000 cash in the company's checking account.
2	Paid $2,400 rent in advance for office space.
3	Purchased office equipment costing $1,800 by signing a note due in 1 year.
14	Office supplies costing $420 were purchased on account.
20	Performed services for customer and collected $1,400.
27	Purchased land for $3,000.
31	Paid $600 for employee's salary.
31	Paid utilities bill of $100 for May.
31	S. Watts withdrew $750 cash for personal use.

At the end of May, the following adjusting entry information was available:

1. Office supplies used, $32.

2. Prepaid rent expired on office space, $200.

3. Depreciation on office equipment, $30.

4. Interest accrued on note payable, $18.

REQUIRED   1. Read the information in the Appendix to the chapter regarding the EDP system for Exercise 6-14.

2. Enter the necessary information into your computer to record May's transactions and ending adjustments.

3. Print out an adjusted trial balance as of May 31, 1991.

4. Print out: (a) an income statement for the month ended May 31, 1991, (b) a statement of changes in owner's equity for the month ended May 31, 1991, and (c) a balance sheet as of May 31, 1991.

Problems

Part A

PROBLEM 6-1A   **Internal Control Terms.**   The following is a list of key terms in internal control, as well as a list of statements describing or relating to these terms:

A. Accountability   E. Purchase requisition

B. Accounts payable account   F. Control account

C. Execution   G. Rules for control of assets

D. Internal auditing   H. Internal control

_____ 1. Set of steps needed to complete the exchange of assets or use of assets in the company.

_____ 2. Internal document requesting that certain items of inventory be purchased.

_____ 3. Credit balance must always be equal to credit total of related subsidiary ledger on balance sheet date.

_____ 4. Policies and procedures used to safeguard a company's assets and to ensure that reliable financial statements are the end result of an efficient accounting system.

_____ 5. Keeping track of assets from the time of their acquisition in one transaction until their disposal or use in another transaction.

_____ 6. Deposit all cash receipts daily in the company's bank.

_____ 7. Review of operations to ensure procedures are being followed.

_____ 8. Takes the place of the individual accounts that have been removed from the general ledger and placed in a subsidiary ledger.

REQUIRED   Place the letter of the key term on the line in front of the statement describing or relating to the term.

PROBLEM 6-2A   **Internal Control and Purchases.**   The Anibonita Company is a retail store with several sales departments. It also has an accounting department, a purchasing department, and a receiving department. All inventory is kept in the sales departments. When the inventory of a specific item is low, the manager of the sales department that sells the item notifies the purchasing department, which then orders the merchandise. All purchases are made on credit. Anibonita Company pays the freight charges on all its purchases after being notified of the cost by the freight company. When the inventory is delivered, it is checked in by the receiving department and then sent to the sales department where it is placed on the sales shelves. The company uses special journals and subsidiary ledgers.

REQUIRED

1. Briefly explain what is meant by authorization, execution, recording, and accountability in relation to internal control over the Anibonita Company's purchasing process.

2. Describe what source documents are needed, as well as how they should be used, to maintain internal control over the purchasing process.

PROBLEM 6-3A **Internal Control Principles.** Internal control is concerned with promoting an efficient accounting system and safeguarding a company's assets. Several general principles have been developed to help in establishing and maintaining good internal control.

REQUIRED List and discuss the general principles of internal control presented in this chapter.

PROBLEM 6-4A **Cash Receipts Journal.** During the month of February Mobac Sound Systems entered into the following transactions related to cash receipts:

Date	Transaction
Feb. 1	The owner, T. Mobac, invested an additional $6,000 cash in the business.
3	Sold $700 of merchandise for cash.
3	Returned $50 of defective merchandise to supplier for cash refund.
5	Collected $530 from B. Teer for payment on account.
8	Sold $450 of merchandise for cash.
11	Received $650 less 2% discount from T. Beem for payment on account.
13	Sold land at cost, $7,000.
14	Received $1,015 in payment of a $1,000 note receivable, plus current interest revenue of $15.
16	Collected $375 from R. Cooke in payment of account.
20	Sold $250 of merchandise for cash.
23	Received $700 less 2% discount from Q. Tempe for payment on account.
28	Borrowed $1,800 from local bank by signing a 3-month note.

The company uses a subsidiary ledger for its accounts receivable and on January 31 showed the following accounts (and selected account balances) in its books:

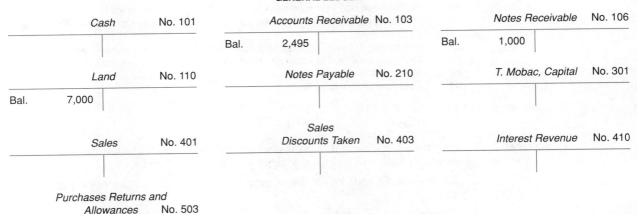

GENERAL LEDGER

Cash	No. 101		Accounts Receivable	No. 103		Notes Receivable	No. 106
		Bal.	2,495		Bal.	1,000	
Land	No. 110		Notes Payable	No. 210		T. Mobac, Capital	No. 301
Bal. 7,000							
Sales	No. 401		Sales Discounts Taken	No. 403		Interest Revenue	No. 410
Purchases Returns and Allowances	No. 503						

**ACCOUNTS RECEIVABLE
SUBSIDIARY LEDGER**

T. Beem		R. Cooke	
Bal.	650	Bal.	375

B. Teer		Q. Tempe	
Bal.	770	Bal.	700

REQUIRED Set up a cash receipts journal and record the Mobac Sound Systems transactions. Make all the necessary daily and monthly postings to its accounts.

PROBLEM 6-5A **Special Journals with Subsidiary Ledgers.** The Twaddler Hot Tub Company entered into the following transactions during the month of April:

Date	Transaction
Apr. 1	Purchased merchandise on credit from the Loone Company, $750, invoice dated March 30. Terms 2/15, n/30.
1	Paid April rent of $500 and recorded as rent expense.
2	Sold merchandise on credit to Norm Waters, Invoice No. 302, $400. Terms 2/10, n/30.
3	Received $50 credit on account from Loone Company for defective merchandise purchased on April 1.
5	Sold merchandise for cash, $1,500.
6	Purchased store equipment on credit from XYZ Supply Company, $800.
8	Purchased $900 of merchandise for cash.
9	Received payment from Norm Waters for Invoice No. 302, less cash discount.
10	Sold merchandise on credit to Lee Dillard, Invoice No. 303, $600. Terms 2/15, n/30.
10	Paid balance due on merchandise purchased from Loone Company on April 1, less cash discount.
12	Sold store equipment at cost, $50.
12	Purchased merchandise on credit from Scroggs Company, invoice dated today, $1,200. Terms 2/10, n/30.
14	Purchased land by paying $2,000 cash and signing an $8,000 note payable.
16	Sold merchandise for cash, $300.
18	Borrowed $6,000 from local bank, issuing a 90-day note payable.
19	Paid balance due on merchandise purchased from Scroggs Company on April 12, less cash discount.
20	The owner, T. Twaddler, invested an additional $2,500 cash in the business.
24	Received balance due from Lee Dillard for Invoice No. 303, less cash discount.
28	Paid monthly salaries, $3,000.
30	Paid April utility bill, $100.

REQUIRED
1. Prepare a sales journal, a purchases journal, a cash receipts journal, a cash payments journal, and a general journal as shown in the text.
2. Record the Twaddler Hot Tub Company transactions in the appropriate journals.
3. Prepare subsidiary ledgers for accounts receivable and accounts payable.
4. Make the daily postings to the subsidiary ledgers.

PROBLEM 6-6A   **Special Journals, Journalizing and Posting.** The transactions that the Boco Sporting Goods Store completed during the month of May are as follows:

Date	Transaction
May 1	Paid May rent of $600 and recorded as rent expense.
2	Sold merchandise on credit to T. Crone, Invoice No. 80, $500. Terms 2/10, n/30.
4	Purchased merchandise for cash, $300.
5	Sold merchandise for cash, $100.
7	Purchased merchandise on credit from Barnum Supply Company, $900, invoice dated May 6. Terms 2/10, n/30.
9	Received payment from T. Crone for Invoice No. 80, less cash discount.
11	Sold land at cost, $2,000.
12	Paid Barnum Supply Company for merchandise received on May 7, less cash discount.
14	Sold merchandise on credit to R. Holen, Invoice No. 81, $350. Terms 2/10, n/30.
15	Purchased merchandise on credit from Walthem's Company $1,600, invoice dated today. Terms n/30.
18	Received $100 credit on account with Walthem's Company for defective merchandise purchased on May 15.
20	Received payment from R. Holen for Invoice No. 81, less cash discount.
24	Purchased store equipment by paying $500 cash and signing a note payable for $1,000.
28	Sold merchandise for cash, $280.
30	Paid May utilities bill, $120.

The company shows the following T-accounts in its general ledger:

Account Titles	Account Number
Cash	101
Accounts Receivable	103
Land	110
Store Equipment	114
Accounts Payable	201
Notes Payable	210
Sales	401
Sales Discounts Taken	403
Purchases	501
Purchases Discounts Taken	503
Purchases Returns and Allowances	506
Utilities Expense	521
Rent Expense	523

REQUIRED   1. Prepare a sales journal, purchases journal, cash receipts journal, cash payments journal, and general journal as shown in the text.

2. Record the Boco Sporting Goods Store transactions in the appropriate journals.

3. Set up the general ledger accounts and subsidiary ledgers for accounts receivable and accounts payable.

4. Make all the necessary postings during and at the end of the month.

PROBLEM 6-7A   **EDP Terms.**   The following is a list of key terms in EDP systems, as well as a list of statements describing or relating to these terms:

A. EDP   E. Mainframe

B. Memory unit   F. Printer

C. Software   G. Computer

D. Input device   H. Hardware

____ 1. High-speed electronic machine that can record, retain, process, and report information on the basis of a set of stored instructions.

____ 2. Stores program instructions and accounting information in a CPU.

____ 3. Used to print output in whatever form programmed into the computer.

____ 4. Used to transfer information and instructions to a computer.

____ 5. Equipment of an EDP system.

____ 6. Using a computer to record, retain, and report a company's financial and managerial accounting information.

____ 7. Largest and most powerful computer.

____ 8. Set of computer programs used to operate a computer.

REQUIRED   Place the letter of the key term on the line in front of the statement describing or relating to the term.

PROBLEM 6-8A   **(Appendix) EDP Accounting System.**   The Hurn Consulting Company was established on January 2, 1991. It created the following chart of accounts:

Acct. No.	Account Title	Acct. No.	Account Title
101	Cash	221	Interest Payable
105	Office Supplies	301	B. Hurn—Capital
110	Land	302	B. Hurn—Withdrawals
112	Building	401	Consulting Revenue
113	Accumulated Depreciation: Building	501	Salary Expense
		502	Utilities Expense
115	Office Equipment	503	Office Supplies Expense
116	Accumulated Depreciation: Office Equipment	505	Depreciation Expense: Building
		506	Depreciation Expense: Office Equipment
201	Accounts Payable		
220	Notes Payable	510	Interest Expense

During January, the company engaged in the following transactions:

Date	Transaction
Jan. 2	B. Hurn set up the company by investing $40,000 cash in the company's checking account.
3	Acquired land and a building at a cash price of $6,000 and $24,000, respectively.
5	Purchased office equipment costing $3,000 by signing a note due in 1 year.
10	Office supplies costing $735 were purchased on account.
21	Performed consulting services for customer and collected $2,020.
31	Paid $650 for employee's salary.
31	Paid utilities bill of $88 for January.
31	B. Hurn withdrew $900 cash for personal use.

At the end of January, the following adjusting entry information was available:

1. Office supplies used, $42.

2. Depreciation on building, $100.

3. Depreciation on office equipment, $50.

4. Interest accrued on note payable, $30.

REQUIRED

1. Read the information in the Appendix to the chapter regarding the EDP system for Exercise 6-14 as it applies to Problem 6-8A.

2. Enter the necessary information into your computer to record January's transactions and ending adjustments.

3. Print out an adjusted trial balance as of January 31, 1991.

4. Print out: (a) an income statement for the month ended January 31, 1991, (b) a statement of changes in owner's equity for the month ended January 31, 1991, and (c) a balance sheet as of January 31, 1991.

Problems

Part B

PROBLEM 6-1B   **Internal Control Terms.** The following is a list of key terms in internal control, as well as a list of statements describing or relating to these terms.

A. Internal control

B. Purchase order

C. Subsidiary ledger

D. Separation of duties

E. Recording

F. Accounts receivable account

G. Authorization

H. Well-designed source documents

_____ 1. Permission to exchange or use assets for specific purposes under given conditions.

_____ 2. Preprinted, serially numbered invoices.

_____ 3. One person should not be responsible for both recording a transaction involving an asset and controlling that asset.

_____ 4. Policies and procedures used to safeguard a company's assets and to ensure that reliable financial statements are the end result of an efficient accounting system.

_____ 5. Debit balance must always be equal to debit total of related subsidiary ledger on balance sheet date.

_____ 6. Business document authorizing a supplier to ship the items listed at a specific price.

_____ 7. Group of similar accounts taken out of general journal that show the detail of one specific accounting activity.

_____ 8. Journalizing and posting transactions, and keeping up-to-date records of a company's assets.

REQUIRED   Place the letter of the key term on the line in front of the statement describing or relating to the term.

PROBLEM 6-2B   **Internal Control and Sales.** The JeBean Company is a wholesale company that makes only sales on account to retail customers who order through the mail. The company has an accounting department, credit department, inventory department, and shipping department. After approval of the order by the credit department, the merchandise is assembled in the inventory department and then sent to the shipping department. The shipping department packs the merchandise in cardboard boxes after which it is picked up by the freight company and shipped to the customer. JeBean Company pays for freight charges on all items shipped to customers after being notified of the cost by the freight company. The company uses special journals and subsidiary ledgers.

REQUIRED   1. Briefly explain what is meant by authorization, execution, recording, and accountability in relation to internal control of the JeBean Company's sales process.

           2. Describe what source documents are needed, as well as how they should be used, to maintain internal control over the sales process.

PROBLEM 6-3B   **Cash Payments Journal.** The Shoer Specialty Import Store entered into the following transactions during the month of January:

Date	Transaction
Jan. 2	Purchased new equipment by signing a $900 note payable and paying $600 cash.
2	Purchased $1,500 of merchandise for cash.
4	Paid January rent of $500 and recorded as rent expense.
6	Paid balance due to Willis Company, $800, less 2% discount.
12	Refunded $80 cash to customer upon return of defective merchandise sold earlier in the month.
12	Paid $600 to Value Suppliers on account.
15	Paid $70 for advertisement in local newspaper.
19	Paid Quine Supply Company $1,000, less 2% discount.
20	Purchased $200 of merchandise for cash.
25	Paid Tailer Company $700 on account.
30	Paid January utility bill in the amount of $110.
31	Paid monthly salaries of $2,500.

The company uses a subsidiary ledger for accounts payable and shows the following accounts (and selected account balances) on its books:

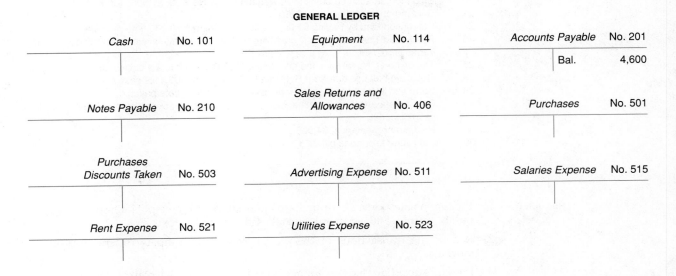

GENERAL LEDGER

Cash	No. 101	Equipment	No. 114	Accounts Payable	No. 201
				Bal.	4,600

Notes Payable	No. 210	Sales Returns and Allowances	No. 406	Purchases	No. 501

Purchases Discounts Taken	No. 503	Advertising Expense	No. 511	Salaries Expense	No. 515

Rent Expense	No. 521	Utilities Expense	No. 523

ACCOUNTS PAYABLE
SUBSIDIARY LEDGER

Quine Supply Company		Tailer Company	
Bal.	1,000	Bal.	1,500

Value Suppliers		Willis Company	
Bal.	1,300	Bal.	800

REQUIRED Set up a cash payments journal and record the transactions of the Shoer Specialty Import Store. Make all the necessary daily and monthly postings to its accounts.

PROBLEM 6-4B **Special Journals with Subsidiary Ledgers.** The Noval Waterbed Company entered into the following transactions during the month of June:

Date	Transaction
June 1	Paid June rent of $450 and recorded as rent expense.
3	Sold merchandise for cash, $500.
5	Purchased equipment on credit from Ziemar Company for $700.
7	Purchased merchandise on credit from the Kaas Company, $1,400, invoice dated June 5. Terms 2/10, n/30.
8	Sold merchandise on credit to B. Coton, Invoice No. 501, $900. Terms 2/10, n/30.
10	Received $100 credit on account from Kaas Company for faulty merchandise purchased on June 7.
12	Sold equipment at cost, $250.
15	Received payment from B. Coton for Invoice No. 501, less cash discount.

18	Purchased $1,200 of merchandise for cash.
19	Paid balance due on merchandise purchased from Kaas Company on June 7, less cash discount.
20	Sold merchandise on credit to R. Hagin, Invoice No. 502, $1,600. Terms 2/10, n/30.
21	Sold merchandise for cash, $750.
23	Purchased land by paying $3,000 cash and signing a $9,000 note payable.
25	Purchased merchandise on credit from Peol Company, invoice dated today, $1,800. Terms 2/10, n/30.
26	The owner T. Noval invested an additional $5,000 cash in the business.
28	Received balance due from R. Hagin for Invoice No. 502, less cash discount.
28	Borrowed $10,000 from local bank, issuing a 6-month note payable.
29	Paid balance due for merchandise purchased from Peol Company on June 25, less cash discount.
30	Paid monthly salaries, $4,000.
30	Paid June telephone bill, $85.

REQUIRED

1. Prepare a sales journal, a purchases journal, a cash receipts journal, a cash payments journal, and a general journal as shown in the text.

2. Record the transactions of the Noval Waterbed Company in the appropriate journals.

3. Prepare subsidiary ledgers for accounts receivable and accounts payable.

4. Make the daily postings to the subsidiary ledgers.

PROBLEM 6-5B   **Special Journals, Journalizing and Posting.** The transactions completed by the Photope Mattress and Bedding Store during the month of June are as follows:

Date	Transaction
June 1	Sold merchandise on account to R. Crush, Invoice No. 180, $500. Terms 2/15, n/30.
3	Paid June rent of $400 and recorded as rent expense.
6	Sold merchandise for cash, $225.
8	Refunded $50 cash for defective merchandise sold on June 6.
10	Purchased merchandise on account from LT Supply Company, $1,500; invoice dated today. Terms 2/15, n/30.
12	Received payment of Invoice No. 180 from R. Crush, less cash discount.
16	Sold delivery equipment at cost, $200.
19	Purchased merchandise on account from Prones Company $1,100, invoice dated June 17. Terms n/30.
21	Paid LT Supply Company for merchandise purchased on June 10, less cash discount.
22	Purchased delivery equipment on account from Peats', $400. Terms n/30.
25	Sold merchandise on account to L. Lind, Invoice No. 181, $300. Terms 2/10, n/30.
27	Sold merchandise for cash, $520.
29	Purchased land by paying $1,000 cash and issuing a $2,000 note payable.
29	Paid June telephone bill, $90.
30	Received payment from L. Lind for Invoice No. 181, less cash discount.
30	Purchased merchandise for cash, $500.

The company shows the following T-accounts in its general ledger:

Account Titles	Account Number
Cash	101
Accounts Receivable	103
Land	110
Delivery Equipment	114
Accounts Payable	201
Notes Payable	210
Sales	401
Sales Discounts Taken	403
Sales Returns and Allowances	406
Purchases	501
Purchases Discounts Taken	503
Telephone Expense	521
Rent Expense	525

REQUIRED

1. Prepare a sales journal, purchases journal, cash receipts journal, cash payments journal, and general journal as shown in the text.

2. Record the transactions of the Photope Mattress and Bedding Store in the appropriate journals.

3. Set up the general ledger accounts and subsidiary ledgers for accounts receivable and accounts payable.

4. Make all the necessary postings during and at the end of the month.

PROBLEM 6-6B

EDP Terms. The following is a list of key terms in EDP systems, as well as a list of statements describing or relating to these terms.

A. Computer

B. Output device

C. Spreadsheet

D. Scanner

E. Control unit

F. EDP

G. Personal computer

H. Computer program

_____ 1. Electronic worksheet.

_____ 2. Detailed instructions to a computer about how to record, retain, process, and report information.

_____ 3. Used to read uniform product codes.

_____ 4. Using a computer to record, retain, and report a company's financial and managerial accounting information.

_____ 5. Used to transfer information out of the computer.

_____ 6. Smallest and least expensive computer.

_____ 7. Reads, interprets, and carries out instructions in a CPU.

_____ 8. High-speed electronic machine that can record, retain, process, and report information on the basis of a set of stored instructions.

REQUIRED

Place the letter of the key term on the line in front of the statement describing or relating to the term.

PROBLEM 6-7B   **EDP Software.**   A friend of yours is familiar with accounting but not computers. She asks, "What is software, what are the common financial accounting software packages, and what are they designed to do?"

REQUIRED   Prepare a written answer for your friend's question.

PROBLEM 6-8B   **(Appendix) EDP Accounting System.**   The Sutton Service Company was established on April 1, 1991. It created the following chart of accounts:

Acct. No.	Account Title	Acct. No.	Account Title
101	Cash	221	Interest Payable
105	Office Supplies	301	S. Sutton—Capital
110	Land	302	S. Sutton—Withdrawals
112	Building	401	Financial Service Revenue
113	Accumulated Depreciation: Building	501	Salary Expense
		502	Utilities Expense
115	Office Equipment	503	Office Supplies Expense
116	Accumulated Depreciation: Office Equipment	505	Depreciation Expense: Building
		506	Depreciation Expense: Office Equipment
201	Accounts Payable		
220	Notes Payable	510	Interest Expense

During April, the company engaged in the following transactions:

Date	Transaction
April 1	S. Sutton set up the company by investing $30,000 cash in the company's checking account.
4	Acquired land and a building at a cash price of $5,000 and $18,000, respectively.
8	Purchased office equipment costing $2,400 by signing a note due in 1 year.
15	Office supplies costing $900 were purchased on account.
23	Performed financial services for customer and collected $1,800.
30	Paid $700 for employee's salary.
30	Paid utilities bill of $92 for April.
30	S. Sutton withdrew $1,000 cash for personal use.

At the end of April, the following adjusting entry information was available:

1. Office supplies used, $39.

2. Depreciation on building, $75.

3. Depreciation on office equipment, $40.

4. Interest accrued on note payable, $24.

REQUIRED   1.   Read the information in the Appendix to the chapter regarding the EDP system for Exercise 6-14 as it applies to Problem 6-8B.

2.   Enter the necessary information into your computer to record April's transactions and ending adjustments.

3.   Print out an adjusted trial balance as of April 30, 1991.

4.   Print out:
   (a)   an income statement for the month ended April 30, 1991,
   (b)   a statement of changes in owner's equity for the month ended April 30, 1991, and
   (c)   a balance sheet as of April 30, 1991.

Decision Cases

DECISION CASE 6-1   **Evaluation of Internal Control.**   You are a consultant for several companies. The following are several independent situations you have discovered, each of which may or may not have one or more internal control weaknesses.

(a)   Company A has purchased several small calculators for use by the office and sales employees. So that these hand calculators will be available to any employee who needs one they are kept in an unlocked storage cabinet in the office. Anyone who takes and uses a calculator "signs out" the calculator by writing his or her name on a sheet of paper posted near the cabinet. When the calculator is returned the employee crosses out his or her name on the sheet.

(b)   In Company B one employee is responsible for counting and recording all the receipts received in the mail from customers paying their accounts. Usually customers pay by check but occasionally they mail cash. Every day after the mail is delivered this employee opens the envelopes containing payments by customers. She carefully counts all remittances and places the checks and cash in a bag. She then lists the amount of each check or cash received and the customer's name on a sheet of paper. After totaling the cash and checks received she records the receipts in the cash receipts journal, endorses the checks in the company's name, and deposits the checks and cash in the bank.

(c)   Company C owns a delivery van for deliveries of sales to customers. No mileage is kept of the deliveries, although all gas and oil receipts are carefully checked before being paid. To advertise the store, two signs with the store's name have been printed and hung on each side of the van. These signs are easily removable so that the van can be periodically cleaned without damaging the signs. The company allows employees to borrow the van at night or on the weekends if they need the van for personal hauling. No mileage is kept of the personal hauling, but the employee who borrowed the van must fill the gas tank before returning the van.

(d)   Employee Y is in charge of employee records for Company D. Whenever a new employee is hired, the new employee's name, address, salary, and other relevant information are properly recorded. Every payday all employees are paid by check. At this time Employee Y makes out each employee's check, signs it, and gives it to each employee. After distributing the paychecks, Employee Y makes an entry in the general journal debiting Salaries Expense and crediting Cash for the total amount of the salary checks.

(e) To reduce the paperwork in Company E, orders for purchases of inventory from suppliers are made by phone. No purchase order is prepared. When the goods arrive at the company they are immediately brought to the sales floor. An employee then authorizes payment based on the supplier's invoice, writes and signs a check, and mails payment to the supplier. Another employee uses the paid invoice to record the purchase and payment in the general journal.

(f) All sales made by Company F, whether they are for cash or on account, are "rung up" on a single cash register. Employee X is responsible for collecting the cash receipts from sales and customer charge slips at the end of each day. The employee carefully counts the cash, preparing a "cash receipts" slip for the total. The employee compares the total of the cash receipts slip and the customer charge slips to the total sales on the cash register tape to verify the total sales for the day. The cash register tape is then discarded and the cash is deposited in the bank. The cash receipts slip and the customer charge slips are turned over to a different employee who records the cash and credit sales in the general journal.

REQUIRED

1. List the internal control weakness or weaknesses you find in each of the preceding independent situations. If no weakness can be found explain why the internal control is good.

2. Describe how you would remedy each situation in which there is an internal control weakness to improve the internal control.

DECISION CASE 6-2

Internal Control over Purchases.   Oliver Bauer, owner of Bauer's Retail Store, has been very careful to establish good internal control over purchases for his store. The store has several employees and since Ollie cannot devote as much time as he would like to running the store, he has entrusted a long-time employee with the task of purchasing inventory. This employee has worked for Ollie for 15 years and knows all of the store's suppliers. Whenever inventory must be purchased the employee prepares a purchase order and mails it to the supplier. When a rush order is needed the employee occasionally calls in the order and does not prepare a purchase order. This procedure is acceptable to the suppliers because they know the employee. When the goods are received from the supplier this employee carefully checks in each item to verify the correct quantity and quality. This job is usually done at night after the store is closed, thus allowing the employee to help with sales to customers during regular working hours. After checking in the items the employee initials the copy of the supplier invoice received with the goods, staples the copy to the purchase order (if there is one), journalizes the purchase, and prepares a check for payment. Oliver Bauer examines the source documents (purchase order and initialed invoice) at this point, signs the check, and the employee journalizes the payment. Ollie has become concerned about the store's gross profit, which has been steadily decreasing even though he has heard customers complaining that the store's selling prices are too high. In a discussion with the employee, the employee says, "I'm doing my best to hold down costs. I will continue to do my purchasing job as efficiently as possible (even though I am overworked). However, I think you should hire another salesperson and spend more on advertising. This will increase your sales and, in turn, your gross profit."

REQUIRED   Why do you think the gross profit of the store has gone down? Prepare a report for Oliver Bauer that summarizes any internal control weaknesses existing in the purchasing procedure and explain what the end result might be. Make suggestions for improving any weaknesses you uncover.

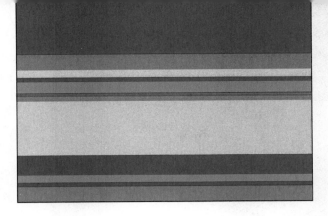

P A R T T W O

ACCOUNTING
FOR ASSETS
AND LIABILITIES

7

Cash

LEARNING OBJECTIVES

1. Identify the components of cash.

2. Explain the basic concepts underlying the internal control of cash.

3. Describe a voucher system.

4. Record the transactions of a petty cash fund.

5. Prepare a bank reconciliation.

6. Explain cash equivalents.

7. Prepare the disclosure of cash and cash equivalents on the balance sheet.

ash is the asset that is listed first on a balance sheet because it is the most liquid current asset. **Current assets are cash and other assets that are expected to be converted into cash, sold, or consumed within 1 year or the normal operating cycle, whichever is longer.** Current assets are usually listed on the balance sheet in the order of their liquidity. **Liquidity is the measure of the time in which the asset will be converted into cash.** The most liquid asset is the asset that will be converted into cash in the shortest time period. Cash is a very important resource for a company in the same way that it is for an individual. Other major types of current assets are marketable securities, accounts receivable, notes receivable, and inventories. In this chapter we discuss the nature of cash and cash equivalents, procedures used to control cash, petty cash, and the bank reconciliation. Accounts and notes receivable are discussed in Chapter 8; inventories are discussed in Chapter 9; and marketable securities are discussed in Chapter 17 along with other investments.

Cash

1. Identify the components of cash.

Cash includes coins and currency on hand, deposits in checking and savings accounts, and checks and money orders that have been received but not yet deposited. A simple rule is that **cash includes anything that a bank will accept as a deposit.** Thus postage stamps and postdated checks (checks that are dated in the future and cannot be deposited) are not cash, but they should be classified as supplies and accounts receivable, respectively.

The management of cash includes:

1. The receipt of cash from many sources, including customers who have purchased goods or services, bank loans, and investments by owners.

2. The payment of cash for many purposes, including making payments to suppliers, employees, and taxing authorities; purchasing new assets; repaying loans; and making withdrawals.

3. The maintenance of the appropriate amount of cash to make the necessary payments and cover unexpected emergencies, while investing excess funds to earn additional revenue.

4. The maintenance of a system of internal control to prevent losses from errors, fraud, or theft.

In addition to being such an integral part of a business, cash is also the most likely asset for employees and others to steal. For example, cash received from customers in a retail store has no identification marks that have been recorded by the store, and therefore once the money has been removed from the store it is very difficult to prove that it was stolen or who stole it. Cash that is illegally transferred from a company bank account involves no physical possession of the cash by the thief, and if the records can be concealed or destroyed the money may not be traceable. Although internal control procedures are necessary for all phases of a company's business, they are usually most important for cash.

Internal Control of Cash

2. Explain the basic concepts underlying internal control of cash.

Internal control of cash consists of the policies and procedures developed by management to ensure that transactions are handled and recorded correctly to prevent theft or other loss of cash and to ensure the correct processing of transactions that involve cash. In addition to the general principles of internal control discussed in Chapter 6, special procedures are used to control the receipt and payment of cash.

Internal control procedures for cash are intended to prevent both the unintentional loss and the theft of cash. **The basic rule for good internal control of cash is to have all payments made by check.** A very small business that is operated by the owner may have little need for additional internal control procedures. The owner is involved in purchasing goods, signing checks for payment, and paying employees by check. Perhaps the only other control procedure that may be needed is in regard to the cash register to ensure that each sale is rung up, a receipt is given to each customer, and that the amount of cash collected is matched against the cash register tape at the end of each employee's work shift.

As a business grows, the owner delegates authority and responsibility and loses direct knowledge of all aspects of operations. The internal control procedures must grow along with this increased delegation. As already discussed, the internal control procedures should prevent fraud and theft, but they should also ensure that employees comply with management policies in an efficient manner and prepare accurate and useful accounting information in a timely fashion. There is no universal set of internal control procedures for cash because each company needs to have policies that are suitable for its particular operating environment and management style. There are several principles that should be included in all systems for the control of cash, however. These principles are:

1. The establishment of responsibilities
2. The maintenance of good records
3. The separation of duties
4. The use of mechanical devices and established routines
5. The necessity of physical safety and insurance
6. The use of special rules for cash receipts and payments

Establishment of Responsibilities

The responsibilities of every person involved with cash in the operation of an accounting system must be clearly established and the procedures to be followed should be defined. An example is discussed in the section on cash receipts. Unfortunately there is usually a conflict between establishing an accounting system in which every procedure is clearly and completely defined and a system in which individuals are allowed discretion in solving problems caused by unusual situations. The first type of accounting system may establish better internal control, whereas the second type may provide greater motivation to employees and perhaps lead to a less expensive overall system because of greater efficiency. In general, an accounting system is only as good as the people who run it. For a cash system, however, it is usually necessary to define responsibilities very clearly and to establish controls that continuously monitor the activities of the employees.

Maintenance of Good Records

A sound internal control system for cash requires that accurate and complete records be maintained so that management can determine whether the system is actually operating in compliance with the established procedures, and so that employees know that documents are available for reviewing their activities. For example, copies of invoices can be reviewed to ensure that unauthorized payments have not been made. Such reviews should be performed periodically on a routine basis, and also whenever a special investigation is warranted, so that the correct operation of the system can be verified. Of course, the records must be maintained outside the control of the employees who are performing the functions. For example, the employee responsible for preparing checks should not have routine access to paid invoices to prevent possible changes being made to the invoices.

The maintenance of good records for cash receipts and payments is desirable for reasons other than internal control. For example, good records assist in the preparation of financial statements and, in the case of corporations, income tax returns. If an audit is performed by the Internal Revenue Service the availability of good records may prevent the assessment of additional taxes.

Separation of Duties

A fundamental characteristic of a good internal control system for cash is that the duties to be performed in the company involving cash should be separated so that more than one employee is involved in each transaction. When cash record keeping is the responsibility of a different employee from the employee performing the activity, there is a separation of duties. For example, a person who authorizes an expenditure should not be the same person who prepares the check, and preferably still another person should sign the check. In this way each employee monitors another employee, which is similar to the double-entry system in which one entry acts as a check on another entry. Also, custody of the cash should be clearly separated from the recording of transactions. For example, the bookkeeper should not have access to cash.

Separation of duties enhances internal control of cash because it is more likely that errors will be discovered as a result of employees monitoring the activities of other employees than by any other method. In addition, fraud or theft of cash would require collusion among employees, and it is therefore less likely than when one employee performs all the duties.

Mechanical Devices and Established Routines

The use of mechanical devices, such as cash registers and check-writing machines, enhances internal control over cash because these devices reduce the likelihood of error from the unintentional loss of cash as well as the opportunities for employees to alter records to conceal the theft of cash. A cash register records the amount of each sale, which can then be totaled and compared to the cash received. A check-writing machine is a device used to print the amounts and signatures on the checks. Its use under the control of a single employee should prevent the unauthorized writing of checks.

The establishment of certain routines is also a useful aspect of internal control over cash. For example, sequential numbering of checks assists in the tracing of all checks written. Employees who operate cash registers should keep the money given to them by the customer out of the cash register until change has been given to minimize errors in determining the correct change. In this way the customer cannot dispute either the original amount given or the amount of change received.

Physical Safety and Insurance

Assets such as cash, which are subject to theft or destruction by an accident such as a fire, should be kept in a physically secure place like a safe to reduce the likelihood of loss. Similarly, a checkbook should be kept in a physically secure place like a locked drawer to prevent unauthorized use.

Insurance should be considered on all assets including cash in case of loss. In addition, employees should be **bonded** because bonding provides insurance against employee theft. When an employee is bonded the company pays an insurance premium to the bonding company, which then pays for any losses caused by the bonded employees. Bonding is particularly important for employees who have access to cash.

Cash Received from Cash Sales

In a retail company, cash is collected from many customers as the sales are made. At the beginning of each sales employee's daily work period, a set amount of cash (for giving change) should be placed in each cash register. Cash sales should be rung up on a cash register as each sale is made. Note that cash refers to both currency and checks. The amount of the sale should be clearly visible to the customer and a receipt should be given to the customer. Each cash register should have a locked-in tape on which each sale is recorded and which is checked against the cash in the register every time there is a change in the employee operating the register. If large amounts of cash are collected during the day, it may be desirable for a supervisor to remove the cash from the cash register periodically during the day. This procedure should not be performed by the person who operates the register, although it may be useful for that employee to count the cash before turning it over to the supervisor to be counted again. In this way two people count the cash, and the employee who operates the cash register also has some protection against theft by the supervisor. If possible, a third employee should be the only person to have access to the tape, thus creating further separation of duties.

At the end of each day cash should be removed from the cash registers and deposited in the bank. Banks have night deposit boxes so that deposits can be made at any time. The cash received from customers should never be used by the company to make payments of any kind. All payments should be made by check except for some minor items that can be paid out of a petty cash fund, which is discussed later in the chapter.

Cash Received by Mail

In a wholesale company or a mail order company, many customers make purchases on account and then pay the invoice by mail. The system for handling the receipt of checks in the mail for payment of these accounts receivable should involve three people. An employee should open the mail and prepare a list of the checks (customer payments by cash should be discouraged) received along with the name of the sender (customer) and the reason for the payment. This information should be available because the person or the company sending the check should include a copy of the invoice with the payment. A copy of this list should be kept by the employee so that a review of the receipts can be made later. The list of the checks received is also sent to the cashier and to the bookkeeper. The cashier is responsible for depositing the cash and the bookkeeper for updating the cash receipts journal, which was discussed in Chapter 6. In this way the bookkeeper never has control of the cash and the cashier never has control of the accounting records. A bank reconciliation, which is discussed later in the chapter, provides a further check on the accuracy of the process.

Cash Payments

Control over cash payments is perhaps more important than control over receipts because many cases of theft have involved payment of fictitious invoices after which the checks are deposited in bank accounts controlled by employees. **All payments should be made by check except for payments from the petty cash fund** (as discussed later in the chapter). Each payment should be based upon adequate source documents that provide verification of the obligation. The authorization, check preparation, and check-signing functions should be performed by three different people, and this separation of duties is often accomplished by using a voucher system. Any spoiled checks should be marked "void" and filed in sequence so that information on all checks is maintained.

Voucher System

3. Describe a voucher system.

A voucher system is a method of providing internal control over the function of purchasing goods or services, paying for them, and ensuring that the correct accounts are debited and credited. The elements of a voucher system are:

1.   The voucher
2.   The voucher register
3.   The check register
4.   The unpaid vouchers file
5.   The paid vouchers file

A voucher is a document used to summarize a transaction and approve payment and recording. A typical voucher is illustrated in Exhibit 7-1 and consists of two parts. One part includes the voucher number, the date, the payee's name and address, and the details of the invoice including the net amount payable (discussed in Chapter 5). The other part includes the accounts debited when the payment is made, a payment summary, the check number used in the payment, the date of payment, and the signature of the person approving payment. These aspects are discussed more fully later in the chapter.

EXHIBIT 7-1   Voucher

(FRONT)	(BACK)

(FRONT)

MOUNTAIN RETAIL COMPANY

Voucher No.   **312**

Date: June 1, 1991

Payee: Adams Co.

Street: 1500 Elm St.

City: Denver

State: CO 80222

Date of Invoice	Terms	Invoice Number	Amount
June 1	n/30	60752	320.00

(BACK)

Accounting Distribution

Account Debited	Acct. No.	Amount
Purchases	501	300.00
Transportation-in	504	20.00

Payment Summary

Total cost   320.00

Discount   –0–

Net payment $320.00

Check No.   573

Date of Check   6/10/91

Payment Approved

David Jackson

Correct use of the voucher system ensures that a procedure for incurring and paying obligations is established. The operation of a typical voucher system involves the sequence of events illustrated in Exhibit 7-2. The procedures for incurring and paying obligations using a voucher system are discussed here and in the following sections.

1. *Approval for Incurring an Obligation (An Acquisition).* Only specified departments and individuals are allowed to incur obligations that result in cash payments. For example, in a retail store only the purchasing department may be allowed to incur obligations for the purchase of merchandise. Although requests for purchases may come from employees in many different areas of the company, all of them must be routed through the purchasing department. A purchase order is prepared by the purchasing department and sent to the supplier.

2. *Receipt of the Goods Ordered.* When goods that have been ordered are received, they must be checked against the purchase order to ensure that the

EXHIBIT 7-2   Operation of Voucher System

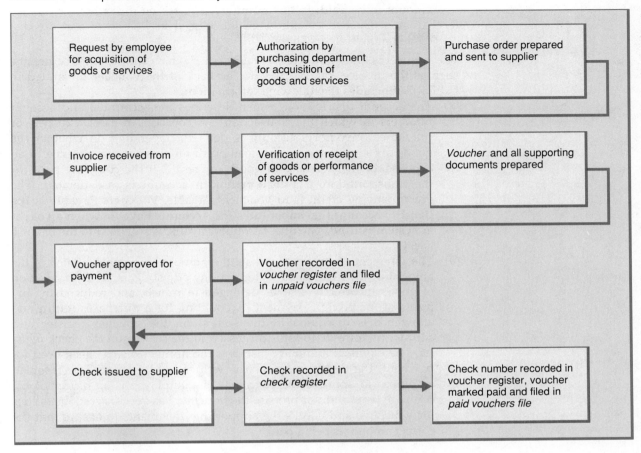

correct items have been sent by the supplier. In addition, the supplier sends an invoice, as illustrated in Chapter 5 (Exhibit 5-1), which includes a description of the goods, the amount that must be paid, freight terms, discount terms, and payment dates. A copy of the invoice is typically included with the goods that are shipped and should also be compared with the purchase order when the goods are received to verify the quantities, prices, and terms of the purchase.

3. *Preparation of the Voucher.* When the ordered goods are received a voucher is prepared. As shown in Exhibit 7-1 the front of the voucher typically includes the following information:

    (a) The voucher number. The vouchers should be sequentially numbered so that reference to, and checking of, vouchers can be accomplished easily.

    (b) The date the voucher is prepared.

    (c) The name of the company (or individual) to which payment is to be made.

    (d) The terms such as the date of the invoice, the invoice number, the cash discount available, the last date for payment if the cash discount is to be received (the date of the invoice plus the discount period), and the amount to be paid. In this example there are no discounts for prompt payment. Such discounts were introduced in Chapter 5 and are discussed more fully in Chapter 9.

The voucher is often in the form of a jacket in which supporting documents, such as the invoice, can be placed. The back of the voucher illustrated in Exhibit 7-1 includes the following information:

(a) The account distribution, which describes the account(s) and account numbers in which the transaction is recorded. An asset, expense, or purchases (inventory) account is debited, depending on whether the goods are considered the acquisition of an asset, the incurrence of an expense, or the purchase of goods for resale. If the company pays for the transportation, a Transportation-In account is also debited. The accompanying credit is to Vouchers Payable. **Vouchers Payable is the liability account that substitutes for Accounts Payable when a voucher system is used.** The title Accounts Payable is still used in the balance sheet.

(b) The payment summary that lists the amount to be paid, which is the amount of the invoice, corrected for any adjustments, such as rejection of goods incorrectly sent or damaged in transit, and reduced by any discount for prompt payment. Accounting for a purchases return and allowance is discussed in the section on the voucher register and accounting for a discount is discussed in the section on the check register. The payment summary also lists the number of the check used for payment, the date the check was written, and includes space for an employee to approve the payment. The employee is an officer of the company who did not prepare the voucher, has specific responsibilities for vouchers, and checks the supporting documents to ensure that the correct amount is being paid.

EXHIBIT 7-3
Voucher Register

				VOUCHER REGISTER			
Date		Voucher No.	Payee	Date Paid	Check No.	Vouchers Payable Credit	Purchases Debit
June	1	312	Adams Company	June 10	573	320.00	300.00
	8	313	David Finney	June 8	570	600.00	
	8	314	Karen Miles	June 8	571	800.00	
	8	315	Steven Smith	June 8	572	400.00	
	10	316	Mountain Telephone	June 20	574	120.00	
	15	317	Falstaff Company	June 25	575	140.00	
	22	318	Sherman Company	July 1	577	850.00	800.00
	26	319	First Bank	June 26	576	75.00	
	30	320	Castle Company	July 15	578	410.00	400.00
	30		Totals			3,715.00	1,500.00

Voucher Register

A voucher register is a multicolumn journal used to record all the vouchers that are prepared. A voucher register is illustrated in Exhibit 7-3. The vouchers are listed in numerical order. One voucher is listed on each line. The date each voucher is prepared is listed first, followed by the voucher number, the name of the payee, the date paid, and the check number. The vouchers payable column lists the amounts of all vouchers approved for payment. The remainder of the register includes columns for the accounts that are regularly debited; the totals of these columns are posted monthly. Each amount in the Other Accounts Debit column is posted daily. The voucher register is very similar to the cash payments journal (discussed in Chapter 6) and replaces this journal when a voucher system is used.

Purchases Returns and Allowances. When purchases returns and allowances are made *before* the voucher is entered in the register the amount of the return or allowance is entered on the voucher and the net amount owed is entered in the register. When an item is returned or an allowance is received *after* the voucher is recorded, a general journal entry is made as follows (amount assumed):

Vouchers Payable	**30**
Purchases Returns and Allowances	30

To record return of defective unit.

The amount of the return is shown on the voucher so that the correct amount will be paid. A reference is made to the general journal entry and the Purchases Returns and Allowances debit memo is placed in the voucher jacket.

Transpor-tation-In Debit	Wages Expense Debit	Adminis-trative Expense Debit	Other Accounts Debit		
			Account Name	Acct. No.	Amount Debit
20.00					
	600.00				
	800.00				
	400.00				
		120.00			
		140.00			
50.00					
			Interest Expense	550	75.00
10.00					
80.00	1,800.00	260.00			75.00

Check Register

A check register is a special journal in which all the checks issued are recorded. A check register for June is illustrated in Exhibit 7-4. The date of payment, the check number used for payment, and the payee are recorded first along with the voucher number. The amount of the debit to the Vouchers Payable account is listed and should be equal to the vouchers payable credit amount listed in the voucher register. When a purchases discount is taken it is recorded in a separate column. The amount of the check is recorded in the final column. The totals of the columns would be posted monthly.

EXHIBIT 7-4
Check Register

				CHECK REGISTER			
Date		Check No.	Payee	Voucher No.	Vouchers Payable Debit	Purchases Discounts Taken Credit	Cash Credit
June	8	570	David Finney	313	600.00		600.00
	8	571	Karen Miles	314	800.00		800.00
	8	572	Steven Smith	315	400.00		400.00
	10	573	Adams Company	312	320.00		320.00
	20	574	Mountain Telephone	316	120.00		120.00
	25	575	Falstaff Company	317	140.00	2.80	137.20
	26	576	First Bank	319	75.00		75.00
	30		Totals		2,455.00	2.80	2,452.20

Unpaid Vouchers and Paid Vouchers Files

In a voucher system some vouchers are paid as soon as they are recorded, as for example the wages in the voucher register in Exhibit 7-3. Vouchers that are not paid immediately are placed in an **unpaid vouchers file.** This file takes the place of the Accounts Payable subsidiary ledger discussed in Chapter 6. The vouchers in the file should be organized by the date they are due to be paid to ensure that all discounts are taken and no accounts become past due. For internal control purposes, at the end of the period the total of the unpaid vouchers file is compared with the Vouchers Payable account balance to be sure that they are in agreement. A **paid vouchers file** is maintained for all the vouchers that have been paid. This file is useful in the case of an audit or a question about a payment.

The specific procedures followed by companies depend on their particular organizational structure and policies. The illustration just discussed is a simple example of a typical system and indicates how internal control over the acquisition and payment for goods or services is established.

Petty Cash Fund

Although a voucher system, or a similar set of procedures, is necessary for establishing good internal control, it is a costly and time-consuming system. Therefore it is inefficient to use a voucher system for various small expenditures that can be better paid in cash. Instead, an **imprest system** is used in which a cash fund is established and reimbursed periodically for documented expenditures that have been made out of the fund. A common example of an imprest system is a petty cash fund. **A petty cash fund is a cash fund established under the control of an employee and is used for making small cash expenditures not included in the voucher system.** A petty cash fund is also used because some payments, such as for taxi fares, collect telegrams, and small amounts of supplies, can be made only in cash, or because writing a check would be cumbersome. There is obviously less control over such expenditures, but the allowable amount for spending should be sufficiently small so that an employee will not be tempted to steal. In addition, we will see that the procedures used in a petty cash fund discourage both intentional and unintentional loss of cash.

A typical petty cash system includes the following elements:

4. Record the transactions of a petty cash fund.

1. ***The Petty Cash Fund Is Established.*** An employee is appointed to control the cash fund and make disbursements. A check is approved for payment to the employee. The amount of the check is based on an estimate of the cash that will be needed for approved payments over a short period of time, for example, a month. If this amount is $200, the journal entry to record this transaction is as follows:

Petty Cash Fund	200	
Cash		200

To establish the petty cash fund.

The employee controlling the petty cash fund cashes the check and places the cash in a secure place such as a locked drawer.

2. *Petty Cash Vouchers.* **Petty cash vouchers are the source documents to record payments made from the petty cash fund.** A petty cash voucher is illustrated in Exhibit 7-5. It requires the recording of the date, an explanation of the reason for the payment, the account to be debited, and the amount of the payment; and it must be signed by the person approving the payment and the recipient of the money.

   Internal control can be readily exercised because the cash remaining in the fund after some payments have been made, plus the amount of the petty cash vouchers, should always be equal to the amount of the petty cash fund ($200 in this example). Therefore the fund can be checked at any time to ensure that it is not being misused.

   It should be noted that journal entries are *not* made in the accounting system when a payment is made from the petty cash fund. In addition, the petty cash vouchers are prenumbered and should always be filed in numerical order to lessen the possibility of the loss or misuse of a voucher.

EXHIBIT 7-5
Petty Cash Voucher

NO. 101	DATE	January 9 , 1991

PETTY CASH VOUCHER

EXPLANATION   Taxi Fare

DEBIT TO   Transportation Expense   ACCOUNT

AMOUNT $25.42

APPROVED BY: PAYMENT RECEIVED BY:

Karen S. Miles   *Carmen J. Mangis*

3. *Replenishment of the Petty Cash Fund.* When the cash in the petty cash fund becomes low the fund must be replenished, and it is also necessary to determine the categories of expenses that have been incurred so that the accounting system is properly updated. **The petty cash fund must also be replenished and the expenses recorded at the end of each accounting period so that the financial statements will be correct.** To illustrate the replenishment of the fund and recording the appropriate amounts in the various accounts, suppose that an examination of the petty cash vouchers indicates that the following payments had been made:

Postage	$55.27
Office Supplies	82.68
Taxi Fares	25.42

The journal entry to record these expenses is as follows:

Postage Expense	55.27	
Office Supplies	82.68	
Transportation Expense	25.42	
Cash		163.37

To record replenishment of the petty cash fund.

A check for $163.37 is written to the employee controlling the petty cash fund, who then cashes it and places the cash in a secure place. Note that the expense accounts are debited and *not* the Petty Cash Fund account. Therefore the accounting system indicates that there is always $200 in the petty cash fund, and every time the fund is replenished the cash payment and the appropriate amounts in the various accounts are recorded. The petty cash vouchers should be "canceled" so that they cannot be resubmitted for a second payment.

4. *Errors in the Petty Cash Fund.* Because the petty cash fund operates on a day-to-day basis it is inevitable that some mistakes will be made. An error

will become known when the sum of the vouchers plus the remaining cash does not equal the amount of the petty cash fund. If the error cannot be traced and collected, the amount of the error is charged to a Cash Over and Short account. **The Cash Over and Short account is used to record the unresolved errors that are the result of a difference between the cash held and the cash recorded in the accounting records.** For example, suppose that after the previously mentioned replenishment the balance in the fund is only $198.45 and no reason for the error can be determined. The shortage of $1.55 is recorded as follows:

Cash Over and Short	1.55	
Cash		1.55

To record shortage of petty cash fund and to replenish fund.

In reality, this journal entry would normally be combined with the earlier entry to record the expenses. Therefore a check for a total of $164.92 would be issued to the employee who controls the fund and the following journal entry would be made (*instead* of the previous two entries):

Postage Expense	55.27	
Office Supplies	82.68	
Transportation Expense	25.42	
Cash Over and Short	1.55	
Cash		164.92

To record replenishment of the petty cash fund.

Although a shortage in the fund may be caused by errors, it may also result from theft. Thus the size of the shortage should be reviewed periodically to see if there is a pattern to the shortages that might indicate theft.

The Cash Over and Short account may *also* be used to record any unexplained difference between the cash collected in the cash register and the amount recorded in the register tape. For example, if cash sales of $826.55 are "rung up" and $830.55 is in the cash register, the journal entry to record the sales is as follows:

Cash	830.55	
Cash Over and Short		4.00
Sales		826.55

To record cash sales.

Although this overage is possible, it is more likely that shortages occur because customers are less likely to report being given too much change than they are to report being given too little change. Therefore the Cash Over and Short account usually has a *debit* balance. It is closed at the end of each accounting period and, if it has a debit balance, this amount is included as a miscellaneous expense on the income statement. If it has a credit balance, this amount would be included as a miscellaneous revenue on the income statement.

Despite all the procedures used to control the receipt and payment of cash, errors in a company's records can still occur. In addition, there are differences between the timing of receipts and payments recorded by the bank and the company. Therefore a bank reconciliation is necessary to determine the accuracy of a company's cash balance.

Bank Reconciliation

The cash account is a company's only account that is also kept independently by another party, the bank. Therefore it is possible, and desirable, to use one as a check on the other. **A bank reconciliation is a schedule prepared to analyze the difference between the ending cash balance in the company's accounting records and the ending cash balance reported by the bank in a bank statement in order to discover errors and to adjust for timing differences in the recorded cash receipts and cash payments.** The bank reconciliation enables the company's correct cash balance to be determined for inclusion in the balance sheet.

Every month banks send canceled checks and a statement to each depositor summarizing the activities that have taken place in the depositor's account. These activities include deposits, checks written, miscellaneous items, and the ending balance in the checking account. Each company has a checking account and maintains its own accounting records for its deposits and checks. Because of the various causes of the difference discussed next, it can be expected that the bank statement and the company's accounting records will not be in complete agreement. When the bank statement is received each month, the company prepares a bank reconciliation to compare the bank statement balance and the company's cash balance so that they may be reconciled. For good internal control, the employee who prepares the bank reconciliation should not be responsible for writing checks or for recording cash transactions. An example of a bank reconciliation is shown in the lower portion of Exhibit 7-7 on page 333. Before discussing this example in detail, it is important to understand several items that affect the reconciliation.

Causes of the Difference

The causes of the difference between the cash balance listed on the bank statement and the balance shown in the company's cash account include the following factors:

1. *Outstanding Checks.* **An outstanding check is a check that has been written by the company and deducted from the company's cash balance but has not yet been deducted from the balance reported in the bank statement.** On the date a company issues a check, it records a reduction in the balance of the Cash account in its general ledger. A period of time is necessary for the check to be received by the payee (the recipient of the check), to be deposited in the payee's bank, and to be forwarded by the payee's bank to the company's bank to be subtracted from the company's bank balance. Therefore a company has a certain number of outstanding checks at the end of each month that causes the company's cash account balance to be less than the balance on the bank statement.

2. *Deposits in Transit.* **A deposit in transit is a cash receipt that has been added to the company's cash balance but has not yet been added to the balance reported on the bank statement.** When a company receives a check it records an addition to its Cash account. A period of time may pass before the check is deposited by the company and is recorded by the bank. At the

end of each month there may be deposits in transit (either cash or checks) that cause the company's cash balance to be greater than the balance reported on the bank statement.

3. *Charges Made Directly by the Bank.* A bank frequently imposes a service charge for a depositor's checking account and deducts this charge directly from the account. Banks also charge for the cost of printing checks according to an agreed price and for stopping payment on checks. The company is informed of the amount of the charge when it receives the bank statement, which includes a document stating the amount of the deduction.

When a customer's check is received by the company it is deposited in the company's bank account for collection. The company (as well as the bank) records this check as a cash receipt even though the cash has not been transferred from the customer's bank account to the company's bank account. The company's bank is occasionally unable to collect the amount of the customer's check. That is, the customer's check has "bounced." **NSF (not sufficient funds) is the term used for a customer's check that has been deposited in a company's bank account but has not been paid by the customer's bank because there are insufficient funds in the customer's account.** Because the bank has not received payment from the customer it deducts this amount from the company's bank account. Although the bank should inform the company immediately of each NSF check and the company should update its accounting records, there may be some NSF checks included in the bank statement that have not been recorded by the company.

At the end of the month each of the previously mentioned charges made directly by the bank are listed as deductions from the company's cash balance on the bank statement even though they may not have been deducted from the company's cash balance in its accounting records. Therefore the bank statement balance is less than the balance in the company's cash account in this case.

4. *Deposits Made Directly by the Bank.* A bank often acts as a collecting agency for its customers on items such as notes receivable. In addition, many checking accounts now earn interest. When a note is collected the bank records the principal and interest as an increase in the company's bank account. Although the bank should immediately inform the company of the deposit and the company should update its records, the bank statement may include notes received by the bank that have not yet been recorded in the company's accounting records. The amount of interest earned by a company on its checking account is typically not known by the company until it receives the bank statement. In both these situations the bank statement balance is greater than the balance in the company's cash account.

5. *Errors.* Despite the internal control procedures established by the bank and the company, errors may arise in either the bank's records or the company's records and they may not be discovered until the bank reconciliation is performed. For example, a bank may include a deposit or a check in the wrong customer's account or make an error in recording an amount. A company may similarly make an error in recording an amount. For example, a common error is to transpose two numbers so that the correct amount of $426 is recorded as $462.

To bring the bank statement balance and the balance in the company's Cash account into agreement, the additions and subtractions shown in Exhibit 7-6 must be made.

EXHIBIT 7-6
Adjustments Required
for a Bank
Reconciliation

Ending Balance in the Company's Cash Account
+ Unrecorded Deposits Made Directly by the Bank
− Unrecorded Charges Made Directly by the Bank
± Errors Made by the Company
= **Ending Reconciled Cash Balance**

Ending Cash Balance from the Bank Statement
+ Deposits in Transit
− Outstanding Checks
± Errors Made by the Bank
= **Ending Reconciled Cash Balance**

The ending reconciled cash balance calculated in these two ways must be equal, otherwise the reconciliation is not complete. The ending reconciled cash balance is the correct cash balance that should be reported in the company's balance sheet.

Procedures for Preparing a Bank Reconciliation

Now that we have identified the items that might cause a difference between the ending balance in the company's cash account and the ending cash balance from the bank statement, we can develop a list of procedures to be followed in preparing a bank reconciliation:

5. Prepare a bank
reconciliation.

1. *Compare the deposits listed on the company's records with the deposits shown on the bank statement.* Determine whether the deposits in transit included in the *last* month's bank reconciliation are included in this month's bank statement. These deposits do not need any adjustment in the bank reconciliation. If they are not shown on the bank statement, an immediate investigation should be made. Any deposits for the current month that are not listed on the bank statement are included in the bank reconciliation. In the reconciliation the amounts of the deposits in transit are added to the ending cash balance of the bank statement.

2. *Compare the checks listed on the company's records with the checks shown on the bank statement.* Determine that the outstanding checks included in last month's bank reconciliation are included in this month's bank statement. These checks do not need any adjustment in the bank reconciliation. Identify any checks not deducted in the current bank statement. The amounts of these outstanding checks are subtracted from the ending cash balance of the bank statement in the reconciliation.

3. *Note any deposits or charges made directly by the bank that are not included on the company's records.* These items include collections of notes receivable, interest earned on the checking account, service charges, NSF checks, and so on, which are listed on the bank statement. The collections or charges

must be added to or subtracted from the company's ending cash balance in the bank reconciliation.

4. *Determine the effect of any errors.* If an error is found the nature of the error determines whether the error is added to or subtracted from the company's ending cash balance or from the ending cash balance of the bank statement.

5. *Complete the bank reconciliation and accompanying journal entries* (which are illustrated next).

Illustration of a Bank Reconciliation

The Perrin Company is performing a bank reconciliation on June 30, 1991. The facts shown in the upper part of Exhibit 7-7 are determined from a review of the company's records, canceled checks, and bank statement. The bank reconciliation is shown in the lower part of Exhibit 7-7. For ease of reference, the items in the bank reconciliation are numbered to correspond to the listed facts (an actual bank reconciliation would not include these numbers).

EXHIBIT 7-7
Preparation of a
Bank Reconciliation

1. Balance in the cash account, June 30	$1,575
2. Cash balance from the bank statement, June 30	1,542
3. Outstanding checks issued in June or prior months: No. 165	130
No. 168	80
4. Deposit in transit, June 30	272
5. Bank service charge unrecorded by the company	10
6. NSF check from David Johnson unrecorded by the company	112
7. Note of $180 collected by the bank, plus interest of $10 and less collection fee of	
$12 (unrecorded by the company)	178
8. The bank recorded a deposit of $242 as $224.	
9. The company recorded check No. 160, written for $132, as $123. The check was for the purchase of supplies.	

PERRIN COMPANY
Bank Reconciliation
June 30, 1991

(1)	Cash balance from the company's records, June 30		$1,575
	Add:		
(7)	Unrecorded collection of $180 note, plus interest of $10, less collection fee of $12	178	$1,753
	Deduct:		
(5)	Bank service charge unrecorded by the company	$ 10	
(6)	NSF check unrecorded by the company	112	
(9)	Error: Check No. 160 written for $132 recorded as $123	9	(131)
	Reconciled Cash Balance, June 30		$1,622
(2)	Cash balance from the bank statement, June 30		$1,542
	Add:		
(4)	Deposit in transit	272	
(8)	Error: Deposit of $242 recorded as $224	18	$1,832
	Deduct:		
(3)	Outstanding checks: No. 165	$ 130	
	No. 168	80	(210)
	Reconciled Cash Balance, June 30		$1,622

Since the Perrin Company has a recorded cash balance of $1,575 but the correct cash balance is $1,622, it must make adjustments to its accounting records. For both outstanding checks and deposits in transit no adjustment to the company's books is necessary. The passage of time will resolve the differences between the bank balance and the company's cash balance because each item will be included in the bank statement in the next period(s). The company does not need to make adjustments to its records for errors made by the bank, but the bank would need to make adjusting journal entries. The remaining items in the bank reconciliation do require that the company make adjusting entries. Charges and deposits made directly by the bank that have not yet been recorded by the company, as well as errors made by the company, require adjusting journal entries. Adjusting entries are needed because each contains new information that is not currently included in the company's accounting system. For the Perrin Company four journal entries are required. The note collected by the bank must be recorded as follows:

Cash	178	
Collection Expense	12	
Interest Revenue		10
Note Receivable		180
To record collection of note by bank.		

The previously unrecorded bank service charge is recorded as follows:

Miscellaneous Expense	10	
Cash		10
To record the bank service charge.		

The check from David Johnson that subsequently became an NSF check would have been recorded as a collection of an account receivable when it was originally deposited. The fact that the check was not collected is recorded by reversing the journal entry used to record the apparent collection as follows:

Accounts Receivable: David Johnson	112	
Cash		112
To record an NSF check.		

Of course the company will continue to attempt to collect the $112 from David Johnson.

The error in recording check No. 160 means that a payment of $132 was recorded as only $123. Since this check was for payment of supplies, the supplies are understated by $9. The journal entry to correct this error is as follows:

Supplies	9	
Cash		9
To correct the recording of check No. 160.		

Instead of the four separate journal entries, a single compound entry could be made as follows:

Cash	47	
Collection Expense	12	
Miscellaneous Expense	10	
Accounts Receivable: David Johnson	112	
Supplies	9	
Interest Revenue		10
Note Receivable		180

To record adjustments from the bank reconciliation.

These four separate entries, or the single compound entry, will bring the company's cash balance to its correct ending amount of $1,622. This amount would be listed on the June 30, 1991, balance sheet.

Cash Equivalents

6. Explain cash equivalents.

The banking and securities industries have experienced considerable changes in recent years. As a result companies are earning interest in a greater variety of ways and at a higher rate than before by investing in cash equivalents. **Cash equivalents are investments that are short-term, highly liquid, and involve very little risk.** For example, many banks offer "money market" accounts, which pay interest daily on the balance in the account. In addition, checks may be written against the account, although there may be a limit on the number allowed. Therefore the account operates as a checking account that pays interest on its daily balance. Companies also invest in such items as commercial paper issued by other companies and treasury bills issued by the federal government.

Companies usually maintain a typical non-interest-bearing checking account because cash equivalents are not as liquid or as easily accessible. When these cash equivalents are purchased, the cost must be recorded in a separate account as follows (amounts assumed):

Cash Equivalents	50,000	
Cash		50,000

To record acquisition of cash equivalent.

The related interest revenue must be recorded each period as follows (amounts assumed):

Cash Equivalents	450	
Interest Revenue		450

To record interest earned.

If the cash equivalent is a money market account, the company receives a statement each period from the bank indicating the checks written, deposits made, and interest earned. A bank reconciliation should be performed, after which journal entries should be made to bring the account balance up to date, as discussed earlier in the chapter.

Disclosure of Cash and Cash Equivalents

7. Prepare the disclosure of cash and cash equivalents on the balance sheet.

The three elements that we have discussed in this chapter must be included in the company's balance sheet. The balance in the petty cash account, the reconciled cash balance of the checking account, and the cash equivalents are all included as the current asset, Cash and Cash Equivalents, in the company's balance sheet. Although a single amount is typically reported, the three components could be disclosed as follows (amounts assumed):

Current Assets		
Petty cash	$ 200	
Cash in checking account	1,470	
Cash equivalents	73,300	
Total cash and cash equivalents		$74,970

Because of its liquidity, the total cash and cash equivalents of $74,970 is included as the first item in the balance sheet as a current asset.

Chapter Summary

Review of Learning Objectives

1. **Identify the components of cash.**
   Cash includes coins and currency on hand, deposits in checking and savings accounts, and checks and money orders that have been received but not yet deposited. Essentially, cash includes anything that a bank will include as a deposit. Therefore such items as postage stamps and postdated checks are not cash.

2. **Explain the basic concepts underlying the internal control of cash.**
   Internal control of cash consists of the policies and procedures developed by management to ensure that transactions are handled and recorded correctly to prevent theft or other loss of cash and to ensure the correct processing of transactions. Elements of internal control of cash include (1) the establishment of responsibilities, (2) the maintenance of good records, (3) the separation of duties, (4) the use of mechanical devices and established routines, (5) the necessity of physical safety and insurance, and (6) the use of special rules for control of cash receipts and payments.

3. **Describe a voucher system.**
   A voucher system is a method of providing internal control over the function of purchasing goods or services, paying for them, and ensuring that the correct accounts are debited and credited. The elements of a voucher system are (1) the voucher, (2) the voucher register, (3) the check register, (4) the unpaid vouchers file, and (5) the paid vouchers file.

> 4. **Record the transactions of a petty cash fund.**
>   A petty cash fund is established under the control of an employee by issuing
>   a check to the employee. It is used for making small cash expenditures not
>   included in the voucher system. When the fund is replenished, the cate-
>   gories of expenses are recorded.

> 5. **Prepare a bank reconciliation.**
>   A bank reconciliation is a schedule prepared to analyze the difference
>   between the ending cash balance in the company's accounting records and
>   the ending cash balance reported by the bank in the bank statement. The
>   items included in the reconciliation are (1) outstanding checks which are
>   subtracted from the bank statement cash balance, (2) deposits in transit
>   which are added to the bank statement cash balance, (3) unrecorded charges
>   made directly by the bank which are subtracted from the company's cash
>   balance, (4) unrecorded deposits made directly by the bank which are added
>   to the company's cash balance, and (5) errors.

> 6. **Explain cash equivalents.**
>   Cash equivalents are investments that are short-term, highly liquid, and
>   involve very little risk. Examples are "money market" accounts, commercial
>   paper, and treasury bills.

> 7. **Prepare the disclosure of cash and cash equivalents on the balance sheet.**
>   The total amount of cash and cash equivalents is usually disclosed as a sin-
>   gle amount on the balance sheet. It includes the amount of petty cash, the
>   reconciled amount of the checking account, and the amount of any cash
>   equivalents. It is usually the first current asset listed because of its liquidity.

Review Problem

The Wellshire Company established a $200 petty cash fund on September 7, 1991. On
December 31, 1991, there was $30.12 in the fund. Check No. 488 was issued to replen-
ish the fund. At that time, the following vouchers had been issued:

Freight charges on purchases	$ 63.97
Postage	48.37
Office supplies	32.45
Reimbursements of employees for taxi fares	24.00
	$168.79

On December 31, 1991, the company had cash equivalents of $2,000. In addition, an
examination of the accounting records and the bank statement of the Wellshire
Company at December 31, 1991, provides the following information:

(a) The cash account has a balance of $1,460.25.

(b) The bank statement shows a bank balance of $1,723.20.

(c) Checks issued in December but not included among the checks listed on the bank statement were:

Check No. 453 .... $357.74
Check No. 489 .... 296.58

(d) The December 31 cash receipts of $783.45 were deposited at the bank on that date but were not recorded by the bank until January 1.

(e) Interest of $34.50 earned on the checking account had not been recorded by the company.

(f) A check received from a customer for $236.42 and deposited by the Wellshire Company was returned marked NSF. The nonpayment had not been previously recorded by the Wellshire Company.

(g) The bank collected a note of $400 with interest of $15 and charged a collection fee of $10. The cash receipt had not previously been recorded by the Wellshire Company.

(h) The Wellshire Company discovered that Check No. 469, which was written for the December utilities, was recorded on its books as $365, although it had been correctly written as $356.

(i) The bank recorded a deposit of $686 as $866.

REQUIRED

1. Prepare the journal entries to record the activities of the Wellshire Company's petty cash fund.

2. Prepare a bank reconciliation on December 31, 1991, for the Wellshire Company.

3. Prepare the separate journal entries that the Wellshire Company should record as a result of the reconciliation.

4. Show how the Wellshire Company would report its cash on the December 31, 1991, balance sheet.

Solution to Review Problem

REQUIREMENT 1

1991			
Sept. 7	Petty Cash Fund	200.00	
	Cash		200.00
	To establish the petty cash fund.		
Dec. 31	Transportation-In	63.97	
	Postage Expense	48.37	
	Office Supplies	32.45	
	Transportation Expense	24.00	
	Cash Over and Short		
	[($200 − $30.12) − $168.79]	1.09	
	Cash ($200 − $30.12)		169.88
	To record replenishment of the petty cash fund.		

REQUIREMENT 2

WELLSHIRE COMPANY
Bank Reconciliation
December 31, 1991

Cash balance from the company's records, December 31	$1,460.25	
Add:		
Unrecorded collection of $400 note, plus interest of $15, less collection fee of $10	405.00	
Unrecorded interest earned by the company	34.50	
Error: Check No. 469 written for $356 recorded as $365	9.00	$1,908.75
Deduct:		
NSF check unrecorded by the company		(236.42)
Reconciled Cash Balance, December 31		$1,672.33
Cash balance from the bank statement, December 31	$1,723.20	
Add:		
Deposit in transit	783.45	$2,506.65
Deduct:		
Outstanding checks: No. 453	$ 357.74	
No. 489	296.58	
Error: Deposit of $686 recorded as $866	180.00	(834.32)
Reconciled Cash Balance, December 31		$1,672.33

REQUIREMENT 3

1991				
Dec. 31	Cash		405	
	Collection Expense		10	
	Interest Revenue			15
	Note Receivable			400
	To record collection of note by bank.			
	Cash		34.50	
	Interest Revenue			34.50
	To record interest earned on checking account.			
	Cash		9	
	Utilities Expense			9
	To correct the recording of Check No. 469.			
	Accounts Receivable		236.42	
	Cash			236.42
	To record an NSF check.			

REQUIREMENT 4

Current Assets		
Petty cash	$ 200.00	
Cash in checking account	1,672.33	
Cash equivalents	2,000.00	
Total cash and cash equivalents		$3,872.33

Glossary

Bank Reconciliation.   A schedule prepared to analyze the difference between the ending cash balance in a company's accounting records and the ending cash balance reported by the bank in a bank statement in order to determine the correct ending cash balance.

Cash.   An asset that includes coins and currency on hand, deposits in checking and savings accounts, and checks and money orders received but not yet deposited.

Cash Equivalents.   Investments that are short-term, highly liquid, and involve very little risk.

Cash Over and Short.   An account used to record the unresolved errors that are the result of a difference between the cash held and the cash recorded in the accounting records.

Check Register.   A special journal in which all the checks issued are recorded.

Deposit in Transit.   A deposit added to a company's cash account that has not yet been recorded by the bank.

Internal Control of Cash.   Policies and procedures developed by management to ensure that transactions are handled and recorded correctly to prevent theft or other loss of cash and to ensure the correct processing of transactions that involve cash.

NSF (Not Sufficient Funds).   The term used for a customer's check that has been deposited in a company's bank account but has not been paid by the customer's bank because there are insufficient funds in the customer's account.

Outstanding Check.   A check that has been written by a company and deducted from its cash account but has not yet been recorded as a deduction by the bank.

Paid Vouchers File.   A file in which all paid vouchers are stored.

Petty Cash Fund.   A cash fund used for the payment of small expenditures.

Petty Cash Voucher.   The source document used to record payments from the petty cash fund.

Unpaid Vouchers File.   A file in which all unpaid vouchers are stored.

Voucher.   A document used to summarize a transaction and approve payment and recording.

Voucher Register.   A journal that is used to record all the vouchers that are prepared.

Vouchers Payable.   The liability account that substitutes for the Accounts Payable account in a voucher system.

Voucher System.   An accounting system used to provide internal control over the function of purchasing goods or services, paying for them, and ensuring that the correct accounts are debited and credited.

Questions

QUESTION 7-1   What items are included in the Cash account balance on a balance sheet? Give examples of two items that are similar to cash but would be excluded from cash.

QUESTION 7-2   What is the purpose of internal control for cash? List the main principles used in a good internal control system for cash.

QUESTION 7-3   Why is the separation of duties a common element of internal control?

QUESTION 7-4   What is the purpose of bonding employees?

QUESTION 7-5   What is the purpose of a voucher system? List the basic elements of a voucher system.

QUESTION 7-6   Why does a company have a petty cash fund?

QUESTION 7-7   When are the payments made out of a petty cash fund recorded as an expense? How often is a debit made to the petty cash fund?

QUESTION 7-8   What is the purpose of a Cash Over and Short account? Will it normally have a debit or credit balance? What happens to the balance in the account at the end of the period?

QUESTION 7-9   Why does a company perform a bank reconciliation? Name five items that might appear in a bank reconciliation.

QUESTION 7-10   What are the procedures that should be followed in performing a bank reconciliation?

QUESTION 7-11   Why might a company make journal entries after performing a bank reconciliation?

QUESTION 7-12   What are cash equivalents?

QUESTION 7-13   How does a money market account differ from a regular checking account? How does such an account affect a company's balance sheet and income statement?

QUESTION 7-14   What are the components of a company's cash balance reported on its balance sheet?

Exercises

EXERCISE 7-1   **Items Included in Cash.**   The accountant of the Sherman Machine Tool Company is considering whether or not the following items should be included in the company's cash balance at December 31, 1991:

(a)   The Sherman Machine Tool Company bid on a contract on December 14, 1991. It included a "good faith" check of $5,000 dated January 14, 1992, with the bid. The bid was rejected on January 10, 1992, and the check was returned.

(b)   A petty cash fund has been established in the amount of $250. At December 31 a count of the cash in the fund showed a balance of $48, and a count of the petty cash vouchers totaled $200. The correct year-end adjusting entry has been made.

(c)   Two checks of $140 were received in December from a customer for payment of its $140 account balance. One of the checks was returned in January.

(d)   A check was received and deposited for $175 in December. The check was returned by the bank in January marked NSF.

(e)   A check from a customer for $87 was received and deposited in December. In January it was discovered that it was in payment of an invoice in the amount of $78. A check for $9 was issued and mailed by the Sherman Machine Tool Company to the customer.

REQUIRED   For each of the items indicate what dollar amount, if any, should have been included in the total cash balance sheet at December 31, 1991. Assume that all the information was obtained from the bank reconciliation for the month ending December 31, 1991.

EXERCISE 7-2   **Internal Control.**   The following independent policies have been developed by a company:

(a) The mail is delivered to the bookkeeper who distributes it unopened to various employees around the company, including the cash receipts clerk.

(b) Cash is often received in the mail without an accompanying invoice for credit purchases made by customers. The bookkeeper opens this mail.

(c) A manager prepares the invoices and signs the checks for items purchased.

(d) The cash in the cash register is not counted before each employee's work period.

(e) The company does not perform a bank reconciliation because it trusts that the bank will not make a mistake.

REQUIRED   For each of the situations explain to management the weakness in the internal control and suggest how it could be overcome.

EXERCISE 7-3   **Voucher System.**   The Stone Metal Stamping Company uses a voucher system. During July, the following transactions occurred:

Date	Transaction
July 2	Recorded Voucher No. 140 for $240 for machinery repairs performed by Megan Company.
10	Recorded Voucher No. 141 for $200 for office supplies purchased from the Cheesman Company on terms of 2/10, n/30.
15	Issued Check No. 764 in payment for Voucher No. 140.
18	Issued Check No. 765 in payment for Voucher No. 141.
31	Recorded Voucher No. 142 and issued Check No. 766 for $950 as payment of salary to D. Stahl.

REQUIRED   1. Prepare a voucher register for July.

2. Prepare a check register for July.

EXERCISE 7-4   **Voucher System.**   The Palas Picture Frame Company uses a voucher system. During March 1991 the following vouchers were prepared:

Date	Voucher No.	Payee	Amount	Check No.	Date Paid	Explanation
5	574	Thomas Co.	$ 300	414	March 12	Purchase
7	575	INP Co.	250	413	March 11	Rent for month
8	576	Peter Jay	350	412	March 8	Travel
15	577	Catch Co.	500	417	April 5	Typewriter
30	578	David Finch	1000	415	March 30	Salary
30	579	Rose Hill	950	416	March 30	Salary

The purchase from the Thomas Company was on terms of 2/10, n/30. The discount was taken.

REQUIRED   1. Prepare a voucher register for March.

2. Prepare a check register for March.

EXERCISE 7-5   **Petty Cash Fund.**   The Huron Typesetting Company maintains a petty cash fund of $500. On June 30 the fund contained cash of $368.45 and the following petty cash vouchers:

Taxi fares	$55.50
Payment to employee for entertainment expenses	50.00
Office supplies	27.50

REQUIRED   1. If the company's fiscal year ends on June 30 should the petty cash fund be replenished on June 30?

2. Prepare the journal entry to record the reimbursement of the petty cash fund on June 30.

EXERCISE 7-6   **Petty Cash Fund.**   The Crestone Welding Company established a $150 petty cash fund on January 9. On September 28 there was $20.53 in the fund, along with the following vouchers:

Freight charge on purchases	$38.68
Office supplies	50.39
Postage	18.72
Miscellaneous	21.68

REQUIRED   1. How much cash is needed to replenish the fund?

2. How much are the expenses for the period?

3. Prepare the journal entry needed to record the reimbursement of the petty cash fund on September 28.

EXERCISE 7-7   **Bank Reconciliation.**   A company is performing a bank reconciliation and discovers the following items:

(a) Outstanding checks.

(b) Deposits in transit.

(c) Unrecorded charges made directly by the bank.

(d) Unrecorded deposits made directly by the bank.

(e) The erroneous underrecording by the bank of a deposit.

(f) The erroneous underrecording by the company of a check written.

REQUIRED   Indicate how each of these items would be used to adjust:

1. The company's cash balance.

2. The bank balance to calculate the reconciled cash balance.

EXERCISE 7-8   **Bank Reconciliation.**   At the end of March 1991 the Elbert Company's books showed a cash balance of $6,943. When comparing the March 31, 1991, bank statement with the company's cash account, it was discovered that outstanding checks totaled $862, deposits in transit were $725, unrecorded bank service charges were $28, and unrecorded NSF checks totaled $175.

REQUIRED

1. Compute the March 31, 1991, reconciled cash balance of the Elbert Company.
2. Compute the unadjusted cash balance listed on the March 31, 1991, bank statement.
3. Prepare appropriate journal entries for the Elbert Company on March 31, 1991.

EXERCISE 7-9 **Bank Reconciliation.** At the end of September 1991 the Bross Bicycle Company's books showed a cash balance of $3,496. When comparing the September 30, 1991, bank statement, which showed a cash balance of $1,860, with the company's cash account, it was discovered that outstanding checks were $462, unrecorded bank service charges were $23, and unrecorded NSF checks totaled $89.

REQUIRED

1. Compute the September 30, 1991, reconciled cash balance of the Bross Bicycle Company.
2. Compute the September deposits in transit.
3. Prepare the appropriate journal entries for the Bross Bicycle Company on September 30, 1991.

EXERCISE 7-10 **Bank Reconciliation.** On September 30, 1991, the Wells Company is preparing a bank reconciliation for the month of September. The following information is available for September:

(a) The cash account has an ending balance of $796.24.
(b) The bank statement shows an ending bank balance of $1,196.39.
(c) Outstanding checks total $277.42.
(d) A deposit in transit of $142.27.
(e) A bank service charge of $25 had not been recorded by the company.
(f) The bank collected a note of $300 and charged a collection fee of $10.

REQUIRED Prepare a bank reconciliation at September 30, 1991.

EXERCISE 7-11 **Bank Reconciliation: Unknown Amounts.** The following five situations (columns 1–5) are independent:

	1	2	3	4	5
Ending balance in the company's cash account	a	$2,000	$4,000	$12,000	$3,000
Unrecorded deposits made directly by the bank	$ 200	b	300	450	200
Deposits in transit	600	800	c	500	900
Outstanding checks	450	1,200	600	d	1,000
Ending cash balance from the bank statement	6,000	3,000	4,100	12,000	e

REQUIRED Compute each of the unknown amounts, items a through e.

EXERCISE 7-12   **Cash Equivalents.**   On January 1, 1991, the Romenesk Company had $70,000 cash in its checking account. The management decided that it was desirable to earn additional revenues by investing in cash equivalents. Therefore the company put $20,000 in a money market account and purchased treasury bills of $40,000. During the year the company earned interest of $1,500 on the money market account and $3,600 on the treasury bills. The interest was added to the respective accounts.

REQUIRED   1. Assuming no other changes in the company's cash, prepare the disclosure of the company's cash and cash equivalents for the December 31, 1991, balance sheet.

2. Evaluate the management's decision.

EXERCISE 7-13   **Money Market Account.**   At the beginning of January, the Floye Company opened a money market account by transferring $5,500 from its checking account. During January, the following transactions occurred related to the money market account:

(a) Wrote a check for $3,500 for a microcomputer.

(b) Transferred an additional $5,000 into the account.

(c) Earned interest of $70 on the account.

REQUIRED   Prepare the journal entries to record all the preceding events.

EXERCISE 7-14   **Disclosure of Cash.**   On December 31, 1991, the Bighorn Condominium Management Company had a balance in its petty cash account of $250, a reconciled cash balance from its checking account of $784.41, cash equivalents of $6,792.80, and unused postage stamps of $10.56.

REQUIRED   Prepare the disclosure of the cash balance in the company's balance sheet, assuming all the components are disclosed.

Problems

Part A

PROBLEM  **Petty Cash Fund.**   On October 10 the Dixon Chemical Company established a petty cash fund of $300 under the control of an employee. During the year the following transactions occurred:

Date	Transaction
Oct. 15	Purchased office supplies, $25.
27	Paid floral maintenance service for the office plants, $14.
Nov. 5	Purchased postage stamps, $9.
15	Paid UPS delivery charges, $10.
29	Purchased office supplies, $20.
Dec. 1	Reimbursed employee for taxi fare, $11.
5	Paid COD delivery charges, $5.
12	Paid for office cleaning, $25.
24	Paid for employee taxi fares, $50.
31	Replenished petty cash fund.

REQUIRED

1. How much is required to replenish the petty cash fund assuming no cash is over or short?

2. If $130 was in the petty cash fund before it was replenished, prepare the journal entry on December 31 to record the expenses and replenish the petty cash fund.

PROBLEM 7-2A

Bank Reconciliation. An examination of the accounting records and the bank statement of the Evans Company at March 31, 1991, provides the following information:

(a) The cash account has a balance of $6,137.38.

(b) The bank statement shows a bank balance of $3,901.81.

(c) The company's petty cash account has a balance of $300 and was replenished on March 31.

(d) The March 31 cash receipts of $3,260.95 were deposited at the bank that day but were not recorded by the bank until April 1.

(e) Checks issued and mailed in March but not included among the checks listed on the bank statement were:

Check No. 706	$869.38
Check No. 717	212.00

(f) A bank service charge of $30 for March had not been recorded by the company.

(g) A check received from a customer for $185 and deposited by the Evans Company was returned marked NSF. The nonpayment had not been previously recorded by the Evans Company.

(h) The bank collected a note of $192 plus current interest of $8, and charged a collection fee of $5. The cash receipt had not previously been recorded by the Evans Company.

(i) The Evans Company discovered that Check No. 701, which was correctly written as $562 for the March rent, was recorded as $526 on the company's books.

REQUIRED

1. Prepare a bank reconciliation at March 31, 1991.

2. Prepare the journal entries required to correct the Evans Company's cash account.

PROBLEM 7-3A

Bank Reconciliation. The Carson Company received the following bank statement for February 1991:

Carson Company
1313 Williams St.
Denver, Co. 80218

Mid-Town Bank
Denver, Co. 80222

Date	Checks	Deposits	Balance
Feb. 1			$4,524.80
5	$2,700.33	$8,642.61	
8	3,484.81		
12	6.00SC	350.00CM	
15	274.09		
19	4,133.60	3,385.49	
23	74.25NSF		
28			$6,229.82

SC = Service Charge
CM = Credit Memo

NSF = Check Returned
DM = Debit Memo

The receipt of $350 on February 12 was for a note of $345 collected by the bank, plus $10 current interest, less a $5 service charge. The company's accounting records contained the following information:

Cash Balance on February 28 from the books: $2,610.42

Cash Disbursements		*Cash Receipts*	
Check No. 155	$2,700.33	Feb. 4	$8,624.61
156	3,484.81	18	3,385.49
157	274.09		
158	589.02	All receipts are verified and correct.	
159	4,133.60		
160	2,742.63		

REQUIRED

1. Prepare a bank reconciliation on February 28 for the Carson Company.

2. Prepare the journal entries that the Carson Company should record as a result of the reconciliation.

PROBLEM 7-4A

Voucher System. The Warfield Irrigation Company uses a voucher system. During May, the following transactions occurred:

Date	Transaction
May 3	Recorded Voucher No. 326 for $160 for office supplies purchased from the Duran Company on terms of 2/10, n/30.
11	Recorded Voucher No. 327 for $500 for office equipment purchased from the Reidel Company.
11	Issued Check No. 580 in payment for Voucher No. 326.
19	Issued Check No. 581 in payment for Voucher No. 327.
23	Recorded Voucher No. 328 for $180 for office equipment repairs performed by the Zall Company.
28	Recorded Voucher No. 329 for $200 for advertisements in the Sunday Dispatch.
31	Recorded Voucher No. 330 and issued Check No. 582 for $1,250 as payment of salary to D. Smolen.

REQUIRED

1. Prepare a voucher register for May.

2. Prepare a check register for May.

3. What is the balance in the company's vouchers payable account on May 31?

PROBLEM 7-5A

Bank Reconciliation: Computing the Company's Cash Balance. The following information is available from the accounting records and the bank statement of the Newton Company for the month of August:

(a) The bank statement shows an ending bank balance of $342.29.

(b) The August 31 cash receipts of $1,658.31 were deposited at the bank that day but were not recorded by the bank until September 1.

(c) Checks issued and mailed in August but not included among the checks listed on the bank statement totaled $690.37.

(d) Interest earned on the account of $35.90 had not been recorded by the company.

(e) A check received from a customer for $329.75 and deposited by the Newton Company was returned marked NSF. The nonpayment had not previously been recorded by the Newton Company.

REQUIRED

1. Compute the Newton Company's reconciled cash balance on August 31, 1991.

2. Compute the Newton Company's cash balance in its accounting records on August 31, 1991, before any adjustments are made.

3. Prepare the journal entries required to correct the Newton Company's cash account.

Problems

Part B

PROBLEM 7-1B   **Petty Cash Fund.**   On November 6 the Checker Taxidermist Company established a petty cash fund of $600 under the control of an employee. During the year the following transactions occurred:

Date	Transaction
Nov. 10	Purchased postage stamps, $15.
21	Paid COD charges, $5.
24	Paid for office cleaning, $20.
30	Paid janitorial service, $13.
Dec. 5	Purchased office supplies, $10.
9	Paid UPS delivery charges, $7.
12	Paid employee's taxi fare, $12.
18	Paid floral maintenance service for the office plants, $25.
20	Purchased office supplies, $23.
31	Replenished petty cash fund.

REQUIRED

1. How much is required to replenish the petty cash fund assuming that there is no cash over or short?

2. If $450 was in the petty cash fund before it was replenished, prepare the journal entry on December 31 to record the expenses and replenish the petty cash fund.

PROBLEM 7-2B   **Bank Reconciliation.**   An examination of the accounting records and the bank statement of the Rancher Company at May 31, 1991, provides the following information:

(a) The cash account has a balance of $7,536.42.

(b) The bank statement shows a bank balance of $3,831.04.

(c) The company's petty cash account has a balance of $450 and was replenished on May 31.

(d) The May 31 cash receipts of $4,926.18 were deposited that day but were not recorded by the bank until June 1.

(e) Checks issued and mailed in May but not included among the checks listed on the bank statement were:

Check No. 949	$518.65
Check No. 957	699.95

(f) A bank service charge of $27 for May had not been recorded by the company.

(g) A check received from a customer for $241 and deposited by the Rancher Company was returned marked NSF. The nonpayment had not been previously recorded by the Rancher Company.

(h) The bank collected a note of $280 plus current interest of $20, and charged a collection fee of $10. The cash receipt had not been previously recorded by the Rancher Company.

(i) The Rancher Company discovered that Check No. 941, which was correctly written as $647.21 for the May utilities bill, was recorded as $627.41 on the company's books.

REQUIRED
1. Prepare a bank reconciliation at May 31, 1991.

2. Prepare the journal entries required to correct the Rancher Company's cash account.

PROBLEM 7-3B   **Bank Reconciliation.**   The Oomph Company received the following bank statement for the month of August 1991:

Oomph Company Denver, Co. 80223		Downtown Bank Denver, Co. 80001	
Date	Checks	Deposits	Balance
Aug. 1			$4,357.25
5	$1,314.88	$4,769.32	
12	773.56		
14	10.00SC	1,000.00CM	
20	3,200.00		
24	6,198.43	9,703.22	
26	290.00NSF		
29			$8,042.92
SC = Service Charge	CM = Credit Memo	NSF = Check Returned	DM = Debit Memo

The receipt of $1,000 on August 14 was for a note of $940 collected by the bank, plus current interest of $75, less a $15 service charge. The company's accounting records contained the following information:

Cash Balance on August 31 from the books: $5,088.08

Cash Disbursements		Cash Receipts	
Check No. 311	$1,314.88	Aug. 3	$4,679.32
312	773.56	20	9,703.22
313	3,200.00		
314	1,751.98	All receipts are verified and correct.	
315	6,198.43		
316	427.86		

REQUIRED

1. Prepare an August 31 bank reconciliation for the Oomph Company.

2. Prepare any journal entries necessary after the reconciliation.

PROBLEM 7-4B   **Voucher System.**   The Karpas Cable Company uses a voucher system. During June, the following transactions occurred:

Date	Transaction
June 4	Recorded Voucher No. 601 for $360 for machinery repairs performed by Lawton Company.
9	Recorded Voucher No. 602 for $230 for office supplies purchased from the Goldstein Company on terms of 1/10, n/30.
18	Issued Check No. 646 in payment for Voucher No. 601.
19	Issued Check No. 647 in payment for Voucher No. 602.
25	Recorded Voucher No. 603 and issued Check No. 648 to Phyllis Parker (the employee in charge of petty cash) for $150.24 to replenish the petty cash fund for the following: office supplies, $27.40; travel, $62.58; and entertainment, $60.26.
27	Recorded Voucher No. 604 for $430 for advertisements in the Daily Post.
30	Recorded Voucher No. 605 and issued Check No. 649 for $1,100 as payment of salary to L. Stone.

REQUIRED

1. Prepare a voucher register for June.

2. Prepare a check register for June.

3. How much is the balance in the company's vouchers payable account on June 30?

PROBLEM 7-5B   **Bank Reconciliation: Computing the Bank Statement Cash Balance.**   The cashier of the Gonner Company, I. Cheat, has notified you that the bank statements for the year have been misplaced. In reviewing selected accounting records from the past year, you discover the following journal entry that was made after the reconciliation of the company's bank account on July 31, 1991:

Accounts Receivable	1,600.00	
Miscellaneous Expense	15.00	
Notes Receivable		250.00
Interest Revenue		20.00
Cash		1,345.00

REQUIRED

1. Since there is no explanation accompanying the journal entry, describe the events that might have caused the reconciling items to occur.

2. Compute the amount that would have appeared as the "cash balance from the bank statement, July 31" on the bank reconciliation if the "cash balance from the company's books, July 31" was $1,386.90, the deposit in transit was $308.24, outstanding checks were $267.91, and your explanations in Requirement 1 are correct.

3. If you contact the bank and discover that a cash balance of $1,368.30 had been reported on the July 31, 1991, bank statement, what would you conclude? What steps would you take to begin investigating your suspicions?

Decision Cases

DECISION CASE 7-1   **Internal Control.**   Sam Lewis has been operating a service station for several years. Although he has occasionally employed students part-time, he has collected the cash for gas and service work himself. He has now decided to open a second service station and put himself more in the role of a manager, and therefore he will hire employees to run the service stations and to pump gas and do repair work.

REQUIRED   How could Sam Lewis implement the principles of internal control for cash? If any of the principles are not applicable in this situation, does it mean that Sam Lewis has to accept that he cannot have control over the financial aspects of the business?

DECISION CASE 7-2   **Reporting Cash on the Balance Sheet.**   The Kleping Company is nearing the end of the year and the preparation of its balance sheet is being planned. The controller is concerned about how to report the amounts of cash and cash equivalents. She is considering reporting cash separately from cash equivalents. The following information is obtained from its accounting system:

1. Balance in First State Bank checking account	$2,000
2. Balance in First Federal Bank checking account	3,500
3. Balance in First Interstate Bank savings account	7,000
4. Employee's IOU	250
5. Employees' travel advances	750
6. Undeposited checks from customers	3,000
7. Traveler's checks	1,500
8. Customer's postdated check	6,000
9. Postage stamps	100
10. Treasury bills	9,000

REQUIRED   Prepare a report for the controller which:

1. lists the amount that would be included in (a) cash and (b) cash equivalents.

2. recommends whether cash should be reported separately from cash equivalents.

3. suggests any changes in policies that could increase the amounts of cash and cash equivalents in the balance sheet.

DECISION CASE 7-3   **Cash.**   General Electric included the following information in its 1988 financial statements (in millions of dollars):

	1988	1987
Cash (Note 12)	$2,187	$2,543

Note 12: Deposits restricted as to usage and withdrawal or used as partial compensation for short-term borrowing arrangements were not material.

REQUIRED   1. Why were the amounts of the items described in Note 12 not disclosed?

2. If the items included in Note 12 were material, how should they be disclosed on the balance sheet?

3. The company's cash decreased by $356 million. Where would you find an explanation of the decrease?

8

Accounts Receivable and Notes Receivable

LEARNING OBJECTIVES

1. Explain the reasons for credit sales.

2. Explain credit card sales.

3. Describe the allowance method of accounting for bad debts.

4. Describe the direct write-off method of accounting for bad debts.

5. Compute the amount of bad debt expense under (a) the percent of sales method and (b) the aging method.

6. Describe a promissory note (receivable) and how to calculate interest on it.

7. Determine the maturity date of a note.

8. Explain the discounting of a note.

9. Describe how accounts receivable and notes receivable are disclosed in financial statements.

ne of the major changes in the economies of numerous countries has been the development of credit transactions. The use of credit has become so common that cash transactions have become relatively rare. One of the reasons for this change is the added convenience of credit transactions, such as the use of credit cards by many individual purchasers. The other reason is that credit allows some transactions to occur that would not otherwise be possible, such as the purchase of a house or car by the typical purchaser. Thus most companies are involved in making credit sales to their customers.

In this chapter we discuss some of the accounting issues associated with the receivables that result from making sales on credit. These issues include the valuation of accounts receivable and the bad debt expense resulting from the noncollection of accounts receivable. Also included is accounting for notes receivable, which involves discussions of calculating and recognizing interest, discounting a note at a bank, and dishonored notes.

Credit Sales and Collections

1. Explain the reasons for credit sales.

Companies make sales on credit for two primary reasons. The first is that it may be more convenient to sell on credit than for cash (as discussed in the last chapter checks received at the time of a sale are considered to be cash). For example, when a company is selling a product that has to be shipped it is a common business practice for the purchaser to pay for the goods after receiving them. Between the time that the purchaser acquires title to the goods and the time payment is received by the seller, credit has been extended by the seller to the purchaser (as discussed in Chapter 5).

The second reason why credit sales are made is that management may believe that offering credit will encourage a purchaser to acquire an item that would not otherwise be purchased. This is particularly common in retail sales when the purchaser may not have sufficient cash available to make the purchase. The seller, or retail store, offers credit terms so that the purchaser will agree to the sale. The disadvantage of credit sales is that they may require a significant management effort because the company must make credit investigations, prepare and mail bills, and ensure collection from the customers. All of these activities involve a cost to the company in money and employee time.

When credit sales are made to facilitate or encourage sales there is always a chance that the seller will not collect the full amount of its accounts receivable because the purchaser does not pay. It should be recognized that the existence of uncollectible accounts does not indicate that the company should not have made credit sales. As long as the gross profit earned from the additional credit sales less the cost of operating the credit activities exceeds the loss from not collecting certain accounts, the policy of offering credit sales may be considered to be advantageous. Suppose that because a company offers credit terms its sales increase by $80,000 and the following results occur:

Gross profit on the increased sales	$15,000	
Less: Costs of operating the credit department	(10,000)	
Increase in profit	$ 5,000	
Less: Uncollectible additional credit sales	(1,600)	(2% × $80,000)
Net increase in profit	$ 3,400	

Therefore even though the amount of the uncollectible accounts increased, the decision to offer credit terms on its sales increased the company's profits. Accounting for the uncollectible accounts receivable is discussed in a later section of the chapter.

Credit Card Sales

2. Explain credit card sales.

Many retail companies make agreements with credit card companies, such as VISA and MasterCard, which enable them to sell products or services to customers who use those credit cards to pay for their purchases. Credit card sales and collections follow several steps. First, the retail company records the credit card sale and bills the credit card company. The retail company then receives payment from the credit card company less a service charge, which is generally between 1% and 5%. The credit card company bills the customer, who makes the payment directly to the credit card company. This arrangement is advantageous from the retail company's perspective because it (1) enables the company to attract customers who might not otherwise make purchases, (2) enables the company to collect cash from the credit card company sooner than it could collect from the customer, and (3) frees the company from being concerned with the problems of credit investigation, billing, and collection. The company must, however, check each credit card against a "lost or stolen" list to avoid the possible rejection of the sale by the credit card company. The company may also be required to obtain permission from the credit card company for large charges to ensure that the customer's credit limit is not exceeded.

There is a time period, which is perhaps very short, between the sale to the customer and the collection of cash from the credit card company. If the customer pays with a bank credit card, such as VISA or MasterCard, the retailer may be able to deposit the credit card receipt along with checks and cash in its bank account and therefore the sale can be immediately recorded as a cash sale rather than as an account receivable. The receipt for other types of credit cards, such as American Express or Diner's Club, which are typically accepted by companies operating airlines, hotels, and restaurants, cannot be deposited directly in the bank and results in an account receivable because there is a period of time before the cash is received. In both situations a credit card expense generally is also recognized at the same time as the transaction is recorded.

Suppose that the Carson Travel Agency sells an airline ticket for $100 to a customer who pays with a credit card. If the service charge is 4% the company will receive only $96 and the $4 is considered to be a credit card expense. This transaction is recorded at the time of sale as follows:

Credit Card Accounts Receivable (or Cash)	96	
Credit Card Expense	4	
Sales		100

To record a credit card sale less the service charge.

When sales discounts were discussed in Chapter 5 the accounts receivable amount was recorded at the full amount. When the customer took the discount (and less cash was received) the difference between the cash and the accounts receivable balance was recorded as a Sales Discount Taken. This procedure was followed because it was not known at the time of the sale whether or not the discount would be taken. In contrast, with credit card sales it is known at the time of the sale that a lesser amount will be received by the retail company, and therefore it is appropriate to record the lesser amount when the sale is made. A company may also find it more convenient to record the account receivable at the full amount and recognize the expense when payment is received. Although this procedure is not as accurate and also is not consistent with the matching principle, it may be more desirable if it lessens record keeping because an expense does not have to be computed for every sale.

Uncollectible Accounts Receivable

Uncollectible accounts receivable are the accounts receivable that a company will not collect. At the time of the credit sales, the company does not know which customers will not pay because, of course, if it knew then that a particular customer would not pay, it would never have made the sale in the first place. Although a company agrees to sell on credit based on a customer's credit references, the references indicate only the past record of the customer's payments and do not guarantee that the customer will pay in the future. Thus a period of time, perhaps several months or even years, may pass before the company decides that it will not collect a particular account. When this decision is made the account is *written off*, which means that continuing attempts are not made to collect the account even though hope for eventual collection may continue.

Whether credit sales are made for convenience or to attract customers the costs associated with making these sales should be an expense. **Bad debt expense is the expense for the accounting period due to the eventual noncollection of accounts receivable.** Recording these costs as bad debt expense is consistent with the treatment of other costs associated with the sale that are also treated as expenses. Although there is no rule that specifies how a company must classify the expense in the income statement, it is more common to include the amount as an operating expense in the category of general and administrative expenses. Since the decision to grant credit is normally made by the credit department rather than by the selling department, it is appropriate to classify bad debt expense as an administrative expense rather than a selling expense.

Accounting for bad debt expense and uncollectible accounts receivable raises two basic questions. The first relates to the period in which the expense should be recognized. The second is the amount of the expense that should be recognized and the value that should be shown for accounts receivable on the balance sheet at the end of the accounting period. Each of these questions is discussed in the next two sections.

When Should the Uncollectibility Be Recognized?

As mentioned, a period of time elapses between recording the sale and knowing that the particular receivable will not be collected. Sometimes these two events occur in the same accounting period, in which case there is no problem. More often, however, the sale is recorded in one accounting period and the knowledge of the uncollectibility of the related account occurs in a later period. This suggests two alternatives for the time period in which the bad debt expense could be recognized. The expense could be recognized in the time period in which the sale is made or in the time period in which the uncollectibility is known, that is, the period of the write-off, as shown in the following diagram.

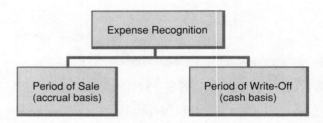

The accrual basis is discussed now and the cash basis is discussed later in the chapter. To illustrate the logic of the accrual basis, suppose that the Marlin Company sells a product for $150 to John Jones in August 1991. John Jones later encounters financial difficulty and declares bankruptcy in July 1992 before he has paid Marlin. Should Marlin recognize this expense in 1991 or 1992?

A review of the matching principle, which was first discussed in Chapter 3, should make it very clear which answer is correct. **The matching principle requires that the cost of generating sales revenue be matched against the revenue in the period in which the revenue is recognized.** We have clearly seen this principle being applied when the cost of the product sold (the cost of goods sold) is matched against the sales revenue in the period of the sale even though the purchase may have been made in an earlier period and the cash payment made in an earlier or later period. The cost of goods sold is *not* recognized in, for example, the period of the purchase or the cash payment, but rather the period in which the product is sold. Similarly, the bad debt expense that is associated with the sales of a period should be matched against the sales of that period.

In order to adhere to the matching concept the allowance method of accounting for uncollectible accounts receivable is used. **The allowance method requires the recognition of the bad debt expense in the period of the sale and *not* in the period of write-off.** Referring to the example in the previous paragraph, the Marlin Company has a bad debt expense in 1991 and *not* in 1992. Since the uncollectibility will not be known until 1992, however, the bad debt expense for 1991 must be *estimated* (this estimate is discussed in the next section).

3. Describe the allowance method of accounting for bad debts.

Once again the recognition of accounting expenses is being separated from the related cash flow, or in this case the lack of a cash flow.

Recognition of Bad Debt Expense

Before explaining in the next section the problem of estimating the amount of the bad debt expense (before the write-off occurs) under the allowance method, let us review how the financial statements are affected by the recognition of a bad debt expense in the period of sale.

When the bad debt expense is recognized the company is accepting the fact that a portion of the accounts receivable will not be collected. Therefore the value of the accounts receivable should also be reduced because otherwise the value of the asset would be overstated. An allowance for uncollectible accounts is used for this purpose. **Allowance for Uncollectible Accounts is a contra-asset account in which a company records its estimate of the amount of accounts receivable that it will not collect.** The Allowance account is subtracted from Accounts Receivable to give net accounts receivable, which is reported in the balance sheet. In the Marlin Company example we discussed the uncollectibility in terms of a single account; in actual practice, however, companies evaluate the uncollectibility of their entire accounts receivable at one time. Thus a single journal entry is used to recognize the expense for the period and the reduction of the asset value at the end of the period for all the company's estimated uncollectible accounts. An adjusting entry is made at the end of the period as follows (using assumed amounts):

Bad Debt Expense	2,500	
Allowance for Uncollectible Accounts		2,500

To record the estimated bad debt expense for the period.

Note that the credit (increase) to the Allowance account has the same effect as a credit (decrease) to the Accounts Receivable account would have; that is, because the Allowance account is increased net accounts receivable is decreased. The advantage of using the contra-asset account is that the Accounts Receivable account will still include the total amount that the company is legally entitled to receive. In addition, if the Accounts Receivable account were credited directly it would not have the same balance as the accounts receivable subsidiary ledger. This result would occur because it is not possible to write down individual accounts in the subsidiary ledger since the individual customers who will not pay in the future are not known now. If the individual customers who failed to pay could have been known, the company would never have made the sales to them. The net accounts receivable, the balance of the Accounts Receivable less the balance of the Allowance for Uncollectible Accounts, indicates the company's *estimate* of the amount of cash it will actually receive. Since the net accounts receivable is generally expected to be collected within 1 year, it is also the amount that is disclosed in the current asset section on the ending balance sheet as follows (using assumed numbers):

Accounts receivable	$95,000
Less: Allowance for uncollectible accounts	(3,200)
Net accounts receivable	$91,800

Write-Off of an Uncollectible Account

Eventually certain specific customer accounts will be judged to be uncollectible. When a company writes off an account receivable it is recognizing the noncollection of an amount that was included in its previous estimation of uncollectible accounts. Therefore **the write-off does *not* affect the total assets or expenses of the company.** The expense and the reduction in the asset were both recorded at the time of the estimate by means of the adjusting entry. Therefore the write-off of a specific uncollectible account receivable of Ann Blake of $220 is recorded in the following journal entry:

Allowance for Uncollectible Accounts	220	
Accounts Receivable: Ann Blake..		220

To record the write-off of uncollectible account receivable.

Note that the effect of this entry is to reduce (debit) a contra asset, Allowance for Uncollectible Accounts, and reduce (credit) an asset, Accounts Receivable. Therefore the net effect on the assets of the company is zero as follows:

	Before the Write-off	After the Write-off
Accounts receivable	$95,000	$94,780
Less: Allowance for uncollectible accounts	(3,200)	(2,980)
Net accounts receivable	$91,800	$91,800

At the same time as this journal entry is made, the specific customer's account in the accounts receivable subsidiary ledger will be credited for the nonpayment of the account. Since a company usually refers to its customer accounts in the subsidiary ledger when deciding whether or not to extend additional credit, this write-off should have the effect of causing the company to refuse credit to this customer in the future.

Direct Write-Off Method

4. Describe the direct write-off method of accounting for bad debts.

Although the allowance method is required by generally accepted accounting principles, some companies use the direct write-off method. **The direct write-off method recognizes the bad debt expense in the period when the account is written off because it is uncollectible.** Therefore no estimate of bad debt expense is made in the period of sale. The direct write-off method is *not* a generally accepted accounting principle for several reasons.

1. It violates the matching principle and causes income to be overstated in the period of sale and understated in the period of the write-off.

2. The accounts receivable are recorded in the balance sheet at an amount greater than the cash that is expected to be collected.

3. The method provides an opportunity for management to manipulate income because it selects the period of write-off.

The method may be used, however, in three circumstances. First, it may be used if the effect on the financial statements is not materially different from using the allowance method (materiality was discussed in Chapter 1). Thus if the effect of using the direct write-off method instead of the allowance method does not result in a materially different measure of income or assets, its use is acceptable.

Second, many companies are not required to follow generally accepted accounting principles in the preparation of their financial statements and therefore may use the direct write-off method. For example, sole proprietorships, partnerships, and corporations whose stock is not publicly traded are not *required* to follow generally accepted accounting principles. It may be a very shortsighted policy, however, not to follow generally accepted accounting principles. Whenever the company comes into contact with third parties such as banks and various regulatory authorities, the absence of generally accepted accounting principles may cause considerable difficulties. In addition, the eventual conversion to generally accepted accounting principles may be expensive and time-consuming. Third, the direct write-off method is used for federal income tax reporting.

Accounting for the direct write-off method is simpler than for the allowance method. No estimate of bad debt expense is made, and no allowance account is used. When an account receivable is judged to be uncollectible, the bad debt expense is recognized and the account receivable written off. For example, if a company writes off a $300 account receivable from Carl Norbeck, the following journal entry is made:

Bad Debt Expense	**300**	
Accounts Receivable: Carl Norbeck		**300**
To record the bad debt expense.		

Although the direct write-off method may be simpler for a smaller company that is not required to follow generally accepted accounting principles, management should be careful to keep track of accounts receivable to avoid incurring unnecessary losses. In the rest of the chapter we will assume that the allowance method is being used.

Measurement of Bad Debt Expense

An obvious problem arises when the bad debt expense is recognized in the period of the sale and not in the period that the account is written off. How is the amount that is eventually to be written off known in the period the sale is made? The amount is not known for certain, but the company can *estimate* how much it will not collect in the future. Two methods of estimation are used. The percent of sales method uses an estimate that is based on the sales of the current period. The aging method uses an estimate that is based on the balance in accounts receivable.

Percent of Sales Method of Estimating Bad Debt Expense

A company can estimate its bad debt expense by using the percent of sales method. **The percent of sales method requires the company to estimate the bad debt expense by multiplying the net credit sales of the period by the percent estimated to be uncollectible.** The method is based on the question, "How much of this year's net credit sales will not be collected?" Net credit sales are credit sales less sales discounts and sales returns and allowances. The estimate can be based on the past experience of the company or on the experiences of other companies published in a trade journal and updated for any changes in economic conditions, such as a general deterioration in the economy. For example, suppose that a company has the following information related to its credit sales for 1991:

Sales	$210,000	(credit)
Sales returns and allowances	(8,000)	(debit)
Sales discounts taken	(2,000)	(debit)
Net credit sales	$200,000	

5(a). Compute the amount of bad debt expense under the percent of sales method.

The company's past experience indicates that $1\frac{1}{2}\%$ of its net credit sales are never collected. Therefore in order to match expenses against revenues the company must recognize a bad debt expense of $3,000 ($1\frac{1}{2}\% \times \$200,000$) in 1991. The adjusting entry at the end of the year to record this expense is as follows:

Bad Debt Expense	3,000	
Allowance for Uncollectible Accounts		3,000

To record the estimated bad debt expense for 1991.

The effect of this entry is to reduce income for 1991 and reduce the value of accounts receivable. If a specific account should be considered uncollectible the write-off is recorded as discussed earlier by reducing (debiting) the Allowance for Uncollectible Accounts and reducing (crediting) Accounts Receivable. The write-off would also be recorded in the accounts receivable subsidiary ledger. Note that this procedure does not give any consideration to the balance in the Allowance account, since the bad debt expense is based solely upon net credit sales for the period.

While the percent of sales method matches the bad debt expense against the sales revenue in the current period, a major disadvantage is that there is no verification of the reasonableness of the balance of the Allowance for Uncollectible Accounts. Recall that the account is increased (credited) when the estimate is made and reduced (debited) when the write-off occurs. Therefore if the company overestimates the bad debts (the estimated amount exceeds the write-offs) the allowance account will have a credit balance remaining in it that exceeds the value of the accounts that will be written off in the future. If this overestimation is not offset by an equal underestimation in subsequent periods, the balance will never be removed. Such a *permanent* balance leads to an incorrect valuation of the accounts receivable and indicates that the bad debt expense of previous periods has been estimated incorrectly. While it is possible for the company to periodically eliminate any balance that has accumulated in the allowance account, the aging method of estimating the bad debt expense prevents such an incorrect balance from being created in the account.

Aging Method of Estimating Bad Debt Expense

Instead of basing the estimate of bad debt expense on net credit sales, the aging method bases the estimate of the balance in the Allowance for Uncollectible Accounts on the age of the individual accounts included in the ending balance of Accounts Receivable. The method is based on the question, "How much of the accounts receivable at the end of the year will not be collected?" The rationale for this method is that the bad debts result from the accounts receivable that are outstanding rather than from the sales themselves. Therefore an excessive bal-ance cannot build up in the Allowance for Uncollectible Accounts because each period's estimate of the amounts uncollectible is based on the particular accounts receivable balance at the end of that period. The aging method is also generally considered to be more accurate for valuing the net accounts receivable collectible at the end of the period because the estimate is based on the age of the specific customer's accounts receivable outstanding. As the length of time a cus-tomer's account has been outstanding increases, the likelihood of the account not being collected is increased. For example, a company is much more likely to collect an account that is 30 days old than an account that is 360 days old. Therefore as the proportion of old accounts increases, the balance in the Allowance for Uncollectible Accounts should also increase in proportion to the larger expected write-offs.

5(b). Compute the amount of bad debt expense under the aging method.

The aging method requires a company to categorize each individual account into age groups based on the length of time it has been outstanding. The total in each age group is then multiplied by an historically based esti-mated percent uncollectible to estimate the amount uncollectible in the age group. The amounts in each age group are summed to give the required end-ing balance in the Allowance for Uncollectible Accounts. As with the percent of sales method these estimates would be based on the past experience of the company and adjusted for changes in economic conditions or on the experiences of other companies that have been published in a trade journal. To illustrate the application of the aging method suppose that the Joyce Company makes credit sales during 1991 and has a balance in accounts receivable of $100,000 at the end of 1991. This total balance is made up of amounts within each age group and percents expected to be uncollectible as follows:

Age Group	Amount	Estimated Percent Uncollectible	Estimated Amount Uncollectible
Not yet due	$ 40,000	$\frac{1}{2}$%	$ 200
1–30 days past due	25,000	1	250
31–60 days past due	20,000	2	400
61–120 days past due	10,000	5	500
More than 120 days past due	5,000	20	1,000
Total	$100,000		$2,350

Since the Joyce Company has accounts receivable of $40,000 that are not yet due, and the company's experience shows that $\frac{1}{2}$% of these accounts will become uncollectible, the expected amount uncollectible is $200 ($\frac{1}{2}$% × $40,000). Applying this analysis to each age group provides a total estimated amount uncollectible of $2,350. Therefore the expected collectible amount is $97,650 ($100,000 − $2,350) and is shown as a current asset in the balance sheet as follows:

Accounts receivable	$100,000
Less: Allowance for uncollectible accounts	(2,350)
Net accounts receivable	$ 97,650

Note that the amount of $2,350 is the required *balance* of the Allowance for Uncollectible Accounts and *not* the amount of the Bad Debt Expense. The Bad Debt Expense is the amount that is needed to increase the existing balance of the Allowance for Uncollectible Accounts up to the required ending balance of $2,350.[1] Therefore if it is assumed that the Joyce Company had a credit balance in the account of $400 before it performed the aging analysis, the bad debt expense for the year is $1,950 ($2,350 − $400) and is recorded by an adjusting entry at year end as follows:

Bad Debt Expense	1,950	
Allowance for Uncollectible Accounts		1,950

To record the estimated bad debt expense for 1991.

It is important to understand why there is a $400 credit balance in the Allowance for Uncollectible Accounts before the year-end adjusting entry. The balance results from the estimates of uncollectible accounts from previous years less the amounts written off to date. It exists because the company may wait more than one year before writing off certain accounts or because actual experience has not been equal to the percentage estimated to be uncollectible. The addition of $1,950 to the credit balance of $400 in the Allowance account results in the correct ending balance of $2,350. Thus the ending accounts receivable is properly valued at the expected amount collectible of $97,650. The analysis of the balance in the Allowance for Uncollectible Accounts may be summarized as follows:

Allowance for Uncollectible Accounts

Actual amounts written off during the year	Beginning balance reflects the estimated amount of the related Accounts Receivable that will not be collected in the current and future periods.
If a debit balance results, the actual amount written off to date exceeded the estimated amount. The debit balance is added to the desired ending credit balance to calculate the expense for the period.	If a credit balance results, the estimated amount exceeded the actual amount written off to date. The credit balance is subtracted from the desired ending credit balance to calculate the expense for the period.

Also note that use of the aging method does *not* consider the sales for the period. Consequently, the use of the aging method avoids the possibility of creating an incorrect ending balance in the Allowance for Uncollectible Accounts as is possible with the percent of sales method.

---

[1] If the Allowance account has a debit balance because the actual amounts written off during the year were greater than the estimate at the end of the previous year, the balance in the account would be *added* to the required balance to compute the bad debt expense. For example, if the Joyce Company had a debit balance of $500 in the Allowance account, the bad debt expense would be $2,850 ($2,350 + $500).

While the aging method is a more accurate method for valuing accounts receivable than the percent of sales method, it requires more information for its application. This added knowledge of the estimated percent of uncollectibles by age groups, however, is useful information that management should know for effective control of its credit operations. As individual accounts move to older age groups the credit department should make increasing efforts to collect the accounts.

When a company (e.g., a bank) has a relatively small number of large receivables, it may be appropriate to analyze each account and estimate its uncollectibility. This procedure is more costly but may be desirable for certain types of companies.

Recovery of Accounts Written Off

Now that we have seen how to estimate and account for bad debt expense and the write-off of accounts receivable, an additional item needs to be considered. After a company has written off an account receivable, the receivable may later be collected. This recovery of a previously written off account receivable requires a two-step process. First, the journal entry used to write off the account must be reversed. Second, the collection of cash on the reinstated account receivable must be recognized. Suppose that the Joyce Company recovers the $150 account of Thomas Martin that it had previously written off. The following journal entries are required:

Accounts Receivable: Thomas Martin	150	
Allowance for Uncollectible Accounts		150

To reverse the write-off of the account of Thomas Martin.

Cash	150	
Accounts Receivable: Thomas Martin		150

To record collection of past due account of Thomas Martin.

Note that these two entries have no effect on total assets although one asset, cash, has been increased and another asset, accounts receivable, has been decreased. The first entry increases (debits) an asset, accounts receivable, and increases (credits) a contra asset, allowance for uncollectible accounts, thereby having no effect on net accounts receivable. The second entry increases (debits) an asset, cash, and decreases (credits) another asset, accounts receivable.

Since the net effect of the two entries is to increase cash and decrease accounts receivable, it is important to recognize why two entries are made instead of a single combined entry (debiting cash and crediting accounts receivable). When a debit or credit entry is made in the **accounts receivable control account,** an entry is also made in the **accounts receivable subsidiary ledger.** The first entry is necessary to reinstate the balance in the customer's subsidiary account and the second entry is necessary to record the account as paid. **This two-entry process provides a complete record of the customer's account that may be useful in determining whether or not to offer credit to this customer in the future.**

In the previous example if the company had used the direct write-off method to write off the Thomas Martin account initially, the subsequent recovery of this account would be recorded as follows:

| Accounts Receivable: Thomas Martin .... | 150 | |
| Bad Debt Expense .... | | 150 |

To reverse the write-off of the account of Thomas Martin.

| Cash .... | 150 | |
| Accounts Receivable: Thomas Martin .... | | 150 |

To record collection of past due account of Thomas Martin.

Summary of Percent of Sales and Aging Methods

In summary, it can be said that the percent of sales method is an income statement approach that properly matches expenses against revenues, although it tends to ignore the valuation of the accounts receivable in the ending balance sheet. In contrast, the aging method focuses on the valuation of the account receivable in the balance sheet, although it puts less emphasis on the expense in the income statement. Whichever method is used the entries that are made in the two accounts, Accounts Receivable and the Allowance for Uncollectible Accounts, can be summarized in general ledger form as follows:

Accounts Receivable		*Allowance for Uncollectible Accounts*	
Beginning balance	Cash received	Accounts written off	Beginning balance
Credit sales	Accounts written off		Amount recorded as bad debt expense
Amounts recovered from write-offs			Amounts recovered from write-offs
Ending balance			Ending balance

Customers sometimes overpay their accounts in anticipation of future purchases or by error. Such credit balances should be shown as liabilities because the company is obligated to the customers for those amounts; that is, they should not be deducted from the accounts receivable that have debit balances.

Notes Receivable

When a company sells on credit in the routine course of business it expects to receive payment in a relatively short time. Many companies, however, also sell to customers under an agreement in which payment will not be received for a much longer period. In this situation the selling company usually requires the purchaser to sign a promissory note. This note can be referred to if there is a legal dispute over the collection of the note. In addition, a major reason for requiring a note is that it can be converted into cash by selling it to a bank.

Promissory Note

6. Describe a promissory note (receivable) and how to calculate interest on it.

A promissory note is a written legal document in which one party (the maker) makes an unconditional promise to pay another party a certain amount of money on demand or on an agreed future date. Exhibit 8-1 includes an example of a note in which John Burgen agrees to pay the Morgan Company $10,000, plus interest of 12% on the maturity date. **The principal (also known as the face value) is the amount that is stated on the face of the note.** In this example the principal is $10,000. **The maturity date is the date on which the note and any interest are due and payable.** In our example the maturity date is February 1, 1992, which is 6 months after the date the note was signed on August 1, 1991. **The maker of the note is the person or company that signs the note and agrees to pay it on the maturity date. The payee is the person or company to whom the note is payable.** In this example John Burgen is the maker (or issuer) of the note and the Morgan Company is the payee.

Notes Receivable is the account used to record promissory notes held by the company. Thus when the Morgan Company makes the sale and receives the note it records sales revenue and a note receivable as follows:

Notes Receivable	10,000	
Sales		10,000

To record note received in a sale to John Burgen.

This entry is identical to the entry made to record a credit sale except for the change in the title of the asset account from Accounts Receivable to Notes Receivable. In addition, a company generally does not use a subsidiary ledger for notes receivable because it can use the physical existence of the note for the necessary supporting documentation.

It is stated on the note that interest of 12% will be paid. It should always be assumed that the quoted interest rate is an *annual* rate, unless otherwise stated. The interest is paid on the principal of the note. Consequently, John Burgen has

EXHIBIT 8-1   Promissory Note

PROMISSORY NOTE

$10,000   August 1, 19 91

Six months   after date, for value received, I, we (and each of us) promise to pay to ___the Morgan Company___ or order

Ten Thousand   Dollars with interest from

August 1, 1991 ___ at the rate of ___12___ per cent, per ___annum___ payable

___--___ annually. Principal payable and interest payable at ___February 1, 1992___

IT IS AGREED that if this note is not paid when due or declared due hereunder, the entire principal and accrued interest thereon shall draw interest at the rate of ___15___ per cent per annum, and that failure to make any payment of principal or interest when due or any default under any encumbrance or agreement securing this note shall cause the whole note to become due at once, or the interest to be counted as principal, at the option of the holder of the note. The makers and endorsers hereof severally waive presentment for payment, protest, notice of non-payment and of protest, and agree to any extension of time of payment and partial payments before, at or after maturity, and if this note or interest thereon is not paid when due, or suit is brought, agree to pay all reasonable costs of collection, including attorney's fees.

John Burgen

Due ___February 1,___ 19 92

No. 125

This Note is Secured by Property located at 1500 Elm Street Boulder, Colorado

No. 1028. Rev. 2-85.   Bradford Publishing, 5825 W. 6th Ave., Lakewood, CO 80214 — (303) 233-6900

2-85

agreed to pay annual interest of 12% for a 6-month period. Since the annual interest would be $1,200 (12% × $10,000), on the maturity date John Burgen will pay $600 ($1,200 × $\frac{6}{12}$) interest for the 6 months. **The maturity value of a note is the principal plus the interest due on the maturity date.** In this example the maturity value is $10,600 ($10,000 principal plus $600 interest).

The payment of interest represents an expense to John Burgen and interest revenue to the Morgan Company. A complication arises, however, because at the end of the Morgan Company's fiscal year (December 31, 1991) the company has earned interest revenue for the period it has held the note even though it has not received any cash. It is important to understand that interest is **earned** continuously over time even though it may only be **collected** periodically. In this situation, the interest earned is for 5 months, from August through December, and therefore is equal to $\frac{5}{12}$ of the annual interest, or $500 ($1,200 × $\frac{5}{12}$). The interest is recorded as follows by an adjusting entry at the end of the year:

Interest Receivable	500	
Interest Revenue		500

To record accrual of interest on John Burgen's note.

In the journal entry the company has recognized revenue because the interest was earned over a 5-month period; it also has recognized a receivable because John Burgen has a legal obligation to pay the interest. The Interest Revenue would be included in the Other Revenues and Expenses category of the income statement, and the Interest Receivable would be listed as a Current Asset in the balance sheet.

The note is due on February 1, 1992, and at that time the Morgan Company will receive $10,600 cash from John Burgen, consisting of the $10,000 principal and interest for 6 months of $600. In 1992, however, interest for only 1 month is earned, which is equal to $\frac{1}{12}$ of the annual interest, or $100 ($1,200 × $\frac{1}{12}$). The remaining $500 is the collection of the interest earned in 1991 and recorded as Interest Receivable at the end of 1991. Therefore the following journal entry is used to recognize the receipt of the $10,600 cash:

Cash	10,600	
Interest Receivable		500
Interest Revenue		100
Notes Receivable		10,000

To record receipt of principal and interest on John Burgen's note.

In summary, the Morgan Company is increasing its assets by $100 ($10,600 − $10,500), recognizing revenue of $100, and exchanging two assets, notes receivable and interest receivable, for cash.

General Rule for Computing Interest and the Maturity Date

The previous example used a simple situation in which the note was outstanding for exactly 6 months. In many situations, however, notes are outstanding for periods that include partial months. When the note is issued with the life of the note stated but the maturity date not specified, two computations are necessary. First, the maturity date of the note must be determined, and second, the interest must be computed for the correct period of time.

7. Determine the maturity date of a note.

Maturity Date. The maturity date of a note may be stated in terms of a specific number of months or days. For example, a 3-month note issued on October 9 matures on January 9. In contrast, when the maturity of a note is stated in terms of a certain number of days, the maturity date is computed by counting the exact number of days between the date the note was signed and the date it is due. In this calculation the day the note is signed is omitted, but the day the note is paid is included. To illustrate this rule suppose that a $2,000, 10%, 90-day note is signed on October 9 and is due 90 days after the signing. The maturity date is calculated as follows:

Life of the note		90
Number of days in October	31	
Minus the day of the note	9	
Number of days for the note in October	22	
Number of days in November	30	
Number of days in December	31	
		83
Maturity date in January		7

The maturity date of the note is determined to be January 7.

Computing Interest. The general rule for computing interest is:

$$\text{Interest} = \begin{array}{c}\textbf{Principal of} \\ \textbf{the Note}\end{array} \times \begin{array}{c}\textbf{Annual Rate} \\ \textbf{of Interest}\end{array} \times \begin{array}{c}\textbf{Period of Time the Note} \\ \textbf{Is Outstanding in Years} \\ \textbf{or Fraction of a Year}\end{array}$$

When a note is outstanding for several whole months the fraction of the year may be expressed by the number of months divided by 12, or in the earlier example of a $10,000, 12%, 6-month note:

$$\text{Interest} = \$10,000 \times 12\% \times \frac{6}{12}$$

$$= \$600$$

A simple rule for the computation of interest for a period other than a whole number of months is to assume that the year consists of 360 days (12 months of 30 days each).[2] Using this 360-day rule the interest on the $2,000, 90-day, 10% note is computed as follows:

$$\text{Interest} = \$2,000 \times 10\% \times \frac{90}{360}$$

$$= \$50$$

There may appear to be some inconsistency in computing *interest* on the basis of a 360-day year and the *maturity date* on the basis of the exact number of days.

---

[2]A 360-day year was commonly used in business transactions. However, in recent years the 365-day year has been used much more frequently.

Nevertheless these procedures are typical business practices and do not result in material errors in the interest calculation.[3]

Accrual of Interest.   At the end of each accounting period the interest that has accrued on any note must be recognized. The number of days the note has been outstanding must be determined and the interest computed according to the rule just explained. To continue the earlier example, on December 31 interest on the note must be accrued. At that time the $2,000 note will have been outstanding for 83 days (22 days in October + 30 days in November + 31 days in December) and 10% interest is computed as follows:

$$\text{Interest} = \$2,000 \times 10\% \times \frac{83}{360}$$
$$= \$46.11$$

The year-end adjusting entry to record the interest is as follows:

Interest Receivable	46.11	
Interest Revenue		46.11

To record accrual of interest on a $2,000, 10% note.

Interest on Accounts Receivable

If a retail company chooses to operate its own credit department rather than accepting national credit cards, interest may be charged on the outstanding accounts receivable balance. The recognition of interest revenue would then follow the same principles as discussed for notes receivable.

Factors Affecting Interest Rates

An interest rate determines the amount received when money is loaned for a period of time. Therefore it is the price charged for the service of making a loan and it changes frequently, just as other prices in the economy change in response to changes in supply and demand. Also, interest rates are affected by several additional factors.

1. The Federal Reserve Board influences interest rates as part of its activities in managing the activity of the entire United States economy.

2. The amount of risk associated with the loan will affect the interest rate. A bank will charge the lowest interest rate to its largest and most secure customers, such as large corporations. This rate is known as the **prime rate.** The bank will charge a higher rate to its smaller and less secure customers. Many credit cards charge interest of $1\frac{1}{2}\%$ a month because of the greater risk associated with those loans.

---

[3]A simple method that was often used to calculate interest is known as the 60-day, 6% rule. The rule is based on the fact that interest at 6% for 60 days is 1% (6% × 60/360). Therefore if a 6% note is outstanding for 60 days, the total interest is computed by multiplying the face value by 1% (or, in other words, by moving the decimal point 2 places to the left). For example, the interest on a note with a face value of $3,682 at 6% for 60 days is $36.82. While this calculation may be a useful "rule of thumb," it is rarely used today because of the ease of making calculations with computers or calculators.

3. Interest rates are affected by the length of the loan because risk increases as the length of the loan increases. For example, if you deposit money in a savings account that gives you the right of immediate withdrawal, you would receive interest of approximately 6% at the time of writing this book. However, if you are willing to loan the bank the money for a longer period, such as 6 months, a year, or even 5 years, the interest rate could go as high as 10%. A bank issuing a 30-year mortgage would receive interest of about 11%.

4. The expected rate of inflation over the life of the loan will affect the interest rate. Since a loan is repaid with dollars that have less purchasing power because of inflation, the bank will increase the interest rate to compensate for the inflation.

Dishonored Notes Receivable

Just as accounts receivable are not always paid, notes receivable are sometimes not paid. **A dishonored note is a note that the maker has failed to pay at the maturity date.** The maker is still responsible for payment, of course, but it is desirable for the payee to classify dishonored notes receivable separately from notes receivable that have not yet become due. For example, if John Burgen had failed to pay his note on February 1, 1992, he would have owed the Morgan Company $10,600 (the $10,000 principal plus the $600 interest). Since the interest for 1992 of $100 would not yet have been recorded in the accounts, the entry to record the dishonored note is as follows:

Notes Receivable Dishonored	10,600	
Notes Receivable		10,000
Interest Receivable		500
Interest Revenue		100

To record John Burgen's note as dishonored.

Apart from the recognition of interest revenue, this entry has no effect on total assets. Nevertheless, it is a useful reclassification of the accounts. As an alternative to using the Notes Receivable Dishonored account, it may be desirable to debit the Accounts Receivable account and establish John Burgen's subsidiary ledger account so that this account may be charged with the dishonored amount. This entry should prevent the Morgan Company from extending additional credit to John Burgen.

It is questionable whether interest revenue should be recognized when collection is in doubt. However, since the maker of the note owes interest as well as the principal and the note is a legal document, which should increase the probability of collection, it is normal to record the interest revenue so that the Notes Receivable Dishonored asset amount reflects the current amount owed. If the note is collected, additional interest may be charged to the maker and recorded as interest revenue. If the note receivable is not collected, the Notes Receivable Dishonored account is written off (credited) and Allowance for Uncollectible Notes Receivable is reduced (debited), if the company has recorded bad debts expense for notes receivable. Otherwise, the company is using the direct write-off method, and Bad Debt Expense would be debited.

Discounting a Note Receivable

8. Explain the
discounting of a note.

One of the advantages of a note that was mentioned earlier is that it can be converted into cash before maturity. Thus management has the opportunity of obtaining additional cash without having to apply for a loan. This is accomplished by discounting the note with a bank. **Discounting a note is a process in which the payee of a note assigns it over to a bank in exchange for cash.** The bank will then collect the note and interest from the maker on the maturity date. The payee, however, usually remains responsible to the bank for the ultimate payment of the note, should the maker default. That is, if the maker fails to pay the bank, the payee must pay the bank. This liability of the payee is known as a contingent liability. **A contingent liability is a liability that may or may not be paid depending on whether or not a future event occurs.** Discounting a note creates a contingent liability because the legal obligation the payee has to the bank is a liability, and the liability is contingent because it will have to be paid only if the maker fails to pay.

When a note is discounted at a bank the proceeds are computed as follows:

$$\text{Proceeds} = \text{Maturity Value} - \text{Discount}$$

Therefore, it is first necessary to compute the maturity value at the maturity date. The maturity value is the sum of the principal and the interest. Since the maturity value is the amount the bank will receive from the maker on the maturity date, the bank then computes interest on this amount for the period between the date the note is discounted to the bank and the maturity date. This interest (often referred to as the *discount*) is deducted from the maturity value to determine the amount to pay the payee. It should be noted that the interest rate charged by the bank bears no relation to the rate listed on the note.

To illustrate the discounting of a note suppose that Susan Davis signs a $1,000, 10%, 6-month note on March 31 payable to the Williams Company as payment for a purchase of furniture. At that time the Williams Company recorded the transaction by increasing (debiting) Notes Receivable and increasing (crediting) Sales for $1,000. The Williams Company holds the note until April 30 when it is discounted at the bank. The bank charges the Williams Company 12% interest on the maturity value of the note. The bank will collect the maturity value of the note from Susan Davis on September 30. The $1,050 maturity value is calculated by adding the interest to maturity of $50 ($1,000 × 10% × 6/12) to the $1,000 face value. Since the bank will collect the $1,050, 5 months after receipt of the note, it charges the Williams Company interest on the maturity value for 5 months at 12%. The $52.50 interest (discount) is computed as $1,050 × 12% × 5/12. Therefore the bank pays to the Williams Company the maturity value less the interest (discount) it charges, or $997.50 ($1,050 − $52.50). The calculation of the discounting of the note may be illustrated in tabular form as follows:

Principal	$1,000.00
Add: Interest to maturity ($1,000 × 10% × 6/12)	50.00
Maturity value	$1,050.00
Less: Discount ($1,050 × 12% × 5/12)	(52.50)
Proceeds	$ 997.50

The elements included in the discounting calculation may be illustrated as follows:

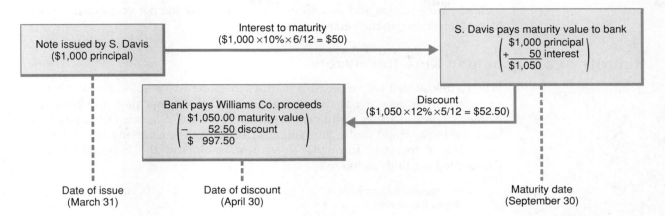

Since the $997.50 total payment on the note is less than the $1,000 principal, there is an interest expense to the Williams Company of $2.50. The Williams Company records the discounting of the note as follows:

Cash	997.50	
Interest Expense	2.50	
Notes Receivable Discounted		1,000

To record the discounting of the Susan Davis note.

Two points should be observed. First, the Williams Company has a *net* interest expense because the interest cost ($52.50) to the company from discounting the note is higher than the interest earned ($50) on the note. The interest expense of $2.50 consists of the following components:

Interest charged on the note, April 30 – September 30	
($1,050 \times 12\% \times \frac{5}{12}$)	$52.50
Less: Interest given up, April 30 – September 30	
($1,000 \times 10\% \times \frac{5}{12}$)	(41.67)
Interest cost	$10.83
Less: Interest earned, March 31 – April 30	
($1,000 \times 10\% \times \frac{1}{12}$)	(8.33)
Net interest expense	$ 2.50

It is entirely possible that the proceeds from discounting the note will exceed the principal of the note, in which case Interest Revenue would be recognized (credited) for the net difference.

The second point is that the credit in the preceding journal entry is made to a Notes Receivable Discounted account rather than to the Notes Receivable account. **The Notes Receivable Discounted account is a contra account to Notes Receivable and is deducted from Notes Receivable on the balance sheet.** (An example of this is shown later.) The purpose of this separate classification is to recognize the existence of the contingent liability discussed earlier. If the Notes Receivable account had been credited instead, the note would no longer be recorded anywhere in the accounting system. Using the Notes Receivable Discounted account retains two references to the note in the accounting system. The net value of the Notes Receivable less the Notes Receivable Discounted for a *particular* note is zero and therefore does not increase the net value of the asset, Notes Receivable, in the balance sheet.

Maturity of a Discounted Note Receivable

When a discounted note receivable matures there are two possibilities: the maker either pays the note as scheduled or defaults. If the maker pays the bank, the payee is relieved of its contingent liability. Therefore if Susan Davis pays the note, the bank would notify the Williams Company. The company then removes the value of the note from the Notes Receivable and the Notes Receivable Discounted accounts as follows:

Notes Receivable Discounted	1,000	
Notes Receivable		1,000

To remove contingent liability for the Susan Davis note.

There is no interest to recognize at the maturity date because the interest was accounted for when the note was discounted.

If the note is dishonored the bank will claim payment from the payee. The payment will include the principal and interest, plus a service charge for processing the dishonored note. Therefore if Susan Davis defaults on her note the bank will claim the $1,000 principal of the note, the $50 interest accrued, plus a service charge from the Williams Company. If the service charge is $10 the total amount will be $1,060 ($1,000 + $50 + $10), and the Williams Company records its payment to the bank on the dishonored note as follows:

Notes Receivable Dishonored	1,060	
Cash		1,060

To record payment on the Susan Davis dishonored note.

As discussed earlier it may be desirable to record the asset as Accounts Receivable rather than Notes Receivable Dishonored. In addition, since the note and the contingent liability are no longer outstanding, the Williams Company eliminates the related accounts as follows:

Notes Receivable Discounted	1,000	
Notes Receivable		1,000

To remove contingent liability for the Susan Davis note.

On receipt of the cash the bank will deliver the dishonored note to the Williams Company. Susan Davis, of course, is still legally obligated to pay the company, which will make every attempt to collect the full amount owed to it, including the service charge imposed by the bank and additional interest on the *total* amount from the maturity date to the date of collection. If the note is collected 1 month after the maturity date, the following entry is made:

Cash	1,068.83	
Notes Receivable Dishonored		1,060.00
Interest Revenue ($1,060 × 0.10 × $\frac{1}{12}$)		8.83

To record collection of the Susan Davis note.

If a company has doubts about its ability to collect notes receivable, a Bad Debt Expense and an Allowance for Uncollectible Notes Receivable should be established in exactly the same way as accounts receivable. If the note is not collected, it is then written off in the same way as an uncollectible account receivable. If an Allowance account has not been established, the Note Receivable is written off (credited) and a Bad Debt Expense is recorded (debited).

Disclosure of Accounts and Notes Receivable in the Financial Statements

9. Describe how accounts receivable and notes receivable are disclosed in financial statements.

As we have seen, both accounts receivable and notes receivable have an impact on the financial statements. Both the bad debt expense and interest revenue are included in the income statement. The balance sheet includes the net value for each type of receivable. For example, if the Aspen Company has accounts receivable of $30,000, an allowance for uncollectible accounts of $2,000, and notes receivable of $20,000, of which $15,000 have been discounted, the balance sheet would typically include the following items in current assets (assuming all items are expected to be collected within one year or the operating cycle, whichever is longer):

Current Assets

Accounts receivable	$30,000	
Less: Allowance for uncollectible accounts	(2,000)	
Net accounts receivable		$28,000
Notes receivable	$20,000	
Less: Notes receivable discounted	(15,000)	
Net notes receivable		5,000

Alternatively, instead of showing both the Notes Receivable and the Notes Receivable Discounted accounts in the balance sheet, the notes receivable can be included in the balance sheet at their net value of $5,000 ($20,000 – $15,000). The contingent liability associated with the discounted notes receivable then would be disclosed in the footnotes as follows:

Footnotes to the Financial Statements
The Aspen Company is contingently liable for $15,000 of notes receivable that have been discounted.

Chapter Summary

Review of Learning Objectives

1. **Explain the reasons for credit sales.**
   Credit sales are made for two reasons. First, it may be more convenient to sell on credit. Second, credit sales may increase a company's profits.

2. **Explain credit card sales.**
   Credit card sales have the advantage of making credit sales without the disadvantage of evaluating credit risks and experiencing bad debts. Most credit

card sales are treated as cash sales, although some do result in recording a receivable.

3. **Describe the allowance method of accounting for bad debts.**
   The allowance method requires the recognition of the bad debt expense in the period of the sale and *not* in the period of write-off. When the bad debt expense is recognized, the Allowance for Uncollectible Accounts is increased. When the write-off occurs in a subsequent period, the Allowance account and the Accounts Receivable are reduced.

4. **Describe the direct write-off method of accounting for bad debts.**
   The direct write-off method recognizes the bad debt expense in the period when the account is written off because it is uncollectible. Therefore no estimate of bad debt expense is made in the period of the sale and no allowance is recorded for uncollectible accounts.

5. **Compute the amount of bad debt expense under (a) the percent of sales method and (b) the aging method.**
   Under the *percent of sales method*, the company estimates the bad debt expense by multiplying the net credit sales of the period by the percent estimated to be uncollectible. It is often referred to as an income statement approach. Under the *aging method*, a company categorizes each individual account into groups based on the length of time it has been outstanding. The total in each age group is then multiplied by an historically based estimated percent uncollectible to estimate the amount uncollectible in the age group. The amounts in each age group are summed to give the required ending balance in the Allowance for Uncollectible Accounts.

6. **Describe a promissory note (receivable) and how to calculate interest on it.**
   A promissory note is a written legal document in which the maker (issuer) gives an unconditional promise to pay the payee a certain amount of money on demand or on an agreed future date. Interest is computed by multiplying the principal amount by the annual interest rate and the period of time the note is outstanding in years or fraction of a year.

7. **Determine the maturity date of a note.**
   The maturity date of a note may be stated in terms of a specific number of months or days. When stated in days, the day the note is signed is omitted, but the day the note is paid is included.

8. **Explain the discounting of a note.**
   Discounting a note is the process in which the payee of a note assigns it over to a bank in exchange for cash. The cash proceeds are equal to the maturity value less the discount.

9. **Describe how accounts receivable and notes receivable are disclosed in financial statements.**
   Accounts receivable are reported net of the allowance for uncollectible accounts and the notes receivable are reported net of the notes receivable discounted. Alternatively, the notes receivable can be reported at their net value and the contingent liability for the discounted notes can be disclosed in the footnotes to the financial statements..

Review Problem

On December 31, 1991, the Holstrum Company had the following balances in selected accounts:

Accounts Receivable	$50,000
Allowance for Uncollectible Accounts	3,000
Interest Receivable	1,400
Notes Receivable	20,000

The note was a 12%, 1-year note due on May 31, 1992. During 1992, the company made credit sales of $120,000 and collected $124,000. In addition, the following transactions occurred in 1992:

Date	Transaction
Jan. 15	Wrote off an uncollectible account of $4,000 due from Donald Eastwood.
Mar. 1	Sold goods worth $10,000 and received a 6-month, 10% note as payment (not included in the credit sales of $120,000).
July 1	Discounted the note received on March 1 to a bank that charged 14% interest.
Aug. 20	Half of the account written off on January 15 was collected.
Sept. 1	The March 1 note was dishonored. The bank made a service charge of $20.
Oct. 1	The dishonored note was collected, along with the service charge and additional interest for 1 month on the total amount.
Dec. 31	The age of the accounts receivable and the percentage estimated to be uncollectible was as follows:

Age Group	Amount	Estimated Percentage Uncollectible
Not yet due	$20,000	1%
1–30 days past due	8,000	3
31–90 days past due	4,000	6
More than 90 days past due	10,000	10

REQUIRED

1. Prepare journal entries to record these events.
2. Show how the net amount of the accounts receivable would be reported on the December 31, 1992, balance sheet.

Solution to Review Problem

REQUIREMENT 1 Summary journal entries for sales and cash collections:

Accounts Receivable[a]	120,000	
Sales		120,000

To record the sale of merchandise on account.

[a]For the summary journal entries individual account names are omitted.

	Cash	124,000	
	Accounts Receivable		124,000

To record collection of accounts receivable during the year.

Jan. 15	Allowance for Uncollectible Accounts	4,000	
	Accounts Receivable: Donald Eastwood ...		4,000

To record the write-off of uncollectible account receivable.

Mar. 1	Notes Receivable	10,000	
	Sales		10,000

To record sale of goods and receipt of 6-month, 10% note.

May 31	Cash	22,400	
	Notes Receivable		20,000
	Interest Receivable		1,400
	Interest Revenue		1,000[a]

To record collection of 12% note and accrued interest.

[a]$20,000 \times 12\% \times \frac{5}{12}$

July 1	Cash	10,255[a]	
	Interest Revenue		255
	Notes Receivable Discounted		10,000

To record the discounted note.

[a]Maturity value = $10,000 + ($10,000 \times 10\% \times \frac{6}{12}) = \$10,500$
Proceeds = $\$10,500 - (\$10,500 \times 14\% \times \frac{2}{12}) = \$10,255$

Aug. 20	Accounts Receivable: Donald Eastwood	2,000	
	Allowance for Uncollectible Accounts		2,000

To reverse the write-off of half the account of Donald Eastwood.

	Cash	2,000	
	Accounts Receivable: Donald Eastwood ...		2,000

To record collection of half the account of of Donald Eastwood previously written off.

Sept. 1	Notes Receivable Dishonored	10,520	
	Cash		10,520

To record payment on the dishonored note.

	Notes Receivable Discounted	10,000	
	Notes Receivable		10,000

To remove contingent liability for the discounted note.

Oct. 1	Cash	10,607.67	
	Notes Receivable Dishonored		10,520.00
	Interest Receivable ($10,520 \times 0.10 \times \frac{1}{12}$)		87.67

To record collection of the dishonored note receivable.

Dec. 31	Bad Debt Expense	680	
	Allowance for Uncollectible Accounts		680

To record the bad debt expense for the year.

Age Group	Amount	Estimated Percent Uncollectible	Estimated Amount Uncollectible
Not yet due	$20,000	1%	$ 200
1–30 days past due	8,000	3	240
31–90 days past due	4,000	6	240
More than 90 days past due	10,000	10	1,000
Total	$42,000		$1,680

Bad debt expense = Required balance − Existing balance
= $1,680 − $1,000
= $680

REQUIREMENT 2

Current Assets
Accounts receivable $42,000
Less: Allowance for uncollectible accounts .... (1,680)
Net accounts receivable $40,320

Glossary

Aging Accounts Receivable. A method of estimating the allowance for uncollectible accounts, and therefore the bad debt expense. Accounts receivable are classified into age groups, and the balance in each age group is multiplied by the estimated percentage of the accounts that are uncollectible. The resulting amounts are summed to determine the ending balance in Allowance for Uncollectible Accounts.

Allowance for Uncollectible Accounts. A contra-asset account in which a company records its estimate of the amount of accounts receivable that it will not collect.

Allowance Method. A method of accounting for uncollectible accounts in which bad debt expense is recognized in the period of the sale.

Bad Debt Expense. The expense for the accounting period due to the eventual non-collection of accounts receivable. It is recorded by means of an adjusting entry at the end of the period.

Contingent Liability. A liability that may or may not be paid depending on whether or not a future event occurs.

Direct Write-Off Method. A method of accounting for uncollectible accounts in which bad debt expense is recognized at the time an account is written off. This method is inconsistent with the accrual concept of accounting and the matching principle.

Discounting a Note. A process in which the payee of a note assigns it to a bank in exchange for cash. The bank then collects the maturity value of the note from the maker on the maturity date.

Dishonored Note. A note that the maker has failed to pay at the maturity date.

Maker of a Note.   The person or company that signs a note and agrees to pay the maturity value on the maturity date. Also called *issuer*.

Maturity Date of a Note.   The date on which a note and any interest are due and payable.

Maturity Value of a Note.   The principal of the note plus the interest due on the maturity date.

Notes Receivable.   The asset account used to record promissory notes held by a company.

Payee.   The person or company to whom a note is payable.

Percent of Sales Method.   A method of estimating bad debt expense. The amount is computed by multiplying the net credit sales for the accounting period by the percent estimated to be uncollectible.

Principal of a Note.   The amount stated on the face of a note. Also called the *face value*.

Promissory Note.   A written legal document in which one party makes an unconditional promise to pay another party a certain sum of money on demand or on an agreed future date.

Questions

QUESTION 8-1   For what two reasons might a company choose to make credit sales? If a company does not collect some of its accounts receivable does it mean that the company's policy of making credit sales is wrong?

QUESTION 8-2   How do credit card sales differ from other types of sales on credit?

QUESTION 8-3   Where is bad debt expense classified in the income statement? Why?

QUESTION 8-4   How can the use of the direct write-off method be justified?

QUESTION 8-5   What accounting principle supports the use of an estimate of bad debt expense? Explain.

QUESTION 8-6   Why is it desirable to keep the amount of a company's uncollectible accounts in the Allowance for Uncollectible Accounts?

QUESTION 8-7   Explain how the financial statements are affected by recording the estimated accounts receivable that will not be collected. How are the financial statements affected by recording the eventual write-off of an account receivable? By the recovery of a receivable previously written off?

QUESTION 8-8   How is bad debt expense estimated when the percent of sales method is used? When the aging method is used?

QUESTION 8-9   Which method of estimating bad debt expense is considered to be an income statement approach? Which is considered to be a balance sheet approach? Why?

QUESTION 8-10   What is a promissory note? Who is the maker? Who is the payee? What are the principal and the maturity date?

QUESTION 8-11   Why might a company prefer to hold a note receivable rather than an account receivable?

QUESTION 8-12   Describe how interest on a note receivable is computed.

QUESTION 8-13   What is meant by the term *dishonored note receivable?*

QUESTION 8-14   Why might a company discount a note receivable?

QUESTION 8-15   How does a bank determine the cash it will pay on a discounted note?

QUESTION 8-16   What is a contingent liability? Why should it be reported differently from a liability such as an account payable?

QUESTION 8-17   How is a discounted note receivable disclosed on a company's balance sheet?

Exercises

EXERCISE 8-1   **Percent of Sales Method.**   The Redford Optical Supplies Company uses the percent of sales method for estimating its bad debt expense. In 1991 the company sold on credit $350,000 of glasses and lenses, and had sales returns and allowances for credit of $20,000. In past years approximately 2% of net credit sales have been uncollectible. At the end of the year, before the bad debt expense is recorded, the accounts receivable balance was $45,000 and the credit balance in the allowance for uncollectible accounts was $300.

REQUIRED   1. Compute the bad debt expense for 1991 using the percent of sales method.
2. Prepare journal entries to record all these events in 1991, including the bad debt expense.
3. Show how the net accounts receivable would be reported in the balance sheet at the end of 1991.

EXERCISE 8-2   **Credit Card Sales.**   On June 10 the Sweep Chimney Cleaning Company made a sale of $500 to a customer who used a bank credit card. The credit card company makes a service charge of 3%, and the company deposited the credit card receipts in the bank along with its deposit of cash from cash sales. The company also made a sale of $800 to a customer who used a VISA credit card. The credit card company makes a service charge of 4%, and the credit card receipt had to be sent to the credit card company to obtain reimbursement.

REQUIRED   Prepare journal entries to record the two sales.

EXERCISE 8-3   **Aging Method.**   Use the facts for the Redford Optical Supplies Company in Exercise 8-1. In addition, the company has found that 2% of accounts receivable that are not overdue at the end of any particular year are never collected and 4% of accounts receivable that are overdue at year end are never collected. Of the accounts receivable balance at the end of 1991, 40% are not overdue.

REQUIRED

1. Compute the bad debt expense for 1991 using the aging method.

2. Prepare the journal entry to record the bad debt expense.

3. Show how the net accounts receivable would be reported in the balance sheet at the end of 1991.

EXERCISE 8-4　　**Aging Method.**　At the end of the year the accounts receivable of the Andrews Company were categorized as follows:

Age Group	Amount	Estimated Percentage Uncollectible
Not yet due	$ 80,000	$\frac{1}{2}$%
1–30 days past due	45,000	1
31–60 days past due	20,000	2
61–90 days past due	12,000	4
More than 90 days past due	8,000	7
	$165,000	

Before recording the bad debt expense the credit balance in the Allowance for Uncollectible Accounts was $800.

REQUIRED

1. Prepare the journal entry to record the bad debt expense.

2. Show how the net accounts receivable would be reported in the balance sheet at the end of the year.

EXERCISE 8-5　　**Direct Write-Off Method.**　The Newman Casting Company made credit sales of $100,000 during the year. In addition, the company wrote off $4,500 of uncollectible accounts receivable in 1991 and uncollectible accounts receivable have averaged 4% of the ending balance of accounts receivable in recent years. The ending balance of accounts receivable is $25,000.

REQUIRED

1. Compute the bad debt expense for 1991 using the direct write-off method.

2. Show how the net accounts receivable would be reported in the balance sheet at the end of 1991.

EXERCISE 8-6　　**Sales Transactions.**　During 1991 the Hopkins International Sales Company made credit sales of $80,000 and gave sales returns and allowances on credit of $4,500. In addition, sales discounts taken by credit customers were $200, which was 2% of the accounts collected. At the end of the year the company estimated that 4% of net credit sales would be uncollectible. The company uses the percent of sales method for estimating bad debts.

REQUIRED　　Prepare journal entries to record these events.

EXERCISE 8-7　　**Write-Off and Recovery of Uncollectible Accounts.**　During 1991 the Ross Company wrote off uncollectible accounts of $600 and recovered accounts of $400 that had been written off in 1990. In addition, the following information is available:

	December 31, 1990	December 31, 1991
Accounts receivable	$30,000	$40,000
Allowance for uncollectible accounts	1,000	1,500

REQUIRED

1. Prepare the journal entries to record the write-off and recovery of the uncollectible accounts in 1991.

2. How much bad debt expense was recorded in 1991?

EXERCISE 8-8   **Interest Revenue.**   The Nicholson Paving Company has the following current notes receivable during 1991:

Amount	Date Issued	Date Due	Interest Rate
$ 5,000	January 5	March 15	10%
8,000	May 13	August 3	12%
10,000	September 17	November 12	9%

REQUIRED   Compute the interest revenue earned by the Nicholson Paving Company during 1991.

EXERCISE 8-9   **Maturity Date and Interest Revenue.**   The Cunningham Company has the following notes receivable during 1991:

Amount	Date Issued	Life	Interest Rate
$3,000	October 18	90 days	12%
5,000	November 5	45 days	8%
2,000	December 12	80 days	9%

REQUIRED

1. What is the maturity date of each note?

2. Compute the interest revenue earned by the Cunningham Company during 1991.

EXERCISE 8-10   **Notes Receivable.**   On April 1, 1991, the O'Neill Farm Equipment Company sold a tractor to Klemme Farms for $60,000 and agreed to delay collection of the selling price for 6 months until after the harvest. Klemme Farms issued a note dated April 1, 1991, that had a stated interest rate of 10%. The note was paid on schedule.

REQUIRED   Prepare the journal entries for the O'Neill Farm Equipment Company during 1991.

EXERCISE 8-11   **Dishonored Notes Receivable.**   Use the facts in Exercise 8-10.

REQUIRED   Prepare the journal entries that the O'Neill Farm Equipment Company would make if Klemme Farms did not pay the note as scheduled.

EXERCISE 8-12   **Discounting Notes Receivable.**   The Gome Company received a 6-month, 10% note of $70,000 dated May 1, 1991, as a result of a current sale. The company discounted the note at a bank on July 1, 1991. The bank charges 12% interest. The issuer of the note pays it on the maturity date and the bank notifies the Gome Company.

REQUIRED   Prepare the journal entries for the Gome Company for 1991.

Problems

Part A

PROBLEM 8-1A   **Accounts Receivable and Percent of Sales Method.**   During January 1991 the following events occurred for the Radner Clothing Company:

Jan. 1	Accounts Receivable balance $30,000; Allowance for Uncollectible Accounts balance, $300 (credit).
2	Wrote off the $500 account of Kevin Habit when he declared bankruptcy.
12	Recovered the $300 account of Patricia Brake that had previously been written off.
18	Accepted a 10% note for the $800 account of Brent Gray that was overdue.
31	Sales for the month were as follows:

Cash	$ 6,000
Credit	65,000
Credit cards	18,000 (The credit card company charges a 3% fee.)

The credit card receipts had to be sent to the credit card company for reimbursement. The Radner Clothing Company estimates that 2% of its net credit sales (excluding credit card sales) will be uncollectible.

REQUIRED   *1.* Prepare journal entries for January for the Radner Clothing Company including the accrual of interest.

2. Explain how each of the events affects the financial statements for January.

PROBLEM 8-2A   **Credit Card Sales.**   The Beatty Department Store had the following selected transactions involving the Christie Credit Card Company for 1991:

Date	Transaction
Feb. 21	Sold merchandise for $500 to a customer using a Christiecard. Christie Credit Card Company charges a fee of 5%.
Mar. 11	Received reimbursement from Christie.

Aug.	7	Sold merchandise for $700 to a customer using a Christiecard.
Aug.	15	Received notification from the Christie Credit Card Company that the card used for the $700 purchase was a stolen card. Because the Beatty Department Store had not called Christie to check the card at the time of the sale, no reimbursement will be made by Christie until it collects payment.
Nov.	20	Received payment of the $700 account from Christie. Owing to the difficulty and expense of collecting this payment, Christie charged an extra 15% fee.
Dec.	3	Sold merchandise for $400 to a customer using a Christiecard. Under a new arrangement with the Christie Credit Card Company, the receipt was deposited directly in Beatty Department Store's bank account.

REQUIRED

1. Prepare the journal entries to record these transactions.

2. Considering that a seller does not receive the full price of merchandise sold to customers using a credit card, why do sellers accept credit cards?

PROBLEM 8-3A **Accounts Receivable and the Aging Method.** The Newman Scientific Instrument Company operates a retail store in which most of its sales are made on credit. In 1991 the company had credit sales of $575,000, sales returns and allowances on credit sales of $15,000, and gave sales discounts of $560 on collections of accounts receivable of $28,000. Additional collections of accounts receivable were made with no sales discounts. During 1991 the company has written off accounts amounting to $1,500 and recovered accounts of $300 that had been written off in 1990. In addition, the following information is available:

	December 31, 1990	December 31, 1991
Accounts receivable	$80,000	$103,000
Allowance for uncollectible accounts	500 (credit)	?

The accounts receivable at the end of 1991 were classified as follows:

Age Group	Balance	Estimated Percentage Uncollectible
Not yet due	$50,000	$\frac{1}{2}$%
1–30 days past due	28,000	1
31–60 days past due	9,000	2
61–120 days past due	4,000	5
More than 120 days past due	12,000	20

REQUIRED

1. Prepare the journal entries to record these events, including the bad debt expense.

2. Show how the net accounts receivable would be reported on the December 31, 1991, balance sheet.

3. Is the aging method or the percent of sales method more desirable to use in the financial statements?

PROBLEM 8-4A **Notes Receivable.**   The Reynolds Company had the following transactions affecting its notes receivable during 1991:

Date		Transaction
Jan.	5	Sold merchandise for $20,000 to the Fields Company and received a 6-month, 10% note.
Mar.	5	Discounted the note from the Fields Company at a bank that charged interest of 12%.
Mar.	18	Sold merchandise on credit for $5,000 to the Shore Company.
Apr.	15	Sold merchandise for $30,000 to the Clayburgh Company and received an 8-month, 12% note.
June	1	Sold merchandise for $6,000 to the Carne Company and received a 12-month, 9% note.
July	1	Received a $5,000, 12-month, 10% note from the Shore Company when it was unable to pay its overdue account.
Aug.	1	Discounted the note from the Carne Company at a bank that charged interest of 8%.

The interest on each note is due on the maturity date.

REQUIRED
1. Prepare the journal entries to record the preceding transactions for the Reynolds Company. The Fields and Clayburgh notes were paid on their due dates.

2. Show how the preceding events would be reported on the financial statements for 1991.

PROBLEM 8-5A **Notes Receivable Discounted and Dishonored.**   Use the facts in Problem 8-4A, except that the Fields and Clayburgh notes were dishonored. The bank charged a $10 fee on the Fields note. The Clayburgh note was paid in full plus $\frac{1}{2}$ month additional interest on December 30. The Fields Company declared bankruptcy on December 10, and the Reynolds Company did not expect to collect any amount on the note.

REQUIRED   Prepare the journal entries to record the events related to the dishonored notes.

Problems

Part B

PROBLEM 8-1B **Accounts Receivable and the Percent of Sales Method.**   During August 1991 the following events occurred for the Olivier Theatrical Supplies Company:

Aug.	1	Accounts Receivable balance $46,000; Allowance for Uncollectible Accounts balance, $750 (credit).
	5	Accepted a 13% note for the $3,000 account of Erin Dudley that was overdue.
	10	Wrote off the $6,000 account of Darcy Mitchell when she declared bankruptcy.
	21	Recovered the $3,000 account of John Gatti that had previously been written off.
	31	Sales for the month were:

           Credit $100,000

           Credit cards   120,000 (The credit card company charges a 6% fee.)

The credit card receipts had to be sent to the credit card company for reimbursement. The Olivier Theatrical Supplies Company estimates that 4% of its net credit sales (excluding credit card sales) will be uncollectible.

REQUIRED

1. Prepare journal entries for August including the accrual of interest.

2. Explain how each of the events affects the financial statements for August.

PROBLEM 8-2B **Credit Card Sales.** The Campbell Discount Store had the following transactions involving the Tucker Credit Card Company during 1991:

Date	Transaction
Mar. 7	Sold merchandise for $400. The customer charged the goods on his Tucker card. Tucker charges a fee of 4%.
Mar. 20	Received reimbursement from Tucker.
July 15	Sold merchandise for $500 to a customer using a Tucker card.
July 22	Received notification from Tucker that the card used for the $500 purchase on July 15 had been a stolen card. Because the Campbell Discount Store had not called to verify the card at the time of the sale, no reimbursement will be made by Tucker until it collects payment.
Dec. 7	Received payment of the $500 account from Tucker. Owing to the trouble and expense of collecting this payment, Tucker charged an extra 20% fee.
Dec. 9	Sold merchandise for $200 to a customer using a Tucker card. Under a new arrangement with the Tucker Credit Card Company, the receipt was deposited directly in the Campbell Discount Store's bank account.

REQUIRED

1. Prepare the journal entries to record these transactions.

2. Why would a seller accept credit cards when it does not collect the full amount of a sale?

PROBLEM 8-3B **Accounts Receivable and the Aging Method.** The Gere Company operates a wholesale outlet that makes most of its sales on credit. In 1991 the company had credit sales of $900,000, sales returns and allowances on credit sales of $21,000, and gave sales discounts of $400 on collections of accounts receivable of $40,000. Additional collections of accounts receivable were made with no sales discounts. During 1991 the company has written off accounts totaling $35,000 and recovered accounts of $18,000 that had been written off in 1990. In addition, the following information is available:

	December 31, 1990	December 31, 1991
Accounts receivable	$190,000	$320,000
Allowance for uncollectible accounts	5,000 (credit)	?

The accounts receivable at the end of 1991 were classified as follows:

Age Group	Amount	Estimated Percentage Uncollectible
Not yet due	$110,000	3%
1–30 days past due	75,000	5
31–60 days past due	60,000	8
61–120 days past due	30,000	15
More than 120 days past due	45,000	30

REQUIRED

1. Prepare the journal entries to record these events, including the 1991 bad debt expense.

2. Show how the net accounts receivable would be reported on the December 31, 1991, balance sheet.

3. Do you think that the Gere Company's credit policy is adequate? What, if any, changes would you suggest? Explain.

PROBLEM 8-4B

Notes Receivable. The Charles Company had the following transactions affecting its notes receivable during 1991:

Date	Transaction
Feb. 1	Received a $120,000, 12-month, 10% note from the Duncan Company in payment for merchandise sold on this date.
Apr. 1	Sold merchandise to the Wells Company and received a $90,000, 6-month, 8% note.
June 1	Discounted the Duncan and Wells notes at a bank that charged interest of 12%.
July 18	Received a $33,000, 2-month, 13% note from the Munroe Company when it was unable to pay its overdue account.

The interest on each note is due on the maturity date.

REQUIRED

1. Prepare the journal entries to record these transactions for the Charles Company. The notes were paid when due.

2. Show how the preceding events would be reported on the financial statements for 1991.

PROBLEM 8-5B   **Notes Receivable Discounted and Dishonored.**   Use the facts in Problem 8-4B, except that the Wells and Munroe notes were dishonored. The bank charges a $20 fee on all dishonored notes. The Munroe Company declared bankruptcy on November 1, and the Charles Company did not expect to collect any amount on the note. The Wells note was paid in full plus 2 months additional interest on December 1.

REQUIRED   Prepare the journal entries to record the events related to the dishonored notes.

Decision Cases

DECISION CASE 8-1   **Accounts Receivable.**   The Midler Boutique has expanded its sales significantly in recent years by offering a liberal credit policy. As a result bad debt losses have also increased. The following summarized income statements have been prepared:

	1987	1988	1989	1990
Sales on credit	$32,000	$50,000	$70,000	$90,000
Cost of goods sold	(12,000)	(19,000)	(26,000)	(33,000)
Bad debt expense	(1,302)	(2,250)	(3,260)	(4,320)
Other expenses	(10,000)	(12,000)	(14,000)	(16,000)
Net Income	$ 8,698	$16,750	$26,740	$36,680
Accounts written off	$ 200	$ 1,000	$ 1,600	$ 2,000

The company uses the percent of sales method to calculate its bad debt expense. The accounts written off each year relate to credit sales made in the previous period.

REQUIRED   Prepare a report for Ms. Midler that explains the trend in bad debts as compared to other items in the income statement. Does it appear that the liberal credit policy is successful? What do you think the bad debt expense for 1991 should be if credit sales were $120,000 that year?

DECISION CASE 8-2   **Accounting for Bad Debts.**   Your friend has been operating a business for two years and has been making many sales on credit. His accountant has told him that an esti- mate of amounts that will be uncollectible in the future must be included in this year's financial statements. Your friend is upset because he does not want "guesses" appearing in the financial statements and he knows that accounting information should be objective and verifiable. Since he knows that you are currently studying accounting, he buys you dinner and before picking up the check asks you for your opinion.

REQUIRED   How would you answer your friend? Explain in detail why the accountant is sug- gesting that an estimate of uncollectible accounts be included in this year's financial statements and why your friend's concerns are not critical.

DECISION CASE 8-3   **Accounts Receivable.**   Eastman Kodak Company reported the following in its 1988 financial report relating to accounts receivable (amounts in millions of dollars):

	1988	1987
Receivables	$4,071	$3,144

Current receivables are shown after deducting an allowance of $111 (1987: $68)

REQUIRED

1. How could you determine if the 1988 allowance for uncollectible accounts is reasonable? (Hint: No calculations are required.)

2. Sales in 1988 were $17,034. Assume that all sales were made on credit and that the bad debt expense for 1988 was $90. Compute the cash collected from sales in 1988 and the amount of bad debts written off in 1988. (Hint: Use T-accounts.)

DECISION CASE 8-4

Credit Card and Credit Sales.   Three years ago, Trevor and Jill Davey formed a company called The Bicycle Boutique. Sales have slowly increased each year and the reputation of the company in the community has steadily improved. However, because of limited resources the company has only made cash sales. With the increase in the prices for modern sophisticated bikes, the Daveys have decided that it would be desirable to offer credit card sales and to sell on credit.

Sales for the last three years have been $100,000, $140,000, and $190,000 respectively. The gross profit has consistently been 40% of sales. The Daveys believe that sales would increase by 50% next year if the policy is not changed, but would double under the new policy. They expect only 30% of the sales to be cash sales with the remaining sales to be equally split between credit card sales and credit sales. The credit card receipts will be deposited immediately in a local bank. The fee on credit card sales will be 4%. It is expected that credit sales will be made evenly throughout the year, will be collected on average after 2 months, and that 2% will not be collectible.

To be able to implement the new policy regarding credit sales, the company has applied for a bank loan of $150,000. The bank will charge interest of 12% and has asked for certain financial information.

REQUIRED

1. Prepare a schedule that shows the cash inflows expected for the next year under the old policy and the new policy.

2. Should the company prefer credit card sales or credit sales?

3. Should the company implement the new policy?

9

Inventories and Cost of Goods Sold

LEARNING OBJECTIVES

1. Determine inventory quantities using (a) the periodic inventory system and (b) the perpetual inventory system.

2. Describe why a physical inventory is taken.

3. Determine the cost of inventory.

4. Explain (a) the gross method and (b) the net method of accounting for purchases discounts.

5. Compute ending inventory and cost of goods sold under the alternative cost flow assumptions, including (a) specific identification, (b) FIFO, (c) average, and (d) LIFO.

6. Evaluate the alternative cost flow assumptions.

7. Explain the lower of cost or market method.

8. Estimate the cost of inventory by (a) the gross profit method and (b) the retail inventory method.

9. Compute the effects of errors in the recording of inventory.

nventory is the category of assets of a company that are being held for sale in the ordinary course of business. For a manufacturing company, inventory also includes materials being held for use in the production process or goods that are in the process of production. In this chapter we discuss inventory by using the example of a merchandising company. A merchandising company is a company engaged in a retail or wholesale business; it does not manufacture the goods it sells. Generally, the principles discussed also apply to a manufacturing company (that does change the physical characteristics of the goods).

In this chapter we consider the factors that affect the calculation of the cost of the ending inventory. We discuss the computation of the quantity of units in the ending inventory and the cost assigned to each unit acquired during the period. We will see that accounting in this area is well defined, and that all companies should follow the same principles. Finally, we discuss the method by which the costs of the units are included in the cost of goods sold and the ending inventory. Here we will see that several alternatives are allowed, and therefore the management of a company can select one from several methods that each gives significantly different amounts of net income and assets on its financial statements.

The Importance of Inventory

Inventory, sometimes called *merchandise inventory*, is a very important asset for many companies and is of particular interest to users of the company's financial statements. Inventory is typically the largest current asset (except for a service company) and represents a source of revenue in the near future through sales of the merchandise. The major issues for inventory are to determine correctly (a) the quantities of items that should be included in the inventory, (b) the cost to attach to each unit included in the inventory, and (c) the method of including these costs in the income statement and the balance sheet; that is, the way that the costs are matched against the revenue of the current and subsequent periods and the costs that are recorded as assets. Before we discuss each of these tasks in detail, however, it is important to realize the significant impact that the inventory figure has on the financial statements.

As discussed in Chapter 5 the cost of goods available for sale is the sum of the beginning inventory for the period and the costs of the net purchases made during the period. In a periodic inventory system when the cost of the ending inventory is determined, it is subtracted from the cost of goods available for sale to compute the cost of the goods sold. The cost of the goods sold is then subtracted from net sales to determine the gross profit. These relationships may be stated in the following three equations:

$$\text{Cost of Goods Available for Sale} = \text{Beginning Inventory} + \text{Purchases (Net)}$$

$$\text{Cost of Goods Sold} = \text{Cost of Goods Available for Sale} - \text{Ending Inventory}$$

$$\text{Gross Profit} = \text{Sales (Net)} - \text{Cost of Goods Sold}$$

Once the cost of goods available for sale has been found, any change in the costs assigned to the ending inventory will change the cost of goods sold, and vice versa (how the cost of the inventory is determined is discussed later in the chapter). Any change in the cost of goods sold, in turn, will have a corresponding effect on gross profit. In addition, since the ending inventory of one accounting period is the beginning inventory of the next period, the cost assigned to the ending inventory will also affect the cost of goods available for sale, the cost of goods sold, and the gross profit of the next period. Thus we can see that the determination of the cost of the ending inventory has a major impact on current and future balance sheets and income statements of the company and therefore may affect the perceptions that the users of the financial statements have of the company. In summary, if ending inventory is overstated (understated) income for the period is overstated (understated).

For example, suppose that a company has the partial income statement shown in Alternative 1 of Exhibit 9-1. Now suppose that ending inventory was computed instead as $1,200, which is an increase of $200 or 20%. As can be seen from Alternative 2, gross profit is increased by $200, which is an increase of 40% ($700 ÷ $500 = 1.40). In this case a percentage change in the value of ending inventory has had a *proportionately* much larger percentage impact on the gross profit.

EXHIBIT 9-1
Effect of Ending
Inventory Valuation
on the Gross Profit

	Alternative 1		Alternative 2	
Sales (net)		$10,000		$10,000
Beginning inventory	$ 800		$ 800	
Purchases (net)	9,700		9,700	
Cost of goods available for sale	$10,500		$10,500	
Less: Ending inventory	(1,000)		(1,200)	
Cost of goods sold		(9,500)		(9,300)
Gross Profit		$ 500		$ 700

In addition to the accounting considerations, proper management of inventory is important for effective management of the company. For example, it is important to have appropriate amounts of inventory on hand to fill customer orders while preventing inadequate or excessive inventory.

Now that we have examined the importance of inventory and its valuation, we discuss the components of this valuation.

Alternative Inventory Systems

The first step in the computation of the cost of the inventory of a company is the determination of the quantity of inventory that is on hand during and at the end of the period. The management of the company may select either the periodic system or the perpetual system to account for inventory.

Periodic Inventory System

1(a). Determine inventory quantities using the periodic inventory system.

The periodic inventory system is a system of accounting for inventory in which a continuous record is *not* kept of the physical quantities (or costs) of inventory on hand during the period. A record of the cost of goods sold is *not* made each time a sale is made (revenue from the sale is recorded in the normal manner). The only time that the physical quantity of inventory on hand (and therefore the quantity sold) is known is when a physical inventory is taken. **A physical inventory is the counting by employees of the physical quantity of each item held in inventory.** A physical inventory enables the quantity sold to be computed as follows:

$$\text{Quantity Sold} = \text{Quantity in Beginning Inventory} + \text{Quantity Purchased} - \text{Quantity in Ending Inventory}$$

At a minimum, a physical inventory must be taken at the end of the annual accounting period so that the financial statements can be prepared. The cost of the ending inventory, and therefore the cost of goods sold, is then found by attaching costs to these physical quantities based on the cost flow assumptions used (as discussed later in the chapter).

For example, if a company has an inventory on January 1, 1991, of 20,000 units and then purchases 70,000 units, the number of units available for sale is 90,000. Although the company has made sales, and therefore has incurred a cost of goods sold, the number of units sold is not known until the physical inventory is taken at the end of the year. If the physical inventory at the end of the year is found to be 30,000 units, the cost of goods sold would include 60,000 units (90,000 – 30,000). The costs attached to these units are discussed later in the chapter. If interim financial statements are prepared during the period (e.g., quarterly financial statements), a physical inventory is usually *not* taken. The cost of the quarterly ending inventory can be found by using one of the estimation methods discussed later in the chapter.

The Purchases Account. The beginning inventory of a period that is recorded in the Inventory account is the ending inventory from the previous period. The cost of inventory purchased during the current period usually is not added (debited) directly to the Inventory account in the periodic system. Such a procedure would lead to the account showing more inventory on hand than the company actually had because the account is not reduced (credited) during the period in which sales of the inventory items are made. Therefore the Purchases account is used to record purchases of inventory in a periodic system. The account is a temporary account to which acquisitions of inventory are added (debited) while the beginning inventory remains in the Inventory account. For example, the purchase of merchandise inventory on account is recorded[1] as follows (using assumed amounts):

Purchases	....	3,200
Accounts Payable	....	3,200
To record purchase of merchandise.		

---

[1]Recall from Chapter 6 that we are not using subsidiary ledger accounts in these subsequent chapters (except for Chapters 8 and 10). If a subsidiary ledger were being used, an entry would be made in the accounts payable subsidiary ledger at the same time.

If a company returns some of the items it has purchased during the period or is granted a reduction in the purchase price due to damaged or inferior goods, it would record these returns or allowances by a credit (increase) to a separate account, Purchases Returns and Allowances. The advantage of recording purchases returns and allowances in a separate account is that management can keep track of the returns and allowances as a proportion of purchases. This relationship gives an indication of the quality of the goods provided by its various suppliers, thereby enabling the effectiveness of the company's purchasing activities to be monitored. Purchases on account that are returned are recorded as follows:

Accounts Payable	600	
Purchases Returns and Allowances		600
To record return of purchases.		

The net purchases for the period are the debit balance in the Purchases account less the credit balance in the Purchases Returns and Allowances account. In addition, as discussed in Chapter 5 Transportation-In is added, whereas Purchases Discounts Taken is subtracted, to obtain net purchases.

At the end of the period the Inventory account will have a balance that is still equal to the beginning inventory for the period, and the Purchases and Purchases Returns and Allowances accounts will have balances that reflect the activities for the period. All these accounts are closed at the end of the period as first discussed in Chapter 5.

Perpetual Inventory System

1(b). Determine inventory quantities using the perpetual inventory system.

A perpetual inventory system is a system of accounting for inventory in which a continuous record is kept of the physical quantities in inventory and the number of units sold. In addition, a continuous record of the cost of the units in inventory and the units sold is frequently maintained. A system that operates only in terms of quantities is simpler, and less expensive, and may provide sufficient information for management. The inclusion of costs facilitates the preparation of financial statements and is assumed in the remaining discussion. The inclusion of costs is becoming more common with the increased sophistication and lower cost of computer-based accounting systems. Many retail stores (e.g., J. C. Penney and Sears) use "point-of-sale" systems in which each item of inventory has a unique code that is entered into the system through the cash register as every unit is sold. Although the perpetual inventory system provides a continual update of the inventory, it is still necessary to verify the amount and cost of the ending inventory by taking a physical inventory periodically.

When a perpetual inventory system is used to maintain a record of the cost of the inventory, purchases and the cost of inventory sold are recorded directly in the Inventory account. Each purchase and related transportation charge is added (debited) directly to the Inventory account. Each time a sale is made the reduction (credit) in the Inventory account and the addition (debit) to the Cost of Goods Sold account are recorded. Thus the journal entries to record the sale and the cost of the sale are made at the same time. If a company has purchases returns and allowances during the period, the Inventory account is usually reduced (credited) directly; these returns and allowances can be maintained in a separate Purchases Returns and Allowances account that has a credit balance, however.

Differences Between the Periodic and Perpetual Inventory Systems

The differences between the periodic and perpetual systems can be illustrated by the equations shown here (using the assumed amounts from the following discussion). Note from the equations that the cost of goods sold and the ending inventory are the same in the two methods. The sequence of their computation is different, however.

PERPETUAL INVENTORY SYSTEM

Ending Inventory	=	Beginning Inventory	+	Net Purchases	−	Cost of Goods Sold
$4,000	=	$3,500	+	$10,000	−	$9,500

PERIODIC INVENTORY SYSTEM

Cost of Goods Sold	=	Beginning Inventory	+	Net Purchases	−	Ending Inventory
$9,500	=	$3,500	+	$10,000	−	$4,000

The net purchases of $10,000 are computed in the same way for both systems by adding the $10,100 purchases and the $300 transportation charges and then subtracting the $400 purchases returns and allowances. Under the perpetual system the cost of goods sold of $9,500 is obtained directly and recorded at the time of sale. The ending inventory of $4,000 is computed by adding the $10,000 net purchases to the $3,500 beginning inventory and subtracting the $9,500 cost of goods sold. In the periodic system the $4,000 ending inventory is determined by a physical count, and the $9,500 cost of goods sold is computed by adding the $10,000 net purchases to the $3,500 beginning inventory and subtracting the $4,000 ending inventory. The cost of goods sold is recorded as the net amount of the closing entries, as discussed in Chapter 5.

Evaluation of the Two Methods

Both the periodic and perpetual inventory systems result in approximately the same ending inventory and cost of goods sold for the year, and therefore the financial statements are not significantly affected by the choice of either method.[2] The selection by management of the periodic or perpetual system depends on other factors.

The advantages of the periodic system are:

1. It is less expensive and simpler to operate.

---

[2]In the preceding example the ending inventory and cost of goods sold were the same for both systems because the first-in, first-out cost flow method (discussed later) was used. When other inventory cost flow methods are used, the periodic and perpetual inventory systems will result in a slightly different ending inventory and cost of goods sold.

2. It is most appropriate for relatively low-cost inventory items because in these cases it is not as important for management to continually know the physical inventory for control and reordering purposes.

The advantages of the perpetual system are:

1. It allows management to exercise better control over the operations of the company because the cost of goods sold and inventory are continually known and can be used for inventory control. Also, management can evaluate the performance of the company whenever it chooses to do so.

2. The difference between the ending inventory according to the balance in the inventory account and the ending inventory determined when the physical inventory is taken provides a measure of the amount of theft, breakage, and spoilage that has occurred during the period. Management may consider this information to be useful in that it will help in the control of the company's activities.

Taking a Physical Inventory

2. Describe why a physical inventory is taken.

As we have seen, taking a physical inventory is essential under either the perpetual or periodic inventory system. The purpose of taking the inventory varies according to the system used. When the periodic system is used the physical inventory is necessary to determine the ending inventory and the cost of goods sold. When the perpetual system is used the taking of a physical inventory acts as a check on the accuracy of the ending inventory included in the perpetual records and indicates the extent of losses from theft, breakage, or spoilage. At a minimum, the taking of a physical inventory occurs at the end of each fiscal year. In many businesses a physical inventory is taken more frequently, perhaps as often as each month, although this count may be for only part of the inventory. Management must evaluate the tradeoff between the cost of taking the inventory and the information that results.

It is usual to take the inventory outside of regular business hours so that the counting is not affected by goods being sold or received while the count is in progress. The taking of a physical inventory should be carefully planned and supervised to prevent some items being omitted from the count, or other items being counted twice. The physical location of the items must be identified (e.g., on the sales floor, in the warehouse, or in the department responsible for receiving the goods), and movement of the items must be prevented during the count. It is usual to plan the inventory count so that one person checks the accuracy of the work of another person. Accuracy can be achieved by counting all the merchandise twice, but a less expensive way is to double check the counts of selected samples of merchandise, perhaps placing special emphasis on high-cost items.

Inventory counts are often performed by two-person teams. One person counts the merchandise and tells the other person the quantity and description. The second person records this information on an inventory sheet, or perhaps on a tape recorder. **Inventory tags are tags attached to each item of merchandise counted during a physical inventory to ensure that each item is counted and only counted once.** The person making the count of each item initials the inventory tag. Similarly, if a second count is made the tag is initialed a second time.

After completion of the individual counts all the tags are collected. The items on each tag are listed and summed on a master sheet to determine the total physical count of the inventory.

Items in Transit and on Consignment

The taking of a physical inventory determines the quantity of inventory actually in the possession of a company in its stores and warehouses. The company may also own additional units of inventory that are in transit or have been sent out on consignment. If the company is the legal owner of such items, they should be included in inventory.

Goods may be purchased or sold under terms of FOB (free on board) shipping point or FOB destination. **FOB shipping point means that transfer of ownership from the seller to the buyer occurs at the place of sale (shipping point).** The selling company should exclude such items in transit from its inventory because they have been sold, whereas the purchasing company should include such items in its inventory. For goods shipped FOB shipping point the purchasing company is responsible for any transportation charges incurred to deliver the goods. The cost of the transportation would be recorded in the Transportation-In account of the purchaser. **FOB destination means that transfer of ownership occurs when the items are delivered to the purchaser.** The selling company should include such items in transit in its inventory until delivery takes place, whereas the purchasing company should exclude them. For goods shipped FOB destination the selling company is responsible for any transportation charges incurred to deliver the goods. The cost of the transportation would be recorded in the Transportation-Out account of the seller. The terms are normally agreed to by the purchaser and the seller at the time the sale is negotiated and are listed on the sales invoice of the seller.

Some companies choose to sell on consignment. In this situation the company (the consignor) ships the goods to a retailer (the consignee) who acts as a selling agent. The retailer does not purchase the goods, and therefore the consignor must include such items in its inventory until they are sold by the retailer, or returned. The retailer does not include these goods in its inventory because it is not the legal owner. Accounting for consignments is beyond the scope of the book.

Determination of the Cost of Inventory

3. Determine the cost of inventory.

The cost of inventory includes all the costs incurred in bringing the items to their existing condition and location. Thus the cost of inventory includes the purchase price (giving consideration to purchases discounts), sales tax, transportation costs, insurance, customs duties, and similar costs. When a cost is difficult to associate with a particular inventory item, such as the cost of ordering the inventory, it may be allocated to each purchase, or as is more common the cost may be expensed directly as a general and administrative expense.

When a purchases discount is offered by the seller of the merchandise, the purchaser can use either the gross method or the net method to account for the discount.

Purchases Discounts: The Gross Method

4(a). Explain the gross method of accounting for purchases discounts.

Purchases discounts, which are offered by sellers to encourage prompt payment of amounts owed, should be deducted from the cost of purchases. One method of accounting for discounts is the gross method. **The gross method requires the purchases (inventory) and accounts payable to be recorded at their gross amounts and the purchases discount to be recorded when the discount is taken at the time of cash payment.** For example, suppose that the Wembley Company purchases merchandise for $1,000 and the seller offers a 2% discount if payment is made within 10 days. If the discount is not taken, full payment is required within 30 days. These terms are usually abbreviated as 2/10, n/30. The purchase and payment within 10 days are recorded in a periodic system as follows (the account titles in parentheses indicate the accounts used in the perpetual system):

Purchases (or Inventory)	1,000	
Accounts Payable		1,000

To record purchase of merchandise using the gross method.

Accounts Payable	1,000	
Purchases Discounts Taken (or Inventory)		20
Cash		980

To record payment within 10 days.

If purchases returns and allowances occur before payment is made, they are recorded at the gross amount before computing the discount. The Purchases Discounts Taken account is a contra account to Purchases (Inventory) and therefore has a credit balance. It represents a reduction in the cost of purchases and is included in the calculation of net purchases. The discounts taken are normally recorded in a separate account so that management will know the total amount of the discounts taken. For example, if the discounts taken decrease over time as a proportion of purchases, it may indicate that the company is being less efficient in its payments and is losing discounts that it should have taken. If payment was not made within 10 days, it is recorded as follows:

Accounts Payable	1,000	
Cash		1,000

To record payment after the discount period has expired.

The Purchases Discounts Taken account is closed at the same time as the Purchases, Purchases Returns and Allowances, and Transportation-In accounts are closed.

Purchases Discounts: The Net Method

4(b). Explain the net method of accounting for purchases discounts.

An alternative method of accounting for purchases discounts is the net method. **The net method requires the purchases discount available to be deducted at the time of the purchase and the purchases and accounts payable to be recorded at their net amounts.** The net amount is the gross amount less the purchases discounts available. For example, the Wembley Company records the purchase of merchandise for $1,000 on terms of 2/10, n/30 at the net amount of $980 [$1,000 – (2% × $1,000)] as follows:

Purchases (or Inventory)	980	
Accounts Payable		980

To record purchase of merchandise using the net method.

If payment is made within the discount period of 10 days, the payment is recorded as follows:

Accounts Payable	980	
Cash		980

To record payment within 10 days.

If payment is not made within the discount period, the cash paid is greater than the balance in the Accounts Payable account and the difference is recorded in the Purchases Discounts Lost account as follows:

Accounts Payable	980	
Purchases Discounts Lost	20	
Cash		1,000

To record payment after the discount period has expired.

If purchases returns and allowances occur before payment is made, they are recorded at the *net* amount in the usual manner. The balance in the Purchases Discounts Lost account would be included in the Other Revenues and Expenses section of the income statement as a financing expense (similar to interest expense).

The computation of the net purchases may be summarized as follows:

Gross Method	*Net Method*

Purchases (at *gross*)
 + Transportation-in
 − Purchases returns and allowances
    (at *gross*)
 − Purchases discounts taken
 = Net purchases
	Purchases (at *net*)
	 + Transportation-in
	 − Purchases returns and allowances
	    (at *net*)
	 = Net purchases

Implications for Management

Although the gross method is used more frequently, the net method has definite advantages for the management of a company. The decision not to take advantage of a purchases discount is very costly. Consider the Wembley Company example. If the company does not take advantage of the discount, it delays payment by 20 days (the 30 days allowed as a maximum minus the 10-day discount period). For this privilege it pays 2% extra. Therefore the company is incurring a cost of 2% to delay payment by 20 days. This is an approximate annual cost of 36% (2% × 360 ÷ 20). It would be less expensive for the company to borrow money from a bank to pay for the purchases within the discount period.

Given the high cost of not taking a discount, management should be very interested in knowing if any discounts have not been taken. The net method indicates this fact directly because any discounts not taken are included in the

Purchases Discounts Lost account. In contrast, the gross method includes in the Purchases Discounts Taken account only the discounts that were available and were taken. It does not indicate the discounts that were available but *not* taken.

Trade Discounts

It is important to distinguish between cash discounts for prompt payment and trade discounts. **A trade discount is a reduction in the invoice price from a catalog or list price.** In order to assist in the sale of merchandise, trade discounts are given to preferred customers, to customers who purchase large quantities, and to wholesalers. Trade discounts are quoted as percentages of the list price. For example, the price might be quoted as $50 less 20%, 10%. This quoted price indicates that the list price of $50 is subject to discounts of 20% and 10% under certain circumstances. Each discount applies to the net price *after* deducting any previous discounts. For example, if a purchaser is allowed both discounts, the invoice price would be:

List price	$50
Less 20% discount ($50 × 0.2)	(10)
	$40
Less 10% discount ($40 × 0.1)	(4)
Net Invoice Price	$36

Trade discounts are *not* recognized for financial reporting purposes because they are used to establish a pricing policy. The purchase of goods subject to trade discounts is recorded at the net invoice price, or $36 in our example. A cash discount for prompt payment would be applied to the net invoice price.

Inventory Cost Flow Assumptions

The cost of each unit of inventory is determined by a review of the source documents (e.g., invoices) used to record the initial acquisition of the inventory. Once a company has determined the number of units in the ending inventory and the cost of the units purchased during the period, it is necessary to determine how the total cost of the units for the period (the cost of goods available for sale) will be divided among the ending inventory (balance sheet) and the cost of goods sold (income statement). This relationship is shown by the following diagram:

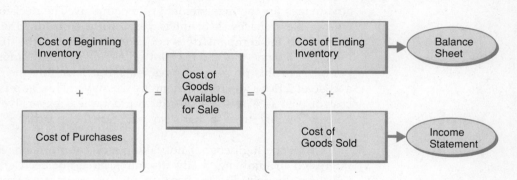

The difficulty of determining the costs to be included in the ending inventory and the cost of goods sold arises when costs incurred to acquire the units in inventory have changed during the period. Such changes (usually increases) occur frequently in the current economic environment. The four alternative cost flow assumptions that are commonly used are:

1. Specific identification
2. First-in, first-out (FIFO)
3. Average cost
4. Last-in, first-out (LIFO)

The method selected by the management of the company must be disclosed in the financial statements, and must be used consistently each year. Each of the methods is discussed for the Davis Company using the information in Exhibit 9-2. For simplicity, the example uses a month rather than the more common quarterly, or annual, period used by actual companies.

EXHIBIT 9-2
Inventory Information

DAVIS COMPANY Inventory Information		
Beginning inventory, January 1	100 units @ $5.00 per unit	$ 500
January 10, purchase	50 units @ $5.50 per unit	275
January 22, purchase	90 units @ $6.00 per unit	540
Cost of goods available for sale	240 units	$1,315
Sales during January	(130) units	
Ending inventory, January 31	110 units	

Notes: 1. The units are sold for $13 per unit.
2. The Davis Company uses the periodic inventory system. For computational simplicity, it is assumed that the physical inventory is taken monthly.

The company has a beginning inventory of $500 and has made two purchases during January with a total cost of $815 ($275 + $540). Therefore the cost of goods available for sale is $1,315 ($500 + $815), which must be divided between the 130 units sold (the cost of goods sold) and the ending inventory of 110 units. It is assumed that the Davis Company uses the *periodic inventory system* (except for LIFO, when the perpetual system is also illustrated).

Each of the four inventory cost flow methods produces different amounts for the cost of goods sold and ending inventory. Note that each of the methods is based on actual costs incurred and is an acceptable interpretation of the historical cost principle. It is also important to understand that these **cost** flow assumptions are *not* related to the actual **physical** flow of the goods in inventory. Typically a company will use a FIFO physical flow to reduce the risk of obsolescence, but may still use any of the cost flow assumptions. The computations to determine the cost of goods sold and ending inventory under each method are discussed in the following sections.

Specific Identification

5(a). Compute ending inventory and cost of goods sold under the specific identification method.

Specific identification is a method of assigning costs to cost of goods sold and ending inventory by identifying a specific cost incurred with each unit sold and each unit in ending inventory. If a unit has been sold, the related cost is included in cost of goods sold; if a unit remains in inventory, the related cost is included in the cost of the ending inventory. For example, when the Davis Company sells a unit at the end of January, the following three alternatives are possible:

	Sell a Unit from the Beginning Inventory	Sell a Unit from the January 10 Purchase	Sell a Unit from the January 22 Purchase
Sales	$13.00	$13.00	$13.00
Cost of goods sold	(5.00)	(5.50)	(6.00)
Gross Profit	$ 8.00	$ 7.50	$ 7.00

Depending on the unit selected, the gross profit can vary from a low of $7 to a high of $8, which is a difference of 14.3% ($8 ÷ $7 = 1.143). Although the specific identification method is often referred to as a cost flow assumption, it may be more accurate to state that it is an actual cost flow rather than a cost flow assumption. The method is particularly appropriate for a company with a small volume of separately identifiable units in inventory, such as an automobile dealership. When a company has an inventory consisting of large quantities of similar items, however, the method may be inefficient, time-consuming, and perhaps impossible to use. For example, the specific identification method would not be suitable for the inventory of frozen peas of a large grocery store. When identical units are carried in inventory, the specific identification method is very arbitrary and perhaps may be manipulated by management to change gross profits as particular units with different costs are selected for sale. Although the specific identification method could be used with the periodic inventory system, it is more compatible with the perpetual system, in which the cost of each unit is identified as it is sold.

First-In, First-Out

5(b). Compute ending inventory and cost of goods sold under FIFO.

In the first-in, first-out (FIFO) cost flow assumption, the earliest costs incurred are included in the cost of goods sold and the latest costs are included in the ending inventory. That is, the first costs incurred are assumed to be the first costs of units sold. Under this method the Davis Company computes the ending inventory to be $650 and the cost of goods sold to be $665, as shown in Exhibit 9-3. (Note that since the company is using the periodic inventory system the ending inventory is computed first.)

The Davis Company has an ending inventory of 110 units and the costs of these units are assumed in the FIFO method to be the latest costs incurred, which

EXHIBIT 9-3
Davis Company: FIFO

> **DAVIS COMPANY**
> **First-In, First-Out Cost Flow Assumption**
> **(Periodic Inventory System)**
>
> Ending Inventory (110 units)
>
> | | |
> |---|---|
> | 90 units @ $6.00 per unit (from January 22 purchase) | $540 |
> | 20 units @ $5.50 per unit (from January 10 purchase) | 110 |
> | 110 | $650 |
>
> Cost of Goods Sold = Beginning Inventory + Purchases − Ending Inventory
> $665 = $500 + $815 − $650

(handwritten: FIFO; Latest → costs; → ASSET)

include the cost of the 90 units from the purchase on January 22 ($540) and the cost of the 20 units remaining from the purchase on January 10 ($110). Consequently, the cost of goods sold ($665) includes the earliest costs, that is, the cost of the 100 units from the beginning inventory and the cost of the 30 units from the purchase made on January 10.

Average Cost

5(c). Compute ending inventory and cost of goods sold under the average cost method.

The average cost flow assumption allocates the average cost for the period to both the ending inventory and the cost of goods sold. That is, the costs of all the units available for sale are commingled, and the resulting average cost is used for both the ending inventory and the cost of goods sold. As shown in Exhibit 9-4, the average cost per unit of $5.48 for the Davis Company is calculated by dividing the total cost of goods available for sale ($1,315) by the number of units available for sale (240, which includes the 100 units in the beginning inventory plus the 140 units purchased).

The ending inventory is computed as $603 for the 110 units on hand at the average cost of $5.48 per unit and the cost of goods sold as $712, which includes the 130 units sold at the average cost of $5.48 per unit.

EXHIBIT 9-4
Davis Company:
Average Cost

> **DAVIS COMPANY**
> **Average Cost Flow Assumption**
> **(Periodic Inventory System)**
>
> Average Cost per Unit = Cost of Goods Available for Sale ÷ Number of Units Available for Sale
> = $1,315 ÷ 240
> = $5.48 per Unit (rounded)
>
> Ending Inventory = Number of Units × Average Cost per Unit
> = 110 × $5.48
> = $603 (rounded to the nearest dollar)
>
> Cost of Goods Sold = Beginning Inventory + Purchases − Ending Inventory
> $712 = $500 + $815 − $603

Last-In, First-Out (Periodic)

5(d). Compute ending inventory and cost of goods sold under LIFO.

In the last-in, first-out (LIFO) cost flow assumption, the latest costs incurred are included in the cost of goods sold and the earliest costs (part or all of which are costs incurred in previous periods) are included in the ending inventory. That is, the last costs incurred are assumed to be the first costs of units sold. The Davis Company computes the ending inventory to be $555 and the cost of goods sold to be $760, as shown in Exhibit 9-5. The company has an ending inventory of 110 units and the costs of these units are assumed in the LIFO method to be the earliest costs incurred, which include the cost of the entire beginning inventory and the cost of the 10 units remaining from the January 10 purchase. Consequently, the cost of goods sold includes the latest costs, that is, the cost of the goods from the January 22 purchase ($540) and the cost of 40 units from the January 10 purchase ($220).

EXHIBIT 9-5
Davis Company:
LIFO Periodic

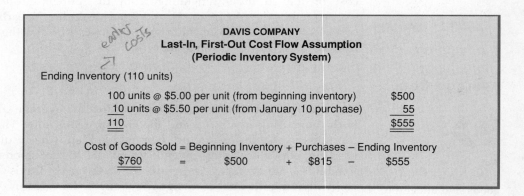

DAVIS COMPANY
Last-In, First-Out Cost Flow Assumption
(Periodic Inventory System)

Ending Inventory (110 units)

100 units @ $5.00 per unit (from beginning inventory)	$500
10 units @ $5.50 per unit (from January 10 purchase)	55
110	$555

Cost of Goods Sold = Beginning Inventory + Purchases − Ending Inventory
$760 = $500 + $815 − $555

Last-In, First-Out (Perpetual)

The previous illustrations of inventory cost flow assumptions assumed the use of the *periodic* inventory system. In that system cost of goods sold is determined by subtracting the ending inventory from cost of goods available for sale. When a company uses the *perpetual* inventory system, cost of goods sold is determined each time units are sold, and the ending inventory is calculated by subtracting cost of goods sold from cost of goods available for sale, as shown on page 395. When FIFO is used cost of goods sold and ending inventory are the same amounts under both the periodic and perpetual inventory systems. This is not true for LIFO because different amounts are obtained depending on the inventory system being used.

The application of LIFO under a perpetual inventory system is illustrated in Exhibit 9-6. This illustration uses the same information as Exhibit 9-2 except that the 130 units were sold as follows: 40 units on January 6, 60 units on January 18, and 30 units on January 25. Note that the cost of goods sold and the ending inventory are different under the LIFO perpetual method ($705 and $610, as shown in Exhibit 9-6) and the LIFO periodic method ($760 and $555, as shown in Exhibit 9-5). The differences result from the difference in the assumptions about the timing of the sales. Under the periodic system the whole accounting period (a month in this example) is treated as a single unit, and the sales are assumed to occur after all the units have been purchased during the period. Therefore the cost of goods sold includes the costs of the *latest purchases of the period*. Under the perpetual system the cost of goods sold is calculated when each sale is made and therefore includes the costs of the *most recent purchase(s) at that time*. For example, the first sale occurs on January 6, and under the perpetual system we assume that the cost of those units is taken from the beginning inventory of $5.00 per unit. Under the periodic system, however, since the number of units purchased by the company exceeds the number of units sold for the month, none of the cost of the beginning inventory is included in the cost of goods sold. Instead, the cost of the 130 units sold is taken from the cost of the purchases during the period.

EXHIBIT 9-6
Davis Company:
LIFO Perpetual

DAVIS COMPANY
LIFO with a Perpetual Inventory System
Inventory Information

Beginning inventory, January 1	100 units @ $5.00 per unit	$ 500
January 6, sale	40 units	
January 10, purchase	50 units @ $5.50 per unit	275
January 18, sale	60 units	
January 22, purchase	90 units @ $6.00 per unit	540
January 25, sale	30 units	
		$1,315

Calculations

Cost of Goods Sold (130 units):

January 6	40 units @ $5.00 per unit	$ 200
January 18	60 units: 50 units @ $5.50	275
	10 units @ $5.00	50
January 25	30 units @ $6.00 per unit	180
		$ 705

Ending Inventory (110 units):

Ending Inventory = Beginning Inventory + Purchases − Cost of Goods Sold

$610	=	$500	+	$815	−	$705

Additional Periodic Illustration

To further illustrate the differences among FIFO, average cost, and LIFO, we continue the Davis Company example through February. The inventory information for the Davis Company for February is shown in Exhibit 9-7. The cost of the ending inventory on February 28 and the cost of goods sold for February are shown for the FIFO, average, and LIFO cost flow assumptions. It is important to note that the beginning inventory for February is the ending inventory for January, and therefore the amount is different for each cost flow assumption. The calculations otherwise follow the same procedures as for January.

EXHIBIT 9-7
Davis Company:
February

DAVIS COMPANY
Ending Inventory and Cost of Goods Sold for February
(Periodic Inventory System)

Additional Information

Beginning Inventory, February 1	110 units	
February 5, purchase	40 units @ $6.20 per unit	$248
February 20, purchase	80 units @ $6.40 per unit	$512
	230 units	
Sales during February	(100) units	
Ending inventory, February 28	130 units	

First-In, First-Out

Beginning Inventory = 20 units @ $5.50 per unit + 90 units @ $6.00 per unit
(from Exhibit 9-3)
= $650

Ending Inventory = 80 units @ $6.40 per unit
+ 40 units @ $6.20 per unit
+ 10 units @ $6.00 per unit
= $820

Cost of Goods Sold = Beginning Inventory + Purchases − Ending Inventory
= $650 + $760 (i.e., $248 + $512) − $820
= $590

Average Cost

Average Cost per Unit $= \dfrac{\text{Cost of Goods Available for Sale}}{\text{Number of Units Available for Sale}}$
= [$603 (from Exhibit 9-4) + $760] ÷ [110 + 120]
= $5.93 per unit (rounded)

Ending Inventory = Number of Units × Average Cost per Unit
= 130 × $5.93
= $771 (rounded to the nearest dollar)

Cost of Goods Sold = Beginning Inventory + Purchases − Ending Inventory
= $603 + $760 − $771
= $592 (or 100 units × $5.93 allowing for a $1 rounding error)

Last-In, First-Out

Beginning Inventory = 100 units @ $5 per unit + 10 units @ $5.50 per unit
= $555   (from Exhibit 9-5)

Ending Inventory = 100 units @ $5 per unit
+ 10 units @ $5.50 per unit
+ 20 units @ $6.20 per unit
= $679

Cost of Goods Sold = Beginning Inventory + Purchases − Ending Inventory
= $555 + $760 − $679
= $636

Evaluation of the Three Alternatives

The advantages and disadvantages of the FIFO, average, and LIFO cost flow assumptions are discussed in this section (the advantages and disadvantages of the specific identification method were discussed earlier).

Effects on the Financial Statements

↑costs LIFO = ↓Income ↓Inventory
FIFO = ↑Income ↑Inventory

6. Evaluate the alternative cost flow assumptions.

The choice made by management to adopt any one of the three cost flow assumptions has an impact on both the income statement and the balance sheet. If costs are rising income will be highest under FIFO and will be lowest under LIFO, whereas ending inventory will be highest under FIFO and lowest under LIFO. The average cost figures will be between those of FIFO and LIFO. If costs are falling the relationships are reversed. Using the Davis Company example, the following comparative gross profit figures result from selling 130 units for $1,690 in *January* (assuming a selling price of $13 per unit):

	FIFO		Average Cost		LIFO	
Sales		$1,690		$1,690		$1,690
Cost of goods available for sale	$1,315		$1,315		$1,315	
Ending inventory	(650)		(603)		(555)	
Cost of goods sold		(665)		(712)		(760)
Gross profit		$1,025		$ 978		$ 930

Since this is a situation of rising costs, we can see that the cost of goods sold is lowest under FIFO and therefore the gross profit is highest. In contrast, LIFO results in the highest cost of goods sold and the lowest gross profit. It is often said that FIFO takes a balance sheet approach by recording the inventory at a cost close to the replacement cost (and therefore understates cost of goods sold). In contrast, LIFO takes an income statement approach by matching current costs against revenues (and therefore understates ending inventory).

It should be noted that there is a simplifying assumption included in the Davis Company example for January that has made the differences less than they might otherwise be. It was assumed that the beginning inventory consisted of 100 units at $5 under all three alternatives. Recall, however, that the beginning inventory of the period is the ending inventory of the previous period. Therefore if each method had been used in the previous period and costs had changed during that period, the beginning inventory would be different under each of the alternatives, just as the ending inventory for January is different under each method. This relationship can be clearly seen in the calculations for February in which the beginning inventory is different in all three situations. This factor can become very significant when the LIFO cost flow assumption is used. If the number of units in the inventory increases during each period, the costs included in the beginning inventory are carried over for each period. As years pass, however, these costs may become very outdated. For example, many companies adopted LIFO in the late 1930s and others during the period of high inflation in the middle of the 1970s. Therefore the inventories disclosed in the balance sheets of today may include elements of costs from many years ago.

Impact of Tax Rules

Why would the management of a company select LIFO when it results in lower reported income? *If the company is a corporation, LIFO is allowable for income tax purposes only if it is also used for the financial statements.* (Any of the other methods discussed may be used for calculating corporate taxable income regardless of which method is used for financial reporting.) If we assume rising costs the use of LIFO results in lower taxable income and consequently in the payment of less income taxes. For instance, according to their recent annual reports, three long-time LIFO users—Amoco, General Electric, and US Steel—have together saved more than $3 billion in taxes compared to what they would have paid using FIFO. This tax saving is a very strong, practical argument in favor of LIFO because companies avoid cash payments for taxes and therefore have more cash available than they otherwise would for such things as withdrawals (dividends); paying employees; investing in property, plant, and equipment; or reducing liabilities.

Income Measurement

Many users of financial statements argue that LIFO results in a better measure of income. To illustrate this point, consider the Davis Company in *January*. If the company uses the FIFO method, it would be selling units and recording a cost of $5 per unit and a gross profit of $8 per unit during January (the $13 selling price less the $5 cost). The company has to replace the inventory during the month by paying $5.50 or $6 per unit, however. Therefore, $.50 or $1 of the profit must be used to buy the replacement units of inventory, and only $7.50 or $7 represents the real profit of the Davis Company. **A holding gain, or inventory profit, is the illusory profit that results from recording cost of goods sold at lower historical costs than the replacement cost of the unit sold.** In this example the holding gain is $.50 or $1 per unit sold. Since the holding gain cannot be distributed to the owners as withdrawals (dividends) without reducing the ability of the company to replace the units of inventory sold, many users argue that the holding gain should be excluded from income. An additional discussion of the problems of accounting under conditions of changing prices is included in Chapter 20.

Although a company is able to select one of the four cost flow assumptions to account for its inventory, it is expected that once the selection is made the method will be consistently applied from period to period. If a change is made the effects of the change must be fully disclosed in the financial statements. A company may also use more than one method by selecting a different cost flow assumption for different types of inventory. For example, if a retail company is selling one type of inventory that has rising costs and another type that has falling costs, the company may select LIFO for the first type of inventory and FIFO for the second.

Inventory Valuation

The LIFO method produces a lower ending inventory value (again assuming rising costs) because the oldest costs remain in this inventory. The balance sheet value of this inventory often bears little or no relationship to the costs of the current period or the costs that will be incurred to replace the inventory. This low valuation affects the computation and evaluation of current assets, working capital, and any financial ratios (discussed in Chapter 19) that include inventory, thereby reducing comparability between companies using LIFO and those using FIFO. Furthermore comparability between two or more companies using LIFO is impaired because the inventory valuation depends on the year in which LIFO was adopted by each company. For example, if companies in the same industry adopted LIFO in different years, the beginning inventory in the year LIFO was adopted will include costs of different years. In addition, if the companies increase their inventories by different amounts in later years, the additional LIFO layers will have been added at different costs.

The FIFO method produces a higher ending inventory value (assuming rising costs) because it includes the latest costs. This value tends to approximate the costs that will be incurred to replace the inventory, but how closely depends on when the purchases included in the ending inventory were made and how fast costs are rising.

Lower of Cost or Market Rule

The requirement that inventory be recorded at its historical cost is modified in one situation. When the market value of the inventory falls below the cost, the inventory should be written down to its market value and the corresponding loss should be included in the income statement.[3] The use of the term *market value* may lead to confusion. It should be clearly understood that it refers to the cost of replacing the item and *not* the selling price.

The cost of replacing the item is known as the replacement cost. **The replacement cost is the cost that would have to be paid at the present time to purchase an item of inventory in normal quantities from the usual suppliers, including any transportation costs ordinarily incurred.** A decline in the replacement cost of the inventory may result from physical deterioration, obsolescence, or perhaps a declining price level.

7. Explain the lower of cost or market method.

For example, suppose that the Barnhill Company has 100 units of inventory for which it paid $50 per unit. If the replacement cost declines to $40 per unit, the inventory should be included in the balance sheet at $40 per unit because the $50 cost is an overstatement of the value of the inventory. Similarly, the company has lost $10 per unit by owning the inventory while its cost declined. If it had delayed the purchase, it could have acquired the inventory for only $40 per unit. The lower of cost or market method is an example of the application of the conservatism principle.

---

[3]There are upper and lower limits to the market value that can be used. See Nikolai and Bazley, *Intermediate Accounting*, 4th ed. (Boston: PWS-KENT Publishing Co., 1988), chapter 9.

The conservatism principle holds that accounting principles should be developed so that there is little likelihood that assets or income are overstated. Therefore losses are recognized when there is evidence to support their existence, whereas gains are recognized when an actual transaction occurs. This principle does *not* state that assets or income should be understated, but when there is a doubt about the likely effect of an accounting method the bias should be toward the conservative method. The rationale for the conservatism principle is that the users of financial statements are least likely to be misled if the least favorable alternative valuation is used; conservatism also tends to offset the optimistic view of management. Many users disagree with the conservatism principle, however, because they believe that accounting should strive to obtain the best valuation with a bias neither toward nor against conservatism. It is also possible that conservatism may be unfair to present stockholders and biased in favor of prospective stockholders because of the lower valuation. Furthermore since the long-term income of the company is the same whether conservatism is applied or not, reducing income or asset values in the current period will inevitably result in higher income in the future than would otherwise have been reported. Nevertheless the conservatism principle has affected several accounting practices, including the lower of cost or market method.

The use of the lower of cost or market rule is also consistent with the matching principle. The loss associated with the decline in value is recorded in the period of the decline, not in the period in which the inventory is ultimately sold.

Another argument in favor of the lower of cost or market method is based on the assumption that the relationship between cost and selling price remains fairly constant. That is, a common practice is to set the selling price at a certain percentage (called the *markup*) above the cost of the inventory. For example, if the Barnhill Company normally sells for $100 the units that cost $50, it is receiving a markup of 100% of cost. If the replacement cost of the inventory drops to $40, it might be expected that the selling price will drop to $80, thus maintaining the 100% markup on cost. Use of the lower of cost or market method thus separates the loss on holding the inventory ($10) from the gross profit that results from selling the inventory ($80 – $40).

The lower of cost or market method is normally applied separately to each item in inventory as indicated in the following example:

	Quantity	Unit Cost	Unit Market	Total Cost	Total Market	Lower of Cost or Market
Item A	100	$20	$18	$ 2,000	$ 1,800	$ 1,800
Item B	200	30	31	6,000	6,200	6,000
Item C	200	25	20	5,000	4,000	4,000
Item D	100	40	43	4,000	4,300	4,000
				$17,000	$16,300	$15,800

The value of the inventory under the lower of cost or market method applied to individual items is $15,800. In this case a loss of $1,200 ($17,000 – $15,800) is recorded as follows:

Loss on Reduction of Inventory to Market	1,200	
Allowance for Reduction of Inventory to Market		1,200

To record valuation of inventory at lower of cost or market.

The inventory is included in the current asset section of the balance sheet at its cost less the allowance as follows:

Inventory, at cost	$17,000
Less: Allowance for reduction to market value	(1,200)
	$15,800

A less conservative method of application is to record the lower of cost or market of the inventory as a whole (this method is not allowed for income tax purposes). The inventory would be valued at $16,300 and a loss of $700 recorded under this alternative. In either case the loss would be included in the Other Revenues and Expenses section of the income statement.

When the conservatism principle was discussed earlier, it was pointed out that the reduction in income in the current period is offset by higher income in later periods than would otherwise have been reported. In the first example income in the second year will be $1,200 higher than it would otherwise have been because the beginning inventory is $1,200 lower, resulting in a lower cost of goods sold (if it assumed that the market value of the inventory is *not* less than the cost at the end of the second year).

Methods of Estimating Inventory Costs

It is sometimes necessary to estimate the cost of inventory. If a company is using the periodic inventory system, the management may need to estimate the cost of the inventory during the year for the preparation of interim financial statements without going to the expense of taking a physical inventory. If a company experiences a loss of inventory in a fire or theft, or if the accounting records are destroyed, it may also need to estimate the remaining inventory (and corresponding loss) without taking a physical inventory. There are two commonly used methods of estimating the cost of inventory. The gross profit method is often used in the special situations just described, whereas the retail inventory method is routinely used by retailing companies, such as supermarkets and department stores.

Gross Profit Method

The gross profit method is used to estimate the cost of inventory by applying a gross profit rate (gross profit ÷ net sales) based on the income statements of previous periods to the net sales of the current period. The resulting estimated gross profit is deducted from the net sales to determine the estimated cost of goods sold. The estimated cost of goods sold is then subtracted from the cost of goods available for sale to provide the estimate of the ending inventory.

For example, suppose that the beginning inventory of a company for the current period is $12,000, net purchases are $48,000, and net sales are $70,000. If the gross profit rate based on the company's income statements of previous peri-

8(a). Estimate the cost of inventory by the gross profit method.

ods is 40%, the ending inventory of the current period is computed by four steps as follows:

STEP 1:   **Gross Profit = Gross Profit Rate × Net Sales**
$$= 40\% \times \$70,000$$
$$= \$28,000$$

STEP 2:   **Cost of Goods Sold = Net Sales – Gross Profit**
$$= \$70,000 - \$28,000$$
$$= \$42,000$$

STEP 3:   **Cost of Goods Available for Sale = Beginning + Net**
                                                Inventory   Purchases
$$= \$12,000 + \$48,000$$
$$= \$60,000$$

STEP 4:   **Ending Inventory = Cost of Goods Available – Cost of Goods**
                             for Sale   Sold
$$= \$60,000 - \$42,000$$
$$= \underline{\$18,000}$$

These relationships can be illustrated in income statement format as follows (Steps 1–4 are listed in parentheses):

Net sales		$70,000 (100%)
Cost of goods sold:		
Beginning inventory	$12,000	
Net purchases	48,000	
Cost of goods available for sale (actual)	(3) $60,000	
Less: Ending inventory (estimated)	(4) (18,000)	
Cost of goods sold (estimated)		(2) (42,000) (60%)
Gross Profit (estimated)		(1) $28,000 (40%)

The validity of the gross profit method depends on the reasonableness of the estimate of the gross profit rate. Since the rate is based on the gross profit and net sales relationships of past periods, it is a valid indicator of the gross profit rate of the current period only if the gross profit relationships are largely unchanged. If it is known that conditions have changed, the gross profit rate should be adjusted so that the estimate of the cost of the ending inventory will be more accurate.

If the company is using the gross profit method to estimate a casualty loss, the amount of the loss would be calculated by subtracting the cost of any salvaged inventory from the estimated cost of the ending inventory.

Retail Inventory Method

Retail companies generally find it easier and less expensive to base their inventory accounting system on the retail value of the inventory being sold. The merchandise is marked and put on display at the retail price; it is then easier to count the inventory at retail prices than to attempt to identify the cost of each item. The *cost* of the inventory must be included in the financial statements, however.

The retail inventory method is used to estimate the cost of inventory by multiplying the retail value of the ending inventory by the cost-to-retail ratio of the current period. To apply this method, the following steps are necessary:

8(b). Estimate the cost of inventory by the retail inventory method.

1. The total goods available for sale (beginning inventory plus net purchases) is computed at both cost and retail value (selling price). Detailed records of the beginning inventory and the net purchases at both cost and retail prices are necessary to establish this rate. Net purchases at cost are purchases at cost minus purchases returns and allowances at cost, whereas net purchases at retail are purchases at retail minus purchases returns and allowances at retail.

2. A cost-to-retail ratio is computed by dividing the cost of the goods available for sale by the retail value of the goods available for sale.

3. The ending inventory at retail is computed by subtracting net sales (sales minus sales returns and allowances) for the period from the retail value of the goods available for sale.[4]

4. The ending inventory at cost is computed by multiplying the ending inventory at retail by the cost-to-retail ratio.

These steps for the retail inventory method are illustrated by the following example, using the same information as in the gross profit method (Steps 1 through 4 are listed in parentheses):

	Cost	Retail	
Beginning inventory	$12,000	$ 20,000	
Purchases (net)	48,000	80,000	
Goods available for sale	$60,000	$100,000	(1)
Cost-to-retail ratio $\dfrac{\$ 60,000}{\$100,000} = 0.60$			(2)
Less: Sales (net)		(70,000)	
Ending Inventory at Retail		$ 30,000	(3)
Ending Inventory at Cost (0.60 × $30,000)	$18,000		(4)

Goods with a retail value of $100,000 were available for sale during the period, and net sales of $70,000 were made. Therefore the ending inventory has a retail value of $30,000. Since costs are 60% of the retail value, the cost of the ending inventory is $18,000, and this cost is reported on the ending balance sheet.

The use of a single ratio of 0.60 implies that the retail value of every item consists of 60% cost and 40% gross profit. Obviously, that is unlikely to be true, but the method develops an acceptable cost of the inventory if it can be assumed that the weighted average of the items included in the goods available for sale and the ending inventory is the same. If this is an unreasonable assumption, separate cost-to-retail ratios should be developed and applied to the items in each category of inventory.

It should be noted that the retail inventory method is an estimating procedure and is useful for interim financial statements. It does not eliminate the need

---

[4]Markups and markdowns are commonly used in the retail industry. **Markups** are increases in price above the original sales price, and **markdowns** are decreases in price below the original sales price. In the most commonly used retail method, markups are added to the retail value of the purchases and therefore are included in the computation of the cost-to-retail ratio. Markdowns are added to net sales in the computation of the value of the ending inventory at retail. Other variations are beyond the scope of this book. See Nikolai and Bazley, *Intermediate Accounting*, 4th ed. (Boston: PWS-KENT Publishing Co., 1988), chapter 9.

for taking a periodic physical inventory, however, especially at the end of the fiscal year. For example, if the company in the preceding example took a physical inventory and found that the retail value of the inventory was $28,000, the cost of the inventory included in the balance sheet would be $16,800 (0.60 × $28,000), because this figure is more accurate than the amount of $18,000 that was computed earlier. The difference of $1,200 would be included in cost of goods sold for the period.

Summary of Estimating Methods

The gross profit method and the retail inventory method are similar because they both estimate the cost of inventory by using a profit percentage. However, the retail inventory method is more sensitive to price changes because it uses a current period estimate of the profit percentage, whereas the gross profit method uses an estimate based on past periods. The two methods may be summarized as follows:

Gross Profit Method	Retail Inventory Method
Cost of goods available for sale Less: Cost of goods sold 　　　　(sales × gross profit rate) Ending inventory at cost	Retail value of goods available Less: Sales Ending inventory at retail × Cost-to-retail ratio Ending inventory at cost

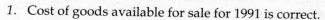

Errors in Recording Inventory

9. Compute the effects of errors in the recording of inventory.

As an additional way of understanding the interrelationships among inventory valuation, income, and assets, we can consider the effects of errors in the valuation of inventory on the income and assets. For example, suppose that at the end of 1991 a company overstates its inventory; that is, it erroneously records the ending inventory at $60,000 instead of $50,000. If the company is using the periodic inventory system the following effects result:

1. Cost of goods available for sale for 1991 is correct.
2. Ending inventory for 1991 is overstated by $10,000.
3. Cost of goods sold for 1991 is understated by $10,000.
4. Gross profit for 1991 is overstated by $10,000.
5. Net income for 1991 is overstated by $10,000.
6. Cost of goods available for sale for 1992 is overstated by $10,000 because the beginning inventory (the ending inventory for 1991) is overstated.
7. Ending inventory for 1992 is correct (because the company took a physical inventory).
8. Cost of goods sold is overstated for 1992 by $10,000.

9. Gross profit for 1992 is understated by $10,000.

10. Net income for 1992 is understated by $10,000.

These relationships can also be stated in equation form as follows:

1991

Beginning Inventory + Purchases – Ending Inventory = Cost of Goods Sold
(correct)   (correct)   (overstated by   (understated by
                                      $10,000) $10,000)

1992

Beginning Inventory + Purchases – Ending Inventory = Cost of Goods Sold
(overstated by   (correct)   (correct)   (overstated by
$10,000) $10,000)

Note that by the end of 1992 the error has counterbalanced. The overstatement of the gross profit and net income in 1991 has been counterbalanced by the understatement of the gross profit and net income in 1992. The inventory in the balance sheet at the end of 1992 is correct, and therefore the future financial statements are unaffected by the error. It should be remembered that if the financial statements for 1991 and 1992 are presented in the future for comparative purposes, however, they should be corrected for the effects of the error. Users of the financial statements who make an analysis of trends over time would be misled if such corrections were not made.

The effects of errors in the valuation of inventory on the net income of the current period may be summarized as follows:

1. If the ending inventory is overstated, net income for the current period is overstated.

2. If the ending inventory is understated, net income for the current period is understated.

3. If the beginning inventory is overstated, net income for the current period is understated.

4. If the beginning inventory is understated, net income for the current period is overstated.

For a corporation, the dollar amount of the effect on net income will not be the same as the dollar amount of the effect on inventory. The difference arises because of the income tax effect on the change in the gross profit. For example, if ending inventory is overstated by $10,000, the gross profit is overstated by $10,000. If the corporate income tax rate is 40%, income tax expense (and liability) is overstated by $4,000, and therefore net income will be overstated by only $6,000.

Disclosure in the Financial Statements

Inventory is included in the current assets section of the balance sheet, usually immediately after receivables. The inventory cost flow assumption (FIFO, average, or LIFO) and the method of valuing the inventory (cost or lower of cost or market) should be disclosed either by a parenthetical note in the balance sheet or

EXHIBIT 9-8
Alternative Forms
of Disclosure

Compaq Computer Corporation
Footnotes (in part):
   Inventories — Inventories are stated at the lower of cost or market, cost being determined on a first-in, first-out basis.

IBM Corporation
   Raw materials, operating supplies, finished goods, and work in process are included at the lower of average cost or market.

United Technologies Corporation
Footnotes (in part):
   A substantial portion of the Corporation's inventories in its building systems industrial products businesses is valued under the LIFO method. If these inventories had been valued at the lower of replacement value or cost under the first-in, first-out method, they would have been higher by $111.3 million at December 31, 1988 ($183.7 million at December 31, 1987).

---

in a footnote to the financial statements. Similarly, cost of goods sold is reported in the income statement. Exhibit 9-8 includes examples of alternative forms of disclosure of the inventory cost flow assumption.

Chapter Summary

Review of Learning Objectives

1. **Determine inventory quantities using (a) the periodic inventory system and (b) the perpetual inventory system.**

   Under the *periodic* inventory system a continuous record is *not* kept of the physical quantities (or costs) of inventory on hand during the period. A record of the cost of goods sold is *not* made each time a sale is made. The amount of inventory and the cost of goods sold are only known when a physical inventory is taken. Under the *perpetual* inventory system a continuous record is kept of the physical quantities in inventory and the number of units sold.

2. **Describe why a physical inventory is taken.**

   When the *periodic* system is used, a physical inventory is necessary to determine the ending inventory and the cost of goods sold. When the *perpetual* system is used, the taking of a physical inventory acts as a check on the accuracy of the ending inventory included in the perpetual records and indicates the extent of losses from theft, breakage, or spoilage.

3. **Determine the cost of inventory.**

   The cost of inventory includes all the costs incurred in bringing the items to their existing condition and location, including the purchase price, sales tax, transportation costs, insurance, customs duties, and similar costs.

4. **Explain (a) the gross method and (b) the net method of accounting for purchases discounts.**

   The *gross* method requires the purchases (inventory) and accounts payable to be recorded at their gross amounts and the purchases discount to be recorded when the discount is taken at the time of cash payment. The *net* method requires the purchases discount available to be deducted at the time of the purchase and the purchases and accounts payable to be recorded at their net amounts. A purchases discount lost is recorded if the available discount is not taken.

5. **Compute ending inventory and cost of goods sold under the alternative cost flow assumptions, including (a) specific identification, (b) FIFO, (c) average, and (d) LIFO.**

   Specific identification is a method of assigning costs to cost of goods sold and ending inventory by identifying a specific cost incurred with each unit sold and each unit in ending inventory. In the first-in, first-out (*FIFO*) cost flow assumption, the earliest costs incurred are included in the cost of goods sold and the latest costs are included in the ending inventory. The *average cost* flow assumption allocates the average cost for the period to both the ending inventory and the cost of goods sold. In the last-in, first-out (*LIFO*) cost flow assumption, the latest costs incurred are included in the cost of goods sold and the earliest costs (part or all of which are costs incurred in previous periods) are included in the ending inventory.

6. **Evaluate the alternative cost flow assumptions.**

   If costs are rising, income will be highest under FIFO and lowest under LIFO, whereas ending inventory will be highest under FIFO and lowest under LIFO. The average cost figures will be between those of FIFO and LIFO. If costs are falling, the relationships are reversed. LIFO is allowable for income tax purposes only if it is also used for the financial statements. Many users of financial statements argue that LIFO results in a better measure of income because it excludes holding gains from income.

7. **Explain the lower of cost or market method.**

   The lower of cost or market rule requires that the ending inventory be recorded in the balance sheet at the lower of its cost (as determined by the cost flow assumption selected) or its market value (replacement cost).

8. **Estimate the cost of inventory by (a) the gross profit method and (b) the retail inventory method.**

   The *gross profit method* is used to estimate the cost of inventory by multiplying the historical gross profit rate times the net sales of the current period. The resulting estimated gross profit is deducted from the net sales to determine the estimated cost of goods sold. The estimated cost of goods sold is then subtracted from the cost of goods available for sale to provide the estimate of the ending inventory. The *retail inventory method* is used to estimate the cost of inventory by first dividing the cost of goods available by the retail value of the goods available to determine the cost-to-retail ratio. Then the ending inventory at retail is computed by subtracting the net sales from the retail value of the goods available. Finally, the estimate of the ending inventory is computed by multiplying the cost-to-retail ratio times the ending inventory at retail.

9. **Compute the effects of errors in the recording of inventory.**

   If the ending inventory is over(under)stated, net income for the current period is over(under)stated. If the beginning inventory is over(under)stated, net income for the current period is under(over)stated.

Review Problem

The Peters Company made the following purchases and sales in 1991 and 1992:

Purchases, 1991	100 units @ $40 per unit = $ 4,000
	120 units @ $41 per unit = 4,920
	220 $ 8,920
Sales, 1991	200 units
Purchases, 1992	150 units @ $42 per unit = $ 6,300
	90 units @ $43 per unit = 3,870
	240 $10,170
Sales, 1992	220 units

The FIFO, average, and LIFO cost per unit of the 1991 beginning inventory of 60 units is $39, $38, and $30, respectively. The company uses the periodic inventory system.

REQUIRED

1. Compute the units in inventory at the end of 1991 and 1992.

2. Compute the ending inventory and cost of goods sold for 1991 and 1992 if the company uses:
   (a) The FIFO cost flow assumption.
   (b) The average cost flow assumption.
   (c) The LIFO cost flow assumption.

Solution to Review Problem

REQUIREMENT 1

1991: $\text{Quantity in Ending Inventory} = \text{Quantity in Beginning Inventory} + \text{Quantity Purchased} - \text{Quantity Sold}$
       = 60 + 220 − 200
       = 80 units

1992: Quantity in Ending Inventory = 80 + 240 − 220 = 100 units

REQUIREMENT 2   (a) First-in, First-out

1991: Beginning Inventory = 60 units @ $39 per unit
                            = $2,340

       Purchases   = 100 units @ $40 per unit + 120 units @ $41 per unit
                          = $8,920

       Ending Inventory   = 80 units @ $41 per unit
                          = $3,280

       Cost of Goods Sold = Beginning Inventory + Purchases − Ending Inventory
                          = $2,340 + $8,920 − $3,280
                          = $7,980

1992: Beginning Inventory = 80 units @ $41 per unit
                            = $3,280

       Purchases   = 150 units @ $42 per unit + 90 units @ $43 per unit
                          = $10,170

       Ending Inventory   = 90 units @ $43 per unit + 10 units @ $42 per unit
                          = $4,290

       Cost of Goods Sold = Beginning Inventory + Purchases − Ending Inventory
                          = $3,280 + $10,170 − $4,290
                          = $9,160

(b) *Average cost*

1991:	Average Cost per Unit	= Cost of Goods Available for Sale ÷ Number of Units
		Available for Sale
		= [(60 × $38) + (100 × $40) + (120 × $41)] ÷ (60 + 100 + 120)
		= $11,200 ÷ 280
		= $40

Ending Inventory = Number of Units × Average Cost per Unit
                  = 80 × $40
                  = $3,200

Cost of Goods Sold = Beginning Inventory + Purchases − Ending Inventory
                   = $2,280 + $8,920 − $3,200
                   = $8,000 (or 200 units × $40)

1992: Average Cost per Unit = [(80 × $40) + (150 × $42) + (90 × $43)] ÷ (80 + 150 + 90)
                             = $13,370 ÷ 320
                             = $41.78 (rounded)

Ending Inventory = Number of Units × Average Cost per Unit
                  = 100 × $41.78
                  = $4,178

Cost of Goods Sold = Beginning Inventory + Purchases − Ending Inventory
                   = $3,200 + $10,170 − $4,178
                   = $9,192 (or 220 units × $41.78)

(c) *Last-in, First-out*

1991: Beginning Inventory = 60 units @ $30 per unit
                           = $1,800

Purchases = 100 units @ $40 per unit + 120 units @ $41 per unit
           = $8,920

Ending Inventory = 60 units @ $30 per unit + 20 units @ $40 per unit
                  = $2,600

Cost of Goods Sold = Beginning Inventory + Purchases − Ending Inventory
                    = $1,800 + $8,920 − $2,600
                    = $8,120

1992: Beginning Inventory = 60 units @ $30 per unit + 20 units @ $40 per unit
                           = $2,600

Purchases = 150 units @ $42 per unit + 90 units @ $43 per unit
           = $10,170

Ending Inventory = 60 units @ $30 per unit + 20 units @ $40 per unit + 20 units
                    @ $42 per unit
                  = $3,440

Cost of Goods Sold = Beginning Inventory + Purchases − Ending Inventory
                    = $2,600 + $10,170 − $3,440
                    = $9,330

Glossary

Average Cost. An inventory cost flow assumption in which an average cost for the period is calculated and assigned to the number of units in cost of goods sold and ending inventory.

Consignee. The company that receives goods to sell on consignment without taking ownership.

Consignor.   The company that ships goods to a retailer to sell on consignment without relinquishing ownership.

FIFO.   An inventory cost flow assumption in which the first costs incurred (including the beginning inventory) during a period are assigned to cost of goods sold, and the latest costs are assigned to ending inventory.

FOB Destination.   Terms for shipping goods in which transfer of ownership occurs at the point of destination.

FOB Shipping Point.   Terms for shipping goods in which transfer of ownership occurs at the original shipping point.

Gross Profit Method.   A method of estimating the cost of ending inventory by applying the historical gross profit rate to net sales of the current period to compute the estimated gross profit. The estimated gross profit is deducted from the net sales to determine the estimated cost of goods sold. The estimated cost of goods sold is deducted from cost of goods available for sale to give the estimated ending inventory.

Holding Gain.   The illusory profit that results from recording cost of goods sold at lower historical costs than the replacement cost of the items sold. Also called *inventory profit*.

Inventory.   Items being held for sale in the ordinary course of business. Sometimes called *merchandise inventory*. In the case of a manufacturing company, inventory also includes items being held for use in the production process or items that are in the process of production.

Inventory Tags.   Attached to items of inventory during the taking of a physical inventory to ensure that each item is counted only once.

LIFO.   An inventory cost flow assumption in which the latest costs incurred during a period are assigned to cost of goods sold, and the earliest costs are assigned to ending inventory.

Periodic Inventory System.   A system of accounting for inventory in which a continuous record of the physical quantities (and costs) is not maintained.

Perpetual Inventory System.   A system of accounting for inventory in which a continuous record of the physical quantities (and costs) on hand and sold is maintained.

Physical Inventory.   The counting of the physical quantity of each item held in inventory.

Replacement Cost.   The cost of replacing (purchasing) an item of inventory.

Retail Inventory Method.   A method of accounting for inventory commonly used by retail companies in which the ending inventory is calculated on the basis of retail prices, and is then converted to cost by use of a cost-to-retail ratio.

Specific Identification.   A method of assigning costs to cost of goods sold and ending inventory by identifying a specific cost incurred with each unit sold and on hand.

Trade Discount.   A reduction in invoice price below the catalog or list price.

Questions

QUESTION 9-1   If the ending inventory of 1991 is understated, what effect does the understatement have on the financial statements for 1991 and 1992?

QUESTION 9-2   Describe the periodic inventory system. How does it differ from the perpetual inventory system? What are the advantages of each system?

QUESTION 9-3   In which of the following types of businesses would a perpetual inventory system be practical: (a) an automobile dealer, (b) an auto parts store, (c) a bookstore, and (d) a restaurant?

QUESTION 9-4   What is the Purchases account used for? Is it used with the periodic or perpetual inventory system?

QUESTION 9-5   What is the Purchases Returns and Allowances account used for? How does the amount in the account affect the income statement?

QUESTION 9-6   What is the purpose of taking a physical inventory? How often should a physical inventory be taken?

QUESTION 9-7   Company X purchases units of inventory under terms FOB destination from Company Y, and the goods are still in transit. Which company should include the units in inventory? How would your answer change if the purchase had been made under terms of FOB shipping point?

QUESTION 9-8   A company purchases inventory for $10,000 under terms of 1/10, n/30. How much is the discount that is available? When must payment be made to receive the discount?

QUESTION 9-9   Describe the difference between the gross method and the net method of accounting for purchases discounts. Which method provides more useful information to management? Explain.

QUESTION 9-10   How is the cost of the ending inventory determined under the FIFO cost flow assumption? Average cost? LIFO? Does the use of a particular method affect the quantities included in the ending inventory?

QUESTION 9-11   If costs are rising, which cost flow assumption will give the lowest net income in the current accounting period? The highest net income? The lowest ending inventory cost? The highest ending inventory cost? An ending inventory cost closest to the current replacement cost?

QUESTION 9-12   What are the advantages and disadvantages of the specific identification method?

QUESTION 9-13   Why might the management of a company choose the LIFO cost flow assumption even though its use causes the company's net income to be lower?

QUESTION 9-14   What is a holding gain? Why do some users of financial statements believe holding gains should be excluded from net income?

QUESTION 9-15   If the ending inventory for 1991 is valued at market under the lower of cost or market rule, what is the effect on the financial statements for 1991? 1992? What is the meaning of the term *market?*

QUESTION 9-16   Describe how ending inventory is estimated using the gross profit method. When might this method be used?

QUESTION 9-17   Describe how ending inventory is computed under the retail inventory method. What is the advantage of this method?

QUESTION 9-18   What is meant by the phrase "inventory errors correct themselves"? If the errors correct themselves, why are users of financial statements concerned with them?

Exercises

EXERCISE 9-1   **Cost of Goods Sold.** The following information for the Clark Racquetball Equipment Company is available:

Beginning inventory	$12,000
Sales	62,000
Purchases	33,000
Purchases returns and allowances	1,100
Purchases discounts taken	700
Transportation-in	500
Ending inventory	10,000

REQUIRED   Compute the cost of goods available for sale, the cost of goods sold, and the gross profit.

EXERCISE 9-2   **Beginning Inventory.** The following information of the Mears Garden Bulb Company is available:

Sales	$80,000
Purchases	35,000
Purchases discounts taken	600
Sales returns and allowances	1,000
Ending inventory	22,000
Cost of goods sold	38,000

REQUIRED   Compute the beginning inventory and the gross profit.

EXERCISE 9-3   **Perpetual and Periodic Inventory.** The financial statements of the Steward Retail Cement Company include the following information:

Beginning inventory	$20,000
Sales	70,000
Purchases	45,000
Ending inventory	10,000

REQUIRED   Assuming that all purchases and sales are for cash, prepare journal entries to record the purchases, sales, and closing entries for the period if the company uses (1) the perpetual inventory system and (2) the periodic inventory system.

EXERCISE 9-4   **Items Included in Inventory.** While taking a physical inventory for the Hawthorn Jewelry Company you discover the following items:

1. Purchases ordered FOB destination are in transit.

2. Purchases ordered FOB shipping point are in transit.

3. Items for sale are being held on consignment by the company.

4. An item of inventory is ready for shipment on the last day of the fiscal year. A completed order for the product from the customer had been received.

REQUIRED   Indicate whether each item should be included in the ending inventory. Explain your reasoning.

EXERCISE 9-5   **Purchases Discounts.**   The Collins Garage Door Company purchased $57,000 of doors during the year on terms of 2/10, n/30. The company took advantage of the discount on 70% of the purchases. It paid for the remainder after the discount period had expired. The company uses the periodic inventory system.

REQUIRED   1.   Prepare journal entries to record the purchases and both payments under (a) the gross method and (b) the net method.

2.   If half the purchases are still in the inventory at the end of the year, what is the cost of the ending inventory under both methods?

EXERCISE 9-6   **Alternative Cost Flow Assumptions.**   The Moss Picture Frame Company uses the perpetual inventory system and makes the following purchases and sales of frames during March:

March	1	Inventory	100 units @ $ 9 = $ 900
	5	Purchases	50 units @ $10 = 500
	12	Sales	40 units
	23	Purchases	80 units @ $13 = 1,040
	26	Sales	70 units

REQUIRED   Compute the cost of goods sold and ending inventory if the company uses:

1.   The FIFO cost flow assumption.

2.   The LIFO cost flow assumption.

EXERCISE 9-7   **Alternative Cost Flow Assumptions.**   The Foyt Pottery Company uses the periodic inventory system and makes the following purchases and sales of pots during September:

Sept.	1	Inventory	310 units @ $27 = $8,370
	10	Purchases	100 units @ $30 = 3,000
	15	Sales	150 units
	22	Purchases	90 units @ $33 = 2,970
	28	Sales	150 units

REQUIRED   Compute the ending inventory and cost of goods sold if the company uses:

1.   The FIFO cost flow assumption.

2.   The average cost flow assumption.

3.   The LIFO cost flow assumption.

EXERCISE 9-8   **Periodic and Perpetual Inventory Systems and FIFO and LIFO.**   The Schukter Tape Company makes the following purchases and sales of tapes during May:

May	1	Inventory	250 units @ $10 = $2,500
	5	Purchases	150 units @ $11 = 1,650
	12	Sales	160 units
	22	Purchases	150 units @ $12 = 1,800
	25	Sales	80 units

REQUIRED   Compute the ending inventory and the cost of goods sold if the company uses:

1. The periodic inventory system and the FIFO cost flow assumption.
2. The periodic inventory system and the LIFO cost flow assumption.
3. The perpetual inventory system and the FIFO cost flow assumption.
4. The perpetual inventory system and the LIFO cost flow assumption.

EXERCISE 9-9   **Lower of Cost or Market.**   The Brabham Kite Company had the following costs and replacement cost of kites in its inventory:

Item	Number of Units	Unit Cost	Unit Replacement Cost
804	100	$10	$11
603	150	12	10
331	320	8	5
928	70	20	22

REQUIRED
1. Compute the value of the ending inventory under the lower of cost or market method, applied to the individual items.
2. How will the financial statements be affected by the application of the lower of cost or market method?
3. Show how the ending inventory would be reported on the balance sheet.

EXERCISE 9-10   **Gross Profit Method.**   On March 31, 1991, the Ireland Peat Company needed to estimate its ending inventory for preparation of its first quarter's financial statements. The following information is available:

Inventory, January 1, 1991	$30,000
Purchases (net)	40,000
Sales (net)	85,000

An examination of past income statements indicates that a gross profit rate of 25% of net sales is appropriate.

REQUIRED   Compute the cost of goods sold and the ending inventory.

EXERCISE 9-11   **Retail Inventory Method.**   The Hunt Hat Boutique uses the retail inventory method. At the end of the year, the following information is available:

	Cost	Retail
Beginning inventory	$10,000	$20,000
Purchases (net)	20,000	40,000
Sales (net)		30,000

REQUIRED Compute the cost of the ending inventory and the gross profit using the retail inventory method.

EXERCISE 9-12   **Errors.**   The Jones Drilling Company had a beginning inventory of $30,000, net purchases of $50,000, an ending inventory of $25,000, and sales of $80,000.

REQUIRED   1. Compute the cost of goods sold.

2. If an error was made in the physical inventory and the ending inventory should have been $32,000, what is the correct cost of goods sold? What is the percentage change in the gross profit?

3. What is the effect of the error in Requirement 2 on the financial statements of the next year?

Problems

Part A

PROBLEM 9-1A   **Cost of Goods Sold.**   The Redman Company uses the FIFO cost flow assumption, and the following summary information was available at the end of the year:

Purchase discounts

Beginning inventory	$25,000
Purchases	60,000
Sales	92,000
Transportation-in	1,500
Sales discounts taken	3,000
Purchases returns and allowances	4,500
Sales returns and allowances	2,000
Ordering costs	500
Ending inventory	28,000

 30,000

The company followed a policy of expensing the ordering costs rather than allocating them to the units of inventory. Discounts of 2/10, n/30 were available on all the purchases, but the company took advantage of only half of them. The purchases returns and allowances were for items on which discounts were not taken. The company uses the gross method of accounting for discounts.

REQUIRED   1. Prepare an income statement through to the calculation of gross profit.

2. The management of the company is considering changing from the FIFO method. It estimates that the ending inventory under average cost and LIFO would have been $20,000 and $15,000 respectively. What would the percentage increase or decrease in the gross profit be from changing to each alternative?

PROBLEM 9-2A   **Purchases Discounts.** The Gurney Gravel Company purchased inventory for $20,000 on terms of 2/10, n/30. The company paid for half the purchase within 10 days and paid for the remainder after the discount period had expired. The company uses the periodic inventory system.

REQUIRED

1. Prepare journal entries to record the preceding events using (a) the gross method and (b) the net method of accounting for purchases discounts.

2. If the company sold half the inventory for $25,000, how much would its gross profit be under each method?

3. How much would the gross profit be if the company deducted all the discounts available from the cost of the inventory under each method?

PROBLEM 9-3A   **Alternative Cost Flow Assumptions: Periodic.** The Ginther Power Tool Company made the following purchases and sales of air compressors during January and February and uses the periodic inventory system:

Jan. 1	Inventory	100 units
10	Purchases	50 units for $100 each
20	Purchases	40 units for $102 each
Feb. 5	Purchases	20 units for $104 each
18	Purchases	60 units for $108 each

Sales during January and February were 80 units and 100 units, respectively. The FIFO, average, and LIFO cost of each unit in the beginning inventory was $97, $95, and $62, respectively.

REQUIRED

1. Compute the ending inventory and the cost of goods sold for each month if the company uses:
   (a) The FIFO cost flow assumption.
   (b) The average cost flow assumption.
   (c) The LIFO cost flow assumption.

2. Which cost flow assumption provides the more realistic balance sheet valuation? Which provides the more realistic measure of income? Why?

PROBLEM 9-4A   **Alternative Cost Flow Assumptions: Perpetual.** The Russell Video Company made the following purchases and sales of videos during April and May, and uses the perpetual inventory system.

Apr. 1	Inventory	200 units
9	Purchases	20 units for $15 each
17	Sales	30 units
24	Purchases	50 units for $16 each
26	Sales	20 units
May 8	Sales	30 units
15	Purchases	60 units for $17 each
22	Sales	50 units

The FIFO and LIFO cost of each unit in the beginning inventory was $12 and $8, respectively.

1. Compute the cost of goods sold and the ending inventory for each month if the company uses:
   (a) The FIFO cost flow assumption.
   (b) The LIFO cost flow assumption.

2. Which cost flow assumption provides the more realistic balance sheet valuation? Which provides the more realistic measure of income? Why?

PROBLEM 9-5A **Lower of Cost or Market.** The Seaman Company's ending inventory of vacuum cleaner parts included the following items:

Item	Number of Units	Unit Cost	Unit Replacement Cost
A12B	50	$100	$90
L15C	150	76	82
P27X	200	60	55
W08S	400	10	9

1. Compute the value of the ending inventory under the lower of cost or market rule applied to individual items.

2. Prepare the journal entry to record the reduction of the inventory to its market value.

3. Show how the ending inventory would be reported on the balance sheet.

4. If the lower of cost or market method is applied to the inventory as a whole, how would your answer to Requirement 1 change?

5. If at the end of the next year none of the items in inventory has a market value below cost, how will the financial statements for the second year be affected by the application of the lower of cost or market method in the first year?

PROBLEM 9-6A **Retail Inventory Method.** The Scheckter Department Store uses the retail inventory method. At the end of the first quarter, the following information was available:

	Cost	Retail
Inventory, Jan. 1	$15,000	$18,000
Purchases	47,000	86,000
Purchases returns	3,000	4,000
Sales		90,000
Sales returns		5,000

1. Compute the cost of the ending inventory and the gross profit for the first quarter.

2. If the company took a physical inventory at the end of the first quarter and the retail value was $12,000, what is the cost of the ending inventory?

3. What may have caused the difference in the answers for Requirements 1 and 2?

PROBLEM 9-7A   **Gross Profit Method.**   The Lotus Tire Company estimates its ending inventory for its quarterly financial statements by using the gross profit method. The following information is available:

	First Quarter	Second Quarter
Inventory, Jan. 1	$30,000	
Purchases	38,000	$50,000
Purchases returns	3,000	5,000
Sales	70,000	80,000
Sales returns	3,000	2,000

The company uses a gross profit rate of 30% of net sales.

REQUIRED   Compute the cost of goods sold and the ending inventory for each quarter.

PROBLEM 9-8A   **Errors.**   The accounting records of the Hill Water Heater Company, which uses the periodic inventory system, showed the following information at the end of the year:

Beginning inventory	$ 21,500
Purchases	42,000
Purchases returns	1,500
Sales	110,000
Sales returns	3,000
Ending inventory	22,000

REQUIRED   1. Using an income statement format compute the cost of goods sold and the gross profit.

2. Suppose a mistake was made in taking the physical inventory and the ending inventory should be $18,000. Using an income statement format compute the resulting cost of goods sold and the gross profit.

3. A purchase of $2,500 was erroneously recorded at $5,200. What is the effect of the error on the financial statements of the current year? (The answer to Requirement 3 is independent of the answer to Requirement 2.)

Problems

Part B

PROBLEM 9-1B   **Cost of Goods Sold.**   The Perth Company uses the LIFO cost flow assumption and the periodic inventory system. The following summary information was available at the end of the year:

Beginning inventory	$15,000
Purchases	75,000
Sales	97,000
Transportation-in	1,500
Sales discounts taken	1,000
Purchases returns and allowances	3,000
Sales returns and allowances	4,000
Ordering costs	500
Ending inventory	28,000

The company followed a policy of expensing its ordering costs rather than allocating them to the units of inventory. Discounts of 1/10, n/30 were available on all the purchases, but the company took advantage of only 60% of them. The purchases returns and allowances were for items on which discounts were not taken. The company uses the gross method of accounting for discounts.

REQUIRED

1. Prepare an income statement through to the calculation of gross profit.

2. The management at Perth is considering changing from the LIFO method. It estimates that the ending inventory would have been $34,000 under FIFO and $30,000 under average cost. What would be the percentage increase or decrease in the gross profit from changing to each alternative?

PROBLEM 9-2B   **Purchases Discounts.**   The Bellemere Baby Clothes Company purchased inventory for $80,000 on terms of 2/10, n/30. The company paid for one-half the purchases within 10 days and paid for the remainder after the discount period had expired. The company uses the periodic inventory system.

REQUIRED

1. Prepare journal entries to record the preceding events using (a) the gross method and (b) the net method of accounting for purchases discounts.

2. If the company sold half the inventory for $50,000, how much would its gross profit be under each method?

3. How much would the gross profit be if the company deducted all the discounts available from the cost of the inventory under each method?

PROBLEM 9-3B   **Alternative Cost Flow Assumptions: Periodic.**   The Johnson Company made the following purchases and sales of watches during July and August, and uses the periodic inventory system:

July 1	Inventory	300 units
8	Purchases	40 units for $20 each
27	Purchases	100 units for $21 each
Aug. 18	Purchases	50 units for $22 each
24	Purchases	60 units for $23 each

Sales during July and August were 200 units and 150 units, respectively. The FIFO, average, and LIFO inventory cost of each unit in the beginning inventory was $19, $18, and $13, respectively.

REQUIRED

1. Compute the ending inventory and the cost of goods sold for each month if the company uses:
   (a) The FIFO cost flow assumption.
   (b) The average cost flow assumption.
   (c) The LIFO cost flow assumption.

2. Which cost flow assumption provides the more realistic balance sheet valuation? Which provides the more realistic measure of income? Why?

PROBLEM 9-4B   **Alternative Cost Flow Assumptions: Perpetual.**   The Caldwell Company made the following purchases and sales of electric motors during November and December and uses the perpetual inventory system.

Nov. 1	Inventory	50 units
12	Sales	40 units
20	Purchases	100 units for $65 each
29	Sales	80 units
Dec. 4	Purchases	100 units for $75 each
10	Purchases	50 units for $80 each
16	Sales	140 units

The FIFO and LIFO cost of each unit in the beginning inventory was $64 and $50, respectively.

REQUIRED   1. Compute the cost of goods sold and the ending inventory for each month if the company uses:
    (a) The FIFO cost flow assumption.
    (b) The LIFO cost flow assumption.

2. Which cost flow assumption provides the more realistic balance sheet valuation? Which provides the more realistic measure of income? Why?

PROBLEM 9-5B   **Lower of Cost or Market.**   The Thodes Company's ending inventory of electrical equipment included the following items:

Item	Number of Units	Unit Cost	Unit Replacement Cost
SP5	30	$500	$400
CX3	300	65	70
TL9	95	220	180
FN6	250	80	90

REQUIRED   1. Compute the value of the ending inventory under the lower of cost or market rule applied to the inventory as a whole.

2. Prepare the journal entry to record the reduction of the inventory to its market value.

3. Show how the ending inventory would be reported on the balance sheet.

4. If the lower of cost or market method is applied to the inventory on an individual item basis, how would your answer to Requirement 1 change?

5. If at the end of the next year none of the items in inventory has a market value below cost, how will the financial statements for the second year be affected by the application of the lower of cost or market method in the first year?

PROBLEM 9-6B **Retail Inventory Method.** The Burris Department Store uses the retail inventory method. At the end of the first quarter, the following information was available:

	Cost	Retail
Inventory, January 1	$ 5,000	$ 9,000
Purchases	35,000	68,000
Purchases returns	2,000	3,000
Sales		65,000
Sales returns		2,000

REQUIRED

1. Compute the cost of the ending inventory and the gross profit for the first quarter.

2. If the company took a physical inventory at the end of the first quarter and the retail value was $10,000, what is the cost of the ending inventory?

3. What may have caused the difference in the answers for Requirements 1 and 2?

PROBLEM 9-7B **Gross Profit Method.** The Williams Fire Alarm Company estimates its ending inventory for its quarterly financial statements by using the gross profit method. The following information is available:

	First Quarter	Second Quarter	Third Quarter
Inventory, January 1	$20,000		
Purchases	50,000	$55,000	$ 64,000
Purchases returns	1,000	2,000	1,000
Sales	98,000	94,000	102,000
Sales returns	3,000	1,000	2,000

The company used a gross profit rate of 40% of net sales in the first two quarters, but in the third quarter the company's estimated gross profit rate decreased 10%. The company did not increase its prices, however.

REQUIRED Compute the cost of goods sold and the ending inventory for each quarter.

PROBLEM 9-8B **Errors.** The accounting records of the Kirkpatrick Foam Insulation Company, which uses the periodic inventory system, showed the following information at the end of the year:

Beginning inventory	$ 35,000
Purchases	85,000
Purchases returns	3,000
Sales	160,000
Sales returns	2,000
Ending inventory	46,000

REQUIRED

1. Using an income statement format compute the cost of goods sold and the gross profit.

2. Suppose a mistake was made in taking the physical inventory and the ending inventory has a cost of $40,000. Using an income statement format compute the resulting cost of goods sold and the gross profit.

3. A purchase of $6,200 was erroneously recorded at $2,600. What is the effect of the error on the cost of goods sold, gross profit, and ending inventory? (The answer to Requirement 3 is independent of the answer to Requirement 2.)

Decision Cases

DECISION CASE 9-1   **Estimate of Inventory Lost in Theft.**   When Janet Guthrie arrived at her dress shop on the morning of June 15, 1992, she found that thieves had broken in overnight and stolen much of her merchandise. The agent of the Alright Insurance Company agreed to visit in the afternoon and promised he would write a check for the amount of the loss if she could verify it. Since it would be very time-consuming to take a physical inventory, Ms. Guthrie needed to make an estimate of the loss so that she could collect the insurance money and buy new merchandise. She asked for your help and you agreed to look at her accounting records. She told you that the store had been in business since January 1, 1991, and she does not use the retail method of accounting. You obtain the following information:

Inventory, January 1, 1991	$ 7,000
Purchases, 1991	43,000
Purchases, 1992	30,000
Sales (net), 1991	80,000
Sales (net), 1992	50,000
Delivery charges on purchases, 1991	2,000
Delivery charges on purchases, 1992	1,500
Inventory, January 1, 1992	16,000

REQUIRED   How much would you recommend that Ms. Guthrie settle for with the insurance company? What is the major assumption underlying your answer?

DECISION CASE 9-2   **Inventory and Holding Gains.**   The Birkin Company uses the FIFO inventory cost flow assumption. The following amounts are included in the company's financial statements:

Inventory, January 1	$100,000
Purchases	300,000
Cost of goods sold	250,000
Inventory, December 31	150,000

The company sells only one product, and purchases and sales are made evenly throughout the year. The replacement cost of the inventory at January 1 and December 31 is $125,000 and $187,500, respectively. The cost of the company's purchases was 25% higher at the end of the year than at the beginning.

REQUIRED   The owner of the Birkin Company asks you to analyze the preceding information and tell her the following:

1. How much would the cost of goods sold be if it were computed on the basis of the average replacement cost for the period?

2. What is the holding gain (inventory profit) included in the income computed on a FIFO basis?

3. Did the number of units in inventory increase or decrease during the year?

DECISION CASE 9-3 **Alternative Cost Flow Assumptions.** K Mart Corporation reported the following information in its 1988 financial statements relating to inventories (amounts in millions of dollars):

A summary of inventories by method of pricing and the excess of current cost over stated LIFO values follows:

	January 25, 1989	January 27, 1988
Last-in, first-out (cost not in excess of market)	$5,090	$5,104
Lower of cost (first-in, first-out) or market	581	467
Total	$5,671	$5,571
Excess of current cost over stated LIFO value	$ 898	$ 738

REQUIRED

1. Why does K Mart use the end of January, rather than December 31, for its balance sheet date?

2. Why does K Mart use both the LIFO and FIFO cost flow assumptions? Is this permissible under generally accepted accounting principles?

3. Why does K Mart only report the excess of current cost over the LIFO inventory value and not the FIFO value?

DECISION CASE 9-4 **Classification of Inventories.** UST reported the following information in its 1988 financial statements (amounts in thousands of dollars):

Inventories	1988	1987
Leaf tobacco	$ 85,934	$ 76,208
Products in process and finished goods	72,225	70,764
Other materials and supplies	16,663	15,275
	$174,822	$162,247

Leaf tobacco and wine inventories are included in current assets . . . notwithstanding the fact that such inventories are carried for several years for the purpose of curing and aging.

REQUIRED

1. Is the treatment of leaf tobacco and wine as a current asset in accordance with generally accepted accounting principles?

2. How would the alternative treatment as a noncurrent asset affect the evaluation of a user of the financial statements?

10

Current Liabilities
and Payrolls

LEARNING OBJECTIVES

1. Describe unearned revenue.

2. Record accrued liabilities including (a) warranty liability, (b) sales tax payable, (c) property taxes payable, and (d) income taxes payable.

3. Explain how to account for contingencies.

4. Describe a note payable and compute interest on the note.

5. Explain how to account for money borrowed from a bank.

6. Explain (a) payroll accounting, including (b) federal income taxes, (c) social security taxes, and (d) unemployment taxes.

7. Describe how to record the payroll, including use of the payroll register.

n the previous three chapters the current assets of cash, accounts and notes receivable, and inventory were discussed. The concept of working capital (current assets minus current liabilities) was introduced earlier in the book. In this chapter current liabilities are discussed. **Current liabilities are liabilities that will be paid, or eliminated, within one year or the normal operating cycle, whichever is longer.**

In the normal course of their operating activities companies incur many current liabilities. Some of these liabilities have been discussed previously as they arose through purchases, such as accounts payable, or through accruing expenses at the end of the year. Others include unearned revenue, warranty liabilities, and sales tax payable. To finance operations companies often borrow money for short periods of time. Accounting for these notes payable is also discussed in this chapter. Finally, accounting for payroll and the accompanying liabilities is discussed.

Purchasing on Credit

As explained in Chapter 8 companies often sell on credit to customers. These credit sales result in accounts receivable. Similarly, companies often make purchases on credit, which give rise to either accounts payable or notes payable. (Accounting for purchases was discussed in Chapter 9.) The reasons for purchasing on credit are similar to the reasons for selling on credit. The first reason is that it is often more convenient to purchase on credit than for cash. For example, if a company places an order with a supplier and the supplier ships the goods, the purchaser records the inventory when it acquires legal ownership. At this point a liability is also created and remains outstanding until the purchaser pays the supplier, usually by mailing a check.

The second reason for purchasing on credit is to delay paying for purchases and, by so doing, obtaining a short-term "loan" from the supplier. Many companies, particularly small companies, often suffer from a cash shortage and find it difficult to pay for their purchases immediately. The management of the company therefore tries to delay payment until the cash is received from the eventual sale of the product; it then uses this cash to pay the liability created by the purchase. This delay is the reason why many suppliers offer cash discounts to encourage prompt payment.

Since accounts payable and notes payable for one company are accounts receivable and notes receivable for another company, the accounting for the liabilities is virtually a "mirror image" of accounting for the assets. Accounting for accounts and notes receivable was discussed in Chapter 8, and it may be useful to refer to this chapter to reinforce the similarities. In addition, accounts payable and accrued liabilities have been included in parts of previous chapters, and therefore only a brief review of these items is included in this chapter. It is useful for the reader, however, to understand clearly the nature of these current liabilities which appear on the balance sheet.

Accounts Payable

Accounts payable is the title of the liability created by the normal activities of a company in purchasing items such as inventory and supplies. The liability is recorded at the same time as the inventory is recorded, as discussed in Chapter 9; that is, when the inventory (or invoice) is received if the terms are FOB destination, or when it is shipped if the terms are FOB shipping point. When the liability is recorded, the Purchases (or Inventory) account is increased (debited) and Accounts Payable is increased (credited). If the gross method of accounting for purchases discounts is used, the purchases and the accounts payable are recorded at the gross amount. If the purchases discounts lost method (the net method) is used, they are recorded at the net amount.

Unearned Revenue and Accrued Liabilities

Many of the operating activities of a company lead to current liabilities being incurred. Interest payable and wages payable are discussed later in the chapter in the sections on notes payable and payroll accounting. One type of current liability is unearned revenue. **Unearned revenue is the liability representing an obligation to provide goods and services in the future as a result of receiving cash in advance.** Another type of current liability is an accrued liability. **An accrued liability represents an obligation at the end of the period that has arisen during the accounting period but has not yet been paid or recorded.** Several accrued liabilities have arisen in transactions discussed earlier in the book. These liabilities were called accrued expenses in Chapter 4 because then we were focusing on matching expenses and revenues. In this chapter we use the term *accrued liabilities* because we are focusing on the liability portion of the journal entry. Unearned revenue and commonly occurring accrued liabilities are discussed in the following sections.

Unearned Revenue

1. Describe unearned revenue.

A company usually receives payment from a customer at the time of the sale or after the sale. A company, however, may require payment in advance for an item it will sell in the future. In this situation revenue should not be recorded by the company at the time of the cash receipt because the service or product has not yet been provided. A liability, unearned revenue, is created instead because the company has an obligation to provide goods or services in the future. When the goods are sold or the services are provided in the future the revenue is recognized.

A common example involves magazine publishing companies, which require the subscriber to pay the subscription in advance. When the cash is received by the company it has performed no service because it has not sent any magazines to the subscriber; therefore it should not recognize any revenue. Instead, when the cash is received by the company a liability (unearned revenue) is created that represents the obligation to deliver magazines in the future.

The liability is reduced each time the publishing company delivers a magazine. As the liability is reduced, revenue could be recognized. As discussed in Chapter 4, however, it may be more efficient for the company to wait until the end of the accounting period and record all of the revenue earned by that date by means of an adjusting entry. For example, suppose that the Outdoors

Publishing Company receives a check for $36 from Susan Chamberlain for a subscription for 12 issues of Outdoor magazine. The journal entry to record the cash receipt is:

Cash	36	
Subscriptions Collected in Advance		36
To record subscription received for 1 year from Susan Chamberlain.		

The Subscriptions Collected in Advance account is a current liability representing the unearned revenue related to the subscription. At the end of the period the liability is reduced based on the number of magazines delivered. If five issues have been delivered to Susan Chamberlain, the liability is reduced by $15 ($36 × 5/12) and is recorded as follows:

Subscriptions Collected in Advance	15	
Subscriptions Revenue		15
To record revenue at year end.		

Subscriptions Revenue would be included in the revenues section of the income statement and the remaining $21 ($36 – $15) balance in Subscriptions Collected in Advance is a current liability in the ending balance sheet. This illustration is for a single subscriber, but in practice the company would make a single adjusting entry to recognize revenue for the period from delivering magazines to all its customers.

Other examples are the collection of premiums by an insurance company and the collection of advance payments for air fares by an airline.

Warranties

2(a). Record warranty liability.

When a company offers a warranty on a product it sells, it agrees to repair or replace the product for a specified period of time. **The cost of providing the warranty should be matched against the revenues in the period of the sale.** For example, suppose that a company incurs warranty costs of $8,000 in the same period as the sales were made. The journal entry is as follows:

Warranty Expense	8,000	
Cash (or Inventory)		8,000
To record fulfillment of warranty.		

If the warranties on the products sold during the current period have not expired at the end of the period, the expected cost of fulfilling the warranties in future periods should be recognized as an expense of the current period. Again, matching requires that a cost associated with making a sale should be recognized as an expense in the period in which the sale is made. The costs of fulfilling the terms of the unexpired warranty are not known in the period of the sale, however, and therefore must be estimated. For example, suppose the company has 540 warranties still outstanding at the end of the current period and it expects to incur an average cost of $10 on each. The journal entry at the end of the year to record these estimated future warranty costs is as follows:

Warranty Expense (540 x $10)	5,400	
Warranty Liability		5,400
To record liability for future warranty costs.		

The warranty expense is included in the income statement as a selling expense, and the balance in the warranty liability account is included as a current liability on the ending balance sheet.

Sales Tax

2(b). Record sales tax payable.

Most states impose a sales tax on many types of products sold in the state. The tax is typically collected by the seller from the customer at the time of the sale and is paid to the state at a later date. Since the company is acting as a collection agency for the state, at the time of the sale there is no revenue or expense to the company with respect to the sales tax. The collection of the tax from the customer creates a liability for the company because it has received cash that it owes to the state. The liability is eliminated when payment is made to the state. For example, if a company makes sales of $20,000 and there is a sales tax of 5%, the summary journal entries to record the collection of the sales tax from customers at the time of the sale and the later payment of the tax to the state are as follows:

Cash (or Accounts Receivable)	21,000	
Sales		20,000
Sales Tax Payable ($20,000 x 0.05)		1,000
To record sales and related sales tax.		
Sales Tax Payable	1,000	
Cash		1,000
To record sales tax remitted to the state.		

Any unremitted Sales Tax Payable at the end of the period is reported as a current liability in the ending balance sheet.

Property Taxes

2(c). Record property taxes payable.

Property taxes are assessed by municipal, county, and some state governments on the value of property owned, such as land and buildings. On the date that the taxes are legally assessed the company owning the property has incurred a liability. The property taxes are assessed for the governmental agency's fiscal year, although this fiscal year may not coincide with a company's accounting period. Furthermore the taxes may not be assessed until the middle of the fiscal year. Whatever the taxing situation the expense associated with the taxes should be recognized over the accounting period of the *company*. For example, the city of Denver has a fiscal year of July 1 to June 30. The city assesses taxes on January 1, which is in the middle of its fiscal year. For a company with an accounting period ending December 31, this company must include a property tax expense in its calendar year income statement and also report a liability at the end of its accounting period. To do so it may have to accrue the expense before the actual assessed taxes are known. Fortunately, because tax rates are well publicized and not subject to sudden changes, a company can usually make an accurate estimate of its future property taxes. In the previous example, at December 31, 1991, it is necessary to recognize an expense for the July 1 to December 31, 1991, portion of the property taxes. (The January 1 to June 30, 1991, property taxes would be known and would already have been expensed on the basis of the tax assessment paid from the previous year.) If the company estimates its annual property taxes to be $5,000, one-half, or $2,500, would be recorded as follows:

Property Tax Expense	2,500	
Property Tax Payable		2,500

To accrue property taxes.

The property tax expense should be included on the income statement in the same section of the statement as the depreciation expense of the asset on which the taxes are being paid. Thus it might be included as a selling or as a general and administrative expense. Property Tax Payable is a current liability on the ending balance sheet. When the property taxes are paid in the next accounting period, the liability is eliminated and the remaining part of the payment is an expense for that accounting period. The payment is recorded as follows:

Property Tax Payable	2,500	
Property Tax Expense	2,500	
Cash		5,000

To record payment of assessed property taxes.

Income Taxes

A corporation is required to compute the income tax expense related to its *income before income taxes* for the accounting period. Since the payment usually takes place after the end of the accounting period, the company accrues an expense and a liability through an adjusting entry at the end of the period as follows (using assumed amounts):

Income Tax Expense	9,200	
Income Taxes Payable		9,200

To accrue income taxes.

2(d). Record income taxes payable.

Individuals typically pay income taxes each pay period (as discussed later) and settle their income tax obligation once a year. In contrast, corporations usually are required to pay income taxes every quarter. Since corporations often prepare quarterly financial statements, the expense and amount payable are recognized each quarter. The income tax expense is deducted from income before income taxes to determine the quarterly net income. The income tax liability would be included as a current liability on the balance sheet at the end of the quarter. When the income taxes are paid the liability is eliminated. Income taxes are discussed more fully in Chapter 15.

Contingencies

A contingency is an existing condition that involves uncertainty as to a possible gain or loss that will ultimately be resolved when a future event occurs (or fails to occur). Two contingencies have already been covered in this book. In Chapter 8 accounting for bad debts was discussed. Selling on credit creates a contingency because there is an existing condition (the receivable is owed by the customer) and there is uncertainty as to a possible loss (the amount of the bad debts expense). Earlier in this chapter warranties were discussed. Offering a

3. Explain how to account for contingencies

warranty creates a contingency because there is an existing condition (the warranty is in effect) and there is uncertainty as to a possible loss (the amount of the warranty expense).

Generally accepted accounting principles focus on *loss* contingencies (such as the bad debts and warranty expenses). The likelihood of the future event occurring has three levels, as follows:

1. *Probable*. The chance of the future event occurring is *likely*.
2. *Reasonably possible*. The chance of the future event occurring is *more* than remote but *less* than likely.
3. *Remote*. The chance of the future event occurring is *slight*.

The two methods of accounting for loss contingencies depend on the degree of certainty that is associated with the future event, as follows:

1. *Recognition in the Financial Statements*. An estimated loss from a loss contingency *must* be reported in the financial statements as a reduction of income (loss or expense) and a liability (or a reduction of an asset) if *both* of the following conditions are met:
   (a) It is probable that an asset has been impaired or a liability has been incurred.
   (b) The amount of the loss can be reasonably estimated.
2. *Disclosure in the Notes to the Financial Statements*. An estimated loss from a loss contingency is reported in the notes if it is *reasonably possible* that an asset has been impaired or a liability has been incurred.

The two examples of bad debt and warranty expenses are recognized in the financial statements (as discussed earlier in the book) because they meet both criteria.

Another very commonly occurring contingency for companies results from lawsuits. When a company is a defendant in a lawsuit, a contingency exists because there is an existing condition (the lawsuit) and there is uncertainty as to a possible loss (win or loss of the lawsuit, along with the amount of any payments). Lawsuits are usually only disclosed in the notes to the financial statements because the company is either unwilling to admit that the likelihood of losing is probable or argues that the amount of any loss *cannot* be reasonably estimated.

Gain contingencies are *not* recorded in the financial statements and are rarely disclosed, regardless of the likelihood of the future event occurring. This practice follows the conservatism principle (discussed in Chapter 9).

Notes Payable

Just as companies sometimes require a note to be signed by a customer, thus creating a note receivable, so are companies also at times the customers at the other end of the transaction. That is, the officers of the company sign and deliver a note to make a purchase, borrow money, or extend the time for payment of an account payable, thus creating a liability for the company. As discussed in

4. Describe a note payable and compute interest on the note.

Chapter 8 a promissory note is a written legal document in which one party makes an unconditional promise to pay another party a certain amount of money on demand or an agreed future date. Notes payable is the account used to record promissory notes issued by a company. Another common way in which a note payable is created is when a company borrows money from a bank for a short period. Again in this situation, a note is signed and delivered to the bank when the cash is received. Each of these situations is discussed in the following sections.

Note Given to Make a Purchase or Extend Payment Time on an Account Payable

When a note is given to a supplier either to make a purchase or to extend the time allowed for payment, a note payable is recorded as a liability accompanied by recording purchases or inventory, or the removal of a liability (accounts payable). For example, suppose that on July 16, 1991, the Simba Company has a $700 account payable with the Avanti Company that is overdue and the Avanti Company agrees to accept a 12%, 90-day note. The Simba Company records the issuance of the note as follows:

1991			
July 16	Accounts Payable: Avanti Company	700	
	Notes Payable		700

To record issuance of 12%, 90-day note to extend payment on an account with Avanti Company.

Simba has not paid the debt but has simply transformed it into a more formal liability and has agreed to pay interest on the liability. When the note is paid in 90 days, interest of $21 ($700 × 12% × 90/360) is paid. At that time the following journal entry is made to record the payment of the note:

1991			
Oct. 14	Notes Payable	700	
	Interest Expense	21	
	Cash		721

To record payment of note and interest due to the Avanti Company on maturity date.

Note Given to Borrow Money from a Bank

5. Explain how to account for money borrowed from a bank.

When a bank loans money to a company, the bank requires that the interest either be paid at the maturity date of the note or be deducted from the amount of money that is paid to the company. To illustrate the accounting for the two types of loans, suppose that the Simba Company borrows $20,000 at 10% for 6 months on August 1, 1991.

Interest Paid When the Note Matures. If interest is to be paid at the maturity date of the note, the journal entry by Simba to record its borrowing is as follows:

1991			
Aug. 1	Cash	20,000	
	Notes Payable		20,000

To record issuance of 10%, $20,000, 6-month note.

No interest is recorded at the date of issuance because the Simba Company is not legally liable for interest at this time. The liability for interest accrues each day for the life of the loan. Therefore interest must be accrued at the end of the Simba Company's fiscal year on December 31, 1991, even though it will not be paid until 1992. The interest expense for 5 months and the accompanying liability are recognized as follows:

```
1991
Dec. 31   Interest Expense  ...........................................    833
              Interest Payable  .........................................           833
          To record interest expense ($20,000 × 10% × 5/12).
```

The interest expense is included in Other Revenues and Expenses on the income statement. The $833 interest payable and the $20,000 notes payable, as shown in the following T-accounts, are included as current liabilities on the ending balance sheet.

Notes Payable		Interest Payable	
8/1/91	20,000	12/31/91	833

When the note becomes due on February 1, 1992, a payment of $21,000 must be made, consisting of the principal of $20,000 and interest of $1,000 ($20,000 × 10% × 6/12). Since an interest expense of $833 has been recognized in 1991 only $167 ($20,000 × 10% × 1/12) is interest expense for 1992. The journal entry to record the payment is as follows:

```
1992
Feb. 1   Interest Payable  ...........................................    833
         Interest Expense  ...........................................    167
         Notes Payable  ..............................................  20,000
             Cash  .....................................................         21,000
         To record payment of note and interest due on maturity
         date.
```

Interest Deducted at Time of Issuance.   As shown in the preceding example, Simba Company paid $21,000 to the bank when the note matured, consisting of the $20,000 principal and interest of $1,000. Alternatively, the bank can deduct the interest from the amount owed by the borrower. In this case the note has a face value of the total principal and interest to be paid at maturity ($21,000), and the bank issues a check to the Simba Company for the net amount ($20,000) of the maturity value ($21,000) less interest ($1,000). The difference of $1,000 represents the interest to be incurred in the future over the life of the note. Since this interest is *not* an expense at the time the note is signed (remember that interest accrues over time), it is recorded in a Discount on Notes Payable account as follows:

```
1991
Aug. 1   Cash  ......................................................  20,000
         Discount on Notes Payable  ..............................   1,000
             Notes Payable  ..........................................         21,000
         To record issuance of $20,000 note at 10% for 6 months
         with interest deducted in advance.
```

The Discount on Notes Payable account (in which future interest costs on a note are recorded) is a contra-liability account because the amount borrowed is only $20,000. It is *not* a prepaid expense because the $1,000 has not yet been paid. The net amount of the liability is $20,000 and is reported in the balance sheet on the date of issuance as follows:

Notes payable	$21,000
Less: Discount on notes payable	(1,000)
	$20,000

Because the Discount on Notes Payable represents the future interest charges on the note, the Discount account is reduced whenever interest expense is recorded and therefore the balance in the account represents the future interest that still remains to be recognized. On December 31, 1991, Simba recognizes interest of $833 (calculated in the same way as before) by reducing the Discount account as follows:

1991			
Dec. 31	Interest Expense	833	
	Discount on Notes Payable		833
	To record interest expense.		

At this point the net amount of the notes payable is $20,833, which consists of the Notes Payable account of $21,000 less the remaining balance in the Discount on Notes Payable account of $167 ($1,000 − $833), as shown in the following T-accounts.

Notes Payable			*Discount on Notes Payable*		
	8/1/91 21,000	8/1/91 1,000	12/31/91 833		
		Balance 167			

This amount ($20,833) is reported as a current liability on the balance sheet. Although the $20,833 is listed as the net amount of the liability, it effectively represents the amount borrowed ($20,000) plus the interest payable to date ($833).

When the note is paid at maturity the remaining interest expense is recognized and the remaining Discount is removed because no future interest remains. The face value of the note is also eliminated by the payment of $21,000, which is recorded as follows:

1992			
Feb. 1	Interest Expense	167	
	Notes Payable	21,000	
	Discount on Notes Payable		167
	Cash		21,000
	To record payment of note on maturity date.		

Comparison of the Two Types of Loans

The two types of loans have the same effect on the financial statements because the same amount ($20,000) is borrowed for the same period at the same rate. The interest expense shown on the income statement is the same under both situations since it amounts to $167 per month, or $833 for the 5 months from August 1 through December 31, 1991, and $167 in January 1992.

The net amount of the liability included in the balance sheet is the same under both situations, but there is a slightly different classification for each type of loan as illustrated by the following partial disclosures:

Interest Paid When the Note Matures		Interest Deducted at Time of Issuance	
		August 1, 1991	
Current liabilities:		Current liabilities:	
Notes payable	$20,000	Notes payable	$21,000
		Less: Discount on notes payable	(1,000)
			$20,000
		December 31, 1991	
Current liabilities:		Current liabilities:	
Notes payable	$20,000	Notes payable	$21,000
		Less: Discount on notes payable	(167)
Interest payable	833		$20,833
	$20,833		

Payroll Accounting

6(a). Explain payroll accounting.

Payroll accounting is a very important, and often complex, aspect of a company's operations. Initially an employee's gross pay must be determined, which is based on either the length of the pay period for a salaried employee, or on the hours worked and the hourly rate of pay for an employee paid on an hourly basis. Numerous deductions are made from gross pay for such items as the employee's federal and state income taxes, federal social security taxes, and contributions to pension plans, union dues, medical insurance, and charitable contributions. These deductions are withheld from the employee, who is then paid the *net pay*. The deductions are later paid by the company to the appropriate agencies on behalf of the employees. In addition, the employer must itself pay federal social security taxes and federal and state unemployment taxes. It also may make contributions to pension plans, hospital insurance, and may match charitable contributions on behalf of employees. Each of these items is illustrated in the following diagram and discussed here.

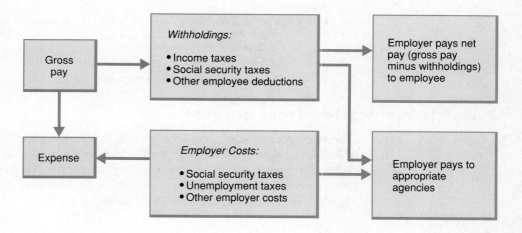

Federal and State Income Taxes

The computation of the federal and state income taxes that must be paid by individuals is very complex. The determination of the amount of the income taxes owed, as well as the payment of the income taxes, is the responsibility of the employee, not the employer. The employer, however, is required to withhold federal and state income taxes from the employee's pay and to send the money withheld at periodic intervals to the appropriate tax authorities. The purpose of this pay-as-you-go withholding of income taxes is to increase the likelihood that the taxing authorities will collect the taxes from the individual taxpayer, because if there were no withholding of taxes many individuals would not save enough to pay their taxes. Since state income tax laws vary from state to state, the discussion will focus on the federal income tax.

6(b). Explain federal income taxes.

The amount of federal income tax to be withheld from an employee's pay is a function of two factors. First, the number of exemptions (or withholding allowances) claimed by the employee affects the amount withheld. **An exemption is an exclusion of earned income from taxable income.** An individual is allowed an exemption for him- or herself (and for the spouse if a joint return is filed), and an additional exemption for each dependent. At the time of writing, each exemption results in $2,000 being exempted from taxable income. Thus an employee who earns $30,000 and claims four exemptions has a taxable income of $22,000. Each employee is required to file an Employee's Withholding Allowance Certificate, called a Form W-4, with the employer. **The Employee's Withholding Allowance Certificate (Form W-4) reports the number of the exemptions claimed by the employee.** It is illustrated in Exhibit 10-1.

The second factor that affects the amount of federal income tax to be withheld is the pay level of the employee. Since tax rates are higher for higher

EXHIBIT 10-1   Employee's Withholding Allowance Certificate (W-4)

Form **W-4** Department of the Treasury Internal Revenue Service	**Employee's Withholding Allowance Certificate** ► **For Privacy Act and Paperwork Reduction Act Notice, see reverse.**	OMB No. 1545-0010 **1988**

1 Type or print your first name and middle initial	Last name	2 Your social security number

Home address (number and street or rural route) City or town, state, and ZIP code	3 Marital Status	☐ Single ☐ Married ☐ Married, but withhold at higher Single rate. **Note:** *If married, but legally separated, or spouse is a nonresident alien, check the Single box.*

4 Total number of allowances you are claiming (from line G above or from the Worksheets on back if they apply) . . . **4**

5 Additional amount, if any, you want deducted from each pay . . . . **5** $

6 I claim exemption from withholding because (check boxes below that apply):

  a ☐ Last year I did not owe any Federal income tax and had a right to a full refund of **ALL** income tax withheld, **AND**

  b ☐ This year I do not expect to owe any Federal income tax and expect to have a right to a full refund of **ALL** income tax withheld.

  c If both **a** and **b** apply and you satisfy the additional conditions outlined above under "Exemption From Withholding," enter the year effective and "EXEMPT" here. Do not complete lines 4 and 5 above . . . . . ► Year 19

7 Are you a full-time student? (**Note:** *Full-time students are not automatically exempt.*) ☐ Yes ☐ No

Under penalties of perjury, I certify that I am entitled to the number of withholding allowances claimed on this certificate or, if claiming exemption from withholding, that I am entitled to claim the exempt status.

Employee's signature ►   Date ►   , 198

8 Employer's name and address **(Employer: Complete 8, 9, and 10 only if sending to IRS)**	9 Office code	10 Employer identification number

EXHIBIT 10-2
Excerpt from
Federal Income Tax
Withholding Table

BIWEEKLY Payroll Period—Employee MARRIED—Effective January 1, 1988

And the wages are-		And the number of withholding allowances claimed is—										
At least	But less than	0	1	2	3	4	5	6	7	8	9	10 or more
		The amount of income tax to be withheld shall be—										
$860	$880	$113	$102	$90	$79	$68	$57	$45	$34	$23	$12	$0
880	900	116	105	93	82	71	60	48	37	26	15	3
900	920	119	108	96	85	74	63	51	40	29	18	6
920	940	122	111	99	88	77	66	54	43	32	21	9
940	960	125	114	102	91	80	69	57	46	35	24	12
960	980	128	117	105	94	83	72	60	49	38	27	15
980	1,000	131	120	108	97	86	75	63	52	41	30	18
1,000	1,020	134	123	111	100	89	78	66	55	44	33	21
1,020	1,040	137	126	114	103	92	81	69	58	47	36	24
1,040	1,060	140	129	117	106	95	84	72	61	50	39	27
1,060	1,080	143	132	120	109	98	87	75	64	53	42	30
1,080	1,100	146	135	123	112	101	90	78	67	56	45	33
1,100	1,120	149	138	126	115	104	93	81	70	59	48	36
1,120	1,140	152	141	129	118	107	96	84	73	62	51	39
1,140	1,160	155	144	132	121	110	99	87	76	65	54	42
1,160	1,180	158	147	135	124	113	102	90	79	68	57	45
1,180	1,200	161	150	138	127	116	105	93	82	71	60	48
1,200	1,220	164	153	141	130	119	108	96	85	74	63	51
1,220	1,240	167	156	144	133	122	111	99	88	77	66	54
1,240	1,260	170	159	147	136	125	114	102	91	80	69	57
1,260	1,280	174	162	150	139	128	117	105	94	83	72	60
1,280	1,300	180	165	153	142	131	120	108	97	86	75	63
1,300	1,320	185	168	156	145	134	123	111	100	89	78	66
1,320	1,340	191	171	159	148	137	126	114	103	92	81	69
1,340	1,360	196	175	162	151	140	129	117	106	95	84	72
1,360	1,380	202	181	165	154	143	132	120	109	98	87	75
1,380	1,400	208	187	168	157	146	135	123	112	101	90	78
1,400	1,420	213	192	171	160	149	138	126	115	104	93	81
1,420	1,440	219	198	177	163	152	141	129	118	107	96	84
1,440	1,460	224	203	182	166	155	144	132	121	110	99	87
1,460	1,480	230	209	188	169	158	147	135	124	113	102	90
1,480	1,500	236	215	194	173	161	150	138	127	116	105	93
1,500	1,520	241	220	199	178	164	153	141	130	119	108	96
1,520	1,540	247	226	205	184	167	156	144	133	122	111	99
1,540	1,560	252	231	210	189	170	159	147	136	125	114	102

incomes, progressively larger amounts are withheld at higher pay levels. An excerpt from the federal income tax withholding table is shown in Exhibit 10-2. For example, if a married employee with two exemptions (withholding allowances) earns $1,000 biweekly, income taxes of $111 are withheld from each biweekly paycheck.

Once the appropriate federal income taxes are withheld, employers must periodically remit the income taxes to the Internal Revenue Service. Each quarter they must also file a report showing the taxes withheld. After the end of the year a Wage and Tax Statement, Form W-2, is prepared by the company.

The Wage and Tax Statement (Form W-2) is a form provided by the employer to the employee and the Internal Revenue Service that reports the employee's total wages and salary, wages and salary subject to FICA taxes, state and federal income taxes withheld, and FICA taxes withheld. (FICA taxes are discussed next.) The W-2 form is illustrated in Exhibit 10-3.

Federal Social Security Taxes

At the time of writing the Social Security Act provides that qualified participants will receive monthly retirement benefits after reaching the age of 62, certain medical benefits after reaching the age of 65, and benefits to the family of the participant in the case of death. The benefits are based on the average earnings during the employee's (participant's) years of employment. The Social Security System is basically a pay-as-you-go system, which means that the money collected during the current period from employed people is used to pay benefits to retired people in the same period. **Social security taxes are assessed against**

EXHIBIT 10-3
Wage and Tax
Statement

1 Control number					
		OMB No. 1545-0008			
2 Employer's name, address, and ZIP code			3 Employer's identification number	4 Employer's state I.D. number	
			5 Statutory employee ☐ Deceased ☐ Pension plan ☐ Legal rep. ☐ 942 emp. ☐ Subtotal ☐ Deferred compensation ☐ Void ☐		
			6 Allocated tips	7 Advance EIC payment	
8 Employee's social security number	9 Federal income tax withheld		10 Wages, tips, other compensation	11 Social security tax withheld	
12 Employee's name, address, and ZIP code			13 Social security wages	14 Social security tips	
			16	16a Fringe benefits incl. in Box 10	
			17 State income tax	18 State wages, tips, etc.	19 Name of state
			20 Local income tax	21 Local wages, tips, etc.	22 Name of locality

Form **W-2 Wage and Tax Statement 1988**
Employee's and employer's copy compared ☐

Copy 1 For State, City, or Local Tax Department

6(c). Explain social
security taxes.

employees and employers under the Federal Insurance Contributions Act (FICA) to pay for benefits of retired employees. They are often referred to as *FICA taxes.* They are levied at a set rate on annual wages and salaries up to a maximum amount *(limit).* In 1989, these taxes were at a 7.51% rate and the annual maximum compensation per employee subject to the tax was $48,000. The maximum compensation increases each year as inflation occurs.

The employer is required to withhold the employee's social security tax at the appropriate rate from each employee's pay until the annual salary limit is reached. The employer must also pay its equal share of the tax. It must periodically remit both amounts to the Internal Revenue Service. Periodic reports have to be filed, and the taxes withheld are reported on Form W-2.

Federal and State Unemployment Taxes

6(d). Explain unemployment taxes.

The federal and state governments participate in a joint unemployment insurance program. The state government operates the program to provide benefits to the unemployed in the form of cash payments made for a specified period of time. **The Federal Unemployment Tax Act (FUTA) taxes are assessed at a maximum rate of 6.2% levied on the employer on the basis of the first $7,000 paid to each employee in each year.** These taxes are often referred to as *FUTA taxes.* Of the 6.2%, 5.4% is paid to the state if the state levies an approved unemployment insurance tax; thus 0.8% is left for the federal government. Most states allow for a reduction of the 5.4% tax through merit-rating plans for employers who do not lay off employees, because steady employment reduces the unemployment funds paid by the state.

Other Employee Deductions

Often employees pay for programs such as medical insurance, union dues, and charitable contributions (e.g., United Fund) through payroll deductions. The employer must keep track of the appropriate deductions from each employee's pay and remit the correct amounts to the various agencies. In addition, the company itself may contribute to the cost of the program and therefore must calculate and pay its share.

Recording the Payroll

The procedures followed in accounting for payroll vary from company to company, although they have some common elements. These elements are discussed in the following sections. Although most companies have automated payroll accounting systems, the elements are described in the form of a nonautomated record-keeping system. The information contained in either type of system is essentially the same.

Payroll Register

7. Describe how to record the payroll, including use of the payroll register.

The payroll register is a record in which details of each employee's pay and deductions for the period are entered. A typical payroll register is illustrated for the Kasper Company in Exhibit 10-4. The register includes each employee's name, social security number, pay rate, total hours worked, and hours of overtime, which in this case are paid at 150% of the regular rate. The gross pay is determined from the hours worked and the pay rate. Federal and state income tax deductions, FICA tax deductions (at an assumed 7.51% rate), and medical insurance deductions are all listed. The total deductions subtracted from the gross pay indicate the net amount to be paid to the employee. Upon payment,

EXHIBIT 10-4
Payroll Register

KASPER COMPANY
Payroll Register
For Week Ended March 8, 1991

Employee Name and Social Security Number	Hours Worked	Overtime Hours	Pay Rate	Earnings Regular Pay	Overtime Pay	Gross Pay
Linda Jones 453-61-5261	40		5.00	200.00		200.00
David Kennedy 523-06-9143	40		8.00	320.00		320.00
Peter Morgan 468-21-6842	45	5	6.00	240.00	45.00	285.00
Kathleen Thomas 521-26-0374	40		7.50	300.00		300.00
Michael Williams 621-55-3164	40		6.00	240.00		240.00
Total				1,300.00	45.00	1,345.00

the number of the check used for payment is recorded. The last column indicates the distribution of the cost; that is, the expense account in which the pay will be recorded.

Recording the Journal Entry for the Payroll

When the Kasper Company has completed the payroll register for all its employees, it prepares a journal entry at the time of the cash payment for the employees' salaries:

Office Salaries Expense ($200 + $240)	440.00	
Sales Salaries Expense	320.00	
Maintenance Salaries Expense	285.00	
Accounting Salaries Expense	300.00	
Federal Income Tax Payable		172.90
State Income Tax Payable		19.92
FICA Taxes Payable		101.00
Medical Insurance Payable		83.00
Cash		968.18

To record payroll for week ending March 8, 1991.

Note that the amount of each salary expense is based on the *gross* pay because that is the cost to the company of each employee. When the company remits the appropriate amounts withheld to the various agencies the related liability is reduced (debited) as the cash is paid (credited).

Frequently the date of payment of the wages and salaries does not coincide with the end of the accounting period. In this case it is necessary to calculate the wages and salaries earned between the last payment date and the end of the

		Deductions				Payment		
Federal Income Tax	State Income Tax	FICA Taxes	Medical Insurance	Total Deductions	Net Pay	Check No.	Distribution
21.30	3.20	15.02	15.00	54.52	145.48	609	Office Salaries Expense
50.60	5.15	24.03	15.00	94.78	225.22	610	Sales Salaries Expense
44.20	4.85	21.40	18.00	88.45	196.55	611	Maintenance Salaries Expense
36.20	3.82	22.53	15.00	77.55	222.45	612	Accounting Salaries Expense
20.60	2.90	18.02	20.00	61.52	178.48	613	Office Salaries Expense
172.90	19.92	101.00	83.00	376.82	968.18		

period in order to record the related expense and liability. For example, if salaries were last paid on December 27, any salaries earned between that date and December 31 should be recognized by an adjusting entry. The adjusting entry would have the same format as the preceding entry, except that Salaries Payable would be credited instead of Cash because payment will not be made until January of the next year. When payment is made the Salaries Payable account is debited and Cash is credited.

Payroll Taxes Incurred by the Employer

As discussed earlier some payroll taxes are levied directly on the employer. These taxes include the employer's share of social security taxes and unemployment taxes. In addition, although they are not really taxes, the employer may pay a share (or all) of such items as medical insurance and pension plan payments.

Continuing the preceding example, the Kasper Company would have to pay FICA taxes of $101 (7.51% × $1,345.00), assuming the salary levels of the employees have not reached the FICA limit; federal unemployment taxes of $10.76 (0.8% × $1,345.00), assuming that the salary levels of the employees have not reached the $7,000 FUTA limit; state unemployment taxes of $72.63 (5.4% × $1,345.00), assuming that the company has no merit-rating reduction; and medical insurance of $83.00, assuming that the Kasper Company matches the employee's insurance payment. The journal entry to record the payroll taxes expense is:

Payroll Taxes Expense	267.39	
FICA Taxes Payable		101.00
Federal Unemployment Taxes Payable		10.76
State Unemployment Taxes Payable		72.63
Medical Insurance Payable		83.00

To record payroll taxes expense for week ended March 8, 1991.

The total expense for the employees' salaries for the Kasper Company is the sum of the expenses recorded in the two journal entries. Thus for the week of March 8, 1991, the total is $1,612.39 ($440 + $320 + $285 + $300 + $267.39).

As an alternative to the treatment of the payroll taxes expense just discussed the company could divide the $267.39 among each salary expense category in the same way as the payments made to employees. For example, a portion of the payroll taxes expense related to David Kennedy could be recorded as a $58.87 debit to Sales Salaries Expense, calculated as follows:

FICA Taxes	$24.03	(7.51% × $320)
Federal Unemployment Taxes	2.56	(0.8% × $320)
State Unemployment Taxes	17.28	(5.4% × $320)
Medical Insurance	15.00	
	$58.87	

The effect of this practice would be to increase the expense in each categorized expense account, but the total expenses for the period would be the same.

Chapter Summary

Review of Learning Objectives

> **1. Describe unearned revenue.**
> Unearned revenue is a liability that arises when a company receives cash in advance for an item it will sell in the future. When the goods are sold or the services are provided in the future, the revenue is recognized and the liability is reduced.

> **2. Record accrued liabilities including (a) warranty liability, (b) sales tax payable, (c) property taxes payable, and (d) income taxes payable.**
> The cost of providing a *warranty* is recognized as an expense in the period of the sale of the product. A warranty liability is recorded as a current liability and reduced as warranty costs are incurred in future periods. The company acts as a collection agency for *sales tax* and the collection of the tax from the customer creates a current liability which is eliminated when payment is made to the state in the next period. *Property taxes payable* is a current liability created before the taxes are assessed on the company and is eliminated when the taxes are paid. A corporation is required to compute the *income tax* expense related to its income before income taxes. A current liability is created because the company pays the taxes in the next period.

> **3. Explain how to account for contingencies.**
> A contingency is an existing condition that involves uncertainty as to a possible gain or loss that will be resolved when a future event occurs (or fails to occur). Loss contingencies are recognized in the financial statements when it is probable that an asset has been impaired or a liability has been incurred and the amount of the loss can be reasonably estimated. Loss contingencies are disclosed in the notes if it is reasonably possible that a loss has been incurred. Gain contingencies are not recorded in the financial statements and are rarely disclosed.

> **4. Describe a note payable and compute interest on the note.**
> A note payable is a written legal document which the officers of the company sign in order to make a purchase, borrow money, or extend the time for payment of an account payable. Interest is computed by multiplying the principal amount of the note by the annual interest rate and the fraction of that for which the note is outstanding.

> **5. Explain how to account for money borrowed from a bank.**
> The note payable is recorded as a current liability. If the interest is to be paid when the note matures, interest expense is recognized and interest payable is recorded as a current liability. Alternatively, the interest may be deducted at the time of issuance of the note. In this case a Discount on Notes Payable is recorded as a contra-liability and reduced as interest expense is recognized.

6. **Explain (a) payroll accounting, including (b) federal income taxes, (c) social security taxes, and (d) unemployment taxes.**

   Payroll accounting involves the computation of the payments to employees after appropriate deductions have been made, and the computation of the company's payroll costs. *Federal income taxes* of the employees are withheld by the company for subsequent payment. *Social security taxes* (FICA) are assessed against employees and employers. *Unemployment taxes* (FUTA) are assessed only against the employer.

7. **Describe how to record the payroll, including use of the payroll register.**

   A payroll register is a record in which details of each employee's pay and deductions for the period are entered. The company records the payroll with two journal entries, one for the employees' salaries and one for its payroll taxes, as shown here in summary form:

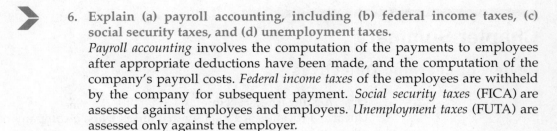

Employees		
Salaries Expense	xx	
Federal Income Tax Payable		xx
FICA Taxes Payable		xx
Medical Insurance Payable		xx
Cash		xx
Payroll Taxes		
Payroll Taxes Expense	xx	
FICA Taxes Payable		xx
Federal Unemployment Taxes Payable		xx
State Unemployment Taxes Payable		xx
Medical Insurance Payable		xx

Review Problem

During 1991 the Cameron Company engaged in the following summarized transactions:

1. The company received $12,000 during the year for subscriptions to a trade magazine it publishes monthly. This amount represented payment for 200 one-year subscriptions. By December 31, 1991, the company had delivered 800 copies of the magazine to the various subscribers.

2. The company offers a warranty on its products. It expects to receive 200 claims at an average amount of $20 on the items it sold in 1991. During 1991, 30 of these claims were satisfied at a total cost of $600.

3. The company collected a sales tax of 6% from customers on its cash sales of $210,000. Of the amount collected for the sales tax 80% has been remitted to the state.

4. The company paid property taxes on April 5 of $20,000. These property taxes covered the period July 1, 1990, to June 30, 1991. The company estimates that property taxes for July 1, 1991, to June 30, 1992, will be $22,000.

5. On September 1 the company borrowed $10,000 for 6 months from a bank that charged 12% interest. The company issued a $10,600 note. The bank deducted interest at the time the note was issued and issued a check to the company for $10,000.

6. During 1991, the company paid salaries as follows:

Sales clerks	$ 80,000
Office employees	60,000
	$140,000

FICA taxes were assessed at a rate of 7.51%, and none of the employees exceeded the annual maximum amount on which taxes are assessed. The company's FUTA taxes are 2.0%, of which 1.2% is paid to the state. Total salaries subject to FUTA taxes were $54,000. The federal income tax withholding rate is 15% of gross pay. Union dues paid by the employees and withheld from their paychecks totaled $6,000. All the deductions and payroll costs have been paid.

7. The company estimated that its income tax expense for 1991 is $12,000. The taxes will be paid in April 1992.

REQUIRED   Prepare journal entries to record the preceding events.

Solution to Review Problem

1.
	During Year		
Cash	12,000	
Subscriptions Collected in Advance		12,000

To record subscriptions received.

	At End of Year		
Subscriptions Collected in Advance	4,000	
Subscriptions Revenue [800/(12 × 200)		
x $12,000]		4,000

To record revenue at year end.

2.
	During Year		
Warranty Expense	600	
Cash		600

To record fulfillment of warranty.

	At End of Year		
Warranty Expense [$20 × (200 – 30)]	3,400	
Warranty Liability		3,400

To record liability for future warranty costs.

3.
	During Year		
Cash	222,600	
Sales		210,000
Sales Tax Payable ($210,000 × 0.06)		12,600

To record sales and related sales taxes.

Sales Tax Payable ($12,600 × 0.80)	10,080	
Cash		10,080

To record remittance of sales tax to the state.

4.

1991

Apr.   5   Property Tax Payable[a]   10,000

         Property Tax Expense   10,000

           Cash   20,000

         To record payment of property taxes.

[a]Accrued at the end of 1990.

1991

Dec. 31   Property Tax Expense ($22,000 × 6/12)   11,000

           Property Tax Payable   11,000

         To accrue property taxes.

5.

1991

Sept. 1   Cash   10,000

         Discount on Notes Payable

            ($10,000 × 12% × 6/12)   600

           Notes Payable   10,600

         To record borrowing of $10,000 from the bank by
issuing 6-month note with interest deducted in
advance.

1991

Dec. 31   Interest Expense ($10,000 × 12% × 4/12)   400

           Discount on Notes Payable   400

         To record interest expense.

6.

Payroll entry

Sales Salaries Expense   80,000

Office Salaries Expense   60,000

     Federal Income Taxes Payable ....   21,000[a]

     FICA Taxes Payable ....   10,514[b]

     Union Dues Payable   6,000

     Cash   102,486

To record payroll for the year.

[a]$140,000 × 15%

[b]$140,000 × 7.51%

Payroll tax entry

Payroll Taxes Expense ....   11,594[a]

     FICA Taxes Payable ....   10,514[b]

     Federal Unemployment Taxes Payable ....   432[c]

     State Unemployment Taxes Payable ....   648[d]

To record payroll tax expenses for the year.

[a]($140,000 × 7.51%) + ($54,000 × 0.8%) + ($54,000 × 1.2%)

[b]$140,000 × 7.51%

[c]$54,000 × 0.8%

[d]$54,000 × 1.2%

Payroll tax payment entry

Federal Income Taxes Payable   21,000

Union Dues Payable   6,000

FICA Taxes Payable ($10,514 + $10,514)   21,028

Federal Unemployment Taxes Payable   432

State Unemployment Taxes Payable   648

     Cash   49,108

To record remittance of payroll tax withholdings.

7.

Income tax entry

Income Tax Expense	12,000	
Income Taxes Payable		12,000

To accrue income taxes.

Glossary

Accrued Liability. A liability outstanding at the end of the period that has arisen during the accounting period but has not yet been paid. Also called an *accrued expense.*

Contingency. An existing condition that involves uncertainty as to a possible gain or loss that will ultimately be resolved when a future event occurs (or fails to occur).

Current Liability. Liability that will be paid, or eliminated, within one year or the normal operating cycle, whichever is longer.

Discount on Notes Payable. A contra-liability account in which the future interest costs on a note are recorded. It arises only when the Notes Payable account is recorded at the maturity value (principal plus interest) of the note.

Employee's Withholding Allowance Certificate (Form W-4). A form filed by the employee with the employer that reports the number of exemptions claimed by the employee.

Exemption. An exclusion of earned income from taxable income.

Federal Unemployment Tax Act (FUTA). Federal unemployment taxes assessed at 6.2% of the first $7,000 of each employee's income in a given year; 5.4% is paid to the state, leaving 0.8% for the federal government.

Notes Payable. The liability account used to record promissory notes issued by a company.

Payroll Register. A record in which details of each employee's pay and deductions for the period are entered.

Social Security Taxes (FICA Taxes). Taxes assessed against employees and employers to pay for benefits of retired employees. The amount of the tax is determined by multiplying a set rate times the annual wages and salaries earned by an employee, up to a maximum amount.

Unearned Revenue. A liability representing an obligation to provide goods and services in the future as a result of receiving cash in advance.

Wage and Tax Statement (Form W-2). A form provided by the employer to the employee and to the Internal Revenue Service that reports the employee's total wages and salary, wages and salary subject to FICA taxes, state and federal income taxes withheld, and FICA taxes withheld.

Questions

QUESTION 10-1 Why do companies often purchase merchandise on credit?

QUESTION 10-2 Why is a liability created when cash is received in advance for rent charged on a building that is being leased to others?

QUESTION 10-3 If a company offers a warranty on a product it sells, why may a liability exist at the end of the accounting period?

QUESTION 10-4   "Since sales taxes are paid by the customer and not by us, there cannot be a liability on our balance sheet for sales taxes payable." Do you agree with this statement? Explain.

QUESTION 10-5   What problem may a company face in determining the correct amount of property tax expense for the current accounting period?

QUESTION 10-6   Under what conditions is a contingency recognized in the financial statements?

QUESTION 10-7   If a company borrows money from a bank and issues a note, describe the difference between a note on which the interest is paid at maturity and a note on which the interest is deducted when the money is borrowed. Is there any difference in how these notes and the related interest are reported in the company's financial statements?

QUESTION 10-8   Why does the employer deduct federal and state income taxes from the employee's paycheck if it is the employee's responsibility to pay these taxes?

QUESTION 10-9   What is an exemption for federal income tax purposes? For what is an exemption given?

QUESTION 10-10   What is the purpose of an Employee's Withholding Allowance Certificate? What information does it include?

QUESTION 10-11   What is the purpose of a Wage and Tax Statement? What information does it include?

QUESTION 10-12   What is the purpose of social security taxes (FICA)? Who pays these taxes?

QUESTION 10-13   Who pays federal unemployment taxes (FUTA)? At what rate are FUTA taxes paid? How may the portion paid to the state be reduced by a company?

QUESTION 10-14   A company paid its employees' salaries on December 26. What must the company do in regard to the payroll if its accounting period ends on December 31?

Exercises

EXERCISE 10-1   **Purchase with Discount Available.**   The Sherman Fertilizer Company uses a periodic inventory system and purchased inventory costing $7,500 on terms of 2/15, n/30. Purchases of $700 were returned during the discount period. Payment was made within 15 days.

REQUIRED   1. Prepare journal entries to record the preceding events using each of the following methods to account for cash discounts:
   (a)   The gross method.
   (b)   The net method.

2. Prepare the journal entry to record the payment under each method if payment was made in 30 days.

EXERCISE 10-2 **Subscriptions.** On March 1, 1991, the Booton Publishing Company received payment for 1,000 subscriptions for a monthly magazine on crocheting. Each annual subscription was $48. On March 1, 1992, the company received payment for 600 annual renewals and 800 new subscriptions. Only July 1, 1992, the company received another 300 subscriptions.

REQUIRED
1. Compute the amount of revenue the company should recognize in (a) 1991 and (b) 1992.

2. Compute the amount of the liability at the end of (a) 1991, and (b) 1992.

EXERCISE 10-3 **Subscriptions Received in Advance.** On June 20 the Madison Publishing Company received $70 for a 2-year subscription to a monthly fishing magazine. The first copy is delivered on July 10.

REQUIRED
1. Prepare the journal entry to record the receipt of the cash.

2. Prepare the adjusting entry necessary at the end of the year. Where would any resulting liability be disclosed?

EXERCISE 10-4 **Warranties.** During 1991 the Ryan Company sold electric toasters with 1-year warranties. It was expected that 600 of the toasters would be returned for repair and that each repair would cost $8. By the end of the year, 300 toasters had been repaired at an average cost of $8 each.

REQUIRED
1. Prepare journal entries to record the preceding events for 1991.

2. What is the amount of the liability at the end of the year? Where would it be disclosed?

EXERCISE 10-5 **Sales Tax.** During 1991 the Caran Cutlery Company made sales of $90,000 on which a 6% sales tax was imposed. The sales tax was collected from the customer at the time of each sale. By the end of the year, 75% of the sales taxes collected had been remitted to the state.

REQUIRED
1. Prepare journal entries to record the preceding events for 1991.

2. What is the amount of the liability at the end of the year? Where would it be disclosed?

EXERCISE 10-6 **Property Taxes.** On December 31, 1991, the Adams Advertising Company was preparing its financial statements and estimated that its property taxes for the period from July 1, 1991, to June 30, 1992, would be $50,000. On February 10, 1992, it received its property tax bill for $50,000 and the bill was paid.

REQUIRED
Prepare journal entries to record the preceding events.

EXERCISE 10-7 **Contingencies.** The Traction Tire Company sold $300,000 of a special high-performance tire during 1991. The company offers a warranty that each tire will last for 60,000 miles. The company estimates that, because of improper care by the buyers, 5% of the tires will be returned for replacement under the warranty. During 1991, the company was sued by a customer who had a tire burst on her Jaguar, causing the car to be wrecked. She is requesting $100,000 in damages. The company agrees that the tire caused the accident but is defending the case because the driver was negligent in exceeding the speed for which the tire was designed.

REQUIRED
How should the company account for the preceding events? Prepare any journal entries that are required.

EXERCISE 10-8

Note Given to Make a Purchase. On August 1, 1991, the Taft Trailer Company purchased inventory for $60,000 and gave a 10%, 6-month note to the seller. The company uses the periodic inventory system.

REQUIRED

1. Prepare the journal entries to record the purchase, the accrual of interest at year end, and the repayment of the note.

2. What are the amounts of the liabilities at the end of the year? Where would they be disclosed?

EXERCISE 10-9

Interest Deducted at Borrowing. On September 1, 1991, the Wilson Dairy Company borrowed $20,000 cash from a bank that charges 12% interest. The company issued a 6-month note in the amount of $21,000 and the bank remitted $20,000 to the company when the note was issued.

REQUIRED

1. What is the face value of the note?

2. Prepare journal entries to record the borrowing, the interest expense at year end, and the repayment of the money.

3. What is the amount of the liability at the end of 1991? Where would it be disclosed?

EXERCISE 10-10

Calculation of Net Pay. For employees of the McKinley Plastics Company, the gross pay and the federal income tax withheld in the first week of February 1991 were as follows:

Employee	Gross Pay	Federal Income Tax Withheld
Carver, James	$300	$42
Webb, Steve	350	54
Bailey, Doreen	400	77

FICA taxes were withheld at a 7.5% rate. FUTA taxes are 3.5%, of which 2.7% is paid to the state. Each employee has a $5 union fee deducted from every paycheck.

REQUIRED

Assuming that no maximum amounts (limits) have been reached, compute the net amount paid to each employee.

EXERCISE 10-11

Calculation of Payroll Expense.   Use the information in Exercise 10-10.

REQUIRED

1. Compute the total salaries expense incurred by the McKinley Plastics Company for the first week of February.

2. Prepare a journal entry to record the salaries, assuming that Carver is a salesman and the other two employees are office employees.

EXERCISE 10-12

Net Pay and Payroll Expense. Anthony Hopkins is an employee of the Seasons Catering Company. His annual salary is $84,000, which is earned evenly over the year. During November the federal income tax withheld was $700. FUTA taxes are 4%, of which 3.2% is paid to the state. For simplicity assume the FICA tax rate is 7.5% up to a maximum salary of $50,000. Hopkins pays $50 per month for medical insurance; the company withholds this amount and also contributes an equal amount.

REQUIRED

1. Compute the net amount paid to Hopkins in November.

2. Compute the salary expense of Hopkins for the Seasons Catering Company in November.

Problems

Part A

PROBLEM 10-1A **Purchases.** During 1991 the Keel Plating Company purchased steel plating inventory at a cost of $60,000 on terms of 2/10, n/30; $6,000 of the purchases were returned during the discount period. The company paid for 60% of the net purchases within the discount period and the remainder was paid after the discount period had expired. The company also purchased inventory that cost $25,000 on terms of n/30; $2,500 of these purchases were returned. Payment of the remainder was made within 30 days. The company uses the periodic inventory system and the gross method of accounting for cash discounts.

REQUIRED Prepare journal entries to record the preceding events.

PROBLEM 10-2A **Accrued Liabilities.** The following events occurred for the Brake Game Company during 1991:

(a) Recorded cash sales of outdoor games in the amount of $130,000. A sales tax of 5% was collected on these sales. Three-quarters of these taxes have been remitted to the state.

(b) Offered a 1-year warranty on its sales of outdoor games. It is expected that the cost of fulfilling the warranty on the games sold in (a) will amount to 5% of the sales price. During 1991, $4,000 costs (all cash) were incurred to fulfill the terms of the warranty.

(c) A property tax bill of $12,000 was received and paid early in 1991 for the period July 1, 1990, to June 30, 1991. Of this amount $6,000 had been accrued at the end of 1990. It is expected that the bill to be received in 1992 will be for $15,000.

(d) Recorded credit sales of electronic games in the amount of $250,000. It is probable that the company will not collect $4,000 of this total.

(e) On September 30 a building owned by the company was rented to another company for $300 per month. A year's rent was received in advance.

REQUIRED Prepare journal entries to record all the preceding events. Where possible record the initial event separately from any adjusting entry required at year end.

PROBLEM 10-3A **Notes Payable.** During 1991 the Birch Company engaged in the following transactions:

Date	Transaction
Aug. 12	Purchased a warehouse for $50,000. Paid 25% down and gave a 10% note due February 8 for the balance.
Sept. 3	Gave a 10%, 90-day note to the Maple Company to extend an overdue account of $2,000.
Oct. 15	Borrowed $15,000 at 12% from the First State Bank. The interest will be paid when the note is repaid on April 13, 1992.
Nov. 1	Borrowed $6,000 for 120 days at 12% from the MetroBank. Issued a $6,240 note and the bank remitted $6,000 since interest was deducted by the bank when the note was signed.

REQUIRED

1. Prepare journal entries to record the preceding events for 1991 and 1992, including the accrual of interest at December 31, 1991. Assume that all notes are paid on schedule. All interest rates are annual rates, and the company computes interest based on a 360-day year for the exact number of days.

2. Show how the notes would be disclosed on the December 31, 1991, balance sheet.

PROBLEM 10-4A   **Payroll Register.**   The Linden Company has three employees. The payroll information about them is as follows:

Name	Pay Rate per Hour	Medical Insurance per Week	Charitable Contributions per Week	Gross Pay Year to Date	Department
A. Snap 40	$11	$5	$2	$11,000	Sales
D. Crackle 40	12	3	3	12,000	Office
Z. Pop 42	9	5	1	6,000	Maintenance

During the first week of July 1991, each employee worked 40 hours except for Pop, who worked 42 hours. Overtime is paid at 150% of the regular rate. For simplicity assume that FICA taxes are assessed at 7.5%, FUTA taxes are 2.8% (0.8% is paid to the federal government and 2.0% is paid to the state), the federal income tax withholding is 15% of gross pay, and the state income tax withholding is 2% of gross pay. The company matches both the medical insurance costs and the charitable contributions paid by the employees as listed in the preceding schedule.

REQUIRED

1. Prepare a payroll register for the Linden Company for the first week of July.

2. Compute the total payroll expense for the Linden Company in the first week of July.

3. Prepare journal entries to record the salaries expense for the first week of July.

PROBLEM 10-5A   **Accrued Liabilities.**   The following events occurred for the Ryan Company during 1991 (the company uses a periodic inventory system):

(a) Purchased $750,000 of climbing equipment on account on terms of n/30, of which one-half has been paid for.

(b) Cash sales of $1 million were made. Sales tax collected was 4%, of which half had been remitted to the state by the end of 1991.

(c) The company is a defendant in a lawsuit resulting from injuries incurred by a customer who purchased a defective climbing rope. The management of the company agrees that it is reasonably possible that a settlement of $500,000 will be necessary.

(d) Income taxes for the year were estimated to be $100,000. None of this amount has been paid yet.

(e) Warranty costs were expected to amount to 3% of sales. Of this amount, half would require a cash refund and half would require replacement of the product.

REQUIRED

1. Prepare journal entries to record the preceding events. Where possible record the initial entry separately from any adjusting entry required at year end.

2. What is the total amount of current liabilities at year end?

Problems

Part B

PROBLEM 10-1B **Purchases.** During 1991 the Mast Fiber Glass Company purchased inventory at a cost of $50,000 on terms of 1/10, n/30; $1,000 of the purchases were returned within the discount period. The company paid for 80% of the net purchases within the discount period and the remainder was paid after the discount period had expired. The company also purchased inventory that cost $20,000 on terms of n/30; $2,000 of these purchases were returned. Payment of the remainder was made within 30 days. The company uses the periodic inventory system and the net method of accounting for cash discounts.

REQUIRED Prepare journal entries to record the preceding events.

PROBLEM 10-2B **Accrued Liabilities.** The following events were recorded by the Poundloss Weight Control Company in 1991:

(a) Sold 7,000 take-home Poundloss kits to customers. The kits sold for $25 each and were subject to a 5% sales tax. All the sales tax collected has been remitted to the state.

(b) Offered a money-back guarantee that weight loss will be maintained for 6 months after a week's stay at a Poundloss residential program. It is expected that the cost of fulfilling the guarantee will amount to 10% of service revenues. During 1991, 6,000 people paid $1,000 each for a week at Poundloss, and $200,000 was paid to customers who did not maintain their weight loss.

(c) A property tax bill of $57,000 was received and paid in January for the period September 1, 1990, to August 31, 1991. One-third of the property taxes had been accrued at the end of 1990. It is expected that the bill to be received in 1992 will be for $90,000.

(d) Recorded credit sales of a calorie counter in the amount of $100,000. It is probable that the company will not collect $1,500 of this total.

(e) By December 31, 1991, 3,000 people had made reservations for the 1992 Poundloss season. A total of $250,000 had been received as deposits.

REQUIRED Prepare journal entries to record all the preceding events. The company's accounting period ends on December 31. Where possible record the initial event separately from any adjusting entry required at year end.

PROBLEM 10-3B **Notes Payable.** During 1991 the Sycamore Company engaged in the following transactions:

Date	Transaction
Jan. 17	Purchased a tract of land for $90,000. Paid 20% down and gave an 8% note due October 14 for the balance.
July 6	Borrowed $60,000 at 10% from Second State Bank. Issued a $63,000 note and the bank remitted $60,000 since the interest was deducted when the note was signed. The note is due on January 2, 1992.
19	Borrowed $30,000 at 9% for 90 days from Outer Metro Bank. The interest will be paid at maturity.
Nov. 4	Gave a 6% note, due January 3, 1992, to the Waze Company to extend an overdue account of $8,000.

REQUIRED

1. Prepare journal entries to record all the preceding events for 1991 and 1992, including the accrual of interest at year end. Assume that all the notes were paid on schedule. All interest rates are annual rates, and the company computes interest based on a 360-day year for the exact number of days.

2. Show how the notes would be disclosed on the December 31, 1991, balance sheet.

PROBLEM 10-4B   **Payroll Register.**   The Ash Company has three employees. The payroll information about them is as follows:

Name	Pay Rate per Hour	Medical Insurance per Week	Charitable Contributions per Week	Gross Pay Year to Date	Department
Jones	$13	$5.33	$2	$12,000	Sales
Smith	12	3.33	2	3,000	Maintenance
Zinski	17	4.00	1	5,000	Office

From June 2 through June 6 each employee worked 40 hours except for Jones, who worked 42. Overtime is paid at 200% of the regular rate. For simplicity, assume that FICA taxes are assessed at 7.5%. FUTA taxes are 2.9% (0.8% is paid to the federal government and 2.1% is paid to the state), the federal income tax withholding rate is 15% of gross pay, and the state income tax withholding rate is 2% of gross pay. The company contributes an additional 50% of the amount of medical insurance costs listed and matches the charitable contributions paid by the employees as shown in the preceding schedule.

REQUIRED

1. Prepare a payroll register for the week of June 2 through June 6.

2. Compute the total payroll expense for the Ash Company during the week of June 2 through June 6.

3. Prepare journal entries to record the salaries expense for the week of June 2 through June 6.

PROBLEM 10-5B   **Accrued Liabilities.**   The following events occurred for the Eastman Drug Company during 1991 (the company uses the periodic inventory system):

(a) Purchased $600,000 of inventory on account, of which one-fourth has been paid.

(b) Cash sales of $950,000 were made. Sales tax collected was 8%; by the end of 1991, one-half has been remitted to the state.

(c) The company is a defendant in a lawsuit resulting from injuries incurred by a customer who purchased a contaminated drug. The management of the company agrees that it is probable that the company will be found liable. However, the company is unsure of the amount that a jury will decide is an appropriate judgment. There has been speculation in the local newspaper that it may be as much as $1 million.

(d) Income taxes for the year were estimated to be $40,000. None of this amount has been paid yet.

(e) Warranty costs were expected to amount to 1% of sales. Of this amount, 75% would require a cash refund and 25% would require replacement of the product.

REQUIRED
1. Prepare journal entries to record the preceding events. Where possible record the initial entry separately from any adjusting entry required at year end.

2. What is the total amount of the current liabilities at year end?

Decision Cases

DECISION CASE 10-1
Payroll Costs. The Zanzibar Company has a significant increase in business around Christmas. In past years it has hired 10 extra employees for December, with each employee working 200 hours. As a result of using seasonal employees, the company pays the full 5.4% of the 6.2% FUTA tax to the state on these salaries as well as on the salaries of its 20 year-round employees. The company is confident that if it did not have this seasonal employment problem, it could achieve a merit rating and pay only 4.6% to the state for the FUTA tax. The company estimates that it costs $50 in interviewing and processing costs to hire each employee.

As an alternative for 1991 the Zanzibar Company is considering using employees provided by Temphelp, a company that specializes in providing temporary employees. Zanzibar would have to pay Temphelp $6 per hour per employee, but Temphelp would pay all social security and federal and state unemployment taxes.

REQUIRED
Using the rates provided in this chapter for 1991, what is the company wage rate at which it would make no difference to the Zanzibar Company if it hired its own employees or used Temphelp? Provide supporting calculations for your answer.

DECISION CASE 10-2
Current Liabilities. Westinghouse Corporation's balance sheet at the end of a recent year included the following current liabilities (amounts in millions of dollars):

Short term debt	$1,955.0
Accounts payable	738.0
Accrued employee compensation	335.1
Accrued product warranty	127.3
Income taxes currently payable	182.5
Estimated future costs of uranium settlements	16.2

REQUIRED
For each of the current liabilities, describe the nature of the liability, name the other account that was recorded when the liability was created, and indicate how and when the liability will be eliminated.

DECISION CASE 10-3
Current Liabilities. The Clark Company has decided to expand its operations as a result of receiving a new order for golf clubs from a distributor. On July 1, 1991, the company acquired a new machine for manufacturing the clubs from a supplier at a cost of $500,000. The supplier offers to accept either immediate payment or a 9-month note with interest of 10%. The company expects to produce 5,000 clubs during the remaining 6 months of the year and to sell them to the distributor for $30 each evenly over the period. Since the distributor will not sell them to the public until the spring of 1992, the company offers terms of immediate payment less a 5% discount if paid within 10 days, or full payment within 2 months, or delayed payment until 1992 with interest charged at 12% after 2 months until full payment is received. The company expects that 2% of the clubs will be found to be defective during their use and returned to it for replacement.

REQUIRED
Compute the amount of the liabilities that the company will have on December 31, 1991, under each of the alternative situations. (Assume a 360-day year.)

11

Property, Plant, and Equipment: Acquisition and Depreciation

LEARNING OBJECTIVES

1. Identify the characteristics of property, plant, and equipment.

2. Compute the acquisition cost of property, plant, and equipment.

3. Explain the concept of depreciation.

4. Compute the amount of depreciation under the (a) straight-line method, (b) double-declining balance method, (c) sum-of-the-years'-digits method, and (d) activity methods.

5. Compute depreciation for fractional periods.

6. Calculate depreciation for income tax purposes.

7. Explain the accounting for expenditures incurred after the acquisition of property, plant, and equipment.

T he title Property and Equipment was used in a classified balance sheet to disclose the operational assets for a service or merchandising company in Chapter 5. The title of Property, Plant, and Equipment is more general because it also applies to manufacturing companies that own plant facilities for manufacturing. An alternative title that is often used is Fixed Assets.

Property, plant, and equipment are very important components of a company's operating activities. In physical terms they include assets that are necessary for a merchandising company to conduct its business, such as land, office buildings, stores, warehouses, and delivery vehicles. A manufacturing company has similar assets, including factory buildings, machinery, and equipment, that are generally accounted for in a way similar to a merchandising company. In financial terms property, plant, and equipment are usually a major portion of the total assets of a company, and therefore an understanding of the accounting principles used is essential to an understanding of financial statements.

Characteristics of Property, Plant, and Equipment

Property, plant, and equipment are the long-term physical assets acquired for use in the operations of a company. These assets include such items as land, buildings, machinery, furniture, office equipment, and automobiles. An asset classified as property, plant, and equipment must have the following three characteristics:

1. Identify the characteristics of property, plant, and equipment.

1. *The asset must be used in the operating activities of the company.* To be included in property, plant, and equipment an asset does not have to be used continuously, and therefore machinery owned for standby purposes in case of breakdowns would be included. It is also possible that a particular asset may be categorized as property, plant, and equipment by one company and as inventory by another. For example, an automobile owned by a car dealer that is intended for resale is included in inventory. The same type of automobile used by an employee of a company would be a part of property, plant, and equipment. Land owned by a real estate company that is intended for resale is included in inventory, whereas similar land on which a company builds a warehouse is categorized as property, plant, and equipment. Land held for speculative purposes or for future use as a building site would be classified as an investment.

2. *The asset must have a life of more than 1 year.* The asset represents a bundle of future services that will be received by the company over the life of the asset. To be included in property, plant, and equipment the benefits must extend for more than 1 year, and therefore the asset is distinguished from other assets, such as supplies or inventory, that are expected to be consumed within 1 year or the operating cycle, whichever is longer. For example, a truck may have an expected life of 100,000 miles and the company will receive the benefits from operating the truck over more than a year. In addition, a company owning a building can expect to receive benefits from that building for more than a year.

3. *The asset must be tangible in nature.* The asset must have a physical substance that can be seen and touched. Intangible assets, in contrast, which are discussed in Chapter 12, do not have a physical substance.

There are several accounting issues associated with property, plant, and equipment. In this chapter we are concerned with the initial cost of such assets, the treatment of subsequent expenditures on these assets, and the depreciation of the assets.

Acquisition Cost of Property, Plant, and Equipment

2. Compute the acquisition cost of property, plant, and equipment.

The acquisition cost of an asset includes all the expenditures that are necessary and reasonable to acquire the asset and prepare the asset for its intended use. For an asset included in property, plant, and equipment these costs include the following:

1. The contract price less any discounts available
2. Transportation costs
3. Sales tax
4. Installation and testing costs
5. Other related necessary and reasonable costs.

The contract (invoice) price is used rather than the list price because it represents the actual cost paid for the asset. The list price may only be an advertised price that is used as a basis for negotiating the contract price. Cash discounts *should* be subtracted from the contract price, whether or not they are taken. If they are not taken, they should be treated as an interest (or financing) expense because management decided to forego early payment. The added cost should not be included in the cost of the asset because it was not a necessary cost of the acquisition. To avoid unnecessary detail, however, some companies do not deduct discounts that are not taken from the acquisition cost. This inconsistency is similar to the inconsistency that arises when some companies use the gross method of recording cash discounts on purchases and other companies use the net method.

Transportation costs incurred by the company are included in the cost of the asset if it is shipped FOB shipping point. If the asset is shipped FOB destination, the supplier pays the transportation costs and they are not explicitly included in the cost of the asset. Installation and testing costs include the cost of salaries and materials directly associated with these activities. Thus these costs are included in the cost of the asset and not in salaries expense or cost of goods sold. Costs that are unnecessary and unreasonable, such as damage during transportation, are excluded from the cost of the asset and are recorded as an expense of the period (unless reimbursed by the transportation company or the supplier).

A company often purchases many low-cost items, such as typewriters and filing cabinets, that benefit future periods. These items should be included as property, plant, and equipment and then depreciated over their useful lives (as discussed later). Many companies, however, expense such items in the period of acquisition because the cost is not *material* and the *benefits do not exceed the costs* involved in the accounting procedures. Companies typically develop a policy that defines a minimum dollar amount for an acquisition to be recorded as an asset.

A company may also construct an asset for its own use. For example, utilities often construct their own generating plants over a period of several years or a manufacturing company may make a special-purpose machine for its own use. All the costs directly related to the construction should be included in the cost of the asset. These costs include those related to materials, labor, and architects' and engineering fees. In addition, companies may add to the asset the cost of interest on amounts borrowed to finance its construction. This topic is beyond the scope of the book.

Types of Property, Plant, and Equipment

There are several types of property, plant, and equipment, including land, buildings, machinery and equipment, leased assets, and leasehold improvements.

Land.   The acquisition cost of land includes: (1) the contract price, (2) the cost of closing the transaction and obtaining title, including real estate commissions, legal fees for examining the correct ownership of the property, and past-due taxes, (3) the costs of surveys, and (4) the costs of preparing the land for its particular use, such as clearing, grading, and razing old buildings (net of the proceeds for any salvaged items), when such improvements have an indefinite life. The costs of improvements with a limited economic life, such as landscaping, streets, sidewalks, and sewers, should be recorded (debited) to a Land Improvements account and depreciated over their economic lives (depreciation is discussed later in the chapter).

Buildings.   The acquisition cost of buildings includes: (1) the contract price, (2) the costs of excavation for the specific building (if not included in the contract price), (3) architectural costs and the cost of building permits, and (4) legal fees associated with the acquisition. If a used building is purchased, the costs of remodeling and reconditioning necessary to prepare the building for its intended use are included in the acquisition cost.

Machinery and Equipment.   The acquisition cost of machinery and equipment includes: (1) the contract price, and (2) installation and testing costs that are necessary to prepare the machinery and equipment for its intended use.

Leased Assets.   Many companies lease property, plant, and equipment rather than purchase these assets. Although these leases do not transfer legal ownership of the asset, they do enable the company to obtain the use of the asset for an extended period of time. Consequently, many leases result in the recording of an asset that is included in property, plant, and equipment on the balance sheet. Leases are discussed briefly in Chapter 12 and more fully in Chapter 16.

Leasehold Improvements.   When leased assets are improved by the lessee the expenditures should be recorded as an asset in a separate Leasehold Improvements account and expensed over the life of the lease or the life of the improvements, whichever is shorter. This procedure is necessary because the company no longer has the use of the leasehold improvements after the end of the life of the lease, and therefore it does not receive any more benefits.

Illustration of Accounting for Acquisition Cost

To illustrate the journal entries necessary to record the acquisition of an asset, suppose that the Gentry Company purchases a machine with a contract price of $10,000 on terms of 2/10, n/30. It incurs transportation costs of $1,500 and installation and testing costs of $1,000. The cash discount of $200 (2% × $10,000) is deducted and the net invoice price is $9,800 ($10,000 – $200). Remember that the discount should be deducted whether or not it is taken. (Note that this procedure is different from the gross method that is often used for discounts on purchases of inventory.) In this example it is assumed that the discount is taken, and therefore, the cash payment is $9,800. Sales tax is 5% of the invoice price, or $500 (5% × $10,000). During the transportation of the machine uninsured damages of $100 were incurred in an accident, and they were paid by the company. The following summary journal entry is made to record these items:

Machine	12,800	
Repair Expense	100	
Cash		12,900

To record acquisition of machine and damages incurred.

The cost of the machine is calculated as follows:

Contract price	$10,000
Transportation costs	1,500
Sales tax	500
Installation and testing costs	1,000
Less: Cash discounts available	(200)
	$12,800

The transportation, sales tax, and installation and testing costs are included in the cost of the asset because they are necessary for the asset to be able to produce the benefits for which it was purchased. The cost of repairing the damages is excluded from the cost of the asset and therefore recorded as an expense because it was not necessary to incur these costs to receive the benefits associated with the machine. If the cash discount of $200 had not been taken, the cash payment would have increased by $200 and interest expense of $200 would have been recorded (debited). As mentioned earlier, for convenience some companies would include the extra $200 in the cost of the asset. Note that although these costs are incurred at various times, all the costs associated with the asset are included in a single account.

Acquisition Cost in a Lump-Sum Purchase

Frequently, land and buildings are purchased in a single package. In this case it is necessary to separate the cost of the land from the cost of the buildings because the buildings have a limited economic life and are depreciated, whereas land is considered to have an indefinite life and is not depreciated. The cost of each component is determined by its relative fair market value, which may be implicit in the purchase contract or may have to be determined by an appraisal. For example, suppose that land and a building are purchased for $200,000 and an independent appraisal shows that the land would be worth $100,000 and the building $140,000 if they were acquired separately. The cost at which to record each asset is determined as follows:

	Appraisal Value	Relative Fair Market Value	×	Total Cost	=	Allocated Cost
Land	$100,000	$100,000 ÷ $240,000	×	$200,000	=	$ 83,333
Building	140,000	140,000 ÷ 240,000	×	200,000	=	116,667
	$240,000					$200,000

The journal entry to record the acquisition is:

Land	83,333	
Building	116,667	
Cash		200,000

To record the acquisition of land and building.

Note that the sum of the costs recorded for the land and the building is $200,000, which is the total acquisition cost and *not* the total appraisal value of $240,000.

In the preceding situation it was assumed that the company intended to use the building. However, if a company purchases land and a building with the intent to demolish the building and erect a new one, the total cost is assigned to the Land account because the existence of the building was incidental to the acquisition of the land. In addition, the costs of demolishing the old building, net of any salvageable materials, are also added to the Land account.

Depreciation

3. Explain the concept of depreciation.

As we have already discussed, assets included in property, plant, and equipment provide benefits to the company owning (or leasing) the items for more than one year. The *matching* principle, which was discussed in Chapter 3, requires that the costs of generating revenue be matched against the revenue in the accounting period when the revenue is earned. As we saw in Chapter 9 the cost of inventory (cost of goods sold) is matched against the sales revenue in each accounting period, and therefore the amount of the income provides a fair measurement of the success of the company. Similarly, the cost of using the property, plant, and equipment (except land) acquired by a company must be matched in each accounting period against the revenue that these assets help to produce. This cost is the depreciation expense. **The depreciation expense is the portion of the cost of a long-term physical asset allocated as an expense to each accounting period in the asset's service (useful) life.** For a merchandising company, the store, the warehouse, the checkout equipment, and delivery vehicles are all examples of items of property, plant, and equipment that are necessary for making sales, and therefore their depreciable (defined later) cost should be matched against the sales revenue they help to produce over their productive lives.

It may be helpful to consider a property, plant, and equipment asset as a "bundle of services" which are to be used up over the life of the asset. These services are used to provide benefits which are recognized as revenue. When the asset is purchased, the company is paying in advance for those services to be received over several years. Therefore the asset is conceptually the same as other assets, such as prepaid rent or inventory, because each will provide benefits in the future. The differences are that the property, plant, and equipment asset will provide the benefits over a much longer time period and in a less well-defined manner. For example, a factory building may be expected to provide a bundle of services for 30 years. However, the benefits may arise in future years from products that have not even been invented yet. Depreciation is the process of matching the cost of the bundle of services against the benefits produced by those services.

To illustrate depreciation expense, first we review a simple and commonly used method for computing depreciation expense, the straight-line method, which was introduced in Chapter 3, and then we discuss several principles that affect our understanding of depreciation. Finally, we explain the other methods of computing depreciation that are used in practice.

Straight-Line Depreciation

4(a). Compute the amount of depreciation under the straight-line method.

The straight-line depreciation method is a method of depreciating an asset in which the cost of an asset less its estimated residual value is allocated equally to each period of the asset's service (useful) life. It is the simplest and most commonly used way of calculating the amount of depreciation expense. There are three factors involved in the calculation of the amount of depreciation: **(1) the cost of the asset; (2) the estimated service life of the asset, which is the life over which the asset is expected to be useful; and (3) the estimated residual value of the asset, which is the estimated proceeds from the sale or disposal of an asset at the end of its estimated service life.** The service life is often referred to as the *economic life,* and the residual value as the *salvage value.* The cost of the asset is determined according to the principles discussed earlier. The service life and the residual value must be estimated by management when the asset is acquired. The factors affecting these estimates are discussed later, but it should be recognized that these estimates may be difficult to make in practice and they may involve some fairly arbitrary assumptions. The amount of the straight-line depreciation was first discussed in Chapter 3 and is computed as follows:

$$\text{Depreciation per Year} = \frac{\text{Cost} - \text{Estimated Residual Value}}{\text{Estimated Service Life}}$$

The numerator of this depreciation equation is known as the depreciable cost. **The depreciable cost is the cost less the estimated residual value.** It is the estimated total portion of the acquisition cost that will be allocated to depreciation expense over the service life.

For example, suppose that the Marbal Company buys a copying machine for $12,000 on January 1, 1991, and estimates that it will be sold for $1,000 (the residual value) after being used for 5 years (the service life). The depreciable cost of the copying machine to the company is the acquisition cost of $12,000 less the $1,000 it expects to obtain when the asset is sold after 5 years. This $11,000 is allocated equally to each year of the asset's life, or at the rate of $2,200 per year. The straight-line depreciation expense is computed as follows:

$$\text{Depreciation per Year} = \frac{\$12,000 - \$1,000}{5 \text{ years}} = \$2,200$$

Each year the recording of the depreciation expense and the accumulated depreciation reduces the income of the company and the book value of the asset. **Accumulated depreciation is the total depreciation recorded on an asset to date. The book value of an asset is the cost of the asset less the accumulated depreciation.** A summary of the straight-line depreciation over the life of the asset is as follows:

STRAIGHT-LINE DEPRECIATION SCHEDULE

Year	Depreciation Expense	Accumulated Depreciation	Book Value at the End of the Year
1991	$2,200	$ 2,200	$9,800
1992	2,200	4,400	7,600
1993	2,200	6,600	5,400
1994	2,200	8,800	3,200
1995	2,200	11,000	1,000

The amount of straight-line depreciation expense may also be expressed as a percentage of the cost of the asset. In this example it would be expressed as 18.33% ($2,200 ÷ $12,000).

Effects of Depreciation on the Financial Statements

The journal entry required to record the preceding annual depreciation calculation is as follows:

Depreciation Expense: Machine 2,200
    Accumulated Depreciation: Machine 2,200

To record depreciation for the year on the copying machine.

Recording depreciation has two effects on the financial statements. The cost that is matched against the revenues in a particular accounting period is included as an expense in the income statement. Therefore it is debited to the Depreciation Expense account. This expired cost also represents a reduction in the book value of the asset (acquisition cost minus accumulated depreciation). Rather than reduce (credit) the asset account directly, the normal procedure is to increase (credit) a contra-asset account, Accumulated Depreciation (contra-asset accounts were first discussed in Chapter 4). Either procedure has the same effect of reducing the book value of the asset, but the use of the contra-asset account is preferable because it aids in preparing the financial statements, in which both the acquisition cost and the sum of the accumulated depreciation to date have to be disclosed in the balance sheet (or in the notes). For example, the Marbal Company would disclose the following information in its balance sheet for December 31, 1991 and 1992:

	1991	1992
Machinery, cost	$12,000	$12,000
Less: Accumulated depreciation	(2,200)	(4,400)
	$ 9,800	$ 7,600

Recording the cost and the accumulated depreciation in separate accounts makes the information more readily available.

Each year the Depreciation Expense account balance is closed to Income Summary, and the balance in the Accumulated Depreciation account grows until the asset is fully depreciated. Therefore at the end of the estimated service life the book value of the asset is equal to its expected residual value. For example, in the straight-line depreciation situation the book value at the end of 1995 is $1,000, the same as the estimated residual value.

As a reminder, the debit to Depreciation Expense is included as an expense that is matched against sales revenue in the income statement, and the credit to Accumulated Depreciation reduces the book value of the asset in the balance sheet. Separate depreciation expense and accumulated depreciation accounts should be maintained for each class of asset.

Causes of Depreciation

The service life of an asset, which is the period over which the asset is expected to provide benefits, may be limited by several factors, which can be divided into the categories of physical causes and functional causes, as shown in the following illustration:

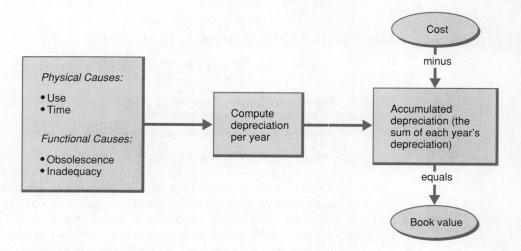

Physical Causes.   Physical causes include wear and tear due to operational *use*, deterioration and decay caused by the passage of *time*, and damage and destruction.

Functional Causes. Functional causes limit the life of the asset, even though the physical life is not exhausted. *Obsolescence* is a common occurrence in a technologically advanced economy when an asset is made obsolete by the introduction of new technology. *Inadequacy* occurs when an asset is no longer suitable for the company's operations even though it may still be physically sound.

The lives of most assets are not limited by a single factor operating alone. In most cases a primary cause can be identified, however. For example, the life of a delivery truck is primarily limited by physical causes, in which wear and tear, deterioration and decay, and damage and destruction may all be expected to contribute. In contrast, the useful life of a computer is likely to be limited by a functional cause, whether it be obsolescence resulting from the availability of newer, more efficient computers, or inadequacy resulting from the needs of the company outgrowing the capacity of the computer.

The straight-line method of depreciation discussed earlier is appropriate when the usefulness of the asset is expected to be equal each period. If the benefits are equal each period, the total *remaining* benefits decline equally each period. This pattern of depreciation occurs when physical deterioration and decay occur at a steady rate over the life of the asset, or when the usefulness is reduced by a functional cause. Then it is reasonable to record an equal amount of depreciation expense each period by using the straight-line method.

Service Life and Residual Value

The estimated service life of an asset is affected by the perceptions of the company's management of the various causes discussed earlier. This estimated service life also directly affects the estimate of the residual value. In some cases it may be management's intention to keep the asset until its physical life is exhausted. In this case the estimated residual value will be close to zero (or it may even be negative if disposal costs are significant and exceed the value of any salvaged material, such as for a nuclear power plant). Alternatively, management may dispose of the asset well before its physical life is exhausted, in which case the estimated residual value may be very large. For example, airlines often sell their planes long before the end of their physical lives. In practice, it may be difficult to estimate the service life and residual value of an asset, but management must make realistic estimates using the best information available.

Allocation of Cost Not Valuation

As we discussed earlier, the process of depreciation involves the matching of the acquisition cost of the asset as an expense against the revenue. **Depreciation is not an attempt to provide an estimate of the value of the asset at any given time.** As we saw with the straight-line method, the purpose of depreciation is to allocate the cost of an asset as an expense over its service life and in so doing reduce the book value of the asset to its estimated residual value (which is an estimate of the market value of the asset at the *end* of its life). Depreciating an asset, however, is *not* an attempt to estimate the market value of an asset *during* its life. Therefore it is only at the time of acquisition and at the end of the life of an asset (if the original estimate of the residual value is accurate) that the book value can be expected to equal the asset's market value. During the life of the asset, the book value is the cost of the remaining "bundle of services" that the company expects to obtain from the asset, and *not* the value of those services. However, certain supplemental disclosures of the current values of property, plant, and equipment may be included in the annual reports of some companies. We will discuss these disclosures in Chapter 20.

Systematic and Rational Allocation of Costs

Since depreciation is not an attempt to measure the value of an asset, it is reasonable to ask, "What is the purpose?" Remember the discussion of matching expenses with revenues with which we introduced the subject of depreciation. The cost of the asset should be matched as an expense against the revenues (benefits) it helps to produce. Since it is usually impossible to measure precisely the benefits that a particular asset provides, the underlying principle is that costs should be matched in a "systematic and rational"[1] manner against revenues. **The term systematic is used to indicate that the calculation should follow a formula and not be determined in an arbitrary manner.** The straight-line method and the alternative methods discussed next are all considered systematic. **The term rational is used to indicate that the amount of the depreciation should relate to the benefits that the asset produces in any period.** Thus the straight-line method should be used when it may be reasonably assumed that the asset produces equal benefits each period over its life. Then an equal cost each period is matched as an expense against an equal benefit (revenues) each period. An accelerated method should be used when it is considered that the benefits generated by an asset are highest early in the life of the asset and decline in each succeeding period. **An accelerated depreciation method is a method of depreciation in which a higher amount of depreciation is recognized in the first year of the asset's life and lesser amounts are recognized in each subsequent year.**

It is sometimes suggested that the management of a company has a free hand in the selection of a depreciation method. The preceding discussion should have made it clear that the selection of a particular method is based on specific criteria that management should follow.

Accelerated Depreciation Methods

Two accelerated depreciation methods, the double-declining balance and the sum-of-the-years'-digits methods, are often used. These methods are also known as *declining charge* methods because the amount of depreciation declines in each succeeding period. The early recognition of a higher depreciation expense, however, is offset by recognizing less depreciation expense later in the life of the asset, and therefore the *total* depreciation expense recognized over the life of the asset is always the same (the total expense equals the depreciable cost, which is the cost less the estimated residual value). Each of these accelerated methods is discussed here.

---

[1]*Accounting Terminology Bulletin No. 1* (New York: AICPA, 1953), par. 56.

4(b). Compute the amount of depreciation under the double-declining balance method.

Double-Declining Balance Method. **The double-declining balance method is an accelerated depreciation method in which the depreciation expense is computed by multiplying the book value of the asset at the beginning of the period by twice the straight-line rate.** Note that the method uses twice the *rate* that is used for the straight-line method (*not* twice the amount) and that the residual value is *not* considered in the calculation of the depreciation expense. The asset, however, should never be depreciated below the estimated residual value, as discussed later. The depreciation expense on an asset in any year is computed as follows:

$$\text{Depreciation per Year} = 2 \times \text{Straight-Line Rate} \times \text{Book Value at the Beginning of the Year}$$

$$= 2 \times \frac{1}{\text{Life}} \times \text{Book Value at the Beginning of the Year}$$

For example, consider the Marbal Company example introduced when straight-line depreciation was discussed. The copying machine was purchased at the beginning of 1991 and had the following characteristics:

Cost	$12,000
Estimated residual value	1,000
Estimated service life	5 years

Since the asset has a life of 5 years, the straight-line depreciation rate is 20% per year. Therefore the double-declining balance depreciation rate is 40% per year, and the depreciation expense each year is calculated as follows:

DOUBLE-DECLINING BALANCE DEPRECIATION SCHEDULE

Year	Book Value at the Beginning of the Year	Depreciation Calculation	Depreciation Expense	Accumulated Depreciation	Book Value at the End of the Year
1991	$12,000	40% × $12,000	$4,800	$ 4,800	$7,200
1992	7,200	40% × 7,200	2,880	7,680	4,320
1993	4,320	40% × 4,320	1,728	9,408	2,592
1994	2,592	40% × 2,592	1,037	10,445	1,555
1995	1,555		555[a]	11,000	1,000

[a] 40% × $1,555 = $622, but depreciation expense is limited to $555. See following discussion.

Note that the calculation of the depreciation in the first year was based on the total acquisition cost of $12,000 and *not* on the acquisition cost less the estimated residual value. In 1995 a modification has to be made to the usual calculations because the asset should not be depreciated below its estimated residual value. Therefore in 1995 the depreciation expense should be only $555 (instead of 40% × $1,555, or $622), which reduces the book value to $1,000 at the end of the year so that it is equal to the estimated residual value.

The double-declining balance method is the most accelerated method of depreciation that is allowed under generally accepted accounting principles.

Another accelerated method that is sometimes used is the 150% declining balance method. This method is applied in exactly the same way as the double-declining method, except that, as the name implies, the rate that is used is $1\frac{1}{2}$ times the straight-line rate. If the Marbal Company used this method it would depreciate the book value of the copying machine at the rate of 30% per year ($1\frac{1}{2} \times 20\%$), and the depreciation expense in 1991 would be $3,600 (30% × $12,000).

4(c). Compute the amount of depreciation under the sum-of-the-years'-digits method.

Sum-of-the-Years'-Digits Method. **The sum-of-the-years'-digits method is an accelerated depreciation method in which the depreciation is computed by multiplying the depreciable cost by a fraction that declines each year.** Thus the depreciation expense on an asset in any year is computed as follows:

$$\text{Depreciation per Year} = (\text{Cost} - \text{Residual Value}) \times \text{Fraction}$$

The fraction each year is calculated as follows:

$$\text{Fraction} = \frac{\text{Number of Years Remaining in the Asset's Life at the Beginning of the Year}}{\text{Sum of the Years' Digits}}$$

The sum of the years' digits for an asset with a 5-year life is $5 + 4 + 3 + 2 + 1 = 15$.[2] The annual depreciation expense and the book value at the end of each year for the Marbal Company's copying machine with a depreciable cost of $11,000 ($12,000 – $1,000) would be computed as follows:

SUM-OF-THE-YEARS'-DIGITS DEPRECIATION SCHEDULE

Year	Depreciation Calculation	Depreciation Expense	Book Value at the End of the Year
1991	$11,000 × 5/15	$3,667	$8,333
1992	11,000 × 4/15	2,933	5,400
1993	11,000 × 3/15	2,200	3,200
1994	11,000 × 2/15	1,467	1,733
1995	11,000 × 1/15	733	1,000

Note that the book value at the end of the last year of the asset's life equals $1,000, which is the estimated residual value of the asset. This value results because the sum of the fractions used in the calculation of the depreciation total 15/15, and the amount being depreciated is the cost less the estimated residual value.

The effect of the straight-line and two accelerated depreciation methods on depreciation expense and book value for the Marbal Company's machine is illustrated by the diagrams in Exhibit 11-1.

---

[2]The general formula to compute the sum of the years' digits is $n(n + 1) \div 2$. Thus for an asset with a 20-year life, the sum is $(20 \times 21) \div 2 = 210$.

EXHIBIT 11-1
Depreciation Expense
and Book Value for
Alternative
Depreciation
Methods

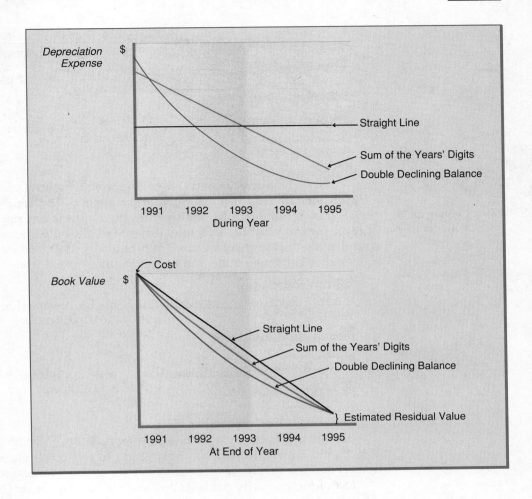

The depreciation methods discussed so far—the straight-line, double-declining balance, and the sum-of-the-years'-digits methods—are all based on the life of the asset measured in years. It may be more reasonable, however, to measure the life of the asset in terms of its expected physical activity, and therefore to base the depreciation expense on that activity.

Activity Depreciation Methods

An activity method is a depreciation method in which the depreciation expense is based on the level of physical activity of the asset. The activity (or use) of an asset may be measured in terms of the number of units the asset is expected to produce, or perhaps the number of hours it is expected to operate. For example, the Marbal Company might estimate that its copying machine would be expected to produce 500,000 copies or operate for 10,000 hours during its useful life. The depreciation *rate* could be computed on the basis of the number of copies or the hours as follows:

$$\text{Depreciation Rate} = \frac{\text{Cost} - \text{Estimated Residual Value}}{\text{Total Lifetime Activity Level}}$$

$$= \frac{\$12,000 - \$1,000}{500,000 \text{ copies}} = \$0.022 \text{ per copy}$$

or

$$\text{Depreciation Rate} = \frac{\$12,000 - \$1,000}{10,000 \text{ hours}} = \$1.10 \text{ per hour}$$

4(d). Compute the amount of depreciation under activity methods.

When the depreciation is based on the activity level of the asset it is sometimes referred to as the *units-of-production* method. **The depreciation expense for the year is computed by multiplying the depreciation rate times the activity level for the year.** For example, if the Marbal Company makes 110,000 copies and operates the machine for 1,900 hours in 1991, the depreciation expense would be computed under the two alternatives, as follows:

$$\text{Depreciation Expense} = \text{Rate per Copy} \times \text{Number of Copies}$$
$$= \$0.022 \times 110,000 \text{ copies}$$
$$= \$2,420$$

or

$$\text{Depreciation Expense} = \text{Rate per Hour} \times \text{Number of Hours}$$
$$= \$1.10 \times 1,900 \text{ hours}$$
$$= \$2,090$$

Although in this example we illustrate depreciation based on both activity levels, it should be noted that the company has to select one measure of the activity level and use that measure consistently for its computation of depreciation. The effect of these activity methods on the financial statements should be compared to the straight-line method. The activity methods produce a constant depreciation rate per *unit* (hour or copy in this example), but the total depreciation expense will vary per *year* as the activity level varies. In contrast, the straight-line method produces a constant depreciation expense per *year*, but the amount will vary per *unit* as the activity level varies. It can be seen from this comparison that an activity method is more appropriate when the service life of the asset is limited by physical reasons (especially wear and tear) and the level of activity varies from period to period.

Use of Alternative Depreciation Methods

The relative use of alternative depreciation methods for 600 surveyed companies is shown in Exhibit 11-2. There are more than 600 responses because many companies use more than one method of depreciation. However, it is very clear that the straight-line method is by far the most widely used method because most companies have assets that provide equal benefits each period.

EXHIBIT 11-2
Use of Alternative
Depreciation Methods

	Number of Companies				
	1987	*1986*	*1985*	*1984*	*1983*
Straight-line	559	561	563	567	564
Declining balance	44	49	53	54	57
Sum-of-the-years' digits	12	14	16	15	17
Accelerated method—not specified	76	77	73	76	74
Activity	51	48	54	60	65
Other	12	12	12	13	12

Source: Accounting Trends and Techniques (New York: AICPA, 1988).

Additional Depreciation Considerations

Several additional considerations are discussed in this section. The calculation of depreciation expense when an asset is acquired or disposed of during a period, the effect of depreciation on income taxes, the relationship between depreciation and replacement of an asset, and a revision of the estimate of residual value or service life are all discussed.

Depreciation and Fractional Periods

5. Compute depreciation for fractional periods.

In the discussion of depreciation so far, we have implicitly assumed that the asset was acquired at the beginning of the year and therefore a full year's depreciation expense was recorded in the year of acquisition. Assets are usually purchased throughout the year, however, and rules have to be developed for determining the amount of depreciation to record for each period in such situations. Three of the commonly used alternatives are as follows:

1. *Compute depreciation expense to the nearest whole month.* An asset purchased on or before the 15th of the month is depreciated for the whole month, and an asset purchased after the 15th of the month is not depreciated in the month of acquisition. For example, if an asset is purchased on May 20, depreciation is recorded in the first year for June through December, or 7 months.

2. *Compute depreciation expense to the nearest whole year.* A full year's depreciation is recorded in the year of acquisition if the asset is acquired in the first half of the fiscal year and no depreciation is recorded in that year if the asset is acquired in the second half of the fiscal year. A full year's depreciation is recorded in the year of disposal if the asset is disposed of in the second half of the fiscal year and no depreciation is recorded in that year if the asset is disposed of in the first half of the fiscal year.

3. *Record one-half year's depreciation expense on all assets purchased or sold during the year.* No matter when the asset is acquired or disposed of during the fiscal year, one-half year's depreciation is recorded in both the year of acquisition and the year of disposal.

To illustrate these three alternatives, suppose that a company with an accounting period ending on December 31 purchases a machine on September 28, 1991, for $6,000. The machine has an estimated life of 3 years and no estimated residual value. The asset is disposed of on September 20, 1994. Straight-line depreciation expense would be computed as follows:

Year	Compute Depreciation to the Nearest Whole Month	Compute Depreciation to the Nearest Whole Year	Record One-Half Year's Depreciation on All Assets Purchased or Sold During the Year
1991	$ 500[a]	$ 0[d]	$1,000[f]
1992	2,000[b]	2,000	2,000
1993	2,000	2,000	2,000
1994	1,500[c]	2,000[e]	1,000[f]

[a] $3/12 \times [(\text{Cost} - \text{Residual}) \div \text{Life}] = 3/12[(\$6,000 - \$0) \div 3]$.
[b] $(\$6,000 - \$0) \div 3$.
[c] $9/12 \times [(\$6,000 - \$0) \div 3]$.
[d] Asset acquired in the second half of the year; depreciation expense is zero.
[e] Asset sold in second half of the year; depreciation expense is for full year, or $2,000.
[f] Asset acquired or sold during the year; depreciation expense is $2,000 \times \frac{1}{2}$.

Depreciation and Income Taxes

Depreciation is an expense that is deducted in the income statement shown in a corporation's annual report, and it is also deducted by a corporation in reporting its taxable income under the provisions of the Internal Revenue Code. Because the depreciation rules are different for income tax purposes than for accounting purposes **the amounts of depreciation expense in any year for financial reporting and for income tax reporting are different** (as discussed next). It should not be surprising that the amounts can be different because the objectives of financial reporting and the Internal Revenue Code are quite different. An objective of the generally accepted accounting principles used in financial reporting is to prepare income statements that fairly present the income-producing activities of the company and are useful to decision makers. In contrast, the objectives of the Internal Revenue Code, among others, are to obtain revenue for the operation of the federal government and to provide certain kinds of investment incentives for business activity.

Management has a responsibility to minimize the income taxes paid by the corporation without violating the law. Therefore it is desirable for a corporation to record, for income tax purposes, as much depreciation as possible early in the life of an asset. Higher depreciation reduces the corporation's taxable income, thereby reducing the income taxes paid. In 1981 the Accelerated Cost Recovery System (ACRS) was introduced by Congress as the method to be used for depreciating assets for income tax purposes; in 1984 and 1986 revisions were made.[3]

---

[3]Assets acquired in years prior to 1981 are depreciated for income tax purposes by different rules that may use the accelerated depreciation methods discussed earlier. Assets acquired in years prior to 1987 are depreciated for income tax purposes by the ACRS method, but the lives and methods used are different.

6. Calculate depreciation for income tax purposes.

There are three ways in which the depreciation deducted for income tax purposes under ACRS may be different than depreciation deducted in the financial statements:

1. *Different Life.* All assets are depreciated over a tax life which is defined for each type of asset by the Internal Revenue Code. These tax lives are used no matter what the service life is estimated to be for the computation of depreciation for financial reporting purposes. Typically the tax life is shorter than the service life.

2. *No Residual Value.* The residual value is ignored, and the asset is depreciated to a zero residual value, thereby making the total depreciation over an asset's life equal to its cost.

3. *Specified Method.* ACRS requires the use of the double-declining balance method for assets with a tax life of 3, 5, 7, or 10 years. The 150% declining balance method is used for assets with a tax life of 15 or 20 years. Buildings are depreciated by the straight-line method over $27\frac{1}{2}$ years (residential) or $31\frac{1}{2}$ years (nonresidential). (Alternatively, a company may select the use of the straight-line method for any asset.)

All the depreciation calculations for income tax purposes are based on the half-year convention; that is, depreciation for half a year is recorded both in the year of acquisition and in the final year of depreciation. Also when an accelerated method is used, a change is made to the straight-line method in the period in which the straight-line depreciation exceeds the amount calculated under the accelerated method. To simplify the calculation of ACRS depreciation, tables have been prepared as illustrated in Exhibit 11-3.

EXHIBIT 11-3
ACRS Depreciation as a Percentage of the Cost of the Asset

Year of Life	3	5	7	10	15	20
			Tax Life of Asset in Years			
1	33.33%	20.00%	14.29%	10.00%	5.00%	3.750%
2	44.45	32.00	24.49	18.00	9.50	7.219
3	14.81	19.20	17.49	14.40	8.55	6.677
4	7.41	11.52	12.49	11.52	7.70	6.177
5		11.52	8.93	9.22	6.93	5.713
6		5.76	8.92	7.37	6.23	5.285
7			8.93	6.55	5.90	4.888
8			4.46	6.55	5.90	4.522
9				6.56	5.91	4.462
10				6.55	5.90	4.461
11				3.28	5.91	4.462
12					5.90	4.461
13					5.91	4.462
14					5.90	4.461
15					5.91	4.462
16					2.95	4.461
17						4.462
18						4.461
19						4.462
20						4.461
21						2.231

The use of ACRS will result in tax depreciation being different than depreciation for financial reporting.[4] Companies are required to disclose the effects of the resulting differences in depreciation in the notes to the financial statements. To illustrate the differences in the two methods assume that the Arc Company purchased an asset on January 1, 1991. Information about the asset is given in Exhibit 11-4 along with the calculation of the depreciation for income tax purposes. The calculations of the depreciation for financial statements is also shown for comparison. Thus it can be seen that the depreciation each year on the financial statements is very different from that reported on the income tax return. However, note that the total depreciation for income tax purposes is $13,500 over the three-year tax life, whereas in the financial statements the total depreciation expense is $12,500 over the five-year service life of the machine. If the machine is sold for $1,000 (the estimated residual value) at the end of 1995, a gain of $1,000 is recognized for income tax purposes, whereas no gain would be recognized in the financial statements because the asset was sold for an amount equal to its book value at the time (gains and losses on disposals of assets are discussed in Chapter 12). Therefore after the sale of the asset the total deductions recorded to date on the company's income statements ($12,500 total depreciation expense) are equal to the total net deductions reported for income tax purposes ($13,500 total depreciation expense less the $1,000 gain on the sale). The use of the ACRS procedures, however, accelerates the deductions taken for income tax purposes, thereby delaying the payment of income taxes until later in the life of the asset. The effect of the differences between the income tax expense and the income taxes paid is briefly discussed in Chapter 16.

EXHIBIT 11-4
Computation of
Depreciation for Income
Taxes and Financial
Statements

ARC COMPANY	
Computation of Depreciation for Income Tax Reporting	**Computation of Depreciation for Financial Statements**
Cost of asset: $13,500	Cost of asset: $13,500
Purchased: January 1, 1991	Purchased: January 1, 1991
ACRS life: 3 years	Service life: 5 years
Residual value: Zero	Residual value: $1,000
ACRS Depreciation Amounts[a]	*Financial Statement Depreciation Amounts*
1991 $4,500 ($13,500 × 33.33%)	1991 $2,500 {($13,500 − $1,000) ÷ 5 years}
1992 $6,000 ($13,500 × 44.45%)	1992 $2,500
1993 $2,000 ($13,500 × 14.81%)	1993 $2,500
1994 $1,000 ($13,500 × 7.41%)	1994 $2,500
1995 $0	1995 $2,500

[a]Percentages from Exhibit 11-3. Amounts are rounded.

[4]Some small companies do use ACRS in their financial statements. Such financial statements are, however, in violation of generally accepted accounting principles unless the difference from an acceptable method is not material.

Depreciation and the Replacement of an Asset

As we have seen, depreciation expense is based on the acquisition cost, estimated residual value, and estimated service life of the asset. It is sometimes suggested, however, that one of the purposes of recording depreciation is to ensure that sufficient cash will be available to replace the asset. When an asset is depreciated, a company has more cash than it *would have had* if no depreciation expense was recorded, because income taxes paid are reduced and therefore the cash held by the company is increased. It should be clearly recognized, however, that this does *not* mean that sufficient cash is available at the end of the life of the asset to replace it. First, the cash would have to be on hand for the replacement of the asset. The cash saved by the company in income taxes, however, may have been used for other purposes. Second, the cash saved is much less than the cost of the asset. Third, the effects of inflation are likely to cause the cost of replacing the asset to be considerably higher than the cash saved in income taxes. It should be clear that planning for the replacement of an asset and also for financing the acquisition require explicit decisions by management.

Revision of Estimates

As we have seen, the calculation of depreciation depends on making estimates of the service life and the residual value of an asset. Sometimes these estimates have to be revised because new knowledge is acquired or operating conditions change. **When estimates are changed, depreciation is computed on the basis of the revised amounts and therefore the remaining undepreciated cost is depreciated over the remaining service life.** For example, suppose that a building has the following characteristics at the time of acquisition:

Acquisition cost	$90,000
Date of purchase	January 1, 1989
Estimated residual value	$10,000
Estimated service life	40 years
Annual depreciation expense (straight line)	$2,000 [($90,000 − $10,000) ÷ 40]

At December 31, 1993, the accumulated depreciation and book value are:

Accumulated depreciation	$10,000 (5 × $2,000)
Book value	$80,000 ($90,000 − $10,000)

At the beginning of 1994 (after 5 years), the following revised estimates are made:

Estimated residual value	$20,000
Estimated remaining service life	20 years (for a total life of 25 years)

The depreciation per year is computed, using the remaining book value and the revised estimates, as follows:

$$\text{Depreciation per Year} = \frac{\text{Book Value} - \text{Estimated Residual Value}}{\text{Estimated Remaining Service Life}}$$

$$= \frac{\$80,000 - \$20,000}{20}$$

$$= \$3,000 \text{ per year}$$

This revised amount of depreciation expense would be recorded each year for the remainder of the asset's life.

Subsequent Expenditures

7. Explain the accounting for expenditures incurred after the acquisition of property, plant, and equipment.

After an asset has been acquired further expenditures on the asset are often made during its economic life. These expenditures and their appropriate accounting treatment can be categorized as follows:

1. *Capital expenditures.* **Capital expenditures are expenditures that increase the benefits to be obtained from an asset and should be capitalized. Capitalization is the recording of the cost as an increase in the book value of the asset.** An increase in the book value of an asset may be accomplished by an increase (debit) in the asset account or a decrease (debit) in the related accumulated depreciation account, as discussed next. If the expenditure increases the usefulness of the asset, it should be added (debited) to the asset account; and if it extends the life of the asset, it should be subtracted from (debited to) the accumulated depreciation account.

2. *Operating expenditures.* **Operating expenditures are expenditures that only maintain the benefits that were originally expected to be obtained from the asset and should be expensed.** Operating expenditures are sometimes called *revenue* expenditures.

Capital Expenditures

Examples of capital expenditures are additions, improvements, replacements, and extraordinary repairs such as adding a new wing to a building, installing additional insulation, replacing the roof of a building so that the life of the building is longer than originally expected, or repairing a boiler in such an extensive way that its life is extended. All costs associated with these items, which are often called "renewals and betterments," should be capitalized.

Ideally, capital expenditures should be accounted for by removing from the accounts (in the manner discussed in the next chapter) the cost and accumulated depreciation that relate to the part of the old asset being replaced or improved. Then the expenditure would be added (or debited) to the appropriate asset account. Since the cost and accumulated depreciation on the part of the asset being replaced or improved are often impossible to determine, however, the common practice is to **add the cost to the asset account if the expenditure is being made to increase the usefulness of the asset.** Alternatively, **subtract the cost from the Accumulated Depreciation account if the expenditure is being made to extend the life of the asset.** The effect of this latter entry is to *decrease* the Accumulated Depreciation account, thereby *increasing* the book value of the asset by the amount of the expenditure. For example, a capital expenditure of $20,000 to replace a roof on a warehouse, thereby extending the life of the warehouse, is recorded as follows:

Accumulated Depreciation: Warehouse	20,000	
Cash		20,000

To record replacement of roof on warehouse.

Alternatively, if an expenditure of $20,000 to enlarge a warehouse increases the usefulness of the warehouse, the cost is added to the asset account as follows:

Warehouse	20,000	
Cash		20,000

To record enlargement of warehouse.

It should be noted that the net effect of both entries is to increase the book value of the asset by $20,000. One entry decreases the accumulated depreciation, and the other entry increases the balance in the asset account.

Operating Expenditures

Expenditures that maintain the benefits that were originally expected from the asset should be expensed when incurred. These expenditures are known as operating (or revenue) expenditures. The major item in this category is routine repair and maintenance costs. For example, if a company buys an automobile that it expects to use for 60,000 miles, it knows that it will have to perform repairs and maintenance during that time. Consequently, each routine repair merely maintains the ability of the car to last for 60,000 miles and does not extend its life beyond the 60,000 miles. To illustrate, if a company had a tuneup on one of its cars at a cost of $60, it is recorded as follows:

Repair Expense	60	
Cash		60

To record tuneup on car.

Some items that should be considered capital expenditures are often accounted for as operating expenditures because the dollar amounts are so small as to be considered immaterial. For example, the company owning the car mentioned earlier might decide to buy a new engine for the car at 50,000 miles so that the car can be used for another 30,000 miles. This is a capital expenditure because it extends the life of the car beyond the original 60,000 miles, although it is often accounted for as an operating expenditure (i.e., it is recorded as an expense) because it is not material.

Effects of Errors If Capital and Operating Expenditures Are Incorrectly Classified. Care must be taken to ensure that an expenditure is properly recorded as a capital or operating expenditure. An erroneous classification that is material may have a significant impact on the financial statements. For example, suppose that the cost of a new machine is incorrectly recorded as a repairs expense. Therefore the repairs expense will be overstated on the income statement and net income will be understated. Also the asset, machinery, on the balance sheet will be understated. If the error is not corrected, depreciation expense in future years will be understated and net income overstated.

Alternatively, suppose that repairs to machinery are incorrectly recorded as a capital expenditure for machinery. Repairs expense will be understated on the income statement and net income will be overstated. Also the asset, machinery, on the balance sheet will be overstated. If the error is not corrected, depreciation expense in future years will be overstated and net income understated. Therefore it can be seen that the correct classification of subsequent expenditures is important to the measurement of income.

Disclosure in the Financial Statements

We have used the title Property, Plant, and Equipment in this chapter because it is the most frequently used caption in the balance sheet. Variations of this title are sometimes used, however, such as Plant and Machinery, Land and Buildings, or for a merchandising company, Property and Equipment. Companies are required to disclose the following items in the financial statements or in the notes accompanying these statements:

1. Depreciation expense for the period.
2. Balances of major classes of depreciable assets by nature (such as land, buildings, equipment) or function (such as petroleum exploration, chemical, construction) at the balance sheet date.
3. Accumulated depreciation, either by major classes of assets or in total, at the balance sheet date.
4. A general description of the method or methods used in computing depreciation with respect to the major classes of depreciable assets.

For example, the United Technologies Corporation satisfies these disclosure requirements as shown in Exhibit 11-5. It should be noted that a company may use different depreciation methods for different types of assets because of differences in the patterns of benefits generated by each group.

EXHIBIT 11-5
Example of Disclosure

UNITED TECHNOLOGIES CORPORATION Consolidated Balance Sheets (Partial) December 31, 1988 and 1987		
Assets (in millions of dollars)	1988	1987
Fixed Assets, at cost:		
Land	$ 119.2	$ 144.5
Buildings and improvements	1,913.6	1,916.5
Machinery, tools and equipment	4,277.7	4,149.3
Under construction	489.0	510.8
	$ 6,799.5	$ 6,721.1
Less accumulated depreciation and amortization	(3,392.9)	(3,367.9)
	$ 3,406.6	$ 3,353.2

Consolidated Statements of Cash Flows (Partial)
Years ended December 31, 1988 and 1987

Depreciation (in millions of dollars)	536.4	505.1

Notes to Financial Statements (in part)

Provisions for depreciation of plant and equipment related to the Corporation's aerospace operations have generally been made on accelerated methods. Provisions for depreciation of other plant and equipment have generally been made on the straight-line method. Wherever possible, accelerated methods are used for income tax purposes. Generally, estimated useful lives used for financial statement depreciation purposes range from 30 to 50 years for buildings and improvements, from 8 to 20 years for machinery and equipment, and from 5 to 10 years for office equipment.

Chapter Summary

Review of Learning Objectives

> 1. **Identify the characteristics of property, plant, and equipment.**
> Property, plant, and equipment are the long-term physical assets acquired for use in the operations of a company. To be included in this category the asset must be used in the operating activities of the company, must have a life of more than 1 year, and must be tangible in nature.

> 2. **Compute the acquisition cost of property, plant, and equipment.**
> The acquisition cost of property, plant, and equipment includes all the expenditures that are necessary and reasonable to acquire the asset and prepare it for its intended use. These costs include the contract price (less any discounts available), transportation costs, sales tax, installation and testing costs, and other related necessary and reasonable costs.

> 3. **Explain the concept of depreciation.**
> The depreciation expense is the portion of the cost of a long-term physical asset allocated as an expense to each accounting period in the asset's service (useful) life. The depreciation expense for each period is therefore matched against the revenues earned.

> 4. **Compute the amount of depreciation under the (a) straight-line method, (b) double-declining balance method, (c) sum-of-the-years'-digits method, and (d) activity methods.**
> The *straight-line* method is a depreciation method in which the depreciation expense is computed by dividing the cost of an asset less its estimated residual value by the asset's service life. The *double-declining balance* method is an accelerated method in which the depreciation expense is computed by multiplying the book value of an asset at the beginning of the period by twice the straight-line rate. The *sum-of-the-years'-digits* method is an accelerated depreciation method in which the depreciation is computed by multiplying the depreciable cost of an asset by a fraction that declines each period. The numerator of the fraction is the number of years remaining in the asset's life at the beginning of the year and the denominator is the sum of the years' digits. An *activity* method is a depreciation method in which the depreciation expense is based on the level of physical activity of the asset.

> 5. **Compute depreciation for fractional periods.**
> When computing depreciation for a fractional period, depreciation expense may be computed to the nearest whole month or to the nearest whole year, or one-half year's depreciation may be recorded on all assets purchased or sold during the year.

> 6. **Calculate depreciation for income tax purposes.**
> Depreciation expense for income tax purposes is computed under the Accelerated Cost Recovery System (ACRS). The system defines the life of the asset, ignores the residual value, and specifies a depreciation method to be used for each defined life.

7. Explain the accounting for expenditures incurred after the acquisition of property, plant, and equipment.

Capital expenditures increase the benefits to be obtained from an asset and should be capitalized. *Operating* expenditures only maintain the benefits that were originally expected to be obtained from the asset and should be expensed.

Review Problem

On January 1, 1991, the Matt Company purchased a machine for $70,000. The machine had an estimated service life of 6 years and an estimated residual value of $7,000.

REQUIRED

1. Prepare a schedule to show the depreciation expense, the accumulated depreciation, and the book value at the end of each year for the following methods:
   a. Straight line.
   b. Sum of the years' digits.
   c. Double declining balance.

2. If the machine has a life for income tax purposes of 3 years, prepare a schedule to compute the ACRS depreciation for each year of the asset's tax life.

Solution to Review Problem

1. a. *Straight line*

Year	Depreciation Expense	Accumulated Depreciation	Book Value at the End of the Year
1991	$10,500[a]	$10,500	$59,500
1992	10,500	21,000	49,000
1993	10,500	31,500	38,500
1994	10,500	42,000	28,000
1995	10,500	52,500	17,500
1996	10,500	63,000	7,000

[a] $\dfrac{\$70,000 - \$7,000}{6}$

b. *Sum of the years' digits*

The total of the sum of the years'
digits for a life of 6 years $= 6 + 5 + 4 + 3 + 2 + 1$
                                      $= 21$
or $n(n + 1) \div 2 = 21$

Year	Depreciation Calculation	Depreciation Expense	Accumulated Depreciation	Book Value at the End of the Year
1991	$63,000 × 6/21	$18,000	$18,000	$52,000
1992	63,000 × 5/21	15,000	33,000	37,000
1993	63,000 × 4/21	12,000	45,000	25,000
1994	63,000 × 3/21	9,000	54,000	16,000
1995	63,000 × 2/21	6,000	60,000	10,000
1996	63,000 × 1/21	3,000	63,000	7,000

c. *Double-declining balance (rounded to the nearest dollar)*

$$\text{Straight line rate} = 1/6 = 16\tfrac{2}{3}\%$$
$$\text{Double declining rate} = 2 \times 16\tfrac{2}{3}\%$$
$$= 33\tfrac{1}{3}\%$$

Year	Book Value at the Beginning of the Year	Depreciation Calculation	Depreciation Expense	Accumulated Depreciation	Book Value at the End of the Year
1991	$70,000	$33\tfrac{1}{3}\% \times \$70,000$	$23,333	$23,333	$46,667
1992	46,667	$33\tfrac{1}{3}\% \times \$46,667$	15,556	38,889	31,111
1993	31,111	$33\tfrac{1}{3}\% \times \$31,111$	10,370	49,259	20,741
1994	20,741	$33\tfrac{1}{3}\% \times \$20,741$	6,914	56,173	13,827
1995	13,827	$33\tfrac{1}{3}\% \times \$13,827$	4,609	60,782	9,218
1996	9,218		2,218[a]	63,000	7,000

[a]The depreciation expense is $2,218 rather than $3,073 ($33\tfrac{1}{3}\% \times \$9,218$) to reduce the book value to the expected residual value of $7,000.

2. *ACRS depreciation*

1991	$23,331	($70,000 × 33.33%)
1992	31,115	($70,000 × 44.45%)
1993	10,367	($70,000 × 14.81%)
1994	5,187	($70,000 × 7.41%)
1995	—	
1996	—	

Glossary

Accelerated Depreciation Methods. Methods of depreciation in which a higher amount of depreciation is recognized in the first year of the asset's life and lesser amounts are recognized in each subsequent year. Examples are double-declining and sum-of-the-years'-digits depreciation. Also known as *declining-charge methods.*

Accumulated Depreciation. The total depreciation recorded on an asset to date.

Acquisition Cost. The total expenditures that are necessary and reasonable to acquire an asset and prepare it for its intended use.

Activity Depreciation Methods. Methods of depreciation that are based on the level of physical activity of the asset. The depreciation rate is determined by dividing the depreciable cost by the total lifetime activity level. The depreciation expense is computed by multiplying the depreciation rate times the activity level for the period. Examples are the units-of-production method based on the number of units the asset is expected to produce or the number of hours the asset is expected to operate.

Book Value. The cost of an asset less the accumulated depreciation to date.

Capital Expenditure. An expenditure that increases the benefits to be obtained from a productive asset. It is capitalized.

Capitalization. Recording a cost as an increase in the book value of an asset.

Depreciable Cost. The acquisition cost less the estimated residual value.

Depreciation Expense. The portion of the cost of an asset allocated as an expense to each accounting period in the asset's service life.

Double-Declining Balance Depreciation. An accelerated depreciation method in which the depreciation expense is computed by multiplying the book value of the asset at the beginning of the period by twice the straight-line rate.

Operating Expenditure.   An expenditure that maintains the benefits that were originally expected to be derived from a productive asset and which is expensed. Also known as a *revenue* expenditure.

Property, Plant, and Equipment.   Long-term physical assets that are held for use in the operations of a company.

Residual Value.   The estimated proceeds from the sale (disposal) of an asset at the end of its estimated service life. Also known as *salvage value*.

Service Life.   The estimated life over which an asset will be useful. Also known as *economic life*.

Straight-Line Depreciation.   A method of depreciating an asset in which the cost of an asset less its estimated residual value (the depreciable cost) is allocated equally to each period of the asset's service life.

Sum-of-the-Years'-Digits Depreciation.   An accelerated depreciation method in which the depreciation is computed by multiplying the depreciable cost by a fraction that declines each year. The numerator of the fraction is the number of years remaining in the life of the asset at the beginning of the year. The denominator of the fraction is the sum of the years' digits.

Questions

QUESTION 11-1   What are the characteristics that an asset must have to be included in property, plant, and equipment?

QUESTION 11-2   What items are normally included in the acquisition cost of land? Of a building?

QUESTION 11-3   If a company purchases an asset for $20,000 on terms of 2/10, n/30 and does not take advantage of the discount, what is the acquisition cost of the asset? How should the purchases discount lost be treated?

QUESTION 11-4   Describe how the acquisition cost of each asset is calculated when a lump-sum purchase occurs. Why is it necessary to determine the cost of each asset?

QUESTION 11-5   What criteria should a company use to choose a depreciation method?

QUESTION 11-6   What is the nature of the Accumulated Depreciation account? What is meant by the term *book value*? How is the book value disclosed in the balance sheet?

QUESTION 11-7   Is the life of a truck more likely to be affected by physical or functional causes? The life of a computer? Explain.

QUESTION 11-8   What is the equation used for computing depreciation under (1) the straight-line method, (2) the sum-of-the-years'-digits method, and (3) the double-declining balance method?

QUESTION 11-9   Is the estimated residual value included in the calculation of sum-of-the-years'-digits depreciation? Double declining balance? Straight line?

QUESTION 11-10   If a company uses an accelerated method of depreciation for a building rather than the straight-line method, what effect does that choice have on the financial statements in the year of acquisition?

QUESTION 11-11   Does the straight-line method produce a constant or variable depreciation amount per unit as the level of activity changes? Is your answer different for the units-of-production method?

QUESTION 11-12   What factors affect the amount of depreciation recorded per year on an asset?

QUESTION 11-13   "Depreciation is an attempt to measure the value of an asset." Do you agree with this statement? Why or why not? Should depreciation on a building be recorded in a year when the market value of the building rises? Discuss.

QUESTION 11-14   If a company purchases an asset in the middle of the year and uses the straight-line method, what alternative approaches may be used to record the first year's depreciation?

QUESTION 11-15   For a corporation, is the same depreciation method used for financial statements in its annual report and the calculation of federal income taxes? Why or why not? If different methods are used, what must the corporation disclose in a note to the financial statements?

QUESTION 11-16   "We will be able to buy the new machine that costs $80,000 because we have over $100,000 of accumulated depreciation." Do you agree?

QUESTION 11-17   If a company changes its estimate of the residual value or service life of an asset, how is the change accounted for?

QUESTION 11-18   What is an operating expenditure? How does it differ from a capital expenditure? Give an example of each type of expenditure. Why might a capital expenditure not be capitalized?

Exercises

EXERCISE 11-1   **Assets Included in Property, Plant, and Equipment.**   The Young Outdoor Clothing Company owned the following assets at the end of its accounting period:

  (a) Land on which a warehouse had been built.

  (b) Land on which it is planning to build a new store two years from now.

  (c) A retail store.

  (d) Shelving in the store used for the display of products.

  (e) Old cash registers that had been replaced by point-of-sale systems and will be sold next year.

  (f) Goods held in a warehouse for later sale.

REQUIRED   Which of the assets should be considered as property, plant, or equipment? Explain your reasoning.

EXERCISE 11-2   **Acquisition Cost of an Asset.**   The Hawkins Publishing Company acquired a new copying machine. The machine had a contract price of $6,000 and was purchased on terms of 2/10, n/30. The bill was paid within 10 days. The sales tax rate is 6% on the contract price. Delivery costs paid by the company were $200. Modifications to the room in which the copier was installed were $150, of which $20 was the result of damage caused by an accident. After a month of use, a service representative repaired damage caused by an employee unfamiliar with the machine at a cost of $50.

REQUIRED   What is the acquisition cost of the copying machine? Justify why you did not include an item(s).

EXERCISE 11-3   **Lump Sum Purchase.**   An acre of land and a building were acquired by the Evans Fireplace Company for $80,000 cash. The land and building were appraised for $30,000 and $70,000, respectively.

REQUIRED   Prepare the journal entry to record the acquisition.

EXERCISE 11-4   **Lump Sum Purchase.**   The Gibson Musical Instrument Company purchased a building and some machinery on January 1, 1991, by paying $100,000 cash. The building was appraised for $90,000 and the machinery for $30,000. The estimated lives of the building and machinery were 20 years and 8 years, respectively, and the estimated residual values were zero. The straight-line depreciation method is used.

REQUIRED   1.   Prepare the journal entry to record the acquisition of the building and machinery on January 1, 1991.

2.   Prepare the journal entry to record the depreciation expense for 1991.

EXERCISE 11-5   **Acquisition Cost of Assets.**   The Jarrett Heating Engineering Company purchased three machines. The machines had list prices totaling $70,000, but the company was able to acquire them for $68,000 because it purchased all three of them at once. Machines A, B, and C had list prices of $35,000, $28,000, and $7,000, respectively. Delivery costs of $1,000 were paid in cash. A discount of 1/10, n/30 was offered, but the company did not pay until 30 days after the receipt of the invoice.

REQUIRED   Prepare the journal entry to record the acquisition of the machines.

EXERCISE 11-6   **Depreciation Methods.**   The Mingus Ice Cream Company purchased a delivery truck on January 1, 1991, for $20,000. The truck was expected to be used for 8,000 hours, be driven 100,000 miles, and be sold for $3,000 at the end of 1994. The truck was used for 1,800 hours and driven 20,000 miles in 1991.

REQUIRED   Compute the depreciation for 1991 under each of the following methods:

1.   Straight line.

2.   Units of production based on (a) hours and (b) miles driven.

EXERCISE 11-7   **Depreciation Methods.**   The Jackson Company purchased a milling machine on January 1, 1991, for $60,000. The machine had an expected life of 10 years or 40,000 hours and a residual value of $2,000. During 1991 and 1992 the machine was used for 3,500 and 4,200 hours, respectively.

REQUIRED   Compute the depreciation for 1991 and 1992 under each of the following methods:

1.   Units of production: hours used.

2.   Straight line.

3.   Double declining balance.

EXERCISE 11-8 **Depreciation Methods.** The Tatum Tax Service Company purchased a minicomputer on January 1, 1991, for $50,000. The computer was expected to be used for 4 years and have a residual value of $6,000.

REQUIRED Prepare a depreciation schedule for the life of the asset under each of the following methods:

1. Straight line.
2. Double declining balance.
3. Sum of the years' digits.

EXERCISE 11-9 **Depreciation and Partial Periods.** The Monk Pawnbroking Company purchased a typewriter for $1,800 on March 31, 1991. The estimated life and residual value of the typewriter were 4 years and $200, respectively. The straight-line depreciation method is used. The company sells the typewriter on March 31, 1995.

REQUIRED Compute the depreciation for each fiscal year over the life of the typewriter under each of the following conditions:

1. Depreciation is computed to the nearest month.
2. One-half year's depreciation is recorded in the year of acquisition and the year of disposal.
3. Depreciation is computed to the nearest whole year.

EXERCISE 11-10 **Depreciation and Income Taxes.** The Paul Cleaning Company purchased an industrial cleaning machine on January 1, 1991, for $60,000. The asset had an expected life of 5 years, a residual value of zero, and a life of 3 years under the Accelerated Cost Recovery System.

REQUIRED Compute the depreciation expense recorded (a) on the company's financial statements (using the straight-line method) and (b) on its income tax returns for each year of the asset's service life.

EXERCISE 11-11 **Revision of Estimates.** The Peterson Sign Company purchased a computer on January 1, 1991, for $30,000. The economic life and the residual value are estimated to be 10 years and $5,000, respectively. The straight-line depreciation method is used. In January 1992, because of advances in technology, the company adjusts its estimates to a 6-year total life and a residual value of $500.

REQUIRED Compute the depreciation expense for 1992.

EXERCISE 11-12 **Capital and Operating Expenditures.** The following events occurred in a company during the year:

(a) Installed a solar energy collector in a warehouse.
(b) Installed a hydraulic lift door in a delivery truck.
(c) Put a new roof on a warehouse.
(d) Painted a new advertising logo on the fleet of the company trucks.
(e) Redecorated offices.
(f) Repaired a company car involved in an accident; the car was not covered by insurance.

REQUIRED Classify the preceding items as capital or operating expenditures. Explain your reasoning.

Problems

Part A

PROBLEM 11-1A   **Acquisition Cost of Assets.**   The Goodman Tie Company purchased land to build a new retail store. The following costs were incurred in regard to the land and building:

Land	$50,000
Legal fees to purchase land	1,000
Cost incurred to cut down trees cleared from land	800 L
Proceeds from sale of trees	200 L
Architect's fee for building	7,000 D
Payment to building contractor for construction	70,000 B
Payment for landscaping	4,000 L
Paving parking lot	3,000 B

REQUIRED
1. Indicate whether each of the preceding costs should be recorded in the land or building account.

2. Calculate the total cost to be recorded in the land and building accounts.

3. Prepare the journal entries to record each of the preceding costs if all the transactions were paid in cash.

PROBLEM 11-2A   **Lump Sum Purchase.**   On January 1, 1991, the Morton Corporation purchased land, a warehouse, and a retail store for $220,000 cash. An appraisal shows that the land, warehouse, and retail store were valued at $50,000, $70,000, and $130,000, respectively. The estimated lives of the warehouse and retail store were 20 years and 15 years, respectively, and each had an estimated residual value of $5,000. The land was expected to be sold in 5 years for $60,000. The company uses straight-line depreciation.

REQUIRED
1. Prepare the journal entry to record the acquisition.

2. Why is it necessary to record the separate components of the acquisition?

3. The president of the corporation wants to record the assets at $250,000. Why do you think the president wants to do this? Is this procedure acceptable?

4. Prepare the journal entries to record the depreciation expense for 1991.

5. Prepare the Property and Equipment section of the balance sheet on December 31, 1991.

PROBLEM 11-3A   **Capital and Operating Expenditures.**   The Jackson Fruit Company paid for the following items in cash during 1991:

(a)   Rearrangement of the office layout, $2,000.

(b)   Uninsured repairs to company truck after accident, $600.

(c)   Routine service on company car, $150.

(d)   Overhaul of machine to extend its life by 2 years, $4,000.

(e)   Repainting the showroom, $800.

(f)   Installation of facilities for handicapped employees, $1,300.

REQUIRED Prepare journal entries to record the preceding events. Explain your reason for the method of recording each item.

PROBLEM 11-4A **Depreciation Methods.** The Desmond Photo Developing Company purchased a machine for printing pictures on January 1, 1991, for $60,000. The estimated life and residual value are 10 years and $10,000, respectively. It is expected that the machine will operate for 20,000 hours and produce 100,000 pictures.

During 1991 the machine was operated for 2,200 hours and produced 10,500 pictures. During 1992 there was a strike and the machine operated for only 1,600 hours and produced only 7,500 pictures.

REQUIRED
1. Compute the depreciation expense for 1991 and 1992 under each of the following methods:
   (a) Activity level: units produced.
   (b) Activity level: hours used.
   (c) Straight line.
   (d) Sum of the years' digits.
   (e) Double declining balance.

2. Show how the asset would be disclosed in the balance sheet at December 31, 1991, under each method.

3. Should the strike affect the application of any of the preceding depreciation methods? Explain.

PROBLEM 11-5A **Depreciation and Changes in Estimates.** The Davis Film Company purchased a building at the beginning of 1987 for $75,000. It was estimated that the building would be used for 20 years, after which it would be sold for $20,000. Straight-line depreciation is used.

REQUIRED
1. Compute the depreciation expense for 1991 and prepare the related journal entry.

2. At the beginning of 1992 management decided that the building would be used for another 25 years. Compute the depreciation expense for 1992 and prepare the related journal entry.

3. Ignore the change in Requirement 2. At the beginning of 1992, because of the increase in real estate prices, management expected that the building would be sold for $30,000 at the end of its life. Compute the depreciation expense for 1992. Show how the asset would be disclosed in the balance sheet at December 31, 1992.

PROBLEM 11-6A **Comprehensive.** The Terry Piano Company purchased a building for $170,000 on January 1, 1991. The building had an estimated service life and residual value of 20 years and $20,000, respectively. The company uses straight-line depreciation. On January 1, 1993, the company spent $10,000 to replace the roof and therefore estimated that the building would have a total economic life of 25 years.

REQUIRED Prepare all the necessary journal entries for the Terry Piano Company in 1991, 1992, and 1993.

PROBLEM 11-7A **Comprehensive.** On August 1, 1991, the Ellington Pen Company purchased two used machines, A and B, at an auction for $120,000. Machine A was newer and worth twice as much as Machine B. It also had an expected remaining life of 10 years compared to 4 years for B. The company decided to use the sum-of-the-years'-digits depreciation method for Machine B and the straight-line method for Machine A with no residual value on either machine.

On October 10, 1991, maintenance was done on both machines. The costs were $800 and $300 for A and B, respectively. On February 1, 1994, the company spent $4,000 on a major overhaul of A and thereby extended its life by an extra 2 years. The company's accounting period ends on December 31, and it computes depreciation to the nearest whole year.

REQUIRED   Prepare journal entries for 1991 through the end of 1994.

Problems

Part B

PROBLEM 11-1B   **Acquisition Cost of Assets.**   The Hughes Camping Equipment Company purchased land to build a warehouse. The following costs were incurred in regard to the land and building:

Land	$70,000
Legal fees to purchase land	2,000
Real estate commission on land	400
Cost to demolish old building	600
Salvage proceeds from old building	200
Architect's fee for building	15,000
Payment to building contractor for construction	80,000
Payment for landscaping	9,000
Paving parking lot	3,000

REQUIRED   1. Indicate whether each of the preceding costs should be recorded in the land or building account.

2. Calculate the total cost to be recorded in the land and building accounts.

3. Prepare the journal entries to record each of the preceding costs if all the transactions were paid in cash.

PROBLEM 11-2B   **Lump Sum Purchase.**   On January 1, 1991, the Stewart Pool Table Corporation purchased three machines, A, B, and C, for $330,000 on terms of 2/10, n/30. An appraisal shows that they were worth $200,000, $160,000, and $40,000, respectively. Sales tax of $3,000 was added to the invoice. The company paid shipping charges of $20,000, and it paid for the machines 2 weeks after delivery. The estimated lives of machines A, B, and C were 10 years, 6 years, and 8 years, respectively. Each machine had a residual value of $1,000. The company uses straight-line depreciation.

REQUIRED   1. Prepare the journal entries to record the acquisition.

2. Why is it necessary to record the separate components of the acquisition?

3. The president of the corporation wants to record the assets at $400,000. Why do you think the president wants to do this? Is this procedure acceptable?

4. Prepare the journal entries to record the depreciation expense for 1991.

5. Prepare the Property and Equipment section of the balance sheet on December 31, 1991.

PROBLEM 11-3B   **Capital and Operating Expenditures.**   The Brooks Legal Services Company paid for the following items in cash during 1991:

(a)   Installation of energy-efficient windows in office, $6,500.

(b)   Overhaul of machine to extend its original life by 3 years, $1,000.

(c)   Replacement of dead trees on landscaping around office building, $700.

(d)   Repair of all office typewriters, $2,000.

(e)   Installation of facilities for handicapped employees, $900.

(f)   Replacement of tires on all company trucks, $5,300.

REQUIRED   Prepare journal entries to record the preceding events. Explain your reason for the method of recording each item.

PROBLEM 11-4B   **Depreciation Methods.**   The Prentiss Poster Company purchased a printing machine on January 1, 1991, for $26,000. The estimated life and residual value are 4 years and $2,000, respectively. The machine is expected to operate for 30,000 hours and produce 200,000 posters. During 1991 the machine was operated for 6,500 hours and produced 50,000 posters. During 1992 there was a strike and the machine operated for only 3,300 hours and produced only 24,000 posters.

REQUIRED   1.   Compute the depreciation expense for 1991 and 1992 under each of the following methods:
   (a)   Activity level: units produced.
   (b)   Activity level: hours used.
   (c)   Straight line.
   (d)   Sum of the years' digits.
   (e)   Double declining balance.

2.   Prepare the journal entries to record depreciation in 1991 and 1992 under each method.

3.   Should the strike affect the application of any of the preceding depreciation methods? Explain.

PROBLEM 11-5B   **Depreciation and Changes in Estimates.**   The Bauer Mapping Company purchased an airplane at the beginning of 1989 for $250,000. It was estimated that the airplane would be used for 10 years, after which it would be sold for $50,000. The company uses straight-line depreciation.

REQUIRED   1.   Compute the depreciation expense for 1991 and prepare the related journal entry.

2.   At the beginning of 1992 it was decided that the airplane would be used for only 2 more years. Compute the depreciation expense for 1992 and prepare the related journal entry.

3.   Ignore the change in Requirement 2. Because of an increase in the demand for this type of airplane, it was decided at the beginning of 1992 that the plane's residual value would be $80,000 at the end of its life. Compute the depreciation expense for 1992. Show how the asset would be disclosed in the balance sheet at December 31, 1992.

PROBLEM 11-6B   **Comprehensive.**   The Roland Radiator Company purchased a machine for $50,000 on January 1, 1989. The estimated service life and residual value were 10 years and $5,000, respectively. The company uses the sum-of-the-years'-digits depreciation method. On January 1, 1992, the company modifies the machine at a cost of $6,000 so that it can be used in a new production process.

REQUIRED

1. What is the book value of the machine on January 1, 1992?

2. Prepare all the necessary journal entries for the Roland Radiator Company in 1992.

Decision Cases

DECISION CASE 11-1   **Choice of Depreciation Method.**   Coltrane Corporation is a newly formed company and has purchased a building, office equipment, a machine to be used in production, and three company cars. The company is considering which depreciation method to select for each asset for financial reporting.

The president wants to report the highest possible net income and pay the lowest possible income taxes. He also argues that the building is unlikely to go down in value in the next five years, so there is no need to depreciate for that time. He wants to "save the depreciation" until later in the life of the building when the value will go down. The chief accountant agrees that it is possible to minimize the payment of income taxes, but argues that it is incorrect to select a depreciation method in order to maximize net income or to relate to the value of an asset.

REQUIRED

1. Evaluate the correctness of each argument.

2. Which depreciation method is it likely that the chief accountant would suggest for each asset? Explain.

DECISION CASE 11-2   **Depreciation and Replacement of Assets.**   Ten years ago, the Davis Corporation purchased some equipment for $200,000. The equipment has been depreciated on a straight-line basis and is now about to be replaced. The income tax rate has been 40%. The president is shocked to find out that the company does not have enough cash available to replace the equipment because the selling price has doubled. The president lends the company enough money to buy the new equipment, but says that "now we will record twice as much depreciation as before so that we don't have this problem again."

REQUIRED

1. Considering only the preceding facts, by how much will the cash balance of the company have changed over the life of the equipment?

2. Can the company implement the president's proposed depreciation policy? Do you agree that it would be desirable?

DECISION CASE 11-3   **Effect of Depreciation on Financial Statements.**   Charles Parker is considering purchasing either the Gordon Company or the Rollins Company. Both companies started business 5 years ago, and at that time each company purchased property, plant, and equipment for $110,000 that are being depreciated over 10 years with no residual value. The Gordon Company is using straight-line depreciation and the Rollins Company is using sum-of-the-years'-digits depreciation. The two companies have very similar products and reputations, and their total assets (other than property, plant, and equipment) and total liabilities on the balance sheet are also very similar.

REQUIRED

1. Compute the book value of the property, plant, and equipment for each company at the end of 5 years.

2. Which company represents the more desirable purchase? Explain your reasoning. Ignore income taxes.

3. Would your answer to Requirement 2 change if income taxes are considered and both companies are corporations?

DECISION CASE 11-4   **Depreciation.** Westinghouse Electric Corporation reported that its depreciable property, plant, and equipment assets at December 31, 1988, had a cost of $4,803.7 million and accumulated depreciation of $2,302.4 million. The company uses the straight-line method of depreciation. Assume that the average life of the assets is 15 years.

REQUIRED   1. What is the average age of the assets on December 31, 1988? Round your answer to the nearest whole year.

2. If the company used the sum-of-the-years'-digits method instead, what would be the amount of accumulated depreciation on December 31, 1988?

3. How much depreciation expense would be recorded in 1989 under the straight-line and sum-of-the-years'-digits methods?

12

Property, Plant, and Equipment: Disposals, Intangibles, and Natural Resources

LEARNING OBJECTIVES

1. Account for the disposal by sale of property, plant, and equipment.

2. Account for the disposal by exchange of (a) dissimilar and (b) similar productive assets.

3. Identify the characteristics of intangible assets.

4. Explain the nature of research and development costs.

5. Describe (a) patents, (b) copyrights, (c) trademarks and tradenames, (d) franchises, (e) computer software costs, and (f) organization costs.

6. Explain the rules for the amortization of intangible assets.

7. Describe the nature of goodwill.

8. Identify the characteristics of natural resource assets.

9. Explain the differences between cost depletion and percentage depletion.

ontinuing the discussion of the previous chapter, we are initially concerned here with accounting for the disposal of tangible assets included in property, plant, and equipment. Disposal may be in the form of a sale of an asset, or an exchange of one asset for another. The discussion then moves to intangible assets, which are another type of economic resource essential to the operation of many companies. Finally, the special accounting issues that arise with regard to natural resource assets are discussed.

Disposals of Property, Plant, and Equipment

1. Account for the disposal by sale of property, plant, and equipment.

The recording of the acquisition cost of an asset included in property, plant, and equipment and the depreciation of that asset over its useful life were discussed in the previous chapter. When the asset is disposed of at the end of its useful life to the company, the disposal must be properly recorded. Three alternative situations may arise: the asset may be sold for an amount equal to the book value; sold for an amount greater or less than the book value, in which case a gain or loss is recognized; or exchanged for a similar asset, in which case a loss but no gain may be recognized.

All disposals have some characteristics in common. Depreciation for the fraction of the year up to the date of disposal should be recorded. In the following discussion it is assumed that the necessary depreciation entries, which were discussed in the previous chapter, have been made. At the time of the disposal the balances in the asset account and its related accumulated depreciation account must be removed. This is accomplished by reducing (crediting) the Asset account by an amount equal to its recorded acquisition cost and reducing (debiting) the Accumulated Depreciation account by an amount equal to the current (credit) balance in the account. Both the Asset and the Accumulated Depreciation accounts will then have a zero balance because the respective (debit and credit) amounts in the journal entry at disposal exactly offset the balance being carried in each account before disposal. These debit and credit entries may comprise all or part of the disposal journal entry. Disposals range from the very simple, where there is no cash involved and the book value is zero, to more complex transactions in which gains or losses on the disposal must be recognized because the actual selling price is not equal to the book value.

Disposal of a Fully Depreciated Asset with No Cash Proceeds

In the simplest situation an asset that is fully depreciated to a zero residual value is discarded. That is, it is disposed of and no cash is received. For example, suppose that a machine that originally cost $10,000 and is fully depreciated to a zero residual value is discarded and no cash is received. The asset and the related accumulated depreciation are removed from the books by the following journal entry:

Accumulated Depreciation: Machine 10,000
    Machine 10,000
To record disposal of machine.

Note that this journal entry has no effect on the total assets in the balance sheet. The entry simply reduces (credits) an asset account and reduces (debits) a contra-asset account for the same amount.

Sale at an Amount Equal to the Residual Value

Suppose that the machine in the previous example had an estimated residual value of $1,000, is fully depreciated to that amount, and is sold for $1,000 cash. Then the following journal entry is made to record the sale:

Cash	1,000	
Accumulated Depreciation: Machine	9,000	
Machine		10,000

To record sale of machine for $1,000.

In this situation an asset with a book value of $1,000 ($10,000 − $9,000) that is included in property, plant, and equipment is removed and another asset, cash, is increased (debited) for $1,000. Thus a noncurrent asset has been replaced by a current asset of equal value.

In addition, it should be noted that a journal entry to record the disposal is recorded only when an asset is sold, *not* when it is fully depreciated to its estimated residual value. An asset that is fully depreciated but is still being used is kept in the accounting records at a book value equal to the estimated residual value (the asset minus the accumulated depreciation equals the estimated residual value). This provides evidence of the continued existence of the asset and is necessary for the operation of the internal control function, which ensures that assets listed in the accounting records are in the physical control of the company, and for the reporting of property taxes.

Sale Price Above Book Value (Gain)

In most practical situations assets are not sold for an amount equal to the book value. Therefore suppose that the same machine discussed earlier, which had an estimated residual value of $1,000, is sold for $1,500 instead of $1,000. The following diagram shows the relationships among the various dollar amounts:

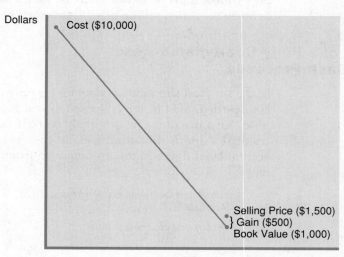

Based on the information in the diagram, the following journal entry is required to record the sale:

Cash..	1,500	
Accumulated Depreciation: Machine......................................	9,000	
Machine..		10,000
Gain on Sale of Machine		500

To record sale of machine with a book value of $1,000 for $1,500.

In this situation a machine with a book value of $1,000 is sold for $1,500 and a gain of $500 is recognized on the sale; the gain is computed by comparing the cash received ($1,500) to the book value ($1,000). The gain arises because the original estimate of the residual value, made at the time the asset was acquired, was incorrect. This is not surprising given the difficulty of making such estimates, but it does mean that the amount of depreciation recorded in previous years is technically incorrect. Changing the amount of depreciation recorded in the financial statements of previous years, however, might be very confusing to the users of the statements. Therefore the gain is considered to be an increase in income for the period of the sale. The total amount included in the income statements over the life of the asset by recording depreciation each period and reporting the gain on the sale in the period of the sale, is the difference between the acquisition cost and the actual disposal value. The gain is recorded by a credit to an account, Gain on Sale of Machine. When the financial statements are prepared, the gain is included in the income statement in the Other Revenues and Expenses section. It should *not* be included as sales revenue because it is not part of the sale of goods or services in the normal course of business.

Sale Price Below Book Value (Loss)

If the machine just discussed is sold for $700, the company incurs a loss of $300 ($1,000 book value – $700 proceeds) on the sale, as shown in the following diagram:

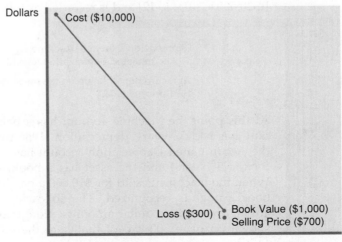

Based on the information in the diagram the sale is recorded as follows:

Cash	700	
Accumulated Depreciation: Machine	9,000	
Loss on Sale of Machine	300	
Machine		10,000

To record the sale of machine with a book value of $1,000 for $700.

The loss is included in the income statement as a negative component of Other Revenues and Expenses.

Sale Before the End of the Estimated Service Life

It was assumed in the preceding examples that the asset had been depreciated to its estimated residual value before disposal. Therefore the book value at the time of disposal was equal to the estimated residual value. However, a company may decide to sell an asset earlier than originally anticipated, before it has been fully depreciated. In this case the book value is not equal to the estimated residual value. The principles underlying the recording of the disposal are not changed. The depreciation must be brought up to date using one of the fractional period methods discussed in the previous chapter. The Asset account and the Accumulated Depreciation account must be credited and debited, respectively, to remove the balances in these accounts. The gain or loss on the sale is still the difference between the book value of the asset and the cash received. For example, suppose that a company sells a machine with the following characteristics:

Original cost	$20,000
Date of purchase	Jan. 1, 1986
Estimated life	10 years
Estimated residual value	Zero
Depreciation method	Straight line
Cash proceeds from sale	$10,000
Date of disposal	July 10, 1991

If the company computes depreciation to the nearest month, it is necessary to record depreciation for 6 months in 1991. The amount of depreciation is $1,000 $[(\$20,000 \div 10) \times 6/12]$ and is recorded as follows:

1991			
July 10	Depreciation Expense: Machine	1,000	
	Accumulated Depreciation: Machine		1,000

To record depreciation on the machine for 6 months in 1991 prior to sale.

At this point the Machine account has a balance of $20,000. Since the machine now has had $5\frac{1}{2}$ years' depreciation (1986 through half of 1991) recorded on it, the Accumulated Depreciation account has a balance of $11,000 ($2,000 per year for the $5\frac{1}{2}$ years) and the asset has a book value of $9,000 ($20,000 − $11,000). When the machine is sold for $10,000 a gain of $1,000 ($10,000 proceeds − $9,000 book value) is recognized. The following diagram shows the relationships among the various dollar amounts. Note that this diagram is similar to the one shown on page 502 except that here the gain is computed by comparing the selling price to the book value instead of the residual value because the asset is sold before the end of its estimated service life.

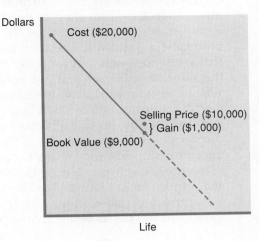

Based on the information in the diagram, the sale is recorded as follows:

1991			
July 10	Cash	10,000	
	Accumulated Depreciation: Machine	11,000	
	Machine		20,000
	Gain on Sale of Machine..................................		1,000
	To record the sale of a machine with a book value of $9,000 for $10,000.		

If the disposal occurs because the asset has been stolen or destroyed by an accident or fire, the procedures are the same as those described earlier except that the gain or loss account would have an appropriate title, such as Loss Due to Fire, or Gain Due to Accident. Note that this latter title does not indicate that the company has "gained" from the accident, but only that the recovery value of the asset, the cash received from the insurance company, is greater than its book value at the time of the accident. Although the insurance company pays the fair value of the used asset, the company may not have gained anything. The company will almost certainly have suffered an economic loss because of other costs related to the accident, such as a disruption of its normal activities. Also, the company may have to replace the used asset with a new asset that is likely to require a greater cash outlay than the amount received from the insurance company.

Exchange of Property, Plant, and Equipment

When a company decides to dispose of an asset it may choose to trade in the asset for a new asset. For example, a used delivery van is often exchanged for a new van. The trade-in allowance (assumed to be equal to the fair market value of the asset) is deducted from the cost of the new delivery van, and the balance owed is paid according to the terms of the agreement. **Boot is the cash paid in the exchange of assets.** Thus the company acquires a new asset by giving up an old asset and paying boot.

Exchange of Dissimilar Productive Assets

2(a). Account for the disposal by exchange of dissimilar productive assets.

Productive assets are assets such as inventory, property, and equipment that are used in the production of goods and services.[1] Productive assets may be classified as similar or dissimilar. The accounting for the exchange of dissimilar productive assets is discussed first because it is less complex. **Dissimilar productive assets are assets that are not of the same general type, that do not perform the same function, or that are not employed in the same line of business.** When dissimilar productive assets are exchanged (e.g., trading in a delivery van toward the acquisition of a building), the exchange is considered as two separate transactions. The disposal of the old asset is recorded as discussed earlier in this chapter (with the proceeds being the fair market value of the old asset rather than the cash paid), and the acquisition of the new asset is recorded as discussed in the previous chapter (i.e., at the acquisition cost), although both the disposal and acquisition are recorded in one journal entry. For example, suppose that a delivery van is traded in for a building (a dissimilar productive asset) and the transaction has the following characteristics:

Original cost of van	$10,000
Accumulated depreciation to date of exchange	6,000
Cost of building	40,000
Cash paid (boot)	37,000

Since the van and cash of $37,000 are exchanged for the building, which costs $40,000, the van must be worth $3,000. The van has a book value of $4,000 (the cost of $10,000 less the accumulated depreciation of $6,000), and therefore there is a loss of $1,000 on the disposal of the van ($4,000 book value – $3,000 fair market value). The journal entry to record the exchange is:

Building	40,000	
Accumulated Depreciation: Delivery Van	6,000	
Loss on Disposal of Delivery Van	1,000	
Delivery Van		10,000
Cash		37,000

To record acquisition of building in exchange for delivery van and cash.

Gains on exchanges of dissimilar productive assets are recorded in the same way as losses. In other words, they are recognized in full in the period in which they occur.

Exchange of Similar Productive Assets

Similar productive assets are assets of the same general type, that perform the same function, or that are employed in the same line of business. When similar productive assets are exchanged, special accounting practices are used. For example, the trade of player contracts by professional sports organizations or the

---

[1]"Accounting for Nonmonetary Transactions," *APB Opinion No. 29* (New York: AICPA, 1973), par. 3.

trade of a used delivery truck for a new delivery truck would be considered exchanges of similar productive assets.

2(b). Account for the disposal by exchange of similar productive assets.

The special accounting procedure for an exchange of similar productive assets is that a gain on the trade-in of the old asset is *not* recognized. This is justified by the argument that the earning process on the old asset has not been completed. For example, suppose that a company buys a warehouse that has an expected life of 20 years. The expectation is that the company will get 20 years of benefits. Suppose that the company exchanges the warehouse for another warehouse after 5 years. Since the 20-year productive life of the original warehouse will be completed by the new warehouse, any "gain" on the trade is ignored.

To illustrate the accounting for similar asset exchanges, suppose that the following facts relate to the exchange of two delivery trucks by a company:

Original cost of old truck	$20,000
Accumulated depreciation on old truck	4,500
Book value of old truck	15,500
Invoice price for new truck	22,000
Cash paid	4,000

Since the new delivery truck has an invoice price of $22,000 but only $4,000 is paid, the trade-in allowance on the old truck must be $18,000. Therefore the seller has an implied gain of $2,500 (trade-in of $18,000 – book value of $15,500) on the old truck, but *this gain is ignored,* and the new truck is recorded as follows:

Book Value of New Asset = Book Value of Old Asset + Cash Paid
= $15,500 + $4,000
= $19,500

The journal entry to record the exchange is:

Truck (New)	19,500	
Accumulated Depreciation: Truck	4,500	
Truck (Old)		20,000
Cash		4,000

To record the exchange of an old truck for a new truck.

The effect of ignoring the gain at the time of the exchange is to reduce the cost of the new asset and therefore the amount of depreciation to be recorded over the life of the newly acquired asset. Thus the "gain" is spread out over the life of the new asset because the lower recorded cost results in lower depreciation expense and higher net income over that life.

Many users of financial statements disagree with this procedure because they argue that the substance of the transaction (the gain) is ignored. If similar productive assets are exchanged in the future and no loss is ever incurred, a virtually permanent nonrecognition of subsequent gains may be possible. It must be emphasized that this special procedure applies only when there is an implicit gain on the exchange. A *loss* is recognized by the same procedure discussed earlier for the exchange of dissimilar productive assets. The recognition of a loss is justified by the conservatism principle, which was discussed in Chapter 9.

Federal Income Tax and the Exchange of Productive Assets

For corporate income tax purposes the Internal Revenue Code requires that either a gain or a loss be recognized when dissimilar productive assets are exchanged. On the other hand the Code requires that either a loss or a gain be *ignored* when similar productive assets are exchanged and cash is *paid* by the company acquiring the asset. (Special procedures, which are beyond the scope of this text, apply when cash is *received* by the company that has a gain. These special procedures also apply to financial reporting.) These similarities and differences are summarized here:

	Dissimilar Productive Assets		Similar Productive Assets	
	Accounting	*Tax*	*Accounting*	*Tax*
Gain	Recognized	Recognized	Not recognized*	Not recognized*
Loss	Recognized	Recognized	Recognized	Not recognized

*Special rules exist when cash is received (beyond the scope of the text)

Thus it can be seen that there is a difference between financial reporting and income tax reporting for the exchange of similar productive assets. This difference occurs because a loss is not recognized for income tax purposes, whereas, as we have seen, it is recognized for financial reporting purposes. This difference would be disclosed in the notes to the financial statements and would also affect the income taxes paid as discussed in Chapter 16.

Intangible Assets

In addition to property, plant, and equipment, many companies have another category of noncurrent assets called intangible assets. **Intangible assets are noncurrent assets that do not have a physical substance.** Their value to the company typically results from the use of the *legal rights* associated with the intangible asset rather than from physical use. Examples of intangibles are patents, copyrights, trademarks and tradenames, franchises, computer software costs, organization costs, and goodwill. It should be noted that the recording of intangibles does not change the accounting principles discussed earlier in this book. For example, advertising costs are expensed in the period incurred and are not considered to be an intangible asset, because it is presumed that they do not provide benefits that could be reliably measured beyond the period of the expenditure. Also, of course, they provide no legal rights to the company. Even though accounts receivable and prepaid items do not have a physical substance they are not intangible assets because they are not long term. If a company had a long-term receivable, it could be argued that the receivable should be classified as an intangible asset because it meets the appropriate criteria. The receivable would not be classified as an intangible asset, however, because the nature of the asset is very different from the other intangibles.

Intangible assets are similar in many ways to the tangible assets, property, plant, and equipment, because (1) they are used in activities related to the production process and they are not held for investment; (2) they have an expected life of more than one year; (3) they derive their value from their ability to generate revenue for their owners; and (4) they should be expensed in the periods in which their benefits are received.

3. Identify the characteristics of intangible assets.

Intangible assets generally have five characteristics that distinguish them from tangible assets:

1. Intangible assets do not have a physical substance but more often, though not exclusively, result from legal rights.

2. There is generally a higher degree of uncertainty regarding the future benefits that can be expected to be derived from them.

3. Their value is subject to wider fluctuations because it may depend to a considerable extent on competitive conditions.

4. They may have value only to a particular company.

5. They may have expected lives that are very difficult to determine.

The cost of an intangible asset is expensed over its life much like property, plant, and equipment. However, this expense is called amortization expense rather than depreciation expense, as discussed later.

Before each kind of intangible asset is explained, accounting for research and development is discussed because it may affect the dollar amounts included as intangible assets.

Research and Development Costs

Many companies engage in research and development (R&D) to improve their products. Expenditures on R&D by technologically oriented companies may represent a significant part of their total expenditures each period.

4. Explain the nature of research and development costs.

Research is a planned search or critical investigation aimed at discovery of new knowledge; development is the translation of research findings into a plan or design for a new product or process.[2] The costs included in R&D are those for such items as materials, equipment, and facilities used in R&D projects, the salaries of R&D employees, and a reasonable allocation of general and administrative costs. **Costs incurred for research and development are required to be expensed as incurred, and the amount must be disclosed directly in the financial statements or in the notes to these financial statements.**

Each year many companies spend large amounts of money on R&D because they expect to receive total future benefits that exceed the total costs incurred; however, not all R&D projects are successful. Some projects will be unsuccessful (costs exceed benefits), and others will be successful (benefits exceed costs) so that, overall, the benefits are expected to exceed the costs. If benefits are expected to exist for many periods in the future, it could be argued that the cost of acquir-

---

[2]"Accounting for Research and Development Costs," *FASB Statement No. 2* (Stamford, Conn.: FASB, 1974), par. 8.

ing these benefits should be recorded as an asset. The decision to require the expensing of all R&D costs was made to avoid the complexity of capitalizing (recording as an asset) any such costs expected to provide future benefits. For example, if accounting principles required the capitalization of R&D projects that were expected to be successful and the expensing of unsuccessful projects, many difficult problems would arise. How reliable would such decisions be on the expected success of projects? Who would make the decisions? How would the accountant verify the decisions? What is the expected life of the benefits? What is the pattern of the expected benefits? It was because of the difficulty of answering these kinds of questions that the FASB required the expensing of all R&D costs. This requirement has the advantage of providing uniformity among all companies even though it may not be the most conceptually sound alternative when future benefits are expected. The creation of uniformity should enhance comparability between companies and therefore help users of financial statements.

To illustrate the accounting for R&D suppose that a company incurs the following costs for R&D activities:

Materials used from inventory	$ 50,000
Wages and salaries	120,000
Allocation of general and administrative costs	20,000
Depreciation on building housing R&D activities	25,000

All these costs are included in R&D expenses, and therefore the journal entry is as follows:

Research and Development Expenses	215,000	
Cash, Payables, etc.		140,000
Inventory		50,000
Accumulated Depreciation: Building		25,000
To record research and development costs.		

Patents

5(a). Describe patents.

A patent is an exclusive right granted by the federal government giving its owner the control of the manufacture, sale, or other use of an invention for 17 years. Patents cannot be renewed, but their effective life is often extended by obtaining new patents on modifications and improvements to the original invention. As a general rule the costs of obtaining a patent are capitalized; that is, they are recorded in an intangible asset account, entitled Patents. Since all the research and development costs associated with the internal development of an invention are expensed, however, the costs that are capitalized primarily consist of the costs of acquiring the patent, such as the costs of processing the patent application and any legal costs incurred. Alternatively, if a patent is purchased from another company, the entire acquisition cost is capitalized. If a company incurs a cost for the successful defense of a patent against infringement by another company, the cost is added (debited) to the Patent account. Of course, if the patent defense is unsuccessful, the costs would have to be expensed and the remaining balance in the Patent account would have to be removed (credited) and a loss recognized (debited) because the patent would no longer provide benefits.

Copyrights

5(b). Describe copyrights.

A copyright is an exclusive right granted by the federal government covering the right to publish, sell, or otherwise control literary or artistic products for the life of the author plus an additional 50 years. Copyrights cover such items as books, music, and films. As with patents, the costs of obtaining the copyright are capitalized in a Copyrights account. The cost of producing the item under copyright would be accounted for separately. For example, the costs of producing a film are accounted for separately from the copyright on the film and therefore are recorded as an asset entitled, say, Film Production. This asset would be depreciated over its revenue-producing life.

Trademarks and Tradenames

5(c). Describe trademarks and tradenames.

A trademark or tradename is registered with the U.S. Patent Office and establishes a right to the exclusive use of a name, symbol, or other device used for product identification. Pepsi and Kleenex, for example, are tradenames. The right lasts for 20 years and is renewable indefinitely as long as the trademark or tradename is used continuously. Again, only the costs directly associated with obtaining the trademark or tradename are capitalized. The costs of promoting the name and producing the product are accounted for separately as advertising expense and inventory, respectively.

Franchises

5(d). Describe franchises.

A franchise is an agreement entered into by two parties in which, for a fee, one party (the franchisor) gives the other party (the franchisee) rights to perform certain functions or sell certain products or services. In addition, the franchisor may agree to provide certain services to the franchisee. For example, many McDonald's restaurants are locally owned and operated under a franchise agreement with the McDonald's Company. As with other intangibles, the cost incurred by the franchisee to acquire the franchise is capitalized as an intangible asset.

Computer Software Costs

5(e). Describe computer software costs.

Until the early 1980s, most companies expensed the cost of software development. At that time many companies started to adopt a policy of capitalizing software costs. In 1985 the FASB adopted accounting principles that clarified the accounting for computer software costs. For accounting purposes there are three categories of costs associated with software that is to be sold, leased, or otherwise marketed directly or indirectly as part of a product, process, or service. First, there are *software production costs* such as design, coding, testing, documentation, and preparation of training materials. These costs are recorded as research and development expenses until technological feasibility of the product is established. **Technological feasibility** is established on the date of the completion of a detail program design or, in its absence, on completion of a working model of the product. After this date, all software production costs are capitalized until the product is available for sale to customers. Any software production costs incurred after the product is ready for sale are expensed. The capitalized software production costs are amortized over the expected life of the product. The amount of the amortization expense is the greater of either (1) the ratio of current gross revenues to the total amount of current and anticipated future gross revenues or (2) the straight-line method. If the market value of the software product becomes lower than the asset's book value, the asset is written down to this value and a loss is recognized. The lower value is then recognized as the new cost and the write-down may not be recovered.

The second category of costs is the *unit cost* of producing the software, such as costs of the disks and duplication of the software, packaging, documentation, and training materials. These unit costs are recorded as inventory and expensed as cost of goods sold when the related revenue is recognized. The third category of costs is the *maintenance and customer support costs* incurred after the software is released. These costs are expensed as incurred.

Note that these rules do *not* apply to the costs of software that is developed for internal use. If such an activity is considered to be research and development, the costs are expensed until it can be concluded that the software project no longer is research or development. Also, the costs of developing or improving software used in a company's selling or administrative activities, such as an airline's computer reservation system or a company's management information system, are not included as research and development. Therefore such costs may be capitalized or expensed, although most companies do follow the practice of expensing them.

Organization Costs

5(f). Describe organization costs.

Organization costs are the costs associated with the formation of a corporation. When a corporation is formed (incorporated) certain costs are incurred, such as legal fees, stock certificate costs, accounting fees, and fees associated with promoting the sale of the stock. These organization costs are also capitalized as an intangible asset entitled Organization Costs. While it may be argued that this asset has an expected life equal to the life of the company, Organization Costs must be amortized over a period not to exceed 40 years, as discussed later. In practice, however, most corporations amortize organization costs over 5 years, because this is the shortest time period allowed by the Internal Revenue Service for federal income tax purposes.

Leases and Leasehold Improvements

A lease (or a leasehold) **is an agreement conveying the right to use property, plant, or equipment without transferring legal ownership of the item.** A **lessee** is the company that acquires the right to use the property, plant, and equipment; a **lessor** is the company giving up the right. Therefore a lease is an intangible asset to the lessee because a right to use property is held by the lessee, while the property is still legally owned by the lessor. A lease may be accounted for as a capital lease or an operating lease by the lessee, as discussed in Chapter 16. Capital leases are typically included on the balance sheet of the lessee within property, plant, and equipment rather than under intangible assets. **A leasehold improvement is an improvement made to the leased property, plant, or equipment by the lessee.** An example is an improvement to the interior design of a leased retail store. Leasehold improvements are also typically classified on the balance sheet of the lessee within property, plant, and equipment. Since the improvement would become the property of the lessor at the end of the lease, a leasehold improvement is amortized over its economic life or the life of the lease, whichever is shorter.

Amortization of Intangibles

Recall that R&D costs are expressed as incurred. On the other hand, since the costs of the intangible assets discussed earlier are capitalized, they must be expensed over the expected service life of the benefits they produce. **Amortization expense is the portion of the acquisition cost of an intangible asset allocated as an expense to each accounting period in the asset's life.** Therefore it is exactly the same concept as depreciation expense, with only a change in the title. Exhibit 12-1 illustrates the differences between the expensing of R&D costs and other intangible assets:

EXHIBIT 12-1
Expensing of Cost of
Intangibles

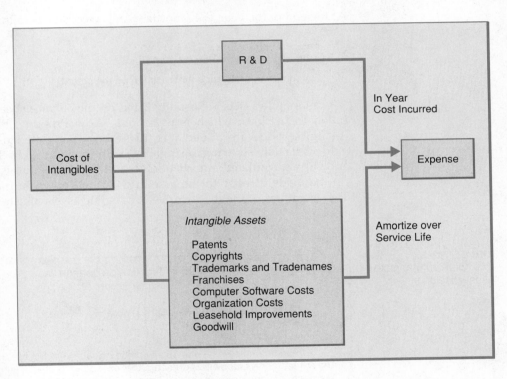

Note that the cost of an intangible is amortized over its expected *service* life and not necessarily over its legal life. For example, although a patent has a maximum legal life of 17 years, its expected service life may be less than 17 years. The patent would be expensed over the lesser of the two periods, its actual service life or its legal life of 17 years. As we have seen, some intangibles have very long lives, and in the case of trademarks and tradenames a potentially indefinite life. Because of the difficulty of determining the likelihood of benefits so far into the future, however, an arbitrary maximum economic life of 40 years has been

6. Explain the rules
for the amortization of
intangible assets.

imposed. **The general rule for amortization of intangibles, therefore, is that the expected life of the intangible is the lesser of the service life or the legal life, up to a maximum of 40 years.** In addition, the *straight-line* amortization method should be used unless there is convincing evidence that an alternative method provides a better matching of expenses against revenues. Since it is unlikely that an intangible asset will have a residual value, none will be used in this chapter.

To illustrate, suppose that a company acquires a patent on a new type of production process at the beginning of the year for $10,000. The production process is expected to be useful for 10 years, after which newer technology will replace it. For this reason the patent is amortized over the 10-year expected service life rather than the 17-year legal life. The acquisition of the patent is recorded as follows:

Patent..	10,000	
Cash...		10,000

To record the acquisition of a patent.

At the end of the year, the amortization is recorded as follows:

Amortization Expense ($10,000 ÷ 10)....................................	1,000	
Patent (or Accumulated Amortization)..............................		1,000

To record the first year's amortization on the patent.

Intangible assets are usually listed on the balance sheet in a separate section called Intangibles, which is presented below Property, Plant, and Equipment. Intangible assets are valued at cost less the accumulated amortization. This book value is usually shown as a single net amount because disclosure of both the cost and the accumulated amortization is not required. That is why the credit entry can be made directly to the asset account as shown in the preceding example. Two examples of the disclosure of intangible assets are shown in Exhibit 12-2. It

EXHIBIT 12-2
Examples of Intangible
Asset Disclosure

SCHERING-PLOUGH CORPORATION		
Balance Sheets (Partial)		
(amounts in millions of dollars)	*1988*	*1987*
Intangible assets (net)	191.1	126.3

Footnotes (in part):

Intangible assets — principally include goodwill, purchased patents, licenses, and trademarks. Goodwill represents the excess of cost over the fair value of net assets of companies purchased, and is amortized on the straight-line method, generally over 40 years. Other intangible assets are recorded at cost and amortized over their expected useful lives on the straight-line method.

GOODYEAR TIRE AND RUBBER COMPANY

Footnotes (in part):

Research and development cost included in cost of goods sold for 1988, 1987, and 1986 was $304.8 million, $266.5 million, and $290.4 million, respectively.

should be recognized that the market value of intangibles is often much greater than their book value disclosed on the balance sheet.

Although an intangible asset is amortized on the basis of its expected service life at the time of acquisition, this life should be reviewed periodically to ensure that it is reasonable. For example, before the trucking industry was deregulated in 1980, many trucking companies included in their balance sheets an intangible asset relating to the franchises they owned allowing them to engage in interstate trucking. When the industry was deregulated these franchises became worthless, and therefore the asset had to be removed from the accounts and a loss recognized.

Goodwill

7. Describe the nature of goodwill.

Goodwill is another intangible asset that might appear on the balance sheet. Goodwill is recorded when a company purchases another company or a significant portion of another company. Goodwill is often called "excess of cost over net assets of acquired companies." **Goodwill is the difference between the price paid to buy a company and the fair market value of the identifiable net assets (assets minus liabilities) acquired.** The reason why a purchaser may be willing to pay more than the market value of the identifiable net assets is that there are some "assets" that are not recorded under generally accepted accounting principles, and therefore the purchaser can expect to obtain higher than normal earnings. For example, a company may have established a reputation for high-quality products and service on those products, or it may have recruited and trained employees who are above average. Such characteristics make the company more valuable than the sum of the recorded net assets, and so the purchaser of the company should be willing to pay more than the fair market value of the net assets that are included on the balance sheet. The following steps should be completed to determine the goodwill involved in the acquisition of another company:

Step 1. Identify any assets and liabilities that are not included on the financial statements of the company being acquired, but which should be recorded (under generally accepted accounting principles).

Step 2. Determine the fair market value of the assets and liabilities recorded on the financial statements of the company being acquired, as well as the fair market value of the assets and liabilities identified in Step 1.

Step 3. Compute the value of goodwill as the difference between the purchase price of the company and the total of the amounts determined from Step 2.

For example, suppose that the balance sheet of the Windsor Company includes assets of $200,000 and liabilities of $75,000. Thus the book value of the recorded net assets (assets minus liabilities) is $125,000. Furthermore assume that the fair market value of these net assets is $185,000 and that the company has unrecorded intangible assets with a fair market value of $25,000. If the Castle Company decides to purchase the Windsor Company for $240,000 the goodwill is computed as follows:

Purchase price		$240,000
Book value of the recorded net assets	$125,000	
Excess of fair market value over book value of recorded net assets ($185,000 – $125,000)	60,000	
Fair market value of unrecorded identifiable intangible assets	25,000	
Less: Value of identifiable net assets		(210,000)
Value of Goodwill Purchased		$ 30,000

The identifiable tangible and intangible net assets are individually recorded at their respective fair market values totaling $210,000, and the purchased goodwill is separately recorded as an intangible asset at its purchase price of $30,000. It is then amortized over its expected service life (not to exceed 40 years). Amortization of goodwill is not an expense that can be deducted when computing corporate federal income taxes. The acquisition of one company by another is discussed further in Chapter 17.

It is important to distinguish the purchased goodwill discussed here from what is often referred to as "internally developed goodwill." For example, many companies develop reputations for exceptionally reliable products, good customer service, high-quality research and development, and good management. None of these components of internally developed goodwill is recognized as an asset; instead the costs associated with these items are expensed in the period that they are incurred. No asset is recognized because there has been no transaction with another entity to establish the value of the asset, as there has been when purchased goodwill is recorded.

Natural Resource Assets

8. Identify the characteristics of natural resource assets.

In addition to property, plant, and equipment and intangible assets, many companies have natural resource assets (sometimes called wasting assets). **A natural resource asset is a productive asset that is used up as it is converted into inventory.** Examples of natural resource assets are oil, coal, gravel, and timber. Natural resource assets are usually disclosed in a separate section of the balance sheet. They may appear above or below property, plant, and equipment, depending on the relative importance of the two categories of assets to the particular company. These assets are accounted for in the same manner as the other categories of productive assets. That is, their acquisition costs are capitalized and expensed over their expected service lives. **Depletion expense is the portion of the acquisition cost (less the estimated residual value) of a natural resource asset allocated as an expense** to each accounting period in the asset's service life. Thus we see that one concept has three different titles — depreciation for property, plant, and equipment, amortization for intangible assets, and depletion for natural resource assets. There are three special aspects of natural resource assets that require further consideration.

Method of Computing Depletion Expense

Depletion expense is computed using the units-of-production method discussed in Chapter 11. That is, the depletable cost (cost minus estimated residual value) is expensed according to the estimate of the production to be obtained from the asset. This method is usually considered appropriate because it results in an equal depletion expense for every unit produced. For example, suppose that a coal mine is purchased for $100,000. The following journal entry is used to record the acquisition:

Coal Mine.. 100,000
    Cash   100,000

To record the purchase of a coal mine.

If the mine is expected to produce 10,000 tons of coal and the estimated residual value is zero, the depletion per ton of coal mined would be computed as follows:

$$\text{Depletion per Unit} = \frac{\text{Cost} - \text{Estimated Residual Value}}{\text{Units of Production}}$$

$$= \frac{\$100,000 - \$0}{10,000 \text{ tons}}$$

$$= \$10 \text{ per ton}$$

If the company produces and sells 1,200 tons in the first year, the following journal entry would be made:

Depletion Expense ($10 × 1,200) 12,000
    Coal Mine (or Accumulated Depletion)............................   12,000

To record depletion of the first year's production.

Note that the credit is often made directly to the asset account, Coal Mine, because separate disclosure in the financial statements of the accumulated depletion is not required.

Often a company purchases or builds tangible assets that have a life that is dependent on the life of the natural resource asset. Such assets should be depreciated over the life of the natural resource. For example, if a company builds housing that has a life of 20 years at a mine that has a life of 10 years, the housing should be depreciated over the expected life of the mine, or 10 years, because the housing will have no use after the mine is exhausted. The depreciation expense on the housing may also be calculated by using the units-of-production method since the usefulness of the housing expires as the coal is mined rather than through the passage of time.

Revised Estimates of Productive Capacity

Because it is often difficult to measure the expected lifetime productive capacity of a natural resource asset, revisions in the estimates are frequently required. Continuing the preceding example, suppose that at the beginning of the second year the company discovers that by spending an additional $14,600 it can increase the capacity of the mine by 2,000 tons. Assuming this additional cost is incurred, the new depletion rate is computed as follows:

$$\text{Depletion per Year} = \frac{\text{Book Value} + \text{Additional Costs} - \text{Estimated Residual Value}}{\text{Remaining Units of Production (including additional units)}}$$

$$= \frac{(\$100,000 - \$12,000) + \$14,600 - \$0}{(10,000 - 1,200) + 2,000 \text{ tons}}$$

$$= \frac{\$102,600}{10,800 \text{ tons}}$$

$$= \$9.50 \text{ per ton}$$

If the company produces and sells 1,300 tons in the second year, the depletion expense will be $12,350 ($9.50 × 1,300).

Cost Depletion and Percentage Depletion

9. Explain the differences between cost depletion and percentage depletion.

For financial statement purposes, depletion expense is based on the cost of the asset, and over the life of the asset the total depletion expense is limited to the cost less the expected residual value. It is known as *cost* depletion and is related to the expected pattern of benefits produced by the asset. This is the method discussed previously.

For corporate federal income tax purposes, depletion expense involves a different concept. **Percentage (or statutory) depletion is computed by multiplying a corporation's "gross income" from a natural resources asset by a statutory percentage.** Gross income is essentially the selling price of the natural resource; the statutory percentage varies, depending on the type of natural resource, from a minimum of 5% to a maximum of 22% (complexities in the computation of the percentage depletion expense are beyond the scope of this book). Since the percentage depletion expense is based only on the stated percentage and gross income, the total percentage depletion expense over the life of the asset for federal income tax purposes is *not* limited by the depreciable cost of the asset.

The special income tax laws for depletion are intended to encourage exploration and development of natural resources, whereas depletion expense for financial statement purposes is intended to match the costs against the benefits derived from the asset. There has been much discussion about whether or not percentage depletion encourages exploration and development, with the natural resource companies supporting the method and many consumer groups objecting to it. Although there does not appear to be any definitive evidence of its success, the percentage depletion method is still allowed for income tax purposes. Therefore most corporations compute a different amount of depletion expense for income tax purposes than for financial statements. The difference between cost depletion and percentage depletion is required to be disclosed in the notes to the financial statements.

Chapter Summary

Review of Learning Objectives

1. **Account for the disposal by sale of property, plant, and equipment.**
   Depreciation for the fraction of the year up to the date of disposal should be recorded. At the time of disposal the balances in the asset account and its related accumulated depreciation account are removed. Disposals include those situations in which no cash is involved, the sale price is equal to the residual value, the sale price is above book value (gain is recorded), and the sale price is below book value (loss is recorded).

2. **Account for the disposal by exchange of (a) dissimilar and (b) similar productive assets.**
   When *dissimilar* productive assets are exchanged, gains and losses are recognized in full. When *similar* productive assets are exchanged, gains are not recognized, whereas losses are recognized in full.

> **3. Identify the characteristics of intangible assets.**
> Intangible assets are noncurrent assets that do not have a physical substance. Intangible assets generally have five characteristics that distinguish them from tangible assets: (1) they do not have a physical substance but more often result from legal rights, (2) there is generally a higher degree of uncertainty regarding their future benefits, (3) their value is subject to wider fluctuations, (4) they may have value only to a particular company, and (5) their expected lives may be difficult to determine.

> **4. Explain the nature of research and development costs.**
> *Research* is a planned search or critical investigation aimed at discovery of new knowledge. *Development* is the translation of research findings into a plan or design for a new product or process. Research and development costs are expensed as incurred.

> **5. Describe (a) patents, (b) copyrights, (c) trademarks and tradenames, (d) franchises, (e) computer software costs, and (f) organization costs.**
> A *patent* is an exclusive right granted by the federal government giving its owner the control of the manufacture, sale, or other use of an invention for 17 years. A *copyright* is an exclusive right granted by the federal government covering the right to publish, sell, or otherwise control literary or artistic products for the life of the author plus an additional 50 years. A *trademark* or *tradename* is registered with the U.S. Patent Office and establishes a right to the exclusive use of a name, symbol, or other device used for product identification. A *franchise* is an agreement entered into by two parties in which, for a fee, the franchisor gives the franchisee rights to perform certain functions or sell certain products or services. *Computer software costs* include software production costs, such as design, coding, testing, documentation, and preparation of training materials. *Organization costs* are the costs associated with the formation of a corporation.

> **6. Explain the rules for the amortization of intangible assets.**
> Intangible assets are amortized over the lesser of the service life or the legal life, up to a maximum of 40 years. The straight-line method is typically used.

> **7. Describe the nature of goodwill.**
> Goodwill is the difference between the price paid to buy a company and the fair market value of the identifiable net assets acquired. The calculation of goodwill is summarized as follows:

Purchase price		$xx
Book value of the recorded net assets	$xx	
Excess of fair market value over book value of recorded net assets	xx	
Fair market value of unrecorded identifiable intangible assets	xx	
Less: Value of identifiable net assets		(xx)
Value of goodwill purchased		$xx

> **8. Identify the characteristics of natural resource assets.**
> A natural resource asset is a productive asset that is used up as it is converted into inventory.

9. **Explain the differences between cost depletion and percentage depletion.**
Cost depletion is the allocation of a portion of the acquisition cost (less the estimated residual value) of a natural resource asset as an expense. Cost depletion is computed by multiplying the depletion per unit times the number of units produced and sold. *Percentage* (or statutory) *depletion* is computed by multiplying a corporation's "gross income" from a natural resource asset by a statutory percentage. Cost depletion is used in financial statements, whereas percentage depletion is used in the computation of federal income taxes.

Review Problem

Note: This review problem includes material from Chapters 11 and 12.

On December 31, 1991, the Vail Company owned the following assets:

Asset	Date of Purchase	Cost	Accumulated Depreciation	Life in Years	Residual Value	Depreciation Method
Building	1/1/1989	$50,000	$ 3,750	40	$ 0	Straight line
Office machinery	1/1/1989	20,000	9,760	10	2,000	Double declining balance
Office fixtures	1/1/1989	30,000	20,000	5	5,000	Sum of the years' digits

The company computes depreciation and amortization expense to the *nearest whole year* (explained in Chapter 11). During 1992, the following events occurred:

Date	Transaction
Jan. 2	Extended the building at a cost of $10,000. As a result, the total useful life of the building is extended to 50 years. (Debit the Building account.)
Mar. 6	Sold a piece of office machinery that had originally cost $4,000 and that had accumulated depreciation of $1,952 on December 31, 1991. The machine was sold for $3,000.
Apr. 28	The company obtained a patent on an invention by paying $2,000. It was expected that the patent would provide protection against competition for 10 years.
May 15	Purchased office fixtures and office machinery for $9,200. The supplier reduced the price because of the joint purchase. If purchased separately, the office fixtures would have cost $6,000 and the office machinery $4,000. Delivery charges paid by Vail were $200. The machinery was accidentally damaged during installation and cost $120 to repair. The office fixtures have an estimated life of 5 years and a residual value of $250. The office machinery has an estimated life of 10 years and a residual value of $500.
Aug. 10	The president's desk (classified as office fixtures) was exchanged for another desk. The desk had cost $600 and had accumulated depreciation on December 31, 1991, of $400 and an estimated residual value of $100. The new desk had a list price of $900 and $700 cash was paid.
Oct. 20	A manufacturer's representative serviced and adjusted the office machinery at a cost of $75.

REQUIRED

1. Check the accuracy of the accumulated depreciation balances at December 31, 1991.

2. Prepare journal entries to record the preceding events in 1992 as well as the year-end recording of depreciation expense.

3. Prepare an accumulated depreciation account for each category of assets, enter the beginning balance, post the journal entries from Requirement 2, and compute the ending balance.

Solution to Review Problem

REQUIREMENT 1

Each category of assets has been depreciated from January 1, 1989, to December 31, 1991, a total of 3 years.

Building:

$$\text{Annual Depreciation Expense} = \frac{\text{Cost} - \text{Estimated Residual Value}}{\text{Estimated Service Life}}$$

$$= \frac{\$50,000 - \$0}{40}$$

$$= \$1,250 \text{ per year}$$

$$\text{Accumulated Depreciation at December 31, 1991} = 3 \times \$1,250$$
$$= \underline{\$3,750}$$

Office Machinery:

$$\text{Double-Declining Rate} = 2 \times \text{Straight-Line Rate}$$
$$= 2 \times 1/10 = 20\%$$

$$\text{Depreciation Expense, 1989} = \text{Double-Declining Rate} \times \text{Book Value at the Beginning of the Year}$$
$$= 20\% \times \$20,000^a = \$4,000$$

$$\text{Depreciation Expense, 1990} = 20\% \times (\$20,000 - \$4,000) = \$3,200$$
$$\text{Depreciation Expense, 1991} = 20\% \times (\$20,000 - \$7,200) = \$2,560$$

$$\text{Accumulated Depreciation at December 31, 1991} = \$4,000 + \$3,200 + \$2,560$$
$$= \underline{\$9,760}$$

ªEstimated residual value is disregarded in computing double-declining balance depreciation.

Office Fixtures:

$$\text{Sum of the Years' Digits} = n(n + 1)/2$$
$$= (5 \times 6)/2 = 15$$

$$\text{Depreciation Expense, 1989} = 5/15 \times (\$30,000 - \$5,000) = \$\ 8,333$$
$$\text{Depreciation Expense, 1990} = 4/15 \times (\$30,000 - \$5,000) = \$\ 6,667$$
$$\text{Depreciation Expense, 1991} = 3/15 \times (\$30,000 - \$5,000) = \underline{\$\ 5,000}$$
$$\text{Accumulated Depreciation at December 31, 1991} = \underline{\$20,000}$$

REQUIREMENT 2

1992

Jan.	2	Building	10,000	
		Cash (or other accounts)		10,000

To record payment for extension of the building. The new estimated total life is 50 years.

Mar. 6	Cash	3,000	
	Accumulated Depreciation: Office Machinery[a]	1,952	
	Office Machinery		4,000
	Gain on Disposal of Office Machinery		952

To record sale of office machinery.

[a]No depreciation expense is recorded because the asset is sold in the first half of the year. Accumulated depreciation is 20% ($4,000 cost ÷ $20,000 total office machinery) × $9,760 total accumulated depreciation (from Requirement 1).

| Apr. 28 | Patent .... | 2,000 | |
| | Cash .... | | 2,000 |

To record acquisition of patent.

May 15	Office Fixtures	5,640[a]	
	Office Machinery	3,760[a]	
	Repair Expense	120	
	Cash		9,520

To record purchase of office fixtures and office machinery and incurrence of repair expense on damage during installation.

$$
\begin{aligned}
^a\text{Total acquisition cost} &= \text{Purchase price} + \text{delivery charges} \\
&= \$9,200 + \$200 = \$9,400 \\
\text{Cost of office fixtures} &= (\$6,000/\$10,000) \times \$9,400 = \$5,640 \\
\text{Cost of office machinery} &= (\$4,000/\$10,000) \times \$9,400 = \$3,760
\end{aligned}
$$

| Aug. 10 | Depreciation Expense: Office Fixtures .... | 67[a] | |
| | Accumulated Depreciation: Office Fixtures .... | | 67 |

To record depreciation on the asset being exchanged.

[a]The exchange of office fixtures occurred in the second half of the year; therefore a full year's depreciation is recorded on the original asset. Depreciation expense on office fixtures purchased on 1/1/1989 = 2/15 ($600 − $100) = $67 (rounded).

Aug. 10	Office Fixtures	833[a]	
	Accumulated Depreciation: Office Fixtures	467[b]	
	Cash		700
	Office Fixtures		600

To record exchange of office fixtures and payment of $700.

[a]Since boot is given, the new asset is recorded at the $133 book value of the old asset ($600 − $467) plus the cash paid ($700).
[b]$400 accumulated depreciation (12/31/1991) + $67.

| Oct. 20 | Repair Expense .... | 75 | |
| | Cash .... | | 75 |

To record service of office machinery.

Dec. 31	Depreciation Expense: Building	1,197[a]	
	Depreciation Expense: Office Machinery	2,390[b]	
	Depreciation Expense: Office Fixtures	5,064[c]	
	Accumulated Depreciation: Building		1,197
	Accumulated Depreciation: Office Machinery		2,390
	Accumulated Depreciation: Office Fixtures		5,064

To record depreciation expense for the year.

$$
^a\ \frac{(\$50,000 - \$3,750) + \$10,000 - \$0}{47^*} = \underline{\underline{\$1,197}} \text{ (rounded)}
$$

*Total life is extended to 50 years. Since the asset has been depreciated for 3 years, 47 years remain.

[b]The sale of office machinery on March 6 occurred in the first half of the year, and therefore no depreciation is recorded on that item.

Cost of remaining office machinery purchased on 1/1/1989 = $20,000 − $4,000 = $16,000.

Accumulated depreciation on remaining office machinery = $9,760 − $1,952 = $7,808.

Depreciation expense on remaining office machinery purchased on 1/1/1989 = 20% ($16,000 − $7,808) = $1,638 (rounded).

The purchase of office machinery on May 15 occurred in the first half of the year, and therefore a full year's depreciation is recorded.

Depreciation expense on office machinery purchased on 5/15/1992 = 20% × $3,760 = $752.

Total depreciation expense on office machinery = $1,638 + $752 = $2,390.

ᶜThe purchase of office fixtures on May 15 occurred in the first half of the year, and therefore a full year's depreciation is recorded.

Depreciation expense = 5/15 × ($5,640 − $250) = $1,797 (rounded).

Depreciation on the office fixtures acquired by exchange is not recorded because the asset was acquired in the second half of the year, and depreciation on the asset disposed of was recorded on August 10.

Depreciation on the office fixtures acquired at 1/1/1989 is
2/15 × [($30,000 − $600) − ($5,000 − $100)] = $3,267 (rounded).

Total depreciation expense on office fixtures = $1,797 + $3,267 = $5,064.

Dec. 31	Amortization Expense	200	
	Patent		200

To record amortization of patent (acquired in the first half of the year) over the estimated economic life of 10 years.

REQUIREMENT 3

Accumulated Depreciation: Building

		Bal. 12/31/91	3,750
		12/31/92	1,197
		Bal. 12/31/92	4,947

Accumulated Depreciation: Office Machinery

3/6/92	1,952	Bal. 12/31/91	9,760
		12/31/92	2,390
		Bal. 12/31/92	10,198

Accumulated Depreciation: Office Fixtures

8/10/92	467	Bal. 12/31/91	20,000
		8/10/92	67
		12/31/92	5,064
		Bal. 12/31/92	24,664

Glossary

Amortization Expense. The portion of the acquisition cost of an intangible asset allocated as an expense to each accounting period in the asset's service life.

Boot. Cash paid as part of an exchange of assets.

Copyright. An exclusive right granted by the federal government for publishing, selling, or controlling literary or artistic products for the life of the author plus an additional 50 years. The cost of acquiring the copyright is recorded as an asset.

Depletion Expense. The portion of the acquisition cost (less the estimated residual value) of a natural resource asset allocated as an expense to each accounting period in the asset's service life. Also called *cost* depletion.

Development. The translation of research findings into a plan or design for a new product or process. Development costs are expensed in the period incurred.

Dissimilar Productive Assets. Productive assets that are not of the same general type, that do not perform the same function, or that are not employed in the same line of business.

Franchise. Agreement in which the franchisor assigns to the franchisee rights to perform certain functions or sell certain products or services. The cost of acquiring a franchise is recorded as an asset.

Gain (Loss) on Sale (Disposal) of an Asset. The amount by which the proceeds from the sale exceed (are less than) the depreciated cost (book value) of an asset.

Goodwill. An intangible asset representing the excess of the cost of acquiring a company over the fair market value of the identifiable net assets.

Intangible Assets. Noncurrent assets that do not have a physical substance. Their value typically results from the use of the legal rights associated with the intangible asset rather than from physical use.

Lease. An agreement conveying the right to use property, plant, or equipment without transferring legal ownership of the item.

Leasehold Improvement. An improvement made to leased property, plant, or equipment by the lessee.

Natural Resource Asset. A productive asset that is used up as it is converted into inventory. Also called a *wasting asset*.

Organization Costs. Costs associated with the formation of a corporation. Recorded as an asset.

Patent. An exclusive right granted by the federal government giving its owner the control of the manufacture, sale, or other use of an invention for 17 years. The cost of acquiring a patent is recorded as an asset.

Percentage Depletion Expense. A method of computing depletion expense as a percentage of the gross income produced by a natural resource asset; it is used for corporate federal income tax purposes.

Productive Assets. Assets such as inventory, property, and equipment that are used in the production of goods and services.

R&D Costs. An abbreviation for research and development costs.

Research. Planned search or critical investigation aimed at discovery of new knowledge. Research costs are expensed in the period incurred.

Similar Productive Assets. Productive assets that are of the same general type, that perform the same function, or that are employed in the same line of business.

Trademark or Tradename. A right to the exclusive use of a name, symbol, or other device that is used for product identification. The cost is recorded as an asset.

Questions

QUESTION 12-1 How is the gain or loss from the disposal of an asset determined when the asset is sold in the middle of the year?

QUESTION 12-2 Are gains and losses from disposals of assets reported in the income statement in the same way as depreciation expense? If not, how are they reported?

QUESTION 12-3 If a corporation traded in a machine on a new model and the trade-in value of the old machine is greater than its book value, would the corporation recognize a gain? If the trade-in value is less than the book value, would the corporation recognize a loss? Would your answer change for the corporation's federal income tax reports?

QUESTION 12-4   How is an exchange of dissimilar assets recorded?

QUESTION 12-5   When a gain is not recognized on the exchange of similar productive assets will the company's financial statements be affected in the long run because the company did not include a gain in the income statement?

QUESTION 12-6   An asset cost $50,000 and had an estimated residual value of $5,000. The accumulated depreciation account has a balance of $45,000. If the asset is still being used, should depreciation be recorded on the asset? Should the asset and accumulated depreciation amounts be removed from the financial statements?

QUESTION 12-7   What is meant by the terms *research* and *development?*

QUESTION 12-8   What characteristics distinguish intangible assets from tangible assets? What characteristics are similar?

QUESTION 12-9   Define the terms: (a) patent; (b) copyright; (c) franchise; (d) trademark; and (e) organization costs.

QUESTION 12-10   What is the correct life to use for the amortization of intangible assets?

QUESTION 12-11   Which amortization method should be used for intangible assets?

QUESTION 12-12   What is the maximum life over which the following intangible assets should be amortized: (a) patent; (b) copyright; (c) franchise; and (d) goodwill?

QUESTION 12-13   What is meant by the term *goodwill?* Describe two factors that might cause a purchaser to pay more than the fair market value of the net assets of a company.

QUESTION 12-14   Under what conditions is goodwill recorded?

QUESTION 12-15   What is a natural resource asset? How is it accounted for?

QUESTION 12-16   What are the similarities and differences among the terms depreciation, amortization, and depletion?

QUESTION 12-17   Describe how depletion expense is calculated under the cost depletion method. How does the calculation differ under percentage depletion?

Exercises

EXERCISE 12-1   **Disposal of an Asset.** The Brown Hydraulic Engineering Company owns a machine that had originally cost $25,000. The accumulated depreciation account now has a balance of $18,000.

REQUIRED   Prepare journal entries to record the disposal of the machine if it is sold for:

1. $7,000.

2. $1,000.

3. $12,000.

EXERCISE 12-2   **Disposal of an Asset.** The Snowdon Mining Company purchased a machine for $80,000 on January 1, 1988. It is being depreciated on a straight-line basis over 5 years to a zero residual value. On December 31, 1991, the machine is sold.

REQUIRED   Prepare journal entries to record the depreciation expense for 1991 and the disposal of the machine if it is sold for:

1. $16,000.

2. $11,000.

3. $17,000.

EXERCISE 12-3   **Exchange of Similar Productive Assets.** The Whillans Sanitary Engineering Company owns a machine that had an original cost of $46,000 and accumulated depreciation of $30,000. The company trades in the machine on a new model, which has an invoice price of $25,000 and pays cash of $8,000.

REQUIRED
1. What is the acquisition cost of the new machine? Prepare the journal entry to record the acquisition.

2. If instead the company traded in the old machine and paid $17,000 in the exchange, what is the acquisition cost of the new machine? Prepare the journal entry to record the acquisition.

EXERCISE 12-4   **Exchange of Dissimilar Productive Assets.** The Scafell Die Cutting Company owns a machine that had an original cost of $70,000 and accumulated depreciation of $12,000. The company trades in the machine on a piece of land and pays $6,000. The machine has a fair market value of $46,000.

REQUIRED
1. What is the acquisition cost of the land? Prepare the journal entry to record the exchange.

2. If the company paid $11,000 on the exchange, what is the acquisition cost of the land? Prepare the journal entry to record the exchange.

EXERCISE 12-5   **Exchange of Dissimilar Productive Assets.** The Everst Sweater Company owns a delivery truck that had an original cost of $20,000 and accumulated depreciation of $12,000. The company trades in the truck on a machine that has a cost of $30,000.

REQUIRED
1. Prepare the journal entry to record the transaction if the company pays $18,000 cash.

2. Prepare the journal entry to record the transaction if the company pays $25,000 cash.

EXERCISE 12-6   **Intangible Assets.** The Noyce Company was involved in the following transactions:

(a) Purchased a patent from another company.

(b) Developed a design for a new type of machine for use in its production process.

(c) Purchased a franchise for exclusive regional sale of a product.

(d) Developed an advertising campaign for a new product.

(e) Purchased another company for more than the fair market value of its identifiable net assets.

REQUIRED Explain whether each of the preceding items requires the company to record an intangible asset. If not, how would each item be recorded?

EXERCISE 12-7 **Accounting for Intangible Assets.** The Langdale Company incurred the following costs:

(a) Purchased a patent from the Pike Company for $30,000.

(b) Developed a design for a new product at a cost of $80,000.

(c) Paid $75,000 to an actor to promote the company's new products.

REQUIRED 1. Prepare the journal entries to record the preceding events assuming all payments are in cash.

2. For each item recorded as an asset indicate the maximum life over which it may be amortized.

EXERCISE 12-8 **Accounting for Intangible Assets.** The Patey Food Company incurred and paid for the following costs:

(a) Obtained legal services associated with the formation of the company, $18,000.

(b) Purchased a Giantburger franchise for $50,000.

(c) Advertised the opening of its new restaurant at a cost of $12,000.

REQUIRED 1. Prepare the journal entries to record the preceding events.

2. For each item recorded as an asset indicate the maximum life over which it may be amortized.

EXERCISE 12-9 **Amortization of Intangible Assets.** The Nevis Company held the following intangible assets:

(a) Organization costs, $5,000.

(b) A patent purchased for $34,000.

(c) A copyright purchased for $16,000.

(d) A trademark purchased for $35,000.

(e) A franchise purchased for $55,000.

The company amortizes the assets by using the straight-line method over the maximum allowable life.

REQUIRED Prepare journal entries to record the amortization in the first year of each asset's life.

EXERCISE 12-10 **Natural Resources.** The Skiddaw Company purchased land for $11 million. The company expected to be able to mine 1 million tons of molybdenum from this land over the next 20 years, at which time the residual value would be zero. During the first 2 years of the mine's operation 30,000 tons were mined each year and sold for $80 per ton. The estimate of the total lifetime capacity of the mine was raised to 1.2 million tons at the beginning of the third year and the residual value was estimated to be $1 million. During the third year, 50,000 tons were mined and sold for $85 per ton.

REQUIRED   Compute the depletion expense for each of the 3 years and prepare the journal entry to record the depletion expense in each year.

EXERCISE 12-11   **Natural Resources.**   The Bonnington Company purchased land for $1.4 million. The company expected to be able to mine 500,000 tons of coal from this land over the next 10 years, after which the land would be sold for $200,000. During the first year of the mine's operation 20,000 tons of coal were mined and sold for $50 per ton. The estimate of the total lifetime capacity of the mine was raised to 600,000 tons at the beginning of the second year, and 40,000 tons were mined and sold for $60 per ton during the year.

REQUIRED   Compute the depletion expense for the first and second years and prepare the journal entry to record the depletion expense in each year.

EXERCISE 12-12   **Cost and Percentage Depletion.**   In a given year a copper mine owned by the Eskdale Corporation that had a cost of $880,000 and had an expected residual value of $160,000 produced 40,000 tons of ore out of its lifetime expected capacity of 320,000 tons. The ore was sold for $25 per ton. The percentage depletion rate is 15%.

REQUIRED   1. Compute the cost depletion expense and the percentage depletion expense for the year.

2. If the selling price and costs remain constant, is it advantageous for the corporation to use percentage depletion for federal income tax purposes over the life of the mine?

Problems

Part A

PROBLEM 12-1A   **Disposal of Assets.**   On January 1, 1991, the Hillary Turbine Company owns the following two assets:

(a) The president's car, which was purchased in 1988 for $15,000; the car was being depreciated on the basis of the miles driven. The original estimate was that the car would be driven for 50,000 miles and then sold for $4,000. On January 1, 1991, the car had been driven 40,000 miles. By May 20 it had been driven another 5,000 miles and was sold for $4,000.

(b) A machine purchased on January 1, 1986, for $40,000; it was being depreciated to a residual value of $4,000 over a period of 6 years by using the straight-line method. On August 31, 1991, it was sold for $8,000 and depreciation for 8 months was recorded.

REQUIRED   1. Prepare journal entries to record the preceding events in 1991.

2. Show how the relevant items would affect the financial statements for 1991.

PROBLEM 12-2A   **Exchange of Similar Productive Assets.**   On January 1, 1991, the Haston Wind Chime Corporation owns two cars. Both cars were purchased on January 1, 1988. The president's car cost $15,000 and the salesman's car cost $8,000. The expected residual values at the end of their expected lives of 4 years are $5,000 and $2,000, respectively. The straight-line depreciation method is used for both cars. On December 31, 1991, both cars are traded for new cars. The president's car is exchanged for a new car with a cost of $24,000, and $12,000 cash is paid. The salesman's car is exchanged for a new car with a cost of $15,000, and $13,500 cash is paid.

REQUIRED

1. Prepare journal entries to record the preceding events in 1991.

2. Show how the relevant items would affect the financial statements for 1991.

3. Prepare the journal entries to record depreciation in 1992 if an expected life of 5 years and a zero residual value is assumed for each new car.

4. State how your computation for Requirement 1 would change for federal income tax reporting (do not prepare journal entries).

PROBLEM 12-3A

Accidental Destruction of Assets. On December 30, 1991, a building and machinery owned by the Messner Electroplating Company were destroyed in a fire. The building had cost $125,000 at the beginning of 1983 and was being depreciated over 40 years to a zero residual value by the straight-line method. The machinery had been purchased at the beginning of 1988 for $50,000 and was being depreciated to a zero residual value over a 10-year life by the sum-of-the-years'-digits method. The salvageable materials from the fire were sold for $22,000 and the company collected $100,000 from its insurance company.

REQUIRED

1. Prepare journal entries for 1991.

2. What is the meaning of the gain or loss that is recognized?

PROBLEM 12-4A

Intangible Assets. The Shipton Publishing Company was involved in the following transactions during the current year:

(a) Developed a design for a new production process at a cost of $90,000. Legal costs to apply for a patent were $8,500.

(b) Paid $20,000 to employees who worked on the development of the design for the new production process.

(c) Paid $12,000 legal costs to successfully defend a copyright against infringement by another company. The original copyright was purchased 4 years ago at a cost of $30,000 and was being amortized over a 10-year life.

(d) Agreed to pay $70,000 to a racing driver to have the company name prominently displayed on his car for the year.

(e) Acquired the copyright to a novel for $35,000.

REQUIRED

1. Prepare journal entries to record the preceding transactions.

2. Prepare journal entries to record the first year's amortization of intangible assets. Use the maximum life allowable unless a shorter life is indicated.

PROBLEM 12-5A

Goodwill. The Caraway Seed Company acquired the Forester Flower Company for $150,000. The balance sheet of the Forester Flower Company showed assets of $80,000 and liabilities of $30,000. The fair market value of the assets was $25,000 higher than the book value. In addition, an intangible asset that was not included on the balance sheet had a fair market value of $6,000.

REQUIRED

1. How much goodwill would the Caraway Seed Company record in regard to the purchase of the Forester Flower Company?

2. Where would the goodwill appear in the financial statements of the Caraway Seed Company?

3. Over what life should the goodwill be amortized?

PROBLEM 12-6A   **Natural Resource Assets.** On January 1, 1991, the Eiger Company purchased a developed mine for $11 million. The expected capacity of the mine was 1 million tons. The cost of restoring the land at the end of the life of the mine was estimated to be $2 million. In addition, the company built housing for the miners for $120,000 that had a life of 20 years but which would have no value after the capacity of the mine has been exhausted. In 1991 the company incurred labor costs of $500,000 to mine 100,000 tons, which it sold at $26 per ton. The company also incurred administrative costs of $350,000.

     In January 1992 additional costs of $250,000 were incurred, which resulted in the capacity of the mine being increased to 100,000 tons greater than originally expected. In 1992 the company mined 150,000 tons, which it sold at $28 per ton, and incurred related labor costs of $700,000 and administrative costs of $400,000.

     The labor costs are expensed each period. Ignore income taxes.

REQUIRED   Prepare income statements for 1991 and 1992.

Problems

Part B

PROBLEM 12-1B   **Disposal of Assets.** On January 1, 1991, the Double Entries rock band owns the following two assets:

(a) A guitar, purchased in 1988 for $9,000, which was being depreciated on the basis of hours played. The original estimate was that the guitar would be played for 2,500 hours and then be sold for $2,000. By January 1, 1991, the guitar had been played for 2,000 hours. By June 3 it had been played for another 200 hours and was sold for $3,000.

(b) A sound system purchased on January 1, 1988, for $650,000, which was being depreciated to a residual value of $100,000 over a period of 5 years by using the straight-line method. On June 30, 1991, it was sold for $200,000 and depreciation for 6 months was recorded.

REQUIRED   *1.* Prepare journal entries to record the preceding events in 1991.

     2. Show how these events would affect the financial statements for 1991.

PROBLEM 12-2B   **Exchange of Similar Productive Assets.** On January 1, 1991, the Townsend Real Estate Corporation owns two airplanes, both of which were purchased on January 1, 1988. The president's jet cost $1.1 million and the regional manager's biplane cost $140,000. The expected residual values at the end of their expected lives of 4 years are $200,000 and $30,000, respectively. The straight-line depreciation method is used for both planes. On December 31, 1991, both planes are traded for new planes. The president's new jet has a cost of $1.5 million, and $1.4 million cash is paid. The regional manager's biplane is exchanged for another plane with a cost of $60,000, and $20,000 cash is paid.

REQUIRED   *1.* Prepare journal entries to record the preceding events in 1991.

     2. Show how these events would affect the financial statements for 1991.

     3. Prepare the journal entries to record depreciation in 1992 if an expected life of 5 years and a zero residual value is assumed for both new planes.

     4. State how your computation for Requirement 1 would change for federal income tax reporting (do not prepare journal entries).

PROBLEM 12-3B   **Accidental Destruction of Assets.**   On December 30, 1991, a movie theater and projection machinery owned by the Emerson Company were destroyed by a tornado. The building had cost $350,000 at the beginning of 1983 and was being depreciated over 40 years to a zero residual value by means of the straight-line method. The projection machinery had been purchased at the beginning of 1988 for $55,000 and was being depreciated to a zero residual value over a 10-year life by means of the sum-of-the-years'-digits method. After the tornado the salvageable materials were sold for $20,000, and the company collected $280,000 from its insurance company.

REQUIRED   1. Prepare journal entries for 1991.

     2. What is the meaning of the gain or loss that is recognized?

PROBLEM 12-4B   **Intangible Assets.**   The Richards Cereal Company was involved in the following transactions during the current year:

(a) Developed a process for producing a new type of breakfast cereal at a cost of $200,000. Legal costs to apply for a patent were $50,000.

(b) Paid $40,000 to employees who worked on the development of the process for producing the breakfast cereal.

(c) Paid $28,000 legal costs to successfully defend a copyright, which was purchased 3 years ago, against infringement by another company. The original copyright cost $20,000 and was being amortized over a 20-year life.

(d) Agreed to pay $100,000 to have the company name flashed on the scoreboard at football games during this season.

(e) Acquired the copyright to a comic strip for $30,000.

REQUIRED   1. Prepare journal entries to record the preceding transactions.

     2. Prepare journal entries to record the first year's amortization of the intangible assets. Use the maximum allowable life unless a shorter life is indicated.

PROBLEM 12-5B   **Goodwill.**   The Floyd Electronics Company acquired the Palmer Software Company for $320,000. The balance sheet of the Palmer Software Company showed assets of $380,000 and liabilities of $200,000. The fair market value of the assets was $40,000 higher than the book value. In addition, an intangible asset that was not included on the balance sheet had a fair market value of $20,000.

REQUIRED   1. How much goodwill would the Floyd Electronics Company record in regard to the purchase of the Palmer Software Company?

     2. Where would the goodwill appear in the financial statements of the Floyd Electronics Company?

     3. Over what life should the goodwill be amortized?

PROBLEM 12-6B   **Natural Resource Assets.**   On January 1, 1991, the Newton Company purchased a developed mine for $5.5 million. The expected capacity of the mine was 500,000 tons. The cost of restoring the land after the mine would be exhausted was estimated to be $100,000. In addition, the company built housing for the miners for $70,000 that had a life of 20 years but which would have no value after the capacity of the mine has been exhausted. In 1991 the company incurred labor costs of $100,000 to mine 65,000 tons, which it sold at $18 per ton. The company also incurred administrative costs of $140,000.

     In January 1992 additional costs of $70,000 were incurred, which resulted in the capacity of the mine being increased to 100,000 tons greater than originally expected.

In 1992 the company mined 100,000 tons, which it sold at $20 per ton, and incurred related labor costs of $200,000 and administrative costs of $300,000.

The labor costs are expensed each period. Ignore income taxes.

REQUIRED Prepare income statements for 1991 and 1992.

Decision Cases

DECISION CASE 12-1   **Intangible Assets.**   The Internal Revenue Service has the following rules regarding the amortization of intangibles for federal income tax purposes:

Patents:	17 years maximum
Copyrights:	40 years maximum
Franchises:	Length of franchise
Research and development:	Write off in period incurred

Intangible assets that have indefinite lives may not be amortized (including good-will).

REQUIRED
1. Explain clearly how the preceding rules differ from the rules for the preparation of financial statements.

2. In each case in which there is a difference, explain how net income and income computed for federal income tax purposes by a corporation would differ.

3. In each case in which there is a difference which alternative do you think is best for financial reporting?

DECISION CASE 12-2   **Goodwill.**   The Fastgro Company has increased its profits to five times the level of 6 years ago. The board of directors is meeting to discuss the sale of the company to a larger competitor. The following comments are made during the meeting:

- "We should add some goodwill on the balance sheet, and then we can sell the company at a price equal to the net assets" (assets minus liabilities).

- "We can't add goodwill to the balance sheet because that would violate generally accepted accounting principles. However, the company that buys us will record goodwill. I don't see why they can and we can't."

- "It doesn't matter whether we add goodwill or not, because the price paid to buy this company will not be affected by the goodwill being on the balance sheet or not."

- "You mentioned that the buyer will record goodwill on its balance sheet. I was wondering how they will decide how much the goodwill is, how they will decide whether or not to amortize it, and over what life?"

REQUIRED Explain how you would respond to each of the comments.

DECISION CASE 12-3   **Intangible Assets.**   The Wewel Company reported the following in its 1991 financial statements (amounts in thousands of dollars):

	1991	*1990*
Patents (net)	$240	$280
Goodwill (net)	880	800

Patents are amortized over their legal lives of 17 years and goodwill is amortized over 40 years. The straight-line method is used for both assets.

REQUIRED
1. Assume that no patents were purchased in 1991 and goodwill of $100,000 was purchased at the end of 1991. What was the original cost of each of the intangible assets?

2. What would have been the impact on the income statement for 1991 if the company had selected a life of 10 years for both assets?

DECISION CASE 12-4 **Goodwill.** Sheri Clark has extensive experience working in shops that sell greeting cards and small gifts. She decided that she wanted to purchase her own store and found two that had the appropriate characteristics. The balance sheets of the two stores at December 31, 1991, were as follows:

	Store A	*Store B*
Cash	$ 10,000	$ 20,000
Accounts receivable	40,000	70,000
Inventory	30,000	100,000
Furniture and fixtures	62,500	125,000
Less: Accumulated depreciation	(40,000)	(25,000)
Intangible assets	10,000	0
	$112,500	$290,000
Accounts payable	$ 25,000	$ 50,000
Bank loan	40,000	80,000
Owner's equity	47,500	160,000
	$112,500	$290,000

Both owners are willing to sell their companies for 125% of the value of the net assets as recorded on their balance sheets. An investigation of the two balance sheets reveals the following:

- *Accounts receivable:* Store B has appropriately provided for uncollectible accounts whereas Store A uses the direct write-off method. It appears that $5,000 of Store A's receivables may not be collectible.

- *Inventory:* Store A uses the LIFO cost flow assumption whereas Store B uses FIFO. The replacement cost of Store A's inventory is $20,000 higher than its balance sheet amount.

- *Furniture and fixtures:* Store A uses the ACRS method to prepare its financial statements whereas Store B uses the straight-line method. Each store purchased its furniture and fixtures two years ago.

- *Intangible assets:* Store B's intangible asset is the cost of the promotional campaign that was undertaken when the store opened.

REQUIRED Prepare a report for Sheri Clark that recommends which of the two stores she should buy.

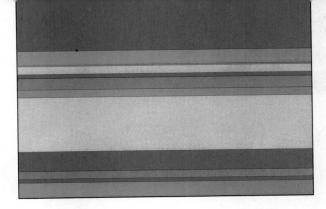

P A R T   T H R E E

BUSINESS ENTITIES

13

Partnership Accounting

LEARNING OBJECTIVES

1. Describe the characteristics of a partnership.

2. Explain the reasons for the formation of a partnership.

3. Account for partnership equity.

4. Compute the distribution of partnership earnings among partners.

5. Prepare the financial statements of a partnership.

6. Account for the admission of a new partner.

7. Account for the withdrawal of a partner.

8. Account for the liquidation of a partnership.

T
here are three principal forms of business organization: the sole proprietorship, the partnership, and the corporation. The discussion in the first five chapters of this book was based on a sole proprietorship, although the differences between a sole proprietorship and a corporation were briefly explained in Chapter 5. Chapters 6 through 12 and 16 through 20 discuss areas of accounting that are independent of the form of business organization. In Chapters 14 and 15 accounting for the corporation is explained. In this chapter the accounting principles that relate to partnerships are discussed. In order to help in understanding these principles it is useful to consider some of the characteristics of partnerships and the reasons for their existence.

Characteristics of a Partnership

1. Describe the characteristics of a partnership.

A partnership is an association of two or more persons to carry on as co-owners a business for profit. Two or more people engaging in business transactions with other parties, therefore, could be operating as a partnership without realizing it and without having made any formal agreement about how to operate their business. In such cases any disputes would be resolved by reference to the Uniform Partnership Act. **The Uniform Partnership Act is an act adopted by most states that governs the formation, operation, and liquidation of partnerships.** However, most individuals who form a partnership prefer to specify in writing the terms of their business relationship in order to limit the potential for disagreements.

Partnership Agreement

A partnership agreement is an agreement among the partners that specifies the terms of the formation, operation, and liquidation of a partnership. The terms of the agreement supersede the Uniform Partnership Act, which is used only in areas not covered by the agreement. The agreement should define the nature of the business, the types and number of partners, the capital contributions required, the duties of each partner, the conditions for admission or withdrawal of a partner, the method of distributing earnings to each partner, and the allocation of assets in the liquidation of the partnership. Many of these topics are discussed in this chapter. Whatever the specific terms included in the partnership agreement, there are several characteristics common to all partnerships.

General and Limited Partners

Unless otherwise specified, all partners of the partnership are designated as general partners. **A general partner is a partner who has unlimited liability with respect to the debts of the partnership.** In most states partnerships are allowed to have limited partners. **A limited partner is a partner whose liability is limited to the assets contributed to the partnership by the specific partner.** The status of a limited partner is especially attractive to wealthy individuals who can contribute assets to the partnership without risking all of their personal assets. All partnerships must have at least one general partner.

Unlimited Liability

Unlimited liability is a characteristic of a partnership meaning that *each* general partner is liable for *all* the debts of the partnership. A creditor's claim on the partnership would first be satisfied by the assets of the partnership, but if these assets are insufficient to pay the claim, each partner's personal assets may be used to satisfy the claim. The only personal assets of a partner that are excluded are assets protected by bankruptcy laws. If one of the partners uses personal assets to pay the debts of the partnership, that partner has a right to claim a share of the payment from the other partners. This unlimited liability is a distinct contrast to the limited liability feature of a corporation discussed in the next chapter.

Income Tax

One of the primary reasons that an individual might prefer to invest in a partnership rather than a corporation is to avoid the double taxation imposed on a corporation. Double taxation refers to the taxing of the income earned by the corporation and the additional taxing of the dividends *paid* to the owners of the corporation. This is discussed more fully in Chapter 15. In contrast, federal income taxes are not assessed against the income of a partnership. Instead, the total earnings (including losses) of the partnership (*not* the withdrawals of the partners) are allocated to each partner, who then includes the allocated amount in his or her personal income for the computation of individual income tax for the year.

Voluntary Association

A partnership is a voluntary association that a person cannot be forced into against his or her will. Since a partner is responsible for the acts of fellow partners and has unlimited liability, it is reasonable that such responsibilities should be accepted only voluntarily. Thus a partner can leave a partnership at any time, unless the partnership agreement prevents it.

Mutual Agency

Each partner is an agent of the partnership. **An agent is a person who has the authority to act for another.** Thus a partner has the power to enter into and bind the partnership, and therefore all the partners, to any contract within the apparent scope of the business. For example, a partner in a grocery store can bind the partnership to contracts to purchase merchandise, hire employees, lease a building, purchase fixtures, and borrow money, because these activities are all within the normal scope of a grocery business. The partner, however, could not bind the partnership to contracts to buy an airplane or manage a musical group because these activities are outside the normal activities of a grocery business.

To provide protection for all the partners, they may agree to limit the type or size of contracts that an individual partner can enter into without prior consultation with the other partners. While such an agreement is binding on the partners and outsiders who know of its existence, outsiders who are unaware of it are not bound by its terms and can therefore assume that each partner acts as an unrestricted agent of the partnership.

Co-Ownership of Partnership Property

The property owned by the partnership is owned jointly by all the partners. Therefore if a partner contributes his or her own property to the partnership, it no longer belongs to that partner.

Limited Life

The life of every partnership is limited. The admission of a new partner, or the death, bankruptcy, incapacity, or withdrawal of an existing partner, automatically terminates the partnership. In addition, if the purpose for which the partnership was formed is completed, the partnership is terminated. If the partnership agreement is for a specified period of time, the partnership ends at the specified date. Finally, if there is no specified time limit and the purpose for which the business was formed continues indefinitely, the partnership may be terminated at any time by the withdrawal of a partner. The characteristic of a limited life is in contrast to the unlimited life of a corporation discussed in Chapter 14.

Reasons for the Formation of a Partnership

2. Explain the reasons for the formation of a partnership.

Partnerships are formed in two common situations. First, partnerships exist in many professional fields, such as accountancy, medicine, and law. In these professions the accountant, doctor, or lawyer has a personal responsibility to the client, and this responsibility is strengthened because the partnership has unlimited liability. Many states prohibit, or limit, the ability of professionals in many fields to form corporations, and therefore they must either be sole practitioners or form partnerships. Partnerships of this type may become very large. For example, some of the international accounting firms have over 1,000 partners as well as thousands of employees. The second common situation occurs when a sole proprietor is expanding his or her business and requires additional capital, or desires to attract another individual who has useful skills to participate in the business. A partnership rather than a corporation will be formed in these situations if the advantages of a partnership exceed the disadvantages.

The **advantages of a partnership** are that it is a very flexible form of organization, is easier and less expensive to form than a corporation, is less likely to be required to report to state and federal regulatory agencies, and avoids double taxation. The **disadvantages of a partnership** are the unlimited liability and the limited life which enables a partner at any time to terminate the partnership and withdraw his or her assets.

Accounting for Partnership Equity

Accounting for a partnership differs primarily from that of a sole proprietorship or a corporation in the way in which owners' equity is treated. Because ownership is divided among the partners and each partner engages in separate transactions with the partnership, it is necessary to have both a Capital account and a Withdrawals account for each partner.

Capital and Withdrawals Account for Each Partner

3. Account for
partnership equity.

A separate Capital account is maintained for each partner. **The Capital account is used to record the capital balance of each partner.** Each capital account is affected by the investments the partner makes, the partner's share of the net income of the partnership, and the partner's withdrawals.

A separate Withdrawals account is maintained for each partner. **The Withdrawals account is used to record the assets withdrawn by each partner during the accounting period.** All withdrawals of assets from the partnership made by each partner during the accounting period are recorded in that partner's withdrawals account. The balance of each partner's withdrawals account is closed to the partner's capital account at the end of each accounting period.

The effect of investments, net income, and withdrawals on the partner's capital and withdrawals accounts is shown here (using assumed amounts).

1. *Investments by the Partner Increase the Capital Account.* The initial investment and any subsequent investments by the partner are recorded as follows:

Cash (or other asset accounts)	40,000	
J. Jones, Capital		40,000

To record investment by J. Jones into partnership.

2. *The Partner's Share of the Net Income (or Loss) of the Partnership Increases (or Decreases) the Capital Account.* Each partner's share of the net income is recorded in the process of closing the Income Summary account as follows:

Income Summary	22,000	
J. Jones, Capital		11,000
F. Smith, Capital		11,000

To close the Income Summary account and distribute
the earnings.

If there is a loss, the entry will be the reverse of the entry shown. The share of the net income (or loss) is determined by the partnership agreement, and the computation may be complex as discussed later in this chapter.

3. *The Partner's Withdrawals During the Period Are Recorded in the Withdrawals Account.* The withdrawal of assets from the partnership by a partner is recorded as follows:

J. Jones, Withdrawals	18,000	
Cash (or other assets)		18,000

To record withdrawal of cash by J. Jones for personal use.

The balance of the Withdrawals account is closed to the Capital account at the end of the period as illustrated next. Of course, the partnership agreement should specify the conditions under which withdrawals can be made and the allowable amounts that may be withdrawn. If merchandise (or other assets) may be withdrawn, the agreement should specify whether the cost (in which case an asset account such as inventory is credited) or the market value (in which case the sales account is credited) should be used.

4. *Withdrawals by the Partner Decrease the Capital Account.* One of the closing entries of the partnership is used to close each partner's Withdrawals account and reduce the partner's Capital account as follows:

| J. Jones, Capital | 18,000 | |
| J. Jones, Withdrawals | | 18,000 |

To close the Withdrawals account.

The balance in the Capital account of each partner at the end of the period is the sum of the investments made by the partner plus the partner's share of net income (or loss) of the partnership, less the amount withdrawn by the partner.

Partnership Earnings

4. Compute the distribution of partnership earnings among partners.

Partnership earnings may be distributed in any proportions agreed to by the partners. In the absence of an agreement the Uniform Partnership Act requires that net income be distributed equally. Most partnerships have an earnings agreement that involves one or all of three basic factors: (1) allocation by a set ratio, (2) provision for interest on each partner's capital balance, and (3) recognition of salaries for each partner.

A particular ratio may be appropriate when the total contribution of each partner is approximately equal. Partners do not invest in a partnership to earn interest, but the distribution of earnings may include a component that represents interest on the capital invested by the partner in the partnership. Similarly, as a member of a partnership, a partner cannot enter into an employer-employee relationship with him- or herself. Therefore no salary can be paid in the legal sense of the term. The distribution of partnership earnings, however, may recognize a payment for services provided to the partnership during the period and be effectively the same as a salary. These allowances for salary and interest on capital may be necessary for a fair distribution of net income. For example, one partner may contribute much more capital than another, whereas another partner may contribute more valuable services to the operations of the partnership. Losses may be divided in a different ratio than profits, but in the absence of a specific agreement it is assumed that losses are divided in the same way as profits. Each of the three basic methods of distributing earnings is discussed in the following sections.

Earnings Distributed According to an Agreed Ratio

The simplest method of distributing earnings is according to an agreed ratio. Examples of the ratios that might be used by the partners are:

1. Equally among all partners
2. A ratio other than equal
3. The ratio of partners' beginning (or ending) capital balances
4. The ratio of partners' weighted average capital balances

To illustrate these alternatives, we will use the facts given in Exhibit 13-1 for the Lyme and Dorset partnership.

Earnings Distributed Equally.   In this situation each partner would receive an equal share of the net income of the partnership. Since there are two partners,

EXHIBIT 13-1   Information for Lyme and Dorset Partnership

		Investments		Withdrawals		Capital December 31, 1991 (before earnings distribution)
Partners	Capital January 1, 1991	Date	Amount	Date	Amount	
H. Lyme	$30,000	Apr. 12	$10,000	July 1	$15,000	$25,000
R. Dorset	50,000	May 31	20,000	Apr. 19	10,000	
				Aug. 30	12,000	48,000

Partnership net income for 1991: $40,000

each would receive half the total 1991 net income of $40,000, or $20,000 each. The journal entry to record the distribution of net income is as follows:

Income Summary	40,000	
H. Lyme, Capital		20,000
R. Dorset, Capital		20,000

To close the Income Summary account and distribute the earnings.

In each of the subsequent earnings distributions, the accounts that are debited and credited are the same and only the amounts distributed to each partner are different. Therefore the journal entry will not be repeated.

A Ratio Other Than Equal.   Suppose instead that the partners agree to distribute net income on the basis of three-fifths to Lyme and two-fifths to Dorset. In this situation, Lyme will be allocated $24,000 ($40,000 × $\frac{3}{5}$) and Dorset will be allocated $16,000 ($40,000 × $\frac{2}{5}$) of the $40,000 net income.

The Ratio of Partners' Beginning Capital Balances.   Suppose instead that the partners agree to distribute net income on the basis of each partner's capital balance at the beginning of the period. Lyme and Dorset have capital balances on January 1, 1991, of $30,000 and $50,000, respectively, or a total of $80,000. Therefore Lyme will be allocated $15,000 [$40,000 × ($30,000 ÷ $80,000)] and Dorset will be allocated $25,000 [$40,000 × ($50,000 ÷ $80,000)].

The Ratio of Partners' Weighted Average Capital Balances.   Suppose instead that the partners agree to distribute net income on the basis of each partner's weighted average capital balance during the period. In this example we will assume that the weighted average capital balance will be computed to the nearest whole month. Thus the investment by Lyme on April 12 will be treated as if it occurred on April 1. To apply this alternative it is first necessary to compute the weighted average capital balance of each partner. Withdrawals are deducted in determining capital balances at the time of the withdrawal even though they would not be closed to the capital account until the end of the period. Thus the

April 19 withdrawal of Dorset (treated as if it occurred on May 1) reduces his capital balance for the computation by $10,000 (from $50,000 to $40,000) even though this amount would be recorded in the Withdrawals account. The weighted average capital balances are computed as follows:

Lyme

Capital Balance		Months		
$30,000	×	3	=	$ 90,000
40,000	×	3	=	120,000
25,000	×	6	=	150,000
		12		$360,000

Weighted average capital balance = $30,000 ($360,000 ÷ 12)

Dorset

Capital Balance		Months		
$50,000	×	4	=	$200,000
40,000	×	1	=	40,000
60,000	×	3	=	180,000
48,000	×	4	=	192,000
		12		$612,000

Weighted average capital balance = $51,000 ($612,000 ÷ 12)

Based on these weighted average calculations, the average total capital is $81,000 ($30,000 + $51,000). The partnership net income of $40,000 will be allocated in the amounts of $14,815 [$40,000 × ($30,000 ÷ $81,000)] to Lyme and $25,185 [$40,000 × ($51,000 ÷ $81,000)] to Dorset.

Interest Provided on Capital

When partners have provided unequal amounts of capital to the partnership, they may agree to include a provision for interest on the capital balances of each partner in the earnings distribution calculation and specify the interest rate. It is important to note that the interest is a distribution of earnings and is *not* an expense of the partnership. If the partnership agreement does not specify an interest provision on the partners' capital balances, no interest is computed. After the provision for interest on capital, the remaining net income is divided among the partners in an agreed ratio. The distribution of the income is recorded by a single journal entry, as illustrated earlier.

The interest may be computed on the basis of the capital balances at the beginning of the period or on the average capital balance. To illustrate these two alternatives, assume that the Lyme and Dorset partnership earnings agreement stipulates an initial allocation of earnings at an interest rate of 10% and that the remaining net income is to be distributed equally after the interest provision has been deducted.

Interest Provided on Beginning Capital Balances.   When the interest is provided on the beginning capital balances, the distribution of the net income of $40,000 is computed as follows:

	Lyme	Dorset	Total
Interest			
Lyme (10% × $30,000)	$ 3,000		
Dorset (10% × $50,000)		$ 5,000	
Total			$ 8,000
Balance allocated equally			
Lyme ($32,000^a × $\frac{1}{2}$)	16,000		
Dorset ($32,000 × $\frac{1}{2}$)		16,000	
Total			32,000
Income Distribution	$19,000	$21,000	$40,000

^{a}$40,000 net income − $8,000 interest provision.

Interest Provided on Average Capital Balances.   It is usually more equitable to compute interest on the basis of the average capital balances during the period because this is a better measure of the investment of each partner. In this case the average capital balances of $30,000 and $51,000 for Lyme and Dorset, respectively, are computed by the weighted average calculation illustrated earlier. The distribution of net income of $40,000 is computed as follows:

	Lyme	Dorset	Total
Interest			
Lyme (10% × $30,000)	$ 3,000		
Dorset (10% × $51,000)		$ 5,100	
Total			$ 8,100
Balance allocated equally			
Lyme ($31,900^a × $\frac{1}{2}$)	15,950		
Dorset ($31,900 × $\frac{1}{2}$)		15,950	
Total			31,900
Income Distribution	$18,950	$21,050	$40,000

^{a}$40,000 net income − $8,100 interest provision.

Recognition of Salaries for Partners

Partners may agree to allocate a portion of earnings as salaries to provide rewards for different levels of performance. Such allocations are *not* expenses of the partnership but are distributions of earnings. If the partnership agreement does not specify that salaries may be allocated to partners, no salary distribution is then made.

To illustrate, suppose that Lyme and Dorset are allocated salaries of $18,000 and $15,000, respectively. Assuming that the remaining balance of the $40,000 net income is distributed equally, the total distribution is computed as follows:

	Lyme	Dorset	Total
Salaries	$18,000	$15,000	$33,000
Balance allocated equally			
Lyme ($7,000^a × $\frac{1}{2}$)	3,500		
Dorset ($7,000 × $\frac{1}{2}$)		3,500	
Total			7,000
Income Distribution	$21,500	$18,500	$40,000

^{a}$40,000 net income – $33,000 salaries provision.

Salaries and Interest

The partners may agree to make provisions for the allocation of both salaries and interest in the earnings distribution, with the balance of the net income to be distributed in a set ratio. To illustrate, suppose that Lyme and Dorset agreed to distribute earnings based upon 8% interest on the average capital balances during the period, salaries of $12,000 and $10,000, respectively, with the remainder being distributed 40% to Lyme and 60% to Dorset. The distribution of the $40,000 net income is as follows:

	Lyme	Dorset	Total
Salaries	$12,000	$10,000	$22,000
Interest			
Lyme (8% × $30,000)	2,400		
Dorset (8% × $51,000)		4,080	
Total			6,480
Balance allocated			
Lyme ($11,520^a × 0.40)	4,608		
Dorset ($11,520 × 0.60)		6,912	
Total			11,520
Income Distribution	$19,008	$20,992	$40,000

^{a}$40,000 net income – $22,000 salaries provision – $6,480 interest provision.

It is important to recognize that when salaries and interest are included in the distribution of earnings, they are typically allocated even if they exceed the net income of the partnership. The resulting "loss" is then distributed in the agreed ratio. For example, assume the same facts as in the preceding example, except that the partnership net income is only $20,000. After allocation of the salaries and interest, which total $28,480 ($22,000 + $6,480), there is a "loss" of $8,480 ($20,000 – $28,480), which is divided in the agreed ratio as follows:

Lyme ($8,480 × 0.40) .... $3,392 loss allocation
Dorset ($8,480 × 0.60) .... $5,088 loss allocation

Therefore the total distributions to each partner are:

	Lyme	Dorset	Total
Salaries	$12,000	$10,000	$22,000
Interest	2,400	4,080	6,480
Balance	(3,392)	(5,088)	(8,480)
Income Distribution	$11,008	$ 8,992	$20,000

It should be noted that even though the "loss" of $8,480 was distributed to the partners in accordance with the earnings agreement, the total net income of $20,000 is closed to the partners' capital accounts in the usual fashion and no "loss" is shown in the partnership income statement. The journal entry to record the distribution is:

Income Summary	20,000	
H. Lyme, Capital		11,008
R. Dorset, Capital		8,992

To close the Income Summary account and distribute the earnings.

Salaries and interest are typically allocated even when the partnership has a net loss. To illustrate this more extreme situation, assume the same facts as in the preceding example except that the partnership has incurred a net *loss* of $10,000. After allocation of salaries and interest, which again total $28,480, there is a total "loss" of $38,480. This "loss" is divided in the agreed ratio as shown here:

Lyme ($38,480 × 0.40)	$15,392 loss allocation
Dorset ($38,480 × 0.60)	$23,088 loss allocation

Therefore the total distributions to each partner are:

	Lyme	Dorset	Total
Salaries	$12,000	$10,000	$ 22,000
Interest	2,400	4,080	6,480
Balance	(15,392)	(23,088)	(38,480)
Income Distribution	$ (992)	$ (9,008)	$(10,000)

Since a net loss has been incurred, the journal entry to record the distribution is as follows:

H. Lyme, Capital	992	
R. Dorset, Capital	9,008	
Income Summary		10,000

To close the Income Summary account and distribute the net loss.

It should be emphasized that the alternative distributions of net income discussed here are distributions that are commonly used in practice, but partners may agree to a distribution in any way they wish.

Financial Statements of a Partnership

The financial statements of a partnership are very similar to the financial statements of a sole proprietorship engaged in the same type of business. The differences between these statements that do occur are discussed for each financial statement in the following sections.

Income Statement

5. Prepare the financial statements of a partnership.

Remember that salaries allocated to partners and interest distributed on capital balances in accordance with the partnership earnings agreement are *not* considered to be expenses, and therefore they are not included in the computation of net income in the income statement. It is common to add a section to the bottom of the income statement that shows the allocation of the income to the partners. To illustrate, refer to the prior example of the Lyme and Dorset partnership in which it earned $20,000. This additional section of the income statement is illustrated in Exhibit 13-2.

EXHIBIT 13-2
Partial Income
Statement

LYME AND DORSET
Partial Income Statement
For Year Ended December 31, 1991

Revenues			$xx,xxx
Expenses			xx,xxx
Net Income			$20,000

Allocation of net income to the partners

	Lyme	Dorset	Total
Salary allowances	$12,000	$10,000	$22,000
Interest at 8% on average capital balances	2,400	4,080	6,480
Distribution of remainder (40%; 60%)	(3,392)	(5,088)	(8,480)
Income Distribution	$11,008	$ 8,992	$20,000

Balance Sheet

The only difference between the balance sheet of a partnership and the balance sheet of a sole proprietorship is that the owners' equity section of a partnership balance sheet includes a separate capital account for each partner. If the number of partners is so large that including each partner's capital account in the balance sheet becomes unwieldy, a single partnership capital balance could be presented. In this case the amount of each partner's capital account would be listed on a separate schedule.

Statement of Changes in Partners' Equity

At the end of each accounting period a statement of the changes in partners' equity should be prepared. **The statement of changes in partners' equity is a supplementary statement that lists the investments, withdrawals, and earnings distribution for each partner during the accounting period.** It is similar to the statement of changes in owner's equity for a sole proprietorship illustrated in Chapter 5. The statement for Lyme and Dorset is shown in Exhibit 13-3, using the information listed in Exhibits 13-1 and 13-2. The statement shows greater detail than could be included conveniently in the balance sheet. Only the partners' ending capital balances are shown in the balance sheet.

EXHIBIT 13-3
Statement of Changes
in Partners' Equity

LYME AND DORSET Statement of Changes in Partners' Equity For Year Ended December 31, 1991			
	Lyme	*Dorset*	*Total*
Balances, January 1, 1991	$30,000	$50,000	$80,000
Add: Additional investments	10,000	20,000	30,000
Less: Withdrawals	(15,000)	(22,000)	(37,000)
Capital balances before earnings distribution	$25,000	$48,000	$73,000
Earnings distribution:			
Salary allowances	12,000	10,000	22,000
Interest allocation	2,400	4,080	6,480
Distribution of remainder	(3,392)	(5,088)	(8,480)
Balances, December 31, 1991	$36,008	$56,992	$93,000

The distribution of earnings and withdrawals by partners are typical changes in the partners' equity. Other changes may be caused by the admission of a new partner, the withdrawal of an existing partner, or the liquidation of the partnership. Each of these factors is discussed in the following sections.

Admission of a New Partner

As discussed earlier an existing partnership is ended whenever there is a change in the partners, either by the admission of a new partner or the withdrawal of an existing partner. From an accounting perspective, however, the business entity is assumed to continue, with the only change being reflected in the capital balances of the partners affected by the change of ownership. In this section we discuss the admission of a new partner; the withdrawal of a partner is discussed in the next section. Liquidation of a partnership is discussed in the final section of the chapter.

Four alternatives may arise when a new partner is admitted to a partnership:

6. Account for the admission of a new partner.

1. The new partner purchases an interest from an existing partner.

2. The new partner invests assets in the partnership and is assigned a capital balance equal to the assets contributed.

3. The new partner invests assets in the partnership and is assigned a capital balance less than the assets contributed. Therefore a "bonus" is assigned to the continuing partners.

4. The new partner invests assets in the partnership and is assigned a capital balance greater than the assets contributed. Therefore a "bonus" is assigned to the new partner.

New Partner Purchases Interest from Existing Partner

When a new partner purchases an interest from an existing partner, the transaction is directly between the two partners, usually with the agreement of all the other partners. **The new partner contributes no assets to the partnership, and therefore the assets and the liabilities of the partnership remain unchanged.** The only payment by the new partner is to the existing partner. In accordance with the business entity concept, the only effect on the accounts of the partnership is the assignment of a part or all of the balance in the capital account from the name of the selling partner to the name of the new partner.

For example, suppose that Hardy and Laurel are partners with capital balances of $50,000 and $60,000, respectively. If Chaplin purchases a $20,000 interest in the partnership from Laurel, the journal entry on the partnership's books is as follows:

Laurel, Capital	20,000	
Chaplin, Capital		20,000

To record the transfer of a $20,000 interest in the partnership from Laurel to Chaplin.

Note that no mention has been made of the price paid by Chaplin to Laurel. It could be less than, equal to, or more than $20,000. In any case, the price paid has no effect on the partnership because it is simply a transfer of personal assets between two individuals. In addition to the preceding journal entry, some of the partnership agreement (e.g., the earnings distribution agreement) must be changed to reflect the admission of the new partner.

Existing partners cannot prevent the sale of a partnership interest by one partner to another individual. If the existing partners do not accept the new partner, one of two alternatives may apply. Under common law the partnership must be liquidated, and the new partner receives only the liquidation rights of the selling partner. In many states the Uniform Partnership Act has replaced common law, and the Act requires that the new partner share in the profits and losses and liquidation of the partnership, but the new partner cannot participate in management.

New Partner Assigned Capital Balance Equal to Assets Contributed

A partner may be admitted to a partnership by contributing assets to the partnership. In this situation **the assets and the total partnership equity increase by the same amount.** In the simplest case the new partner is assigned a capital balance equal to the assets contributed to the partnership. In the following examples it is assumed that the new partner contributes cash to the partnership, but any asset could be contributed, such as inventory or a building.

EXHIBIT 13-4
Balance Sheet

HARDY AND LAUREL			
Balance Sheet			
January 1, 1991			
Assets		*Liabilities and Owners' Equity*	
Cash.............................	$ 25,000	Liabilities	$ 25,000
Other assets....................	110,000	Hardy, capital	50,000
		Laurel, capital	60,000
		Total Liabilities and	
Total Assets..................	$135,000	Owners' Equity	$135,000

To illustrate, assume that the Hardy and Laurel partnership has the condensed balance sheet shown in Exhibit 13-4. If Hardy and Laurel agree to admit Chaplin to a 20% interest in the partnership upon payment of a certain amount of cash, and Chaplin is to be assigned a capital balance equal to the cash amount, how much must Chaplin invest? The existing capital of the partnership is $110,000 ($50,000 + $60,000), but Chaplin is purchasing a 20% interest in the new partnership, *after* the contribution of Chaplin's assets to the partnership. Since Chaplin's share is to be 20%, the existing partners will own 80% of the new partnership. Their total capital balances of $110,000 therefore represent an 80% share of the new partnership, and the total capital of the new partnership is $137,500 ($110,000 ÷ 0.80). Thus Chaplin must contribute $27,500, which increases the partnership assets by that amount and increases the partnership capital by $27,500 to $137,500 ($110,000 + $27,500). This calculation is summarized as follows:

Capital of existing partners	$110,000
Investment of new partner	27,500
Total Capital of New Partnership	$137,500
New Partner's Capital (20% × $137,500)	$ 27,500

The journal entry that is used by the partnership to record the admission of Chaplin is:

Cash	27,500	
Chaplin, Capital		27,500

To record admission of Chaplin to the partnership.

After the admission, the condensed balance sheet of the partnership is as shown in Exhibit 13-5.

EXHIBIT 13-5
Balance Sheet After
Admission of New
Partner

HARDY, LAUREL, AND CHAPLIN			
Balance Sheet			
January 1, 1991			
Assets		*Liabilities and Owners' Equity*	
Cash	$ 52,500	Liabilities	$ 25,000
Other assets	110,000	Hardy, capital	50,000
		Laurel, capital	60,000
		Chaplin, capital	27,500
		Total Liabilities and	
Total Assets	$162,500	Owners' Equity	$162,500

While Chaplin has a 20% ownership in the partnership, he does not have a right to 20% of the earnings. The division of net income is subject to a separate earnings agreement among the partners and may be completely unrelated to the capital balances. If the partnership agreement does not specify the distribution of earnings, it is assumed the partners intend to share profits and losses equally.

Bonus to Existing Partners

If the capital balance assigned to the new partner is not equal to the assets contributed by that partner, a bonus exists. **A bonus is the difference between the assets contributed by a new partner and the capital balance assigned to the new partner.** The bonus is assigned either to the existing partners or to the new partner as follows:

- Bonus is assigned to the *existing* partners if the capital balance assigned to the new partner is *less* than the assets contributed by the new partner.
- Bonus is assigned to the *new* partner if the capital balance assigned to the new partner is *greater* than the assets contributed by the new partner.

To illustrate a bonus assigned to the existing partners, assume that Chaplin invests $30,000 for a 20% share of the partnership and that Hardy and Laurel share net income on the basis of 60% and 40%, respectively. Chaplin's investment raises the capital of the partnership to $140,000 ($110,000 + $30,000), but Chaplin's capital is only $28,000 ($140,000 × 0.20). The difference between the investment and the capital balance is $2,000 ($30,000 investment − $28,000 Chaplin's capital) and is the bonus assigned to the existing partners. The bonus is divided according to the earnings distribution ratio, and therefore Hardy is assigned $1,200 ($2,000 × 0.60) and Laurel is assigned $800 ($2,000 × 0.40). The journal entry used by the partnership to record the admission of Chaplin is:

Cash	30,000	
Chaplin, Capital		28,000
Hardy, Capital		1,200
Laurel, Capital		800

To record admission of Chaplin to the partnership.

It is fairly common for a bonus to be assigned to the existing partners because the new partner has the advantage of entering an ongoing partnership with an established business.

Bonus to New Partner

Sometimes a new partner brings unusual benefits to the partnership, perhaps in the form of special skills or business contacts. In such situations **a bonus may be assigned to the new partner.** For example, assume that Chaplin invests $30,000 for a 30% share of the partnership. The capital assignment to Chaplin is calculated as follows:

Capital of existing partners	$110,000
Investment of new partner	30,000
Total Capital of New Partnership	$140,000
New Partner's Capital ($140,000 × 0.30)	$ 42,000

Under these terms Chaplin is assigned a bonus of $12,000 ($42,000 Chaplin's capital – $30,000 investment). This bonus is subtracted from (debited to) the capital balances of the existing partners in their earnings distribution ratios. Hardy's share is $7,200 ($12,000 × 0.60) and Laurel's share is $4,800 ($12,000 × 0.40). The journal entry used by the partnership to record the admission of Chaplin is:

Cash	30,000	
Hardy, Capital	7,200	
Laurel, Capital	4,800	
Chaplin, Capital		42,000

To record admission of Chaplin to the partnership.

Again, the distribution of net income in the earnings agreement is a separate decision of the partners.

Withdrawal of a Partner

The partnership agreement should specify the procedures to be followed in the event of the withdrawal of a partner from the partnership. Usually the agreement calls for an audit and a revaluation of the partnership's assets to their market value. Instead of this revaluation process, the withdrawing partner may be allowed to withdraw assets less than, or greater than, the book value of his or her capital. Each of these three alternatives is discussed in the following sections:

Assets Revalued and Partner Receives the Book Value of Equity

7. Account for the withdrawal of a partner.

When the assets of the partnership are revalued, **the difference between the market value and the book value is allocated to the partners' capital accounts in their earnings distribution ratios.** The partners' capital accounts then reflect the current value of their equity, and **the withdrawing partner receives assets equal to the value in his or her capital account.**

To illustrate this procedure, assume that Palmer is retiring from the partnership of Lake, Palmer, and Emerson on January 9, 1991. The partners have shared earnings in the ratio of 50%, 25%, and 25%, respectively. The balance sheet of the partnership before the audit and revaluation is shown in Exhibit 13-6.

EXHIBIT 13-6
Balance Sheet

LAKE, PALMER, AND EMERSON
Balance Sheet
January 9, 1991

Assets		Liabilities and Owners' Equity	
Cash	$ 60,000	Liabilities	$ 10,000
Accounts receivable	20,000		
Inventory	35,000		
Property and equipment	90,000	Lake, capital	80,000
Less: Accumulated		Palmer, capital	50,000
depreciation	(25,000)	Emerson, capital	40,000
		Total Liabilities and	
Total Assets	$180,000	Owners' Equity	$180,000

The audit and revaluation indicate that an allowance for uncollectible accounts of $2,000 should be established and that the fair market value of the property and equipment is $10,000 greater than the book value. The net increase in the value of the assets of $8,000 is divided among the partners in their earnings sharing ratio. It is fair to allocate the net increase in the earnings sharing ratio because the impact of the revaluation will eventually appear in the income statement through changes in the expenses recorded in future periods. The journal entry to record these revaluations is as follows:

Property and Equipment	10,000	
Allowance for Uncollectible Accounts		2,000
Lake, Capital		4,000
Palmer, Capital		2,000
Emerson, Capital		2,000

To record revaluation of the assets.

After the revaluation the balance sheet is as shown in Exhibit 13-7.

EXHIBIT 13-7
Balance Sheet
After Revaluation

LAKE, PALMER, AND EMERSON
Balance Sheet
January 9, 1991

Assets		*Liabilities and Owners' Equity*	
Cash	$ 60,000	Liabilities	$ 10,000
Accounts receivable	20,000		
Less: Allowance for			
uncollectible accounts ...	(2,000)		
Inventory	35,000		
Property and equipment	100,000	Lake, capital	84,000
Less: Accumulated		Palmer, capital	52,000
depreciation	(25,000)	Emerson, capital	42,000
		Total Liabilities and	
Total Assets	$188,000	Owners' Equity	$188,000

Palmer withdraws from the partnership and receives cash equal to his equity of $52,000, which is recorded as follows:

Palmer, Capital	52,000	
Cash		52,000

To record withdrawal of Palmer from the partnership.

The withdrawing partner does not have to take cash as settlement but may take any combination of assets or receive a promissory note from the partnership.

Partner Receives Assets Less Than the Book Value of Equity

The partnership agreement may specify that a withdrawing partner receive less than the book value of his or her equity. The assets may, or may not, be revalued first in the same way as shown in the preceding example. Receipt of less than the book value may have been agreed on, for example, to discourage withdrawals. Alternatively, the partners may believe the assets to be overvalued or the partner may be very anxious to withdraw from the partnership. When withdrawing assets that are less than his or her equity, the partner is leaving part of his or her equity in the partnership. The amount left is distributed among the remaining partners in their earnings distribution ratio.

For example, suppose instead that Palmer withdraws from the partnership *without* a revaluation of the assets and receives assets of $41,000. This leaves $9,000 ($50,000 capital balance – $41,000) to be allocated to the remaining partners. Since the original earnings distribution ratio was 50%, 25%, 25% or 2 : 1 : 1, the remaining partners will distribute net income on a 2 : 1 ratio or $66\frac{2}{3}\%$ to $33\frac{1}{3}\%$. Thus Lake would be allocated $6,000 ($9,000 × $66\frac{2}{3}\%$) and Emerson $3,000 ($9,000 × $33\frac{1}{3}\%$). The journal entry to record the withdrawal of Palmer is:

Palmer, Capital	50,000	
Cash		41,000
Lake, Capital		6,000
Emerson, Capital		3,000

To record withdrawal of Palmer from the partnership.

After the withdrawal of Palmer, Lake and Emerson could change the earnings distribution agreement or any other aspect of the partnership agreement.

Partner Receives Assets Greater Than the Book Value of Equity

The partnership agreement may specify that a withdrawing partner receive more than the book value of his or her equity. This may be done to avoid the expense of revaluing the assets while attempting to approximate the market value of the partner's equity. Alternatively, the remaining partners may be so anxious for the partner to withdraw that they are willing to pay more than the book value of his or her equity. The effect of withdrawing assets greater than the book value of the equity is that the withdrawing partner is also withdrawing a portion of the equity of the other partners.

For example, suppose that Palmer withdraws from the partnership *without* a revaluation of the assets and receives assets of $62,000. The excess of $12,000 ($62,000 – $50,000 capital balance) is removed from the capital accounts of the remaining partners in their earnings distribution ratios. Therefore $8,000 ($12,000 × $66\frac{2}{3}\%$) will be deducted from Lake's capital account and $4,000 ($12,000 × $33\frac{1}{3}\%$) from Emerson's capital account. The journal entry to record the withdrawal of Palmer is:

Palmer, Capital	50,000	
Lake, Capital	8,000	
Emerson, Capital	4,000	
Cash		62,000

To record withdrawal of Palmer from the partnership.

Liquidation of a Partnership

Liquidation is the dissolution of a partnership by selling the assets, paying the liabilities, and closing each partner's capital account. The liquidation of a partnership may occur for one of the following five reasons:

8. Account for the liquidation of a partnership.

1. The purpose for which the partnership was formed is accomplished.
2. The time for which the partnership was formed has expired.
3. An agreement among the partners has been made to terminate the partnership.
4. A partner has declared bankruptcy.
5. A partner has died or withdrawn from the partnership.

Regardless of the reason for liquidation, the following sequence of events occurs:

1. The noncash assets are sold or converted into cash and the gain or loss is distributed among the partners.
2. The liabilities of the partnership are paid.
3. The remaining cash (or assets not sold) is distributed to the partners and the partnership accounts are closed.

A liquidation may take place over a long period of time, in which case several partial distributions of cash may be made. Because the procedures to be followed are beyond the scope of this book, it will be assumed in the following examples that a single distribution of cash is made after all the assets have been converted into cash.

When a liquidation occurs the assets may be sold at a gain or a loss, there may or may not be sufficient cash to pay the liabilities, or a partner may have a negative capital balance. Each of these three situations is discussed in the following sections, using the balance sheet of the Lowe and Lerner partnership in Exhibit 13-8. Lowe and Lerner are allocated 60% and 40% of the partnership's earnings, respectively.

EXHIBIT 13-8
Balance Sheet

LOWE AND LERNER Balance Sheet July 15, 1991			
Assets		*Liabilities and Owners' Equity*	
Cash	$10,000	Accounts payable	$20,000
Accounts receivable	8,000		
Inventory	25,000		
Property and equipment	70,000		
Less: Accumulated		Lowe, capital	38,000
depreciation	(35,000)	Lerner, capital	20,000
		Total Liabilities and	
Total Assets	$78,000	Owners' Equity	$78,000

Assets Sold at a Gain

If the assets are sold at a gain, the gain is allocated to the partners in their earnings distribution ratio. The liabilities are paid off and the remaining cash is distributed to the partners in accordance with their capital balances and *not* in the earnings distribution ratio.

To illustrate, assume that the Lowe and Lerner partnership sold the assets *other than cash* for $80,000, resulting in a gain of $12,000 ($80,000 − $68,000). The gain allocated to Lowe is $7,200 ($12,000 × 0.60) and to Lerner is $4,800 ($12,000 ×

0.40). Note that it is the gain, and *not* the proceeds, from the sale of the assets that is allocated to the partners. The journal entry to record the sale of the assets and the distribution of the gain is as follows:

Cash	80,000	
Accumulated Depreciation	35,000	
Accounts Receivable		8,000
Inventory		25,000
Property and Equipment		70,000
Lowe, Capital		7,200
Lerner, Capital		4,800

To record sale of assets.

Normally assets would be sold individually and would result in many gains and losses. For simplicity the preceding journal entry assumes a single sale and therefore a single gain or loss. The journal entry to record the payment of the liabilities is:

Accounts Payable	20,000	
Cash		20,000

To record payment of liabilities.

At this point the partnership has cash of $70,000 ($10,000 + $80,000 − $20,000) and the capital balances of Lowe and Lerner are $45,200 ($38,000 + $7,200) and $24,800 ($20,000 + $4,800), respectively. The cash is distributed to the partners according to their capital balances as follows:

Lowe, Capital	45,200	
Lerner, Capital	24,800	
Cash		70,000

To record distribution of cash to partners.

A schedule of the steps contained in the liquidation is illustrated in Exhibit 13-9. The schedule is based on the journal entries but with the changes in the account

EXHIBIT 13-9   Liquidation Schedule

LOWE AND LERNER PARTNERSHIP
Liquidation Schedule

	Cash	Accounts Receivable	Inventory	Property and Equipment	Accumulated Depreciation	Accounts Payable	Lowe, Capital	Lerner, Capital
Balances, July 15, 1991	$ 10,000	$ 8,000	$ 25,000	$ 70,000	$(35,000)	$(20,000)	$(38,000)	$(20,000)
Sale of assets	80,000	(8,000)	(25,000)	(70,000)	35,000	$ 0	(7,200)	(4,800)
	$ 90,000	$ 0	$ 0	$ 0	$ 0	$(20,000)	$(45,200)	$(24,800)
Payment of liabilities	(20,000)					20,000		
	$ 70,000					$ 0		
Distribution to partners	(70,000)						45,200	24,800
	$ 0						$ 0	$ 0

balances listed in the respective columns. Credit amounts are shown in parentheses. It should be noted that the amounts in each line have a net total of zero because at all times the debit balances equal the credit balances.

Assets Sold at a Loss

When assets are sold at a loss the same procedures are followed except that the loss on the sale (as opposed to the gain) is allocated among the partners in their earnings distribution ratio. For example, suppose that the assets *other than cash* are sold for $50,000, resulting in a loss of $18,000 ($68,000 − $50,000). The loss allocated to Lowe is $10,800 ($18,000 × 0.60) and to Lerner is $7,200 ($18,000 × 0.40). The journal entries to record the liquidation are as follows:

Cash	50,000	
Accumulated Depreciation	35,000	
Lowe, Capital	10,800	
Lerner, Capital	7,200	
Accounts Receivable		8,000
Inventory		25,000
Property and Equipment		70,000

To record sale of assets.

Accounts Payable	20,000	
Cash		20,000

To record payment of liabilities.

Lowe, Capital ($38,000 − $10,800)	27,200	
Lerner, Capital ($20,000 − $7,200)	12,800	
Cash		40,000

To record distribution of cash to the partners.

Partner Has Negative Capital Balance

In some situations the loss on the sale of assets is so large that a partner's capital balance is negative after the share of the loss has been allocated to it. After payment of the liabilities the cash available for distribution to the partners with positive (credit) capital balances will be insufficient until the partner with the negative (debit) capital balance has contributed cash to the partnership equal to the balance. If the partner with the negative balance is unable to pay the amount owed because of personal bankruptcy, the remaining partners must allocate this loss among themselves in their profit and loss sharing ratios.

For example, suppose that the Lowe and Lerner partnership could sell their assets other than cash for only $8,000, resulting in a loss of $60,000 ($68,000 − $8,000). The loss allocated to Lowe is $36,000 ($60,000 × 0.60) and to Lerner is $24,000 ($60,000 × 0.40). The journal entry to record the sale of the assets is as follows:

Cash	8,000	
Accumulated Depreciation	35,000	
Lowe, Capital	36,000	
Lerner, Capital	24,000	
Accounts Receivable		8,000
Inventory		25,000
Property and Equipment		70,000

To record sale of assets.

At this point Lerner's capital account has a negative (debit) balance of $4,000 ($20,000 – $24,000). Lerner must therefore contribute cash to the partnership to remove the negative balance. If this occurs the journal entry to record the additional contribution is as follows:

Cash	4,000	
Lerner, Capital		4,000
To record contribution by Lerner.		

After the additional contribution the partnership would have the following account balances:

Cash $22,000 ($10,000 + $8,000 + $4,000)
Accounts payable $20,000
Lowe, capital $2,000 ($38,000 – $36,000)
Lerner, capital $0 ($20,000 – $24,000 + $4,000)

The cash is used to pay the liabilities and Lowe. The journal entry to record the payment is as follows:

Accounts Payable	20,000	
Lowe, Capital	2,000	
Cash		22,000
To record payment of liabilities and cash distribution to Lowe.		

If Lerner is unable to pay the $4,000 to the partnership to cover the negative capital balance, the debit balance in Lerner's capital account is allocated to the remaining partners, Lowe in this case. The journal entry to record the allocation is:

Lowe, Capital	4,000	
Lerner, Capital		4,000
To assign Lerner's deficit to Lowe.		

Lowe's capital account now has a negative balance of $2,000 ($38,000 – $40,000), which Lowe must remove by paying $2,000 to the partnership:

Cash	2,000	
Lowe, Capital		2,000
To record contribution by Lowe.		

Lowe's capital account now has a zero balance and the remaining cash is used to pay off the liabilities:

Accounts Payable	20,000	
Cash		20,000
To record payment of liabilities.		

Now all the accounts of the partnership have zero balances.

Insufficient Cash to Pay the Liabilities

The previous two examples have illustrated the concept of unlimited liability. **The partners had to contribute assets to the partnership to cover negative bal-**

ances in their capital accounts and to cover the negative balances in the capital accounts of partners who were personally insolvent. The effect is that the partner is paying cash from his or her personal resources to cover his or her "debts" to the partnership, either for payment to other partners or to pay the liabilities.

A more extreme situation might arise in which none of the partners is able to contribute sufficient assets to the partnership so that the liabilities can be paid. In a situation such as this any payments by the partnership to the liability holders would be decided under the provision of the bankruptcy laws applied to the partners.

Chapter Summary

Review of Learning Objectives

1. **Describe the characteristics of a partnership.**
   A partnership is an association of two or more persons to carry on as co-owners a business for profit. A partnership should have a partnership agreement, may have limited partners as well as at least one general partner, has unlimited liability, is not subject to income tax, is a voluntary association, has mutual agency, has co-ownership of partnership property, and has a limited life.

2. **Explain the reasons for the formation of a partnership.**
   Partnerships exist in many professional fields and may also be created when a sole proprietor wants to expand his or her business. The advantages of a partnership are flexibility, ease of formation, fewer reporting requirements, and avoidance of double taxation. The disadvantages are unlimited liability and the limited life.

3. **Account for partnership equity.**
   Partnership equity includes a capital account for each partner, which is increased by the partner's investments and share of net income (based on the earnings distribution agreement) and decreased by withdrawals. The withdrawals account is used to record the withdrawals during the period and is closed to the capital account.

4. **Compute the distribution of partnership earnings among partners.**
   Partnerships usually have an agreement to distribute earnings based on one or all of three factors: (a) allocation by a set ratio, (b) provision for interest on each partner's capital balance, and (c) recognition of salaries for each partner.

5. **Prepare the financial statements of a partnership.**
   The financial statements of a partnership differ from those of a sole proprietorship because (a) the allocation of net income to partners should be included at the bottom of the income statement, (b) the balance sheet includes a separate capital account for each partner, and (c) a statement of changes in partners' equity is prepared.

6. **Account for the admission of a new partner.**
   Four alternatives arise when a new partner is admitted to a partnership: (a) the new partner purchases an interest from an existing partner, (b) the new partner invests assets in the partnership and is assigned a capital balance equal to the assets contributed, (c) the new partner invests in the partnership and is assigned a capital balance less than the assets contributed (a bonus is assigned to the continuing partners), or (d) the new partner invests assets in the partnership and is assigned a capital balance greater than the assets contributed (a bonus is assigned to the new partner).

7. **Account for the withdrawal of a partner.**
   When a partner withdraws, the assets should be revalued and the partner may receive (a) the book value of the equity, (b) less than the book value of the equity (the difference is distributed among the capital accounts of the remaining partners), or (c) more than the book value of the equity (the difference is deducted from the capital accounts of the remaining partners).

8. **Account for the liquidation of a partnership.**
   When a partnership is liquidated, (a) the noncash assets are sold and the gain or loss is distributed among the partners, (b) the liabilities of the partnership are paid, and (c) the remaining cash is distributed to the partners. A partner with a negative capital balance should contribute cash equal to the balance. If the partner is unable to pay, the remaining partners allocate the loss among themselves.

Review Problem

On December 31, 1991, the balance sheet of the partnership of Spice and Sugar, who share earnings in a 2 to 1 ratio, was as follows:

SPICE AND SUGAR
Balance Sheet
December 31, 1991

Assets		Liabilities and Owners' Equity	
Cash	$ 50,000	Accounts payable	$ 25,000
Accounts receivable	30,000		
Property and equipment	60,000		
Less: Accumulated		Spice, capital	60,000
depreciation	(25,000)	Sugar, capital	30,000
		Total Liabilities and	
Total Assets	$115,000	Owners' Equity	$115,000

On January 1, 1992, Salt was admitted to the partnership. She paid $15,000 for a 10% share of the partnership. On June 30 the three partners each withdrew $10,000. During 1992 the partnership had sales of $90,000 on account, paid wages to employees of $22,000, and collected accounts receivable of $80,000. Depreciation expense for

1992 was $8,000. Assume accounts payable remained unchanged. The partners distribute earnings as follows:

> Salaries: Spice, $10,000; Sugar, $8,000; Salt, $5,000
> Interest: 10% of capital balances on January 1 (after admission of Salt)
> Balance: In the new earnings distribution ratio of 6 : 3 : 1

On January 1, 1993, the partnership was liquidated. The assets other than cash were sold for $47,000, the accounts payable were paid, and the remaining cash was distributed to the partners.

REQUIRED

1. Prepare journal entries to record the preceding events in 1992.
2. Prepare a balance sheet for the partnership at December 31, 1992.
3. Prepare journal entries to record the liquidation.

Solution to Review Problem

REQUIREMENT 1

1992
Jan. 1	Cash		15,000	
	Salt, Capital			10,500[a]
	Spice, Capital ($\frac{2}{3} \times$ $4,500)			3,000
	Sugar, Capital ($\frac{1}{3} \times$ $4,500)			1,500

To record admission of Salt to partnership.

[a]Capital of existing partners	$ 90,000
Investment of new partner	15,000
Total Capital of New Partnership	$105,000
New Partner's Capital (10% × $105,000)	$ 10,500

June 30	Spice, Withdrawals		10,000	
	Sugar, Withdrawals		10,000	
	Salt, Withdrawals		10,000	
	Cash			30,000

To record withdrawals by partners.

During 1992	Accounts Receivable		90,000	
	Sales			90,000

To record sales for the year.

During 1992	Wages Expense		22,000	
	Cash			22,000

To record wages paid for the year.

During 1992	Cash		80,000	
	Accounts Receivable			80,000

To record cash collections for the year.

Dec. 31   Depreciation Expense   8,000
               Accumulated Depreciation   8,000

           To record depreciation for the year.

Dec. 31   Sales 90,000
               Income Summary   90,000

           To close the sales account.

Dec. 31   Income Summary 30,000
               Wages Expense   22,000
               Depreciation Expense   8,000

           To close the expense accounts.

Dec. 31   Income Summary[a] 60,000
               Spice, Capital   32,200
               Sugar, Capital   19,100
               Salt, Capital   8,700

           To close the Income Summary account and distribute
           the earnings.

[a]Schedule for Distribution of Income

	Spice	Sugar	Salt	Total
Salaries	$10,000	$ 8,000	$5,000	$23,000
Interest:				
Spice ($60,000 + $3,000) × 10%	6,300			
Sugar ($30,000 + $1,500) × 10%		3,150		
Salt ($10,500 × 10%)			1,050	
Total				10,500
Balance Allocated:				
Spice ($26,500* × 60%)	15,900			
Sugar ($26,500 × 30%)		7,950		
Salt ($26,500 × 10%)			2,650	
Total				26,500
Income Distribution	$32,200	$19,100	$8,700	$60,000

*$60,000 − $23,000 − $10,500 = $26,500

Dec. 31   Spice, Capital 10,000
           Sugar, Capital 10,000
           Salt, Capital 10,000
               Spice, Withdrawals   10,000
               Sugar, Withdrawals   10,000
               Salt, Withdrawals   10,000

           To close the withdrawals accounts.

REQUIREMENT 2

SPICE AND SUGAR
Balance Sheet
December 31, 1992

Assets		*Liabilities and Owners' Equity*	
Cash	$ 93,000[a]	Accounts payable	$ 25,000
Accounts receivable	40,000[b]		
Property and equipment	60,000	Spice, capital	85,200[d]
Less: Accumulated		Sugar, capital	40,600[e]
depreciation	(33,000)[c]	Salt, capital	9,200[f]
		Total Liabilities and	
Total Assets	$160,000	Owners' Equity	$160,000

[a] $50,000 + $15,000 − $30,000 − $22,000 + $80,000
[b] $30,000 + $90,000 − $80,000
[c] $25,000 + $8,000
[d] $60,000 + $3,000 − $10,000 + $32,200
[e] $30,000 + $1,500 − $10,000 + $19,100
[f] $10,500 − $10,000 + $8,700

REQUIREMENT 3

```
1993
Jan.  1  Cash  .......................................................  47,000
         Accumulated Depreciation  ................................  33,000
         Spice, Capital [($67,000 − $47,000) × 60%]  .................  12,000[a]
         Sugar, Capital [($67,000 − $47,000) × 30%]  .................   6,000
         Salt, Capital [($67,000 − $47,000) × 10%]  ...................   2,000
             Accounts Receivable  .....................................          40,000
             Property and Equipment  ..................................          60,000

         To record the sale of the assets and loss of $20,000.
```

[a]Since the liquidation occurs on January 1, no recognition of salaries or interest is necessary. Therefore the loss is distributed in the ratio of 6 : 3 : 1.

```
Jan.  1  Accounts Payable  ..........................................  25,000
             Cash  ...................................................          25,000

         To record the payment of liabilities
```

```
Jan.  1  Spice, Capital ($85,200 − $12,000)  .........................  73,200
         Sugar, Capital ($40,600 − $6,000)  ...........................  34,600
         Salt, Capital ($9,200 − $2,000)  .............................   7,200
             Cash  ...................................................         115,000

         To record the distribution of remaining cash to the partners.
```

Glossary

Agent. A person who has the authority to act for another person.

Bonus. The difference between the assets contributed by a new partner and the capital balance assigned to the new partner.

Earnings Distribution Ratio. The ratio agreed by the partners that is used to distribute the earnings of the partnership to each partner (after the provisions for salaries and interest, if any).

General Partner.   A partner who has unlimited liability.

Interest Allocated to Partners.   A method of distributing a portion of the earnings of a partnership that compensates each partner for the capital contributed. Not an expense of the partnership.

Limited Partner.   A partner who has limited liability.

Liquidation.   The dissolution of a partnership by selling the assets, paying the liabilities, and closing the partners' capital accounts.

Partner's Capital Account.   An account used by a partnership to record the capital balance of each partner.

Partnership.   An association of two or more persons to carry on as co-owners a business for profit.

Partnership Agreement.   An agreement among the partners specifying the formation, operation, and liquidation of a partnership.

Partner's Withdrawal Account.   An account used by a partnership to record the assets withdrawn by each partner during the accounting period.

Salaries Distributed to Partners.   A method of distributing a portion of the earnings of a partnership that compensates each partner for his or her contribution to the operations of the partnership. Not an expense of the partnership.

Statement of Changes in Partners' Equity.   A supplementary statement that lists the investments, withdrawals, and earnings distribution for each partner during the accounting period.

Uniform Partnership Act.   An act adopted by most states that governs the formation, operation, and liquidation of a partnership. It is superseded by the partnership agreement.

Unlimited Liability.   A characteristic of a partnership meaning that *each* general partner is liable for *all* the debts of the partnership.

Questions

QUESTION 13-1   What is a partnership? Can a partnership exist without a written agreement?

QUESTION 13-2   What is a partnership agreement? What is typically included in the agreement?

QUESTION 13-3   What are the characteristics that are common to all partnerships?

QUESTION 13-4   What is meant by *unlimited liability?* How does this affect a partner as compared to a person with an ownership interest in a corporation?

QUESTION 13-5   What is the difference between a general and a limited partner?

QUESTION 13-6   Does a partnership have to pay income taxes on its earnings? Explain.

QUESTION 13-7   What is an *agent?* Can an agent bind other partners to all contracts?

QUESTION 13-8   A partner in a legal firm orders a tractor. Can the seller force the partnership to pay? Would your answer change if the partnership was involved in farming?

QUESTION 13-9   When does the life of a partnership end? Does a corporation have a limited life?

QUESTION 13-10   Why might two people form a partnership? What are the disadvantages?

QUESTION 13-11   What transactions directly affect the Capital account of each partner?

QUESTION 13-12   What is the purpose of the Withdrawals account of each partner?

QUESTION 13-13   What factors might be used to determine the distribution of the earnings of a partnership?

QUESTION 13-14   What are the alternatives that may arise when a new partner is admitted to a partnership?

QUESTION 13-15   Upon admission of a new partner, when is a bonus assigned to the existing partners? To the new partner?

QUESTION 13-16   When a partner withdraws from a partnership does it affect the capital balances of the other partners? If so, how?

QUESTION 13-17   A partner is withdrawing from a partnership. He claims that in addition to receiving assets equal to his capital balance, he should also receive an amount equal to a reasonable salary and interest on the capital he invested while a partner. Is this a valid claim? Explain.

QUESTION 13-18   Why might a partnership to be liquidated? After the assets have been sold and the liabilities paid, will the remaining cash balance equal the sum of the partners' capital accounts?

QUESTION 13-19   If a partner has a negative capital balance when a partnership is liquidated, what is the correct procedure to follow?

Exercises

EXERCISE 13-1   **Capital Account.**   During 1991 Susan Chambers was admitted to a law partnership on payment of $50,000. She received a capital balance equal to her investment. During the year her share of the net income of the partnership was $20,000 and she withdrew $15,000.

REQUIRED   Prepare journal entries to record the preceding events. The partnership uses a Withdrawals account for each partner.

EXERCISE 13-2   **Earnings Distribution.**   During 1991 the Clark, Hill, and Chapman medical partnership had a net income of $45,000.

REQUIRED   Prepare the journal entry to close the income summary account and distribute the net income if:

1. Earnings are divided equally.
2. Earnings are divided in the ratio 4 : 3 : 3 to Clark, Hill, and Chapman, respectively.

EXERCISE 13-3 **Earnings Distribution Based on Capital Balances.** The following information is for the Simon and Art partnership:

Partner	Capital 1/1/1991	Investments		Withdrawals	
		Amount	Date	Amount	Date
Simon	$60,000	$10,000	June 30	$24,000	Nov. 1
Art	40,000	4,000	Apr. 1	18,000	Oct. 1

REQUIRED

1. Prepare the journal entry to close the income summary account and distribute the net income of $50,000 if:
   (a) The partnership earnings are divided on the basis of beginning capital balances.
   (b) The partnership earnings are divided on the basis of average capital balances.

2. Prepare a statement of changes in partners' equity when the earnings distribution is based on the average capital balances.

EXERCISE 13-4 **Interest on Capital Balances.** Use the same information as in Exercise 13-3. The partnership's net income in 1991 was $50,000. Interest of 10% was allowed on capital balances, with the remaining earnings being divided equally.

REQUIRED

1. Prepare the journal entry to close the income summary account and distribute the net income if:
   (a) Interest is allowed on the beginning capital balances.
   (b) Interest is allowed on the average capital balances.

2. Is the interest recorded as interest expense on the partnership's income statement? Why or why not?

EXERCISE 13-5 **Recognition of Salaries.** During 1991 the Carter and Hawkins accounting partnership had a net income of $90,000. Salaries of $30,000 and $20,000 are allowed to Carter and Hawkins, with the remaining earnings being distributed equally.

REQUIRED

1. Prepare the journal entry to close the income summary account and distribute the net income.

2. Instead, prepare the closing entry assuming the partnership had a net income of $40,000.

3. Are the salaries recorded as salaries expense on the partnership's income statement? Why or why not?

EXERCISE 13-6 **Admission of a New Partner.** The Chamberlain and Cambridge law partnership decides to admit a new partner, Hart. Hart will pay $50,000 and will be assigned a capital balance of the same amount. Chamberlain and Cambridge have capital balances of $75,000 and $50,000, respectively, and share earnings equally.

REQUIRED   Prepare the journal entry to record the admission of Hart if:

1. Hart contributes cash of $50,000 to the partnership.

2. Hart purchases two-thirds of Chamberlain's interest directly from him.

EXERCISE 13-7   **Admission of a New Partner.**   Use the information in Exercise 13-6, except that Hart does not receive a capital balance equal to $50,000.

REQUIRED   1. Prepare the journal entry to record the admission of Hart if:
   (a) Hart purchases a 25% share of the partnership.
   (b) Hart purchases a 40% share of the partnership.

   2. What is the justification for Hart not receiving a capital balance equal to the assets contributed?

EXERCISE 13-8   **Withdrawal of a Partner.**   Cameron decides to withdraw from the Taylor, Durrant, and Cameron medical partnership. He will receive cash equal to his capital balance after revaluation. The partners have an audit and revaluation that indicates that the inventory should be reduced by $2,000 and property and equipment increased by $14,000. Taylor, Durrant, and Cameron share in earnings 50%, 30%, and 20% and have capital balances of $70,000, $30,000 and $15,000, respectively.

REQUIRED   Prepare journal entries to record the revaluation and withdrawal.

EXERCISE 13-9   **Withdrawal of a Partner.** Use the information in Exercise 13-8, except that Cameron does not receive cash equal to his capital balance.

REQUIRED   Prepare journal entries to record the revaluation and withdrawal if:

   1. Cameron receives cash of $10,000.

   2. Cameron receives cash of $20,000.

EXERCISE 13-10   **Liquidation of a Partnership.**   The Upps and Downs engineering partnership has the following balance sheet on November 10, 1991:

UPPS AND DOWNS
Balance Sheet
November 10, 1991

Assets		*Liabilities and Owners' Equity*	
Cash	$10,000	Accounts payable	$15,000
Inventory	30,000		
Property and equipment	40,000	Upps, capital	25,000
Less: Accumulated		Downs, capital	20,000
depreciation	(20,000)	Total Liabilities and	
Total Assets	$60,000	Owners' Equity	$60,000

The partners, who share earnings equally, decide to liquidate the partnership. The inventory is sold for $35,000 and the property and equipment for $25,000.

REQUIRED   Prepare journal entries to record the liquidation.

EXERCISE 13-11   **Statement of Changes in Partners' Equity.**   Snowdon and Peak had capital balances on January 1, 1991, of $30,000 and $50,000, respectively. During 1991 Snowdon and Peak made additional investments of $15,000 and $14,000 and withdrawals of $9,000 and $10,000, respectively. In the distribution of earnings at the end of the year, Snowdon received a salary allowance of $12,000 and an interest allocation of $3,000.

Peak received a salary allowance of $11,000 and an interest allocation of $5,000. The remaining $6,000 of partnership earnings were divided equally.

REQUIRED   Prepare a statement of changes in partners' equity for 1991.

Problems

Part A

PROBLEM 13-1A   **Distribution of Earnings.**   Carson and Rickles had capital balances on January 1, 1991, of $50,000 and $30,000, respectively. On June 1 Carson contributed $10,000 cash to the partnership. On August 1, 1991, Rickles contributed a car worth $8,000 to the partnership. On March 31, 1991, Carson and Rickles withdrew $10,000 and $8,000, respectively. On September 30, 1991, they withdrew $12,000 and $9,000, respectively. The net income for 1991 was $25,000.

REQUIRED

1. Prepare journal entries to record the closing of the income summary account and distribution of the partnership net income under each of the following independent alternatives:
   (a) Earnings are divided equally.
   (b) Earnings are divided 60% to Carson and 40% to Rickles.
   (c) Earnings are divided in the ratio of the partners' average capital balances.
   (d) Interest of 10% is provided on the average capital balances with the remainder divided equally.
   (e) Salaries of $18,000 and $15,000 are allocated to Carson and Rickles, with the remainder divided equally.
   (f) Salaries of $12,000 and $8,000 are allocated to Carson and Rickles, interest of 10% is provided on beginning capital balances, and the remainder is divided equally.

2. For your answer to Requirement 1, part f, prepare a partial income statement showing the allocation of net income to the partners for 1991.

PROBLEM 13-2A   **Admission of a New Partner.**   Howard and Castle are partners in a company with capital balances of $75,000 and $50,000, respectively. The partnership has assets consisting of cash of $40,000, inventory of $45,000, and property and equipment of $80,000. Liabilities total $40,000. Howard receives 70% of the partnership's earnings, with the remainder going to Castle. A new partner, Duke, is admitted to the partnership by paying $30,000.

REQUIRED

1. Prepare journal entries to record the admission of Duke to the partnership under each of the following independent alternatives:
   (a) Duke pays $30,000 to Howard and Castle directly for 20% of each of their interests.
   (b) Duke pays $30,000 to the partnership and is assigned a capital balance of $30,000.
   (c) Duke pays $30,000 to the partnership and is assigned a capital balance of $25,000.
   (d) Duke pays $30,000 to the partnership and is assigned a capital balance of $34,000.

2. Prepare a condensed balance sheet for the partnership immediately after the admission of Duke for each of the alternatives.

PROBLEM 13-3A **Withdrawal of a Partner.** The balance sheet of the Mays, Young, and Hodges engineering partnership on June 30, 1991, is as follows:

MAYS, YOUNG, AND HODGES
Balance Sheet
June 30, 1991

Assets		*Liabilities and Owners' Equity*	
Cash	$15,000	Accounts payable	$10,000
Accounts receivable	20,000	Note payable	5,000
Inventory	10,000		
Property and equipment	40,000	Mays, capital	20,000
Less: Accumulated		Young, capital	10,000
depreciation	(10,000)	Hodges, capital	30,000
		Total Liabilities and	
Total Assets	$75,000	Owners' Equity	$75,000

Earnings are distributed among Mays, Young, and Hodges in a 2 : 1 : 3 ratio. Young decides to withdraw from the partnership. An audit reveals that an allowance for uncollectible accounts of 8.5% of accounts receivable should be established and that the property and equipment is worth $35,000.

REQUIRED
1. Prepare the journal entry to record the revaluation.

2. Prepare the journal entry to record the withdrawal of Young under each of the following independent alternatives:
   (a) Young receives partnership cash equal to her capital balance.
   (b) Young receives partnership cash equal to 80% of her capital balance.
   (c) Young receives partnership cash equal to 120% of her capital balance.
   (d) Young receives partnership cash equal to her capital balance and also receives inventory with a cost of $4,000.
   (e) Young sells her interest to Mays who pays her $45,000.

PROBLEM 13-4A **Liquidation of a Partnership.** The balance sheet of the Evans and Monk law partnership on April 15, 1991, is as follows:

EVANS AND MONK
Balance Sheet
April 15, 1991

Assets		*Liabilities and Owners' Equity*	
Cash	$ 5,000	Accounts payable	$ 5,000
Accounts receivable	10,000	Notes payable	7,000
Prepaid rent	2,000		
Equipment	30,000		
Less: Accumulated		Evans, capital	8,000
depreciation	(25,000)	Monk, capital	2,000
		Total Liabilities and	
Total Assets	$22,000	Owners' Equity	$22,000

The amount shown in accounts receivable is for services performed for a client who is now in jail and the amount is unlikely to be paid. The prepaid rent is for the next 2 months, and the partners do not expect to be able to rent the building to others. The equipment is sold for $7,500. Interest on the notes payable is accrued to date and is included in the notes payable balance. The partners share earnings equally.

REQUIRED

1. Prepare journal entries to record the liquidation of the partnership if both partners can contribute cash to the partnership.

2. Prepare journal entries to record the liquidation of the partnership if Monk cannot contribute cash to the partnership.

PROBLEM 13-5A   **Comprehensive.** The balance sheet of the Haston, Brown, and Ward industrial design partnership on January 1, 1991, is as follows:

HASTON, BROWN, AND WARD
Balance Sheet
January 1, 1991

Assets		*Liabilities and Owners' Equity*	
Cash	$30,000	Accounts payable	$35,000
Accounts receivable	15,000		
Inventory	40,000		
Property and equipment	30,000	Haston, capital	30,000
Less: Accumulated		Brown, capital	18,000
depreciation	(20,000)	Ward, capital	12,000
		Total Liabilities and	
Total Assets	$95,000	Owners' Equity	$95,000

Haston, Brown, and Ward share earnings in the ratio 50%, 30%, and 20%, respectively, after a salary allocation of $14,000, $10,000, and $11,000, respectively, and an interest provision of 10% on beginning capital balances. The following summarized events occurred during 1991.

(a) Made sales of $93,000 on account.

(b) Collected accounts receivable of $90,000.

(c) Purchased inventory on account for $32,000.

(d) Paid accounts payable of $33,000.

(e) Paid wages to employees of $15,000.

(f) The property and equipment is being depreciated on a straight-line basis over 15 years to a zero residual value.

(g) Ending inventory was $46,000.

On January 1, 1992, Haston withdrew from the partnership. At that time the value of the accounts receivable was reduced by $3,000 and the value of the property and equipment increased by $8,000. Haston received cash equal to 90% of the value of her equity after revaluation.

On January 2, 1992, Gold was admitted to the partnership by paying $17,600 to the partnership for a capital balance of $16,000. His share of the earnings is to be 30%

after a salary allocation of $5,600 and an interest provision of 10% on his beginning capital balance. Brown's and Ward's salary allocations and interest provisions remain the same as in 1991. Their share of the earnings after the salary allocations and interest provisions are 42% and 28%, respectively. Between January 1, 1992, and March 31, 1992, the following summarized events occurred:

(a) Sales of $35,000 on account.

(b) Wages paid to employees were $4,000.

(c) Ending inventory was $4,000.

On March 31, 1992, the partnership was liquidated. All noncash assets were sold at an auction for $63,000. All three partners were able to contribute cash to the partnership to cover any negative capital balances. Salary distributions and interest allocations were made on a proportional basis for the partial year. Gold receives an interest allocation on the basis of his $16,000 initial capital balance. The partnership uses the periodic inventory system.

REQUIRED
1. Prepare journal entries (including closing entries) to record the preceding events for each year.

2. Prepare the 1991 partnership income statement, the 1991 statement of changes in partners' equity, and the balance sheet at December 31, 1991.

Problems

Part B

PROBLEM 13-1B

Distribution of Earnings. Peters and Ladd had capital balances of $120,000 and $180,000, respectively, on January 1, 1991. On April 1 Peters and Ladd withdrew $30,000 and $60,000, respectively. On July 1 Peters contributed $12,000 cash to the partnership. On September 1 Ladd contributed a machine worth $51,000 to the partnership. On October 1 Ladd contributed $25,000 to the partnership. The net income for 1991 was $250,000.

REQUIRED
1. Prepare journal entries to close the income summary account and distribute the partnership net income under each of the following independent alternatives:
   (a) Earnings are distributed equally.
   (b) Earnings are distributed 40% to Peters and 60% to Ladd.
   (c) Earnings are distributed in the ratio of the partners' average capital balances.
   (d) Interest of 20% is provided on the average capital balances, with the remainder distributed equally.
   (e) Salaries of $50,000 and $75,000 are allocated to Peters and Ladd, with the remainder divided 40% to Peters and 60% to Ladd.
   (f) Salaries of $53,000 and $77,000 are allocated to Peters and Ladd, interest of 20% is provided on average capital balances, and the remainder is divided equally.

2. For your answer to Requirement 1, part f, prepare a partial income statement showing the allocation of net income to the partners for 1991.

PROBLEM 13-2B   **Admission of a New Partner.**   Dreves and Guthrie are partners in a consulting firm with capital balances of $50,000 and $35,000, respectively. The partnership has assets consisting of cash of $10,000, inventory of $33,000, and property and equipment of $49,000. Liabilities total $7,000. Dreves receives 60% of the partnership's earnings, with the remainder going to Guthrie. A new partner, Dolph, is admitted to the partnership by paying $15,000.

REQUIRED

1. Prepare journal entries to record the admission of Dolph to the partnership under each of the following independent alternatives:
   - *(a)* Dolph pays $15,000 to Dreves and Guthrie directly for 30% of each of their interests.
   - *(b)* Dolph pays $15,000 to the partnership and is assigned a capital balance of $15,000.
   - *(c)* Dolph pays $15,000 to the partnership and is assigned a capital balance of $11,000.
   - *(d)* Dolph pays $15,000 to the partnership and is assigned a capital balance of $23,000.

2. Prepare a condensed balance sheet for the partnership immediately after the admission of Dolph for each of the alternatives.

PROBLEM 13-3B   **Withdrawal of a Partner.**   The balance sheet of the Webster, Reeves, and Koontz architectural partnership on April 30, 1991, is as follows:

WEBSTER, REEVES, AND KOONTZ
Balance Sheet
April 30, 1991

Assets		Liabilities and Owners' Equity	
Cash	$ 70,000	Accounts payable	$ 44,000
Accounts receivable	30,000	Rent payable	13,000
Inventory	26,000		
Property and equipment	95,000	Webster, capital	62,000
Less: Accumulated		Reeves, capital	30,000
depreciation	(31,000)	Koontz, capital	41,000
		Total Liabilities and	
Total Assets	$190,000	Owners' Equity	$190,000

Earnings are distributed among Webster, Reeves, and Koontz in a $2:1:2$ ratio. Koontz decides to withdraw from the partnership. An audit reveals that an allowance for uncollectible accounts of 10% of accounts receivable should be established, that the inventory is worth $21,000, and that property and equipment is worth $67,000.

REQUIRED

1. Prepare the journal entry to record the revaluation.

2. Prepare the journal entry to record the withdrawal of Koontz under each of the following independent alternatives:
   - *(a)* Koontz receives partnership cash equal to her capital balance.
   - *(b)* Koontz receives partnership cash equal to 75% of her capital balance.
   - *(c)* Koontz receives partnership cash equal to 130% of her capital balance.
   - *(d)* Koontz receives $25,000 cash and inventory with a cost of $20,000.
   - *(e)* Koontz sells 30% of her interest to Reeves and 70% to Webster and receives $20,000 from Reeves and $30,000 from Webster.

PROBLEM 13-4B   **Liquidation of a Partnership.**   The balance sheet for the Price and Iverson medical partnership on September 15, 1991, is as follows:

PRICE AND IVERSON
Balance Sheet
September 15, 1991

Assets		*Liabilities and Owners' Equity*	
Cash	$ 50,000	Accounts payable	$ 23,000
Accounts receivable	15,000	Notes payable	27,000
Prepaid rent	8,000		
Equipment	110,000		
Less: Accumulated		Price, capital	43,000
depreciation	(83,000)	Iverson, capital	7,000
		Total Liabilities and	
Total Assets	$100,000	Owners' Equity	$100,000

The amount shown in accounts receivable is for services performed for a company that has since declared bankruptcy and is unlikely to be paid. The prepaid rent is for next month, and the partners do not expect to be able to rent their office space to others. The equipment is sold for $5,000. Interest on the notes payable is accrued to date and is included in the notes payable balance. Price and Iverson share earnings in a 3 : 1 ratio.

REQUIRED   *1.* Prepare journal entries to record the liquidation of the partnership if both partners can contribute cash to the partnership.

2. Prepare journal entries to record the liquidation of the partnership if Iverson cannot contribute cash to the partnership.

PROBLEM 13-5B   **Comprehensive.**   The balance sheet for the Larson, Hayes, and Little industrial engineering partnership on January 1, 1991, is as follows:

LARSON, HAYES, AND LITTLE
Balance Sheet
January 1, 1991

Assets		*Liabilities and Owners' Equity*	
Cash	$100,000	Accounts payable	$130,000
Accounts receivable	120,000		
Inventory	60,000		
Property and equipment	80,000	Larson, capital	92,000
Less: Accumulated		Hayes, capital	73,000
depreciation	(40,000)	Little, capital	25,000
		Total Liabilities and	
Total Assets	$320,000	Owners' Equity	$320,000

Larson, Hayes, and Little share earnings in a 3 : 1 : 1 ratio, respectively, after a salary distribution of $30,000, $20,000, and $10,000, respectively, and an interest allocation of 10% on beginning capital balances. The following summarized events occurred during 1991:

(a) Made sales of $405,000 on account.

(b) Collected accounts receivable of $455,000.

(c) Purchased inventory on account for $210,000.

(d) Paid accounts payable of $240,000.

(e) Paid wages to employees of $130,000.

(f) The property and equipment is being depreciated on a straight-line basis over 20 years to a zero residual value.

(g) Ending inventory was $90,000.

On January 1, 1992, Hayes withdrew from the partnership. At that time the value of the inventory was increased by $11,000 and the value of the property and equipment was reduced by $22,000. Hayes received cash equal to 110% of the value of her equity after revaluation. On January 2, 1992, Grant was admitted to the partnership by paying $55,000 to the partnership for a capital balance of $40,000. His share of the earnings is to be one-fifth after a salary distribution of $15,000 and an interest provision of 10% on his beginning capital balance. Larson and Little's salary allocations and interest provisions remain the same as in 1991. Their share of the earnings after the salary allocations and interest provisions are 50% and 30%, respectively. Between January 1, 1992, and April 30, 1992, the following summarized events occurred:

(a) Sales of $80,000 on account.

(b) Wages paid to employees were $40,000.

(c) Ending inventory was $10,000.

On April 30, 1992, the partnership was liquidated. All noncash assets were sold at an auction for $120,000. All three partners were able to contribute cash to the partnership to cover any negative capital balances. Salary distributions and interest allocations were made on a proportional basis for the partial year. Grant receives an interest allocation on the basis of his $40,000 initial capital balance. The partnership uses the periodic inventory method.

REQUIRED

1. Prepare journal entries (including closing entries) to record the preceding events for each year.

2. Prepare the 1991 partnership income statement, the 1991 statement of changes in partners' equity, and the balance sheet at December 31, 1991.

Decision Cases

DECISION CASE 13-1   **Admission to a Partnership.**   Anton and Derek have operated a partnership for many years. Anton's capital balance is $60,000, and she receives a salary allocation of $16,000. Derek's capital balance is $50,000, and he receives a salary allocation of $12,000. Interest of 10% is provided each year on each partner's beginning capital balance. Remaining earnings and losses are distributed 60% to Anton and 40% to Derek. The net income of the partnership has averaged $80,000 per year in recent years.

Tiegs has worked for the partnership for 10 years and has built an excellent relationship with the customers. She is currently being paid a salary of $16,000, but she has received an offer from a competitor for $20,000.

Since they are anxious to retain Tiegs in the business, Anton and Derek offer her a share of the partnership under the following terms:

1. She will be admitted to the partnership by paying $24,000 cash. She will be assigned a capital balance of $25,000.

2. Interest of 10% on her capital balance will be provided, and she will receive a salary allocation of $12,000. Anton and Derek will continue to receive the same interest and salary allocations as before.

3. Remaining earnings will be distributed to Anton, Derek, and Tiegs in the ratio of 50%, 30%, and 20%, respectively.

REQUIRED   Tiegs has come to you for advice on whether she should become a partner or take the offer from the competitor. Prepare a report for Tiegs that analyzes the advantages and disadvantages of becoming a partner.

DECISION CASE 13-2   **Withdrawal from a Partnership.**   Andrews and Moore have operated a partnership for a few years. Andrews and Moore receive salary allocations of $12,000 and $10,000, respectively, and interest of 10% is provided on their capital balances of $9,000 and $6,000, respectively. The remaining earnings are shared in the ratio of 60% and 40%, respectively.

The partnership has never been very successful, and this year there has been a loss of $1,000. The partnership agreement does not specify how losses are to be distributed. Moore decides to withdraw from the partnership and suggests the following two alternatives:

1. The loss will be distributed equally with no interest or salary allocations being made.

2. The $14,000 assets of the partnership remaining after payment of the liabilities will be distributed according to the capital balances of the partners.

REQUIRED   Prepare a report for Andrews advising him which alternative he should accept.

DECISION CASE 13-3   **Partnership Earnings.**   David Jackson and Edward Olmos have decided to go into the business of customizing cars. They have been told that they need a formal partnership agreement and have asked you for help in deciding on how to distribute the earnings of the partnership. David Jackson is currently earning $35,000 per year, will contribute $50,000 of his savings on which he is currently earning 10% per year, and will be responsible for the work done on the cars. Edward Olmos is currently earning $50,000 per year, will contribute $100,000 which he is borrowing interest-free from a relative, and will be responsible for marketing, hiring employees, and customer relations. They expect that the partnership will lose $30,000 the first year, but expect to improve that by $20,000 per year for the next 7 years.

REQUIRED   Prepare a recommendation for the distribution of partnership earnings.

14

Corporations: Capital Stock and Contributed Capital

LEARNING OBJECTIVES

1. Define capital stock, stock certificate, and stockholder.

2. List the rights of stockholders.

3. State the (a) advantages and (b) disadvantages of a corporation.

4. Define stockholders' equity and identify its two components.

5. Explain (a) legal capital and (b) additional paid-in capital.

6. Record capital stock issued (a) for cash, (b) in subscriptions, and (c) in noncash exchanges.

7. Record (a) donated capital and (b) stock splits.

8. Explain convertible, callable, and redeemable preferred stock.

9. Describe treasury stock.

10. Record the (a) reacquisition and (b) reissuance of treasury stock.

11. Prepare a statement of changes in stockholders' equity.

n the earlier chapters we focused primarily on accounting for sole proprietorships. In Chapter 13 we discussed the specific accounting issues of partnerships. Although sole proprietorships and partnerships outnumber corporations in the number of existing entities, corporations produce and sell far more goods and services. For instance, according to recent government statistics, corporations comprised only 19% of the number of companies in the United States but provided 90% of the total revenues of all companies. To accumulate sufficient capital to finance its activities, a corporation may enter into many different transactions involving the issuance of its capital stock. In this chapter the main focus is on understanding corporations, their capital stock transactions, and the impact of these transactions upon the owners' equity of a corporation.

Corporate Form of Organization

In 1819 Chief Justice John Marshall defined a corporation as "an artificial being, invisible, intangible, and existing only in contemplation of the law." Today, although a corporation is a collection of individual owners, it is treated as a separate entity according to the law. **A corporation is a separate legal entity, with a continuous life, that is independent of its individual owners.** Thus ownership in a corporation may be transferred from one individual to another. An owner has no personal liability for the corporation's debts and frequently plays no active part in the management of the corporation. As a result, the success of the corporation depends on its ability to attract large amounts of capital (often from a diverse set of owners), which is controlled by its professional management group for an indefinite period of time.

Procedures for Incorporation

To operate as a corporation in the United States, a business entity must incorporate in one of the states. **Incorporation is the process of filing the necessary documents and obtaining permission to operate as a corporation.** Each state has its own laws of incorporation; many of these laws are uniform throughout the country, whereas others are not. Normally one or more individuals may apply to the appropriate state officials for approval to form a corporation. The application includes the names of the individual incorporators; the corporate name, address, and nature of business; the types, legal value (if any), and number of capital shares to be authorized for issuance; and any other information required by the state's laws. The application may also include the names and addresses of the initial subscribers (subscriptions are discussed later) to the capital stock, the number of subscribed shares, the subscription price, and the down payment (if any). **The articles of incorporation (or corporate charter) is an approved application to form a corporation.** A meeting may then be held at which the initial issuance of capital stock is made to the incorporators, a board of directors is elected, a set of rules (bylaws) regulating the corporate operations is established, and the executive officers (i.e., the *top management*) of the corporation are appointed by the board. These terms are discussed more fully later in the chapter.

In order for a corporation to conduct its operations, the state gives it various rights and powers, including the right to enter into contracts, to hold, buy, and sell property, to sue and be sued, and to have a continuous life. These rights and powers are accompanied by a number of responsibilities. A corporation may engage only in the activities for which it was established; it must safeguard the corporate capital; it must adhere to all state and federal laws; it must adhere to state regulations concerning the distribution of net income; it must pay its debts; and it must pay local, state, and federal taxes.

Ownership and Management of a Corporation

1. Define capital stock, stock certificate, and stockholder.

Capital stock is the ownership unit in a corporation. A stock certificate is evidence of ownership in a corporation. **A stock certificate is a serially numbered legal document that indicates the number of shares of capital stock owned by a stockholder and the par (legal) value, if any.** It may also include additional information concerning the method of transferring the capital stock to any other owner. An illustration of a stock certificate is presented in Exhibit 14-1. **The owners of a corporation are referred to as the stockholders (or shareholders).**

EXHIBIT 14-1   Illustration of Stock Certificate

Reprinted by permission.

Since shares of stock are transferable between individuals, the owners of a corporation may be a diverse set of stockholders who are not involved in the management of the corporation. Because of this separation of ownership and management, each stockholder may be given five rights. These rights are:

2. List the rights of stockholders.

1. The right to attend stockholders' meetings and to vote in setting and approving major policies and actions of the corporation. Included are policies and actions concerning such items as mergers with other companies, acquisitions of other companies, sales of major portions of the corporation, and the issuance of additional stock and bonds (discussed in Chapter 16).

2. The right to vote in the election of the board of directors. **A board of directors is a group of individuals that has the responsibility and authority to supervise the corporation's ordinary business activities, make future plans, and take whatever action is necessary in the current management of the corporation.** Voting to elect the board of directors (and the *chairman of the board*) also takes place at the stockholders' meetings.

3. The right to share in net income by receiving dividends from the corporation. The payment of dividends, however, is determined by the board of directors.

4. The right to purchase additional capital stock if it is issued. This is called the preemptive right. **The preemptive right is the right to maintain a proportionate percentage of ownership of the corporation by purchasing a proportionate (pro rata) share of additional capital stock if it is issued.** This right is often very significant for small, privately held companies for which control is very important. It may be waived by a stockholder, for example, to allow the corporation to acquire another company by issuing a large number of additional shares of stock.

5. The right to share in the distribution of the assets of the corporation if it is liquidated (terminated). If a corporation is terminated creditors are given first priority in the collection of their claims; any remaining assets are then distributed to stockholders.

The separation of ownership and management has resulted in the need for an organizational structure for operating and managing the corporation. A corporation's organizational structure is shown in its organization chart. An **organization chart is a diagram that shows the lines of responsibility and authority among the officers in the corporation.** No two corporations will have the same organization chart because of their different structures. However, a typical organizational structure is illustrated in the organization chart presented in Exhibit 14-2.

Stockholders vote on major corporate policies and actions. They also vote in the election of the board of directors, thus indirectly influencing the supervision of the corporation's business activities. The board of directors appoints the president, who is usually the top (chief) executive officer in the organization. The president is responsible for the planning and control of all the corporate activities. Several vice presidents usually assist the president in the planning and control of operations, however. For instance, the vice president of marketing deals with sales, advertising, and marketing research. The vice president of production is responsible for purchasing, manufacturing, and quality control. The vice president of finance may oversee both the treasurer and controller. The trea-

EXHIBIT 14-2 Typical Corporate Organization Chart

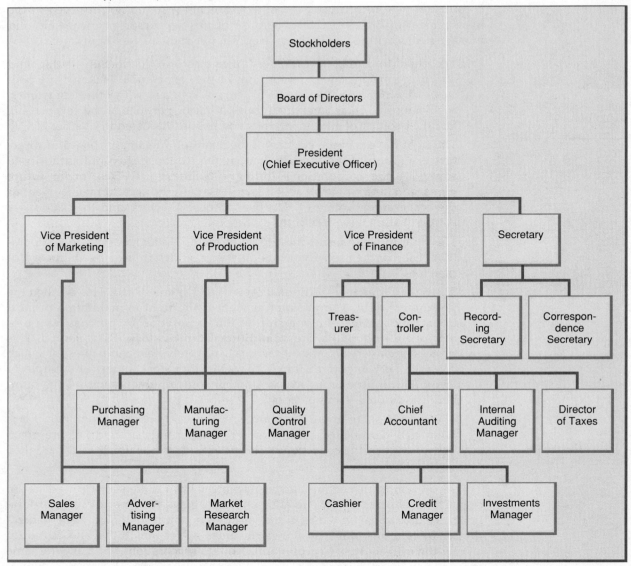

surer is responsible for short- and long-term financing, credit and collections, and short- and long-term investments. The controller is responsible for the general supervision of accounting, internal auditing (and internal control), and management of corporate taxes. The secretary is responsible for the corporate records, including keeping the minutes of the stockholders' meetings and the board of directors' meetings, corresponding with stockholders, and maintaining the stockholders' records.

Because stock certificates may be transferred from one individual to another, state laws require that each corporation maintain records of its stockholders. **The stockholders' ledger contains a record of each stockholder's name, address,**

and number of shares held. This information enables the corporation to notify stockholders of all stockholders' meetings and to pay the correct amount of dividends to the proper stockholders. Whenever new shares are issued or shares are exchanged between stockholders, the stockholders' ledger must be updated. Exchanges of stock are initially recorded in a stock transfer journal. **A stock transfer journal contains the names and addresses of the new and former stockholders involved in each stock transfer, the date of exchange, the stock certificate numbers, and the number of shares exchanged.** Many corporations employ an independent *transfer agent* to issue the stock certificates as well as a *registrar* to maintain the stockholder records.

Advantages of a Corporation

3(a). State the advantages of a corporation.

The corporation has become so prominent because it offers five primary advantages:

1. *Limited Liability.* Under the law a corporation is a separate legal entity, independent of its owners, and responsible for paying its obligations. Stockholders normally cannot be held personally responsible for the corporation's debts. This difference is the most important advantage over sole proprietorships and partnerships, in which creditors may be able to satisfy their claims by use of the owner's personal assets.

2. *Ease of Transferring Ownership.* The capital stock of many corporations sells on organized stock markets like the New York Stock Exchange and the American Stock Exchange. Because shares of stock are transferable, it is relatively easy for an owner to dispose of his or her ownership should the need arise. This is not the case in a sole proprietorship or partnership.

3. *Ability to Attract Large Amounts of Ownership Capital.* The operation of a major corporation requires a large amount of capital invested by owners. Because ownership in a corporation is transferable and stockholders have limited liability, corporations usually are able to attract the large amounts of capital necessary for their operations.

4. *Ability to Attract Top-Quality Management.* Most owners of a corporation have neither the talent nor the desire to manage its operations. These owners willingly give these management duties to the corporation's board of directors. The directors, in turn, can hire the highest quality *management team* necessary to ensure successful operations.

5. *Continuity of Life.* As a separate legal entity a corporation has a continuous life. In contrast to a sole proprietorship or partnership, the activities of a corporation are normally not affected or disrupted by the death or withdrawal of an owner.

Disadvantages of a Corporation

Although the advantages of a corporation generally are very important, there are three primary disadvantages:

1. *Significant Taxation.* Sole proprietorships and partnerships, as business entities, are not subject to income taxes. The owners of a sole proprietorship

3(b). State the disadvantages of a corporation.

or partnership are taxed on their personal income from the business. Corporations, however, are treated as separate legal entities subject to federal and state income taxes. Since the maximum federal income tax rate for corporations is currently 34%, and many of them pay state income taxes, it is not unusual for income taxes to approach or exceed 40% of a corporation's income before income taxes. When the earnings of the corporation are distributed to stockholders as dividends, the stockholders may again be taxed on this personal income. This is referred to as *double taxation* and is the most significant disadvantage of a corporation.

2. *Government Control and Regulation.* In order to protect creditors and stockholders, laws have been enacted to control and regulate corporations. For instance, the payment of dividends by a corporation is usually limited to a specified amount established by the laws of the state in which it is incorporated. In addition, corporations are restricted in the purchase of their own stock. If a corporation's capital stock is sold on a stock market, certain reports must be filed by the corporation. Additional reports are required to be filed for such items as employees' safety and health and the corporation's environmental activities.

3. *Restricted Ability to Attract Creditor Capital.* For a sole proprietorship or partnership the creditors may use the personal assets of the owners to satisfy their claims. The owners of a corporation have limited liability, however. As a result a corporation (particularly a smaller one) may find it more difficult to borrow money on a short- or long-term basis because creditors may perceive their investment to be less safe.

The advantages of a corporation usually exceed the disadvantages when a business grows to a reasonable size. It should be noted, however, that the earlier statements about the characteristics of corporations (and the statements in the next section about capital stock) are general statements. In any particular state, or for any particular corporation, these generalities may not hold.

Because a corporation's management has the responsibility to abide by state and federal laws and to safeguard and ensure the proper use of capital invested by a diverse set of owners, accounting for the invested capital has become an important activity in itself. The remainder of this chapter deals with this accounting process.

Corporate Capital Structure

In a sole proprietorship there is a single owner and in a partnership there are usually only a few owners. An owner's capital account is used for each owner, to report the owner's equity on the balance sheet. The ending balance of each owner's capital account includes the investments by the owner, plus the owner's share of the net income earned to date less the owner's withdrawals. There are usually many owners of a corporation and frequent changes in ownership, making it almost impossible to establish separate capital accounts for each owner like those of a sole proprietorship or partnership. Furthermore state laws require special accounting procedures for the owners' equity of a corporation; these laws have been established to protect the absentee owners of a corporation as well as its creditors.

4. Define stockholders' equity and identify its two components.

Stockholders' equity is the term used for the owners' equity of a corporation. The stockholders' equity on a corporation's balance sheet is usually separated into two components: contributed capital and retained earnings. This division of stockholders' equity is established in adherence to state laws. The basic format (with assumed numbers of shares and dollar amounts) of the stockholders' equity section on a corporation's balance sheet is shown here:

Stockholders' Equity

Contributed capital
    Capital stock, $5 par, 20,000 shares
        authorized, 10,000 shares issued and outstanding $50,000
    Additional paid-in capital 70,000
        Total contributed capital $120,000
Retained earnings 90,000
        Total Stockholders' Equity $210,000

The total amount of investments made by stockholders into the corporation is reported in the contributed capital section. Each of the accounts (capital stock and additional paid-in capital) and the information about the characteristics (e.g., par value) and the number of shares (authorized, issued, and outstanding) included in this section are discussed in the following sections. **The balance in retained earnings reports the total lifetime corporate earnings that have been reinvested in the corporation and not distributed to stockholders as dividends.** The accounting issues relating to retained earnings were briefly introduced in Chapter 5 and are discussed in Chapter 15.

Capital Stock and Legal Capital

Capital stock refers to the ownership units in the corporation. Capital stock may be issued by the corporation for cash, in installment sales, in noncash exchanges, and in other transactions. The dollar amount recorded in the Capital Stock account by a corporation for each capital stock transaction depends on the laws of the state in which it is incorporated. Because capital stockholders have a *limited liability,* to protect creditors state laws usually set a legal capital for all corporations. **Legal capital is the amount of stockholders' equity that cannot be distributed to stockholders.** A corporation may not pay dividends or reacquire capital stock if these activities will reduce the legal capital. The definition of legal capital varies from state to state. In most states, however, the total par value or stated value of the issued capital stock is the legal capital.

5(a). Explain legal capital.

Par Value Stock. Historically, the usual way legal capital has been established is by requiring that all capital stock have a par value. **The par value of capital stock is a monetary amount that is designated as the legal capital per share in the articles of incorporation and is printed on each stock certificate.** The total legal capital of a corporation is determined by multiplying the par value per share times the number of shares issued. Generally, states require that a separate accounting be made of the legal capital. Consequently, as we will see shortly, for each issuance of capital stock the total dollar amount of the par value is recorded in a capital stock account.

No-Par Stock.   Most states also allow the issuance of no-par capital stock. **No-par capital stock does not have a par value.** When no-par stock is issued, some states require that the entire proceeds received by the corporation for the issued shares be designated as legal capital, and accounting practices have been established for this situation. Many states, however, allow the corporation's board of directors to establish a stated value per share of no-par stock. **The stated value of no-par stock is the legal capital per share of stock.** The stated value per share, when multiplied times the number of shares issued, is the total amount of legal capital. Accounting for stated value, no-par stock is very similar to accounting for par value stock, and the total dollar amount of the stated value is recorded in a capital stock account.

The concept of legal capital has had a significant impact upon corporate accounting practices, particularly as they apply to stockholders' equity. Capital stock accounts are established to record the legal capital, and additional paid-in capital accounts are used for the remainder of the total amount of capital contributed by stockholders.

Additional Paid-In Capital

The par value of a share of capital stock often is set very low—perhaps $10, $2, or even less per share. Note that the par value of the General Motors' stock in Exhibit 14-1 is $1\frac{2}{3}$ per share. Since capital stock normally is issued at a price far in excess of par value, the legal capital is usually only a small part of the total proceeds received. The total proceeds received is the *market* value, the price at which the stock is issued. It is very important to understand that the par value of capital stock has *no* direct relationship to its market value at any time.

5(b). Explain additional paid-in capital.

A corporation may issue capital stock in a variety of transactions. In addition to following state laws for recording the par or stated value in a capital stock account, it is also sound accounting practice (as well as state law in certain states) to record the excess value received. The excess value received is called additional paid-in capital. **Additional paid-in capital is the difference between the market value and the par (or stated) value in each stock transaction and is recorded in an Additional Paid-in Capital account.** (How this is recorded is discussed later.) This account is alternatively entitled *Additional Paid-in Capital on Capital Stock, Additional Paid-in Capital in Excess of Par (or Stated) Value, Premium on Capital Stock,* or *Contributed Capital in Excess of Par (or Stated) Value.* Additional paid-in capital sometimes arises from transactions not involving the original issuance of capital stock. These transactions are discussed later in the chapter.

Classes of Capital Stock

Corporations may issue two classes of capital stock, common stock and preferred stock. If a corporation issues only one class of capital stock, it is generally referred to as common stock. **Common stock is capital stock that shares in all the stockholders' rights.** If a corporation issues more than one class of stock, the other class of stock (in addition to common stock) is called preferred stock. **Preferred stock is capital stock for which certain additional rights are given to the stockholders in exchange for giving up some of the usual stockholders' rights.** The additional rights may involve the right to receive a dividend before any dividend is paid to common stockholders and the right to convert the preferred stock to common stock at a later date. The right to vote may be given up in exchange for these additional rights. Alternatively, the preferred stock may be callable or redeemable. Dividends on preferred stock are discussed more fully in Chapter 15. The conversion of preferred stock to common stock and the recall or redemption of preferred stock are briefly discussed later in this chapter.

Preferred stock is typically issued with a par value. When a corporation issues both common stock and preferred stock, it will use a Common Stock account and a Preferred Stock account to record the legal capital of each kind of stock. It will also use an Additional Paid-in Capital on Common Stock account and an Additional Paid-in Capital on Preferred Stock account for the differences between the market values received and the par (or stated) values, respectively. We also use these account titles in this book. When a corporation issues both classes of stock, the contributed capital component of stockholders' equity would be expanded to include the additional accounts as shown next (using assumed numbers of shares and dollar amounts):

Stockholders' Equity		
Contributed capital		
Preferred stock, $100 par, 2,000 shares authorized,		
600 shares issued and outstanding	$60,000	
Common stock, $10 par, 30,000 shares authorized,		
9,000 shares issued and outstanding	90,000	
Additional paid-in capital on preferred stock	72,000	
Additional paid-in capital on common stock	43,000	
Total contributed capital		$265,000
Retained earnings		173,000
Total Stockholders' Equity		$438,000

With this background in mind, we now turn to recording the various types of capital stock transactions. Since most capital stock is common stock, our examples are in terms of common stock. The journal entries shown would be the same for preferred stock, however, except for the necessary changes in the account titles. The review problem at the end of the chapter includes transactions involving preferred stock.

Capital Stock Transactions

Common stock is authorized for issuance in the articles of incorporation after which it may be issued for cash, in installment sales, in noncash exchanges, and in other transactions. Each of these alternatives is discussed next.

Authorization

The corporate charter contains the authorization to issue capital stock. This authorization lists the classes of stock that may be issued, the par or stated value, the number of authorized shares, and in the case of preferred stock, any preference provisions. Once a corporation has issued all of its authorized stock, it must obtain stockholder approval and reapply to the state to issue more shares. Consequently, a corporation usually obtains authorization to issue more stock than it initially plans to sell.

It is important to understand the difference between authorized capital stock and issued capital stock. **Authorized capital stock is the number of shares of capital stock (both common and preferred) that the corporation *may* legally issue.** On the other hand, **issued capital stock is the number of shares of capital stock that a corporation has legally issued to its stockholders on a specific date.** As shown earlier the numbers of shares authorized and issued for each class of stock are reported in the stockholders' equity section of a corporation's balance sheet.

Issuance for Cash

Capital stock may be issued with a par value, as no-par stock with a stated value, or as true no-par stock. In the case of par value stock issued for cash, when the cash received is equal to the par value, the journal entry is simply a debit (increase) to cash and a credit (increase) to the capital stock account for the amount of cash received. In the more usual case, when the cash received is more than the total par value, the difference is recorded in an additional paid-in capital account. To illustrate, assume that a corporation issues 300 shares of its $10 par common stock for $16 per share. The following journal entry is made to record the transaction:

6(a). Record capital stock issued for cash.

Cash ($16 × 300)	4,800	
Common Stock, $10 par ($10 × 300)		3,000
Additional Paid-in Capital on Common Stock		1,800
To record issuance of common stock.		

If, instead, the stock were no-par stock with a stated value of $10 per share, the preceding transaction would be recorded as follows:

Cash	4,800	
Common Stock, $10 stated value		3,000
Additional Paid-in Capital on Common Stock		1,800
To record issuance of common stock.		

Note that, except for the title of the capital stock account, accounting for the issuance of no-par stock with a stated value is identical to that of par value stock.

Alternatively, the company may be authorized to issue no-par stock without a stated value. In this case the entire amount of the cash received is the legal capital and is recorded in the capital stock account. If the preceding transaction had involved no-par common stock, with no stated value, the following journal entry would have been made:

Cash	4,800	
Common Stock, no-par		4,800

To record issuance of 300 shares of common stock.

Note that in the explanation of this journal entry the number of *shares* issued was included. This was necessary because the number of shares issued in this transaction could not be determined by dividing the total increase in the Common Stock account by the par value per share. The remaining examples of stock issuances assume a par value.

Although typically prohibited, capital stock might be issued at a price *below* its par or stated value. In this case the stock sells at a *discount,* and the original stockholder may be required to pay into the corporation the amount of the discount should the corporation be unable to meet its financial obligations. When the stock is issued the difference between the cash received and the par value would be *debited* to an account entitled Discount on Common Stock. The Discount on Common Stock account would be listed as a contra (negative) account in the Contributed Capital section of stockholders' equity.

Miscellaneous costs may be incurred for the issuance of common stock. They include legal fees, accounting fees, stock certificate costs, and other costs. As discussed in Chapter 12 these costs associated with the *initial* issuance of stock at incorporation should be recorded (debited) as an intangible asset entitled Organization Costs. When these costs are associated with *subsequent* issuances of common stock they reduce the proceeds received and should be debited to the Additional Paid-in Capital account.

Stock Subscriptions

Investors sometimes agree to purchase capital stock on an "installment" basis. In this case the corporation and the future stockholder enter into a legally binding subscription contract. **In a subscription contract the subscriber (investor) agrees to buy a certain number of shares at a set price, with the payment spread over a specified time period.** The contract often requires a down payment and may contain provisions for any defaults (nonpayments) by the subscriber. The shares of capital stock are not issued to a subscriber until the subscriber has completed full payment of the subscription price.

To illustrate, assume that a corporation and several subscribers enter into a subscription contract that involves the purchase of 400 shares of $5 par common stock at a price of $9 per share. The contract requires a down payment of $2 per share, with the remaining $7 per share collectible at the end of 1 month. The stock will be issued to each subscriber upon full payment. The journal entry to record the subscription is as follows:

6(b). Record capital stock issued in subscriptions.

Cash ($2 × 400)	800	
Subscriptions Receivable: Common Stock ($7 × 400)	2,800	
Common Stock Subscribed ($5 × 400)		2,000
Additional Paid-in Capital on Common Stock		
[($9 – $5) × 400]		1,600

To record subscription to common stock.

Note that the balance to be received ($2,800) is recorded in a Subscriptions Receivable account. This account is usually listed as a current asset on the balance sheet because the subscription contract ordinarily requires full payment within a year.

The Common Stock Subscribed account is increased (credited) for the $2,000 par value of the shares subscribed. This account is used because the shares have not yet been legally issued, although the corporation has contracted to issue additional stock. If a balance sheet is issued after a subscription contract but before the subscribed shares have been issued, the Common Stock Subscribed account is listed in the Contributed Capital section of stockholders' equity. Additional Paid-in Capital is increased (credited) for the entire difference ($1,600) between the subscription price (the proceeds) and the par value of the subscribed stock under the assumption that the legal contract will be completed and the stock fully paid for.

To illustrate the reporting of common stock subscribed in stockholders' equity, assume that the previously mentioned corporation had issued 1,000 shares of the $5 par common stock for $6 per share prior to entering into the subscription. If a balance sheet were prepared immediately after entering into the subscription contract, stockholders' equity would appear as follows:

Stockholders' Equity

Contributed capital		
Common stock, $5 par, 10,000 shares authorized,		
1,000 shares issued and outstanding	$5,000	
Common stock subscribed (400 shares)	2,000	
Additional paid-in capital on common stock	2,600[a]	
Total contributed capital		$ 9,600
Retained earnings (assumed)		6,000
Total Stockholders' Equity		$15,600

[a][($6 − $5) × 1,000] + $1,600

If no-par common stock with no stated value is used in a stock subscription, the entire subscription price is credited to the Common Stock Subscribed account. No-par stock with a stated value and preferred stock are accounted for as in the example, with suitable changes in account titles.

When the remaining payments on the stock subscription are received, Cash is increased (debited) and Subscriptions Receivable is decreased (credited). At the final payment by a subscriber, stock certificates are issued to the subscriber for the number of fully paid subscribed shares. At that time a journal entry is made decreasing (debiting) Common Stock Subscribed and increasing (crediting) Common Stock for the par value of the issued shares. To illustrate, assume that the $7 per share final payment on the 400 shares was received at the end of the month. The journal entries to record both the receipt and the issuance of the shares are as follows:

Cash ($7 × 400)	2,800	
Subscriptions Receivable: Common Stock		2,800
To record receipt of final payment on subscription contract.		

Common Stock Subscribed	2,000	
Common Stock, $5 par		2,000
To record issuance of fully paid subscribed shares.		

Occasionally a subscriber will not make payments required by the subscription contract. When a default occurs the accounting is determined by the subscription contract provisions, such as (1) return to the subscriber the entire amount paid in; (2) return to the subscriber the amount paid in, less any costs incurred by the corporation to reissue the stock; (3) issue to the subscriber a lesser number of shares based upon the total amount of payment received; or (4) require the forfeiture of all amounts paid in. If the subscription contract does not include a provision for subscription defaults, the laws of the state in which the corporation is incorporated usually provide for one of these alternatives. The procedures are beyond the scope of this textbook.

Noncash Issuance of Stock

Sometimes capital stock is issued for assets other than cash, or for services performed. When this occurs a correct value must be used to record the transaction. This is a thorny issue when it involves intangible assets such as patents, copyrights, or organization costs because of the difficulty in valuing these assets. **The general rule is to record the transaction at the fair market value of the stock issued or the assets received, whichever is more reliable.** For instance, at the time of the transaction the stock may be selling on the stock market at a specified price. In this case the stock has a known value (the stock market price), and therefore this value would be used to record the transaction.

To illustrate, suppose that a corporation issues 100 shares of $10 par common stock in exchange for a patent. The stock is currently selling for $18 per share on the stock market. A value of $1,800 would be used to record the transaction as follows:

6(c). Record capital stock issued in noncash exchanges.

Patent	1,800	
Common Stock, $10 par ($10 × 100)		1,000
Additional Paid-in Capital on Common Stock		
[($18 – $10) × 100]		800

To record issuance of common stock for patent.

Alternatively, the corporation's stock may not be actively traded on a stock market. In this case the fair market value of the assets received may be more reliable and should be used to record the transaction. This value may be based on a review of recent transactions involving similar assets or on an appraisal by a competent, independent appraiser. To illustrate, assume that a corporation issues 1,000 shares of $4 par common stock that is not widely traded in exchange for an acre of land. An independent appraiser indicates the land has a value of $16,000. The journal entry to record the transaction is as follows:

Land	16,000	
Common Stock, $4 par ($4 × 1,000)		4,000
Additional Paid-in Capital on Common Stock		
($16,000 – $4,000)		12,000

To record issuance of common stock for land.

Sometimes shares of capital stock are issued by a corporation as payment for legal or accounting services performed in its incorporation process. As we indicated earlier, the costs of these services are recorded as an intangible asset Organization Costs because these services will benefit the corporation in the future. The transaction should be recorded at the agreed-upon contract price for the services by increasing (debiting) Organization Costs for the contract price, increasing (crediting) Common Stock for the par value of the shares issued, and recording the difference between the contract price and the par value as an increase (credit) to Additional Paid-in Capital.

It is important to understand the impact on the financial statements of an error in recording the noncash issuance of capital stock. Suppose, for instance, that stock was issued for equipment and the transaction was recorded at too high a value. In this case both the assets and stockholders' equity of the corporation would be overstated. In addition, since equipment is a depreciable asset the initial error would cause an overstatement each year in the depreciation expense, resulting in an understatement of net income. The financial statements would be correct only at the end of the asset's useful life. If the equipment was initially recorded at too low a value, opposite errors would result. Good judgment must be used in recording noncash issuances of capital stock to avoid errors in the financial statements of current and later periods.

Transfer of Stock Between Stockholders

The preceding discussions involving the sale of stock for cash, in subscription contracts, and in noncash exchanges only dealt with the *initial* issuance of stock to stockholders. Later, the corporation's stock may be "traded" (i.e., purchased and sold) among stockholders. In such a case the corporation is not directly involved in the transaction, and no stockholders' equity accounts are affected. Therefore the corporation makes no journal entry, but does update its stock transfer journal and stockholders' ledger as discussed earlier in the chapter.

Other Changes in Contributed Capital

Several other items may affect contributed capital. These items include donated capital, stock splits, and the conversion, recall, or redemption of preferred stock. Each of these items is discussed in the sections that follow.

Donated Capital

7(a). Record donated capital.

In a few instances a corporation may increase contributed capital for events not related to the issuance of capital stock. These increases are rare because they generally do not conform to the historical cost principle. For example, it is possible for a corporation to receive donated assets, such as a plant site, to induce it to locate in an "industrial park" of a community. Some communities do this to increase the employment opportunities for their citizens and to increase the collection of property taxes. In this case the corporation should record the donation as an increase (debit) in its assets at the fair market value (as determined by, say, an independent appraisal). The credit portion of the journal entry would involve an increase (credit) to an account entitled Additional Paid-in Capital from

Donations. This is appropriate because the assets of the corporation have increased without an increase in liabilities; the entire value belongs to the stockholders. To illustrate, suppose that a community donated land worth $8,000 to a corporation. The corporation records the event as follows:

Land 8,000	
Additional Paid-in Capital from Donations	8,000
To record donated land at its fair market value.	

Note that this transaction does *not* affect the income statement. Whether cash or noncash assets are received as a result of donations, the balance of the Additional Paid-in Capital from Donations account is listed as an item in the contributed capital section of the balance sheet. It is added to the balances of the capital stock and other additional paid-in capital accounts to determine the total contributed capital.

Stock Splits

Sometimes the market price of a corporation's common stock increases to the point where it is not as attractive to certain investors. Many corporations believe a wide distribution of ownership increases the demand for their stock, improves their public image, and increases their product sales to their stockholders. To reduce the market price so that it falls within the *trading range* (the price per share investors are willing to pay for common stock) of most investors, the board of directors may authorize a stock split. **A stock split is a decrease in the par value per share of stock and a proportional increase in the number of shares authorized and issued.** For example, in May 1989, Johnson & Johnson issued a 2 for 1 stock split of its common stock.

Since a stock split affects the number of authorized shares and the legal capital, each stock split must be approved by the state in which the corporation is incorporated. To illustrate a stock split, suppose a corporation that has issued 50,000 shares of $10 par common stock at $13 per share declares a 2 for 1 stock split with a reduction to a $5 par value. After the split a total of 100,000 shares of $5 common stock have been issued. A stockholder who previously owned 40 shares of $10 par common stock will own 80 shares of $5 par common stock after the stock split. The additional number of shares participating in the same amount of corporate earnings will cause a proportional decrease in the market price per share.

A stock split has no impact upon the dollar amount of any element of stockholders' equity and consequently it has no effect on total stockholders' equity. Even though a stock split does not affect the balance of any account, a memorandum entry[1] is necessary to maintain a chronological history of the corporation's financial activities in the general journal. For the previously mentioned stock split, the memorandum entry in the general journal might appear as follows

---

[1]**A memorandum entry is a written description of an event involving the corporation's financial activities.** It is recorded in the general journal but does not involve a debit or credit amount.

(assuming the corporation was authorized to issue 80,000 shares before the stock split):

7(b). Record stock splits.

> On January 1, 1991, with approval by the state, the board of directors authorized a 2 for 1 stock split, reducing the par value of the common stock from $10 per share to $5 per share. The number of authorized shares increased from 80,000 to 160,000 shares, and the issued common stock increased from 50,000 to 100,000 shares.

The effect of this stock split on contributed capital is shown in the following schedule:

Before Stock Split		*After Stock Split*	
Contributed capital		Contributed capital	
Common stock, $10 par, 80,000 shares authorized, 50,000 shares issued and outstanding	$500,000	Common stock, $5 par, 160,000 shares authorized, 100,000 shares issued and outstanding	$500,000
Additional paid-in capital on common stock	150,000	Additional paid-in capital on common stock	150,000
Total contributed capital	$650,000	Total contributed capital	$650,000

Note in the schedule that the stock split has no effect on the $650,000 total stockholders' equity. The total par value of the common stock is $500,000 before and after the stock split. Furthermore the $150,000 of additional paid-in capital remains unchanged.

Convertible, Callable, and Redeemable Preferred Stock

Earlier we mentioned that a corporation may issue two classes of stock, common and preferred. One of the preferences that might be extended to preferred stockholders is the right to exchange (convert) the preferred stock for common stock at a later date. **Convertible preferred stock is preferred stock that is exchangeable into common stock at the option of the stockholders.** Usually the number of common shares into which each preferred share is convertible is established at the time the preferred stock is issued. For instance, at the end of 1988, General Telephone & Electronics Corporation (GTE) had issued 239,538 shares of $50 par convertible preferred stock that were convertible into 316,190 shares of common stock.

8. Explain convertible, callable, and redeemable preferred stock.

Another feature of preferred stock involves the right to a set dividend. Both the conversion preference and the dividend feature are advantages to the preferred stockholder. Since the preferred stock is convertible into a specified amount of common stock, the market price of the convertible preferred stock tends to rise in proportion to any rise in the market price of the common stock. When the market price of the common stock is falling, however, the right to a set dividend on the preferred stock tends to stabilize the market value of the preferred stock.

Preferred stock may also be callable or redeemable. **Callable preferred stock may be retired (recalled) by the corporation at its option.** The call price is stated on the stock certificate and is usually several dollars above the issuance price. Stockholders owning nonconvertible preferred stock must give up their shares when called by the corporation. Stockholders owning convertible preferred stock usually have the choice of conversion or recall. **Redeemable preferred stock is subject to mandatory retirement at a specified maturity date and price.**[2] The primary difference between callable preferred stock and redeemable preferred stock is that callable preferred stock *may* be retired while redeemable preferred stock *must* be retired. The primary reason why a corporation issues callable or redeemable preferred stock relates to dividends. Retirement of the preferred stock enables the corporation to save its preferred stock dividend payments, thereby increasing its cash available for common stock dividends or other purposes.

The issuance of convertible, callable, or redeemable preferred stock is accounted for in the same manner as the issuance of common stock. After issuance, the conversion, call, or redemption feature is disclosed in a note to the financial statements. Accounting for the conversion of preferred to common stock is very straightforward. The par value of the converted preferred stock and the additional paid-in capital on the preferred stock are eliminated (debited) and replaced (credited) with the par value of the common stock and the additional paid-in capital on the common stock. Thus the conversion of preferred stock to common stock affects the components of contributed capital but not the total contributed capital.

To illustrate, assume that at incorporation a corporation issues 40 shares of $100 par convertible preferred stock for $110 per share and 1,000 shares of $5 par common stock for $20 per share. Each share of preferred stock is convertible into 6 shares of common stock. Later, all the shares of preferred stock are converted into common stock. The impact on contributed capital before and after the conversion of all the preferred stock is shown in the following schedule:

Before Conversion		*After Conversion*	
Contributed capital		Contributed capital	
Preferred stock, $100 par	$4,000	Common stock, $5 par	6,200[a]
Additional paid-in capital		Additional paid-in capital	
on preferred stock	400	on common stock	18,200[b]
Common stock, $5 par	5,000	Total contributed	
Additional paid-in capital		capital	$24,400
on common stock	15,000		
Total contributed capital	$24,400		

[a]$5,000 + (40 × 6 × $5)
[b]$15,000 + [$4,400 − (40 × 6 × $5)]

Note in the preceding schedule that the $24,400 total contributed capital was not affected by the conversion because the $4,400 of contributed capital for the preferred stock was replaced by the same amount for the common stock.

Accounting for the recall or redemption of preferred stock is also straightforward. The par value of the retired preferred stock and the related additional paid-in capital are eliminated (debited) and cash is reduced (credited) for the call price. Since the cash paid to retire the stock is greater than the original issuance

---

[2]Some redeemable preferred stock may be retired at any time at the *option* of the stockholder.

price, Retained Earnings is reduced (debited). (Note that a *loss* is not recorded; this procedure restricts a corporation from influencing its net income by transactions involving its own stock.) Thus the recall or redemption of preferred stock reduces both the contributed capital and retained earnings components of stockholders' equity. The income statement is not affected.

Treasury Stock

In most states a corporation may reacquire its own previously issued capital stock, after which the stock is held by the corporation in its treasury. **Treasury stock is a corporation's own capital stock that (1) has been fully paid for by stockholders, (2) has been legally issued, (3) is reacquired by the corporation, and (4) is being held by the corporation.** For instance, at the end of its 1988 fiscal year Campbell Soup Company held 6,584,035 shares of its capital stock as treasury stock.

Overview

A corporation may acquire treasury stock for various reasons:

1. to have shares available for employee purchase plans;
2. to issue stock in the conversion of convertible preferred stock;
3. to invest excess cash and help to maintain the market price of its stock;
4. to issue stock in the acquisition of other companies;
5. to reduce the number of shares outstanding and increase the earnings per share (discussed in Chapter 15);
6. to use in the issuance of a stock dividend (discussed in Chapter 15);
7. to concentrate ownership of the shares to assist in the defense against hostile takeovers.

Each of these transactions is subject to legal, governmental, and stock exchange regulations.

Treasury stock is clearly *not* an asset; a corporation cannot own itself. A corporation cannot recognize a gain or loss when reacquiring its own stock, which restricts a corporation from influencing its net income by buying and selling its own stock. Consequently, treasury stock is accounted for as a reduction of stockholders' equity as discussed next. Treasury stock generally does not have the stockholders' rights discussed earlier; it has no voting or preemptive rights, cannot participate in dividends, and has no rights at liquidation. It does participate in stock splits, however, since the par value must be reduced. When treasury stock is acquired, the amount of retained earnings available for dividends must ordinarily be restricted by the cost of the treasury stock held so that the payment of dividends will not reduce contributed capital.

Just as the original issuance of capital stock represents an increase in stockholders' equity and the number of shares outstanding, its reacquisition has an opposite effect. Stockholders' equity (and the number of shares outstanding) is reduced. It is important to understand the difference between issued capital stock and outstanding capital stock. Recall that issued capital stock is the num-

9. Describe treasury stock.

ber of shares that a corporation has issued to stockholders. **Outstanding capital stock is the number of shares that have been issued to stockholders and that are still being held by them as of a specific date.** Thus the difference between issued capital stock and *outstanding* capital stock is the number of shares being held by a corporation as *treasury* stock. Treasury stock may be reissued by a corporation for the purposes cited earlier. Upon reissuance stockholders' equity and the number of shares outstanding are again increased.

Accounting for Reacquisition

When capital stock is reacquired, the *cost* of the reacquisition[3] is recorded as an increase (debit) to an account entitled Treasury Stock and a decrease (credit) to Cash. Since treasury stock is capital stock that has already been legally issued, the par value of the stock is disregarded in recording the reacquisition. During the period between reacquisition and reissuance, the Treasury Stock account is treated as a contra-stockholders' equity account. If a balance sheet is issued during this period, the cost of the treasury stock would be deducted from the total of contributed capital and retained earnings.

10(a). Record the reacquisition of treasury stock.

To illustrate, suppose that a corporation has previously issued 5,000 shares of $10 par common stock for $12 per share. The corporation decides to reacquire 400 shares of this common stock, and it purchases these shares on the stock market at a cost of $14 per share. The journal entry to record the reacquisition of the stock is as follows:

Treasury Stock ($14 × 400)	5,600	
Cash		5,600

To record reacquisition of 400 shares of common stock as treasury stock.

Note that the treasury stock was recorded at its *cost* per share and that the stock's original par value was disregarded. Note also that the explanation indicates the number of shares reacquired. If the corporation prepared a balance sheet before reissuing these shares, the stockholders' equity would appear as follows:

Stockholders' Equity		
Contributed capital		
Common stock, $10 par, 40,000 shares authorized,		
5,000 shares issued, 4,600 shares outstanding	$50,000	
Additional paid-in capital on common stock	10,000	
Total contributed capital		$60,000
Retained earnings (assumed) [see *Note*]		35,000
Total contributed capital and retained earnings		$95,000
Less: Treasury stock (400 shares at $14 per share)		(5,600)
Total Stockholders' Equity		$89,400

Note: Retained earnings are restricted regarding dividends in the amount of $5,600, the cost of the treasury stock.

---

[3]This cost method is the most common way of accounting for treasury stock. Other accounting methods (e.g., the *par value* method) are sometimes used, but they are much less common and are not discussed in this text.

In the example, the $5,600 cost of the treasury stock is subtracted from the $95,000 total of contributed capital and retained earnings to determine the $89,400 total stockholders' equity. The numbers of shares authorized, issued, and outstanding are shown after the common stock account. The amount of retained earnings available for dividends must be restricted in the amount of the cost of the treasury stock so that the payment of dividends will not reduce contributed capital. This is typically disclosed in a note to the financial statements as shown. Restrictions of retained earnings are discussed more in Chapter 15.

Accounting for Reissuance

When treasury stock is reissued it may be reissued at a price above, below, or equal to the cost of reacquisition. Upon reissuance the Treasury Stock account is reduced (credited) for the *cost* of the shares reissued, and the difference between the proceeds received and this cost is treated as an adjustment of stockholders' equity. When the proceeds exceed the cost of the reissued treasury stock, the excess is treated as an increase (credit) in an account entitled Additional Paid-in Capital from Treasury Stock. The balance of this account is included in the contributed capital section in the balance sheet. If the proceeds are less than the cost, this Additional Paid-in Capital from Treasury Stock account is reduced by the amount of the difference. If this account does not exist or has a balance too small to absorb the difference, the remainder is recorded as a reduction in retained earnings. Since treasury stock may be reacquired at different dates and costs, companies keep records so the cost information is on hand when the stock is reissued.

To illustrate the reissuance, assume that 300 shares of the treasury stock from our earlier example are reissued at $15 per share. The journal entry to record this reissuance is as follows:

10(b). Record the reissuance of treasury stock.

Cash ($15 × 300)	4,500	
Treasury Stock ($14 × 300)		4,200
Additional Paid-in Capital from Treasury Stock		300

To record reissuance of 300 shares of treasury stock.

In this journal entry the Treasury Stock account was reduced by the $4,200 cost of the reissued shares, and the difference between the $4,500 proceeds and this cost was credited to Additional Paid-in Capital from Treasury Stock. The number of shares reissued was identified in the explanation for the journal entry. After this transaction the stockholders' equity appears as follows:

Stockholders' Equity		
Contributed capital		
Common stock, $10 par, 40,000 shares authorized,		
5,000 shares issued, 4,900 shares outstanding	$50,000	
Additional paid-in capital on common stock	10,000	
Additional paid-in capital from treasury stock	300	
Total contributed capital		$60,300
Retained earnings (assumed) [see *Note*]		35,000
Total contributed capital and retained earnings		$95,300
Less: Treasury stock (100 shares at $14 per share)		(1,400)
Total Stockholders' Equity		$93,900

Note: Retained earnings are restricted regarding dividends in the amount of $1,400, the cost of the treasury stock.

In this stockholders' equity section observe that the Additional Paid-in Capital from Treasury Stock is included in contributed capital. As long as this account has an ending balance, it is included in contributed capital even if a company has reissued all of its treasury stock. This is because stockholders have contributed more to the company than the company paid for its treasury stock and this excess is a part of contributed capital. Also observe that the number of shares outstanding has increased (to 4,900) from the previous example.

To continue, suppose that the remaining 100 shares of treasury stock were reissued at $13 per share. The journal entry to record this reissuance is as follows:

Cash ($13 × 100)	1,300	
Additional Paid-in Capital from Treasury Stock	100	
Treasury Stock ($14 × 100)		1,400

To record reissuance of treasury stock.

In this case the $1,300 proceeds were less than the $1,400 cost of the treasury stock and therefore Additional Paid-in Capital from Treasury Stock was reduced for the $100 difference.

No-Par or Preferred Treasury Stock

In the previous examples we used common stock with a par value to illustrate the accounting for the reacquisition and reissuance of treasury stock. The reacquisition and reissuance of no-par common stock with or without a stated value is accounted for in the same manner. Companies also may occasionally reacquire preferred stock as treasury stock. The same accounting principles also apply to the reacquisition and reissuance of preferred shares as treasury stock.

Summary of Treasury Stock Characteristics

For treasury stock the following items are important:

1. Treasury stock is not an asset; it is accounted for as a reduction in stockholders' equity.
2. Treasury stock has no vote, has no preemptive right, does not share in dividends, and does not participate in assets at liquidation, but does participate in stock splits.
3. Treasury stock transactions do not result in gains or losses on the income statement so that a corporation cannot influence its net income by buying and selling its own stock.
4. Treasury stock reissuances increase additional paid-in capital when the proceeds exceed the cost of the reissued shares.
5. Treasury stock reissuances decrease additional paid-in capital (and occasionally retained earnings) when the proceeds are less than the cost of the reissued shares.
6. The cost of treasury stock is deducted from the sum of contributed capital and retained earnings to determine total stockholders' equity on the balance sheet.
7. Retained earnings usually must be restricted as to dividends by the cost of treasury stock held.

Statement of Changes in Stockholders' Equity

As can be seen from the discussion in this chapter, in a single accounting period a corporation may have many transactions affecting some component of contributed capital. In addition, as we briefly introduced in Chapter 5 the retained

EXHIBIT 14-3   Statement of Changes in Stockholders' Equity

BARTH CORPORATION
Statement of Changes in Stockholders' Equity
Schedule A
For Year Ended December 31, 1991

Explanation	Common Stock Shares Issued	Common Stock $10 Par Value	Common Stock Subscribed	Additional Paid-in Capital On Common Stock	Additional Paid-in Capital From Treasury Stock	Additional Paid-in Capital From Donations	Retained Earnings	Treasury Stock
Balances, 1/1/1991	6,000	$60,000	-0-	$24,000	$2,000	-0-	$67,000	$(4,500)
Issued for cash	1,000	10,000		8,000				
Reissued treasury stock (100 shares at $17, cost $15)					200			1,500
Subscription to 500 shares at $18 per share			$5,000	4,000				
Accepted donated land for plant site						$6,000		
Net income							49,000	
Dividends							(20,000)	
Balances, 12/31/1991	7,000	$70,000	$5,000	$36,000	$2,200	$6,000	$96,000	$(3,000)

EXHIBIT 14-4
Stockholders' Equity

BARTH CORPORATION
Stockholders' Equity
December 31, 1991

Contributed capital (see Schedule A)		
Common Stock, $10 par, 30,000 shares authorized, 7,000 shares issued, 6,800 shares outstanding	$70,000	
Common stock subscribed (500 shares)	5,000	
Additional paid-in capital on common stock	36,000	
Additional paid-in capital from treasury stock	2,200	
Additional paid-in capital from donations (land)	6,000	
Total contributed capital		$119,200
Retained earnings (see Note and Schedule A)		96,000
Total contributed capital and retained earnings		$215,200
Less: Treasury stock (200 shares at a cost of $15 per share)		(3,000)
Total Stockholders' Equity		$212,200

Note: Retained earnings are restricted regarding dividends in the amount of $3,000, the cost of the treasury stock.

earnings of a corporation are increased by the net income and decreased by the dividends of the accounting period. To disclose its corporate capital activities, each corporation reports the changes in the different classes of capital stock (including the number of shares issued), in each additional paid-in capital account, in capital stock subscribed, in treasury stock, and in retained earnings. Most corporations disclose this information on a statement of changes in stockholders' equity. **A statement of changes in stockholders' equity is a supporting schedule to the stockholders' equity section of the balance sheet.**

The statement of changes in stockholders' equity of the Barth Corporation is shown in Exhibit 14-3, using assumed figures. In Exhibit 14-3 the stockholders' equity account titles are listed across the top of the schedule, and the beginning balances are listed in the respective columns. Then each of the transactions that affected the components of stockholders' equity is briefly explained in the explanation column. The shares issued and dollar amounts are included under the appropriate column. For instance, the second line indicates that the $18,000 proceeds received from issuing 1,000 shares of common stock were allocated in the amounts of $10,000 to the common stock account and $8,000 to additional paid-in capital. Note that the amounts in the treasury stock column are listed in parentheses because treasury stock is a negative component of stockholders' equity. The columns are then totaled, and the column headings and totals are included in the stockholders' equity section of the balance sheet, as shown in Exhibit 14-4. Note that the items and amounts listed in stockholders' equity in Exhibit 14-4 correspond to the columns and totals in Exhibit 14-3, as shown by the arrow.

11. Prepare a statement of changes in stockholders' equity.

Chapter Summary

Review of Learning Objectives

1. **Define capital stock, stock certificate, and stockholder.**
   Capital stock is the ownership unit in a corporation. Ownership is shown by a *stock certificate*, which is a serially numbered legal document that indicates the number of shares of capital stock owned and the par (legal) value, if any. The owners of a corporation are called *stockholders* (or shareholders).

2. **List the rights of stockholders.**
   The five rights of stockholders usually are the right to: (1) attend stockholders' meetings and vote regarding policies and actions of the corporation, (2) vote to elect the board of directors, (3) share in net income by receiving dividends, (4) purchase additional capital stock on a proportionate basis if it is issued (preemptive right), and (5) share in the distribution of the assets of the corporation if it is liquidated.

3. **State the (a) advantages and (b) disadvantages of a corporation.**
   There are five primary *advantages* of a corporation: (1) limited liability, (2) ease of transferring ownership, (3) ability to attract large amounts of ownership capital, (4) ability to attract top-quality management, and (5) continuity

of life. There are three primary *disadvantages:* (1) significant taxation, (2) government control and regulation, and (3) restricted ability to attract creditor capital.

4. Define stockholders' equity and identify its two components.

Stockholders' equity is the owners' equity of a corporation. It consists of two components: *contributed* capital, which includes the total amount of investments made by stockholders, and *retained earnings,* which includes the total lifetime corporate earnings that have been reinvested in the corporation and not distributed to stockholders as dividends.

5. Explain (a) legal capital and (b) additional paid-in capital.

Legal capital is the amount of stockholders' equity that cannot be distributed to stockholders. For most stock, legal capital is the *par value* of the stock printed on the stock certificate. Some stock may be *no-par stock,* in which case the entire proceeds received for the issued stock is the legal capital. For other no-par stock a *stated value* may be assigned, and this amount is the legal capital. *Additional paid-in capital* is the difference between the market value and the par (or stated) value of stock in each stock transaction.

6. Record capital stock issued (a) for cash, (b) in subscriptions, and (c) in noncash exchanges.

Summary journal entries for these common stock transactions are as follows:

Stock Transaction	*Illustration of Journal Entry*		
Cash sale	Cash	x	
	Common Stock (par)		x
	Additional Paid-in Capital on Common Stock		x
Installment sale	Cash	x	
	Subscriptions Receivable: Common Stock	x	
	Common Stock Subscribed (par)		x
	Additional Paid-in Capital on Common Stock		x
Noncash issuance	Patent (fair value)	x	
	Common Stock (par)		x
	Additional Paid-in Capital on Common Stock		x

7. Record (a) donated capital and (b) stock splits.

An asset acquired by a *donation* is recorded by an increase (debit) in the asset account at the fair market value and an increase (credit) to an account Additional Paid-in Capital from Donations. A stock split is a decrease in the par value per share of stock and a proportional increase in the number of shares authorized and issued. It is recorded by a memorandum entry describing the event. A donation increases contributed capital while a stock split has no effect on total stockholders' equity.

8. **Explain convertible, callable, and redeemable preferred stock.**
   Convertible preferred stock is exchangeable into common stock at the option of the stockholders. *Callable* preferred stock may be retired (recalled) by the corporation at its option. *Redeemable* preferred stock is subject to mandatory retirement at a specified maturity date and price. The conversion of preferred stock to common stock affects the components of, but not the total, contributed capital. The recall or redemption of preferred stock reduces both contributed capital and retained earnings.

9. **Describe treasury stock.**
   Treasury stock is a corporation's own stock that has been fully paid for and legally issued, is reacquired by the corporation, and is being held by the corporation. Treasury stock is not an asset; it is treated as a reduction of stockholders' equity. Treasury stock has no stockholders' rights, although it participates in stock splits. A corporation cannot record gains or losses on treasury stock transactions. The cost of treasury stock is deducted from the sum of contributed capital and retained earnings on the balance sheet. Retained earnings must be restricted as to dividends for the cost of the treasury stock.

10. **Record the (a) reacquisition and (b) reissuance of treasury stock.**
    When treasury stock is reacquired, the treasury stock is recorded at the cost of acquisition. When treasury stock is reissued, additional paid-in capital is increased when the proceeds are more than the cost, and decreased when the proceeds are less than the cost. Summary journal entries for these transactions are as follows:

Treasury Stock Transaction	*Illustration of Journal Entry*		
Reacquisition	Treasury Stock (cost)	x	
	Cash		x
Reissuance for more than cost	Cash	x	
	Treasury Stock		x
	Additional Paid-in Capital from Treasury Stock		x
Reissuance for less than cost	Cash	x	
	Additional Paid-in Capital from Treasury Stock	x	
	Treasury Stock		x

11. **Prepare a statement of changes in stockholders' equity.**
    To prepare the statement, first list each stockholders' equity account in a column across the top of the statement. Then list the beginning number of shares and beginning balance in each respective column. Next give a brief explanation of each transaction that affected stockholders' equity during the year, and list the amounts in the appropriate columns. Finally, total the columns to determine the ending balances. Include the column headings and ending balances in the stockholders' equity section of the balance sheet.

Review Problem

Coral Corporation is authorized to issue 5,000 shares of $100 par preferred stock and 20,000 shares of $5 par common stock. Its December 31, 1990, stockholders' equity accounts showed the following balances.

Common stock, $5 par	$50,000
Additional paid-in capital on common stock	30,000
Retained earnings	60,000

During 1991 it entered into the following capital stock transactions:

Date	Transaction
Jan. 3	Issued 400 shares of preferred stock for $120 per share.
Mar. 11	Issued 600 shares of common stock in exchange for land valued at $5,400.
June 24	Reacquired 500 common shares as treasury stock for $10 per share.
Sept. 6	Reissued 300 shares of treasury stock for $11 per share.
Nov. 15	Agreed to a subscription contract for 800 shares of common stock for $12 per share. The subscription contract requires a down payment of $2 per share and a $4 per share payment on December 16. The balance is due on January 16, 1992, after which the stock will be issued.
Dec. 16	Collected the $4 per share payment on the subscription contract.

REQUIRED

1. Prepare journal entries to record the preceding transactions.

2. Prepare a statement of changes in stockholders' equity (assume 1991 net income of $40,000 and dividends of $18,000).

3. Prepare the stockholders' equity section of the December 31, 1991, balance sheet.

Solution to Review Problem

REQUIREMENT 1

1991				
Jan. 3	Cash ($120 × 400)		48,000	
		Preferred Stock, $100 par ($100 × 400)		40,000
		Additional Paid-in Capital on Preferred Stock		8,000
	To record issuance of preferred stock.			
Mar. 11	Land		5,400	
		Common Stock, $5 par ($5 × 600)		3,000
		Additional Paid-in Capital on Common		
		Stock ($5,400 − $3,000)		2,400
	To record issuance of common stock for land.			

June 24	Treasury Stock	5,000		
	Cash ($10 × 500)		5,000	

To record reacquisition of 500 shares of common stock as treasury stock.

Sept. 6	Cash ($11 × 300)	3,300		
	Treasury Stock ($10 × 300)		3,000	
	Additional Paid-in Capital from Treasury Stock		300	

To record reissuance of 300 shares of treasury stock.

Nov. 15	Cash ($2 × 800)	1,600		
	Subscriptions Receivable: Common Stock			
	($10 × 800)	8,000		
	Common Stock Subscribed ($5 × 800)		4,000	
	Additional Paid-in Capital on Common Stock		5,600	

To record subscription to common stock.

Dec. 16	Cash ($4 × 800)	3,200		
	Subscriptions Receivable: Common Stock		3,200	

To record receipt of payment on stock subscription.

REQUIREMENT 2

CORAL CORPORATION
Statement of Changes in Stockholders' Equity
Schedule A
For Year Ended December 31, 1991

Explanation	Preferred Stock Shares Issued	Preferred Stock $100 Par Value	Common Stock Shares Issued	Common Stock $5 Par Value	Common Stock Subscribed	Additional Paid-in Capital On Preferred Stock	Additional Paid-in Capital On Common Stock	Additional Paid-in Capital From Treasury Stock	Retained Earnings	Treasury Stock
Balances, 12/31/1990	-0-	-0-	10,000	$50,000	-0-	-0-	$30,000	-0-	$60,000	-0-
Issued for cash	400	$40,000				$8,000				
Issued for land			600	3,000			2,400			
Reacquired 500 common shares as treasury stock										$(5,000)
Reissued 300 shares of treasury stock								$300		3,000
Subscription to 800 common shares at $12 per share					$4,000		5,600			
Net income									40,000	
Dividends									(18,000)	
Balances, 12/31/1991	400	$40,000	10,600	$53,000	$4,000	$8,000	$38,000	$300	$82,000	$(2,000)

REQUIREMENT 3

Stockholders' Equity

Contributed capital (see Schedule A):		
Preferred stock, $100 par, 5,000 shares authorized,		
400 shares issued and outstanding	$40,000	
Common stock, $5 par, 20,000 shares authorized,		
10,600 shares issued, 10,400 shares outstanding	53,000	
Common stock subscribed (800 shares)	4,000	
Additional paid-in capital on preferred stock	8,000	
Additional paid-in capital on common stock	38,000	
Additional paid-in capital from treasury stock	300	
Total contributed capital		$143,300
Retained earnings (see *Note* and Schedule A)		82,000
Total contributed capital and retained earnings		$225,300
Less: Treasury stock (200 shares at $10 per share)		(2,000)
Total Stockholders' Equity		$223,300

Note: Retained earnings are restricted regarding dividends in the amount of $2,000, the cost of the treasury stock.

Glossary

Additional Paid-in Capital on Common (or Preferred) Stock.   Difference between the legal capital and the proceeds received from the issuance of common (preferred) stock.

Articles of Incorporation.   Legal document containing information about a corporation, including the names of the incorporators, the corporate name, address, and nature of business, the types, legal value, and number of capital shares authorized for issuance. Also called a *corporate charter.*

Callable Preferred Stock.   Preferred stock that may be retired (recalled) by the corporation at its option.

Capital Stock.   Unit of ownership in a corporation. There are two classes of capital stock, preferred stock and common stock.

Common Stock.   Class of capital stock that shares in all the stockholders' rights including the preemptive right, right to vote, right to share in net income, and right to share in assets upon liquidation.

Common Stock Subscribed.   A contributed capital account used to record the par value of common stock that has been subscribed to but not yet fully paid for. A Preferred Stock Subscribed account is used in the same manner.

Contributed Capital.   Component of stockholders' equity listing the balances of the capital stock accounts and the additional paid-in capital accounts. Represents the total capital invested by stockholders.

Convertible Preferred Stock.   Preferred stock that is exchangeable into common stock at the option of the stockholders.

Corporation.   Business entity with a continuous life that is treated legally as independent and separate from its owners, called stockholders.

Legal Capital.   The amount of stockholders' equity that cannot be distributed to stockholders. Intended to protect the corporation's creditors.

Memorandum Entry.   Written description of a financial event of a company, not involving a debit or credit amount. Recorded in the general journal.

No-Par Stock.   Capital stock that does not have a par value. May have a *stated value* that is treated like par value.

Organization Chart.   Diagram that shows the lines of responsibility and authority among the officers of a corporation.

Par Value.   Monetary amount that is designated as the legal capital per share. Total legal capital of a corporation is determined by multiplying the par value per share times the number of shares issued.

Preemptive Right.   Stockholder's right to maintain a proportionate percentage of ownership of a corporation by purchasing a pro rata share of additional capital stock, should it be issued.

Preferred Stock.   Class of capital stock for which certain additional rights are given to its stockholders in exchange for giving up some of the usual stockholders' rights. Additional rights may include the right to a set dividend or to convert the preferred stock to common stock. May also be callable or redeemable.

Redeemable Preferred Stock.   Preferred stock that is subject to mandatory retirement at a specified maturity date and price.

Stated Value.   Legal capital assigned to a share of no-par stock.

Statement of Changes in Stockholders' Equity.   Schedule in which a corporation reports the changes in all of its stockholders' equity accounts and the changes in the number of capital shares issued during each accounting period.

Stock Certificate.   Serially numbered legal document that indicates the number of capital shares owned by a stockholder, the legal value per share, and other relevant information.

Stockholders.   Holders of capital stock. Owners of a corporation. Also called *shareholders*.

Stockholders' Equity.   Owners' equity section in a corporate balance sheet. Consists of two parts, contributed capital and retained earnings.

Stockholders' Ledger.   Corporate record in which are kept the name, address, and number of shares owned by each stockholder.

Stock Split.   Decrease in the par value of a corporation's capital stock and a proportional increase in the number of shares authorized and issued.

Stock Transfer Journal.   Corporate record containing the names, addresses, stock certificate numbers, and other pertinent information for the exchange of capital stock between old and new stockholders.

Subscription Contract.   Contract in which an investor (subscriber) agrees to purchase a certain number of shares of capital stock at an agreed-upon price, with the payment spread over a specified time period.

Subscriptions Receivable.   Asset account used to record the amount owed by subscribers in a subscription for capital stock.

Treasury Stock.   A corporation's own capital stock that (1) has been fully paid for by stockholders, (2) has been legally issued, (3) is reacquired by the corporation, and (4) is being held by the corporation.

Questions

QUESTION 14-1   What information is included in a corporation's articles of incorporation?

QUESTION 14-2   Define the following terms: (a) stock certificate, (b) stockholders' ledger, (c) stock transfer journal.

QUESTION 14-3   What is capital stock? How does preferred stock differ from common stock?

QUESTION 14-4   List the basic rights of a stockholder. Which right do you consider to be the most important?

QUESTION 14-5   What is stockholders' equity? Identify the two major components of stockholders' equity.

QUESTION 14-6   Identify the accounts included in contributed capital.

QUESTION 14-7   What is legal capital and why is it important?

QUESTION 14-8   How is the total legal capital of a corporation determined, assuming capital stock has (a) a par value, (b) a stated value, or (c) no-par or stated value?

QUESTION 14-9   What is the meaning of the following terms: (a) authorized capital stock, (b) issued capital stock, (c) outstanding capital stock, and (d) treasury stock? What is the difference between issued and outstanding capital stock?

QUESTION 14-10   What is a stock subscription? How are the accounts Common Stock Subscribed and Subscriptions Receivable classified in a balance sheet? Why are they so classified?

QUESTION 14-11   If capital stock is issued for an asset other than cash, what amount would you use to record the transaction?

QUESTION 14-12   How would you record the donation of an asset to a corporation on the corporation's books? Why?

QUESTION 14-13   What is convertible preferred stock? How does the conversion of preferred stock to common stock affect contributed capital?

QUESTION 14-14   What is callable preferred stock? Redeemable preferred stock? How does the recall of preferred stock affect stockholders' equity?

QUESTION 14-15   What is a stock split? How does a corporation record a stock split? What impact does a stock split have on the dollar amounts of the elements and the total of stockholders' equity?

QUESTION 14-16   What is treasury stock? Why might a corporation wish to acquire treasury stock?

QUESTION 14-17   Briefly explain the accounting for the reacquisition and reissuance of treasury stock.

QUESTION 14-18   How is treasury stock reported in a balance sheet? What note is included for retained earnings in regard to treasury stock?

QUESTION 14-19   What is a statement of changes in stockholders' equity? What changes in specific accounts are reported in this statement?

Exercises

EXERCISE 14-1   **Par Value and No-Par Issuance.**   Ryland Carpet Corporation is authorized to issue 100,000 shares of common stock. It sells 30,000 at $14 per share.

REQUIRED   Prepare the journal entires to record the sale of the common stock, given the following independent assumptions:

1. The stock has a par value of $5 per share.

2. The stock is no-par stock, but has been assigned a stated value of $4 per share.

3. The stock has no-par and no stated value.

EXERCISE 14-2   **Stock Subscription.** On July 1 the Mark Razor Corporation enters into a subscription contract with subscribers for 9,000 shares of $5 par common stock at a price of $8 per share. The contract requires a down payment of $2 per share, with the remaining balance to be paid in full on December 1. The stock will be issued to each subscriber upon full payment.

REQUIRED   Prepare journal entries to record the following:

    1. The July 1 receipt of the down payment upon the signing of the contract.

    2. The December 1 receipt of the remaining balance of $6 per share.

    3. The issuance of the stock upon full payment.

EXERCISE 14-3   **Noncash Issuance of Stock.** The Antley Company issued 200 shares of $100 par preferred stock in exchange for 5 acres of land.

REQUIRED   Prepare the journal entry to record the acquisition of the land for each of the following independent situations.

    1. The preferred stock is currently selling on the market for $150 per share. No appraisal is available on the land.

    2. The land is appraised at $29,000. The preferred stock is not actively traded on the stock market.

EXERCISE 14-4   **Various Journal Entries.** Webster Scaffolding Corporation is authorized to issue 50,000 shares of $3 par common stock. During the current period it engaged in the following transactions:

    (a) Entered into a subscription contract for 7,000 shares of common stock at $10 per share and received a 20% down payment.

    (b) Collected the remaining balance of the subscription contract and issued the common stock.

    (c) Acquired 30 acres of land by issuing 10,000 shares of common stock. The common stock was selling on the market for $14 per share. No appraisal value was available for the land.

    (d) Sold 1,000 shares of common stock at $13 per share.

REQUIRED   Prepare the journal entries to record the preceding transactions.

EXERCISE 14-5   **Various Journal Entries.** Thompson Corporation is authorized to issue 60,000 shares of no-par, $5 stated value common stock and 3,000 shares of $100 par preferred stock. It enters into the following transactions:

    (a) Sells 10,000 shares of common stock at $13 per share.

    (b) Sells 1,000 shares of preferred stock at $123 per share.

    (c) Acquires a building by paying $10,000 cash and issuing 5,000 shares of common stock and 500 shares of preferred stock. Common stock is currently selling for $15 per share; preferred stock is selling for $125 per share. No appraisal value is available for the building.

    (d) Enters into a subscription contract for 15,000 shares of common stock at $17 per share and receives a $6 per share down payment.

    (e) Collects the remaining balance of the subscription contract and issues the common stock.

REQUIRED   Prepare the journal entries to record the preceding transactions.

EXERCISE 14-6   **Donated Capital.** The community of Happy Rock donated land to the Jipem Window Corporation for the site of a new factory. The land was valued at $18,000.

REQUIRED   Prepare the journal entry to record the donation of the land on the Jipem Window Corporation's books.

EXERCISE 14-7   **Stock Split.** Bloom Company is authorized to issue 30,000 shares of $4 par common stock. To date it has issued 10,000 shares for $10 per share. On May 8, 1991, the board of directors authorized a 2 for 1 stock split with a reduction in par value to $2 per share.

REQUIRED   1. Prepare the entry to record the stock split.

2. What is the effect on the stockholders' equity accounts as a result of the stock split?

EXERCISE 14-8   **Convertible Preferred Stock.** At incorporation the Gasser Furnace Corporation issued 75 shares of $100 par preferred stock for $108 per share and 2,000 shares of $10 par common stock for $36 per share. Each share of preferred stock was convertible into three shares of the common stock. One year later, the preferred stockholders elected to exercise the conversion option on 50 shares of preferred stock.

REQUIRED   1. Prepare the contributed capital section of Gasser Furnace Corporation's balance sheet at the time of incorporation.

2. Prepare the same contributed capital section immediately after the conversion.

EXERCISE 14-9   **Callable Preferred Stock.** On January 1, 1991, the Roberts Alarm Company issued 200 shares of $100 par callable preferred stock at $116 per share. The call price is $120 per share. On January 4, 1993, all of the preferred stock was recalled.

REQUIRED   1. Prepare the journal entry to record the issuance of the preferred stock.

2. Prepare the journal entry to record the recall of the preferred stock.

EXERCISE 14-10   **Treasury Stock.** On January 1, 1991, the Amitroy Company had 10,000 shares of $5 par common stock outstanding. These shares were originally issued at a price of $12 per share. During 1991 the following stock transactions occurred:

(a) March 4: The company reacquired 2,000 shares of its common stock at a cost of $12 per share.

(b) April 23: The company sold 1,000 shares of the treasury stock for $13 per share.

(c) July 25: The company sold the remaining 1,000 shares of the treasury stock for $11 per share.

REQUIRED   Prepare the journal entries to record the preceding transactions.

EXERCISE 14-11   **Treasury Stock and Stockholders' Equity.** On January 1, 1991, the Rollo Awning Corporation had 5,000 shares of $10 par common stock outstanding. These shares were originally issued at $25 per share. During 1991 the Rollo Awning Corporation entered into the following transactions:

(a) Reacquired 2,500 shares of its common stock for $26 per share.

(b) Sold 1,250 shares of the treasury stock for $28 per share.

(c) Sold 750 shares of the treasury stock for $23 per share.

REQUIRED

1. Prepare journal entries to record the preceding stock transactions.

2. Prepare, in good form, the stockholders' equity section of the Rollo Awning Corporation's balance sheet at December 31, 1991 (assume 40,000 shares are authorized and retained earnings is $40,000).

EXERCISE 14-12   **Contributed Capital.** The following is a list of selected accounts and ending account balances taken from the accounting records of the Dean Company on December 31, 1991:

Account Title	Amount
Additional paid-in capital on preferred stock	$ 9,700
Common stock	80,000
Subscriptions receivable: preferred stock	6,750
Additional paid-in capital from treasury stock	1,000
Preferred stock	50,000
Treasury stock	6,000
Preferred stock subscribed	10,000
Retained earnings	90,000
Additional paid-in capital on common stock	30,000

Additional Information:

(a) Common stock has a $10 par value, 10,000 shares are authorized, 8,000 shares have been issued and are outstanding.

(b) Preferred stock has a $100 par value, 1,000 shares are authorized, 500 shares have been issued and are outstanding. One hundred shares have been subscribed at $120 per share.

(c) During 1991, 1,500 shares of common stock were reacquired at $12 per share; 1,000 shares were reissued at $13 per share.

REQUIRED   Prepare the contributed capital section of the December 31, 1991, balance sheet for the Dean Company.

EXERCISE 14-13   **Changes in Stockholders' Equity.** Fliter Drilling Company is authorized to issue 10,000 shares of $10 par common stock. On January 1, 1991, 6,200 shares of common stock were outstanding. These shares had been issued at $21 per share. The retained earnings account has a beginning balance of $95,000. During 1991 the following transactions took place:

Date	Transaction
Jan. 15	Issued 400 shares of common stock at $23 per share.
Mar. 29	Purchased land by issuing 2,100 shares of common stock. The stock had a current market price of $22 per share, which was used to record the transaction.
June 10	Reacquired 250 shares of common stock at $21 per share.

REQUIRED   Prepare a statement of changes in stockholders' equity for the year ended December 31, 1991 (assume net income for 1991 was $14,000 and dividends were $1,600).

EXERCISE 14-14   **Changes in Stockholders' Equity.**   Clook Corporation is authorized to issue 25,000 shares of $5 stated value common stock. At the beginning of 1991, 14,000 shares were outstanding. These shares had been issued at $35 per share. The retained earnings account has a beginning balance of $560,000. During 1991 the following transactions took place:

Date	Transaction
Jan. 14	Issued 1,000 shares of common stock for $38 per share.
Apr. 17	Reacquired 850 shares of its common stock for $39 per share.
July 25	Issued 1,200 shares of common stock in exchange for a patent. The stock was selling at $40 per share on the market, and this price was used to record the transaction.
Sept. 12	Sold 850 shares of the treasury stock for $42 per share.

REQUIRED

1. Prepare a statement of changes in stockholders' equity for the year ended December 31, 1991 (assume net income was $93,000 and dividends were $43,000).

2. Prepare the stockholders' equity section of the December 31, 1991, balance sheet for the Clook Corporation.

Problems

Part A

PROBLEM 14-1A   **Stock Transactions.**   The Cary Furniture Company is authorized to issue 100,000 shares of $7 par common stock. At the beginning of 1991, 28,000 shares of common stock were issued and outstanding. These shares had been issued at $14 per share. During 1991 the company entered into the following transactions:

Date	Transaction
Jan. 16	Issued 1,600 shares of common stock at $15 per share.
Mar. 21	Exchanged 12,000 shares of common stock for a building. The common stock was selling at $16 per share.
May 7	Reacquired 500 shares of its common stock at $17 per share.
July 3	Accepted subscriptions to 1,000 shares of common stock at $18 per share. The contract called for a 10% down payment, with the balance due December 3.
Sept. 20	Sold 500 shares of treasury stock at $19 per share.
Dec. 3	Collected the balance due on the July 3 subscriptions and issued the stock.

REQUIRED

1. Prepare the journal entries to record the preceding transactions.

2. Prepare the stockholders' equity section of the December 31, 1991, balance sheet (assume ending retained earnings for 1991 is $122,000).

PROBLEM 14-2A **Stock Transactions.** The Crane Heavy Equipment Corporation was organized and started business on January 1, 1991. It is authorized to issue 100,000 shares of $2 par common stock and 50,000 shares of $100 par preferred stock. During 1991 the Crane Heavy Equipment Corporation entered into the following stock transactions:

Date	Transaction
Jan. 1	Issued 20,000 shares of common stock at $16 per share and 5,000 shares of preferred stock at $127 per share.
Jan. 7	Issued 10,000 shares of common stock in payment of various organization costs totaling $150,000. Since the stock had not been on the market long enough to establish a price, the total amount of $150,000 was used to record the transaction.
Mar. 6	Issued 30,000 shares of common stock at $17 per share and 10,000 shares of preferred stock at $130 per share.
June 24	Purchased land by issuing 1,000 shares of common stock and 500 shares of preferred stock. Common and preferred stock were selling on the market at $16 and $129 per share, respectively, and these prices were used to record the purchase.
Sept. 11	Issued 5,000 shares of common stock at $18 per share.
Oct. 18	Issued 600 shares of preferred stock at $128 per share.

REQUIRED *1.* Prepare the journal entries to record the preceding transactions.

2. Prepare the contributed capital section of the December 31, 1991, balance sheet.

PROBLEM 14-3A **Treasury Stock.** Mulky Company reported the following data on its December 31, 1990 balance sheet:

Preferred stock, $100 par (4,000 shares authorized)	$100,000
Additional paid-in capital on preferred stock	10,000
Common stock, $10 par (30,000 shares authorized)	80,000
Additional paid-in capital on common stock	40,000
Retained earnings	112,000

During 1991 the company entered into the following transactions:

(a) Reacquired 300 shares of its own preferred stock at $112 per share.

(b) Reacquired 500 shares of its own common stock at $16 per share.

(c) Sold 200 shares of preferred treasury stock at $114 per share.

(d) Sold 300 shares of common treasury stock at $19 per share.

(e) Sold 200 shares of common treasury stock at $14 per share.

The company maintains separate treasury stock accounts and related additional paid-in capital accounts for each class of stock.

REQUIRED *1.* Prepare the journal entries required to record the preceding treasury stock transactions.

2. Assuming the company earned a net income in 1991 of $30,000 and declared and paid dividends of $10,000, prepare the stockholders' equity section of the balance sheet at December 31, 1991.

PROBLEM 14-4A   **Contributed Capital.** A partial list of the accounts and ending account balances taken from the post-closing trial balance of the Harley Transport Company on December 31, 1991, is shown as follows:

Account Title	Amount
Retained earnings	$ 30,000
Accounts payable	9,000
Common stock subscribed	30,000
Accounts receivable	125,000
Additional paid-in capital on common stock	520,000
Additional paid-in capital from treasury stock	2,500
Common stock	200,000
Subscriptions receivable: common stock	95,000
Additional paid-in capital on preferred stock	98,500
Preferred stock	400,000

Additional Information:

(a) Common stock is no-par, with a stated value of $5 per share. 80,000 shares are authorized, 40,000 shares have been issued and are outstanding, and 6,000 shares have been subscribed at a price of $19 per share.

(b) 500 shares of common stock were reacquired in 1991 at $18 per share, and reissued later at $23 per share.

(c) Preferred stock has a $100 par value; 7,000 shares are authorized, and 4,000 shares have been issued and are outstanding.

REQUIRED   Prepare the contributed capital section of the December 31, 1991, balance sheet for the Harley Transport Company.

PROBLEM 14-5A   **Changes in Stockholders' Equity.** The Fife Office Equipment Corporation is authorized to issue 20,000 shares of $10 par common stock and 1,000 shares of $100 par preferred stock. The December 31, 1990, stockholders' equity accounts showed the following balances:

Common stock, $10 par	$80,000
Additional paid-in capital on common stock	61,000
Retained earnings	38,000

During 1991 the corporation engaged in the following capital stock transactions:

Date	Transaction
Jan. 15	Issued 250 shares of preferred stock at $104 per share.
Apr. 1	Issued 3,000 shares of common stock at $22 per share.
July 5	Accepted donated land valued at $11,000 for a plant site.
Sept. 30	Reacquired 650 shares of common stock at $15 per share.
Nov. 18	Accepted subscription contract for 1,000 shares of common stock at $22 per share. The contract calls for a 25% down payment and for the balance to be paid on December 16.
Dec. 16	Received balance due on November 18 subscription contract.

| REQUIRED | Prepare a statement of changes in stockholders' equity for the year ended December 31, 1991 (assume net income was $29,000 and dividends were $8,000). |

PROBLEM 14-6A **Various Journal Entries.** The Walt-Ben Clock Corporation is authorized to issue 8,000 shares of $100 par convertible preferred stock and 60,000 shares of $10 stated value common stock. As of December 31, 1990, there were 3,500 shares of preferred stock and 30,000 shares of common stock outstanding. These shares had been issued at $132 and $22 per share for the preferred and common stock, respectively. During 1991 the following transactions took place:

Date	Transaction
Jan. 4	Issued 1,200 shares of common stock at $24 per share.
Jan. 21	Issued 800 shares of preferred stock at $136 per share.
Mar. 6	Holders of 600 shares of preferred stock converted their shares to common stock in a ratio of 6 to 1 (i.e., six common shares for every one preferred share held). The 600 shares had originally been issued at $132 per share.
June 13	Accepted donation of four acres of land for future building site. The land had a fair market value of $10,000.
Sept. 3	Issued 550 shares of common stock at $25 per share.
Dec. 31	Declared a 2 for 1 stock split on the common stock, reducing the stated value to $5 per share and increasing the authorized shares to 120,000.

REQUIRED

1. Prepare the journal entries to record the preceding transactions.

2. Prepare the contributed capital section of the December 31, 1991, balance sheet for the Walt-Ben Clock Corporation.

PROBLEM 14-7A **Stock Subscriptions.** On September 2, 1991, the Tonley Company accepts separate subscriptions for 500 shares of $100 par preferred stock at $118 per share and 2,000 shares of $10 par common stock at $32 per share. The subscription contracts call for a 25% down payment, with the balance due on December 2, 1991. Shares are to be issued to each subscriber upon full payment.

On December 2 the company received the remaining balances due on all the preferred stock and common stock. The shares were issued on this date.

REQUIRED Prepare journal entries to record all the transactions related to:

1. Preferred stock.

2. Common stock.

Problems

Part B

PROBLEM 14-1B **Stock Transactions.** The Rane Steel Fencing Corporation is authorized to issue 100,000 shares of $10 par common stock. At the beginning of 1991, 40,000 shares of common stock were issued and outstanding. These shares had been issued at $26 per share. The following are the stock transactions entered into by the corporation during 1991:

Date	Transaction
Jan. 1	Issued 3,000 shares of common stock at $28 per share.
Mar. 4	Purchased a patent by issuing 2,000 shares of common stock. Common stock was selling at $29 per share, and no value was available for the patent.
Apr. 15	Reacquired 800 shares of common stock at $27 per share.
June 3	Accepted subscription contract for 1,500 shares of common stock at $28 per share. The contract calls for a $12 per share down payment and the balance to be paid in two equal payments on September 3, 1991, and January 3, 1992, respectively.
Aug. 19	Sold 600 shares of treasury stock at $29 per share.
Sept. 3	Collected payment due on June 3 subscription.

REQUIRED

1. Prepare the journal entries to record the preceding transactions.

2. Prepare the stockholders' equity section of the December 31, 1991, balance sheet (assume retained earnings is $279,200).

PROBLEM 14-2B   **Stock Transactions.**   The Bain Publishing Company was organized and started business on January 1, 1991. It is authorized to issue 45,000 shares of $50 par preferred stock and 100,000 shares of $5 stated value common stock. During 1991, the company entered into the following stock transactions:

Date	Transaction
Jan. 1	Issued 7,000 shares of common stock in payment of miscellaneous organization costs. The stated value was used in recording the transaction.
Jan. 2	Issued 14,000 shares of common stock at $6 per share and 9,000 shares of preferred stock at $76 per share.
Jan. 9	Purchased printing equipment by issuing 13,000 shares of common stock. The equipment was valued at $78,000, and this amount was used to record the purchase.
May 24	Issued 30,000 shares of common stock at $11 per share.
July 25	Issued 16,000 shares of preferred stock at $78 per share.
Oct. 30	Acquired a building by issuing 2,000 shares of common stock and 575 shares of preferred stock. Common and preferred stock were selling on the market for $13 and $80 per share, respectively, and these prices were used to record the purchase.
Dec. 4	Issued 2,500 shares of common stock at $14 per share.

REQUIRED

1. Prepare the journal entries to record the preceding transactions.

2. Prepare the contributed capital section of the December 31, 1991, balance sheet.

PROBLEM 14-3B   **Treasury Stock.**   Langy Electronics Corporation is authorized to issue 40,000 shares of $5 par common stock and 5,000 shares of $100 par preferred stock. At the beginning of 1991 there were 14,000 shares of common stock and 3,600 shares of preferred stock issued and outstanding. These shares had been issued at $15 and $105 per share for the common and preferred stock, respectively. During 1991 the corporation entered into the following transactions:

Date	Transaction
Jan. 14	Reacquired 800 shares of its common stock at $16 per share.
Mar. 25	Reacquired 500 shares of its preferred stock at $108 per share.
May 6	Sold 300 shares of preferred treasury stock at $18 per share.
June 17	Sold 350 shares of preferred treasury stock at $111 per share.
Aug. 20	Sold 150 shares of preferred treasury stock at $107 per share.

The company maintains separate treasury stock accounts and related additional paid-in capital accounts for each class of stock.

REQUIRED
1. Prepare the journal entries to record the preceding treasury stock transactions.

2. Prepare the stockholders' equity section of the balance sheet at December 31, 1991 (assume retained earnings is $260,000).

PROBLEM 14-4B **Contributed Capital.** A partial list of the accounts and ending account balances taken from the post-closing trial balance of the Suitcom Clothing Corporation on December 31, 1991 follows.

Account Title	Amount
Common stock	$ 520,000
Subscriptions receivable: common stock	22,500
Additional paid-in capital on preferred stock	49,500
Common stock subscribed	12,000
Equipment	1,000,000
Additional paid-in capital from treasury stock	2,000
Preferred stock	630,000
Additional paid-in capital on common stock	780,000
Wages payable	145,000
Retained earnings	40,000

Additional Information:

(a) 1,000 shares of common stock were reacquired in 1991 at $24 per share. The treasury stock was later resold at $26 per share.

(b) Preferred stock has a $100 par value, 10,000 shares are authorized, and 6,300 shares have been issued and are outstanding.

(c) Common stock has a $10 par value, 100,000 shares are authorized, and 52,000 shares have been issued and are outstanding. 1,200 shares have been subscribed at $25 per share.

REQUIRED Prepare the contributed capital section of the December 31, 1991, balance sheet for the Suitcom Clothing Corporation.

PROBLEM 14-5B   **Changes in Stockholders' Equity.**   The Dought Corporation is authorized to issue 2,000 shares of $100 par preferred stock and 50,000 shares of $5 stated value common stock. As of December 31, 1990, Dought's stockholders' equity accounts showed the following balances:

Preferred stock, $100 par	$130,000
Common stock, $5 stated value	150,000
Additional paid-in capital on preferred stock	16,900
Additional paid-in capital common stock	480,000
Retained earnings	90,000

During 1991 Dought entered into the following transactions affecting stockholders' equity:

(a)   Issued 200 shares of preferred stock at $115 per share.

(b)   Reacquired 500 shares of common stock for $20 per share.

(c)   Sold 250 shares of the treasury stock for $20 per share.

(d)   Issued 1,300 shares of common stock in exchange for 10 acres of land. At this time the common stock was selling for $23 per share, and no appraisal value was available for the land.

REQUIRED   1.   Prepare a statement of changes in stockholders' equity for the year ended December 31, 1991 (assume 1991 net income was $113,000 and dividends were $23,000).

2.   Prepare the stockholders' equity section of the December 31, 1991, balance sheet for the Dought Corporation.

PROBLEM 14-6B   **Various Journal Entries.**   The GoGro Fertilizer Company is authorized to issue 80,000 shares of $10 par common stock and 10,000 shares of $100 par convertible preferred stock. Each share of preferred stock is convertible into four shares of common stock. At the beginning of 1991, 50,000 shares of common stock (issued at $27 per share) and 6,000 shares of preferred stock (issued at $109 per share) were outstanding. During 1991 the following transactions took place:

Date	Transaction
Jan. 1	Accepted donation of a building and land to open a new warehouse. The building was valued at $58,000 and the land at $9,000.
Apr. 2	Issued 400 shares of preferred stock at $112 per share.
May 15	Holders of 1,000 shares of preferred stock converted their shares to common stock. The preferred stock had been originally issued at $109 per share.
Sept. 6	Issued 1,000 shares of preferred stock at $104 per share.
Dec. 31	Declared a 2 for 1 stock split on the common stock, reducing the par value to $5 per share and increasing the authorized shares to 160,000.

REQUIRED   1.   Prepare the journal entries to record the preceding transactions.

2.   Prepare the contributed capital section of the December 31, 1991, balance sheet for the GoGro Fertilizer Company.

PROBLEM 14-7B **Various Journal Entries.** The stockholders' equity section of the January 1, 1991, balance sheet for the M-T Corporation is shown as follows:

Stockholders' Equity	
Contributed capital	
Preferred stock, $100 par, 5,000 shares authorized, 3,000	
shares issued and outstanding	$300,000
Common stock, no-par, 50,000 shares authorized, 13,000	
shares issued and outstanding	273,000
Additional paid-in capital on preferred stock	60,000
Total contributed capital	$633,000
Retained earnings	228,000
Total Stockholders' Equity	$861,000

During 1991 the corporation entered into the following transactions:

Date	Transaction
Mar. 4	Issued 400 shares of preferred stock at $122 per share.
June 18	Issued 200 shares of preferred stock and 1,000 shares of common stock in exchange for a patent. At the time of the exchange the preferred and common stock were selling at $124 and $20 per share, respectively. The total value of the stock was used to record the exchange.
July 23	Reacquired 500 shares of common stock at $22 per share.
Sept. 5	Issued 900 shares of common stock at $23 per share.
Oct. 14	Sold 450 shares of treasury stock at $23 per share.
Dec. 20	Issued 250 shares of preferred stock at $126 per share.

REQUIRED
1. Prepare the journal entries to record the preceding transactions.

2. Prepare the stockholders' equity section of the December 31, 1991, balance sheet for the M-T Corporation (assume 1991 net income was $65,000 and dividends were $22,000).

Decision Cases

DECISION CASE 14-1 **Exchange of Stock for Asset.** At the beginning of the current year the Blong Chocolate Company issued common stock in exchange for equipment. The president of the company has asked your advice. He states, "I don't know how the company should record this transaction. However, even if the company recorded the transaction at too high or too low a price, it should not make any difference. This transaction does not affect net income for the current accounting period because it does not involve a revenue or expense account. Furthermore, since it occurs during the current accounting period, the future financial statements of the company will not be affected."

REQUIRED   Prepare a written evaluation of the president's comments. Include a suggestion for recording the transaction.

DECISION CASE 14-2   **Stock Subscriptions.**   The Downs Pool Table Company is considering whether or not to issue more common stock. One of the executives of the company has been advised that the company should sell its stock on the "installment basis," in which the investor agrees to buy a certain number of shares, makes a down payment, and then agrees to pay the remainder in the future. The executive has not heard of this procedure and makes the following statement, "I don't see how this installment sale would work. It seems to me that it would result in an understatement of assets at the time of the agreement because the company would show only the cash down payment. Furthermore since the stock is issued at the time of the agreement, we would have too many shares outstanding for the amount of money paid in. And, on top of all this, what if an investor decides not to pay in full? How would we handle this and how would we get our stock back?"

REQUIRED   Prepare a written explanation of installment sales of stock, responding to each of the issues raised by the executive.

DECISION CASE 14-3   **Treasury Stock.**   At the beginning of 1991 the Zing Corporation reacquired 500 shares of its own common stock for $20 per share. During 1991 it reissued 200 of these treasury shares for $25 per share. As of December 31, 1991, the company had not yet reissued the remaining treasury stock.

The president of Zing Corporation has suggested that the 300 shares of treasury stock be shown as an asset on the corporation's December 31, 1991, balance sheet and that the $1,000 "gain" be shown in the income statement. He also feels the treasury stock should be considered as outstanding shares and should not be distinguished from common stock issued.

REQUIRED   1. Define treasury stock.

2. Why would a corporation acquire treasury stock?

3. What is common stock outstanding? What is the difference between common stock issued and common stock outstanding?

4. Identify how the president of Zing Corporation arrived at the $1,000 gain. Explain why he is wrong in suggesting that treasury stock be shown as an asset and that the gain be shown in the income statement.

5. In response to the suggestions by Zing Corporation's president, how would you recommend that the treasury stock and the gain be disclosed on the corporation's 1991 financial statements?

DECISION CASE 14-4   **Reconstruct Journal Entries.**   At the end of its first year of operations the Lynn Company had a fire that destroyed many of its accounting records. It was able to save information on the following accounts and ending account balances related to stock transactions and dividends.

| | Balance | |
Amount	Debit	Credit
Cash (from stock and dividends paid)	$65,400	
Subscriptions receivable: common stock	22,000	
Equipment	77,000	
8% preferred stock, $100 par		$70,000
Additional paid-in capital on preferred stock		7,000
Common stock subscribed (2,000 shares)		10,000
Common stock, $5 par value (7,000 shares)		35,000
Additional paid-in capital on common stock		55,000
Retained earnings		7,400

In addition, the company's management was able to recall that during the first year the following events occurred:

1. Subscription contracts were entered into for common stock at $11 per share. The stock subscriptions required no down payment. Shares were issued to each subscriber upon full payment by that subscriber.

2. One thousand shares of common stock were sold for $11 per share, and the stock was issued to stockholders.

3. Equipment with an appraised value of $77,000 was acquired by issuing 700 shares of preferred stock.

4. Net income of $20,000 was closed to Retained Earnings from Income Summary at the end of the year.

5. Dividends of $8 per share on all the preferred stock outstanding and $1 per share on all the common stock outstanding were distributed at the end of the year (the company debited Retained Earnings and credited Cash for *each* dividend).

The management has asked for your help in reassembling its accounting information related to the preceding items.

REQUIRED   On the basis of the preceding information, reconstruct all the journal entries that the company made to record the stock transactions, net income, and dividends.

DECISION CASE 14-5   **Stockholders' Equity.**   Review the financial statements and related notes of the Black & Decker Corporation that are shown in Appendix A at the end of the textbook.

REQUIRED   Answer the following questions. (Note: You do not need to make any calculations. All answers can be found in Appendix A.) Indicate on what page of the annual report you located the answer.

1. What was the total stockholders' equity on September 25, 1988? September 27, 1987?

2. How many shares of common stock are authorized? How many shares were outstanding on September 25, 1988? September 27, 1987?

3. What is the par or stated value per share of common stock? What was the total par value of the common stock outstanding on September 25, 1988?

4. What was the capital in excess of par value on September 25, 1988? September 27, 1987? What was the major reason for this change?

15

Corporations: Earnings, Retained Earnings, and Dividends

LEARNING OBJECTIVES

1. Identify the major components of net income.
2. Calculate and report income from continuing operations.
3. Allocate income taxes in an income statement.
4. Report the results of discontinued operations.
5. Describe and disclose extraordinary items.
6. Compute and disclose earnings per share.
7. State the important dates for a dividend and prepare the journal entries.
8. Define a stock dividend and explain the difference between a small and large stock dividend.
9. Identify the dividend rights of preferred stockholders.
10. Make correcting entries.
11. Describe an appropriation of retained earnings.
12. Prepare a statement of retained earnings.

he stockholders' equity section of a corporate balance sheet includes a contributed capital component and a retained earnings component. Contributed capital reports the total amount of investments made by stockholders into the corporation. The transactions involving the issuance of capital stock and the resulting impact on contributed capital and stockholders' equity were discussed in Chapter 14. In this chapter the focus is on retained earnings. Retained earnings includes the lifetime earnings of the corporation not distributed as dividends to stockholders. Corporate earnings are reported differently from the earnings of a sole proprietorship or partnership because of the effect of income taxes, discontinued operations, extraordinary items, and the disclosure of earnings per share. Dividends may be distributed to both preferred and common stockholders, after having been "declared" at an earlier date. Dividends may be paid out in cash or distributed as stock dividends. Retained earnings may also be affected by corrections of errors made in the computation of previous earnings and by appropriations. Each of these topics is discussed in this chapter.

Corporate Earnings

Net income (loss) is the amount of earnings transferred to the Retained Earnings account as a result of a corporation's income-producing activities during its accounting period. This net income is reported in the corporation's income statement for the period. In contrast to the income statements of a sole proprietorship or partnership, the income statement of a corporation has several major components. An outline of these components[1] and the items within each follows:

1. Identify the major components of net income.

1. Income from continuing operations
   (a) Operating income
   (b) Nonoperating income (other revenues and expenses)
   (c) Income tax expense related to continuing operations
2. Results of discontinued operations
   (a) Income (loss) from operations of a discontinued segment (net of income taxes)
   (b) Gain (loss) on disposal of discontinued segment (net of income taxes)
3. Extraordinary gains or losses (net of income taxes)
4. Net income (the sum of items 1, 2, and 3)
5. Earnings per share

Not every corporate income statement contains each of these components. An example of a corporate income statement that includes each component is shown in Exhibit 15-1; these components are discussed next.

---

[1]Another possible component of a corporate income statement is the "cumulative effect of a change in accounting principle." Because this element is both uncommon and complex, it is not discussed further in this textbook.

EXHIBIT 15-1   Income Statement

GLANTON CORPORATION
Income Statement
For Year Ended December 31, 1991

	Sales (net)		$100,000
	Cost of goods sold		(60,000)
	Gross profit		$ 40,000
	Operating expenses		
	Selling expenses	$16,000	
	General and administrative expenses	13,000	
	Total operating expenses		(29,000)
Income from Continuing Operations	Operating income		$ 11,000
	Other revenues and expenses		
	Gain on sale of equipment	$ 500	
	Interest revenue	700	
	Interest expense	(200)	
	Nonoperating income		1,000
	Pretax income from continuing operations		$ 12,000
	Income tax expense of continuing operations		(4,800)
	Income from continuing operations		$ 7,200
Results of Discontinued Operations	Results of discontinued operations		
	Loss from operations of discontinued		
	Segment X (net of $200 income tax credit)	$ (300)	
	Gain on sale of discontinued Segment X		
	(net of $600 income tax expense)	900	600
	Income before extraordinary loss		$ 7,800
Extraordinary Loss	Extraordinary loss from tornado (net of $800 income		
	tax credit)		(1,200)
Net Income →	Net Income		$ 6,600
Earnings per Share	Earnings per common share (see *Note A*)		
	Income from continuing operations		$ 2.61
	Results of discontinued operations		.26
	Extraordinary loss from tornado		(.52)
	Earnings per common share		$ 2.35

Note A: Preferred dividends of $1,200 were deducted from net income and income from continuing operations in computing earnings per share. The weighted average number of common shares outstanding is 2,300 shares.

Income from Continuing Operations

2. Calculate and report income from continuing operations.

This component of a corporate income statement is similar to that of any business entity. Included here is operating income, determined by subtracting cost of goods sold from net sales to obtain gross profit, and then deducting the selling expenses and general and administrative expenses. Also included is the nonoperating income (or expense), which is the sum of the other revenues and expenses. These other revenues and expenses include significant recurring items, such as interest expense and revenue, which are not part of the corporation's primary operations. They also include ordinary (as opposed to extraordinary) gains and losses (discussed later) such as those related to the sale of equipment or to the writedown of inventory to its lower of cost or market value.

The total of the operating income and the nonoperating income is entitled "income before income taxes" *if* the corporation does not report results of discontinued operations or extraordinary items (discussed later). If either of these items is reported, the total of the operating income and nonoperating income is entitled "pretax income from continuing operations." For instance, Gerber Products Company reported pretax income from continuing operations of $84,042,000 in 1988. In Exhibit 15-1 the Glanton Corporation's operating income is $11,000, its nonoperating income is $1,000, and its pretax income from continuing operations totals $12,000.

Income Taxes

The earnings (net income) of sole proprietorships and partnerships are not subject to income taxes because, for tax purposes, these business entities are not considered to be independent of their owners. The owners of sole proprietorships and partnerships are, of course, taxed as individuals on their personal earnings from the business. A corporation, on the other hand, is considered to be a legal entity that is separate and distinct from its owners. Consequently, the earnings of a corporation are subject to federal and, in many cases, state and foreign income taxes. Since the maximum federal corporate income tax rate is 34% at the time of writing, it is not unusual for a corporation's income tax rate to approach or exceed 40% of its income before income taxes. Because actual income tax computations are very complex, for simplicity we will assume an income tax rate of 40% for all discussion and homework materials.

Income taxes are imposed on a corporation's "taxable income," which consists of the sum of its pretax income from continuing operations, results of discontinued operations, and extraordinary items.[2] To determine a corporation's *total* income taxes, its taxable income is multiplied times the income tax rate. Because it is necessary to report on the income statement the income tax expense (or income tax credit in the case of a loss) related to each of these components, a separate income tax computation for each component is required.

To illustrate, assume that in 1991 the Glanton Corporation reports pretax income from continuing operations of $12,000, a pretax loss from operations of discontinued Segment X of $500, a pretax gain on the sale of discontinued Segment X of $1,500, and a pretax extraordinary loss of $2,000. It computes its total income taxes and the income taxes related to each item as shown in Exhibit 15-2 (assuming a 40% income tax rate). Note that the two items of loss reduced the income taxes in the amounts of $200 and $800, respectively. These amounts are called *income tax credits*.

Income taxes are an expense for a corporation. Because this expense is usually so large in total and the amount is determined on the basis of several items, the components are separately reported on the income statement by income tax allocation. **Income tax allocation in an income statement is the process of matching a portion of the total income tax expense against the**

---

[2]It is not necessary to understand the meaning of both *results of discontinued operations* and *extraordinary items* for computing income taxes. It may be helpful, however, to read the later sections of this chapter dealing with these items in conjunction with the remainder of this section.

EXHIBIT 15-2
Income Tax
Computation

GLANTON CORPORATION Computation of Income Taxes for 1991					
	Pretax Amount	×	Income Tax Rate	=	Income Taxes
Pretax income from continuing operations	$12,000	×	.40	=	$4,800
Pretax loss from operations of discontinued segment	(500)	×	.40	=	(200)
Gain (pretax) on sale of discontinued segment	1,500	×	.40	=	600
Extraordinary loss (pretax)	(2,000)	×	.40	=	(800)
Taxable Income and Income Taxes	$11,000	×	.40	=	$4,400

3. Allocate income taxes in an income statement.

pretax: (1) income from continuing operations, (2) income (loss) from the operations of a discontinued segment, (3) gain (loss) from the disposal of a discontinued segment, and (4) gain (loss) from an extraordinary item. The reason for this allocation is to give a fair presentation of the after-tax impact of the major components of net income.

The portion of the income tax expense for continuing operations is listed as a *separate* item on the income statement and is deducted from pretax income from continuing operations (or income before income taxes if there are no additional components of net income) to determine income from continuing operations. (If there are no additional components the resulting amount is the net income.) As shown in Exhibit 15-1 for the Glanton Corporation, the $4,800 income tax expense of continuing operations, as computed in Exhibit 15-2, is deducted from the $12,000 pretax income from continuing operations to determine the $7,200 income from continuing operations.

Any items included in the results from discontinued operations or as extraordinary items are shown *net* of income taxes. That is, for each of these items the income tax expense (or income tax credit, in the case of a loss) is deducted *directly* from each item, and only the *after-tax* amount is included in the computation of net income. The income tax expense or credit is shown parenthetically on the income statement, however. In Exhibit 15-1 the loss from operations of discontinued Segment X is shown at its after-tax amount of $300 ($500 less the income tax credit of $200 from Exhibit 15-2), the gain on sale of discontinued Segment X is listed at $900 ($1,500–$600), and the extraordinary loss at $1,200 ($2,000–$800). The income tax expense or credit related to each item, as computed in Exhibit 15-2, is shown parenthetically in Exhibit 15-1.

A corporation, like an individual, is required to *pay* income taxes several months after the end of the accounting period.[3] In recording the amount of the income taxes in the general journal, an Income Tax Expense account is increased (debited) for the *total* income taxes and Income Taxes Payable is increased (cred-

---

[3]Some corporations are required to pay income taxes four times a year but this situation is beyond the scope of this chapter. For convenience, in this section we will assume that the entire amount of corporate income taxes is paid at one time, as indicated.

ited) for a like amount.[4] The Income Taxes Payable account is classified on a corporate balance sheet as a current liability because it will be paid within 1 year. The journal entry to record the Glanton Corporation income taxes based on the computations in Exhibit 15-2 is as follows:

```
1991
Dec. 31   Income Tax Expense ..........................................  4,400
              Income Taxes Payable .....................................          4,400
          To record income taxes for the year.
```

When the corporate income taxes are paid in the next year, the Income Taxes Payable account is decreased (debited) and Cash is decreased (credited) for the amount of the payment.

Results of Discontinued Operations

Many corporations, sometimes called *conglomerates*, have several major divisions (segments) that sell different products or services. A corporation occasionally disposes of one of these segments; this is referred to as a *disposal of a discontinued segment*. The disposal is usually made because the segment is not making a sufficient profit (or is operating at a loss), or because the corporation is restructuring its activities. **A segment is a component of a corporation whose activities involve a separate major line of business and whose assets, results of operations, and activities can be clearly separated from the rest of the corporation.**[5] Examples of transactions involving the disposal of a segment include the sale by a communications company of all its radio stations or the disposal by a food distributor of its wholesale supermarket division.

The disposal of a discontinued segment is an important event for a corporation because the disposal potentially affects its future earnings potential. For this reason certain information about the discontinued segment is reported separately on the corporation's income statement. This information is reported in a section entitled **"Results of discontinued operations." Two items are included in this section:**

4. Report the results of discontinued operations.

1. **the income (or loss) from the operations of the discontinued segment for the accounting period and**

2. **the gain (or loss) from the disposal of the discontinued segment.**

For instance, Gerber Products Company disposed of its juvenile furniture operations in 1988. The company reported an operating loss of $4,245,000 from the operation of this segment and a $15,000,000 loss from the disposal of this segment in the results of discontinued operations section of its 1988 income statement.

---

[4]For simplicity, we are assuming that a corporation's "taxable income" for income tax reporting and its "pretax accounting" for financial statements are the same. This may not be the case, however, when the income tax rules differ from accounting principles. When this occurs the amount of income tax expense is not equal to the amount of income taxes payable, and the difference is recorded as "deferred income taxes." Deferred income taxes are a complex topic and are briefly discussed in Chapter 16.

[5]"Reporting the Results of Operations," *APB Opinion No. 30* (New York: AICPA, 1973), par. 13.

When the corporation operates the segment for part of the accounting period before its disposal the pretax income (loss) from these operations must be calculated. The related income taxes are deducted from this pretax income (loss), and the after-tax income (loss) from the operations of the discontinued segment is shown on the income statement. As we discussed earlier, in Exhibit 15-1 the Glanton Corporation reported a $300 loss (after an income tax credit of $200) from the operations of discontinued Segment X.

When the assets of the discontinued segment are sold a gain or loss (the difference between the selling price and the book value of the assets) is recorded. This gain or loss is computed in the same way as for an individual asset as discussed in Chapter 12. The related income taxes are deducted from this pretax gain (loss) and the after-tax gain (loss) is shown on the income statement. The after-tax gain (loss) on the disposal and the operating income (loss) of the discontinued segment are added together in the results of discontinued operations section of the income statement. For the Glanton Corporation, in Exhibit 15-1 the $900 gain (after income taxes of $600) is added to the $300 operating loss (net of an income tax credit of $200) to determine the $600 results of discontinued operations. The $600 is added to the $7,200 income from continuing operations to determine the income before extraordinary loss of $7,800.

Extraordinary Gains and Losses

5. Describe and disclose extraordinary items.

Sometimes an event or transaction occurs that causes a gain or loss for a corporation and that is defined as an extraordinary item. **An extraordinary item is an event or transaction that is both unusual in nature *and* infrequent in occurrence, taking into consideration the political, legal, and physical environment within which the corporation operates.** Both criteria (unusual and infrequent) must be met in order to classify an event or transaction as extraordinary in nature.[6]

Examples of events that are likely to be extraordinary items are an earthquake, tornado, flood, expropriation of assets by a foreign country, and a prohibition under a newly enacted law. These extraordinary items are so abnormal in regard to a corporation's current and potential earnings that the related gains or losses are reported separately on its income statement. **Extraordinary gains or losses result from extraordinary items and are shown, net of income taxes, in a separate section of the income statement.** This section is located directly below the results of discontinued operations section (or, if there is no such section, after income from continuing operations). For instance, in its income statement for 1988, Robinson Nugent, Inc. reported an extraordinary gain of $1,379,000 net of income taxes, as a result of collecting insurance proceeds in excess of the carrying value of its assets damaged in a fire in Switzerland. In Exhibit 15-1, the Glanton Corporation shows a $1,200 extraordinary loss from a tornado (after deducting an $800 income tax credit).

Most gains and losses are *not* considered to be extraordinary. For example, the writedown of receivables or inventories and the sale of property, plant, and

---

[6]Ibid, par. 20.

equipment results in ordinary gains and losses.[7] These are listed in the nonoperating income section as other revenues and expenses and are included in pretax income from continuing operations.

Earnings per Share

The owners (stockholders) of a corporation hold shares of stock as evidence of ownership. Because these shares are readily transferable, the stock of many corporations sells on organized stock markets like the New York Stock Exchange and the American Stock Exchange. In these stock exchanges, daily prices are listed for these shares of stock to help current and potential stockholders determine whether to buy, sell, or hold capital stock. Stockholders invest (or sell their investments) in a corporation for many reasons, including the likelihood of receiving future dividends or participating in any future increase in the stock market price. Both these factors are influenced by the corporation's current and future earnings.

To predict a corporation's future earnings, dividends, and stock market price, investors prepare many kinds of analyses (discussed in Chapter 19). One of the items of financial information that is used in these analyses is the corporation's *earnings per share*. Each corporation discloses its earnings per share (abbreviated as EPS) on its income statement, directly below the net income. For instance, Whirlpool Corporation reported earnings per share of $1.36 on its income statement for 1988, based on net earnings of $94.1 million and common shares of 69.3 million.

The figure for earnings per share is probably the most frequently cited information in a financial analysis of a corporation. **Earnings per share is a corporation's net income per share available to its common stockholders.** In its simplest form, earnings per share is computed by dividing the corporation's net income by the number of common shares outstanding throughout the entire year. Many corporations, however, report several components of net income and have preferred stock outstanding that has first priority to dividends (discussed later in the chapter). They also may have shares of common stock outstanding for only a portion of a year as a result of stock issuances during the year.

Earnings per share computations can be very complicated; only the basic earnings per share computations are discussed here.[8] The earnings per share computation may be expressed in the following equation. A discussion of each element of the equation follows.

$$\text{Earnings per Common Share Outstanding} = \frac{\text{Net Income} - \text{Preferred Dividends}}{\text{Weighted Average Number of Common Shares Outstanding}}$$

Net Income and Preferred Dividends. Common stockholders are considered to be the *residual* owners of the corporation. Therefore earnings per share applies *only* to common shares, and only the earnings available to common stockholders are used in the numerator of the earnings per share computation. If a corpora-

---

[7]Ibid, par. 23.

[8]For a more complete discussion, see Nikolai and Bazley, *Intermediate Accounting*, 4th ed. (Boston: PWS-KENT Publishing Co., 1988), Ch. 18.

tion has no preferred shares outstanding, the net income is used as the numerator in computing earnings per share. If there is outstanding preferred stock, however, the preferred dividends for the current period are deducted from the net income to determine the earnings available to common stockholders. To illustrate the computation of the numerator, suppose that the Glanton Corporation (from Exhibit 15-1) had preferred stock outstanding during all of 1991 and the dividends on this preferred stock amounted to $1,200. The numerator of the Glanton Corporation's 1991 earnings per share is $5,400, computed by subtracting the $1,200 preferred dividends from the $6,600 net income. These computations are summarized later in Exhibit 15-4.

Weighted Average Common Shares.   Since a corporation earns its net income over the entire year, the earnings should be related to the weighted average number of common shares outstanding during the year. If a corporation has not issued any common shares during the year, the common shares outstanding for the entire year are used as the denominator. When common shares have been issued during the year these shares are multiplied times the fraction of the year (in months) they are outstanding. The result is added to the beginning number of shares to determine the weighted average number of common shares outstanding during the year. This number is used as the denominator in the earnings per share calculation.

To illustrate, assume the Glanton Corporation had 1,800 common shares outstanding during all of 1991. On August 1, 1991, it issued an additional 1,200 common shares so that it had 3,000 common shares outstanding at the end of the year. Its weighted average number of common shares outstanding during 1991 is 2,300, determined by adding 1,800 + 500 (1,200 × 5/12). These computations are shown in Exhibit 15-3, and included as the denominator in Exhibit 15-4.

EXHIBIT 15-3
Weighted Average
Common Shares

Months Shares Are Outstanding	Shares Outstanding	×	Fraction of Year Outstanding	=	Weighted Average
January-December	1,800		$\frac{12}{12}$		1,800
August-December	1,200		$\frac{5}{12}$		500
			Total Weighted Average Common Shares		2,300

Computation and Disclosure.   The earnings per share figure is computed by dividing the earnings available to common stockholders (i.e., net income less preferred dividends) by the weighted average number of common shares outstanding. This earnings per share figure is disclosed on the income statement directly below net income. In addition, the earnings per share related to the major components of net income are also disclosed. The earnings per share for the income from continuing operations is calculated by subtracting the preferred dividends from the income from continuing operations and dividing the result by the weighted average common shares. The earnings per share figures for the results of discontinued operations and extraordinary items are computed by

6. Compute and disclose earnings per share.

dividing the respective amounts (disregarding the preferred dividends) by the weighted average common shares. The amount of the preferred dividends deducted from the numerator and the weighted average number of common shares used in the denominator should be disclosed in a note to the income statement.

The earnings per share of the Glanton Corporation for 1991 are $2.35, as calculated in Exhibit 15-4. Also shown are the earnings per share for each component of the income statement. The earnings per share figures, of course, total $2.35 and are shown on the Glanton Corporation's income statement in Exhibit 15-1. The note to the Glanton Corporation income statement discloses the preferred dividends and weighted average shares.

EXHIBIT 15-4
Earnings per Share
Computations

Item	Computations		EPS
Earnings per share	$\dfrac{\$6,600 - \$1,200}{2,300}$	=	$2.35
Components:			
Income from continuing operations	$\dfrac{\$7,200 - \$1,200}{2,300}$	=	$2.61
Results of discontinued operations	$\dfrac{\$600}{2,300}$	=	.26
Extraordinary loss from tornado	$\dfrac{\$(1,200)}{2,300}$	=	(.52)
			$2.35

Dividends

Cash dividends are the most common type of dividends distributed by a corporation. (Stock dividends are another "type" of dividend, discussed later in the chapter.) Whereas net income increases the assets of the corporation and this increase is recorded in retained earnings, the distribution of cash dividends has the opposite effect. The distribution reduces the *assets* of the corporation and is also recorded as a reduction in retained earnings. Thus the phrase, "retained earnings paid out in dividends," which is often used in discussing dividends, is somewhat misleading. Cash dividends are paid out of *cash* and retained earnings are reduced because the payment is a return of capital to the stockholders.

In order to pay dividends a company must meet legal requirements and have enough cash available. The setting of a corporation's dividend policy is the responsibility of the board of directors. The board determines the amount and timing of the dividends, considering legal requirements, compliance with contractual agreements, and the financial well-being of the corporation.

Legal requirements vary from state to state, with most states requiring a positive (credit) balance in retained earnings before dividends may be declared and limiting dividends to the amount of this credit balance. (**A deficit is the term used to describe a *negative* retained earnings balance.** This occurs when the account has a *debit* balance, the result of accumulated prior net losses or dividends in excess of prior earnings.) Usually the amount of retained earnings available for dividends is also restricted by the cost of the treasury shares held.

In considering the financial well-being of the corporation, the board of directors should consult the corporate financial personnel, including the accountants. Consideration should be given to the impact of the payment of a dividend upon cash, current assets, and working capital, the ability to finance corporate expansion projects with the remaining assets, and the effect of the dividend on the stock market price per share. Payment of dividends should be in the financial long- and short-term best interests of the corporation and its stockholders.

In this section we discuss the important dates and journal entries for cash dividends, contrast these dividends with stock dividends, and examine the impact of preferred stock characteristics upon dividends.

Cash Dividends

Withdrawals in a sole proprietorship or partnership can be made very quickly. When the owner wants to withdraw cash, a check is written to the owner from the company's checking account, a journal entry is made to record (debit) the withdrawal and reduction (credit) in cash, and the owner cashes the check for personal use. In contrast, the distribution of dividends by a corporation cannot be made so quickly. There may be many stockholders of a corporation, and therefore extensive record keeping may be required by the corporation for its dividends. As a result the dividend process is usually spread out over a period of several weeks.

Three dates are significant for a cash dividend (or any type of dividend):

1. the date of declaration,
2. the date of record, and
3. the date of payment.

For instance, on February 14, 1989, Sears Roebuck & Company declared a 50¢ per share quarterly dividend, payable on April 1, 1989, to stockholders of record on February 24, 1989.

7. State the important dates for a dividend and prepare the journal entries.

On the date of declaration, the board of directors formally declares that a dividend will be paid to stockholders of record on a specified future date, typically 4 to 6 weeks later. On the declaration date the corporation becomes legally liable to pay the future dividend, and a journal entry is made to reduce retained earnings and establish the current liability. It normally takes a corporation some time to process the dividend checks and for investors to determine whether they desire to buy or sell the stock based on the dividends. Thus a *cut-off* date is needed—the date of record. **On the date of record, only investors listed as stockholders of the corporation (the stockholders of record) can participate in the dividend.** The date of record usually occurs several weeks after the declaration date and several weeks before the payment date, as specified in the dividend provisions. On the date of record no journal entry is necessary, although the corporation may make a memorandum entry in the general journal indicating that the date of record has been reached; it also begins processing the dividend checks. **On the date of payment, the corporation mails the dividend checks.** A journal entry is also made on this date to eliminate the liability and reduce the cash.

On the date of declaration the total amount of the dividend liability to common stockholders, as well as any dividend liability to preferred stockholders (discussed later), is determined. Dividends are normally declared on a *per share basis.* That is, a set dollar amount per common share outstanding is established at the time of declaration. The total amount of the dividend liability is determined by multiplying the dividends per share times the number of common shares outstanding on the date of declaration. The Retained Earnings account is usually reduced (debited) directly. (Some companies prefer to increase (debit) a contra-retained earnings account entitled Dividends Declared; however, this procedure will not be used in this chapter.) A liability, Dividends Payable, is also established (credited).

To illustrate, assume that on November 15, 1991, a corporation declared a 60¢ per share dividend on its 4,000 outstanding common shares. These dividends are payable on December 30, 1991, to stockholders of record as of December 15, 1991. The journal entry to record the declaration of the $2,400 dividends (4,000 × $0.60) is as follows:

```
1991
Nov. 15   Retained Earnings .............................................   2,400
              Dividends Payable .........................................              2,400
          To record the declaration of cash dividends.
```

The journal entry to record the payment of the dividends is as follows:

```
1991
Dec. 30   Dividends Payable .............................................   2,400
              Cash ......................................................              2,400
          To record the payment of dividends.
```

If a Dividends Declared account had been used to record the declaration of the dividends, this account would be closed at the end of the year by a debit to Retained Earnings and a credit to the Dividends Declared account. If the accounting period had ended between the date of declaration and the date of payment, the Dividends Payable account would be classified as a current liability on the corporate balance sheet.

Stock Dividends

8. Define a stock dividend and explain the difference between a small and large stock dividend.

Occasionally a corporation may declare and distribute a stock dividend. **A stock dividend is a pro rata (proportional) distribution of additional shares of a corporation's own stock to its stockholders.** For instance, early in 1989 Tootsie Roll Industries, Inc., issued a 3% stock dividend to its common stockholders.

A stock dividend usually consists of the same class of shares; that is, a common stock dividend is declared on common stock outstanding. Stock dividends most frequently are issued out of authorized but unissued shares, although treasury stock shares may be used. Unlike cash dividends, the declaration of a stock dividend can usually be legally rescinded.

A stock dividend differs from a cash dividend in that *no* corporate assets are distributed. After a stock dividend, each stockholder holds the same percentage of ownership in the corporation as was held prior to the distribution. For instance, assume that a corporation has 10,000 common shares outstanding, one stockholder owns 2,000 shares, and the corporation issues a 10% stock dividend. After the stock dividend 11,000 shares will be outstanding (10,000 × 1.10), and the stockholder will now own 2,200 (2,000 × 1.10) shares. The stockholder owned 20% of the outstanding common stock *both prior to and after* the stock dividend. What occurs, from an accounting standpoint, is a rearrangement of stockholders' equity. Total stockholders' equity does not change, but retained earnings is decreased by the amount of the dividend and contributed capital is increased by the same amount because of the additional number of shares issued. *A stock dividend also differs from a stock split* (discussed in Chapter 14). Although both transactions increase the number of shares outstanding and neither causes any change in total stockholders' equity, a stock dividend does not affect the par value, whereas a stock split does not affect total retained earnings or total contributed capital.

Stock dividends are often viewed favorably by stockholders even though:

1. they receive no corporate assets;

2. theoretically, the total market value of their investment will not increase because the increased number of shares will be offset by a decrease in the stock market price per share due to a larger number of shares participating in the same corporate earnings; and

3. future cash dividends may be limited because retained earnings is decreased by the amount of the stock dividend, and most states set legal dividend restrictions based on positive retained earnings.

Some stockholders, however, welcome stock dividends because:

1. they see them as evidence of corporate growth and sound financial policy;

2. other investors may also look favorably on the stock dividends and purchase the stock, causing the stock market price *not* to decrease proportionally;

3. the corporation may continue to pay the same cash dividend per share, in which case stockholders will receive higher total dividends; and

4. the market price may decrease to a lower trading range, making the stock more attractive to additional investors.

In accounting for a stock dividend by a corporation, a distinction is made between a *small* and a *large* stock dividend and generally accepted accounting principles have been established for each of them. **A small stock dividend is less than or equal to 20% of the previously outstanding common shares.**[9] It is argued that for a small stock dividend the size of the dividend does not significantly affect the stock market price of the outstanding shares. Thus the "value" of the stock issued in the stock dividend is considered to be the current stock market price, and therefore the stock dividend is recorded at this price. For a small stock dividend, retained earnings is reduced and contributed capital is increased by an amount equal to the current market value on the date of declaration for the additional shares of the stock dividend.

A large stock dividend is greater than 20% of the previously outstanding common shares. The size of a large stock dividend is likely to cause a substantial decrease in the stock market price of the outstanding shares. Therefore the current market price is *not* appropriate for recording such a stock dividend. The *par* (or *stated*) value of the stock is used instead. For a large stock dividend, retained earnings is reduced and contributed capital is increased by the total par value for the additional shares of the stock dividend.

The following diagram shows the effect of a small and large stock dividend on the various items of stockholder equity.

---

[9]Generally accepted accounting principles state that a small stock dividend is less than 20% or 25%. For simplicity, we will use 20%.

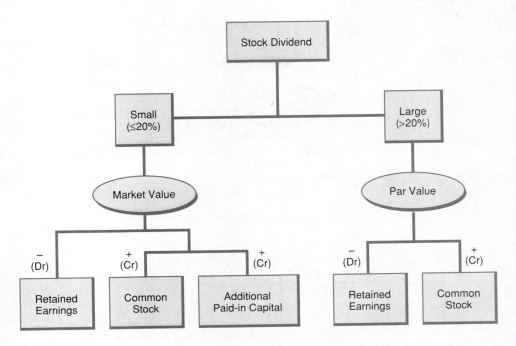

To illustrate the accounting for the two sizes of stock dividends, assume that a corporation has the following stockholders' equity prior to a stock dividend:

Stockholders' Equity

Contributed capital
  Common stock, $10 par, 40,000 shares authorized,
    10,000 shares issued and outstanding $100,000
  Additional paid-in capital on common stock 70,000
    Total contributed capital $170,000
Retained earnings 80,000
    Total Stockholders' Equity $250,000

Small Stock Dividend.   Assume that the corporation declares and issues a 10% stock dividend. On the date of declaration the stock is selling for $19 per share. The 1,000 share (10,000 shares × 10%) stock dividend is recorded at the current market value of $19,000 as follows:

Date of Declaration

Retained Earnings (1,000 × $19) 19,000
   Common Stock To Be Distributed (1,000 × $10) 10,000
   Additional Paid-in Capital from Stock Dividend 9,000

To record declaration of small stock dividend.

Date of Issuance

Common Stock To Be Distributed 10,000
   Common Stock, $10 par 10,000

To record issuance of stock for stock dividend.

The resulting stockholders' equity is as follows:

Stockholders' Equity

Contributed capital

Common stock, $10 par, 40,000 shares authorized,
11,000 shares issued and outstanding $110,000

Additional paid-in capital on common stock 70,000

Additional paid-in capital from stock dividend 9,000

    Total contributed capital $189,000

Retained earnings 61,000

    Total Stockholders' Equity $250,000

On the date of declaration, since the common stock will not be issued until later, a temporary contributed capital account, Common Stock To Be Distributed, is used to record the par value of the stock. If a balance sheet is prepared after the declaration but prior to the issuance of the stock dividend, the Common Stock To Be Distributed account would be listed in stockholders' equity as a component of contributed capital. The account is *not* a liability like the dividend payable account for cash dividends because no assets will be distributed in a stock dividend. It is a temporary stockholders' equity item showing the legal capital of the stock to be issued. As illustrated, it is eliminated when the stock is issued. The Additional Paid-in Capital from Stock Dividend is also added to the other additional paid-in capital accounts in the contributed capital section. Note that there is no difference in the $250,000 total stockholders' equity prior to and after the stock dividend. Only the components are changed, with retained earnings decreasing by $19,000 and contributed capital increasing by the same amount (and the issued shares increasing to 11,000).

Large Stock Dividend. Assume, *instead*, that the corporation declares and issues a 30% stock dividend when the stock is selling for $19 per share. In this case the market value is disregarded, and the par value of $30,000 for the 3,000 shares (10,000 shares × 30% × $10) is used to record the stock dividend. The declaration and issuance of the large stock dividend are recorded as follows:

Date of Declaration

Retained Earnings (3,000 × $10) 30,000

    Common Stock To Be Distributed 30,000

To record declaration of large stock dividend.

Date of Issuance

Common Stock To Be Distributed 30,000

    Common Stock, $10 par 30,000

To record issuance of stock for stock dividend.

The resulting stockholders' equity is as follows:

Stockholders' Equity	
Contributed capital	
Common stock, $10 par, 40,000 shares authorized,	
13,000 shares issued and outstanding	$130,000
Additional paid-in capital on common stock	70,000
Total contributed capital	$200,000
Retained earnings	50,000
Total Stockholders' Equity	$250,000

Again there is no difference between the $250,000 total stockholders' equity prior to and after the stock dividend. Only the components are changed, with retained earnings decreasing by $30,000 and contributed capital increasing by the same amount (and the number of issued shares increasing by 3,000 to 13,000).

Dividends on Preferred Stock

As we indicated in the previous chapter some investors consider certain stockholder rights to be more important than others. To appeal to these investors, preferred stock may be issued. The rights of preferred stockholders are included on the stock certificate. Three of these rights are important for dividends. They include: (1) a preference to dividends, (2) accumulation of dividends, and (3) participation in excess dividends. Preferred stock may be issued with one or a combination of these rights. Each of these rights is discussed next.

9. Identify the dividend rights of preferred stockholders.

Preference as to Dividends. Holders of preferred stock have a preference as to dividends. **A dividend preference is a right of preferred stockholders to receive a dividend before a dividend can be paid to common stockholders.** Preferred stock is usually issued with a par or stated value and the dividends are expressed as a percentage of this value. For instance, assume that a corporation has outstanding 1,000 shares of 10%, $50 par preferred stock. The corporation must pay $5 per share ($50 par × 10%), which totals $5,000 ($5 × 1,000 shares), as dividends to preferred stockholders before it can pay *any* dividends to common stockholders.

Such a preference to dividends does *not* guarantee that a preferred dividend will be paid in any given year since the board of directors can decide not to pay any dividends. To protect preferred stockholders further, a provision may be included on the preferred stock certificate that requires the accumulation of dividends.

Cumulative Preferred Stock. Stockholders are not legally entitled to share in dividends unless these dividends have been declared by the corporate board of directors. If dividends are not declared in a given year, a holder of noncumulative preferred stock will never be paid that dividend. For this reason noncumulative preferred stock is seldom issued, because investors consider this feature to be a distinct disadvantage.

Most preferred stock is cumulative. **Cumulative preferred stock is preferred stock that must be paid all dividends of the current and past periods**

before any dividends can be paid to common stockholders. Any dividends not declared on cumulative preferred stock in a given period become dividends in arrears. Dividends in arrears accumulate from period to period. The dividends in arrears are *not* a liability to the corporation because no liability exists until the dividend declaration. Any dividends in arrears, however, are very important to investors and other interested parties and should be disclosed in a note to the financial statements.

To illustrate dividends in arrears, assume that a corporation has 2,000 shares of 8%, $100 par cumulative preferred stock outstanding. Each share of stock is entitled to an $8 annual dividend (computed by multiplying the 8% by the $100 par value). If dividends are not declared in 1989 and 1990, preferred stockholders would be entitled to dividends in arrears of $16,000 (2,000 × $8) at the end of 1989 and $32,000 (2,000 × $8 × 2 years) at the end of 1990. At the end of 1991 dividends of $48,000 (for 3 years) would have to be paid to preferred stockholders before any dividend payments could be made to common stockholders.

Participating Preferred Stock.   **Participating preferred stock is preferred stock that shares with the common stock in any *extra* dividends on a proportional basis.** Extra dividends are paid only after preferred stockholders have been paid their stated dividend rate (on the *preferred* par value) and common stockholders have been paid at a rate (on the *common* par value) equal to that paid on the preferred stock. For example, if a corporation has 9%, $50 par participating preferred stock and $10 par common stock outstanding, it must first pay preferred stockholders $4.50 per share (9% times the $50 par) and common stockholders 90¢ per share (9% times the $10 par). If the total dividend to be paid then exceeds the amount needed to meet these dividend requirements, an extra dividend arises. Participating preferred stock shares with common stock in this extra dividend on a proportional basis. Participating preferred stock is rare. Corporations generally agree that preferred stockholders receive too many rights if they are given first preferences to dividends and are also allowed to participate in all dividends.

Accounting for Preferred Dividends.   Cash dividends on preferred stock are usually declared and paid at the same time as the cash dividends on common stock. When both classes of stock are outstanding, separate dividends payable accounts should be used for each class of stock. For instance, if a corporation declared and paid preferred and common dividends of $2,000 and $3,000 respectively, the following journal entries would be made:

Date of Declaration

Retained Earnings	5,000	
Dividends Payable: Preferred		2,000
Dividends Payable: Common		3,000

To record the declaration of cash dividends.

Date of Payment

Dividends Payable: Preferred	2,000	
Dividends Payable: Common	3,000	
Cash		5,000

To record the payment of dividends.

Prior Period Adjustments: Corrections of Errors

Corporations sometimes make changes in their accounting practices that require an adjustment of their accounting records of prior years. Some of these adjustments are called prior period adjustments. They include certain changes in accounting principles (e.g., a change from LIFO to FIFO for inventory) or a correction of an error made in a prior period. We discuss only error corrections here.

A corporation may make an error in the revenue or expense accounts (with a related error in the asset or liability accounts) of one accounting period that is not discovered until a later period. These errors may result from an oversight, the incorrect use of existing facts, or a mistake in mathematics. Such errors are corrected with correcting entries.

Correcting Entries

10. Make correcting entries.

The correction of an error made in a previous period is recorded as a prior period adjustment to the beginning retained earnings balance in the accounting period when the error is discovered. That is, the asset or liability account balance in error at the beginning of the period is corrected (debited or credited) and the offsetting debit or credit is recorded directly in the Retained Earnings account. This is because the error in the prior year's revenue or expense accounts was closed to retained earnings and the error does not affect the revenues or expenses of the current period. Any related impact on the prior year's income taxes should also be recorded in a similar way.

To illustrate, suppose that in 1991 the Slusher Corporation discovered that it inadvertently recorded too much depreciation expense in the amount of $5,000 in 1990. This error understated 1990 income before income taxes by $5,000 (which was closed to Retained Earnings). Thus retained earnings must be increased by $5,000 in the correcting entry. Assuming a 40% income tax rate, the 1990 income tax expense (previously closed to retained earnings) was understated, and therefore the corporation also owes an additional $2,000 of income taxes for 1990. The journal entries that are made *in 1991* to record the corrections to the accounts are as follows:

Accumulated Depreciation	5,000	
Retained Earnings		5,000

To record the correction of the overstatement
of the 1990 depreciation.

Retained Earnings	2,000	
Income Taxes Payable		2,000

To record the additional income taxes resulting from the correction
of the 1990 depreciation overstatement.

The debit to Accumulated Depreciation in the first entry reduces the account balance for the overstatement recorded in 1990. The credit to Retained Earnings increases the account to correct it for the understatement of 1990 income before income taxes (remember that 1990 net income has been closed to retained earnings). The second entry records the effect of the error correction on prior income taxes. The debit to Retained Earnings reduces the account for the additional income tax expense related to 1990 income. The credit to Income Taxes Payable shows the additional taxes owed for 1990 but not yet paid.

Alternatively, if the depreciation had been understated in 1990, the correcting entry in 1991 would reduce (debit) Retained Earnings and increase (credit) Accumulated Depreciation. The correction for taxes would involve an increase (credit) in Retained Earnings (to correct for the prior overstatement of income tax expense) and an increase (debit) in a current asset account entitled Income Tax Refund Receivable for the overpayment of 1990 income taxes.

Financial Statement Disclosure

Prior period adjustments (e.g., error corrections) are reported, in the year of the correction, as an adjustment to the corporation's beginning retained earnings in its statement of retained earnings (discussed at the end of this chapter). The prior period adjustment, net of income taxes (the income taxes are shown in parentheses), is added to (or subtracted from) the beginning retained earnings balance to determine the *adjusted* beginning retained earnings. The correction of the overstatement of depreciation in our example is shown as a prior period adjustment in Exhibit 15-6 at the end of the chapter.

Appropriations of Retained Earnings

When setting dividend policy the board of directors of a corporation should consider both legal requirements and sound financial practice. Stockholders sometimes look at only the legal requirements, and as the Retained Earnings account balance increases, they may expect to receive more dividends. The assets of the corporation, however, must be used for a variety of corporate activities, including financing ongoing operations and long-term expansion projects, meeting principal and interest payments on bonds (discussed in Chapter 16), and making dividend payments.

11. Describe an appropriation of retained earnings.

To indicate that a part of retained earnings is unavailable for dividends, a corporation may appropriate (restrict) retained earnings. **An appropriation of retained earnings is the restriction of an amount of retained earnings by the board of directors so that this amount is not available for the declaration of dividends.** It is important to note that such a policy does *not* directly restrict the use of any assets; it merely requires that the corporation not distribute any assets that would reduce the restricted retained earnings. A corporation may still declare and pay dividends, reducing unappropriated retained earnings.

Reasons for Appropriations

A board of directors may appropriate retained earnings (1) to meet *legal* requirements, (2) to meet *contractual* restrictions, or (3) because of *discretionary* actions. Corporations must follow the laws of the state in which they are incorporated. States usually require restrictions of retained earnings when a corporation reacquires its own stock as treasury stock, the appropriation of retained earnings being an amount equal to the cost of the treasury shares. The argument for this appropriation is that the corporation, by acquiring treasury stock, reduces the amount of invested (permanent) capital. By restricting retained earnings for an equal amount, permanent capital is protected.

Retained earnings may also be restricted as a result of a contractual agreement. Such an agreement is often made when a corporation issues long-term bonds. To provide some assurance that excessive dividends will not be distributed which would endanger bondholders' claims, the bond provisions may require the periodic appropriation of a certain amount of retained earnings.

Finally, retained earnings may be appropriated as a result of management discretion. This type of restriction may be related to planning for future expansion. That is, a company may be planning to build a new plant or to add to existing facilities. It may be desirable to finance this activity through internally generated funds (i.e., funds that the corporation already holds or will receive from operations in the near future) rather than seek external funding from creditors or through the issuance of more capital stock. To indicate that these internal funds are being held as assets within the corporation for this purpose and are unavailable for dividends, the board of directors may appropriate a portion of retained earnings.

Accounting for Appropriations

Appropriations of retained earnings generally are accounted for by reporting the restrictions in a note to the financial statements.[10] When a note is used, a clear description of the legal, contractual, or discretionary provisions and the amount of the restriction is necessary. To illustrate, assume a corporation has a $200,000 retained earnings balance when it acquires treasury stock for $40,000. The retained earnings balance and the note to the financial statements for the treasury stock would appear as follows:

Retained earnings (see *Note A*) **$200,000**

Note A: Retained earnings are restricted regarding dividends in the amount of $40,000, the cost of the treasury stock.

If the appropriation is canceled, the note is removed from the financial statements.

Statement of Retained Earnings

The statement of retained earnings is an important part of the financial statements. This schedule reports the impact of the net income, dividends, and prior period adjustments for the accounting period on retained earnings. To show the impact of these items, the format in Exhibit 15-5 is used.

---

[10]Occasionally a company may make a journal entry for an appropriation, debiting Retained Earnings and crediting Appropriated Retained Earnings. This procedure is not discussed further in this textbook.

EXHIBIT 15-5
Format for Statement
of Retained Earnings

Statement of Retained Earnings
For Year Ended December 31, 1991

Retained earnings, January 1, 1991
Plus (minus): Prior period adjustments (net of income tax effect)
Adjusted retained earnings, January 1, 1991
Plus (minus): Net income (net loss)
Minus: Cash dividends (identified for each class of stock, including per share amounts)
　　　　Stock dividends
Retained earnings, December 31, 1991

**12. Prepare a
statement of retained
earnings.**

The retained earnings statement may be prepared as a separate schedule to the balance sheet, as a schedule directly beneath the income statement, or as is common, included in the statement of changes in stockholders' equity discussed in Chapter 14. Any restrictions (appropriations) of retained earnings would be disclosed by means of a note to the financial statements.

Exhibit 15-6 provides an illustration of a retained earnings statement (all amounts are assumed).

EXHIBIT 15-6　Statement of Retained Earnings

SLUSHER CORPORATION
Statement of Retained Earnings
For Year Ended December 31, 1991

Retained earnings, January 1, 1991		$78,000
Prior Period Adjustment — Add: Correction of understatement in 1990 net income due to overstatement of depreciation (net of $2,000 income tax expense)		3,000
Adjusted retained earnings, January 1, 1991		$ 81,000
Net Income → Add: Net income		39,000
		$120,000
Dividends — Less: Cash dividend on common stock ($4 per share)	$9,300	
Cash dividend on preferred stock ($6 per share)	7,200	
Stock dividend on common stock	2,500	(19,000)
Retained earnings, December 31, 1991		$101,000

Chapter Summary

Review of Learning Objectives

1. **Identify the major components of net income.**
The major components of net income are (1) income from continuing operations, which includes operating income, nonoperating income, and the relat-

ed income tax expense; (2) results of discontinued operations, which includes the income (loss) from operations of a discontinued segment and the gain (loss) on disposal of the segment (both shown net of income taxes), and (3) extraordinary gains or losses (net of income taxes). Earnings per share is also reported for each component.

2. **Calculate and report income from continuing operations.**
Income from continuing operations is reported as the first component of net income. It includes operating income (revenues less cost of goods sold, selling expenses, and general and administrative expenses), nonoperating income (other revenues and expenses), and the related income tax expense.

3. **Allocate income taxes in an income statement.**
Income taxes are allocated in an income statement by matching a portion of the total income tax expense against pretax income from continuing operations, the two components of results of discontinued operations, and extraordinary gains and losses. The portion of income tax expense for continuing operations is listed as a separate item in that section. Any items included in the results of discontinued operations or as extraordinary items are shown net of income taxes.

4. **Report the results of discontinued operations.**
For a discontinued segment of a business, two items are included in the *results of discontinued operations* section of the income statement. This section is included directly after income from continuing operations. The items included are: (1) the income (loss) from the operations of the discontinued segment for the accounting period, and (2) the gain (loss) from the disposal of the discontinued segment. Both items are shown net of income taxes.

5. **Describe and disclose extraordinary items.**
An extraordinary item is an *unusual and infrequent* event or transaction, resulting in a gain or loss. Extraordinary gains or losses are disclosed, net of income taxes, in a separate section of the income statement directly after any results of discontinued operations.

6. **Compute and disclose earnings per share.**
Earnings per share is computed by dividing net income (less any preferred dividends) by the weighted average number of common shares outstanding during the accounting period. The earnings per share is reported on the income statement directly below net income. In addition, the earnings per share related to each of the major components of net income is also disclosed.

7. **State the important dates for a dividend and prepare the journal entries.**
There are three important dates for a dividend. The date of *declaration* is the date on which the board of directors formally declares a dividend. The date of *record* is the date on which an investor must be listed as a stockholder of record to participate in the dividend. The date of *payment* is the date on which the corporation mails the dividend checks. For a cash dividend, the declaration of a dividend is recorded by a debit to Retained Earnings and a credit to Dividends Payable. The payment of the dividend is recorded by a debit to Dividends Payable and a credit to Cash.

8. **Define a stock dividend and explain the difference between a small and large stock dividend.**

A stock dividend is a pro rata (proportional) distribution of a corporation's own stock to its stockholders. A *small* stock dividend is less than or equal to 20% of the previously outstanding common shares. A *large* stock dividend is greater than 20% of the previously outstanding common shares. A small stock dividend is recorded at the current stock market price, while a large stock dividend is recorded at the par value of the stock.

9. **Identify the dividend rights of preferred stockholders.**

There are three possible dividend rights of preferred stockholders. A dividend *preference* is the right of preferred stockholders to receive a dividend before dividends can be paid on common stock. *Cumulative* preferred stock must be paid all dividends of the current and past periods (dividends in arrears) before dividends can be paid on common stock. *Participating* preferred stock shares in any extra dividends with common stock on a proportional basis.

10. **Make correcting entries.**

Correcting entries are journal entries made in the current period to correct an error of a prior period. A correcting entry involves a debit (or credit) to the asset or liability account that is in error, and an offsetting credit (or debit) to the Retained Earnings account. Any related impact on the prior year's income taxes is also corrected in a similar way.

11. **Describe an appropriation of retained earnings.**

An appropriation of retained earnings is the restriction of an amount of retained earnings so that this amount is not available for dividends. An appropriation generally is accounted for by reporting the restriction in a note to the financial statements.

12. **Prepare a statement of retained earnings.**

A retained earnings statement starts with the beginning retained earnings balance. Then any prior period adjustments (error corrections), net of taxes, are added or subtracted to determine the adjusted beginning retained earnings balance. To this balance net income is added and then the amounts of all the types of dividends are subtracted to determine the ending retained earnings balance.

Review Problem

On January 1, 1991, the Fairview Corporation had 1,200 shares of common stock outstanding and a retained earnings balance of $50,800. On that date the company issued 300 shares of 8%, $100 par preferred stock. On March 1, 1991, the company issued an additional 960 shares of common stock. During 1991 the company discovered it had not recorded bad debt expense of $3,000 in 1990. The company properly recorded the correction (including the effect on prior income taxes). At the end of 1991 the company records showed the following alphabetical list of items. The company is subject to a 40% income tax rate.

Cost of goods sold	$52,000
Dividends declared and paid: Common stock	2,160
Dividends declared and paid: Preferred stock	2,400
General and administrative expenses	8,000
Interest expense	1,400
Interest revenue	400
Sales	90,000
Selling expenses	14,000

REQUIRED   Prepare for 1991 (1) an income statement and (2) a statement of retained earnings.

Solution to Review Problem

REQUIREMENT 1

FAIRVIEW CORPORATION
Income Statement
For Year Ended December 31, 1991

Sales		$90,000
Cost of goods sold		(52,000)
Gross profit		$38,000
Operating expenses		
Selling expenses	$14,000	
General and administrative expenses	8,000	
Total operating expenses		(22,000)
Operating income		$16,000
Other revenues and expenses		
Interest revenue	$ 400	
Interest expense	(1,400)	
Nonoperating loss		(1,000)
Income before income taxes		$15,000
Income tax expense (40%)		(6,000)
Net Income		$ 9,000
Earnings per common share (see *Note A*)		$ 3.30

Note A: Preferred dividends of $2,400 were deducted from net income in computing earnings per share. The weighted average number of common shares outstanding is 2,000 shares [(1,200 × 12/12) + (960 × 10/12)].

REQUIREMENT 2

FAIRVIEW CORPORATION
Statement of Retained Earnings
For Year Ended December 31, 1991

Retained earnings, January 1, 1991		$50,800
Less: Correction of overstatement of 1990 net income due to		
understatement of bad debt expense (net of $1,200 income		
tax credit)		(1,800)
Adjusted retained earnings, January 1, 1991		$49,000
Add: Net income		9,000
		$58,000
Less: Cash dividends on common stock ($1 per share)	$2,160	
Cash dividends on preferred stock ($8 per share)	2,400	(4,560)
Retained earnings, December 31, 1991		$53,440

Glossary

Appropriation of Retained Earnings. Restriction by board of directors of amount of retained earnings so that this amount is not available for the declaration of dividends. Retained earnings is appropriated for legal requirements, contractual restrictions, or discretionary actions. Reported in a note to the financial statements.

Common Stock To Be Distributed. Account used on the date of declaration to record the total par value of common stock to be issued in a stock dividend. Temporary contributed capital account.

Cumulative Preferred Stock. Preferred stock that must be paid all preferred dividends from current and past periods (dividends in arrears) before dividends can be paid to common stockholders.

Date of Declaration. Date on which a dividend is declared by the corporate board of directors. Dividend becomes legal liability of corporation at this time.

Date of Payment. Date on which dividends are paid to stockholders.

Date of Record. Date on which an investor must be listed as a stockholder of the corporation in order to participate in the payment of the corporation's dividends.

Deficit. Term used for a negative (debit) balance in the Retained Earnings account.

Dividend. Cash or capital stock distributed to stockholders as a return on their investment in a corporation.

Dividends in Arrears. Dividends on cumulative preferred stock that have not been declared.

Dividends Payable. Current liability account used to record the amount of cash dividends owed on the date of declaration of the dividends.

Dividend Preference. Right of preferred stockholders to receive a dividend before a dividend is paid to common stockholders.

Earnings per Share. Net income per share available to common stockholders. Computed by dividing net income (less preferred dividends) by weighted average number of common shares outstanding. Disclosed on the income statement below net income.

Extraordinary Gain or Loss. Gain or loss resulting from extraordinary event or transaction that is both *unusual* in nature and *infrequent* in occurrence. Shown on the income statement as a separate item (net of income taxes) below results of discontinued operations.

Income from Continuing Operations. Component of income statement showing the net amount of the operating income, nonoperating income, and the income tax expense of operations.

Income Tax Allocation. Process of matching the total corporate income tax expense in an income statement against pretax income from continuing operations, the results of discontinued operations, and extraordinary gains or losses.

Income Taxes Payable. Current liability showing the total amount of income taxes owed to federal, state, and foreign governments.

Income Tax Expense. Account showing total amount of corporate income tax expense for the year. Allocated to components of net income.

Income Tax Expense of Continuing Operations. The portion of total income tax expense that is matched against pretax income from continuing operations.

Large Stock Dividend. Stock dividend greater than 20% of the previously outstanding common shares. Recorded at par (or stated) value of the stock.

Participating Preferred Stock. Preferred stock that participates with common stock in any extra dividends (dividends paid in excess of the preferred rate on preferred and common stock) on a proportional basis.

Prior Period Adjustment. Adjustment of the beginning retained earnings balance for the correction of an error of a prior period. Shown, net of income taxes, on statement of retained earnings.

Results of Discontinued Operations. Component of income statement showing the after-tax income (loss) from the operations of a discontinued segment and the after-tax gain (loss) from the disposal of the discontinued segment.

Retained Earnings. Account used to accumulate the total lifetime earnings of a corporation that have not been distributed to stockholders as dividends. Component of stockholders' equity on the balance sheet of a corporation.

Small Stock Dividend. Stock dividend of less than or equal to 20% of the previously outstanding common shares. Recorded at current market value of the stock.

Statement of Retained Earnings. Schedule that reports the impact on retained earnings of the net income, dividends, and prior period adjustments for the accounting period.

Stock Dividend. Dividend in which a pro rata (proportional) distribution of additional shares of a corporation's own common stock is made to its stockholders.

Questions

QUESTION 15-1 What are the major components and the items in each component on a corporate income statement?

QUESTION 15-2 What is income tax allocation in an income statement? Why is it necessary?

QUESTION 15-3 What is a segment of a corporation? What information for a discontinued segment is disclosed on an income statement and where is it disclosed?

QUESTION 15-4 What is an extraordinary item? Where and how are gains or losses from extraordinary items disclosed on an income statement?

QUESTION 15-5 How is earnings per common share outstanding computed? How is it disclosed on a corporate income statement?

QUESTION 15-6 What is the weighted average number of common shares outstanding for computing earnings per share and how is it determined?

QUESTION 15-7 What are the three dates of importance in regard to dividends? What journal entry is made on each date?

QUESTION 15-8 What is a stock dividend? Distinguish between a large and a small stock dividend and explain what amounts are used to record the declaration of each dividend.

QUESTION 15-9 How are a stock dividend and a stock split alike? How are they different?

QUESTION 15-10 Define the following terms regarding preferred stock: (a) dividend preference, (b) cumulative, (c) participating.

QUESTION 15-11 What does it mean when preferred dividends are "in arrears"? What journal entry is made to record dividends in arrears?

QUESTION 15-12 How does the declaration and payment of cash dividends on preferred stock differ from that for cash dividends on common stock?

QUESTION 15-13 What two journal entries must be made in the current period to record a correction of an error made in a prior period?

QUESTION 15-14   How is a correction of an error made in a prior period reported in the current period's financial statements?

QUESTION 15-15   What is an appropriation of retained earnings? For what reasons would retained earnings be appropriated?

QUESTION 15-16   How is an appropriation of retained earnings accounted for?

QUESTION 15-17   What is the format used for the statement of retained earnings?

Exercises

EXERCISE 15-1   **Income Statement.**   The records of the Gliten Dental Instruments Corporation for the year ended December 31, 1991, show the following items:

Operating income	$16,000
Nonoperating income	3,000

Additional Information:

(a) The weighted average number of common shares outstanding for the year is 6,000 shares.

(b) The company is subject to a 40% income tax rate.

(c) There is no preferred stock outstanding and the company has no discontinued segments or extraordinary items.

REQUIRED   Prepare the lower portion of the income statement of the Gliten Dental Instruments Corporation for 1991, starting with operating income. Be sure to include earnings per share.

EXERCISE 15-2   **Income Statement.**   The records of the Crowney Trailer Corporation for the year ended December 31, 1991, show the following items:

Pretax income from continuing operations	$74,000
Loss from operations of discontinued	
Segment Z (pretax)	(2,000)
Gain on sale of discontinued Segment Z (pretax)	2,200
Extraordinary loss from flood (pretax)	(30,000)

Additional Information:

(a) The corporation had 10,000 shares of common stock outstanding during all of 1991.

(b) There is no preferred stock outstanding.

(c) The corporation is subject to a 40% income tax rate.

REQUIRED   Prepare the lower portion of the income statement of the Crowney Trailer Corporation for 1991, starting with pretax income from continuing operations. Be sure to include earnings per share.

EXERCISE 15-3   **Income Statement.**   The following information is available for the Teresa Textile Corporation for the year ended December 31, 1991: (1) pretax income from continuing operations, $29,000; (2) loss from operations of discontinued Segment B (pretax), $6,500; (3) extraordinary gain (pretax), $4,200; and (4) loss on sale of discontinued Segment B (pretax), $5,000.

The corporation is subject to a 40% tax rate. It had no preferred stock outstanding and 6,000 shares of common stock outstanding during all of 1991.

REQUIRED Prepare the lower portion of the Teresa Textile Corporation's 1991 income statement, starting with pretax income from continuing operations. Be sure to include earnings per share.

EXERCISE 15-4 **Weighted Average Shares.** At the beginning of the current year the Stepher Saw Corporation had 3,000 shares of $10 par common stock outstanding. During the year it engaged in the following transactions related to its common stock:

Date	Transaction
Apr. 1	Issued 800 shares of stock
July 1	Issued 460 shares of stock

REQUIRED Determine the weighted average number of common shares outstanding for computing the earnings per share.

EXERCISE 15-5 **Computation of Earnings per Share.** The Neese Corporation reported net income in 1991 of $35,000. The company paid dividends for the current year on 200 shares of 7%, $100 par preferred stock and had 12,000 shares of common stock outstanding for the entire year.

REQUIRED Compute the earnings per share of the Neese Corporation for 1991.

EXERCISE 15-6 **Disclosure of Earnings per Share.** The Rondale Supply Corporation reported net income in 1991 of $26,000, consisting of income from continuing operations of $24,400, results of discontinued operations (net of tax) of $4,000, and an extraordinary *loss* (net of tax) of $2,400. The corporation paid dividends for the current year on 100 shares of 8%, $100 par preferred stock and had 10,000 shares of common stock outstanding for the entire year.

REQUIRED Compute the earnings per share of the Rondale Supply Corporation for 1991 and show how it would be reported on the income statement.

EXERCISE 15-7 **Earnings per Share.** At the beginning of 1991 the Davels Corporation had 1,000 shares of 9%, $100 par preferred stock and 16,500 shares of common stock outstanding. On June 1 Davels issued 3,000 additional shares of common stock. On December 31, 1991, Davels reported net income of $37,105 and paid the dividends for the current year on preferred stock.

REQUIRED Compute the earnings per share of the Davels Corporation for 1991.

EXERCISE 15-8 **Cash Dividends.** On October 1, 1991, the Sewel Corporation declared a cash dividend on its 1,600 outstanding shares of 9%, $100 par preferred stock. These dividends are payable on December 2, 1991, to stockholders of record as of November 15, 1991. On November 1, 1991, the company declared an 80¢ per share cash dividend on its 9,000 outstanding shares of common stock. These dividends are payable on December 16, 1991, to stockholders of record as of November 30, 1991.

REQUIRED Prepare the journal entries for the Sewel Corporation to record the declaration and the payment of each of the previously mentioned dividends.

EXERCISE 15-9 **Stock Dividend.** The stockholders' equity section of the January 1, 1991, balance sheet for the Turner Tennis Corporation follows:

Contributed capital	
Common stock, $10 par, 60,000 shares authorized,	
30,000 shares issued and outstanding	$300,000
Additional paid-in capital on common stock	100,000
Total contributed capital	$400,000
Retained earnings	325,000
Total Stockholders' Equity	$725,000

On June 3, 1991, the corporation declared a 15% stock dividend to be distributed on July 15, 1991. The market value of the stock on June 3 was $16 per share. No additional shares of common stock were issued between January 1 and June 3, 1991.

REQUIRED
1. Prepare the journal entry at the date of declaration.

2. Prepare the journal entry at the date of issuance.

3. Prepare the stockholders' equity section of the July 15, 1991 balance sheet for the Turner Tennis Corporation after the issuance of the stock dividend.

EXERCISE 15-10 **Stock Dividend.** The stockholders' equity section of the January 1, 1991, balance sheet for the Rutler Lock Corporation follows:

Contributed capital	
Common stock, $5 par, 80,000 shares authorized,	
40,000 shares issued and outstanding	$200,000
Additional paid-in capital on common stock	370,000
Total contributed capital	$570,000
Retained earnings	320,000
Total Stockholders' Equity	$890,000

On June 3, 1991, the corporation declared a 40% stock dividend to be distributed on July 1, 1991. On the date of declaration the stock had a current market value of $22 per share. No additional shares of common stock were issued between January 1 and June 3, 1991.

REQUIRED
1. Prepare the journal entries to record the declaration and issuance of the stock dividend.

2. Prepare the stockholders' equity section of the July 1, 1991 balance sheet for the Rutler Lock Corporation after the issuance of the stock dividend.

EXERCISE 15-11 **Dividends in Arrears.** The Ithaca Corporation has 4,000 shares of 10%, $100 par cumulative preferred stock outstanding. Dividends on this stock have *not* been declared for the past 4 years. This year the corporation wishes to pay dividends to its common stockholders.

REQUIRED   What amount of preferred dividends must be paid before the Ithaca Corporation can pay dividends on common stock? Show your calculations.

EXERCISE 15-12   **Prior Period Adjustment.**   In 1991 the Closel Corporation discovered that it had not recorded $7,000 of depreciation expense in 1990. The corporation is subject to a 40% income tax rate.

REQUIRED   1. Prepare the journal entries for the Closel Corporation in 1991 to correct its accounting records.

2. Where would the correction be disclosed in the corporation's financial statements for 1991?

EXERCISE 15-13   **Retained Earnings Statement.**   The Donner Tape Corporation began 1991 with a retained earnings balance of $82,000. During the year the following events occurred:

(a) The corporation earned net income of $69,000.

(b) Current dividends totaling $8,000 on common and $4,000 on preferred stock were declared and paid.

(c) The corporation discovered that the depreciation expense had been overstated by $6,000 in 1990. The correcting entry increased retained earnings by $3,600 after related income taxes of $2,400.

REQUIRED   Prepare a statement of retained earnings for the Donner Tape Corporation for the year ended December 31, 1991.

EXERCISE 15-14   **Appropriations.**   On January 1, 1991, the Bloner Corporation had a retained earnings balance of $125,000. On June 1, 1991, the corporation acquired treasury stock at a cost of $31,000. The treasury stock is still being held at the end of 1991.

REQUIRED   1. Prepare the note for the appropriation to accompany the December 31, 1991, balance sheet.

2. During 1992 all of the treasury stock was reissued and the appropriation of retained earnings was canceled. How would the cancellation be handled?

Problems

Part A

PROBLEM 15-1A   **Income Statement.**   The records of the Stringer Cable Corporation show the following items on December 31, 1991:

Cost of goods sold	$42,000
Extraordinary loss from tornado (pretax)	1,500
General and administrative expenses	8,000
Interest revenue	700
Interest expense	200
Gain on sale of discontinued Segment R (pretax)	1,000
Loss from operations of discontinued Segment R (pretax)	3,000
Selling expenses	13,000
Sales	78,000

Additional Information:

(a) There were 2,000 shares of common stock outstanding on January 1, 1991. On July 1, 1991, the corporation issued 4,000 common shares.

(b) The corporation paid dividends for the current year on 200 shares of 8%, $100 par preferred stock outstanding. No dividends were paid to common stockholders.

(c) The corporation is subject to a 40% income tax rate.

REQUIRED   Prepare the income statement of the Stringer Cable Corporation for 1991.

PROBLEM 15-2A   **Income Statement, Lower Portion.** On January 1, 1991, the Eshroe Plastics Corporation had 2,200 shares of common stock outstanding and a retained earnings balance of $60,200. On June 1, 1991, another 2,400 shares of common stock were issued. On December 31, 1991, the company's records showed the following items:

Nonoperating income	$ 4,500
Loss from operations of discontinued Segment Y (pretax)	2,000
Operating income	19,000
Gain on sale of discontinued Segment Y (pretax)	2,500
Extraordinary loss from flood (pretax)	3,500
Dividends declared and paid: Preferred stock	3,000
Dividends declared and paid: Common stock	2,880

During 1991 it was discovered that the depreciation expense for 1990 had been overstated by $3,000 (pretax). Correcting entries were made for the error and related income taxes.

REQUIRED   Assuming the Eshroe Plastics Corporation is subject to a 40% income tax rate, prepare:

1. The lower portion of the income statement for 1991 starting with operating income.

2. A statement of retained earnings for 1991.

PROBLEM 15-3A   **Dividends.** The stockholders' equity accounts of the Quiser Corporation on January 1, 1991, follow:

Preferred stock, 9%, $100 par (5,000 shares authorized)	$100,000
Common stock, $10 par (80,000 shares authorized)	200,000
Additional paid-in capital on preferred stock	12,000
Additional paid-in capital on common stock	37,000
Retained earnings	172,000
	$521,000

The company entered into the following transactions during 1991:

Date	Transaction
Jan. 1	Declared the annual cash dividend on the outstanding preferred stock and a 95¢ per share dividend on the outstanding common stock. These dividends are to be paid on February 15, 1991.
Feb. 15	Paid the cash dividend declared on January 1.

May 15	Declared a 15% stock dividend on the common stock outstanding on this date. The stock is to be distributed on June 28. The common stock is currently selling for $18 per share.
June 28	Issued the stock dividend declared on May 15.
July 1	Split the common stock 2 for 1, reducing the par value to $5 per share and increasing the authorized shares to 160,000.
Aug. 5	Declared a 35% stock dividend on the common stock outstanding on this date. The stock is to be distributed on September 25, 1991.
Sept. 25	Issued the stock dividend declared on August 5.
Dec. 31	Discovered that the 1990 depreciation expense had been understated by $2,500.

REQUIRED

1. Prepare the journal entries of the Quiser Corporation to record the preceding transactions (the corporation is subject to a 40% income tax rate).

2. Prepare the stockholders' equity section of the December 31, 1991, balance sheet for the Quiser Corporation (assume that 1991 net income was $101,000).

PROBLEM 15-4A **Retained Earnings.** The records of the Warner Import-Export Corporation show the following items as of December 31, 1991:

Income from continuing operations	$39,000
Loss from operations of discontinued Segment P (net of tax)	3,000
Gain on sale of discontinued Segment P (net of tax)	6,500
Extraordinary loss from expropriation of assets (net of tax)	2,500
Dividends declared and paid: Preferred stock	3,800
Dividends declared and paid: Common stock	7,900
Prior period adjustment: Overstatement of 1990 depreciation (net of $2,160 income tax)	3,240
Additional paid-in capital: Treasury stock	10,000
Stock dividend declared and issued	20,000
Treasury stock	12,000

REQUIRED Prepare a statement of retained earnings for the Warner Import-Export Corporation for the year ended December 31, 1991 (assume that the beginning retained earnings balance for 1991 was $66,100).

PROBLEM 15-5A **Dividends.** The Gunther Corporation has outstanding 1,000 shares of 10%, $100 par preferred stock and 40,000 shares of $10 par common stock. The company has $70,000 to distribute in dividends.

REQUIRED

1. Assuming that the preferred stock is cumulative and that dividends have been paid each year, (a) compute the amount of the preferred and common dividends and (b) prepare the journal entries to record the declaration and payment of the dividends.

2. Assuming, instead, that the preferred stock is cumulative and that dividends are 2 years in arrears, (a) compute the amount of the preferred and common dividends and (b) prepare the journal entries to record the declaration and payment of the dividends.

PROBLEM 15-6A **Income and Retained Earnings Statements.** The Grotwohl Pre-Fab Building Corporation lists the following items on December 31, 1991:

Cost of goods sold	$142,000
Extraordinary loss from earthquake (net of tax)	4,000
General and administrative expenses	11,000

Interest revenue	1,750
Interest expense	650
Gain on sale of discontinued Segment L (net of tax)	1,200
Loss from operations of discontinued Segment L (net of tax)	400
Selling expenses	24,900
Sales (net)	267,000

Additional Information:

(a) There were 18,000 shares of common stock outstanding on January 1, 1991. On September 1, 1991, the company issued 6,000 more common shares.

(b) The company paid current cash dividends on 850 shares of 8%, $100 par preferred stock outstanding and an 80¢ per share dividend on the common stock outstanding on December 31, 1991.

(c) During 1991 a mathematical error was discovered in the computation of a gain on the sale of machinery recorded in 1990. The 1990 gain was understated by $900 (net of tax). The correcting entry was made for the error and related income taxes.

REQUIRED
1. Prepare the income statement of the Grotwohl Pre-Fab Building Corporation for the year ended December 31, 1991. Include earnings per share information (assume a 40% income tax rate).

2. Prepare a statement of retained earnings for the year ended December 31, 1991 (assume the beginning retained earnings for 1991 was $75,000).

Problems

Part B

PROBLEM 15-1B   **Income Statement.** The records of the Lundgren Motors Corporation show the following items on December 31, 1991:

Cost of goods sold	$ 65,000
Extraordinary loss from flood (pretax)	2,250
General and administrative expenses	12,000
Interest revenue	700
Interest expense	300
Loss on sale of discontinued Segment Q (pretax)	250
Income from operations of discontinued Segment Q (pretax)	800
Selling expenses	23,000
Sales	119,400

Additional Information:

(a) There were 3,000 shares of common stock outstanding on January 1, 1991. On July 1, 1991, the company issued 6,000 common shares.

(b) The company paid dividends for the current year on 500 shares of 7%, $100 par preferred stock outstanding. No dividends were paid on common stock.

REQUIRED   Prepare the income statement of the Lundgren Motors Corporation for 1991. Assume a 40% income tax rate.

PROBLEM 15-2B **Income Statement, Lower Portion.** On January 1, 1991, the Conler Outdoor Lighting Corporation had 3,600 shares of common stock outstanding and a retained earnings balance of $76,400. On April 1, 1991, another 1,600 shares of common stock were issued. During 1991 it was discovered that the depreciation expense for 1990 had been understated by $1,500 (pretax). Correcting entries were made for the error and related income taxes. On December 31, 1991, the company's records showed the following items:

Dividends declared and paid: Common stock	$ 5,000
Nonoperating income	3,500
Income from operations of discontinued Segment C (pretax)	1,950
Operating income	39,000
Loss on sale of discontinued Segment C (pretax)	2,750
Extraordinary loss from earthquake (pretax)	4,500
Dividends declared and paid: Preferred stock	4,200

REQUIRED Assuming the Conler Outdoor Lighting Corporation is subject to a 40% income tax rate, prepare:

1. The lower portion of the income statement for 1991 starting with operating income.

2. A statement of retained earnings for 1991.

PROBLEM 15-3B **Dividends.** The stockholders' equity accounts of the Kahler Corporation on January 1, 1991, follow:

Preferred stock, 8%, $100 par (8,000 shares authorized)	$ 300,000
Common stock, $10 par (200,000 shares authorized)	450,000
Additional paid-in capital on preferred stock	28,000
Additional paid-in capital on common stock	255,000
Retained earnings	400,000

The company entered into the following transactions during 1991:

Date	Transaction
Jan. 1	Declared the annual cash dividend on the outstanding preferred stock and an 80¢ per share dividend on the outstanding common stock, to be paid on January 30, 1991.
Jan. 30	Paid the cash dividend declared on January 1.
Mar. 1	Declared a 30% stock dividend on the common stock outstanding on this date. The stock is to be distributed on April 15, 1991.
Apr. 15	Issued the stock dividend declared on March 1.
May 15	Split the common stock 2 for 1, reducing the par value to $5 per share and increasing the authorized shares to 400,000.
June 3	Declared a 10% stock dividend on the common stock outstanding on this date. The stock is to be distributed on July 1, 1991. The common stock is currently selling for $15 per share.
July 1	Issued the stock dividend declared on June 1.
Dec. 31	Discovered that an error was made in calculating the 1990 depreciation expense. This error understated 1990 net income by $3,000 (pretax).

REQUIRED

1. Prepare the journal entries of the Kahler Corporation to record the preceding transactions (the corporation is subject to a 40% income tax rate).

2. Prepare the stockholders' equity section of the December 31, 1991, balance sheet for the Kahler Corporation (assume that the 1991 net income was $320,000).

PROBLEM 15-4B   **Retained Earnings.**   The records of the Borg Chemicals Corporation show the following items as of December 31, 1991.

Income from continuing operations	$73,000
Loss from operations of discontinued Segment B (net of tax)	5,500
Gain on sale of discontinued Segment B (net of tax)	11,000
Extraordinary loss from explosion (net of tax)	5,000
Dividends declared and paid: Preferred stock	4,800
Dividends declared and paid: Common stock	9,200
Accounts receivable	26,000
Additional paid-in capital from treasury stock	41,000
Stock dividend declared and issued	12,000
Prior period adjustment: Understatement of 1990 depreciation (net of $1,480 income tax credit)	2,220

REQUIRED   Prepare a statement of retained earnings for the Borg Chemicals Corporation for the year ended December 31, 1991 (assume that the beginning retained earnings balance for 1991 was $95,500).

PROBLEM 15-5B   **Dividends.**   The stockholders' equity of the Landers Corporation is as follows:

Contributed capital	
Preferred stock, 9%, $100 par	$ 300,000
Common stock, $10 par	900,000
Additional paid-in capital on preferred stock	24,000
Additional paid-in capital on common stock	360,000
Total contributed capital	$1,584,000
Retained earnings	716,000
Total Stockholders' Equity	$2,300,000

The company wishes to distribute $150,000 in dividends this year.

REQUIRED

1. Assuming that the preferred stock is noncumulative and that no dividends have been paid for 3 years, (a) compute the amount of dividends to be distributed to preferred and common stock and (b) prepare the journal entries to record the declaration and payment of the dividends.

2. Assuming, instead, that the preferred stock is cumulative and that dividends are 2 years in arrears, (a) compute the amount of dividends to be distributed to preferred and common stock and (b) prepare the journal entries to record the declaration and payment of the dividends.

Decision Cases

DECISION CASE 15-1   **Dividends.**   The Small Corporation shows the following items of stockholders' equity:

Common stock, $10 par (40,000 shares authorized, 10,000 shares issued and outstanding)	$100,000
Additional paid-in capital on common stock	80,000
Retained earnings	160,000

The company's common stock is currently selling for $30 per share on the stock market. The board of directors is considering the following *alternative* actions in regard to "dividends":

(a) Payment of a $3 per share cash dividend.

(b) Distribution of a 15% stock dividend.

(c) Distribution of a 40% stock dividend.

(d) Distribution of a 2 for 1 stock split, reducing the par value to $5 per share.

The board has always paid a cash dividend and is not very familiar with stock dividends and stock splits. It is also unsure of the effect of each of these alternatives upon stockholders' equity and has asked for your advice.

REQUIRED
1. Explain what is meant by a stock dividend and a stock split, including which, if any, is really a "dividend."

2. Explain what is likely to happen to the market price per share of common stock as a result of a stock dividend or stock split.

3. For each *alternative*, determine the amount of each item of stockholders' equity for the Small Corporation immediately *after* the cash payment or the issuance of the common stock. Show your calculations for each amount that changed.

DECISION CASE 15-2 **Misclassifications.** The bookkeeper for the Cortez Company prepared the following income statement and retained earnings statement for the year ended December 31, 1991:

CORTEZ COMPANY
December 31, 1991
Expense and Profits Statement

Sales (net)		$220,000
Less: Selling expenses		(27,200)
Net sales		$192,800
Add: Interest revenue		1,300
Add: Gain on sale of equipment		4,900
Gross sales revenues		$199,000
Less: Costs of operations		
Cost of goods sold	$139,100	
Correction of overstatement in last year's income due to error (net of $2,200 income tax credit)	3,300	
Dividend costs ($0.50 per share for 8,300 common shares outstanding the entire year)	4,150	
Extraordinary loss due to earthquake (net of $2,400 income tax credit)	3,600	(150,150)
Taxable revenues		$ 48,850
Less: Income tax on continuing income		(14,800)
Net income		$34,050
Miscellaneous deductions:		
Loss from operations of discounted Segment L (net of $1,200 income tax credit)	$ 1,800	
Administrative expenses	21,800	(23,600)
Net Revenues		$ 10,450

CORTEZ COMPANY
Retained Revenues Statement
For Year Ended December 31, 1991

Beginning retained earnings	$65,000
Add: Gain on sale of Segment L (net of $1,800 income tax expense)	2,700
Recalculated retained earnings	$67,700
Add: Net revenues	10,450
	$78,150
Less: Interest expense	(1,100)
Ending retained earnings	$77,050

You determine that the preceding account *balances* are correct but, in certain instances, have been incorrectly titled or classified.

REQUIRED

1. Review both statements and indicate where each incorrectly classified item should be classified. Also indicate any other errors you find.

2. Prepare a corrected 1991 income statement and retained earnings statement for the Cortez Company.

DECISION CASE 15-3 **Various Income Statements Items.** Baker Company reports a retained earnings balance of $54,600 at the beginning of 1991. The following information is available pertaining to 1991:

1. The company declared and paid a 62-cent cash dividend per share on the 5,000 shares of common stock that were outstanding the entire year.

2. The company found and corrected a pretax $4,000 understatement of 1990 depreciation expense due to a mathematical error.

3. The company incurred a pretax $10,000 loss as a result of an earthquake, which is unusual and infrequent for the area.

4. The company sold division P in May. From January through May division P had incurred a pretax loss from operations of $6,000. A pretax gain of $5,500 was recognized on the sale of division P.

5. The company reported sales (net) of $99,600, cost of goods sold of $57,900, and operating expenses of $18,200.

The company is unclear about how to report the various preceding items in its financial statements and has asked for your advice.

REQUIRED Assuming that all "pretax" items are subject to a 40% income tax rate:

1. Prepare the Baker Company's income statement for 1991.

2. Prepare an accompanying retained earnings statement for 1991.

DECISION CASE 15-4 **Earnings and Retained Earnings.** Review the financial statements and related notes of the Black & Decker Corporation that are shown in Appendix A at the end of the textbook.

REQUIRED Answer the following questions. (Note: You do not need to make any calculations. All answers can be found in Appendix A.) Indicate on what page of the annual report you located the answer.

1. What were the net earnings for the year ended September 25, 1988? September 27, 1987? On what was the earnings growth based?

2. What were the earnings per share for the year ended September 25, 1988? September 27, 1987?

3. What was the income tax expense for the year ended September 25, 1988? What was the reason for and amount of the extraordinary item for the year ended September 28, 1986?

4. What were the (a) total dividends paid to shareholders and (b) the dividends per share for the year ended September 25, 1988? September 28, 1986?

5. In addition to dividends, what item(s) caused retained earnings to change for the year ended September 25, 1988?

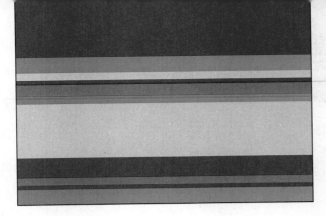

PART FOUR

FINANCIAL STATEMENTS: ADDITIONAL ASPECTS OF FINANCIAL REPORTING

16

Noncurrent Liabilities

LEARNING OBJECTIVES

1. Describe a bond.

2. Explain why bonds may be issued.

3. Account for bonds sold at par.

4. Explain why bonds are sold at a discount or premium.

5. Describe the straight-line method of accounting for a (a) discount or (b) premium.

6. Explain the concepts of present value and future value.

7. Compute present values and future values.

8. Describe the effective interest method of amortizing a (a) discount or (b) premium.

9. Record the retirement of bonds (a) at maturity or (b) prior to maturity.

10. Explain (a) leases, (b) mortgages, (c) deferred income taxes, and (d) pensions.

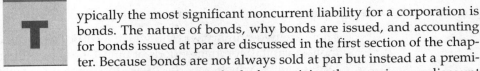

ypically the most significant noncurrent liability for a corporation is bonds. The nature of bonds, why bonds are issued, and accounting for bonds issued at par are discussed in the first section of the chapter. Because bonds are not always sold at par but instead at a premium or discount, the straight-line method of amortizing the premium or discount is explained next. The concepts of present and future value are then discussed. An understanding of these concepts is essential when evaluating decisions involving amounts of money received or paid at different time periods. In addition, the concept of present value is used in several areas of financial accounting, one of which, bonds payable (the selling price and the effective interest method of amortizing a premium or a discount), is discussed in this chapter. Four other noncurrent liabilities, leases, pensions, mortgages, and deferred income taxes, are briefly discussed.

Bonds Payable

1. Describe a bond.

Companies frequently borrow money. When such a borrowing is for a large amount of money for a long period of time, it usually involves the issuance of bonds by the company. **A bond is a type of note in which a company agrees to pay the holder the face value at the maturity date and to pay interest periodically at a specified rate on the face value.** Thus the company that issues the bonds is borrowing money from the holder of the bonds, who is the lender. **The face value (also called the par value) is the amount of money that the issuer promises to pay at maturity.** It is the same concept as the principal of a note. **The maturity date is the date on which the issuer of the bond agrees to pay the face value to the holder.** The issuer also agrees to pay interest each period. **The contract rate is the rate at which the issuer of the bond pays interest each period until maturity.** The contract rate is also called the *stated* or *nominal* rate. This information is printed on a bond certificate, which is held by the owner of the bond. **A bond certificate is a serially numbered legal document that specifies the face value, the annual interest rate, the maturity date, and other characteristics of the bond issue.** Since bond issues are usually intended to borrow large amounts of money, corporations (and government entities) are the most common issuers of bonds. Each bond issue usually has a bond indenture. **A bond indenture is a document that defines the rights of the bondholders.** Corporate bonds are nearly always issued so that each bond has a face value of $1,000. The entire bond issue may be sold to one purchaser or to numerous individual purchasers. Thus a $1 million dollar bond issue will consist of 1,000 bonds, each with a $1,000 face value. In addition, interest is usually paid twice each year (semiannually), although the interest rate is expressed in annual terms. Therefore the annual rate must be halved to obtain the interest rate per semiannual period. For example, a 10%, $1,000 bond will pay interest of $100 (10% × $1,000) per year in two installments of $50 (10% × $\frac{1}{2}$ × $1,000) every 6 months. A face value of $1,000 per bond and semiannual interest payments will be assumed throughout this chapter.

Why Bonds Are Issued

There are two primary ways in which a corporation can obtain large amounts of money (capital) for long periods of time. One is by selling common stock (or preferred stock), which was discussed in Chapter 14. Selling common stock provides the company with permanent capital since there is no obligation to repay the stockholders. In addition, there is no legal obligation to make periodic dividend payments although many companies choose to do so. Because the stockholders are owners, selling additional stock spreads ownership, voting rights, and the earnings over more shares. The second way of obtaining long-term capital is to issue bonds, which obligates the company to repay the amount borrowed and also to pay interest each period. The payment of interest is a legal obligation, and if the company issuing the bonds (the borrower) fails to pay the interest on the principal, the holder of the bonds (the lender) can take legal action to enforce payment, which may cause the borrower to declare bankruptcy. The bondholders are creditors of the company, do not become owners, and have no voting rights.

2. Explain why bonds may be issued.

The primary reason why the management of a company may decide to issue bonds instead of common stock is that the earnings available to the common stockholders can be increased through leverage. **Leverage is the use of borrowing by a company to increase the return to common stockholders.** It is also called *trading on equity*. If a corporation can borrow money by issuing bonds and using the money to invest in a project that provides greater income than the interest that must be paid on the bonds, the company and its stockholders will be better off (they will earn a higher income). One measure of the return to common stockholders is earnings per share, which was discussed in Chapter 15. When a company successfully uses leverage, earnings per share will increase.

To illustrate this concept, assume that a corporation currently has 10,000 shares of common stock outstanding, income before income taxes of $100,000, and an income tax rate of 40%. The management has decided to expand its operations by building a factory for $200,000. The factory will provide additional pre-tax income of $40,000 per year. The company is considering selling 5,000 additional shares for $40 each or issuing bonds at par with a face value of $200,000 and a 10% interest rate. The effects of the two alternatives are illustrated in Exhibit 16-1.

The interest expense on the bonds is an expense on the income statement, and therefore income before income taxes is reduced when bonds are used for financing. Income tax expense is also reduced so that the net effect of the bond

EXHIBIT 16-1
Use of Leverage

	Before Expansion	Bond Financing	Stock Financing
Earnings before interest and income taxes	$100,000	$140,000	$140,000
Interest expense	—	(20,000)	—
Income before income taxes	$100,000	$120,000	$140,000
Income tax expense	(40,000)	(48,000)	(56,000)
Net Income	$ 60,000	$ 72,000	$ 84,000
Earnings per share	$6.00	$7.20	$5.60

financing alternative is that net income is increased by $12,000 ($72,000 − $60,000) when bond financing is used. When stock financing is used, although net income increases by $24,000 ($84,000 − $60,000), the number of common shares is increased to 15,000 so that earnings per share declines from $6.00 to $5.60 ($84,000 ÷ 15,000 = $5.60). The company may choose to pay dividends to the stockholders, but the payments do not affect the computation of net income and may not be deducted in the computation of income taxes. When bond financing is used, earnings per share increases to $7.20 ($72,000 ÷ 10,000 = $7.20). Therefore although financing by issuing bonds does not increase net income by as much as selling common stock does, in this case it has a more favorable impact on earnings per share of present stockholders and is of greater benefit to the stockholders.

The reason for this advantageous result is that the new factory is expected to earn a pretax return (earnings ÷ investment) of 20% ($40,000 ÷ $200,000), whereas the pretax interest cost on the bonds is only 10%. Borrowing money at 10% to earn a return of 20% provides the leverage that is advantageous to the owners of the company. While it may be advantageous to borrow money, there is a limit to the amount of money a company can borrow. As the amount of money borrowed increases, the risk of default increases and therefore the interest rate the company will have to pay increases. At some point the interest rate will exceed the rate that can be earned from an investment, lenders will refuse to lend more money, or management will decide the risk of borrowing has become too high. Thus all companies have a limit on the amount of borrowing that they can undertake.

It should be recognized that the issuing of bonds can result in lower earnings per share if the project is not successful. For example, suppose that the expansion turns out to be disastrous and the earnings before interest expense and income taxes are reduced to $50,000. The earnings per share if stock financing is used is reduced to $2.00 ($30,000 ÷ 15,000), whereas if bond financing is used earnings per share is only $1.80 ($18,000 ÷ 10,000) as shown in Exhibit 16-2.

EXHIBIT 16-2
Lower Earnings per Share Through Bond Financing

	Bond Financing	Stock Financing
Earnings before interest and income taxes	$50,000	$50,000
Interest expense	(20,000)	—
Income before income taxes	$30,000	$50,000
Income tax expense	(12,000)	(20,000)
Net Income	$18,000	$30,000
Earnings per share	$1.80	$2.00

Characteristics of Bonds

Companies issue bonds that may have different characteristics. Some of the more common types of bonds and their characteristics are:

1. *Debenture bonds are bonds that are not secured by specific property.* That is, the holder of the bonds (the lender of the money) is considered as a general

creditor with the same rights as others creditors if the issuer fails to pay the interest or principal and declares bankruptcy.

2. *Mortgage bonds are bonds that are secured with specific property.* That is, the lender has a priority right to the specific property if the company fails to pay the interest or principal.

3. *Registered bonds are bonds whose ownership is registered with the company.* That is, the company maintains a record of the holder of each bond, and therefore payment of the interest and principal can be made without such payment being requested by the holder.

4. *Coupon bonds are unregistered bonds on which interest is claimed by the holder presenting a coupon to the company.* Currently, coupon bonds are rarely issued because bonds issued after December 31, 1982, must be registered for the related interest expense to be deductible for income tax purposes.

5. *Zero-coupon bonds are bonds on which the interest is not paid until the maturity date.* That is, the bonds are sold at a price considerably below their face value, interest accrues until maturity, and then the bondholders are paid the face value, which includes the interest, at maturity. Series E U.S. Savings Bonds are examples of zero-coupon bonds.

6. *Serial bonds are bonds issued at one time, but portions of the total face value mature at different future dates.* For example, a bond issued in 1991 may have a face value of $50,000 and bonds with a face value of $10,000 mature each year from 1998 through 2002.

7. *Sinking fund bonds are bonds for which the company must pay into a sinking fund over the life of the bonds.* The amount paid in should be sufficient to retire the bonds at maturity. *Sinking fund* is the term used to describe the account into which the cash is paid.

8. *Callable bonds are bonds that are callable by the company at a predetermined price for a specified period.* That is, the company has a right to require the holder to return the bonds before the maturity date, with the company paying the predetermined price and interest to date.

9. *Convertible bonds are bonds that are convertible into a predetermined number of common shares.* That is, the owner of each bond may exchange it for a predetermined number of shares of the company.

The characteristics of a particular bond issue are listed on the bond certificates for that issue. Although companies may issue bonds with these various characteristics, we focus on the accounting for debenture bonds in this chapter.

Bonds Issued at Par

3. Account for bonds sold at par.

If bonds are sold at par (i.e., at face value), the accounting is relatively simple because the cash received from the sale equals the face value. The semiannual interest expense also equals the interest paid.

Suppose that the Homestake Company issues 10%, 5-year bonds with a face value of $100,000 for $100,000. When bonds are issued, the face value of the bonds is recorded in a Bonds Payable account, as follows:

Cash	100,000	
Bonds Payable		100,000

To record issuance of 10% bonds at par.

The bonds payable are reported as a noncurrent liability in the balance sheet.

The interest must be computed on each interest payment date. Since bonds pay interest semiannually, the semiannual interest payment is computed as follows:

$$\text{Semiannual interest payment} = \text{Face value of bonds} \times \left(\text{Annual contract rate} \div \text{Number of interest payments per year} \right)$$

For the Homestake Company, the calculation is as follows:

$$\begin{aligned} \text{Semiannual interest payment} &= \$100,000 \times (10\% \div 2) \\ &= \$5,000 \end{aligned}$$

The journal entry to record the semiannual interest expense and cash payment is as follows:

Interest Expense	5,000	
Cash		5,000

To record interest paid on bonds.

The interest expense is included in the Other Revenues and Expenses section in the income statement.

Interest Rates

In the preceding example of a bond issued at par, it was assumed that a 10% interest rate is appropriate. The determination of an appropriate interest rate depends on several factors and may vary significantly from the 10% rate assumed for our example.

An interest rate paid on bonds is affected by many factors such as the policies of the Federal Reserve Board, which affect the supply and demand for money in the national economy, federal regulations, and the budget surplus or deficit of the federal government. Long-term interest rates, however, are generally considered to include three primary factors:

- The risk-free rate
- The risk premium
- The expected inflation rate

The risk-free rate is the rate that would be paid by a borrower, and received by a lender, in a situation in which there is no risk of default by the borrower and no inflation is expected. **The risk premium** is the additional interest that must be paid when there is a possibility of default by the borrower. The higher the risk of default, of course, the higher the risk premium. The third component is **the expected inflation rate,** which is included so that additional interest must be paid by the borrower to compensate for the expected inflation over the life of the borrowing. Inflation causes the value of the dollar that is eventually repaid to be worth less than the dollar that was originally lent, and the added interest compensates for this decline.

To illustrate the nature of these three components, at the time of writing this book the following rates, called *yields* (discussed later), were being incurred on selected borrowings:

Maturity Date	Borrower	Interest Rate
2004	Federal government	9.0%
2004	Citicorp	9.3%
2007	Citicorp	9.7%
2007	AT&T	9.6%

Since the United States is not inflation free, there are no situations in which only risk-free borrowings occur. Thus we can see only the effect of the risk-free rate plus the expected inflation rate. This is illustrated by borrowings of the federal government, which are considered to be risk free but occur in an inflationary environment. Thus the risk-free rate plus the inflation expectation is 9%. Since Citicorp does have some risk of default, the risk premium associated with the borrowing that will mature in 2004 is 0.3%. The risk premium for the 2007 borrowing of Citicorp is 0.7% because there is a longer time period in which Citicorp can have financial problems. The risk premium for AT&T is 0.6%, which indicates the lower likelihood that AT&T rather than Citicorp will default. While it is not expected that the reader will be able to compute an interest rate for a particular situation, an understanding of the components should increase the understanding of bonds and the present and future value calculations later in the chapter.

Bonds Issued at a Discount or Premium

When a company decides to issue bonds it may offer them to the public or offer them privately to an institution such as an insurance company or a pension fund. When the bonds are offered to the public the company usually deals with a securities broker (or an investment banker). The broker, or a group of brokers, agrees on a price for the bonds and pays the company for them. The broker then sells the bonds to its clients. The broker, of course, hopes to make a profit on this service, but the company issuing the bonds avoids the problem of having to find the purchasers and be involved in cash transactions with each purchaser.

There are certain steps a company must follow when it issues bonds. The company must receive approval from the regulatory authorities such as the Securities and Exchange Commission. It must also set the terms of the bond issue such as the contract rate and the maturity date. It must also make a public announcement of its intent to sell the bonds on a particular date and print the bond certificates. At the time of the sale the broker negotiates with the company to determine an appropriate selling price. The selling price is based on the terms of the bond issue and the components of the interest rate as discussed earlier. The broker determines the rate that it believes best reflects current market conditions. This market rate of interest is called a yield. **The yield is the market rate at**

which the bonds are issued.[1] Although the yield is stated as a percentage, it is usually referred to as a yield instead of a yield rate. The yield is also sometimes called the *effective rate.* The yield on the bonds may be different from the contract rate set by the company and printed on the bond certificates. The contract rate on the bonds is determined by the management of the company, whereas the yield is determined by the marketplace. Sometimes the interest rate and the yield are equal, in which case the bonds sell at par (face value). However, often they are not equal, in which case the bonds sell at a discount or premium. The difference between the contract rate and the yield may result from a difference of opinion between the broker and the company about the yield at which the bonds will be sold, or a change of economic conditions between the date the company announced the bond issue, set the contract rate and had the rate printed on the bond certificates, and the date it was issued.

4. Explain why bonds are sold at a discount or premium.

Once the terms of the bond issue have been set and the yield determined, the selling price of the bonds may be calculated. The calculation is illustrated later in the chapter. **If the yield is *more* than the contract rate, the purchasers of the bonds will pay *less* than the face value of the bonds; that is, the bonds are sold at a *discount*.** Alternatively, **if the yield is *less* than the contract rate, the purchasers of the bonds will pay *more* than the face value of the bonds; that is, the bonds are sold at a *premium*.** The issuance price of bonds sold at a premium or discount is usually quoted as a percentage of the face value. For example, bonds with a face value of $10,000 that are quoted at 102 (i.e., 102% of the face value) sell for $10,200 ($10,000 × 1.02), whereas bonds with a face value of $20,000 that are quoted at 97 sell for $19,400 ($20,000 × 0.97).

It is important to understand why bonds sell at a price different from the face value when the yield is different from the contract rate. This is because the difference between the price paid and the face value will enable the purchaser to earn a return on the bonds equal to the yield required by the market at the date of purchase. For instance, bonds are sold at a discount because the yield is higher than the contract rate. The "savings" (i.e., the discount) between the lower selling price and the face value, coupled with the contract interest received by the purchaser each interest period, results in a return equal to the higher yield. Alternatively, bonds are sold at a premium because the yield is lower than the contract rate. The "excess" (i.e., the premium) between the higher selling price and face value, coupled with the contract interest received by the purchaser each interest period, results in a lower yield.

Because purchasers of bonds are effectively earning a yield either higher (for bonds sold at a discount) or lower (for bonds sold at a premium) than the contract rate, the interest *expense* recorded by the issuing company each period is different from the interest *paid*. When bonds are sold at a *discount* the interest expense is *more* than the interest paid. When bonds are sold at a *premium* the interest expense is *less* than the interest paid. The difference between the interest expense and the interest payment is the amount of the discount or premium amortized in the period.

---

[1]After bonds have been issued, the yield on them will fluctuate in the bond market as changes occur in the risk premium and expected inflation rate. It is the yield at the time of issuance, however, that is relevant to a company in accounting for the bonds.

Straight-Line Amortization

The two methods of computing the interest expense and the amortization of the bond discount or premium are (1) the effective interest method of computing interest expense and (2) the straight-line method of amortization. The effective interest method focuses on the computation of the interest expense with the amortization being the balancing amount. In contrast, the straight-line method focuses on the computation of the amortization with the interest expense being the balancing amount. Although the effective interest method is the preferred method, its use requires an understanding of present value concepts and therefore is discussed later in the chapter, after those concepts have been introduced. In this section of the chapter, straight-line amortization is explained.

Bonds Issued at a Discount

To illustrate the sale of bonds at a discount, the computation of the interest expense, and the amortization of the discount, suppose that the Homestake Company sells a bond issue with the following characteristics:

Date of sale	January 1, 1991
Maturity date	December 31, 1995
Face value	$100,000
Contract rate	10%
Interest payment dates	June 30 and December 31

If the yield on the bonds is 12%, the selling price of the 10% bonds is $92,639.93 (the calculation is explained later in the chapter). Thus the bonds sell at a discount because the yield required by investors is higher than the contract rate.

When a company issues bonds at a discount it receives cash and incurs a liability for the same amount. It is customary, however, to record the liability in two accounts. The face value is recorded in the Bonds Payable account. **A discount is the excess of the face value over the selling price and is recorded in the Discount on Bonds Payable account.** Therefore the journal entry to record the issue of the Homestake Company bonds on January 1, 1991, is:

1991			
Jan. 1	Cash	92,639.93	
	Discount on Bonds Payable	7,360.07	
	Bonds Payable		100,000.00
	To record issuance of 10% bonds at a discount.		

The Discount on Bonds Payable is a contra account to Bonds Payable and is subtracted from the Bonds Payable account in the balance sheet to determine the book value of the bonds. **The book value of the bonds is the balance in the Bonds Payable account less the balance in the Discount on Bonds Payable account.**

If the Homestake Company prepared a balance sheet immediately after selling the bonds, the following information would be disclosed in the noncurrent liability section:

10% Bonds payable, due 12/31/1995	$100,000.00
Less: Discount on bonds payable	(7,360.07)
	$ 92,639.93

5(a). Describe the straight-line method of accounting for a discount.

As mentioned earlier, when bonds are sold at a discount the interest expense each period is higher than the interest paid, the difference being the amount of the discount amortized in the period. **Amortization is the process of writing off the discount (or premium) as an adjustment of interest expense over the life of the bonds. The straight-line method is a method of amortizing a discount or premium by an equal amount each period.** The amount of the semiannual interest payment, the semiannual discount amortization, and the semiannual interest expense are computed as follows:

Semiannual interest payment = Face value × (Annual contract ÷ Number of interest rate / payments per year)

= $100,000 × (10% ÷ 2)

= $5,000

Semiannual discount amortization = Total discount at issuance of bonds ÷ (Number of years in life of bonds × Number of interest payments per year)

= $7,360.07 ÷ (5 × 2)

= $736.01 (rounded)

Semiannual interest expense = Semiannual interest payment + Semiannual discount amortization

= $5,000 + $736.01

= $5,736.01

The journal entry to record the interest expense on June 30, 1991, is as follows:

1991			
June 30	Interest Expense	5,736.01	
	Discount on Bonds Payable		736.01
	Cash		5,000.00

To record interest paid on bonds and discount amortization by the straight-line method.

The remaining balance in the Discount account is often referred to as the *unamortized* Discount on Bonds Payable. At this point, the Discount account has a balance of $6,624.06 ($7,360.07 − $736.01), and the book value of the bonds has *increased* from $92,639.93 to $93,375.94 ($100,000 − $6,624.06).

Since the company is using the straight-line method of amortization, an identical journal entry is made on December 31, 1991, as follows:

1991			
Dec. 31	Interest Expense	5,736.01	
	Discount on Bonds Payable		736.01
	Cash		5,000.00

To record interest paid on bonds and discount amortization by the straight-line method.

The balance in the Discount on Bonds Payable account is now $5,888.05 ($6,624.06 – $736.01) and the book value of the bonds is now $94,111.95. These amounts would be reported on the December 31, 1991, balance sheet in the non-current liability section as follows:

10% Bonds payable, due 12/31/1995	$100,000.00
Less: Discount on bonds payable	(5,888.05)
	$ 94,111.95

The total interest expense of $11,472.02 (2 × $5,736.01) would be shown on the income statement for 1991 in the Other Revenues and Expenses section.

To summarize the interest expense for each 6-month period, a discount amortization schedule can be prepared as shown in Exhibit 16-3. The amounts in the columns are based on the equations presented earlier. At the end of the life of the bonds on December 31, 1995, the discount has been completely amortized so that the book value of the bonds is equal to the face value of $100,000.

EXHIBIT 16-3
Bond Discount
Amortization Schedule

		HOMESTAKE COMPANY Bond Discount Amortization Schedule Straight-Line Method		
Date	Cash Paid[a] (credit)	Amortization of Discount on Bonds Payable[b] (credit)	Interest Expense[c] (debit)	Book Value of Bonds[d]
1/1/1991				$ 92,639.93
6/30/1991	$5,000	$736.01	$5,736.01	93,375.94
12/31/1991	5,000	736.01	5,736.01	94,111.95
6/30/1992	5,000	736.01	5,736.01	94,847.96
12/31/1992	5,000	736.01	5,736.01	95,583.97
6/30/1993	5,000	736.01	5,736.01	96,319.98
12/31/1993	5,000	736.01	5,736.01	97,055.99
6/30/1994	5,000	736.01	5,736.01	97,792.00
12/31/1994	5,000	736.01	5,736.01	98,528.01
6/30/1995	5,000	736.01	5,736.01	99,264.02
12/31/1995	5,000	735.98[e]	5,735.98	100,000.00

[a]Face value × (Annual contract rate ÷ Number of interest payments per year), or $100,000 × (10% ÷ 2).
[b](Face value – Selling price) ÷ (Life of the bond in years × Number of interest payments per year), or ($100,000 – $92,639.93) ÷ (5 × 2).
[c]Cash paid + Amortization of discount on bonds payable, or $5,000 + $736.01.
[d]Previous book value + Amortization of discount on bonds payable.
[e]Adjusted for rounding error of $.03.

Bonds Issued at a Premium

As we saw in the preceding example, a bond may be sold at a price below its face value. A bond may also be sold at a price above its face value, that is, at a premium. **A premium is the excess of the selling price over the face value.** As discussed earlier, bonds sell at a premium when the yield required by investors is lower than the contract rate.

To illustrate a bond sold at a premium consider the same bond issue by the Homestake Company, except that instead the yield is 8%. The selling price of the 10% bonds is assumed to be $108,110.88 (the calculation is explained later in the chapter). When bonds are sold at a premium it is customary to record the liability in two accounts. The face value is recorded in the Bonds Payable account and **the excess of the selling price over the face value (i.e., the *premium*) is recorded in the Premium on Bonds Payable account.** The journal entry to record the issue of the Homestake Company bonds on January 1, 1991, is as follows:

```
1991
Jan. 1   Cash  ...............................................  108,110.88
              Bonds Payable  ....................................         100,000.00
              Premium on Bonds Payable  ....................          8,110.88
```

To record issuance of 10% bonds at a premium.

The Premium on Bonds Payable is an adjunct account to the Bonds Payable account. **An adjunct account is an account added to another account to determine the book value.** This account is in contrast to a contra account, which is subtracted from another account to determine the book value. Thus **the book value of the bonds is the balance in the Bonds Payable account plus the balance in the Premium on Bonds Payable account.** If the Homestake Company prepared a balance sheet immediately after selling the bonds, the following information would be disclosed in the noncurrent liability section:

```
10% Bonds payable, due 12/31/1995  .......................................   $100,000.00
Plus: Premium on bonds payable  ..........................................        8,110.88
                                                                              $108,110.88
```

5(b). Describe the straight-line method of accounting for a premium.

As mentioned earlier, when bonds are sold at a premium the interest expense each period is lower than the interest paid, the difference being the amount of the premium amortized in the period. Under the straight-line method, the amounts of the semiannual interest payment, the semiannual premium amortization, and the semiannual interest expense are computed as follows:

Semiannual interest payment = Face value × $\left(\begin{array}{l}\text{Annual contract} \div \text{Number of interest} \\ \text{rate} \qquad\qquad \text{payments per year}\end{array}\right)$

= $100,000 × (10% ÷ 2)

= $5,000

Semiannual premium amortization = Total premium at issuance of bonds ÷ $\left(\begin{array}{l}\text{Number of years} \times \text{Number of interest} \\ \text{in life of bonds} \qquad \text{payments per year}\end{array}\right)$

= $8,110.88 ÷ (5 × 2)

= $811.09 (rounded)

Semiannual interest expense = Semiannual interest – Semiannual premium
payment   amortization

= $5,000 – $811.09

= $4,188.91

The journal entries to record the interest expense on June 30 and December 31, 1991, are as follows:

1991

June 30   Interest Expense 4,188.91
         Premium on Bonds Payable 811.09
              Cash 5,000.00

         To record interest paid on bonds and premium
         amortization by the straight-line method.

Dec. 31   Interest Expense 4,188.91
         Premium on Bonds Payable 811.09
              Cash 5,000.00

         To record interest paid on bonds and premium
         amortization by the straight-line method.

The balance in the Premium on Bonds Payable account on December 31, 1991, is $6,488.70 ($8,110.88 − $811.09 − $811.09), and the book value of the bonds is $106,488.70. These amounts are reported on the December 31, 1991, balance sheet in the noncurrent liability section as follows:

10% Bonds payable, due 12/31/1995 .... $100,000.00
Plus: Premium on bonds payable 6,488.70
                                                                           $106,488.70

The total interest expense of $8,377.82 (2 × $4,188.91) is shown on the income statement for 1991 in the Other Revenues and Expenses section.

To summarize the interest expense for each 6-month period, a premium amortization schedule can be prepared as shown in Exhibit 16-4. The amounts in

EXHIBIT 16-4
Bond Premium
Amortization Schedule

HOMESTAKE COMPANY **Bond Premium Amortization Schedule** **Straight-Line Method**				
Date	Cash Paid[a] (credit)	Amortization of Premium on Bonds Payable[b] (debit)	Interest Expense[c] (debit)	Book Value of Bonds[d]
1/1/1991				$108,110.88
6/30/1991	$5,000	$811.09	$4,188.91	107,299.79
12/31/1991	5,000	811.09	4,188.91	106,488.70
6/30/1992	5,000	811.09	4,188.91	105,677.61
12/31/1992	5,000	811.09	4,188.91	104,866.52
6/30/1993	5,000	811.09	4,188.91	104,055.43
12/31/1993	5,000	811.09	4,188.91	103,244.34
6/30/1994	5,000	811.09	4,188.91	102,433.25
12/31/1994	5,000	811.09	4,188.91	101,622.16
6/30/1995	5,000	811.09	4,188.91	100,811.07
12/31/1995	5,000	811.07[e]	4,188.93	100,000.00

[a]Face value × (Annual contract rate ÷ Number of interest payments per year), or $100,000 × (10% ÷ 2).
[b](Selling price − Face value) ÷ (Life of the bond in years × Number of interest payments per year), or ($108,110.88 − $100,000) ÷ (5 × 2).
[c]Cash paid − Amortization of premium on bonds payable, or $5,000 − $811.09.
[d]Previous book value − Amortization of premium on bonds payable.
[e]Adjusted for rounding error of $.02.

the columns are based on the equations presented earlier. At the end of the life of the bonds on December 31, 1995, the premium has been completely amortized so that the book value of the bonds is equal to the face value of $100,000.

Recording Accrued Interest Under Straight-Line Method

The interest expense on bonds payable is typically recorded by a company on each interest payment date. In many cases, however, an interest payment date does not coincide with the end of a company's accounting period because a company may issue bonds at any time during the year. In such a case, **the company must make an adjusting entry at the end of the accounting period to record the interest that has accrued since the last interest payment date.** This enables the company to report the correct total interest expense for the period on its income statement and the correct book value of the liability on its ending balance sheet. For example, suppose the Homestake Company in the previous example had instead issued the bonds on September 30, 1991, and the bonds pay interest each March 31 and September 30. When the company's accounting period ends on December 31, 1991, it must record the interest that has accrued on its bonds from September 30, 1991, through the end of December. The interest expense for these 3 months under the straight-line method is determined by computing the interest for 6 months, as discussed earlier, and then allocating this amount proportionately over the 6 months as follows:

Interest expense for = **Semiannual interest expense** × **Fraction of period since**
fraction of period   **previous recognition of**
                                                                interest expense

$$= \$5,736.01 \times 3/6$$
$$= \$2,868 \text{ (rounded)}$$

In the situation in which the bonds were issued at a discount, the amortization of the discount is calculated as follows:

Amortization of discount = **Semiannual amortization** × **Fraction of period since**
on bonds payable   **previous recognition of**
for fraction of period   **interest expense**

$$= \$736.01 \times 3/6$$
$$= \$368 \text{ (rounded)}$$

The amount of interest owed at this date is calculated as follows:

Interest payable for = **Semiannual interest payment** × **Fraction of period**
fraction of period   **since previous payment**

$$= \$5,000 \times 3/6$$
$$= \$2,500$$

The journal entry to record the interest at December 31, 1991, is:

1991			
Dec. 31	Interest Expense	2,868.00	
	Discount on Bonds Payable		368.00
	Interest Payable		2,500.00

To accrue interest at the end of the year.

On March 31, 1992, the first semiannual interest payment of $5,000 is made. The interest expense to be recognized at this time is the remaining portion of the semiannual interest expense not recognized at December 31, 1991, which amounts to $2,868.01 ($5,736.01 – $2,868.00). Therefore the journal entry to record the interest payment is:

1992			
Mar. 31	**Interest Expense**	**2,868.01**	
	Interest Payable	**2,500.00**	
	Discount on Bonds Payable		**368.01**
	Cash		**5,000.00**

To record interest paid on bonds and discount amortization by the straight-line method.

In the situation in which the bonds were issued at a premium, the accrual of interest on December 31, 1992, is computed in a similar way as the discount example. The interest expense would be $2,094.46 ($4,188.91 × 3/6) and the amortization of the premium would be $405.55 ($811.09 × 3/6).

Because of its simplicity, many companies use the straight-line method to compute the interest expense and amortize the premium or discount on bonds payable. This is acceptable when the results are not materially different from the effective interest method.[2] The effective interest method requires an understanding of present value concepts, discussed next.

Present Value and Future Value

Would you rather receive $1 today or $1 next year? The answer to this question should be that you would rather receive $1 today because a dollar held today is worth more than a dollar to be received a year from now. The difference between the two amounts is *interest*, or more generally, there is a *time value of money*. The components of the interest rate were discussed earlier in the chapter; they are the factors that cause money to have a time value.

To illustrate the time value of money suppose that Peter Cameron has $100 on January 1, 1991, and can invest it at 10%. This money will grow over the next three years as shown in the following table:

	Principal Amount at Beginning of the Year	Interest at 10%	Principal Amount at End of the Year
1991	$100	$10.00	$110.00
1992	110	11.00	121.00
1993	121	12.10	133.10

---

[2]"Interest on Receivables and Payables," *APB Opinion No. 21* (New York: AICPA, 1971), par. 15.

Therefore a person would rather have $100 today than $100 in one year, because the $100 today grows to $110 in one year. Alternatively, the analysis tells us that the following amounts, given the 10% interest rate and their respective dates, have *equivalent* values:

- $100 at the beginning of 1991
- $110 at the end of 1991
- $121 at the end of 1992
- $133.10 at the end of 1993

Since these amounts have equivalent values, if you were asked which amount you wanted to receive, you would be indifferent between the four alternatives, given the 10% rate. It is essential to note, however, that the dollar amounts have a time attached to them. Whenever we are considering the time value of money we must always know the date at which the dollar amount is measured. A dollar received or paid in 1991 does not have the same value as a dollar received or paid in 1992.

Definitions of Present Value and Future Value

6. Explain the concepts of present value and future value.

There are two important terms that are widely used whenever the value of money is being considered. **Present value is the value today of a certain number of dollars measured in the future.** The present value concept can be used analytically by either the payor or receiver of money. In the preceding example, therefore, $100 is the present value at the beginning of 1991 of $133.10 at the end of 1993 when the interest rate is 10%. **Future value is the value at a future date of a certain number of dollars measured today.** Therefore $133.10 at the end of 1993 is the future value of $100 at the beginning of 1991 when the interest rate is 10%. Again, this analytical concept can be used by either the payor or receiver.

Although present value and future value are both widely used concepts, present value is a much more useful accounting concept than future value because it is often necessary to include in the financial statements the value of cash flows that will occur in the future. Therefore the discussion in this chapter concentrates on present value although future value is also discussed.

Simple Interest and Compound Interest

Simple interest was discussed in Chapter 8; remember that simple interest is calculated by the formula:

$$\textbf{Interest = Principal} \times \textbf{Rate} \times \textbf{Time}$$

Therefore simple interest on $100 for 3 years at 10% would be:

$$\text{Interest} = \$100 \times 10\% \times 3 \text{ years}$$
$$= \$30$$

This simple interest is different from the interest in the preceding example, which amounted to $33.10 ($133.10 − $100.00), because the example uses compound interest. **Compound interest is interest that accrues on both the principal and past accrued (unpaid) interest.** Thus during 1991 interest of 10% is accrued on the principal of $100, making a total of $110 at the end of 1991. In 1992 interest of 10% is accrued on the principal of $100 *and* the 1991 interest of $10, or on a total of $110. The interest amounts to $11 in 1992. In 1993 interest is similarly accrued on the principal of $100 plus the interest for 1991 and 1992 of $21. The interest on the $121 is $12.10. Thus the total compound interest is $33.10 ($10 + $11 + $12.10) compared to the simple interest of $30. Compound interest is the process that underlies the concepts of present and future value.

Calculations of present and future values are essential in many situations. If a company enters into a transaction which creates an obligation to pay a certain number of dollars in the future, the present value of those dollars should be disclosed as a liability in the balance sheet. Application of this present value concept in accounting for bonds payable is discussed later in this chapter. Accounting for leases, mortgages, and pensions also utilizes present value concepts and each of these topics is briefly discussed later in the chapter. In addition, present and future values are necessary for many types of investment decisions, such as the acquisition of property, plant, and equipment. To assist these types of accounting disclosures and management decisions, formulas and tables are frequently used.

Formulas and Tables

Instead of preparing a year-by-year calculation of present and future values, a formula or a table may be used. The general relationship between present and future value is as follows:

$$FV = PV(1 + i)^n \text{ or } PV = \frac{FV}{(1 + i)^n}$$

where

> PV = **Present value**
> FV = **Future value**
> i = **Interest rate**
> n = **Number of periods**

Using the same example of 10% and 3 years, if we know the present value of $100, the future value is calculated as follows:

$$
\begin{aligned}
FV &= PV(1 + i)^n \\
&= \$100(1 + 0.10)^3 \\
&= \$100(1.331) \\
&= \$133.10
\end{aligned}
$$

7. Compute present values and future values.

Alternatively, if the future value of $133.10 is known, the present value is calculated as follows:

$$
\begin{aligned}
PV &= \frac{FV}{(1 + i)^n} \\[6pt]
&= \frac{\$133.10}{(1 + 0.10)^3} \\[6pt]
&= \frac{\$133.10}{1.331} \\[6pt]
&= \quad \$100
\end{aligned}
$$

Tables have been developed that simplify the calculation process even more. Table 1 in Appendix B is entitled the Future Value of $1. **Table 1 is used to compute the future value of a single amount when the present value is known.** A future value is computed by using the table as follows:

$$FV = PV \times \textbf{Future value of \$1 factor}$$

A *factor* is an arithmetic amount for a certain time period and rate. Thus each arithmetic amount included in Table 1 is a future value factor for a certain time period and rate. If you look up the factor for 10% and 3 periods in Table 1, you will find that it is 1.331000. Therefore the future value at the end of 3 years of $100 received or paid today using a 10% interest rate is as follows:

$$\begin{aligned} FV &= PV \times \text{Future value of \$1 factor for 3 periods at 10\%} \\ &= \$100 \times 1.331000 \\ &= \$133.10 \end{aligned}$$

Table 2 in Appendix B is entitled the Present Value of $1. **Table 2 is used to compute the present value of a single amount when the future value is known.** A present value is computed by using the table as follows:

$$PV = FV \times \textbf{Present value of \$1 factor}$$

If you look up the factor for 10% and 3 periods in Table 2, you will find that it is 0.751315. Therefore the present value of $133.10 received or paid at the end of 3 years, using a 10% interest rate is:

$$\begin{aligned} PV &= FV \times \text{Present value of \$1 factor for 3 periods at 10\%} \\ &= \$133.10 \times 0.751315 \\ &= \$100 \end{aligned}$$

The process of converting a future value to a smaller present value is known as *discounting,* and the rate used is often called the **discount rate.** Thus the $133.10 future value is discounted to the $100 present value by multiplying it times the 0.751315 factor for 3 periods at the 10% discount rate.

Tables 1 and 2 are following exactly the same procedures as the formulas. They simply provide the answers that would be obtained by using the formulas for the various rates and time periods. Thus the Future Value of $1 table is based on the formula $(1 + i)^n$ and the Present Value of $1 table is based on the formula $1/(1 + i)^n$.

In summary, the Present Value of $1 table is used to convert (discount) a future value back to the present. Note that all numbers in the table are less than 1.0. The calculation of the present value can be diagrammed as follows:

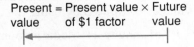

The Future Value of $1 table is used to convert a present value to a future value. Note that all the numbers in the table are greater than 1.0. The calculation of the future value may be diagrammed as follows:

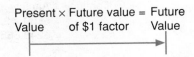

An Annuity

In many situations we are not concerned with the present or future value of a single amount as in the preceding examples, but with an annuity. **An annuity is a series of equal periodic cash flows.** These cash flows may be either received or paid. For example, a 3-year $100 annuity consists of a cash flow of $100 per year for 3 years. In this book we will assume that the first cash flow in an annuity occurs at the *end* of the first time period. Thus if an annual annuity begins on January 1, 1991, the first cash flow occurs on December 31, 1991.

We could compute the present value on January 1, 1991, of a 3-year $100 annuity at 10% by treating it as three separate single amounts and using the factors from Table 2 as follows:

PV of $100 paid or received on Dec. 31, 1991 = $100 × 0.909091 = $ 90.9091
PV of $100 paid or received on Dec. 31, 1992 = $100 × 0.826446 =   82.6446
PV of $100 paid or received on Dec. 31, 1993 = $100 × 0.751315 =   75.1315
PV of $100, 3-year annuity at 10% on Jan. 1, 1991   = $248.6852

This computation can also be illustrated by using a time diagram as follows:

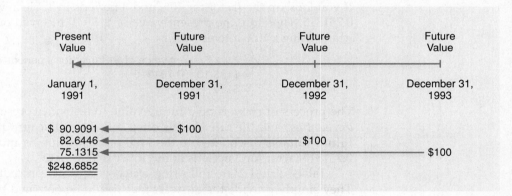

Instead of using Table 2 and completing the numerous calculations shown, using Table 4 in Appendix B makes the calculation process much simpler. The table is entitled Present Value of Ordinary Annuity of $1 and is developed on the basis of the assumption that the first cash flow occurs at the *end* of the first time period. **Table 4 is used to compute the present value of an annuity.** The present value is computed by using the table as follows:

PV of annuity = Periodic amount of the annuity × Present value of annuity factor

If you look up the factor for 10% and 3 periods in Table 4, you will find that it is 2.486852. Therefore the present value of the annuity of $100 received or paid at the end of each year for 3 years using a 10% interest rate is as follows:

PV of annuity = Annuity × Present value of annuity for 3 periods at 10%
            = $100 × 2.486852
            = $248.6852

Another way of saying this is that the annuity of $100 received or paid at the end of each year for 3 years is discounted to a present value of $248.6852. This process enables the present value to be computed by a single multiplication rather than three multiplications and an addition. It is important to realize, however, that exactly the same present value concept is involved. The purpose of Table 4 is to simplify the calculations.

Table 3 in Appendix B is entitled Future Value of Ordinary Annuity of $1. **Table 3 is used to compute the future value of an annuity.** The future value is computed by using the table as follows:

FV of annuity = Periodic amount of the annuity × Future value of annuity factor

The future value of a 3-year annuity of $100 received or paid at the end of each year for 3 years using a 10% interest rate is calculated by looking up the factor for 3 periods at 10% in Table 3, which is 3.310000:

$$FV \text{ of annuity} = \text{Annuity} \times \text{Future value of annuity for 3 periods at 10\%}$$
$$= \$100 \times 3.310000$$
$$= \$331.00$$

Many electronic calculators have the capacity to compute present and future values. The calculation process follows exactly the same concepts discussed earlier. The calculator uses formulas to determine each factor whenever a calculation is made (we have not illustrated the formulas for the annuity calculations), and thus the user avoids the need to look up the factor in a table as is usually done when a calculator is not available.

Interest Periods Other Than One Year

It is often necessary to calculate present and future values for situations in which interest periods other than 1 year are used. Remember, however, that *interest rates are expressed in terms of an annual rate unless specified otherwise.* For example, a savings account may pay 8% interest, compounded quarterly. This means that the interest is 2% each quarter and that the interest accrues each quarter on the principal plus interest of the previous quarters. Thus, in this example, if we are computing a present value or future value for a 3-year period, we would look up in the appropriate table the factor for 2% for 12 periods (3 years × 4 quarters) rather than 8% for 3 years. **The general rule is that if there are *n* compounding periods in the year, the interest rate per period is the annual interest rate divided by *n* and the number of interest periods is the number of years multiplied by *n*.**

To illustrate, suppose that we need to compute the present value of $1,000 that will be received at the end of 4 years. The annual interest rate is 10%, but interest accrues *semiannually.* Therefore the appropriate rate to use is 5% (10% ÷ 2) per period; and there are 8 (4 years × 2) time periods. The calculation (using the factor from Table 2) is as follows:

$$\text{Present value} = \text{Future value} \times \text{Present value of \$1 factor for 8 periods at 5\%}$$
$$= \$1,000 \times 0.676839$$
$$= \$676.84 \text{ (rounded)}$$

In contrast, the present value calculated with *annual* compounding would be as follows:

Present value = Future value × Present value of $1 factor for 4 periods at 10%
= $1,000 × 0.683013
= $683.01 (rounded)

It should be expected that the semiannual compounding would result in a lower *present value* ($676.84 as compared with $683.01) than would annual compounding because of the added interest that will accrue. That is, a smaller present value will accrue to the same future value when interest is compounded more often. Similarly, if the future value is being calculated from a present value, compounding more frequently than once a year will result in a higher future value.

Bond Selling Prices and Effective Interest Method

The selling price of a bond issue may be calculated by a present value computation if the maturity date, the face value, the contract rate, and the yield are known. **The selling price is the present value of the cash flows that the company is committed to pay under the terms of the bond issue.** The cash flows consist of the semiannual interest payments and the face value at the end of the life of the bonds. The selling price is calculated as follows:

**Selling price of the bond issue = Present value of + Present value of
face value   interest payments**

The present value of the face value is computed as follows:

Present value of face value = Face value × Present value of $1 factor

The present value of the interest payments is computed as follows:

**Present value of interest payments = Periodic interest × Present value of
payment   annuity factor**

and

Periodic interest payment = Face value of bonds × Periodic interest rate

and

**Periodic interest rate = Annual contract rate ÷ Number of interest
payments per year**

The present value factors in each calculation are based on the *yield* and the life of the bonds. Recall from our earlier discussion that the yield on the bonds is the market rate of interest when the bonds are *issued*; it is the return that will be earned by the purchaser of the bonds on the purchase price and is also the cost to the company of the money it borrows. Although bond yields are stated in terms of annual rates, in reality the actual yield for each interest period is half the annual yield because bonds pay interest semiannually. Thus the semiannual yield is determined as follows:

Semiannual yield = Annual yield ÷ 2

Since the yield is stated in terms of a semiannual rate, the periods must also be semiannual as follows:

Number of semiannual periods = Life of the bonds in years × 2

Therefore the cash payments to which the company is committed are discounted at the semiannual yield for the number of semiannual periods in the life of the bonds.

Selling Price Less Than Face Value (Discount)

To illustrate the calculation of the selling price of a bond issue by using present value concepts, consider the Homestake Company example used earlier in the chapter. The bond issue has the following characteristics:

Date of sale	January 1, 1991
Maturity date	December 31, 1995
Face value	$100,000
Contract rate	10%
Interest payment dates	June 30 and December 31

The selling price of the 10% bonds is the present value of the future cash payments to which Homestake is committed. These payments are the face value of $100,000 at the maturity date and the interest payment of $5,000 ($100,000 × 10% × $\frac{1}{2}$) every 6 months.

If the bonds are sold to yield 12%, the cash payments to which Homestake is committed should *not* be discounted at 12% per year for 5 years. They should instead be discounted at 6% per semiannual period for 10 semiannual periods. The present value is calculated as follows:

**Present value of face value = Face value × Present value of $1 factor
for 10 periods at 6%**
= $100,000 × 0.558395 (from Table 2)
= $55,839.50

**Present value of semiannual = Semiannual interest × Present value of annuity
interest payments   payment   factor for 10 periods at 6%**
= $5,000 × 7.360087 (from Table 4)
= $36,800.43

**Selling price of the bonds = Present value of + Present value of semiannual
face value   interest payments**
= $55,839.50 + $36,800.43
= $92,639.93

In this case the bonds sell at a discount; that is, at a selling price that is *less* than the face value. The discount occurs because the yield is *higher* than the contract rate. The purchasers of the bonds are obtaining a 12% return (6% semiannually) on the $92,639.93 they are lending the company, and the company is borrowing $92,639.93 at a cost of 12% (6% semiannually).

As discussed earlier, the liability for the bonds is separated into two accounts when the sale is recorded. The face value is recorded in the Bonds Payable account, and the difference between the face value and the selling price is recorded in the Discount on Bonds Payable account. The journal entry to record the issue of the Homestake Company bonds on January 1, 1991 is the same as the one illustrated earlier in the chapter:

1991			
Jan. 1	Cash	92,639.93	
	Discount on Bonds Payable	7,360.07	
	Bonds Payable		100,000.00
	To record issuance of 10% bonds to yield 12%.		

Interest Expense and Interest Payment

The Homestake Company makes its first interest payment of $5,000 on June 30, 1991, as indicated earlier. This amount is *not* the interest expense for the period, however. **The effective interest method is a method of recognizing interest expense in which the expense is based on the amount of money borrowed and the rate (yield) at which it is borrowed.** The effective interest method is the preferred method of recognizing interest expense and is an alternative to the straight-line method discussed earlier in the chapter. The two methods are compared later in the chapter. **Under the effective interest method, the interest expense for a period is calculated by multiplying the book value of the bonds at the beginning of the period by the yield per period.** The yield per period is computed by dividing the annual yield by the number of interest periods in the year. For the Homestake Company, the book value at the beginning of the first period is the issuance price and the yield is 6% (12% ÷ 2) per semiannual interest period. **When bonds are sold at a discount the interest expense each period is greater than the interest paid.** The semiannual interest expense and the semiannual interest payment are calculated as follows:

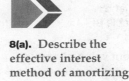

8(a). Describe the effective interest method of amortizing a discount.

$$\text{Semiannual interest expense} = \left(\text{Annual yield} \div \begin{matrix} \text{Number of interest} \\ \text{payments per year} \end{matrix} \right) \times \begin{matrix} \text{Book value of the} \\ \text{bonds at the} \\ \text{beginning of the} \\ \text{period} \end{matrix}$$

$$= (12\% \div 2) \times (\$100,000 - \$7,360.07)$$
$$= 6\% \times \$92,639.93$$
$$= \$5,558.40$$

$$\text{Semiannual interest payment} = \text{Face value} \times \left(\begin{matrix} \text{Annual contract} \\ \text{rate} \end{matrix} \div \begin{matrix} \text{Number of interest} \\ \text{payments per year} \end{matrix} \right)$$

$$= \$100,000 \times (10\% \div 2)$$
$$= \$5,000$$

Since the company has an interest *expense* of $5,558.40 but is only *paying* interest of $5,000, it is increasing its liability by the difference of $558.40. The company increases its bond liability by amortizing a portion of the discount. Using the effective interest method the amount of the amortization may be expressed as follows:

Semiannual discount amortization = Semiannual interest – Semiannual interest
expense   payment
$$= \$5,558.40 - \$5,000$$
$$= \$558.40$$

The amount of the discount amortization is subtracted from (credited to) the Discount on Bonds Payable account, thereby *increasing* the book value of the liability. The journal entry to record the interest expense, discount amortization, and interest payment on June 30, 1991, using the effective interest method is:

```
1991
June 30   Interest Expense  .........................................   5,558.40
              Discount on Bonds Payable  ......................                558.40
              Cash  .................................................              5,000.00

          To record interest paid on bonds and interest
          expense by the effective interest method.
```

At this point the Discount on Bonds Payable account has a balance of $6,801.67 ($7,360.07 – $558.40) and the book value of the bonds has increased from $92,639.93 to $93,198.33 ($100,000 – $6,801.67).

The second interest payment is made on December 31, 1991. The semiannual interest expense is computed as follows:

$$\text{Semiannual interest expense} = (12\% \div 2) \times (\$100,000 - \$6,801.67)$$
$$= 6\% \times \$93,198.33$$
$$= \$5,591.90$$

Since the interest payment is $5,000, the discount amortization is $591.90 and the following journal entry is made:

```
1991
Dec. 31   Interest Expense  .........................................   5,591.90
              Discount on Bonds Payable  ......................                591.90
              Cash  .................................................              5,000.00

          To record interest paid on bonds and interest
          expense by the effective interest method.
```

The balance in the Discount on Bonds Payable account is now $6,209.77 ($6,801.67 – $591.90) and the book value of the bonds is $93,790.23. These amounts would be reported on the December 31, 1991, balance sheet as follows:

```
10% Bonds payable, due 12/31/1995  .......................................   $100,000.00
Less: Discount on bonds payable  ..........................................      (6,209.77)
                                                                            $ 93,790.23
```

The total interest expense of $11,150.30 ($5,558.40 + $5,591.90) is shown on the income statement for 1991 in the Other Revenues and Expenses section.

To summarize the interest expense each 6-month period, a discount amortization schedule can be prepared as shown in Exhibit 16-5. The amounts in the columns are based on the equations presented earlier. At the end of the life of the bonds on December 31, 1995, the discount has been completely amortized so that the book value of the bonds is equal to the face value of $100,000.

EXHIBIT 16-5
Bond Discount
Amortization Schedule

			Amortization of	
		Interest	Discount on	Book Value
	Cash Paid[a]	Expense[b]	Bonds Payable[c]	of Bonds[d]
Date	(credit)	(debit)	(credit)	
1/1/1991				$ 92,639.93
6/30/1991	$5,000	$5,558.40	$558.40	93,198.33
12/31/1991	5,000	5,591.90	591.90	93,790.23
6/30/1992	5,000	5,627.41	627.41	94,417.64
12/31/1992	5,000	5,665.06	665.06	95,082.70
6/30/1993	5,000	5,704.96	704.96	95,787.66
12/31/1993	5,000	5,747.26	747.26	96,534.92
6/30/1994	5,000	5,792.10	792.10	97,327.02
12/31/1994	5,000	5,839.62	839.62	98,166.64
6/30/1995	5,000	5,890.00	890.00	99,056.64
12/31/1995	5,000	5,943.36[e]	943.36	100,000.00

HOMESTAKE COMPANY
Bond Discount Amortization Schedule
Effective Interest Method
(10% bonds to yield 12%)

[a]Face value × (Annual contract rate ÷ Number of interest payments per year), or $100,000 × (10% ÷ 2).
[b](Annual yield ÷ Number of interest payments per year) × Book value of bonds at beginning of period (from previous line); at 6/30/1991 (12% ÷ 2) × $92,639.93.
[c]Interest expense – Cash paid; at 6/30/1991, $5,558.40 – $5,000.00.
[d]Book value of bonds from previous line + Amortization of discount on bonds payable (this is equal to the face value of the bonds payable – the unamortized discount on bonds payable); at 6/30/1991, $92,639.93 + $558.40.
[e]Adjusted for rounding error of $.04.

Selling Price More Than Face Value (Premium)

As we saw in the preceding example, a bond may be sold at a price below its face value. A bond may also be sold at a price above its face value, that is, at a premium. This will occur when the yield required by investors is less than the contract rate.

To illustrate a bond sold at a premium, consider the same bond issue by the Homestake Company, except that now the yield is 8%, or 4% each 6 months. The selling price of the 10% bonds is computed as follows:

Present value of face value = Face value × Present value of $1 factor
for 10 periods at 4%
= $100,000 × 0.675564
= $67,556.40

Present value of semiannual = Semiannual interest × Present value of annuity
interest payments   payment   factor for 10 periods at 4%
= $5,000 × 8.110896
= $40,554.48

Selling price of the bonds = Present value + Present value of semiannual
of face value   interest payments
= $67,556.40 + $40,554.48
= $108,110.88

As discussed earlier the liability for the bonds is separated into two accounts when the sale is recorded. The face value is recorded in the Bonds Payable account and the excess of the selling price over the face value is recorded in the Premium on Bonds Payable account. The journal entry to record the sale of the bonds on January 1, 1991, is:

```
1991
Jan. 1  Cash ...................................................  108,110.88
            Bonds Payable .....................................              100,000.00
            Premium on Bonds Payable .....................                8,110.88
```

To record issuance of 10% bonds to yield 8%.

The interest expense using the effective interest method and the related premium amortization are computed in a similar way as for a discount as follows:

8(b). Describe the effective interest method of amortizing a premium.

$$\text{Semiannual interest expense} = \left(\text{Annual yield} \div \text{Number of interest payments per year}\right) \times \begin{array}{l}\text{Book value of the bonds at the beginning of the period}\end{array}$$

$$\text{Semiannual interest payment} = \text{Face value} \times \left(\text{Annual contract rate} \div \text{Number of interest payments per year}\right)$$

$$\text{Semiannual premium amortization} = \text{Semiannual interest payment} - \text{Semiannual interest expense}$$

A premium amortization schedule may be prepared for these bonds and is shown in Exhibit 16-6. The amounts in the columns are based on the equations presented earlier. We can see from the exhibit that the journal entry to record the interest expense on June 30, 1991, is:

EXHIBIT 16-6
Bond Premium
Amortization Schedule

	HOMESTAKE COMPANY			
	Bond Premium Amortization Schedule			
	Effective Interest Method			
	(10% bonds to yield 8%)			
Date	Cash Paid[a] (credit)	Interest Expense[b] (debit)	Amortization of Premium on Bonds Payable[c] (debit)	Book Value of Bonds[d]
1/1/1991				$108,110.88
6/30/1991	$5,000	$4,324.44	$675.56	107,435.32
12/31/1991	5,000	4,297.41	702.59	106,732.73
6/30/1992	5,000	4,269.31	730.69	106,002.04
12/31/1992	5,000	4,240.08	759.92	105,242.12
6/30/1993	5,000	4,209.68	790.32	104,451.80
12/31/1993	5,000	4,178.07	821.93	103,629.87
6/30/1994	5,000	4,145.19	854.81	102,775.06
12/31/1994	5,000	4,111.00	889.00	101,886.06
6/30/1995	5,000	4,075.44	924.56	100,961.50
12/31/1995	5,000	4,038.50[e]	961.50	100,000.00

[a]Face value × (Annual contract rate ÷ Number of interest payments per year), or $100,000 × (10% ÷ 2).
[b](Annual yield ÷ Number of interest payments per year) × Book value of bonds at beginning of period (from previous line); at 6/30/1991, (8% ÷ 2) × $108,110.88.
[c]Cash paid − Interest expense; at 6/30/1991, $5,000 − $4,324.44.
[d]Book value of bonds from previous line − Amortization of premium on bonds payable (this is equal to the face value of the bonds payable + the unamortized premium on bonds payable); at 6/30/1991, $108,110.88 − $675.56.
[e]Adjusted for rounding error of $.04.

```
1991
June 30   Interest Expense .......................................   4,324.44
          Premium on Bonds Payable  ..........................    675.56
              Cash .................................................           5,000.00
          To record interest paid on bonds and interest
          expense by the effective interest method.
```

When bonds are sold at a premium the interest expense each period is less than the interest paid. Therefore the company is repaying some of its liability with each interest payment. This is recognized by reducing the amount in the Premium on Bonds Payable account, which in turn reduces the book value of the liability (Bonds Payable plus Premium on Bonds Payable).

The second interest payment is made on December 31, 1991. The semiannual interest expense is computed as follows:

$$
\begin{aligned}
\text{Semiannual interest expense} &= (8\% \div 2) \times (\$100{,}000 + \$7{,}435.22) \\
&= 4\% \times \$107{,}435.22 \\
&= \$4{,}297.41
\end{aligned}
$$

Since the interest payment is $5,000, the premium amortization is $702.59 ($5,000 − $4,297.41) and the following journal entry is made:

```
1991
Dec. 31   Interest Expense .......................................   4,297.41
          Premium on Bonds Payable  ..........................    702.59
              Cash .................................................           5,000.00
          To record interest paid on bonds and interest
          expense by the effective interest method.
```

At the end of the life of the bonds on December 31, 1995, the premium is completely amortized. At this point the book value of the bonds equals the face value of $100,000.

Recording Accrued Interest Under Effective Interest Method

As discussed earlier in regard to straight-line amortization, an interest payment date may not coincide with the end of a company's accounting period. In such a case, the company must make an adjusting entry at the end of the accounting period to record the interest that has accrued since the last interest payment date. For example, assume that the Homestake Company instead issued bonds on September 30, 1991, and the bonds pay interest each March 31 and September 30. When the company's accounting period ends on December 31, 1991, it must record the interest that has accrued on its bonds from September 30, 1991, through the end of December. Under the effective interest method, the interest expense for these 3 months is determined by computing the interest for 6 months and then allocating this amount proportionately over the 6 months. In the situation in which the bonds were issued at a discount, the calculations are as follows:

$$
\begin{aligned}
\text{Semiannual interest} &= \left(\begin{array}{c}\text{Annual} \div \text{Number of interest}\\ \text{yield} \qquad \text{payments per year}\end{array}\right) \times \begin{array}{c}\text{Book value of}\\ \text{the bonds}\end{array}\\
&= (12\% \div 2) \times (\$100{,}000 - \$7{,}360.07)\\
&= 6\% \times \$92{,}639.93\\
&= \$5{,}558.40
\end{aligned}
$$

$$
\begin{aligned}
\text{Interest expense for} &= \text{Semiannual interest} \times \begin{array}{c}\text{Fraction of period since}\\ \text{previous recognition of}\\ \text{interest expense}\end{array}\\
\text{fraction of period} &\quad \text{expense}\\
&= \$5{,}558.40 \times 3/6\\
&= \$2{,}779.20
\end{aligned}
$$

The amount of interest owed at this date is calculated as follows:

$$
\begin{aligned}
\text{Interest payable for} &= \text{Semiannual interest} \times \begin{array}{c}\text{Fraction of period since}\\ \text{previous interest payment}\end{array}\\
\text{fraction of period} &\quad \text{payment}\\
&= \$5{,}000 \times 3/6\\
&= \$2{,}500
\end{aligned}
$$

The difference between the interest expense and the interest payable is again a reduction in the Discount on Bonds Payable account. The year-end accrual of the interest expense would be recognized as follows:

```
1991
Dec. 31   Interest Expense ........................................  2,779.20
              Discount on Bonds Payable ........................              279.20
              Interest Payable ....................................            2,500.00
          To accrue interest at the end of the year.
```

On March 31, 1992, the first semiannual interest payment of $5,000 is made. The interest expense to be recognized at this time is the remaining portion of the semiannual interest expense not recognized at December 31, 1991. This expense is calculated as follows:

$$
\begin{aligned}
\text{Interest expense} &= \text{Semiannual interest} \times \begin{array}{c}\text{Fraction of period since}\\ \text{previous recognition of}\\ \text{interest expense}\end{array}\\
&\quad \text{expense}\\
&= \$5{,}558.40 \times 3/6\\
&= \$2{,}779.20
\end{aligned}
$$

Therefore the journal entry to record the interest payment is:

```
1992
Mar. 31   Interest Expense ........................................  2,779.20
          Interest Payable ........................................  2,500.00
              Discount on Bonds Payable ........................              279.20
              Cash ...................................................            5,000.00
          To record interest paid on bonds and interest
          expense by the effective interest method.
```

In the situation in which the bonds were issued at a premium, the accrual of interest on December 31, 1992 is computed in a similar way as the discount example. The interest expense would be $2,162.22 ($4,324.44 × 3/6) and the amortization of the premium would be $337.78 ($2,500 − $2,162.22).

Additional Considerations

Several additional aspects of bonds need to be discussed. Bonds are frequently issued between interest payment dates; bonds are retired at the maturity date, and some bonds are retired prior to the maturity date. Each of these topics is discussed in the following sections.

Bonds Issued Between Interest Payment Dates

As we have seen, the dates on which the company issuing bonds agrees to pay interest are included in the terms of the bond and are printed on the bond certificate. These payments are usually semiannual, and at the end of each semiannual period the company pays a full 6 months' interest. As we discussed and illustrated earlier an interest payment date may not coincide with the end of a company's accounting period, in which case interest must be accrued at the end of the period. In another situation, **a company may issue the bonds between the specified interest dates because of the time that may elapse between the announcement of the bond issue and the actual sale of the bonds.** In such a case the purchasers of bonds are entitled to receive interest only for the period the bonds are owned, which on the first interest payment date is the period from the purchase date to the first interest payment date. To reduce record keeping and to allow the company to make a complete interest payment to each purchaser, **at the time of issuance the purchasers of the bonds pay accrued interest in addition to the purchase price of the bond.** The accrued interest is the interest that has accumulated from the interest payment date preceding the sale of the bonds to the date of the sale of the bonds. At the next interest payment date the company then pays the full 6 months' interest.

To illustrate, suppose that on March 1, 1992, the Lowland Company sells 5-year, 10% bonds with a face value of $24,000 at par value plus accrued interest. The bonds pay interest on June 30 and December 31. Two months have elapsed, therefore, between the interest payment date preceding the sale (December 31) and the date of the sale (March 1). On March 1 accrued interest of $400 ($24,000 × 10% × 2/12) is paid by the purchasers of the bonds in addition to the par value of $24,000.

The journal entry to record the sale on March 1 is:

1992			
Mar. 31	Cash	24,400	
	Interest Payable		400
	Bonds Payable		24,000

**To record issuance of 10% bonds at par plus
accrued interest for 2 months.**

The accrued interest is recorded as a liability because it will be paid on June 30, 1992, when the next semiannual interest payment is made. This payment will be $1,200 ($24,000 × 10% × 6/12), although only $800 is the interest expense for the 4 months the bonds have been outstanding while the remaining $400 is the payment of the liability recorded on March 1. The journal entry to record the first semiannual interest payment on June 30, 1992, is:

```
1992
June 30   Interest Expense ............................................   800
          Interest Payable ...........................................   400
             Cash ....................................................          1,200
```

To record interest paid on bonds.

The preceding sequence of events may be illustrated by the following diagram:

```
December 31,        March 1,                                June 30,
   1991          1992 (sale)                                 1992
  ├─────────────────┼───────────────────────────────────────┤

         Accrued                   Interest                  Interest
        Interest      +            Expense        =            Paid
          $400                      $800                     $1,200
```

It may seem confusing for a company to charge bond purchasers for accrued interest and then return this accrued interest when the first interest payment is made. The primary purpose for this practice is that if the bonds were sold on different dates to different purchasers and the company did not charge accrued interest, it would have to record separately the date of each sale and calculate the exact amount of interest it has to pay each purchaser on the first interest payment date. By charging accrued interest at the time of the sale, the company can make a full semiannual interest payment to all purchasers. It should also be noted that for amortizing any premium or discount (none, in this example), the bonds will not be outstanding for the full 5 years, but only for 4 years and 10 months.

Retirement of Bonds at Maturity

9(a). Record the retirement of bonds at maturity.

As discussed earlier in the chapter, the process of computing the interest expense and amortizing the discount or premium over the life of the bonds by either the straight-line or effective interest method means that at the maturity date the balance in the Discount or Premium account will have been eliminated. On the maturity date, therefore, the Bonds Payable account is the only account with a remaining balance and reflects the maturity value, which is the amount of cash that must be paid to the holders of the bonds. The journal entry to record the retirement of the bonds of the Homestake Company on December 31, 1995, is:

```
1995
Dec. 31   Bonds Payable ............................................   100,000
             Cash ....................................................          100,000
```

To record redemption of bonds payable at maturity date.

Retirement of Bonds Prior to Maturity

As mentioned earlier in the chapter, bonds may be issued with a call provision that allows a company to retire (*call*) the bonds before they mature by paying an amount to the holders that was specified at the time the bonds were sold. Alternatively, if the bonds are being traded on a bond market, the company can purchase the bonds and retire them.

Before accounting for the retirement, the company must first accrue the interest expense and pay the interest for the period since the last interest payment or accrual. This is done by using the method discussed for accruing the interest on December 31, 1991, for the bonds issued by the Homestake Company on September 30, 1991, at a discount or premium. That is, the semiannual interest is calculated in the normal way (for either the straight-line or effective interest method, whichever method the company is using), and this amount is multiplied by the fraction of the 6 months that has passed.

9(b). Record the retirement of bonds prior to maturity.

After recognizing the interest expense the company has to account for the retirement of the bonds. **When the cash used to retire the bonds is less than the book value of the bonds, the company recognizes a *gain* on the retirement.** Or, **if the cash payment is greater than the book value of the bonds, the company recognizes a *loss*.** If such gains and losses are material, they must be classified as *extraordinary* items on the income statement (discussed in Chapter 15), even though they did not meet the criteria of being unusual in nature and occurring infrequently.[3]

To illustrate the early retirement of bonds, suppose that a company calls bonds with a face value of $10,000 when they have a book value of $9,800 (we will assume that the recording of interest is up to date). The cost to retire the bonds is $10,200. This can be stated as *a call price* of 102 because, as discussed earlier, bond prices are quoted as a percentage of the face value. The face value of $10,000 multiplied by the call price of 102 stated as a fraction gives the cost of retiring the bonds ($10,000 × 1.02 = $10,200). The $400 extraordinary loss on retirement of the bonds is the cost of retiring the bonds minus the book value of the bonds ($10,200 − $9,800). The journal entry to record the retirement is:

Bonds Payable	10,000	
Extraordinary Loss on Retirement of Bonds	400	
Discount on Bonds Payable		200
Cash		10,200

To record retirement of bonds at a call price of 102.

The extraordinary loss would be disclosed, net of applicable income taxes, in the extraordinary items section of the income statement.

Straight-Line and Effective Interest Methods

Accounting principles require the use of the effective interest method unless the results obtained by the straight-line method are not materially different. Since the two methods do not produce material differences for bonds issued at a value close to par, many companies use the straight-line method. The advantage of using the straight-line method is that it is simpler to apply because the same journal entry is made every semiannual period. It does not lead to a rational measure of interest expense, however, because the expense stays constant even though the book value of the bonds increases (decreases) each period as the dis-

---

[3]"Reporting Gains and Losses from Extinguishment of Debt," *FASB Statement No. 4* (Stamford, Conn.: FASB, 1975), par. 8.

count (premium) is amortized. Therefore, the *effective rate* of interest changes each period under the straight-line method.

In contrast, the effective interest method records an interest expense each semiannual period that is based on the yield and the book value of the bonds. Since the yield represents the interest rate on the money borrowed by the company and the book value is the outstanding balance of the amount borrowed during the period, the interest expense is a rational measure of the cost of borrowing money for the period. The interest expense increases (decreases) as the book value of the bonds increases (decreases) as the discount (premium) is amortized.

In summary, under the straight-line method the amount of the semiannual interest expense is calculated by adding (subtracting) the discount (premium) amortized to the cash paid. Under the effective interest method the semiannual interest expense is computed by multiplying the semiannual yield times the book value of the bonds, and the difference between the interest expense and the cash payment is the amount of the discount or premium amortization.

Leases

10(a). Explain leases.

A lease is an agreement conveying the right to use property, plant, or equipment without transferring legal ownership of the item. For example, when a company leases a computer from IBM the company acquires the right to use the computer for the period of the lease, but it does not acquire legal ownership. IBM remains the legal owner of the computer. **The lessee is the company that acquires the right to use the property, plant, or equipment. The lessor is the company that gives up the use of the property, plant, or equipment.** (For instance, IBM is the lessor in this example.)

Before discussing how to account for leases, it is useful to compare leasing an asset to purchasing an asset on credit. For example, if a company purchases a building for use in its operations by issuing a 30-year mortgage, there is no doubt about how the transaction should be recorded. An operating asset, the building, and a liability, the mortgage payable, are both recognized. Although the company owns the building, the mortgage company has a legally secured interest in the building to protect its financial interests.

Now suppose that another company leases a building for 30 years for use in its operations. It does not acquire legal ownership of the building but agrees to make lease payments for 30 years. In both the lease and the mortgage situations, the company purchasing the building and the company leasing the building will use the building in their operations and each is committed to make payments for 30 years. Users of financial statements are not particularly concerned with the legal differences between a purchase and a lease. It would not be relevant to those users to report no asset for the lessee in the lease situation because there is no legal ownership, and to report no liability to make payments. Instead it is more relevant to report that there is an asset because the lessee has use of the building for 30 years, and to report a liability because the lessee has a 30-year commitment to make lease payments. In other words, it is most helpful for users if financial statements focus on the economic substance of the transaction. That is, the purchaser of the building and the lessee of the building have engaged in substantially similar economic transactions to acquire operating assets. Therefore the lease should result in the lessee recording both an operating asset and a liability.

Accountants have generally concluded that **economic substance is more important than legal form.** Therefore generally accepted accounting principles require that the lessee record an operating asset and a liability for a lease when substantially all the risks and benefits of ownership have been transferred by the lessor to the lessee. The specific criteria used to determine whether the risks and benefits of ownership have been transferred are beyond the scope of this book.

There are two types of leases for financial reporting purposes, a capital lease and an operating lease.[4] **A lease is a capital lease if the risks and benefits of ownership have been transferred from the lessor to the lessee.** On the other hand **a lease is an operating lease if it does not transfer the risks and benefits of ownership.** Accounting for capital and operating leases for the lessee are discussed in the following sections. This discussion focuses only on the basic principles involved because accounting for leases is a very complex area involving numerous rules. These rules, as well as accounting for leases by the lessor, are beyond the scope of the book.

Capital Lease

If a lease is classified as a capital lease, the lessee records an operating asset and a liability. **Both the asset and the liability are valued at the present value of the lease payments agreed to in the lease. D**etermination of the appropriate interest rate to use in the present value calculation is a complex procedure beyond the scope of this book, and therefore a rate will always be assumed. For example, suppose that the Adams Company enters into a capital lease for a computer from the Binary Company under the following terms:

Inception of lease	January 1, 1991
Life of lease	8 years
Annual lease payments at the end of each year	$5,000
Date of first payment	December 31, 1991
Interest rate	10%

The value at which to record the asset and liability is computed as follows:

Present value of = **Annual payment** × **Present value of**
lease payments   **annuity factor for**
                                             8 periods at 10%

= $5,000 × 5.334926
= $26,675 (rounded)

---

[4]"Accounting for Leases," *FASB Statement No. 13 as Amended and Interpreted through May 1980* (Stamford, Conn.: FASB, 1980).

The asset and liability are recorded by the lessee (Adams Company) on January 1, 1991, as follows:

```
1991
Jan. 1   Leased Property ................................................ 26,675
             Obligation Under Capital Lease ........................           26,675
         To record acquisition of computer under lease from
         Binary Company.
```

The leased property is listed in the Property, Plant, and Equipment section of the balance sheet. The portion of the Obligation liability to be paid in the next year is included as a current liability, with the remaining portion classified as a noncurrent liability.[5]

Since the Adams Company has recorded an asset, the cost must be amortized as an expense over its useful life (the term *amortization* is used more commonly than *depreciation* for leased property but the concept is exactly the same). The life of the lease is 8 years, and if it is assumed that straight-line amortization is used with no residual value, the amortization each year is calculated as follows:

$$\text{Annual amortization} = \frac{\text{Cost of leased property} - \text{Estimated residual value}}{\text{Estimated life}}$$

$$= \frac{\$26,675 - \$0}{8}$$

$$= \$3,334 \text{ (rounded)}$$

The Adams Company records this amortization in the normal manner on December 31, 1991, as follows:

```
1991
Dec. 31   Amortization Expense ........................................ 3,334
              Accumulated Amortization: Leased Property ........           3,334
          To record annual amortization on leased computer.
```

This journal entry would be repeated for each year of the asset's life. The amortization expense is classified as an operating expense on the income statement. The accumulated amortization is deducted from the Leased Property on the balance sheet to show the remaining book value of the asset.

Each $5,000 lease payment consists of a payment of both interest and principal. Every year when the Adams Company records the payment, it must separate the payment into the Interest Expense portion and the portion involving a reduction in the Obligation liability. The procedure used for this purpose is the effective interest method described earlier in the chapter, except that if the lease payment is made annually as assumed in this example, the *annual* interest rate is used in the interest expense computation.

---

[5]For simplicity, in this book we include the entire amount payable in the next year as a current liability of the lessee. In reality, if material, only the principal portion of the next year's lease payment(s) would be reported by the lessee as a current liability, since the interest has not yet accrued. This topic is beyond the scope of the text.

The interest expense and the reduction in the liability are computed as follows:

$$\text{Interest expense} = \text{Interest rate} \times \text{Book value of liability}$$
$$= 10\% \times \$26,675$$
$$= \$2,667 \text{ (rounded)}$$

$$\text{Reduction of liability} = \text{Cash payment} - \text{Interest expense}$$
$$= \$5,000 - \$2,667$$
$$= \$2,333$$

Therefore the journal entry to record the lease payment by the Adams Company on December 31, 1991, is:

1991			
Dec. 31	Interest Expense	2,667	
	Obligation Under Capital Lease	2,333	
	Cash		5,000
	To record lease payment for computer.		

The book value of the liability is now $24,342 ($26,675 − $2,333), and this amount is reported on the balance sheet. The amount payable in the next year ($5,000) is included as a current liability and the remaining portion ($19,342) as a noncurrent liability. The interest expense is included in the Other Revenues and Expenses section of the income statement.

A journal entry similar to 1991 would be made at the end of each year of the lease, with the amount based on the same equations. The calculation of the interest expense and reduction in liability for 1992 is as follows:

$$1992 \text{ Interest expense} = \text{Interest rate} \times \text{Book value of liability}$$
$$= 10\% \times \$24,342$$
$$= \$2,434 \text{ (rounded)}$$

$$1992 \text{ Reduction of liability} = \text{Cash payment} - \text{Interest expense}$$
$$= \$5,000 - \$2,434$$
$$= \$2,566$$

By using this procedure, the Obligation Under Capital Lease liability will be reduced to zero at the end of the life of the lease.

Operating Lease

When a lease does not transfer the risks and benefits of ownership, it is classified as an operating lease and the lessee does *not* record the "purchase" of an operating asset or a noncurrent liability. If the lease of the computer were considered an operating lease, the Adams Company would record nothing at the inception of the lease. When the payment is made each December 31, the company would record the payment as an expense, commonly called Rent Expense, because the lease is being accounted for as a rental. The payment on December 31, 1991 (and each successive year) would be recorded as follows:

1991			
Dec. 31	Rent Expense	5,000	
	Cash		5,000
	To record lease payment for computer.		

The rent expense is included as an operating expense in the income statement.

Mortgages Payable

A mortgage payable is a long-term debt for which the lender has a specific claim against an asset of the borrower. For example, most homeowners purchase their homes by issuing a mortgage. That is, they borrow the money from a lender and the lender is assigned a secured claim on the home. Companies also acquire assets through mortgages.

The typical mortgage requires equal monthly payments (an annuity), and these payments are determined according to present value principles as follows:

10(b). Explain mortgages.

> **Monthly payment = Amount borrowed ÷ Present value of annuity factor based on the interest rate and the life of the mortgage**

Each payment consists of two components: (1) interest expense based on the periodic interest rate and the book value of the loan at the beginning of the period and (2) a portion of the principal balance. This is similar to the lease payments discussed earlier, and these components are calculated as follows:

> **Interest expense = Periodic interest rate × Book value of loan at the beginning of the period**

> **Repayment of principal = Monthly payment − Interest expense**

To illustrate how to account for a mortgage suppose that the Joma Company purchases a building for $100,000. It agrees to pay $20,000 at acquisition and to pay the remainder under the terms of a 30-year mortgage at 12%. The journal entry to record the acquisition is:

Building	100,000	
Cash		20,000
Mortgage Payable		80,000

To record purchase of building with $20,000 cash payment and a 30-year, 12% mortgage.

Since the payments are to be monthly, the annual rate of 12% and time period of 30 years must be converted into their monthly equivalents of 1% and 360 periods. This factor is not included in Table 4 of Appendix B but it is 97.218331. The monthly payment is computed as follows:

> **Monthly payment = Amount borrowed ÷ Present value of annuity factor**
> = $80,000 ÷ 97.218331
> = $822.89

The interest expense for the *first* month is calculated as follows:

> **Interest expense = Periodic interest rate × Book value of loan at the beginning of the month**
> = 1% × $80,000
> = $800

The remaining portion of the monthly payment is $22.89 ($822.89 − $800.00) and is the reduction of the principal. The journal entry to record the first monthly payment is:

Interest Expense	800.00	
Mortgage Payable	22.89	
Cash		822.89

To record monthly mortgage payment.

Each month the balance in the Mortgage Payable account is reduced so that the balance in the account is eliminated when the final monthly payment is made.

At the end of each year, depreciation is recorded on the building in the usual manner. The depreciation expense and interest expense are reported on the Joma Company's income statement in the Operating Expenses and Other Revenues and Expenses sections, respectively. The mortgage payable is split into the current liability and long-term liability amounts on the company's year-end balance sheet in a similar way as discussed for leases.

Deferred Income Taxes

In Chapter 15, for simplicity we assumed that the amount of income tax expense for a corporation was the same as its income taxes payable. In many chapters, we have explained that the rules for computing taxable income are different than those for computing pretax accounting income. One of the major differences is depreciation. In Chapter 11 we explained that most companies use the straight-line method for financial reporting (although other methods are allowed), whereas all companies must use the Accelerated Cost Recovery System (ACRS) for income tax reporting (unless the asset was acquired before 1981). As a result pretax accounting income is different from taxable income in any given year. Although the two amounts of depreciation in any year are different, the total expense over the life of the asset is the same (assuming a zero residual value), and therefore the yearly difference in depreciation is known as a temporary difference.

10(c). Explain deferred income taxes.

A temporary difference occurs when an expense (or a revenue) is recognized in a different period for financial statement reporting than for income tax reporting, but the total lifetime expense (or revenue) is the same for both. In the case of depreciation, in the early years of an asset's life ACRS depreciation is usually *greater* than financial statement depreciation. However, in future years the temporary difference will reverse and ACRS depreciation will be less than financial statement depreciation, causing taxable income to be greater than pretax accounting income. These differences in future years will cause the company to owe additional taxes because of the higher taxable income. **Deferred income taxes is the account used to record the amount of the liability for the future additional income taxes resulting from temporary differences.**

To determine its total deferred income taxes in a given year, a company multiplies its expected future yearly temporary differences times the expected future income tax rate in each year. An adjustment is then made for the deferred income taxes of the current year. (These computations are complex and beyond the scope of the book.) The company's income tax expense is the sum of its income tax obligation and its deferred income taxes for the year. For example, if for 1991, a company's income taxes payable is $9,000 and the increase in its deferred income taxes for the year is $480, the company would record these amounts in the following journal entry:

```
1991
Dec. 31  Income Tax Expense  ......................................  9,480
             Deferred Income Taxes  ...............................          480
             Income Taxes Payable  ..................................       9,000
         To record income tax expense and
         income taxes owed.
```

The income tax expense of $9,480 ($9,000 + $480) would be reported on the company's 1991 income statement. The income taxes payable would be reported as a current liability on the company's 1991 ending balance sheet. The deferred income taxes would also be reported as a liability on the company's 1991 ending balance sheet.

Considerable controversy surrounds deferred income tax accounting because of the effect these procedures can have over many years. Typically, over time a company increases its assets which are subject to depreciation, either because the company is getting larger and requires more assets or because the company replaces its assets at a higher cost, or both. When assets increase, depreciation for income tax purposes is consistently greater than depreciation for the financial statements. In this situation taxable income is always less than pretax accounting income; therefore the deferred income taxes will accumulate and never be paid. For this reason many users of financial statements argue that the deferral of income taxes does not create a real liability and that the deferred income tax procedures should *not* be used. Instead they suggest that the income tax expense recorded in the company's income statement should be equal to the income taxes payable.

Although this section has discussed depreciation because it is usually the greatest single cause of deferred income taxes for a company, note that many other temporary differences also cause income taxes to be deferred. There are also permanent differences between pretax accounting income and taxable income that do not result in deferred income taxes. As a result, accounting for income taxes is very complex, and only the basic issues have been discussed here.

Pensions

10(d). Explain pensions.

A person who retires typically has three sources of income: savings, social security (which was discussed in Chapter 10), and a pension. Many companies, especially large ones, have a pension plan for their employees. **A pension plan is an agreement by a company to provide an income to its employees during retirement.** For example, an employee might receive an annual pension income as follows:

Average of last 5 years' pay × Number of years of service × 0.02

Therefore an employee who worked for 40 years for a company and had an average salary of $60,000 for the last 5 years of service would receive $48,000 per year ($60,000 × 40 × 0.02) during retirement until death.

To pay each employee's retirement income, a company generally contributes an annual amount during each year the employee works to a "funding agency," which is responsible for safeguarding and investing the pension assets and for making payments to the retired employees. The determination of the amount that the company contributes is made by an *actuary*, who is trained to calculate insurance risks and premiums. The computations involve present value and future value analyses and are based on assumptions concerning future pay rates, life expectancies, and expected rates of return.

The agreement to pay future retirement income causes the company to incur an expense in each year the employee works. The computation of the pension expense is very complex and beyond the scope of this book. Typically a company pays the same amount to the funding agency that it records as an expense. In such a situation, the company would make the following journal entry (amounts assumed):

```
1991
Dec. 31   Pension Expense  ..........................................   40,000
              Cash  ......................................................              40,000
          To record the pension expense and
          payment for 1991.
```

In those situations in which a company pays less (more) to the funding agency than it records as an expense, a liability (asset) would be recorded and reported on the balance sheet.

The procedures to account for pensions are controversial. We have only discussed the basic issues in this section.

Chapter Summary

Review of Learning Objectives

1. **Describe a bond.**
   A bond is a type of note in which a company agrees to pay the holder the face value at the maturity date and to pay interest periodically at a specified rate on the face value.

2. **Explain why bonds may be issued.**
   The primary reason why the management of a company may decide to issue bonds instead of common stock is that the earnings of the company may be increased through leverage. Leverage is advantageous when the company can earn a higher return than the rate of interest incurred on the bonds.

3. **Account for bonds sold at par.**
   When bonds are sold at par the cash received is equal to the face value of the bonds. The interest expense each period is equal to the interest payment.

4. **Explain why bonds are sold at a discount or premium.**
   Bonds are sold at a discount when the yield is more than the contract rate. Bonds are sold at a premium when the yield is less than the contract rate.

5. **Describe the straight-line method of accounting for a (a) discount or (b) premium.**

    Under the straight-line method of amortization, the premium or discount is amortized by an equal amount each period. For a discount the interest expense is greater than the cash payment each period. For a premium the interest expense is less than the cash payment each period. The calculations may be summarized as follows:

    Semiannual interest payment = Face value × $\left(\begin{array}{l}\text{Annual contract} \\ \text{rate}\end{array} \div \begin{array}{l}\text{Number of interest} \\ \text{payments per year}\end{array}\right)$

    Semiannual discount (premium) amortization = $\begin{array}{l}\text{Total discount} \\ \text{(premium) at} \\ \text{issuance of} \\ \text{bonds}\end{array} \div \left(\begin{array}{l}\text{Number of} \\ \text{years in} \\ \text{life of} \\ \text{bonds}\end{array} \times \begin{array}{l}\text{Number of} \\ \text{interest} \\ \text{payments} \\ \text{per year}\end{array}\right)$

    Semiannual interest expense = $\begin{array}{l}\text{Semiannual interest} \\ \text{payment}\end{array} + \begin{array}{l}\text{Semiannual discount} \\ \text{amortization} \\ \text{or} \\ -\text{Semiannual premium} \\ \text{amortization}\end{array}$

6. **Explain the concepts of present value and future value.**

    Present value is the value today of a certain number of dollars measured in the future. Future value is the value at a future date of a certain number of dollars measured today.

7. **Compute present values and future values.**

    Table 1 in Appendix B is used to compute the future value of a single amount when the present value is known. Table 2 is used to compute the present value of a single amount when the future value is known. Table 3 is used to compute the future value of an annuity. Table 4 is used to compute the present value of an annuity.

8. **Describe the effective interest method of amortizing a (a) discount or (b) premium.**

    The effective interest method is a method of recognizing interest expense in which the expense is based on the amount of money borrowed and the rate at which it is borrowed. The calculations may be summarized as follows:

    Semiannual interest expense = $\left(\begin{array}{l}\text{Annual yield} \\ \end{array} \div \begin{array}{l}\text{Number of} \\ \text{interest} \\ \text{payments} \\ \text{per year}\end{array}\right) \times \begin{array}{l}\text{Book value of the} \\ \text{bonds at the} \\ \text{beginning of the} \\ \text{period}\end{array}$

    Semiannual interest payment = Face value × $\left(\begin{array}{l}\text{Annual contract} \\ \text{rate}\end{array} \div \begin{array}{l}\text{Number of interest} \\ \text{payments per year}\end{array}\right)$

    Semiannual discount amortization = $\begin{array}{l}\text{Semiannual interest} \\ \text{expense}\end{array} - \begin{array}{l}\text{Semiannual interest} \\ \text{payment}\end{array}$

    Semiannual premium amortization = $\begin{array}{l}\text{Semiannual interest} \\ \text{payment}\end{array} - \begin{array}{l}\text{Semiannual interest} \\ \text{expense}\end{array}$

9. **Record the retirement of bonds (a) at maturity or (b) prior to maturity.**
When bonds are retired at maturity the cash paid is equal to the face value of the bonds. When bonds are retired prior to maturity and the cash paid is less than the book value of the bonds, the company recognizes an extraordinary gain on the retirement. If the cash payment is greater than the book value, the company recognizes an extraordinary loss.

10. **Explain (a) leases, (b) mortgages, (c) deferred income taxes, and (d) pensions.**
A *lease* is an agreement conveying the right to use property, plant, or equipment without transferring legal ownership of the item. For a *capital* lease, the lessee records an *asset and liability* at the present value of the lease payments. The *asset* is amortized over its useful life. For the liability, *interest expense* is recorded at the end of each period at an amount equal to the interest rate multiplied by the book value of the liability at the beginning of the period. The *liability* is reduced at the end of each period by an amount equal to the cash payment minus the interest expense. For an *operating* lease, the lessee recognizes rent expense when payments are made. For payments on a *mortgage,* the *interest expense* is equal to the periodic interest rate multiplied by the book value of the loan at the beginning of the period. The *repayment of principal* is equal to the monthly payment minus the interest expense. *Deferred income taxes* are caused by temporary differences. A *temporary difference* occurs when an expense (or a revenue) is recognized in a different period for financial statement reporting than for income tax reporting, but the total lifetime expense (or revenue) is the same for both. Deferred income taxes is the account used to record the amount of the liability for future additional income taxes. A *pension plan* is an agreement by a company to provide an income to its employees during retirement. Typically a company pays to the funding agency an amount equal to the pension expense. In situations in which a company pays less (more) to the funding agency than it records as an expense, a liability (asset) would be recognized.

Review Problem

On January 1, 1991, the Cleese Company sold 6-year, 12% bonds with a face value of $20,000. The bonds were sold for $21,772.64. The bonds pay interest on June 30 and December 31 each year.

REQUIRED

1. If the company uses the straight-line method:
   (a) Prepare a bond premium amortization schedule.
   (b) Prepare journal entries to record the sale and interest expense for the bonds during 1991.
   (c) Show how the bonds would be reported in the balance sheet on December 31, 1991.

2. If the company uses the effective interest method:
   (a) Compute the selling price of the bonds if the yield is 10%.
   (b) Prepare a bond premium amortization schedule.
   (c) Prepare journal entries to record the sale and interest expense for the bonds during 1991.
   (d) Show how the bonds would be reported in the balance sheet on December 31, 1991.

Solution to Review Problem

REQUIREMENT 1(a)

CLEESE COMPANY
Bond Premium Amortization Schedule
Straight-Line Method

Date	Cash Paid[a] (credit)	Amortization of Premium on Bonds Payable[b] (debit)	Interest Expense[c] (debit)	Book Value of Bonds[d]
1/1/1991				$21,772.64
6/30/1991	$1,200	$147.72	$1,052.28	21,624.92
12/31/1991	1,200	147.72	1,052.28	21,477.20
6/30/1992	1,200	147.72	1,052.28	21,329.48
12/31/1992	1,200	147.72	1,052.28	21,181.76
6/30/1993	1,200	147.72	1,052.28	21,034.04
12/31/1993	1,200	147.72	1,052.28	20,886.32
6/30/1994	1,200	147.72	1,052.28	20,738.60
12/31/1994	1,200	147.72	1,052.28	20,590.88
6/30/1995	1,200	147.72	1,052.28	20,443.16
12/31/1995	1,200	147.72	1,052.28	20,295.44
6/30/1996	1,200	147.72	1,052.28	20,147.72
12/31/1996	1,200	147.72	1,052.28	20,000.00

[a]$20,000 \times (12\% \div 2)$.
[b]$(\$21,772.64 - \$20,000) \div (2 \times 6)$.
[c]$1,200 - \$147.72$.
[d]Book value of bonds from previous line − $147.72; at 6/30/1991, $21,772.64 − $147.72.

REQUIREMENT 1(b)

```
1991
Jan.   1   Cash ...................................   21,772.64
               Bonds Payable ...................                20,000.00
               Premium on Bonds Payable ....................                 1,772.64

           To record issuance of 12% bonds at a premium.


June  30   Interest Expense ......................    1,052.28
           Premium on Bonds Payable .........................      147.72
               Cash .............................................                 1,200.00

           To record interest paid on bonds and premium
           amortization by the straight-line method.


Dec.  31   Interest Expense ......................    1,052.28
           Premium on Bonds Payable .........................      147.72
               Cash .............................................                 1,200.00

           To record interest paid on bonds and premium
           amortization by the straight-line method.
```

REQUIREMENT 1(c)

Noncurrent liabilities
12% Bonds payable, due 12/31/1996 .... $20,000.00
Plus: Premium on bonds payable .... _1,477.20_
$21,477.20

REQUIREMENT 2(a)

Selling = Present value of + Present value of semiannual
price   face value   interest payments
= ($20,000 × 0.556837) + ($1,200 × 8.863252)
= $21,772.64

Note: Each present value factor is for 12 periods (6 years × 2) and 5% (10% ÷ 2).

REQUIREMENT 2(b)

CLEESE COMPANY
Bond Premium Amortization Schedule
Effective Interest Method
(12% bonds to yield 10%)

Date	Cash Paid[a] (credit)	Interest Expense[b] (debit)	Amortization of Premium on Bonds Payable[c] (debit)	Book Value of Bonds[d]
1/1/1991				$21,772.64
6/30/1991	$1,200	$1,088.63	$111.37	21,661.27
12/31/1991	1,200	1,083.06	116.94	21,544.33
6/30/1992	1,200	1,077.22	122.78	21,421.55
12/31/1992	1,200	1,071.08	128.92	21,292.63
6/30/1993	1,200	1,064.63	135.37	21,157.26
12/31/1993	1,200	1,057.86	142.14	21,015.12
6/30/1994	1,200	1,050.76	149.24	20,865.88
12/31/1994	1,200	1,043.29	156.71	20,709.17
6/30/1995	1,200	1,035.46	164.54	20,544.63
12/31/1995	1,200	1,027.23	172.77	20,371.86
6/30/1996	1,200	1,018.59	181.41	20,190.45
12/31/1996	1,200	1,009.55[e]	190.45	20,000.00

[a]$20,000 × (12% ÷ 2).
[b](10% ÷ 2) × Book value of bonds at beginning of period (from previous line); at 6/30/1991, (10% ÷ 2) × $21,772.64.
[c]Cash paid − Interest expense; at 6/30/1991, $1,200 − $1,088.63.
[d]Book value of bonds from previous line − Amortization of premium on bonds payable; at 6/30/1991, $21,772.64 − $111.37.
[e]Adjusted for rounding error of $.03.

REQUIREMENT 2(c)

1991
Jan. 1 Cash 21,772.64
            Bonds Payable 20,000.00
            Premium on Bonds Payable 1,772.64

        To record issuance of 12% bonds to yield 10%.

June	30	Interest Expense	1,088.63	
		Premium on Bonds Payable	111.37	
		Cash		1,200.00

To record interest paid on bonds and interest expense by the effective interest method.

Dec.	31	Interest Expense	1,083.06	
		Premium on Bonds Payable	116.94	
		Cash		1,200.00

To record interest paid on bonds and interest expense by the effective interest method.

REQUIREMENT 2(d)

Noncurrent liabilities
12% Bonds payable, due 12/31/1996	$20,000.00
Plus: Premium on bonds payable	1,544.33
	$21,544.33

Glossary

Adjunct Account. An account added to another account to determine the book value.

Amortization. The process of writing off the discount, or premium, on bonds payable as an adjustment of interest expense over the life of the bond issue.

Annuity. A series of equal periodic cash flows. The tables in Appendix B used to compute the present or future value of an annuity are prepared on the assumption that the first cash flow occurs at the end of the first time period.

Bond Certificate. A serially numbered legal document that specifies the face value, the annual interest rate, the maturity date, and other characteristics of the bond issue.

Bond Indenture. A document that defines the rights of the bondholders.

Bonds Payable. A type of note payable in which the issuer (borrower) makes an unconditional promise to pay the holder (lender) the face value at the maturity date and to pay interest periodically at a specified rate on the face value.

Book Value of Bonds Payable. The face value of the bonds less the unamortized discount or plus the unamortized premium.

Callable Bonds. Bonds that are callable by the issuer at a predetermined price for a specified period. That is, the issuer has a right to require the holder to return the bonds before the maturity date and the issuer pays the predetermined price and interest to date.

Capital Lease. A lease in which the risks and benefits of ownership are considered to have been transferred from the lessor to the lessee. It is recorded as the acquisition of an asset and a liability by the lessee.

Compound Interest. Interest that accrues on both the principal and past accrued interest.

Contract Rate. The rate at which an issuer of a bond pays interest. Also called the *stated rate*, the *face rate*, or the *nominal rate*.

Convertible Bonds. Bonds that are convertible into a predetermined number of shares of common stock.

Coupon Bonds. Unregistered bonds on which interest is claimed by the holder by presenting a coupon to the issuer.

Debenture Bonds. Unsecured bonds. That is, the holder is considered as a general creditor if the issuer fails to pay the interest or principal.

Deferred Income Taxes. The account used to record the amount of the liability for the future additional income taxes resulting from temporary differences.

Discount on Bonds Payable. A contra account in which is recorded the amount by which the book value of the bonds payable is less than the face value.

Effective Interest Method. A method of recognizing interest expense in which the semiannual expense for a period is based on the semiannual yield times the book value of the bonds at the beginning of the period.

Face Value. The amount of money that the issuer of the bonds promises to pay on the maturity date. Also called *par value*.

Future Value. The value in the future of a certain number of dollars.

Lease. An agreement conveying the right to use property, plant, and equipment (without passage of legal title).

Leased Property. An asset recognized by the lessee of a capital lease. It is reported at the present value of the total lease payments, less the accumulated amortization. Included in Property, Plant, and Equipment in the balance sheet.

Lessee. The company that acquires the right to use property, plant, and equipment in a lease agreement.

Lessor. The company that gives up the right to use property, plant, and equipment in a lease agreement.

Leverage. The use of borrowing by a company to increase the return to the common stockholders. Also called *trading on equity*.

Maturity Date. The date on which the issuer of a bond agrees to pay the face value to the holder.

Mortgage Bonds. Bonds that are secured with specific property. That is, the holder of the bonds has a priority right to the specific property if the issuer fails to pay the interest or principal.

Mortgage Payable. A long-term debt for which the lender has a specific claim against an asset of the borrower.

Obligation Under Capital Lease. A liability recognized by the lessee under a capital lease. It is recorded at the present value of the remaining lease payments.

Operating Lease. A lease in which substantially all the risks and benefits of ownership have not been transferred from the lessor to the lessee.

Pension Plan. An agreement by a company to provide an income to its employees during retirement.

Premium on Bonds Payable. An adjunct account in which is recorded the amount by which the book value of the bonds payable exceeds the face value.

Present Value. The value today of a certain number of dollars in the future.

Registered Bonds. Bonds for which ownership is registered with the issuer. That is, the issuer maintains a record of the holder of each bond so that payment of interest and principal can be made without such payment being requested by the holder.

Serial Bonds. Bonds issued at one time but portions of the total face value mature at different future dates.

Sinking Fund Bonds. Bonds for which the issuer must pay an agreed amount each period into a sinking fund to be used to retire the bonds at maturity. *Sinking fund* is the term used to describe the account into which the cash is paid.

Straight-Line Method. A method of amortizing a discount or premium on bonds payable by an equal amount each period.

Temporary Difference. A difference that occurs when an expense (or a revenue) is recognized in a different period for financial statement reporting than for income tax reporting, but the total lifetime expense (or revenue) is the same for both.

Unamortized Discount (or Premium) on Bonds Payable. The amount of the discount (or premium) that has not yet been amortized.

Yield. The market (or effective) interest rate at which bonds are issued. The rate of return earned by the purchaser of bonds, and the cost of the money borrowed by the issuer. Also called *effective rate*.

Zero-Coupon Bonds. Bonds on which interest accrues, but the interest is not paid until the maturity date.

Questions

QUESTION 16-1   Define the following terms as they relate to bonds: (a) face value; (b) maturity date; and (c) contract rate.

QUESTION 16-2   Why would a company issue bonds when it is obliged to pay interest each period instead of issuing stock for which dividend payments are discretionary?

QUESTION 16-3   Distinguish between the following types of bonds: (a) debenture and mortgage bonds; (b) registered and coupon bonds; (c) serial bonds and callable bonds.

QUESTION 16-4   Why may a bond's contract rate differ from its yield?

QUESTION 16-5   What are the factors that affect an interest rate?

QUESTION 16-6   Under what condition will a bond be sold at a discount? At a premium?

QUESTION 16-7   What type of accounts are the Discount on Bonds Payable account and the Premium on Bonds Payable account? How is each included in the financial statements?

QUESTION 16-8   What is meant by the time value of money?

QUESTION 16-9   What is the difference between present value and future value?

QUESTION 16-10   Explain the difference between simple interest and compound interest.

QUESTION 16-11   What is an annuity? Why is an annuity a useful financial concept?

QUESTION 16-12   In calculating compound interest, how are the number of periods and the interest rate computed for interest periods other than 1 year?

QUESTION 16-13   Explain how interest expense is computed under the effective interest and straight-line methods.

QUESTION 16-14   Assume that a company has issued bonds at a discount and is using the straight-line amortization method, and that the interest payment does not coincide with the end of its accounting period. How does the company compute the interest expense, interest payable, and discount amortization which are recorded at the end of the accounting period? Would your answer change if the company were using the effective interest method?

QUESTION 16-15   How does a company record the selling price of bonds issued at par plus accrued interest when the bonds are sold between the interest payment dates?

QUESTION 16-16   If a bond is retired prior to its maturity date, under what condition will the issuing company report a loss on its income statement? A gain? Is the loss or gain ordinary or extraordinary?

QUESTION 16-17   If there is a capital lease, how does the lessee compute its interest expense? How does the lessee compute the reduction in its liability?

QUESTION 16-18   What are the two components of each monthly mortgage payment? How is each calculated?

QUESTION 16-19   How does a temporary difference occur? If a company's ACRS depreciation is greater than its straight-line depreciation, describe the differences between the company's financial statements and income tax calculations.

QUESTION 16-20   What is included in a company's deferred income tax account? Does it typically have a debit or credit balance? Why?

QUESTION 16-21   Where are deferred income taxes disclosed on a company's financial statements? Why do some users of financial statements disagree with this disclosure?

QUESTION 16-22   What is a pension plan? Why does a company record an expense if it will not pay its employees until after they have retired?

Exercises

EXERCISE 16-1   **Bonds Sold at Par.**   On January 1, 1991, the Miles Shredding Machine Company issued 20-year, 10% bonds with a face value of $200,000 at par. Interest is to be paid semiannually on June 30 and December 31.

REQUIRED   1. How much interest expense is recorded in 1991?

2. What is the book value of the bonds in the December 31, 1991, balance sheet? Show how this is disclosed.

EXERCISE 16-2   **Straight-Line Method.**   Use the same information as in Exercise 16-1, except that the company uses the straight-line amortization method and the bonds were issued at 102.

REQUIRED   1. How much interest expense does the Miles Shredding Machine Company recognize in 1991?

2. What is the book value of the bonds in the December 31, 1991, balance sheet? Show how this is disclosed.

EXERCISE 16-3   **Straight-Line Method.**   Use the same information as in Exercise 16-1, except that the company uses the straight-line amortization method and the bonds were issued at 99.

REQUIRED   1. How much interest expense does the Miles Shredding Machine Company recognize in 1991?

2. What is the book value of the bonds in the December 31, 1991, balance sheet? Show how this is disclosed.

EXERCISE 16-4   **Bonds Sold at a Premium.**   On January 1, 1991, the Mark Paint Company issued 2-year, 12% bonds with a face value of $100,000 at 102. The bonds pay interest semiannually on June 30 and December 31, and the company uses the straight-line amortization method.

REQUIRED   Prepare all the journal entries for the life of the bonds.

EXERCISE 16-5   **Present Value of a Single Sum.**   The following are amounts to be received or paid in the future:

(a) $2,000 to be received at the end of 4 years; interest rate of 6%.

(b) $5,000 to be received at the end of 5 years; interest rate of 8%.

(c) $10,000 to be paid at the end of 10 years; interest rate of 12%.

(d) $15,000 to be paid at the end of 15 years; interest rate of 5%.

(e) $3,000 to be received at the end of 6 years; interest rate of 6%.

REQUIRED   Compute the present value of each amount.

EXERCISE 16-6   **Future Value of a Single Sum.**   The following are present value amounts, numbers of periods, and interest rates:

(a) $2,000; 3 years; interest rate of 5%.

(b) $5,000; 5 years; interest rate of 10%.

(c) $10,000; 10 years; interest rate of 12%.

(d) $20,000; 15 years; interest rate of 5%.

(e) $3,000; 9 years; interest rate of 6%.

REQUIRED   Compute the future value of each amount at the end of the given number of periods.

EXERCISE 16-7   **Present Value of an Annuity.**   The following are annuities to be received or paid in the future:

(a) A 3-year annuity of $2,000 at 6%.

(b) A 5-year annuity of $5,000 at 10%.

(c) A 10-year annuity of $10,000 at 12%.

(d) A 15-year annuity of $15,000 at 5%.

(e) A 9-year annuity of $3,000 at 6%.

REQUIRED   Compute the present value of each annuity.

EXERCISE 16-8   **Future Value of an Annuity.**   Use the information in Exercise 16-7.

REQUIRED   Compute the future value of each annuity.

EXERCISE 16-9   **Bonds Sold at a Discount.**   On January 1, 1991, the Loveland Tractor Company issued 10-year, 9% bonds with a face value of $100,000. The bonds pay interest semi-annually and were issued to yield 10%. The company uses the effective interest method.

REQUIRED   *1.* What is the selling price of the bonds? What is the amount of the discount?

2. How much interest expense does the Loveland Tractor Company record in 1991?

3. What is the book value of the bonds in the December 31, 1991, balance sheet? Show how this is disclosed.

EXERCISE 16-10   **Bonds Sold at a Premium.**   Use the same information as Exercise 16-9, except that the bonds were issued to yield 6%. The company uses the effective interest method.

REQUIRED   *1.* What is the selling price of the bonds? What is the amount of the premium?

2. How much interest expense does the Loveland Tractor Company recognize in 1991?

3. What is the book value of the bonds in the December 31, 1991, balance sheet? Show how this is disclosed.

EXERCISE 16-11

Bonds Sold at a Discount.   On January 1, 1991, the James Wood Stove Company issued 2-year, 10% bonds with a face value of $100,000 for $96,534.93. The bonds pay interest semiannually on June 30 and December 31 and were issued to yield 12%. The company uses the effective interest amortization method.

REQUIRED   Prepare all the journal entries for the life of the bonds.

EXERCISE 16-12

Retirement of Bonds at Maturity.   Use the same information as Exercise 16-9.

REQUIRED   Prepare the journal entry to record the retirement of the bonds at their maturity date.

EXERCISE 16-13

Bonds Issued Between Interest Payment Dates.   On August 1, 1991, the Linjo Insecticide Company issued 10-year, 12% bonds with a face value of $15,000 at par plus accrued interest. The bonds pay interest on June 30 and December 31.

REQUIRED

1. How much accrued interest do the purchasers of the bonds pay to the Linjo Insecticide Company on August 1, 1991?

2. How much cash does the Linjo Insecticide Company receive at the sale?

3. Prepare the journal entry for the Linjo Insecticide Company to record the payment of interest on December 31, 1991.

EXERCISE 16-14

Bonds Issued Between Interest Payment Dates.   On May 1, 1991, the Duran Furniture Company issued 6-year, 12% bonds with a face value of $60,000 at par plus accrued interest. The bonds pay interest on June 30 and December 31.

REQUIRED

1. How much accrued interest do the purchasers of the bonds pay to the Duran Furniture Company on May 1, 1991?

2. How much cash does the Duran Furniture Company receive at the time of sale?

3. Prepare the journal entries for the Duran Furniture Company to record the sale of the bonds on May 1, 1991, and the interest payment on June 30, 1991.

EXERCISE 16-15

Retirement of Bonds Before Maturity.   The Porter Luggage Company has 10% bonds outstanding with a face value of $40,000. The bonds pay interest on June 30 and December 31. On July 1, 1991, when the bonds have a book value of $41,000, the Porter Luggage Company calls them at 101.

REQUIRED   Prepare the journal entry to record the redemption of the bonds.

EXERCISE 16-16

Expense from Capital Lease.   On January 1, 1991, the Thompson Cement Company leased a computer from the Hexad Computer Company. The lease was a capital lease, and the asset and liability were recorded by the Thompson Cement Company at $84,000 based on a 10% interest rate and a 12-year life. The lease payment of $12,328 is made at the end of each year. The company uses the straight-line amortization (depreciation) method for the leased asset and no residual value is expected.

REQUIRED   What is the interest expense and the amortization expense for the Thompson Cement Company in 1991?

EXERCISE 16-17

Operating Lease. Using the information in Exercise 16-16 assume the lease was classified as an operating lease.

REQUIRED

1. How much expense due to the lease will the Thompson Cement Company recognize in 1991?

2. On which company's balance sheet will the computer be recorded at the end of 1991? Why?

EXERCISE 16-18

Capital Lease. On January 1, 1991, the Eton Horse Breeding Company leased a Rolls Royce from Elite Cars for the president's use. The lease specified that $20,000 was to be paid at the end of each year for 5 years. The lease was classified as a capital lease. The interest rate is 10%. The straight-line amortization (depreciation) method and a zero residual value are used.

REQUIRED

1. Show how the leased asset would be reported on the balance sheet of the Eton Horse Breeding Company at December 31, 1991.

2. What is the amount of the liability on the balance sheet of the Eton Horse Breeding Company at December 31, 1991?

EXERCISE 16-19

Mortgage. The Holliday Company purchased a hotel for $180,000 and paid 20% down. The remainder was financed by a 20-year mortgage at 12%, with payments to be made monthly. The present value of an annuity of 1% for 240 periods is 90.819416.

REQUIRED

1. Compute the amount of the monthly mortgage payment.

2. Prepare journal entries to record the acquisition of the building and to record each of the first two mortgage payments.

EXERCISE 16-20

Deferred Income Taxes. At the end of 1991, the Lucero Child Care Company reported taxable income for the year of $27,000. It is subject to a 40% income tax rate. The company computes its deferred income taxes for the year to be $700.

REQUIRED

Prepare the journal entry to record income taxes for the Lucero Child Care Company at the end of 1991.

EXERCISE 16-21

Deferred Income Taxes. At the end of 1991, the Karpas Fire Alarm Company reported taxable income for the year of $40,000. It is subject to a 40% income tax rate. The company computes its deferred income taxes for the year to be $2,400.

REQUIRED

Prepare the journal entry to record income taxes for the Karpas Fire Alarm Company at the end of 1991.

EXERCISE 16-22

Pensions. The Mullen Rafting Company operates a pension plan for the benefit of its employees. The company computed its pension expense for 1991 to be $60,000 and paid that amount to a funding agency at the end of the year.

REQUIRED

1. Prepare the journal entry to record the pension expense.

2. If the company had paid more than $60,000, how would the financial statements be affected?

EXERCISE 16-23

Pensions. The Martin Insurance Company operates a pension plan for the benefit of its employees. The company computed its pension expense for 1991 to be $95,000 and paid that amount to a funding agency at the end of the year.

REQUIRED   *1.* Prepare the journal entry to record the pension expense.

2. If the company had paid less than $95,000, how would the financial statements be affected?

Problems

Part A

PROBLEM 16-1A   **Straight-Line Amortization.**   On January 1, 1991, the Myrtle Furniture Company issued 10-year, 9% bonds with a face value of $100,000 at 98. Interest is paid on June 30 and December 31 each year. The company uses the straight-line method of amortization.

REQUIRED   *1.* Prepare an amortization schedule for the discount or premium.

2. Prepare the journal entries to record all the events for the bonds during 1991.

3. Compute the book value of the bonds on the December 31, 1991, balance sheet and show how it is disclosed.

4. Compute the interest expense for 1991 and show how it is disclosed on the 1991 income statement.

PROBLEM 16-2A   **Present and Future Values.**   The following are four independent situations:

(a) Jane Seymour invests $7,500 on January 1, 1991, in a savings account that earns interest at 8% compounded quarterly. How much will be in the account on December 31, 1995?

(b) David Jones wants to put enough money in a fund to pay for his son's college education for 4 years. The fund will pay $3,000 every 6 months, starting September 1, 1991, and it is expected that the fund can be invested to earn 12% compounded semiannually. How much money must be put in the fund on March 1, 1991?

(c) Peter Morgan is saving to buy a house. On December 31, 1991, a relative dies and leaves him $20,000, which he immediately puts into a savings account. He believes he can also put $5,000 per year into the account starting on December 31, 1992. If the savings account pays 6% compounded annually, how much will Peter Morgan have available on January 1, 1997?

(d) Anne Boleyn purchases a 10-year annuity on January 1, 1991, for $100,000. The annuity will pay her an equal amount each year for 10 years. If she wants a 10% return on her investment, how much will each annuity payment be? Assume that the annuity is paid once each year beginning on December 31, 1991.

REQUIRED   Using the appropriate present and future value tables in Appendix B, solve each of the preceding situations.

PROBLEM 16-3A   **Effective Interest Method of Amortization.**   On January 1, 1991, the Mussel Hardware Company issued 9% bonds with a face value of $70,000. Interest on the bonds is paid on June 30 and December 31 each year, and the bonds mature on December 31, 1996. The bonds are sold to yield 8% and the company uses the effective interest method of amortization.

REQUIRED
1. Compute the selling price of the bonds.
2. Prepare an amortization schedule for the premium or discount.
3. Prepare the journal entries to record all the events for the bonds in 1991.
4. Prepare the journal entry to retire the bonds at the maturity date.

PROBLEM 16-4A   **Effective Interest Method of Amortization.**   Use the same information as Problem 16-3A, except that the bonds were sold to yield 10%.

REQUIRED
1. Compute the selling price of the bonds.
2. Prepare an amortization schedule for the premium or discount.
3. Prepare the journal entries to record all the events for the bonds in 1991.
4. Prepare the journal entry to retire the bonds at the maturity date.

PROBLEM 16-5A   **Retirement of Bonds Before Maturity.**   On December 31, 1991, the following information appeared in the balance sheet of the Zoom Boat Company:

7% Bonds payable, due December 31, 1997	$50,000
Less: Discount on bonds payable	2,346
	$47,654

Interest is paid on June 30 and December 31. The bonds were originally sold to yield 8%. On January 1, 1992, the Zoom Boat Company retired bonds with a face value of $30,000 by purchasing them at 101 on the bond market. On July 1, 1992, the company called the remaining bonds at 102. The company uses the effective interest method.

REQUIRED
1. Prepare journal entries to record all the events for the bonds during 1992.
2. Prepare a partial income statement for 1992 for the Zoom Boat Company relating to the preceding information.

PROBLEM 16-6A   **Capital Lease.**   On January 1, 1991, the Odoms Ink Company leased a building from the Weese Development Company. The lease is for 20 years and requires a payment of $15,000 on December 31 of each year. An interest rate of 10% is used and the lease is classified as a capital lease. The company uses the straight-line amortization (depreciation) method and no residual value is expected.

REQUIRED
1. Prepare the journal entries to record the lease for the Odoms Ink Company during 1991.
2. Prepare a partial income statement for 1991 and a partial balance sheet at December 31, 1991, for the Odoms Ink Company relating to the lease.

PROBLEM 16-7A   **Mortgage.**   On November 1, 1991, the Williams Pipe Company purchased an office building for $120,000 and paid 20% down. The remainder was financed by a 25-year mortgage at 12% with payments to be made monthly. The present value of an annuity of 1% for 300 periods is 94.946551. The building has an estimated service life and residual value of 40 years and $20,000, respectively. The company uses the straight-line depreciation method.

REQUIRED
1. Compute the amount of the monthly mortgage payment.
2. Prepare journal entries to record all of the events for the building and the mortgage in 1991.
3. Prepare the required disclosures in the financial statements for 1991.

Problems

Part B

PROBLEM 16-1B

Straight-Line Amortization. On January 1, 1991, the Golden Jewelry Company sold 5-year, 10% bonds with a face value of $400,000 at 102. Interest is paid on June 30 and December 31 each year. The company uses the straight-line method of amortization.

REQUIRED

1. Prepare an amortization schedule for the discount or premium.

2. Prepare the journal entries to record all the events for the bonds during 1991.

3. Compute the book value of the bonds on the December 31, 1991, balance sheet and show how it is disclosed.

4. Compute the interest expense for 1991 and show how it is disclosed on the 1991 income statement.

PROBLEM 16-2B

Present and Future Values. The following are four independent situations:

(a) Steven Stunning is saving to build a weight room in his home. On July 1, 1991, he sells his motorcycle for $1,000 and immediately puts the money into his savings account. He believes that he can also put $1,100 per year into this account starting on July 1, 1992. If the savings account pays 8% compounded annually, how much will Steve have in the account on July 1, 1995?

(b) Laurie Lightly purchases a 20-year annuity on January 1, 1991, for $200,000. The annuity will pay her an equal amount each year for 20 years. If she wants an 8% return on her investment, how much will the annuity payment be each December 31 if the first payment is received on December 31, 1991?

(c) Rhonda Ritz puts $300,000 in a savings account on June 1, 1991. If the account pays 10% interest compounded annually, how much will be in the account on May 31, 1996?

(d) Brian Bright wants to put enough money in a fund to pay for his daughter's college education for four years. The fund will pay $2,500 every 4 months starting September 1, 1991, and the fund will earn 12% compounded every four months. How much money must Brian put in the fund on May 1, 1991?

REQUIRED

Using the appropriate present and future value tables in Appendix B, solve each of the preceding situations.

PROBLEM 16-3B

Effective Interest Method of Amortization. On January 1, 1991, the Adobe Brick Company issued 10% bonds with a face value of $60,000. Interest on the bonds is paid on June 30 and December 31 each year, and the bonds mature on December 31, 1996. The bonds were sold to yield 8% and the company uses the effective interest method of amortization.

REQUIRED

1. Compute the selling price of the bonds.

2. Prepare an amortization schedule for the premium or discount.

3. Prepare the journal entries to record all the events for the bonds in 1991.

4. Prepare the journal entry to retire the bonds at the maturity date.

PROBLEM 16-4B **Effective Interest Method of Amortization.** Use the same information given in Problem 16-3B, except that the bonds were sold to yield 12%.

REQUIRED
1. Compute the selling price of the bonds.

2. Prepare an amortization schedule for the premium or discount.

3. Prepare the journal entries to record all the events for the bonds in 1991.

4. Prepare the journal entry to retire the bonds at the maturity date.

PROBLEM 16-5B **Retirement of Bonds Before Maturity.** On December 31, 1991, the following information appeared in the balance sheet of the Bix Glass Company:

9% Bonds payable, due December 31, 2009	$75,000
Plus: Premium on bonds payable	4,747
	$79,747

Interest on the bonds is paid on June 30 and December 31. The bonds were originally sold to yield 8%. On July 1, 1992, the Bix Glass Company retired bonds with a face value of $25,000 by purchasing them at 99 on the bond market. On December 31, 1992, the company called the remaining bonds at 101. The company uses the effective interest method.

REQUIRED
1. Prepare journal entries to record all events for the bonds during 1992.

2. Prepare a partial income statement for 1992 for the Bix Glass Company relating to the preceding information.

PROBLEM 16-6B **Capital Lease.** On January 1, 1991, the Ventrello Shoe Company leased a jet from the Cate Aviation Company. The lease is for 6 years and requires a payment of $150,000 on December 31 each year. The lease is classified as a capital lease and the interest rate is 12%. The company uses the straight-line amortization (depreciation) method and no residual value is expected.

REQUIRED
1. Prepare journal entries to record the lease for the Ventrello Shoe Company during 1991.

2. Prepare a partial income statement for 1991 and a partial balance sheet at December 31, 1991, for the Ventrello Shoe Company in regard to the lease.

PROBLEM 16-7B **Mortgage.** On November 1, 1991, the Blossom Signal Company purchased a building for $110,000 and paid 10% down. The remainder was financed by a 15-year mortgage at 15% with payments to be made monthly. The present value of an annuity of 1.25% for 180 periods is 71.449643. The building has an estimated service life and residual value of 30 years and $10,000, respectively. The company uses the straight-line depreciation method.

REQUIRED
1. Compute the amount of the monthly mortgage payment.

2. Prepare journal entries to record all of the events for the building and the mortgage in 1991.

3. Prepare the required disclosures in the financial statements for 1991.

Decision Cases

DECISION CASE 16-1

Financing by Stocks or Bonds.   The Underhill Ski Company has been operating at a very stable level, consistently earning a pretax income of $200,000. The company is evaluating the possibility of expanding its operations to include snowboards. It has calculated that it would cost $1 million to build a new plant. It is expected that pretax income would increase by $150,000 as a result of the expansion. The company currently has 100,000 shares of $10 par value common stock outstanding. Its income tax rate is 40%. The company is considering whether to finance the expansion by selling 10% bonds at par or by selling 70,000 shares of common stock to obtain the $1 million.

REQUIRED

1. How much will earnings per share be using each of the alternative methods of financing?

2. Which method of financing would you recommend?

DECISION CASE 16-2

Sale of Bonds at a Premium or Discount.   At a board meeting of the Temple Battery Company to discuss the issuance of bonds with a face value of $100,000, the following comments were made:

- "At current market rates, I think the bonds will sell to yield 10%. Therefore, we should have a contract rate of 11% so that the bonds will sell at a premium. Like anyone else, investors view premiums as favorable, and we should do anything we can to get favorable reactions."

- "I agree that the yield will be 10%, but I think we should have a contract rate of 8%, so that the bonds will be sold at a discount. We all know people like to get a good deal, and if they can buy the bonds for less than the face value, I'm sure they will sell very easily."

- "If the yield is 10%, we should have a contract rate of 10%. Since we need exactly $100,000 to finance our expansion, that is the best alternative."

REQUIRED   Critically evaluate each of the comments.

DECISION CASE 16-3

Bonds.   Colgate Palmolive reported the following in its 1988 financial statements (amounts in thousands of dollars):

	December 31, 1988	December 31, 1987
$150,000 face amount debentures due 2017 (less amortized discount of $3,535 and $3,660) at an effective interest rate of 9.98%	$146,465	$146,340

Assume that the bonds were issued on December 31, 1987 and pay interest annually on December 31.

REQUIRED

1. Compute the interest paid in 1988.

2. Compute the interest expense for 1988 if the company used the straight-line method instead.

DECISION CASE 16-4   **Leasing.**   The Byrne Bus Company is planning to acquire some office machinery. It is considering three different methods of acquiring the machinery, which has a 6-year life and no residual value.

(a) Buy the machinery for $50,000, pay $10,000 down, and borrow the balance from a bank at 10% for 6 years. Interest is to be paid on December 31 each year.

(b) Lease the machinery under a 6-year lease, which would be classified as a capital lease. The lease would require a payment of $15,000 at the end of each year. There is no option to buy the machinery included in the lease.

(c) Lease the machinery under a 1-year lease, which would be classified as an operating lease. The company intends to renew the lease each year for 6 years. The lease payment, which is due when the lease is signed, is $15,000.

REQUIRED   *1.* Prepare an analysis (using assumptions that you think are appropriate) of the cash flows the company would pay over the 6 years under each alternative.

2. Explain how each of the alternatives would affect the financial statements.

3. Which alternative would you recommend?

DECISION CASE 16-5   **Leases.**   Kimberly-Clark is a large manufacturer and marketer of natural and synthetic products for personal and health care. The following excerpts are from its 1988 financial statements related to leases (in millions of dollars):

Note 7. Leases (in part):
   Future minimum rental payments under operating leases as of December 31, 1988 were:

	(in millions)
Year ending December 31:	
1989	$ 19.9
1990	16.0
1991	13.1
1992	9.4
1993	5.7
Thereafter	45.2
Total minimum rental payments	$109.3

REQUIRED   Using T-accounts, compute the effect on the balance sheet at December 31, 1988, and the income statement for 1989 if the operating leases were recorded as capital leases instead. Assume each year's payments are made at the end of the year. Use a 10% interest rate and straight-line amortization. Assume the "thereafter" payments are due in equal amounts over the next ten years after 1993.

17

Investments

LEARNING OBJECTIVES

1. Identify marketable securities.

2. Account for the (a) acquisition cost, (b) subsequent valuation using the lower of cost or market method, (c) revenue on, and (d) sale of current marketable securities—stocks.

3. Account for the (a) acquisition cost and (b) subsequent valuation using the lower of cost or market method for noncurrent marketable securities—stocks.

4. Account for the (a) acquisition cost, (b) subsequent valuation using the cost method, (c) revenue on, and (d) sale of current marketable securities—bonds.

5. Record noncurrent investments in bonds under the (a) straight-line method and (b) effective interest method.

6. Identify when to use the lower of cost or market method, the equity method, and consolidation.

7. Explain the characteristics of the equity method.

8. Describe consolidated financial statements.

9. Explain the elimination of the investment account in consolidations.

10. Explain the elimination of intercompany transactions.

11. Describe the goodwill recorded in consolidations.

12. Describe the nature of minority interest.

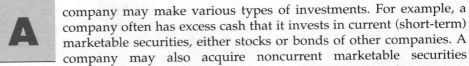

A company may make various types of investments. For example, a company often has excess cash that it invests in current (short-term) marketable securities, either stocks or bonds of other companies. A company may also acquire noncurrent marketable securities because excess cash is available for more than one year. Noncurrent investments in bonds of other companies may be acquired, either to develop a financial relationship with another company or to obtain a relatively safe source of continuing revenue. Noncurrent investments in the stocks of other companies may be purchased. These acquisitions may be made either because they appear to be more profitable than investing in property, plant, or equipment, or for operating reasons. For example, a company can obtain a certain degree of influence, or even control, over the operations of other companies from which it purchases inventory or to which it sells products by purchasing common stock of these companies, voting at the stockholders' meeting, and being represented on the board of directors. A company may also invest in the stocks of companies that tend to have a business cycle different from its own. In this way it is hoped that the income earned on the stock will help to offset any declines in the income from the company's own business, and therefore a smoother trend of earnings may result. Each of these investments is discussed in this chapter.

Marketable Securities

When a company acquires stocks or bonds of other companies it may intend to sell them soon or hold them for a longer period. If for a short period a company has excess cash that it does not need for its current operations, it may not wish to invest in long-term physical assets or reduce liabilities because the company realizes that it will need the money in the near future for operations. Instead of investing the excess cash in cash equivalents (discussed in Chapter 7) that earn relatively low interest, many companies invest in marketable securities that may provide a higher rate of return. **Marketable securities are investments in common stocks or bonds that are readily saleable.** (Marketable securities may also include preferred stocks but, for simplicity, these are not discussed in this book.) Examples of marketable securities are:

1. Identify marketable securities.

1. **Common Stocks of Other Companies.** The common stock of a corporation (discussed in Chapter 14) may be purchased on the stock market by another company. Common stock is the stock that shares in all the stockholders' rights. Any dividends paid on the common stock are received by the company (or individual) holding the stock.

2. **Bonds of Other Companies.** A bond (as discussed in Chapter 16) is a written promise by a company to repay a specific amount (the face value) at some specified date (the maturity date) and to pay interest (usually semiannually) each year. In addition, federal, state, and local governments also issue bonds to finance their activities. The company (or individual) holding these bonds receives the interest.

These securities are classified as *current* if, to obtain extra cash as needed, the company's intent is to sell the securities (or the securities mature) within 1 year or the operating cycle, whichever is longer. These securities are classified as *noncurrent* if the intent is to hold the security for *more* than 1 year or the normal operating cycle, whichever is longer. The classification as current or noncurrent is simply based on management intent. Also, since the classification is only important when the financial statements are issued, the criterion of a year extends from the balance sheet date.

Two general issues arise in accounting for marketable securities. First, how should the asset be reported in the balance sheet? Second, when is the revenue from the investment recognized? The answers to both questions unfortunately vary between stocks and bonds. Marketable securities—stocks are reported in the balance sheet at the lower of cost or market, whereas current marketable securities—bonds are reported at cost.[1] Dividends paid by the corporation issuing the stock are recorded as revenue by the owner of the stock when the dividends are received. Interest paid by the corporation issuing the bonds is recorded as revenue by the owner of the bonds for the period they are owned. To put it simply, interest accrues continuously over time, whereas dividends are discretionary periodic payments.

In the first part of the chapter accounting for current and noncurrent marketable securities—stocks is discussed. Next current marketable securities—bonds and noncurrent investments in bonds are discussed. Later in the chapter the equity method for investments in stocks is explained. Finally, accounting for a controlling interest is discussed.

Market Prices of Stocks and Bonds

An investment in stocks or bonds of publicly traded companies can be made very easily by dealing through a stockbroker. A stockbroker is a person or company that buys and sells (*trades*) stocks, bonds, and similar types of investments for other people or companies. The stocks and bonds of large companies are traded on organized securities exchanges, such as the New York Stock Exchange or the American Stock Exchange. The stocks and bonds of smaller companies are traded in the over-the-counter market in which brokers deal directly with each other rather than through a stock exchange.

The market prices of such stocks and bonds are quoted daily and reported in many newspapers. For example, the stock of IBM was recently listed as follows:

| 52 Weeks | | | | | | | | |
High	Low	Dividend	Yield, %	Volume, 100s	High	Low	Close	Net Change
$129\frac{1}{2}$	$104\frac{1}{2}$	4.40	3.6	4629	$123\frac{1}{2}$	$122\frac{3}{4}$	$123\frac{3}{8}$	$+\frac{7}{8}$

---

[1]Current marketable securities—bonds may also be reported at lower of cost or market. In this book, however, we assume that these securities are reported at cost.

This information indicates that the stock has sold at a high of $129\frac{1}{2}$ per share and a low of $104\frac{1}{2}$ per share in the last 52 weeks. The annual dividend is $4.40 per share, which is a yield of 3.6% (the dividend as a percentage of the market price) on the closing market price. On the date of this quotation, 462,900 shares were traded, the high price for the day was $123\frac{1}{2}$ per share, the low price $122\frac{3}{4}$ per share, and the closing price $123\frac{3}{8}$ per share, which was an increase in price of $\frac{7}{8}$ over the closing price of the previous day.

Bonds of IBM were also listed as follows:

Bonds	Current Yield	Volume	Close	Net Change
$9\frac{3}{8}$ 04	9.4	55	$99\frac{3}{8}$	$+\frac{1}{8}$

This information indicates that the bonds have an interest rate of $9\frac{3}{8}\%$ and mature in the year 2004. The bonds currently yield 9.4% (the annual interest as a percentage of the market price) and on the date of this quotation 55 bonds were traded. The closing price was $99\frac{3}{8}$, which represents an increase of $\frac{1}{8}$ from the closing price of the previous day. This bond price is quoted as a percentage of the face value of the bond and not as a dollar amount. Since bonds have a face value of $1,000 this quote represents a price of $993.75 ($99\frac{3}{8}\% \times \$1,000$).

These quoted market prices indicate the price an investor company would have to pay to purchase the securities or the price at which they can be sold. In addition, it would have to pay a fee to the stockbroker to make a purchase or a sale, and for bonds the investor company will also have to pay accrued interest since the last interest payment date.

Marketable Securities—Stocks

Accounting for the acquisition, valuation, revenue from, and sale of current and noncurrent marketable securities—stocks is discussed in the following sections.

Acquisition of Current Marketable Securities—Stocks

2(a). Account for the acquisition cost of current marketable securities—stocks.

All marketable securities are recorded at the cost of acquisition, which is the purchase price, including commissions to the stockbroker, and any transfer taxes that are imposed.

Suppose that on October 1, 1991, the Lennon Company purchases as a current investment 100 shares of the common stock of General Motors when the market price is $40 per share and 50 shares of the common stock of United Airlines when the market price is $20 per share. Stockbroker's fees and transfer taxes are ignored in this example. The total acquisition cost of $5,000 [(100 × $40) + (50 × $20)] is recorded as follows:

1991

Oct. 1   Current Marketable Securities—Stocks   5,000

               Cash   5,000

               **To record acquisition of 100 shares of General Motors and
50 shares of United Airlines.**

Thus the Lennon Company has exchanged one current asset, cash, for another current asset, marketable securities.

Subsequent Valuation of Current Marketable Securities— Stocks: Lower of Cost or Market Method

2(b). Account for the subsequent valuation of current marketable securities—stocks using the lower of cost or market method.

On each balance sheet date, the current marketable securities—stocks must be properly valued for inclusion as a current asset on the balance sheet. This valuation of current marketable securities—stocks uses the lower of cost or market method based on the current portfolio of stocks owned.[2] **A company's portfolio includes all of its investments in stock of other companies. The current portfolio includes the investments in stock that are classified as current. As applied to the current portfolio, the lower of cost or market method is a valuation method in which the portfolio is valued at the lower of its original cost or its current market value.** That is, if the total cost of the current portfolio of investments in stock is less than the total market value of the portfolio on the balance sheet date, the Current Marketable Securities—Stocks are carried at cost. Alternatively, if the market value of the portfolio is less than the cost of the portfolio, the Current Marketable Securities—Stocks are carried at market value. This procedure is consistent with the conservatism principle, discussed in Chapter 9.

To illustrate the application of the lower of cost or market method, suppose that the Lennon Company's current investments in capital stock had the following values at December 31, 1991, determined from current stock market prices as discussed earlier:

Company	Number of Shares	Cost per Share	Market Value per Share	Total Cost	Total Market Value
General Motors	100	$40	$30	$4,000	$3,000
United Airlines	50	20	25	1,000	1,250
				$5,000	$4,250

Since the total market value of the current portfolio is $4,250 and the cost was $5,000, the portfolio must be valued at $4,250 in the balance sheet and a loss of $750 ($5,000 − $4,250) included in the income statement. A loss is reported because there is a decline in the value of the assets of the company, and this

---

[2]"Accounting for Certain Marketable Securities," *FASB Statement No. 12* (Stamford, Conn.: FASB, 1975).

decline in value accrues to the owners of the company. Furthermore this procedure is consistent with the matching concept because the loss in value is recognized in the period in which it occurs and not in the period in which the securities are ultimately sold. The loss is included in the income statement in the Other Revenues and Expenses section. The journal entry on December 31, 1991, to record the decline in value is as follows:

```
1991
Dec. 31   Unrealized Loss on Decline in Value of Current
              Marketable Securities—Stocks ...........................   750
          Allowance for Decline in Value of Current Marketable
              Securities—Stocks ........................................          750
          To record current marketable securities—stocks at lower
          of cost or market.
```

The Unrealized Loss on Decline in Value of Current Marketable Securities—Stocks is the loss from holding current marketable securities (stocks) that has not been realized through a sale. Therefore the loss is called an *unrealized loss*. The Allowance for Decline in Value of Current Marketable Securities—Stocks is a contra-asset account used to record the amount by which the market value of Current Marketable Securities—Stocks is less than the cost. The account has the effect of reducing the asset value in the balance sheet. The cost of the portfolio of Current Marketable Securities—Stocks, however, is also reported (usually on the face of the balance sheet) so that the users of the financial statements know both the cost and the market value. For example, the Lennon Company might disclose its current marketable securities as follows:

```
Current Assets
    Marketable securities—stocks, at cost .....................................   $5,000
    Less: Allowance for decline in value ........................................    (750)
    Marketable securities—stocks, at lower of cost or market ..............   $4,250
```

If the market price of the portfolio continues to fall, a loss must again be recognized at the end of the next period. The loss would be equal to the additional decline in value and would be the amount necessary to obtain the correct balance in the Allowance account. The general rule is that the loss in any period is equal to the decline in the recorded value of the portfolio during the period under the lower of cost or market method. For example, suppose that the Lennon Company is preparing its quarterly financial statements on March 31, 1992, and the portfolio has the following market values:

Company	Number of Shares	Cost per Share	Market Value per Share	Total Cost	Total Market Value
General Motors	100	$40	$27	$4,000	$2,700
United Airlines	50	20	26	1,000	1,300
				$5,000	$4,000

Note that although the market price of the United Airlines stock went up from $25 to $26 per share, it is the *total* market value of the current portfolio that is compared to the previously recorded value of the portfolio. Since the previously recorded market value was $4,250, the journal entry on March 31, 1992, to record the additional $250 decline in value to $4,000 is as follows:

```
1992
Mar. 31   Unrealized Loss on Decline in Value of Current
               Marketable Securities—Stocks  ...........................    250
             Allowance for Decline in Value of Current Marketable
               Securities—Stocks  ........................................            250
          To record current marketable securities—stocks at lower
          of cost or market.
```

If the market price of the portfolio subsequently rises, the gain (loss recovery) in value is recognized at the end of the next period, but the gain cannot exceed previously recognized losses. That is, the portfolio cannot be valued above cost. The general rule is that the gain in any period is equal to the increase in the recorded value of the portfolio during the period provided that the recorded value does not exceed cost. For example, suppose that the Lennon Company is preparing its quarterly financial statements on June 30, 1992. At this time the portfolio has the following market values:

Company	Number of Shares	Cost per Share	Market Value per Share	Total Cost	Total Market Value
General Motors	100	$40	$33	$4,000	$3,300
United Airlines	50	20	26	1,000	1,300
				$5,000	$4,600

Before discussing the journal entry required on June 30, 1992, let us review the entries that have been made in the following related accounts:

Current Marketable Securities—Stocks		Allowance for Decline in Value of Current Marketable Securities—Stocks	
10/1/91 5,000		12/31/1991 750	
		3/31/1992 250	

Since the Current Marketable Securities account has a balance of $5,000 and the Allowance account has a balance of $1,000, the book value of the portfolio of current marketable securities in stock is $4,000. At June 30, 1992, the $4,600 market value of the portfolio is still less than the $5,000 cost, and therefore the securities should be carried at their market value of $4,600 in the balance sheet. This requires an ending balance in the Allowance account of $400 ($5,000 – $4,600). Since the existing balance is $1,000, this balance has to be reduced by $600 ($1,000 – $400) to $400 by the following journal entry:

```
1992
June 30   Allowance for Decline in Value of Current
                  Marketable Securities—Stocks ...........................   600
          Unrealized Gain on Increase in Value of Current
                  Marketable Securities—Stocks ..........................          600

          To record current marketable securities—stocks at lower
          of cost or market.
```

The gain of $600 appears in the income statement for the quarterly period in the Other Revenues and Expenses section and the balance sheet includes the value of the portfolio as follows:

```
Current Assets
   Marketable securities—stocks, at cost .....................................   $5,000
   Less: Allowance for decline in value .......................................    (400)
   Marketable securities—stocks, at lower of cost or market ..............   $4,600
```

If the total market value of the current marketable securities (stocks) is $5,500 on September 30, 1992, when the next quarterly financial statements are prepared, a gain of only $400 is recorded and therefore the Allowance account is eliminated. That is, when the market value of the portfolio goes *above* the cost, the gain is computed by the company as the difference between the previous market value ($4,600) and the cost ($5,000) of the portfolio. Therefore the marketable securities are now recorded at their cost of $5,000 and *not* at the market value of $5,500 because the market value is *higher* than the cost. The Lennon Company would disclose the following information in its balance sheet:

```
Current Assets
   Marketable securities—stocks, at cost
      (market value is $5,500) ...............................................   $5,000
```

Revenue on Current Marketable Securities—Stocks

2(c). Account for the revenue on current marketable securities—stocks.

A corporation has no obligation to pay dividends on its issued common stock. Dividends are a discretionary payment that must be voted by the board of directors as discussed in Chapter 15. Thus the purchaser of stock has no right to receive dividends, and therefore earns no revenue, until the dividends are *declared* by the corporation. When a corporation decides to pay dividends it first declares that it will pay dividends. This act creates a legal obligation to pay the dividends. The dividends are actually paid about a month later. The reasons for different declaration and payment dates were discussed in Chapter 15. Most companies recognize revenue when the dividend is received. Suppose United Airlines pays a dividend of $1 per share. The Lennon Company now has revenue of $50 (50 shares × $1), which is recorded as follows:

```
Cash ........................................................................   50
   Dividend Revenue ......................................................        50

To record dividend received on the current investment
in United Airlines stock.
```

The Dividend Revenue is included in the Other Revenues and Expenses section in the income statement. Some companies record dividend revenue when the dividend is declared by the investee company. Then a Dividends Receivable account is debited and the Dividend Revenue account is credited when the dividend is declared. Cash is debited and Dividends Receivable is credited when the cash is received.

Sale of Current Marketable Securities—Stocks

When additional cash is needed for a company's operations, an individual security included in current marketable securities—stocks may be sold. A gain or loss may arise from the sale, which is the difference between the selling price and the *cost* of the particular stock. That is, the balance in the Allowance account is *ignored*. The gain or loss is *not* measured as the difference between the selling price of the security and its most recent market value because *individual* stocks are not carried at their market value. It is the *total* portfolio that is being carried at the lower of cost or market. After the sale, at the end of the period the portfolio of stocks is valued again, and the balance in the Allowance account is adjusted accordingly. Suppose the Lennon Company sells the 100 shares of General Motors common stock for $35 per share (ignoring the stockbroker's commission and transfer taxes). The Lennon Company receives $3,500 (100 × $35) and recognizes a loss of $500 (the $4,000 original cost – $3,500) as follows:

2(d). Account for the sale of current marketable securities—stocks.

Cash	3,500	
Loss on Sale of Current Marketable Securities—Stocks	500	
Current Marketable Securities—Stocks		4,000

To record sale of 100 shares of General Motors stock.

The Loss on Sale is included in the Other Revenues and Expenses section on the income statement.

Noncurrent Marketable Securities—Stocks

As mentioned earlier, accounting for the noncurrent portfolio of marketable securities—stocks is very similar to that used for the current portfolio. That is, the noncurrent portfolio (acquisitions that are intended to be held for *more* than 1 year or the operating cycle, whichever is longer) is initially recorded at the acquisition cost. Furthermore the portfolio is valued on the balance sheet at the lower of its cost or market value.[3] The "loss" caused by a decline in the value of the noncurrent portfolio, however, is included directly as a reduction in stockholders' equity on the balance sheet.[4] This procedure is in contrast to the lower of cost or market method for current marketable securities where the unrealized loss caused by the decline in value is included in the income statement. This dif-

---

[3]This procedure is used for investments of less than 20% ownership interest. For larger investments, different methods are used that are discussed later in the chapter.

[4]"Accounting for Certain Marketable Securities," *op. cit.*, par. 11.

ference is illustrated in the following diagram. Note that the impact on the balance sheet is the same for both the current and noncurrent portfolio because the asset value and stockholders' equity on the balance sheet are both reduced.

Decline in Value (–)	Income Statement	Stockholders' Equity (–)
Current portfolio ⟶	Unrealized loss ⟶	Retained earnings
Noncurrent portfolio ⟶		Unrealized decline

The reason for not including the reduction in market value of a noncurrent portfolio in the income statement is that, since the portfolio is to be held for at least a year, there is a reasonable possibility that the decline will be reversed before a sale is made. Including these declines and reversals in the income statement might tend to distort the results of the ongoing operating activities of the company. It seems just as likely, however, that the user of the financial statements will be confused by the placement of this decline on noncurrent marketable securities—stocks in the stockholders' equity section of the balance sheet and the loss on current marketable securities—stocks in the income statement.

As with the current marketable securities—stocks, the Allowance account balance is subtracted from the cost of the noncurrent marketable securities—stocks to report the market value of these securities in the balance sheet. The unrealized decline in the value of the securities that is included in stockholders' equity would be reported in the balance sheet in the following manner (amounts assumed):

Stockholders' Equity		
Contributed capital		
Common stock, $5 par	$10,000	
Additional paid-in capital	25,000	
Total contributed capital		$35,000
Retained earnings		42,000
Total contributed capital and retained earnings		$77,000
Less: Unrealized decline in value of noncurrent marketable securities — stocks		(2,000)
Total Stockholders' Equity		$75,000

As discussed earlier, recoveries in the market value *up to* the cost of the portfolio are recognized. Remember that marketable securities—stocks cannot be carried at a value in excess of their cost. This recovery of value for noncurrent marketable securities—stocks, in contrast to current marketable securities—stocks, is *not a gain* reported on the income statement. Instead, it is treated as a *reduction* of the unrealized decline on the balance sheet.

To illustrate the application of the lower of cost or market method to noncurrent marketable securities—stocks, we will assume that the Lennon Company purchased in 1991 a portfolio of noncurrent marketable securities—stocks for $5,000. The acquisition would be recorded on October 1, 1991, as follows:

1991
Oct. 1   Noncurrent Marketable Securities—Stocks 5,000
           Cash   5,000

           To record acquisition of 100 shares of General Motors and
           50 shares of United Airlines.

On December 31, 1991, the securities had a value of $4,250. The $750 ($5,000 – $4,250) decline in the value of the portfolio of noncurrent marketable securities—stocks is recognized by the following journal entry:

1991
Dec. 31   Unrealized Decline in Value of Noncurrent
           Marketable Securities—Stocks   750
           Allowance for Decline in Value of Noncurrent
           Marketable Securities—Stocks   750

           To record noncurrent marketable securities—stocks at lower
           of cost or market.

Therefore the carrying value of the securities in the December 31, 1991, balance sheet would be $4,250 as follows:

Long-Term Investments
    Noncurrent marketable securities—stocks, at cost $5,000
    Less: Allowance for decline in value ....   (750)
    Noncurrent marketable securities—stocks,
       at lower of cost or market $4,250

The unrealized decline of $750 would be included in the stockholders' equity section of the balance sheet, as illustrated earlier.

Assume that there are no purchases or sales of stock in 1992 and that the market value of the noncurrent portfolio has increased to $4,750 at the end of 1992. The increase of $500 ($4,750 – $4,250) is recorded as follows:

1992
Dec. 31   Allowance for Decline in Value of Noncurrent
           Marketable Securities—Stocks   500
           Unrealized Decline in Value of Noncurrent
           Marketable Securities—Stocks   500

           To record noncurrent marketable securities—stocks at lower
           of cost or market.

Note that no gain is recognized in this journal entry. Instead, the entry is the reverse of the entry used to record the decline and therefore it has the effect of reducing the amount of the Unrealized Decline included in the stockholders' equity on the balance sheet. The Allowance account now has a balance of $250 ($750 – $500) and the carrying value of the portfolio is $4,750 ($5,000 cost – $250 allowance) as illustrated earlier. The Unrealized Decline of $250 is included in stockholders' equity as also illustrated earlier. If the market value of the portfolio increases to an amount *above* cost, the recovery is limited to the amount of the Unrealized Decline. That is, the portfolio cannot be recorded at higher than cost.

For noncurrent marketable securities—stocks, revenue from dividends and the sale of an individual security are both recognized in the same way as for the current portfolio. That is, revenue is recognized as dividends are received by debiting Cash and crediting Dividend Revenue, and the gain or loss on a sale is the difference between the selling price and the cost of the security. The dividend revenue and the gain or loss on the sale are reported in the Other Revenues and Expenses section of the income statement. At this point, it may be helpful to refer back and observe the similarities between applying the lower of cost or market method to current and noncurrent marketable securities—stocks.

Additional Considerations

Income Tax Rules for Marketable Securities—Stocks

Federal income tax rules do not allow the use of the lower of cost or market method for income tax reporting purposes. Thus an unrealized loss on a decline in the value of current marketable securities—stocks is not a tax deduction, and subsequent gains up to the original cost are not taxable income. Similarly, an unrealized decline in the value of noncurrent marketable securities—stocks is also not a tax deduction. The gain or loss on the sale of marketable securities—stocks for tax purposes is the difference between the selling price and the cost and therefore is the same amount as we discussed in this chapter. Such a gain is taxable income and a loss is deducted from taxable income.

Evaluation of Lower of Cost or Market Method

The lower of cost or market method is consistent with the historical cost and conservatism concepts discussed in Chapters 1 and 9, respectively. Many users of financial statements criticize this method, however, and argue that marketable securities—stocks should always be reported in a company's balance sheet at their market value and cost should be ignored. If such market values were recognized, gains in value above cost would have to be recognized. Since such a gain can easily be realized through a sale, many users argue that it should be included in the income statement of the period. The major arguments in favor of using market values are:

1. The current market price is a better indicator than cost of the eventual amount of cash to be received from the sale.
2. The market value of the securities may be received easily through a sale without interfering with the productive operations of the company.
3. Changes in market value are an indicator of the success of the investment strategy of the management of the company, and the resulting gains and losses should be reported in the income statement.
4. The market price can be easily determined and is reliable.

Although companies are not allowed to use market value in the financial statements,[5] the market value of each portfolio of marketable securities should be disclosed in the financial statements as shown earlier. The market value may be disclosed in parentheses on the face of the balance sheet or in the notes to the financial statements.

Those who support the lower of cost or market method suggest that including the asset at market value would violate the historical cost concept and confuse the users of financial statements by valuing different assets in different ways. In addition, it is argued that an increase in value should not be recognized until there is a transaction (the sale of the stock), so that this increase can be measured with more reliability. Also, it may be argued that the use of the lower of cost or market method may be less relevant for the noncurrent portfolio because the intent is for the company to own the investment for at least a year. Therefore the current market value may not be a relevant indicator of the expected selling price at some future date.

Current Marketable Securities—Bonds

Accounting for the acquisition, valuation, revenue from, and sale of current marketable securities—bonds is discussed in the following sections.

Acquisition of Current Marketable Securities—Bonds

4(a). Account for the acquisition of current marketable securities—bonds.

As with stocks an investment in Current Marketable Securities—Bonds is recorded at the acquisition cost. For example, suppose that on August 30, 1991, the Lennon Company purchased 12 Exxon Company bonds when they were selling at 98. Remember that, as discussed in Chapter 16, bonds have a face value of $1,000 and the selling price is quoted as a percentage of the face value. Thus the company is purchasing bonds with a face value of $12,000 for 98% of the face value, or $11,760. If stockbrokers' fees of $150 are also paid, the cost of the bonds is $11,910. An additional complication arises with the acquisition of bonds, however, because interest on the bonds accrues continuously but is paid periodically. Therefore when purchasing the bonds the Lennon Company will be charged by the previous owner for the interest that has accrued to the owner since the last interest payment date. Suppose that the Exxon Company bonds have an annual interest rate of 10% and pay interest semiannually on June 30 and December 31. On August 30 (the purchase date) 2 months of interest has accrued since June 30, which amounts to $200 ($12,000 \times 10\% \times \frac{2}{12}$). The previous owner of the bonds has earned the interest for 2 months, but the Lennon Company will receive the interest payment for the entire 6 months at December 31, 1991. Therefore the Lennon Company pays the previous owner of the bonds for the 2 months interest and would pay a total of $12,110 ($11,910 + $200). The acquisition is recorded as follows:

---

[5]Some companies in special industries, such as mutual funds and brokerage companies, report investments in securities at their current market value.

1991
Aug. 30   Current Marketable Securities—Bonds 11,910
            Interest Receivable 200
               Cash   12,110

To record acquisition of 12 Exxon 10% bonds and
payment of 2 months accrued interest.

The interest is recorded as a receivable because the interest accrues over time and the Lennon Company will receive the interest when Exxon makes the next interest payment on December 31. Note that in accordance with the accrual basis of accounting the Lennon Company is recognizing interest *revenue* on a separate basis from interest *received*. This procedure is discussed in greater detail later.

Subsequent Valuation of Current Marketable Securities—Bonds

4(b). Account for the subsequent valuation of current marketable securities—bonds using the cost method.

On each balance sheet date, the current marketable securities—bonds must be properly valued for inclusion as a current asset on the balance sheet. The accounting principles used for this valuation and reporting of Current Marketable Securities—Bonds are not as clearly defined as the principles for stocks. Most companies use the *cost method*, which simply means that the investment is reported in the balance sheet at the acquisition cost no matter whether the market value is higher or lower. Therefore no adjusting entry is required at the end of the period. The lower of cost or market method, however, is allowed for current investments in bonds, in which case the adjustment procedure described for stocks would be used. In this textbook we use the cost method. Thus on the December 31, 1991, balance sheet the investment in the Exxon bonds would be shown as follows:

Current Assets
     Marketable securities—bonds, at cost $11,910

In addition, the market value of the bonds should be disclosed. Since the interest receivable on the bonds will have been collected on December 31, 1991 (as discussed in the following section), it is not shown as a current asset.

Revenue on Current Marketable Securities—Bonds

4(c). Account for the revenue on current marketable securities—bonds.

As discussed earlier interest on bonds accrues continuously over time, and therefore the investor in Current Marketable Securities—Bonds earns revenue continuously. Whenever financial statements are prepared the investor must recognize the correct amount of interest revenue for the period. Continuing with the example in the previous section, Exxon will pay 6 months' interest of $600 ($12,000 × 10% × $\frac{6}{12}$) on December 31, 1991, to the Lennon Company. Since the Lennon Company has owned the bonds for only 4 months, however, interest for only 4 months should be recognized as revenue. The receipt of the other 2 months' interest would be payment of the Interest Receivable recorded at the time of acquisition. The receipt of the interest is recorded on December 31, 1991, as follows:

```
1991
Dec. 31  Cash ...........................................................  600
              Interest Receivable ......................................         200
              Interest Revenue ..........................................         400
```
To record receipt of interest payment on Exxon bonds.

Thus of the $600 cash received only $400 is included in revenue of the period, and the remaining $200 is receipt of an asset recognized at the time of the acquisition of the bonds. The Interest Revenue is included in the Other Revenues and Expenses section of the income statement.

Sale of Current Marketable Securities—Bonds

When additional cash is needed for the operations of a company a current investment in bonds may be sold. Because interest accrues over time it is necessary to recognize the interest earned between the last interest payment date and the date of the sale. Suppose that the Lennon Company sells its investment in the Exxon bonds on January 31, 1992, at 102 plus accrued interest. The company will receive $12,240 ($12,000 × 1.02) for the bonds plus the interest that has been earned since the last payment date. The company has earned interest of $100 ($12,000 × 10% × $\frac{1}{12}$) since the last interest payment on December 31, 1991. Since the company sells the bonds for $12,240 plus accrued interest, and interest revenue of $100 had been earned during January, total cash of $12,340 is received. Because the bonds were being carried at their cost of $11,910, the Lennon Company has a gain of $330 on the sale ($12,240 – $11,910). The journal entry on January 31, 1992, to record the sale is as follows:

4(d). Account for the sale of current marketable securities— bonds.

```
1992
Jan. 31  Cash ...........................................................  12,340
              Gain on Sale of Current Marketable Securities—
                   Bonds ..........................................................         330
              Interest Revenue ..........................................         100
              Current Marketable Securities—Bonds ................         11,910
```
To record sale of Exxon bonds.

Both the Gain on Sale and the Interest Revenue are included in the Other Revenues and Expenses section on the income statement. It is important to differentiate between the two amounts because they result from different causes. The gain on the sale is the result of advantageous buying and selling decisions whereas the interest revenue is the amount earned on the investment over time.

The treatment of the interest at the acquisition of the bond, during its ownership, and at its sale may be summarized as follows:

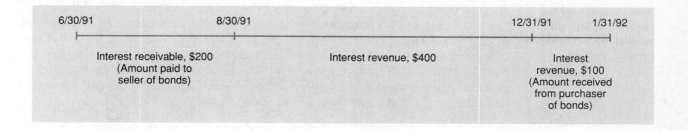

Noncurrent Investments in Bonds

Accounting for noncurrent investments in bonds does not follow the same principles as for current marketable securities—bonds, but instead parallels the accounting for bonds payable discussed in Chapter 16. A noncurrent investment in bonds is classified as such if management's intent is *not* to sell the bonds within 1 year or the operating cycle, whichever is longer.

An investor company would purchase the bonds of another company as a noncurrent investment to acquire a relatively safe source of continuing revenue or to establish a financial relationship with another company, perhaps a company whose stock it already owns. Insurance companies and companies with investments in pension funds often purchase bonds for the former reason. Because they can plan their cash payments to the insurance policyholders or the recipients of the pensions over a long period of time, they can plan to hold the bonds until maturity and avoid having to sell the bonds if their market price should become depressed.

Bonds Purchased at a Discount or Premium

Bonds are purchased at the current market price as an investment in order to earn periodic interest revenue and receive the face value on the maturity date. Bonds purchased at a discount or premium (i.e., at an amount below or above face value) are recorded at their acquisition cost, which includes the cost of the bonds, broker's fees, and transfer taxes. **The cost is recorded in an Investment in Bonds account, and generally no separate discount or premium account is used.**

Even though a separate discount or premium account is not used, the discount or premium (the difference between the purchase price and the face value) is amortized as an adjustment to interest revenue over the remaining life of the bonds. Thus the balance of the Investment account will increase (in the case of a purchase at a discount) or decrease (in the case of a purchase at a premium) over the life of the bonds until the balance equals the face value on the maturity date of the bonds. As with accounting for bonds payable **the effective interest method should be used, although the straight-line method is acceptable if the results are not materially different.** The related interest revenue is recognized periodically when cash is received and must also be accrued at the end of the accounting period. The interest revenue is included in the Other Revenues and Expenses section in the income statement.

To illustrate the accounting for a bond investment assume that the Wilkens Company purchased bonds issued by the Homestake Company with the following characteristics:

Date of purchase	January 1, 1991
Maturity date	December 31, 1995
Face value	$100,000
Contract rate	10%
Interest payment dates	June 30 and December 31
Yield	12%

Accounting for these bonds by the Homestake Company was discussed in Chapter 16, and it may be useful to refer to that chapter and compare the accounting by the Wilkens Company and the Homestake Company.

The purchase price of the bonds is $92,639.93, as discussed in Chapter 16 (brokerage fees and transfer taxes are ignored in this example).[6] The Wilkens Company records the acquisition on January 1, 1991, as follows:

```
1991
Jan. 1   Investment in Bonds  ...................................   92,639.93
            Cash  ...................................................                92,639.93
         To record purchase of 10% Homestake Company
         bonds to yield 12%.
```

The total purchase price is recorded in one account, instead of the two accounts used by the Homestake Company. Although not recorded separately, there is a discount of $7,360.07 ($100,000 − $92,639.93), which can be amortized by either the straight-line method or the effective interest method each time the interest revenue is recorded.

Straight-Line Method

When a company uses the straight-line method to amortize a premium or discount for an investment in bonds the amount of the semiannual interest receipt, the semiannual discount (premium) amortization, and the semiannual interest revenue are computed as follows:

Semiannual interest receipt	$=$ Face value $\times \left(\begin{array}{c} \text{Annual contract} \\ \text{rate} \end{array} \div \begin{array}{c} \text{Number of interest} \\ \text{payments per year} \end{array} \right)$
Semiannual discount (premium) amortization	$=$ Total discount (premium) at purchase of bonds $\div \left(\begin{array}{c} \text{Number of} \\ \text{years in} \\ \text{life of} \\ \text{bonds} \end{array} \times \begin{array}{c} \text{Number of} \\ \text{interest} \\ \text{receipts} \\ \text{per year} \end{array} \right)$
Semiannual interest revenue	$=$ Semiannual interest receipt $+$ Semiannual discount amortization or $-$ Semiannual premium amortization

If the Wilkens Company amortizes the discount by using the straight-line method, the discount of $7,360.07 would be amortized evenly over 10 semiannual periods, or $736.01 ($7,360.07 ÷ 10, rounded) each period. Since the interest received on June 30, 1991, is $5,000 [$100,000 × (10% ÷ 2)] the interest revenue is $5,736.01 ($5,000 + $736.01). The receipt of the first interest payment on June 30, 1991, is recorded as follows:

---

[6]The present value of the bonds is computed as follows:

$$\begin{aligned} \text{Present value} &= \text{Present value of face value} + \text{Present value of interest payments} \\ &= (\$100,000 \times 0.558395) + (\$5,000 \times 7.360087) \\ &= \$55,839.50 + \$36,800.43 \\ &= \$92,639.93 \end{aligned}$$

5(a). Record noncurrent investments in bonds under the straight-line method.

1991			
June 30	Cash	5,000.00	
	Investment in Bonds	736.01	
	Interest Revenue		5,736.01

To record receipt of interest on investment in Homestake Company bonds and discount amortization by the straight-line method.

When the straight-line method is used the Wilkens Company recognizes the same amount of interest revenue each semiannual period. Therefore the journal entry to record the interest received on December 31, 1991, is:

1991			
Dec. 31	Cash	5,000.00	
	Investment in Bonds	736.01	
	Interest Revenue		5,736.01

To record receipt of interest on investment in Homestake Company bonds and discount amortization by the straight-line method.

At the end of the year the Investment in Bonds account would be included in the Noncurrent Assets section of the balance sheet at a book value of $94,111.95 ($92,639.93 + $736.01 + $736.01). Interest revenue of $11,472.02 ($5,736.01 + $5,736.01) is included in the Other Revenues and Expenses section of the 1991 income statement. To facilitate the recording of the interest revenue each period the Wilkens Company could prepare a discount or premium amortization schedule similar to Exhibits 16-3 and 16-4, except that the headings would be labeled Cash Received (debit), Increase (Decrease) in Investment (debit or credit), Interest Revenue (credit), and Book Value of Investment, and the amounts would be based on the equations presented earlier.

Effective Interest Method

When a company uses the effective interest method to amortize a premium or discount for an investment in bonds the amount of the semiannual interest revenue, the semiannual interest receipt, and the semiannual discount (premium) amortization are computed as follows:

Semiannual interest revenue = (**Annual yield** ÷ **Number of interest payments per year**) × **Book value of the bond investment at the beginning of the period**

Semiannual interest receipt = **Face value** × (**Annual contract rate** ÷ **Number of interest receipts per year**)

Semiannual discount amortization = **Semiannual interest revenue** − **Semiannual interest receipt**

or

Semiannual premium amortization = **Semiannual interest receipt** − **Semiannual interest revenue**

If the Wilkens Company uses the effective interest method to amortize the discount, the interest revenue recognized on June 30, 1991, is $5,558.40 [(12% ÷ 2) ×

5(b). Record noncurrent investments in bonds under the effective interest method.

$92,639.93], the cash received is $5,000 [(10% × $\frac{1}{2}$) × $100,000], and the difference of $558.40 is the amortization of the discount that increases the book value of the Investment in Bonds. The journal entry on June 30, 1991, to record the interest revenue is:

1991			
June 30	Cash	5,000.00	
	Investment in Bonds	558.40	
	Interest Revenue		5,558.40

To record receipt of interest on investment in Homestake Company bonds and discount amortization by the effective interest method.

At December 31, 1991, the Wilkens Company recognizes interest revenue for the second 6-month period. The interest revenue is $5,591.90 [(12% ÷ 2) × ($92,639.93 + $558.40)]. Since the interest received is $5,000 [(10% ÷ 2) × $100,000], the increase in the value of the Investment is $591.90 ($5,591.90 − $5,000). The journal entry to record this interest on December 31, 1991, is recorded as follows:

1991			
Dec. 31	Cash	5,000.00	
	Investment in Bonds	591.90	
	Interest Revenue		5,591.90

To record receipt of interest on investment in Homestake Company bonds and discount amortization by the effective interest method.

At the end of the year the Investment account is included in the Noncurrent Assets section on the balance sheet at a book value of $93,790.23 ($92,639.93 + $558.40 + $591.90). Interest revenue of $11,150.30 ($5,558.40 + $5,591.90) is included in the Other Revenues and Expenses section of the 1991 income statement. Recognition of interest revenue in subsequent years would parallel the recording of the Homestake Company's interest expense. To facilitate the recording of the interest revenue each period the Wilkens company could prepare a discount or premium amortization schedule similar to Exhibits 16-5 and 16-6, except that the headings would be labeled Cash Received (debit), Interest Revenue (credit), Increase (Decrease) in Investment (debit or credit), and Book Value of Investment, and the amounts would be based on the equations presented earlier.

Under either the effective interest or straight-line method, the book value of the bonds in the balance sheet will increase (for bonds purchased at a discount) or decrease (for bonds purchased at a premium) until the book value equals the face value on the maturity date. The book value of the bonds under either method is not affected by any changes in the market value of the bonds.

Noncurrent Acquisitions of Stock

Earlier we discussed investments in noncurrent marketable securities—stocks for which the lower of cost or market method is used. At that time we assumed that the investment was a small percentage of the shares outstanding. However, acquisitions of stock may involve large percentages. Accounting for these acquisitions is complex but can be made easier if it is understood that the accounting method used by the investor for a particular acquisition depends on the ownership interest in the investee measured in terms of the proportion of the common stock owned. **The investor is the company purchasing the stock. The investee is the company whose stock is being purchased.** The ownership interest of the investor company in the investee company and the accounting methods used are as follows:

Ownership Interest in Outstanding Common Stock	Accounting Method Used
Less than 20%	Lower of cost or market
20% to 50%	Equity
More than 50%	Consolidation

6. Identify when to use the lower of cost or market method, the equity method, and consolidation.

The **lower of cost or market method is used when less than 20% of the outstanding common stock of the investee company is owned by the investor company.** This method was discussed earlier in this chapter. **The equity method is used when the investor company has significant influence over the investee company. Significant influence is presumed to exist when 20% or more of the outstanding common stock is owned by the investor company.** Significant influence, however, can be indicated by other factors, such as representation on the board of directors, participation in the policy-making process, significant intercompany transactions, interchange of managerial personnel, or technological dependency. If the other evidence outweighs the ownership interest, the 20% rule can be ignored. For example, a company with 10% of the common stock might be able to elect 4 of the 10 members of the board of directors, in which case it would be appropriate to use the equity method. In this book we will use the equity method only when the ownership interest is 20% or more.

The **consolidation method is used when the investor company owns more than 50% of the outstanding common stock of the investee company.** In this case, the investor company uses the equity method to account for the investment *during* the period. However, because the investor company has *control* over the investee company, *consolidated* financial statements must be prepared at the *end* of the period. This is a very complex area of accounting and is discussed briefly at the end of the chapter after the equity method is discussed.

How the Investment Is Made

Before discussing the equity method and consolidations, it is important to understand how the investor company acquires the shares of the investee company. In most situations, the investor buys the shares on the stock market from existing owners who are willing to sell their shares. This transaction has no direct effect on the investee company whose shares are being purchased and sold, and therefore there is no effect on its financial statements (the investee company does have to record the name and address of the new owners in its stockholders' ledger, however, so that dividend checks and other shareholder information can be correctly mailed).

Occasionally an investor company purchases shares that are being newly issued. In this situation the financial statements of the investee company whose shares are being sold are affected. The issuance of new shares was discussed in Chapter 14. In this chapter it is assumed that the investor company is purchasing shares that are already outstanding. Therefore the transaction has no effect on the financial statements of the investee company whose shares are being purchased. No matter how the acquisition is made, the investor company records (debits) an Investment (asset) account for the cost of acquisition, which includes the purchase price, commissions to the stockbroker, and any transfer taxes that are imposed, as discussed earlier.

The Equity Method

As discussed earlier, the equity method of accounting for noncurrent investments in common stock is used when the investor company has the ability to exercise significant influence over the investee company but does not have control. Significant influence is presumed to exist when the ownership interest is at least 20% of the common stock of the investee and less than 50%, at which point control can be exercised.

At this level of ownership there are several reasons why the lower of cost or market method is not appropriate.

1. It can be expected that the investment will be for a long period of time and therefore the cost may become outdated.

2. The market value of the shares of the investee company will not necessarily represent a good measure of the total value of the investment. The price of a share on the stock market on any given day is the result of the supply and demand on that day. The sale of over 20% of the shares of a company would almost certainly be at a different market price than the sale of a small quantity of shares.

3. Income is not best measured by the dividends received. For example, suppose that an investee company earns $40,000 and pays dividends of $4,000. If an investor company owns 25% of the shares it would receive dividends of $1,000, but this amount does not represent the income accumulation of the investor company in the sense that it is not the best measure of the increase in its wealth. Since the investee has earned $40,000 and the investor owns 25% of the income, the investor should instead recognize income of $10,000.

4. The investor may be able to influence the dividend policy and thereby affect the cash payments received. Therefore recognition of income on an accrual basis (equity method) is preferable to the recognition of income on the basis of the cash dividends received (lower of cost or market method).

The equity method uses an approach for recording the value of the investment and recognizing income different from the lower of cost or market method. The investor company accounts for the investment and income as follows:

$$\text{Investment} = \text{Cost} + \text{Income earned} - \text{Dividends received}$$

where:

$$\text{Income earned} = \text{Investee's net income} \times \text{Ownership \%}$$

and:

$$\text{Dividends received} = \text{Total dividends paid by investee} \times \text{Ownership \%}$$

7. Explain the characteristics of the equity method.

The investor company recognizes as income its share of the investee company's net income. When this income is recognized the value of the Investment (asset) account is increased by the same amount. The receipt of dividends does *not* involve recognition of income, but instead the investor company records this receipt as a *reduction* in the book value of the Investment account. The accounting by the investor company parallels the accounting by the investee company. When the investee company earns income there is an increase in its stockholders' equity, and when it pays dividends its stockholders' equity is decreased. The book value of the investor company's Investment account is increased as its share of the investee company's stockholders' equity increases (as income is earned) and is decreased as its share of the investee company's stockholders' equity decreases (as dividends are received). For the investor company to record dividends received as income would involve double counting because the investee company's income, out of which the dividends are received, has already been recognized as income by the investor company.

Comprehensive Example

To illustrate the equity method, suppose that the Davis Company purchases 25% of the outstanding common shares of the Bristol Company on January 1, 1991, for $50,000. The investment would be recorded by the Davis Company on this date as follows:

```
1991
Jan. 1   Investment in Bristol Company ..............................   50,000
              Cash ......................................................                50,000
         To record acquisition of 25% of the outstanding
         common stock of Bristol Company
```

On January 1, 1991, the Bristol Company's condensed balance sheet was as shown in Exhibit 17-1.

EXHIBIT 17-1
Balance Sheet

BRISTOL COMPANY Balance Sheet January 1, 1991			
Assets		*Liabilities*	
Current assets $120,000		Current liabilities	$ 40,000
Noncurrent assets 280,000		Noncurrent liabilities	160,000
		Total Liabilities	$200,000
		Stockholders' Equity	
		Common stock, no par	$ 30,000
		Retained earnings	170,000
		Total Stockholders' Equity ...	$200,000
		Total Liabilities and	
Total Assets $400,000		Stockholders' Equity	$400,000

At the end of 1991 the Bristol Company reported net income of $60,000 and paid dividends of $20,000. The income from the investment that is included in the Davis Company's income statement is:

$$\text{Income earned} = \text{Investee's net income} \times \text{Ownership \%}$$
$$= \$60,000 \times 25\%$$
$$= \underline{\$15,000}$$

The dividends that are received by the Davis Company are:

$$\text{Dividends received} = \text{Total dividends paid by the investee} \times \text{Ownership \%}$$
$$= \$20,000 \times 25\%$$
$$= \underline{\$5,000}$$

The Davis Company recognizes its share of the Bristol Company's net income as follows:

1991			
Dec. 31	**Investment in Bristol Company**	15,000	
	Income from Investment in Bristol Company		15,000
	To recognize 25% of Bristol Company's net income.		

The receipt of the dividends from Bristol Company is recorded by the Davis Company as follows:

Dec. 31	**Cash**	5,000	
	Investment in Bristol Company		5,000
	To record dividends received from Bristol Company.		

The book value of the Davis Company's investment at the end of 1991 is:

Cost of investment	**$50,000**
+ Share of Bristol Company's net income (25% × $60,000)	15,000
− Dividends received (25% × $20,000)	(5,000)
Book Value of Investment at Year End	**$60,000**

In order to further emphasize the rationale of the equity method, consider the balance sheet of the Bristol Company (the investee) after the preceding events have been recorded. The investment by the Davis Company has no effect on the balance sheet of the Bristol Company because the Davis Company purchased 25% of the *existing* outstanding shares. The earning of income and the payment of dividends by the Bristol Company do affect its balance sheet. By using the basic accounting equation (Assets = Liabilities + Stockholders' Equity) we can examine the effect of these events. For simplicity, we will assume that liabilities remain unchanged. The income and dividends have the following impact on Bristol Company's accounting equation (and balance sheet):

	Assets	=	Liabilities	+	Stockholders' Equity
Earning income	+$60,000	=	0		+$60,000
Payment of dividends	– 20,000	=	0		– 20,000
Net Effect	+$40,000	=	0		+$40,000

The net effect is an increase in the assets and the stockholders' equity of the Bristol Company of $40,000. The assets of the Bristol Company are now $440,000 ($400,000 at the beginning of the period plus the increase of $40,000) and the liabilities are $200,000 (it is assumed they remain unchanged), and therefore the net assets (stockholders' equity) are $240,000 ($440,000 – $200,000). Since the Davis Company owns 25% of the Bristol Company, it effectively owns 25% of the net assets of the company. The value of this 25% share is $60,000 (25% × $240,000). Note that this is exactly the balance of the Davis Company's account, Investment in Bristol Company.

The fact that the book value in the Investment account of the investor company parallels the book value of the ownership interest in the net assets (stockholders' equity) of the investee company is the primary justification for the equity method. It should be recognized that the values are *equal* only because the Davis Company made the original purchase of the shares at a cost ($50,000) that was equal to the book value of the ownership interest in the net assets of the Bristol Company on January 1, 1991 [25% × ($30,000 common stock + $170,000 retained earnings) or 25% × ($400,000 assets – $200,000 liabilities)]. That is, the market price of Bristol's shares was equal to the book value on that date. If the Davis Company had made the purchase for an amount different from $50,000, the book value of the Investment in Bristol Company account at year end would not be equal to the ownership interest in the net assets of the Bristol Company. The increase in the book value of the Investment account ($10,000), however, would be equal to the Davis Company's share of the increase in the net assets of the Bristol Company (25% × $40,000).

Evaluation of Equity Method

Some users of financial statements criticize the equity method because the investor company recognizes income in excess of the cash received as dividends (assuming that the investee's income is more than the dividends it pays). They argue that the cash received from dividends is a more useful measure of the investor company's income. This criticism is not consistent with the accrual concept which has such a strong influence on accounting. In accrual accounting income is recognized in the period in which it is earned and therefore income flows and cash flows are seldom, if ever, equal. The equity method is another example of the recognition of income on the accrual basis. An understanding of the preceding discussion of the equity method should enable the reader to recognize why generally accepted accounting principles require the use of the equity method when the investor company can exercise significant influence over the investee company.

Accounting for a Controlling Interest

When an investor company owns more than 50% of the common stock of another company the investor has control over the investee. **The parent company is the investor company that owns more than 50% of the outstanding common stock of the investee.** On the other hand, **the subsidiary company is the investee company that has more than 50% of its outstanding common stock owned by the investor (parent) company.** The companies remain separate legal entities and maintain separate accounting records during the accounting period. Users of financial statements, however, are interested in financial statements that report the activities of the parent company and all the entities in which the parent company has a controlling interest. At the end of the accounting period, therefore, the results of operations and the ending financial position are accounted for in the parent company's annual report as if the separate legal entities are a single accounting entity. That is, a single set of financial statements called consolidated financial statements is published. **Consolidated financial statements are the financial statements prepared by the parent company that owns more than 50% of the outstanding common stock of the subsidiary company.** The financial statements are the result of bringing together, or consolidating, the financial statements of the separate companies.

8. Describe consolidated financial statements.

For example, the Ford Motor Company's financial statements represent the consolidated results of at least 45 separate companies. The individual who owns shares in Ford does not receive (or want) financial statements that report separately on the activities of each of the 45 companies. Instead a single set of consolidated financial statements is prepared. **The separate legal entities are treated as a single accounting entity for financial reporting.** Ideally, the investor in Ford should receive a set of financial statements that would be identical to the statements that would be prepared if the entire operations of Ford consisted of only one company. Although the consolidated financial statements are not identical, the principles used to prepare consolidated financial statements ensure that the consolidated financial statements are prepared in such a way that they are essentially the same as if there is only one company.

Although consolidated financial statements are prepared when the ownership of a parent company in a subsidiary exceeds 50%,[7] for simplicity, we will assume that the parent company owns 100% of the subsidiary. Even when there is 100% ownership it is common for the subsidiary to continue to exist as a separate legal entity. A major advantage of this continued separate legal identity is that the principle of limited liability applies to each corporation. Thus the parent company is not responsible for the debts of the subsidiary. There may also be other reasons, such as tax advantages, for maintaining the separate legal entities.

In principle the consolidated financial statements are the sum of the financial statements of the separate companies. Thus the assets and liabilities of the separate companies are added together in the consolidated balance sheet, and the revenues and expenses of the separate companies are combined in the consolidated income statement (except for the items discussed next). It is common, however, for the parent and subsidiary to buy and sell from each other and

---

[7]There are some exceptions to this rule. Subsidiaries are not consolidated if the parent company cannot exercise control.

engage in other kinds of intercompany transactions. Since they are separate legal entities, they would record these transactions in their own accounting records. To avoid double counting, certain items that are included in the separate financial statements must be eliminated (excluded) from the consolidated financial statements. A diagram of these relationships is as follows:

Parent		Subsidiary			Consolidated Financial Statements
Balance Sheet		*Balance Sheet*			*Balance Sheet*
Assets	+	Assets			Assets
Liabilities	+	Liabilities	– Eliminations =		Liabilities
Stockholders' Equity	+	Stockholders' Equity			Stockholders' Equity
Income Statement		*Income Statement*			*Income Statement*
Revenues	+	Revenues	– Eliminations =		Revenues
Expenses	+	Expenses			Expenses
Net Income		Net Income			Net Income

Since consolidated financial statements are the only ones available to users, the companies do not make the eliminations directly on the financial statements. Furthermore, since each company maintains its own accounting records, there is no set of consolidated financial records. Thus there is no consolidated general journal or consolidated general ledger. The consolidated financial statements are prepared by using a worksheet. The adjusted trial balances of the parent and subsidiaries are listed on the worksheet and certain items are eliminated. **Eliminations are items that must be removed from the investor company's and the investee company's financial statements to avoid double counting in the consolidated financial statements.** The consolidated financial statements are prepared by adding together each company's financial statements after the eliminations. Some of the items that must be eliminated are discussed in the following sections.

Investment of Parent and Stockholders' Equity of Subsidiary

The parent company accounts for its investment in the subsidiary in its own accounting records by the equity method, as discussed earlier. Thus the parent company has an asset, Investment in Subsidiary, on its individual balance sheet. This asset represents the ownership of the assets of the subsidiary. When the assets of both companies are combined in the consolidated balance sheet, the Investment account must be eliminated to avoid double counting.

Furthermore the stockholders' equity of the subsidiary is entirely owned by the parent (assuming 100% ownership). To include the stockholders' equity of

9. Explain the elimination of the investment account in consolidations.

both the parent and the subsidiary in the consolidated balance sheet would also result in double counting. Since the consolidated financial statements are prepared for the use of the stockholders of the parent company, the stockholders' equity of the subsidiary is eliminated.

In summary, to avoid double counting the parent company's Investment account and the subsidiary company's stockholders' equity accounts must not be included (they must be eliminated) in the consolidated balance sheet. To illustrate this process consider the balance sheets of the Parent Company and the Subsidiary Company on December 31, 1991, which are shown in worksheet form[8] in Exhibit 17-2.

EXHIBIT 17-2   Preparation of Consolidated Balance Sheet

Parent Company and Its Subsidiary **Worksheet for Preparation of Consolidated Balance Sheet** **December 31, 1991**				

			Eliminations		
Account Titles	Parent Company	Subsidiary Company	Debit	Credit	Consolidated Balance Sheet
Cash	$ 70,000	$ 10,000			$ 80,000
Notes receivable	30,000	20,000		(b) 10,000	40,000
Inventory	80,000	30,000			110,000
Investment in subsidiary company	150,000			(a) 150,000	
Property, plant, and equipment (net)	270,000	160,000			430,000
	$600,000	$220,000			$660,000
Notes payable	$ 25,000	$ 20,000	(b) 10,000		$ 35,000
Bonds payable	100,000	50,000			150,000
Common stock, no par	200,000	100,000	(a) 100,000		200,000
Retained earnings	275,000	50,000	(a) 50,000		275,000
	$600,000	$220,000	$160,000	$160,000	$660,000

On January 1, 1991, the Parent Company had purchased all the common stock of the Subsidiary Company for $130,000 on the stock market, and the Parent Company's investment was recorded at the purchase price. At that time the Subsidiary Company's no-par common stock totaled $100,000 and its retained earnings totaled $30,000. During 1991 the Subsidiary earned income of $20,000 and no dividends were paid. This increased its Retained Earnings to $50,000. Since the Parent Company owns 100% of the common stock of the Subsidiary Company, it recorded its share of the Subsidiary's income (100% × $20,000) in its Investment account (in accordance with the principles described for the equity method), thereby increasing the Investment account balance to $150,000. The $150,000 balance in the Investment account of the Parent Company and the Subsidiary's Common Stock and Retained Earnings balances of $100,000 and $50,000, respectively, must be eliminated from the consolidated financial

[8]For simplicity, only the ending balance sheets are included in Exhibit 17-2. The adjusted trial balances and income statements are not included because many complexities involving these items are beyond the scope of this book.

statements. Therefore the Investment account is reduced (credited) by $150,000 and the Subsidiary's Common Stock and Retained Earnings accounts are reduced (debited) by $100,000 and $50,000, respectively. This elimination entry, labeled (a) in Exhibit 17-2, is included only in the worksheet used to prepare the consolidated financial statements. It is not recorded in the accounting system of either company. Two examples of other eliminations are discussed next.

Intercompany Transactions

Parent and subsidiary companies often engage in transactions with each other. **Intercompany transactions are transactions between a parent and a subsidiary company.** These transactions must be eliminated when preparing consolidated financial statements.

10. Explain the elimination of intercompany transactions.

Intercompany Loans.   One company may loan money to the other, or one company may owe money as a result of a transaction. For example, suppose that in addition to the purchase of the common stock the Parent Company lent $10,000 to the Subsidiary Company. Therefore the Subsidiary Company has a note payable of $10,000 and the Parent Company has a note receivable of $10,000. Whereas each individual company has an asset and a liability, the consolidated entity has neither an asset nor a liability because no cash receipt or payment will occur with an outside entity. To avoid double counting both the note payable and the note receivable must be eliminated. This is accomplished by reducing (debiting) the note payable of the Subsidiary Company and reducing (crediting) the note receivable of the Parent Company. This is shown as entry (b) in Exhibit 17-2.

The consolidated balance sheet is prepared by adding together the amounts from the individual balance sheets less the amounts eliminated, as shown in the last column in Exhibit 17-2.

Sales Between the Parent and Subsidiary.   When a sale is made between the parent and subsidiary, the sale must be eliminated from the consolidated income statement. This elimination is required because no sale has occurred for the consolidated entity. It is only when a sale has been made outside the consolidated entity that sales revenue is recognized. Along with the elimination of the sale, the cost of the inventory recorded as cost of goods sold by the other company must be eliminated.

For example, suppose that the Parent Company purchases inventory for $5,000 from the Subsidiary Company and sells it to outsiders for $9,000. The Subsidiary Company had originally purchased the inventory for $3,000. On their separate income statements, the two companies would include the following information:

	Parent	Subsidiary
Sales	$9,000	$5,000
Cost of goods sold	(5,000)	(3,000)
Gross Profit	$4,000	$2,000

For the consolidated entity, however, the sales to outsiders are only $9,000 and the cost of the goods sold to outsiders is only $3,000. Therefore when the consolidated income statement is prepared by adding together the income statements of the two companies, sales of $5,000 and cost of goods sold of $5,000 must be eliminated to avoid double counting.

Although sales between parent and subsidiary companies are usually the most significant elimination in the consolidated income statement, other eliminations may also be necessary. For example, interest revenue and interest expense on a loan between the companies would also have to be eliminated.

Purchase Price Greater Than Market Value of Net Assets

In the earlier example the purchase price of $130,000 equaled the book value (net assets) of the Subsidiary Company. It was also assumed that the market value of the net assets was equal to the book value of the net assets. Neither of these conditions typically exists in a real transaction, however. Usually the purchase price exceeds the market (and book) value of the net assets of the Subsidiary Company.

11. Describe the goodwill recorded in consolidations.

In these situations the net assets of the subsidiary included in the consolidated balance sheet must be adjusted to their market value and goodwill must be recorded. It is appropriate to record the net assets at their market values because they represent the purchase prices of those individual assets. **Goodwill is recorded as the difference between the purchase price of the subsidiary company and the market value of its net assets** (goodwill was discussed in Chapter 12). Remember that the accounting records of the subsidiary are *not* adjusted to record the market values. For example, suppose that in the earlier example the following values existed at the time of acquisition:

Price paid by Parent Company $200,000
Market value of net assets of Subsidiary Company 170,000

Although the book value of the net assets of the Subsidiary Company at the time of acquisition was $130,000 ($100,000 common stock + $30,000 retained earnings), the market value of the net assets of the Subsidiary Company is $170,000 and would be included in the ending consolidated balance sheet. Goodwill of $30,000 would also be recognized and included in the consolidated balance sheet. Goodwill is measured as the difference between the purchase price of $200,000 and the market value of the net assets. It is therefore valued at $30,000 ($200,000 − $170,000). Under these conditions the consolidated balance sheet of Parent Company would be as shown in Exhibit 17-3.

Comparing this balance sheet to the balance sheet shown in Exhibit 17-2, it may be seen that the cash is only $10,000 because the Parent Company would have $70,000 less cash since it paid that much more for the investment in the second example ($200,000 purchase price compared to $130,000). The property, plant, and equipment are $470,000 (instead of the $430,000 shown in Exhibit 17-2), because it is assumed that all of the $40,000 excess of the market value of the net assets above their book value ($170,000 compared to $130,000) is attributable to property, plant, and equipment. In addition, the goodwill of $30,000 is included on the consolidated balance sheet.

EXHIBIT 17-3
Consolidated
Balance Sheet

PARENT COMPANY AND ITS SUBSIDIARY
Consolidated Balance Sheet
December 31, 1991

Assets			*Liabilities*		
Current assets			Current liabilities		
Cash	$ 10,000		Notes payable	$ 35,000	
Notes receivable	40,000		Noncurrent liabilities		
Inventory	110,000		Bonds payable	150,000	
Noncurrent assets			Total Liabilities	$185,000	
Property, plant, and					
equipment (net)	470,000		*Stockholders' Equity*		
Goodwill	30,000		Common stock, no par	$200,000	
			Retained earnings	275,000	
			Total Stockholders' Equity	$475,000	
			Total Liabilities and		
Total Assets	$660,000		Stockholders' Equity	$660,000	

Minority Interest

12. Describe the nature of minority interest.

All the preceding examples have assumed that the parent purchased 100% of the common stock of the subsidiary. When the parent buys more than 50% but less than 100% of the stock, consolidated financial statements are prepared by using the same general principles discussed earlier. In this case, however, the subsidiary has other stockholders who own a minority interest in its net assets. **Minority interest is the ownership of other stockholders when the parent company owns less than 100% of the common stock of the subsidiary company.** The minority interest is included in the consolidated balance sheet. The amount of the minority interest is computed by multiplying the percentage ownership interest of the minority stockholders by the total stockholders' equity of the subsidiary.

To illustrate minority interest, suppose that in the first example the Parent Company purchased 70% of the common stock of the Subsidiary Company for $91,000 (70% × $130,000). The Parent Company would record its $14,000 (70% × $20,000) share of the Subsidiary's net income of $20,000, and therefore its investment account balance on December 31, 1991, would be $105,000 ($91,000 + $14,000 or 70% × $150,000 total stockholders' equity of subsidiary). The minority interest at December 31, 1991, is $45,000 (30% × $150,000). In this case the elimination of the stockholders' equity of the subsidiary at December 31, 1991, can be illustrated in journal entry form as follows (remember this is only recorded on a worksheet):

Common Stock, no par (subsidiary)	100,000	
Retained Earnings (subsidiary)	50,000	
Investment in Subsidiary (parent)		105,000
Minority Interest		45,000

The minority interest is often listed in the stockholders' equity section of the consolidated balance sheet, although it is sometimes listed in a separate section between liabilities and stockholders' equity.

Chapter Summary

Review of Learning Objectives

> **1. Identify marketable securities.**
> Marketable securities are investments in common stocks or bonds that are readily saleable.

> **2. Account for the (a) acquisition cost, (b) subsequent valuation using the lower of cost or market method, (c) revenue on, and (d) sale of current marketable securities—stocks.**
> Current marketable securities—stocks are recorded at their cost, which includes the purchase price, commissions paid to the stockbroker, and any transfer taxes that are imposed. On each balance sheet date the lower of cost or market method is applied to the current portfolio and the unrealized loss or the unrealized gain are included in the income statement. Revenue is recognized when the dividend is received. A gain or loss on the sale of an individual security is the difference between the selling price and the cost of the particular stock.

> **3. Account for the (a) acquisition cost and (b) subsequent valuation using the lower of cost or market method for noncurrent marketable securities—stocks.**
> Noncurrent marketable securities—stocks are recorded at their cost. On each balance sheet date the lower of cost or market method is applied to the noncurrent portfolio and the unrealized decline is included as a negative element of the stockholders' equity section of the balance sheet. Subsequent increases in the value of the portfolio (up to cost) increase stockholders' equity by reducing (or eliminating) the negative component. Dividends received and sales of stock are recorded in a way similar to the recording for current marketable securities—stocks.

> **4. Account for the (a) acquisition cost, (b) subsequent valuation using the cost method, (c) revenue on, and (d) sale of current marketable securities—bonds.**
> Current marketable securities—bonds are recorded at their cost, but the total cash paid is the cost plus the interest that has accrued since the last interest payment date. The cost method is used to value current marketable securities—bonds. Interest revenue is earned continuously through the passage of time and is accrued on each balance sheet date. A gain or loss on the sale of bonds is the difference between the selling price and the cost of the particular bonds. The cash received also includes the interest revenue that has accrued since the last interest payment date.

> **5. Record noncurrent investments in bonds under the (a) straight-line method and (b) effective interest method.**
> Under the *straight-line* method the semiannual interest revenue is equal to the interest received plus the semiannual discount amortized or minus the semiannual premium amortized. The semiannual discount or premium amortized is the total discount or premium at acquisition divided by the

number of semiannual periods in the life of the bonds. Under the *effective interest* method the semiannual interest revenue is computed by multiplying the semiannual yield by the book value of the investment at the beginning of the period. The semiannual discount or premium amortized is the difference between the interest revenue and the interest received.

6. **Identify when to use the lower of cost or market method, the equity method, and consolidation.**
The *lower of cost or market method* is used when less than 20% of the outstanding common stock of the investee company is owned by the investor company. The *equity method* is used when the investor company has significant influence over the investee company (20% to 50% ownership). *Consolidated financial statements* are prepared when control exists because the investor company owns more than 50% of the outstanding common stock of the investee company.

7. **Explain the characteristics of the equity method.**
The investment is recorded at its cost plus the income earned less the dividends received. The income earned is computed by multiplying the investee's net income times the ownership percentage. The dividends received are determined by multiplying the investee's total dividends paid times the ownership percentage.

8. **Describe consolidated financial statements.**
Consolidated financial statements are the financial statements prepared by the parent company that owns more than 50% of the outstanding common stock of the subsidiary company. Consolidated financial statements are prepared because users are interested in the statements that report on the activities of the parent company and all the entities in which the parent has a controlling interest.

9. **Explain the elimination of the investment account in consolidations.**
The investment of the parent is eliminated against the stockholders' equity of the subsidiary to avoid double counting in the consolidated financial statements. The worksheet entry involves a debit to the subsidiary's Common Stock and Retained Earnings accounts and a credit to the parent's Investment account.

10. **Explain the elimination of intercompany transactions.**
Intercompany transactions between the parent and subsidiary are eliminated to avoid double counting in the consolidated financial statements. For example, for a loan made by a parent company to its subsidiary the note receivable (asset) of the parent and the note payable (liability) of the subsidiary must be eliminated from the consolidated balance sheet.

11. **Describe the goodwill recorded in consolidations.**
Goodwill is recorded in the consolidated balance sheet as an intangible asset when the purchase price of the subsidiary company is greater than the market value of its net assets.

12. **Describe the nature of minority interest.**
Minority interest is the ownership of other stockholders when the parent company owns less than 100% of the common stock of the subsidiary com-

pany. The amount of the minority interest is computed by multiplying the percentage ownership interest of the minority stockholders by the total stockholders' equity of the subsidiary.

Review Problem

The Drake Company invests its temporary excess cash in marketable securities. At the end of 1991 Drake's portfolio of current marketable securities is as follows:

Company	Number of Shares or Bonds	Cost per Share or Bond	Market Value per Share or Bond
Texaco	200 shares	$ 45	$ 44
Coca Cola	100 shares	35	36
DuPont	300 shares	40	38
U.S. Steel	Twelve 10% bonds	950	940

All securities were purchased during the last quarter of 1991, and no securities had previously been owned during the year. During the first quarter of 1992 the company engaged in the following transactions:

Date	Transaction
Feb 5	Sold the Coca Cola shares for $33 each.
Mar. 2	Purchased 100 shares of Anheuser-Busch for $30 each.
31	Dividends of $200 were received, interest was recorded, and the market prices on this date were:

Security	Market Value per Share or Bond
Texaco	$ 42
Anheuser-Busch	25
DuPont	41
U.S. Steel	930

During the second quarter of 1992 the company engaged in the following transactions:

Date	Transaction
Apr. 6	Sold the Texaco shares for $47 each.
June 1	Sold the U.S. Steel bonds at 98 plus accrued interest.
June 30	Dividends of $250 were received, and the market prices on this date were:

Security	Market Value per Share
DuPont	$39
Anheuser-Busch	31

The company records dividend revenue when the cash is received and uses the cost method to account for its investments in bonds. The bonds pay interest on June 30 and December 31.

REQUIRED

1. What is the balance in the Allowance for Decline in Value of Current Marketable Securities—Stocks on December 31, 1991?

2. Prepare journal entries to record the preceding events for 1992.

3. Show how the income recognized for each period and the value of the marketable securities reported in the balance sheet at the end of each period would be disclosed on the interim financial statements for 1992.

4. Explain how your answers would differ if the portfolio of stocks was classified as noncurrent. Include a revised answer to Requirement 3.

Solution to Review Problem

REQUIREMENT 1

The balance in the Allowance for Decline in Value of Current Marketable Securities—Stocks on December 31, 1991, may be calculated as follows (because all the securities were purchased in the last quarter of 1991 and no securities had previously been owned during the year):

Company	Number of Shares	Cost per Share	Market Value per Share	Total Cost	Total Market Value
Texaco	200	$45	$44	$ 9,000	$ 8,800
Coca Cola	100	35	36	3,500	3,600
DuPont	300	40	38	12,000	11,400
				$24,500	$23,800

The balance in the Allowance account is $700 ($24,500 − $23,800) at December 31, 1991. (Note: Only the shares are included because the bonds are accounted for by the cost method.)

REQUIREMENT 2

Feb. 5	Cash	3,300	
	Loss on Sale of Current Marketable Securities—Stocks	200	
	Current Marketable Securities—Stocks		3,500
	To record sale of 100 Coca Cola shares.		
Mar. 2	Current Marketable Securities—Stocks	3,000	
	Cash		3,000
	To record purchase of 100 shares of Anheuser-Busch.		
Mar. 31	Cash	200	
	Dividend Revenue		200
	To record receipt of dividends on current marketable securities.		

Mar. 31	Interest Receivable	300
	Interest Revenue	300

To record interest revenue ($12,000 × 10% × $\frac{3}{12}$).

31	Unrealized Loss on Decline in Value of Current Marketable Securities—Stocks[a]	100
	Allowance for Decline in Value of Current Marketable Securities—Stocks	100

To record current marketable securities—stocks at the lower of cost or market.

[a]Company	Number of Shares	Cost per Share	Market Value per Share	Total Cost	Total Market Value
Texaco	200	$45	$42	$ 9,000	$ 8,400
DuPont	300	40	41	12,000	12,300
Anheuser-Busch	100	30	25	3,000	2,500
				$24,000	$23,200

The balance in the Allowance account needs to be $800. The balance before the adjusting entry is $700, and therefore an unrealized loss of $100 is recognized.

Apr. 6	Cash	9,400
	Current Marketable Securities—Stocks	9,000
	Gain on Sale of Current Marketable Securities—Stocks	400

To record sale of 200 Texaco shares.

June 1	Cash	12,260[c]
	Gain on Sale of Current Marketable Securities—Bonds :...................................	360[d]
	Interest Receivable	300
	Interest Revenue	200[a]
	Current Marketable Securities—Bonds	11,400[b]

To record sale of U.S. Steel bonds.

[a]$12,000 × 10% × $\frac{2}{12}$.   [c]($12,000 × $\frac{98}{100}$) + $500.
[b]12 × $950.   [d]12 × ($980 − $950).

June 30	Cash	250
	Dividend Revenue	250

To record receipt of dividends.

30	Allowance for Decline in Value of Current Marketable Securities—Stocks	600
	Unrealized Gain on Increase in Value of Current Marketable Securities—Stocks[a]	600

To record current marketable securities at the lower of cost or market.

[a]Company	Number of Shares	Cost per Share	Market Value per Share	Total Cost	Total Market Value
DuPont	300	$40	$39	$12,000	$11,700
Anheuser-Busch	100	30	31	3,000	3,100
				$15,000	$14,800

The balance in the Allowance account needs to be $200. The balance before the adjusting entry is $800, and therefore an unrealized gain of $600 is recognized.

REQUIREMENT 3

Income Statement	First Quarter	Second Quarter
Other revenues and expenses		
Gain (loss) on sale of current marketable securities ...	$ (200)	$ 760
Revenue on current marketable securities	500[a]	450[b]
Unrealized gain (loss) on increase (decline) in value		
of current marketable securities.	(100)	600
	$ 200	$ 1,810

Balance Sheet	First Quarter	Second Quarter
Current Assets		
Marketable securities—stocks, at cost	$24,000	$15,000
Less: Allowance for decline in value	(800)	(200)
Marketable securities—stocks, at the lower		
of cost or market	$23,200	$14,800
Marketable securities—bonds at cost	11,400	—
Total marketable securities	$34,600	$14,800

[a]Dividends, $200 plus interest, $300.
[b]Dividends, $250 plus interest, $200.

REQUIREMENT 4

The asset account, the allowance account, the loss on sale account, and the gain on sale account would have appropriate changes made in their titles to reflect the non-current securities being accounted for. The entries on March 31 and June 30 to recognize the changes in the value of the portfolio would be to an account, Unrealized Decline in Value of Noncurrent Marketable Securities—Stocks, rather than to "Unrealized Loss . . . " and "Unrealized Gain . . . " accounts.

The answer to Requirement 3 would be as follows:

Income Statement	First Quarter	Second Quarter
Other revenues and expenses		
Gain (loss) on sale of noncurrent marketable		
securities	$ (200)	$ 760
Revenue on current marketable securities	500	450
	$ 300	$ 1,210

Balance Sheet	First Quarter	Second Quarter
Current Assets		
Marketable securities—bonds, at cost	$11,400	—
Long-term Investments		
Noncurrent marketable securities—		
stocks, at cost	$24,000	$15,000
Less: Allowance for decline in value	(800)	(200)
Noncurrent marketable securities—		
stocks, at lower of cost or market	$23,200	$14,800
Total marketable securities	$34,600	$14,800
Stockholders' Equity		
Unrealized decline in value of noncurrent		
marketable securities—stocks	$ (800)	$ (200)

Glossary

Allowance for Decline in Value of Marketable Securities.   A contra-asset account used to record the amount by which the market value of Marketable Securities—Stocks is less than cost (see lower of cost or market).

Consolidated Financial Statements.   Financial statements prepared by an investor company (the parent) that owns more than 50% of the outstanding common stock of an investee company (the subsidiary). The financial statements of each company are combined into consolidated financial statements.

Eliminations.   Items that must be removed from the investor company's and investee company's financial statements to prevent double counting in consolidated financial statements.

Equity Method.   A method of accounting for a long-term investment in the common stock of an investee company that is used when the investor company has significant influence over the investee (e.g., 20% or more ownership). The investor company recognizes income based on the percentage ownership in the investee.

Intercompany Transactions.   Transactions between a parent and a subsidiary company. These transactions must be eliminated when consolidated financial statements are prepared.

Investee Company.   The company whose common stock has been purchased by another company (the investor).

Investor Company.   The company that has acquired the common stock of another company (the investee).

Lower of Cost or Market Method.   A method of accounting for an investment in the common stock of an investee company that is used when the investor does not have significant influence over the investee (e.g., less than 20% ownership). The portfolios of current and noncurrent marketable securities—stocks are reported at the lower of cost or the aggregate market value of the portfolio on the balance sheet date.

Marketable Securities.   Investments in securities, such as common stock or bonds that are readily saleable. They are classified as current (noncurrent) if it is intended that they be sold (not be sold) within 1 year or the operating cycle, whichever is longer.

Minority Interest.   The ownership interest of other stockholders when the parent company owns less than 100% of the common stock of the subsidiary company. Included in a consolidated balance sheet.

Parent.   The investor company that owns more than 50% of the outstanding common stock of the investee (subsidiary) company.

Portfolio.   All the investments in stock of other companies. May be classified as either current or noncurrent.

Significant Influence.   The criterion that must exist for the equity method of accounting to be used. Significant influence is presumed to exist when the investor owns 20% or more of the outstanding common stock of the investee.

Subsidiary.   The investee company that has more than 50% of its outstanding common stock owned by the investor (parent) company.

Unrealized Decline in Value of Noncurrent Marketable Securities—Stocks. The cumulative amount by which the market value of the portfolio of noncurrent marketable securities—stocks is less than the cost. It is included in stockholders' equity as a negative amount.

Unrealized Gain or Loss on Decline in Value of Current Marketable Securities—Stocks   A gain or loss from holding current marketable securities—stocks during a period that has not been realized through a sale. It is measured by the difference between the cost and the market value of the portfolio of current marketable securities—stocks.

Questions

QUESTION 17-1   Why does a company invest in current marketable securities? Give examples of the securities in which a company might invest.

QUESTION 17-2   Why does a purchaser of bonds pay for "accrued interest" whereas a purchaser of stocks does not pay for "accrued dividends"?

QUESTION 17-3   How is an investment in current marketable securities—stocks accounted for subsequent to acquisition? An investment in current marketable securities—bonds?

QUESTION 17-4   What is an Unrealized Loss on Decline in Value of Current Marketable Securities—Stocks account and where is it disclosed on the financial statements?

QUESTION 17-5   What is an Allowance for Decline in Value of Current Marketable Securities—Stocks account and where is it disclosed on the financial statements?

QUESTION 17-6   How is revenue on current marketable securities—stocks accounted for? Revenue on current marketable securities—bonds?

QUESTION 17-7   How is the gain or loss on the sale of marketable securities—stocks determined? Current marketable securities—bonds?

QUESTION 17-8   When the lower of cost or market method is used for noncurrent marketable securities—stocks, how is a decline in the value of the securities included in the financial statements?

QUESTION 17-9   Are unrealized losses on the valuation of current marketable securities—stocks included in the determination of taxable income? Explain.

QUESTION 17-10   Why do some users of financial statements criticize the lower of cost or market method?

QUESTION 17-11   Why may a company make a noncurrent investment in the bonds of another company?

QUESTION 17-12   How does the recording of a noncurrent investment in bonds differ from the recording of bonds payable?

QUESTION 17-13   What are the two methods by which a premium or discount on a noncurrent investment in bonds may be amortized? Explain how interest revenue is calculated for each method.

QUESTION 17-14   Why may a company make a long-term investment in the stock of another company rather than a short-term investment in the same stock?

QUESTION 17-15   Define the terms *investor company* and *investee company*.

QUESTION 17-16   What are the three methods that may be used to account for a noncurrent acquisition of the common stock of another company? When is each used?

QUESTION 17-17   What characteristics may be used to indicate that the investor company has significant influence over the investee company?

QUESTION 17-18   An investor may purchase shares on the stock market or from the investee company itself. How does each of these methods of acquisition affect the investee company's financial statements?

QUESTION 17-19   Why is the equity method considered to be a better accounting method than the lower of cost or market method for certain types of investments?

QUESTION 17-20　When the equity method is used, how does the investor company record the value of its investment? How does the investor company record the income earned on its investment?

QUESTION 17-21　When the equity method is used, what is the relationship between the change in the balance of the investor company's investment account and the change in the balance sheet of the investee company?

QUESTION 17-22　When a consolidated balance sheet is prepared, why is it necessary to eliminate certain items? Give two examples of items that might be eliminated.

QUESTION 17-23　When a consolidated income statement is prepared, why is it necessary to eliminate certain items? Give two examples of items that might be eliminated.

QUESTION 17-24　What is minority interest? Where would it appear in a consolidated balance sheet? How is it computed?

Exercises

EXERCISE 17-1　**Current Marketable Securities—Stocks.**　The Castle Brush Company purchased a portfolio of current marketable securities—stocks on January 14, 1991. The company bought and sold shares during the next year, and the portfolio had the following costs and market values at the end of each quarter during the year:

	Cost	Market Value
March 31, 1991	$87,500	$88,200
June 30, 1991	83,000	80,000
September 30, 1991	92,000	87,000
December 31, 1991	64,000	66,000

REQUIRED　*1.* How much unrealized loss or gain will be reported in each of the quarterly income statements prepared on the preceding dates?

2. Prepare the journal entries required on each of the preceding dates.

EXERCISE 17-2　**Current Marketable Securities—Stocks.**　On January 7, 1991, the Belford Buckle Company purchased a portfolio of current marketable securities—stocks for $41,000. At the end of the company's fiscal year on June 30, 1991, the market value of the portfolio was $35,000. On August 26, 1991, the company sold one of the stocks in its portfolio, which had cost $10,000, for $12,000. On June 30, 1991, this security had a market value of $9,500.

REQUIRED　*1.* How much income will the Belford Buckle Company recognize from January 7, 1991, through August 26, 1991, as a result of these events?

2. Prepare journal entries required to record these events.

EXERCISE 17-3　**Noncurrent Marketable Securities—Stocks.**　On September 15, 1991, the Morton Tile Corporation purchased shares of common stock (all less than 20% of the outstanding stock) in three companies and classified the portfolio as noncurrent. No dividends were declared or received on any of the shares during 1991. The costs and the market values on December 31, 1991, were as follows:

Company	Number of Shares	Cost per Share	Market Value per Share
Moses Company	100	$21	$23
Upchurch Company	250	40	42
Jensen Company	500	11	8

REQUIRED   Show all of the items that will appear in the Morton Tile Corporation's financial statements in 1991 relating to the securities.

EXERCISE 17-4   **Noncurrent Marketable Securities—Stocks.** Use the same information as in Exercise 17-3. Assume that the Morton Tile Corporation sold the shares of the Jensen Company on December 10, 1992, for $9 per share.

REQUIRED   1. How much is the gain or loss that is recognized on the sale?

   2. If the prices of the shares in the other two companies have not changed since December 31, 1991, show all of the items that will appear in the Morton Tile Corporation's 1992 financial statements relating to the securities.

EXERCISE 17-5   **Current Marketable Securities—Bonds.** On February 1, 1991, the Grays Turbine Company purchased 9 Torres Company 8% $1,000 bonds at 105 plus accrued interest, and paid stockbroker's fees of $200. The bonds pay interest on June 30 and December 31 each year. On September 1, 1991, the company sold the bonds at 106 plus accrued interest.

REQUIRED   1. Compute the total amount paid for the bonds.

   2. Compute the interest earned on the bonds by the Grays Turbine Company during 1991.

   3. For the sale of the bonds, compute the amount received and the gain or loss.

   4. Prepare the journal entries required to account for the bonds during 1991.

EXERCISE 17-6   **Current Marketable Securities—Bonds.** On March 1, 1991, the Harsh Hat Company purchased Elm Company bonds with a face value of $12,000. The bonds pay interest at a 10% annual interest rate on June 30 and December 31 each year. The Harsh Hat Company paid 97 plus accrued interest, plus a stockbroker's commission of $150. The Harsh Hat Company sold the bonds on November 1, 1991, at 101 plus accrued interest.

REQUIRED   1. Compute the amount paid for the bonds.

   2. Compute the interest earned on the bonds by the Harsh Hat Company during 1991.

   3. For the sale of the bonds, compute the amount received and the gain or loss.

   4. Prepare the journal entries required to account for the bonds during 1991.

EXERCISE 17-7   **Noncurrent Investment in Bonds and the Straight-Line Method.** On January 1, 1991, the Porter Rug Company purchased 8%, 20-year bonds with a face value of

$100,000 for $95,000. Interest is paid on June 30 and December 31. The company uses the straight-line amortization method and classified the bonds as noncurrent.

REQUIRED

1. Compute the interest revenue recorded during 1991.

2. What would be the balance of the Investment in Bonds account on the Porter Rug Company's December 31, 1991, balance sheet?

EXERCISE 17-8   **Noncurrent Investment in Bonds and the Effective Interest Method.** On January 1, 1991, the Robinson Steel Company purchased 12%, 10-year bonds with a face value of $100,000 for $112,462.16. At this price the bonds yield 10%. Interest on the bonds is paid on June 30 and December 31. The company uses the effective interest method of amortization and classified the bonds as noncurrent.

REQUIRED

1. Compute the interest revenue recorded during 1991.

2. What would be the balance of the Investment in Bonds account on the Robinson Steel Company's December 31, 1991, balance sheet?

EXERCISE 17-9   **Equity Method.** On January 1, 1991, the Jackson Pen Company purchased 10,000 shares of the Rizzo Pencil Company, which represented 40% of its outstanding common stock. On that date the book value of the net assets of the Rizzo Pencil Company was $125,000. The total cost of the shares was $50,000. At the end of 1991 the Rizzo Pencil Company reported net income of $35,000 and paid total dividends of $16,000.

REQUIRED

1. How much does the Jackson Pen Company recognize as income for 1991?

2. What is the book value of the investment reported in the balance sheet of the Jackson Pen Company on December 31, 1991?

EXERCISE 17-10   **Equity Method.** On January 1, 1991, the Foley Aircraft Company purchased 20,000 shares of the Preston Helicopter Company for $105,000. This represents 25% of the Preston Helicopter Company's outstanding shares. On that date the book value of the net assets of the Preston Helicopter Company was $420,000. On December 31, 1991, the Foley Aircraft Company reported a balance in its investment account of $120,000. The Preston Helicopter Company did not pay dividends during 1991.

REQUIRED

1. How much did the Foley Aircraft Company report as 1991 income on its investment?

2. What was the total net income of the Preston Helicopter Company during 1991?

EXERCISE 17-11   **Consolidated Balance Sheet.** On January 1, 1991, the Kyle Company had total assets of $310,000, including cash of $30,000, a note receivable of $35,000, inventory of $75,000, property, plant, and equipment of $120,000, and investment in the Swensen Company of $50,000; liabilities of $210,000; and stockholders' equity of $100,000. The Swensen Company had assets of $140,000, consisting of cash of $15,000, inventory of $55,000, and property, plant, and equipment of $70,000; liabilities of $90,000; and stockholders' equity of $50,000. The Kyle Company owns 100% of the outstanding common stock of the Swensen Company.

REQUIRED   Prepare a consolidated balance sheet on January 1, 1991, for the Kyle Company and its subsidiary.

EXERCISE 17-12   **Consolidated Income Statement.** During 1991 the Merman Company had sales of $60,000, cost of goods sold of $24,000, and operating expenses of $15,000. During 1991 the Harrison Company had sales of $40,000, cost of goods sold of $19,000, and operating expenses of $10,000. The Merman Company owns 100% of the outstanding common stock of the Harrison Company. Included in the previously mentioned sales were goods costing the Harrison Company $6,000 which it sold to the Merman Company for $8,000. The Merman Company has resold the goods to its outside customers.

REQUIRED   Prepare a consolidated income statement for the Merman Company and its subsidiary for 1991.

EXERCISE 17-13   **Minority Interest.**   On January 1, 1991, the Norel Company purchased 90% of the common stock of the Weir Company for $135,000. At that date the Weir Company had common stock of $70,000 and retained earnings of $80,000.

REQUIRED   1. How much is the minority interest on the January 1, 1991, consolidated balance sheet?

2. Prepare the necessary elimination entry for the worksheet in general journal form.

Problems

Part A

PROBLEM 17-1A   **Current Marketable Securities—Stocks.**   The Wilson Textile Company invests its temporary excess funds in marketable securities. At the end of 1991 the company's portfolio of current marketable securities—stocks is as follows:

Security	Number of Shares	Cost per Share	Market Value per Share
Bierstadt Company	500	$25	$28
Lindsey Company	400	35	37
Pyramid Company	900	20	20

During the first quarter of 1992 the company engaged in the following transactions:

Date	Transaction
Feb 10	Sold one-half of the Pyramid shares for $24 per share.
Mar. 18	Purchased 800 shares of Maroon Company stock for $18 per share.
Mar. 31	Received dividends of $1,400 on the marketable securities during the period for which the market values on this date are:

Security	Market Value per Share
Bierstadt Company	$24
Lindsey Company	31
Pyramid Company	22
Maroon Company	17

During the second quarter of 1992 the company engaged in the following transactions:

Date	Transaction
Apr. 17	Purchased 300 shares of the Huron Company stock for $31 per share.
May 15	Sold the Lindsey Company shares for $38 per share.
June 30	Received dividends of $1,800 on the marketable securities during the period for which the market values on this date are:

Security	Market Value per Share
Bierstadt Company	$26
Pyramid Company	19
Maroon Company	21
Huron Company	32

REQUIRED

1. Prepare journal entries to record these events. The company records dividend revenue when the cash is received.

2. Show how the income recognized each quarter and the value of the marketable securities reported in the balance sheet at the end of each quarter would be disclosed on the interim financial statements.

PROBLEM 17-2A   **Current Marketable Securities (Comprehensive).**   The Windom Freight Company purchased and sold several marketable securities that were classified as current. The acquisitions, sales, and market values were as follows:

Security	Acquisition Date	Cost	Market Value 12/31/1991	Market Value 12/31/1992	Sale Date	Selling Price
1,000 shares	1/10/1991	$11,000	$ 9,000	–	1/10/1992	$12,000
2,000 shares	3/25/1991	16,000	14,000	–	2/11/1992	13,000
Twenty 10% bonds	4/1/1991	22,000	21,000	$23,000	3/1/1993	25,000
500 shares	3/10/1992	11,000	–	12,000	4/20/1993	9,000
Ten 9% bonds	6/1/1992	9,000	–	6,000	4/30/1993	6,000
100 shares	10/4/1993	5,000	–	–	6/6/1994	8,000

Assume that the bonds are accounted for by the cost method and pay interest on June 30 and December 31 of each year. The cost of the bonds excludes the accrued interest that was also paid at the time of purchase. The selling price listed previously for the bonds excludes the accrued interest collected at the time of the sale. The last purchase of 100 shares has a market value on December 31, 1993, of $6,000. No dividends have been paid or declared on the shares.

REQUIRED

1. Prepare journal entries to record these events for the period 1991 through 1994.

2. Show how the income reported each year by the Windom Freight Company as a result of these transactions would be disclosed on its income statement.

3. Show how the value of the Current Marketable Securities would appear in the balance sheet at the end of each year.

4. Some of the securities were held for more than a year. Does this mean that they should not have been included in the current portfolio?

PROBLEM 17-3A **Noncurent Marketable Securities—Stocks.** The Prestridge Corporation had the following transactions for its noncurrent marketable securities—stocks:

January 2, 1991. Purchased common stock as follows:
  Wright Company, 700 shares for $21 per share
  Armstrong Company, 500 shares for $30 per share
  Keyworth Company, 1,000 shares for $14 per share

December 31, 1991:

	Cost per Share	Market Value per Share	Dividends Received per Share
Wright Company	$21	$19	$1
Armstrong Company	30	28	2
Keyworth Company	14	16	1

June 10, 1992. Sold 500 shares of Wright Company for $19 per share.

August 14, 1992. Sold 400 shares of Keyworth Company for $17 per share.

December 31, 1992:

	Cost per Share	Market Value per Share	Dividends Received per Share
Wright Company	$21	$22	$1
Armstrong Company	30	35	2
Keyworth Company	14	17	1

REQUIRED 1. Prepare journal entries to record the preceding events for the Prestridge Corporation. The corporation records dividend revenue when the cash is received.

2. Prepare partial income statements for 1991 and 1992 and also partial balance sheets at December 31, 1991, and December 31, 1992, relating to the preceding events for the Prestridge Corporation.

PROBLEM 17-4A **Noncurrent Investments in Bonds and the Straight-Line Method.** On January 1, 1991, the Andrews Bus Company purchased noncurrent investments in the bonds of two companies:

	Damar	Ackerman
Cost	$87,600	$65,400
Face value	$90,000	$60,000
Maturity date	Dec. 31, 1998	Dec. 31, 1996
Contract rate	9%	12%

Both bonds pay interest on June 30 and December 31. The company uses the straight-line method to amortize any premiums or discounts in regard to the investments in bonds.

REQUIRED

1. Prepare journal entries for the Andrews Bus Company to record all the events for the investments in 1991.

2. Show how the balance of the Investments account would be reported on the December 31, 1991, balance sheet of the Andrews Bus Company.

PROBLEM 17-5A   **Noncurrent Investments in Bonds and the Effective Interest Method.**   On January 1, 1991, the Nairne Gas Company purchased noncurrent investments in the bonds of two companies:

	Simon Company	Fraser Company
Face value	$50,000	$40,000
Maturity date	Dec. 31, 1996	Dec. 31, 2000
Contract rate	9%	7%
Yield	8%	8%

Both bonds pay interest on June 30 and December 31. The company uses the effective interest method to amortize any premiums or discounts in regard to the investments in bonds.

REQUIRED

1. Compute the purchase price of each bond issue.

2. Prepare journal entries for the Nairne Gas Company to record all the events for the investments during 1991.

3. Compute the book value of each investment at December 31, 1991.

PROBLEM 17-6A   **Equity Method.**   The Carter Company purchased, on the stock market, 48,000 of the 120,000 outstanding shares of the Chavous Company on January 1, 1991, for $240,000. The condensed balance sheet of the Chavous Company on January 1, 1991, is as follows:

CHAVOUS COMPANY
Consolidated Balance Sheet
January 1, 1991

Assets		*Liabilities*	
Current assets	$ 400,000	Current liabilities	$ 100,000
Noncurrent assets	600,000	Noncurrent liabilities	300,000
		Total Liabilities	$ 400,000
		Stockholders' Equity	
		Common stock, no par	$ 250,000
		Retained earnings	350,000
		Total Stockholders' Equity .	$ 600,000
		Total Liabilities and	
Total Assets	$1,000,000	Stockholders' Equity	$1,000,000

At the end of 1991 the Chavous Company reported net income of $150,000 and paid dividends of $40,000.

REQUIRED
1. Prepare journal entries to record the preceding events in 1991 for the Carter Company.

2. Prepare a partial income statement for 1991 and a partial balance sheet at December 31, 1991, for the Carter Company relating to the preceding events.

3. Assuming that noncurrent assets increased by $60,000, and liabilities and common stock are unchanged, prepare a condensed balance sheet for the Chavous Company at December 31, 1991.

4. What is the relationship between the change in the balance of the Investment account of the Carter Company since the purchase of the investment and the change in the balance sheet of the Chavous Company?

PROBLEM 17-7A   **Consolidation.**   On June 30, 1991, the Milo Company purchased 100% of the common stock of the Alpha Company. In addition, on the same date the Alpha Company borrowed $20,000 from the Milo Company by issuing a note. After these transactions the balance sheet accounts of the two companies on June 30, 1991, were as follows:

Assets	Milo Company	Alpha Company
Cash	$ 10,000	$ 9,000
Accounts receivable	30,000	6,000
Notes receivable	50,000	30,000
Inventory	80,000	40,000
Investment in Alpha Company	70,000	—
Property, plant, and equipment (net)	120,000	80,000
Total Assets	$360,000	$165,000

Liabilities and Stockholders' Equity		
Accounts payable	$ 55,000	$ 27,000
Notes payable	65,000	68,000
Common stock, no par	100,000	40,000
Retained earnings	140,000	30,000
Total Liabilities and Stockholders' Equity	$360,000	$165,000

REQUIRED   Prepare the consolidated balance sheet for the Milo Company and its subsidiary at June 30, 1991.

Problems

Part B

PROBLEM 17-1B   **Current Marketable Securities—Stocks.**   The Streeter Hot Tub Company invests its temporary excess funds in marketable securities. At the end of 1991 the company's portfolio of current marketable securities—stocks is as follows:

Security	Number of Shares	Cost per Share	Market Value per Share
Parham Company	500	$20	$23
Beckman Company	400	30	32
Traub Company	800	15	15

During the first quarter of 1992 the company engaged in the following transactions:

Date	Transaction
Mar. 11	Sold one-half of the Parham shares for $24 per share.
17	Purchased 600 shares of Gilman Company stock for $10 per share.
31	Received dividends of $1,500 on the marketable securities during the period, and the market values on this date are:

Security	Market Value per Share
Parham Company	$18
Beckman Company	28
Traub Company	17
Gilman Company	9

During the second quarter of 1992 the company engaged in the following transactions:

Date	Transaction
May 15	Purchased 300 shares of the Hagge Company stock for $26 per share.
June 9	Sold the Beckman Company stock for $31 per share.
June 30	Received dividends of $2,000 on the marketable securities during the period, and the market values on this date are:

Security	Market Value per Share
Parham Company	$21
Traub Company	14
Gilman Company	13
Hagge Company	27

REQUIRED

1. Prepare journal entries to record these events. The company records dividend revenue when the cash is received.

2. Show how the income recognized each quarter and the value of the marketable securities reported in the balance sheet at the end of each quarter would be disclosed on the interim financial statements.

PROBLEM 17-2B   **Current Marketable Securities (Comprehensive).** The Martell Clock Company purchased and sold several marketable securities that were classified as current. The acquisitions, sales, and market values were as follows:

Security	Acquisition Date	Cost	Market Value 12/31/1991	Market Value 12/31/1992	Sale Date	Selling Price
1,000 shares	2/18/1991	$16,000	$12,000	–	2/17/1992	$17,000
2,500 shares	4/5/1991	21,000	19,000	–	3/11/1992	17,000
Fifteen 11% bonds	5/1/1991	16,000	15,000	$17,000	4/1/1993	18,000
600 shares	3/19/1992	12,000	–	13,000	4/30/1993	9,000
Twenty 8% bonds	6/1/1992	18,000	–	15,000	6/1/1993	17,000
120 shares	10/19/1993	6,000	–	–	7/8/1994	8,000

Assume that the bonds are accounted for by the cost method and pay interest on June 30 and December 31 of each year. The cost of the bonds excludes the accrued interest, which was also paid at the time of purchase. The selling price listed previously for the bonds excludes the accrued interest collected at the time of the sale. The last purchase of 120 shares has a market value on December 31, 1993, of $7,000. No dividends have been paid or declared on the shares.

REQUIRED

1. Prepare journal entries to record these events for the period 1991 through 1994.

2. Show how the income reported each year by the Martell Clock Company as a result of these transactions would be disclosed on its income statement.

3. Show how the value of the Current Marketable Securities would appear in the balance sheet at the end of each year.

4. Some of the securities were held for more than a year. Does this mean that they should not have been included in the current portfolio?

PROBLEM 17-3B **Noncurrent Marketable Securities—Stocks.** The Adams Corporation had the following transactions for its noncurrent marketable securities—stocks:

March 21, 1991. Purchased common stock as follows:
  Stephens Company, 300 shares for $31 per share
  Wheaton Company, 800 shares for $15 per share
  White Company, 500 shares for $19 per share

December 31, 1991:

	Cost per Share	Market Value per Share	Dividends Received per Share
Stephens Company	$31	$32	$2
Wheaton Company	15	13	1
White Company	19	18	1

July 2, 1992. Sold 100 shares of Stephens Company stock for $33 per share.

September 9, 1992. Sold 400 shares of White Company stock for $16 per share.

December 31, 1992:

	Cost per Share	Market Value per Share	Dividends Received per Share
Stephens Company	$31	$33	$2
Wheaton Company	15	14	1
White Company	19	16	1

REQUIRED

1. Prepare journal entries to record the preceding events for the Adams Corporation. The corporation records dividend revenue when the cash is received.

2. Prepare partial income statements for 1991 and 1992 and partial balance sheets at December 31, 1991, and December 31, 1992, relating to the preceding events for the Adams Corporation.

PROBLEM 17-4B   **Noncurrent Investments in Bonds and the Straight-Line Method.**   On January 1, 1991, the Gooch Concrete Company purchased noncurrent investments in the bonds of two companies:

	Tanner	Carew
Cost	$46,500	$97,200
Face value	$50,000	$90,000
Maturity date	Dec. 31, 1997	Dec. 31, 2002
Contract rate	8%	11%

Both bonds pay interest on June 30 and December 31. The company uses the straight-line method to amortize any premium or discount in regard to the investments in bonds.

REQUIRED

1. Prepare journal entries for the Gooch Concrete Company to record all of the events for the investments in 1991.

2. Show how the balance of the Investments account would be reported on the December 31, 1991, balance sheet of the Gooch Concrete Company.

PROBLEM 17-5B   **Noncurrent Investments in Bonds and the Effective Interest Method.**   On January 1, 1991, the Winfrey Silicone Company purchased noncurrent investments in the bonds of two companies:

	Bates Company	Clevett Company
Face value	$90,000	$70,000
Maturity date	Dec. 31, 1995	Dec. 31, 2000
Contract rate	9%	11%
Yield	10%	10%

Both bonds pay interest on June 30 and December 31. The company uses the effective interest method to amortize any premium or discount in regard to the investments in bonds.

REQUIRED

1. Compute the purchase price of each bond issue.

2. Prepare journal entries for the Winfrey Silicone Company to record all of the events for the investments during 1991.

3. Compute the book value of each investment at December 31, 1991.

PROBLEM 17-6B   **Equity Method.**   The Wild Company purchased, on the stock market, 60,000 of the 200,000 outstanding shares of the Dynan Company on January 1, 1991, for $270,000. The condensed balance sheet of the Dynan Company on January 1, 1991, is as follows:

DYNAN COMPANY
Balance Sheet
January 1, 1991

Assets		Liabilities	
Current assets	$ 600,000	Current liabilities	$ 200,000
Noncurrent assets	900,000	Noncurrent liabilities	400,000
		Total Liabilities	$ 600,000
		Stockholders' Equity	
		Common stock, no par	$ 400,000
		Retained earnings	500,000
		Total Stockholders' Equity .	$ 900,000
		Total Liabilities and	
Total Assets	$1,500,000	Stockholders' Equity	$1,500,000

At the end of 1991 the Dynan Company reported net income of $300,000 and paid dividends of $60,000.

REQUIRED   *1.* Prepare journal entries to record the preceding events in 1991 for the Wild Company.

2. Prepare a partial income statement for 1991 and a partial balance sheet at December 31, 1991, for the Wild Company relating to the investment.

3. Assuming that noncurrent assets increased by $100,000, and liabilities and common stock are unchanged, prepare a condensed balance sheet for the Dynan Company at December 31, 1991.

4. What is the relationship between the change in the balance of the Investment account of the Wild Company since the purchase of the investment and the change in the balance sheet of the Dynan Company?

PROBLEM 17-7B   **Consolidation.**   On January 1, 1991, the Bashor Company purchased 100% of the common stock of the Cohen Company. It paid $120,000, which was equal to the book value of the Cohen Company at that time. During the year the Cohen Company earned income of $30,000 and no dividends were paid. In addition, the Bashor Company sold goods costing $10,000 to the Cohen Company for $18,000 on account. The account has not yet been paid. The Cohen Company sold these goods to its outside customers for $25,000 cash. At December 31, 1991, the balance sheets of the two companies were as follows:

Assets	Bashor Company	Cohen Company
Cash	$ 35,000	$ 15,000
Accounts receivable	52,000	25,000
Notes receivable	43,000	13,000
Inventory	90,000	57,000
Investment in Cohen Company	150,000	—
Property and equipment (net)	100,000	75,000
Total Assets	$470,000	$185,000

Liabilities and Stockholders' Equity

Accounts payable	$ 75,000	$ 20,000
Notes payable	50,000	15,000
Common stock, no par	120,000	60,000
Retained earnings	225,000	90,000
Total Liabilities and Stockholders' Equity	$470,000	$185,000

REQUIRED   1. Develop a worksheet for the preparation of a consolidated balance sheet for the Bashor Company and its subsidiary on December 31, 1991.

2. What items would be eliminated on a consolidated income statement for 1991?

Decision Cases

DECISION CASE 17-1   **Current Marketable Securities—Stocks.**   The Board of Directors of the Oxford Company is discussing the method that should be used for the valuation of the company's current marketable securities—stocks. Some of the comments are as follows:

- "We should use cost, because until we sell the securities we don't know if we have made any money."

- "If we use cost we are effectively misleading the users of the financial statements, and as a member of the Board of Directors I don't feel I'm fulfilling my responsibilities."

- "Market value is too pessimistic. If the price is up in one period and down in the next, we will report a loss in the second period although we may have a profit over all. That's misleading."

REQUIRED   Describe what the speaker of each of these comments means and prepare a counterargument for each of them. (Ignore the requirements of generally accepted accounting principles.)

DECISION CASE 17-2   **Investments in Common Stock.**   When a company buys common stock of another company the acquisition can be accounted for under one of four alternative methods: lower of cost or market with the loss on the decline in market value included in the income statement; lower of cost or market with the "loss" included in stockholders' equity; the equity method; or consolidation. Each method results in different amounts appearing in various sections of the financial statements.

REQUIRED   1. In what situation is each of the four methods used?

2. Explain how the results of the four methods appear on the financial statements.

3. Explain the justification for requiring the use of each of the four different methods from the perspective of the user of the financial statements.

DECISION CASE 17-3   **Equity Method.**   Scott Paper Company disclosed the following in its 1988 financial statements with respect to the equity method used for investments in supplier and other affiliates (amounts in millions of dollars):

	1988	*1987*
Cost	$ 43.0	$ 9.5
Equity in undistributed earnings	0.1	29.8
	$ 43.1	$39.3
Changes		
Share of earnings	$ 3.8	$ 6.2
Cash distributions paid to Scott	(149.1)	(6.3)
New investments	191.1	-0-
Dispositions	(42.0)	-0-
Increase (decrease) in investment	$ 3.8	$(0.1)

REQUIRED   Analyze all the impacts on the financial statements from investments in supplier affiliates in 1988 using T-accounts.

DECISION CASE 17-4   **Various Accounting Methods for Investments.** American Express reported the following in its 1988 financial statements (amounts in millions of dollars):

	1988	*1987*
Investment securities—at cost		
Total (market: 1988, $28,625; 1987, $23,166)	$28,929	$23,167
Investment securities—at lower of aggregate cost or		
market		
Total (cost: 1988, $2,638; 1987, $2,402)	$ 2,514	$ 2,265
Investment securities—at market		
Total	$17,704	$15,939
Shareholders' equity		
Net unrealized security losses	$ (74)	$ (41)

Note 1. Summary of Significant Accounting Policies [in part]:
Investment Securities. Debt securities and investment mortgage loans, other than trading securities of Shearson Lehman Hutton Holdings Inc. (Shearson), are carried at amortized cost, except where there is a permanent impairment of value, in which case they are carried at estimated realizable value. All trading securities owned by Shearson and all nonredeemable preferred and common stocks owned by the life insurance subsidiaries are carried at market. Other preferred and common stocks are generally carried at the lower of aggregate cost or market except that preferred stock that either must be redeemed by the issuer or may be redeemed by the issuer at the holder's request are carried at cost. Unrealized appreciation or depreciation on Shearson's trading securities is included in net income.

    Net income excludes net unrealized gains (losses) of securities carried at market and the lower of aggregate cost or market, except that unrealized gains (losses) of trading securities held by Shearson are included in net income. Net unrealized gains (losses) relating to securities carried at market and at the lower of aggregate cost or market, excluding trading securities held by Shearson, are included in shareholders' equity.

REQUIRED   *1.* Explain why American Express uses three different accounting methods for its investment securities.

    2. Use T-accounts to explain all the 1988 changes in the investment security accounts listed. Assume that there was only one aggregate sale of $800 million investment securities (carried at market) for $900 million cash and that $1,000 million investment interest income was earned in 1988. Also assume 1988 purchases of $236 million and $2,000 million of investment securities at LCM and at market, respectively.

18

Statement of Cash Flows

LEARNING OBJECTIVES

1. Define a statement of cash flows.

2. List several cash flows from operating, investing, and financing activities.

3. Identify the sections of the statement of cash flows.

4. Classify changes in balance sheet accounts as to their impact on cash flows.

5. Identify and report investing and financing activities not affecting cash.

6. Describe the (a) direct method and (b) indirect method for reporting the net cash provided by operating activities.

7. List the seven steps in the visual inspection method.

8. Prepare a worksheet for the statement of cash flows.

APPENDIX

A-1. List the categories of operating cash (a) inflows and (b) outflows under the direct method.

A-2. Describe the modification in the visual inspection approach under the direct method.

T hroughout this textbook we have studied two major financial statements: the income statement, which summarizes the results of the operating activities of a company during the accounting period, and the balance sheet, which shows the financial position of the company at a specific time in the accounting period. Both of these statements are prepared under *accrual* accounting. With just these two financial statements, a vital link between the company's activities and the information reported to the users of accounting information is missing. A financial statement is needed to report a summary of the cash flows from the company's operating, investing, and financing activities during the accounting period. The statement should report such items as how much cash was increased because of operations, what proceeds were received from the issuance of stocks or bonds, how much cash was paid for dividends and interest, and how the acquisition of equipment was financed. This financial statement, known as the statement of cash flows, is the subject of this chapter.

Conceptual Overview and Reporting Guidelines

Companies have prepared versions of the statement of cash flows for a long time. These reports were mainly used to assist the managers of the business in its day-to-day operations, however. These reports were referred to by many names, including the "sources and uses statement," the "cash flow statement," and the "funds statement." Prior to 1987, companies were required to show a "statement of changes in financial position" whenever a balance sheet and income statement were issued for external users. In preparing the statement of changes in financial position, however, a company could define "funds" from operations as either cash or working capital (current assets minus current liabilities). Furthermore there were differences among companies in the formats of and classifications in this statement. To improve comparability and reduce these differences, in 1987 the Financial Accounting Standards Board (FASB) required that a "statement of cash flows" be provided whenever a company presents an income statement and balance sheet.

A company cannot continue operating unless it has sufficient cash to do so. The information in a statement of cash flows, if used with information in the other two major financial statements (i.e., the income statement and balance sheet), should help external users to assess: (a) a company's ability to obtain positive future net cash flows, (b) a company's ability to meet its obligations and pay dividends, (c) a company's need for external financing, (d) the reasons for differences between a company's net income and related cash receipts and payments, and (e) both the cash and noncash aspects of a company's financing and investing transactions during the accounting period.

Definition and Components of Statement

1. Define a statement of cash flows.

A statement of cash flows is a financial statement that shows the inflows and outflows of cash from the operating, investing, and financing activities of a company during an accounting period, in a manner that reconciles the beginning and ending cash balances. *Operating activities* include all transactions and other events that are not investing and financing activities. These transactions involve acquiring, selling, and delivering goods for sale, as well as providing services. Cash inflows from and cash outflows for operating activities are:

1. Receipts from cash sales
2. Receipts from collections of accounts receivable from credit sales
3. Receipts from collections of interest revenue and dividend revenue
4. Payments for inventory and supplies
5. Payments for employees' salaries and other expenses
6. Payments for interest and income taxes

Investing activities include transactions involving lending money and collecting on the loans, acquiring and selling investments (both short-term and long-term), and acquiring and selling property and equipment. Cash inflows from and cash outflows for investing activities are:

1. Receipts from selling investments in stocks and bonds
2. Receipts from selling property and equipment
3. Payments for investments in stocks and bonds
4. Payments for purchases of property and equipment

Financing activities include transactions involving obtaining resources from owners and providing them with a return on their investment, as well as obtaining resources from creditors and repaying the amounts borrowed. Cash inflows from and cash outflows for financing activities are:

1. Receipts from the issuance of stocks and bonds
2. Receipts from the issuance of notes and mortgages
3. Payments of dividends
4. Payments to retire stocks and bonds
5. Payments to retire notes and mortgages

The statement of cash flows is intended to provide useful information to external users about the preceding items. Owners, potential investors, creditors, and potential creditors may use the information in the statement to evaluate how effectively the management of the company obtains and uses its cash. It is important, therefore, to have an agreement about what to include in the statement. The statement of cash flows for the accounting period should clearly show:[1]

1. The cash provided by or used in the company's operating activities.
2. The cash provided by or used in the company's investing activities.
3. The cash provided by or used in the company's financing activities.
4. The net increase or decrease in cash.
5. A reconciliation of the beginning cash balance to the ending cash balance.

2. List several cash flows from operating, investing, and financing activities.

3. Identify the sections of the statement of cash flows.

---

[1]A company may have had important financing and investing activities that did not affect cash during the period. The results of these activities are shown in a separate schedule that accompanies the statement of cash flows as described later in the chapter.

Many companies invest excess cash in short-term highly liquid investments, such as money market funds. These investments are called *cash equivalents*. When a company makes such investments the purpose of the statement of cash flows is to explain the change during the period in *cash and cash equivalents*. In this chapter, however, we will focus only on changes in *cash*.

Illustration

A typical statement of cash flows for the Rainey Corporation is illustrated in Exhibit 18-1 and discussed next. Note that the statement of cash flows in Exhibit 18-1 is divided into three sections entitled: (1) net cash flow from operating activities, (2) cash flows from investing activities, and (3) cash flows from financing activities. These are the titles generally used in a statement of cash flows.

The net cash provided by or used in a company's operating activities is shown in the first section of a statement of cash flows. It is unlikely that a company will continue to be successful unless it is able to obtain most of its cash from its operations. This occurs when the cash received from selling goods or services exceeds the cash paid to provide the goods or services. Obtaining cash from operations is generally considered to be the most important cash flow activity of a company. The Rainey Corporation provided a net cash inflow of

EXHIBIT 18-1
Statement of Cash
Flows: Rainey
Corporation

RAINEY CORPORATION Statement of Cash Flows For Year Ended December 31, 1991		
Net Cash Flow From Operating Activities		
Net Income	$ 6,000	
Adjustments for differences between net income and cash flows from operating activities:		
Add: Depreciation expense	4,000	
Increase in salaries payable	400	
Increase in accounts payable	1,300	
Less: Increase in accounts receivable	(3,500)	
Net cash provided by operating activities		$ 8,200
Cash Flows From Investing Activities		
Payment for purchase of building	$(14,000)	
Payment for purchase of equipment	(2,000)	
Proceeds from sale of land, at cost	5,000	
Net cash used for investing activities		(11,000)
Cash Flows From Financing Activities		
Proceeds from issuance of common stock	$ 9,000	
Proceeds from issuance of bonds	6,000	
Payment of dividends	(4,000)	
Payment of note payable	(7,000)	
Net cash provided by financing activities		4,000
Net Increase in Cash		$ 1,200
Cash, January 1, 1991		6,300
Cash, December 31, 1991		$ 7,500

$8,200 from its operating activities during 1991, as shown in Exhibit 18-1. This $8,200 amount was determined by adjusting the $6,000 net income for several items; this procedure is explained later in the chapter. External users can compare the company's net cash flow from operating activities for a given year with the same information from previous years in order to detect favorable or unfavorable *trends* in the company's operating activities. This information can also be compared with the same information from other companies for the same purposes.

The cash inflows and outflows from a company's investing activities are reported in the second section of the statement of cash flows. Each investing cash inflow and outflow is listed and the amounts are subtotaled to determine the net cash used for (or provided by) investing activities. During 1991 the Rainey Corporation had a cash outflow of $14,000 to purchase a building and a cash outflow of $2,000 to purchase equipment. It received a cash inflow of $5,000 from the sale of land, at cost. The net result was that $11,000 of cash was used for its investing activities.

The cash inflows and outflows from a company's financing activities are reported in the third section of the statement of cash flows. Each financing cash inflow and outflow is listed and the amounts are subtotaled to determine the net cash provided by (or used for) financing activities. During 1991 the Rainey Corporation had cash inflows of $9,000 and $6,000 from the issuance of common stock and bonds, respectively. It had a cash outflow of $4,000 for the payment of dividends, and a $7,000 cash outflow for the payment of a note. The net result was that $4,000 of cash was provided by its financing activities.

The net increase or decrease in cash is the next amount on the statement of cash flows. It is determined by combining the amounts of the net cash flow from operating activities, the net cash flow from investing activities, and the net cash flow from financing activities. The $8,200 net cash provided by operating activities, combined with the $11,000 net cash used for investing activities and the $4,000 net cash provided by financing activities, resulted in a $1,200 net increase in cash for the Rainey Corporation in 1991. This $1,200 net increase in cash reconciles the $6,300 beginning cash balance to the $7,500 ending cash balance. These amounts were reported on the beginning and ending balance sheets, respectively, for 1991.

By reviewing the financing and investing sections of the statement of cash flows, external users can see how (in addition to operations) a company obtained and used its cash. They can compare the relative amounts in each section to see if important changes have occurred. A comparison with other companies can also reveal, for instance, whether the company is obtaining or using a greater proportion of its cash from financing or investing activities rather than from operating activities. External users can evaluate the likelihood of future cash dividends as well as the need for additional cash to finance existing operations or the expansion of operations. They can also evaluate the ability of the company to make continual interest payments and to pay off debt when the debt reaches its maturity date.

Management, too, as internal users, are able to use the information in the statement of cash flows in much the same way as external users. They can determine whether the net cash flow from operating activities is large enough to finance existing operations, whether excess cash from operating activities may be sufficient to finance expansion projects, or whether additional capital must be obtained from external sources. In addition, management uses a form of the statement of cash flows in its budgeting process.

Cash Inflows and Outflows

Before discussing how to prepare the statement of cash flows, it is helpful to understand the major inflows and outflows of cash from a company's activities. These cash flows are shown in Exhibit 18-2. On the statement of cash flows, these inflows and outflows must be classified into the operating, investing, and financing sections. To do so, it is necessary to analyze the relationships between the changes in balance sheet accounts and a company's cash flows.

EXHIBIT 18-2
Major Inflows and Outflows of Cash

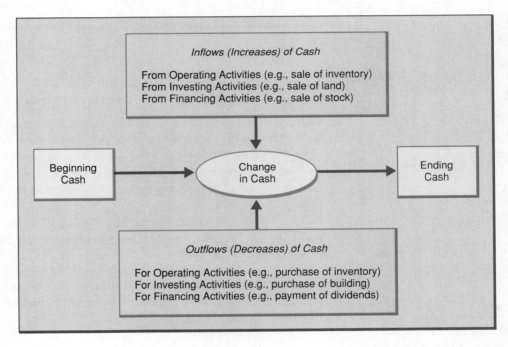

Inflows of cash are caused by decreases in assets (other than cash), increases in liabilities, and increases in stockholders' equity during an accounting period. Outflows of cash are caused by increases in assets (other than cash), decreases in liabilities, and decreases in stockholders' equity during the accounting period. The difference between the inflows and outflows is the change in cash during the accounting period. This relationship is further illustrated by the equations shown in Exhibit 18-3. Each equation is a modification of the previous equation to eventually show the increases and decreases in cash. Note that these relationships are derived from the basic accounting equation. With this background in mind, we can refine the relationships shown in the last two equations of Exhibit 18-3.

EXHIBIT 18-3
Equations for
Change in Cash

		Assets	=	Liabilities	+	Stockholders' Equity		
		Changes in Assets	=	Changes in Liabilities	+	Changes in Stockholders' Equity		
Changes in Cash	+	Changes in Assets Other Than Cash	=	Changes in Liabilities	+	Changes in Stockholders' Equity		
		Changes in Cash	=	Changes in Liabilities	+	Changes in Stockholders' Equity	−	Changes in Assets Other Than Cash
Where:		Increases in Cash	=	Increases in Liabilities	+	Increases in Stockholders' Equity	+	Decreases in Assets Other Than Cash
And:		Decreases in Cash	=	Decreases in Liabilities	+	Decreases in Stockholders' Equity	+	Increases in Assets Other Than Cash

Inflows of Cash

There are three categories of inflows (increases) of cash.

1. *Decreases in Assets Other Than Cash.* The sale or other disposal of assets (other than cash) causes an inflow (increase) of cash because cash is received in exchange for the assets.

2. *Increases in Liabilities.* The issuance or other incurrence of liabilities causes an inflow (increase) of cash because cash is received in exchange for the liabilities.[2]

3. *Increases in Stockholders' Equity.* Stockholders' equity increases mainly because of net income and additional investments by owners. Additional investments cause an inflow (increase) of cash because cash is usually received in exchange for the stock issued. Net income is slightly more complicated because the inflows and outflows of cash for operating activities do not usually equal the revenues and expenses included in net income (this topic is discussed later).

Outflows of Cash

There are also three categories of outflows (decreases) of cash.

1. *Increases in Assets Other Than Cash.* The acquisition of assets (other than cash) causes an outflow (decrease) of cash because cash is paid in exchange for the assets.[3]

---

[2]Alternatively, as discussed later, the increase in a liability such as accounts payable results in a "savings" (i.e., increase) in cash because of a smaller cash outflow.

[3]Alternatively, as discussed later, the increase in an asset such as accounts receivable results, in effect, in a decrease in cash because of a smaller cash inflow.

2. *Decreases in Liabilities.* The payment of liabilities causes an outflow (decrease) of cash because cash is usually paid to satisfy the liabilities.

3. *Decreases in Stockholders' Equity.* Stockholders' equity may decrease as a result of several transactions. Two common transactions are the payment of dividends and the acquisition of treasury stock. In each case a decrease in stockholders' equity is accompanied by an outflow (decrease) of cash.

Classifications of Cash Flows

The categories of inflows and outflows of cash discussed in the previous section can be further classified as relating to operating, investing, and financing activities.

4. Classify changes in balance sheet accounts as to their impact on cash flows.

1. *Operating Cash Flows*
   A. *Inflows:* Increases in stockholders' equity (i.e., retained earnings) due to certain revenues, adjusted for changes in certain current assets (related to operating cycle) and for changes in certain current liabilities (related to operating cycle).
   B. *Outflows:* Decreases in stockholders' equity (i.e., retained earnings) due to certain expenses, adjusted for changes in certain current assets (related to operating cycle) and for changes in certain current liabilities (related to operating cycle).

2. *Investing Cash Flows*
   A. *Inflows:* Decreases in noncurrent assets and certain current assets (e.g., notes receivable, marketable securities).
   B. *Outflows:* Increases in noncurrent assets and certain current assets (e.g., notes receivable, marketable securities).

3. *Financing Cash Flows*
   A. *Inflows:* Increases in noncurrent liabilities, stockholders' equity, and certain current liabilities (e.g., notes payable).
   B. *Outflows:* Decreases in noncurrent liabilities, stockholders' equity, and certain current liabilities (e.g., notes payable).

Note that the listing of the operating cash flows is more general than that of the investing and financing cash flows, and involves several adjustments for items relating to the operating cycle. The net cash flow from operating activities is further explained in a later section.

Investing and Financing Activities Not Affecting Cash Flows

5. Identify and report investing and financing activities not affecting cash.

Changes (increases or decreases) in assets (other than cash), liabilities, and stockholders' equity may also be the result of investing and financing activities *not* affecting cash. For instance, a company might acquire land by issuing common stock, it might purchase equipment by exchanging other equipment, or it might convert bonds payable into common stock. Although these transactions are rare, they do involve "simultaneous" investing and financing transactions not affecting cash. For example, take the case of the acquisition of land by the issuance of common stock. In this situation, the acquisition of the land is an investing activity not affecting cash, while the issuance of the common stock is a financing activity not affecting cash.

Because of their potential importance to users of financial statements, companies are required to report any investing and financing transactions not affecting cash in a separate schedule that accompanies the statement of cash flows. (This schedule is discussed later in the chapter.) In other words, companies must report on the results of *all* investing and financing activities, regardless of whether or not cash was affected.

Net Cash Flow From Operating Activities

The calculation of the net cash flow from operating activities is usually the most difficult part of the statement of cash flows. To prepare this section, it is useful to understand how sales revenues, expenses, and cash flows are related in a company's operating cycle.

Remember that a company's operating cycle is the average time taken to spend cash for inventory, sell the inventory, and collect the accounts receivable, converting them back into cash. To begin a company's operating cycle, the company purchases inventory for cash or on account. To make cash or credit sales, it has cost of goods sold and selling expenses, and reduces inventory, pays cash, or incurs current liabilities. In its operations, the company has general and administrative expenses and either pays cash, incurs current liabilities, or uses up prepaid expenses. Finally, the company collects its accounts receivable and converts them back into cash. This step completes the operating cycle. These revenues, expenses, and related cash flows in the operating cycle are illustrated in Exhibit 18-4.

As seen in Exhibit 18-4 each phase of the operating cycle has an impact on both net income and the net cash flow from operating activities. The impact is not likely to be the same for both items, however, because of differences in the recording of revenues and expenses and the timing of cash flows. For instance, when inventory is purchased for cash an outflow of cash occurs but no expense is recorded. A purchase of inventory on credit increases accounts payable (a current liability) but involves no immediate expense or cash outflow. Later, when the accounts payable is paid no expense is recorded but a cash outflow occurs. The expense is recorded (as cost of goods sold) when the inventory is sold even though no cash outflow occurs at that time. When a cash sale is made revenue is recorded and there is a cash inflow. However, when a credit sale is made both revenue and accounts receivable (a current asset) are increased but no inflow of cash occurs. Later, when the accounts receivable is collected no revenue is recorded but a cash inflow occurs. Some accounts receivable are not collected so an expense (bad debts) is incurred even though no cash outflow occurs. In addition, throughout the accounting period when selling expenses and general and administrative expenses are paid in cash, expenses are recorded and cash outflows occur. However, when these expenses are accrued at the end of the period, both the expenses and current payables are recorded but no cash outflows occur. The cash outflows are made in the next accounting period when the payables are paid. Furthermore cash outflows for some of these expenses may occur and be

EXHIBIT 18-4
Operating Cycle:
Revenues, Expenses,
and Related Cash Flows

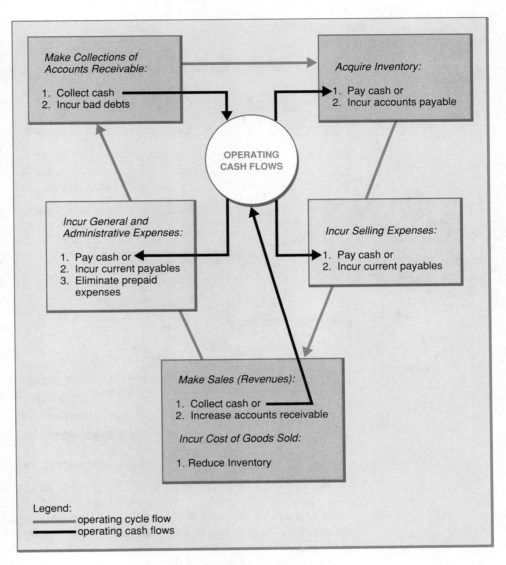

recorded as a current asset in the accounting period before the expenses are recorded (e.g., prepaid insurance).

Exhibit 18-5 illustrates the basic differences between revenues and cash inflows from operating activities, and between expenses and cash outflows for the operating activities that are discussed in this section. For example, assume for simplicity that the Jones Company made cash sales of $30,000 and credit sales of $42,000 during its first year of operations, and collected $37,000 of the related accounts receivable. At the end of the year the Sales Revenue account would show a credit balance of $72,000 and the Accounts Receivable account would show a debit balance of $5,000. As shown in Exhibit 18-6 an analysis of the related T-accounts shows an increase of $67,000 in the cash inflows from operating

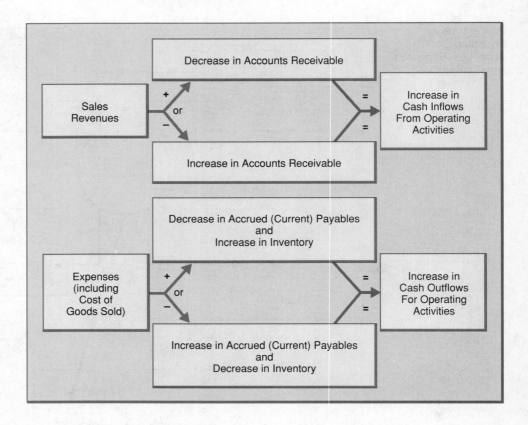

activities. (This $67,000 is equal to the cash sales of $30,000 plus the collections on accounts receivable of $37,000.)

Similarly, assume that Jones Company paid salaries of $13,000 and recorded accrued salaries of $1,000 during its first year of operations. At the end of the year the Salaries Expense account would show a debit balance of $14,000 and the Salaries Payable account would show a credit balance of $1,000. As shown in Exhibit 18-6 an analysis of the related T-account shows an increase of $13,000 in the cash outflows for operating activities. There are additional changes in other current asset and current liability accounts that may affect the net cash flow from operating activities and each of these changes must be analyzed to determine the impact on operating cash inflows and outflows.

There are also changes in certain noncurrent asset accounts that affect net income but do not result in a cash inflow or outflow for operating activities. For instance, when depreciation is recorded the journal entry involves a debit to Depreciation Expense and a credit to Accumulated Depreciation (a noncurrent contra-asset account). Although depreciation expense reduces net income (and noncurrent assets), there is no cash outflow for operating activities. The recording of amortization expense for intangible assets (such as patents) has the same effect. That is, there is a reduction in net income (and noncurrent assets) but no operating cash outflow. Each of the changes in these noncurrent asset accounts must also be analyzed to determine the impact on the net cash flow from operating activities.

EXHIBIT 18-6   Calculation of Cash Flows From Operating Activities

Sales Revenue		
	30,000	
	42,000	
Bal	72,000	

Accounts Receivable		
42,000	37,000	
Bal 5,000		

Sales Revenues	−	Increase in Accounts Receivable	=	Increase in Cash Inflows from Operating Activities
$72,000	−	$5,000	=	$67,000

Salaries Expense		
13,000		
1,000		
Bal 14,000		

Salaries Payable		
	1,000	
Bal	1,000	

Expenses	−	Increase in Accrued (Salaries) Payables	=	Increase in Cash Outflows for Operating Activities
$14,000	−	$1,000	=	$13,000

Direct Method

6(a). Describe the direct method for reporting the net cash provided by operating activities.

There are two methods of calculating and reporting a company's net cash flow from operating activities on its statement of cash flows. One alternative is called the *direct* method. **Under the direct method the operating cash outflows are deducted from the operating cash inflows to determine the net cash provided by operating activities.** The operating cash inflows are computed first, based on an analysis like that shown in the upper portion of Exhibit 18-6. The operating cash outflows are computed next, based on an analysis like that shown in the lower portion of Exhibit 18-6. The operating cash outflows are then deducted from the operating cash inflows to determine the net cash provided by operating activities. To illustrate, suppose the Rainey Corporation presents the following income statement information for the year ended December 31, 1991:

Sales revenue (cash and accounts receivable)		$ 36,000
Less:		
Cost of goods sold (cash and accounts payable)	$15,000	
Salaries expense (cash and salaries payable)	7,000	
Depreciation expense	4,000	(26,000)
Income before income taxes		$ 10,000
Income tax expense (cash)		(4,000)
Net income		$ 6,000

A further analysis reveals the following changes in current asset and current liability accounts: accounts receivable increased by $3,500, accounts payable increased by $1,300, and salaries payable increased by $400. Under the direct method the net cash flow from operating activities section of the statement of cash flows would be reported as follows:

Cash Flows From Operating Activities		
Cash Inflows:		
Cash received from customers	$32,500	
Cash inflows from operating activities		$ 32,500
Cash Outflows:		
Cash paid to suppliers	$13,700	
Cash paid to employees	6,600	
Cash paid for income taxes	4,000	
Cash outflows for operating activities		(24,300)
Net cash provided by operating activities		$ 8,200

The $32,500 cash received from customers was computed by deducting the increase in accounts receivable ($3,500) from the sales revenue ($36,000). This was the only cash receipt, so that cash inflows from operating activities were $32,500. The $13,700 cash paid to suppliers was computed by deducting the increase in accounts payable ($1,300) from the cost of goods sold ($15,000). The $6,600 cash paid to employees was computed by deducting the increase in salaries payable ($400) from the salaries expense ($7,000). The entire amount of income tax expense ($4,000) was paid in cash. These cash outflows for operating activities totaled $24,300, so that the net cash provided by operating activities was $8,200. Note that the depreciation expense was *not* included because it did *not* result in an outflow of cash.

The direct method is criticized because it does not "tie" the net income reported on a company's income statement to the net cash provided by operating activities reported on the company's statement of cash flows. Also, the direct method does not show how the changes in the parts (i.e., current assets and current liabilities) of a company's operating cycle affected its operating cash flows.

Indirect Method

6(b). Describe the indirect method for reporting the net cash provided by operating activities.

Use of the *indirect* method to report a company's net cash flow from operating activities on its statement of cash flows resolves the two criticisms of the direct method. **Under the indirect method net income is adjusted to the net cash flow from operating activities.** To do so, net income is listed first and then adjustments (additions or subtractions) are made to net income: (1) to eliminate certain amounts (such as depreciation expense) that were included in net income but did not involve a cash inflow or cash outflow for operations, and (2) to include any changes in the current assets (other than cash) and current liabilities involved in the company's operating cycle that affected cash flows differently than net income. In other words, under the indirect method income flows are converted from an *accrual* basis to a *cash* basis.

To illustrate, refer to the Rainey Corporation's income statement and additional information presented earlier. Under the indirect method the net cash flow from operating activities section of the statement of cash flows would be reported as follows:

Net Cash Flow From Operating Activities

Net Income	$ 6,000	
Adjustments for differences between net income and cash flows from operating activities:		
Add: Depreciation expense	4,000	
Increase in accounts payable	1,300	
Increase in salaries payable	400	
Less: Increase in accounts receivable	(3,500)	
Net cash provided by operating activities		$8,200

It is important to understand the nature of each adjustment to convert net income to the net cash provided by operating activities. First, the $4,000 depreciation expense is *added* to the $6,000 net income because initially it had been deducted to determine net income but did not result in an outflow of cash. The increases in the current liabilities, accounts payable ($1,300) and salaries payable ($400), resulted in an increase in expenses (salaries expense and other operating expenses) and a decrease in net income. Both are *added* to net income because they did not result in an outflow of cash. On the other hand, the $3,500 increase in the current asset accounts receivable resulted in an increase in revenues and net income. The amount is *deducted* from net income because it did not result in an inflow of cash. Note that by using either the direct method or the indirect method, the result is the same because net cash provided by operating activities is $8,200. The indirect method is the method used by the Rainey Corporation in Exhibit 18-1 at the beginning of the chapter.

The indirect method is used by most companies and is the method we will use in the main part of this chapter, although we will further explain the direct method in the appendix to this chapter. *(You should use the indirect method for all homework, unless otherwise indicated.)* In the previous example, we made only a few simple adjustments to convert net income to the net cash flow from operating activities. Furthermore our adjustments for changes in current assets and current liabilities focused on increases in these items. In reality, there may be many adjustments involving both increases and decreases in current assets and current liabilities, as well as other accounts. To help in understanding, Exhibit 18-7 lists the major adjustments needed to convert net income to the net cash provided by operating activities.[4] These adjustments will be explained in the examples that follow.

Procedures for Preparation of Statement

When beginning to prepare the statement of cash flows for a company it is helpful to remember that the statement is used to report the cash inflows and cash outflows from the company's operating, investing, and financing activities. It is also useful to recall the three categories of inflows (or outflows) of cash:

---

[4]Net income may also need to be adjusted for other items such as the amortization of premiums and discounts on bonds payable, the amortization of premiums and discounts on investments in bonds, changes in deferred income taxes and extraordinary items. These adjustments, however, involve a complex analysis and are not discussed further in this chapter.

EXHIBIT 18-7
Adjustments to Convert
Net Income to Net Cash
Flow Provided by
Operating Activities

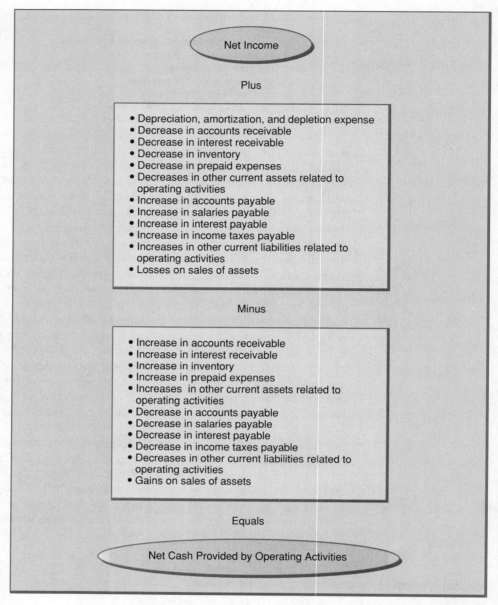

(1) decreases (increases) in assets other than cash, (2) increases (decreases) in liabilities, and (3) increases (decreases) in stockholders' equity.

Information Requirements

When preparing the statement of cash flows, information from the following financial statements is required:

1. The income statement

2. The retained earnings statement

3. The beginning and ending balance sheets

In addition, other supplementary information is usually needed concerning the reasons for the changes in the balance sheet accounts (other than cash).

Steps in Preparation (Visual Inspection)

The statement of cash flows may be prepared using the visual inspection method or the worksheet method (discussed later in the chapter). Under the **visual inspection method,** the financial statements are visually inspected and the statement of cash flows is prepared without the use of a worksheet. This method may be used when the financial statements are not complex and when the relationship between changes in account balances can be easily observed and analyzed.

There are seven steps in the visual inspection method.

7. List the seven steps in the visual inspection method.

1. Prepare the heading for the statement of cash flows and list the three major sections: (a) net cash flow from operating activities, (b) cash flows from investing activities, and (c) cash flows from financing activities.

2. Calculate the net change in cash that occurred during the accounting period. This is a major subtotal, or "target figure," on the statement of cash flows.

3. Determine the company's net income and list this amount as the first item in the net cash flow from operating activities section.

4. Calculate the increase or decrease that occurred during the accounting period in each balance sheet account (except cash).

5. Determine whether the increase or decrease in each balance sheet account (except cash) caused an inflow or outflow of cash, and if so, whether the cash flow was related to an operating, investing, or financing activity.

6. If no cash flow occurred in Step 5, then determine the adjustment (addition or subtraction) necessary to help convert net income to the net cash provided by operating activities.

7. Complete the various sections of the statement of cash flows (based on the analysis in Steps 5 and 6). Be sure to check that the changes in all the balance sheet accounts have been accounted for, that the subtotals of the sections sum to the net change (increase or decrease) in cash (from Step 2), and that the sum of the net change in cash and the beginning cash balance is equal to the ending cash balance reported on the balance sheet.

Illustration

To illustrate the visual inspection method, review the condensed financial information of the Jay Company for the year ended December 31, 1991, shown in Exhibit 18-8. The statement of cash flows that was prepared from that information is shown in Exhibit 18-9. After preparing the heading and listing the three sections of the statement, the $1,100 increase in cash was determined. This increase was computed by comparing the $4,000 cash balance on the beginning balance sheet to the $5,100 cash balance on the ending balance sheet. Then the $12,000 net income was obtained from the income statement and listed as the first item in the net cash flow from operating activities section. The following discussion explains the remaining steps in the preparation by reviewing the items in each section of the statement.

EXHIBIT 18-8
Condensed Financial
Information:
Jay Company

JAY COMPANY
Condensed Financial Information

1. Income statement information for 1991:

Sales revenue		$ 44,300
Operating expenses		
Depreciation expense	$ 4,800	
Other expenses	19,500	
Total expenses		(24,300)
Income before income taxes		$ 20,000
Income tax expense		(8,000)
Net income		$ 12,000

2. Retained earnings information for 1991:

Beginning retained earnings	$ 21,300
Add: Net income	12,000
	$ 33,300
Less: Dividends	(5,000)
Ending retained earnings	$ 28,300

3. Balance sheet information:

	Balances	
Accounts	1/1/1991	12/31/1991
Cash	$ 4,000	$ 5,100
Accounts receivable	7,300	12,500
Land	8,000	5,000
Buildings and equipment	50,000	69,000
Accumulated depreciation	(12,500)	(17,300)
Total Assets	$ 56,800	$ 74,300
Accounts payable	$ 6,500	$ 9,000
Bonds payable, 12%	10,000	18,000
Common stock, no par	19,000	19,000
Retained earnings	21,300	28,300
Total Liabilities and Stockholders' Equity	$ 56,800	$ 74,300

4. Additional information: (a) a building was purchased for cash during the year, (b) land was sold (at cost) for cash during the year, (c) no buildings or equipment were sold during the year, and (4) bonds payable were issued at the end of the year.

Net Cash Flow From Operating Activities. In this section there are three adjustments to convert net income to the net cash provided by operating activities. The first adjustment involves the $4,800 depreciation expense. This amount was obtained from the income statement in Exhibit 18-8. It is also the $4,800 increase (from $12,500 to $17,300) in the accumulated depreciation account on the balance sheets during the year.[5] Because depreciation was deducted in the computation of net income but did not cause a cash outflow, the $4,800 depreciation expense was added to net income.

The second adjustment involves the $2,500 increase (from $6,500 to $9,000) in accounts payable. Accounts payable increased during the year because other

---

[5]Note that this is the case because no buildings or equipment had been sold during the year. In a later example, we will explain how to account for a sale of buildings or equipment, where accumulated depreciation is decreased.

EXHIBIT 18-9
Statement of
Cash Flows:
Jay Company

JAY COMPANY
Statement of Cash Flows
For Year Ended December 31, 1991

Net Cash Flow From Operating Activities		
Net Income	$ 12,000	
Adjustments for differences between net income		
and cash flows from operating activities:		
Add: Depreciation expense	4,800	
Increase in accounts payable	2,500	
Less: Increase in accounts receivable	(5,200)	
Net cash provided by operating activities		$ 14,100
Cash Flows From Investing Activities		
Payment for purchase of building	$(19,000)	
Proceeds from sale of land, at cost	3,000	
Net cash used for investing activities		(16,000)
Cash Flows From Financing Activities		
Proceeds from issuance of bonds	$ 8,000	
Payment of dividends	(5,000)	
Net cash provided by financing activities		3,000
Net Increase in Cash		$ 1,100
Cash, January 1, 1991		4,000
Cash, December 31, 1991		$ 5,100

operating expenses recorded during the year exceeded the cash payments for these items. Therefore the expenses deducted to compute net income were greater than the related cash outflows. Consequently the $2,500 increase in accounts payable was added to net income to show the lesser cash outflows.

The third adjustment involves the $5,200 increase (from $7,300 to $12,500 in Exhibit 18-8) in accounts receivable. Accounts receivable increased during the year because sales on account exceeded the cash collections on account. Therefore sales revenue and net income were greater than the related cash inflows. Consequently, the $5,200 increase in accounts receivable was *deducted* from net income to show the lesser cash inflows.

As a result of the preceding adjustments the net cash flow provided by operating activities was $14,100 for the Jay Company in 1991, as shown in Exhibit 18-9. Note that, with the exception of depreciation, the adjustments to net income involved changes in current assets (except cash) and current liabilities.

Cash Flows From Investing Activities.   There are only two cash flows from investing activities, one cash outflow and one cash inflow. During 1991, the buildings and equipment account increased by $19,000, from $50,000 to $69,000 as shown on the balance sheets in Exhibit 18-8. This increase was the result of the purchase of a building, an investing activity, which required a cash outflow of $19,000. This cash outflow was listed as the first item in this section. During 1991, the land account decreased by $3,000, from $8,000 to $5,000. This decrease was the result of the sale of land, an investing activity. Because the land was sold at cost, there was no gain or loss.[6] The resulting $3,000 cash inflow was listed as

---

[6]The reporting of the sale of noncurrent assets at a gain or loss is discussed in a later example.

the second item in this section. As a result of these two cash flows net cash of $16,000 was used for investing activities by the Jay Company in 1991, as shown in Exhibit 18-9.

Cash Flows From FInancing Activities.   There are two cash flows from financing activities, one cash inflow and one cash outflow. During 1991, the bonds payable account increased by $8,000, from $10,000 to $18,000 as shown in Exhibit 18-8. This increase was the result of the issuance of bonds, a financing activity, which provided a cash inflow of $8,000. This cash inflow was listed as the first item in this section. During 1991, the company declared and paid dividends of $5,000. The amount of the dividends was obtained from the retained earnings statement in Exhibit 18-8. (Note also that the $12,000 net income, offset by the $5,000 dividends, accounts for the $7,000 increase in the retained earnings account shown on the balance sheets.) The payment of dividends, an investing activity, caused a cash outflow of $5,000. This cash outflow was listed as the second item in this section. As a result of these two cash flows, net cash of $3,000 was provided by the financing activities of the Jay Company during 1991.

Summary.   Note that in the preparation of the three sections we accounted for all of the changes in the asset, liability, and stockholders' equity accounts during 1991, as shown in Exhibit 18-8. Note also that, with the exception of depreciation, all of the adjustments to net income in the net cash flow from operating activities section involved changes in current asset (except cash) and current liability accounts. On the other hand, all of the cash flows from investing activities involved changes in noncurrent asset accounts, while all of the cash flows from financing activities involved changes in noncurrent liability and stockholders' equity accounts. This is generally the case. The $14,100 net cash provided by operating activities, less the $16,000 net cash used for investing activities, plus the $3,000 net cash provided by financing activities equals the $1,100 net increase in cash. And, the $1,100 net increase in cash plus the $4,000 beginning cash balance is equal to the $5,100 ending cash balance (as reported on the December 31, 1991 balance sheet in Exhibit 18-8). The statement of cash flows shown in Exhibit 18-9 is now complete.

Worksheet Method

The visual inspection method is not suitable when a company's financial statements are complex and when it has many different types of operating, investing, and financing transactions. In this case the worksheet method is used. Under the *worksheet method* a worksheet is prepared first, before preparing the statement of cash flows. In this approach the cash flow effects of operating, investing, and financing activities during the accounting period are first analyzed. Then they are entered on the worksheet in a way that accomplishes three goals: (1) to record the cash inflows and outflows according to the major sections of the statement of cash flows, (2) to record any investing and financing activities not affecting cash, and (3) to account for the change in each asset, liability, and stockholders' equity account. Because the worksheet method is used in more complex situations, it is helpful to follow a series of steps. Each of these steps is explained in the following section.

Steps in Preparation (Worksheet Method)

Like the visual inspection method, financial information from the company's income statement, retained earnings statement, and beginning and ending balance sheets of the accounting period is required to prepare the worksheet. Generally, however, more supplementary information is needed to complete the worksheet because of the more complex analysis that must be made. This additional information is obtained from a review of the company's accounting records.

After gathering the preceding information, six steps must be completed to prepare the worksheet and the statement of cash flows. These steps are summarized next, after which a comprehensive example is used to explain each step.

8. Prepare a worksheet for the statement of cash flows.

Step 1:   Prepare the column headings on a worksheet (see Exhibit 18-11 later in the chapter). Then enter the account title Cash on the first line of the account titles column. From a review of the company's balance sheet information, list the beginning balance, ending balance, and change in cash in the respective columns beside the cash account title.

Step 2:   Enter the titles of all the remaining accounts from the balance sheet on the worksheet. List each beginning account balance, ending account balance, and the change in the account balance directly below the cash information. The accounts with debit balances are listed first, followed by the accounts with credit balances (see Exhibit 18-11). Total the amount columns to check your work, being sure that the debit totals equal the credit totals.

Step 3:   Directly below these accounts add the following headings:
  A.   Net Cash Flow From Operating Activities
  B.   Cash Flows From Investing Activities
  C.   Cash Flows From Financing Activities
  D.   Investing and Financing Activities Not Affecting Cash

  Leave sufficient room (about 6 lines for the first heading, 4 lines for the other headings) below each heading so that each cash flow may be listed where appropriate.

Step 4   Account for all the changes in the noncash accounts that occurred during the current period. *Reconstruct* the journal entries that caused the changes in the noncash accounts directly on the worksheet, making certain modifications to show the cash inflows and outflows related to the company's operating, investing, and financing activities. Remember that you are preparing this worksheet at the *end* of the accounting period. The actual journal entries that caused the changes have already been made and recorded in the accounts. In this step you are simply reconstructing the journal entries on the worksheet to prepare the statement of cash flows. Use the following general rules to reconstruct the journal entries:
  A.   Start with net income. The net income is a summary of all the journal entries from operating activities affecting current assets or current lia-

bilities and retained earnings. The net income must be adjusted on the worksheet to change it to the net cash provided by operating activities. Therefore the proper entry on the worksheet to list net income and to explain the impact upon retained earnings is a debit to the caption Net Income under the heading Net Cash Flow From Operating Activities and a credit to Retained Earnings.[7] This *worksheet entry* (and later entries in this section) is illustrated in general journal form[8] here (the amounts shown are from the comprehensive example, which is discussed later):

Net Cash Flow From Operating Activities: Net Income 3,600
    Retained Earnings 3,600

B. Account for the changes in the current asset (except cash) and current liability accounts. Since nearly all the changes in the current assets and current liabilities are part of the company's *operating cycle*, the impacts of these changes on cash are listed as *adjustments to net income* in the net cash flow from operating activities section of the worksheet. The intent is to convert net income to net cash flow provided by operating activities. Review each current asset (except cash) and current liability account. Make an entry on the worksheet that records the change (debit or credit) in that account and the adjustment credit (deduction) and debit (addition) to net income. For example, to account for a decrease in accounts receivable during the year, the following worksheet entry would be made:

Net Cash Flow From Operating Activities: Decrease in
    Accounts Receivable 500
    Accounts Receivable 500

C. Account for the changes in the noncurrent accounts. Review each noncurrent account and determine the journal entry responsible for its change. Identify whether the transaction involves an operating, investing, or financing activity. If the transaction involves an investing or financing activity, make the entry on the worksheet with the following changes:

(1) If the entry affects cash, replace a debit to cash with either an investing or financing cash inflow caption, and list the item as a debit (inflow) under the proper heading of the worksheet. Replace a credit to cash with a proper cash outflow caption, and list the item as a credit (outflow) under the proper heading of the worksheet. For example, if bonds payable were issued for cash during the year, the following worksheet entry would be made:

---

[7]The entry to show a net loss would involve a debit to Retained Earnings and a credit to Net Cash Flow From Operating Activities: Net Loss. Any adjustments for noncash items included in net income such as in Step 4C(2) would be made as usual.

[8]In the text, for each entry we will always first list the heading of the worksheet and then indicate the caption to write under the heading. Thus in this case the caption, Net Income, is to be written under the heading, Net Cash Flow From Operating Activities, on the worksheet.

Cash Flows From Financing Activities: Proceeds From
  Issuance of Bonds 4,000
  Bonds Payable   4,000

(2)   If the entry involves an operating activity and affects a non-cash income statement item (e.g., depreciation, gain, or loss), replace the debit or credit to this noncash item in the worksheet entry with an adjustment to net income under the Net Cash Flow From Operating Activities heading. For example, to adjust net income for depreciation (a noncash expense), the following worksheet entry would be made:

Net Cash Flow From Operating Activities: Depreciation
  Expense 1,700
  Accumulated Depreciation   1,700

(3)   If the entry does not affect an operating activity or cash, it is a "simultaneous" financing and investing transaction. For this type of transaction, create "expanded" entries on the worksheet to record both the financing and investing activities. For example, if common stock were exchanged for land, the following two worksheet entries would be made:

Investing and Financing Activities Not Affecting Cash:
  Issuance of Common Stock for Land 2,000
  Common Stock, $10 par   500
  Additional Paid-in Capital   1,500

Land 2,000
  Investing and Financing Activities Not Affecting Cash:
  Acquisition of Land by Issuance of Common Stock   2,000

The first entry shows the financing aspect of the exchange while the second entry shows the investing aspect. These types of transactions are not common but are required to be disclosed on a schedule accompanying the statement of cash flows.

Step 5: Make a final worksheet entry to record the net change in cash. The worksheet entries must account for all the changes in the noncash accounts recorded in Step 2. The difference between the total cash inflows and outflows must be equal to the change in the Cash account. A final entry to record an increase in cash would be made as follows:

Cash 600
  Net Increase in Cash   600

For a net decrease in cash, an opposite entry (a debit to Net Decrease in Cash and a credit to Cash) would be made. Total the debit and credit worksheet entries in the upper and lower portions of the worksheet to check your work, being sure that the respective totals are equal.

Step 6: Prepare the statement of cash flows and accompanying schedule. Use the information developed in the *lower* portion of the worksheet (and the beginning and ending cash balances). Under the major sections of the statement list the various cash inflows and outflows. Subtotal the items under each major section and add or subtract the subtotals to determine the net change in cash. Add the net change in cash to the beginning cash balance to determine the ending cash balance. In an accompanying schedule, list the various investing and financing activities not affecting cash.

Note several aspects of the worksheet. First, other than usually starting with net income, there is no particular order in which the worksheet entries are reconstructed. You should develop a method so that you can account for all the changes in the noncash accounts in an orderly way. Second, you may have to make more than one worksheet entry to account for the change in an account. For instance, the change in the Land account may be the result of both a sale and purchase of land. In such cases, both the cash inflow and cash outflow must be accounted for separately. Third, remember that these worksheet entries are *not* posted to any accounts. They are recorded on the worksheet for only one reason, to help in preparing the statement of cash flows. Finally, you do not always have to prepare a worksheet. Other working papers may also be used. For instance, instead of preparing a worksheet, T-accounts may be used. In this case the change in cash and in each noncash account is entered in separate T-accounts. The major cash flow headings are also set up as T-accounts, and then the reconstructed entries are recorded directly in the T-accounts. Because the worksheet is a more efficient way of preparing the information, it is the method used in this book.

Comprehensive Example

It is easier to understand the process of preparing a worksheet and the statement of cash flows by studying an example, as shown next. The example includes a detailed discussion of each step presented earlier. As you study this example it will be helpful to reread these steps. The condensed financial information in Exhibit 18-10 is used in the example.

Steps 1, 2, and 3: Setting Up the Worksheet

Steps 1 and 2 involve setting up the worksheet; entering the account titles, their beginning and ending balances, and changes in the appropriate columns of the worksheet; and totaling the columns to check your work. In Step 3, the major headings, Net Cash Flow From Operating Activities, Cash Flows From Investing Activities, Cash Flows From Financing Activities, and Investing and Financing Activities Not Affecting Cash, are then listed on the worksheet. Enough space is left under each heading so that the cash flows may be listed accordingly. These accounts and headings are shown in Exhibit 18-11.

Step 4: Completion of the Worksheet

The worksheet entries to account for all the changes in the noncash accounts are entered directly on the worksheet in Step 4, as shown in Exhibit 18-11. To explain them better, however, each of the entries in Exhibit 18-11 is also presented in journal entry *form* here. The following entries are listed (a) through (l) to correspond to the entries on the worksheet. You should review each entry and explanation and then trace the entry back to the corresponding entry on the worksheet.

EXHIBIT 18-10
Condensed Financial
Information:
Symes Company

SYMES COMPANY
Condensed Financial Information

1. Income statement information for 1991:

Sales revenue		$ 40,000
Cost of goods sold		(24,300)
Gross profit		$ 15,700
Operating expenses:		
Depreciation expense	$ 1,700	
Other expenses	8,300	(10,000)
Operating income		$ 5,700
Other revenues:		
Gain on sale of equipment		300
Income before income taxes		$ 6,000
Income tax expense		(2,400)
Net income		$ 3,600

2. Retained earnings information for 1991:

Beginning retained earnings	$ 5,300
Add: Net income	3,600
	$ 8,900
Less: Dividends	(700)
Ending retained earnings	$ 8,200

3. Balance sheet information:

	Balances	
Accounts	*1/1/1991*	*12/31/1991*
Cash	$ 500	$ 1,100
Accounts receivable	1,400	900
Inventory	2,000	2,850
Land	5,200	7,200
Buildings and equipment	25,700	32,200
Accumulated depreciation	(3,000)	(4,300)
Total Assets	$ 31,800	$ 39,950
Accounts payable	$ 2,100	$ 1,150
Salaries payable	400	600
Bonds payable, 10%	-0-	4,000
Common stock, $10 par	8,000	8,500
Additional paid-in capital	16,000	17,500
Retained earnings	5,300	8,200
Total Liabilities and Stockholders' Equity	$ 31,800	$ 39,950

4. Additional information for 1991: (a) equipment was purchased for cash at a cost of $7,600, (b) ten-year bonds payable with a face value of $4,000 were issued for $4,000 at the beginning of the year, (c) land was acquired through the issuance of 50 shares of $10 par common stock when the stock was selling at a market price of $40 per share, and (d) equipment with a cost of $1,100 and a book value of $700 was sold for $1,000 cash.

The usual procedure is to start with the net income amount (because it is a summary amount that includes the results of both cash and noncash operating activities). Net income caused an increase in retained earnings. To list net income and to record the impact on retained earnings, the following entry is made on the worksheet:

(a)	Net Cash Flow From Operating Activities: Net Income	3,600	
	Retained Earnings		3,600

EXHIBIT 18-11   Worksheet: Symes Company

SYMES COMPANY
Worksheet for Statement of Cash Flows
For Year Ended December 31, 1991

	Balances			Worksheet Entries			
Account Titles	1/1/1991	12/31/1991	Change		Debit		Credit
Debits							
Cash	$ 500	$ 1,100	$ 600	(l)	$ 600		
Noncash Accounts:							
Accounts receivable	1,400	900	(500)			(c)	$ 500
Inventory	2,000	2,850	850	(d)	850		
Land	5,200	7,200	2,000	(i-2)	2,000		
Buildings and equipment	25,700	32,200	6,500	(g)	7,600	(k)	1,100
Totals	$34,800	$44,250	$ 9,450				
Credits							
Accumulated depreciation	$ 3,000	$ 4,300	$ 1,300	(k)	400	(b)	1,700
Accounts payable	2,100	1,150	(950)	(e)	950		
Salaries payable	400	600	200			(f)	200
Bonds payable	-0-	4,000	4,000			(h)	4,000
Common stock, $10 par	8,000	8,500	500			(i-1)	500
Additional paid-in capital	16,000	17,500	1,500			(i-1)	1,500
Retained earnings	5,300	8,200	2,900	(j)	700	(a)	3,600
Totals	$34,800	$44,250	$ 9,450		$13,100		$13,100

Net Cash Flow From Operating Activities							
Net Income				(a)	3,600		
Add: Depreciation expense				(b)	1,700		
Decrease in accounts receivable				(c)	500		
Increase in salaries payable				(f)	200		
Less: Increase in inventory						(d)	850
Decrease in accounts payable						(e)	950
Gain on sale of equipment						(k)	300
Cash Flows From Investing Activities							
Payment for purchase of equipment						(g)	7,600
Proceeds from sale of equipment				(k)	1,000		
Cash Flows From Financing Activities							
Proceeds from issuance of bonds				(h)	4,000		
Payment of dividends						(j)	700
Investing and Financing Activities Not Affecting Cash							
Issuance of common stock for land				(i-l)	2,000		
Acquisition of land by issuance of common stock						(i-2)	2,000
Net Increase in Cash						(l)	600
Total					$13,000		$13,000

To adjust net income to the net cash flow from operating activities, adjustments for depreciation and for the changes in the current assets (except cash) and current liabilities must be made. Generally, depreciation is treated first. During the year Depreciation Expense was increased (debited) for $1,700, and this amount was shown as a deduction on the income statement to determine net income. The noncurrent account, Accumulated Depreciation, was also increased (credited) for $1,700. Although the depreciation expense reduced net income, there was no outflow of cash for operating activities. Therefore this depreciation deduction must be *added* back to net income to help adjust it to show the net cash provided by operating activities. To do this, as well as to show the increase in the Accumulated Depreciation account, the following worksheet entry is made:

(b) **Net Cash Flow From Operating Activities: Depreciation
      Expense** 1,700
      Accumulated Depreciation 1,700

It is important to understand that depreciation is *not* a cash inflow from operating activities! It is added back to net income because when depreciation was originally deducted in computing the amount of net income, there was no corresponding outflow of cash. It is also important to note that entry (b) does not account for the change ($1,300 increase) in Accumulated Depreciation. This is because another transaction, entry (k), also affected the Accumulated Depreciation account, as discussed later.

The next adjustments all deal with the changes in the current assets (except cash) and current liabilities. The Accounts Receivable decreased $500 during the year. This is because cash collections exceeded credit sales by this amount (see Exhibit 18-5). To adjust for the additional cash inflow from operating activities, the following worksheet entry is made:

(c) **Net Cash Flow From Operating Activities: Decrease in
      Accounts Receivable** 500
      Accounts Receivable 500

Inventory increased by $850 during the year, indicating that purchases exceeded the cost of goods sold. To show the additional operating cash outflow due to the purchase of inventory, the net cash flow from operating activities must be decreased. The following worksheet entry is made:

(d) **Inventory** 850
      **Net Cash Flow From Operating Activities:
      Increase in Inventory** 850

Accounts Payable decreased by $950 during the year, indicating that cash payments for operating activities exceeded expenses. This additional cash outflow must be shown as a decrease in the net cash flow from operating activities as follows:

(e) **Accounts Payable** 950
      **Net Cash Flow From Operating Activities:
      Decrease in Accounts Payable** 950

Salaries Payable increased by $200 during the year, indicating that less cash was paid than that shown as salaries expense (included in operating expenses on Exhibit 18-10) for the year. To adjust net income to show a higher net cash flow from operating activities, the following worksheet entry is made:

(f) **Net Cash Flow From Operating Activities: Increase in
      Salaries Payable** 200
      Salaries Payable 200

At this point, all of the changes in the current assets (except cash) and current liabilities have been accounted for. We now turn to the noncurrent accounts; the investing and financing transactions affecting these accounts are summarized in Item 4 of Exhibit 18-10.

During the year the company purchased equipment at a cost of $7,600. The purchase was an investing activity and required a cash outflow (i.e., a debit to Buildings and Equipment and a credit to Cash). The worksheet entry to record the purchase is as follows (note that the credit to Cash is replaced with the caption Payment for Purchase of Equipment under the heading Cash Flows From Investing Activities):

(g)   Buildings and Equipment 7,600
       Cash Flows From Investing Activities: Payment for
         Purchase of Equipment 7,600

Note that entry (g) does not account for the change (increase of $6,500) in the Buildings and Equipment account. This is because another transaction (k) also affected the account.

The issuance of long-term bonds was a financing activity that caused an increase in Bonds Payable and an inflow of cash (e.g., debit to Cash and credit to Bonds Payable). The worksheet entry to record the issuance is as follows (the debit to the current asset Cash is replaced by the caption, Proceeds from Issuance of Bonds, under the heading Cash Flows From Financing Activities):

(h)   Cash Flows From Financing Activities: Proceeds From
       Issuance of Bonds 4,000
       Bonds Payable 4,000

When the company issued shares of its common stock in exchange for land, the exchange was recorded at the market price of the 50 shares of stock. At that time the Land account was increased (debited) by $2,000, the Common Stock, $10 par account was increased (credited) for the par value of $500, and the Additional Paid-in Capital account was increased (credited) for the excess of the market value over par value, $1,500. Although this transaction did not affect cash, it did involve a simultaneous financing and investing activity. The company invested in land and financed this investment by the issuance of common stock. Both the financing and the investing information must be disclosed on a schedule accompanying the statement of cash flows. To do so, the original transaction is "expanded" into two transactions, a financing transaction and an investing transaction, which are recorded on the worksheet as:

(i-1)   Investing and Financing Activities Not Affecting
         Cash: Issuance of Common Stock for Land 2,000
         Common Stock, $10 par 500
         Additional Paid-in Capital 1,500

(i-2)   Land 2,000
         Investing and Financing Activities Not Affecting
         Cash: Acquisition of Land by Issuance of
         Common Stock 2,000

The recording of these expanded entries on the worksheet accounts for the changes in the Land, Common Stock, and Additional Paid-in Capital accounts and shows both the investing and financing parts of the original transaction.

Retained earnings and cash were reduced by the declaration and payment of cash dividends (i.e., a debit to Retained Earnings and a credit to Cash). This is a financing activity. The following worksheet entry accounts for the decrease in retained earnings as well as the cash outflow for dividends (note that the credit to the current asset Cash is replaced with the caption Payment of Dividends under the heading Cash Flows From Financing Activities):

(j)	Retained Earnings	700	
	Cash Flows From Financing Activities: Payments of		
	Dividends		700

The increase in Retained Earnings of $3,600 because of net income, reduced by the decrease of $700 because of dividends, accounts for the $2,900 change in Retained Earnings.

During the year, the company sold equipment. At that time it recorded an increase (debit) in Cash of $1,000, a decrease (debit) in Accumulated Depreciation of $400, and a decrease (credit) in Buildings and Equipment of $1,100. Since the $1,000 proceeds were more than the $700 ($1,100 − $400) book value, the company also recorded (credited) a Gain on Sale of Equipment of $300. As shown on the income statement in Exhibit 18-10, this gain caused net income to increase even though there was no cash inflow from *operating* activities. The only cash inflow was the $1,000 proceeds, and this inflow was from an *investing* activity. In preparing the worksheet entry for this transaction, two modifications must be made: (1) instead of debiting Cash, the caption Proceeds From Sale of Equipment under the heading Cash Flows From Investing Activities must be debited for the $1,000 proceeds, and (2) instead of crediting the Gain account, the caption Gain on Sale of Equipment must be *credited* under the heading Net Cash Flow From Operating Activities to *deduct* the gain from net income in order to avoid double counting and to correctly show the cash provided by operating activities.[9] The worksheet entry is:

(k)	Cash Flows From Investing Activities: Proceeds from		
	Sale of Equipment	1,000	
	Accumulated Depreciation	400	
	Net Cash Flow From Operating Activities: Gain on		
	Sale of Equipment		300
	Buildings and Equipment		1,100

After recording this worksheet entry and combining the results with those from entry (b), it may be seen that the change ($1,300 increase) in Accumulated Depreciation has now been accounted for. In addition, combining the results of this worksheet entry with the results from entry (g) accounts for the change ($6,500 increase) in the Buildings and Equipment account. It is often necessary to record the results of two (or more) unrelated transactions before accounting for the change in an account.

---

[9]If the equipment had been sold at a loss, the loss would have decreased net income even though there was no outflow of cash for operating activities. In this case the worksheet entry would be modified as discussed, except instead of debiting the Loss account, the heading and caption Net Cash Flow From Operating Activities: Loss on Sale of Equipment would be debited to *add* back the loss to net income in a manner similar to depreciation expense.

Step 5: Final Worksheet Entry

In Step 5 a doublecheck of the debit and credit entries on the worksheet shows that all changes in the noncash accounts on the balance sheet have been accounted for. A final worksheet entry is made to record the increase in cash and to bring the debit and credit columns into balance. It is recorded as follows:

(I)	Cash	600	
	Net Increase in Cash		600

The debit and credit columns in the upper and lower portions of the worksheet are now totaled. As shown in Exhibit 18-11, the columns in the upper portion total $13,100, and the columns in the lower portion total $13,000. The worksheet is now complete.

Step 6: Preparation of Statement

When the worksheet is complete, the statement of cash flows and accompanying schedule of investing and financing activities not affecting cash are prepared (Step 6). The statement of cash flows for the Symes Company and accompanying

EXHIBIT 18-12
Statement of
Cash Flows:
Symes Company

SYMES COMPANY Statement of Cash Flows For Year Ended December 31, 1991		
Net Cash Flow From Operating Activities		
Net Income	$ 3,600	
Adjustments for differences between net income and cash flows from operating activities:		
Add: Depreciation expense	1,700	
Decrease in accounts receivable	500	
Increase in salaries payable	200	
Less: Increase in inventory	(850)	
Decrease in accounts payable	(950)	
Gain on sale of equipment	(300)	
Net cash provided by operating activities		$ 3,900
Cash Flows From Investing Activities		
Payment for purchase of equipment	$(7,600)	
Proceeds from sale of equipment	1,000	
Net cash used for investing activities		(6,600)
Cash Flows From Financing Activities		
Proceeds from issuance of bonds	$ 4,000	
Payment of dividends	(700)	
Net cash provided by financing activities		3,300
Net Increase in Cash (see Schedule 1)		$ 600
Cash, January 1, 1991		500
Cash, December 31, 1991		$ 1,100
Schedule 1: Investing and Financing Activities Not Affecting Cash		
Investing Activities Acquisition of land by issuance of common stock	$(2,000)	
Financing Activities Issuance of common stock for land	2,000	

schedule are shown in Exhibit 18-12. The information developed in the lower portion of the worksheet (Exhibit 18-11) is used to list the items in each section of the statement of cash flows and in the schedule. The $3,900 net cash provided by operating activities, less the $6,600 net cash used for investing activities, plus the $3,300 net cash provided by financing activities equals the $600 net increase in cash. The $600 net increase in cash plus the $500 beginning cash balance equals the $1,100 ending cash balance. In the schedule, the amount of the investing activity not affecting cash (acquisition of land by issuance of common stock) is offset by the amount of the financing activity not affecting cash (issuance of common stock for land), in order to report on all the company's investing and financing activities.

After studying the six steps and the completed worksheet of the comprehensive example you should be well on your way to understanding the procedures involved in preparing the statement of cash flows. Not all the possible operating, investing, and financing activities transactions were included in this example. Additional transactions are shown in the review problem at the end of this chapter.

APPENDIX: Direct Method for Reporting Operating Cash Flows

Throughout the main part of the chapter, the *indirect* method was used to report the net cash flow from operating activities on the statement of cash flows. This is the method that has been used by most companies. Under this method, we started with net income and adjusted it for any noncash items and for changes in current assets (except cash) and current liabilities to convert net income to net cash provided by (or used in) operating activities. This approach has the advantage of providing information about the differences between net income and operating cash flows.

Although the FASB allows use of both the indirect method and the direct method, it encourages the use of the *direct method* to report the cash flows from operating activities on the statement of cash flows. As briefly discussed earlier in the chapter, **under the direct method the operating cash outflows are deducted from the operating cash inflows to determine the net cash provided by (or used in) operating activities.** This approach has the advantage of directly reporting operating cash receipts and cash payments, which may be useful in estimating future cash flows. Because of the FASB's support for the direct method, use of this method is likely to increase. Consequently, application of the direct method is explained in this appendix.

Under the direct method the cash flows from *investing* activities and the cash flows from *financing* activities are reported on the statement of cash flows in exactly the same manner as under the indirect method. Therefore the focus in this appendix is on determining and reporting the cash flows from *operating* activities of a company. However, because there are some slight differences in *preparing* the information concerning the investing and financing activities, this analysis is discussed as well.

Operating Cash Flows

Under the direct method a company must report its operating cash inflows separately from its operating cash outflows. Each of these classifications is discussed next.

Operating Cash Inflows

Under the direct method a company should report its cash inflows from operating activities in three categories: (1) collections from customers, (2) interest and dividends collected, and (3) other operating receipts, if any. Generally, these cash inflows from operating activities are calculated by an analysis of income statement and balance sheet items as follows:

A-1(a). List the categories of operating cash inflows under the direct method.

1. *Collections from customers:* Sales revenue, plus decrease in accounts receivable or minus increase in accounts receivable.

2. *Interest and dividends collected:* Interest revenue and dividend revenue, plus decrease in interest/dividends receivable or minus increase in interest/dividends receivable.

3. *Other operating receipts:* Other revenues, plus increase in unearned revenues or minus decrease in unearned revenues, minus gains on disposals of assets and liabilities.

Most of the adjustments relate to the company's operating cycle. One adjustment was illustrated earlier in Exhibit 18-6. These adjustments are further discussed and illustrated later in this appendix.

Operating Cash Outflows

A company should report its cash outflows for operating activities in five categories: (1) payments to suppliers, (2) payments to employees,[10] (3) payments of interest, (4) other operating payments (if any), and (5) payments of income taxes. Generally, these cash outflows for operating activities are calculated by an analysis of income statement and balance sheet items as follows:

1. *Payments to suppliers:* Cost of goods sold, plus increase in inventory or minus decrease in inventory, plus decrease in accounts payable or minus increase in accounts payable.

---

[10]The FASB requires that payments to suppliers and payments to employees be combined into one category. It does, however, encourage further breakdowns when useful; we separate these cash payments in this appendix. In a manufacturing company, a separation of payments to suppliers and payments to employees may not be practical because various manufacturing costs may be combined. In such a case, reporting the combined payments may be the only practical disclosure.

A-1(b). List the categories of operating cash outflows under the direct method.

2. *Payments to employees:* Salaries expense, plus decrease in salaries payable or minus increase in salaries payable.

3. *Payments of interest:* Interest expense, plus decrease in interest payable or minus increase in interest payable.

4. *Other operating payments:* Other expenses, plus increase in prepaid expenses or minus decrease in prepaid expenses, minus depreciation, depletion, and amortization expense, minus losses on disposals of assets and liabilities.

5. *Payments of income taxes:* Income tax expense, plus decrease in income taxes payable or minus increase in income taxes payable.

Like the operating cash inflows, most of the adjustments relate to the company's operating cycle. One adjustment was illustrated earlier in Exhibit 18-6. These adjustments are further discussed and illustrated later in this appendix.

Diagram of Operating Cash Flows

To summarize the discussion in the preceding sections, the cash inflows from operating activities for the statement of cash flows may be computed by adjusting the various revenue accounts for changes in certain asset accounts (primarily current assets involved in the operating cycle) and to eliminate certain "noncash" revenues. The cash outflows for operating activities may be computed by adjusting the various expense accounts for changes in certain liability (and asset) accounts (primarily current liabilities and current assets in the operating cycle) and by eliminating certain "noncash" expenses. These adjustments are shown in Exhibit 18-13. It should be noted that these adjustments may have to be modified depending on the manner in which a company reports and classifies the related items in its financial statements. Net cash provided by (or used in) operating activities is the difference between the cash inflows from operating activities and the cash outflows for operating activities, as computed according to Exhibit 18-13.

Procedures for Statement Preparation

When using the direct method to prepare the information for the statement of cash flows, either the visual inspection method or the worksheet method may be used depending on the complexity of the accounting information. The information may be obtained, however, in a slightly different manner. Normally, the information for the statement of cash flows under the direct method is obtained from the following accounting working papers:

1. *Post-closing trial balance (or balance sheet) from **previous** period:* Recall from Chapter 3 that a post-closing trial balance contains the debit and credit balances of all the *permanent* accounts in a company's general ledger. In other words, a post-closing trial balance of the previous period contains the same information as the *ending balance sheet* of the previous period.

EXHIBIT 18-13   Major Adjustments to Convert Income Statement Amounts to Operating Cash Flows

Income Statement Amounts	Adjustments		Cash Flows From Operating Activities	Net Operating Cash Flows
Sales revenue	+ Decrease in accounts receivable or − Increase in accounts receivable	=	Collections from customers	Cash Inflows From Operating Activities
Interest revenue and dividend revenue	+ Decrease in interest receivable or − Increase in interest receivable	=	Interest and dividends collected	
Other revenues	+ Increase in unearned revenues or − Decrease in unearned revenues − Gains on disposals of assets and liabilities*	=	Other operating receipts	
Cost of goods sold	+ Increase in inventory or − Decrease in inventory + Decrease in accounts payable or − Increase in accounts payable	=	Payments to suppliers	
Salaries expense	+ Decrease in salaries payable or − Increase in salaries payable	=	Payments to employees	
Interest expense	+ Decrease in interest payable or − Increase in interest payable	=	Payments of interest	Cash Outflows For Operating Activities
Other expenses	+ Increase in prepaid expenses or − Decrease in prepaid expenses − Depreciation, depletion, and amortization expense* − Losses on disposals of assets and liabilities*	=	Other operating payments	
Income tax expense	+ Decrease in income taxes payable or − Increase in income taxes payable	=	Payments of income taxes	

*Unless listed as separate items on income statement

2. *Adjusted trial balance of **current** period:* Recall that an adjusted trial balance contains the debit and credit balances (after adjustments but before closing) of all the temporary and permanent accounts in a company's general ledger. In other words, an adjusted trial balance of the current period contains the *balance sheet, income statement,* and *retained earnings statement* information for the current period.

In addition, other supplemental information is usually needed concerning the reasons for the changes in the balance sheet (permanent) accounts (other than cash). This information is obtained from a review of the accounting records.

Then the statement of cash flows is prepared. For simplicity, in this appendix we focus on the visual inspection method for the statement preparation.

Visual Inspection Method

Under the visual inspection approach the steps to complete the statement of cash flows using the direct method are virtually the same as for the indirect method, with one exception. This exception deals with determining the information for the operating activities section of the statement. After preparing the heading for the statement, listing the three major sections, and determining the change in cash as the "target figure" for the statement, the information for the cash flows from operating activities section should be computed as follows:

A-2. Describe the modification in the visual inspection approach under the direct method.

- Make adjustments to the applicable revenues for the period (e.g., to sales revenue for change in accounts receivable) to determine the amounts of collections from customers, interest and dividend receipts, and other operating receipts, if any. Make adjustments to the applicable expenses for the period (e.g., to cost of goods sold for change in accounts payable) to determine the amounts of payments to suppliers, payments to employees, payments of interest, other operating payments, if any, and payments of income taxes. Use of the schedule in Exhibit 18-13 is helpful for these adjustments.

Once the operating activities section is completed, the investing activities section and the financing activities section are completed by analyzing the changes in the other balance sheet accounts, as discussed earlier in the chapter.

Example. To illustrate preparation of the operating activities section, assume the following income statement items were taken from the adjusted trial balance of the Green Company at the end of 1991:

	Debit	Credit
Sales		$84,000
Interest revenue		6,200
Cost of goods sold	$40,000	
Salaries expense	17,500	
Depreciation expense	11,000	
Interest expense	8,400	
Other expenses	4,300	
Income tax expense	3,600	

Also assume that a comparison of the post-closing trial balance for 1990 with the adjusted trial balance for 1991 reveals the following *changes* in selected balance sheet accounts:

Accounts receivable	$ 8,000	credit
Interest receivable	1,200	debit
Inventory	7,300	debit
Prepaid expenses	600	debit
Accumulated depreciation	11,000	credit
Accounts payable	4,800	credit
Salaries payable	500	debit
Interest payable	200	credit
Income taxes payable	300	credit

EXHIBIT 18-14   Schedule to Compute Operating Cash Flows: Green Company

Income Statement Amounts		Adjustments		Operating Cash Flows	
Sales	$ 84,000	+ Decrease in accounts receivable of	$8,000 =	$ 92,000	Collections from customers
Interest revenue	6,200	− Increase in interest receivable of	1,200 =	5,000	Interest collected
				$ 97,000	Operating cash inflows
Cost of goods sold	$(40,000)	+ Increase in inventory of	7,300		
		− Increase in accounts payable of	4,800 =	$(42,500)	Payments to suppliers
Salaries expense	(17,500)	+ Decrease in salaries payable of	500 =	(18,000)	Payments to employees
Interest expense	(8,400)	− Increase in interest payable of	200 =	(8,200)	Payments of interest
Other expenses	(4,300)	+ Increase in prepaid expenses of	600 =	(4,900)	Other operating payments
Income tax expense	(3,600)	− Increase in income taxes payable of	300 =	(3,300)	Payments of income taxes
				$(76,900)	Operating cash outflows
				$ 20,100	Net cash provided by operating activities

Based upon the preceding information, Exhibit 18-14 has been prepared to determine each of the operating cash inflows and outflows. In Exhibit 18-14, the $84,000 sales revenue is increased by the $8,000 decrease (credit) in accounts receivable to determine the $92,000 collections from customers. This is because cash collections exceeded sales during the year. On the other hand, the $6,200 interest revenue is decreased by the $1,200 increase (debit) in interest receivable to determine the $5,000 interest collected because less cash was received than accrued as interest revenue. The total operating cash inflows were $97,000 in 1991.

The $40,000 cost of goods sold is adjusted for two items. It is increased for the $7,300 increase (debit) in inventory because purchases exceeded cost of goods sold by that amount. It is decreased by the $4,800 increase (credit) in accounts payable because cash payments were less than purchases. Thus payments to suppliers totaled $42,500 in 1991. The $17,500 salaries expense is increased by the $500 decrease (debit) in salaries payable to determine the $18,000 paid to employees, because salaries paid exceeded salaries expense. Note that the $11,000 depreciation expense (debit) is the same as the $11,000 credit to accumulated depreciation. Since this is a "noncash" income statement item and is listed separately from other operating expenses, *no* adjustment is made for operating cash flows. The $8,400 interest expense is decreased by the $200 increase (credit) in interest payable to determine the $8,200 payments of interest, because less interest was paid than recorded as expense. The $4,300 other expenses are increased by the $600 increase (debit) in prepaid expenses to determine the $4,900 other operating payments because cash payments for prepaid items exceeded expenses. The $3,600 income tax expense is decreased by the $300 increase (credit) to income taxes payable to determine the $3,300 payments of income taxes because less taxes were paid than recorded as expense. The total operating cash outflows were $76,900 in 1991, so that $20,100 net cash was provided by operating activities during 1991.

EXHIBIT 18-15
Statement of
Cash Flows (Partial):
Green Company

GREEN COMPANY
Statement of Cash Flows (Partial)
For Year Ended December 31, 1991

Cash Flows From Operating Activities
  Cash Inflows:
    Collections from customers .... $ 92,000
    Interest collected 5,000
    Cash inflows from operating activities .... $ 97,000

  Cash Outflows:
    Payments to suppliers .... $(42,500)
    Payments to employees .... (18,000)
    Payments of interest .... (8,200)
    Other operating payments .... (4,900)
    Payments of income taxes .... (3,300)
    Cash outflows for operating activities .... (76,900)
Net cash provided by operating activities .... $ 20,100

The cash flows from operating activities section of the Green Company's statement of cash flows, under the direct method, is shown in Exhibit 18-15. The cash flows from investing activities and the cash flows from financing activities would be included in the usual manner to complete the statement of cash flows.

Chapter Summary

Review of Learning Objectives

1. **Define a statement of cash flows.**
   A statement of cash flows is a financial statement that shows the inflows and outflows of cash from the operating, investing, and financing activities of a company during an accounting period, in a manner that reconciles the beginning and ending cash balances.

2. **List several cash flows from operating, investing, and financing activities.**
   The cash flows from *operating* activities include receipts from cash sales, collections of accounts receivable from credit sales, and collections of interest and dividend revenue, as well as payments for inventory and supplies, employees' salaries and other expenses, and interest and income taxes. The cash flows from *investing* activities include receipts from selling investments in stocks and bonds and from selling property and equipment, as well as payments for investments in stocks and bonds and for purchases of property and equipment. The cash flows from *financing* activities include receipts

from the issuance of stocks, bonds, notes, and mortgages, as well as payments of dividends and payments to retire stocks, bonds, notes and mortgages.

3. **Identify the sections of the statement of cash flows.**
   The sections of the statement of cash flows include the net cash flow from operating activities, the cash flows from investing activities, the cash flows from financing activities, the net increase or decrease in cash, and the reconciliation of the beginning cash balance to the ending cash balance.

4. **Classify changes in balance sheet accounts as to their impact on cash flows.**
   Operating cash inflows (outflows) are caused by increases (decreases) in stockholders' equity due to certain revenues (expenses), adjusted for changes in certain current assets and current liabilities. Investing cash inflows (outflows) are caused by decreases (increases) in noncurrent assets and certain current assets (e.g., marketable securities). Financing cash inflows (outflows) are caused by increases (decreases) in noncurrent liabilities, stockholders' equity, and certain current liabilities (e.g., notes payable).

5. **Identify and report investing and financing activities not affecting cash.**
   Investing and financing activities not affecting cash cause changes (increases or decreases) in assets (other than cash), liabilities, or stockholders' equity. For example, equipment may be purchased (an investing activity) by issuing bonds payable (a financing activity). Any investing and financing transactions not affecting cash are reported in a separate schedule that accompanies the statement of cash flows.

6. **Describe the (a) direct method and (b) indirect method for reporting the net cash provided by operating activities.**
   Under the *direct* method the operating cash outflows are deducted from the operating cash inflows to determine the net cash provided by operating activities. Under the *indirect* method net income is adjusted to the net cash flow from operating activities by: (1) the elimination of certain amounts included in net income that did not involve operating cash flows, and (2) the inclusion of any changes in current assets and current liabilities involved in the operating cycle that affected cash flows differently than net income.

7. **List the seven steps in the visual inspection method.**
   The seven steps to prepare the statement of cash flows are: (1) prepare the heading and list the three major sections; (2) calculate the net change in cash; (3) determine the net income and list it as the first item in the net cash flow from operating activities section; (4) calculate the increase or decrease in each balance sheet account (except cash); (5) determine whether the increase or decrease in step 4 caused an inflow or outflow of cash related to an operating, investing, or financing activity; (6) if no cash flow occurred in step 5, then determine the adjustment to convert net income to the net cash

provided by operating activities; and (7) complete the various sections of the statement of cash flows, and reconcile the beginning cash balance to the ending cash balance with the net change in cash.

8. **Prepare a worksheet for the statement of cash flows.**
    To prepare the worksheet, the following steps must be completed: (1) prepare the column headings, then list Cash, the beginning and ending balance, and the change in the cash account balance in the respective columns; (2) list the account titles, respective beginning and ending balances, and changes for the period of the remaining balance sheet accounts; (3) list the major headings of the statement of cash flows, along with the heading Investing and Financing Activities Not Affecting Cash (when necessary), leaving room for listing the specific cash flows under each heading; (4) account for the changes in all the noncash accounts that occurred during the accounting period by reconstructing the journal entries that caused the changes directly on the worksheet, making modifications to show the cash inflows and outflows related to operating, investing, and financing activities; (5) make a final worksheet entry to record the net change in cash; total the upper and lower portions of the debit and credit columns being sure the respective totals are equal; and (6) prepare the statement of cash flows and accompanying schedule (if necessary).

A-1. **List the categories of operating cash (a) inflows and (b) outflows under the direct method.**
       Under the direct method the operating cash *inflows* include: (1) collections from customers, (2) interest and dividends collected, and (3) other operating receipts. The operating cash *outflows* include: (1) payments to suppliers, (2) payments to employees, (3) payments of interest, (4) other operating payments, and (5) payments of income taxes.

A-2. **Describe the modification in the visual inspection approach under the direct method.**
       When the direct method is used to report the operating cash flows the necessary information is obtained from the post-closing trial balance (or balance sheet) of the previous period and the adjusted trial balance of the current period. At this point, the steps to complete the statement of cash flows by visual inspection under the direct method are almost the same as under the indirect method. There is one exception to the steps listed in Review of Learning Objective 7. After completing steps 1 through 3, make adjustments to the applicable revenues to determine the amounts of collections from customers, interest and dividend receipts, and other operating receipts (if any). Make adjustments to the applicable expenses to determine the amounts of payments to suppliers, payments to employees, payments of interest, other operating payments, if any, and payments of income taxes. Once the operating activities section is completed, analyze the changes in the other balance sheet accounts to prepare the investing activities and financing activities sections, and complete the statement of cash flows.

Review Problem

LAMB COMPANY
Condensed Financial Information

1. Balance sheet information:

	Balances	
Accounts	1/1/1991	12/31/1991
Cash	$ 800	$ 2,000
Accounts receivable	1,200	2,200
Inventory	3,200	3,000
Land	4,800	3,800
Buildings and machinery	16,500	22,500
Accumulated depreciation	(1,400)	(2,800)
Patents (net)	2,300	2,200
Total Assets	$ 27,400	$ 32,900
Accounts payable	$ 2,300	$ 2,800
Bonds payable	2,000	-0-
Notes payable (long-term)	-0-	1,000
Common stock, $5 par	6,000	7,000
Additional paid-in capital	11,000	13,400
Retained earnings	6,100	8,700
Total Liabilities and Stockholders' Equity	$ 27,400	$ 32,900

2. Income statement information:

Revenues		$ 6,000
Expenses:		
Depreciation expense	$ 1,400	
Patent amortization expense	100	
Other expenses	1,000	(2,500)
Operating income		$ 3,500
Other items:		
Loss on sale of land		(300)
Net income		$ 3,200

3. Retained earnings information:

Beginning retained earnings	$ 6,100
Add: Net income	3,200
	$ 9,300
Less: Dividends	(600)
Ending retained earnings	$ 8,700

4. Supplementary information for 1991 (including data from the preceding items):
   (a) Net income was $3,200.
   (b) Depreciation expense for the year was $1,400.
   (c) Patent amortization expense for the year was $100. No patents were sold or acquired during the year.
   (d) Dividends declared and paid were $600.
   (e) Two hundred shares of $5 par common stock were issued for $17 per share.
   (f) Bonds payable with a book value of $2,000 were retired for $2,000.
   (g) Machinery with a value of $1,000 was acquired through the issuance of a long-term note.
   (h) A building was purchased for $5,000.
   (i) Land with a cost of $1,000 was sold for $700.

REQUIRED

1. Prepare a worksheet for a 1991 statement of cash flows of the Lamb Company.
2. Prepare the 1991 statement of cash flows.

Solution to Review Problem

REQUIREMENT 1

LAMB COMPANY
Worksheet for Statement of Cash Flows
For Year Ended December 31, 1991

Account Titles	Balances 1/1/1991	Balances 12/31/1991	Change	Worksheet Entries Debit		Worksheet Entries Credit	
Debits							
Cash	$ 800	$ 2,000	$ 1,200	(m)	$ 1,200		
Noncash Accounts:							
Accounts receivable	1,200	2,200	1,000	(d)	1,000		
Inventory	3,200	3,000	(200)			(e)	$ 200
Land	4,800	3,800	(1,000)			(l)	1,000
Buildings and machinery	16,500	22,500	6,000	(j-2)	1,000		
				(k)	5,000		
Patents (net)	2,300	2,200	(100)			(c)	100
Totals	$28,800	$35,700	$ 6,900				
Credits							
Accumulated depreciation	$ 1,400	$ 2,800	$ 1,400			(b)	1,400
Accounts payable	2,300	2,800	500			(f)	500
Bonds payable	2,000	-0-	(2,000)	(i)	2,000		
Notes payable (long-term)	-0-	1,000	1,000			(j-1)	1,000
Common stock, $5 par	6,000	7,000	1,000			(h)	1,000
Additional paid-in capital	11,000	13,400	2,400			(h)	2,400
Retained earnings	6,100	8,700	2,600	(g)	600	(a)	3,200
Totals	$28,800	$35,700	$ 6,900		$10,800		$10,800

	Debit		Credit	
Net Cash Flow From Operating Activities				
Net Income	(a)	3,200		
Add: Depreciation expense	(b)	1,400		
Patent amortization expense	(c)	100		
Decrease in inventory	(e)	200		
Increase in accounts payable	(f)	500		
Loss on sale of land	(l)	300		
Less: Increase in accounts receivable			(d)	1,000
Cash Flows From Investing Activities				
Payment for purchase of building			(k)	5,000
Proceeds from sale of land	(l)	700		
Cash Flows From Financing Activities				
Payment of dividends			(g)	600
Proceeds from issuance of stock	(h)	3,400		
Payment to retire bonds			(i)	2,000
Investing and Financing Activities Not Affecting Cash				
Issuance of note payable to acquire machinery	(j-1)	1,000		
Acquisition of machinery by issuance of note payable			(j-2)	1,000
Net Increase in Cash			(m)	1,200
Totals		$10,800		$10,800

REQUIREMENT 2

LAMB COMPANY
Statement of Cash Flows
For Year Ended December 31, 1991

Net Cash Flow From Operating Activities

Net income	$ 3,200	
Adjustments for differences between net income and cash flows from operating activities:		
Add: Depreciation expense	1,400	
Patent amortization expense	100	
Decrease in inventory	200	
Increase in accounts payable	500	
Loss on sale of land	300	
Less: Increase in accounts receivable	(1,000)	
Net cash provided by operating activities		$ 4,700
Cash Flows From Investing Activities		
Payment for purchase of building	$(5,000)	
Proceeds from sale of land	700	
Net cash used for investing activities		(4,300)
Cash Flows From Financing Activities		
Proceeds from issuance of stock	$ 3,400	
Payment of dividends	(600)	
Payment to retire bonds	(2,000)	
Net cash provided by financing activities		800
Net Increase in Cash (see Schedule 1)		$ 1,200
Cash, January 1, 1991		800
Cash, December 31, 1991		$2,000

Schedule 1: Investing and Financing Activities Not Affecting Cash

Investing Activities	
Acquisition of machinery by issuance of note payable	$(1,000)
Financing Activities	
Issuance of note payable to acquire machinery	1,000

Glossary

Cash Flows From Financing Activities.   A section of the statement of cash flows that reports the cash receipts from and cash payments for financing activities.

Cash Flows From Investing Activities.   A section of the statement of cash flows that reports the cash receipts from and cash payments for investing activities.

Direct Method.   Method of computing the net cash provided by operating activities on the statement of cash flows. The amount is computed by deducting the operating cash outflows from the operating cash inflows.

Financing Activities.   Activities (transactions) involving obtaining resources from owners and providing them with a return on their investment, as well as obtaining resources from creditors and repaying the amounts borrowed.

Indirect Method.   Method of computing the net cash provided by operating activities on the statement of cash flows. The amount is computed by adjusting net income for any noncash income statement items and for changes in current assets (other than cash) and current liabilities related to operating activities. Most common method used.

Investing Activities.   Activities (transactions) involving lending money and collecting on loans, acquiring and selling investments, and acquiring and selling property and equipment.

Net Cash Flow From Operating Activities.   A section of the statement of cash flows that reports the net cash provided by operating activities.

Operating Activities.   Activities (transactions) involving acquiring, selling, and delivering goods for sale, as well as providing services.

Operating Cash Inflows.   Cash inflows from operating activities computed under the direct method. These inflows include collections from customers, interest and dividends collected, and other operating receipts (if any).

Operating Cash Outflows.   Cash outflows for operating activities computed under the direct method. These outflows include payments to suppliers, payments to employees, payments of interest, other operating payments (if any), and payments of income taxes.

Schedule of Investing and Financing Activities Not Affecting Cash.   A schedule that accompanies the statement of cash flows that reports on the investing and financing activities that did not affect cash.

Statement of Cash Flows.   A financial statement that shows the inflows and outflows of cash from the operating, investing, and financing activities of a company during the accounting period, in a manner that reconciles the beginning and ending cash balances.

Questions

QUESTION 18-1   What is a statement of cash flows?

QUESTION 18-2   Briefly describe the three types of activities reported in a statement of cash flows.

QUESTION 18-3   What does the information in a statement of cash flows help external users to assess?

QUESTION 18-4   Name the five items a statement of cash flows should clearly show. What items are reported in a separate schedule accompanying the statement?

QUESTION 18-5   What are the three categories of inflows of cash?

QUESTION 18-6   What are the three categories of outflows of cash?

QUESTION 18-7   Briefly describe a company's operating cycle and the related cash inflows and outflows.

QUESTION 18-8   What is the direct method of calculating a company's net cash flow from operating activities? What is the indirect method?

QUESTION 18-9   Show the usual way of reporting the net cash provided by operating activities. Include several common additions to and deductions from net income.

QUESTION 18-10   Give two examples of cash inflows from investing activities.

QUESTION 18-11   Give two examples of cash outflows for investing activities.

QUESTION 18-12   Give two examples of cash inflows from financing activities.

QUESTION 18-13   Give two examples of cash outflows for financing activities.

QUESTION 18-14   Give two examples of investing and financing activities not affecting cash. Where are these activities disclosed?

QUESTION 18-15   What is the visual inspection method? List the steps in this method.

QUESTION 18-16   Briefly describe the worksheet method to help prepare the statement of cash flows. (Do *not* list the steps in preparation.)

QUESTION 18-17   *(Appendix)*. Define the *direct* method of reporting the cash flows from operating activities.

QUESTION 18-18   *(Appendix)*. List the three operating cash inflows reported under the direct method.

QUESTION 18-19   *(Appendix)*. List the five operating cash outflows reported under the direct method.

QUESTION 18-20   *(Appendix)*. Briefly describe how to determine each of the operating cash inflows and operating cash outflows under the direct method.

Exercises

EXERCISE 18-1   **Types of Cash Flows.**   The following are several transactions and events of a company:

    (a)   Proceeds from sale of building

    (b)   Payment of dividends

    (c)   Net income

    (d)   Proceeds from issuance of bonds

    (e)   Increase in accounts receivable

    (f)   Payment for purchase of investments

    (g)   Increase in salaries payable

REQUIRED   Indicate in which section of the statement of cash flows each of the preceding items would appear. Also indicate whether it would be an inflow (addition) or outflow (subtraction).

EXERCISE 18-2   **Types of Cash Flows.**   The Ace Bearing Company had the following transactions and events during the last year:

    (a)   Payment for purchase of equipment

    (b)   Net income

    (c)   Decrease in inventory

    (d)   Proceeds from issuance of stock

    (e)   Decrease in accounts payable

    (f)   Proceeds from sale of investments

    (g)   Payment to retire bonds

REQUIRED   Indicate in which section of the statement of cash flows each of the preceding items would appear. Also indicate whether it would be an inflow (addition) or outflow (subtraction).

EXERCISE 18-3   **Operating Activities.**   The following are selected items taken from the accounting records of the Wilson Book Company for 1991:

(a) Net income, $5,300

(b) Depreciation expense, $800

(c) Increase in accounts receivable, $500

(d) Payment of dividends, $2,000

(e) Decrease in wages payable, $360

(f) Increase in accounts payable, $220

(g) Proceeds from issuance of bonds, $2,000

(h) Decrease in inventory, $640

REQUIRED   Prepare the net cash flow from operating activities section of the Wilson Book Company's statement of cash flows for 1991.

EXERCISE 18-4   **Operating Activities.**   Selected items that were taken from the accounting records of the Rocky Shoe Company for 1991 are as follows:

(a) Depreciation expense, $1,200

(b) Decrease in accounts payable, $790

(c) Payment to retire bonds, $3,000

(d) Net income, $8,200

(e) Increase in inventory, $1,500

(f) Decrease in accounts receivable, $180

(g) Increase in prepaid expenses, $230

(h) Increase in salaries payable, $310

(i) Proceeds from issuance of stock, $4,000

(j) Loss on sale of land, $450

REQUIRED   Prepare the net cash flow from operating activities section of the Rocky Shoe Company's statement of cash flows for 1991.

EXERCISE 18-5   **Statement of Cash Flows.**   The following is a list of items to be included in the 1991 statement of cash flows of the Brockman Lawn Sprinklers Company:

(a) Increase in accounts receivable, $700

(b) Payment for purchase of trenching equipment, $6,000

(c) Depreciation expense, $900

(d) Payment of dividends, $2,500

(e) Decrease in accounts payable, $400

(f) Decrease in inventory, $800

(g) Net income, $6,200

(h) Proceeds from issuance of stock, $4,000

(i) Increase in salaries payable, $500

(j) Proceeds from sale of land (at cost), $1,000

(k) Beginning cash balance, $1,200

REQUIRED   Prepare the statement of cash flows.

EXERCISE 18-6   **Statement of Cash Flows.**   The items to be included in the Garcia Hardware Company's 1991 statement of cash flows are as follows:

(a) Payment of dividends, $1,800

(b) Net income, $3,900

(c) Increase in inventory, $930

(d) Payment for purchase of warehouse, $9,200

(e) Depreciation expense, $720

(f) Decrease in salaries payable, $100

(g) Proceeds from issuance of bonds, $3,000

(h) Increase in accounts payable, $460

(i) Proceeds from sale of marketable securities (at cost), $1,300

(j) Decrease in accounts receivable, $810

(k) Ending cash balance, $7,350

REQUIRED   Prepare the statement of cash flows.

EXERCISE 18-7   **Erroneous Statement of Cash Flows.**   The 1991 statement of cash flows for the Frye Company, as developed by its bookkeeper, is as follows:

FRYE COMPANY
Cash Flows Statement
December 31, 1991

Inflows of Cash

Operating Activities		
Net income		$ 12,500
Add: Proceeds from sale of equipment		3,800
Proceeds from issuance of stock		4,300
Less: Payment of note		(1,000)
Net cash inflows from operations		$ 19,600
Other Inflows		
Decrease in accounts receivable	$ 2,100	
Depreciation expense	5,000	
Total other inflows of cash		7,100
Total inflows of cash		$ 26,700
Outflows of Cash		
Payment for purchase of land	$(16,400)	
Decrease in accounts payable	(3,000)	
Payment of dividends	(2,500)	
Total outflows of cash		(21,900)
Net Increase in Cash		$ 4,800
Cash, December 31, 1991		11,000
Cash, January 1, 1991		$ 6,200

You determine that the *amounts* of the items listed on the statement are correct, but in certain circumstances, incorrectly classified.

REQUIRED   Prepare a correct 1991 statement of cash flows for the Frye Company.

EXERCISE 18-8   **Visual Inspection.**   The beginning and ending balance sheet accounts of the Tyler Health Spa for 1991 are shown next:

Accounts	1/1/1991	12/31/1991
Cash	$ 3,000	$ 2,700
Accounts receivable	5,000	4,700
Property and equipment	76,000	85,000
Accumulated depreciation	(12,000)	(13,400)
Totals	$ 72,000	$ 79,000
Accounts payable	$ 4,000	$ 2,500
Common stock, $5 par	12,000	13,500
Additional paid-in capital	36,000	40,500
Retained earnings	20,000	22,500
Totals	$ 72,000	$ 79,000

Additional Information for 1991:

1. Net income was $7,000, including depreciation expense of $1,400.

2. Three hundred shares of common stock were issued for $20 per share.

3. Dividends of $4,500 were declared and paid.

4. Exercise equipment was acquired at a cost of $9,000.

REQUIRED Prepare a statement of cash flows for 1991. A worksheet is not required.

EXERCISE 18-9 **Visual Inspection.** The following are the beginning and ending balance sheet accounts of the Anita Company for 1991:

Accounts	1/1/1991	12/31/1991
Cash	$ 2,000	$ 3,500
Accounts receivable	4,000	7,000
Land	6,000	10,500
Buildings and equipment	37,000	37,000
Accumulated depreciation	(10,000)	(11,000)
Totals	$ 39,000	$ 47,000
Accounts payable	$ 2,000	$ 2,500
Bonds payable	-0-	3,000
Common stock, no par	17,000	18,500
Retained earnings	20,000	23,000
Totals	$ 39,000	$ 47,000

Additional Information for 1991:

1. Net income was $5,500. Included in net income was depreciation expense of $1,000.

2. Dividends were $2,500.

3. Land was purchased for $4,500.

4. Ten-year, $3,000 bonds payable were issued at face value.

5. Two hundred shares of no-par common stock were issued for $7.50 per share.

REQUIRED Without using a worksheet, prepare a statement of cash flows for 1991.

EXERCISE 18-10 **Ending Balance Sheet.** The following beginning balance sheet and the statement of cash flows for 1991 are available for the Wolfe Company:

WOLFE COMPANY
Balance Sheet
January 1, 1991

Assets

Cash	$ 1,000
Accounts receivable	6,000
Land	9,000
Buildings and equipment	22,000
Accumulated depreciation	(7,000)
Total Assets	$ 31,000

Liabilities and Stockholders' Equity

Accounts payable	$ 3,000
Total Liabilities	$ 3,000
Common stock, no par	$ 16,000
Retained earnings	12,000
Total Stockholders' Equity	$ 28,000
Total Liabilities and Stockholders' Equity	$ 31,000

WOLFE COMPANY
Statement of Cash Flows
For Year Ended December 31, 1991

Net Cash Flow From Operating Activities		
Net income	$ 7,500	
Adjustments for differences between net income and cash flows from operating activities:		
Add: Depreciation expense	1,700	
Increase in accounts payable	300	
Less: Increase in accounts receivable	(900)	
Net cash provided by operating activities		$ 8,600
Cash Flows From Investing Activities		
Payment for purchase of equipment	$(7,000)	
Proceeds from sale of land (at cost)	1,200	
Net cash used for investing activities		(5,800)
Cash Flows From Financing Activities		
Proceeds from issuance of common stock	$ 5,000	
Payment of dividends	(4,000)	
Net cash provided by financing activities		1,000
Net Increase in Cash		$ 3,800
Cash, January 1, 1991		1,000
Cash, December 31, 1991		$ 4,800

REQUIRED   Based on the preceding information prepare a balance sheet as of December 31, 1991, for the Wolfe Company.   Hint: Combine the information from the statement of cash flows with the information from the beginning balance sheet to determine the ending account balances.

EXERCISE 18-11   **Worksheet.** A partially completed worksheet for the 1991 statement of cash flows of the Ment Tent Company is as follows:

| | | Worksheet Entries | |
Account Titles	Change	Debit	Credit
Debits			
Cash	$ 3,300		
Noncash Accounts:			
Accounts receivable	(350)		
Inventory	700		
Property and equipment	10,000		
Totals	$13,650		
Credits			
Accumulated depreciation	$ 1,600		
Accounts payable	750		
Bonds payable	5,000		
Common stock, no par	2,000		
Retained earnings	4,300		
Totals	$13,650		
Net Cash Flow From Operating Activities			
Net Income			
Add:			
Less:			
Cash Flows From Investing Activities			
Cash Flows From Financing Activities			
Net Increase in Cash			
Totals			

Additional Information for 1991:

(*a*) Net income was $7,100.

(*b*) Depreciation expense was $1,600.

(*c*) Twenty-year, $5,000 bonds payable were issued at face value.

(d) Delivery equipment was purchased at a cost of $10,000.

(e) One hundred shares of common stock were issued for $20 per share.

(f) Dividends of $2,800 were declared and paid.

REQUIRED   Complete the worksheet.

EXERCISE 18-12   **(Appendix) Operating Cash Flows.**   The following are the operating cash flows of the Northshore Company for 1991:

(a) Payments to employees, $10,300

(b) Interest and dividends collected, $3,000

(c) Payments of income taxes, $3,100

(d) Other operating payments, $500

(e) Collections from customers, $34,900

(f) Payments to suppliers, $16,000

(g) Payment of interest, $4,400

(h) Other operating receipts, $600

REQUIRED   Using the direct method, prepare the cash flows from operating activities section of the Northshore Company's statement of cash flows for 1991.

EXERCISE 18-13   **(Appendix) Statement of Cash Flows.**   The following is a list of items to be included in the 1991 statement of cash flows of the Brown Company:

(a) Payments to suppliers, $32,500

(b) Payments of dividends, $4,000

(c) Payments of income taxes, $5,000

(d) Collections from customers, $66,200

(e) Payment for purchase of equipment, $18,500

(f) Payments to employees, $19,300

(g) Interest and dividends collected, $7,100

(h) Proceeds from issuance of bonds, $11,300

(i) Payments of interest, $8,400

(j) Proceeds from the sale of investments, $7,000

(k) Beginning cash balance, $8,300

REQUIRED   Prepare the 1991 statement of cash flows, using the direct method for operating cash flows.

Problems

Part A

PROBLEM 18-1A   **Operating Cash Flows.**   The Natton Container Company had the following changes in current assets and current liabilities during 1991:

Current Assets	Increase (Decrease)	Current Liabilities	Increase (Decrease)
Accounts receivable	$ (900)	Accounts payable	$(2,600)
Notes receivable	5,000	Notes payable	(6,000)
Interest receivable	750	Interest payable	(800)
Inventory	3,300	Salaries payable	500

Additional Information for 1991: (a) Net income $13,800; (b) Depreciation expense, $4,100; (c) Patent amortization expense, $1,300; (d) Loss on sale of equipment, $1,000.

REQUIRED

1. Prepare the net cash flow from operating activities section of the Natton Container Company's 1991 statement of cash flows.

2. Are there any items that you did not include in this section? If so, where would they be reported?

PROBLEM 18-2A   **Statement of Cash Flows.** The following is a list of the items to be included in the 1991 statement of cash flows of the Bartle Brewing Company:

(a) Depreciation expense, $7,400

(b) Proceeds from sale of land, $6,200

(c) Increase in inventory, $3,700

(d) Payment of dividends, $7,500

(e) Net income, $15,600

(f) Issuance of common stock for equipment, $5,600

(g) Decrease in accounts payable, $1,500

(h) Proceeds from issuance of bonds, $10,000

(i) Increase in interest payable, $490

(j) Gain on sale of land, $1,300

(k) Payment for purchase of storage building, $19,900

(l) Decrease in accounts receivable, $2,600

(m) Increase in salaries payable, $510

(n) Beginning cash balance, $14,200

REQUIRED   Prepare the statement of cash flows.

PROBLEM 18-3A   **Visual Inspection.** The following changes in account balances and other information for 1991 were taken from the accounting records of the Watts Racket Company:

	Net Changes for 1991	
	Debits	Credits
Cash	$ 1,700	
Accounts receivable		$ 1,200
Inventory	2,000	
Property and equipment	8,800	
Accumulated depreciation		2,800
Accounts payable	900	
Common stock, no par		5,500
Retained earnings		3,900
	$13,400	$13,400

Additional Information for 1991: Net income was $7,900. Dividends were declared and paid. Stringing equipment was purchased for $13,800. Land was sold at cost for $5,000. One hundred shares of common stock were sold for $55 per share. The beginning cash balance was $8,200.

REQUIRED
1. Using visual inspection, prepare a 1991 statement of cash flows for the Watts Racket Company.

2. What would have happened to the company's cash if it had not issued common stock during the year?

PROBLEM 18-4A **Worksheet and Statement of Cash Flows.** The following are the beginning and ending balance sheet accounts of the Pierce Axe Company for 1991:

Accounts	1/1/1991	12/31/1991
Cash	$ 4,700	$ 9,600
Accounts receivable	6,000	5,000
Inventory	15,100	20,000
Prepaid insurance	-0-	700
Land	7,200	11,600
Buildings and equipment	60,100	77,000
Accumulated depreciation	(16,200)	(21,300)
Totals	$ 76,900	$102,600
Accounts payable	$ 5,500	$ 7,800
Salaries payable	1,300	700
Bonds payable	8,000	14,000
Common stock, $10 par	22,000	27,000
Additional paid-in capital	15,000	19,000
Retained earnings	25,100	34,100
Totals	$ 76,900	$102,600

Additional Information for 1991:

1. Net income was $18,200, which included $5,100 of depreciation.

2. Dividends of $9,200 were declared and paid.

3. Land and sharpening equipment were purchased at $8,400 and $16,900, respectively.

4. Long-term bonds were issued at their face value of $6,000.

5. Five hundred shares of $10 par common stock were issued at $18 per share.

6. Land that had cost $4,000 was sold for $3,100.

REQUIRED
1. Prepare a worksheet for the 1991 statement of cash flows of the Pierce Axe Company.

2. Prepare the statement of cash flows.

PROBLEM 18-5A **Complex Worksheet and Statement of Cash Flows.** The following are the comparative condensed balance sheets and the condensed income statement of the McVey Table Company for 1991:

McVEY TABLE COMPANY
Comparative Balance Sheets

	January 1, 1991	December 1, 1991
Cash	$ 3,200	$ 6,600
Accounts receivable	6,800	11,600
Inventory	8,000	8,400
Land	9,200	15,200
Buildings	75,100	100,300
Accumulated depreciation: buildings	(26,700)	(30,600)
Equipment	33,900	34,600
Accumulated depreciation: equipment	(10,300)	(11,100)
Patents (net)	8,500	7,800
Total Assets	$107,700	$142,800
Accounts payable	$ 11,000	$ 17,300
Wages payable	700	500
Bonds payable (due 12/31/2001)	-0-	9,000
Premium on bonds payable	-0-	400
Common stock, $10 par	22,000	27,500
Additional paid-in capital	31,000	38,100
Retained earnings	43,000	50,000
Total Liabilities and Stockholders' Equity	$107,700	$142,800

McVEY TABLE COMPANY
Income Statement
For Year Ended December 31, 1991

Sales	$ 73,000
Cost of goods sold	(43,800)
Depreciation expense: buildings	(3,900)
Depreciation expense: equipment	(2,100)
Patent amortization expense	(700)
Other expenses	(8,200)
Operating income	$ 14,300
Loss on sale of equipment	(1,500)
Net income	$ 12,800

Additional Information for 1991:

1. Dividends declared and paid were $5,800.

2. Three hundred shares of $10 par common stock were sold for $22 per share.

3. Equipment and a building were purchased for $8,700 and $25,200, respectively.

4. Equipment with a cost of $8,000 and accumulated depreciation of $1,300 was sold for $5,200.

5. Ten-year bonds payable with a face value of $9,000 were issued for $9,400 on December 31, 1991. (Hint: Record the issuance of the bonds at a premium in the usual manner.)

6. Two hundred and fifty shares of $10 par common stock with a current market value of $24 per share were issued in exchange for land.

REQUIRED
1. Prepare a worksheet for a 1991 statement of cash flows of the McVey Table Company.

2. Prepare the statement of cash flows for 1991.

PROBLEM 18-6A   **(Appendix) Statement of Cash Flows.** The following is a list of the items to be included in the 1991 statement of cash flows for the Blue Company:

(a) Proceeds from sale of land, $3,100

(b) Payment of interest, $5,000

(c) Proceeds from issuance of common stock, $11,000

(d) Other operating payments, $2,300

(e) Interest and dividends collected, $4,700

(f) Payments to employees, $19,800

(g) Payment for purchase of investments, $13,300

(h) Collections from customers, $56,800

(i) Payments of income taxes, $3,900

(j) Payment of dividends, $5,200

(k) Other operating receipts, $1,600

(l) Payments to suppliers, $30,500

(m) Beginning cash balance, $16,500

REQUIRED   Prepare the statement of cash flows, using the direct method for operating cash flows.

PROBLEM 18-7A   **(Appendix) Visual Inspection.** The following is accounting information taken from the adjusted trial balance of the Railwood Chain Saw Company for 1991:

	Debit	Credit
Sales		$71,000
Interest revenue		4,500
Cost of goods sold	$35,500	
Salaries expense	23,600	
Interest expense	6,400	
Income tax expense	4,000	

During 1991, the following *changes* occurred in selected accounts:

Accounts receivable	$6,100	credit
Inventory	7,800	debit
Accounts payable	8,000	credit
Salaries payable	900	debit
Interest payable	400	credit

A review of the accounting records also reveals the following information for 1991:

1. Investments were sold for $2,700.

2. Dividends of $6,200 were declared and paid.

3. Land was purchased for $13,000.

4. Common stock was issued for $12,000.

5. Beginning cash balance was $44,100.

REQUIRED Prepare the statement of cash flows of the Railwood Chain Saw Company for 1991, using the direct method for operating cash flows.

Problems

Part B

PROBLEM 18-1B **Operating Cash Flows.** The following are the changes in current assets and current liabilities of the Fox Mining Company for 1991:

Current Assets	Increase (Decrease)	Current Liabilities	Increase (Decrease)
Accounts receivable	$2,700	Accounts payable	$1,500
Notes receivable	(3,000)	Notes payable	2,000
Interest receivable	(840)	Interest payable	600
Inventory	(2,100)	Wages payable	(590)
Prepaid expenses	430		

Additional Information for 1991: (a) Net income, $16,800; (b) Depreciation expense, $6,400; (c) Gain on sale of land, $3,200; (d) Depletion expense, $1,300.

REQUIRED
1. Prepare the net cash flow from operating activities section of the Fox Mining Company's statement of cash flows for 1991.

2. Are there any items that you did not include in this section? If so, where would they be reported?

PROBLEM 18-2B **Statement of Cash Flows.** The following is a list of the items to be included in the 1991 statement of cash flows of the Topps Glass Company:

(a) Proceeds from sale of cutting equipment, $2,100

(b) Decrease in inventory, $3,000

(c) Net income, $18,300

(d) Payment for purchase of building, $35,000

(e) Depreciation expense, $9,300

(f) Proceeds from issuance of stock, $5,000

(g) Increase in interest receivable, $650

(h) Loss on sale of cutting equipment, $500

(i) Payment of dividends, $3,900

(j) Increase in accounts receivable, $2,700

(k) Issuance of bonds for land, $4,700

(l) Increase in accounts payable, $1,800

(m) Decrease in wages payable, $390

(n) Ending cash balance, $18,400

REQUIRED Prepare the statement of cash flows.

PROBLEM 18-3B **Visual Inspection.** The following changes in account balances and other information for 1991 were taken from the accounting records of the Harmon Company:

	Net Changes for 1991	
	Debits	*Credits*
Cash		$ 1,800
Accounts receivable	$ 2,000	
Land		3,400
Buildings and equipment	23,000	
Accumulated depreciation		4,500
Accounts payable		2,100
Salaries payable	500	
Bonds payable		5,000
Common stock, no par		-0-
Retained earnings		8,700
	$25,500	$25,500

Additional Information for 1991: Net income was $13,100. Dividends were declared and paid. Land was sold for $3,400; a building was purchased for $23,000. No land was purchased and no buildings and equipment were sold. Bonds payable were issued at face value. The ending cash balance was $22,400.

REQUIRED

1. Using visual inspection, prepare a 1991 statement of cash flows for the Harmon Company.

2. Assume the company's common stock had been selling for $9 per share during 1991. How many shares would the company have had to issue to avoid having a decrease in cash during the year? Where would this issuance have been reported on the statement of cash flows?

PROBLEM 18-4B   **Worksheet and Statement of Cash Flows.**   The beginning and ending balance sheet accounts of the Johnson Paint Company for 1991 are as follows:

Accounts	*1/1/1991*	*12/31/1991*
Cash	$ 2,500	$ 7,600
Accounts receivable	3,100	6,700
Marketable securities	1,000	5,100
Inventory	7,400	6,100
Land	5,800	3,000
Buildings and equipment	41,300	50,400
Accumulated depreciation	(11,900)	(16,600)
Totals	$ 49,200	$ 62,300
Accounts payable	$ 4,900	$ 2,700
Wages payable	1,100	1,600
Notes payable	-0-	3,000
Common stock, $10 par	13,000	15,800
Additional paid-in capital	8,700	11,500
Retained earnings	21,500	27,700
Totals	$ 49,200	$ 62,300

Additional Information for 1991:

1. Net income was $11,200; dividends declared and paid were $5,000.

2. Depreciation expense was $4,700.

3. Marketable securities were purchased for $4,100.

4. Cash of $3,000 was borrowed by issuing a note payable.

5. Stirring equipment was purchased at a cost of $9,100.
6. Two hundred eighty shares of common stock were issued for $20 per share.
7. Land that had cost $2,800 was sold for $3,700.

REQUIRED
1. Prepare a worksheet for the 1991 statement of cash flows of the Johnson Paint Company.
2. Prepare the statement of cash flows.

PROBLEM 18-5B **Complex Worksheet and Statement of Cash Flows.** The following are condensed balance sheets, a condensed income statement, and the retained earnings of the Fite Company for 1991:

FITE COMPANY
Comparative Balance Sheets

	1/1/1991	12/31/1991
Cash	$ 2,700	$ 2,800
Accounts receivable	7,100	9,200
Inventory	8,200	8,000
Land	10,100	18,700
Buildings and machinery	105,300	135,300
Accumulated depreciation	(42,400)	(45,000)
Copyrights (net)	9,400	7,900
Total Assets	$100,400	$136,900
Accounts payable	$ 8,100	$ 9,200
Salaries payable	1,300	1,000
Note payable (due 12/31/1996)	-0-	8,600
Bonds payable	-0-	10,000
Common stock, $5 par	25,000	30,000
Additional paid-in capital	29,000	36,000
Retained earnings	38,000	45,300
Treasury stock (at cost)	(1,000)	(3,200)
Total Liabilities and Stockholders' Equity	$100,400	$136,900

FITE COMPANY
Income Statement
For Year Ended December 31, 1991

Sales	$ 81,000
Cost of goods sold	(48,800)
Depreciation expense	(6,800)
Copyright amortization expense	(1,500)
Other expenses	(12,200)
Operating income	$ 11,700
Gain on sale of machinery	1,700
Net Income	$ 13,400

FITE COMPANY
Retained Earnings Statement
For Year Ended December 31, 1991

Beginning retained earnings	$ 38,000
Add: Net income	13,400
	$ 51,400
Less: Cash dividends	(6,100)
Ending Retained Earnings	$ 45,300

Additional Information for 1991:

1. Long-term bonds were issued at their face value of $10,000.

2. A building was purchased at a cost of $42,200.

3. Machinery with a cost of $12,200 and accumulated depreciation of $4,200 was sold for $9,700.

4. One thousand shares of $5 par common stock were issued for $12 per share.

5. On December 31, 1991, a 5-year note for $8,600 was issued in exchange for an acre of land.

6. Two hundred shares of the company's common stock were reacquired as treasury stock for $11 per share.

REQUIRED

1. Prepare a worksheet for the 1991 statement of cash flows for the Fite Company.

2. Prepare the statement of cash flows for 1991.

PROBLEM 18-6B   **(Appendix) Statement of Cash Flows.**   A list of the items to be included in the 1991 statement of cash flows for the Cross Glove Company is as follows:

(a) Proceeds from sale of land, $2,300

(b) Payment of interest, $4,000

(c) Proceeds from issuance of common stock, $8,500

(d) Other operating payments, $1,100

(e) Interest and dividends collected, $3,500

(f) Payments to employees, $16,800

(g) Payment for purchase of sewing equipment, $9,300

(h) Collections from customers, $48,300

(i) Payments of income taxes, $2,000

(j) Payment of dividends, $4,200

(k) Other operating receipts, $1,200

(l) Payments to suppliers, $22,400

(m) Ending cash balance, $33,300

REQUIRED   Prepare the statement of cash flows, using the direct method for operating cash flows.

PROBLEM 18-7B   **(Appendix) Visual Inspection.**   The following is accounting information taken from the adjusted trial balance of the Lake Company for 1991:

	Debit	Credit
Sales		$65,000
Interest revenue		5,600
Cost of goods sold	$33,200	
Salaries expense	16,400	
Interest expense	8,000	
Income tax expense	5,200	

During 1991, the following changes occurred in selected accounts:

Accounts receivable	$5,100	debit
Inventory	9,800	debit
Accounts payable	7,000	credit
Salaries payable	1,000	credit
Interest payable	700	debit

A review of the accounting records also reveals the following transactions during 1991:

1. Dividends of $4,000 were declared and paid.
2. Land was sold for $6,000.
3. Equipment was purchased for $10,500.
4. Bonds payable were issued for $10,200.
5. Ending cash balance was $14,000.

REQUIRED Prepare the statement of cash flows of the Lake Company for 1991, using the direct method for operating cash flows.

Decision Cases

DECISION CASE 18-1 **Misleading Statement.** The president of Tide Corporation has come to your bank for a loan. He states: "Each of the last three years our cash has gone down. This year we need to increase our cash by $7,000 so that we have a $20,000 cash balance at year end. We have never borrowed any money on a long-term basis and are reluctant to do so. However, we definitely need to purchase some new, more advanced equipment to replace the old equipment we are selling this year. We also want to acquire some treasury stock because it would be a good investment. In addition, we would like to pay dividends of 50% of net income instead of our usual 40%. Given our expected net income and the money we will receive from our depreciation expense and the gain on the sale of the old equipment, I estimate we will have to borrow $12,000, based on the following schedule."

SCHEDULE OF CASH FLOWS FOR 1991

Inflows of cash:		
Sources from net income		$ 20,000
Other sources:		
Depreciation expense		6,000
Decrease in accounts receivable		2,000
Gain on sale of old equipment		3,000
Proceeds from sale of old equipment		8,000
Bank loan (estimated)		12,000
Total inflows		$ 51,000
Outflows of cash:		
Purchase equipment	$(30,000)	
Decrease in accounts payable	(4,000)	
Pay dividends (50% of net income)	(10,000)	
Total outflows		(44,000)
Increase in Cash		$ 7,000

The president explains that the $5,000 expected cost of acquiring the treasury stock was not included because it would involve only a transaction between the corporation and the existing stockholders and would be of no interest to "outsiders." He also states that "if his figures are off a little bit," the most the corporation wants to borrow is $16,000. You determine that the amounts he has listed for each item (except the bank loan) are accurate.

REQUIRED

1. Prepare a statement of cash flows for the Tide Corporation that shows the necessary bank loan in order to increase cash by $7,000.

2. Explain to the president why his $12,000 estimate of the bank loan is incorrect.

3. Suggest ways to reduce the necessary bank loan and still increase cash.

DECISION CASE 18-2 **Outline and Discussion.**   A friend of yours is having difficulty understanding the statement of cash flows and has asked for your assistance.

REQUIRED Prepare an outline (including all the possible major headings) of the statement. Include examples of items that would be disclosed under each major heading. Finally, discuss the financial information that is disclosed in the income statement, balance sheet, and statement of cash flows, respectively, that is not disclosed on the other statements.

DECISION CASE 18-3 **Erroneous Statement of Cash Flows.**   The 1991 statement of cash flows for the Lakes Company, as developed by its bookkeeper, follows:

LAKES COMPANY
Cash Flows Statement
December 31, 1991

Inflows of Cash

Operating Activities		
Net income		$ 10,200
Add: Proceeds from sale of equipment		3,900
Proceeds from issuance of stock		4,600
Less: Payment for investment in bonds		(6,000)
Payment of long-term note		(5,000)
Net cash inflows from operations		$ 7,700
Other Inflows		
Decrease in accounts receivable	$ 2,100	
Depreciation expense	4,700	
Total other inflows of cash		6,800
Total inflows of cash		$ 14,500
Outflows of Cash		
Payment for purchase of land	$(5,400)	
Decrease in accounts payable	(2,800)	
Payment of dividends	(3,000)	
Gain on sale of equipment	(700)	
Total outflows of cash		(11,900)
Net Increase in Cash		$ 2,600
Cash, December 31, 1991		11,400
Cash, January 1, 1991		$ 8,800

You determine the *amounts* of the items listed on the statement are correct, but in certain circumstances, incorrectly classified.

REQUIRED   Prepare a corrected 1991 statement of cash flows for the Lakes Company.

DECISION CASE 18-4   **Analysis of Cash Flows.**   Review the statement of cash flows and related notes of
the Black & Decker Corporation that are shown in Appendix A at the end of this textbook.

REQUIRED   Answer the following questions. (*Note:* You do not need to make any calculations.
All answers can be found in Appendix A.) Indicate on what page of the annual
report you located the answer.

1. By how much did cash and cash equivalents increase for the year ended
   September 25, 1988? September 27, 1987?

2. What was the cash flow from operating activities for the year ended September
   25, 1988? September 27, 1987? What was the reason for most of the improvement
   from 1987 to 1988?

3. What was the cash flow from investing activities for the year ended September
   25, 1988? September 27, 1987?

4. How much was spent on capital expenditures and how much was received from
   disposals of property, plant and equipment for the year ended September 25,
   1988?

5. What was the cash flow from financing activities for the year ended September
   25, 1988? September 27, 1987?

6. What were the proceeds from borrowings for the year ended September 25,
   1988? How much involved an increase in long-term debt, and why did this borrowing occur?

19

Analysis and Interpretation
of Financial Statements

LEARNING OBJECTIVES

1. Identify the important items in financial analysis evaluations.

2. Describe (a) intracompany and (b) intercompany comparisons.

3. Define an industry segment and identify the information to be reported about each reportable industry segment.

4. (a) Define interim financial statements and (b) prepare an interim income statement.

5. Describe horizontal analysis.

6. Describe vertical analysis.

7. Identify and calculate the (a) stockholder profitability, (b) company profitability, (c) liquidity, (d) activity, and (e) stability ratios.

A company's financial statements are intended to summarize the results of its operations, its cash flows, and its ending financial position. The information in the statements is studied and related to other information by external users for several reasons. Current stockholders, for example, are concerned about their investment income, as well as about the company's overall profitability and stability. Some potential investors are interested in "solid" companies, that is, companies whose financial statements indicate stable earnings and dividends with little growth in operations. Others prefer companies whose financial statements indicate a trend for rapid growth in different lines of business. Short-term creditors are interested in a company's short-run liquidity—its ability to pay current obligations as they become due. Long-term creditors are concerned about the safety of their interest income and the company's ability to continue its earnings and cash flows to meet its financial commitments. And these are only a few of the users, and uses, of financial statements.

Companies prepare their financial statements on an annual basis (many also prepare statements on a shorter basis, for instance, quarterly). These companies often include certain supplementary schedules and analyses with their annual financial statements. Additional analyses of the financial statement information may be made by the external users of the information, such as lending institutions, current and potential bondholders and stockholders, and other groups. Whether a person is an accountant who prepares the financial statement information for the company or an external user who uses the information in decision making, it is necessary to understand the content, uses, and limitations of these analyses.

The purpose of this chapter is to discuss the various types of financial analyses that might be made and reported in addition to the financial statements. They include: (1) reports on the results of business segments, (2) interim financial reports, (3) horizontal and vertical percentage analyses, and (4) ratio analyses.

Financial Analysis Evaluations

Before discussing the various financial analyses it is helpful to review what information is useful and how this information is used. Recall from Chapter 1 that decision making consists of several stages, including recognition of the problem, identification of the alternatives, evaluation of the alternatives, and the decision itself. Financial accounting information is especially useful in the evaluation stage for external users. In this stage external users study the various data of importance to them in financial reports in order to evaluate the data and make their decisions. They usually make comparisons within the same or related industries. These comparisons are important in financial analysis.

Useful Information

In the evaluation stage of decision making, the external user is concerned with evaluating the results of a company's current operations and financial position. In this evaluation, information about several items is important. As discussed in

Chapters 2 and 3, these items include (1) return on investment, (2) risk, (3) financial flexibility, (4) liquidity, and (5) operating capability.

1. Identify the important items in financial analysis evaluations.

- *Return on investment* occurs when a company provides earnings on the capital invested by its owners. Before a company can provide a return on capital, the owners' capital must first be maintained. Once this capital is maintained, any earnings may be distributed to the owners or reinvested in the company.

- *Risk* is the uncertainty about the future earnings potential of a company. Risk is caused by many factors, such as unpredictability of demand and technological change. In general, the greater the risk, the higher the expected return on investment.

- *Financial flexibility* is the ability of a company to adapt to change. It is important because it allows a company to increase or reduce operations as needed. Financial flexibility comes from, for instance, the ability of a company to obtain cash from the issuance of bonds or the sale of additional capital stock.

- *Liquidity* refers to the nearness to cash of a company's assets. It is important because a company must be able to pay its liabilities as they come due in order to remain solvent.

- *Operating capability* refers to a company's ability to maintain a given physical level of operations. Information about operating capability is important in understanding a company's current and past performance, and in predicting future changes in volume.

Each of the financial analyses discussed in this chapter is used to provide information about the preceding issues so that comparisons, evaluations, and decisions can be made.

Intracompany Comparisons

2(a). Describe intracompany comparisons.

One method of evaluating the results of a company's current operations and its financial position is to compare them with the company's past results. These are referred to as intracompany comparisons. **Intracompany comparisons are comparisons *within* the company.** Important in these comparisons is the evidence of *trends*—indications that a company's performance is stable, is improving, or is declining, not only in the short run but also in the longer run. Most companies now present at least 2 years of comparable data in their financial statements. That is, they include the current and previous year's income statements, balance sheets, and statements of cash flows. Most companies show the current year's information in the left column. Some companies, however, show the current year's information in the right column, so care should be taken to check the dates before any analysis is performed. Many companies also include 5-, 10-, or 15-year summaries of key data from these financial statements.

An important point to remember when preparing and using financial analysis information in these comparisons is to be consistent over time. Whether business segment information, interim data, percentage analyses, or ratios are prepared, each year's information should be presented in a similar manner so that valid comparisons and reliable trends may be obtained. When making these comparisons, consideration should be given to how changes in the general, regional, or industry economy might have affected the company's results from year to year.

Intercompany Comparisons

2(b). Describe intercompany comparisons.

A second method of evaluation involves the use of intercompany comparisons. **Intercompany comparisons are comparisons of a company's performance with that of competing companies, with the industry as a whole, or with the results in related industries.** Intercompany comparisons may be made for a single period or for several past periods. Competing companies' financial information may be obtained from their financial statements. Information on the performance of the industry as a whole or of related industries may be based on financial information provided by such financial analysis companies as Moody's Investors Service, Standard and Poor's, Dun and Bradstreet, and Robert Morris and Associates, available in most college and public libraries. These companies not only provide information from annual reports but also publish monthly and quarterly updates and supplements. Other organizations and trade associations provide similar information.

Anyone preparing or using financial analysis information in intercompany comparisons must be concerned with the consistency of data across companies. For instance, they should take into consideration the impact of different generally accepted accounting principles (e.g., LIFO versus FIFO for inventories, or accelerated versus straight-line depreciation for property and equipment) upon the results. When making these comparisons the impact of changes in the general, regional, or industry economy should also be considered.

Relationships

Both intracompany comparisons and intercompany comparisons of financial information are made to provide information on a company's return on investment, risk, financial flexibility, liquidity, and operating capability. A diagram of these relationships is shown in Exhibit 19-1.

EXHIBIT 19-1
Relationship of Financial
Comparisons to
Useful Information

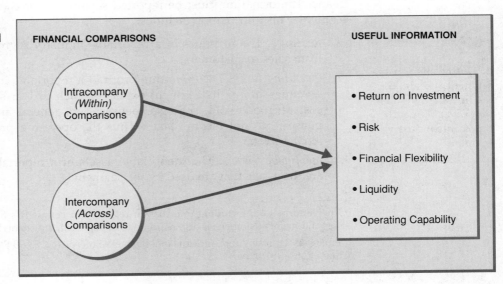

Segment Reporting

Many financial statements of large corporations with several subsidiaries and divisions are prepared on a *consolidated* basis. That is, the accounting results of the various segments are combined into a set of financial statements for the entire economic entity. Consolidated financial statements were briefly discussed in Chapter 17. Although investors and creditors think that consolidated financial statements are important in evaluating the overall performance of each corporation, they also like to know information about the corporation's operating segments. These users feel that evaluations of the operations and assets of the separate segments of a corporation are useful in determining each segment's return on investment and operating capability.

Because of the need for such data, a company's financial statements must include information about its operations in different segments.[1] The required information, how it is prepared, and the way it is reported are discussed next.

Information to Be Reported

Company operations are reported by *segments*. **An industry segment is a component (e.g., department, division, or subsidiary) of a company that provides a product or service to customers for a profit.** To determine its industry segments, a company might consider its products (e.g., appliances, chemicals), its geographic sales territories (e.g., East Coast, Midwest), or its methods of sales (e.g., discount stores, department stores). For instance, General Mills reports its segment information separately for three segments: consumer foods, restaurants, and specialty retailing.

A company need not report separate financial information about all of its industry segments, however. Only information about a company's reportable industry segments must be separately reported. **A reportable industry segment has revenues, operating profits,** or **identifiable assets that are 10% or more of the company's total revenues, operating profits,** *or* **identifiable assets.**[2] Certain financial information must be reported separately for each reportable industry segment. This information includes:

3. Define an industry segment and identify the information to be reported about each reportable industry segment.

1. *Revenues.* The revenues of a reportable industry segment include revenues from sales to customers.

2. *Operating Profit.* The operating profit of a reportable industry segment is its revenues minus its segment expenses. Included in segment expenses are cost of goods sold, selling expenses, and general and administrative expenses, but not income taxes. Thus the operating profit is reported *before income taxes.*

3. *Identifiable Assets.* The identifiable assets of a reportable industry segment are the assets that are used by the segment.

---

[1]Other information, including information related to a company's foreign operations, export sales, and major customers, is also required to be reported, but is not discussed in this chapter.

[2]"Financial Reporting for Segments of a Business Enterprise," *FASB Statement No. 14* (Stamford, Conn.: FASB, 1976), par. 1.

This information is also reported for the rest of the company's industry segments that have not met at least one of the criteria for reportable segments. That is, the remaining other industry segments are combined and their combined revenues, operating profits, and identifiable assets are reported.[3] Note that there are no requirements for disclosing the cash flow of industry segments.

Thus to provide more useful information a company's consolidated financial statements are "broken down" into segment reports. These segment reports include information on each reportable industry segment's revenues, operating profit, and identifiable assets. A diagram of this relationship is shown in Exhibit 19-2.

EXHIBIT 19-2   Relationship of Consolidated Financial Statements to Segment Reports

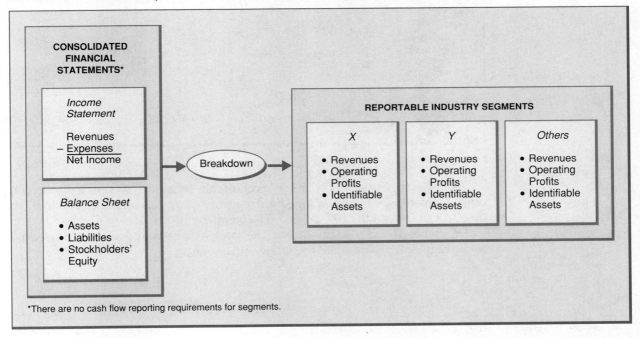

*There are no cash flow reporting requirements for segments.

Preparation and Reporting of Segment Information

The revenues, operating profits, and assets of the reportable industry segments and the combined remaining segments are reported in a schedule accompanying the financial statements. On the schedule the revenues listed for the reportable industry segments and the other combined industry segments must sum to the total sales revenue reported in the company's income statement; the operating profit of the segments must sum to the income before income taxes; and the identifiable assets of the segments must sum to the company's total assets reported in its balance sheet.

---

[3]Certain items, such as *general corporate revenues* (e.g., interest revenue), *general corporate expenses* (e.g., interest expense), and general corporate assets (e.g., marketable securities) are *not* allocated to *any* segments. These items are not considered further in this chapter.

On the schedule the revenues for each segment and in total are listed first. Next the operating profit is listed for each segment and in total. Finally, the identifiable assets are listed for each segment and in total.

Illustration. To illustrate, suppose that the Baxter Corporation presents the income statement shown in Exhibit 19-3.

EXHIBIT 19-3
Income Statement

BAXTER CORPORATION Income Statement For Year Ended December 31, 1991		
Sales		$100,000
Cost of goods sold		(60,000)
Gross profit		$ 40,000
Operating expenses		
Selling expenses	$ 8,000	
General and administrative expenses	13,000	
Total operating expenses		(21,000)
Income before income taxes		$ 19,000
Income tax expense		(7,600)
Net Income		$ 11,400

The Baxter Corporation has two reportable segments, A and B. Its several other segments are to be combined for reporting purposes because none of them meet at least one of the 10% criteria. The company lists total assets of $146,000 on its December 31, 1991 balance sheet. The sales, expenses, and assets are assigned to the segments according to the following amounts:

	Amounts Identified with		
	Segment A	*Segment B*	*Other Segments*
Sales	$30,000	$50,000	$20,000
Cost of goods sold	17,000	32,000	11,000
Selling expenses	2,000	4,400	1,600
General and administrative expenses	4,200	6,000	2,800
Identifiable assets	46,000	70,000	30,000

The schedule that the Baxter Corporation would use to report its segment information is shown in Exhibit 19-4.

In Exhibit 19-4 the revenues are listed first and total $100,000, the amount of sales reported in Exhibit 19-3. The operating profit of each segment and in total are listed next. Reportable industry segments A and B earned operating profits of $6,800 and $7,600, respectively, while the other industry segments earned a combined operating profit of $4,600. These operating profits total $19,000, the income before income taxes listed in Exhibit 19-3. The identifiable assets are allo-

EXHIBIT 19-4
Industry Segment
Financial Information

BAXTER CORPORATION
Industry Segment Financial Information
For Year Ended December 31, 1991

	Reportable Industry Segments		Other Industry Segments	Totals
	A	*B*		
Revenues (sales)	$30,000	$50,000	$20,000	$100,000
Operating profit	$ 6,800	$ 7,600	$ 4,600	$ 19,000
Identifiable assets	$46,000	$70,000	$30,000	$146,000

cated to each segment, and the $146,000 total identifiable assets reconcile with the total assets reported on the company's December 31, 1991 balance sheet.

Uses of Segment Information

The reporting of segment information by companies provides useful information for investors and creditors. Intracompany comparisons of revenues and operating profits of each reportable industry segment can be made. These comparisons can show how well one segment is performing as compared to another segment. For instance, comparisons can be made of each segment's operating profits to its sales and to its identifiable assets to see how well each segment is using its resources (e.g., in Exhibit 19-4 Segment A earned an operating profit of $6,800 using assets of $46,000, or a 15% "return" on the resources used by this segment, while Segment B earned $7,600 using $70,000 assets, only an 11% return). Or the results of one segment for several years can be compared to identify any trends in its operating performance. Intercompany comparisons can also be made, although care must be taken to be sure that each company has identified its reportable industry segments in the same manner. If not, valid comparisons cannot be made because there is a lack of *comparability*. Later in the chapter we use certain ratios to make these comparisons easier.

Interim Financial Statements

4(a). Define interim financial statements.

External users often want more frequent accounting information than is provided in a company's annual financial statements. As a result, interim reports called interim financial statements are prepared. **Interim financial statements are reports for periods of less than a year.** Interim financial statements are normally issued four times a year. Hence the term *quarterly report* is often used for these interim statements. Accounting principles have been established for interim financial statements. Basically, each interim (quarterly) period is considered to be part of the annual accounting period. Certain principles are modified, however, so that the results will be more useful.

Principles of Interim Reporting

The accounting principles for interim financial statements apply primarily to income statement items. They are summarized here:

1. *Revenues.* Revenues should be recognized during an interim period in the same manner as during the annual accounting period. If revenues are subject to seasonal variations (e.g., toy sales), the company should report the seasonal nature of its activities.

2. *Cost of Goods Sold.* Companies that use a periodic inventory system may use the *gross profit method* or *retail inventory method* (discussed in Chapter 9) to estimate their interim inventory. The method used should be disclosed.

3. *Expenses.* Expenses that affect the operating activities of more than one interim period should be allocated among the interim periods. This allocation should be based on, say, the time expired or some activity related to the periods. For instance, depreciation expense might be based on the units produced in each interim period. Expenses such as utilities that affect only one interim period should be assigned *only* to that period. Gains and losses on the sale of land or equipment, for example, should also be recognized in the interim period when they occur. Income tax expense for each interim period should be based on the income tax rate applicable for the entire year.

4. *Extraordinary Items and Disposals of Business Segments.* Extraordinary items (net of income taxes) and the results from the disposal of a business segment (net of income taxes) should be disclosed in the interim period during which the events occur.

5. *Earnings per Share.* Earnings per share should be computed for each interim period and reported on the face of the interim income statement. A breakdown of earnings per share related to continuing income, the disposal of a business segment, and extraordinary items should also be disclosed.

6. *Interim Income.* The income for the current interim period is reported in that interim income statement. In addition, a current *year-to-date* (i.e., from the beginning of the year until the end of the interim period) income statement is also provided. Thus in the second quarter of a company's fiscal year, the company prepares an income statement for the second quarter as well as an income statement for the first 6 months of the year. These income statements are shown beside each other.

Preparation and Disclosure of Interim Financial Statements

4(b). Prepare an interim income statement.

The procedures involved in preparing the interim financial statements are similar to those for annual statements. A year-to-date adjusted trial balance is developed, from which the year-to-date interim financial statements are prepared in the usual manner. There are two areas of difference, however. First, for companies using a periodic inventory system, the ending inventory for the interim financial statements is usually determined by using an *estimate* instead of taking a physical inventory. The gross profit method or retail inventory method (discussed in Chapter 9) is typically used to estimate the ending interim inventory. Second, in an interim period after the first period, amounts from previous interim periods must *not* be included in the revenues and expenses on the current interim income statement. To avoid this problem, companies usually prepare the interim income statement on a year-to-date basis and then deduct out the income statement results from any previous interim periods. For example, at the end of 6 months a company must report an income statement for the second quarter (as well as for 6 months). To do so the company prepares an income statement for 6 months and then deducts out (subtracts) the first-quarter income statement results to determine the second-quarter income statement.

Illustration. Although companies are encouraged to include all financial statements in their interim reports, many companies only include an income statement, along with selected balance sheet and statement of cash flow items. To conserve space only the preparation of an interim income statement is shown here. Suppose that the Baker Corporation reported the income statement shown in Exhibit 19-5 at the end of its first quarter of 1991. The corporation is now preparing its interim income statements for the second quarter and first 6 months of 1991. To do so, the corporation prepares an adjusted trial balance on June 30, 1991, that includes the revenue and expense accounts[4] shown in Exhibit 19-6.

EXHIBIT 19-5
Interim Income
Statement

BAKER CORPORATION Income Statement For First Quarter Ended March 31, 1991		
Sales (net)		$8,000
Cost of goods sold		
Inventory (1/1/1991)	$2,100	
Purchases (net)	5,100	
Cost of goods available for sale	$7,200	
Less: Inventory (3/31/1991, estimated)	(2,400)	
Cost of goods sold		(4,800)
Gross profit		$3,200
Operating expenses		
Selling expenses	$1,000	
General and administrative expenses	1,200	
Total operating expenses		(2,200)
Income before income taxes		$1,000
Income tax expense		(400)
Net Income		$ 600
Earnings per share (2,000 shares)		$ .30

Based upon the information in Exhibit 19-6, the interim income statement for 6 months is prepared first in the usual manner, except for the ending inventory in the cost of goods sold section. This income statement is shown in the right-hand columns of Exhibit 19-7. Note here that the $2,100 beginning inventory is the same as the January 1, 1991 inventory shown in Exhibit 19-5.

---

[4]Normally, the income before income taxes must be known *before* determining the $1,000 income tax expense shown in Exhibit 19-6. This complexity is beyond the scope of this textbook. To simplify any related homework, the year-to-date income tax expense is always provided.

EXHIBIT 19-6
Partial Adjusted
Trial Balance

BAKER CORPORATION
Adjusted Trial Balance (Partial)
June 30, 1991

	Debits	Credits
Sales (net)		$18,000
Interest revenue		60
Purchases (net)	$11,300	
Selling expenses	2,160	
General and administrative expenses	2,600	
Income tax expense	1,000	

The $2,600 ending inventory on June 30, 1991, is estimated by using the gross profit method instead of taking a physical inventory, as follows. Based on experience, Baker Corporation estimates its gross profit is 40% of net sales, or $7,200 ($18,000 × 0.40). Cost of goods sold is estimated to be $10,800 ($18,000 net sales less $7,200 gross profit). Finally, the $2,600 ending inventory is found by deducting the $10,800 cost of goods sold from the cost of goods available for sale ($2,100 beginning inventory plus $11,300 net purchases).

The interim income statement for the second quarter (April 1–June 30) of 1991 is shown in the center of Exhibit 19-7. Except for the beginning and ending

EXHIBIT 19-7
Interim Income
Statements

BAKER CORPORATION
Income Statements

	For Periods	
	Apr. 1–June 30, 1991	Jan. 1–June 30, 1991
Sales (net)	$10,000	$18,000
Cost of goods sold		
Inventory (beginning)	$2,400	$ 2,100
Purchases (net)	6,200	11,300
Cost of goods available for sale	$8,600	$13,400
Less: Ending inventory (estimated)	(2,600)	(2,600)
Cost of goods sold	(6,000)	(10,800)
Gross profit	$ 4,000	$ 7,200
Operating expenses		
Selling expenses	$1,160	$ 2,160
General and administrative expenses	1,400	2,600
Total operating expenses	(2,560)	(4,760)
Operating income	$ 1,440	$ 2,440
Other revenues		
Interest revenue	60	60
Income before income taxes	$ 1,500	$ 2,500
Income tax expense	(600)	(1,000)
Net Income	$ 900	$ 1,500
Earnings per share (2,000 shares)	$ .45	$ .75

inventories, each amount was determined by subtracting the first quarter amount (shown in Exhibit 19-5) from the 6-month amount. For instance, the $10,000 second quarter sales was determined by subtracting the $8,000 first quarter sales from the $18,000 6-month amount. On the other hand, the $60 interest revenue for the 6 months was all applicable to the second quarter because there was no interest revenue in the first quarter. The $2,400 beginning inventory for the second quarter was the estimated ending inventory from the first quarter, while the $2,600 ending inventory is the same for both the second quarter and the 6 months.

Interim Balance Sheet.   For a company that includes an ending interim balance sheet in its interim report[5] the procedures are straightforward. Except for the ending inventory and retained earnings, the amounts are obtained from the year-to-date adjusted trial balance. The ending inventory is the same as that used in the interim income statement. The ending retained earnings is computed by adding the net income to (and subtracting any dividends from) the beginning retained earnings.

Uses of Interim Financial Statements

Interim reports provide more timely information than annual reports for external users in decision making. The same intercompany and intracompany comparisons can be made with interim financial statements as are made with annual financial statements, although on a more frequent basis. This more timely information helps to reduce the risk associated with investing in or lending money to a company. For instance, trends in a company's sales, operating expenses, and earnings over time can be more quickly detected in interim reports. Or for seasonal industries, the current sales and earnings of a company can be compared either to its own past results or to the results of other companies in the interim "peak sales" periods and in the "low-volume" interim periods to identify differences in operating activities. For instance, Eastman Kodak Company reported sales and net earnings of $4,543 million and $312 million in the fourth quarter of 1988, respectively, as compared to $3,328 million sales and $260 million net earnings for the first quarter. It is likely that these increases were due, in part, to the greater demand for photographic equipment around Christmas. Managers, as internal users, can also use interim financial statement information in their planning and control functions. It should be noted, however, that interim financial statements are *not* audited.

Percentage Analyses

The evaluation of current operating results and the comparison of a company's operating results, cash flows, and financial position across several accounting periods or with other companies may be improved by converting the monetary

---

[5]A company may also include an interim statement of cash flows in its interim report. For simplicity, this statement is not discussed in this chapter.

relationships within the financial statements to percentage relationships.[6] The three types of analyses that use percentage relationships are referred to as horizontal analysis, vertical analysis, and ratio analysis. The first two types are discussed in this section; ratio analysis is discussed in the following section.

Horizontal Analysis

5. Describe horizontal analysis.

Horizontal analysis shows the changes in a company's operating results over time in percentages as well as in dollar amounts. Horizontal analysis is usually done for each item on the income statement. It is less often used for balance sheet comparisons. Two years of income statement data are usually shown in dollars. The earlier year is used as the base year, and the amount of change in each item on the income statement is expressed as a *percentage* of that item's base year amount. That is, the percentage change in each item is computed by dividing the dollar amount of the change by the base year dollar amount of the item.

Exhibit 19-8 shows a horizontal analysis of the 1991 and 1992 income statements of the Trumbell Company. Note that the 10.0% increase in sales is computed by dividing the $10,000 increase ($110,000 in 1992 compared to $100,000 in 1991) by the $100,000 sales for 1991. The other percentage changes are computed in a similar way.

EXHIBIT 19-8
Horizontal Analysis
of Income Statements

	TRUMBELL COMPANY Comparative Income Statements (Horizontal Analysis)			
	For Years Ended December 31		Year-to-Year Increase (Decrease) 1991 to 1992	
	1992	*1991*	*Amount*	*Percent*
Sales	$110,000	$100,000	$10,000	10.0%
Sales returns	(9,200)	(10,000)	(800)	(8.0)
Sales (net)	$100,800	$ 90,000	$10,800	12.0
Cost of goods sold	(69,000)	(60,000)	9,000	15.0
Gross profit	$ 31,800	$ 30,000	$ 1,800	6.0
Selling expenses	(9,000)	(8,000)	1,000	12.5
General expenses	(10,800)	(11,400)	(600)	(5.3)
Interest expense	(1,000)	(600)	400	66.7
Total expenses	$ (20,800)	$ (20,000)	$ 800	4.0
Income before income taxes	$ 11,000	$ 10,000	$ 1,000	10.0
Income tax expense	(4,400)	(4,000)	400	10.0
Net Income	$ 6,600	$ 6,000	$ 600	10.0
Number of common shares	3,500	3,000	500	16.7
Earnings per share[a]	$ 1.63	$ 1.70	$ (.07)	(4.1)

[a]Earnings per share = $\dfrac{\text{Net income} - \text{Preferred dividends (\$900)}}{\text{Average common shares outstanding}}$

---

[6]Although percentage relationships may be developed for the information in the statement of cash flows, for simplicity these analyses are excluded from this chapter.

By analyzing the horizontal percentage changes, several observations can be made that are not readily apparent from the absolute dollar amounts. First, net income has increased by the same percentage (10.0) as sales. Cost of goods sold, however, increased at a greater percentage (15.0), resulting in gross profit increasing by only 6.0%. Selling expenses also increased by 12.5%, which was more than the increase in revenues. Only by a *reduction* of 5.3% in general expenses was the company able to increase its net income at the same rate as sales. Even though net income increased by 10.0%, earnings per share *decreased* by 4.1% because the percentage increase in the number of common shares outstanding was greater than the percentage increase in net income.

Whenever horizontal analysis is used care must be taken in computing and evaluating percentage changes. For instance, an amount may be shown in parentheses on the income statement because it is a deduction. In this case, the parentheses should be ignored in computing the amount of change and percentage change. In addition, if a base figure is zero, although an *amount* of the change may be shown, *no percentage* change may be validly expressed. Furthermore if horizontal changes are shown as percentages, no addition or subtraction of the percentages can be made because the percentage changes result from the use of a different base for each item. Finally, for items of small base amounts (such as interest expense in Exhibit 19-8) a small dollar change may result in a very high percentage change. This may lead users to attach more importance to the item than they should.

Vertical Analysis

6. Describe vertical analysis.

Vertical analysis shows the items on the financial statements of a given *period* or *date* in percentages as well as in dollar amounts. When vertical analysis is used for comparisons of financial statements from several periods, trends or changes in the relationships between items are more easily identified. **Financial statements expressed only in percentages are referred to as common-size statements.**

Vertical analysis may be used for the income statement or balance sheet. On the income statement, *net* sales usually are shown as 100% and all the other items are expressed as a percentage of net sales. That is, the dollar amount of each item is divided by the dollar amount of net sales to determine the percentage. On the balance sheet, total assets as well as total liabilities and stockholders' equity are shown as 100%.

Vertical analyses for the Trumbell Company are shown in Exhibits 19-9 and 19-10. Note in Exhibit 19-9 that the 66.7% cost of goods sold in 1991 is computed by dividing the $60,000 cost of goods sold by the $90,000 net sales. In Exhibit 19-10 the 8.6% inventory in 1992 is computed by dividing the $8,200 inventory by the $95,000 total assets. The other percentages are computed in a similar way.

The vertical percentage changes from the 1991 to the 1992 income statement in Exhibit 19-9 reveal that although net income has increased in dollars, it has decreased slightly as a percentage of net sales. This is primarily due to the increase in cost of goods sold as a percent of 1992 sales being offset by a decrease in general expenses as a percent of 1992 sales, while the percentage of selling expenses to 1992 sales remained unchanged as compared to 1991. The vertical

EXHIBIT 19-9
Vertical Analysis
of Income Statements

TRUMBELL COMPANY
Comparative Income Statements
For Years Ended December 31, 1991, and 1992
(Vertical Analysis)

	1992		1991	
	Amount	*Percent*	*Amount*	*Percent*
Sales	$110,000	109.1%	$100,000	111.1%
Sales returns	(9,200)	(9.1)	(10,000)	(11.1)
Sales (net)[a]	$100,800	100.0	$ 90,000	100.0
Cost of goods sold	(69,000)	(68.5)	(60,000)	(66.7)
Gross profit	$ 31,800	31.5	$ 30,000	33.3
Selling expenses	(9,000)	(8.9)	(8,000)	(8.9)
General expenses	(10,800)	(10.7)	(11,400)	(12.7)
Interest expense	(1,000)	(1.0)	(600)	(.6)
Total expenses	$(20,800)	(20.6)	$(20,000)	(22.2)
Income before income taxes	$ 11,000	10.9	$ 10,000	11.1
Income tax expense	(4,400)	(4.4)	(4,000)	(4.4)
Net Income	$ 6,600	6.5	$ 6,000	6.7
Number of common shares	3,500		3,000	
Earnings per share	$ 1.63		$ 1.70	

[a]Seventy percent of the net sales were credit sales (used in the ratio analysis discussed later).

EXHIBIT 19-10
Vertical Analysis
of Balance Sheets

TRUMBELL COMPANY
Comparative Balance Sheets
December 31, 1991, and December 31, 1992
(Vertical Analysis)

	1992		1991	
	Amount	*Percent*	*Amount*	*Percent*
Cash	$ 2,000	2.1%	$ 2,200	2.7%
Marketable securities (short-term)	2,900	3.0	2,700	3.4
Accounts receivable (net)	6,900	7.3	6,300	7.9
Inventory	8,200	8.6	7,800	9.8
Prepaid items	1,000	1.1	1,200	1.5
Total current assets	$21,000	22.1	$20,200	25.3
Noncurrent assets (net)	74,000	77.9	59,800	74.7
Total Assets	$95,000	100.0	$80,000	100.0
Current liabilities	$10,000	10.5	$ 9,000	11.2
Long-term liabilities (8%)	12,500	13.2	7,500	9.4
Total Liabilities	$22,500	23.7	$16,500	20.6
Preferred stock, 6%, $100 par	$15,000	15.8	$15,000	18.8
Common stock, $5 par[a]	17,500	18.4	15,000	18.8
Additional paid-in capital	17,800	18.7	12,800	16.0
Retained earnings[b]	22,200	23.4	20,700	25.8
Total Stockholders' Equity	$72,500	76.3	$63,500	79.4
Total Liabilities and Stockholders' Equity	$95,000	100.0	$80,000	100.0

[a]December 31, 1992, market price is $20.00 per share.
[b]Retained earnings in 1992 were reduced by dividends of $6 per share on the preferred stock and $1.20 per share on the common stock.

analyses of the ending 1991 and 1992 balance sheets in Exhibit 19-10 reveal a shift in the percentage composition of total assets from 1991 to 1992. The percentage of the more liquid current assets has decreased and the percentage of noncurrent assets has increased. The percentage composition of "equities" has also changed. As compared to 1991, the 1992 creditor equities (total liabilities) have increased while the preferred stockholders' equities have decreased and the common stockholders' equities have remained about the same.

Both vertical and horizontal analysis may be used to a limited extent in analyzing interim reports and reports of the results of business segments. Vertical and horizontal analyses are also used in conjunction with ratio analysis.

Ratio Analyses

Another form of percentage analysis involves the use of financial ratios. **Ratios are computations in which one (or more than one) item on the financial statements is divided by another related item or items.** Ratios are often used to evaluate the financial success of a company. Many ratios have become standardized; they are considered to be useful indicators of financial success (or lack of success) and are routinely computed and published on a company and industry basis by the financial analysis companies mentioned earlier. These ratios become "benchmarks" against which to compare a company's results to evaluate its performance. The ratios are used by different external users in intracompany and intercompany comparisons for numerous economic decisions. Other ratios are developed by individual users or user groups for their own specific needs.

More than 40 different ratios or variations of ratios have been discussed in the financial analysis literature. We shall study only the main standard ratios, however. They are classified into five groups:

1. stockholder profitability ratios,
2. company profitability ratios,
3. liquidity ratios,
4. activity ratios, and
5. stability ratios.

We discuss the use of each ratio and its computation in the following sections. The 1992 data for computing each of these ratios is included in Exhibits 19-9 and 19-10 for the Trumbell Company. Since the numbers used in each calculation are not discussed in the text, you should study these exhibits to identify the information used for each ratio.

For certain ratios an *average* figure is used for the denominator of the ratio. This is because the numerator is an amount flowing into or out of the company (e.g., net income, net credit sales, cost of goods sold) during the accounting period. In these cases the denominator should be expressed as an average amount for the accounting period (e.g., average total assets, average stockholders' equity, average inventory). A simple, unweighted average is usually calculated for the denominator by summing the beginning balance and the ending balance of the item for the period and dividing the result by 2 (e.g., beginning inventory plus ending inventory, divided by 2). Occasionally, only an ending (or a beginning) balance of an item is known, in which case no average can be computed. The known amount must then be used even though it results in a less accurate ratio.

Stockholder Profitability Ratios

Stockholder profitability ratios have been developed to serve as indicators of how effective a company has been (or will be) in meeting the profit objectives of its owners. Several stockholder profitability ratios have been developed; they are shown in Exhibit 19-11, along with the calculations for the Trumbell Company. Each of these ratios is discussed next.

EXHIBIT 19-11   Stockholder Profitability Ratios

Ratio	Formula	Calculations (1992)
1. Earnings per Share	$\dfrac{\text{Net Income} - \text{Preferred Dividends}}{\text{Average Common Shares Outstanding}}$	$\dfrac{\$6,600 - \$900}{3,500} = \$1.63$
2. Price/Earnings	$\dfrac{\text{Ending Market Price per Common Share}}{\text{Earnings per Share}}$	$\dfrac{\$20.00}{\$1.63} = 12.3 \text{ times}$
3. Dividend Yield	$\dfrac{\text{Dividends per Common Share}}{\text{Ending Market Price per Common Share}}$	$\dfrac{\$1.20}{\$20.00} = 6.0\%$

7(a). Identify and calculate the stockholder profitability ratios.

Earnings per Share.   The earnings per share (EPS) information is probably the most frequently cited ratio in a financial analysis. It is considered so important that it is a required disclosure on the face of the income statement. As its name indicates, it shows the amount of a company's earnings for each share of common stock held by stockholders. Earnings per share information is used to evaluate a company's past, current, and potential earnings performance. Because this ratio involves only common stockholders' earnings, in the numerator the net income is reduced by the amount of preferred dividends. The denominator is based on a weighted average of the common shares outstanding. The calculation of this ratio was discussed in Chapter 15.

Price/Earnings.   Although it is not exactly a stockholder profitability ratio, actual and potential stockholders use the price/earnings ratio to evaluate how attractive an investment is in a company's common stock. A higher price/earnings ratio as compared to other companies may indicate that investors see a good chance that the company's earnings will grow faster. Or, it may reflect investors' perceptions of the quality of the company's management or its favorable competitive position. Care must be taken, however, that the comparison is made to other "similar" companies. The price/earnings ratio for companies in certain "growth" industries, such as the software development industry, will be much higher than for, say, companies in the automobile or steel industries. Interpretation of the ratio is also affected by investors' evaluations of the company's quality and trend of earnings, relative risk, use of alternative accounting methods, and economic and other factors.

Dividend Yield.   The market value of common stock is the value a stockholder must forego to continue owning the security. Stockholders are interested in their individual rates of return based on the actual dividends received as compared with the ending market price (or market price on another particular date) of the stock. The dividend yield provides this information. The return from an investment, however, also includes the change in the market price of the stock held during the accounting period. Thus the dividend yield is often combined with the percentage change in the market price of the stock to determine the total annual percentage return on the stockholders' investment.

Company Profitability Ratios

Company profitability ratios are used as indicators of how efficient a company has been in meeting its overall profit objectives, especially in relation to the resources invested (i.e., return on investment). Several overall company profitability ratios are shown in Exhibit 19-12, along with the calculations for the Trumbell Company. Each is discussed next.

EXHIBIT 19-12   Company Profitability Ratios

Ratio	Formula	Calculations (1992)
1. Profit Margin	$\dfrac{\text{Net Income}}{\text{Net Sales}}$	$\dfrac{\$6,600}{\$100,800} = 6.5\%$
2. Return on Total Assets	$\dfrac{\text{Net Income} + \substack{\text{Interest Expense} \\ \text{(net of tax)}}}{\text{Average Total Assets}}$	$\dfrac{\$6,600 + (\$1,000 \times 0.6)}{\dfrac{\$95,000 + \$80,000}{2}} = 8.2\%$
3. Return on Stockholders' Equity	$\dfrac{\text{Net Income}}{\text{Average Stockholders' Equity}}$	$\dfrac{\$6,600}{\dfrac{\$72,500 + \$63,500}{2}} = 9.7\%$

7(b). Identify and calculate the company profitability ratios.

Profit Margin.   The relationship of net income to net sales is commonly used to evaluate a company's efficiency in controlling costs and expenses in relation to sales. That is, the lower a company's expenses relative to sales, the higher the sales dollars remaining for other activities. Extraordinary gains or losses and results of disposals of discontinued segments are typically excluded from the numerator because they are the results of events not directly related to ongoing sales or expenses. The reporting of industry segment information discussed earlier in the chapter permits a variation of this ratio to be computed for the reportable industry segments of a company. For each segment, the profit margin *before* income taxes can be computed by dividing the segment's operating profit by its revenues (sales). A weakness of the ratio is that it does not consider the investment (the total assets or stockholders' equity) required to make the sales and income. A "return on investment" (either total assets or stockholders' equity) overcomes this weakness.

Return on Total Assets.   The management of a company has the responsibility to use the company's assets to earn a satisfactory profit. The amount of net income earned in relation to total assets is an indicator of a company's efficiency in the use of its economic resources. When comparing the return on total assets of one company to the return on total assets of another company consideration should be given to the age of the assets of each company. With increasing prices today, a company utilizing recently purchased assets (at higher prices) will show a lower return on these assets. Extraordinary items and results of disposals of discontinued segments are typically excluded from the numerator because they are the result of infrequent events not directly related to the ongoing economic resources used in a company's operations. Interest expense (after taxes)[7] is added back to net income because it is a financial cost paid to creditors to acquire the assets and not an expense of making sales. Since net income is earned over the entire period, the *average* total assets (beginning plus ending assets divided by 2) for the period are used as the denominator. Reporting the results of industry segments permits the computation of a variation of this ratio for the reportable industry segments of a company. For each segment the *pretax* return on *identifiable* assets can be computed by dividing the segment's operating profit by its identifiable assets.

Return on Stockholders' Equity.   Total assets are financed (provided) by both creditors and owners (stockholders). The management of a company not only has the responsibility of efficiently using the company's assets to earn income, but also to earn a satisfactory return for its stockholders on their equity (investment). Net income may also be divided by stockholders' equity to show the return on the owners' equity. When this return is higher than the return on total assets the company has favorable financial leverage (i.e., it is trading on the equity, discussed in Chapter 16 and later in this chapter, in regard to the debt ratio). A weakness of both ratios, however, is that they do not consider the current values of the assets or investments because both are shown in the financial statements based on the historical cost dollar amounts. Extraordinary items and results of disposals of discontinued segments are not included in the numerator (for the reason cited earlier) and average stockholders' equity is used for the denominator.

Liquidity Ratios

7(c) Identify and calculate the liquidity ratios.

Liquidity ratios (sometimes called *solvency* ratios) are used to evaluate a company's ability to pay its current liabilities. These ratios generally involve all or most of the components of a company's working capital, its current assets less its current liabilities. Current assets include cash, short-term marketable securities, receivables, inventory, and prepaid items. Among current liabilities are items such as accounts payable incurred for goods or services, accruals for wages, taxes, and interest payable, short-term notes payable, and advance collections of unearned revenues. The common liquidity ratios are shown in Exhibit 19-13, along with the calculations for the Trumbell Company. Each is discussed next.

Current Ratio.   The current ratio is probably the most commonly used indicator of a company's short-run liquidity. This ratio is sometimes referred to as the

---

[7]After-tax interest expense is usually computed by multiplying the pretax expense by 1 minus the income tax rate. For the Trumbell Company it is assumed that the income tax rate is 40%, and therefore the $1,000 pretax interest expense is multiplied by 60% (1 − 0.40) to determine the after-tax results.

EXHIBIT 19-13
Liquidity Ratios

Ratio	Formula	Calculations (1992)
1. Current	$\dfrac{\text{Current Assets}}{\text{Current Liabilities}}$	$\dfrac{\$21,000}{\$10,000} = 2.1\text{ to }1$
2. Acid-Test	$\dfrac{\text{Quick Assets}}{\text{Current Liabilities}}$	$\dfrac{\$11,800}{\$10,000} = 1.2\text{ to }1$

working capital ratio. It is considered to be a better indicator of a company's current debt-paying ability than simply using working capital. This is because working capital shows only the absolute difference between a company's current assets and its current liabilities. By computing the current ratio the relative relationship between the current assets and current liabilities is known, and therefore comparisons of different sized companies may be made. In the past, as a "rule of thumb," a 2.0 current ratio was considered satisfactory. Today, however, more attention is given to (1) industry practices, (2) the length of a company's operating cycle, and (3) the mix of the current assets. Too *high* a current ratio as compared to similar companies in the same industry may indicate inefficient management of current assets. The shorter a company's operating cycle, the less likely it will need a large amount of working capital or as high a current ratio to operate efficiently. (A company's operating cycle is evaluated by the use of activity ratios, discussed in the next section.) The proportion of different items that make up the total current assets is called the *mix* of the current assets. This mix has an effect upon how quickly the current assets can be converted into cash. As an extreme, a high proportion of prepaid items within current assets may indicate a weak liquidity position since prepaid assets are consumed in the operating cycle instead of being converted back into cash. The mix of a company's current assets and the impact upon its liquidity are considered in the acid-test ratio.

Acid-Test Ratio. The acid-test or *quick* ratio is a more severe (and more accurate) test of a company's short-term debt-paying abilities. In this ratio only the current assets that may be easily converted into cash are used in the calculation. These assets are referred to as quick assets, and they generally consist of cash, short-term marketable securities, accounts receivable, and short-term notes receivable. Inventory is excluded because it is frequently sold on credit, which means it cannot be quickly converted into cash. Prepaid items are excluded because they are not convertible into cash. Since short-term marketable securities are shown on a company's balance sheet at their lower of cost or market value, if the market value of these securities is *higher* than cost, this market value should be included (instead of cost) in the computation. The acid-test ratio highlights potential liquidity problems resulting from a poor mix of current assets. For instance, the use of this ratio usually shows the lower liquidity of a company with a high investment in inventory that would not be revealed in the current ratio. Care must be taken when thinking about which assets to include, however. Even though inventory is usually not included in the numerator of the acid-test ratio, sometimes inventory is, in fact, more liquid than certain receivables. This may be the case when a company makes a high percentage of its sales for cash. A quick ratio of 1.0 has been used as a general rule of thumb. Today, however, more attention is given to industry practices and the company's typical operations.

Activity Ratios

Activity ratios are used to give a general idea of the length of the segments of a company's operating cycle so that the liquidity of selected current assets may be evaluated. A company's operating cycle is the length of time it takes to invest in inventory, make credit sales, and convert the receivables into cash. The ratios also indicate the efficiency with which the company uses its short-term economic resources. The two common activity ratios are shown in Exhibit 19-14, along with the calculations for the Trumbell Company. Each is discussed next.

EXHIBIT 19-14   Activity Ratios

Ratio	Formula	Calculations (1992)
1. Inventory Turnover	$\dfrac{\text{Cost of Goods Sold}}{\text{Average Inventory}}$	$\dfrac{\$69,000}{\dfrac{\$8,200 + \$7,800}{2}}$ = 8.6 times or 42 days[a]
2. Accounts Receivable Turnover	$\dfrac{\text{Net Credit Sales}}{\text{Average Net Accounts Receivable}}$	$\dfrac{\$100,800 \times 0.70}{\dfrac{\$6,900 + \$6,300}{2}}$ = 10.7 times or 34 days[a]

[a]365-day business year.

7(d). Identify and calculate the activity ratios.

Inventory Turnover.   Inventory is purchased, sold, and replaced as part of a company's normal operations during its accounting period. Dividing a company's cost of goods sold for the period by its average inventory shows the number of times the inventory is *turned over* or sold during that period. As a general rule, the higher the inventory turnover, the more efficient the company is in its operations and the lesser the amount of investment that must be tied up in inventory. A company with a higher turnover is generally using its purchasing, receiving, and sales departments more efficiently. It is also minimizing the chance of having obsolete inventory. The lesser amount needed for investment in inventory means that the company either needs less capital or can invest its capital in other earnings activities.

Too high an inventory turnover, however, may indicate lost sales because there was not enough inventory on hand. Furthermore when a comparison is made of one company to another, both companies should be using similar inventory costing methods. In periods of rising prices, no valid comparison of inventory turnovers can be made when one company is using FIFO and the other company is using LIFO. This is because the company using LIFO will show a higher cost of goods sold and lower inventory than the FIFO company, even though their operations may be similar. The inventory turnover is frequently divided into the number of operating days in a *business year* (companies conduct their business on a 7-day, 6-day, or 5-day work week, resulting in a business year of 365, 300, or 250 days, depending on the industry) so that the inventory segment of the operating cycle may be shown in days. In general, the lower the number of days in which a company's inventory turns over, the more efficient it is.

Accounts Receivable Turnover.   Once inventory has been sold on credit, the company must collect the receivables to complete its operating cycle. Dividing net credit sales by average net accounts receivable shows how many times the average receivables are *turned over* or collected each period. The accounts receivable turnover is a measure of the efficiency with which the company collects its receivables and converts them back into cash. As a general rule, the higher the turnover the better, because the company has less resources tied up in receivables, collects these resources at a faster pace, and usually has fewer uncollectible accounts. The amount of net *credit* sales is the appropriate figure to use in the accounts receivable turnover. Most companies report only total sales without giving a breakdown of credit and cash sales, however. In this case net sales may be used in the ratio.

The accounts receivable turnover is often divided into the business year (365, 300, or 250 days) to show the average collection period (in days). A comparison of a company's average collection period to the days in its typical credit terms gives an indication of how aggressively the company's credit department collects overdue accounts. When comparing the accounts receivable turnovers of different companies consideration also should be given to the length of each company's credit terms. Companies operating in industries where the typical credit terms are 30 days are likely to have shorter turnovers of receivables than companies with 60-day credit terms. When both the inventory turnover and accounts receivable turnover are expressed in days, the days in the inventory turnover may be added to the average collection period for an approximation of the days in the company's operating cycle. The Trumbell Company's operating cycle is approximately 76 days (a 42-day inventory turnover plus a 34-day accounts receivable turnover).

Stability Ratios

Stability ratios are used to indicate the long-run solvency, financial flexibility, and stability of the company. They provide evidence of the safety of the investments in the company by long-term bondholders and stockholders. Several stability ratios are shown in Exhibit 19-15, along with the calculations for the Trumbell Company. Each is discussed next.

EXHIBIT 19-15   Stability Ratios

Ratio	Formula	Calculations (1992)	
1. Debt	$\dfrac{\text{Total Liabilities}}{\text{Total Assets}}$	$\dfrac{\$22,500}{\$95,000}$	= 23.7%
2. Times Interest Earned	$\dfrac{\text{Pretax Operating Income}}{\text{Interest Expense}}$	$\dfrac{\$11,000 + \$1,000}{\$1,000}$	= 12 times
3. Book Value per Common Share	$\dfrac{\text{Common Stockholders' Equity}}{\text{Outstanding Common Shares}}$	$\dfrac{\$72,500 - (\$100 \times 150)}{3,500}$	= $16.43 per Common Share

7(e). Identify and calculate the stability ratios.

Debt Ratio.   The debt ratio shows the percentage of total assets contributed by creditors. This ratio is subtracted from 100% to show the percentage of total assets (i.e., equity ratio) contributed by stockholders.[8] The desired relationship (or *mix*) between the debt and equity ratios depends on the industry. In general, creditors prefer to see a lower debt ratio because if business declines it is more likely that the company will be able to pay its interest costs. Up to a point, stockholders prefer a higher debt ratio, especially when the company is favorably *trading on the equity* or applying favorable *financial leverage*. This occurs when the company borrows money from creditors at an interest rate (net of income taxes) that is lower than the return the company can earn in its operations (discussed in Chapter 16). A very high debt ratio, however, is usually a disadvantage when a company wants to attract additional capital. Investors in both long-term bonds and stocks usually feel that a highly leveraged company is not a very stable or attractive investment.

Times Interest Earned.   The times interest earned ratio (sometimes called the *interest coverage* ratio) is used to show the ability of a company to cover its interest obligations through its annual earnings. It is a measure of the safety of creditors' (especially long-term) investments in the company. As a general rule, the higher the ratio, the better able is the company to meet its interest obligations. While interest obligations are legal commitments, it is also true that continued interest payments are endangered by low earnings over an extended period of time. Because both earnings and interest expense are based on accrual accounting, the times interest earned ratio is slightly inaccurate, since it should include only cash outflows for interest and cash inflows from earnings. Such refinements are not usually made to this ratio, however.

   The numerator of the times interest earned ratio is usually pretax operating income; that is, income before income taxes, to which interest expense is added back. When a company reports income from continuing operations along with the results of discontinued operations and extraordinary gains and losses, interest expense is added back to pretax income from continuing operations to compute pretax operating income. Extraordinary gains and losses and results of disposals of discontinued segments are not included because they generally do not affect the long-run interest-paying ability of a company.

Book Value.   The book value per common share shows the net assets per share of common stock. It is sometimes erroneously called the *liquidation* value per share (liquidation occurs when a company ceases to operate, sells all its assets, and pays off its debts). Although book value is frequently computed, for several reasons it is actually not very useful for showing a company's financial stability. First, most companies are ongoing businesses so that a liquidation value is not important. Second, even if a liquidation value were important, the book value is based on assets recorded primarily at historical costs and not at current liquidation selling prices. Third, the market value per share of a company's common stock is important in evaluating its stability. Since book value is based on historical costs, it also has no direct relationship to a common stock's market value.

---

[8]Total liabilities are sometimes divided by total stockholders' equity to determine the *debt/equity* ratio.

When book value per share is computed and the company has both preferred and common stock outstanding, it is necessary to determine the stockholders' equity belonging to the common stockholders. Of the total stockholders' equity, preferred stock is usually allocated its par value. When preferred dividends are cumulative and in arrears, a portion of retained earnings equal to the dividends in arrears is also assigned as preferred stockholders' equity. The remaining amount of stockholders' equity is then assigned as common stockholders' equity. The book value per common share is computed by dividing the number of common shares outstanding into this remaining stockholders' equity.

Summary

Only the primary standard ratios were identified and discussed in this section. Exhibit 19-16 summarizes these ratios and their computations.

EXHIBIT 19-16
Summary of Ratios

Ratio	Formula
Stockholder Profitability Ratios	
1. Earnings per Share	$\dfrac{\text{Net Income} - \text{Preferred Dividends}}{\text{Average Common Shares Outstanding}}$
2. Price/Earnings	$\dfrac{\text{Ending Market Price per Common Share}}{\text{Earnings per Share}}$
3. Dividend Yield	$\dfrac{\text{Dividends per Common Share}}{\text{Ending Market Price per Common Share}}$
Company Profitability Ratios	
1. Profit Margin	$\dfrac{\text{Net Income}}{\text{Net Sales}}$
2. Return on Total Assets	$\dfrac{\text{Net Income} + \text{Interest Expense (net of tax)}}{\text{Average Total Assets}}$
3. Return on Stockholders' Equity	$\dfrac{\text{Net Income}}{\text{Average Stockholders' Equity}}$
Liquidity Ratios	
1. Current	$\dfrac{\text{Current Assets}}{\text{Current Liabilities}}$
2. Acid-Test	$\dfrac{\text{Quick Assets}}{\text{Current Liabilities}}$
Activity Ratios	
1. Inventory Turnover	$\dfrac{\text{Cost of Goods Sold}}{\text{Average Inventory}}$
2. Accounts Receivable Turnover	$\dfrac{\text{Net Credit Sales}}{\text{Average Net Accounts Receivable}}$
Stability Ratios	
1. Debt	$\dfrac{\text{Total Liabilities}}{\text{Total Assets}}$
2. Times Interest Earned	$\dfrac{\text{Pretax Operating Income}}{\text{Interest Expense}}$
3. Book Value per Common Share	$\dfrac{\text{Common Stockholders' Equity}}{\text{Outstanding Common Shares}}$

Chapter Summary

Review of Learning Objectives

1. **Identify the important items in financial analysis evaluations.**
   These items include return on investment, risk, financial flexibility, liquidity, and operating capability. *Return on investment* occurs when a company provides earnings on the capital invested by its owners. *Risk* involves uncertainty about the future earnings potential of a company. *Financial flexibility* is the ability of a company to adapt to change. *Liquidity* is the nearness to cash of a company's assets. *Operating capability* refers to a company's ability to maintain a given physical level of operations.

2. **Describe (a) intracompany and (b) intercompany comparisons.**
   Intracompany comparisons are comparisons within a company to identify trends in the company's performance. *Intercompany* comparisons are comparisons of a company's performance with other competing companies, with the company's industry, or with related industries. These comparisons may be for the current period or several past periods.

3. **Define an industry segment and identify the information to be reported about each reportable industry segment.**
   An industry segment is a component (e.g., department) of a company that provides a product or service to customers for a profit. The information to be reported about each of a company's reportable industry segments includes: (1) revenues, which are the sales to customers; (2) operating profit, which is segment revenues minus segment expenses; and (3) identifiable assets, which are the assets used by the segment. This information is reported in a schedule accompanying the financial statements.

4. **(a) Define interim financial statements and (b) prepare an interim income statement.**
   Interim financial statements are reports for periods of less than a year. To prepare an interim income statement, the revenue and expense information from a year-to-date adjusted trial balance is used in the usual manner. For a company using the periodic inventory system, however, the ending inventory in the cost of goods sold section is usually estimated by either the gross profit method or retail inventory method.

5. **Describe horizontal analysis.**
   Horizontal analysis shows the changes in a company's operating results *over time* in percentages as well as in dollar amounts. Two years of income statement information is usually shown in dollars. Then the amount of change in each item is shown in dollars and is expressed as a percentage of that item's base year amount.

6. **Describe vertical analysis.**
   Vertical analysis shows the items on the financial statements of a given *period* or *date* in percentages as well as dollar amounts. On the income statement, net sales are shown as 100% and all the other items are expressed as a

percentage of net sales. On the balance sheet, total assets as well as total liabilities and stockholders' equity are shown as 100%.

7. **Identify and calculate the (a) stockholder profitability, (b) company profitability, (c) liquidity, (d) activity, and (e) stability ratios.**
There are three *stockholder profitability* ratios, including earnings per share, price/earnings, and dividend yield. There are also three *company profitability* ratios, including the profit margin, return on total assets, and return on stockholders' equity. The two *liquidity* ratios are the current and acid-test ratios. The two *activity* ratios are the inventory turnover and accounts receivable turnover. There are three *stability* ratios, including the debt, times interest earned, and book value per common share ratios. The formulas for calculating these ratios are summarized in Exhibit 19-16.

Review Problem

Fay Diversified Corporation operates in several different industries. Following is a condensed 1991 income statement of the entire company for the year ended December 31, 1991.

FAY DIVERSIFIED CORPORATION
Income Statement
For Year Ended December 31, 1991

Sales	$100,000
Less: Cost of goods sold	(60,000)
Gross profit	$ 40,000
Less: Selling and general expenses	(25,000)
Income before income taxes	$ 15,000
Income tax expense	(6,000)
Net Income	$ 9,000

The company has two reportable industry segments, L and M. On December 31, 1991, the company has $105,000 total assets. The sales, operating expenses, and assets are assigned to segments according to the following percentages:

	Segment L	Segment M	Other Segments
Sales	46%	34%	20%
Cost of goods sold	43	36	21
Selling and general expenses	50	33	17
Identifiable assets	48	30	22

REQUIRED Based on the preceding information prepare a schedule that reports the 1991 segment financial information for Fay Diversified Corporation.

Solution to Review Problem

FAY DIVERSIFIED CORPORATION
Industry Segment Financial Information
For Year Ended December 31, 1991

	Reportable Industry Segments		Other Industry Segments	Totals
	L	M		
Revenues (sales)	$46,000[a]	$34,000	$20,000	$100,000
Operating profit	$ 7,700	$ 4,150[b]	$ 3,150	$ 15,000
Identifiable assets	$50,400	$31,500	$23,100[c]	$105,000

[a]$100,000 sales × 0.46.
[b]$34,000 − ($60,000 cost of goods sold × 0.36) − ($25,000 selling and operating expenses × 0.33)
[c]$105,000 assets × 0.22

Glossary

Common-Size Statements.   Financial statements that are expressed only in percentages.

Horizontal Analysis.   Shows the changes in a company's operating results *over time* in percentages as well as in dollar amounts.

Industry Segment.   Department, division, or subsidiary of a company that provides a product or service to customers for a profit.

Intercompany Comparisons.   Comparisons of a company's operating results and financial position with those of competing companies.

Interim Financial Statements.   Financial statements for periods of less than a year; usually issued quarterly. Also called *interim reports* or *quarterly reports.*

Intracompany Comparisons.   Comparisons of a company's current operating results and financial position with its past results.

Ratio.   Computation in which one (or more than one) item on the financial statements is divided by another related item or items.

Reportable Industry Segment.   Industry segment that has revenues, operating profits, or identifiable assets that are 10% or more of the company's total revenues, operating profits, or identifiable assets.

Vertical Analysis.   Shows the items on a financial statement for a given *period* or *date* in percentages as well as in dollar amounts.

Questions

QUESTION 19-1   What five items are important in evaluating the results of a company's current operations and financial position? Briefly define each item.

QUESTION 19-2   What two types of comparisons are often made by external users in their financial decision making? What points should be remembered when making these comparisons?

QUESTION 19-3   Why do financial statement users desire financial information about the segments of a company?

QUESTION 19-4   Briefly define the terms (a) revenues, (b) operating profit, and (c) identifiable assets as they apply to a reportable industry segment.

QUESTION 19-5   What are interim financial statements? How often are they usually issued?

QUESTION 19-6   What specific principles may be used by a company using the periodic inventory system in reporting cost of goods sold and inventory in its interim financial statements?

QUESTION 19-7   What principles should be used in accounting for expenses during an interim period?

QUESTION 19-8   Briefly explain how an interim income statement is prepared for a company using the periodic inventory system.

QUESTION 19-9   What is a horizontal analysis and how is it prepared?

QUESTION 19-10   What is a vertical analysis and how does it differ from a horizontal analysis?

QUESTION 19-11   What are ratios and for what are they used?

QUESTION 19-12   Briefly describe how each of the stockholder profitability ratios is computed.

QUESTION 19-13   Briefly describe how each of the company profitability ratios is computed.

QUESTION 19-14   Which financial ratios may be used to evaluate the efficiency of a company's reportable industry segments?

QUESTION 19-15   Briefly describe how each of the liquidity ratios is computed.

QUESTION 19-16   Briefly describe how each of the activity ratios is computed.

QUESTION 19-17   Briefly describe how each of the stability ratios is computed.

Exercises

EXERCISE 19-1   **Segment Reporting.**   Mory Conglomerate Company has total assets of $140,000 at the end of 1991 and lists the following condensed income statement for 1991.

MORY CONGLOMERATE COMPANY	
Income Statement	
For Year Ended December 31, 1991	
Sales	$110,000
Operating expenses	(75,000)
Income before income taxes	$ 35,000
Income tax expense	(14,000)
Net Income	$ 21,000

The company has two reportable industry segments, A and B, and has developed the following information:

| | Segments | | Other | |
	A	B	Segments	Total
Sales	$50,000	$35,000	$25,000	$110,000
Operating expenses	30,000	24,000	21,000	75,000

The company's assets are assigned to the segments as follows: $67,000 to Segment A; $44,000 to Segment B; and $29,000 to the other segments.

REQUIRED   Prepare a schedule to report on the 1991 revenues, operating profits, and identifiable assets of Segments A and B and the other industry segments of the Mory Conglomerate Company.

EXERCISE 19-2   **Determination of Reportable Industry Segments.**   In preparing its segment reporting schedule, the Loxer Diversified Company has developed the following information for each of its five segments:

| | Segments | | | | | |
	1	2	3	4	5	Totals
Sales	$3,520	$3,000	$3,880	$25,800	$3,800	$40,000
Operating expenses	2,200	1,800	1,700	15,480	2,820	24,000
Identifiable assets	6,300	7,500	6,200	40,000	5,000	65,000

REQUIRED   Using the reportable industry segment definition from the text (e.g., the percentage of revenues, operating profits, or identifiable assets rule) determine which of the preceding segments are reportable industry segments and which should be combined for segment reporting. Justify your conclusions.

EXERCISE 19-3   **Segment Reporting.**   York Drug Company has two reportable industry segments, A and B. A 1991 condensed income statement for the entire company is as follows:

YORK DRUG COMPANY
Income Statement
For Year Ended December 31, 1991

Sales	$90,000
Cost of goods sold	(50,000)
Gross profit	$40,000
Operating expenses	(18,000)
Income before income taxes	$22,000
Income tax expense	(8,800)
Net Income	$13,200

Additional Information:

1. Sales are made as follows: Segment A, $52,000; Segment B, $26,000; other segments, $12,000 of the total.

2. Cost of goods sold for each segment is as follows: Segment A, $30,000; Segment B, $12,500; other segments, $7,500.

3. Operating expenses are identified with the segments as follows: Segment A, $10,000; Segment B, $4,500; other segments, $3,500.

4. The company has $110,000 total assets as of December 31, 1991. These assets are assigned to the segments as follows: Segment A, $49,500; Segment B, $38,500; other segments, $22,000.

REQUIRED Prepare a schedule that reports on the 1991 revenues, operating profits, and identifiable assets of Segments A and B and the other segments of the York Drug Company.

EXERCISE 19-4 **Interim Reporting, Gross Profit Method.** The Jolsh Corporation listed the following items on its interim worksheet for the second quarter, ended June 30, 1991:

Inventory (beginning)	$ 4,000
Purchases	22,000
Sales	28,000
Sales returns and allowances	3,000

Based on experience Jolsh Corporation estimates its gross profit is 30% of net sales.

REQUIRED
1. Compute the estimated cost of goods sold of the Jolsh Corporation for the second quarter of 1991 using the gross profit method.

2. Based on your answer to Requirement 1, compute the estimated ending inventory on June 30, 1991.

EXERCISE 19-5 **Interim Income Statement.** The Pellagrini Communications Company prepares interim reports. The following are selected accounts listed on its March 31, 1991 adjusted trial balance:

	Debits	Credits
Inventory (1-1-1991)	$ 5,500	
Sales (net)		$50,000
Purchases (net)	30,000	
Selling expenses	6,325	
General and administrative expenses	5,200	

The company uses the gross profit method to estimate its interim inventory. Historical gross profit has averaged 45% of net sales. The income tax rate is 40%, and 6,000 shares of common stock have been outstanding for the entire 3 months.

REQUIRED Prepare the first quarter 1991 interim income statement of the Pellagrini Communications Company.

EXERCISE 19-6 **Interim Income Statement.** Cruz Recreational Sales, Inc. has accumulated the following information for its first quarter 1991 interim income statement.

(a) Sales (net), $100,000; Interest revenue, $800

(b) Selling expenses, $12,600; Purchases (net), $60,000

(c) Inventory (1-1-1991), $10,000; Historical gross profit, 44% of net sales

(d) General and administrative expenses, 20% of cost of goods sold; Income tax expense, 40% of income before income taxes

(e) Shares of common stock outstanding for entire 3 months, 10,000

REQUIRED Prepare the first quarter 1991 income statement of Cruz Recreational Sales, Inc.

EXERCISE 19-7 **Horizontal Analysis.** The Clovland Company presents the following condensed comparative income statements for 1991 and 1992:

CLOVLAND COMPANY Comparative Income Statements		
	For Years Ended December 31	
	1992	1991
Sales (net)	$108,000	$90,000
Cost of goods sold	(60,000)	(45,000)
Gross profit	$ 48,000	$45,000
Operating expenses	(22,000)	(20,000)
Income before income taxes	$ 26,000	$25,000
Income tax expense	(10,400)	(10,000)
Net Income	$ 15,600	$15,000
Number of common shares	7,000	7,500
Earnings per share	$2.23	$2.00

REQUIRED Based on the preceding information prepare a horizontal analysis for the years 1991 and 1992. Calculate the profit margin for the company for each year. What is this ratio generally used for and what does it indicate about the Clovland Company?

EXERCISE 19-8 **Horizontal Analysis.** The Taboue Cutlery Corporation showed the following information for the years 1991 and 1992:

TABOUE CUTLERY CORPORATION Comparative Income Statements				
	For Years Ended December 31		Year-to-Year Increase (decrease) 1991 to 1992	
	1992	1991	Amount	Percent
Sales (net)	$65,000	$60,000	$ (a)	(b)%
Cost of goods sold	(c)	(33,600)	(d)	(e)
Gross profit	$27,950	$26,400	$ (f)	(g)
Operating expenses	(19,050)	(h)	400	(i)
Income before income taxes	$ 8,900	$ (j)	$1,150	(k)
Income tax expense	(3,560)	(3,100)	(l)	(m)
Net Income	$ (n)	$ 4,650	$ (o)	(p)
Number of common shares	2,700	(q)	(r)	12.5
Earnings per share	$ 1.98	$ 1.94	$ (s)	(t)

REQUIRED   Determine the appropriate percentages and amounts for the blanks lettered (a) through (t). Round to the nearest tenth of a percent. Briefly comment on what your analysis reveals.

EXERCISE 19-9   **Vertical Analysis.**   The Cooke Company presents the following condensed balance sheet information for 1991:

COOKE COMPANY
Balance Sheet
December 31, 1991

Cash	$ 1,500
Accounts receivable	3,500
Inventory	5,500
Long-term investments	10,000
Property and equipment (net)	39,500
Total Assets	$60,000
Current liabilities	$ 5,000
Bonds payable, 8%	20,000
Total Liabilities	$25,000
Common stock, $2 par	$ 6,000
Additional paid-in capital	9,000
Retained earnings	20,000
Total Stockholders' Equity	$35,000
Total Liabilities and Stockholders' Equity	$60,000

REQUIRED   Based on the preceding information prepare a vertical analysis of the Cooke Company balance sheet for 1991. Round to the nearest tenth of a percent. What is the company's current ratio? Based on the "rules of thumb" is it satisfactory?

EXERCISE 19-10   **Vertical Analysis.**   The Anton Electronics Company presents the following condensed income statement for 1991:

ANTON ELECTRONICS COMPANY
Income Statement
For Year Ended December 31, 1991

Sales (net)	$135,000
Cost of goods sold	(75,000)
Gross profit	$ 60,000
Operating expenses	(33,750)
Income before income taxes	$ 26,250
Income tax expense	(10,500)
Net Income	$ 15,750
Earnings per share	$3.00

In addition, the average inventory for 1991 was $10,000.

REQUIRED Based on the preceding information prepare a vertical analysis of the income statement for 1991. What is the company's inventory turnover and what does this ratio tell us about a company?

EXERCISE 19-11 **Ratio Analysis.** The Tomor Export Company listed the following items as of December 31, 1991:

Net income	$ 10,000
Current assets	$ 15,000
Average stockholders' equity	$ 70,000
Cost of goods sold	$ 75,000
Total liabilities	$ 25,000
Preferred dividends paid	$ 1,000
Net sales	$100,000
Current liabilities	$ 6,000
Average inventory	$ 10,000
Total assets	$100,000
Ending market price per common share	$ 24
Average common shares outstanding	3,000 shares

The company uses a 365-day business year.

REQUIRED Based on the preceding information determine the following ratios for the Tomor Export Company:

1. Earnings per share
2. Price/earnings
3. Profit margin
4. Return on stockholders' equity
5. Current
6. Inventory turnover (in days)
7. Debt

EXERCISE 19-12 **Ratio Analysis.** The following are six ratios partially completed for the Yarby Company (assume a 40% income tax rate):

$$\text{Acid Test } \frac{(a)}{\$14,000} = 1.5$$

$$\text{Accounts Receivable Turnover } \frac{\$68,000}{(b)} = 8.5 \text{ times}$$

$$\text{Times Interest Earned } \frac{\$18,000}{(c)} = 10 \text{ times}$$

$$\text{Dividend Yield } \frac{(d)}{\$18.00} = 7\frac{1}{2}\%$$

$$\text{Return on Total Assets } \frac{(e) + (\$2,000 \times 0.6)}{\$100,000} = 12\%$$

$$\text{Book Value per Common Share } \frac{\$74,250}{(f)} = \$14.85 \text{ per common share}$$

REQUIRED Determine the names and correct amounts for the blanks lettered (a) through (f). All the necessary information is provided.

Problems

Part A

PROBLEM 19-1A **Segment Reporting.** The Doxy Diversified Company has total assets of $115,000 at the end of 1991 and the following condensed income statement for 1991:

DOXY DIVERSIFIED COMPANY
Income Statement
For Year Ended December 31, 1991

Sales	$80,000
Operating expenses	(57,600)
Income before income taxes	$22,400
Income tax expense (40%)	(8,960)
Net Income	$13,440

The company has two reportable industry segments, A and B, and has developed the following information to prepare its segmental reporting schedule:

		Segments		
	A	*B*	*Other*	*Totals*
Sales	$51,360	$14,360	$14,280	$ 80,000
Operating expenses	36,780	10,400	10,420	57,600
Identifiable assets	70,320	22,720	21,960	115,000

REQUIRED 1. Based on the preceding information prepare a schedule that reports on the 1991 revenues, operating profits, and identifiable assets of Segments A and B and the other segments of the Doxy Diversified Company.

2. Compute the profit margin *before* income taxes for Segments A and B, and for the other segments. What do these ratio results reveal?

PROBLEM 19-2A **Segment Reporting.** The Slotter Conglomerate Company does business in several different industries. The following is a 1991 condensed income statement for the entire company:

SLOTTER CONGLOMERATE COMPANY
Income Statement
For Year Ended December 31, 1991

Sales		$150,000
Operating expenses		
Cost of goods sold	$70,000	
Selling expenses	15,000	
General and administrative expenses	30,000	(115,000)
Income before income taxes		$35,000
Income tax expense (40%)		(14,000)
Net Income		$ 21,000

Slotter has two reportable industry segments, X and Y. No other segment contributes 10% or more of the company's activities. As of December 31, 1991, the company had assets totaling $500,000. The sales, expenses, and assets are assigned to segment activities according to the following percentages:

	Percent Identified with		
	Segment X	Segment Y	Other Segments
Sales	41%	44%	15%
Cost of goods sold	38	48	14
Selling expenses	39	42	19
General and administrative expenses	35	40	25
Identifiable assets	30	50	20

REQUIRED

1. Prepare a schedule that reports the Slotter Conglomerate Company's industry segment financial information for the year ended December 31, 1991.

2. Compute the *pretax* return on ending *identifiable* assets for Segments X and Y, and for the other segments. What do these ratio results reveal?

PROBLEM 19-3A   **Interim Income Statement.**   The Campbell Tire Company prepares quarterly and year-to-date interim reports. The following is its interim income statement for the quarter ended March 31, 1991:

CAMPBELL TIRE COMPANY
Income Statement
For First Quarter Ended March 31, 1991

Sales (net)		$80,000
Cost of goods sold		(44,000)
Gross profit		$36,000
Operating expenses		
Selling expenses	$11,500	
General expenses	10,800	(22,300)
Operating income		$13,700
Other revenues and expenses		
Interest revenue	$ 300	
Interest expense	(500)	(200)
Income before income taxes		$13,500
Income tax expense		(5,400)
Net Income		$ 8,100
Earnings per share (10,000 shares)		$ .81

On June 30, 1991, the company accountant completed a year-to-date adjusted trial balance to prepare the year-to-date (i.e., 6-month) interim income statement. The following are selected accounts and amounts listed in the debit and credit columns of this adjusted trial balance:

	Debits	Credits
Sales (net)		175,000
Interest revenue		650
Cost of goods sold	94,000	
Selling expenses	24,000	
General expenses	20,000	
Interest expense	1,050	
Income tax expense	14,640	

The company uses a perpetual inventory system. In addition, 10,000 shares of common stock have been outstanding for the entire 6 months.

REQUIRED Based on the preceding information for the Campbell Tire Company, prepare:

1. A year-to-date interim income statement for the first 6 months of 1991.

2. An interim income statement for the second quarter of 1991.

PROBLEM 19-4A **Interim Reporting.** The Ziegler Medical Equipment Supply Corporation presented the following interim income statement for the first quarter of 1991:

ZIEGLER MEDICAL EQUIPMENT SUPPLY CORPORATION
Income Statement
For First Quarter Ended March 31, 1991

Sales (net)		$320,000
Cost of goods sold		
Inventory (1-1-1991)	$ 38,400	
Purchases (net)	192,000	
Cost of goods available for sale	$230,400	
Less: Inventory (3-31-1991, estimated)	(54,400)	
Cost of goods sold		(176,000)
Gross profit		$144,000
Operating expenses		
Selling expenses	$ 52,000	
General and administrative expenses	32,000	
Total operating expenses		(84,000)
Income before income taxes		$ 60,000
Income tax expense		(24,000)
Net income		$ 36,000
Earnings per share (12,000 shares)		$3.00

On June 30, 1991, the accounting department prepared the following adjusted trial balance:

Account Titles	Debits	Credits
Cash	$ 54,400	
Accounts receivable	32,300	
Notes receivable (due 12-31-1991)	16,000	
Inventory (1-1-1991)	38,400	
Property and equipment	100,000	
Accumulated depreciation		$ 22,500
Accounts payable		16,000

Common stock, no par		56,000
Retained earnings		22,600
Sales (net)		600,000
Purchases (net)	320,000	
Selling expenses	97,500	
General and administrative expenses	58,500	
Interest receivable	1,000	
Interest revenue		1,000
Income tax expense	46,000	
Income taxes payable		46,000
Totals	$764,100	$764,100

The company uses the gross profit method to estimate its interim inventory. Historical gross profit has averaged 45% of net sales. No common stock has been issued or retired in 1991.

REQUIRED

1. Prepare interim income statements for the periods April 1–June 30, 1991, and January 1–June 30, 1991.

2. Prepare a June 30, 1991, interim balance sheet (report form).

3. For both the first quarter (January 1–March 31, 1991) and the second quarter (April 1–June 30, 1991) compute the following ratios: (a) earnings per share, (b) inventory turnover, and (c) profit margin. What do your ratio results reveal?

PROBLEM 19-5A   **Horizontal Analysis and Ratios.**   The Shulz Industrial Clothing Company presents the following comparative income statements for 1991 and 1992:

SHULZ INDUSTRIAL CLOTHING COMPANY Comparative Income Statements		
	For Years Ended December 31,	
	1992	*1991*
Sales (net)	$100,000	$85,000
Cost of goods sold	(55,000)	(45,000)
Gross profit	$ 45,000	$40,000
Selling expenses	(12,000)	(10,000)
General expenses	(8,000)	(8,000)
Operating income	$ 25,000	$22,000
Interest revenue	500	200
Interest expense	(1,000)	(500)
Income before income taxes	$ 24,500	$21,700
Income tax expense	(9,800)	(8,680)
Net Income	$ 14,700	$13,020
Average number of common shares	6,000	5,000

Additional Information:

1. There were no shares of preferred stock outstanding in 1991 or 1992.

2. As of December 31, 1992, the company's common stock had a market price of $12.50 per share. The market price on December 31, 1991, was $15.00 per share.

3. Dividends in the amount of $6,000 and $7,500 were paid to common stockholders in 1992 and 1991, respectively.

| REQUIRED | 1. Prepare a horizontal analysis for the Shulz Industrial Clothing Company for 1991 and 1992. |

2. Compute the following ratios for the company for 1991 and 1992:
   (a) Earnings per share
   (b) Price/earnings
   (c) Profit margin
   (d) Dividend yield
   (e) Times interest earned

3. Briefly discuss any important changes in operating results revealed by your horizontal and ratio analyses.

PROBLEM 19-6A   **Vertical Analysis and Ratios.** The Koeppen Company operates a high-volume retail outlet. The following are comparative financial statements for the company for 1991 and 1992.

KOEPPEN COMPANY
Comparative Income Statements

For Years Ended December 31,

	1992	1991
Sales	$180,000	$150,000
Cost of goods sold	(108,000)	(85,500)
Gross profit	$ 72,000	$ 64,500
Operating expenses	(44,600)	(37,300)
Income before income taxes	$ 27,400	$ 27,200
Income tax expense (40%)	(10,960)	(10,880)
Net Income	$ 16,440	$ 16,320
Earnings per share (6,000 shares)	$2.74	$2.72

KOEPPEN COMPANY
Comparative Balance Sheets

December 31,

	1992	1991
Cash	$ 4,200	$ 3,000
Marketable securities (short-term)	2,000	2,100
Accounts receivable (net)	8,600	6,400
Inventory	11,300	9,700
Noncurrent assets (net)	129,900	118,800
Total Assets	$156,000	$140,000
Current liabilities	$ 13,000	$ 12,400
Long-term liabilities (10%)	40,000	35,000
Total Liabilities	$ 53,000	$ 47,400
Common stock, $3 par	$ 18,000	$ 18,000
Additional paid-in capital	30,000	30,000
Retained earnings	55,000	44,600
Total Stockholders' Equity	$103,000	$ 92,600
Total Liabilities and Stockholders' Equity	$156,000	$140,000

Additional Information:

1. At the beginning of 1991 the company had outstanding accounts receivable (net) of $7,600.

2. On January 1, 1991, the inventory totaled $10,100.

3. The beginning balance of stockholders' equity for 1991 was $85,400.

4. Sixty percent of the company's sales were on credit.

REQUIRED

1. Prepare vertical analyses of the Koeppen Company income statements and balance sheets for 1991 and 1992.

2. Compute the following ratios for 1991 and 1992:
   (a) Current
   (b) Inventory turnover (in days, assuming a 365-day business year)
   (c) Accounts receivable turnover (in days, assuming a 365-day business year)
   (d) Return on stockholders' equity

3. Briefly discuss any important changes revealed by your vertical and ratio analyses.

PROBLEM 19-7A   **Ratios.**   The Lobe Insulation Company presents the following condensed income statement for 1991 and condensed December 31, 1991, balance sheet.

LOBE INSULATION COMPANY
Income Statement
For Year Ended December 31, 1991

Sales (net)		$400,500
Less: Cost of goods sold	$240,000	
Operating expenses	88,950	
Interest expense	11,550	
Income taxes	24,000	
Total expenses		(364,500)
Net Income		$ 36,000

LOBE INSULATION COMPANY
Balance Sheet
December 31, 1991

Cash	$ 7,500
Marketable securities (short-term)	15,000
Accounts receivable (net)	23,000
Inventory	86,500
Long-term investments	45,000
Property and equipment (net)	423,000
Total Assets	$600,000
Current liabilities	$ 60,000
Bonds payable, 7%	190,000
Common stock, $10 par	200,000
Additional paid-in capital	67,500
Retained earnings	82,500
Total Liabilities and Stockholders' Equity	$600,000

Additional Information:

1. Common stock was outstanding the entire year and dividends of $1.20 per share were declared and paid in 1991. The common stock is selling for $19 per share on December 31, 1991.
2. Credit sales for the year totaled $260,325.
3. Average net accounts receivable for the year were $26,500.
4. Average stockholders' equity for the year was $343,000.
5. The company operates on a 365-day business year.

REQUIRED On the basis of the preceding information compute the following ratios for the Lobe Insulation Company:

1. Earnings per share
2. Dividend yield
3. Return on stockholders' equity
4. Current
5. Acid-test
6. Accounts receivable turnover (in days)
7. Times interest earned
8. Book value per common share

On the basis of applicable "rules of thumb," what information is revealed by the acid-test ratio for the company that is not disclosed by its current ratio?

Problems

Part B

PROBLEM 19-1B **Segment Reporting.** Steinoff Industries has total assets of $171,000 at the end of 1991 and the following condensed income statement for 1991:

STEINOFF INDUSTRIES Income Statement For Year Ended December 31, 1991	
Sales	$125,000
Operating expenses	(86,400)
Income before income taxes	$ 38,600
Income tax expense (40%)	(15,440)
Net Income	$ 23,160

The company has two reportable industry segments, Q and R, and has developed the following information in preparing its segmental reporting schedule:

	Segments			
	Q	R	Other	Totals
Sales	$ 79,560	$30,400	$15,040	$125,000
Operating expenses	55,170	20,800	10,430	86,400
Identifiable assets	110,000	33,000	28,000	171,000

REQUIRED   *1.* On the basis of the preceding information prepare a schedule that reports on the 1991 revenues, operating profits, and identifiable assets of Segments Q and R, and the other segments of Steinoff Industries.

2. Compute the *pretax* return on ending *identifiable* assets for Segments Q and R, and for the other segments. What do these ratio results reveal?

PROBLEM 19-2B   **Segment Reporting.** The Walters Company does business in several different industries. The following is a 1991 condensed income statement for the entire company:

WALTERS COMPANY Income Statement For Year Ended December 31, 1991		
Sales		$75,000
Cost of goods sold		(35,000)
Gross profit		$40,000
Selling expenses	$ 7,500	
General and administrative expenses	15,000	(22,500)
Income before income taxes		$17,500
Income tax expense		(7,000)
Net Income		$10,500

Walters has two reportable industry segments, 1 and 2. No other segment contributes 10% or more of the company's activities. As of December 31, 1991, the company had assets totaling $285,000. The sales, expenses, and assets are assigned to the segments according to the following percentages:

	Percent Identified with		
	Segment 1	*Segment 2*	*Other Segments*
Sales	48%	35%	17%
Cost of goods sold	44	38	18
Selling expenses	45	40	15
General and administrative expenses	42	40	18
Identifiable assets	52	38	10

REQUIRED   *1.* Prepare a schedule that reports the Walters Company's industry segment financial information for the year ended December 31, 1991.

2. Compute the profit margin *before* income taxes for Segments 1 and 2, and for the other segments. What do these ratio results reveal?

PROBLEM 19-3B   **Interim Income Statement.** The Doley Adhesives Corporation showed the following income statement for the first 6 months of 1991:

DOLEY ADHESIVES CORPORATION
Income Statements

	Jan. 1–June 30, 1991		Percent Applicable to Jan. 1–Mar. 31, 1991
Sales (net)		$28,000	40%
Cost of goods sold			
Inventory (beginning)	$ 5,000		—
Purchases (net)	15,000		35
Cost of goods available for sale	$20,000		
Less: Ending inventory (estimated) .	(5,100)[a]		—
Cost of goods sold		(14,900)	
Gross profit		$13,100	
Operating expenses			
Selling expenses	$ 3,100		42
General and administrative			
expenses	3,250		46
Total operating expenses		(6,350)	
Operating income		$ 6,750	
Other revenues			
Interest revenue		100	50
Income before income taxes		$ 6,850	
Income tax expense		(2,740)[b]	
Net Income		$ 4,110	

[a]The estimated ending inventory on March 31, 1991, was $4,597.
[b]Assume a 40% tax rate for the first and second quarters.

REQUIRED   Prepare an income statement for the second quarter of 1991. Assume that 1,000 shares of common stock have been outstanding for the entire 6 months.

PROBLEM 19-4B   **Interim Reporting.** The Renax Burglar Alarm Company prepared the following interim income statement for the first quarter of 1991:

RENAX BURGLAR ALARM COMPANY
Income Statement
For First Quarter Ended March 31, 1991

Sales (net)		$480,000
Cost of goods sold		
Inventory (1-1-1991)	$ 57,600	
Purchases (net)	288,000	
Cost of goods available for sale	$345,600	
Less: Inventory (3-31-1991, estimated)	(76,800)	
Cost of goods sold		(268,800)
Gross profit		$211,200
Operating expenses		
Selling expenses	$ 78,000	
General and administrative expenses	48,000	
Total operating expenses		(126,000)
Income before income taxes		$ 85,200
Income tax expense		(34,080)
Net income		$ 51,120
Earnings per share (22,000 shares)		$2.32

The accounting department prepared the following adjusted trial balance on June 30, 1991, the end of the second quarter:

Account Titles	Debits	Credits
Cash	$ 77,600	
Accounts receivable	48,450	
Notes receivable (due 12-31-1991)	24,000	
Inventory (1-1-1991)	57,600	
Property and equipment	150,000	
Accumulated depreciation		$ 33,750
Accounts payable		24,000
Common stock, no par		84,000
Retained earnings		33,900
Sales (net)		920,000
Purchases (net)	500,000	
Selling expenses	148,500	
General and administrative expenses	89,500	
Interest receivable	600	
Interest revenue		600
Income tax expense	66,960	
Income taxes payable		66,960
Totals	$1,163,210	$1,163,210

No common stock has been issued or retired in 1991. The company uses the gross profit method to estimate its interim inventory. Historical gross profit has averaged 44% of net sales.

REQUIRED

1. Prepare interim income statements for the periods April 1–June 30, 1991, and January 1–June 30, 1991.

2. Prepare a June 30, 1991, interim balance sheet (account form).

3. For both the first quarter (January 1–March 31, 1991) and the second quarter (April 1–June 30, 1991) compute the following ratios: (a) earnings per share, (b) inventory turnover, and (c) profit margin. What do your ratio results reveal?

PROBLEM 19-5B **Horizontal Analysis and Ratios.** Howale Corporation presented the following comparative income statements for 1991 and 1992.

HOWALE CORPORATION Comparative Income Statements		
	For Years Ended December 31,	
	1992	1991
Sales (net)	$250,000	$262,000
Cost of goods sold	(150,000)	(129,400)
Gross profit	$100,000	$132,600
Selling expenses	(28,000)	(25,500)
General expenses	(23,500)	(21,000)
Operating income	$ 48,500	$ 86,100
Interest revenue	500	400
Interest expense	(1,500)	(500)
Income before income taxes	$ 47,500	$ 86,000
Income tax expense	(19,000)	(34,400)
Net Income	$ 28,500	$ 51,600
Average number of common shares	16,000	15,000

Additional Information:

1. Dividends in the amounts of $20,000 and $53,000 were paid to common stockholders in 1992 and 1991, respectively.

2. There were no preferred shares outstanding in either year.

3. As of December 31, 1992, the company's stock had a market price of $14.00 per share. On December 31, 1991, the stock had a market price of $29.50 per share.

REQUIRED
1. Prepare a horizontal analysis for the Howale Corporation for 1991 and 1992.

2. Compute the following ratios for the company for 1991 and 1992:
   (a) Earnings per share   (c) Profit margin
   (b) Price/earnings   (d) Dividend yield

3. Briefly discuss any important changes in operating results revealed by your horizontal and ratio analyses.

PROBLEM 19-6B   **Vertical Analysis and Ratios.**   The Tuscumber Draperies Company presented the following comparative financial statements for 1991 and 1992.

TUSCUMBER DRAPERIES COMPANY
Comparative Income Statements

For Years Ended December 31,

	1992	1991
Sales	$200,000	$185,000
Cost of goods sold	(120,000)	(124,000)
Gross profit	$ 80,000	$ 61,000
Operating expenses	(52,400)	(38,800)
Income before income taxes	$ 27,600	$ 22,200
Income tax expense (40%)	(11,040)	(8,880)
Net Income	$ 16,560	$ 13,320
Earnings per share (6,000 shares)	$2.76	$2.22

TUSCUMBER DRAPERIES COMPANY
Comparative Balance Sheets

December 31,

	1992	1991
Cash	$ 12,000	$ 10,500
Marketable securities (short-term)	8,000	8,400
Accounts receivable (net)	10,400	12,000
Inventory	17,600	14,300
Noncurrent assets (net)	106,000	104,800
Total Assets	$154,000	$150,000
Current liabilities	$ 25,100	$ 34,700
Long-term liabilities (12%)	52,300	47,300
Total Liabilities	$ 77,400	$ 82,000
Common stock, $3 par	$ 18,000	$ 18,000
Additional paid-in capital	20,000	20,000
Retained earnings	38,600	30,000
Total Stockholders' Equity	$ 76,600	$ 68,000
Total Liabilities and Stockholders' Equity	$154,000	$150,000

Additional Information:

1. At the beginning of 1991 the company had outstanding accounts receivable (net) of $11,600.

2. On January 1, 1991, the inventory totaled $18,000.

3. The beginning balance of stockholders' equity for 1991 was $64,000.

4. Seventy percent of the company's sales were on credit.

REQUIRED

1. Prepare vertical analyses of the Tuscumber Draperies Company income statements and balance sheets for 1991 and 1992.

2. Compute the following ratios for 1991 and 1992:
   (a) Current
   (b) Inventory turnover (in days, assuming a 300-day business year)
   (c) Accounts receivable turnover (in days, assuming a 300-day business year)
   (d) Return on stockholders' equity.

3. Briefly discuss any important changes revealed by your vertical and ratio analyses.

PROBLEM 19-7B   **Ratios.**   The following is a condensed income statement for 1991 and a December 31, 1991, balance sheet for the Mea Company:

MEA COMPANY
Income Statement
For Year Ended December 31, 1991

Sales (net)	$152,200
Cost of goods sold	(91,300)
Gross profit	$ 60,900
Operating expenses	(40,100)
Interest expense	(2,800)
Income before income taxes	$ 18,000
Income taxes	(7,200)
Net Income	$ 10,800

MEA COMPANY
Balance Sheet
December 31, 1991

Cash	$ 3,000
Marketable securities (short-term)	2,100
Accounts receivable (net)	6,350
Inventory	9,650
Property and equipment (net)	97,900
Total Assets	$119,000
Current liabilities	$ 12,400
Bonds payable, 8%	35,000
Common stock, $10 par	40,000
Additional paid-in capital	12,250
Retained earnings	19,350
Total Liabilities and Stockholders' Equity	$119,000

Additional Information:

1. The common stock was outstanding the entire year and is selling for $23 per share at year end.

2. On January 1, 1991, the inventory was $10,950, the total assets were $110,000, and the total stockholders' equity was $62,600.

3. The company operates on a 300-day business year and is subject to a 40% income tax rate.

REQUIRED   Compute the following ratios for the Mea Company:

1. Price/earnings

2. Profit margin

3. Return on total assets

4. Return on stockholders' equity

5. Current

6. Inventory turnover (in days)

7. Debt

Is the company favorably "trading on its equity"? Explain.

Decision Cases

DECISION CASE 19-1   **Financial Analysis and Interpretation.**   Review the financial statements and related financial information of the Black & Decker Corporation in Appendix A at the end of the textbook.

REQUIRED   Answer the following questions. (*Note:* You do not need to make any calculations. All answers can be found in Appendix A.) Indicate on what page of the annual report you located the answer.

1. When is the end of the corporation's fiscal year for 1988?

2. What were the net sales for the year ended September 25, 1988? September 27, 1987? What was the primary cause of the sales growth from 1987 to 1988? By what percent did sales grow in Europe for 1988?

3. What was the total amount of inventories on September 25, 1988? What were the components and related amounts of these inventories on this date? How was the cost determined for inventories in the United States? For all other inventories?

4. What was the increase in cash and cash equivalents for the year ended September 25, 1988? How much of this was due to the issuance of common stock? How much was spent on capital expenditures during 1988? 1987? Why were capital expenditures abnormally low in 1987?

5. What were the (a) earnings before income taxes and extraordinary items and (b) net earnings for the year ended September 25, 1988? By what percents did these two items increase from 1987 to 1988?

6. What was the book value of property, plant and equipment on September 25, 1988? What were the components and related amounts of property, plant and

equipment on this date? How is depreciation computed for financial reporting purposes?

7. What was the cash flow from operating activities for the year ended September 25, 1988? What was the adjustment of net earnings for (a) depreciation and amortization and (b) inventories in the statement of cash flows for the year ended September 25, 1988?

8. What was the cost of products sold for the year ended September 25, 1988? What was the gross margin as a percentage of sales for 1988? How did this compare to 1987 and 1986? What was the primary reason for the improvement?

9. What were the current liabilities on September 25, 1988? How much of this amount was for short-term borrowings? What were the components and related amounts of these short-term borrowings?

10. What was the cash flow from financing activities for the year ended September 25, 1988? How much of this related to proceeds from borrowings? To payments of cash dividends?

11. How many shares of common stock were outstanding on September 25, 1988? What was the par value per share and in total on this date? What were the cash dividends per share during 1988?

12. What was the (a) current ratio, (b) net sales to average total assets, and (c) percent return on average stockholders' equity for 1988?

DECISION CASE 19-2   **Intra- and Intercompany Comparisons.**   A classmate of yours asks, "What is the difference between 'intra' and 'inter' company comparisons? I always thought they meant the same thing because they sound so much alike. Now I'm not so sure. And what information is compared? It seems to me that if each company presents annual financial statements, surely this is enough information for comparison. But now I am told that segment reports, interim financial reports, and horizontal, vertical, and ratio analyses are used for comparisons. What are these analyses anyway? It seems like a lot of extra work to prepare them when the only information investors and creditors are interested in is a company's annual earnings and its financial position at the end of the year."

REQUIRED   Write a brief report to your friend: (1) explaining the differences between intracompany and intercompany comparisons; (2) describing segment reports, interim financial reports, and horizontal, vertical, and ratio analyses; and (3) discussing how the analyses in Requirement 2 are useful for the comparisons in Requirement 1.

DECISION CASE 19-3   **Ratios Provided in Annual Reports.**   Monsanto is a large integrated company. The following data are taken directly from the "financial summary" included in its 1988 annual report.

	1988	1987	1986
Profit margin	7%	6%	6%
Return on shareholders' equity	15%	11%	12%
Earnings per share	$8.27	$5.63	$5.55
Current ratio	1.6	1.7	1.6
Debt/equity ratio	34%	35%	35%
Price/earnings ratio	10	15	14
Book value per share	$55.21	$52.65	$48.69

REQUIRED   1. Evaluate the performance of Monsanto across the three years using the ratio categories discussed in the chapter: (a) stockholder profitability, (b) company profitability, (c) liquidity, (d) activity, and (e) stability.

2. Indicate what additional ratios not provided by Monsanto would be helpful in evaluating performance in each of these categories.

DECISION CASE 19-4   **Segment and Interim Reporting.**   Review the notes to the financial statements of the Black & Decker Corporation that are shown in Appendix A at the end of the textbook.

REQUIRED   Answer the following questions. (*Note:* You do not need to make any calculations. All answers can be found in Appendix A.) Indicate on what page of the annual report you located the answer.

1. What is the one business segment within which Black & Decker operates?

2. What were the sales to unaffiliated customers in the United States for 1988?

3. Where are the subsidiaries included in the Europe operations of the corporation located? What was the operating income of the Europe operations for 1988?

4. Where are the subsidiaries included in the Other operations of the corporation located? What were the identifiable assets of the Other operations for 1988?

5. What were the net sales for the first quarter of 1988? 1987?

6. What were the net earnings (and EPS) for the second quarter of 1988? 1987?

7. What was the gross margin for the fourth quarter of 1988? 1987?

20

Accounting for Changing Prices and International Operations

LEARNING OBJECTIVES

1. Explain the alternative measures of income when prices change.

2. Distinguish between a specific price change and a general price change.

3. Prepare comprehensively adjusted constant purchasing power financial statements.

4. Compute the purchasing power gain or loss on net monetary items.

5. Prepare comprehensively adjusted current cost financial statements.

6. Explain the methods of computing current cost.

7. Evaluate the advantages and disadvantages of the alternative methods.

8. List the discretionary disclosures on the effects of changing prices.

9. Describe an exchange rate.

10. Explain how foreign currency transactions result in the recognition of exchange gains and losses.

11. Define the functional currency.

12. Distinguish between translation and remeasurement.

13. Convert the financial statements of a foreign subsidiary into U.S. dollars.

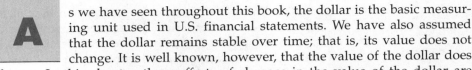

As we have seen throughout this book, the dollar is the basic measuring unit used in U.S. financial statements. We have also assumed that the dollar remains stable over time; that is, its value does not change. It is well known, however, that the value of the dollar does change. In this chapter, three effects of changes in the value of the dollar are explained. One is the change in the overall value of the dollar caused by inflation. The second is the change in the specific prices of individual goods and services. The third is the change in the value of the dollar with respect to foreign currencies.

Furthermore when transactions are expressed in foreign currencies or a company owns a foreign subsidiary, the foreign currency amounts must be converted into U.S. dollars to be included in the company's financial statements. These topics are also discussed in this chapter.

Alternative Measures of Income
When Prices Change

Suppose that a company purchased land at the beginning of 1991 for $50,000. A year later, after there has been inflation of 10%, the land is sold for $65,000. What is the profit on the sale of the land? There are three different answers depending on how profit is measured. Before we discuss the three alternatives, however, we should have a clear understanding of what is meant by the term *profit* or *income*.

A common definition of income in economics is that **income is the amount that could be paid to the owners of the company during a period of time and still enable the company to be as well off at the end of the period as it was at the beginning.** The issue, therefore, is the measurement of the wealth (i.e., how well off is the company) at the beginning and the end of the period.

One answer to the earlier question is that the profit is $15,000 ($65,000 − $50,000). This is the answer if profit is measured according to the generally accepted accounting principles discussed in this book. In this case profit is being measured as the difference between the dollars received from the sale and the historical dollars used to acquire the item being sold. The wealth at the beginning of the period is measured as the *nominal* dollars used to acquire the land, and therefore the profit of $15,000 is the increase in the nominal dollars during the period. **Nominal dollars are dollars that have not been adjusted to reflect changes in prices.** Nominal dollars are used in the historical cost financial statements that have been discussed throughout this book because they are the basis for generally accepted accounting principles.

A second answer is that the profit is $10,000. This is the answer if the wealth at the beginning of the period is measured in terms of the purchasing power at the end of the period of the dollars that were originally used to buy the land. **Purchasing power is the measure of the ability of dollars to purchase goods and services.** Because the land cost $50,000 and there has been inflation of 10% since the purchase, the $50,000 historical dollars have the same value, or purchasing power, as $55,000 ($50,000 × 1.10) at the end of the period. Therefore the purchasing power of the owner of the land has increased by $10,000 ($65,000 −

1. Explain the alternative measures of income when prices change.

$55,000). This is the measure of profit when the wealth at the beginning of the period is measured in terms of the purchasing power of the dollars at the end of the period, or more generally, when profit is measured in terms of constant purchasing power. **Constant purchasing power amounts (constant dollars) are historical (nominal) dollars that have been adjusted for changes in the general purchasing power.**

A third answer is that the profit is zero. If it is accepted that the owner of the land needs to replace it with land of equivalent capacity (e.g., same size and location), there is no profit because the $65,000 obtained from the sale is needed to replace the land. A similar piece of land of the same size and location would, of course, cost $65,000 and therefore there is no profit. This is the measure of profit when the wealth at the beginning of the period is measured in terms of the current cost of the item being sold. **Current cost is the amount that would have to be paid at a certain point in time (e.g., the current period) to purchase an identical, or similar, item.**

Companies may prepare certain constant purchasing power or current cost information for both internal decision making and external reporting. Before discussing this information, it is useful to examine additional characteristics of these two alternative methods of measurement.

The Nature of Price Changes

As all of us are aware the price of virtually everything that is bought and sold changes each year. In recent times most of the price changes have been increases rather than decreases. It can easily be seen, however, that price changes vary with the type of item. For instance, some prices rise much faster than others. However, the prices of energy and housing have tended to fluctuate, whereas the prices of computers and calculators have tended to fall.

A price change is either a specific price change or a general price change. **A specific price change is the measure of the change in the price of a *particular* good or service.** Examples are the price changes in such items as a gallon of unleaded gas or a pound of lean hamburger. Current cost accounting is based upon changes in specific prices. **A general price change is the weighted average of the changes in the individual prices of a *group* of goods and services.** This measure of the change in prices indicates the general inflation rate and therefore the change in the purchasing power of the dollar. **A general price-level index is a measure of general price changes over a period of time stated as an index rather than in dollar amounts.** Constant purchasing power accounting is based on changes in the general price level as measured by a general price-level index.

2. Distinguish between a specific price change and a general price change.

To illustrate the difference between the two concepts of price changes further, consider a general price-level (GPL) index made up of four individual items. To simplify the illustration we are including only four items, whereas the available indexes (discussed later) include thousands of items. The items are included in the index by using amounts that reflect average buying patterns. For example, if the average household buys 40 pounds of hamburger per year, the price of 40 pounds of hamburger will be included when the index is computed. The price per unit of each of the four items and the average amounts purchased per year are used to compute the average total price as follows:

Item	Price per Unit in 1991	Average Amounts Purchased	Average Total Price in 1991
A	$ 2.00	40 units	$ 80
B	5.00	30	150
C	10.00	20	200
D	40.00	10	400
Total			$830

In 1992 the prices of the individual items and the average amounts purchased are used to compute the average total price as follows:

Item	Price per Unit in 1992	Average Amounts Purchased	Average Total Price in 1992
A	$ 3.00	40 units	$120
B	6.00	30	180
C	12.00	20	240
D	40.00	10	400
Total			$940

The change in prices between 1991 and 1992 may be summarized as follows:

Item	Percent Change in Prices	Calculations
A	50%	($3 – $2) ÷ $2 = 0.50
B	20	($6 – $5) ÷ $5 = 0.20
C	20	($12 – $10) ÷ $10 = 0.20
D	0	($40 – $40) ÷ $40 = 0
Overall	13.25%	($940 – $830) ÷ $830 = 0.1325

The prices of individual items, that is, the specific prices, have increased in the range from zero (Item D) to 50% (Item A), whereas the general price change indicates an average increase of 13.25% [($940 — $830) ÷ $830].

Although this is a very simple measure of the change in the general price level, it is possible to use it to develop a general price-level index. If the price of the items in 1991 is assigned an index number of 100, the general price level in 1992 has an index of 113.25:

$$\text{GPL index in 1992} = \frac{\text{Average total price in 1992}}{\text{Average total price in 1991}} \times \text{Index in 1991}$$

$$= \frac{\$940}{\$830} \times 100$$

$$= 113.25$$

To illustrate the index concept further, suppose that in 1993 the average total price for the four items is $1,020. The index in 1993 would be:

$$\text{GPL index in 1993} = \frac{\text{Average total price in 1993}}{\text{Average total price in 1991}} \times \text{Index in 1991}$$

$$= \frac{\$1,020}{\$830} \times 100$$

$$= 122.89$$

Alternatively, the index in 1993 could be calculated as follows:

$$\text{GPL index in 1993} = \frac{\text{Average total price in 1993}}{\text{Average total price in 1992}} \times \text{Index in 1992}$$

$$= \frac{\$1,020}{\$940} \times 113.25$$

$$= 122.89$$

A *specific* price-level index of a particular item can be developed in the same way as the general price-level index, based on a comparison of the specific prices of an individual item in each year. For example, the price of Item A has risen from $2.00 in 1991 to $3.00 in 1992. If the price of $2.00 in 1991 is assigned an index number of 100, the specific price-level index for Item A in 1992 is 150 [($3.00 ÷ $2.00) × 100].

Available Price-Level Indexes

Numerous price-level indexes are developed by various groups and are publicly available. The largest developer of price-level indexes is the federal government, which publishes over 2,700 different indexes. Most of them are specific price-level indexes, although many of them measure the change in the general price level. Of the latter type, there are three indexes that are widely publicized—the Wholesale Price Index, the Gross National Product Implicit Price Deflator, and the Consumer Price Index. The Consumer Price Index is prepared for various types of consumers. **The Consumer Price Index for All Urban Consumers (CPI-U) was used for the constant purchasing power supplementary disclosures that are discussed later in the chapter.** We use the CPI-U as the general price-level index throughout this chapter.

Comprehensively Restated Financial Statements

In the first section of this chapter the basic principles underlying the historical cost, constant purchasing power, and current cost methods of accounting were discussed. A company is required to use the historical cost method to prepare its financial statements. However, a company may prepare a complete set of constant purchasing power or current cost financial statements for use in its internal decision making or for supplementary disclosures in its annual report. To illustrate these three alternatives further, consider the following example of a series of simplified events for a corporation. In this example we use a corporation because the companies that make disclosures of the effects of changing prices are likely to be corporations. Some of the situations and amounts discussed are very simple so that the reader can more easily focus on the concepts and not be distracted by complex arithmetic. A more complex example is included as a review problem at the end of the chapter. A study of that problem will assist in the solution of homework problems.

1. The Triad Company was formed by selling no-par common stock for $100 when the CPI-U index was 100.

2. The company purchased a building for $30 with a 2-year life and no residual value when the CPI-U index was 100.

3. The company purchased three units of inventory for $10, $12, and $14 each when the CPI-U index was 100, 110, and 120 respectively.

4. The company sold two units of inventory for $30 each when the CPI-U index was 110. A FIFO cost flow assumption is used.

5. The average CPI-U index for the year was 110.

6. The current cost at year end was $14 for the inventory and $40 for the building. The CPI-U index at year end was 120.

7. Income taxes are disregarded.

Historical Cost Financial Statements

The income statement and ending balance sheet prepared under the three alternatives are presented in Exhibits 20-1 and 20-2. In Exhibit 20-1 the historical cost

EXHIBIT 20-1
Income Statement

TRIAD COMPANY
Income Statement
For Current Year

	Historical Cost	Constant Purchasing Power	Current Cost
Sales revenue	$60[a]	$60.00[d]	$60.00[g]
Cost of goods sold	(22)[b]	(23.00)[e]	(24.00)[h]
Depreciation expense	(15)[c]	(16.50)[f]	(17.50)[i]
Net Income	$23	$20.50	$18.50

[a] 2 units × $30.
[b] Since a FIFO cost flow assumption is used, the cost of the first two units ($10 + $12) is included in the cost of goods sold.
[c] (Cost − Residual value) ÷ Life = ($30 − $0) ÷ 2.
[d] It is assumed that the sales were made at the average general price level for the year, or $60 × $\frac{110}{110}$ = $60.

[e] $\left(\$10 \times \frac{110}{100}\right) + \left(\$12 \times \frac{110}{110}\right) = \$23.$

[f] $\$15 \times \frac{110}{100}.$

[g] The sales revenue does not require adjusting.

[h] Average current cost × Number of units sold = $\frac{\$14 + \$10}{2} \times 2.$

[i] (Average current cost − Residual value) ÷ Life = $\left(\frac{\$40 + \$30}{2} - \$0\right) \div 2.$

EXHIBIT 20-2
Ending Balance Sheet

TRIAD COMPANY
Balance Sheet
At End of Current Year

	Historical Cost	Constant Purchasing Power	Current Cost
Cash	$ 94[a]	$ 86.17[d]	$ 94[a]
Inventory	14[b]	12.83[e]	14[j]
Building	30	33.00[f]	40[k]
Less: Accumulated depreciation	(15)	(16.50)[g]	(20)[l]
Total Assets	$123	$115.50	$128
Common stock, no par	$100	$110.00[h]	$100
Retained earnings[c]	23	5.50[i]	28[m]
Total Liabilities and Stockholders' Equity	$123	$115.50	$128

[a]$100 (sale of common stock) − $30 (building) − $36 (inventory) + $60 (sales).
[b]Since a FIFO cost flow assumption is used, the cost of the last unit purchased is included in inventory.
[c]Since the beginning retained earnings is assumed to be zero and no dividends are paid, the retained earnings in the ending balance sheet is equal to the results of the calculations in footnotes i and m.
[d]$94 × (110 ÷ 120).
[e]$14 × (110 ÷ 120).
[f]$30 × (110 ÷ 100).
[g]$15 × (110 ÷ 100).
[h]$100 × (110 ÷ 100).
[i]Net income ($20.50) − Purchasing power loss ($15.00).
[j]1 unit × Ending current cost of $14.
[k]Current cost at year end.
[l](Current cost − Residual value) ÷ Life = ($40 − $0) ÷ 2 = $20.
[m]Net income ($18.50) + Holding gains ($9.50).

(or nominal dollar) net income is $23 because sales are $60, the cost of goods sold on a FIFO basis is $22, and the depreciation expense, computed on a straight-line basis, is $15. In Exhibit 20-2 the total assets, measured on a historical cost (nominal dollar) basis, are $123, consisting of cash of $94, inventory of $14, and the building with a book value of $15. In this simple example there are no liabilities. Common stock is $100 and the retained earnings are equal to the net income of the period because there were no beginning retained earnings or dividends paid during the year. The remaining items in the exhibits expressed in constant purchasing power and current costs are discussed in the next section.

Constant Purchasing Power Financial Statements

The underlying principle of constant purchasing power financial statements is to adjust historical costs into dollars of constant purchasing power. The general formula for this adjustment is:

3. Prepare comprehensively adjusted constant purchasing power financial statements.

$$\text{Constant purchasing power} = \text{Historical cost} \times \frac{\text{General price-level index in current period}}{\text{General price-level index at time of historical cost transaction}}$$

For example, in the illustration used at the beginning of the chapter the land was purchased for $50,000 and there was inflation of 10%, which is equivalent to a general price-level index increasing from, for example, 150 to 165 ($150 \times 1.10 = 165$). Therefore the cost of the land in constant purchasing power is measured by:

$$\text{Constant purchasing power cost of land} = \$50,000 \times \frac{165}{150}$$

$$= \$55,000$$

This approach has been used to calculate the constant purchasing power amount of the sales, cost of goods sold, depreciation expense, cash, inventory, building, accumulated depreciation, and common stock for the Triad Company. The amount in the retained earnings account is calculated differently, as is discussed later. In this example the price-level index in the current period that is used for the numerator of the general price-level calculation is the *average* index for the current period, or 110. The average index is used because the financial statements report on the activities of the company for the year. The computations of the constant purchasing power income statement items in Exhibit 20-1 are discussed next.

Sales. The sales were made when the CPI-U index was 110 and therefore do not need adjusting. Alternatively, the formula for the adjustment could be used as follows:

$$\$60 \times \frac{110}{110} = \$60 \text{ Sales}$$

Cost of Goods Sold. Under the FIFO cost flow assumption the cost of goods sold included units with historical costs of $10 and $12, which were purchased when the CPI-U index was 100 and 110, respectively. The cost of goods sold is adjusted as follows:

$$\left(\$10 \times \frac{110}{100}\right) + \left(\$12 \times \frac{110}{110}\right) = \$23 \text{ Cost of goods sold}$$

Note that if the average cost flow assumption had been used, the average historical cost per unit would be $12 [($10 + $12 + $14) ÷ 3] and the cost of goods sold on a historical cost basis would be $24 (2 units × $12). It would be typical to assume that the cost of goods sold on an average cost basis was measured in terms of the average price level for the year and therefore would not need adjusting. The constant purchasing power cost of goods sold would be $24 [$24 × (110 ÷ 110)].

Depreciation Expense. For historical cost depreciation expense the original cost of the asset is depreciated over its expected life (2 years in this example), and therefore depreciation expense is measured in terms of the historical dollars at the time of acquisition of the asset and not in a constant purchasing power amount. Thus the historical cost depreciation of $15 is measured in terms of a CPI-U index of 100 and needs to be adjusted as follows:

$$\$15 \times \frac{110}{100} = \$16.50 \text{ Depreciation expense}$$

Other expenses included in the income statement (such as selling expenses, general and administrative expenses, and income tax expense) are typically assumed to occur at the average price level for the year and therefore do not need adjusting. The computations of the constant purchasing power balance sheet items in Exhibit 20-2 are discussed next.

Cash.   The cash in the historical cost balance sheet is measured in terms of the CPI-U index at that time, which is the year-end index of 120. Therefore the cash needs to be adjusted to the average price level of the year as follows:

$$\$94 \times \frac{110}{120} = \$86.17 \text{ Cash}$$

Other "monetary" assets (defined later), such as accounts receivable, would be adjusted to the average price level by using the same adjustment factor.

Inventory.   Under the FIFO cost flow assumption the unit in the ending inventory cost \$14; it was purchased when the index was 120 and is adjusted as follows:

$$\$14 \times \frac{110}{120} = \$12.83 \text{ Inventory}$$

Building and Accumulated Depreciation.   The building was purchased for \$30 and accumulated depreciation of \$15 has been recorded. Since both of these amounts are measured in terms of the CPI-U index of 100, they have to be adjusted as follows:

$$\$30 \times \frac{110}{100} = \$33.00 \text{ Building}$$

$$(\$15) \times \frac{110}{100} = (\$16.50) \text{ Accumulated depreciation}$$

Liabilities.   The Triad Company has no "monetary" liabilities (defined later), but if it did these monetary liabilities would be adjusted in the same way as cash. That is, they are included in the historical cost balance sheet at the price level of the end of the year, and they must be adjusted to the average price level.

Common Stock.   The common stock was sold when the CPI-U index was 100 and therefore is adjusted as follows:

$$\$100 \times \frac{110}{100} = \$110 \text{ Common stock}$$

Purchasing Power Gain or Loss on Net Monetary Items.   During a period of inflation, holding cash results in a loss of purchasing power. For example, \$10 cash when hamburger is \$2 per pound enables you to buy 5 pounds of hamburger. When the price of hamburger rises to \$2.50 per pound, \$10 will buy only 4 pounds of hamburger. Therefore holding the \$10 cash during the period of inflation has resulted in the loss of purchasing power of 1 pound of hamburger. This loss is 25% of the purchasing power needed to buy 4 pounds of hamburger at the end of the period (1 pound ÷ 4 pounds = 0.25). This loss can also be measured as 25% of the cash held or \$2.50 (\$10 × 0.25 = \$2.50). This result also can be obtained

4. Compute the purchasing power gain or loss on net monetary items.

by noting that at the end of the period it takes $12.50 (or an increase of 25%) to buy 5 pounds of hamburger. More generally, *the purchasing power of cash declines as inflation in the prices of all goods and services occurs.* When constant purchasing power financial statements are prepared this loss of general purchasing power must be recognized.

Cash is only one monetary asset. There are several monetary assets (and liabilities) that a company can own (or owe). **A monetary asset is money or a claim to receive a fixed amount of money in the future.** The principal monetary assets are cash, accounts receivable, and notes receivable. Holding monetary *assets* during a period of inflation results in a purchasing power *loss*. **A monetary liability is an obligation to repay a fixed amount of money in the future.** The principal monetary liabilities include accounts payable, notes payable, and bonds payable. Holding a monetary *liability* during a period of inflation results in a purchasing power *gain* because inflation reduces the purchasing power of the dollars needed to repay these liabilities. The reduction in the purchasing power owed results in a purchasing power gain. **Net monetary items are monetary assets less monetary liabilities.** The purchasing power gain or loss is the combined gain or loss in purchasing power that occurs when net monetary items are held during a period in which the general price level changes. The computation of the purchasing power gain or loss is made more complex because the net monetary items are changed during the period by some of a company's transactions.

In the Triad Company example cash is the only monetary item. The cash balance has decreased from $100 to $94 during the period. The company has incurred a purchasing power loss that is computed as follows. First, all the cash transactions are adjusted to the constant purchasing power represented by the average CPI-U index of 110 as shown here:

	Historical Cost		Adjustment		Constant Purchasing Power
Beginning net monetary items	$100	×	$\frac{110}{100}$	=	$110.00
Sales	60	×	$\frac{110}{110}$	=	60.00
Purchase of building	(30)	×	$\frac{110}{100}$	=	(33.00)
Purchases of inventory	(10)	×	$\frac{110}{100}$	=	(11.00)
	(12)	×	$\frac{110}{110}$	=	(12.00)
	(14)	×	$\frac{110}{120}$	=	(12.83)
Ending Net Monetary Items	$ 94				$101.17

The historical beginning net monetary items (cash) of $100 are measured in beginning-of-the-year purchasing power (CPI-U = 100), whereas the constant purchasing power amount is measured in average purchasing power (CPI-U = 110). Therefore the beginning balance of $100 must be adjusted to the average purchasing power of the period (i.e., constant purchasing power amount) by multiplying times an adjustment factor of 110/100. The sales during the year caused an increase in net monetary items while the payments for the purchases of the building and inventory caused a decrease in net monetary items. Each is adjusted from the general price level at the time the cash was received or paid to the average purchasing power of the period by multiplying times the appropriate adjustment factor. The ending net monetary items at historical cost and at constant purchasing power are computed by adding or subtracting the inflows or outflows.

The historical ending net monetary items of $94 are measured in year-end purchasing power (CPI-U = 120), whereas the constant purchasing power amount of $101.17 is measured in average purchasing power (CPI-U = 110). To complete the computation of the purchasing power loss, the historical ending balance of $94 must be adjusted to the average purchasing power of the period. The purchasing power loss (measured in terms of the average purchasing power of the period) is computed by comparing the constant purchasing power ending balance to the adjusted historical ending balance as shown here:

Constant purchasing power ending balance	$101.17
Historical ending balance adjusted to average price level $\left(\$94 \times \dfrac{110}{120}\right)$ ...	(86.17)
Purchasing Power Loss (at average price level)	$ 15.00

The constant purchasing power ending balance of $101.17 is the average purchasing power that the company's cash balance *should have had*. Since the ending cash balance of $94 had only an average purchasing power of $86.17, there has been a purchasing power loss of $15. If the company had held net monetary liabilities instead of net monetary assets, there would have been a purchasing power gain. Usually all of these computations are shown on a single schedule entitled *schedule to compute purchasing power gain or loss*.

If the company had held monetary liabilities and monetary assets other than cash, the beginning net monetary items (monetary assets less monetary liabilities) would be computed in a separate schedule. This amount would be included as the beginning balance and adjusted to the constant purchasing power amount. The changes in the net monetary items during the period would be recorded in the same way as shown in the preceding example and also adjusted to the constant purchasing power amount. The resulting ending balance of net monetary items in the *historical cost* column would be adjusted to the constant purchasing power amount and subtracted from the ending balance of the *constant purchasing power* column to determine the purchasing power gain or loss.

There is disagreement among users of financial statements about whether the purchasing power gain or loss should be included in the computation of constant purchasing power net income. In this example the loss has been *excluded* from net income but has been *deducted* from retained earnings.

Retained Earnings.   Since there was no beginning balance of retained earnings and no dividends were paid, the amount in the balance sheet ($5.50) is the net income for the period ($20.50) less the purchasing power loss ($15.00). Examples of adjustments to additional items not included in the preceding example are included in the review problem at the end of the chapter.

Current Cost Financial Statements

The current cost financial statements include the current cost of each item. The current cost of an item is the amount it would cost to acquire the item at a certain point in time. Because the income statement is a report on the performance of the company for an entire period, *average* current costs for the period are used in the income statement. The balance sheet, in contrast, is a report of the financial position at year end, and therefore *year-end* current costs are used in the balance sheet. The computations of the current cost income statement items in Exhibit 20-1 are discussed next.

5. Prepare comprehensively adjusted current cost financial statements.

Sales. Sales are typically not adjusted because it is assumed that they are made at the average prices for the period.

Cost of Goods Sold. Cost of goods sold is computed by multiplying the number of units sold by the average current cost for the period. In this example two units are sold during the period, and they are included in the income statement at the average current cost for the period, which is based on the beginning ($10) and ending ($14) current costs for the period. The computation of the $24 cost of goods sold is as follows:

$$\text{Cost of goods sold} = \text{Units sold} \times \text{Average current cost per unit}$$
$$= 2 \times \frac{\$10 + \$14}{2}$$
$$= \$24$$

Depreciation Expense. The depreciation expense is based on the average current cost of the building as follows:

$$\text{Depreciation expense} = \frac{\text{Average current cost} - \text{Residual value}}{\text{Life}}$$
$$= \frac{\left(\dfrac{\$30 + \$40}{2}\right) - \$0}{2}$$
$$= \$17.50$$

Other expenses typically included in the income statement (such as selling expenses, general and administrative expenses, and income tax expense) are assumed to occur at the average cost for the year and therefore do not need adjusting. The computations of the current cost balance sheet items in Exhibit 20-2 are discussed next.

Cash. Cash does not need adjustment because it is already stated in terms of its value at the end of the year. Similarly, all other monetary assets and monetary liabilities are not adjusted.

Inventory. The inventory in the balance sheet is valued at the current cost of the units in the inventory at year end. In our example the ending inventory of $14 is computed as follows:

$$\begin{aligned}
\text{Ending inventory} &= \text{Number of units} \times \text{Ending current cost} \\
&= 1 \times \$14 \\
&= \$14
\end{aligned}$$

Building and Accumulated Depreciation.   The building is valued at the current cost at year end ($40) less accumulated depreciation based on this year-end value. Since the life of the building is half over, the accumulated depreciation is half the current cost:

$$\text{Building} \quad = \$40$$

$$\begin{aligned}
\genfrac{}{}{0pt}{}{\text{Accumulated}}{\text{depreciation}} &= \left(\genfrac{}{}{0pt}{}{\text{Current cost at the}}{\text{end of the period}} - \genfrac{}{}{0pt}{}{\text{Residual}}{\text{value}}\right) \times \frac{\text{Number of years owned}}{\text{Life}} \\
&= (\$40 - \$0) \times \frac{1}{2} \\
&= \$20
\end{aligned}$$

Common Stock.   The common stock is not adjusted because there is no reliable measure of the amount for which all the common stock outstanding could be sold in the current period.

Holding Gains and Losses.   When current cost financial statements are being prepared holding gains and losses arise. **A holding gain (loss) is the increase (decrease) in the current cost of a nonmonetary asset during the period.** Holding gains (losses) may be realized or unrealized. **A realized holding gain (loss) is a gain (loss) that has been recognized on an item that has been included in the historical cost income statement.** On the other hand, **an unrealized holding gain (loss) is a gain (loss) on an item that has not yet been recognized in the historical cost income statement.** In general, the realized and unrealized holding gains (losses) are measured as follows:

$$\text{Realized holding gain (loss)} = \text{Current cost expense} - \text{Historical cost expense}$$
$$\text{Unrealized holding gain (loss)} = \text{Current cost asset value} - \text{Historical cost asset value}$$

In the Triad Company example holding gains arise on the inventory and the building. Therefore the realized and unrealized holding gains are calculated as follows:

$$\begin{aligned}
\genfrac{}{}{0pt}{}{\text{Realized holding gain}}{\text{(inventory)}} &= \genfrac{}{}{0pt}{}{\text{Current cost of the}}{\text{cost of goods sold}} - \genfrac{}{}{0pt}{}{\text{Historical cost of}}{\text{the cost of goods sold}} \\
&= \$24 - \$22 \\
&= \$2
\end{aligned}$$

$$\begin{aligned}
\genfrac{}{}{0pt}{}{\text{Realized holding gain}}{\text{(building)}} &= \genfrac{}{}{0pt}{}{\text{Current cost}}{\text{depreciation expense}} - \genfrac{}{}{0pt}{}{\text{Historical cost}}{\text{depreciation expense}} \\
&= \$17.50 - \$15.00 \\
&= \$2.50
\end{aligned}$$

$$\begin{aligned}
\genfrac{}{}{0pt}{}{\text{Unrealized holding gain}}{\text{(inventory)}} &= \genfrac{}{}{0pt}{}{\text{Current cost of}}{\text{inventory}} - \genfrac{}{}{0pt}{}{\text{Historical cost of}}{\text{inventory}} \\
&= \$14 - \$14 \\
&= \$0
\end{aligned}$$

$$\begin{aligned}
\genfrac{}{}{0pt}{}{\text{Unrealized holding gain}}{\text{(building)}} &= \genfrac{}{}{0pt}{}{\text{Net current cost}}{\text{of building}} - \genfrac{}{}{0pt}{}{\text{Net historical cost}}{\text{of building}} \\
&= (\$40 - \$20) - (\$30 - \$15) \\
&= \$5
\end{aligned}$$

The total holding gains are $9.50 ($2 + $2.50 + $0 + $5). There is disagreement among users of financial statements about whether holding gains and losses should be included in income. In this example the holding gains are *excluded* from income, but they are *added* to retained earnings. No matter how holding gains and losses are included in financial statements it is important to recognize the nature of these gains. They result simply from the rise in price of the respective assets, and they do not increase the wealth of the company if it is agreed that the assets will have to be replaced at the higher cost. It is difficult to argue that the company is better off because it will have to replace assets at the higher cost.

Retained Earnings. Since there is no beginning balance of retained earnings and no dividends were paid, the amount in the balance sheet is the net income for the period ($18.50) plus the holding gain ($9.50), or $28. Examples of the adjustments to additional items not included in the preceding example are included in the review problem at the end of the chapter.

Methods of Computing Current Cost

6. Explain the methods of computing current cost.

As we have seen in the previous examples, the method of computing the constant purchasing power amounts is clearly defined because the CPI-U index was used, and this index is prepared by the federal government.

The method of computing the current cost supplementary disclosures, in contrast, is much less well defined. There are three basic methods of finding the current cost of inventory and property, plant, and equipment.[1]

Direct Pricing

The current cost of the asset is determined directly by using the most recent invoice price, a supplier's price list or other quotations or estimates, or by using standard manufacturing costs. This is an appropriate measurement technique for assets that are frequently purchased or manufactured or that have an established market price, such as inventory and office equipment.

Functional or Unit Pricing

The current cost is calculated by estimating the construction (or acquisition) cost per unit (such as per square foot of building space) and multiplying this figure by the number of units in the asset. For example, if a company owns a building with 5,000 square feet and current construction costs are $100 per square foot, the current cost of the building would be $500,000.

Specific Price Index

The current cost is calculated by adjusting the historical cost by a specific price index appropriate to the asset. Since the federal government publishes more

---

[1]"Financial Reporting and Changing Prices," *FASB Statement No. 33* (Stamford, Conn.: FASB, 1979), par. 60.

than 2,700 price indexes, it should be possible to find an index that is appropriate for each particular asset, or component of an asset. The adjustment process is the same as that used for a general price index:

$$\text{Current cost} = \text{Historical cost} \times \frac{\text{Specific price index in current period}}{\text{Specific price index at time of historical cost transaction}}$$

The second two methods are more likely to be appropriate for property, plant, and equipment. Since any of the methods may be used for any asset, however, and the second two methods do not necessarily result in accurate measures of current cost, there is likely to be much variation in the current cost figures developed by companies. This potential variation is one of the major criticisms of any supplementary current cost disclosures.

Exit Values

The three alternative measurement methods that have been discussed in this chapter use *entry*, or input, values. An historical cost is, of course, the cost measured at the time of the acquisition of an asset. A constant purchasing power amount is an adjusted historical cost amount. A current cost is the amount that would have to be paid to purchase the asset. In contrast, some users of financial statements argue that it would be more appropriate to use exit values. **An exit value is the net cash amount that a company would receive if it sold an asset.** An exit value is often referred to as the *net realizable value* because it is the net amount received from the sale after deducting costs associated with the sale, such as transportation costs and sales commissions. The basic argument in favor of the use of exit values is that the company will have to dispose of each asset at some point in the future and therefore the current measure of the cash to be received from such sales is relevant to users of financial statements.

Many people argue that the use of exit values would not provide relevant information, however. Consider two examples. If a company used an exit value for its inventory, it would record that inventory at its selling price (less costs of disposal) before any sales transaction occurred and therefore would recognize income simply by acquiring inventory. Second, suppose that a company acquired a specialized machine for use in its activities. If the machine has no value to another company, its value would immediately be recorded as zero and its entire purchase price expensed in the period of acquisition.

Evaluation of the Alternative Methods

As has been explained in this chapter the three input methods are based on different concepts. The historical cost method is based on nominal dollars, the constant purchasing power method is based on dollars of the same purchasing power, and the current cost method is based on productive capacity. Since the methods are alternatives, and *not* substitutes, for each other it is impossible to state that one is the best. The user of the information needs to understand the meaning of the information presented under each alternative and therefore decide which method yields the most useful information for any particular purpose.

The historical cost method has the advantage of being the most reliable and widely understood method. It is also the most conservative in terms of the balance sheet valuations, but as we have seen, it does not necessarily produce the most conservative, or lowest, measure of income during periods of inflation. It is difficult to see that it best satisfies the needs of users of financial statements, however. The user only knows that there has been a net inflow of nominal dollars (assuming the company has a positive net income) and that the company's capital measured in nominal dollars has increased. The user has no assurance that the purchasing power of the company's capital is being maintained or that the company can continue to operate at the same capacity level.

Ensuring that the company maintains the purchasing power of its capital would probably be considered desirable by most stockholders. They contributed a certain number of dollars to the company when they invested in it, and are probably more concerned about the purchasing power of those dollars than about the number of dollars originally contributed. Constant purchasing power income statements ensure that the purchasing power of the capital is maintained before income is earned.

In addition, the usefulness of the constant purchasing power balance sheet is increased in two ways. First, the values of all the items in the balance sheet are reported in terms of dollars of constant purchasing power. Thus the amounts can be meaningfully compared. In contrast, the historical cost balance sheet includes costs incurred at many different times, and therefore these costs are very difficult, if not impossible, to compare. For example, the purchasing power of the cash, which is measured in current period dollars, cannot be compared with the purchasing power of the dollars invested in the land, which was purchased in a previous period and is therefore measured in dollars of that period. Second, the comparability of historical cost balance sheets over time is very limited for the same reasons. For example, a valid comparison between a 1987 and a 1991 balance sheet cannot be made because each includes costs of very different purchasing powers. When both balance sheets are converted to 1991 constant dollars, a meaningful comparison can be made.

A company needs specific assets to conduct its operations, and it is possible that the company could be maintaining the general purchasing power of its capital but not its ability to replace these assets. This situation would arise when the costs of the particular assets that the company is using rise faster than the general price level. Use of the current cost concept ensures that the operating capacity of the company is maintained before income is earned. In addition, the current value of the assets reported in the balance sheet represents the value of these assets at that particular balance sheet date, which many users of financial statements consider to be more relevant than a report of the number of nominal dollars that the asset originally cost.

When the three alternatives are compared many users of financial state-

7. Evaluate the advantages and disadvantages of the alternative methods.

ments argue that the current cost method of preparing financial statements is conceptually the most desirable, and therefore it is much more relevant. It must be recognized that the amounts may be less reliable than those produced under the historical cost or constant dollar methods, but it is very difficult to evaluate a tradeoff between relevance and reliability.

Discretionary Supplementary Disclosures

The earlier illustration of the preparation of comprehensive constant dollar and current cost financial statements was based on very simple historical cost financial statements. In practice, however, financial statements are much more complex. Although they may voluntarily do so, no companies are required to prepare *comprehensively* adjusted financial statements. Selected companies (beginning in 1979), however, were required to make certain supplementary disclosures of the effects of changing prices.[2] The original disclosures were simplified in 1984.[3] In 1986, the *requirement* for the disclosures was suspended and companies were instead *encouraged* to make them.[4] These discretionary disclosures include selected information for the current year as well as for 5 years, as follows.

The selected disclosures for the current year are:

8. List the discretionary disclosures on the effects of changing prices.

1. Income from continuing operations based on current cost.
2. Purchasing power gain or loss on net monetary items (excluded from income from continuing operations).
3. Current cost amounts of inventory and of property, plant, and equipment at the end of the current year.
4. Increase or decrease in the current cost amounts of inventory and of property, plant, and equipment, before and after eliminating the effects of inflation (excluded from income from continuing operations).

The selected disclosures included in a 5-year summary are:

1. Net sales and other operating revenues.
2. Income from continuing operations (and related earnings per share) based on current cost.
3. Net assets at year end based on current cost.
4. Increase or decrease in the current cost amounts of inventory and of property, plant, and equipment, after eliminating the effects of inflation.
5. Purchasing power gain or loss on net monetary items.

---

[2]*Ibid.*

[3]"Financial Reporting and Changing Prices: Elimination of Certain Disclosures," *FASB Statement No. 82* (Stamford, Conn.: FASB, 1984).

[4]"Financial Reporting and Changing Prices," *FASB Statement of Financial Accounting Standards No. 89* (Stamford, Conn.: FASB, 1986).

6. Cash dividends declared per common share.

7. Market price per common share at year end.

The methods of computing this information are beyond the scope of this book.

Over the seven years that the selected information was required to be disclosed, there was significant controversy about the usefulness of the disclosures. The FASB considered the arguments in favor of, and against, the disclosures before deciding to make them voluntary rather than mandatory. The arguments in favor of eliminating the required disclosures were as follows:

1. The disclosures were not widely used because of concerns about the relevance and reliability of the information.

2. The costs of preparing the information exceeded the benefits obtained.

3. The disclosures lacked comparability.

4. The disclosures were difficult to understand.

5. Users of financial statements had developed their own methods of adjusting for the effects of changing prices.

6. The significance of the disclosures had decreased because prices were changing much less than in previous years.

The arguments in favor of continuing the required disclosures were as follows:

1. The alternative measures of income are conceptually more logical.

2. Seven years is an insufficient time to assess the usefulness of the information.

3. Suspension of the disclosures would encourage companies to remove the systems used to develop the information.

4. Demand for the disclosures will increase when inflation rates increase at some time in the future.

Whether the FASB made the correct decision is still disputed by many users of financial statements. However, the passage of time may (or may not) provide a better perspective on the decision.

Accounting for International Operations

As U.S. companies expand their operations, they frequently become involved in transactions with customers and suppliers in other countries. For example, a U.S. company may decide that it can purchase inventory at a lower cost or acquire machinery that is more efficient from a company based in a foreign country. Or, a U.S. company may decide to expand its revenue opportunities by selling its products in foreign countries. In each of these situations, the accounting for the transaction by the U.S. company is complicated by the need to record the transaction in U.S. dollars while the price may be expressed in terms of a foreign currency. Furthermore as a U.S. company expands its operations in a foreign country it often sets up (or buys) a foreign subsidiary company, whose financial statements must be consolidated into the U.S. parent company's financial statements, as discussed in the previous section. These types of transactions and events are becoming more common; therefore a basic understanding of international accounting issues is important for students entering today's business world.

Two situations concerning international accounting issues are discussed in the following sections: (1) accounting for the kinds of foreign currency transactions just described and (2) procedures for converting a foreign subsidiary's financial statements (expressed in terms of a foreign currency) into U.S. dollars.

Before we discuss these two situations, it is important to understand the meaning of exchange rates. **An exchange rate measures the value of one currency in terms of another currency.** Unfortunately, some exchange rates are commonly expressed in U.S. dollars whereas others are expressed in terms of the number of foreign units that are equal to the U.S. dollar. To illustrate, recently the British pound was quoted at a rate of $1.80. This rate means that it would take $1.80 to buy 1 British pound; that is, the pound is a larger unit than the U.S. dollar. In contrast, the West German mark was recently quoted at a rate of 1.75 marks to the U.S. dollar. This rate means that it would take 1.75 marks to buy 1 dollar; that is, the mark is a smaller unit than the dollar. To avoid confusion, in this book we will always quote exchange rates in terms of the number of U.S. dollars that is equivalent to 1 unit of the foreign currency. Therefore regarding the British pound and the West German mark, we will use exchange rates of $1.80 for the pound and $0.57 (1 ÷ 1.75) for the mark. The general rule is that a foreign currency is converted into U.S. dollars as follows:

Amount in   = Foreign currency × Exchange rate
U.S. dollars   amount   (stated in dollars)

Some recent exchange rates are illustrated in Exhibit 20-3.

Since an exchange rate represents the price of one currency in terms of another, rates change continuously as supply and demand for currencies change. These changes are often described by terms such as strong (rising) and weak (falling). To illustrate, consider the exchange rate for the pound of $1.80 in Exhibit 20-3. If the dollar is weakening against the pound, the price (exchange rate) of the pound rises when stated in terms of the dollar. For example, a change in the rate to $1.90 would be a weakening of the dollar because it now takes more dollars to buy 1 pound. Saying that the dollar is weakening is the same as saying that the pound is strengthening.

9. Describe an exchange rate.

EXHIBIT 20-3
Selected Foreign Exchange Rates

Country (currency)	Price in U.S. Dollars
Britain (pound)	$1.80
Canada (dollar)	0.83
France (franc)	0.17
Israel (shekel)	0.625
Japan (yen)	0.008
Mexico (peso)	0.00043
Saudi Arabia (riyal)	0.27
Switzerland (franc)	0.67
West Germany (mark)	0.57
Source: The *Wall Street Journal* (December 27, 1988).	

Foreign Currency Transactions

As explained earlier, many U.S. companies conduct transactions with customers and suppliers in foreign countries. Sometimes the transaction is expressed in U.S. dollars. For example, most purchases and sales of crude oil are expressed in terms of the U.S. dollar. In these situations, there is no accounting issue; the transaction is recorded just as we have discussed in the previous chapters of this book. For example, if a U.S. oil company purchases 10,000 barrels of crude oil from Saudi Arabia, the price would be quoted in dollars and not in the equivalent amount of riyals. If the price is $18 per barrel, the company would record a purchase of inventory and the related payment of $180,000 ($18 × 10,000).

In many situations, however, the transaction is expressed in terms of the foreign currency. In these cases the transaction must be recorded by the company in U.S. dollars. Therefore the foreign currency amount must be converted into dollars at the exchange rate on the day of the transaction. For example, suppose a U.S. company purchases inventory of electronic components from a Japanese company for 50 million yen (Y) when the exchange rate is $0.008 (1 yen = $0.008). Assume that the U.S. company pays cash on the same day. The transaction is recorded by the U.S. company as follows (assuming the company uses a perpetual inventory system):

Inventory (Y50,000,000 × $0.008)	400,000	
Cash		400,000

To record the purchase of merchandise.

More often, transactions between companies in different countries involve credit terms, if only to allow time for the processing of the orders and payment across international borders. In addition, currency exchange rates change continuously. As a result, the exchange rate is likely to have changed between the date the U.S. company records, say, a purchase transaction and the date it makes the payment. On the date of payment, then, the company must record an exchange gain or loss to account for the difference between the purchase price and the amount of the payment. **An exchange gain or loss is caused by a change in the exchange rate between the date a payable is incurred or a receivable is acquired and the date of the payment or receipt.** More specifically, exchange gains and losses occur for purchases or sales on account as follows:

10. Explain how foreign currency transactions result in the recognition of exchange gains and losses.

1. An exchange *gain* occurs when the exchange rate *declines* between the date a *payable* is incurred and the date of the cash *payment*.

2. An exchange *gain* occurs when the exchange rate *increases* between the date a *receivable* is acquired and the date of the cash *receipt*.

3. An exchange *loss* occurs when the exchange rate *increases* between the date a *payable* is incurred and the date of the cash *payment*.

4. An exchange *loss* occurs when the exchange rate *declines* between the date a *receivable* is acquired and the date of the cash *receipt*.

To illustrate an exchange gain that occurs when the exchange rate declines between the date a credit purchase is recorded and the date of the cash payment, suppose that in the preceding example the U.S. company made the purchase of the electronic components on account. Because the inventory was purchased when the exchange rate was $0.008, the acquisition is recorded as follows:

```
Inventory  ............................................................  400,000
     Accounts Payable  ...............................................            400,000
```
To record the purchase of merchandise on account.

The Japanese company has a right to receive 50 million yen, and the U.S. company is obligated to pay sufficient dollars that will convert to 50 million yen on the date that the payment is made. Now assume that the exchange rate on the date of payment is $0.0078 (1 yen = $0.0078). In this case, since only $0.0078 now buys 1 yen, the U.S. company will have to pay fewer dollars to buy 50 million yen. That is, the yen has become less expensive. More specifically, the U.S. company has to pay only $390,000 (Y50,000,000 × $0.0078). Therefore the company has incurred an exchange *gain* of $10,000 ($400,000 – $390,000), which it records at the time of payment as follows:

```
Accounts Payable (Y50,000,000 × $0.008)  .........................  400,000
     Cash (Y50,000,000 × $0.0078)  ...................................            390,000
     Exchange Gain ($400,000 – $390,000)  ...........................             10,000
```
To record payment on account and exchange gain.

The exchange gain occurs because the U.S. company has to pay only $390,000 to settle its debt originally recorded at $400,000. The gain can also be computed by multiplying the amount owed by the change in the exchange rate [Y50,000,000 × ($0.008 – $0.0078) = $10,000]. Remember that the Japanese company still receives 50 million yen; it is the U.S. company that has the exchange gain.

To illustrate an exchange loss that occurs when the exchange rate declines between the date a credit sale is recorded and the date of the cash receipt, suppose that a U.S. company sells computer equipment to a West German company on account and agrees to a price of 300,000 marks (DM) rather than a price in dollars. On the date of the sale, the exchange rate is $0.57 (1 mark = $0.57), and therefore the U.S. company records the sale as follows:

```
Accounts Receivable (DM300,000 × $0.57)  .........................  171,000
     Sales Revenue  ......................................................            171,000
```
To record the sale of merchandise on account.

The West German company has an obligation to pay 300,000 marks regardless of the exchange rate on the date of payment. If the exchange rate is $0.55 when it pays the amount owed, the U.S. company can convert those marks into only $165,000 (DM300,000 × $0.55). As a result, it has incurred an exchange *loss* of $6,000 ($165,000 – $171,000), which it records at the time of the cash collection as follows:

```
Cash (DM300,000 × $0.55)  .............................................  165,000
Exchange Loss ($165,000 – $171,000)  .............................    6,000
     Accounts Receivable (DM300,000 × $0.57)  .....................            171,000
```
To record collection of cash on account and exchange loss.

The exchange loss can also be computed by multiplying the amount receivable by the change in the exchange rate [DM300,000 × ($0.57 – $0.55) = $6,000]. For financial reporting purposes, the amounts of the Exchange Loss and the Exchange Gain would typically be combined in one account, entitled Exchange Gains and Losses. The net amount of the Exchange Gains and Losses would be reported in the Other Revenues and Expenses section of the income statement.

This amount is included in the income statement because the exchange gains and losses were caused by fluctuations in the exchange rates that resulted in increased or decreased dollar cash flows during the accounting period.

Note that the U.S. company experienced exchange gains and losses in the preceding situations because it agreed to transactions expressed in terms of foreign currencies. In such situations, the U.S. company accepts the risks associated with exchange rate changes. When the transactions are expressed in U.S. dollars, the foreign company accepts, and the U.S. company avoids, the risks associated with exchange rate changes.

Conversion of the Financial Statements of a Foreign Subsidiary into U.S. Dollars

11. Define the functional currency.

As explained earlier, many U.S. companies establish or purchase foreign companies. If a foreign subsidiary is controlled by a U.S. parent company, the subsidiary company's financial statements must be included in the consolidated financial statements of the U.S. parent company (as discussed in Chapter 17). The subsidiary company's financial statements must be prepared according to U.S. generally accepted accounting principles before consolidation occurs. Since we are assuming that the foreign subsidiary's financial statements are prepared in foreign currency amounts, they must be converted into U.S. dollars for consolidation.

Before we can explain the process of converting the foreign currency amounts into U.S. dollars, we must distinguish between the reporting currency and the functional currency of the subsidiary. **The reporting currency is the currency that a company uses for its financial statements.** Thus a U.S. parent company uses the dollar as its reporting currency. Generally, however, a foreign subsidiary of the U.S. parent company uses the foreign currency as its reporting currency. **The functional currency is the currency of the location in which a company primarily operates.**[5] Normally it is the currency in which the company primarily receives and pays cash. Thus a U.S. parent company uses the dollar as its functional currency. For a foreign subsidiary, the functional currency is the *same* as the reporting currency (i.e., the *foreign currency*) when the subsidiary's operations are relatively self-contained; that is, when the foreign subsidiary primarily receives and pays foreign currency. In contrast, the functional currency of a foreign subsidiary is the *U.S. dollar* when the subsidiary's operations are directly related to, or an extension of, the parent company (e.g., a branch office); that is, when the subsidiary primarily receives and pays U.S. dollars. Note, however, that even though the functional currency of a foreign subsidiary may be the U.S. dollar, the subsidiary's financial statements may still be expressed in a foreign currency. The decision to use a particular reporting currency is made by management for the convenience of the operation of its accounting system. In contrast, the decision regarding the functional currency is determined by generally accepted accounting principles.[6]

The definition of the functional currency of the foreign subsidiary is impor-

---

[5]If a foreign country has a "highly inflationary economy" (defined as cumulative inflation of approximately 100% or more over a 3-year period), the functional currency is defined to be the U.S. dollar.

[6]"Foreign Currency Translation," *FASB Statement No. 52* (Stamford, Conn.: FASB, 1981).

12. Distinguish between translation and remeasurement.

tant because it determines the method used to convert the reporting currency of the foreign subsidiary into U.S. dollars. **If a foreign currency is used for both the reporting currency and the functional currency of the foreign subsidiary, the financial statements of the foreign subsidiary are** *translated* **into U.S. dollars.** After translation into U.S. dollars, the financial statements of the foreign subsidiary are combined with those of the U.S. parent company into consolidated financial statements. Assets and liabilities of the foreign subsidiary are translated using the *current* exchange rate at the date of the consolidated balance sheet. The common stock is translated at the appropriate historical rate at the time the stock was issued. The retained earnings is computed in the normal way as the sum of the beginning balance plus the translated amount of the net income less the translated amount of the dividends distributed. Each is eliminated during the consolidation process. The translation of the asset and liability amounts from the foreign currency into U.S. dollars results in *translation adjustments.* The amount of the translation adjustments is included directly in the stockholders' equity section of the consolidated balance sheet. Revenues, expenses, gains, and losses of the foreign subsidiary are translated at the *average* exchange rate for the period of the consolidated income statement.

If a foreign subsidiary's reporting currency is a foreign currency but its functional currency is the U.S. dollar, the subsidiary's financial statements are *remeasured* **into U.S. dollars.** (Note the use of the term *"remeasured"* instead of *"translated"* which is used when the functional currency is a foreign currency.) After the remeasurement into U.S. dollars, the financial statements of the foreign subsidiary are combined with those of the U.S. parent company into consolidated financial statements. In this case, the *monetary assets* and *monetary liabilities* of the foreign subsidiary are remeasured at the *current* exchange rate at the date of the consolidated balance sheet. A monetary asset is money or a claim to receive a fixed amount of money in the future. The principal monetary assets include cash, accounts receivable, and notes receivable. A monetary liability is an obligation to repay a fixed amount of money in the future. The principal monetary liabilities include accounts payable, notes payable, and bonds payable. Monetary assets and liabilities were discussed in greater detail earlier in the chapter.

Nonmonetary assets and *nonmonetary liabilities* of the foreign subsidiary are remeasured at the *historical* exchange rate at the time the asset was acquired or the liability incurred. The common stock of the foreign subsidiary is remeasured at the appropriate historical rate, and the retained earnings is computed in the normal way as the sum of the beginning balance plus the remeasured amount of the net income less the remeasured amount of the dividends distributed; each is eliminated during the consolidation process. The remeasurement of the monetary assets and liabilities from the foreign currency into U.S. dollars results in *transaction gains and losses,* which are included in the consolidated income statement. Revenues, expenses, gains, and losses of the foreign subsidiary are remeasured at the *average* exchange rate for the period of the consolidated income statement unless they can be related to the acquisition of a specific asset at a *historical* rate. For example, cost of goods sold and depreciation expense should be remeasured at the historical rate at which the inventory and the property, plant, and equipment of the foreign subsidiary were acquired, respectively. The two alternative situations just discussed and the appropriate exchange rates to translate or remeasure are summarized in Exhibit 20-4.

EXHIBIT 20-4
Summary of Translation
and Remeasurement
Process

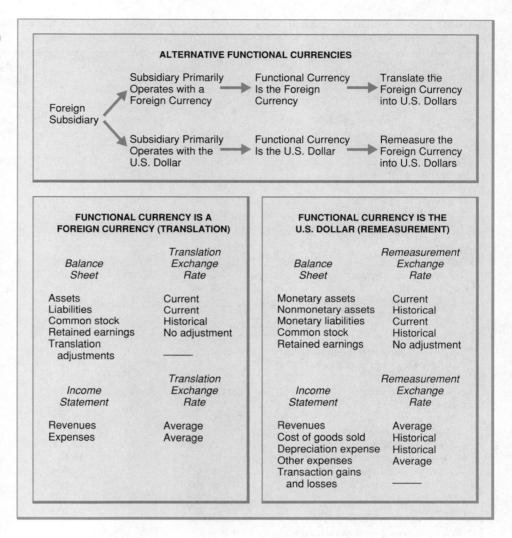

Example of the Conversion of Financial Statements into U.S. Dollars

13. Convert the financial statements of a foreign subsidiary into U.S. dollars.

An example of the conversion of a foreign subsidiary's financial statements is illustrated in Exhibit 20-5. We explain the conversion of the financial statements of the Tenden Company, a foreign subsidiary of a U.S. parent company, from the foreign currency (marks) into U.S. dollars for each of the two methods. After the conversion of the financial statements into dollars, any intercompany transactions would be eliminated and the consolidation procedures discussed in Chapter 17 would be followed. For simplicity, we will not discuss the consolidation of the Tenden Company's financial statements into the statements of its U.S. parent company.

EXHIBIT 20-5 Tenden Company (Foreign Subsidiary) Conversion of Financial Statements from German Marks into U.S. Dollars

		Functional Currency Is the Mark		Functional Currency Is the U.S. Dollar	
Balance Sheet *December 31, 1991*	*Marks*	*Translation Exchange Rate*	*U.S. Dollars*	*Remeasurement Exchange Rate*	*U.S. Dollars*
Cash	DM 50,000	$0.60[a]	$ 30,000	0.60[a]	$ 30,000
Accounts receivable	70,000	0.60	42,000	0.60	42,000
Inventory	120,000	0.60	72,000	0.59[f]	70,800
Property and equipment	250,000	0.60	150,000	0.50[g]	125,000
Less: Accumulated depreciation	(100,000)	0.60	(60,000)	0.50	(50,000)
Total Assets	DM390,000		$234,000		$217,800
Accounts payable	DM100,000	0.60	$ 60,000	0.60	$ 60,000
Bonds payable	60,000	0.60	36,000	0.60	36,000
Common stock, no par	140,000	0.40[b]	56,000	0.40[b]	56,000
Retained earnings	90,000	—	35,000[c]	—	65,800[c]
Translation adjustment (cumulative)	—		47,000[d]		—
Total Liabilities and Stockholders' Equity	DM390,000		$234,000		$217,800
Income Statement *For Year Ended December 31, 1991*					
Sales	DM400,000	$0.58[e]	$232,000	$0.58[e]	$232,000
Cost of goods sold	(170,000)	0.58	(98,600)	0.59[f]	(100,300)
Gross profit	DM230,000		$133,400		$131,700
Operating expenses					
Depreciation expense	(30,000)	0.58	(17,400)	0.50[g]	(15,000)
Selling and administrative expenses	(80,000)	0.58	(46,400)	0.58	(46,400)
Transaction loss	—		—		(16,000)[h]
Income before income taxes	DM120,000		$ 69,600		$ 54,300
Income tax expense	(48,000)	0.58	(27,840)	0.58	(27,840)
Net income	DM 72,000		$ 41,760		$ 26,460

[a]Exchange rate on December 31, 1991
[b]Exchange rate on the date the stock was initially sold
[c]Balancing amount because the beginning balance sheet was not given
[d]Cumulative lifetime adjustment
[e]Average exchange rate for 1991
[f]Exchange rate when the inventory was purchased
[g]Exchange rate when the property and equipment was acquired
[h]Transaction loss for the year

Functional Currency Is the West German Mark.   When the functional currency of the Tenden Company (foreign subsidiary) is the West German mark, all the items (except for the common stock and retained earnings) in the company's December 31, 1991, balance sheet are *translated* at the current exchange rate of $0.60 on that date. The common stock is translated at the historical rate when the stock was initially sold. The retained earnings is a balancing amount because, for simplicity, the beginning balance sheet was not provided in this example. (Both the common stock and the retained earnings of the company would be eliminated if we had completed the consolidation process.) The amount of the translation adjustment is the *cumulative* total of each year's translation adjustments and is caused by the exchange rate change on the company's net assets (assets minus liabilities).[7] All items in the Tenden Company's 1991 income statement are translated at the average exchange rate for 1991 of $0.58. Note that there is no *transaction* gain or loss in the income statement because all *translation* adjustments are included in the stockholders' equity section of the company's balance sheet when the functional currency is a foreign currency.

Functional Currency Is the U.S. Dollar. When the functional currency of the Tenden Company is the U.S. dollar, the monetary assets and liabilities (cash, accounts receivable, accounts payable, and bonds payable) in the company's December 31, 1991, balance sheet are *remeasured* at the current exchange rate of $0.60 on that date. The nonmonetary assets are remeasured at the appropriate historical rate. We assumed that the inventory was purchased when the exchange rate was $0.59 and that the property and equipment was acquired when the exchange rate was $0.50. Therefore these rates are used to remeasure the two items. The common stock is remeasured at the historical rate when the stock was initially sold. The retained earnings is a balancing amount because, for simplicity, the beginning balance sheet was not provided in this example. Note that there is no *translation* adjustment in the company's balance sheet because all *transaction* gains and losses are included in the company's income statement when the U.S. dollar is the functional currency.

In the 1991 income statement, the sales, selling and administrative expenses, and the income tax expense are all remeasured at the average rate for 1991 of $0.58. The items for which a historical rate is appropriate (cost of goods sold and depreciation expense) are remeasured at their appropriate historical rates of $0.59 and $0.50. The transaction loss (amount assumed) is also included in the company's income statement and is caused by the exchange rate change on the company's net monetary assets (monetary assets less monetary liabilities).

Note that in this example, for simplicity, we have assumed that the company has not made any foreign currency transactions that resulted in exchange gains and losses (as discussed earlier). If the company had such gains and losses, they would have been included in its income statement under both functional currency alternatives.

Evaluation of the Conversion of Financial Statements into U.S. Dollars

The two methods of converting the financial statements of a foreign subsidiary from the foreign currency into U.S. dollars may at first seem arbitrary. However, they are based on a logic that relates to the definition of the functional currency. When the functional currency is the foreign currency the subsidiary is relatively self-contained. The foreign currency net cash flows that the foreign subsidiary

---

[7]The amount tends to be added (credit balance) to stockholders' equity when the exchange rates in the countries where the subsidiaries are located have risen and be subtracted (debit balance) when those rates have fallen.

generates may be either reinvested in the subsidiary or converted into U.S. dollars and paid as dividends to the U.S. parent company. For this type of foreign subsidiary, we exclude the translation adjustments from the consolidated income statement because the foreign subsidiary is self-contained and its cash flows and income-producing activities do not directly affect the cash flows and income-producing activities of the U.S. parent company. Instead, they affect the foreign subsidiary's net assets and the U.S. parent's investment, and therefore the translation adjustments are included in the stockholders' equity of the consolidated balance sheet.

In contrast, when the functional currency is the U.S. dollar the foreign subsidiary is an extension of the U.S. parent company. Therefore the changes in the foreign subsidiary's assets and liabilities have a direct impact on the U.S. parent company's cash flows and income-producing activities in U.S. dollars, and so the transaction gains or losses are included in the consolidated income statement. The remeasurement process attempts to include the subsidiary in the consolidated financial statements as if *no foreign currency transactions had occurred*. Indeed, if the subsidiary chose to keep its financial records in U.S. dollars, its financial statements could be consolidated directly without any need for remeasurement.

International Accounting Principles

As discussed in Chapter 1, financial statements are prepared to assist external users in making investment and credit decisions. With the continuing growth of international business activities, more and more investors and creditors are making decisions about companies operating in foreign countries. For example, many U.S. investors purchase shares of European and Japanese companies. Such investors would prefer that companies in all countries use the same accounting principles. Unfortunately, very little conformity exists from country to country. The lack of conformity has been caused by such factors as the different ways the accounting profession in each country has developed, the different legal systems, and the different goals of the governments. In addition, differences in tax laws cause differences in financial reporting. Some countries require that financial statements be prepared according to tax rules, whereas other countries, including the U.S., have financial accounting principles that are not directly related to tax rules.[8]

Two organizations are directly concerned with international accounting activities. The International Accounting Standards Committee (IASC) was formed in 1972 with the intent of developing international accounting principles. By 1988, 100 accounting organizations representing 74 countries were participating in the Committee. To date, the IASC has issued 26 International Accounting Standards. Members of the IASC have committed themselves to introducing these standards in their respective countries. The IASC has no enforcement powers, however, and so the use of these standards is not universal.

The main objective of the International Federation of Accountants (IFAC), which was founded in 1977, is to establish international standards of auditing, ethics, education, and training. By 1988, 100 professional accounting organiza-

---

[8]For a more detailed discussion of international accounting issues, see AlHashim and Arpan, *International Dimensions of Accounting,* Second Edition (Boston: PWS-KENT Publishing Co., 1988).

tions representing 74 countries were members of the IFAC. Like the IASC, the IFAC also has no enforcement powers, but its members are committed to enhancing the quality of accounting in their respective countries.

We hope that through the continued efforts of the IASC and the IFAC a greater uniformity of accounting principles and practices will be developed throughout the world.

Chapter Summary

Review of Learning Objectives

After studying this chapter, you should be able to:

1. **Explain the alternative measures of income when prices change.**
   In historical cost financial statements, income is measured as the increase in nominal dollars. In constant purchasing power financial statements, income is measured as the increase in purchasing power. In current cost financial statements, income is measured as the increase in the operating capacity of the assets.

2. **Distinguish between a specific price change and a general price change.**
   A specific price change is the measure of the change in the price of a *particular* good or service. A general price change is the weighted average of the changes in the individual prices of a *group* of goods and services.

3. **Prepare comprehensively adjusted constant purchasing power financial statements.**
   In these statements each item is adjusted to the average purchasing power of the period as follows:

$$\text{Constant purchasing power} = \text{Historical cost} \times \frac{\text{General price-level index in current period}}{\text{General price-level index at time of historical cost transaction}}$$

4. **Compute the purchasing power gain or loss on net monetary items.**
   The beginning net monetary items and the change in each net monetary item are all converted to the average purchasing power of the period to give the constant purchasing power amount of the ending net monetary items. The historical cost balance of the ending net monetary items is also converted to the average purchasing power of the period. The purchasing power gain or loss is computed as the difference between the two measures of the constant purchasing power amount of the ending net monetary items.

5. **Prepare comprehensively adjusted current cost financial statements.**
   In these statements each item in the income statement is adjusted to the average current cost of the period, and each item in the balance sheet is adjusted to the current cost at the end of the year. Typically, the items that need adjusting are cost of goods sold, depreciation expense, inventory, and property, plant, and equipment.

6. **Explain the methods of computing current cost.**
    The three methods of computing current cost are (1) direct pricing in which an established price is used, (2) functional or unit pricing in which the current construction (or acquisition) cost per unit is multiplied by the number of units in the asset, and (3) the use of a specific price index to adjust the historical cost of the asset.

7. **Evaluate the advantages and disadvantages of the alternative methods.**
    The historical cost method is the most reliable and widely understood method. The constant purchasing power method enhances the comparability of amounts within the financial statements and over time. The current cost method is often considered to be more relevant but less reliable.

8. **List the discretionary disclosures on the effects of changing prices.**
    The supplementary disclosures for the current year include (a) income from continuing operations based on current cost, (b) purchasing power gain or loss on net monetary items, (c) current cost amounts of inventory and of property, plant, and equipment at the end of the current fiscal year, and (d) increases or decreases in the current cost amounts of inventory and property, plant, and equipment, before and after eliminating the effects of inflation. The 5-year summary includes (a) net sales and other operating revenues, (b) income from continuing operations under the current cost basis, (c) net assets at year end under the current cost basis, (d) increases or decreases in the current cost amounts of inventory and property, plant, and equipment, after eliminating the effects of inflation, (e) purchasing power gain or loss on net monetary items, (f) cash dividends declared per common share, and (g) market price per common share at year end. Each item in the 5-year summary is disclosed in terms of the average CPI-U for the current year.

9. **Describe an exchange rate.**
    An exchange rate measures the value of one currency in terms of another currency.

10. **Explain how foreign currency transactions result in the recognition of exchange gains and losses.**
    An exchange gain occurs when the exchange rate declines (increases) between the date a payable is incurred (receivable is acquired) and the date of the cash payment (receipt). An exchange loss occurs when the exchange rate increases (declines) between the date a payable is incurred (receivable is acquired) and the date of the cash payment (receipt).

11. **Define the functional currency.**
    The functional currency is the currency of the location in which a company primarily operates.

12. **Distinguish between translation and remeasurement.**
    Translation is the conversion of financial statements of a foreign subsidiary into U.S. dollars when the functional currency is a foreign currency. *Remeasurement* is the conversion of financial statements of a foreign subsidiary into U.S. dollars when the functional currency is the U.S. dollar.

13. **Convert the financial statements of a foreign subsidiary into U.S. dollars.**
    The financial statements are translated using exchange rates of the current

period. The financial statements are remeasured using exchange rates of the current period for monetary assets and liabilities, as well as revenues and other expenses. Appropriate historical exchange rates are used for nonmonetary assets, as well as cost of goods sold and depreciation expense.

Review Problem

The historical cost financial statements of the Burke Company for 1992 are as follows:

BURKE COMPANY
Income Statement
For Year Ended December 31, 1992

Sales		$150,000
Cost of goods sold		
Beginning inventory	$ 30,000	
Purchases	74,000	
Cost of goods available for sale	$104,000	
Less: Ending inventory	(40,000)	
Cost of goods sold		(64,000)
Gross profit		$ 86,000
Operating expenses		
Depreciation expense	$ 10,000	
Selling expenses	16,000	
General and administrative expenses	24,000	
Total operating expenses		(50,000)
Net Income		$ 36,000

BURKE COMPANY
Balance Sheets

	December 31, 1991	December 31, 1992
Cash	$ 5,000	$ 10,000
Accounts receivable	10,000	15,000
Inventory	30,000	40,000
Property and equipment	90,000	90,000
Less: Accumulated depreciation	(20,000)	(30,000)
Total Assets	$115,000	$125,000
Accounts payable	$ 30,000	$ 4,000
Bonds payable	25,000	25,000
Common stock, no par	20,000	20,000
Retained earnings	40,000	76,000
Total Liabilities and		
Stockholders' Equity	$115,000	$125,000

The following additional information for 1992 is available:

1. Sales, selling expenses, and general and administrative expenses occurred evenly throughout the year. Income taxes are ignored.

2. The inventory was valued on a FIFO cost flow assumption. The December 31, 1991, inventory consisted of 10,000 units purchased at $3 each in September 1991. The December 31, 1992, inventory consisted of 10,000 units purchased at $4 each in September 1992. Purchases of 20,000 units were made in 1992; these purchases were at the average general price level for the year. The current cost of the inventory was as follows:

December 1991	$3.30 per unit
Average 1992	3.80 per unit
December 1992	4.30 per unit

3. The property and equipment included the following items:

Item	Cost	Date of Purchase	Current Cost of Equivalent New Assets December 1991	Current Cost of Equivalent New Assets December 1992	Depreciation Life	Depreciation Method
Land	$10,000	January 1978	$40,000	$44,000	—	—
Building	80,000	January 1990	90,000	96,000	8 years	Straight line (no residual value)

4. The common stock was sold when the company was formed in January 1978.

5. The CPI-U index was as follows:

January 1978	110
January 1990	240
September 1991	254
December 1991	260
Average 1992	275
September 1992	282
December 1992	290

6. Net monetary items were affected by sales, purchases, selling expenses, and general and administrative expenses.

REQUIRED   Complete the following (round each amount to the nearest dollar):

1. Prepare in terms of the average CPI-U for 1992:
   (a) a comprehensively adjusted income statement for 1992
   (b) a schedule of net monetary items and a schedule to compute the purchasing power gain or loss for 1992
   (c) a comprehensively adjusted balance sheet. (Hint: Use the retained earnings as a balancing amount.)

2. Prepare a comprehensively adjusted current cost income statement for 1992 in terms of the average current cost for the year. Do not compute holding gains or losses.

3. Prepare comprehensively adjusted current cost balance sheets in terms of the current cost at the end of 1991 and 1992. (Hint: Use the retained earnings as a balancing amount.)

Solution to Review Problem

REQUIREMENT 1

(a)

BURKE COMPANY
Income Statement
For Year Ended December 31, 1992

Sales		$150,000[a]
Cost of goods sold		
Beginning inventory	$ 32,480[b]	
Purchases	74,000[a]	
Cost of goods available for sale	$106,480	
Less: Ending inventory	(39,007)[c]	
Cost of goods sold		(67,473)[d]
Gross profit		$ 82,527
Operating expenses		
Depreciation expense	$ 11,458[e]	
Selling expenses	16,000[a]	
General and administrative expenses	24,000[a]	
Total operating expenses		(51,458)
Net Income		$ 31,069

[a]No adjustment because the item occurred evenly throughout the year.
[b]$30,000 × 275/254.
[c]$40,000 × 275/282.
[d]Note that if the average cost flow assumption was used, the cost of goods sold on a historical cost basis would have been 20,000 × $3.60 [(10,000 × $3.00 + 20,000 × $3.70 + 10,000 × $4.00) ÷ (10,000 + 20,000 + 10,000)] and no adjustment would have been necessary.
[e]$10,000 × 275/240.

(b)

Schedule of Net Monetary Items

	December 31, 1991 (beginning)	December 31, 1992 (ending)
Cash	$ 5,000	$10,000
Accounts receivable	10,000	15,000
Less: Accounts payable	(30,000)	(4,000)
Bonds payable	(25,000)	(25,000)
Net Monetary Items	($40,000)	($ 4,000)

Schedule to Compute Purchasing Power Gain or Loss for 1992

	Historical Cost	Adjustments	Constant Purchasing Power
Beginning net monetary items	($40,000)	275/260	($42,308)
Sales	150,000	275/275	150,000
Purchases	(74,000)	275/275	(74,000)
Selling expenses	(16,000)	275/275	(16,000)
General and administrative expenses	(24,000)	275/275	(24,000)
Ending net monetary items	($4,000)		
Constant purchasing power ending balance (at average price level)			($ 6,308)
Historical ending balance adjusted to average price level ($4,000 × 275/290)			(3,793)
Purchasing Power Gain for 1992 (at average price level)			($ 2,515)

(c)

BURKE COMPANY
Balance Sheets

	December 31, 1991	*December 31, 1992*
Cash	$ 5,288[a]	$ 9,483[j]
Accounts receivable	10,577[b]	14,224[k]
Inventory	32,480[c]	39,007[l]
Property and equipment	116,667[d]	116,667[d]
Less: Accumulated depreciation	(22,917)[e]	(34,375)[m]
Total Assets	$142,095	$145,006
Accounts payable	$ 31,731[f]	$ 3,793[n]
Bonds payable	26,442[g]	23,707[o]
Common stock, no par	50,000[h]	50,000[h]
Retained earnings	33,922[i]	67,506[i]
Total Liabilities and Stockholders' Equity	$142,095	$145,006

[a] $5,000 × 275/260.
[b] $10,000 × 275/260.
[c] $30,000 × 275/254.
[d] $80,000 × 275/240 + $10,000 × 275/110.
[e] $20,000 × 275/240.
[f] $30,000 × 275/260.
[g] $25,000 × 275/260.
[h] $20,000 × 275/110.

[i] Balancing amount.
[j] $10,000 × 275/290.
[k] $15,000 × 275/290.
[l] $40,000 × 275/282.
[m] $30,000 × 275/240.
[n] $4,000 × 275/290.
[o] $25,000 × 275/290.

REQUIREMENT 2

BURKE COMPANY
Income Statement
For Year Ended December 31, 1992

Sales		$150,000[a]
Cost of goods sold		(76,000)[b]
Gross profit		$ 74,000
Operating expenses		
Depreciation expense	$11,625[c]	
Selling expenses	16,000[a]	
General and administrative expenses	24,000[a]	
Total operating expenses		(51,625)
Net Income		$ 22,375

[a] No adjustment because the item occurred evenly throughout the year.
[b] 20,000 units × $3.80.
[c] [($96,000 + $90,000) ÷ 2] ÷ 8.

REQUIREMENT 3

BURKE COMPANY
Balance Sheets

	December 31, 1991	*December 31, 1992*
Cash	$ 5,000[a]	$ 10,000[a]
Accounts receivable	10,000[a]	15,000[a]
Inventory	33,000[b]	43,000[g]
Property and equipment	130,000[c]	140,000[c]
Less: Accumulated depreciation	(22,500)[d]	(36,000)[h]
Total Assets	$155,500	$172,000

Accounts payable	$ 30,000[a]	$ 4,000[a]
Bonds payable	25,000[a]	25,000[a]
Common stock, no par	20,000[e]	20,000[e]
Retained earnings	80,500[f]	123,000[f]
Total Liabilities and Stockholders' Equity	$155,500	$172,000

[a]No adjustment because the item is at the current cost at the end of the year.
[b]10,000 units × $3.30.
[c]Amount given in original information.
[d][$90,000 × (2 years old ÷ 8-year life)].
[e]Not adjusted because no reliable measure is available.
[f]Balancing amount.
[g]10,000 units × $4.30 per unit.
[h][$96,000 × (3 years old ÷ 8-year life)].

Glossary

Constant Purchasing Power Amounts. Dollars that have been adjusted for changes in the general price level. That is, each dollar is expressed in the same purchasing power.

Current Cost. The amount that would have to be paid at a certain point in time (e.g., the current period) to purchase an identical or similar item.

Exchange Gain or Loss. A gain or loss caused by a change in the exchange rate between the date a payable is incurred or a receivable is acquired and the date of the payment or receipt.

Exchange Rate. The measurement of the value of one currency in terms of another currency.

Exit Value. The net cash amount that a company would receive if it sold an asset. Also referred to as the *net realization value*.

Functional Currency. The currency of the location in which a company primarily operates.

General Price-Level Change. The weighted average of the changes in the individual prices of a group of goods and services. The measure of the general price change used for supplementary disclosures is the Consumer Price Index for All Urban Consumers (CPI-U).

Holding Gain (Loss). The increase (decrease) in the current cost of an item. A realized holding gain (loss) is a gain (loss) on an item that has been included in the historical cost income statement. An unrealized holding gain (loss) is a gain (loss) on an item that has not yet been recognized in the historical cost income statement.

Monetary Asset. Money or a claim to receive a fixed amount of money in the future.

Monetary Liability. An obligation to repay a fixed amount of money in the future.

Net Monetary Items. Monetary assets less monetary liabilities. When monetary assets exceed monetary liabilities, net monetary items are referred to as *net monetary assets*. When monetary liabilities exceed monetary assets, net monetary items are referred to as *net monetary liabilities*.

Nominal Dollars. Dollars that have not been adjusted for changes in prices. Nominal dollars are the dollars used in historical cost financial statements.

Purchasing Power. A measure of the ability of a certain number of dollars to purchase goods and services.

Purchasing Power Gain or Loss on Net Monetary Items. The gain or loss in purchasing power that occurs when net monetary items are held during a period in which the general price level changes. A loss (gain) results when net monetary assets (liabilities) are held during a period of inflation.

Remeasurement.   The process of converting the financial statements of a foreign subsidiary into U.S. dollars, when the reporting currency of the foreign subsidiary is a foreign currency and the functional currency is the U.S. dollar.

Reporting Currency.   The currency that a company uses for its financial statements.

Specific Price Change.   A change in the price of a particular good or service.

Translation.   The process of converting the financial statements of a foreign subsidiary into U.S. dollars, when both the reporting currency and the functional currency of the foreign subsidiary are a foreign currency.

Questions

QUESTION 20-1   Define the following terms: (a) nominal dollars; (b) constant purchasing power amounts; and (c) current cost. Which measure adjusts for the change in specific prices?

QUESTION 20-2   Explain the difference between a general and a specific price change.

QUESTION 20-3   Which general price-level index is required for the discretionary supplementary disclosures of the effect of changing prices?

QUESTION 20-4   Describe how historical costs are adjusted to constant purchasing power.

QUESTION 20-5   Define monetary assets and monetary liabilities. Give two examples of each.

QUESTION 20-6   During a period of inflation does holding net monetary assets result in a purchasing power gain or loss? Why?

QUESTION 20-7   Is the base year of a price index significant to accountants? Why or why not?

QUESTION 20-8   What is a holding gain? Distinguish between a realized and an unrealized holding gain.

QUESTION 20-9   Why is a current cost income statement prepared in terms of the average current costs for the year, whereas a current cost balance sheet is prepared in terms of the current costs at the end of the year?

QUESTION 20-10   What basic methods may be used to determine the current cost of inventory, and property, plant, and equipment? Give an example of an asset for which each method is appropriate.

QUESTION 20-11   When discretionary supplementary disclosures about the effects of changing prices are made, what information about the current year should be included?

QUESTION 20-12   When discretionary supplementary disclosures about the effects of changing prices are made, what information should be included in the 5-year summary?

QUESTION 20-13   Explain what causes an exchange gain or loss and when each occurs.

QUESTION 20-14   Explain the meaning of the terms *reporting currency* and *functional currency*.

QUESTION 20-15   Distinguish between translation and remeasurement.

Exercises

EXERCISE 20-1 **Income Measurement.** A company purchased land for $22,500. Three years later the current cost of the land is $32,000. During the 3 years the general price level rose from 120 to 150.

REQUIRED 1. If the company sells the land how much income would be computed at the time of the sale under each of the following concepts:
(a) Historical cost.
(b) Constant purchasing power.
(c) Current cost.

2. What is the concept of income used in each of the alternatives?

EXERCISE 20-2 **General Price-Level Index.** January 1988 is the base period for a general price-level index. For simplicity, it will be assumed that the price index includes only five items. The following are the average amounts purchased and the prices of the items in January 1988, January 1991, and January 1992:

Item	Average Amounts Purchased	Price per Unit in January 1988	Price per Unit in January 1991	Price per Unit in January 1992
A	30 units	$ 3.00	$ 3.80	$ 4.20
B	25	5.00	5.40	5.20
C	20	8.00	9.25	10.00
D	15	21.00	23.00	23.60
E	10	50.00	58.30	60.00

REQUIRED 1. What is the general price-level index in January 1991 and in January 1992?

2. What is the percentage change in the average total price between January 1991 and January 1992?

3. What would be the general price-level index in each of the three years if January 1991 was the base period?

4. What is the purpose of the average amounts purchased? (Hint: Compute the general price-level index in January 1991, using January 1988 as the base period, if no amounts are used in either year.)

EXERCISE 20-3 **Specific Price-Level Indexes.** Use the information in Exercise 20-2.

REQUIRED Compute a specific price-level index for each of the five items if January 1988 is the base period for each index.

EXERCISE 20-4 **Constant Purchasing Power Income Statement.** The Abaco Company is preparing a comprehensively adjusted constant purchasing power income statement for the year at the average CPI-U index of 132. The following are the historical cost amounts and the index when the amount was recorded:

	Amount	Index
Sales	$80,000	132
Cost of goods sold	37,000	—
Depreciation expense	10,000	—
Selling expenses	12,000	132
Administrative expenses	16,000	132

The depreciation expense was calculated on a straight-line basis for assets purchased when the index was 110. The cost of goods sold was calculated on a FIFO basis. It included inventory that was purchased for $24,000 when the index was 128 and for $13,000 when the index was 130. The CPI-U index at the end of the year is 136.

REQUIRED   Prepare a comprehensively adjusted constant purchasing power income statement for the Abaco Company using the average CPI-U index. Round each amount to the nearest dollar.

EXERCISE 20-5   **Constant Purchasing Power Balance Sheet.**   The Marsh Company is preparing a comprehensively adjusted constant purchasing power balance sheet at the end of the year in terms of the average CPI-U index for the year of 132. The CPI-U index at the end of the year is 136. The following are the historical cost amounts in the various balance sheet accounts and the index when the amount was recorded:

	Amount	Index
Cash	$13,600	136
Accounts receivable	17,000	136
Inventory	25,750	—
Machinery	37,000	110
Accumulated depreciation: machinery	14,000	—
Accounts payable	20,400	136
Common stock, no par	30,000	100
Retained earnings	28,950	—

The machinery is being depreciated on a straight-line basis with no residual value. The company used the FIFO inventory method and the ending inventory for the year included units that had cost $16,750 when the index was 134 and $9,000 when the index was 135.

REQUIRED   Prepare a comprehensively adjusted constant purchasing power balance sheet for the Marsh Company using the average CPI-U index. Round each amount to the nearest dollar. (Hint: Use the retained earnings as a balancing amount.)

EXERCISE 20-6   **Purchasing Power Gain or Loss.**   At the beginning of the year the Baker Woodworking Company had net monetary assets of $42,000. At the end of the year the net monetary assets were $50,000. During the year the following transactions affected the net monetary assets:

(a) Sales of $100,000, which occurred evenly throughout the year.

(b) Purchases of inventory of $44,000, which occurred when the CPI-U index was 122.

(c) Payment of wages of $30,000, which occurred evenly throughout the year.

(d) Purchase of a building for $18,000, which occurred when the CPI-U index was 125.

The beginning, average, and ending CPI-U indexes for the year were 120, 124, and 128, respectively.

REQUIRED   Prepare a schedule to compute the purchasing power gain or loss for the year at the average price level. Round each amount to the nearest dollar.

EXERCISE 20-7   **Current Cost Income Statement.**   The Powell Company is preparing a comprehensively adjusted current cost income statement using average current costs for the current year. The following items are the historical cost amounts in selected accounts:

Sales	$90,000
Cost of goods sold	40,000
Depreciation expense	12,000
Selling expenses	16,000
Administrative expenses	18,000

The cost of goods sold consisted of 10,000 units at $4 each. The cost of the inventory at the beginning of the year was $3.70 per unit and rose by 20% during the year. Selling and administrative expenses were incurred at average costs for the year. The depreciation was calculated by using straight-line depreciation on an asset that cost $60,000, with a 5-year life and no expected residual value. The cost of an equivalent asset at the beginning of the year was $78,000 and rose by 15% during the year.

REQUIRED   Prepare a comprehensively adjusted current cost income statement for the current year.

EXERCISE 20-8   **Current Cost Balance Sheet.**   The Erikson Lighting Company is preparing a comprehensively adjusted current cost balance sheet using ending current costs for the period. The following items are the historical cost amounts in selected accounts:

Cash	$ 8,000
Marketable securities	10,000
Inventory	16,000
Machinery	40,000
Accumulated depreciation: machinery	5,000

The following additional information is available:

1. The market value of the marketable securities at the end of the year is $9,000.

2. The inventory consists of 10,000 units purchased at an average cost of $1.60 per unit. The current cost of the inventory at the beginning and end of the year was $1.50 and $1.75 per unit, respectively.

3. The machinery was purchased at the beginning of the year and is being depreciated on a straight-line basis over an expected life of 8 years with no residual value. At year end the current cost is $46,000.

REQUIRED   At what amount should each item be included in the current cost balance sheet of the Erikson Lighting Company?

EXERCISE 20-9   **Exchange Gains and Losses.**   On January 15, 1991, the Searle Company, a U.S. company, acquired machinery on account from a British company for 12,000 pounds. The company paid for the machine on January 30, 1991. The exchange rates on January 15 and 30 were $1.85 and $1.80, respectively.

REQUIRED   Prepare journal entries to record the acquisition and payment by the Searle Company.

EXERCISE 20-10 **Exchange Gains and Losses.** On June 20, 1991, the Livingstone Company, a U.S. company, sold merchandise on account to a Swiss company for 25,000 francs. The company received payment for the merchandise on July 10, 1991. The exchange rates on June 20 and July 10 were $0.69 and $0.68, respectively.

REQUIRED Prepare journal entries to record the sale and collection by the Livingstone Company.

Problems

Part A

PROBLEM 20-1A **Constant Purchasing Power Financial Statements.** The historical cost financial statements of the Newport Company are shown as follows:

NEWPORT COMPANY
Income Statement
For Year Ended December 31, 1992

Sales		$82,000
Cost of goods sold		
Beginning inventory	$21,000	
Purchases	54,000	
Cost of goods available for sale	$75,000	
Less: Ending inventory	(27,000)	
Cost of goods sold		(48,000)
Gross profit		$34,000
Operating expenses		
Depreciation expense	$ 6,000	
Other operating expenses	18,000	
Total operating expenses		(24,000)
Net Income		$10,000

NEWPORT COMPANY
Balance Sheets

	December 31, 1991	December 31, 1992
Cash	$ 14,000	$ 17,000
Accounts receivable	16,000	22,000
Inventory	21,000	27,000
Property and equipment	80,000	80,000
Less: Accumulated depreciation	(24,000)	(30,000)
Total Assets	$107,000	$116,000
Accounts payable	$ 5,000	$ 4,000
Bonds payable	16,000	16,000
Common stock, no par	40,000	40,000
Retained earnings	46,000	56,000
Total Liabilities and Stockholders' Equity	$107,000	$116,000

The following additional information is available:

1. Sales and other operating expenses occurred evenly throughout the year.

2. Inventory is valued on a FIFO cost flow assumption. Ending inventory each year was purchased in September of that year. Purchases were made at the average price level for the year.

3. The property and equipment consists of land that was purchased for $20,000 in January 1984 and a building that cost $60,000 on January 1, 1988 and is being depreciated using the straight-line method over a 10-year life with no residual value.

4. The common stock was sold when the company was formed in January 1984.

5. The CPI-U index was as follows:

January 1984 160
January 1988 210
September 1991 270
December 1991 275
Average for 1992 290
September 1992 295
December 1992 300

6. Net monetary items were affected by sales, purchases, and other operating expenses.

REQUIRED   Prepare (a) a comprehensively adjusted constant purchasing power income statement for 1992, (b) a schedule of net monetary items and a schedule to compute the purchasing power gain or loss, and (c) a constant purchasing power balance sheet at December 31, 1992, all in terms of the average index for 1992. Ignore income taxes. Round each amount to the nearest dollar. (Hint: In the balance sheet, use the retained earnings as a balancing amount.)

PROBLEM 20-2A   **Current Cost Financial Statements.**   Use the historical cost financial statements for the Newport Company in Problem 20-1A. The following additional information is available:

1. Sales and other operating expenses occurred evenly throughout the year.

2. The ending inventory each year included 10,000 units. The cost of goods sold in 1992 was composed of 20,000 units. The current cost of the inventory was as follows:

December 1991 .... $2.25 per unit
Average 1992 .... 2.50 per unit
December 1992 .... 2.75 per unit

3. The property and equipment includes the following items:

		Current Cost of Equivalent New Assets		
Item	Cost	December 31, 1991	December 31, 1992	Depreciable Life
Land	$20,000	$50,000	$55,000	—
Building	60,000	80,000	95,000	10 years (no residual value)

REQUIRED

1. Prepare a comprehensively adjusted current cost income statement in terms of the average current costs for 1992. Ignore income taxes and holding gains or losses.

2. Prepare a current cost balance sheet at December 31, 1992, in terms of the current costs at that time. (Hint: Use the retained earnings as a balancing amount.)

PROBLEM 20-3A

Translation. The Rozman Company, a foreign subsidiary of a U.S. company, had prepared the following income statement and balance sheet in terms of West German marks:

ROZMAN COMPANY
Income Statement
For Year Ended December 31, 1991

Sales	DM700,000
Cost of goods sold	(300,000)
Gross profit	DM400,000
Operating expenses	
Depreciation expense	(60,000)
Selling and administrative expenses	(80,000)
Income before income taxes	DM260,000
Income tax expense	(104,000)
Net income	DM156,000

ROZMAN COMPANY
Balance Sheet
December 31, 1991

Cash	DM 300,000
Accounts receivable	400,000
Inventory	600,000
Property and equipment	900,000
Less: Accumulated depreciation	(100,000)
Total Assets	DM2,100,000
Accounts payable	DM 300,000
Bonds payable	700,000
Common stock, no par	800,000
Retained earnings	300,000
Total Liabilities and Stockholders' Equity	DM2,100,000

The following additional information is available:

1. The functional currency of the Rozman Company is the West German mark.

2. The average exchange rate for 1991 was $0.52.

3. The exchange rate on December 31, 1991, was $0.54.

4. The common stock was issued when the exchange rate was $0.45.

REQUIRED   Prepare the 1991 income statement and ending balance sheet of the Rozman Company in terms of U.S. dollars. Assume that the company has a cumulative translation adjustment of $40,000. Use the retained earnings as a balancing amount.

PROBLEM 20-4A   **Remeasurement.**   The Chambers Pharmaceutical Company, a French subsidiary of a U.S. company, had prepared the following income statement and balance sheet in francs:

CHAMBERS PHARMACEUTICAL COMPANY
Income Statement
For Year Ended December 31, 1991

Sales	Fr900,000
Cost of goods sold	(150,000)
Gross profit	Fr750,000
Operating expenses	
Depreciation expense	(80,000)
Selling and administrative expenses	(320,000)
Income before income taxes	Fr350,000
Income tax expense	(140,000)
Net income	Fr210,000

CHAMBERS PHARMACEUTICAL COMPANY
Balance Sheet
December 31, 1991

Cash	Fr 50,000
Accounts receivable	150,000
Inventory	270,000
Property and equipment	500,000
Less: Accumulated depreciation	(160,000)
Total Assets	Fr810,000
Accounts payable	Fr100,000
Obligations under capital leases	300,000
Common stock, no par	200,000
Retained earnings	210,000
Total Liabilities and Stockholders' Equity	Fr810,000

The following additional information is available:

1. The functional currency of the Chambers Pharmaceutical Company is the U.S. dollar.

2. The average exchange rate for 1991 was $0.17.

3. The exchange rate on December 31, 1991 was $0.15.

4. The inventory was purchased when the exchange rate was $0.16.

5. The property and equipment was purchased when the exchange rate was $0.20.

6. The common stock was issued when the exchange rate was $0.25.

7. The transaction loss for 1991 was $12,000.

REQUIRED   Prepare the 1991 income statement and ending balance sheet of the Chambers Pharmaceutical Company in terms of U.S. dollars. Use the retained earnings as a balancing amount.

Problems

Part B

PROBLEM 20-1B   **Constant Purchasing Power Financial Statements.** The historical cost financial statements of the Basin Company are shown as follows:

BASIN COMPANY
Income Statement
For Year Ended December 31, 1992

Sales		$155,000
Cost of goods sold		
Beginning inventory	$ 41,000	
Purchases	101,000	
Cost of goods available for sale	$142,000	
Less: Ending inventory	(70,000)	
Cost of goods sold		(72,000)
Gross profit		$ 83,000
Operating expenses		
Depreciation expense	$ 20,000	
Other operating expenses	36,000	
Total operating expenses		(56,000)
Net Income		$ 27,000

BASIN COMPANY
Balance Sheets

	December 31, 1991	December 31, 1992
Cash	$ 23,000	$ 48,000
Accounts receivable	36,000	50,000
Inventory	41,000	70,000
Property and equipment	200,000	200,000
Less: Accumulated depreciation	(80,000)	(100,000)
Total Assets	$220,000	$268,000
Accounts payable	$ 12,000	$ 33,000
Bonds payable	70,000	70,000
Common stock, no par	50,000	50,000
Retained earnings	88,000	115,000
Total Liabilities and		
Stockholders' Equity	$220,000	$268,000

The following additional information is available:

1. Sales and other operating expenses occurred evenly throughout the year.

2. Inventory is valued on a FIFO cost flow assumption. Ending inventory each year was purchased in October of that year. Purchases were made at the average price level for 1992.

3. The property and equipment consists of land that was purchased for $60,000 in May 1983 and a machine that cost $140,000 on January 1, 1988 and is being depreciated using the straight-line method over a 7-year life with no residual value.

4. The common stock was sold when the company was formed in May 1983.

5. The CPI-U index was as follows:

May 1983	140
January 1988	200
October 1991	265
December 1991	270
Average for 1992	285
October 1992	290
December 1992	295

6. The net monetary items were affected by sales, purchases, and other operating expenses.

REQUIRED Prepare (a) a comprehensively adjusted constant purchasing power income statement for 1992, (b) a schedule of net monetary items and a schedule to compute the purchasing power gain or loss for 1992, and (c) a constant purchasing power balance sheet at December 31, 1992, all in terms of the average CPI-U index for 1992. Ignore income taxes. Round each amount to the nearest dollar. (Hint: In the balance sheet use the retained earnings as a balancing amount.)

PROBLEM 20-2B **Current Cost Financial Statements.** Use the historical cost financial statements for the Basin Company in Problem 20-1B. The following additional information is available:

1. Sales and other operating expenses occurred evenly throughout the year.

2. The ending inventory for 1991 and 1992 included 5,000 units and 7,000 units, respectively. The cost of goods sold in 1992 was composed of 8,000 units. The current cost of the inventory was as follows:

December 1991	$ 8.60 per unit
Average 1992	9.50 per unit
December 1992	10.40 per unit

3. The property and equipment includes the following items:

		Current Cost of Equivalent New Asset		Depreciable Life
Item	Cost	December 31, 1991	December 31, 1992	
Land	$ 60,000	$ 95,000	$100,000	—
Building	140,000	180,000	191,000	7 years (no residual value)

REQUIRED 1. Prepare a comprehensively adjusted current cost income statement in terms of the average current costs for 1992. Ignore income taxes and holding gains or losses.

2. Prepare a current cost balance sheet at December 31, 1992, in terms of the current costs at that time. (Hint: Use the retained earnings as a balancing amount in the balance sheet.)

PROBLEM 20-3B **Translation.**   The Fowler Grain Company, a Canadian subsidiary of a U.S. company, had prepared the following income statement and balance sheet in Canadian dollars:

FOWLER GRAIN COMPANY
Income Statement
For Year Ended December 31, 1991

Sales	C$750,000
Cost of goods sold	(400,000)
Gross profit	C$350,000
Operating expenses	
Depreciation expense	(40,000)
Selling and administrative expenses	(150,000)
Income before income taxes	C$160,000
Income tax expense	(64,000)
Net income	C$ 96,000

FOWLER GRAIN COMPANY
Balance Sheet
December 31, 1991

Cash	C$ 40,000
Accounts receivable	200,000
Inventory	300,000
Property and equipment	240,000
Less: Accumulated depreciation	(120,000)
Total Assets	C$660,000
Accounts payable	C$ 50,000
Obligations under capital leases	180,000
Common stock, no par	100,000
Retained earnings	330,000
Total Liabilities and Stockholders' Equity	C$660,000

The following additional information is available:

1. The functional currency of the Fowler Grain Company is the Canadian dollar.

2. The average exchange rate for 1991 was $0.83.

3. The exchange rate on December 31, 1991, was $0.81.

4. The common stock was issued when the exchange rate was $0.90.

REQUIRED   Prepare the 1991 income statement and ending balance sheet of the Fowler Grain Company in terms of U.S. dollars. Assume that the company has a cumulative translation adjustment of $22,000. Use the retained earnings as a balancing amount.

PROBLEM 20-4B   **Remeasurement.**   The Groski Company, a foreign subsidiary of a U.S. company, had prepared the following income statement and balance sheet in terms of British pounds:

GROSKI COMPANY
Income Statement
For Year Ended December 31, 1991

Sales	£ 400,000
Cost of goods sold	(100,000)
Gross profit	£ 300,000
Operating expenses	
Depreciation expense	(20,000)
Selling and administrative expenses	(50,000)
Income before income taxes	£ 230,000
Income tax expense	(92,000)
Net income	£ 138,000

GROSKI COMPANY
Balance Sheet
December 31, 1991

Cash	£ 100,000
Accounts receivable	200,000
Inventory	500,000
Property and equipment	700,000
Less: Accumulated depreciation	(200,000)
Total Assets	£1,300,000
Accounts payable	200,000
Bonds payable	300,000
Common stock, no par	600,000
Retained earnings	200,000
Total Liabilities and Stockholders' Equity	£1,300,000

The following additional information is available:

1. The functional currency of the Groski Company is the U.S. dollar.

2. The average exchange rate for 1991 was $1.90.

3. The exchange rate on December 31, 1991, was $1.85.

4. The inventory was purchased when the exchange rate was $1.88.

5. The property and equipment was purchased when the exchange rate was $2.10.

6. The common stock was issued when the exchange rate was $2.20.

7. The transaction loss for 1991 was $5,000.

REQUIRED   Prepare the 1991 income statement and ending balance sheet of the Groski Company in terms of U.S. dollars. Use the retained earnings as a balancing amount.

Decision Cases

DECISION CASE 20-1

Alternative Income Concepts.   Alan Pierce owns and operates a small company. He has heard about the supplementary disclosures about the effects of changing prices and is interested in having the same disclosures prepared for his company. During a meeting to discuss the disclosures, he makes the following comments:

1. "I understand these alternatives are measuring different types of income because they assume different things about how to measure wealth. I don't understand how that can be, because I invested $50,000 in my business 5 years ago and nobody can change that."

2. "This purchasing power loss is very strange. How can I have a loss when I haven't paid money out, sold something, or had a debit or credit in the accounting system?"

3. "How can it be useful to know the current cost of the building when I have no intention of replacing the building for at least 10 years?"

4. "Net income, after income taxes at 40%, this year was $20,000. Dividends paid by the company to me were $15,000. I thought that the company was $5,000 better off. Now you say that the current cost income before income taxes is $12,000. I still have to pay the taxes, but the company seems to be heading for trouble. . . . "

REQUIRED   Prepare a response to each comment made by Mr. Pierce.

DECISION CASE 20-2

Measuring Current Cost.   A company is preparing its supplementary disclosures on the effects of changing prices. The accountant who has been assigned the task of calculating the current cost of the assets has come to you for help.

"For example," she says, "think about the building we're sitting in. The company paid $60,000 for it when it was brand new 3 years ago. I can go to a real estate agency and find out what they think it's worth. But they're always optimistic. I could go to a builder and ask what it would cost to build today. But they don't build them quite the same way today; different materials, better insulation, and so on. I could look up a government-prepared index for building prices, but that's only an overall average. Or I could apply functional pricing. This building has 2,000 square feet, and I could find out the cost per square foot to build now. But that wouldn't be the same building, and what about all of the improvements the company has made. What should I do?"

REQUIRED   Clearly describe the alternative methods of calculating current costs. Describe the advantages and disadvantages of each method in the context of a building. How would you recommend the current cost of the building be determined?

DECISION CASE 20-3

Changing Prices.   The following excerpts are taken from a discussion of a company's disclosures of the effects of changing prices:

Financial statements are prepared using historical costs as required by generally accepted accounting principles. As a result, these financial statements do not fully reflect the impacts of specific price changes (current cost) or general inflation (constant purchasing power).

Supplementary disclosures are provided in an attempt to remeasure certain historical financial information to recognize the effects of changes on specific prices using current cost indices. For comparative purposes, the current cost information is then expressed in average dollars of the current year to reflect the effects of general inflation based on the U.S. Consumer Price Index. These procedures use assumptions and estimates and therefore should not be interpreted as a very reliable indicator of the effects of inflation. Furthermore, comparisons between companies may not be valid.

Net income has been adjusted for two items. First, depreciation has been remeasured to reflect the current costs of the current year. Because the company uses the LIFO method for valuing its inventories, the cost of goods sold is already reported in current costs. No adjustments have been made to net sales, other operating expenses, or the income tax expense. The effective tax rates are therefore higher than reported in the primary financial statements.

REQUIRED   Evaluate the above statements.

DECISION CASE 20-4   **International Operations.**   Kimberly-Clark disclosed the following information in its 1988 annual report (amounts in millions of dollars):

BALANCE SHEET

	1988	1987
Stockholders' Equity		
Unrealized currency translation adjustments (note 1)	$(50.5)	$(85.9)

Note 5. Foreign currency translation:
Assets and liabilities of foreign operations are translated into U.S. dollars at period-end exchange rates except for operations in the hyper-inflationary economies of Mexico, Brazil, and Colombia where the functional currency for U.S. accounting purposes is considered to be the U.S. dollar. Gains and losses on such translations are reflected as unrealized currency translation adjustments in stockholders' equity. Income and expense accounts are translated into U.S. dollars at rates of exchange in effect each month.

UNREALIZED CURRENCY TRANSLATION ADJUSTMENTS

	1988	1987
Balance, January 1	$(85.9)	$(163.8)
Canadian Dollar	34.7	21.3
British Pound	(5.3)	30.6
French Franc	(8.3)	12.3
German Mark	(3.7)	8.2
Other	18.0	5.5
Total	35.4	77.9
Balance, December 31	$(50.5)	$ (85.9)

The net loss reflected in the determination of net income pertaining to currency transactions and translation of balance sheets of operations in hyper-inflationary economies was $5.2 million in 1988 and $13.4 million in 1987, compared to a gain of $0.7 million in 1986.

REQUIRED   Explain the foreign currency translations and currency exchange transactions in relation to the strength or weakness of the U.S. dollar in 1988 and 1987. Why aren't such translations reflected in the income statement?

APPENDIX A

The Black & Decker Corporation 1988 Annual Report— Financial Section

FINANCIAL INFORMATION TABLE OF CONTENTS

Management Discussion and Analysis

Overview

For the year ended September 25, 1988, the Corporation reported net earnings of $97.1 million or $1.65 per share compared to $55.6 million or $.95 per share for 1987. Sales reached $2.28 billion in 1988 compared to $1.93 billion in 1987. This sales and earnings improvement was broad based, coming from most geographic areas and product lines within these areas. The power tool and household product core businesses were strong and were favorably affected by new product introductions.

The gross margin improvement continued; expenses remained under tight control; return on equity improved significantly; and cash flow before financing activities was substantially improved.

Sales

The following table sets forth an analysis of sales growth for fiscal years 1986 through 1988.

ANALYSIS OF SALES GROWTH (DOLLARS IN MILLIONS)	1988	1987	1986
Consolidated			
Sales	$2,281	$1,935	$1,791
Volume	14 %	3%	(3)%
Price	–	1%	1 %
Currency	4 %	4%	5 %
Total Growth	18 %	8%	3 %
United States			
Sales	$1,185	$1,018	$1,001
Volume	17 %	2%	(4)%
Price	(1)%	–	(1)%
Total Growth	16 %	2%	(5)%
Europe			
Sales	$ 755	$ 612	$ 514
Volume	10 %	1%	(7)%
Price	2 %	3%	3 %
Currency	11 %	15%	22 %
Total Growth	23 %	19%	18 %
Other			
Sales	$ 341	$ 305	$ 276
Total Growth	12 %	11%	10 %

This significant sales growth was primarily the result of numerous successful new product introductions, aggressive new marketing programs, and continued emphasis on improving customer service and product quality. All geographic areas reported double-digit sales growth over 1987. Pricing opportunities were limited as the Corporation concentrated on improving market position. Although foreign exchange translation made a positive contribution to growth, this impact lessened during the latter half of 1988.

Sales volume in the United States improved by 17% over the prior year, continuing the trend which began in 1987. Sales in most major product groups grew at a double-digit pace as compared to last year. New products made a significant contribution to this growth.

Sales in Europe also showed substantially improved volume growth over 1987, up 10% as compared to basically flat volume last year. Most product groups in the major markets of Europe grew at a double-digit pace as compared to 1987. New products, including selective household product introductions in certain major markets, contributed to this growth. The United Kingdom and Italy continued their growth trends of last year. Germany, after several years of declining sales, showed a modest increase in 1988. The strengthening of the U.S. dollar over the latter part of the year against most major European currencies diminished the favorable effect of foreign exchange translation on sales from 22% in 1986 to 11% in 1988.

Sales volume in other areas, including Canada, Latin America, Australasia, and the Far East, also improved compared to last year. Growth came from both power tools and household products, with Australia and Mexico leading the way. Because of the hyperinflationary environment of much of Latin America, it is impracticable to isolate and quantify foreign exchange and pricing actions for operations in this region.

Earnings

Earnings before taxes and extraordinary item were $125.7 million in 1988 compared to $69.8 million in 1987 and $34.7 million in 1986. This represents an 80% earnings increase in 1988 following the 100% earnings growth last year. As was the case with sales, this earnings growth was broad based across all geographic areas and most major markets within these areas.

Gross margin as a percentage of sales was 37.3% for 1988 compared to 36.4% in 1987 and 35.2% in 1986. Most of the improvement over the three-year period can be attributed to the manufacturing restructuring program, which is now substantially complete. As compared to two years ago, the Corporation is operating with five fewer manufacturing facilities worldwide to support the 27% sales growth over the period. Plant utilization improved significantly, reducing costs even with increases in certain raw material and sourced product costs. In addition, focused manufacturing facilities are now producing many products for global markets.

Marketing and administrative expenses declined as a percentage of sales to 30.3% in 1988 from 30.6% in 1987 and 32.1% in 1986. The decline in expense as a percentage of sales resulted primarily from the increased volumes and continued tight expense control. During 1988 as compared to 1987, higher promotional and advertising expense to introduce new products and increased levels of research and development activities necessary to continue the new product effort were more than offset by a lower percentage of general, administrative and selling costs. Most of the 1987 expense reduction as a percentage of sales compared to 1986 was due to the elimination of consumer rebates on most household products, and to reduced administrative expenses resulting from the cost-cutting actions taken during 1986.

Interest expense (net of interest income) was well below both 1987 and 1986 levels as interest income earned increased over the prior two years, primarily the result of favorable cash flow during 1988 as compared to both 1987 and 1986.

Other income for 1988 includes the receipt of $25 million during the third quarter as a result of the Corporation's termination of a tender offer, $16.7 million of expenses associated with that tender offer, and a $7.4 million accrual for the incremental cost of discontinuing certain product lines. Other income for 1987 was at about the same level as 1986 with the exception of an $18.2 million gain on sale of foreign currency exchange agreements included in 1986.

During 1988, the Corporation adopted Statement of Financial Accounting Standard (SFAS) No. 87, "Employer's Accounting for Pensions," for all domestic pension plans as more fully explained in Note 10 of Notes to Consolidated Financial Statements. The effect of adoption was immaterial. The Corporation will adopt SFAS No. 87 for all non-domestic plans in either fiscal 1989

or 1990. The impact of such adoption has not yet been fully quantified, but it is not expected to be material.

Foreign exchange effects included in earnings for 1988, 1987 and 1986 were immaterial except for the aforementioned gain on sale of foreign currency exchange agreements in 1986. However, operating results of foreign subsidiaries were translated at higher foreign exchange rates during 1988 compared to 1987, which had a positive effect on both sales and earnings. The impact on sales is summarized in the chart on page 22. For additional information regarding the Corporation's policy relating to foreign exchange effects, see Note 1 and the column designated "Equity Adjustments From Translation" included in Note 7 of Notes to Consolidated Financial Statements.

The foreign exchange effects described above are not all the effects of foreign currency fluctuations. It is not practicable to isolate price changes, changes in costs structures and interest income and expense that result as management responds to foreign currency movement.

During 1988, the Corporation adopted Statement of Financial Accounting Standard (SFAS) No. 96, "Accounting for Income Taxes." An analysis of the effects of taxes on earnings is included in Note 9 of Notes to Consolidated Financial Statements.

Effects of Inflation
During 1988, inflation continued to have an adverse impact on the Corporation. Although general inflation rates in the United States and certain other countries in which the Corporation operates remained about the same as prior year levels, the price of certain raw materials and sourced products that the Corporation uses in the manufacturing process have increased. The Corporation plans to recover these higher costs through continued cost reduction and increased pricing. There are also other factors which must be considered in assessing the impact of inflation on the Corporation's financial condition and results of operations, particularly in a multinational environment. Such factors include the relative difference in foreign exchange rates and interest rates, competitive pressures, general economic and market conditions, and productivity and technological improvements.

Financial Condition

For 1988, the Corporation generated cash before financing activities of $51.9 million compared to a cash requirement of $21.8 million in 1987. Operating activities generated positive cash flow of $121.1 million for 1988, more than three times last year's positive cash flow of $39.3 million. Significantly improved earnings accounted for most of the improvement compared to last year. Working capital items, particularly accounts receivable, inventory, and accounts payable and accruals have increased above prior-year levels. The receivable increase was directly related to the higher level of sales activity (up 18% over last year). Increases in inventory resulted from the need to build inventory in anticipation of higher sales and to meet the Corporation's customer service objectives. The higher level of accounts payable and accruals was primarily the result of a significantly increased level of sales and production activity and increases in taxes payable.

Investing activities required cash of $69.1 million. As expected, capital expenditures have increased above 1987 levels. Capital expenditures were abnormally low during 1987 as a result of reduced spending during implementation of the manufacturing restructuring program. With restructuring now substantially complete, capital spending returned to anticipated levels during 1988. Cash flows from hedging activities are the result of the Corporation's policy to minimize exposure to foreign exchange rate fluctuations.

Financing activities, including dividends, required cash of $20.2 million. Long-term debt increased by $26 million, primarily due to the Corporation's entering into a 100 million pounds sterling revolving credit facility which extends for a period up to five years. Of the total amount outstanding at September 25, 1988, 15 million pounds sterling has been classified as long-term debt. This increase was offset by a decrease in short-term borrowings.

The Corporation's debt-to-total capital ratio was 40% at September 1988 compared to 42% at September 1987. Under the Corporation's back-to-back transactions, short-term borrowings and deposits of $84.1 million were eliminated from the balance sheet at September 27, 1987. Although the legal right of offset exists as of the balance sheet date on all back-to-back transactions, $37.0 million of these transactions which were eliminated from the balance sheet at September 27, 1987, were of a short duration and the loans and deposits did not have matching maturities. If these amounts had not been eliminated from the balance sheet at September 27, 1987, cash and debt would have increased accordingly and the Corporation's debt-to-total capital ratio for 1987 would have been 44%. At September 25, 1988, back-to-back transactions of a short duration and without matching maturities were not eliminated from the balance sheet.

Variable rate debt as a percentage of total debt was 51% in 1988 compared to 49% in 1987. The average maturity of the Corporation's debt was three years in 1988, four years in 1987, and three years in 1986.

In 1987, cash requirements before financing activities were met primarily by the issuance of long-term debt. During both 1987 and 1986 the Corporation extinguished certain higher-cost, long-term debt with the proceeds from the 1986 equity offering and several long-term debt refinancings. During 1987 these refinancings included the issuance of $100 million aggregate principal amount of 8.375%, ten-year unsecured notes and 100 million deutsche marks (approximately $55 million) of 5.75%, seven-year bonds.

Capital expenditures during 1989 are expected to exceed 1988 levels as the Corporation continues to commit capital for new products, increased productivity and cost reduction. Management believes that internally generated funds and currently available sources of credit will be adequate to meet the Corporation's operational cash requirements in 1989.

The Corporation intends to continue efforts to broaden its earnings base internally and through strategic acquisitions of product line extensions or new businesses that are compatible with the Corporation's profile. Any such acquisition could require the commitment of funds in excess of those internally generated and available through current sources of credit.

Consolidated Statement of Earnings
The Black & Decker Corporation and Subsidiaries

	Year Ended		
(Thousands of Dollars Except Per Share Data)	Sept. 25, 1988	Sept. 27, 1987	Sept. 28, 1986
Net Sales	$2,280,923	$1,934,799	$1,791,194
Costs and expenses:			
Cost of products sold	1,430,764	1,229,989	1,160,379
Marketing and administrative expenses	691,044	592,337	575,490
Interest expense (net of interest income of $27,826 for 1988, $19,216 for 1987, and $12,422 for 1986)	36,502	43,385	43,227
Other (income) expense	(3,082)	(678)	(22,645)
Earnings Before Income Taxes and Extraordinary Item	125,695	69,766	34,743
Income taxes	28,600	14,200	7,200
Net Earnings Before Extraordinary Item	97,095	55,566	27,543
Extraordinary item:			
Loss on early extinguishment of debt	—	—	(21,239)
Net Earnings	$ 97,095	$ 55,566	$ 6,304
Per Share:			
Net earnings before extraordinary item	$ 1.65	$ .95	$ .49
Extraordinary loss	—	—	(.38)
Net earnings	$ 1.65	$ .95	$ .11

See Notes to Consolidated Financial Statements

Consolidated Balance Sheet
The Black & Decker Corporation and Subsidiaries

(Thousands of Dollars)	Sept. 25, 1988	Sept. 27, 1987
Assets		
Cash and cash equivalents	$ 74,356	$ 40,460
Short-term investments	33,183	16,963
Trade receivables, less allowances of $16,883 (1987–$16,549)	553,373	501,686
Inventories	591,060	509,722
Other current assets	50,234	75,348
Total Current Assets	1,302,206	1,144,179
Property, Plant and Equipment	403,395	394,931
Goodwill	70,142	75,190
Other Assets	49,366	53,745
	$1,825,109	$1,668,045
Liabilities and Stockholders' Equity		
Short-term borrowings	$ 215,483	$ 227,958
Accounts payable	160,666	120,039
Other accrued liabilities	370,271	345,532
Total Current Liabilities	746,420	693,529
Long-Term Debt	277,091	250,578
Deferred Income Taxes	28,808	19,929
Other Long-Term Liabilities	47,922	54,895
Stockholders' Equity		
Common stock (outstanding:		
Sept. 25, 1988–58,554,854 shares;		
Sept. 27, 1987–58,363,234 shares)	29,277	29,182
Capital in excess of par value	505,384	502,279
Retained earnings	248,810	175,112
Equity adjustment from translation	(58,603)	(57,459)
Total Stockholders' Equity	724,868	649,114
	$1,825,109	$1,668,045

See Notes to Consolidated Financial Statements

Consolidated Statement of Cash Flows
The Black & Decker Corporation and Subsidiaries

	Year Ended		
(Thousands of Dollars)	Sept. 25, 1988	Sept. 27, 1987	Sept. 28, 1986
Operating Activities			
Net earnings	$ 97,095	$ 55,566	$ 6,304
Adjustments:			
Depreciation and amortization	93,488	99,036	107,370
Trade receivables	(49,299)	(38,389)	19,619
Inventories	(79,339)	8,301	(16,710)
Accounts payable and accrued liabilities	104,825	1,743	17,867
Charges to restructuring reserves	(38,687)	(72,266)	(78,134)
Other assets and liabilities	29,388	3,450	15,790
Investing and financing activities included in net earnings	(36,401)	(18,113)	(5,071)
Cash Flow From Operating Activities	121,070	39,328	67,035
Investing Activities			
Capital expenditures	(98,404)	(58,766)	(82,375)
Disposals of property, plant and equipment	13,203	14,419	19,752
Cash inflow from foreign currency hedging	96,746	39,847	56,797
Cash outflow from foreign currency hedging	(88,998)	(56,668)	(27,407)
Tender offer termination payment received	25,000	–	–
Tender offer expenses	(16,673)	–	–
Cash Flow From Investing Activities	(69,126)	(61,168)	(33,233)
Cash Flow Before Financing Activities	51,944	(21,840)	33,802
Financing Activities			
Proceeds from borrowings	104,405	195,414	117,942
Payments on borrowings	(104,383)	(138,443)	(280,595)
Issuance of common stock	3,200	4,373	141,191
Cash dividends	(23,397)	(23,269)	(32,509)
Cash Flow From Financing Activities	(20,175)	38,075	(53,971)
Effect of exchange rate changes on cash	2,127	2,044	2,885
Increase (Decrease) in Cash and Cash Equivalents	33,896	18,279	(17,284)
Cash and cash equivalents at beginning of year	40,460	22,181	39,465
Cash and Cash Equivalents at End of Year	$ 74,356	$ 40,460	$ 22,181

Income tax payments were $11,339, $9,908 and $9,939 for 1988, 1987 and 1986, respectively.
Interest payments were $64,220, $58,061 and $61,380 for 1988, 1987 and 1986, respectively.

See Notes to Consolidated Financial Statements

Notes to Consolidated Financial Statements
The Black & Decker Corporation and Subsidiaries
(Thousands of Dollars Except Per Share Data)

Note 1: Summary of Accounting Policies

PRINCIPLES OF CONSOLIDATION: The consolidated financial statements include the accounts of the Corporation and its subsidiaries. Intercompany transactions have been eliminated.

RESTATEMENT: Effective for the fiscal year ended September 25, 1988, the Corporation adopted Statement of Financial Accounting Standard (SFAS) No. 95, "Accounting for Cash Flows." All prior years as presented in the Consolidated Statement of Cash Flows have been restated to conform to SFAS No. 95, which requires the reporting of cash flows from operating, investing and financing activities. Also, all cash flows from subsidiaries outside the United States have been converted to U.S. dollars using the exchange rates in effect at the time of the cash flow. In the consolidated statement of cash flows, all earnings effects of investing and financing activities must be adjusted out of the operating section and the cash flow effect shown as a financing or investing activity. This adjustment to the operating section is titled "Investing and Financing Activities Included in Net Earnings" and includes earnings effects of foreign currency hedging, certain foreign exchange effects in hyperinflationary environments, gain or loss on property, plant and equipment, and loss on early extinguishment of debt.

RECLASSIFICATIONS: Certain prior years' amounts in the consolidated financial statements have been reclassified to conform to the presentation used for 1988.

CASH AND CASH EQUIVALENTS: Cash and cash equivalents include cash on hand, demand deposits, and short-term investments with maturities of three months or less.

SHORT-TERM INVESTMENTS: Short-term investments are those with maturities in excess of three months and are valued at cost, which approximates market.

FOREIGN CURRENCY TRANSLATION: The financial position and results of operations of substantially all of the Corporation's subsidiaries outside the United States are measured using local currency as the functional currency except those subsidiaries located in highly inflationary economies, in which case the U.S. dollar is the functional currency. For subsidiaries other than those located in highly inflationary economies, assets and liabilities are translated at the rates of exchange on the balance sheet date. The resultant translation gains or losses are included in the component of stockholders' equity designated as "Equity Adjustment from Translation." Income and expense items of these subsidiaries are translated at average monthly rates of exchange. Gains and losses from foreign currency transactions of these subsidiaries are included in net earnings. For subsidiaries operating in highly inflationary economies, gains and losses on foreign currency transactions and balance sheet translation adjustments are included in net earnings. Interest expense resulting from debt associated solely with the hedging activities of one of the Corporation's subsidiaries outside the United States is classified as foreign currency exchange losses and included in other (income) expense.

Although the Corporation has significant foreign investment, it is the Corporation's policy to reduce substantially the effects of fluctuations in foreign currency exchange rates associated with these investments through its exposure management and foreign currency hedging activities.

INVENTORIES: Inventories are stated at the lower of cost or market. The cost of United States inventories is based on the last-in, first-out (LIFO) method; all other inventories are based on the first-in, first-out (FIFO) method.

PROPERTY AND DEPRECIATION: Property, plant and equipment is stated at cost. Depreciation is computed generally on the straight-line method for financial reporting purposes and on both accelerated and straight-line methods for tax reporting purposes. Depreciation expense charged to operations was $81,459 in 1988, $86,482 in 1987, and $93,112 in 1986.

GOODWILL AND OTHER INTANGIBLES: Goodwill and other intangibles are amortized on the straight-line basis over periods ranging up to 20 years.

DEBT: The Corporation and certain of its subsidiaries participate in various back-to-back transactions with banks whereby funds are borrowed and funds are deposited to support the loans. In the event of default under these arrangements, a legal right of offset permits the use of the deposit to satisfy the defaulted principal and interest. Since the mutual right of offset exists, debt and the equivalent deposits have been eliminated from the balance sheet. Related interest income and interest expense also have been eliminated.

PRODUCT DEVELOPMENT COSTS: Costs associated with the development of new products and changes to existing products are charged to operations as incurred. Product development costs were $50,708 in 1988, $40,480 in 1987, and $39,686 in 1986.

INCOME TAXES: United States income taxes have not been provided on unremitted earnings of subsidiaries located outside the United States as such earnings are considered to be permanently reinvested.

EARNINGS PER SHARE: Earnings per share are based on the average number of shares outstanding during each year. Fully diluted earnings per share are not materially different.

Note 2: Inventories

	1988	1987
FIFO cost		
Raw materials and work-in-process	$121,239	$110,902
Finished products	494,688	418,312
	615,927	529,214
Excess of FIFO cost over LIFO inventory value	(24,867)	(19,492)
	$591,060	$509,722

The cost of United States inventories stated under the LIFO method was approximately 53% of the value of total inventories.

Note 3: Property, Plant and Equipment

	1988	1987
Land and improvements	$ 20,963	$ 20,724
Buildings	160,570	161,962
Machinery and equipment	626,453	575,492
	807,986	758,178
Less accumulated depreciation	404,591	363,247
	$403,395	$394,931

Note 4: Other Accrued Liabilities

	1988	1987
Discounts and allowances	$ 58,874	$ 47,828
Salaries and wages	40,757	32,224
Pension and other benefits	28,361	31,438
Advertising and promotion	27,446	23,642
Accrued restructuring costs	20,057	52,186
All other	194,776	158,214
	$370,271	$345,532

All other for 1988 and 1987 primarily includes accruals for various operating expenses, income and other taxes, warranty, and interest.

Note 5: Short-Term Borrowings

	1988	1987
Bank loans	$197,804	$221,478
Commercial paper	16,685	3,400
Current maturity of long-term debt	994	3,080
	$215,483	$227,958

During 1988, the Corporation entered into a 100 million pound sterling revolving credit facility extending for a period of up to five years with several banks. The facility provides for variable interest rates based on the London interbank borrowing rate. Commitment fees of .125% per annum are payable on the unused balance of the facility for the first year and at .15% per annum thereafter. Of the total amount outstanding at September 25, 1988, 15 million pounds sterling ($25,635) have been classified as long term since the facility extends for a period up to five years, and the Corporation does not intend to repay this amount currently. At September 25, 1988, 10 million pounds sterling were available to the Corporation under this facility.

The Corporation also has a revolving credit facility in the amount of $90,000 with several commercial banks available through December 31, 1988. This facility is at various interest rates at the Corporation's option based on the prime, London interbank borrowing, certificates of deposit, bankers' acceptance, or other negotiated rates; and it can also be used to support the issuance of commercial paper in the United States and in European markets through dealers at the best available open market interest rates. Commitment fees are .25% on the unused balance during the availability period. At September 25, 1988, the entire facility of $90,000 was available to the Corporation.

Under terms of informal line of credit arrangements, the Corporation may borrow up to an additional $229,000 on such terms as may be mutually agreed upon. These arrangements do not have termination dates and are reviewed periodically. No material compensating balances are required or maintained.

During 1987, the Corporation entered into a series of interest rate swap agreements to manage interest rate risk on its 1987 and 1988 seasonal financing needs. The swap agreements cover $75,000 of seasonal financing needs for the periods from July 1 to December 31, in each of these years, at an average fixed interest rate of 6.7% and 8.2% for the periods, respectively. The Corporation has also entered into an interest rate cap agreement for the period July 1 to December 31, 1989. This agreement effectively limits the Corporation's interest rate on $75,000 of seasonal financing needs to a maximum of 8%.

Under the Corporation's back-to-back transactions, short-term borrowings and deposits of $7,616 and $84,102 have been eliminated from the balance sheet as of September 25, 1988 and September 27, 1987, respectively. Although the legal right of offset exists as of the balance sheet date on all back-to-back transactions, $36,951 of these transactions which were eliminated from the balance sheet at September 27, 1987, were of short duration and the loans and deposits did not have matching maturities. At September 25, 1988, back-to-back transactions of a short duration and without matching maturities were not eliminated from the balance sheet.

Due to seasonal cash requirements, the Corporation's short-term borrowings fluctuate during the year with higher requirements in the first and fourth fiscal quarters. The average short-term borrowings outstanding during 1988 and 1987 were $215,000 and $226,000, respectively. The maximum amounts outstanding during 1988 and 1987 were $399,000 and $398,000, respectively.

Note 6: Long-Term Debt

	1988	1987
8.375% notes due 1997	$ 99,080	$ 98,850
Pound sterling loans due in 1990	85,450	80,375
5.75% deutsche mark bonds due 1994	51,489	52,753
Pound sterling revolving credit facility	25,635	—
Other loans due through 2010 at rates from 1.5% to 9.4%	15,437	18,600
	$277,091	$250,578

Principal payments due within the next five fiscal years are as follows: 1989–$994; 1990–$86,432; 1991–$26,653; 1992–$396; 1993–$254.

During 1987, the Corporation issued $100,000 aggregate principal amount of 8.375% unsecured notes at 99.83%. These notes are due in April 1997 and the Corporation has an early redemption option on and after April 1, 1994. Also in 1987, the Corporation issued bonds in the amount of 100 million deutsche marks at 100.75% with interest at a rate of 5.75%. The bonds will mature in March 1994 and the Corporation is entitled to repay all of the bonds before maturity based on certain terms and conditions outlined in the bond indenture agreement. Proceeds from this and from the $100,000 unsecured notes were used to repay short-term debt.

The pound sterling loans are at variable interest rates, at the Corporation's option, of either the London interbank borrowing rate or the rate for pound sterling acceptances eligible for discount at the Bank of England.

The Corporation has complied with restrictions and limitations included in the provisions of various loan agreements. At September 25, 1988, retained earnings were not restricted as to payment of dividends by these provisions.

The Corporation maintains certain long-term loans which it requires for its operations and has implemented its back-to-back policy to offset these loans. Under this policy, $76,610 and $75,900 of long-term debt and deposits have been eliminated from the 1988 and 1987 balance sheets, respectively.

During 1986, the Corporation reported an extraordinary loss of $21,239 ($.38 per share) for costs related to the early retirement of certain long-term debt. Because of the Corporation's net operating loss position, no tax benefits were applicable to these transactions.

Note 7: Stockholders' Equity

	Outstanding Common Shares	$.50 Par Value	Capital in Excess of Par Value	Retained Earnings	Equity Adjustments From Translation
Balance at September 29, 1985	50,783,102	$25,392	$360,505	$169,020	$(50,069)
Net earnings	—	—	—	6,304	—
Cash dividends ($.58 per share)	—	—	—	(32,509)	—
Sale of common stock	7,000,000	3,500	132,637	—	—
Common stock issued under employee benefit plans	311,746	156	4,890	—	—
Valuation changes, less effect of hedging activities	—	—	—	—	(3,175)
Other	561	—	8	—	—
Balance at September 28, 1986	58,095,409	29,048	498,040	142,815	(53,244)
Net earnings	—	—	—	55,566	—
Cash dividends ($.40 per share)	—	—	—	(23,269)	—
Common stock issued under employee benefit plans	266,512	133	4,225	—	—
Valuation changes, less effect of hedging activities	—	—	—	—	(4,215)
Other	1,313	1	14	—	—
Balance at September 27, 1987	58,363,234	29,182	502,279	175,112	(57,459)
Net earnings	—	—	—	97,095	—
Cash dividends ($.40 per share)	—	—	—	(23,397)	—
Common stock issued under employee benefit plans	177,683	88	2,969	—	—
Valuation changes, less effect of hedging activities	—	—	—	—	(1,144)
Other	13,937	7	136	—	—
Balance at September 25, 1988	58,554,854	$29,277	$505,384	$248,810	$(58,603)

The Corporation has one class of $.50 par value common stock with 150,000,000 authorized shares and 5,000,000 authorized shares of Series Preferred Stock of which none has been issued.

The Corporation has a Stockholder Rights Plan under which each stockholder has share purchase rights for each outstanding share of common stock of the Corporation. Each right enables the holder, only under certain conditions, to purchase for $60, subject to adjustment, one one-hundredth of a share of Series A Junior Participating Preferred Stock through April 27, 1996. In addition, under certain conditions, the holder of a right (except for an "Acquiring Person" and certain related parties as defined under the Stockholder Rights Plan) may, subject to adjustment, purchase shares of common stock of the Corporation with a market value of $120 for $60. The Corporation has reserved 1,500,000 shares of the preferred stock for issuance upon exercise of the rights.

Note 8: Business Segment and Geographic Areas

1988	United States	Europe	Other	Corporate & Eliminations	Consolidated
Sales to unaffiliated customers	$1,185,496	$754,581	$340,846	$ —	$2,280,923
Sales and transfers between geographic areas	83,658	81,697	177,229	(342,584)	—
Total sales	$1,269,154	$836,278	$518,075	$(342,584)	$2,280,923
Operating income (loss)	$ 81,670	$ 59,763	$ 23,900	$ (6,218)	$ 159,115
Identifiable assets	$ 961,389	$673,738	$377,946	$(187,964)	$1,825,109
1987					
Sales to unaffiliated customers	$1,017,913	$612,385	$304,501	$ —	$1,934,799
Sales and transfers between geographic areas	39,075	63,346	117,814	(220,235)	—
Total sales	$1,056,988	$675,731	$422,315	$(220,235)	$1,934,799
Operating income (loss)	$ 69,164	$ 41,987	$ 18,626	$ (17,304)	$ 112,473
Identifiable assets	$ 884,312	$625,089	$320,271	$(161,627)	$1,668,045
1986					
Sales to unaffiliated customers	$1,001,404	$513,994	$275,796	$ —	$1,791,194
Sales and transfers between geographic areas	37,462	54,094	91,574	(183,130)	—
Total sales	$1,038,866	$568,088	$367,370	$(183,130)	$1,791,194
Operating income (loss)	$ 34,024	$ 22,886	$ 6,498	$ (8,083)	$ 55,325
Identifiable assets	$ 820,866	$530,115	$268,727	$ (39,137)	$1,580,571

The Corporation operates in one business segment–the manufacturing, marketing and servicing of a wide range of power tools, household products and other labor-saving devices generally used in and around the home and by professional users.

In the above table, the United States includes all domestic operations and an intercompany manufacturing facility outside the United States, which manufactures products predominately for sale in the United States. Europe includes subsidiaries located in Western Europe and the Middle East. Other includes subsidiaries located in Canada, Latin America, Australasia and the Far East.

Transfers between geographic areas are accounted for at cost plus a reasonable profit. Identifiable assets for the geographic areas are those assets identified with the operations in each area. Corporate assets included in corporate and eliminations were $109,375 at September 25, 1988, $115,441 at September 27, 1987, and $108,267 at September 28, 1986, and consist principally of cash and cash equivalents, prepaid expenses, property, sundry items, and intangible assets. The remainder of corporate and eliminations includes intangible amortization as well as amounts to eliminate intercompany sales, income and expense, accounts receivable, and profit in inventory. Net equity of subsidiaries located outside the United States was $672,394 at September 25, 1988, $566,816 at September 27, 1987, and $529,958 at September 28, 1986. Cash balances maintained by these subsidiaries do not have significant legal restrictions as to withdrawal.

Note 9: Income Taxes (Benefits)

The Corporation adopted Statement of Financial Accounting Standards (SFAS) No. 96, "Accounting for Income Taxes," at the beginning of fiscal 1988. The initial adoption and current year net earnings effects were immaterial principally due to the Corporation's net operating loss carryforward position. During fiscal 1988, tax benefits of approximately $18,000 ($.31 per share) were recorded as a result of utilizing net operating loss carryforwards. Under the provisions of SFAS No. 96, these tax benefits are included as a reduction of income tax expense rather than as an extraordinary item. The disclosures for 1988 are calculated and reported under the liability method as defined by SFAS No. 96. The 1987 and 1986 disclosures are calculated and reported using the previous method. Under the liability method, the deferred tax liability is determined based on the differences between the financial and tax bases of assets and liabilities as of the balance sheet date multiplied by the tax rate in effect at the time the differences reverse. The principal types of differences between financial and tax bases assets and liabilities are accelerated depreciation, 1985 restructuring reserve spending, spending for various accrued items and deferred interest expense.

Earnings (Loss) Before Income Taxes and Extraordinary Item:

	Liability Method	Deferred Method	
	1988	1987	1986
United States	$ 45,092	$ 19,174	$(23,372)
Other countries	80,603	50,592	58,115
	$125,695	$ 69,766	$ 34,743

Components of Income Taxes (Benefits):

	Liability Method	Deferred Method	
	1988	1987	1986
Current:			
United States	$ (429)	$ —	$ —
Other countries	19,745	16,415	6,419
Withholding on remittances from other countries	1,304	876	2,017
	20,620	17,291	8,436
Deferred:			
United States	—	—	(1,368)
Other countries	7,980	(3,091)	132
	7,980	(3,091)	(1,236)
	$ 28,600	$ 14,200	$ 7,200

The components of deferred income tax expense are summarized as follows:

	Liability Method	Deferred Method	
	1988	1987	1986
Deferred interest expense	$ 1,324	$(2,779)	$ 3,140
Accelerated depreciation	1,187	(332)	(3,993)
Other	5,469	20	(383)
	$ 7,980	$(3,091)	$(1,236)

Net operating losses of approximately $258,000 will be carried forward to offset future financial statement taxable income and will expire from 1989 to 2017. Tax basis carryforwards at September 25, 1988, consisted of net operating losses of approximately $223,600 expiring from 1989 to 2002 and other tax credits of $15,100 expiring from 1989 to 2002.

At September 25, 1988, unremitted earnings of subsidiaries outside the United States were $476,800 (at current balance sheet exchange rates) on which no United States taxes have been provided. If such earnings were to be remitted without offsetting tax credits in the United States, withholding taxes would be $99,800. The Corporation's intention, however, is to permanently reinvest these earnings or to repatriate such earnings only when tax effective to do so.

A reconciliation of income taxes at the federal statutory rate to the Corporation's income taxes is as follows:

	Liability Method	Deferred Method	
	1988	1987	1986
Income taxes at federal statutory rate	$ 42,700	$ 30,000	$ 16,000
Higher (lower) effective taxes on earnings of other countries	4,200	(12,000)	(23,100)
Book/tax difference on acquired net assets	—	(6,900)	—
Effect of net operating loss carryforwards	(17,600)	3,200	11,600
Withholding on remittances from other countries	1,300	900	2,000
Other—net	(2,000)	(1,000)	700
Income taxes	$ 28,600	$ 14,200	$ 7,200

The Corporation and its subsidiaries have pension plans covering substantially all of their employees. The Corporation's general policy is to fund pension cost in conformity with requirements of local laws and regulations. Benefits are based on age, years of service, and the level of compensation during the final years of employment.

At the beginning of fiscal 1988, the Corporation adopted Statement of Financial Accounting Standards (SFAS) No. 87, "Employer's Accounting for Pensions," for its domestic pension plans. The effect of adoption was immaterial. Pension expense for all plans was $6,634 in 1988, $8,116 in 1987, and $8,200 in 1986, including amortization of prior service costs over periods ranging up to 15 years.

Net domestic pension expense for 1988 includes the following components:

Service cost	$ 4,196
Interest cost on projected benefit obligation	11,556
Actual return on assets	(3,985)
Net amortization and deferral	(11,056)
Net domestic pension expense	$ 711

The funded status of the domestic plans at the date of adoption of SFAS No. 87 and at September 25, 1988 was as follows:

	Sept. 25, 1988	Beginning of Fiscal 1988
Actuarial present value of benefit obligations:		
Vested benefit obligation	$113,203	$104,170
Accumulated benefit	$116,738	$107,171
Projected benefit	$133,755	$119,868
Plan assets at fair value	134,274	134,140
Plan assets in excess of projected benefit obligation	519	14,272
Unrecognized net loss	17,484	–
Unrecognized net asset at date of adoption net of amortization	(15,894)	(17,285)
Net pension asset (liability) recognized in the Consolidated Balance Sheet	$ 2,109	$ (3,013)

Assumptions used in the accounting for domestic defined benefit plans as of September 25, 1988 and date of adoption were:

	Sept. 25, 1988	Beginning of Fiscal 1988
Weighted-average discount rate	9.5%	10.0%
Salary scale	6.0%	6.0%
Expected return on plan assets	10.5%	10.5%

Plan assets consist principally of investments in fixed income and real estate funds and common stock.

Outside of the United States, employees are generally covered by either defined benefit Corporation sponsored plans similar to the domestic plans or by government administered retirement or insured annuity plans. Under the government administered and insured annuity plans, the Corporation expenses payments to the plan on behalf of its employees. Since the Corporation does not participate in the management of the assets, no asset or liability data on these plans is reported.

Under the defined benefit plans outside the United States, at September 25, 1988 and September 27, 1987, the total of fund assets and balance sheet accruals exceeded the actuarially computed present value of vested benefits. The customary practice in some countries outside the

United States is to maintain balance sheet accruals in lieu of funding these pension liabilities. As of September 25, 1988, other long-term liabilities included $15,437 of pension liabilities of subsidiaries located in these countries.

In addition to pension benefits, the Corporation provides post retirement health care and medical benefits to eligible United States employees upon retirement. Retirees in other countries are generally covered by government sponsored programs. The cost of all benefits in the United States is expensed as claims and premiums are paid. For 1988, 1987 and 1986, these costs amounted to $4,388, $2,310 and $1,930, respectively.

Note 11: Stock Option and Purchase Plans

Under various stock option plans, options to purchase common stock may be granted until 1996. Options are granted at 100% of fair market value at the date of grant, are generally exercisable in installments beginning one year from the date granted, and expire ten years after the date of grant. The plans permit the issuance of either incentive stock options or nonqualified stock options which, for certain of the plans, may be accompanied by cash appreciation or stock appreciation rights issued simultaneously with the grant of the stock options.

As of September 25, 1988, 294,682 incentive stock options, 1,413,424 nonqualified stock options without cash appreciation rights, and 1,015,935 nonqualified stock options with cash appreciation rights were outstanding under domestic plans; and 147,625 stock options were outstanding under a United Kingdom plan.

Nonqualified stock options covering 20,825 shares remain outstanding under prior stock option plans. The options expire at the end of ten years from the dates of their respective grant. No further options will be granted under those prior plans.

Under all plans there were 289,061 shares of common stock reserved for future grants as of September 25, 1988. Transactions are summarized as follows:

	Common Shares Under Option	Price Range
September 27, 1987	2,452,426	$13.13–25.63
Granted	618,200	15.63–23.75
Exercised	(28,958)	13.13–21.88
Canceled or expired	(149,177)	13.13–25.63
September 25, 1988	2,892,491	13.13–25.25
Shares exercisable at September 25, 1988	1,384,134	13.13–25.25
Shares exercised in 1987	190,786	13.13–21.88
Shares exercised in 1986	241,312	13.13–20.38

Under the 1986 Employees' Stock Purchase Plan, employees may subscribe through April 1990 to purchase shares of the Corporation's common stock at the lower of 90% of the market value on the date offered or on the date purchased. As of September 25, 1988, there were 321,128 shares of common stock reserved for subscriptions. Transactions are summarized as follows:

	Common Shares Subscribed	Price Range
September 27, 1987	48,775	$ 17.63
Subscriptions	123,018	16.63
Purchases	(45,128)	17.63
Cancellations	(5,311)	17.63–16.63
September 25, 1988	121,354	16.63
Shares purchased in 1987	12,390	17.38
Shares purchased in 1986	18,382	20.25

Note 12: Other (Income) Expense

Other (income) expense primarily includes foreign currency transactions and remeasurement gains and losses and other miscellaneous income and expense items. For 1988, other (income) expense also includes the receipt during the third quarter of $25,000 as a result of the Corporation's termination of a tender offer, $16,673 of expenses associated with that tender offer, and a $7,400 accrual for the incremental cost of discontinuing certain product lines. Other (income) expense for 1986 includes a gain of $18,244 on the sale of foreign currency exchange agreements.

Note 13: Leases

The Corporation leases certain service centers, administrative headquarters, warehouses and equipment. Generally, the leases carry renewal provisions and require the Corporation to pay maintenance costs. Rental payments may be adjusted for increases in taxes and insurance above specified amounts. Rental expense charged to earnings for 1988, 1987 and 1986 amounted to $40,818, $37,065 and $32,691, respectively. Capital leases are immaterial in amount and are treated as operating leases. Future minimum payments under noncancellable operating leases with initial or remaining terms of more than one year as of September 25, 1988, are as follows:

1989	$ 21,803
1990	17,373
1991	14,059
1992	11,254
1993	9,565
Thereafter	46,445
Total	$120,499

These future minimum lease payments have not been reduced for sublease rental income of $5,677 to be received in the future under noncancellable subleases.

Note 14: Quarterly Results (unaudited)

1988	1st Quarter	2nd Quarter	3rd Quarter	4th Quarter
Net sales	$612,279	$537,787	$539,331	$591,526
Gross margin	229,697	202,166	200,857	217,439
Net earnings	31,118	21,145	21,393	23,439
Earnings per share	.53	.36	.36	.40
1987				
Net sales	$529,000	$438,714	$465,008	$502,077
Gross margin	192,608	164,628	166,325	181,249
Net earnings	22,385	9,256	8,991	14,934
Earnings per share	.38	.16	.15	.26

Management Report on Financial Statements

Management has prepared and is responsible for the consolidated financial statements, which were prepared in accordance with generally accepted accounting principles and include amounts that are based on certain estimates and judgments.

To fulfill their responsibility, management maintains a system of internal accounting controls, supported by formal policies and procedures that are communicated throughout the Corporation. Management also maintains a staff of internal auditors who evaluate the adequacy of and investigate the adherence to these controls, policies and procedures.

The Corporation's financial statements have been audited by Ernst & Whinney, independent auditors who were selected by the Board of Directors and whose selection was ratified by the stockholders. During the audit, they review and make appropriate tests of the systems of internal accounting control and of the financial data included in the consolidated financial statements to the extent they consider necessary to render an opinion.

The Board of Directors pursues its oversight role with respect to the Corporation's financial statements through the Audit Committee, which is composed solely of outside directors. The Committee meets periodically with the independent auditors, internal auditors and management to assure that all are properly discharging their responsibilities. Both Ernst & Whinney and the internal auditors have unrestricted access to the Audit Committee.

Report of Independent Auditors

To the Stockholders and Board of Directors
The Black & Decker Corporation

We have audited the accompanying consolidated balance sheets of The Black & Decker Corporation and subsidiaries as of September 25, 1988 and September 27, 1987, and the related consolidated statements of earnings and cash flows for each of the three years in the period ended September 25, 1988. These financial statements are the responsibility of the Company's management. Our responsibility is to express an opinion on these financial statements based on our audits.

We conducted our audits in accordance with generally accepted auditing standards. Those standards require that we plan and perform the audit to obtain reasonable assurance about whether the financial statements are free of material misstatement. An audit includes examining, on a test basis, evidence supporting the amounts and disclosures in the financial statements. An audit also includes assessing the accounting principles used and significant estimates made by management, as well as evaluating the overall financial statement presentation. We believe that our audits provide a reasonable basis for our opinion.

In our opinion, the financial statements referred to above present fairly, in all material respects, the consolidated financial position of The Black & Decker Corporation and subsidiaries at September 25, 1988 and September 27, 1987, and the consolidated results of their operations and their cash flows for each of the three years in the period ended September 25, 1988, in conformity with generally accepted accounting principles.

Ernst & Whinney

Baltimore, Maryland
November 17, 1988

Eleven-Year Summary
The Black & Decker Corporation and Subsidiaries

(Thousands of Dollars Except per Share Data)	1988(f)	1987	1986	1985
Summary of Operations				
Net sales	$2,280,923	$1,934,799	$1,791,194	$1,732,278
% change	17.9	8.0	3.4	13.0
Cost of products sold	1,430,764	1,229,989	1,160,379	1,107,228
Earnings (loss) from continuing operations				
before income taxes and extraordinary item	125,695	69,766	34,743	(159,825)
% of net sales	5.5	3.6	1.9	(9.2)
% change	80.2	100.8	—	—
Income taxes (benefits)	28,600	14,200	7,200	(1,400)
Effective tax (benefit) rate	22.8	20.4	20.7	(.9)
Earnings (loss) from continuing operations				
before extraordinary item	97,095	55,566	27,543	(158,425)
% change	74.7	101.8	—	—
Earnings (loss) from discontinued				
operations	—	—	—	—
Net earnings (loss) before extraordinary item	97,095	55,566	27,543	(158,425)
% change	74.7	101.8	—	—
Extraordinary item	—	—	(21,239)	—
Net earnings (loss)	97,095	55,566	6,304	(158,425)
% change	74.7	781.4	—	—
Per Share Data (b)				
Earnings (loss):				
Continuing operations	1.65	.95	.49	(3.11)
Discontinued operations	—	—	—	—
Extraordinary item	—	—	(.38)	—
Total	1.65	.95	.11	(3.11)
Cash dividends	.40	.40	.58	.64
Stockholders' equity	12.38	11.12	10.61	9.94
Other Data (c)				
Number of stockholders	19,820	19,160	19,593	17,844
Number of employees	20,800	19,700	21,700	22,400
Total assets	1,825,109	1,668,045	1,580,571	1,452,146
Long-term debt	277,091	250,578	195,544	334,501
Total debt	492,574	478,536	407,426	371,983
Stockholders' equity	724,868	649,114	616,659	504,848
Capital expenditures	98,404	58,766	82,375	118,299
Depreciation and amortization	93,488	99,036	107,370	93,338
Working capital	555,786	450,650	355,128	344,684
Current ratio	1.7	1.6	1.5	1.7
Net sales to average total assets	1.31	1.19	1.18	1.18
% return on average stockholders' equity (d)	14.1	8.8	1.1	(26.7)

(a) The Corporation adopted Statement of Financial Accounting Standards No. 52 in 1982. Financial information for the years 1979-1981 has been restated for this change in accounting. In 1979 the Corporation changed its method of determining the cost of United States inventories from the FIFO (first-in, first-out) method to the LIFO (last-in, first-out) method.

(b) Based on the average number of shares of common stock outstanding during each year, except stockholders' equity which is based on shares outstanding at year-end.

(c) Number of employees, capital expenditures and depreciation and amortization relate to continuing operations of the Corporation.

1984(e)	1983	1982	1981	1980	1979(a)	1978
$1,532,883	$1,167,752	$1,160,233	$1,244,510	$1,219,844	$1,027,168	$ 822,325
31.3	.6	(6.8)	2.0	18.8	24.9	17.5
953,841	742,986	730,962	763,633	738,086	618,893	487,570
140,804	38,451	55,481	99,298	136,777	142,735	115,644
9.2	3.3	4.8	8.0	11.2	13.9	14.1
266.2	(30.7)	(44.1)	(27.4)	(4.2)	23.4	22.7
45,400	10,300	14,800	26,300	56,900	60,400	57,000
32.2	26.8	26.7	26.5	41.6	42.3	49.3
95,404	28,151	40,681	72,998	79,877	82,335	58,644
238.9	(30.8)	(44.3)	(8.6)	(3.0)	40.4	27.9
—	16,000	(117,283)	(6,205)	9,408	3,328	7,594
95,404	44,151	(76,602)	66,793	89,285	85,663	66,238
116.1	—	—	(25.2)	4.2	29.3	28.2
—	—	—	—	—	—	—
95,404	44,151	(76,602)	66,793	89,285	85,663	66,238
116.1	—	—	(25.2)	4.2	29.3	28.2
1.95	.65	.97	1.74	1.90	1.96	1.40
—	.37	(2.79)	(.15)	.22	.08	.18
—	—	—	—	—	—	—
1.95	1.02	(1.82)	1.59	2.12	2.04	1.58
.58	.52	.76	.76	.74	.68	.57
13.58	11.79	10.70	13.68	13.82	12.36	10.64
18,697	19,212	22,337	23,321	24,408	23,194	20,862
23,000	14,500	15,700	17,000	18,200	18,600	16,200
1,473,448	985,358	995,329	1,133,254	1,193,223	917,209	797,206
279,540	159,108	263,864	269,032	225,608	90,749	90,604
303,763	179,515	306,239	304,039	317,875	140,417	137,469
683,507	554,416	450,419	576,073	581,397	519,119	446,213
91,835	75,759	80,837	79,948	95,526	58,121	32,459
66,211	51,973	48,444	43,335	34,369	29,805	28,079
461,545	423,809	406,542	420,163	387,354	250,538	250,557
2.2	2.8	2.8	2.8	2.2	1.9	2.1
1.25	1.18	1.09	1.07	1.16	1.20	1.10
15.4	5.2	8.1	14.5	16.6	19.9	16.5

(d) Calculated on an "as reported" basis for 1984 through 1988. For years 1978 through 1983 a pro forma basis was used with earnings from continuing operations and stockholders' equity adjusted to exclude portions allocable to operations sold.

(e) Includes Housewares operations acquired on April 27, 1984.

(f) The Corporation adopted Statement of Financial Accounting Standard No. 96 in 1988. Accordingly, tax benefits recorded in 1988 as a result of utilizing net operating loss carryforwards are included as a reduction of income tax expense rather than as an extraordinary item.

Stockholder Information

Price Range Per Share
(New York Stock Exchange Composite Transactions)

Fiscal Quarter	1988	1987
October–December	$26⅛-$13	$18 -$15⅜
January–March	$22 -$17⅛	$22 -$15⅞
April–June	$23⅞-$18¼	$24¼-$18
July–September	$24¾-$19¼	$26½-$22⅞

Dividends Per Share

Fiscal Quarter	1988	1987
October–December	$ .10	$ .10
January–March	.10	.10
April–June	.10	.10
July–September	.10	.10
	$ .40	$ .40

Stock Listings:
Ticker Symbol: BDK
New York Stock Exchange
Pacific Stock Exchange
London Stock Exchange
Frankfurt Stock Exchange
Basel Stock Exchange
Zurich Stock Exchange

Annual Meeting
The annual meeting of stockholders will be held on January 30, 1989, at the Sheraton Towson Hotel, 901 Dulaney Valley Road, Towson, MD 21204 at 11:00 a.m. A proxy statement will be sent to stockholders on or about December 15, 1988, at which time proxies for the meeting will be requested.

Transfer Agent, Registrar and Dividend Disbursing Agent
Morgan Shareholder Services Trust Company
30 West Broadway
New York, NY 10007-2192
(212) 587-6516

Dividend Reinvestment Plan
All registered owners of Black & Decker common stock are eligible to increase their investment in the Corporation voluntarily through automatic dividend reinvestment or cash payments, without paying brokerage or administrative fees. For additional information about the Dividend Reinvestment Plan, contact:
Morgan Shareholder Services Trust Company
Dividend Reinvestment Plan
Post Office Box 3506
Church Street Station
New York, NY 10008-3506
(212) 587-6516

Additional Information
Additional information about Black & Decker, including copies of Form 10-K Reports to the Securities and Exchange Commission, a description of the Stockholders Rights Plan, and stockholder publications including annual reports, quarterly reports and proxy statements may be obtained without charge from:
The Office of The Secretary
The Black & Decker Corporation
701 East Joppa Road
Towson, MD 21204

General Counsel
Miles & Stockbridge
10 Light Street
Baltimore, MD 21202
(301) 727-6464

Independent Auditors
Ernst & Whinney
One North Charles Street
Baltimore, MD 21201
(301) 539-7940

Trademarks
Use of ® or ™ in this annual report indicates trademarks owned by the Black & Decker Corporation and its subsidiaries.

Corporate Headquarters
Towson, Maryland U.S.A. 21204

APPENDIX B

Present Value and Future Value Tables

TABLE 1
Future Value of $1

N	2.0%	3.0%	4.0%	5.0%	6.0%	8.0%
1	1.020000	1.030000	1.040000	1.050000	1.060000	1.080000
2	1.040400	1.060900	1.081600	1.102500	1.123600	1.166400
3	1.061208	1.092727	1.124864	1.157625	1.191016	1.259712
4	1.082432	1.125509	1.169859	1.215506	1.262477	1.360489
5	1.104081	1.159274	1.216653	1.276282	1.338226	1.469328
6	1.126162	1.194052	1.265319	1.340096	1.418519	1.586874
7	1.148686	1.229874	1.315932	1.407100	1.503630	1.713824
8	1.171659	1.266770	1.368569	1.477455	1.593848	1.850930
9	1.195093	1.304773	1.423312	1.551328	1.689479	1.999005
10	1.218994	1.343916	1.480244	1.628895	1.790848	2.158925
11	1.243374	1.384234	1.539454	1.710339	1.898299	2.331639
12	1.268242	1.425761	1.601032	1.795856	2.012196	2.518170
13	1.293607	1.468534	1.665074	1.885649	2.132928	2.719624
14	1.319479	1.512590	1.731676	1.979932	2.260904	2.937194
15	1.345868	1.557967	1.800944	2.078928	2.396558	3.172169
16	1.372786	1.604706	1.872981	2.182875	2.540352	3.425943
17	1.400241	1.652848	1.947900	2.292018	2.692773	3.700018
18	1.428246	1.702433	2.025817	2.406619	2.854339	3.996019
19	1.456811	1.753506	2.106849	2.526950	3.025600	4.315701
20	1.485947	1.806111	2.191123	2.653298	3.207135	4.660957
21	1.515666	1.860295	2.278768	2.785963	3.399564	5.033834
22	1.545980	1.916103	2.369919	2.925261	3.603537	5.436540
23	1.576899	1.973587	2.464716	3.071524	3.819750	5.871464
24	1.608437	2.032794	2.563304	3.225100	4.048935	6.341181
25	1.640606	2.093778	2.665836	3.386355	4.291871	6.848475
26	1.673418	2.156591	2.772470	3.555673	4.549383	7.396353
27	1.706886	2.221289	2.883369	3.733456	4.822346	7.988061

N	10.0%	12.0%	14.0%	16.0%	20.0%	25.0%
1	1.100000	1.120000	1.140000	1.160000	1.200000	1.250000
2	1.210000	1.254400	1.299600	1.345600	1.440000	1.562500
3	1.331000	1.404928	1.481544	1.560896	1.728000	1.953125
4	1.464100	1.573519	1.688960	1.810639	2.073600	2.441406
5	1.610510	1.762342	1.925415	2.100342	2.488320	3.051758
6	1.771561	1.973823	2.194973	2.436396	2.985984	3.814697
7	1.948717	2.210681	2.502269	2.826220	3.583181	4.768372
8	2.143589	2.475963	2.852586	3.278415	4.299817	5.960464
9	2.357948	2.773079	3.251949	3.802961	5.159780	7.450581
10	2.593742	3.105848	3.707221	4.411435	6.191736	9.313226
11	2.853117	3.478550	4.226232	5.117265	7.430084	11.641532
12	3.138428	3.895976	4.817905	5.936027	8.916100	14.551915
13	3.452271	4.363493	5.492411	6.885791	10.699321	18.189894
14	3.797498	4.887112	6.261349	7.987518	12.839185	22.737368
15	4.177248	5.473566	7.137938	9.265521	15.407022	28.421709
16	4.594973	6.130394	8.137249	10.748004	18.488426	35.527137
17	5.054470	6.866041	9.276464	12.467685	22.186111	44.408921
18	5.559917	7.689966	10.575169	14.462514	26.623333	55.511151
19	6.115909	8.612762	12.055693	16.776517	31.948000	69.388939
20	6.727500	9.646293	13.743490	19.460759	38.337600	86.736174
21	7.400250	10.803848	15.667578	22.574481	46.005120	108.420217
22	8.140275	12.100310	17.861039	26.186398	55.206144	135.525272
23	8.954302	13.552347	20.361585	30.376222	66.247373	169.406589
24	9.849733	15.178629	23.212207	35.236417	79.496847	211.758237
25	10.834706	17.000064	26.461916	40.874244	95.396217	264.697796
26	11.918177	19.040072	30.166584	47.414123	114.475460	330.872245
27	13.109994	21.324881	34.389906	55.000382	137.370552	413.590306

TABLE 2
Present Value of $1

N	2.0%	3.0%	4.0%	5.0%	6.0%	8.0%
1	0.980392	0.970874	0.961538	0.952381	0.943396	0.925926
2	0.961169	0.942596	0.924556	0.907029	0.889996	0.857339
3	0.942322	0.915142	0.888996	0.863838	0.839619	0.793832
4	0.923845	0.888487	0.854804	0.822702	0.792094	0.735030
5	0.905731	0.862609	0.821927	0.783526	0.747258	0.680583
6	0.887971	0.837484	0.790315	0.746215	0.704961	0.630170
7	0.870560	0.813092	0.759918	0.710681	0.665057	0.583490
8	0.853490	0.789409	0.730690	0.676839	0.627412	0.540269
9	0.836755	0.766417	0.702587	0.644609	0.591898	0.500249
10	0.820348	0.744094	0.675564	0.613913	0.558395	0.463193
11	0.804263	0.722421	0.649581	0.584679	0.526788	0.428883
12	0.788493	0.701380	0.624597	0.556837	0.496969	0.397114
13	0.773033	0.680951	0.600574	0.530321	0.468839	0.367698
14	0.757875	0.661118	0.577475	0.505068	0.442301	0.340461
15	0.743015	0.641862	0.555265	0.481017	0.417265	0.315242
16	0.728446	0.623167	0.533908	0.458112	0.393646	0.291890
17	0.714163	0.605016	0.513373	0.436297	0.371364	0.270269
18	0.700159	0.587395	0.493628	0.415521	0.350344	0.250249
19	0.686431	0.570286	0.474642	0.395734	0.330513	0.231712
20	0.672971	0.553676	0.456387	0.376889	0.311805	0.214548
21	0.659776	0.537549	0.438834	0.358942	0.294155	0.198656
22	0.646839	0.521893	0.421955	0.341850	0.277505	0.183941
23	0.634156	0.506692	0.405726	0.325571	0.261797	0.170315
24	0.621721	0.491934	0.390121	0.310068	0.246979	0.157699
25	0.609531	0.477606	0.375117	0.295303	0.232999	0.146018
26	0.597579	0.463695	0.360689	0.281241	0.219810	0.135202
27	0.585862	0.450189	0.346817	0.267848	0.207368	0.125187

N	10.0%	12.0%	14.0%	16.0%	20.0%	25.0%
1	0.909091	0.892857	0.877193	0.862069	0.833333	0.800000
2	0.826446	0.797194	0.769468	0.743163	0.694444	0.640000
3	0.751315	0.711780	0.674972	0.640658	0.578704	0.512000
4	0.683013	0.635518	0.592080	0.552291	0.482253	0.409600
5	0.620921	0.567427	0.519369	0.476113	0.401878	0.327680
6	0.564474	0.506631	0.455587	0.410442	0.334898	0.262144
7	0.513158	0.452349	0.399637	0.353830	0.279082	0.209715
8	0.466507	0.403883	0.350559	0.305025	0.232568	0.167772
9	0.424098	0.360610	0.307508	0.262953	0.193807	0.134218
10	0.385543	0.321973	0.269744	0.226684	0.161506	0.107374
11	0.350494	0.287476	0.236617	0.195417	0.134588	0.085899
12	0.318631	0.256675	0.207559	0.168463	0.112157	0.068719
13	0.289664	0.229174	0.182069	0.145227	0.093464	0.054976
14	0.263331	0.204620	0.159710	0.125195	0.077887	0.043980
15	0.239392	0.182696	0.140096	0.107927	0.064905	0.035184
16	0.217629	0.163122	0.122892	0.093041	0.054088	0.028147
17	0.197845	0.145644	0.107800	0.080207	0.045073	0.022518
18	0.179859	0.130040	0.094561	0.069144	0.037561	0.018014
19	0.163508	0.116107	0.082948	0.059607	0.031301	0.014412
20	0.148644	0.103667	0.072762	0.051385	0.026084	0.011529
21	0.135131	0.092560	0.063826	0.044298	0.021737	0.009223
22	0.122846	0.082643	0.055988	0.038188	0.018114	0.007379
23	0.111678	0.073788	0.049112	0.032920	0.015095	0.005903
24	0.101526	0.065882	0.043081	0.028380	0.012579	0.004722
25	0.092296	0.058823	0.037790	0.024465	0.010483	0.003778
26	0.083905	0.052521	0.033149	0.021091	0.008735	0.003022
27	0.076278	0.046894	0.029078	0.018182	0.007280	0.002418

TABLE 3
Future Value of
Ordinary Annuity of $1

N	2.0%	3.0%	4.0%	5.0%	6.0%	8.0%
1	1.000000	1.000000	1.000000	1.000000	1.000000	1.000000
2	2.020000	2.030000	2.040000	2.050000	2.060000	2.080000
3	3.060400	3.090900	3.121600	3.152500	3.183600	3.246400
4	4.121608	4.183627	4.246464	4.310125	4.374616	4.506112
5	5.204040	5.309136	5.416323	5.525631	5.637093	5.866601
6	6.308121	6.468410	6.632975	6.801913	6.975319	7.335929
7	7.434283	7.662462	7.898294	8.142008	8.393838	8.922803
8	8.582969	8.892336	9.214226	9.549109	9.897468	10.636628
9	9.754628	10.159106	10.582795	11.026564	11.491316	12.487558
10	10.949721	11.463879	12.006107	12.577893	13.180795	14.486562
11	12.168715	12.807796	13.486351	14.206787	14.971643	16.645487
12	13.412090	14.192030	15.025805	15.917127	16.869941	18.977126
13	14.680332	15.617790	16.626838	17.712983	18.882138	21.495297
14	15.973938	17.086324	18.291911	19.598632	21.015066	24.214920
15	17.293417	18.598914	20.023588	21.578564	23.275970	27.152114
16	18.639285	20.156881	21.824531	23.657492	25.672528	30.324283
17	20.012071	21.761588	23.697512	25.840366	28.212880	33.750226
18	21.412312	23.414435	25.645413	28.132385	30.905653	37.450244
19	22.840559	25.116868	27.671229	30.539004	33.759992	41.446263
20	24.297370	26.870374	29.778079	33.065954	36.785591	45.761964
21	25.783317	28.676486	31.969202	35.719252	39.992727	50.422921
22	27.298984	30.536780	34.247970	38.505214	43.392290	55.456755
23	28.844963	32.452884	36.617889	41.430475	46.995828	60.893296
24	30.421862	34.426470	39.082604	44.501999	50.815577	66.764759
25	32.030300	36.459264	41.645908	47.727099	54.864512	73.105940
26	33.670906	38.553042	44.311745	51.113454	59.156383	79.954415
27	35.344324	40.709634	47.084214	54.669126	63.705766	87.350768

N	10.0%	12.0%	14.0%	16.0%	20.0%	25.0%
1	1.000000	1.000000	1.000000	1.000000	1.000000	1.000000
2	2.100000	2.120000	2.140000	2.160000	2.200000	2.250000
3	3.310000	3.374400	3.439600	3.505600	3.640000	3.812500
4	4.641000	4.779328	4.921144	5.066496	5.368000	5.765625
5	6.105100	6.352847	6.610104	6.877135	7.441600	8.207031
6	7.715610	8.115189	8.535519	8.977477	9.929920	11.258789
7	9.487171	10.089012	10.730491	11.413873	12.915904	15.073486
8	11.435888	12.299693	13.232760	14.240093	16.499085	19.841858
9	13.579477	14.775656	16.085347	17.518508	20.798902	25.802322
10	15.937425	17.548735	19.337295	21.321469	25.958682	33.252903
11	18.531167	20.654583	23.044516	25.732904	32.150419	42.566129
12	21.384284	24.133133	27.270749	30.850169	39.580502	54.207661
13	24.522712	28.029109	32.088654	36.786196	48.496603	68.759576
14	27.974983	32.392602	37.581065	43.671987	59.195923	86.949470
15	31.772482	37.279715	43.842414	51.659505	72.035108	109.686838
16	35.949730	42.753280	50.980352	60.925026	87.442129	138.108547
17	40.544703	48.883674	59.117601	71.673030	105.930555	173.635684
18	45.599173	55.749715	68.394066	84.140715	128.116666	218.044605
19	51.159090	63.439681	78.969235	98.603230	154.740000	273.555756
20	57.274999	72.052442	91.024928	115.379747	186.688000	342.944695
21	64.002499	81.698736	104.768418	134.840506	225.025600	429.680869
22	71.402749	92.502584	120.435996	157.414987	271.030719	538.101086
23	79.543024	104.602894	138.297035	183.601385	326.236863	673.626358
24	88.497327	118.155241	158.658620	213.977607	392.484236	843.032947
25	98.347059	133.333870	181.870827	249.214024	471.981083	1054.791184
26	109.181765	150.333934	208.332743	290.088267	567.377300	1319.488980
27	121.099942	169.374007	238.499327	337.502390	681.852760	1650.361225

TABLE 4
Present Value of
Ordinary Annuity of $1

N	2.0%	3.0%	4.0%	5.0%	6.0%	8.0%
1	0.980392	0.970874	0.961538	0.952381	0.943396	0.925926
2	1.941561	1.913470	1.886095	1.859410	1.833393	1.783265
3	2.883883	2.828611	2.775091	2.723248	2.673012	2.577097
4	3.807729	3.717098	3.629895	3.545951	3.465106	3.312127
5	4.713460	4.579707	4.451822	4.329477	4.212364	3.992710
6	5.601431	5.417191	5.242137	5.075692	4.917324	4.622880
7	6.471991	6.230283	6.002055	5.786373	5.582381	5.206370
8	7.325481	7.019692	6.732745	6.463213	6.209794	5.746639
9	8.162237	7.786109	7.435332	7.107822	6.801692	6.246888
10	8.982585	8.530203	8.110896	7.721735	7.360087	6.710081
11	9.786848	9.252624	8.760477	8.306414	7.886875	7.138964
12	10.575341	9.954004	9.385074	8.863252	8.383844	7.536078
13	11.348374	10.634955	9.985648	9.393573	8.852683	7.903776
14	12.106249	11.296073	10.563123	9.898641	9.294984	8.244237
15	12.849264	11.937935	11.118387	10.379658	9.712249	8.559479
16	13.577709	12.561102	11.652296	10.837770	10.105895	8.851369
17	14.291872	13.166118	12.165669	11.274066	10.477260	9.121638
18	14.992031	13.753513	12.659297	11.689587	10.827603	9.371887
19	15.678462	14.323799	13.133939	12.085321	11.158116	9.603599
20	16.351433	14.877475	13.590326	12.462210	11.469921	9.818147
21	17.011209	15.415024	14.029160	12.821153	11.764077	10.016803
22	17.658048	15.936917	14.451115	13.163003	12.041582	10.200744
23	18.292204	16.443608	14.856842	13.488574	12.303379	10.371059
24	18.913926	16.935542	15.246963	13.798642	12.550358	10.528758
25	19.523456	17.413148	15.622080	14.093945	12.783356	10.674776
26	20.121036	17.876842	15.982769	14.375185	13.003166	10.809978
27	20.706898	18.327031	16.329586	14.643034	13.210534	10.935165

N	10.0%	12.0%	14.0%	16.0%	20.0%	25.0%
1	0.909091	0.892857	0.877193	0.862069	0.833333	0.800000
2	1.735537	1.690051	1.646661	1.605232	1.527778	1.440000
3	2.486852	2.401831	2.321632	2.245890	2.106481	1.952000
4	3.169865	3.037349	2.913712	2.798181	2.588735	2.361600
5	3.790787	3.604776	3.433081	3.274294	2.990612	2.689280
6	4.355261	4.111407	3.888668	3.684736	3.325510	2.951424
7	4.868419	4.563757	4.288305	4.038565	3.604592	3.161139
8	5.334926	4.967640	4.638864	4.343591	3.837160	3.328911
9	5.759024	5.328250	4.946372	4.606544	4.030967	3.463129
10	6.144567	5.650223	5.216116	4.833227	4.192472	3.570503
11	6.495061	5.937699	5.452733	5.028644	4.327060	3.656403
12	6.813692	6.194374	5.660292	5.197107	4.439217	3.725122
13	7.103356	6.423548	5.842362	5.342334	4.532681	3.780098
14	7.366687	6.628168	6.002072	5.467529	4.610567	3.824078
15	7.606080	6.810864	6.142168	5.575456	4.675473	3.859263
16	7.823709	6.973986	6.265060	5.668497	4.729561	3.887410
17	8.021553	7.119630	6.372859	5.748704	4.774634	3.909928
18	8.201412	7.249670	6.467420	5.817848	4.812195	3.927942
19	8.364920	7.365777	6.550369	5.877455	4.843496	3.942354
20	8.513564	7.469444	6.623131	5.928841	4.869580	3.953883
21	8.648694	7.562003	6.686957	5.973139	4.891316	3.963107
22	8.771540	7.644646	6.742944	6.011326	4.909430	3.970485
23	8.883218	7.718434	6.792056	6.044247	4.924525	3.976388
24	8.984744	7.784316	6.835137	6.072627	4.937104	3.981111
25	9.077040	7.843139	6.872927	6.097092	4.947587	3.984888
26	9.160945	7.895660	6.906077	6.118183	4.956323	3.987911
27	9.237223	7.942554	6.935155	6.136364	4.963602	3.990329

Index

Boldface numbers refer to pages with definitions; small letter n refers to footnotes.